Masterplots

Fourth Edition

Masterplots

Fourth Edition

Volume 4
Eclogues—Girl with a Pearl Earring

Editor

Laurence W. Mazzeno
Alvernia College

SALEM PRESS
Pasadena, California   Hackensack, New Jersey

Editor in Chief: Dawn P. Dawson

Editorial Director: Christina J. Moose	*Editorial Assistant:* Brett S. Weisberg
Development Editor: Tracy Irons-Georges	*Research Supervisor:* Jeffry Jensen
Project Editor: Desiree Dreeuws	*Research Assistant:* Keli Trousdale
Manuscript Editors: Constance Pollock,	*Production Editor:* Joyce I. Buchea
Judy Selhorst, Andy Perry	*Design and Graphics:* James Hutson
Acquisitions Editor: Mark Rehn	*Layout:* William Zimmerman

Cover photo: Sinclair Lewis (The Granger Collection, New York)

Library of Congress Cataloging-in-Publication Data

Masterplots / editor, Laurence W. Mazzeno. — 4th ed.
  v.   cm.
Includes bibliographical references and indexes.
ISBN 978-1-58765-568-5 (set : alk. paper) — ISBN 978-1-58765-572-2 (v. 4 : alk. paper)
1. Literature—Stories, plots, etc.   2. Literature—History and criticism.   I. Mazzeno, Laurence W.
PN44.M33 2010
809—dc22

2010033931

Fourth Edition
First Printing

PRINTED IN THE UNITED STATES OF AMERICA

Contents

Contents

Complete List of Titles

Volume 1

Volume 2

Contents

Volume 3

Volume 4

Volume 5

Contents clxxi
Complete List of Titles clxxv

Volume 6

Volume 7

Contents ccxlvii
Complete List of Titles ccli

Volume 8

Volume 9

Contents cccxxiii
Complete List of Titles cccxxvii

Volume 10

Contents ccclxi

Volume 11

Volume 12

Contents . . . .

Complete List of Titles. . . . .

Masterplots

Fourth Edition

Eclogues

Author: Vergil (70-19 B.C.E.)
First published: 43-37 B.C.E. (English translation, 1575)
Type of work: Poetry

Principal characters:
TITYRUS, an aging shepherd, sometimes thought to
  represent Vergil
MALIBOEUS, an exile
CORYDON, a lovelorn shepherd boy
DAPHNIS, in the fifth eclogue, a shepherd hero who has
  recently died
GALLUS, a poet and military leader, a friend of Vergil

Vergil's ten eclogues made their young author a renowned figure when they were first made public in approximately 39 B.C.E. Although these poems do not reach the heights of the *Georgics* (c. 37-29 B.C.E.) or the *Aeneid* (c. 29-19 B.C.E.), they are the work of a master, not the hesitant stumblings of an apprentice writer. Vergil made the pastoral form, first popularized by Theocritus, his own and paved the way for many English poets who imitated him, among them Edmund Spenser, Philip Sidney, John Milton, Percy Bysshe Shelley, and Matthew Arnold.

Vergil's pastoral world is not populated by Dresden-china shepherdesses in a never-never landscape; while his shepherds have their lighthearted moments, they inhabit real Italian hills and farms from which they can be evicted by unjust landlords. Exile, loneliness, and poverty threaten many of the characters in the poems. Even the traditional lovelorn shepherds are tied to Vergil's world by the naturalness of the landscape in which they lament; the heat of the Italian summer, the shade of the willow tree, the rocky hillsides where sheep pasture—all are part of the total effect of the eclogues.

Much scholarly effort has been directed toward proving that these poems are allegories that deal with contemporary events. It seems more fruitful and more realistic to accept the fact that Vergil is commenting on conditions of his age. One need not search for disguised poets and government officials. There is no certainty that any shepherd represents the poet's own view, although he has often been identified with Tityrus in the first eclogue.

This poem is one of the most realistic of the group; it reflects the days after Julius Caesar's assassination when residents of northern Italy were dispossessed to provide land for discharged soldiers. Maliboeus, one of the speakers, is among the exiles. He has left his newborn goats on the rocky road as he makes his way toward a new home in Africa, Scythia, or Britain. He laments the fact that the land he has labored to cultivate must fall into the hands of some barbarous

veteran, and he inquires how his friend Tityrus has managed to escape the general desolation. Tityrus explains that he went to Rome to plead for his land and that a youth, whom some have identified with Augustus, granted his request, leaving him free to enjoy the humming of the bees on his neighbor's land. He offers his sympathy and his simple hospitality to the unfortunate Maliboeus.

The second eclogue is the disjointed lament of the Sicilian shepherd, Corydon, for his disdainful beloved, Alexis. Vergil conveys the character of Corydon brilliantly in his passionate, illogical outbursts, uttered as the boy wanders in the hot midday sun, when even lizards have sought shelter, recognizing the futility of his love, yet unable to forget the scornful youth and settle down to care properly for his vines.

Among the most vividly conceived personages of the eclogues are the two brash young shepherds who amicably insult each other in the third poem. Damoetas and Menalcas taunt each other with misdeeds they have witnessed; Damoetas has seen his friend slashing at a farmer's grapevines, while Menalcas suspects Damoetas of trying to steal a goat from Damon's flock. Damoetas spiritedly defends himself; he had won the goat legitimately in a singing match, but Damon refused to pay the prize. Menalcas scoffs at the notion of Damoetas's possessing such skill, and he is immediately challenged to a contest. The ensuing song follows the traditional pattern; the challenger sings one verse, then his opponent adds a second in keeping with the first, and the song moves from invocations to Jove and Apollo to tributes to the sweethearts of each singer to realistic comments on the scene. Each singer concludes with a riddle, and Palaemon, who has been brought in as judge, decides that both deserve prizes, as do all who know the joy or bitterness of love.

The most famous of these poems is the fourth, or Messianic, eclogue, in which Vergil prophesies the birth of a child who will usher in a new golden age when peace will prevail, humanity and nature will become self-sufficient, commerce will cease, and the land will need no further plowing and pruning. The poet laments that he will not survive to see this new age come to fruition, but he rejoices at being able to bid the infant to smile at his mother.

The identity of the expected child has been cause for extensive speculation; both Antony and Augustus became fathers about this time, and Vergil may have refused out of political expediency to single out one or the other. Throughout the Middle Ages, however, Vergil was thought to have foreseen the birth of Christ; for this reason, he became for later ages a kind of pagan saint.

The pastoral elegy, the form of the fifth eclogue, has been imitated more often than any of the other types of poetry in this collection. Readers of English poetry may find many echoes of Mopsus's lament for Daphnis, who is mourned by nymphs, by lions, and by the men whom he taught to celebrate Bacchic rites. Since his death, crops have failed, as if the flowers also lamented; only thorns and thistles grow where the violet and narcissus were planted. Mopsus's elegy concludes with a request for shepherds to build a mound for Daphnis and to carve an epitaph commending his fame and loveliness.

Menalcas rhapsodizes over his friend's verse, then begins his own elegy, in which he places Daphnis, now deified, at the gate of heaven, bringing peace to all the countryside. The mountains and rocks rejoice and the shepherds worship their new god in joyous rites. The contrasting moods of grief and exaltation remained a part of the pastoral tradition throughout succeeding ages, in poems such as Milton's *Lycidas* (1637; published 1638) and Shelley's *Adonais* (1821).

The prologue to the sixth eclogue gives interesting insight into Vergil's poetic ambitions. The speaker, Tityrus, comments that his earliest poetry was in the Sicilian vein, pastoral, but that he had turned to kings and battles for a time, until Apollo cautioned him that a shepherd poet should sing of the countryside. Therefore, he depends on others to celebrate the great deeds of his friend Varus, while he must be content to dedicate to him his rustic song about the old satyr, Silenus, who tells young satyrs and naiads old tales about the creation, the Golden Age, the fate of Prometheus, and many other mythological legends. The reference within the poem to a scene in which the Muses bestow a reed pipe upon Gallus, one of the best-known writers of Vergil's time, has led to the suggestion that, in this eclogue, allusions are made to Gallus's work. The range of subject matter is wide, and there seems to be little connection between the various episodes in Silenus's narrative.

In the seventh eclogue, another singing match is described. The song of Corydon and Thyrsis reflects Vergil's deep love for the countryside and for the simplicity of the life of the shepherds. The reader can almost see the mossy springs, the budding vines of the early spring, and the chestnuts.

The eighth poem is addressed to a Roman hero, variously identified as the consul, Pollio, who is mentioned within the body of the poem, or as Augustus. Vergil will attempt to please this nobleman with the pastoral song he requests, while he waits for a chance to record his heroic exploits. In the lyric itself, Damon and Alphesiboeus recite songs for each other. The first is a lament for the infidelity of Nysa, Damon's beloved, who has married Mopsus. The deserted shepherd is both scornful and sentimental—at one moment, recalling his first childhood meeting with the girl, at another, bitterly berating the bridegroom or mourning the cold cruelty of the god of love. All nature should be upturned, with the wolf fleeing from the lamb and apples growing on oak trees, when such a love does not take its natural course. The singer sees no final recourse but death; he will plunge from the mountaintop into the waves below.

Alphesiboeus's song is a curious one. He speaks as a young girl who is trying to lure her lover home from town by witchcraft, and the song begins with a number of spells. The ashes on the girl's altar flame spontaneously in the last stanza, and she expresses her hope that the absent shepherd is, indeed, coming.

The mood of the first poem is re-created in the ninth as Moeris tells his friend Lycidas that he has been evicted from his property by a new owner. Lycidas expresses surprise; he had heard that Menalcas's poetry had preserved that land. Moeris, made wise in the world's ways by misfortune, replies that there is such a rumor, but that poetry has no force against the soldiers who are taking over the land. He and Menalcas barely escape with their lives. The thought that they might have lost the best of their shepherd poets recalls some of his lines to Lycidas and Moeris, and they quote them as they talk. One passage, referring to the new, beneficent star of "Olympian Caesar," has aroused special interest, since it obviously refers to the recently deceased Julius Caesar. This eclogue ends with an appealing scene, as Lycidas urges Moeris to stop and rest beside the calm lake they are passing and to sing as they watch countrymen pruning their vines.

The final poem is another tribute to Gallus, who was a highly competent military leader as well as a fine poet; he was viceroy of Egypt after the defeat of Marc Antony at the battle of Actium. Unfortunately, his pride led to his political downfall and probably also to the loss of his poetry; readers must rely on Vergil's praise for an estimate of his talents.

Gallus's mistress, Lycoris, to whom most of his love poetry has been addressed, runs away to the north of Italy with another soldier. In Vergil's poem, her betrayed lover laments her loss, followed by sympathetic shepherds. He resolves to seek what comfort he can in writing pastoral verse and hunting the wild boar, yet he cannot restrain a poignant hope that the sharp glaciers of the Alps will not cut the feet of his lost lady. He realizes, finally, that even poetry and hunting are powerless to mollify the god of love; he can only yield and accept his misery. The *Eclogues* present a theme constant throughout Vergil's writings: a longing for a return to a Golden Age. In these verses, he hints at what will become apparent in his magnum opus, the *Aeneid*: the establishment of the Roman Empire as it was to exist under Augustus after the Pax Romana was declared and Roman rule preserved peace throughout the Mediterranean region for more than a century. As early as 39 B.C.E., Vergil saw in the rise of his friend Octavian (the future Augustus) the fulfillment of a form of manifest destiny for the Roman people. The coming age, celebrated in the fourth eclogue, was to be one much like that Arcadian era celebrated in the poems of the Greek writer Theocritus, Vergil's model for his first sustained poetic endeavor.

Vergil borrows heavily from Greek predecessors, especially the poet Theocritus, whose short poems celebrating the pastoral life were models for a number of Roman writers. Like Theocritus, Vergil speaks wistfully of the simple country life where political cares rarely intrude and where love, not war, serves as the primary agent of both discord and harmony. Even in these early compositions, Vergil expresses the sentiment for which he has become famous for two millennia: The *lachrymae rerum*, the "tears in things," a sensitive, melancholy realization that even the most idyllic scenes and experiences possess within themselves the power to move one to sadness when one realizes the transitory nature of existence.

After reading these highly ornate poems, it is easy to find oneself agreeing with critics who complain about the artificiality of their composition and about the forced union of mythology and philosophy. Readers caught up in the beauty and sentiment of individual eclogues may miss an important element that gives further significance to Vergil's composition. The arrangement of the ten poems exhibits a careful pattern, deliberately chosen by the author to provide an implicit contrast between the pastoral world of his shepherds and the political situation in his own country. The references to contemporary events highlight the contrasts between the world of political and military strife of the decades immediately preceding the composition of the *Eclogues*, and the Arcadian world of perpetual peace that Vergil celebrates in these ten poems.

The *Eclogues* are carefully divided into two sets of five poems each: The first five are forward-looking, peaceful, and patriotic; the second five are ambiguous, concerned with the past, and dominated by discussions of unworthy love. Individual eclogues from the first group seem to be paired with complementary (or contrasting) ones in the second. The neat structure gives the work a unity of purpose that transcends the focus of any single eclogue; this pattern is one repeated infrequently in literature until the nineteenth and twentieth centuries, when the assemblage of fragments to create a unified impression becomes an acceptable method for reflecting the concerns of the modern world; Alfred, Lord Tennyson's *Idylls of the King* (1859-1885) and T. S. Eliot's *The Waste Land* (1922) are inheritors of this Vergilian method of composition.

Vergil's *Eclogues* brought a new note of personal feeling and a fresh appreciation of nature into the highly artificial and rhetorical poetic tradition of his time. It is in large part this element of humanity that has sustained the appeal of his pastorals.

Revised by Laurence W. Mazzeno

Further Reading

Griffin, Jasper. *Virgil*. New York: Oxford University Press, 1986. Basic introduction to Vergil's poetry. The second chapter exclusively addresses the *Eclogues* and provides a rewarding discussion of the themes of Arcadia and the tension between nature and the urban life in Rome. Includes index and bibliography.

Leach, Eleanor Winsor. *Vergil's Eclogues: Landscapes of Experience*. Ithaca, N.Y.: Cornell University Press, 1974. Detailed introduction and analysis of the work. Includes a sophisticated reading of poetic symbolism in the *Eclogues* and in Vergil's poetry in general, as well as interpretation of Roman views on nature and the world. Copious illustrations and photographs enhance the text.

Lee, Guy, trans. *Virgil: The Eclogues*, by Vergil. Harmondsworth, England: Penguin Books, 1984. The introduction provides a general but thorough discussion of pastoral poetry, Vergil's contribution to the tradition, and a historical overview of the poet's life and the *Ecologues'* composition. Includes a useful bibliography of primary and secondary sources.

Putnam, Michael C. J. *Virgil's Pastoral Art: Studies in the Eclogues*. Princeton, N.J.: Princeton University Press, 1970. Detailed, scholarly analysis of all important aspects of the *Eclogues*, including themes and their historical context.

Saunders, Timothy. *Bucolic Ecology: Virgil's "Eclogues" and the Environmental Literary Tradition.* London: Duckworth, 2008. Analyzes the importance of nature in defining the ten poems by analyzing their relation to astronomy, geography, topography, landscape, and ecology.

Slavitt, David R. *Virgil.* New Haven, Conn.: Yale University Press, 1991. A solid source. Chapter 1 focuses on the *Eclogues* and provides a straightforward explanation of its relation to ancient poetry and its influence on subsequent and modern literature. Includes a bibliography of primary and secondary sources and an index.

Van Sickle, John. *The Design of Virgil's Bucolics.* 2d ed. London: Bristol Classical, 2004. Argues that the ten Eclogues were conceived as a concerted whole, which Van Sickle calls the *Book of Bucolics.* Analyzes recurring motifs in the *Eclogues,* including the return of a golden age and a new mythology. Describes how *Eclogues* laid the groundwork for Vergil's later works, *Aeneid* and *Georgics.* The second edition contains an updated introduction by the author.

Volk, Katharina, ed. *Vergil's "Eclogues."* New York: Oxford University Press, 2008. Collection of essays about the work, including discussions of their poetic technique, a review of scholarly approaches to the work since the 1970's, and analyses of some of the individual eclogues. An article by Noble Prize-winning poet Seamus Heaney examines the "staying power" of this pastoral.

The Edge of the Storm

Author: Agustín Yáñez (1904-1980)
First published: Al filo del agua, 1947 (English translation, 1963)
Type of work: Novel
Type of plot: Social realism
Time of plot: Spring, 1909, to spring, 1910
Locale: Near Guadalajara, Mexico

Principal characters:
DON DIONISIO, the parish priest
MARÍA and MARTA, his nieces
PADRE ISLAS and PADRE REYES, assistant priests
DAMIÁN LIMÓN, a young man
MICAELA RODRÍGUEZ, a spoiled young woman
VICTORIA, a young widow, visiting from Guadalajara
GABRIEL, a young man reared by Don Dionisio
LUIS GONZAGA PÉREZ, a seminary student
MERCEDES TOLEDO, another young woman
LUCAS MACÍAS, a soothsayer

The Story:

Don Timoteo Limón is finishing his personal devotions when he becomes aware that a dog is howling continuously and that he forgot to pray to several saints. Terrorized by the plaintive sound of the dog, which recalls to him the tragedy of his young daughter Rosalía, Don Timoteo has visions of past events. One such event that makes him feel guilty is his killing a man in self-defense. The officials exonerated him, but the image of the dead man's face still haunts him. He then links the dog's howling to the fate of his son Damián, who went to the United States to seek his fortune. Soon after going to bed, Don Timoteo Limón is disturbed by his visualizations of desirable women and finally gets up to sprinkle holy water over his pillow, sheets, and windows. He concludes that his evil thoughts result from superstitions concerning the dog's howling and decides to attend a religious retreat.

The same night Mercedes Toledo is unable to sleep after receiving Julián's letter. As does Don Timoteo Limón, Mercedes wrestles with horrifying thoughts and contemplates taking refuge in a religious institution. Later that night upon her return from Mexico City, Micaela Rodríguez is restless because of visions of a happy, modern life away from her small hometown. She resolves to scandalize the Daughters of Mary, an organization for unmarried maidens with strict rules, in the following manner: first, arousing envy with her pretty clothes; second, conversing about the interesting life outside the village; and, third, stealing the attractive men away from the maidens. Her plan involves scandalous conduct, and Micaela thinks she will be hated and therefore will have to leave the stagnant, hypocritical people of the village. She is pleased.

At the men's retreat, the principal parish priest, Dionisio Martínez, meets with Father Reyes and five other priests; they hear confessions and meditate on sin, death, judgment, hell, the Lord's Passion, and the parable of the prodigal son. Although Don Timoteo Limón and other villagers feel uneasy because they find themselves standing next to their enemies, Father Reyes uses tact to quell the bitter feelings. The priests frighten the men by talking about the terrible assaults of the devil and end the retreat by depicting the impending days of sadness.

Don Dionisio is caring for his orphaned nieces, María and Marta, as well as for the bell ringer, Gabriel. The priest quits his subscription to a magazine because it stimulates María's interest in travel; he forbids her to read geography books or to visit Micaela Rodríguez since she dresses indecently and converses inappropriately after her trip to Mexico City. Marta loves children and wants to adopt Leonardo's child Martinita after the death of her mother. Marta shows her devotion to her religious beliefs and demonstrates her ability to give helpful advice, but she expresses thoughts and feelings that she cannot understand. Gabriel becomes infatuated with the widow Victoria. As a result of his confused emotions, he rings the church bells excessively and later leaves the village.

Luis Gonzaga Pérez returns from the seminary with strict moral standards and projects that must be implemented on a timetable. Holy Week brings him great joy. His change from a fearful to a happy personality is shown by his desire to create great harmonies, to paint impressive murals, or to compose a poem that will become recognized in world literature. He becomes angered when Father Martínez will not allow him to carry the canopy in the procession. Pérez flees to the mountains as he feels mystical rapture increasing on Good Friday. The hot sun beating down upon his head, he contorts his face to drive away evil thoughts but, overwhelmed with despair, loses consciousness. Shortly thereafter, Pérez's mind becomes permanently impaired.

Father Islas is the chaplain of the Daughters of Mary Immaculate. He advocates the traditional beliefs of the Catholic Church, using the idea of the purity of the maidens in order to discourage the young women from marrying. In spite of his unhealthy appearance, Islas commands the maidens' loyalty, gaining authority through various superstitious devices: amazing examples of prophecy and healing, levitation, trances, and the multiplication of food. The maidens esteem Father Islas as a saint beyond reproach. However, after collapsing from an attack of epilepsy, he leaves the priesthood, disillusioning his parishioners. The highly qualified Don Dionisio is then appointed head priest.

Damián Limón returns home and is castigated for having gone to such a sinful place where Mexicans are mistreated. After precipitating his father's heart attack over a dispute about his inheritance, Damián murders Micaela after an illicit love affair. The light sentence given to him by a corrupt political boss enables him to join the revolutionaries at the end. After learning that Gabriel declared his love for her because of Victoria, who also encouraged him to study music, María chooses to seek love. Condemned by the villagers for protecting the killer Damián, she decides to join the revolutionary army. Lucas Macías, the chronicler, links the appearance of Halley's Comet with the coming of Francisco Madero, the man who is to provide leadership against the tyranny of Porfirio Díaz.

"The Story" by Linda Prewett Davis

Critical Evaluation:

Al filo del agua (literally, on the edge of the water) is a Spanish phrase with two meanings. It signifies the moment that the rain begins. The phrase is also used in reference to something imminent. The imminent in Agustín Yáñez's novel, the Mexican Revolution, was brought on by dissatisfaction with the political situation and by social unrest. The Roman Catholic Church was one of Mexico's institutions on which the unrest was focused; hence the emphasis on religion in the novel. Reform of the political system and land distribution were other causes for the revolution.

By 1910, Porfirio Díaz had been dictator of Mexico for more than thirty years. He had ruled with an iron hand, and only recently had the dream of political freedom and social improvement begun to filter through to the many semi-isolated towns of Mexico. The same few families had always been the social leaders and political bosses in the towns, and Díaz's thirty-odd years of rule had done nothing to lessen this inequity or to improve the lot of the common people. Education was nonexistent except for the privileged few, and superstition was rampant.

Another force that held the people in its grip was the Church, a circumstance especially true in rural areas where Juarez's 1859 Reform Laws seldom reached. These laws had greatly reduced the political power of the church, and such things as processions and public religious festivities were forbidden. In the small towns, however, the priests often continued such ecclesiastical activities in spite of the law.

Yáñez paints against this historical background a series of character studies portraying the effects of a narrow, rigid, dull, and conventional life on people of different ages, with varying degrees of education and exposure to outside influences. These influences, being, in the eyes of the village, outside ones and therefore bad, include such things as freemasonry, bright clothing, strangers, uncensored writings, fun, spiritualists, and people who had been to the United States. The list could go on and on. Yáñez creates a sense of monotonous gloom with the sure hand of an artist who has experienced this kind of life himself. The fictitious but typical town in which the action takes place is set in the state of Jalisco, of which the author was a native.

Each morning the church bells in this town call the people out of their beds as early as four o'clock to begin another dreary, quiet, prayerful day. Life is taken very seriously. The women wear dark, somber colors and do not leave the house except to go to church or to do necessary errands. There is no visiting except in the case of extreme illness or a death in the house of a neighbor. There is little laughter, dancing, or singing. Strangers and strangeness are condemned. Nonconformity, even in small things, starts tongues wagging. At the end of each unvarying day, the church bells send the people to bed, an act that for many means the onset of sleepless hours of anxiety or of wrestling with guilty consciences and of wondering when and in what form God's wrath will be brought down upon their heads.

With this daily pattern providing the atmosphere, broken only by funerals, special fiesta days, and an occasional scandal, the action in the story begins as the people are preparing for their Lenten and Easter activities. The panorama of people and events proceeds through the year, displaying the special religious days of June; the expected deaths, illnesses, and bad luck in August; the celebration of patriotic holidays in September; the scandalous prank of the students home for vacation in November; and the Christmas season with its festivities, which continues on into the New Year, at which time the people are awaiting the appearance of Halley's Comet. This event is being anticipated so intently by Lucas Macías, the soothsayer, that the rest of the people prepare for trouble, for Lucas has from the start associated the appearance of the comet with the stepping onto the scene of Francisco Madero, the man who is to lead the revolution against the tyranny of Díaz.

The person who can most nearly be described as the main character is Don Dionisio, the stern and upright but just and compassionate parish priest. He alone touches in some way upon the lives of all the other characters in the book. His help comes from two assistant priests, who present a vivid contrast to each other. One, Padre Reyes, is liberal and forward-looking; the other, Padre Islas, is narrow and conservative. Although Padre Reyes is much more likable, it is Padre Islas, scurrying along the street from church to home so as to avoid meeting his parishioners on a personal basis, who wields more influence on the lives of the townspeople, for it is he who directs the organization to which all the unmarried girls belong. Into their minds he instills the urgent need to stay pure by remaining single, and he imbues them with a sense of guilt for thinking even wholesome thoughts connected with the opposite sex. This narrow man never uses the chapel of the Holy Family but always the chapel of the Virgin Mary, and Padre Reyes, the other assistant, is not above teasing him by asking if he thinks María and Juan will make a nice couple, or if he is aware that Mercedes is about ready to make someone a good wife. These questions are calculated to enrage Padre Islas. Padre Reyes, with his modern ideas about such things as life insurance—too far removed from the imaginations of the people to be noticed—is largely ignored, while Padre Islas is revered as a saint beyond the temptations and afflictions of ordinary man. Great is the disillusionment when the good Father Islas is found collapsed on the floor of the church in a fit of epilepsy, which results in his having to be removed permanently from the priesthood. The archbishop chooses wisely when Don Dionisio is made head priest, for he approaches the problems of his parishioners with the best elements of the philosophies of his two assistants—an urgent sense of responsibility for their souls accompanied by a forgiving and understanding heart.

Two other personalities who present a study in contrasts are María and Marta, the orphaned nieces of Don Dionisio, who has reared them since they were very small. At the time the story begins, they are in their twenties, unmarried, and on the verge of taking opposite paths in life. Marta is contented with her love for children, her work in the hospital, and other gentle occupations. She is the ideal end product of the social and religious forces at work in her environment. María is rebellious. She has read forbidden literature—for example, *Les Trois Mousquetaires* (1844; *The Three Musketeers*, 1846) and newspapers from the capital—behind her uncle's back. María runs away with a woman of very questionable reputation to follow the revolutionary army. She is a creature of reaction against her unnatural environment.

What happens to María happens, with variations, to nearly all the young people who have had contact in any way with the outside world. Luis Gonzaga Pérez, a young and talented seminary student, is unable to reconcile his inhibitions concerning the opposite sex with his natural desires, and at the end of the novel, he is drawing lewd pictures on the walls of his room in an insane asylum.

Damián Limón, the young son of a fairly prosperous landowner, leaves home, like the prodigal son, and goes to the United States to work. Upon his return home, when criticized for going to such a sinful place, where Mexicans are treated like dogs, he counters by stating that at least there Mexicans are paid in money instead of in promises as in Mexico. Damián becomes scandalously involved in a flagrant love affair and kills the woman, Micaela Rodríguez, after having just caused his father to have a fatal heart attack over an argument about his father's will. A corrupt political boss has a disgracefully light sentence placed upon him, and at the end of the story, he rides away to join the ranks of the revolutionaries.

The parents of Micaela, a spoiled only child, make the mistake of taking her to Mexico City for a few months. There she sees the parties, pretty clothes, and merriment of the capital's young people. Never again is she satisfied to stay in her dreary hometown, and, failing to force her parents to move away to a livelier place, she threatens vengeance on the environment that binds her and shocks the town to its roots with her shameless flirting and indecent dress. She is finally stabbed by a jealous lover but dies forgiving him and putting the blame for her death on her own actions.

Doubt seems to be the villain that causes the downfall of these unfortunate young people. They taste of the world, compare it with their narrow surroundings, and find the surroundings wanting. Being few in number, these unlucky ones fall under the weight of a relentless social system that will tolerate no questioning. They turn their doubt of the system inward and begin to doubt themselves.

In the novel, the time is near at hand, however, when many doubters will join together with enough force to make a crack in the wall of hypocrisy that characterized Mexican society at the time. That crack would become ever wider as education seeped through. This is the meaning of the title of the novel. Yáñez gives the reader an unprejudiced and intricately detailed view of life in a Mexican town shortly after the beginning of the twentieth century. The book is not a call to arms to reform; rather, it presents an understanding, scathingly honest, and touching portrait.

Further Reading

Anderson, Mark D. "Agustín Yáñez's Total Mexico and the Embodiment of the National Subject." *Bulletin of Spanish Studies* 84, no. 1 (January, 2007): 79-99. Argues that *The Edge of the Storm* may be the first "total novel" in Mexico, a term used to describe a Spanish American novel that expresses universal literary values. Examines how in this novel Yáñez rewrites outmoded nineteenth century fiction from a twentieth century perspective.

Brushwood, John S. *The Spanish American Novel: A Twentieth-Century Survey*. Austin: University of Texas Press, 1975. Situates Yáñez's novel in the nineteenth century by discussing the major characteristics and innovations of fiction. Analyzes the contribution of *The Edge of the Storm* to Spanish American literature.

Detjens, Wilma Else. *Home as Creation: The Influence of Early Childhood Experience in the Literary Creation of Gabriel García Márquez, Agustín Yáñez, and Juan Rulfo*. New York: Peter Lang, 1993. Describes how Yáñez's childhood home, the people he knew as a child, and events in Mexican history influenced the geographic setting and other elements of *The Edge of the Storm*.

Harris, Christopher. *The Novels of Agustín Yáñez: A Critical Portrait of Mexico in the Twentieth Century*. Lewiston, N.Y.: E. Mellen Press, 2000. Argues that Yáñez was a social critic as well as an innovative novelist. Demonstrates how in his novels Yáñez denounces government corruption and restrictions on artistic freedom.

Langford, Walter M. *The Mexican Novel Comes of Age*. Notre Dame, Ind.: University of Notre Dame Press, 1971. Explains why the publication of *The Edge of the Storm* marks a significant accomplishment in the development of the Mexican novel. Discusses the structure of Yáñez's work.

Lindstrom, Naomi. *Twentieth-Century Spanish American Fiction*. Austin: University of Texas Press, 1994. Defines the continuities that link the different periods in modern Spanish American literature. Discusses significant elements in *The Edge of the Storm*.

Sommers, Joseph. *After the Storm: Landmarks of the Modern Mexican Novel*. Albuquerque: University of New Mexico Press, 1968. Evaluates the significance of Yáñez's work in the history of the novel. Provides an informative commentary on the novelist's epoch.

Williams, Raymond Leslie. "The Novels of Agustín Yáñez." In *The Modern Latin American Novel*. New York: Twayne, 1998. Discusses Latin American novels that were published since the rise of modernist fiction in the region in the mid-1940's, devoting a brief chapter to the works of Yáñez.

The Edible Woman

Author: Margaret Atwood (1939-   )
First published: 1969
Type of work: Novel
Type of plot: Comedy of manners
Time of plot: Mid-twentieth century
Locale: Toronto, Ontario, Canada

Principal characters:
MARIAN MCALPIN, a young woman
AINSLEY TEWCE, her roommate
PETER WOLLANDER, Marian's fiancé
CLARA BATES, Marian's friend
JOE BATES, Clara's husband
LEN SLANK, Marian's friend
DUNCAN, Marian's friend
FISCHER "FISH" SMYTHE, and
TREVOR, Duncan's roommates

The Story:

Marian McAlpin, a recent college graduate, works for Seymour Surveys, a marketing research company. One hot summer day she and her roommate, Ainsley Tewce, visit Clara and Joe Bates, who live nearby and have two small children. Clara is seven months pregnant, and her house is in disarray. She sits languidly in the garden, holding a baby, while Joe cooks dinner and changes the babies' diapers. Later, Ainsley tells Marian that she has decided to have a child. Although she does not want to get married, she plans to find an appropriate man to father the child. Marian tries unsuccessfully to dissuade her.

Working the next day, Marian conducts a door-to-door survey about a proposed advertisement for Moose Beer. One person who responds to the survey with interesting but ambiguous answers is a mysterious young man named Duncan. Marian meets him unexpectedly in various places: a park, a Laundromat, and a movie theater. Duncan takes her to a mummy exhibition at a museum and invites her for dinner at the apartment he shares with Trevor and Fish, fellow graduate students in English.

Marian's boyfriend, Peter Wollander, is a young lawyer. He is depressed because one of his friends just got married, so Marian hopes to cheer him up by introducing him to her friend Len Slank, who has recently returned from England. They go to a bar and are surprised when they find Ainsley there. She has come to check out Len as a possible father for her child. She has heard that he is attracted to young girls, so she is dressed up to look young, and she orders ginger ale. Peter and Len converse animatedly about hunting and photography. Marian behaves strangely. She cries, although she does not know why. They all go to Len's apartment, and Marian hides under the bed. Upon leaving, she runs away from Peter. He reaches her as a storm is brewing, so she agrees to

get in his car. They watch a lightning storm, and then Peter asks her to marry him.

Meanwhile, Ainsley has decided that Len is an appropriate father for her child. When the time is right, she seduces him. He is horrified to learn that Ainsley is pregnant and tries unsuccessfully to persuade her to have an abortion. She explains that motherhood is necessary for women, and she plans to raise the child herself.

Once engaged to Peter, Marian loses her appetite and feels that she is shrinking or dissolving. She asks Peter to make decisions, such as the day of their wedding or what to order for dinner at restaurants. She stops eating meat and then stops eating other foods as well. When Duncan's friend Trevor invites her for dinner, she tosses her pieces of meat to Duncan, trying to be inconspicuous. The third roommate, Fischer "Fish" Smythe, expounds at great length about birth imagery and the importance of birth, claiming that what is needed is a new pregnant Venus.

In preparation for her child, Ainsley reads books about childcare, attends parenting workshops, and knits baby clothes. One workshop claims that to grow up well adjusted, children need fathers. She hopes Len will agree to marry her for the sake of the child. He refuses.

Peter is holding a party and urges Marian to dress up for it. She invites some of her young coworkers, and Duncan and his two roommates, to attend. She buys a red dress, gets her hair done, and has Ainsley apply dramatic makeup for her. When Duncan arrives at the party he tells her he did not know it was a masquerade, and he does not enter. Instead, he heads for a Laundromat. Both Len and Ainsley attend the party separately. When they encounter each other, they argue, and Ainsley announces to the guests that they are going to have a child. Len responds by angrily pouring his glass of beer over

Ainsley. Duncan's roommate Fish takes off his sweater to dry Ainsley. He is excited to encounter a pregnant woman. Marian is afraid of Peter's camera, as if it will literally shoot or freeze her. She flees his party and goes to the Laundromat to find Duncan.

Duncan has claimed that he is sexually inexperienced, and Marian decides that this is the time for her to initiate him sexually. As she has no money with her and Duncan has little, they find a seedy hotel for the encounter. The next morning, they go out for breakfast, and then Duncan takes her to a snow-covered ravine. Marian asks Duncan to talk to Peter because she does not know what to say to him. However, Duncan says that to do so is impossible and that she must solve her problems herself.

Marian decides she must determine whether her fear of Peter is justified. When he phones her to demand an explanation, he is invited to come to her apartment later. In preparation for their meeting she bakes a cake in the shape of a woman and decorates it with a face, a pink frosting dress, and a bouffant hairdo. Peter arrives, and she presents him with the cake. She tells him that she knows that he had been planning to destroy her, so she made a substitute. Peter leaves hurriedly.

Marian cleans the apartment and invites Duncan over to eat the cake. Duncan is upset because Fish is moving away from his apartment. Marian explains that Fish and Ainsley are getting married and going to Niagara Falls for their honeymoon. Duncan starts to eat the cake, and Marian begins to eat it as well. Duncan pronounces that she is now back to "so-called reality."

Critical Evaluation:

The title of Margaret Atwood's novel *The Edible Woman* exemplifies the theme of commodity and consumption, which is linked to Marian McAlpin's job with a consumer research, or marketing, company. Marian believes that her boyfriend and later fiancé, Peter Wollander, sees her as an item to be consumed, a trophy wife who will be an asset in his climb to success. Food and eating are important patterns of imagery through the novel. There are several dinner parties, and meals are often described in detail. Marian's inability to eat indicates her struggles to make sense of—to digest—a world that often seems ridiculous.

The story is a comedy of manners, a parody of the traditional romance plot in which a young woman rejects an inappropriate suitor to marry the right man. In this novel, neither Peter nor Duncan is the right match for Marian. She becomes engaged to Peter, then breaks off the engagement; her future remains uncertain. The other female characters are caricatures representing different versions of the courtship plot.

The once fragile and beautiful Clara Bates is married and overwhelmed by her family. The three young women in Marian's office are hoping to find mates to marry. Ainsley Tewce is convinced that motherhood is the proper role for a woman. She actively pursues a man to father her child, and to marry her. Similarly, Peter is the stereotyped yuppie, the ambitious lawyer with his carefully chosen wardrobe, fiancé, and proper masculine hobbies of hunting and photography.

The novel incorporates a range of literary allusions, including such fairytales as "The Gingerbread Man" (1875) and "Der Räuberbräutigam" (1812; "The Robber Bridegroom," 1823), in which the groom murders a succession of wives until his last wife outwits him. One of the most important literary intertexts is Lewis Carroll's *Alice's Adventures in Wonderland* (1865), in which a young woman enters a confusing underground world and changes shape, much like the pregnant Clara (or like Marian when she crawls under a bed or stops eating). Fischer "Fish" Smythe discusses *Alice's Adventures in Wonderland* at great length at a dinner party. He claims that the novel is about a young woman struggling to find her feminine identity. This scene is both a parody of pedantic English graduate students and a comment on Marian's struggles in the novel. Both Peter and Ainsley claim that Marian is rejecting her femininity. Rather, she is questioning the ideals of consumerism and female subservience in contemporary Western society.

The novel's narrative strategy reflects Marian's confusion. She narrates part one in the first person. Part two is told in objective third-person, with Marian as the main character. Part three returns to Marian's first-person narration.

Marian's job at Seymour Surveys is to translate the psychological jargon of the marketing questionnaires into understandable prose. Symbolically, Marian is trying to make sense of a confusing society. For help, she often turns to the mysterious Duncan for advice. The waiflike and unkempt graduate student Duncan is the opposite of the practical, well-groomed, ambitious Peter. As a trickster, Duncan provides contradictory and confusing information, but does ultimately prod Marian to resolve her own problems.

The novel ends with a symbolic feast, a celebration of Marian's freedom from the subservient role that marriage to Peter would bring. She regains her independence and eats again.

Karen F. Stein

Further Reading

Bouson, J. Brooks. *Brutal Choreographies: Oppositional Strategies and Narrative Design in the Novels of Marga-*

ret Atwood. Amherst: University of Massachusetts Press, 1993. Bouson's second chapter, "*The Edible Woman*'s Refusal to Consent to Femininity," discusses the courtship process as a predatory hunting ritual. In refusing marriage, Marian rejects subservience to claim her own power.

Howells, Coral Ann. *Margaret Atwood.* New York: St. Martin's Press, 1996. A lively critical and biographical study that elucidates issues that have energized all of Atwood's fiction: feminist issues, literary genres, and her own identity as a Canadian, a woman, and a writer.

_____, ed. *The Cambridge Companion to Margaret Atwood.* New York: Cambridge University Press, 2006. This collection of twelve excellent essays critically examines Atwood's novels, including *The Edible Woman.* Includes a concise biography of the author.

Keith, W. J. *Introducing Margaret Atwood's "The Edible Woman."* Toronto, Ont.: ECW Press, 1989. Intended as a reader's guide, this book provides a chronology of Atwood's life and works and a useful, accessible chapter-by-chapter summary and analysis of the novel.

MacLulich, T. D. "Atwood's Adult Fairy Tale: Lévi-Strauss, Bettelheim, and *The Edible Woman.*" In *Critical Essays on Margaret Atwood,* edited by Judith McCombs. Boston: G. K. Hall, 1988. This essay focuses on the novel's depiction of food and eating. Draws from Claude Lévi-Strauss's analysis of mythic structure as a way of mediating between culture and nature, and then compares *The Edible Woman* to the children's story "The Gingerbread Man."

Stein, Karen F. *Margaret Atwood Revisited.* New York: Twayne, 1999. This book is intended as a guide for the general reader. Stein's third chapter focuses on Atwood's first three novels. Its section on *The Edible Woman* analyzes the book as a darkly comic parody of romance fiction, consumerism, advertising, and courtship.

Stow, Glenys. "Nonsense as Social Commentary in *The Edible Woman.*" *Journal of Canadian Studies / Revue d'etudes Canadiennes* 23, no. 3 (1988): 90-101. Stow compares *The Edible Woman* to Lewis Carroll's *Alice's Adventures in Wonderland.* She points to Atwood's use of techniques of nonsense writing such as distortion and exaggeration to call attention to the oppressive nature of modern society.

Wilson, Sharon Rose. *Margaret Atwood's Fairy-Tale Sexual Politics.* Toronto, Ont.: ECW Press, 1993. Wilson finds that Atwood makes extensive use of fairytale plots in her novels. The chapter "Cannibalism and Metamorphosis in *The Edible Woman:* 'The Robber Bridegroom'" compares a range of fairytales with *The Edible Woman.*

The Education of Henry Adams

Author: Henry Adams (1838-1918)
First published: 1907
Type of work: Autobiography

The Education of Henry Adams intimately traces Henry Adams's thought processes, but it does so on an intellectual plane not generally achieved by most writers. For style and content, this book ranks with the finest of American autobiographies.

Adams was born in Boston in 1838 into the illustrious Brooks and Adams families. He was the grandson and great-grandson of two former U.S. presidents. He matured in a period of mechanical and industrial invention, but he had been raised in a colonial atmosphere. He remembers that his first serious encounter with his grandfather, former president John Quincy Adams, had occurred when the youngster had refused to go to school one day. His grandfather led him there by the hand. For the young Adams, the death of the former president had marked the end of his eighteenth century, colonial environment.

The major theme of *The Education of Henry Adams* is the multiplication and acceleration of mechanical forces. These forces, Adams argued, led to the breakdown of moral relationships among people and to the degeneration of their pursuits into money seeking or complete lassitude. The book also deals with the way in which modern science had produced a view of the universe radically different from the view held before the end of the nineteenth century, so much so that Adams called this new world a multiverse. The term "multiverse" meant, in Adams's day, a universe in chaos, lacking any kind of ordering principle.

Adams's father, Charles Francis Adams, had been instrumental in forming the Free-Soil Party in 1848, and he ran for vice president of the United States on the party's ticket with Martin Van Buren. The younger Adams believed that his own education—Puritan morality, politics, and literary matters—was chiefly an inheritance from his father. In later life, looking back on his formal education, he concluded that this education had been a failure. As an adult, he realized that what he had needed as a student were courses in mathematics, French, German, and Spanish—not Latin and Greek.

Prompted by his teacher, James Russell Lowell, Adams spent nearly two years abroad after his graduation from Harvard. He enrolled in a program to study civil law in Germany, but he found the lecture system atrocious. He then devoted most of his stay in Europe to experiencing art, opera, and theater. When he returned to Boston in 1860, he settled down briefly to study law. In the elections that year, however, his father was chosen to be a U.S. representative. Adams accompanied him to Washington, D.C., as his secretary. There he met John Hay, who became his best friend.

In 1861, U.S. president Abraham Lincoln had chosen Charles Adams, Henry's father, to be minister to England. Henry once again followed his father. The Adams party had barely disembarked when they heard bad news: England had recognized the belligerency of the Confederacy. The North was now England's undeclared enemy. The Battle of Bull Run proved so crushing a blow to American prestige that Charles had believed he was in England on a day-to-day sufferance. He remained in England until 1868.

By the end of the American Civil War, the younger Adams had no means of earning a livelihood. He had earlier developed some taste as a dilettante in art, and he wrote several articles for the *North American Review*. On his return to the United States, Adams noted how he had been impressed by the "movements" of his fellow Americans, who were now harnessing a mechanical energy that led them to "travel," literally and figuratively, in the same direction. In contrast, the Europeans, he believed, were trying to go in several directions at one time. Still, handicapped by his limited education and by his long absence from home, he had difficulty adapting to the new industrial America. He achieved some recognition with his essays on, for example, legal tender, and with his essays in the *Edinburgh Review*. He had hoped that he would be offered a government position in the administration of Ulysses S. Grant. However, Grant, a man of action, was not interested in reformers or intellectuals like Adams.

Adams earned a position as an assistant professor of medieval history at Harvard, and taught there for seven years. During this time, he tried to replace the lecture system with seminars and individual research. He found his students apt and quick to respond to this new style. He resigned his position in 1871 and traveled west to Estes Park, Colorado, with a government geological survey. There he met Clarence King, a member of the survey party, with whom he could not help contrasting himself. King had a systematic, scientific education and had his choice of scientific, political, or literary prizes, leading Adams to reflect on his own limitations.

After his flight from Harvard, Adams made his permanent home in Washington, D.C., where he wrote a series of books on American history. In 1893, he visited the Chicago World's Fair. From his observations of the steamship, the locomotive, and the newly invented dynamo, he concluded that force is the one unifying factor in American thought. Back in Washington, he saw the adoption of the gold standard and concluded that the capitalist system and American intervention in Cuba offered signs of the direction in which the country was headed. During a visit to the Great Exposition in Paris in 1900, Adams formulated an important theory. In observing the dynamo, he decided that history is not merely a series of causes and effects, of people acting upon people, but is the record of forces acting upon people. For him, the dynamo became the symbol of force acting upon his own time, just as the Virgin was the symbol of force acting upon the twelfth century.

Adams believed that his education had been a lifelong process. He found that the tools he had been given as a youth were utterly useless, and he spent all of his days forging new ones. As he aged, he realized that the moral standards of his father's and grandfather's times were disintegrating; corruption and greed now existed at the highest political levels. According to his calculations, the rate of change, due to mechanical force, was accelerating, and that the generation of 1900 could rely only on impersonal forces to teach the generation of 2000. He himself saw no end to the multiplicity of forces that he believed were so rapidly dwarfing humanity into insignificance.

As a work of literature, *The Education of Henry Adams* may be read in at least three ways: first, as a conventional autobiography; second, as a work in the mainstream of the European bildungsroman tradition, a personal narrative of one person's intellectual and emotional coming-of-age; and third, as a critical treatise on Western civilization and culture. Some critics have even called the book a kind of novel, especially given that Adams refers to himself not in the first person but in the third person throughout the book. That is, he presents himself as "Henry Adams," "Adams," and the "private secretary," rather than as "I," and he often changes the actual facts of his life.

In the mode of a critical treatise, Adams anticipates the twentieth century's preoccupation with the relationship of technology and science to social and cultural assumptions. Modern science and technology, he feels, completely destroy traditional views of the relationship between the individual and society. The individual becomes a kind of cog in the wheels of society, like a part of a huge machine—a dynamo.

A key chapter in the book is "The Dynamo and the Virgin." Here, Adams uses the two symbols of the dynamo and the Virgin to spell out his analysis of the shaping forces of civilization; the chapter is a synthesis of ideas reflecting his entire education. This excursion into historiography places Adams in the front rank of nineteenth and early twentieth century historical philosophers, for here he posits the thesis that belief had been, in the past, the guiding force of sociopolitical and cultural phenomena. He adds that he does not know what will be the guiding force in the future.

Just as religious beliefs—the Virgin—had created the great works of the Middle Ages, Adams writes, so also the modern belief in science and technology—the dynamo—will shape the major creations of the modern age. At last, though, he views the modern age with trepidation and anxiety, for he realizes that in most ways the humanistic education he received from his family does not suit him for the age of the dynamo. He sees that the machine is destroying moral values of great worth, values that underlie the significant achievements of his great grandfather, John Adams, second president of the United States; his grandfather, John Quincy Adams, sixth president of the United States; and his father, Charles Adams, a U.S. representative and a minister to England. At last, then, Henry Adams defines the major conflicts of twentieth century American civilization, a drama whose denouement remains undecided.

Adams considers his education to have been a complete failure: "One might as well try to educate a gravel-pit," he writes. He had one of the best educations available in his day, yet he insists that this education had prepared him for life not in the twentieth century but for life in the eighteenth century, a time that ended decades before he was born.

Repeatedly in his autobiography, Adams refers to the story of Adam and Eve and the Garden of Eden. In so doing, he is alluding not only to the biblical story and his own surname; he also is referring to the idea of the American Adam, that is, of the new person in the New World, and an idea common in nineteenth century American literature. Adams, however, gives this idea a new twist: He is a new man in a new multiverse consisting of radium, X rays, dynamos, and other forms of power never before dreamed of. Unlike the American Adam in the New World, who quickly makes a home for himself modeled in many ways on Europe, Adams sees himself as a complete stranger in a new multiverse in which none of his previous ideas are of any value. This is a place in which he will never dwell in comfort.

Revised by Richard Tuerk

Further Reading

Adams, Henry. *The Education of Henry Adams: A Centennial Version.* Edited by Edward Chalfant and Conrad Edick Wright. Boston: Massachusetts Historical Society, 2007. Establishes what the editors feel is the correct text of *The Education of Henry Adams.* Identifies people, places, and things in endnotes, and traces the writing and publishing history of the work. Compares Adams's actual life with his portrayal of himself in the book.

Brookhiser, Richard. *America's First Dynasty: The Adamses, 1735-1918.* New York: Free Press, 2002. Treats Adams's life in the context of the lives of his illustrious ancestors and family members. Examines *The Education of Henry Adams* as a story about the times in which Adams lived rather than a story of his life and times.

Dusinberre, William. *Henry Adams: The Myth of Failure.* Charlottesville: University Press of Virginia, 1980. Argues that Adams's literary career should not be judged from *The Education of Henry Adams* alone, and relates the book to Adams's other historical writings.

Levenson, J. C. *The Mind and Art of Henry Adams.* 1957. Reprint. Stanford, Calif.: Stanford University Press, 1968. One of the first important studies to consider Adams's thought in its entirety. Contains an analysis of how *The Education of Henry Adams* fits in the writing life of its author.

O'Toole, Patricia. *The Five of Hearts: An Intimate Portrait of Henry Adams and His Friends, 1880-1918.* New York: Clarkson N. Potter, 1990. An engaging narrative about Adams and his closest associates. Provides valuable insights into the events and emotions that lie behind the writing of *The Education of Henry Adams.*

Rowe, John Carlos, ed. *New Essays on "The Education of Henry Adams."* New York: Cambridge University Press, 1996. Essays interpret the book in terms of twentieth century ideas about education, historiography, gender, and U.S. foreign policy. Includes discussions of the book during the age of imperialism and examines what Adams calls "Being a 'Begonia' in a Man's World."

Samuels, Ernest. *Henry Adams.* Cambridge, Mass.: Belknap Press, 1989. An excellent one-volume biography of Adams, with a discussion of the writing of *The Education of Henry Adams* that links the book to the events of Adams's life.

Simpson, Brooks D. *The Political Education of Henry Adams.* Columbia: University of South Carolina Press, 1996. Simpson recounts Adams's political career, refuting much of the information contained in *The Education of Henry Adams.* Argues that Adams's book is not a reliable source about post-Civil War politics, nor is it a truthful look at Adams's failed political career.

Edward II

Author: Christopher Marlowe (1564-1593)

First produced: c. 1592, as *The Troublesome Reign and Lamentable Death of Edward the Second, King of England, with the Tragical Fall of Proud Mortimer*; first published, 1594; commonly known as *Edward II*

Type of work: Drama

Type of plot: Historical

Time of plot: Fourteenth century

Locale: England and France

Principal characters:
EDWARD II, king of England
PRINCE EDWARD, his son
EDMUND, earl of Kent, half brother to the king
PIERCE DE GAVESTON, earl of Cornwall
GUY, earl of Warwick
THOMAS, earl of Lancaster
LORD MORTIMER, the elder
LORD ROGER MORTIMER, the younger
HUGH SPENCER, earl of Gloucester
QUEEN ISABELLA, wife of King Edward

The Story:

King Edward II recalls his favorite, Pierce de Gaveston, from exile; Gaveston joyfully returns to England. While hurrying to Westminster to rejoin his monarch, he comes upon the king talking to his courtiers. Secretively, he hides from the royal assemblage and overhears the noblemen discussing his repatriation.

They discuss how Edward, an immature and weak-minded yet stubborn man, nourished for Gaveston an unwholesome and unyielding love, in spite of the fact that Edward's father originally banished the man. The noblemen of England, sworn to uphold the decree of exile, hate the royal favorite. Most passionate in his fury is young Mortimer. Others are not far behind Mortimer in their antipathy, and they threaten the king with revolt if Gaveston remains in England. None but the king's brother Edmund will harbor Gaveston. The fiery discussion ends; the nobles stalk off in haughty displeasure.

Gaveston, still in hiding, rejoices in his knowledge of the king's love, for Edward reveals his pettiness by his unconcern for the welfare of his kingdom as weighed against his desire to clasp Gaveston to his bosom once more. When Gaveston reveals his presence, Edward ecstatically rewards him with a series of titles and honors, the scope of which causes even Edmund to comment wryly that Edward outdid himself. Gaveston claims with a smirk that all he desires is to be near his monarch. To add salt to the kingdom's wounds, Edward sentences the Bishop of Coventry, the instigator of Gaveston's exile, to die in the Tower of London.

This action, coupled with the titles and estates lavishly bestowed upon Gaveston, so incenses the rebellious nobility that under the leadership of the two Mortimers, Warwick, and Lancaster, they plot to kill Gaveston. The Archbishop of Canterbury, protesting the damage inflicted upon the Church by the king's folly, allies himself with the plot. Queen Isabella, who professes to love her lord dearly, complains to the noblemen that since Gaveston's return Edward snubs her beyond endurance. She agrees that Gaveston must be done away with, but she cautions the angry noblemen not to injure Edward.

When the rebellious nobility seize Gaveston, Edward, yielding to the archbishop's threat to enforce his papal powers against the king, can do nothing but stand by and allow his beloved friend to be carried off. A bitter exchange of words between the king and his lords is tempered by the gentle sentiments of Gaveston as he bids Edward farewell. Driven by childish anger, perhaps incensed by an intuitive knowledge, Gaveston attacks the queen and accuses her of a clandestine association with the younger Mortimer, a charge that she denies. Sensing his advantage, Edward seizes upon the accusation as a wedge to undermine his enemies, and he compels the queen to use her influence to save Gaveston. The queen, because of her love for Edward and her hopes for a reconciliation, resolves to mend the rift by abetting her husband.

At first the nobles disdainfully refuse to hear her entreaties. Then, having prevailed upon young Mortimer's sympathy, she discloses to him a plot whereby Gaveston could be overthrown and the king obeyed at the same time. Mortimer then convinces the other nobles that if Gaveston is allowed to remain in England, he will become so unpopular that the common people will rise in protest and kill him. There is peace in England once more. Edward affects renewed love for his queen and the lords humbly repledge their fealty to Edward. An undercurrent of meanness prevails, however, in the bosom of young Mortimer, whose sense of justice is outraged at the fact that Edward chose such a baseborn villain as his minion. He still believes that it would be a service to his country to unseat Gaveston, and thus he plots secretly.

At the ceremonial in honor of Gaveston's return, the lords cannot stomach the presence of the king's minion. Bitter sarcasm showers upon Gaveston, and young Mortimer tries to stab him. Edward is so outraged at this show of independence by his peers that he vows vengeance for his dear Gaveston's sake. Even the loyal Edmund cannot brook this display of pettiness on the part of his brother; he deserts Edward to join the nobles.

Edward renews the smoldering accusation against Isabella that she is Mortimer's lover. Defeated in battle, the king's forces, with Gaveston in flight, are split up to confuse the enemy. Warwick, Lancaster, and others succeed in capturing the king's minion and order his death, but Arundel, a messenger from Edward, pleads that Gaveston be allowed to say farewell to the king. One of the nobles, unable to scorn the king's wishes, arranges to escort Gaveston to Edward. With a servant in charge, Gaveston is conducted to a hiding place to spend the night. Warwick, driven by blind hatred and an irrational patriotism, kidnaps the prisoner.

Meanwhile Valois, king of France and Isabella's brother, takes advantage of the revolt in England and seizes Normandy. Edward, displaying the corruption of his statesmanship, dispatches his son, Prince Edward, and Isabella to negotiate a parley with Valois. Arundel reports to Edward that Warwick beheaded Gaveston. Edward, in a wild rage against his lords, swears to sack their lands and to destroy their families. Characteristically, losing his beloved friend, he also declares that henceforth young Spencer will be his favorite. He continues to resist the rebels, and before long Warwick, Lancaster, and Edmund are captured and sentenced to death.

In France, the earl of Gloucester suspects that Isabella is gathering forces to place her son upon the throne. Isabella, in the meantime, is rejected by Valois. Sir John of Hainault rescues the queen and prince by offering to keep the pair at his estate in Flanders until Edward matures sufficiently to rule England. The young prince is already showing signs of royal character and a depth and a magnitude of personality that promise to make him a suitable monarch.

The condemned Mortimer and Edmund escape to France, where Sir John agrees to help them in levying forces to aid Isabella and the prince. Landing at Harwich, the forces of Mortimer and Edmund rout the king, who flees toward Ireland. Stalwart, sincere, and intellectually honest, Edmund, who broke with his brother only after the king drove him too far, relents in his feelings against Edward; he is further disturbed by a suspicion that Isabella is in love with Mortimer. Mortimer becomes a despot in his triumph. Edward is captured and sent to Kenilworth Castle, a prisoner. There he is prevailed upon to surrender his crown to the prince.

With the queen's consent, Mortimer outlines a crafty scheme to kill Edward. He draws up an ambiguous note that orders the king's death in one sense and abjures it in another. When Prince Edward, Isabella, Edmund, and Mortimer argue fiercely to decide upon the prince's protector, the prince reveals his distrust of Mortimer. Edmund, fearing greater disunion, resolves to rescue the imprisoned king. His attempt fails.

Prince Edward is crowned by the Archbishop of Canterbury. Shortly after the coronation the deposed Edward, tortured cruelly in a dungeon, is murdered by Mortimer's hireling, and Edmund is beheaded. Thereupon Edward III, now monarch, orders Mortimer to be hanged and Isabella, suspected of being the nobleman's accomplice in plotting her husband's death, to be taken to the Tower of London.

Critical Evaluation:

Edward II, probably the last play (the dating of his dramas is conjectural) written by Christopher Marlowe before his untimely death, is a chronicle in its highest form. In fact, the drama was in the past attributed to William Shakespeare. Unlike Marlowe's earlier work, this play is polished in form, sustained in theme, and consistent in characterization. Marlowe's first real success in the field of historical drama, *Edward II* sacrifices for a highly dramatic and tragic ending the lyrical beauty of language and of metaphor present in his other plays. A further accomplishment to be noted here is Marlowe's use of a large group of dominant characters; in his earlier plays he employed only two central figures.

Edward II, regarded by many as Marlowe's finest work, shows tighter structure and greater clarity and unity than his earlier works. Since it was published almost immediately after his death, the text escaped the corruption that his other works suffered, and there are relatively few problems with establishing an accurate text. Scholars also possess the source material for the work, Raphael Holinshed's *Chronicles of England, Scotland, and Ireland*, in the edition of 1577 or 1587. By comparing this play with others of its genre and with its source, it is possible to arrive at an appreciation of Marlowe's achievement.

Holinshed's account of the reign of Edward II (r. 1307-1327) is relatively unstructured and, though providing much material, does not establish clear relationships or a connected series of events. Marlowe, who worked closely enough with Holinshed's text to incorporate actual phrases from the chronicle, nevertheless set about to structure the story and bring out salient features, developing relationships and characterizations, and compressing the events of more than twenty years—from Gaveston's return in 1307 to the execution of Mortimer in 1330—into what seems on stage to be a relatively short span. While this creates some problems in terms of improbably swift shifting of loyalties and changes of policy, it gives the drama a forward movement that underscores the alienation of Edward's associates—his wife, the loyal Edmund, and the outraged barons.

This surging wave of hostility is the central event of the play, which begins with the return of the king's beloved Gaveston from exile. Marlowe makes it quite clear that the two men are lovers, but it is not the homosexual relationship that disturbs the barons—in fact, at one point the elder Mortimer explains "the mightiest kings have had their minions," and lists famous pairs of male lovers in history. Rather it is the fact that Edward ignores his role as king for the sake of Gaveston that enrages the nobles. Gaveston is lowborn, but Edward elevates him to share the throne, and in his infatuation, he forgets his duties to his realm. He is following his personal will and shows this weakness in his inability to give up his personal pleasure for the good of his kingdom. He is childish both in his willfulness and in his stubbornness, and he remains blind to the facts of his own misrule and of the justice of the nobles' grievances.

The Tudor world saw rebellion against an anointed king as a grievous breach of natural law, and the play documents the slow evolution of rebellion. At first it is solely against Gaveston that the hostility is directed. Only gradually does this hostility spread to the king, first after the death of Gaveston, and then when Edward fastens his affections upon new flatterers, primarily Spencer. Whereas the loyalty of Gaveston and Edward, for all its folly, had a touch of nobility about it, Spencer is merely a sycophant, and the king, in listening to him, reveals his fatal weakness of character. His early frivolousness turns to vengeance when the barons move to open revolt, and even his loving queen and the loyal Edmund slowly turn against him. It is perhaps a weakness of the play that neither party in the conflict can arouse the audience's admiration; there is no moral framework to the play, no good side and evil side, or even wisdom to oppose the folly. The misrule of the king is overthrown by a Machiavellian villain, the hypocritical Mortimer. Whereas Shakespeare tended to glorify those who put an end to misrule, as does Bolingbroke in *Richard II* (pr. c. 1595-1596, pb. 1600), which bears many similarities to *Edward II*, Marlowe paints a picture of unrelieved gloom, as the rebels, led by the unfaithful queen and the power-grabbing Mortimer, depose the king. It is only at the very end, as Edward III comes to the throne, executing Mortimer and imprisoning the queen, that rightful rule is restored. Edward III specifically seeks the counsel of his nobles before he acts and in so doing restores the reciprocity upon which the well-being of the realm rests.

Beyond the concept of divine right remains the concept that the king must rule not by whim but with concern for the welfare of his land and in concert with his nobles, who, like him, are born to their station. Though the play has strong political overtones, the absence of any developed conflict between right and wrong robs it of the sort of symbolic value that marks Shakespeare's finest history plays. Indeed, the absence of a figure with whom the audience can identify may be in part responsible for the unpopularity of the play, which perhaps because of its historicity lacks the fascination of the powerfully imaginative *Tamburlaine the Great, Part I* (1587) and *Doctor Faustus* (1588).

Marlowe's genius was at its best when expressing strong emotions and characters with extravagant poetic imaginations. In *Edward II* there is less opportunity for such luxuriant language, and for many, the play does not really come alive until the downfall of the king, when in spite of his unsympathetic character, the pathos of his situation commands the involvement of the audience. To be sure, Gaveston is also very much a Marlowe character, perhaps much like Marlowe himself—impulsive, poetic, a lover of pleasure and beauty, both irresponsible and passionate. It is Edward, however, who sticks in the mind. Aside from his touching and loyal love for Gaveston, he has no redeeming qualities; the extremity of his suffering gives him a nobility that is not destroyed even by his anguish. Even at the end he can exclaim, "I am still king!" Marlowe constructs one of the most harrowing death scenes to be found in Elizabethan drama—though he actually softens the even more horrible historical fact—and the pathos of Edward's intense emotional suffering elevates the play beyond the level of historical chronicle and assures its place among the world's great dramas.

"Critical Evaluation" by Steven C. Schaber

Further Reading

Cheney, Patrick, ed. *The Cambridge Companion to Christopher Marlowe*. New York: Cambridge University Press, 2004. Collection of essays, including discussions of Marlowe's life; his place in the twenty-first century; his literary style; gender and sexuality in his work; and his reception and influence. Thomas Cartelli provides an analysis of *Edward II*.

Deats, Sara Munson, and Robert A. Logan, eds. *Placing the Plays of Christopher Marlowe: Fresh Cultural Contexts*. Burlington, Vt.: Ashgate, 2008. Includes an essay, "Marlowe's *Edward II* and the Early Playhouse Audience" by Ruth Lunney, as well as numerous references to this play that are listed in the index.

Hopkins, Lisa. *Christopher Marlowe, Renaissance Dramatist*. Edinburgh: Edinburgh University Press, 2008. An introduction to Marlowe's plays, discussing their themes, theatrical contexts, and performance histories from 1587 through 2007; Marlowe's relationship to William Shakespeare; and Marlowe's theatrical achievements. The references to *Edward II* are listed in the index.

Levin, Harry. *The Overachiever: A Study of Christopher Marlowe*. Cambridge, Mass.: Harvard University Press, 1952. Discusses how in Marlowe's plays men's passions ultimately betray them. Asserts that whereas William Shakespeare deals with the well-being of the state, Marlowe focuses upon individual tragedies.

Marlowe, Christopher. *Edward the Second*. Edited by Charles R. Forker. New York: Manchester University Press, 1994. Contains an excellent 136-page introduction. Considers the relationship between *Edward II* and Shakespeare's histories.

Oz, Avraham, ed. *Marlowe*. New York: Palgrave Macmillan, 2003. Collection of essays about Marlowe's plays, including "The Terms of Gender: 'Gay' and 'Feminist' *Edward II*" by Dympna Callaghan and "Queer *Edward II*: Postmodern Sexualities and the Early Modern Subject" by Thomas Cartelli.

Ribner, Irving. *The English History Play in the Age of Shakespeare*. Princeton, N.J.: Princeton University Press, 1957. Describes *Edward II* as the first fully developed Elizabethan history play and tragedy of character. Discusses the personalities of Edward and Mortimer and the theoretical underpinning of political issues.

Sales, Roger. *Christopher Marlowe*. New York: St. Martin's Press, 1991. Considers the Elizabethan mentality as revealed in Marlowe's life. In the analysis of *Edward II*, the emphasis is on Mortimer and the difficulties posed by deposing and executing a monarch.

Weil, Judith. *Christopher Marlowe: Merlin's Prophet*. New York: Cambridge University Press, 1977. A study of Marlowe's satiric and tragic irony, examining the playwright's relationship to his public. Argues that Edward becomes sympathetic, one in whom reason is reborn between his defeat and his death.

The Effect of Gamma Rays on Man-in-the-Moon Marigolds

Author: Paul Zindel (1936-2003)
First produced: 1965; first published, 1970
Type of work: Drama
Type of plot: Domestic melodrama
Time of plot: Early 1960's
Locale: Unnamed

Principal characters:
BEATRICE HUNSDORFER, an embittered widow
TILLIE, her younger daughter
RUTH, her older daughter
NANNY, an elderly boarder
JANICE VICKERY, Tillie's classmate

The Story:

The teenaged Tillie Hunsdorfer describes her fascination with the wonder of the atom. Her mother, Beatrice, is in their cluttered home, speaking on the phone with Mr. Goodman, one of Tillie's teachers. Mr. Goodman is concerned about Tillie's withdrawn nature and her repeated absences. It soon becomes apparent that Beatrice is responsible for Tilllie's absences from school, claiming that she needs her to take care of errands around the house. In reality, Tillie finds solace in her science class, and school is an escape from her dismal domestic life.

Beatrice threatens to chloroform the rabbit that Mr. Goodman gave to Tillie unless Tillie takes care of the rabbit droppings immediately. Tillie's older sister Ruth appears, looking for lipstick and referring to it as "Devil's Kiss." She announces that Tillie's appearance at the science assembly was the cause of much laughter in the auditorium. Beatrice offers Ruth a cigarette in exchange for a back-scratch. During this exchange, it is revealed that Ruth spent time in a sanitarium after her father died and is troubled by nightmares.

Tillie's interest in science increases as her teacher gives her some marigold seeds that have been exposed to varying degrees of radiation. While Tillie is tending to her experiment, Beatrice reads the newspaper and speculates wildly about business prospects. The family's elderly boarder, Nanny, appears, supported by her walker. She neither speaks nor shows any signs of comprehending the activity around her. Beatrice addresses Nanny loudly and mocks her to her blank face. Nanny's daughter, a successful business woman, does not have time to take care of her, so Nanny is now in Beatrice's "care."

Nanny is the latest of a string of boarders with terminal illnesses that have been the primary source of the family's income. The boarders' grotesque ailments are also the source of Ruth's recurrent nightmares. One boarder had worms in his legs. Beatrice continues to express her frustration with how her life has turned out. She describes herself as the best dancer in school, smart, and popular until she married the wrong man. Again, she gets Tillie's attention by threatening to kill her pet rabbit. Nanny's shuffling to the bathroom annoys Beatrice, and she explodes at the end of the scene. She says that the half-life of Tillie's cobalt-exposed flowers is nothing compared to Beatrice: She is the original half-life, with a daughter who has half a mind; another who is half a test tube, half a corpse; and a house half-full of rabbit droppings.

Beatrice again speaks with Mr. Goodman on the phone. She flirts with him and expresses her concern about having radioactive flowers in the house, as she has heard radioactivity can cause sterility. At the end of her conversation, a scream is heard from upstairs. Ruth has had another nightmare, and Beatrice calms her down. A storm has caused the electricity to go out, and the two sit in a chair downstairs in the darkness. Ruth begins to describe her dream, but Beatrice does not want to hear anything unpleasant. Ruth begs her to tell the story of the wagon, even though it is clear

that she has heard this story many times. Beatrice describes how she took her father's vegetable cart while he was asleep one afternoon and rode it all over town. This story reveals how attached Beatrice was to her father, a produce vendor who took care of her after her mother died. Beatrice also recounts a recurrent nightmare that is symbolic of her frustrated desires.

At the end of act 1, Ruth exuberantly rushes into the house. She announces that Tillie is a finalist in their school's science fair. Beatrice does not share Ruth's excitement and reluctantly answers the phone to speak to the school's principal. Beatrice's anxiety about joining her daughter on stage with the other mothers comes to a head when she yells at the principal over the phone. Beatrice is afraid that she will be the target of ridicule in the same way as Tillie. She even calls Tillie "ugly." Tillie is in tears and Beatrice, realizing how much she has hurt her daughter, comforts her.

Two weeks later, the family is preparing to attend the science fair. Ruth tells Tillie that the only competition she has to worry about is Janice Vickery's cat skeleton, which she proceeds to describe in grisly detail. Ruth also mentions that she heard two of the teachers talking about Beatrice and how her nickname used to be "Betty the Loon." Ruth manipulates Tillie into giving her the rabbit by promising not to say anything to their mother about what she overheard.

Beatrice has dressed herself up for the occasion. Tillie says she looks beautiful. Beatrice nervously fusses over Tillie's outfit. Ruth has dressed herself in her usual too-tight sweater in the hopes of attending the event, but Beatrice insists that she stay home and look after Nanny. In her frustration, Ruth tells Beatrice that all the teachers are waiting for her to show up so they can laugh at her. A heated exchange follows and Ruth reneges on her promise to Tillie by calling Beatrice "Betty the Loon." Visibly shaken by this revelation, Beatrice orders Ruth to go with Tillie to the school.

Janice Vickery, Tillie's chief competitor in the science fair, describes the process by which she put together a cat skeleton in lurid detail. Meanwhile, Beatrice has been drinking. She calls Nanny's daughter to take Nanny away and proceeds up the stairs carrying the rabbit cage and a bottle of chloroform. Tillie presents the findings of her experiment at the science fair.

When Tillie and Ruth return with the news that Tillie won first prize, Beatrice announces that the rabbit is in Ruth's room and needs to be buried. Ruth has a violent seizure. After the convulsions subside, Tillie affectionately tucks her sister into bed while Beatrice announces that she hates the world. The final scene is Tillie's speech at the science fair, in which she describes the beauty and potential of the atom.

Critical Evaluation:

Clive Barnes wrote in *The New York Times* that *The Effect of Gamma Rays on Man-in-the-Moon Marigolds* was "one of the most discouraging titles yet devised by man." Largely autobiographical, the play had its beginnings in Houston, Texas, in 1965 at the Alley Theater. It then opened Off-Broadway on April 7, 1970, at the Mercer-O'Casey Theatre, with Sada Thompson in the role of Beatrice. *Variety* called it "a masterful, pace-setting drama and the most compelling work of its kind since Tennessee Williams' *The Glass Menagerie*." Indeed, the setting of the cramped Hunsdorfer household, a former vegetable store, recalls the claustrophobic atmosphere of *The Glass Menagerie* (pr. 1944, pb. 1945). Paul Zindel himself acknowledged the influence of Williams's play on *The Effect of Gamma Rays on Man-in-the-Moon Marigolds*: "Tennessee Williams' work attracted me, inspired me, although at the time I didn't have a knowledge of structure or an exposure to the works of other dramatists who had influenced him." While majoring in chemistry in college, Zindel took courses in creative writing, including one course taught by his contemporary playwright, Edward Albee.

In 1971, the play moved to Broadway, where it ran for 819 performances. It won both the Pulitzer Prize in drama and the New York Drama Critics' Circle Award. A film adaptation appeared the following year, directed by Paul Newman and starring Joanne Woodward. Zindel's other plays, most notably *And Miss Reardon Drinks a Little* (pr. 1967, pb. 1972) and *The Secret Affairs of Mildred Wild* (pr. 1972, pb. 1973), also feature complex female characters.

Zindel dedicated his heavily autobiographical play to his mother, Betty Frank, on whom he based the domineering, abusive Beatrice. In the introduction to the 1997 reissue of the play, Zindel acknowledged that he based the life-affirming, science-loving Tillie on himself. Zindel also drew heavily from his ten-year stint as a high school chemistry teacher.

The action of the play is built around Beatrice's frustration with her life and the impact it has on her daughters. At turns abusive and pathetic, Beatrice represents the toxic effect—like that of the radioactive gamma rays—that permeates the household. However, the play does not end on Beatrice's nihilistic "I hate the world" but on Tillie's hopeful note about the beauty of the atom. Zindel based on one of his class lectures this underlying concept that all atoms, in all living things, come from the Sun and that, as a result, all people are linked to the universe and never really die.

In the play's final sequence, Tillie describes the results of her experiment with radiation, "and how dangerous it can be if not handled correctly." Some of the seeds died, some produced double-blooms, and some grew giant stems. Unlike her sister Ruth, Tillie emerges as a positive mutation in spite of Beatrice's potentially damaging influence. A naïve perspective about the benefits of atomic energy may date the play somewhat, but the other issues that Zindel raises—single parenting, child abuse, and alcoholism—are, unfortunately, more relevant today than ever.

Zindel wrote several popular novels for young adults, including *My Darling, My Hamburger* (1969), *I Never Loved Your Mind* (1970), and *The Pigman* (1968) but never succeeded in writing another play that was as acclaimed as *Marigolds*. Zindel died of cancer in 2003 at the age of sixty-six.

Robin Imhof

Further Reading

Forman, Jack Jacob. *Presenting Paul Zindel*. Boston: Twayne, 1988. As part of Twayne's Young Adult Author series, this book discusses Zindel's plays and novels in the context of adolescent issues.

Loomis, Jeffrey B. "Female Freedoms, Dantesque Dreams, and Paul Zindel's Anti-Sexist *The Effects of Gamma Rays on Man-in-the-Moon Marigolds*." *Studies in American Drama, 1945-Present* 6 (1991). Affirms the antisexist message of *The Effects of Gamma Rays on Man-in-the-Moon Marigolds* and finds an imaginative correlation between Zindel's play and Dante's *La divina commedia* (c. 1320; *The Divine Comedy*, 1802).

Thomason, Elizabeth. *Presenting Analysis, Context, and Criticism on Commonly Studied Dramas*. Vol. 12 in *Drama for Students*. Detroit, Mich.: Gale, 2001. *The Effects of Gamma Rays on Man-in-the-Moon Marigolds* is one of the fifteen plays provided with detailed, exemplary analysis in this study that simultaneously provides insights into the works and demonstrates to students of drama the craft of gleaning such insights.

Zindel, Paul. " . . . And Gamma Rays Did It!" Interview by Guy Flatley. *The New York Times*, April 19, 1970, p. 89. Zindel discusses his themes and personal history in the aftermath of the play's Off-Broadway success.

_____. "Paul Zindel." Interview by John L. DiGaetani. In *A Search for a Postmodern Theater: Interviews with Contemporary Playwrights*. New York: Greenwood Press, 1991. Zindel acknowledges his debt to psychoanalytic therapy as a source of inspiration and recovery.

Effi Briest

Author: Theodor Fontane (1819-1898)
First published: 1895 (English translation, 1914)
Type of work: Novel
Type of plot: Domestic realism
Time of plot: Second half of the nineteenth century
Locale: Germany

Principal characters:
EFFI VON BRIEST, the only child of the Briest family
FRAU VON BRIEST, her mother
RITTERSCHAFTSRAT VON BRIEST, her father
BARON VON INNSTETTEN, Effi's husband and a
   government official in Kessin
ANNIE, Effi's daughter
MAJOR VON CRAMPAS, the district commander in Kessin
ROSWITHA, Effi's maid

The Story:

Effi von Briest is sixteen years old when her mother cheerfully announces that Baron von Innstetten has asked for her hand in marriage. Effi had seen Innstetten only once, but she knows he had wanted to marry her mother years before. During a time when Baron von Innstetten was absent for a long period, her mother married Effi's father, Ritterschaftsrat von Briest, for he seemed too good a match to give up. Since then Innstetten has become a government official with a promising future.

Half an hour earlier, Effi was sitting on a swing enjoying her happy childhood. Now she is to be a bride, and in a few weeks, she will be the wife of an important government official. After the excitement of the preparations, the wedding, and a honeymoon trip to Italy, the couple arrives in Kessin, a small town on the Baltic Sea. At first, Effi finds her new surroundings interesting, but soon she begins to feel uncomfortable in the strange house, which was formerly owned by a seafaring captain; his relics and souvenirs give the place a bizarre character. A stuffed shark, stories about the captain's mysterious Chinese servant, and a mentally ill maidservant, who sits in the kitchen with a black chicken on her lap, give Effi nightmares, and she claims that she hears noises in an unoccupied upstairs room. Innstetten is considerate toward his young wife and never fails to show his devotion. A practical man, however, he pays no attention to Effi's tales of supernatural happenings in the house. He is convinced that his wife's childish imagination will soon calm down.

After having paid the obligatory social visits to the local aristocracy, Effi realizes that she will not find friends in that circle. The first friend she makes is the town apothecary. Her second friend is Roswitha, her maid, whom she meets in the graveyard where the girl is grieving for the loss of her former mistress. Effi is pregnant and needs a maid. Once she learns that Roswitha is Catholic, she is convinced that Roswitha's faith will conquer the unexplained noises in the house.

Roswitha never hears ghosts, and her straightforward manner is a relief from the formal stiffness of Effi's social world. The birth of her daughter, Annie, gives Effi new activities, but she continues to be bored in Kessin.

The new military commander in Kessin, Major von Crampas, is another addition to Effi's social world. The major's carefree behavior and witty conversation are quite a contrast to the well-disciplined and formal Innstetten, but the two men respect each other and become friends. Crampas often visits the Innstetten home, and he and Effi ride horses along the seashore and participate in community plays. Effi soon realizes the danger of this situation and tries to avoid him. During a sleigh ride, Crampas oversteps the boundaries of friendship.

One day, Innstetten informs Effi that he has been promoted to a new post in a Berlin ministry, a position that will take them to Berlin. Effi is happy to leave the strange house, the boring people, and above all Crampas, for their relationship, although they keep it secret, increasingly burdens her conscience. Innstetten notices Effi's great joy when he tells her about the transfer to Berlin, and he feels guilty for not having considered leaving sooner.

In Berlin, Innstetten makes a special effort to provide her with a cheerful house and an enjoyable social life. Though Innstetten's duties at the ministry keep them from spending much time together, the years in Berlin are happy ones until Effi is sent to a spa at Ems to recuperate after an illness. Innstetten and Annie remain in Berlin. One day, when Annie falls and cuts her forehead, Roswitha searches through Effi's belongings to find a bandage. When Innstetten thereupon tries to restore order in Effi's room, he finds a bundle of love letters from Crampas, written six years earlier. Innstetten does what he considers his duty regardless of his personal feelings: He calls a friend to make the necessary arrangements for a duel with Crampas. Although his friend points out that the letters are more than six years old, Innstetten, who would prefer to pardon Effi, decides to go through with the duel because he feels the insult to his honor is not diminished by time. The two men fight near Kessin, and Crampas is fatally shot.

While these events take place, Effi is still in the Rhine country, wondering why Innstetten's daily letters have ceased. Finally, a letter from her mother informs her of the duel and of the pending divorce. Innstetten is given custody of Annie. The Briest family is willing to assist Effi financially, but it refuses to allow her to return home. Heartbroken, she goes back to Berlin, where she lives in a small apartment, a social outcast. Only Roswitha remains faithful to her.

Effi's health declines. Once she accidentally sees Annie leaving school, but she avoids meeting the child. Finally, moved by a desire to see her daughter again, Effi requests legal permission to have Annie visit her. When Annie arrives at the apartment, however, she gives only evasive and well-rehearsed answers. Discouraged, Effi sends the child home without the hope of seeing her again. Soon after this, Effi's health declines severely. Her doctor reports her condition to her parents, hinting that their continued rejection could mean her death. When she is finally permitted to return home, her health does improve. Aside from her parents and the local minister, however, Effi has no friends or social intercourse. Roswitha, concerned for her mistress's loneliness, writes to Innstetten asking him to give Effi the family dog. Innstetten is glad to fulfill her desire. He is extremely successful in the ministry, but none of his promotions lessens the pain in his heart, for he still loves Effi.

After a beautiful summer at her parents' home, Effi dies. In her last conversation with her mother, she asks Frau von Briest to tell Innstetten that he did the only correct thing possible for him. She wants to die as Effi Briest, for she did not honor her married name.

Critical Evaluation:

Effi Briest is Theodor Fontane's masterpiece. Surprised at how easily it came to him, he compared it to a psychogram. Based loosely on an actual case, the novel treats sensational topics, including adultery and a duel, but in his tolerant, nonjudgmental stance, Fontane keeps a discreet narrative distance from intimate scenes.

The main theme of the novel, death, is pervasive and eclipses individual incidents. By the end of the novel Effi's death seems inevitable. It is her fate, the accumulation of myriad factors beyond her control. Her inclinations, circumstances, and surroundings combine so that the reader, with Fontane, can only say "Poor Effi."

Effi is a remarkably passive and detached heroine. The plot is advanced not so much by what she does as by what is done to her. The opening scene of Effi playing in the garden with her friends shows her as a carefree child, quite unprepared for the arranged marriage her mother springs on her. As she stands trembling before Innstetten, her friend Hertha calls to her from outside, "Effi, come." Even Innstetten finds the call fraught with meaning, as if Effi is being called away from him to finish her childhood. In the original German edition, these words are given even more weight when near the end of the book Effi's father says exactly the same thing when he calls her to come home. Effi feels at home only in her parents' manor house in Hohen-Cremmen and thinks of herself to the end as Effi Briest, her parents' child, and not as Innstetten's wife.

If violence is done to Effi, figuratively speaking, by interrupting her childhood, then violence is also done to her by moving her as a bride into the very house in Kessin where the previous bride had met with a mysterious end, leaving the house haunted by the ghost of a Chinese man who had presumably been her secret lover. The ghost bodes ill for Effi. It links the house with adultery and death, and it is the point of contention that widens the gap in communication between Effi and Innstetten. Effi wants to move out, but Innstetten is insensitive and insists they stay.

Fontane was a master at writing dialogue and often manages to convey as much through what is not said as through what is said. One such dialogue, at the beginning of chapter 20, reveals that the rift between Effi and Innstetten is beyond repair. After arranging to have Effi ride home from a party with Crampas, who is known to have had illicit affairs, Innstetten expresses suspicion of Effi in their conversation the following morning. Crampas had, in fact, availed himself of the opportunity to make advances, but Effi discloses none of this to her husband and finds herself defending Crampas as the perfect gentleman. The dialogue shows that Effi's loyalty has shifted from Innstetten to Crampas.

It is also through dialogue that Fontane illustrates the rift between Effi and her only child, Annie. Showing rare initiative, Effi arranges for the child to visit her and promises herself much from the meeting. Effi loves nothing more than a good chat, but she despairs when she is confronted with a rigid, uncommunicative little girl who answers like a parrot, repeating the phrase: "Oh yes, if I may." This one effort convinces her of the futility of establishing any sort of meaningful relationship with her daughter. It is another nail in Effi's coffin.

A close reading of the novel reveals that Effi is doomed from the start. Apparently incidental details reinforce one another, forming an artistic web of references to the forces that contribute to her demise. Hertha is not just the girl who calls out to Effi from the garden. In chapter 24, Effi and Innstetten visit Lake Hertha, the site of ancient rites of Hertha worship, which involved sacrificial victims. Seen in this light, the call from Hertha can be interpreted as the call to death, not a good omen at the moment of betrothal. Fontane introduces the topic of adultery as early as the opening scene with Effi and Hertha in which the girls ceremoniously drown discarded gooseberry skins, commenting that in days gone by unfaithful wives were given the same treatment. How ingenious of Fontane to have Effi visit Lake Hertha as an alternative to visiting a town called Crampas. She turns aside from adultery only to face death.

Indeed, it becomes increasingly apparent that Hertha's seemingly harmless call is the more sinister of Effi's two options on that opening day. The choice is between Innstetten, who is indoors, and Hertha, who is outdoors in the fresh air. Effi's mother has already remarked that Effi should always be in the air. Initially, it seems that by going with Innstetten Effi has made the wrong choice, a choice that leads to adultery and ignominy. When her father finally sends his two-word telegram: "Effi, come," the reader would like to think that this would take her life back to the point where she heard those words from Hertha, thus undoing the unhappy marriage and letting Effi take the other option back into her parents' garden where she belongs. Ironically, this is just where she does belong. When she spends the autumn nights sitting at her window, the night air kills her and she is buried in the garden.

The associations built up around Hertha exemplify the exceptionally rich texture of *Effi Briest*. Written when Fontane was over seventy, the novel reflects the wise realization that there is seldom a simple explanation. Life is extraordinarily complex. For those who would seek a single cause for Effi's decline and death, Fontane speaks through her father in the closing words of the novel: "That is *too* big a subject."

"Critical Evaluation" by Jean M. Snook

Further Reading

Chambers, Helen. *The Changing Image of Theodor Fontane.* Columbia, S.C.: Camden House, 1997. Chambers charts the critical reception of Fontane's work from contemporary reviews published when his work first appeared through critical pieces published in the 1990's. She focuses on criticism published since 1980, including feminist and psychoanalytic interpretations of his work. Includes a chapter on Fontane and the realistic novel, as well as notes and a bibliography.

Craig, Gordon Alexander. *Theodor Fontane: Literature and History in the Bismarck Reich.* New York: Oxford University Press, 1999. Craig places Fontane within the context of historical events, authors, and the literature published in nineteenth century Prussia. The book contains chapters on the historical novels and the novels of society, as well as a bibliography and index.

Doebeling, Marion, ed. *New Approaches to Theodor Fontane: Cultural Codes in Flux.* New York: Camden House, 2000. Eight essays examine Fontane's realist approach to literature and explore the difficulty and ultimate impossibility of a true mirroring of realism. Includes bibliography and index.

Greenberg, Valerie D. "The Resistance of Effi Briest: An (Un)told Tale." *PMLA* 103, no. 5 (October, 1988): 770-782. A revisionist interpretation of the novel as Effi's struggle for liberation. A close reading of Effi's last remarks to her mother reveals that each point can be read in opposition to its surface meaning.

Subiotto, Frances M. "The Ghost in *Effi Briest*." *Forum for Modern Language Studies* 21 (1985): 137-150. Analyzes the ghost as a metaphor for all that is absent: suitable living quarters, action, love, and opportunities for women in Prussian society. Sees *Effi Briest* as a paradigm of the solitary state of the individual.

Tucker, Brian. "Performing Boredom in *Effi Briest*: On the Effects of Narrative Speed." *German Quarterly* 80, no. 2 (Spring, 2007): 185-200. Argues that when Fontane depicts boredom in the novel, he imposes boredom upon the reader by deliberately slowing the pace of the narrative.

Turner, David. "Theodor Fontane: *Effi Briest*." In *The Monster in the Mirror*, edited by D. A. Williams. New York: Oxford University Press, 1978. Examines *Effi Briest* in the context of contemporary European literature. Discusses what makes Fontane's treatment of the subject matter realistic, as well as his accurate detail and skillful use of leitmotifs and symbols.

Wansink, Susan. *Female Victims and Oppressors in Novels by Theodor Fontane and François Mauriac.* New York: Peter Lang, 1998. An interesting combination of literary and cultural criticism. Situates Fontane in his time while also reading *Effi Briest* and other novels as complex studies of the interaction between characters and societal norms. Includes notes and bibliography.

Zwiebel, William L. *Theodor Fontane.* New York: Twayne, 1992. Contains a concise summary of important critical observations on the genesis of *Effi Briest*, the four narrative sections, the role of predestination, Fontane's criticism of Prussian society, and the function of the ghost.

Egmont

Author: Johann Wolfgang von Goethe (1749-1832)
First produced: 1789; first published, 1788 (English
    translation, 1837)
Type of work: Drama
Type of plot: Tragedy
Time of plot: Sixteenth century
Locale: Brussels

Principal characters:
COUNT EGMONT, the lord of Gaure
CLÄRCHEN, his beloved
BRACKENBURG, a citizen in love with Clärchen
THE DUKE OF ALVA, an emissary of Philip II
MARGARET OF PARMA, the regent of The Netherlands
WILLIAM, prince of Orange

The Story:

The people of the Netherlands are unhappy in the state of their homeland. Philip II of Spain is tightening his absolute control of the Lowlands, particularly in religious matters, for Philip is the main instrument of the Inquisition. A new regent is appointed to administer his rule. The populace hoped the office would go to Count Egmont, who, after his defeat of the French at Gravelines, has become a national hero. Besides, although Egmont is a Catholic, he treats Protestants with kindness, and he even goes to Madrid to plead with Philip to lessen the strictures of Catholic repression.

The king, however, gives the office to Margaret, his half sister. She, like Philip, tolerates no dissent from the established church, yet by firmness and tact she pacifies the burghers who stubbornly resist any laws but their own. She even manages to conciliate Egmont and William of Orange, so that outwardly at least there is harmony among the nobility.

Margaret summons Machiavel, her secretary, to hear his account of new uprisings. He tells her how throughout Flanders mobs are breaking into cathedrals and despoiling the monuments of the hated foreign religion. He counsels Margaret to be firm but not cruel toward the Protestants. Margaret tells him that her efforts toward conciliation will mean little, for it is rumored that the cruel duke of Alva is on his way to assume control of the provinces. Machiavel reminds her that as regent she will hold the final power, but Margaret is wise in the ways of kings. Officially or not, Alva will rule the Netherlands, and she will be able to circumvent him only by appealing directly to her brother. She is especially fearful of what might happen to Egmont and William of Orange and of the effects of Alva's harsh rule on the people.

In her humble house, Clärchen is happily singing, for she expects Egmont that night. Brackenburg watches her anxiously. He loves her and is certain that no good will come of the love between a count and a commoner. When Clärchen, looking out of her windows, sees a mob in the street, she asks Brackenburg to learn the cause of the disturbance. While he is gone, her mother reproaches Clärchen bitterly for having

rejected Brackenburg's suit. Even now, the mother declares, the burgher will be glad to marry Clärchen. Brackenburg returns to tell them the people are hearing of the outbreaks in Flanders and are heartened by that uprising against their oppressors.

A group of commoners argue about their rights as citizens. One, who can read, tells them of their rights under the constitution and of their forefathers' vigilance in protecting their privileges. Egmont, arriving on the scene, advises them to be moderate in their talk but to preserve their ancient liberties. After he leaves, a keen observer remarks that Egmont's head will make a dainty morsel for the headsman.

In his residence, Egmont attends to duties of state. One of his letters comes from Count Oliva, his old preceptor, who counsels him to be more circumspect in his behavior and less free in his talk. Egmont throws the letter aside, remarking that everyone is different; he himself believes in doing what is right without fear or favor. Let others play the part of fawning courtier.

William of Orange arrives to talk about Alva's coming. William is in favor of caution; they will do nothing until they know what Alva is being sent to accomplish. Egmont reminds him that they are both Knights of the Golden Fleece. As members of that order, they cannot be punished except by a trial by their peers. William is inclined to place little trust in their rights, however, for Philip is a determined and ruthless ruler. William declares that he will remain on his own estate and refuses to meet the duke of Alva. Egmont decides to speak his mind freely. If he has to be a rebel, he will openly do his best to advance the welfare of the Netherlands.

Margaret, in the meantime, receives a dispatch from Philip. The letter is gentle and considerate in tone, a fact ominous in itself. The king informs her officially of Alva's mission and gives details of the formidable army the duke is bringing to garrison the recalcitrant towns. Margaret knows that her authority as regent has been superseded.

In the evening, Clärchen joyfully receives Egmont. For a

time, Egmont is remote, even keeping on his mantle. Then he shows her that he is wearing his full uniform, decorated with the emblem of the Golden Fleece, and says that he comes thus attired because she asked him to do so as a favor. Clärchen, particularly impressed by the decoration of the Golden Fleece, is touched by that evidence of his regard.

The inhabitants of the town grow fearful. Alva's soldiers are stationed at every strategic point and his spies are everywhere, so that the citizens dare not congregate to discuss their new woes. The ordinary people are afraid for Egmont; it is rumored that he will be killed.

In his palace, Alva makes his plans, with his trusted guards forming so tight a cordon around the residence that no one can get in or out. To his natural son Ferdinand he announces that he is expecting Egmont and William. At the end of the audience, Alva will detain Egmont on a pretext. William will be arrested outside. As soon as he is safely in custody, Ferdinand, acting as the duke's messenger, is to return to the reception chamber. His arrival will be the signal to arrest Egmont. Ferdinand, uneasy over the success of the plot, is nevertheless flattered by the part he is to play.

William is too cautious to fall into the duke's trap, however, and he stays away from the audience. Egmont, who knows no fear, goes without hesitation and discusses at great length the troubled situation in the Netherlands. He is a skillful debater. At every point he upholds the dignity of the burghers and wisely counsels patience and tact in dealing with them. At last, Alva becomes impatient and abruptly orders his arrest. He reads a document in which Philip decrees that Egmont was tried and found guilty of treason. Because the king of Spain does not acknowledge the authority of the Knight of the Golden Fleece, Egmont fails in his demand for immunity.

Clärchen is distraught when she hears of Egmont's arrest. Accompanied by the faithful Brackenburg, she wanders about the town in an attempt to incite the citizens to rescue Egmont. Alva did his work well, however; the burghers are afraid even to discuss the matter. Returning to the house, Clärchen thinks of the vial of poison that Brackenburg once showed her when he was disconsolate. Thinking to quiet her temporarily, he gives her the vial. Clärchen immediately drinks the poison.

In the palace prison, Egmont is wakeful. When he finally dozes off he is awakened by Ferdinand and Silva, who reads him his sentence: He is to be executed publicly in the marketplace as a warning to the people. Silva leaves, but Ferdinand remains behind to condole with the count. Although he had a part in the plot, he actually sympathizes with Egmont.

When Egmont sleeps again, a vision appears. Freedom is reclining on a cloud. Her features are those of Clärchen. She holds above his head a wreath of victory. Egmont awakens at dawn to strains of martial music. The guards are at his door.

Critical Evaluation:

Partly a historical drama and partly a character drama, Johann Wolfgang von Goethe's *Egmont* links public and private realms in a way that was somewhat unusual for eighteenth century literature. In his crowd scenes, Goethe provided historical breadth through the comments of ordinary folk, and he made deft and accurate use of the biographies of the important public figures around Count Egmont: the regent, Margaret of Parma, the duke of Alva, and Prince William of Orange. However, it is useful to view the work as at heart a character drama. Count Egmont represents a way of living and a philosophy of life that has continued to fuel controversy about the play. Because most characters in the drama and fiction of Goethe's era were devoted either to public duty or to private desires, Egmont, who integrates the two realms effortlessly, dazzles as an exception. This aspect of Egmont affects the way Goethe treats the essential underlying theme of freedom, and it requires that the plot concerning his political career be complemented by the largely separate (and fictive) story of his love for the commoner Clärchen.

In literary tradition, love between a nobleman and a woman from a lower class usually illustrates class conflict and ends tragically; Goethe's drama *Faust* (1833; *The Tragedy of Faust*, 1838) is one of many examples of this. It is an innovation that for Clärchen and Egmont, class and morality are never at issue. Clärchen resists her mother's suggestion that she will be scorned for engaging in an affair that cannot lead to marriage. Indeed, it was offensive to many of Goethe's contemporaries that the play depicts Clärchen as being virtuous and the bourgeois morality of her mother and the pitifully weak Brackenburg as being deplorable. Clärchen and Egmont illustrate the continuity of the personal and the political. Because she loves Egmont both as the human being and as the hero of her people, her attempt to launch a movement to rescue him is privately as well as publicly justified. When he embraces his sweetheart in full Spanish dress uniform, Egmont shows symbolically the fusion of public and private life. What he wants for himself and what he fights for on behalf of his people are unified: freedom to enjoy life, not just the freedom of speech or assembly. As a further token of the possible union of private and public, the goddess Freedom, who promises national liberation in Egmont's dream, physically resembles Clärchen.

Written between the time of the American and French revolutions, the play *Egmont*, in the spirit of its era, joins liberty to nationalism without being nationalistic. The religious conflict that motivates the rioters to destroy churches and smash images is presented as an aspect of the political struggle for self-rule. Egmont tells Alba that the people consider imposed Catholicism just a façade to hide tyrannous governmental policies. The riots in Flanders are thus less a matter of conscience than a political protest fanned by oppression. Nationalism becomes a forced product of the tyranny of foreign rulers rather than a natural, healthy assertion of common identity, as it was for later German nationalists. Egmont is perfectly content to serve a Spanish king; Margaret is presented as a capable and lenient ruler, praised by Clärchen and the townspeople, despite the fact that she is a Spaniard. Although Goethe's contemporaries were shocked by the political radicalism of the play, Egmont subdues the burgher who advocates revolutionary violence by telling the people that rights cannot be secured by rioting. It is only on the eve of his execution that Egmont can accept the inevitability of a national war for independence from Spain. His desire to prevent the devastations of war is one reason he refuses to flee with William when Alva enters Brussels with Spanish troops.

Structurally, this play is organized to display Egmont's temperament and attitude toward life. The count speaks of his ability to enjoy parties, hunting, and food and drink without letting anxiety for the future hamper him. The burghers of Brussels approve, for it makes them feel that he understands them and is one of them. Several characters speak of Egmont's prowess in past battles, his generous, open nature, and his relative tolerance for Protestant preachers. Those who criticize the count's way of life attack his lavish entertainments, irresponsibility, and lack of circumspection. By walking into the trap set for him by Alva, Egmont demonstrates imprudence and overconfidence; but if this is a flaw, it is also inseparable from his strength and charm. The nobles Margaret, Alva, and William function as foils for Egmont in their caution, practicality, and ability to maneuver better politically. Although Egmont is not like them, he is far happier as a human being for entrusting himself to fate; and his political idealism does him credit. Egmont is neither calculating nor sober, but rather playful and free; because he does not worry about the future, he can enjoy the present moment. It is this freedom to live life to the fullest, as well as political freedoms for his people, for which Egmont claims he is dying.

Some critics take a dim view of Egmont's happy-go-lucky temperament, and others have faulted Goethe's play for the lack of action on stage and for the dream sequence near the end. It is true that the characters tend to talk about their attitudes and values rather than to show these through their actions. Like all Goethe's plays, this one is more reflective and poetic than outright dramatic. Besides the fascination with Egmont's character, the strength of the play lies in its artful exploration of the philosophy and psychology of all the characters, in its absorbing analysis of the historical forces at work, and in its treatment of the issues of nationalism, freedom, and power politics. Although it is true that the count's death sparked the great uprising of the Netherlands, the ironic fact is that Brussels and Egmont's province Flanders, both part of Belgium today, never succeeded in throwing off the foreign yoke as the northern Dutch provinces did several decades after the historical Egmont was executed. That Egmont is consoled in prison by a dream that predicts the future Dutch victory, inspired by his own martyrlike death, perhaps detracts from the realism and tragedy of the play, but poetically it is compelling.

"Critical Evaluation" by Julie D. Prandi

Further Reading

Armstrong, John. *Love, Life, Goethe: Lessons of the Imagination from the Great German Poet.* New York: Farrar, Straus and Giroux, 2007. Goethe's works are analyzed and his life examined in this comprehensive volume. Armstrong discusses a wide range of Goethe's writings, including his lesser known works, and gives a close study of his personal life. Knowing German and English, he provides translations of several key passages, while keeping his writing style plain and clear. This volume offers readers a better understanding of Goethe's writing, and the circumstances that inspired it.

Goethe, Johann Wolfgang von. *Egmont: A Tragedy in Five Acts.* Translated by Charles E. Passage. New York: Ungar, 1985. Included in this careful translation of Goethe's play is a useful ten-page introduction to the work. Provides a good overview of theme, character, style, and structure. Also places the work in its historical and literary context.

Gray, Ronald. *Goethe: A Critical Introduction.* London: Cambridge University Press, 1967. Provides a concise account of Goethe's works, including not only information about sources, influences, and relationship to the author's life and position in German literature but also insightful critical assessment. Chapter 4 discusses Goethe's major dramatic works, including *Egmont.* Includes bibliography and chronology of Goethe's life and works.

Hatfield, Henry C. *Goethe: A Critical Introduction.* Cambridge, Mass.: Harvard University Press, 1964. Provides interpretations of Goethe's works with a minimum of biographical and background material. In chapter 3, "Resolution and Maturity," the author discusses Goethe's turn toward "objective" verse in *Egmont* and several other works. Includes a bibliography.

Kerry, Paul E. *Enlightenment Thought in the Writings of Goethe: A Contribution to the History of Ideas.* Rochester, N.Y.: Camden House, 2001. Kerry analyzes Goethe's works to demonstrate how he was influenced by Voltaire, David Hume, and other Enlightenment philosophers and writers. Chapter 3, "An Enlightenment Coign of Vantage: The Intersection of History, Literature, and Belief in *Egmont*," focuses on this work.

Sharpe, Lesley, ed. *The Cambridge Companion to Goethe.* New York: Cambridge University Press, 2002. Collection of newly commissioned essays analyzing Goethe's prose fiction, poetry, and drama; Goethe and gender, philoso-

phy, and religion; and Goethe's critical reception, among other topics. Includes bibliography and index.

Swales, Martin, and Erika Swales. *Reading Goethe: A Critical Introduction to the Literary Work.* Rochester, N.Y.: Camden House, 2002. A comprehensive critical analysis of Goethe's literary output, which argues that the writer is an essential figure in German modernity. Chapter 4 focuses on his plays.

Wells, G. A. "Criticism and the Quest for Analogies: Some Recent Discussions of Goethe's *Egmont*." *New German Studies* 15, no. 1 (1988-1989): 1-15. Summarizes critical viewpoints on Goethe's play. Among other perspectives, the work is viewed as a drama of innocence versus experience and a conflict between romanticism and social/ moral realities.

The Egoist
A Comedy in Narrative

Author: George Meredith (1828-1909)
First published: 1879
Type of work: Novel
Type of plot: Psychological realism
Time of plot: Nineteenth century
Locale: England

Principal characters:
SIR WILLOUGHBY PATTERNE, the egoist
VERNON WHITFORD, his cousin
COLONEL DE CRAYE, his relative
LAETITIA DALE, a neighbor
CLARA MIDDLETON, Sir Willoughby's betrothed
DR. MIDDLETON, her father
CROSSJAY PATTERNE, Sir Willoughby's distant kinsman

The Story:

On the day of his majority, Sir Willoughby Patterne announces his engagement to Miss Constantia Durham. Laetitia Dale, who lives with her old father in a cottage on Willoughby's estate, loves him, she thinks secretly, but everyone, including Willoughby, is aware of it. Ten days before the wedding day, Constantia astonishes everyone by eloping with Harry Oxford, a military man. For a few weeks after the elopement, Willoughby courts Laetitia, and the neighborhood gossips about her chances to become his wife. There is great disappointment when he suddenly decides to go abroad for three years. On his return, he brings with him his cousin, Vernon Whitford, to advise him in the management of his properties, and a young distant kinsman named Crossjay Patterne.

Laetitia is at first overjoyed at Willoughby's return, but she soon sees that she is to lose him again, for he becomes en-

gaged to Clara Middleton, the daughter of a learned doctor. Middleton and his daughter come to Willoughby's estate to visit for a few weeks. Over Willoughby's objections, Vernon encourages Crossjay to enter the marines, and the young man is sent to Laetitia to be tutored for his examination. Vernon, a literary man, wants to go to London, but Willoughby overrules him. Noting Willoughby's self-centered attitude toward Crossjay, his complete and selfish concern with matters affecting himself, and his attempt to dominate her own mind, Clara begins to feel trapped by her betrothal. She reflects that Constantia escaped by finding a gallant Harry Oxford to take her away, but she sadly realizes that she has no one to rescue her.

When Clara attempts to break her engagement, she finds Willoughby intractable and her father too engrossed in his studies to be concerned. Willoughby decides that Laetitia should become Vernon's wife, so that he will have near him both his cousin and the woman who feeds his ego with her devotion. According to Willoughby's plan, Vernon can retire to one of the cottages on the estate and write and study. When Willoughby asks Clara to help him in his plan, Clara takes the opportunity to ask Vernon's advice on her own problem. He tells her that she must move subtly and slowly.

In desperation, she persuades Dr. Middleton to agree to take a trip to France with her for a few weeks. She hopes never to return to Willoughby, but the wary lover introduces Dr. Middleton to his favorite brand of claret, and after two bottles of the wine, the doctor is putty in Willoughby's hands. When Clara asks him if he is ready to go to London with her, he tells her that the thought is preposterous.

Colonel De Craye, who arrives to serve as best man at the wedding, gradually senses that Clara is not happy at the prospect of her approaching marriage. In desperation, Clara writes to her friend, Lucy Darleton, and receives an invitation to visit her in London.

Clara gives Crossjay the privilege of accompanying her to the train station. A hue and cry rise at her absence from the estate, and Vernon, accidentally discovering her destination, follows her to the station and urges her to come back. She does so only because she believes that her behavior might injure Crossjay's future. Vernon is soon to go to London to follow his writing career, and if she left, too, Willoughby would have full control of the young boy.

Complications result from Clara's attempted escape. At the station, Vernon persuades her to drink some brandy to overcome the effects of the rainy weather. The neighborhood begins to gossip. Willoughby confronts Crossjay, who tells him the truth about Clara's escape. Clara hopes that Willoughby will release her from her engagement, but he again refuses. Dr. Middleton, determined that his daughter should fulfill her pledge, ignores what is happening. In any case, he likes Willoughby's vintage wines and the estate.

Gradually, though, the egoist realizes that his marriage to Clara will not take place. To soothe his wounded vanity, he asks Laetitia to become his wife. She refuses, declaring she no longer loves him. Colonel De Craye shrewdly surmises what happened. He tells Clara the hopeful news. Clara feels that her only remaining obstacle is her father's insistence that she not break her promise to Willoughby. Now, however, she can show that Willoughby broke his promise first by proposing to Laetitia while still pledged to her.

Dr. Middleton announces firmly that Clara need not marry Willoughby. He decides that he admires Vernon's scholarship more than he likes Willoughby's wines. The twice-jilted lover tries to even the score by manipulating Clara to consent to marry Vernon, which he feels will have the ironic touch that will be some measure of recompense to him. He is denied even this satisfaction when Clara tells him it is already her intention to wed Vernon as soon as her engagement to Willoughby is officially broken. The egoist's selfishness and arrogance bring them together.

Defeated, the egoist goes to Laetitia, offering her his hand even if she is willing to marry him only for his money. Laetitia accepts on the condition that Crossjay be permitted to enter the marines. Clara and the doctor plan to leave for Europe. Vernon arranges to meet them in the Swiss Alps, where he and Clara will marry.

Critical Evaluation:

The Egoist by George Meredith is a remarkable depiction of a sensitive and intelligent woman's mental, moral, and emotional agonies as she attempts to free herself from her engagement to an egotistical man. With an unusual degree of self-awareness, honesty, and perceptivity, Meredith identifies with Sir Willoughby Patterne's egoism and convinces his readers that egoism is characteristic of all humans.

Several parallels to Meredith's life are significant. In 1849, when Meredith was twenty-one years old, he married Mary Ellen Nicolls, who was twenty-seven, the widow of a marine officer and the daughter of Thomas Love Peacock. The marriage lasted seven years and was full of tension and quarrels. Meredith believed that his egoism drove her away. The breakup of this relationship underlies the deep psychological probing in the fifty poems of Meredith's *Modern Love and Poems of the English Roadside* (1862). There, Meredith indicates that he, like Willoughby, sought control, expected others to submit to him, entertained an artificial but quite conventionally sentimental conception of femininity, and thought of himself as the center of the universe. In the poems and in the novel, he emphasizes the suffering of the woman and concludes that both men and women are trapped in tragic circumstances by insincerity and lack of mutual understanding.

In *The Egoist*, Clara Middleton, like Mary Ellen Meredith, is caught in a nexus of relationships because of her virtues: purity, docility, and usefulness to men. Meredith allows the reader to share her thought processes as she works her way through a labyrinth of dilemmas. Willoughby is in everyone's eyes the perfect husband; she faces social disgrace. Fortunately Clara escapes before the wedding instead of after and manages to gain her freedom without sacrificing her reputation or hurting anyone.

Meredith not only shared with Willoughby a self-esteem based on thoughtless self-importance but also shared the scholarly interests of Dr. Middleton, Clara's father, who values the opportunity to use the library and to drink the aged wine at Patterne Hall above his responsibility toward his daughter. Dr. Middleton, who is thought to be a fictional portrayal of Peacock, is also an egoist; his confidence in his own judgment blinds him to Clara's needs.

Vernon Whitford is thought to be modeled on two of Meredith's friends, Sir Leslie Stephen, the father of Virginia Woolf—which is particularly interesting in view of the fact that Vernon is portrayed as being fully worthy of Clara—and Meredith's close companion Henry Wallis, with whom Mary Ellen ran away from her marriage. As a writer, Vernon also has several characteristics in common with Meredith, who wrote eight novels and several volumes of poetry before *The Egoist*. After writing this novel, he, like Vernon, turned to periodical journalism and became a literary adviser.

In form, the novel is a comedy that follows the principles Meredith laid out two years earlier in an essay entitled "The Idea of Comedy and the Uses of the Comic Spirit" (1877). Here, he advocated the therapeutic value of laughter in correcting vanity and promoting common sense. In the prelude to the novel Meredith alludes to the feminine comic spirit who "proposes the correction of pretentiousness." Meredith's women conspire with the comic imps who love to "uncover ridiculousness in imposing figures" and gather wherever egoism is found. In the last sentences of the novel, the "grave and sisterly" comic muse accompanies the lovers in their escape to the Alps, which represent all that is natural and freeing.

In many ways, the novel is like a comic drama. "The curtain falls" in the last chapter, and the action follows the unities of place (Patterne Hall), action (Clara's attempts to free herself), and even time, as it takes place over a few days. The women are impishly clever, witty, and wise as well as well bred and well educated, thus resembling Mary Peacock Nicolls, who learned classical languages and attended plays as a child. The women are also superior in unselfishness, intuition, and innate common sense. Their dialogues approach those of a brilliant drawing-room comedy. Laetitia Dale is a writer and a woman of deep thoughts and emotions, who moves from idealistic worship of Willoughby to a more mature and objective view of him. By the end of the novel, she sees his faults, forgives him, and accepts him on her own terms. Constantia Durham, who "had money and health and beauty, the triune of perfect starriness which makes all men astronomers," is intelligent enough to leave Willoughby. The delightful comments of Mrs. Mountstuart Jenkinson and Lady Busshe include clever predictions and sparkling dinner-table conversation. Even Willoughby's de-

voted aunts wield the corrective comic spirit. Significantly, it is the women who comment on the artificiality of the conventional codes of drawing-room conduct and the false values that shape their society.

Meredith's richly poetic narrative is noteworthy for its use of recurrent symbols, including that of the most cherished dinnerware of the nineteenth century, the "willow pattern." The idea of ancient artificial china is echoed in Willoughby's name, in Mrs. Montstuart Jenkinson's references to Clara as a "dainty rogue in porcelain," and in the breaking of a porcelain vase, one of Clara's wedding gifts.

Many of the patterns of imagery suggest the prevalence of Charles Darwin's ideas in contemporary thinking. Willoughby feels that since he is "the fittest" he has a responsibility to help breed the noblest race of men to come. The young Crossjay embodies the animal innocence and natural exuberance of the primitive instinct that still exists in human beings. Meredith implies that culture did not yet totally cut off the primal passions that are restricted by rules of a society in which the supernatural is replaced by the principles of evolution with no regard for the individual. Even Vernon's "holy tree," the double-blossomed cherry, is threatened by scientific breeders, but his appreciation of its beauty indicates that blood, brain, and spirit join in him in joyful wholeness. Crossjay instinctively knows that Vernon is right for Clara, who runs and plays with him as if her "real vitality had been in suspense."

"Critical Evaluation" by Constance M. Fulmer

Further Reading

Fraser, Robert. "Nineteenth-Century Adventure and Fantasy: James Morier, George Meredith, Lewis Carroll, and Robert Louis Stevenson." In *A Companion to Romance: From Classical to Contemporary*, edited by Corinne Saunders. Malden, Mass.: Blackwell, 2004. Fraser's essay about Meredith and three other British writers is included in this study of romance literature, which charts the genre from its beginnings through the twenty-first century.

Handwerk, Gary J. "Linguistic Blindness and Ironic Vision in *The Egoist*." *Nineteenth Century Literature* 39, no. 2 (September, 1984): 163-185. Handwerk discusses the irony of the relationship between self-knowledge and language.

Harris, Margaret. "George Meredith at the Crossways." In *A Companion to the Victorian Novel*, edited by William Baker and Kenneth Womack. Westport, Conn.: Greenwood Press, 2002. An introductory overview of the Victorian novel. Contains essays about Meredith and other authors and discussions of the historical and social context of the Victorian novel, the growth of serialization, and the different genres of Victorian fiction.

Hill, Charles J. "Theme and Image in *The Egoist*." *University of Kansas City Review* 20, no. 4 (Summer, 1954): 281-285. Reprinted in *The Egoist*, edited by Robert M. Adams. New York: W. W. Norton, 1979. Hill reads the novel as a document in Meredith's campaign to encourage men to support women's emancipation.

Jones, Mervyn. *The Amazing Victorian: A Life of George Meredith*. London: Constable, 1999. Jones's biography aims to recover Meredith from obscurity and introduce the author to a new generation of readers. He links Meredith life to his writing and includes a forty-page appendix recounting the plot summaries of all of Meredith's novels.

Mayo, Robert D. "*The Egoist* and the Willow Pattern." *English Literary History* 9 (1942): 71-78. Reprinted in *The Egoist*, edited by Robert M. Adams. New York: W. W. Norton, 1979. This significant article explains how Sir Willoughby Patterne is identified with the unrealistic conventionalism of the willow design as it is so charmingly described by Charles Lamb in his essay "Old China."

Roberts, Neil. *Meredith and the Novel*. New York: St. Martin's Press, 1997. Roberts employs twentieth century literary criticism, especially the ideas of literary critic Mikhail Bakhtin, to analyze all of Meredith's novels. Includes bibliographical references and an index.

Stevenson, Richard C. *The Experimental Impulse in George Meredith's Fiction*. Lewisburg, Pa.: Bucknell University Press, 2004. Stevenson focuses on the novels he considers most representative of Meredith's experimental fiction, including *The Egoist*, in order to demonstrate how these books feature controversial contemporary themes, innovative narrative structures, depictions of human consciousness, and other unconventional elements.

Sundell, Michael C. "The Functions of Flitch in *The Egoist*." *Nineteenth-Century Fiction* 24, no. 2 (September, 1969): 227-235. Reprinted in *The Egoist*, edited by Robert M. Adams. New York: W. W. Norton, 1979. Sundell discusses how Adam Flitch, the coachman at Patterne Hall who was dismissed as a result of Willoughby's brutal egoism, symbolizes the perennial servitor.

Tague, Gregory. *Ethos and Behavior: The English Novel from Jane Austen to Henry James (Including George Meredith, W. M. Thackeray, George Eliot, and Thomas Hardy)*. Bethesda, Md.: Academica Press, 2008. *The Ordeal of Richard Feverel* and *The Egoist* are among the novels Tague analyzes in his examination of English didactic literature. His study includes a discussion of the ethical aspects of these novels and the conduct of their fictional characters.

El Zarco, the Bandit

Author: Ignacio Manuel Altamirano (1834-1893)
First published: El Zarco: Episodios de la vida mexicana en 1861-1863, 1901 (English translation, 1957)
Type of work: Novel
Type of plot: Historical
Time of plot: 1861-1863
Locale: Province of Morelos, Mexico

Principal characters:
NICOLÁS, an Indian blacksmith
EL ZARCO, a bandit
MANUELA, a woman in love with El Zarco
DOÑA ANTONIA, her mother
PILAR, Doña Antonia's godchild, in love with Nicolás
MARTÍN SÁNCHEZ, a rancher and El Zarco's enemy
EL TIGRE, El Zarco's lieutenant

The Story:

During the War of Reform and after, bands of robber outlaws take advantage of the troubled times to overrun those districts of Mexico where the local authorities, in a land still disturbed by civil war, are powerless to make effective reprisals against them. Roaming the countryside in armed bands, the *plateados*, as they are called, waylay and murder travelers, kidnap wealthy estate owners for ransom, and levy tribute on the villages and haciendas. For their amusement, they often wantonly burn the cane fields and inflict brutal tortures on their prisoners.

One town terrorized in this fashion is Yautepec, a pleasant village of the *tierra caliente* in the province of Morelos. By day, the people of the village maintain lookouts in the church towers to give warning of approaching marauders; at night, they barricade themselves in their houses, so that after sunset the little town in the middle of its circling orange groves resembles a place of the dead. The bandits, some five hundred strong, have their headquarters at Xochimancas, a nearby ruined hacienda from which they make forays to ravage the whole district. Their leader is El Zarco, a man of savage temper and cruel disposition whose bloody exploits cause respectable, decent people to fear him. The bandits sometimes enter the town and ride boldly through the streets.

On an evening in August, 1861, Doña Antonia sits in the inner courtyard of her house with her daughter Manuela and Pilar, her godchild. The two girls are plaiting flower garlands for their hair. After a time, Manuela begins to tease Pilar because her friend is making a wreath of orange blossoms, the flower of weddings; Manuela is twining a circlet of roses. When Manuela complains of her dull life, her mother rebukes her sharply, saying that Manuela ought to forget fiestas and dances, and take a husband who will protect her. Doña Antonia's choice is Nicolás, the sober and industrious blacksmith of the estate at Atlihuayan. At this suggestion, Manuela begins to speak scornfully of the Indian, as she calls him, and declares that she would rather have El Zarco as a suitor. She adds that Nicolás might be good enough for Pilar, but she herself will never have him. Pilar blushes but says nothing.

Before Doña Antonia can reprove her daughter further, Nicolás, a nightly caller, arrives with the news that, on the previous night, the *plateados* robbed and killed an English family traveling to Acapulco, and that a cavalry detachment is being sent from Cuernavaca to pursue the bandits. Alarmed at this latest outrage, Doña Antonia decides that she and Manuela will go to Mexico City until times are better; they will travel with the troops as their escort for part of the dangerous journey. Nicolás thinks her decision a wise one for Manuela's sake.

Later, while Nicolás is on his way back to Atlihuayan, another rider is traveling toward Yautepec. The horseman is El Zarco. In the village, he turns down a dark lane that leads to a stone wall surrounding Doña Antonia's orange grove. Drawing rein beneath a giant sapota tree, he whistles twice. An answering whistle comes from the darkness under the tree, where Manuela is waiting for her lover.

El Zarco had met Manuela in Cuernavaca during a brief period when he and his men were aiding the government

forces, and the two were strongly drawn to each other. After he established himself at Xochimancas, the bandit learned that Manuela and her mother had returned to Yautepec. Through his spies in the village, he has arranged to see her regularly. El Zarco finds her wholehearted devotion flattering to his vanity. Manuela, refusing to believe the stories of his violence and cruelty, sees him only as a handsome, brave *caballero*. Now, unwilling to leave Yautepec, she tells him of Doña Antonia's plans and asks him to take her away. Before they part that night, they arrange for him to carry her off to Xochimancas. In parting, El Zarco gives her several small boxes for safekeeping. After his departure, she sees that one of them is bloodstained. The boxes contain a diamond ring, two bracelets, and earrings. Putting the jewelry on, Manuela goes to a pool in the garden and looks at her reflection by the light of a lantern. She buries the jewels with other gems and money that El Zarco has already entrusted to her.

The next night, Manuela flees with El Zarco to his hideout, leaving behind a note in which she tells her mother goodbye. Heartbroken, Doña Antonia asks Nicolás to go with her to beg the cavalry troop from Cuernavaca to hunt down the bandits and rescue Manuela. They approach the cavalry commander, but he refuses, and Nicolás accuses the officer of shirking his duty. The blacksmith is then placed under arrest and ordered held for trial.

Pilar, upset by the news of Nicolás's arrest, tries to visit him in prison but is turned back by his guards. Nicolás, hearing her pleas, realizes that it is Pilar and not Manuela whom he truly loves. The authorities of Yautepec and the manager of Atlihuayan are indignant over the treatment Nicolás has received. When the commander sets out to take his prisoner to the capital, a large party accompanies the troops to see that the blacksmith receives full justice. Through the intercession of the owner of Atlihuayan, Nicolás is finally released. He returns to Yautepec in time to see Doña Antonia on her deathbed, for the poor woman is dying of grief over her daughter's disgrace. After her death, Nicolás continues to ride into the village each evening, but now he visits Pilar.

Meanwhile, at Xochimancas, Manuela lives a different and sordid life of lawlessness and violence. Forced to associate with the disreputable women of the *plateados*, ogled by the men and showered with their lewd comments, she is at first terrified by her new surroundings. She realizes that she was attracted to El Zarco by infatuation and greed, not love. In particular, she is horrified by the condition of a French prisoner whom the bandits torture daily with the aim of extorting a greater ransom. At a fiesta to celebrate one of El Zarco's raids, Manuela is forced to dance with El Tigre, a repulsive creature who tells her that El Zarco will tire of her eventually and turn her over to one of his lieutenants. El Tigre intends to be that man.

A short time before, El Zarco had killed the father and son of a rancher named Martín Sánchez. Swearing revenge, Sánchez sells his property and buys arms and equipment for twenty men whom he recruits to track down the bandits. After he and his men make several successful raids on the outlaws, others are roused from their apathy and fears to join them. In an encounter at La Calavera, in which Nicolás takes part, El Zarco is wounded and taken prisoner. With him is Manuela.

In spite of Sánchez's protests, El Zarco cleverly arranges to have his trial held in Cuernavaca. While the prisoners are being taken there, bandits attack the escorting troops and set El Zarco and Manuela free. Sánchez, determined to end lawlessness in the region, obtains from President Juarez the authority to hang, without trial, any bandit who falls into his hands.

The day of Pilar and Nicolás's wedding arrives at last. After the ceremony, the couple starts by coach for Atlihuayan with friends invited to the wedding feast that is to be held there. On the way, they meet a troop of horsemen led by Martín Sánchez, who asks the party to drive on without stopping. At that moment, Manuela appears from behind the horsemen and begs the help of Nicolás and his bride. El Zarco and El Tigre, she says, have been captured and are to be executed. Sánchez tells them that he has saved the wedding party from an ambush. Pilar, filled with pity for Manuela, wants to take her into the coach, but Manuela cries out that she would rather die with El Zarco than see Pilar in her wreath of orange blossoms. Saddened, the wedding party rides on.

El Zarco is shot down by a firing squad, and his body is then hung from the branch of a tree. Manuela, seeing her lover dangling there, gives a loud cry and falls to the ground. Blood runs from her mouth. Several men try to lift her, but she is already dead.

Critical Evaluation:

Ignacio Manuel Altamirano, who was of Aztec background, became a lawyer and served as a soldier in the War of Reform (1858-1860) and in the resistance to the French occupation of Mexico (1862-1867). In addition to writing novels, he produced poetry, newspaper articles, and essays. He was also an active politician associated with the Liberal Party. In 1889, he became Mexico's consul to Spain. The fact that he never forgot his humble origins is reflected in his active promotion of literacy programs for the lower classes, peasants, and indigenous peoples. His political platform presupposed that Mexico's success depended on its becoming a more intellectually developed country, retaining awareness of its glorious past as its masses became educated.

Altamirano also promoted the study of European cultures in order to incorporate the Mexico of the late nineteenth century into the most innovative intellectual currents. He spoke French fluently, a feat for one who had learned Spanish at fourteen years of age. He was an avid reader of European literatures, which provided him the classical structure for his own literary craft. Contemporary critics praised his works; they considered him a true Mexican novelist who had moved away from the old literary molds inherited from Spain.

In fact, Altamirano displayed no major involvement in Spanish literature, since Spanish culture was associated with the Conservative Party, Altamirano's political opponents. His novels exhibit the carefully studied neoclassical literary design that was much in vogue in eighteenth century Europe. He was also an acclaimed literary critic and chronicler of Mexican literature, both colonial and contemporary.

As a politician, however, Altamirano also understood that his literature served a strong pedagogical purpose in promoting Mexico's political positions. *El Zarco, the Bandit* is the product of a sophisticated political theorist. Its plot is partially founded on historical events that the author witnessed as a soldier. His strong interest in Mexican history made him a forerunner in the promotion of a national literature. The novel continues the Romantic tradition of recapturing folklore; it also seeks to validate Mexican motifs as material worthy of literature. This radical position illustrates Altamirano's strong desire to incorporate autochthonous types, settings, and events into a literature formerly dominated by foreign influences. Because the Mexican illiteracy rate was high, it is probable that Altamirano intended for his literature, full of local color, to be appreciated by international readers.

The peculiar untamed environment of the *tierra caliente* of southern Mexico and the region's native characters stand out in *El Zarco, the Bandit*. In rural settings, Altamirano sets characters against one another in a struggle for the survival of the fittest. Although the struggle is physical, as reflected in the novel's many armed confrontations between outlaws and innocent peasants, it is also moral. The characters in *El Zarco, the Bandit* fall into two distinct groups: The evil of the robbers contrasts with the honesty and the patriotism of the civilians who fight the outlaws. This primal view of human behavior is the central focus of the plot. This archetypal construction makes *El Zarco, the Bandit* read like an epic narration. The novel tells of the clash between good and evil and the consequent destruction of evil. At first, the land in the *tierra caliente* is claimed by the outlaws. When the hard-working peasants triumph, the suggestion is that the land itself will also be tamed by the forces of good.

Altamirano incorporates an important difference in *El Zarco, the Bandit*, however, from what one may expect of an archetypal story. The hero, Nicolás, is an Indian and physically unattractive. Nicolás, a hardworking blacksmith, is a strong and able man, a jack-of-all-trades, and he also has a good heart. El Zarco, who is blond and blue-eyed, has no useful skills except his ability to kill. The contrast of the racial backgrounds of El Zarco and Nicolás defies what might politely be called traditional symbology. The unattractive Indian is an uncommon protagonist in the newly developed Mexican literature. Traditional colonial literature presents natives as a destructive entity; indigenous groups appear aligned with nature, and both are depicted as untamed forces. In *El Zarco, the Bandit*, however, the blond antagonist (whom the reader supposes to be of Spanish descent) is evil. At a time when European influence in Mexico was despised by peasants and light-skinned people were the targets of outlaws, the novel presents a struggle between two typical figures of the New World, the European newcomer and the indigenous laborer.

Another important function of the ethnic contrast is its use to build suspense as several related issues find themselves linked in the plot. The most significant issue is that of interracial love. Nicolás, unaware that El Zarco has been visiting Manuela furtively, expresses his desire to court her. Manuela, who, like El Zarco, is white, openly disdains Nicolás, whom she considers to be a dirty, ugly Indian. Nicolás finds love, however, in Pilar, also an Indian and in love with him. Suspense grows as characters come to know their own feelings and to recognize the emotions of the other characters.

Altamirano's *El Zarco, the Bandit*, with its emphasis on history as a means of understanding modern Mexico, precedes the literature of the Mexican Revolution. Like writers of that movement, Altamirano shows a consistent interest in promoting Mexican folklore and in documenting accounts of armed confrontations. His writing has a strong political and moral purpose. The message is clear: Mexican society, without a detailed account of all the forces involved in its formation, may appear chaotic, but once patterns of behavior are established it is obvious that Mexican society can be examined by objective means. A close understanding of Mexico as

a complex country will help to make possible the building of a more stable society.

"Critical Evaluation" by Rafael Ocasio

Further Reading

Castagnaro, Anthony R. *The Early Spanish American Novel.* New York: Las Américas, 1971. Focuses on the development of the Latin American novel since the nineteenth century. Establishes Altamirano as a precursor of the genre in Mexico.

Duncan, Cynthia. "Ignacio Manuel Altamirano." In *Dictionary of Mexican Literature*, edited by Eladio Cortés. Westport, Conn.: Greenwood Press, 1992. Good introduction to Altamirano presents a survey of his works.

Long, Ryan. "The Cautious Critique of Foundational Violence in Ignacio Manuel Altamirano's *El Zarco*." *Journal of Latin American Cultural Studies* 16, no. 1 (March, 2007): 81-94. Provides a character study of El Zarco and Nicolás, focusing on why Altamirano chose to end El Zarco's life at the hands of Martín Sánchez and not those of Nicolás, who is a more significant character in the novel.

Nacci, Chris. *Ignacio Manuel Altamirano.* New York: Twayne, 1970. Offers a good introduction to Altamirano's life and works. Presents an overview of his fiction along with strong biographical and historical background.

Reyes, Lisa. "The Nineteenth-Century Latin American National Romance and the Role of Women." *Ariel* 8 (1992): 33-44. Provides a comparative study of major nineteenth century novelists' treatment of women in their works. Stresses the influence of the strong Latin American patriarchal social structure on the emerging novel.

Segre, Erica. *Intersected Identities: Strategies of Visualisation in Nineteenth- and Twentieth-Century Mexican Culture.* New York: Berghahn Books, 2007. Asserts that the "visual element" has played a significant role in creating the Mexican national identity since the country gained its independence. Analyzes Mexican literature, periodicals, films, and photographs of the nineteenth and twentieth centuries to demonstrate how this visual element operates. The works of Altamirano are addressed in a chapter titled "An Italicised Ethnicity: Memory, Renascence, and Visuality in the Literary Writings of Ignacio Manuel Altamirano."

The Elder Statesman

Author: T. S. Eliot (1888-1965)
First produced: 1958; first published, 1959
Type of work: Drama
Type of plot: Allegory
Time of plot: Mid-twentieth century
Locale: London

Principal characters:
LORD CLAVERTON, the elder statesman
MICHAEL CLAVERTON-FERRY, his son
MONICA CLAVERTON-FERRY, his daughter
CHARLES HEMINGTON, her fiancé
FEDERICO GOMEZ, formerly Fred Culverwell
MRS. CARGHILL, MAISIE BATTERSON, alias MAISIE
    MONTJOY, a woman out of Lord Claverton's past

The Story:

Lord Claverton's daughter's fiancé, Charles, is protesting that, should he stay for tea in the Claverton town house, he will not be able to have any private conversation with Monica because of her father's presence. Monica worships her father, who was a famous man in the political and financial worlds of England but who is currently, on his doctor's orders, retired from public life. Lord Claverton is preparing for a rest cure at Badgley Court, a nursing home in the country. Lord Claverton enters. He becomes querulous over the emptiness of his future. Like most men of affairs who are compelled to give up their former activities, he realizes the hollowness of his past eminence, yet he cannot endure the prospect of a life devoid of his former important activities. Life becomes a mere waiting for death for him. He recognizes himself as a ghost and, with dramatic irony, remarks that he smiles when he thinks people are frightened of ghosts.

Hardly is this remark uttered when the first ghost from his own past arrives in the form of one Señor Gomez, from the Latin American Republic of San Marco. Almost immediately Gomez is revealed as Fred Culverwell, a friend of Lord Claverton's Oxford days. The unbearably suave expatriate is in possession of a damaging secret. Years before, the two university students were driving at night with two young women when Claverton—then plain Dick Ferry—ran over a man and did not stop because he feared the possible scandal. Culverwell also accuses Claverton of being the cause of Culverwell's ruin in England. By taking Culverwell up at Oxford and teaching him expensive tastes that he, a poor boy, lacked the means to gratify, Claverton forced him to resort to theft and finally to forgery, which led to a prison sentence and flight from England. In San Marco, with its peculiar political situation, he did well. Culverwell is no crude blackmailer and wants only Claverton's friendship, something to give him reality after thirty-five years of homesick exile under an assumed name. He is a realist; he knows that, although a worldly success, he failed, although not so badly as Claverton,

who keeps on pretending to himself that he succeeded. To his credit, Claverton stands the attack well, maintains his dignity, and shows no fear of the moral blackmail that Culverwell is so subtly exercising.

Claverton's doctor orders him to Badgley Court, a nursing home run in a grimly cheerful fashion, for a complete rest. Hardly does he arrive when another ghost from his past appears, this time in the form of Mrs. Carghill. A generation before she was Maisie Montjoy, a star of the music halls. She is currently a prosperous widow. The Dick Ferry of those far-off days was in love with her and she with him—or so she claims. She settled her breach-of-promise suit out of court, and now she retains only sentimental memories and all of his letters. Again Claverton, in spite of her sarcastic comments, maintains his unruffled dignity, even when she points out that there is only a negligible difference between being an elder statesman and posing as one. Twice the ghosts bring home to him his essential emptiness.

The ultimate trial comes in the form of his son Michael, a spendthrift and ne'er-do-well who, even in his effort to see his father, becomes involved in a motor accident, although not a serious one. In a sense, Michael is also a ghost, the ghost of the boy Claverton might have been were he not possessed by a devil who was prudent as well as wayward. The son, although obviously a weakling, has his side of the story. He is desperately eager to get out of England into some country where he can have a life of his own, free from the oppressive shadow of his father's great name. It is clear that the father dominated the son too much. The situation between the two seemed to reach an impasse, but a solution is provided by the two ghosts. Mrs. Carghill suggests to Gomez that he take Michael back with him to the mysterious business in San Marco. The price to be paid for this solution is that Claverton must have all his past errors laid bare before his daughter and her fiancé. This is his act of contrition, after which he receives absolution in the form of Monica's forgiveness and understanding. The ghosts from his past are at last exorcised, to return into the darkness whence they came. Claverton goes out into the grounds of the nursing home to await death, much as Oedipus left the grove at Colonus to find his appointed end. The mask of the "elder statesman" is dropped forever. Claverton is himself, the real man under the mask.

Critical Evaluation:

Although often treated as a minor work, *The Elder Statesman* embodies some of T. S. Eliot's finest achievements in verse drama. As Eliot's final play, this work represents a culmination of many of Eliot's themes and techniques. His ability to make each character on stage an aspect of the central character, his technique of forming characters into competing triangles, and his facility for depicting spiritual conflicts through visible, human struggles all reach a zenith in this play.

Many of the characters in *The Elder Statesman* fit into the recognizable roles of pilgrim, witness, watcher, and tempter, roles used in Eliot's earlier plays, and do so more naturally than in any of Eliot's previous dramas. Lord Claverton is the pilgrim who gains his redemption through facing his past failures. Monica Claverton-Ferry and Charles Hemington serve as witnesses whose love and forgiveness enable Lord Claverton to discover his real self and make peace with his past. These three form a triangle of compassion and of forgiveness. Michael Claverton-Ferry is a watcher who sees much but learns little, and like most of Eliot's watchers is destined to failure. Mrs. Carghill and Federico Gomez are the tempters who haunt Claverton and complete their merciless revenge by tutoring Michael in their diabolical habits. Mrs. Carghill and Señor Gomez entice Michael into a triangle of hate and unforgiveness. The only other prominent character not fitting into one of these triangles is Mrs. Piggott. As the meddlesome manager of Badgley Court, she prods and prompts characters into action or self-expression. Her treatment in the play is too scant to allow the audience to observe her full character, but Mrs. Piggott seems to function as a watcher, an observer who gains little from the events of the play.

Claverton's escape from the triangle of hate involves more than overcoming guilt, a potentially healthy emotion. He struggles against the hate that would use guilt as a weapon for revenge. His cure takes place in two stages. First, Claverton must accept his true self and his past. He must likewise recognize the potential for good his friends once had. Claverton accomplishes this first step when he confesses to Charles and Monica how he has failed his friends Fred and Maisie. Sec-

ond, Claverton must accept only his part of the guilt and refuse the rest. In both of these processes, his daughter's all-accepting love is vital to his final redemption from a deadening past. Through this love he finds the courage to die and, ironically, experience a new life. Claverton's struggle ends in self-acceptance, peace, and completion. His recognition that "in becoming no one, I begin to live" shows that he has grasped the essence of childlike humility. With the yielding of vanity and pride, the ghosts of fear over humiliation also dissipate.

As a completion of Eliot's treatment of Christian community, *The Elder Statesman* illustrates how witnesses can function as agents of redemption for the pilgrim. This pattern of action is the opposite of that in *Murder in the Cathedral* (1935), in which the pilgrim-martyr pours out his life as a blessing upon his contrite parishioners. While Claverton, the pilgrim, remains the focal point of the play throughout, he is dependent upon the love of the two witnesses, Monica and Charles, to make possible his spiritual pilgrimage from ghostly hollowness to wholeness. In this play divine love is portrayed through human love, as reflected in Monica's self-sacrificing love for her father. For the first time in Eliot's works, human love functions as an agent of divine love. Thus the opening and closing love scenes create a fitting frame for the play and mark a high achievement in Eliot's career.

Eliot's treatment of tempters nearly comes full circle in *The Elder Statesman*, for in this final play he used the morality play as a model. Just as Eliot uses characters surrounding Thomas Becket in *Murder in the Cathedral* to portray his inner qualities and struggles, so the playwright uses various characters around Claverton in *The Elder Statesman* to represent his strengths and deficiencies. In Eliot's last play he discovers how to depict spiritual struggles as the visible trials of human beings. Consequently, the tempters are far more natural and believable than in Eliot's earlier plays. As Eliot learned to appreciate the value of the natural world, he also discovered how to use it as the basis for his drama on spiritual themes. In this sense, his plays demonstrate a definite improvement in characterization.

Eliot made use of Sophocles' *Oidipous epi Kolōnōi* (401 B.C.E.; *Oedipus at Colonus*, 1729) as a foundation for *The Elder Statesman*. In *The Elder Statesman* Claverton functions as the aged and dying Oedipus who is aided by his daughter as he seeks a happy death, or translation into a new life. Although some critics find Eliot's use of Greek models too subtle for comparison, these models nevertheless form an important reference point for interpreting the patterns of Eliot's plays. Another element often overlooked in Eliot's dramas is his use of poetry of the common person. In fact, the first viewers of *The Cocktail Party* (1949) and subsequent plays did not perceive that the plays were written in verse at all. Certainly *The Elder Statesman* reads smoothly, and only skillful actors can capture the written music without overplaying it. In this matter, too, Eliot was an experimenter, one who finally achieved his stated objective of writing such natural verse that listeners would declare "I could speak in verse, too."

The Elder Statesman is an excellent example of Eliot's ideals for verse drama. Although this drama is not considered by many to be his best work, it nevertheless points toward a new mode of writing verse drama in which few have excelled as Eliot did.

"Critical Evaluation" by Daven M. Kari

Further Reading

Chiari, Joseph. *T. S. Eliot: Poet and Dramatist.* New York: Barnes & Noble, 1972. Sees *The Elder Statesman* as a fitting culmination of Eliot's verse dramas and offers a positive interpretation of its accomplishments.

Däumer, Elisabeth. "Vipers, Viragos, and Spiritual Rebels: Women in T. S. Eliot's Christian Society Plays." In *Gender, Desire, and Sexuality in T. S. Eliot*, edited by Cassandra Laity and Nancy K. Gish. New York: Cambridge University Press, 2004. Däumer analyzes Eliot's depiction of women in *The Elder Statesman* and several other plays.

Gordon, Lyndall. *T. S. Eliot: An Imperfect Life.* New York: W. W. Norton, 1999. An authoritative, thoroughly researched biography that concedes Eliot's many personal flaws as well as describing his poetic genius.

Hinchliffe, Arnold P., ed. *T. S. Eliot, Plays: "Sweeney Agonistes," "The Rock," "Murder in the Cathedral," "The Family Reunion," "The Cocktail Party," "The Confidential Clerk," "The Elder Statesman": A Casebook.* New York: Macmillan, 1985. A concise selection of critical reviews by prominent critics. Many insights.

Jones, David E. *The Plays of T. S. Eliot.* London: Routledge & Kegan Paul, 1960. Chapter 7 concludes that in this play Eliot has complemented the motifs in *The Family Reunion* (1939) and resolved his dramas into a naturalistic surface. Discusses the Greek model for this play.

Kari, Daven Michael. *T. S. Eliot's Dramatic Pilgrimage: A Progress in Craft as an Expression of Christian Perspective.* Lewiston, N.Y.: Edwin Mellen Press, 1990. Finds the play a fitting completion of Eliot's Christian and artistic ideals. Addresses the criticism that Eliot's poetic skills waned in this work, and instead finds the play a model for future religious verse dramas.

Moody, A. David, ed. *The Cambridge Companion to T. S. Eliot.* New York: Cambridge University Press, 1994. Collection of essays, including discussions of Eliot's life; Eliot as a philosopher, a social critic, and a product of America; and religion, literature, and society in Eliot's work. Also features the essay "Pereira and After: The Cures of Eliot's Theater" by Robin Grove.

Raine, Craig. *T. S. Eliot.* New York: Oxford University Press, 2006. In this examination of Eliot's work, Raine maintains that "the buried life," or the failure of feeling, is a consistent theme in the poetry and plays. Chapter 5 focuses on Eliot's plays.

Smith, Carol H. *T. S. Eliot's Dramatic Theory and Practice: From "Sweeney Agonistes" to "The Elder Statesman."* Princeton, N.J.: Princeton University Press, 1963. Chapter 7 provides a useful summary of the play's main characteristics and concludes that the play succeeds as a theatrical fable designed to project religious insights.

Elective Affinities

Author: Johann Wolfgang von Goethe (1749-1832)
First published: Die Wahlverwandtschaften, 1809 (English translation, 1872)
Type of work: Novel
Type of plot: Love
Time of plot: Eighteenth century
Locale: Germany

Principal characters:
EDWARD, a wealthy nobleman
CHARLOTTE, his wife
OTTILIE, Charlotte's protégé
THE CAPTAIN, Edward's friend
LUCIANA, Charlotte's daughter by a previous marriage
NANNY, a youngster and Ottilie's protégé
HERR MITTLER, a self-appointed marriage counselor

The Story:

Edward, a wealthy nobleman, is long in love with Charlotte, but each is forced to wed someone else. Their first spouses die, however, before many years elapse, and soon afterward Edward and Charlotte are married. With Charlotte's daughter Luciana placed in a good school, the pair, happily married at last, settle down to an idyllic existence at Edward's rural castle. They spend their time working at pleasant tasks about the castle and its park, leading together the kind of life for which they long hoped and dreamed.

One day, a letter comes to the happy couple. The Captain, long a friend of Edward, is out of a position. Edward immediately suggests that his friend be invited to the castle, where the Captain can help in improving the grounds and buildings. At first Charlotte withholds her consent, but finally she agrees to her husband's earnest desire. She reveals that she, too, thinks of inviting someone to the castle, the daughter of a dead friend. Charlotte takes the young woman, Ottilie, as her protégé because of her friendship with the girl's mother. Ottilie, who is at school with Luciana, is not immediately invited for the visit Charlotte plans.

The Captain arrives shortly, and his presence soon makes marked differences in the household. In order that he and Edward might work together undisturbed and with greater convenience, Edward moves from the wing in which Charlotte's rooms are located to the wing in which the Captain is placed. Charlotte sees less and less of her husband. One evening, the three read about the elective affinities of chemical elements and speculate on how people are also attracted to one another in different combinations and in varying degrees. The invitation to Ottilie is again discussed. Since Ottilie is not doing well in school, and because Charlotte clearly needs additional companionship, Ottilie is immediately sent for.

When Edward saw Ottilie and was in her company on previous occasions, Ottilie made no impression on him. Seeing her in the same household, however, he soon becomes aware of her attractiveness. It becomes obvious, too, that Ottilie finds Edward attractive. The two fit together strangely well. When they play duets, Ottilie's mistakes coincide with Edward's. Gradually, as the two spend more and more time together, Charlotte and the Captain often find themselves together, much to their delight. After some weeks pass, Edward realizes the extent of his influence on Ottilie, all of which make him rejoice. Recognizing the force of his passion, he makes efforts to cause it to grow, as it does steadily and swiftly. Although Charlotte notices the attentions he pays Ottilie, she refuses to become upset by them; since she discovers her own regard for the Captain, she can more easily overlook her husband's behavior.

One day, while Charlotte and the Captain are out boating, their passion for each other can no longer be concealed. Considering themselves mature people, however, they immediately control their emotions and resolve, after a few kisses, to adhere strictly to the moral path in their conduct. In addition, during one of their periods together, Ottilie and Edward discover their love for each other. More easily swayed and emotionally immature, they welcome the passion and do not try to curb their emotions.

While the relationships among the four are developing, more guests come to the castle. They are a countess and a baron who are spending a vacation as lover and mistress while away from their respective spouses. On the night of their arrival, Edward shows the baron the way to the countess's rooms, that the lovers might be together. While wishing he could enter Ottilie's room with the same freedom as the baron enters that of his mistress, Edward finds himself at his wife's door. He knocks and is admitted. He remains the night with Charlotte, but when he and his wife embrace they do not think of each other, but of Ottilie and the Captain.

The four people are all working on plans for improving the grounds of the castle, with the hope, especially on Edward's part, that everything might be finished in time for Ottilie's birthday. On the day of the birthday celebration, Edward makes a public spectacle of himself, proving almost a fool in his ardor for Ottilie. Finally, Charlotte suggests that Ottilie be returned to school or be sent to live with other friends. Edward, angry and frustrated in his love, leaves the castle. When he leaves, he vows he will have nothing more to do with Ottilie, as Charlotte wishes, so long as Ottilie remains. On the same day, the Captain, who receives a position that promotes him to the rank of major, also leaves the castle.

Shortly after Edward's departure, Charlotte, discovering that she is pregnant as the result of the night her husband spent in her apartments, calls on the services of Herr Mittler, a volunteer marriage counselor. Herr Mittler, however, is unable even to begin a reconciliation with Edward, whose passion for Ottilie conquers him completely. Edward was accustomed all of his life to doing as he pleased and cannot see why he should not have his way in this matter. When war breaks out, he enters the king's service. He serves gallantly and wins many honors. He believes that if he lives through the war he is fated to have Ottilie.

Meanwhile, Charlotte endures her pregnancy, but she and Ottilie are no longer close to each other, for the younger woman becomes suspicious of Charlotte. For a time life at the castle is enlivened when Luciana arrives for a visit with a large party of her friends. During the entertainment of the visit, Luciana pointedly leaves Ottilie out of the activities arranged for the guests.

Ottilie's friend during the trying weeks after Edward leaves is a young architect hired to supervise the building of a summerhouse. Although his work is completed, Charlotte keeps him on to redecorate the local church. The young man admires Ottilie very much. A young schoolmaster who taught Ottilie also expresses interest in marrying her, but Ottilie can think only of Edward.

At last a son is born to Charlotte. At the christening Ottilie and Herr Mittler, who stand as sponsors for the baby, are surprised to note how much the infant resembles both Ottilie and the Captain, a resemblance soon noted by others. Charlotte, remembering how she dreamed of the Captain while embracing her husband, guesses that Edward was dreaming at the same time of Ottilie. In a sense the child, named Otto, is a symbol of the parents' double adultery.

Edward returns to a nearby farm when the war ends. He meets the Captain and makes a proposal to solve everyone's problems. He suggests that he and Charlotte divorce, so that he can marry Ottilie and Charlotte can marry the Captain. Although the ethics of the plan do not appeal to him, the Captain agrees to take the suggestion to Charlotte. When the Captain sets out for the castle, Edward also visits the grounds in the hope of seeing Ottilie. They meet, and Ottilie is extremely upset, so much so that while returning to the castle alone in a small boat she drops Charlotte's baby overboard. The child drowns. When the Captain arrives at the castle, Charlotte shows him the little corpse that is a miniature of himself.

Ottilie decides to go away. Edward meets her at an inn and persuades her to return to the castle with him. There the four—Edward, Charlotte, Ottilie, and the Captain—try to resume the happy life they knew before. Ottilie, however, seldom speaks and eats her meals in her rooms. One day she dies suddenly, having starved herself to death. It comes out that Nanny, her little protégé, was persuaded to eat the food intended for Ottilie. Edward also begins a fast. When he dies a short time later, although not as the result of his fasting, he is laid in a tomb beside the woman he loved. In death for one, in life for the other, the two couples are finally united.

Critical Evaluation:

Johann Wolfgang von Goethe's middle years as a classicist were bracketed by early and late years dominated by Romantic characteristics. *Elective Affinities* is a product of that late Romanticism. As he aged, however, Goethe was less adamant than he was in his younger days about his own adherence to any set of aesthetic principles. As a consequence, *Elective Affinities* contains elements of both classicism—

primarily in form—and Romanticism—mainly in content. The novel has a classic symmetry of form that complements the symmetrical arrangement of the four protagonists, dividing the married couple, Edward and Charlotte, between their two guests, Ottilie and the Captain. The classic harmonious structure of *Elective Affinities* is created by its cool, formal, generally unemotional style—particularly evident in the distancing between narrator and action evoked by Goethe's use of a third-person narrator. These classical qualities lead to the expectation that the issues with which the novel deals will be rigorously pursued to the necessary logical conclusion.

Such, however, is not the case, because Goethe treats content from a predominantly Romantic perspective. In *Elective Affinities*, the absolute moral imperative of classicism collides with the irresistible force of Romantic natural law. The classical view would mandate that society emerge the victor. Indeed, classic orthodoxy would reject the simultaneous existence of two immutable but antithetical laws in the universe. Romanticism, on the other hand, would argue for the victory of the individual and allows for paradox and contradiction. Rather than affirm a clear-cut endorsement of either law, however, Goethe concludes the novel ambiguously: Although death is the fate of the lovers who defied the moral code of society, those disciples of natural law ironically carry off a moral victory of sorts by wringing sympathetic comments from the narrator, who thinks about the existence of some higher plane where there is no conflict between social order and natural law. The implication—a thoroughly Romantic one—is that the two lovers, buried side by side, may yet reach that plane.

In addition to the fusion of classic and Romantic elements typical of Goethe's works, *Elective Affinities* also illustrates another of the author's lifelong preoccupations: the nature of the learning process. From *Die Leiden des jungen Werthers* (1774; *The Sorrows of Young Werther*, 1779) to *Faust* (1833; *The Tragedy of Faust*, 1838), Goethe was concerned with epistemology and its relation to education, although that concern is most pronounced in the two Wilhelm Meister novels. The bildungsroman, as these novels are called, is a tale of character development and the shaping of one's innate endowments. As such, the term also applies to *Elective Affinities*, since this novel subtly delineates the evolving mental and emotional qualities of the four protagonists as each one's elective affinity—in chemistry, the irresistible mutual attraction between two elements—changes over the course of the story. To be sure, *Elective Affinities* is much more than a novel about the philosophy of learning or a study in classic versus Romantic, but a delicately woven, intense psychological drama.

Further Reading

Armstrong, John. *Love, Life, Goethe: Lessons of the Imagination from the Great German Poet*. New York: Farrar, Straus and Giroux, 2007. Goethe's works are analyzed and his life examined in this comprehensive volume. Armstrong discusses a wide range of Goethe's writings, including his lesser known works, and gives a close study of his personal life. Knowing German and English, he provides translations of several key passages, while keeping his writing style plain and clear. This volume offers readers a better understanding of Goethe's writing and the circumstances that inspired it.

Bishop, Paul. *The World of Stoical Discourse in Goethe's Novel "Die Wahlverwandtschaften."* Lewiston, N.Y.: Edwin Mellen Press, 1999. Examines Goethe's interest in the philosophy of Stoicism and point outs elements of this philosophy in *Elective Affinities*.

Dieckmann, Liselotte. "Novels: The *Elective Affinities*." In *Johann Wolfgang von Goethe*. Boston: Twayne, 1974. Discusses the way irony, symbolism, and other narrative elements shape the novel. Contains an annotated list of Goethe criticism.

Hutchinson, Peter, ed. *Landmarks in the German Novel*. Part 1. New York: Peter Lang, 2007. Traces the development of the German novel from the eighteenth century until 1959 by analyzing thirteen milestone works, including separate essays discussing Goethe's *Elective Affinities*, *The Sorrows of Young Werther*, and *Wilhelm Meister's Apprenticeship*.

Lange, Victor. Introduction to *Elective Affinities*, by Johann Wolfgang von Goethe. Translated by Elizabeth Mayer and Louise Bogan. Chicago: Regnery, 1963. Written by a well-known Goethe scholar, this is an excellent introduction to the philosophical and moral issues raised in the novel. Emphasizes the ambivalence of love and marriage in the story.

Peacock, Ronald. "The Ethics of Goethe's *Die Wahlverwandtschaften*." *Modern Language Review* 71, no. 2 (April, 1976): 330-343. Examines the novel's ethical sensibility regarding marriage as an institution. Places Ottilie at the center of the story as an affirmative ethical statement, despite her tragic life.

Sharpe, Lesley, ed. *The Cambridge Companion to Goethe*. New York: Cambridge University Press, 2002. Collection of newly commissioned essays analyzing Goethe's prose fiction, drama, and poetry; Goethe and gender, philosophy, and religion; and Goethe's critical reception, among other topics. Includes bibliography and index.

Swales, Martin, and Erika Swales. *Reading Goethe: A Critical Introduction to the Literary Work*. Rochester, N.Y.: Camden House, 2002. A comprehensive critical analysis of Goethe's literary output, which argues that the writer is an essential figure in German modernity. Chapter 3, "Narrative Fiction," focuses on Goethe's novels. Includes bibliography and index.

Tanner, Tony. "Goethe's *Die Wahlverwandtschaften*." In *Adultery in the Novel: Contract and Transgression*. Baltimore: Johns Hopkins University Press, 1979. A study of the four main characters. Highly critical of Ottilie, who is usually idolized. Analyzes the symbolic value of particular objects, activities, and landscape descriptions that are prominent in the novel.

Tantillo, Astrida Orle. *Goethe's "Elective Affinities" and the Critics*. Rochester, N.Y.: Camden House, 2001. Traces the critical reception of the novel, which has continually confused critics and spurred debate about its content, style, and tone. Chronicles how Goethe's contemporaries responded to the book and how Goethe tried to shape the novel's reception. Describes how the novel was viewed from different perspectives during the nineteenth and twentieth centuries.

Electra

Author: Euripides (c. 485-406 B.C.E.)

First produced: *Ēlektra*, 413 B.C.E. (English translation, 1782)

Type of work: Drama

Type of plot: Tragedy

Time of plot: After the fall of Troy

Locale: Argos

Principal characters:
ELECTRA, the daughter of Agamemnon
ORESTES, her brother
CLYTEMNESTRA, her mother
AEGISTHUS, the lover of Clytemnestra

The Story:

When Agamemnon, the king of Argos, returns home from the Trojan War, he is murdered in cold blood by his wife, Clytemnestra, and her lover, Aegisthus. Afterward, Aegisthus and Clytemnestra are married, and Aegisthus becomes king. Orestes, the young son of Agamemnon, is sent by a relative to Phocis before Aegisthus can destroy him. Electra, the daughter, remains, but is given in marriage to an old peasant, lest she marry a warrior powerful enough to avenge her father's death.

One day, after Electra and the peasant go out to do the day's work, Orestes comes in disguise with his best friend, Pylades, to the farm to seek Electra. They hear her singing a lament for her fate and for the death of her father. A messenger interrupts her lament with word that a festival is to be held in honor of the goddess Hera and that all Argive maidens are to attend. Electra says she prefers to remain on the farm away from the pitying eyes of the people of Argos. The messenger advises her to honor the gods and to ask their help. Electra mistakes Orestes and Pylades for friends of her brother. She tells them her story and speaks of her wish that Orestes will avenge the death of Agamemnon and the ill treatment of his children. Aegisthus, meanwhile, offers a reward for the death of Orestes.

The peasant returns from his work and asks Orestes and Pylades to remain as his guests. Electra sends her husband to bring the relative who took Orestes away from Argos. On his way to the peasant's cottage, the old foster father notices that a sacrifice was made at the tomb of Agamemnon and that there are red hairs on the grave. He suggests to Electra that Orestes might be in the vicinity, but Electra answers that there is no chance of his being in Argos. When Orestes comes out of the cottage, the old man recognizes a scar on his forehead; thus brother and sister are made known to each other.

At the advice of the old peasant, Orestes plans to attend a sacrificial feast over which Aegisthus will preside. Electra sends her husband to tell Clytemnestra that she gave birth to a

baby. Electra and Orestes invoke the aid of the gods in their venture to avenge the death of their father.

Orestes and Pylades are hailed by Aegisthus as they pass him in his garden. The pair tell Aegisthus that they are from Thessaly and are on their way to sacrifice to Zeus. Aegisthus informs them that he is preparing to sacrifice to the nymphs and invites them to tarry. At the sacrifice of a calf, Orestes plunges a cleaver into Aegisthus's back while Aegisthus is examining the beast's entrails. Orestes then reveals his identity to the servants, who cheer the son of their former master. Orestes carries the corpse of Aegisthus back to the cottage, where it is hidden after Electra reviles it.

At the sight of Clytemnestra approaching the peasant's hut, Orestes has misgivings about the plan to murder her. He fears that matricide might bring the wrath of the gods upon him. Electra is, however, determined to complete the revenge. She reminds Orestes that an oracle told him to destroy Aegisthus and Clytemnestra.

Clytemnestra defends herself before Electra with the argument that Agamemnon sacrificed Iphegenia, their child, as an offering before the Trojan venture and that he returned to Argos with Cassandra, princess of Troy, as his concubine. Electra indicts her mother on several counts and claims that it is only just that she and Orestes murder her. The queen enters the hut to prepare a sacrifice for Electra's supposed firstborn; within, Orestes kills her, though he moans in distress at the violence and bloodshed and matricide in which the gods involved him.

The Dioscuri, twin sons of Zeus and brothers of the half divine Clytemnestra, appear to the brother and sister, who are overcome with mixed feelings of hate, love, pride, and shame at what they did. The twin gods question Apollo's wisdom, whose oracle advised this violent action; they decree that Orestes should give Electra to Pylades in marriage and that Orestes himself should be pursued by the Furies until such a time as he will face a trial in Athens, from which he will emerge a free man.

Critical Evaluation:

Electra is a compelling example of Euripides' dramaturgy. At the same time, it affords a means of comparing his purpose and techniques with those of Aeschylus and Sophocles, for all of them used the same legend and presented roughly the same action. Aeschylus in *Choēphoroi (The Libation Bearers*, 1777), part of the *Oresteia* trilogy (458 B.C.E.); Sophocles in *Electra* (418-410 B.C.E.); and Euripides in his *Electra* all treat Orestes' return to Argos, his presenting himself to his sister Electra, their planning of the revenge against Aegisthus and Clytemnestra, and the execution of that revenge. The different treatments are, however, quite individual and show the distinctions among these three tragedians.

With Aeschylus, the twin murders of Aegisthus and Clytemnestra are the culminating crimes in a family polluted by generations of kin slayings. Regicide and matricide are evils instigated by Apollo to punish and purge the earlier murder of Agamemnon. Orestes alone takes on the burden of these crimes. Electra, a minor character, offers him encouragement to the deeds, but her nature shrinks from being an actual accomplice. Aeschylus shows Orestes' revenge as an act of divine justice, a crime that will in time earn an acquittal. Sophocles takes a different view of the matter. The regicide and matricide are justifiable for him in human terms as the proper retribution for Agamemnon's killing. Electra is portrayed as a hard, bitter, determined young woman who aids her brother as a rightful duty. This perspective is similar to that in Homer's *Odyssey* (c. 725 B.C.E.).

Euripides calls both points of view into question. He sees the murders of Aegisthus and Clytemnestra as wholly unmitigated evils that are neither humanly nor divinely justifiable. Euripides says in effect that no killing is permissible for any reason. He carries this logic to its logical conclusion—that killers have as much right to live as anyone else no matter how twisted their psyche or how questionable their motives. This is a radical stand, but it is based on Euripides' firm conviction of the value of every human life, a belief that shines through the whole of *Electra* and makes the idea of just retribution a mockery. Euripides gives the impression that he would have liked to abolish all courts and prisons, turning justice into a matter of individual conscience. What is interesting is the way he works out these ideas dramatically.

Whereas Aeschylus and Sophocles concentrate on royalty and heroes, Euripides does not hesitate to depict an honorable peasant or to show ignoble blue bloods. In fact, the entire action of *Electra* takes place in front of a peasant's hut. To Euripides, each life has worth, and the index to that worth is strength of character. Position, wealth, power, beauty, and physique are nothing to him. Rather, he is chiefly interested in accurate, realistic psychology.

Each of the main characters is shown as a clearly defined personality in relation to a specific environment. Euripides tends to concentrate on the sordid aspects in *Electra* as the legend would seem to demand, yet it is here that his faith in human dignity reveals its power. It is easy to love good people, but to love people as warped by circumstances as Electra, Orestes, or Clytemnestra requires moral courage. Euripides possessed that courage, and he portrays their pain as though it were his own.

Electra has fallen from lavish prosperity to squalor and a forced, loveless marriage to a peasant, although that peasant is a compassionate man. She is slovenly and full of self-pity and spite. She envies her mother, Clytemnestra, who lives in luxury and power, and she hates Aegisthus. Her single passion is to kill them both, and when she discovers Orestes, she uses him to obtain revenge. Orestes himself is a neurotic vagabond of no status but with authorization from Apollo to kill his mother and her lover, and he declaims pompously about nobility of character. Clytemnestra seems like a housewife in queen's clothing, operating by a retaliatory logic. She takes a lover because her husband has a mistress, and she kills Agamemnon because he killed their daughter Iphigenia. None of this, however, has made her happy, and when she visits Electra out of motherly concern, she is hacked to death by her two children. Even Aegisthus appears to have decent aspects to him. It is precisely the ordinariness of Clytemnestra and Aegisthus that makes the realistic descriptions of their murders so sickening. Euripides convinces his readers and audiences that they deserve to live.

Once their passion for revenge is spent, Orestes and Electra are filled with self-revulsion and feel utterly degraded. Euripides brings two gods on stage, Castor and Polydeuces, to settle the matter, a *deus ex machina* ending that places the action in a new light. Apollo is directly responsible for the murders, just as Zeus is responsible for the Trojan War. These are not wise or just gods by human standards, and Euripides shows those human standards to have infinitely more worth than the abominable edicts of the gods. Euripides is supremely confident in his position, and he does not shrink from judging gods by it.

Consistent with his faith in humanity's value, he allows Orestes and Electra a good measure of compassion in the end. They are both exiled, and Orestes will be driven mad by the Furies, which only he can see. Nevertheless, they, too, deserve to live, Euripides declares, and in time they, too, will win forgiveness. Rarely has the belief in human dignity had such a steadfast champion as Euripides.

"Critical Evaluation" by James Weigel, Jr.

Further Reading

Grube, G. M. A. *The Drama of Euripides.* London: Methuen, 1941. Offers a detailed interpretation of *Electra*, which Grube admires for its psychological insights into all the characters.

Kitto, Humphrey Davy Findley. *Greek Tragedy: A Literary Study.* London: Methuen, 1939. Reprint. New York: Routledge, 2002. Labeling *Electra* a melodrama, Kitto argues that the play succeeds because of its characterization but lacks a universal theme. Compares Euripides' version with what Kitto regards as the more tragic treatment of the story by Sophocles.

Luschnig, C. A. E. *The Gorgon's Severed Head: Studies in "Alcestis," "Electra," and "Phoenissae."* New York: Brill, 1995. Examines three plays from various periods in Euripides' career and concludes that all three demonstrate his use of innovative dramatic techniques and traditional stories, his depiction of characters who create themselves and each other, and his treatment of gender issues. The chapters on *Electra* focus on the displacement of myth.

McDonald, Marianne. *Terms for Happiness in Euripides.* Göttingen, Germany: Vandenhoeck & Ruprecht, 1978. Analyzes *Electra* as a work that stresses the theme of friendship and shows that the traditional view of happiness is mistaken. Wealth, power, and victory do not produce the happiness enjoyed by the peasant who is married to Electra.

Michelini, Ann Norris. *Euripides and the Tragic Tradition.* Madison: University of Wisconsin Press, 1987. The first four chapters offer an overview of Euripidean criticism and discuss the literary conventions he inherited, his audience, and his style. Chapter 7 focuses on *Electra*, which Michelini regards as balancing comedy and tragedy.

Morwood, James. *The Plays of Euripides.* Bristol, England: Bristol Classical, 2002. Morwood provides a concise overview of all of Euripides' plays, devoting a separate chapter to each one. He demonstrates how Euripides was constantly reinventing himself in his work.

Mossman, Judith, ed. *Euripides.* New York: Oxford University Press, 2003. Collection of essays, some providing a general overview of Euripidean drama, others focusing on specific plays. Includes "The Argive Festival of Hera and Euripides' *Electra*" by F. I. Zeitlin.

Electra

Author: Hugo von Hofmannsthal (1874-1929)
First produced: 1903; first published, 1904 (English translation, 1908)
Type of work: Drama
Type of plot: Tragedy
Time of plot: Antiquity
Locale: Mycenae, Greece

Principal characters:
ELECTRA, a daughter of the murdered king Agamemnon
CHRYSOTHEMIS, her younger sister
ORESTES, their brother
CLYTEMNESTRA, the widow of Agamemnon and mother of Electra, Chrysothemis, and Orestes
AEGISTHUS, Clytemnestra's consort

The Story:

As the reddish glow of the setting sun floods the inner courtyard of the palace, five women servants come to fill their pitchers at the well. While they are speaking, Electra, Agamemnon's eldest daughter, appears, dressed in ragged clothing. Startled by their presence, she quickly disappears like a frightened animal. Four of the women exchange contemptuous observations about the mourning rites that Electra practices each evening for her father, and they ridicule both her and the wretched conditions of life that her mother and Aegisthus impose upon her. Disdainfully, they mention that she prefers eating on the ground with the dogs to sharing the servants' table, and that she insults all the servants of the house and stares at them fiercely like a wild cat. When the young fifth servant expresses her admiration for the abused princess, she is ordered inside, where she is promptly beaten for her insolence. Their pitchers filled, the servant women reenter the palace.

Electra returns and, speaking alone, reveals her secret

thoughts and feelings. She recalls in vivid detail the murder of her father who, upon his return from the Trojan War, was at this very twilight hour slaughtered in his bath with an ax by his wife and her lover. She prays for her father's spirit to appear to her again, promising that his blood will one day be avenged. She vows to sacrifice at his grave when that day comes and swears that she, along with her sister Chrysothemis and her brother Orestes, will dance around his tomb in royal pageantry to commemorate his greatness.

Chrysothemis appears in the doorway, interrupting Electra's fantasy, to alert her that she overheard Clytemnestra and Aegisthus plotting to imprison her in a dungeon. Electra replies contemptuously, which leads Chrysothemis to plead with her to understand her personal unhappiness. She explains that if they are to relinquish the hope of Orestes' return and his subsequent revenge, they will both be able to lead relatively normal lives, to love and marry, to bear children, and to experience the joys of family life. She will quite willingly tolerate the injustice of their father's murder in exchange for an ordinary happy life. Not so Electra, who reproaches her sister severely and reassures her that their brother will indeed return one day, and that together they will punish the criminals. Sounds from within alert them of Clytemnestra's approach. Chrysothemis flees, but Electra resolutely awaits a confrontation.

Clytemnestra, covered with jewels and charms that she believes to possess magical powers, appears in the window with her attendants and speaks insultingly to Electra, who answers deceptively, inducing her mother to descend into the courtyard to seek her counsel. Clytemnestra complains that her sleep is often troubled by bad dreams and that a terrible "nothing" torments her soul, causing her to feel horror of sinking alive into chaos; whatever demon is responsible can be appeased by an appropriate sacrifice, and she solicits assistance in discovering it. Electra offers elusive and evasive responses: To dispel the dreams, a man of their house, but yet a stranger, must slay some unidentified impure woman in any place, at any hour. Receiving indifferent answers to her questions about Orestes' return, Electra, overcome by hysterical rage, screams that Clytemnestra herself must be the sacrificial victim and that Orestes will slay her with the same ax she used to kill his father. Taken aback, Clytemnestra shakes with voiceless fear.

A servant enters and whispers something in Clytemnestra's ear, at which the expression on her face changes to one of evil triumph; calling for lights, she sweeps inside. Chrysothemis returns to tell Electra of the arrival of two strangers who announce the death of Orestes. A young manservant comes looking for a horse, so that he might carry such

important news immediately to Aegisthus. Electra now determines to kill the guilty rulers herself, and when her frightened sister refuses to participate in such a deed and runs away, Electra resolves to accomplish it alone. She is digging in the earth for the ax that she buried years before when she notices a stranger enter the courtyard.

She speaks with him cautiously, since he claims to have information about Orestes' death, but when she reveals her name, he discloses that he is indeed Orestes. Brother and sister embrace. Rejoicing at their reunion, Electra explains that the expectation of his return sustained her through terrible times. A servant leads Orestes into the palace to meet the queen, and, soon after, her screams can be heard. The servants become frightened and bewildered. When Aegisthus returns home, Electra meets him with a torch and conducts him to the palace door. Within minutes, he appears at a window crying for help, but he is quickly dragged out of sight.

Chrysothemis enters the courtyard with other women and tells her sister that the wicked are all slaughtered by Orestes and his followers. Electra seems to be able to hear only the triumphant music in her own head, to which she dances like a maenad, arms stretched wide, knees flung high, in a mad dance of triumph. She suddenly falls to the ground, while Chrysothemis pounds on the palace door, calling helplessly for her brother.

Critical Evaluation:

Hugo von Hofmannsthal's poetic tragedy *Electra* is an adaptation of Sophocles' drama *Élektra* (418-410 B.C.E.; *Electra*, 1649). The work adheres closely to the structure and dramatic organization of the original but omits the chorus of women of Mycenae and develops and interprets the poetic materials in an entirely original fashion. In some instances, Hofmannsthal also drew on Aeschylus's *Oresteia* (458 B.C.E.; English translation, 1777) and Euripides' *Élektra* (413 B.C.E.; *Electra*, 1782) for promptings pertaining to diction and poetic imagery.

Hofmannsthal added no new twists to the plot of his Greek sources, but his conception of the characters differs radically from theirs. In Sophocles' play, Electra is overwhelmed by grief and sorrow, and Clytemnestra seeks to justify her crimes with rational explanations. Orestes returns wielding a sword of justice with which to reestablish order within the corrupted kingdom, and he is not tormented by the Furies, as in Aeschylus and Euripides. Hofmannsthal created an Electra possessed by an insane, all-consuming hatred and sustained by the expectation of eventual revenge; his superstitious Clytemnestra is tormented by insomnia produced by a guilty conscience; his Orestes (Hofmannsthal had at one time considered omitting him entirely from the play) is merely an agent of revenge, a character who lacks any strong personal definition. The secondary characters of Aegisthus and Chrysothemis are retained relatively unchanged, though the latter appears somewhat less sympathetic and more willing to serve as a partner in evil in the modern work.

Hofmannsthal's decision to omit the chorus found in all the Greek versions resulted in substantial shifts in the meaning and emotional tone of the drama. In Sophocles, the chorus functioned as sensible representatives of a traditional moral order. There, Electra found the chorus sympathetic to her sorrowful laments, and their commiseration and approval of her grief legitimized her sufferings; the women of Mycenae represented uninvolved persons who could judge morally from a position emotionally outside the framework of the tragic situation. Lacking an anchor in any such continuing moral order, Hofmannsthal's characters struggle in a fundamental moral chaos that remains unredeemed at the play's conclusion by either choral statements affirming the restoration of traditional values, as in Sophocles, or a strong-minded Orestes, who promises to establish a new moral order for his new society. Hofmannsthal thereby enunciates his theme that at the dawn of the twentieth century human beings stand alone in the ruins of their old values yet are powerless to create significant new ones to replace them.

The world of Hofmannsthal's *Electra* is one in which hatred and oppression are the ruling forces in society, and political legitimacy is shown to reside in the effective use of force to gain and maintain power and authority. Other ideas that shape Hofmannsthal's world derive from such sources as Sigmund Freud and Josef Breuer's 1895 study on hysteria and Freud's *Die Traumdeutung* (1900; *The Interpretation of Dreams*, 1913). Like most intellectuals at the time, Hofmannsthal owned both books and was thoroughly familiar with them. His depictions of neurotic obsession in the character of Electra and those of guilt-induced dreams in the character of Clytemnestra rank among the finest early examples of the impact Freud had on literature.

Hofmannsthal employs ordinary, mundane language, similar to that of Sophocles and Aeschylus, which he arranges into simple, clear, and direct lines of free verse that convey the characters' thoughts forcefully and vividly. His frequent use of violent images relating to blood, murder, slaughter, and butchery, which impart this work's gruesome tone, has a precedent in the Greek sources: Where Hofmannsthal has Electra urge her brother on by saying, "Once more, strike!" Sophocles wrote, "Strike her again, strike!" Eschewing any display of feats of poetic virtuosity, Hof-

mannsthal avoids a stilted and convoluted rhetorical style and shuns any images reminiscent of "lofty and sublime" imitations of classical Greek harmony and serenity. His clear, simple style was easily understood by a theater audience, and it proved to be ideal for being set to music in an opera.

When the German composer Richard Strauss saw Max Reinhardt's production of *Electra* in Berlin, he immediately recognized its operatic potential. He had met Hofmannsthal in Paris in 1900, and the two had enthusiastically considered the mutual benefits to be derived from working together. The stage play *Electra*, appropriately modified to meet the musical requirements of an opera libretto, offered an ideal opportunity for collaboration and proved to be the first of several of the greatest musical-dramatic collaborations in operatic history. Serious work on the opera began in 1906. Hofmannsthal's drama of approximately 1,500 lines was too long and was reduced to about 825 lines, including two new short passages Strauss requested from the poet. Hofmannsthal's conception remained intact; cuts merely eliminated elaborations from speeches and insignificant scenes of comic relief, and reduced the importance of minor characters. The opera was first produced in Dresden in 1909 and, though received coolly at first, was soon recognized as a masterpiece. It is the operatic version, rather than Hofmannsthal's spoken drama, that has most consistently held the international stage and become known to a worldwide audience.

Raymond M. Archer

Further Reading

Bottenberg, Joanna. *Shared Creation: Words and Music in the Hofmannsthal-Strauss Operas*. New York: Peter Lang, 1996. Examines the collaboration of Hofmannsthal and Richard Strauss that resulted in the creation of six operas, including *Electra*.

Hamburger, Michael. *Hofmannsthal: Three Essays*. Princeton, N.J.: Princeton University Press, 1972. An excellent introduction to Hofmannsthal's poems, plays, and libretti for English-speaking readers.

_____. *A Proliferation of Prophets: Essays on German Writers from Nietzsche to Brecht*. Manchester, England: Carcanet Press, 1983. Contains a highly readable essay tracing Hofmannsthal's poetic and artistic development, with advice for readers new to his work on how to approach his poetry. Includes a very good section on *Electra*.

Kovach, Thomas A., ed. *A Companion to the Works of Hugo von Hofmannsthal*. Columbia, S.C.: Camden House, 2002. Collection of essays analyzing Hofmannsthal's works, including discussions of his lyric drama, collaborations with Richard Strauss, and his works' reception in the twentieth century.

Puffett, Derrick, ed. *Richard Strauss: "Elektra."* New York: Cambridge University Press, 1989. A collection of eight essays from renowned scholars that examine in depth all aspects of the opera based on Hofmannsthal's drama.

Scott, Jill. "Beyond Tragic Catharsis: Hugo von Hofmannsthal's *Elektra*." In *Electra After Freud: Myth and Culture.* Ithaca, N.Y.: Cornell University Press, 2005. Analyzes the depiction of Electra in Hofmannsthal's play and other literary works in which writers transformed the ancient Greek myth.

Strathausen, Carsten. "Hofmannsthal and the Voice of Language." In *The Look of Things: Poetry and Vision Around 1900.* Chapel Hill: University of North Carolina Press, 2003. A study of German poetry, philosophy, and visual media around 1900. Describes how Hofmannsthal and other writers used language as a means of competing with photography and film.

Ward, Philip. *Hofmannsthal and Greek Myth: Expression and Performance.* New York: Peter Lang, 2002. Examines why and how Hoffmansthal adapted Greek mythology in his works. In one chapter, Ward focuses on how Hoffmansthal used myth to depict women's behavior in *Electra*.

Electra

Author: Sophocles (c. 496-406 B.C.E.)
First published: *Ēlektra*, 418-410 B.C.E. (English translation, 1649)
Type of work: Drama
Type of plot: Tragedy
Time of plot: c. 1250-1200 B.C.E.
Locale: Mycenae, Greece

Principal characters:
PAEDAGOGUS, a servant of Orestes
ORESTES, the son of the murdered King Agamemnon
ELECTRA, the daughter of Agamemnon
CHRYSOTHEMIS, sister of Electra and Orestes
CLYTEMNESTRA, Agamemnon's widow
AEGISTHUS, Agamemnon's cousin and Clytemnestra's lover
CHORUS, women of Mycenae

The Story:

When Clytemnestra and Aegisthus murder King Agamemnon, Electra has her brother, Orestes, spirited away by the Paedagogus, a loyal servant charged with caring for the boy. When Orestes becomes a man, he, the Paedagogus, and Orestes' friend Pylades return to avenge the murder. Urged on by Electra, Orestes is counseled by Apollo to gain vengeance stealthily. Wishing to take the culprits off guard, Orestes pretends that he and his companions are strangers, that Orestes was killed in a chariot accident, and that they come to return the princely ashes to his mother.

Even as Orestes explains his plan to the Paedagogus, intending also to lay an offering at Agamemnon's grave, Electra, wailing, emerges from the palace. The three men leave, and Electra bemoans her lost youth, spent in mourning for her slain father. Oppressed with sorrow, she remains unbedded (a-lectra), a virgin obsessed with vengeance against her adulterous mother and Aegisthus. The Chorus's advice about rea-

sonable limits to mourning and expressions of rage do not sway her from her course. She saw Aegisthus kill her father at his hearth, and she is anguished to see the murderer ruling her father's kingdom, wearing her father's clothes, and sleeping with her father's wife. Electra is now beyond childbearing, beyond marrying, and her life seems incapable of gaining meaning except through avenging the murder.

Electra's sister, Chrysothemis, arrives bearing burial offerings that Clytemnestra, troubled by dreams, orders her to take to Agamemnon's grave. Chrysothemis, though outraged, hopes to live comfortably, and she advises Electra to control herself; otherwise, Electra will be imprisoned, and she will have to live out her life alone. The prospect does not frighten Electra, who relishes the thought that Clytemnestra dreamed that Agamemnon returned, planted his scepter at his hearth, and produced foliage that covered all Mycenae. With the Chorus's approval, she urges Chrysothemis to offer locks of her own hair and Electra's hair and belt rather than what their corrupt mother sent.

Clytemnestra, emerging from the palace, accuses Electra of bringing sorrow upon herself by her insolence. Although the Chorus and Electra believe that Clytemnestra assassinated Agamemnon out of lust for Aegisthus, Clytemnestra claims that she killed him because, on his way to Troy, he sacrificed their daughter Iphigenia. Electra retorts that Iphigenia was sacrificed because Agamemnon, mistakenly killing a stag of Artemis, was doomed with all his crew to be stranded, unable to proceed or retreat, unless he sacrificed the girl. Even if Agamemnon had a wrong motive for the sacrifice, she argues, Clytemnestra's act remains unacceptable.

After Clytemnestra prays to Apollo for a peaceful life with loving children, the Paedagogus enters to report Orestes' death. Clytemnestra claims that she does not know whether to respond with joy at the end of a potential threat or with sorrow at the loss of her child. Actually, however, she is relieved. Electra, on the other hand, is crushed by the report. She resolves to bring on her own death by wasting away at the gate.

Chrysothemis returns with news that Orestes is back. She found a lock of his hair at Agamemnon's grave, along with other offerings. Believing their brother to be dead, however, Electra guesses that someone left the offerings as a tribute to the deceased Orestes. Chrysothemis accepts the explanation.

Electra, devoid of hope of getting help from the outside, resolves to kill Aegisthus herself. She invites Chrysothemis to lend a hand, the rewards being twofold: admiration from the dead, who will honor their piety, and freedom for Chrysothemis to marry someone worthy. Chrysothemis is fearful, however, and argues that justice is sometimes harmful to the just. Electra is undeterred, and the Chorus praises her.

When Orestes arrives, pretending that he is a Phocian, he hands Electra what he claims to be her brother's ashes; she laments the death of the child she saved from being murdered. Orestes, moved to reveal himself, is loath to do so in front of the Chorus, which advises Electra to moderate her mourning. Assured that the Chorus is on Electra's side, however, he identifies himself, cautioning the joyous Electra to restrain herself and focus on what they had to know and to do in order to succeed.

The Paedagogus reappears with the news that Clytemnestra and Aegisthus are relieved by the thought that Orestes is dead. Orestes and Pylades enter the palace, and, after hearing vain cries for mercy from Clytemnestra, the Chorus and Electra hear the queen die. Orestes returns in a sober mood, hoping that Apollo's prophecy and his fulfillment of it will have positive results.

Aegisthus arrives almost immediately, happily expecting more news about Orestes' death. Electra leads him to believe that Orestes' body is in the palace, and he orders the doors to be thrown open, so that any who still hope for Orestes' return can see the proof of his demise. Confronted by Clytemnestra's corpse, Aegisthus thinks that it is Orestes', but he soon recognizes his plight. Orestes forces him to enter the palace where, like Clytemnestra, Aegisthus meets his end.

Critical Evaluation:

Sophocles, the most successful of the ancient Greek playwrights, garnered between eighteen and twenty-four victories in yearly competitions at the Festival of Dionysus. He wrote about 123 tragedies, of which seven are preserved. Three concern the family of Oedipus; one relates the story of Deianira and her husband, Heracles; and three are devoted to the Trojan War and its consequences. *Electra*, Sophocles' only surviving play about the family of Agamemnon, preserves the basic story as Aeschylus revised it from Homer's *Odyssey* (c. 725 B.C.E.; English translation, 1614) but alters the details yet again. The changes help the reader to understand Sophocles' interpretation of the myth and the yield for humanity that he saw in it.

Homer carefully avoids the horror of matricide in his account of Orestes' vengeance, recalling that Orestes murdered Aegisthus and properly buried both him and Clytemnestra. Though a number of alternative explanations for Clytemnestra's death can be advanced, Aeschylus sees matricide implicit in the situation, and in the last two plays of the *Oresteia* (458 B.C.E.; English translation, 1777), his trilogy about the family of Agamemnon, Orestes is plagued by Furies, or in the vernacular of later ages, "driven mad by guilt" for slaying his mother. He is acquitted when the goddess Athena's utterly unjustified vote of not guilty breaks the deadlock of an evenly divided jury. Aeschylus is concerned with exploring matters of state: how personal anguish relates to one's obligations to a slain king and father; how humanity progresses; and what is involved in moving from one system of justice to another, here from blood vengeance to trial by jury.

Sophocles is more interested in the ways in which experience, working with innate qualities, determines a human being's character. The gods hardly figure in his play, and guilt is not the issue. Given their innate proclivities and experiences, his characters do what they think or feel they must do; the worst of them, Clytemnestra, sees and regrets in some measure the horrors she perpetrated, and the best, Electra, is goaded into encouraging and supporting horrors of equal magnitude.

Noble and idealistic Electra, obsessed by the loss of the

father she loved and feeling repugnance for her mother that is tainted with jealousy, abandons all hope of marrying, loving a husband, and bearing children. Instead, she commits herself to the past, to avenging her father's murder. She hates the usurper Aegisthus and her mother because they mistreat her, and, to a degree, that hatred compromises her desire for moral vengeance. She not only wants revenge but also wants to cause her enemies pain. Her great fear is that she may possess traits inherited from her mother, and the fear is justified. Clytemnestra, if her account of her motive for killing Agamemnon carries any weight, is, like Electra, fiercely committed to justice by blood vengeance. Her hatred and lust, too, are implacable. She waits ten years for revenge, and, gaining it, mutilates the corpse of her victim, husband though he was. She celebrates the anniversaries of his death with festivals. Electra's transcendent hatred and the lust for vengeance that she nurtures for years mirror Clytemnestra's; Electra, too, is determined to dishonor the corpse of a culprit, intending to toss the slain Aegisthus as carrion to birds and dogs. Warped by her experiences, the expression of her noble intent is unavoidably impious.

Chrysothemis, Clytemnestra's middle child, who is less proud and determined than her sister, accepts the condition of servitude in the household of her father's murderers. She subordinates her unhappiness and hopes for a better life in the future. Unwilling to risk her life to avenge Agamemnon (presumably she does not know him as well as Electra does), she is not made of the fierce, unyielding stuff that characterizes her sister and her mother. She can be swayed to deliver her mother's offerings to the tomb of her father; she can then be swayed not to do so. Aware of Aegisthus and Clytemnestra's power, however, she will not openly oppose them.

Orestes, on the other hand, knows his father and mother only theoretically. He is taught that his father was treacherously slain, and he is dedicated to vengeance against the murderers, one of whom happens to be a person he does not recall, his mother. The anguish he causes Electra does not deter him from deceiving her when he sees an advantage in doing so. Without the memory of family relationships to impede him, Orestes is neither rash nor timid but calculating and efficient, the perfect killer; he happens to be attached to the side that passes for justice.

Guilt and pollution are endemic to the House of Atreus. As Sophocles sees the conflicts, the issue is how people deal with the problems, what in their characters, compounded of inherited traits and experiences, determines their actions. Clytemnestra, proud, bold, sexual, and vengeful, is the wrong kind of woman to outrage by murdering her child, and the wrong kind, too, to leave "unserviced" for ten years. Her

lover, now husband, Aegisthus, has motives of his own for hating the family of his cousin Agamemnon, whose father, Atreus, killed Aegisthus's brothers and fed them to their father. The untrustworthy scion of an untrustworthy family with a history of savagery and pain, Aegisthus in a minor way reinforces the vision of character that Sophocles presents. Chrysothemis, yielding by nature, is a survivor, a follower who, like her uncle Aegisthus, can swell a scene or two but cannot create or dominate one. Orestes, deprived of the emotional complications engendered by family life, is an instrument of whatever purpose he embraces. Electra, by contrast, is indeed her mother's daughter—and, like her, proud, bold, vengeful, and sexual in her obsession. Tragically twisted into a woman for whom destruction is the only positive prospect, magnificent in both her love and her hatred, Electra stretches beyond the deaths of her enemies in a vain search for peace. Hers is a tragedy about the fruits of the past, the ways in which violence and perversity warp people, and the consequences for their lives.

Albert Wachtel

Further Reading

Beer, Josh. *Sophocles and the Tragedy of Athenian Democracy.* Westport, Conn.: Praeger, 2004. Analyzes Sophocles' plays within the context of Athenian democracy in the fifth century B.C.E., focusing on the political issues in the dramas. Examines Sophocles' dramatic techniques and how they "revolutionized the concept of dramatic space." Chapter 8 discusses *Electra.*

Garvie, A. F. *The Plays of Sophocles.* Bristol, England: Bristol Classical, 2005. Concise analysis of Sophocles' plays, with a chapter devoted to *Electra.* Focuses on Sophocles' tragic thinking, the concept of the Sophoclean hero, and the structure of his plays.

Lloyd, Michael. *Sophocles: "Electra."* London: Duckworth, 2005. A companion to the play, providing information about the myth of Electra before Sophocles adapted it, the theater in Sophocles' time, and the action, stagecraft, and characterization of the play. Discusses the play's depiction of matricide, questioning if it is a just and final act of violence or if it is more problematic than it seems.

Morwood, James. *The Tragedies of Sophocles.* Exeter, England: Bristol Phoenix Press, 2008. Analyzes each of Sophocles' seven extant plays, with chapter 6 devoted to *Electra.* Discusses several modern productions and adaptations of the tragedies.

Reinhardt, Karl. *Sophocles.* Translated by Hazel Harvey and David Harvey. New York: Barnes & Noble, 1979. A structural appreciation of *Electra* as the first of Sophocles' uniquely related last plays.

Ringer, Mark. *"Electra" and the Empty Urn: Metatheater and Role Playing in Sophocles.* Chapel Hill: University of North Carolina Press, 1998. Focuses on elements of metatheater, or "theater within theater," and ironic self-awareness in Sophocles' plays, with special focus on *Electra*. Analyzes plays-within-plays, characters who are in rivalry with the playwright, and characters who assume roles in order to deceive one another. Chapter 7 provides a lengthy discussion of *Electra*.

Sophocles. *Electra*. Translated by William Sale. Englewood Cliffs, N.J.: Prentice-Hall, 1973. Sensitive, detailed analyses of theme, meaning, and structure. Introduced by Eric A. Havelock's excellent general survey and Adam Parry's sketch on metrics.

Webster, T. B. L. *An Introduction to Sophocles.* 2d ed. New York: Methuen, 1969. A challenging portrait of a pious Sophocles, for whom god-inspired matricide is good.

Whitman, Cedric H. *Sophocles: A Study of Heroic Humanism.* Cambridge, Mass.: Harvard University Press, 1966. Sees *Electra* as a play that embraces the Homeric values of the *Odyssey*. Celebrates Electra's suffering, endurance, and wise triumph.

Winnington-Ingram, R. P. "The *Electra* of Sophocles: Prolegomena to an Interpretation." In *Oxford Readings in Greek Tragedy*, edited by Erich Segal. New York: Oxford University Press, 1983. Presents an interpretation in which the Furies were operative on Electra and Clytemnestra before her murder, allowing for both Homeric and Aeschylean interpretations.

The Elegy of Lady Fiammetta

Author: Giovanni Boccaccio (1313-1375)
First published: Elegia di Madonna Fiammetta, 1343-1344 (English translation, 1587)
Type of work: Novel
Type of plot: Love
Time of plot: Fourteenth century
Locale: An Italian city, possibly Naples

Principal characters:
FIAMMETTA, a noble lady
PANFILO, a young man

The Story:

Fiammetta has a dream that a serpent bites her while she is lying in a meadow and that, as darkness comes, the wound festers and brings her close to death. When she awakens, she discovers that she has no injury and, failing to realize that the dream is a warning and a prophecy, she dismisses it from her thoughts.

Fiammetta is admired by the ladies and gentlemen who surround her when she goes to church on a certain festival day, but of all her admirers none strikes her fancy until she sees a young gentleman leaning against a marble pillar of the church. The glances that she and the young man exchange prove that the attraction is mutual.

Realizing that she is overtaken by love, Fiammetta spends hours in her chamber picturing the young man and hoping to see him again. As other chance meetings increase her interest in him, she becomes so disturbed and changed by love that

her nurse comments on it and warns her of the dangers of passion and of betraying her husband. Fiammetta, however, is too much enamored of the young man to heed such warnings; she dreams that Venus comes to her and tells her of the delight and power of love, urging her to ignore her nurse's warnings and to submit to love's promptings.

Encouraged by her fond glances, the young man becomes familiar with Fiammetta's friends and with her husband, so that he and Fiammetta might converse together, hiding their love. The young man teaches her by his example how to converse in the company of others so as to reveal their love only to each other; he pretends to be telling of two lovers, Fiammetta and Panfilo, in order to show how deeply his own passion moves her. Although Fiammetta grows adept at this word game, she knows that their love cannot forever be kept within the bounds of propriety.

Despite Fiammetta's refusals, which Panfilo takes as coy signs of encouragement, he finally gains what all lovers desire. He and Fiammetta spend innumerable nights together, learning new delights of love. Nothing else matters to Fiammetta. She thanks Venus for encouraging her in love, and she laughs at other gentlewomen who imagine that they know what passion is.

Fiammetta's happiness, however, is fated to come to an end. One night, while she and Panfilo are together in her chamber, Fiammetta awakens to find Panfilo weeping. She hesitates to inquire into the cause of his distress for fear that he will reveal some other love for whom he is secretly longing. Pretending that she does not see him weeping, she suddenly cries out as if in her sleep. When he wipes his tears and turns to her, she tells him that she suddenly feared that she lost him. He answers that neither fortune nor death can change his love for her; he then begins to sob and sigh again. Answering her question concerning his sorrow, Panfilo tells her that he has to leave the city for four months because of his father's illness.

Fiammetta argues that if he loves her he will not leave her. She is sure of his love and cannot bear to part with it; as one so desperately in love, she deserves his presence more than his father does. She fears for his health and safety if he leaves her. Finally, she concludes, a storm is coming; no man of sense will go out in such weather.

In spite of her protests, Panfilo insists that it is his duty to see his dying father, but he assures her that he will return at the end of four months. After a long and loving farewell, she accompanies him to the gate. Then, overcome with sorrow, she faints and has to be revived by her maid.

During the four months of Panfilo's absence, Fiammetta spends her days remembering the delights she shared with him, wondering whether he is falling in love with someone else, counting the days and scolding the moon for being slow in its course, and imagining and dreaming that he returns to her.

Even the satisfaction of daydreaming is denied to Fiammetta when she learns from the conversation of a merchant that Panfilo is married. She is plunged into jealousy and grief, but as time goes on, she begins to hope that Panfilo might not find happiness with his wife. She offers prayers to Venus asking that he be stricken again with love for her so that he will return.

Fiammetta's husband notices that she loses her appetite and is having difficulty sleeping. Ignorant of the cause, he at first has medicines prescribed for her and then takes her on a vacation to some beautiful islands. The medicines, however, have no effect on her passion, and the islands only remind her of the delightful times she spent with Panfilo. Feasts and shows fail to please her, and she spends her days sighing and praying to the gods of love and fortune.

Fiammetta learns from one of her servants that Panfilo is not married, as she supposed from the merchant's tale, but rather that he is in love with a beautiful gentlewoman who loves him. Her misery intensifies at this news. She finds no comfort in her husband's loving and compassionate words, and her nurse cannot bring her to her senses. She considers many ways of suicide, all of which seem too painful or too difficult to be considered. She then reasons that if she kills herself she will never see Panfilo again. Finally, fearing that worse torments are to come, she attempts to leap from the house, but she is stopped by the nurse and other servants.

After her nurse tells her that Panfilo is returning, Fiammetta, for a time, hopes to see him again. The rumor, however, confuses Fiammetta's Panfilo with another man having the same name, and Fiammetta is forced to realize that she lost him forever. She compares her condition to that of other betrayed lovers, supposing herself to be more unfortunate than they. She tells her story in order that others might take it as an example of what misery may befall an amorous gentlewoman.

Critical Evaluation:

Giovanni Boccaccio's elegy has often been touted by scholars as the first psychological work of literature written in a modern language. It is an account of specific emotions occurring in an individual's mind, whereas most medieval literature relates physical actions, such as the exploits of knights or pilgrims, or expresses idealized emotions, such as in courtly love poetry. Boccaccio's work is composed as a letter written by the principal character, Fiammetta, to be sent as advice to other women who may find themselves in a similar situation, that is, seemingly duped by a man.

The elegy relates her emotional history from when she first sees and falls in love with her lover, Panfilo, through his leaving her, temporarily as she believes at first, up to her ultimate realization that he must have chosen never to return, thus rejecting her as his lover. Fiammetta seeks to express her feelings; the actions she leaves to readers to imagine. For example, she describes their trysts in only the vaguest of terms, but she expresses fully the emotions she feels during their affair.

Although, by her own account, happily married, she is impressed by the handsomeness of a young man. Becoming acquainted, they fall in love and carry on an affair secret to almost everyone. Even their pretend names for each other reveal the emotional nature of their relationship: Fiammetta ("endearing flame") and Panfilo ("all-loving," or "lover of all"). In a stream-of-consciousness literary style, she expresses the agonies of facing separation from her lover and then of wondering why he has stayed away far longer than he said he would, without communicating. Finally, she describes the despair that paralyzes her life. She blames herself, him, and the misfortune of the circumstances that divided them initially. Her emotions revolve between intense anguish in missing Panfilo and extreme anger because of his presumed rejection of her. She contemplates and even acts on thoughts of suicide. Her letter is meant to warn other women of the dangers of loving a man so deeply as to be as vulnerable to his abandonment as she proves to be.

The Elegy of Lady Fiammetta, although one of Boccaccio's minor works, has become better known as literary critics and historians have paid greater attention to gender-related issues in their research. It is one of only a few works of its time that have a woman as a principal character and of even fewer whose story is actually told through a female voice. Judged by modern social criteria, this work does not stand as a source of enhancing woman's status. Fiammetta's language describes her not only as victimized by a particular man but also more generally as a woman who is by nature vulnerable, culpable, and weak. The impression is one of a woman treated by her lover merely as a sexual object to be discarded after use. As Fiammetta relates so vividly, her beauty, her dignity, and her being dissipate in Panfilo's absence. The reader can choose, however, to evaluate this work in its own historical context. Accordingly, *The Elegy of Lady Fiammetta* stands as a departure from traditional literature. It portrays a woman in a social role beyond mere subservience, someone who desires a man who is not her husband and seeks to gain him. It does not condemn Fiammetta as a mere adulteress or seductress but presents her as an individual with full awareness of her own life and wishes. The account is sympathetic. She schemes to betray her husband and she may be naïve, but Boccaccio depicts her above all as a victim of fortune.

A particular feature of Boccaccio's writing unrelated to either its psychological style or its content deserves mention. Reflecting a familiarity with classical literature, Boccaccio frequently refers to stories and characters from ancient history and mythology. Fiammetta and other speakers in the work often draw parallels between her trials and the relationships of other lovers of the past. In some cases, Boccaccio cites long series of classical references. These would have been readily recognized by his contemporary readers; what a modern reader may take as tedious, esoteric references would

have reinforced the story and increased its impact for earlier readers.

Scholarly consensus has turned away from an earlier autobiographical interpretation of this work, by which Boccaccio seemed to be describing an affair of his own with a noblewoman in Naples in the late 1330's. Instead, Fiammetta appears to have been mostly a literary creation. She appears in other of his works, and the evidence linking her to a specific woman is not wholly persuasive. If one were to prefer a historical approach to the work, considering it as an autobiographical revelation, another interpretation offers itself. Boccaccio had lived most of his early life in Naples before leaving for Florence, where he composed this elegy, and one could view it as an emotional parallel to his travels, because he preferred Naples. He perhaps saw himself as Panfilo, the one who loved his southern city but was constrained by circumstances to leave for the north. Accordingly, he also envisaged Fiammetta (Naples) mourning his absence and torn emotionally over why he was no longer in her presence.

The beauty of *The Elegy of Lady Fiammetta* is in how much Boccaccio leaves to the reader to imagine. Fiammetta's psyche is revealed, but the women recipients of her letter (and all readers of the work) are left to imagine the specifics of the circumstances of the affair. The affair thus is general; it adapts to individual situations. The reader is left not knowing even if Panfilo eventually returns. *The Elegy of Lady Fiammetta* is a work that draws the reader into the mind of its principal character and elicits an emotional response. Whether Fiammetta is indicting men or fortune, whether she is medieval in her behavior or modern, and whether Boccaccio was expressing a male perception of society through a female character or was antedating feminism—these issues remain open to interpretation.

"Critical Evaluation" by Alan Cottrell

Further Reading

Boccaccio, Giovanni. *The Elegy of Lady Fiammetta*. Edited and translated by Mariangela Causa-Steindler and Thomas Mauch. Chicago: University of Chicago Press, 1990. Perhaps the most elegant modern translation into American English. The introduction presents an overview of the author's life, the elegy, and the various sources of its inspiration.

_____. *The Elegy of Madonna Fiammetta Sent by Her to Women in Love*. Translated by Roberta L. Payne and Alexandra Hennessey Olsen. New York: Peter Lang, 1992. Contains a useful, brief introduction to the work's literary features. The translation is of a slightly different original text from Causa-Steindler and Mauch's and thus can serve for comparison.

Gittes, Tobias Foster. *Boccaccio's Naked Muse: Eros, Culture, and the Mythopoeic Imagination.* Toronto, Ont.: University of Toronto Press, 2008. Examines all of Boccaccio's works, including *The Elegy of Lady Fiammetta,* to demonstrate how he used an innovative and coherent system of mythology in order to express his cultural experience and address the needs of his readers.

Hagedorn, Suzanne C. "Abandoned Women and the Dynamics of Reader Response: Boccaccio's Amorosa, Visione, and *Elegia di Madonna Fiammetta.*" In *Abandoned Women: Rewriting the Classics in Dante, Boccaccio, and Chaucer.* Ann Arbor: University of Michigan Press, 2004. A feminist interpretation of medieval literature. Hagedorn examines the theme of the abandoned woman in Boccaccio's work as a means of questioning his assumptions about gender roles.

Smarr, Janet Levarie. *Boccaccio and Fiammetta: The Narrator as Lover.* Champaign: University of Illinois Press, 1986. The chapter on *The Elegy of Lady Fiammetta* discusses the character of Fiammetta as she appears in other works by Boccaccio. Discusses the variety of perspectives found in the voices of reasoned narrators and impassioned characters, who often were the same person playing differing roles.

Elegy Written in a Country Churchyard

Author: Thomas Gray (1716-1771)
First published: 1751; collected in *Poems by Mr. Gray,* 1768
Type of work: Poetry

Thomas Gray probably began "Elegy Written in a Country Churchyard" about 1746. It was originally a somewhat shorter poem than the version he published in 1751, and some have speculated that the poem may have been occasioned by an actual death, perhaps that of Gray's friend Richard West in 1742. When Gray designated his work as an elegy, he placed it in a long tradition of meditative poems that focus on human mortality and sometimes reflect specifically on the death of a single person. By setting his meditation in a typical English churchyard with mounds, gravestones, and yew trees, Gray was also following a tradition. Some of the most popular poems in the middle of Gray's century were set in graveyards and meditated on death.

"Elegy Written in a Country Churchyard" is cast in four-line stanzas, or quatrains, in which the first line rhymes with the third, the second with the fourth. This *abab* pattern, at this time associated with elegiac poetry, gives the poem an appropriately stately pace. The last three stanzas are printed in italic type and given the title "The Epitaph."

In the first three stanzas (lines 1 to 12), Gray sets the scene for his private and quiet meditations. He is far from the city and looking out from a country churchyard at a rural scene, but the sights and sounds of this rural world of men and beasts fade away. Although the scene is beautiful, life is not joyous, and Gray reflects that this day dies just like the one before it, as the plowman plods wearily home. The poet is alone, but he is not tired. The text gives a sense of the vitality of his solitude and of the stillness of the scene by describing the few things that remain to disturb it: the tinkling of the cattle who have returned home, the drone of the beetle, and the sound of an owl from the church tower. This owl—a "moping," secret, solitary ruler over the churchyard since ancient times—strikes an ominous note and protests that the poet is challenging its reign. With these descriptions, Gray creates the backdrop for his melancholy reflections about eternal truths.

In the next four stanzas (lines 13 to 28), Gray uses the churchyard scene to invoke important images: the strength of the elms, death as symbolized by the graves, and the comfort provided by the yews shading bodies that sleep. The poet begins by reflecting that death for the humble and lower class means a cessation of life's simple pleasures: waking up to the songs of birds, sharing life with a wife and children, and enjoying hard and productive work. Gray reflects not on the untimely death of young people but on the death that comes after a normal life span.

In the next four stanzas (lines 29 to 44), the poet addresses the upper classes—those with ambition, grandeur, power, nobility, and pride—and exhorts them not to mock the poor for their simplicity or for not having elaborate statues on their graveyard memorials. He tells the living upper classes (perhaps the people Gray envisions as his readers) that ultimately it does not matter what glory they achieve or how elaborate a tombstone they will have. They will die just like the poor.

The eight stanzas (lines 45 to 76) that follow provide the central message of the poem: The poor are born with the same natural abilities as members of the upper classes. Who can say what humble people might have accomplished in the great world had they not been constrained by their condition and their innate powers not been frozen by "Chill Penury." Gray implies that the innocence and beauty of these souls, wasted in their isolated rural environment, and resembling hidden deserts and ocean caves, could have flourished in better circumstances:

> Full many a gem of purest ray serene,
> The dark unfathomed caves of ocean bear:
> Full many a flower is born to blush unseen,
> And waste its sweetness on the desert air.

The churchyard graves may also contain the remains of a person who had the ability to become a great scholar, a generous national leader, or a man who could have been a great poet but is in the end no more than a "mute inglorious Milton." Gray goes on to speculate, however, that poverty may have prevented some dead men from doing not good but evil; now death has made them (unlike Oliver Cromwell) "guiltless" of shedding blood; they have not been able to slaughter, to refuse mercy, to lie, or to wallow in luxury and pride. Far from the "ignoble strife" of the great world, the village people have led "sober" and "noiseless" lives. Gray implies that, even though the village dead have accomplished nothing in the world, on balance they may be morally superior to their social betters.

Gray returns to the churchyard in the next section (lines 77 to 92), remarking on the graves' simple markers with their badly spelled inscriptions, names, and dates. Some bear unpolished verses or consoling biblical texts; some are decorated with "shapeless sculpture." Gray is touched that such grave markers show the humanity these dead people share with all men and women (including, by implication, the famous who took paths of glory). Those who remain can sense that the dead "cast one long lingering look" back on what they were leaving and were comforted by at least one loved one. Gray reflects that the voice of general human nature can be heard crying from these graves. In the last line of this

section, Gray reflects that what he has learned will apply to himself and his readers: The "wonted fires" of his life and those of his readers will continue to burn in the ashes of all graves.

This more personal line provides a transition to the next six stanzas (lines 93-116), where it seems (the grammar is confusing) that Gray is addressing himself when he writes:

> For thee, who mindful of the unhonoured dead
> Dost in these lines their artless tale relate,
> If chance, by lonely contemplation led,
> Some kindred spirit shall inquire thy fate

Gray imagines an old farmer, who is described as a "hoary-headed swain," replying to this question in lines 98 to 116. The farmer's story describes Gray as a man who does not fit into either of the classes described earlier; he is neither a poor man nor a man of noble achievement. He is a wanderer, a man who vigorously meets the sun at dawn, yet later lies by a favorite tree and gazes listlessly at a brook. He mutters his fancies, resembling a madman or a hopeless lover. He is everything that Gray's contemporaries thought a poet should be—a man of exquisite sensibility, unfit for the world's work, meditative, and sad.

The farmer recounts that he saw the poet's funeral procession to a church, presumably the one where the poem is set. He does not seem to have helped arrange the funeral nor, unlike the reader, can he read the epitaph that concludes the poem (Gray may be indicating that the farmer's social class is not that of the poet and the reader). Perhaps Gray, in indicating that the poet chose to be buried where people of his class are not usually buried, intended to reinforce that the poem's theme applies to all humankind.

In the three stanzas of the epitaph (lines 117 to 128), Gray speaks of his grave being "upon the lap of Earth" and not inside the church. He accords himself modest praise and justifies his life as worthwhile. Despite his "humble birth," he was well educated. Although some may consider the poet's natural melancholy a disadvantage, he himself probably thought it the source of his poetic temperament. Gray describes himself as generous and sincere, for which his reward was not worldly fame or fortune (the "paths of glory") but heavenly "recompense," undoubtedly the "friend" mentioned in line 124. The epitaph concludes by telling the reader not to ask more about the poet's virtues and frailties but to leave him to God.

"Elegy Written in a Country Churchyard" moves from a meditation in a particular place upon the graves of the poor to a reflection on the mortality of all humankind and on some of the benefits of being constrained by poverty. The poem alludes to the wish of all people not to die and to the ways in which each is remembered after death. Gray concludes by imagining his own death and how he hopes to be remembered. If this progression of thought is not entirely logical, it is all the more understandable. One reason for the long popularity of Gray's elegy lies in the universal chord he managed to strike not only with the thoughts he expressed but, perhaps even more important, with the progression he gave those thoughts. Beyond that, the poem contains some of the most striking lines of English poetry.

George Soule

Further Reading

Brady, Frank. "Structure and Meaning in Gray's *Elegy*." In *From Sensibility to Romanticism: Essays Presented to Frederick A. Pottle*, edited by Frederick W. Hilles and Harold Bloom. New York: Oxford University Press, 1965. In his lucid and careful reading of Gray's elegy, Brady stresses the appropriateness of the closing "epitaph." The book contains two other essays on the "Elegy Written in a Country Churchyard."

Brooks, Cleanth. "Gray's Storied Urn." In *The Well Wrought Urn: Studies in the Structure of Poetry*. New York: Reynal & Hitchcock, 1947. In a celebrated and important close reading of the poem, Brooks argues that the "Elegy Written in a Country Churchyard" is rich in irony and implication. Essential reading for any interpreter of the work.

Curr, Matthew. *The Consolation of Otherness: The Male Love Elegy in Milton, Gray, and Tennyson*. Jefferson, N.C.: McFarland, 2002. Compares elegiac verse written by Gray, John Milton, and Alfred, Lord Tennyson, all of whom wrote poetry in response to the death of a young male friend. Discusses Gray's relationship with Richard West, the friend who may have inspired the elegy. Analyzes Gray's use of the Latin vernacular to express his grief and describes how his sense of "otherness" in the poem offers solace for his loss.

Lonsdale, Roger, ed. *The Poems of Thomas Gray, William Collins, Oliver Goldsmith*. London: Longman, 1969. Lonsdale's introduction to Gray's elegy and his notes to the text are invaluable, especially on the difficulties of lines 93 to 96.

Mack, Robert L. *Thomas Gray: A Life*. New Haven, Conn.: Yale University Press, 2000. Mack begins his biography with an examination of "Elegy Written in a Country Churchyard," which he describes as "one of the most moving and effective meditations on death ever to have been written in English." His biography benefits from up-to-date scholarship that offers new insights into Gray's life, and his analysis of Gray's works makes use of gender studies and other modern critical theory.

Sells, A. L. Lytton, assisted by Iris Lytton Sells. *Thomas Gray: His Life and Works*. London: George Allen and Unwin, 1980. This biography includes frequent references to Gray's elegy and features a lengthy discussion of the work. Sells believes that the epitaph refers to Richard West.

Weinfield, Henry. *The Poet Without a Name: Gray's "Elegy" and the Problem of History*. Carbondale: Southern Illinois University Press, 1991. A scholarly book that employs a variety of critical methods to establish the poem's significance. Weinfield, who gives his own intricate reading of the work in chapter 3, considers the "thee" in line 93 to refer to all of humanity.

Ellen Foster

Author: Kaye Gibbons (1960-   )
First published: 1987
Type of work: Novel
Type of plot: Bildungsroman
Time of plot: 1970's
Locale: Southern United States

Principal characters:
ELLEN FOSTER, the narrator and protagonist
BILL, her foster "daddy"
MAMA, her unnamed mother
NEW MAMA, Ellen's foster mother
STARLETTA, Ellen's best friend, who is African American
BETSY, Ellen's maternal aunt
JULIA, Ellen's art teacher
ROY, Julia's husband, an organic gardener
MAMA'S MAMA, Ellen's grandmother
MAVIS, an African American field worker
NADINE, Ellen's maternal aunt
DORA, Nadine's daughter and Ellen's cousin

The Story:

Ellen Foster's life is one of having been abused and or-phaned and of living with generally unwelcoming relatives. She finally chooses a new mama, a woman who takes in foster children. Having at last found a real home, Ellen changes her name to Foster—for her new foster family.

Two years after being welcomed into a new home, a place where she has felt safe and loved, Ellen realizes that her foster parents are desperately unhappy. Ellen's foster mother had married Bill, a man "beneath" her who, even on the night she returns weakened and exhausted from a hospital stay because of heart trouble, treats her cruelly. Ellen takes control of the situation, sending her mother to bed and tending to her drunken father.

The next day, Ellen's mother commits suicide by taking too much of her medication, and her father refuses to intervene. Ellen lies down with her mother after her father claims her mother just needs sleep. Ellen hears her heart stop beating.

After the funeral, Ellen is trapped in the house with her drunken father, dodging his sexual advances and those of his friends; she has to tolerate his tirades as well. She sneaks money from his meager resources, which he uses mostly to buy alcohol, to eat and to save for some kind of escape. The only safety she can find is with her friend Starletta and her parents, who allow Ellen to spend the night with them when she flees her father's sexual abuse. Ellen, raised in a still-racist South, deeply appreciates their kindness, but is not quite comfortable among them.

Because she is afraid to return to her father's house, Ellen first calls her Aunt Betsy, who agrees that she can stay with her. Life is good here. Betsy confides that she has always

wanted a daughter but soon tells Ellen it is time for her to go home. Clearly, her mother's sister is not prepared to take Ellen in and raise her as her own.

Julia, Ellen's art teacher at the elementary school, discovers Ellen's bruises and takes her in. Julia and her husband, Roy, are compassionate and somewhat unconventional people, delighted by the courage Ellen shows in not succumbing to self-pity and by her gifts as an artist. Ellen is happy here, and she celebrates her eleventh birthday with Starletta. Soon, however, Ellen must find another home because Julia is not rehired by the school and decides to move away. Thus continues a series of displacements for Ellen, each situation unhappier than the former.

Ellen's grandmother, mama's mama, is the next person to take her in, for the court has ordered that Ellen is best off with family. Mama's mama hates Ellen's father and blames him for exposing his fragile daughter to a life of misery. She transfers this hatred to Ellen. She sees to her physical needs but speaks cruelly to her, even blaming her granddaughter for her mother's death.

Finally, mama's mama puts Ellen to work in the cotton fields, into hot and backbreaking work fit only, in the eyes of mama's mama, for the African Americans she hires. Ellen endures, however, helped along by Mavis, a field hand who befriends and helps her. Soon, Ellen's father as well as her grandmother dies. She is then sent to another of her mother's sisters, Aunt Nadine.

Life with Aunt Nadine seems fine at first, until it becomes clear that Nadine and her unpleasant daughter, Dora, are determined to keep Ellen in her place. The breaking point occurs when Ellen makes pictures for her aunt and cousin for

Christmas, framing them herself with colored paper and proudly presenting them as gifts on Christmas Eve. Ellen overhears their reactions to the gifts and is angered and humiliated.

The next morning, while Dora opens gift after gift, Ellen is presented with just one gift, the pack of white paper she had asked for, and nothing else. Ellen is furious at their insensitivity and selfishness and retreats to her room. She invents a boyfriend who gives her the microscope she had bought earlier for herself to taunt Dora.

After Nadine accuses Ellen of ingratitude, Ellen packs her things, dresses in her best clothes, and walks to the house of a woman she has seen in church with her daughters, a foster mother, she has been told. She asks the woman to take her in and offers her the $160 she had saved while living with her father. The woman takes her in, and she also arranges to keep her legally. Ellen has at last found a home, and a new mama.

Starletta visits Ellen at her new home. Though Ellen has always loved her friend, she experiences a kind of epiphany, recognizing her own earlier racism. She decides that Starletta has a harder time in life than she has. Ellen not only has survived and endured but also has grown beyond the narrow-mindedness of her society.

Ellen's life in her new foster home is a happy one, a life filled with "normal" childhood things, like going to school, a clean and orderly household, eating nutritious meals, helping with chores, celebrating holidays, riding her horse, and above all, basking in her new mama's warm attention.

Critical Evaluation:

Ellen Foster is Kaye Gibbons's first novel, begun while taking a class with the eminent scholar of southern literature Louis Rubin, at the University of North Carolina at Chapel Hill. Rubin had encouraged her to finish and publish the novel with Algonquin Press. Some autobiographical elements characterize the story: Gibbons was born in the South, in Nash County, North Carolina, in 1960. Her mother committed suicide by overdosing on pills when Gibbons was ten years old, and her abusive and alcoholic father drank himself to death as a young man. She subsequently lived with relatives and foster families, until finally finding a home where she was accepted and happy.

For *Ellen Foster*, Gibbons won the Sue Kaufman Prize for First Fiction and a special citation from the Ernest Hemingway Foundation. She also won the Louis D. Rubin, Jr., Prize in Creative Writing in 1987. The novel was produced by Hallmark Hall of Fame for CBS television in December, 1997, and, together with her novel *A Virtuous Woman* (1989), was selected for Oprah's Book Club in 1998. *Ellen Foster*

then remained on *The New York Times* best-seller list for many weeks.

Gibbons writes within a distinguished tradition of southern literature that extends from the southern renaissance, which, beyond the revolutionary work of William Faulkner, had established a powerful tradition of women writers, including Caroline Gordon, Eudora Welty, Flannery O'Connor, Carson McCullers, Ellen Douglas, Elizabeth Spencer, Lee Smith, and Jill McKorkle.

Ellen Foster also is celebrated as a coming-of-age story like the novels *Adventures of Huckleberry Finn* (1884) by Mark Twain and *The Catcher in the Rye* (1951) by J. D. Salinger. Ellen reminds one of Huck and Holden, with their honest and individual voices and their exposure of the hypocrisies and cruelties of adult society. Like the virtually orphaned Huck, who in his own mind risks damnation to save his friend—the escaped slave Jim—Ellen includes her friend Starletta in her life, despite her own discomfort about the younger child's race, and finally comes to see Starletta as someone who lives a life even more difficult than her own. Ellen regrets and renounces the prejudice she inherited from her family and from life in the South.

Gibbons's subsequent novels have been lauded for their strong, self-reliant women characters, who face the challenges of love and marriage, children, abandonment, poverty, and prejudice—including racism and sexism—without giving in to self-pity. Whether contemporary or historical, these women, like Ellen, speak in a vernacular that captures the cadences and eccentricities of southern and individual speech without the cumbersome spellings of dialect, another of Gibbons's strengths as a writer.

Ellen's is the first of these series of voices. In *Ellen Foster*, quotation marks are absent, as Ellen is allowed to breathlessly tell her story. All of the words are hers, including the words of the other characters (their voices are translated through Ellen). Despite her age and the horror of her experiences, she is a trustworthy narrator. After all, she begins with the admission that she had once thought of ways to "kill" daddy. Such forthrightness could suggest a deranged or a rigorously honest storyteller. As the narrative proceeds, it is clear the latter is the case.

Ellen's grammatical errors and colorful sayings suggest her age and upbringing, her southern heritage, and her particular cast of mind, including her precocity. Sometimes her errors, like her mother's "romantic fever" (rheumatic fever), suggest truths beyond those a child should understand. Her grammatical errors, like "his own self" or "somebody you know good," show the influence of her father's class rather than the class of her mother. Other particulars of her speech are simply southern, "like throw a fit" or "cut the lights off." Still others are just popular slang, like her grandmother's being "off her rocker" or the occasional mild profanity, like "chickenshit." The mix makes for a highly individual, but at the same time clearly regional, voice.

In the narrative structure, Ellen alternately recounts her past and celebrates her present. The juxtapositions are meaningful. In general, they contrast the deprivation, disorder and unpredictability, and suffering of her old life with life in her latest foster mother's home. More specifically, Ellen contrasts feeling trapped between Dora and Dora's mama in a car on the way to her mother's funeral with the freedom of riding all day on her horse, Dolphin.

The theme most discussed with regard to *Ellen Foster* is race. An African American character, Starletta, is central to the story's unfolding, inasmuch as Ellen's friendship with Starletta demonstrates Ellen's growing awareness of racism. The novel depicts the changing South, especially its racial climate, in a realistic way. It is set in a turbulent time, a time in which Martin Luther King, Jr., had been assassinated (1968), in which U.S. president Lyndon B. Johnson had signed the Civil Rights Act (1968), and in which the U.S. Supreme Court had upheld busing as a means of integrating schools (1971). Ellen and Starletta clearly attend an integrated school, though socially the two races at the school remain far apart.

The lingering importance of class distinctions and their painful consequences are embodied in Ellen's parents' tragic marriage. Furthermore, that art teacher Julia, a 1960's "flower child" raised in the East, is not rehired, implies the southern resistance to difference and progress and to outsiders.

The myth of a bucolic, slower-paced South is likewise exploded as Julia and Roy fail to realize their dream of farming in and teaching in the South. Churchgoing has not tempered the various cruelties, hypocrisies, and prejudices Ellen encounters in her relatives. Family, so sacred in the South, helps Ellen find neither refuge nor love.

However, the novel confirms the generous humanity of individual characters, especially Ellen's resilience, humor, self-awareness, and capacity to love beyond her own prejudices. Institutions, too, display a sort of humanity: The elementary school that saves Ellen from her father, finds her a loving temporary home, and even houses the well-meaning, if less than helpful, psychologist, benefits Ellen.

Finally, among the many motifs lending unity to the narrative is food. Ellen is a hungry child in every way. The contrast of the meagerness of meals with her mother and father and of her near starvation with her father, with the plentiful, regular, and even ritual mealtimes with her foster mother, suggests how far Ellen has come in her circumstances and her spirit. During Starletta's visit with Ellen in her new home, Ellen does not fail to remark that soon they will have supper and maybe even some cake. All is well.

Susie Paul

Further Reading

DeMarr, Mary Jean. *Kaye Gibbons: A Critical Companion.* Westport, Conn.: Greenwood Press, 2003. A thorough study of Gibbons's work (to 1998) through the lens of feminist, Marxist, and cultural theory. A chapter is dedicated to each novel and includes analyses of persistent themes, issues of genre, style, and narrative technique.

Folks, Jeffrey J. *From Richard Wright to Toni Morrison: Ethics in Modern and Postmodern American Narrative.* New York: Peter Lang, 2001. In the chapter "Obligations of the Dispossessed: The Ethical Vision of Kaye Gibbons's *Ellen Foster* and *A Virtuous Woman*," Folks characterizes Gibbons's novels as revisionist, creating a world in which the failures and schisms of the southern past are transformed in the direction of hope. Also looks at Ellen's moral development.

Guinn, Matthew. *After Southern Modernism: Fiction of the Contemporary South.* Jackson: University Press of Mississippi, 2000. In a chapter dedicated to Gibbons and to writer Bobbie Ann Mason, Guinn discusses *Ellen Foster.* Compares the novel's protagonist and her journey with the journey of Huck Finn down the Mississippi River. For advanced high school students and college students.

Powell, Dannye Romine. "Kaye Gibbons." In *Parting the Curtains: Interviews with Southern Writers.* Winston-Salem, N.C.: John F. Blair. 1994. A lengthy interview with Gibbons, who discusses several stages of her life and career. Covers her childhood, pertinent to *Ellen Foster* and its autobiographical elements, as well as her marriages and children, her struggles with manic depression (bipolar disorder), and her writing process.

Snodgrass, Mary Ellen. *Kaye Gibbons: A Literary Companion.* Jefferson, N.C.: McFarland, 2007. A thorough study of Gibbons's work that lays out for new readers the characters, plots, dates, allusions, literary motifs, and themes of her novels. An appendix features a time line of historical events in the novels that correspond to actual events in the history of the South.

Elmer Gantry

Author: Sinclair Lewis (1885-1951)
First published: 1927
Type of work: Novel
Type of plot: Satire
Time of plot: 1902-1925
Locale: Midwestern United States

Principal characters:
ELMER GANTRY, a minister
MRS. GANTRY, his mother
CLEO BENHAM GANTRY, his wife
LULU BAINS, his mistress
HETTIE DOWLER, another of his mistresses
OSCAR DOWLER, Hettie's husband
JUDSON ROBERTS, a former football star and state secretary of the YMCA
FRANK SHALLARD, a minister and Elmer's chief antagonist
SHARON FALCONER, an evangelist
MRS. EVANS RIDDLE, AN EVANGELIST AND A NEW THOUGHT LEADER
T. J. RIGGS, a rich associate of Elmer in Zenith

The Story:

Elmer Gantry, known as Hell-cat to his classmates at Terwillinger College in Kansas in 1902, is a large man, six feet one, with a loud, booming voice. He leads the team as football captain and is twice elected class president. Although he is assumed to be popular, Gantry is not really well liked by his classmates. Elmer's father, Logan Gantry, a feed dealer, died at a young age, leaving his widow to support herself and her son with her sewing. She was a religious woman and made Gantry go to church, where he learned about religion but failed to learn decency or kindness.

When the evangelist Judson Roberts speaks at the college for the YMCA Week of Prayer, Gantry is moved to kneel in prayer and announce that he is saved. The crowd cheers for the passionate speech Gantry delivers following his conversion, and the president of the college tells him he is a born preacher. Gantry's mother, who attended the meeting, says it was her happiest moment. College officials and his mother urge Elmer to become a minister.

Gantry attends Mizpah Seminary, where he is ordained as a Baptist minister. While he is preaching in a small town, Gantry meets Lulu Bains, the daughter of a deacon at the church, and seduces her. He promises to marry her but quickly tires of her. When Floyd Naylor and Deacon Bains threaten to beat him if he does not marry Lulu, Gantry claims he always planned to marry her, and they announce the engagement. In a scheme to get out of his commitment, however, he stages a fight with Lulu and then leaves her alone with Floyd. As Floyd innocently embraces Lulu to comfort her, Gantry leads Deacon Bains to the spot and shines a flashlight on the couple. Outraged to see his daughter kissing Floyd, the deacon forces Lulu to marry Floyd. Gantry pre-

tends to be devastated by Lulu's betrayal and asks the dean for a transfer.

On his way to the new church, Gantry gets drunk with a stranger he meets on the train, passes out, and misses the church service. He is fired from the seminary and has to find work as a salesman for a farm implement company. On his travels, he falls under the spell of a female evangelist named Sharon Falconer. Acting as her assistant, Gantry pays people to fake being saved or feigns his own conversion. Following her rise to eminence as a healer of the sick, Sharon buys a resort on the New Jersey coast that she names Waters of Jordan Tabernacle. By holding meetings there, she does not have to share her profits with local churches. When a workman carelessly discards a cigarette, the tabernacle goes up in flames and kills 111 people, including Sharon and her crew. Gantry tries to lead Sharon to safety, but she stubbornly keeps her station, holding a wooden cross in front of her. Only Gantry survives.

Unable to earn a living as an independent evangelist, Gantry works for Mrs. Evans Riddle, another evangelist, until he is fired for stealing from the collection plate. In 1913, Gantry meets the Methodist church leader Bishop Toomis, who is impressed with Gantry's style. Gantry becomes a Methodist, and Toomis arranges for Gantry to serve as a minister in the small town of Banjo Crossing. There he courts and marries Cleo Benham because he thinks she will help his career. Gantry never returns the love Cleo feels for him, and after the birth of their second child, they move into separate bedrooms.

At the age of thirty-nine, Gantry is given a large church in Zenith, a city with a population of 400,000. He becomes friends with T. J. Riggs, a famous trial lawyer and a trustee of the church. Gantry is a popular preacher and soon builds up attendance. Preferring to spend time on church work and organizations, Gantry is seldom home and, when he is, he is so surly and critical that his own children are afraid of him.

One Sunday, Lulu and Floyd show up at Gantry's church. Lulu is still in love with Gantry, and he feels physical attraction for her. Soon Lulu and Gantry are meeting secretly in the church on Tuesday nights.

Gantry meets with other ministers in town on a regular basis, and after he is in Zenith for a year and a half, he organizes a committee on public morals to conduct an attack on the red-light district. He wins attention in the press through a few carefully staged raids on small-time bootleggers and prostitutes.

Gantry's hellfire and damnation sermons continue to attract attention from the public and the press. Gantry also uses his pulpit to denounce the religious views of his former classmate, Frank Shallard, who preaches in the same town. As a result of Gantry's smear attack, Shallard is fired from his church. Later, thugs calling him a heretic beat Shallard so brutally that he loses sight in one eye. Gantry calls to offer condolences and says he will find and punish the offenders, but Shallard never hears from Gantry again.

As Gantry's success continues, he joins the Rotary Club, plays golf with the wealthy men of the community, and spends money on expensive clothes. He convinces the officials of Abernathy College to award him a doctor of divinity degree so that people can call him Dr. Gantry. When his sermons are broadcast on the radio, his audience increases from two thousand to ten thousand. He travels to London, New York, Los Angeles, and Toronto to preach.

Gantry fires his longtime secretary and hires Hettie Dowler, a beautiful young woman who soon becomes his mistress. To get rid of Lulu, Gantry tells her that Cleo found out about the affair and that he has to end their relationship. That leaves Gantry free to concentrate on Hettie. When Hettie and her husband try to blackmail Gantry with the letters that Gantry wrote to her, the press gets hold of the news and denounces Gantry. A detective, hired by Gantry's friend Riggs, investigates Hettie and discovers enough information on her past activities to force her to sign a confession that exonerates Gantry. The newspapers announce Gantry's innocence, and the congregation cheers him on Sunday. Gantry vows to avoid temptation in the future, but even as he kneels in prayer with his congregation, he notices a pretty woman in the choir whom he wants to meet.

"The Story" by Judith Barton Williamson

Critical Evaluation:

Sinclair Lewis wrote *Elmer Gantry* at the height of his fame, in the middle of the 1920's. That decade began for Lewis with *Main Street: The Story of Carol Kennicott* (1920) and ended with *Dodsworth* (1929) and included not only *Babbitt* (1922) and *Arrowsmith* (1925) but also their author's refusal of a Pulitzer Prize. Curiously, *Elmer Gantry* gives the first hint of the waning of Lewis's powers. Before this novel, Lewis had served a long apprenticeship and achieved great success. Between 1915 and 1920, he wrote fifty short stories and five novels, experimenting with his themes and characterizations and sketching out his satiric portraits of various types, not the least of these being religious types. The climax of that kind of portraiture came with *Elmer Gantry*.

Lewis spent years perfecting his method of research to establish the realistic foundation on which his satires rest. *Main Street* was a sensational best seller, and apparently it occurred to Lewis that he could repeat his success if he would, in a programmatic way, turn his satiric eye upon the various aspects of American life in sequence. After his exposure of the village, he next chose Zenith, a middle-sized city, and George F. Babbitt, a middle-class businessman. Thereafter he applied his attention (in collaboration with Dr. Paul de Kruif) to medicine, public health, and medical experimentation. Finally, he found a challenging topic in the ministry. Undertaking an exposure of hypocrisy in religion was a formidable and dangerous task, but Lewis felt confidently ready for it. In *Babbitt*, he had written of Mike Monday, the evangelist; Mrs. Opal Emerson Mudge, leader of the New Thought League; and the Reverend John Jennison Drew, author of *The Manly Man's Religion*.

Following his usual method of research, he sought expert advice to provide the background for his novel. He turned to a minister in Kansas City, with whom he was acquainted, and he hosted a weekly seminar of local pastors of many faiths and sects; after luncheon, there might be a session on "The Holy Spirit," with Lewis challenging, pressing, arguing, and thus absorbing material. Gradually, the characters and plot of his novel took shape. In Elmer Gantry, Lewis created his most extravagant faker: a salesman of religion with no real knowledge of theology and no scruples or morals, a stupid man who would exploit his parishioners as he climbed to success from village to town to city, a seducer of women, and a man of greed.

Lewis gave much of his attention to his portrait of Sharon Falconer, the beautiful and somewhat mad female evangelist who preaches in a majestic temple and then leads Gantry to her retreat in the hills where she allows herself to be seduced on an altar she has built to such pagan goddesses as Astarte.

Sharon says she has visions and confesses that she hates little vices such as smoking and swearing but loves big ones such as lust and murder. Nevertheless, from some confused notions about God, Sharon derives sufficient strength to stand at the pulpit in her burning tabernacle and attempt to quell the panic of the mob of her parishioners. By contrast, Gantry knocks aside dozens of helpless people and is able to escape. Into such scenes as these, and into the final episode in which Gantry is narrowly saved from entrapment in the old badger game, Lewis poured all his vitality. What critics have missed, however, and what seems to suggest the first waning of Lewis's powers, is the lack of any real opposition. In Gantry there seems to be no decency, therefore there are no alternatives contending in his soul. In the "good" characters there is insufficient understanding and fortitude, and they neither supply important alternatives nor force Gantry to any choices. In this book, Lewis displayed his virtuosity as a satirist, but he also indulged it and failed to find for it any opposition in positive values.

Further Reading

Dooley, D. J. "Aspiration and Enslavement." In *The Art of Sinclair Lewis*. Lincoln: University of Nebraska Press, 1967. Examines Elmer's picaresque journey through American religion in the early twentieth century. Charges that the novel fails as satire because it is neither realistic nor witty.

Geismar, Maxwell. "Sinclair Lewis: The Cosmic Bourjoyce." In *The Last of the Provincials: The American Novel, 1915-1925*. New York: Hill and Wang, 1949. Suggests that Lewis has little insight into religious motivation or the commercial exploitation of religion. Criticizes the character of Sharon Falconer as neoprimitive and that of Gantry as an archetypal opportunist and false prophet.

Grebstein, Sheldon Norman. "The Great Decade." In *Sinclair Lewis*. New York: Twayne, 1962. Explores the novel's background and describes its having been written in "the most hotly charged religious atmosphere in America since the Salem witch burnings."

Hilfer, Anthony Channell. "Elmer Gantry and That Old Time Religion." In *The Revolt from the Village, 1915-1930*. Chapel Hill: University of North Carolina Press, 1969. Perceives *Elmer Gantry* as an attack on small-town provincialism. Discusses contemporary social events and issues, such as the Scopes trial, Prohibition, and the hypocrisy and corruption of some religious extremists.

Hutchisson, James M. *The Rise of Sinclair Lewis, 1920-1930*. University Park: Pennsylvania State University Press, 1996. Focuses on Lewis's career in the 1920's, when he wrote *Elmer Gantry* and the other novels that earned him the Nobel Prize in Literature. Hutchisson examines the techniques Lewis used to create his novels, focusing on *Elmer Gantry* in chapter 4.

_____, ed. *Sinclair Lewis: New Essays in Criticism*. Troy, N.Y.: Whitston, 1997. Includes George Killough's essay "Elmer Gantry, Chaucer's Pardoner, and the Limits of Serious Words," as well as essays on many of Lewis's other novels and an annotated bibliography of Lewis studies from 1977 through 1997.

Lingeman, Richard R. *Sinclair Lewis: Rebel from Main Street*. New York: Random House, 2002. A critical biography that includes analysis of Lewis's novels. Lingeman provides a detailed description of Lewis's unhappy life.

Schorer, Mark, ed. *Sinclair Lewis: A Collection of Critical Essays*. Englewood Cliffs, N.J.: Prentice-Hall, 1962. Contains earlier criticism of *Elmer Gantry*, including Rebecca West's famous attack on the novel as ineffective satire and Joseph Wood Krutch's praise of the book, as well as Schorer's classic study, "Sinclair Lewis and the Method of Half-Truths."

Éloges, and Other Poems

Author: Saint-John Perse (1887-1975)
First published: Éloges, 1911 (English translation, 1944)
Type of work: Poetry

Alexis Saint-Léger Léger, who wrote under the name of Saint-John Perse, was born in Guadeloupe and had a long and very distinguished career in both the prewar and postwar French diplomatic service. He thus represents that peculiarly French combination of the public servant and the man of letters. Though his *Anabase* (1924; *Anabasis*, 1930) was translated by so famous a writer as T. S. Eliot, he remained little known outside Europe. It is improbable that his work will ever achieve any wide degree of popularity; nevertheless, because of his marked influence on twentieth century poetry, he remains an important figure.

"Pictures for Crusoe," the earliest of the poems included in the volume, should be read first; they are the clearest and, once understood, provide a sort of key to the other sections. In them, the reader is made immediately aware of the author's childhood spent in the tropics; there is a succession of luxuriant images from the island left behind by Robinson Crusoe and the expression of nostalgia for clean wind, sea, and sand, and for the brilliant colors of dawn and sunset. It is the theme of this series of short poems that Crusoe's real disaster occurs when he returns to the cities of men and leaves forever the lost tropic island. Everything he brings with him, every symbol of the island—the goatskin parasol, the bow, the parrot—decays in the sour dirt of the city; the seed of the purple tropic flower that he plants will not grow; even Goodman Friday, as he steals from the larder, leers with eyes that have become sly and vicious. Crusoe weeps, remembering the surf, the moonlight, and other, distant shores.

The same theme of nostalgia, much less clearly stated, runs through the longer poems "To Celebrate a Childhood" and "Praises." Here the poet tries to recapture, by the same device of a series of pictures, the lost world of a childhood against the background of violent contrasts of brilliant light and shining water and crowding vegetation. The lush images succeed one another with bewildering rapidity until the lost childhood is re-created. Indeed, the images are heaped with such profusion that the poems become almost cloying, like overripe fruit. There is a shift of emphasis here, for no longer is there a contrast between two worlds, the island and the city, but rather an almost total recall of both the beauty and the squalor of the tropics.

The second section of the book, "The Glory of Kings," consists of four poems, two written in 1910 and two in 1924. These poems are much more obscure than those in the first section. In them, Perse seems to have moved from the background of his childhood in Guadeloupe to the world of some primitive people where nameless speakers address praises to their half-human, half-divine rulers—the queen, a mysterious sphinxlike creature, at once the queen and the mother; the prince, with his towering headdress, the healer and enchanter, keeping vigil. It may be that Perse is trying to express something of the spirit in which members of a primitive society identify themselves with their rulers, until the king becomes the symbol, indeed the very soul, of his people and is rejoiced in as such. By implication, this belief is set against the critical, questioning attitude of twentieth century human beings, shorn of reverence, cut off from "the sources of the spirit." "The Glory of Kings" seems to develop further a theme that is already implicit in "Pictures for Crusoe," the cult of the primitive that appears in the work of so many twentieth century writers.

Under the first pen name of their author, these early poems by Perse are referred to by Marcel Proust, who, in *Sodome et Gomorrhe* (1922; *Cities of the Plain*, 1927), gives an appreciation of them and an indication of the likely reaction of the average reader: Lying on the narrator's bed is a book of the admirable but ambiguous poems of Saint-Léger Léger; Madame Celeste Albaret picks up the book and asks if he is sure that they are poems and not riddles. It is natural that Proust, preoccupied as he was with the evocation of the past in all of its subtle ramifications in time and place, would have delighted in a poet bent on the same task of recapturing the totality of the experiences of childhood—including the sights, the sounds, and the odors. Nor is it surprising that these pictures from the tropics, so different from the hothouse, artificial life that Proust knew, should, by their very contrast, have appealed to him.

However, by including the remark of Madame Celeste, so distressing to the narrator, Proust succinctly indicates the probable response of most readers of poetry who approach Perse for the first time. It cannot be denied that these poems make very difficult reading. Eliot, in his preface to his translation of Perse's *Anabasis*, tries to defend the author against the charge of willful obscurity by claiming that their seeming obscurity results from the linkage of explanatory and connecting matter, not from incoherence. Eliot's advice to the reader is to allow the images of the poem to fall into the memory with unquestioning acceptance, each contributing to a total effect that will be apparent at the end of the poem. It is an indication of the contribution that Perse makes to poetic technique that this analysis could equally well be applied to much of Eliot's own work.

It is by means of sequences of images, abruptly shifting into one another, that Perse achieves his total effects. This aspect of his poetry elicited the special praise of Valéry Larbaud, who considers his descriptions far superior to those of François-Auguste-René Chateaubriand because they are concrete, exact, precise, and filled with meaning. The result is a blending of the ugly and the beautiful, the whole a passionate rendering of experience. In his descriptions Perse makes full use of a device so characteristic of contemporary poetry: the sudden juxtaposition of the so-called poetic and the deliberately ugly or grotesque. A coconut, tossed into the street, "diverts from the gutter/ the metallic splendor of the purple waters mottled with grease and urine, where soap weaves a spider's web." It is intriguing to consider that such lines were being written in France in 1910, at a time when English poetry was dominated by the Georgians.

Few modern poets so little known to the reading public have received from their fellow poets such high praise as has Perse. His work has been translated into English, German, Spanish, Italian, Russian, and Romanian. Hugo von Hofmannsthal considered that a direct road leads from Arthur Rimbaud to the early work of Stefan George and to that of Perse. Larbaud maintained that between 1895 and 1925 perhaps a hundred poets appeared in France, of whom at least thirty would continue to be worthy of attention; of these thirty, only a few would survive. To both of these critics, Perse is valuable because of his attempt, through the manipulation of language and his brilliant descriptions, to revivify French lyricism. It may well be, however, that Perse will remain essentially a poets' poet, important to other writers because of what they can learn from his method, rather than a poet for the general reader. It is no longer necessary for the poet to appeal to the community and the wider view. He may now appeal to himself and the urgencies of his private vision.

Further Reading

Galand, René. *Saint-John Perse.* New York: Twayne, 1972. Ideal for serious research. Discusses the themes, symbolism, and influences on Perse's poetry in a systematic and chronological order. Includes a chronology of Perse's life and an extensive bibliography.

Gallagher, Mary. "Seminal Praise: The Poetry of Saint-John Perse." In *An Introduction to Caribbean Francophone Writing: Guadeloupe and Martinique,* edited by Sam Haigh. New York: Berg, 1999. Analyzes the "highly complex connection" between the Caribbean and Perse's poetry.

Little, Roger. *Saint-John Perse.* London: Athlone Press, 1973. Excellent discussion of the collected poems, extremely helpful for beginning a study of the poet. Includes chapters on Perse's other writings and ways in which to interpret his poetry. Bibliography.

Loichot, Valérie. "Saint-John Perse's Shipwrecked Plantation: *Éloges.*" In *Orphan Narratives: The Postplantation Literature of Faulkner, Glissant, Morrison, and Saint-John Perse.* Charlottesville: University of Virginia Press, 2007. Analyzes how *Éloges* and other works of postslavery literature reflect the violence of plantation slavery.

Mehlman, Jeffrey. "Saint-John Perse: Discontinuities." In *Émigré New York: French Intellectuals in Wartime Manhattan, 1940-1944.* Baltimore: Johns Hopkins University Press, 2000. Chronicles the lives of Perse and other French writers who spent World War II living in exile in New York City.

Ostrovsky, Erika. *Under the Sign of Ambiguity: Saint-John Perse/Alexis Léger.* New York: New York University Press, 1984. A chronological discussion of Perse's life in relation to his poetry. Ostrovsky attempts to eliminate the ambiguities inherent in Perse's poetry. Includes a bibliography.

Rigolot, Carol. *Forged Genealogies: Saint-John Perse's Conversations with Culture.* Chapel Hill: Department of Romance Languages, University of North Carolina, 2001. Rigolot likens reading Perse's poetry to "eavesdropping on a telephone conversation in which only one side is audible." She analyzes his use of dialogue in his poetry, focusing on his conversations with a range of historical figures. Chapter 1 focuses on *Éloges.*

Sterling, Richard L. *The Prose Works of Saint-John Perse: Towards an Understanding of His Poetry.* New York: Peter Lang, 1994. A good source for twentieth century French aesthetics, especially in relation to Perse's poetry. Includes a good bibliography.

The Emigrants

Author: W. G. Sebald (1944-2001)

First published: Die Ausgewanderten, 1992 (English translation, 1996)

Type of work: Novel

Type of plot: Historical

Time of plot: 1890's to 1980's

Locale: Continental Europe, England, New Jersey, and New York

Principal characters:

THE NARRATOR, unnamed

HENRY SELWYN, an English physician

PAUL BEREYTER, the narrator's schoolteacher

LUCY LANDAU, Paul's companion

AMBROS ADELWARTH, the narrator's great-uncle

COSMO SOLOMON, a wealthy young man for whom Ambros acts as valet

MAX FERBER, an artist living in Manchester

LUISA LANZBERG, Ferber's mother

The Story:

An unnamed narrator is traveling to the small English town of Hingham in search of lodging. Near the village church, with an ancient graveyard, he discovers a large house with a flat for lease. While he describes the grounds as overgrown, the house in mild disrepair, and its inhabitants eccentric, the narrator moves in and befriends his landlady's husband, Dr. Henry Selwyn. During one conversation, Selwyn tells the narrator about an encounter in his youth, in which he had befriended a sixty-five-year-old alpine guide in Switzerland, whose death, presumably in a glacial crevasse, sent Selwyn into a deep depression.

After moving from the flat, the narrator learns from Selwyn that the doctor is not English by birth, as the narrator had assumed, but a Lithuanian Jew named Hersch Seweryn, whose family had emigrated to London in 1899. Selwyn confesses to a growing homesickness. Not long after, the narrator learns that Selwyn has committed suicide with a hunting rifle. The narrator then reads an article in a Swiss newspaper about the discovery of an alpine guide whose body had recently been released by the glacier—the same man who Selwyn had known and mourned.

The narrator later reads a news report of the suicide of his schoolteacher, Paul Bereyter, in 1984. Because of an unexplained line in the obituary, reporting that during the Third Reich, Bereyter had been forbidden from teaching, the narrator is compelled to uncover the full story. Paul, who was invariably called by his first name by students and townspeople alike, was a freethinking and devoted teacher with little patience for convention or sanctimony.

After describing his own recollections of Paul, the narrator gains a fuller account of his teacher's life when he finds Lucy Landau, Paul's confidant in his later years. Landau discloses that Paul, who was one-quarter Jewish, had left Germany in the 1930's because of persecution but had returned

before the war and had been conscripted. His likely fiancé had been deported, probably to the concentration camp Theresienstadt. It was after his return from the war that Paul had taught the narrator in their provincial town.

The narrator tells a story about his great-uncle, Ambros Adelwarth. He had met his great-uncle only once, when the American branch of the family returned to Germany for a brief visit in 1951. Thirty years later, the narrator visits New Jersey in an effort to understand Uncle Adelwarth, who is elegant and cultured, and who has worked as the manservant for a succession of wealthy families. During the early 1910's, Adelwarth had traveled through Europe as the companion of Cosmo Solomon, an eccentric yet gifted heir. There are hints that their relationship was deeper than appeared, and the narrator hears oblique references to Adelwarth's homosexuality from his uncle.

Cosmo had won considerable amounts of money in the European casinos, money he spent on a journey through Constantinople and Jerusalem. Accounts of the war had troubled Cosmo, and he reported visions of the trenches. After a later breakdown, he had been sent to a sanatorium in New York, where his health declined rapidly. Some decades later, Adelwarth fell into a depression and committed himself to the same sanatorium. He elected to submit to electroconvulsive therapy, which led to his death. The narrator describes a visit to the sanatorium in search of an account of his Uncle Adelwarth.

The narrator arrives in Manchester, England, where he happens upon Max Ferber, an artist who paints primarily through a process of subtraction, adding paint and then scraping it from his canvases. While he becomes close to Ferber, the narrator never questions him about his history. Twenty years after leaving Manchester, the narrator finds a painting by Ferber in the Tate Gallery. He returns to Manchester for a reunion with Ferber, who divulges that his parents had sent him to England before the war, though they had been unable to acquire exit visas to join him.

As the narrator takes his leave of Ferber, the artist gives him a series of notes made by his mother, which he claims to be emotionally unable to read once again. These notes, written after it became clear that she would be unable to join her son, detail the memories of the youth of Luisa Lanzberg. The narrator reconstructs her memories.

Critical Evaluation:

One of the primary concerns of W. G. Sebald's *The Emigrants* is memory, which not only is valued for its ability to suggest meaning to the present but also is potentially destructive. Throughout the novel, characters are lost to their memories of injustices that often have been repressed for many years. The narrator finds himself compelled to uncover the stories of these lives, which he values both for their ordinary human qualities and for their pathos. When Max Ferber bequeaths the narrator a packet of letters he had received from his mother, he says that the letters

had seemed to him like one of those evil German fairy tales in which, once you are under the spell, you have to carry on to the finish, till your heart breaks, with whatever work you have begun—in this case, the remembering, writing and reading.

The novel also points to the ways in which memory can be elliptical and unreliable. The writing itself raises the question of authenticity by calling attention to moments in which the characters' accounts seem suspect or self-contradictory. The novel does not attempt to smooth the seams between its parts, which appear to include fiction, memoir, travel writing, and essay. Though critics have struggled to define their genre, Sebald has called his books prose narratives. He notes, however, that every novelist produces a combination of reality and fiction, and he sees himself as part of the tradition of the modern novel.

The precariousness of memory is also alluded to in the novel's inclusion of photographs. Rather than illustrating the text, these images of less-than-artistic quality, linked in no immediate way to the accounts they accompany, are often simply found objects that prompt the narrator in his search for the past. (In this sense, the images from photo albums that appear in the book are similar to other archival elements, such as newspaper clippings and diaries, which drive the narrator's quest and which are also sometimes reproduced.) Unlike the typical use of photography, which serves as documentary evidence for accounts that require substantiation, these uncaptioned photographs—or snapshots—suggest further uncertainties, as their subject and purpose are not always clear. Some of the photos might even be fabricated.

Despite the instability of memory, that "lagoon of oblivion" that obliterates the characters' recollections of their pasts, the four sections of the novel become unified through the narrator's careful stitching. Though the four accounts initially seem connected only through the narrator's voice and perhaps the belated return of the past in the characters' lives, the recurrence of seemingly coincidental details, images, and language builds to suggest a more systematic linkage. Perhaps the most visible connection between the four parts is that at various points of time in each section, the figure of Vladimir Nabokov appears, not as the celebrated author of *Speak, Memory: An Autobiography Revisited* (1966) but as a lepidopterist carrying his butterfly net.

The fate of European Jews in the twentieth century could be considered one connecting line of the novel. Though the narrator approaches the history of the Holocaust only obliquely or allusively, the historical reality of the war waged by his compatriots is a driving force behind the actions of the characters. Sebald has spoken about his frustration with what he calls a conspiracy of silence in his parents' generation's unwillingness to speak openly about the past. His approach to writing about the events of the war is, he argues, the only legitimate way that he could draw near the atrocities of the Holocaust—not by recapitulating the familiar images of the camps, but peripherally, through the lives of those who were touched by the events. His unwillingness to compromise his stance or to resort to sensationalism or sentimentality is, in itself, a moral stance.

"And so they are ever returning to us, the dead," writes the narrator after discovering the newspaper account of the body of the alpine guide who had been befriended by Dr. Henry Selwyn. The perception recurs in the meandering turns taken by the captivating voice of the narrator. This voice speaks in a rich tone that is, by turns, ironic, wry, melancholic, and perceptive to occasional detail and cultural ephemera. This voice achieves its authenticity through its steady gaze and succeeds in summoning the lives of figures touched by modern history through its honesty to the uncertainties surrounding lived experience.

Todd Samuelson

Further Reading

Aciman, André. "In the Crevasse." *Commentary* 103, no. 6 (June, 1997): 61-64. A review of *The Emigrants* by the novelist and memoirist, which discusses the role of memory in the record of the displaced persons depicted in the novel.

Aliaga-Buchenau, Ana-Isabel. "'The Time He Could Not Bear to Say Any More About': Presence and Absence of the Narrator in W. G. Sebald's *The Emigrants*." In *W. G. Sebald: History—Memory—Trauma*, edited by Scott Denham and Mark McCulloh. Berlin: Walter de Gruyter, 2006. This essay discusses the problem of form in *The Emigrants*, arguing that the issue of the book's hybridity of genre is solved by the unifying voice of the narrator.

Angier, Carole. "Who Is W. G. Sebald?" In *The Emergence of Memory: Conversations with W. G. Sebald*, edited by Lynne Sharon Schwartz. New York: Seven Stories Press, 2007. An interview with the author originally published in the *Jewish Quarterly*. Primarily concerned with the sources of the Jewish characters in *The Emigrants* and Sebald's portrayal of their lives.

Doctorow, E. L. "W. G. Sebald." In *Creationists: Essays, 1993-2006*. New York: Random House, 2006. Focuses on Sebald's *The Emigrants*, praising Sebald for his ability to weave various leitmotifs into the novel to capture the themes of displacement and movement.

Feiereisen, Florence, and Daniel Pope. "The Enigmatic in Sebald's Use of Images in *The Emigrants*." In *Searching for Sebald: Photography After W. G. Sebald*, edited by Lise Patt. Los Angeles: Institute of Cultural Inquiry, 2007. This article attempts to account for the inconsistencies in the connections between the narratives and the photographs in *The Emigrants*, arguing that the relationship adds to an enigmatic quality that intentionally intrudes on the verisimilitude of the novel.

Long, J. J. "Family Albums: *The Emigrants*." In *W. G. Sebald: Image, Archive, Modernity*. New York: Columbia University Press, 2007. This chapter, part of a study that examines Sebald's response to modernity, pays particular attention to the role of photography and the concept of the archive in his work.

Long, J. J., and Anne Whitehead, eds. *W. G. Sebald: A Critical Companion*. Seattle: University of Washington Press, 2004. Collection of essays that explore Sebald's life, his influences, and the themes of his writings.

McCulloh, Mark R. "*The Emigrants*: In Search of the Vividly Present Dead." In *Understanding W. G. Sebald*. Columbia: University of South Carolina Press, 2003. A highly accessible book that provides an excellent student guide to Sebald's life and work. Chapter on *The Emigrants* synthesizes the critical dialogue, section by section, and discusses questions of reception and the novel's relation to the author's oeuvre.

Wachtel, Eleanor. "Ghost Hunter." In *The Emergence of Memory: Conversations with W. G. Sebald*, edited by Lynne Sharon Schwartz. New York: Seven Stories Press, 2007. An interview with the author conducted in 1997, after the publication of the English translation of *The Emigrants*. Discusses the form and origins of the novel.

The Emigrants of Ahadarra
A Tale of Irish Life

Author: William Carleton (1794-1869)
First published: 1848
Type of work: Novel
Type of plot: Regional
Time of plot: 1840's
Locale: Ireland

Principal characters:
BRYAN M'MAHON, an honest young farmer
KATHLEEN CAVANAGH, Bryan's beloved
HYACINTH "HYCY" BURKE, a well-to-do libertine and rascal
JEMMY BURKE, Hycy's father
NANNY PEETY, a beggar girl
KATE HOGAN, Nanny's aunt, a tinker's wife
PATRICK O'FINIGAN, a drunken schoolmaster

The Story:

Hyacinth "Hycy" Burke is the son of a wealthy and respected peasant who has allowed his wife, a woman with social pretensions of her own, to spoil the boy. With his mother's approval, Hycy has become a dissolute young man. Because his father, Jemmy Burke, tries to curb him by reducing his allowance, Hycy enters into partnership with whiskey smugglers to supplement his diminished income.

When one of the prettiest young women in the area, Kathleen Cavanagh, catches Hycy's eye, he determines to seduce her. Unfortunately for his plans, he misdirects two letters. One, intended for Kathleen, goes instead to Bryan M'Mahon, who truly loves Kathleen; another, intended for young M'Mahon, goes to Kathleen. Later, after being publicly snubbed on more than one occasion, Hycy resolves to have revenge on Kathleen and her true admirer. Any additional villainy can scarcely put him in greater danger than he is already in; he has already been an accomplice to burglarizing his father's house, has taken a large sum of money, and has been an active accomplice of smugglers. It is through his fellow smugglers that he plans to get his revenge.

A law in Ireland requires the inhabitants of a township to pay fines for any illegal distillation and smuggling of whiskey in their township if the actual culprits are not known. Bryan M'Mahon's farm at Ahadarra covers an entire township, and if he were to be required to pay such a fine by himself, he would be ruined. To carry out his plan, Hycy enlists the help of the nephew of the local goods inspector. Hycy promises the nephew the chance to lease a fine farm if the latter will press Hycy's suit for his sister's hand. The farm, of course, is Bryan M'Mahon's.

Bryan is not the only member of his family facing tragedy. Both his and his father's farm leases have run out, and death has prevented the absentee landlord from renewing them. The new landlord, a well-meaning but weak and inexperienced young man, is ruled by his agent, who wishes to see the M'Mahons lose their farms, leased by the family for generations.

Hycy carefully makes his plans. What he fails to realize, however, is that he has made enemies while Bryan has made friends; consequently, some persons who know of his villainy are prepared to take measures to thwart him. Nanny Peety, a pretty, virtuous beggar girl, resents Hycy for his many attempts to seduce her. She knows something of his plans, and she was a witness to the burglary that Hycy and his accomplice committed. Nanny's aunt, Kate Hogan, loves her niece and also thinks highly of Kathleen Cavanagh. She is willing and able to help them, because she is married to one of Hycy's smuggling associates. Patrick O'Finigan, a drunken schoolmaster, is also friendly to Kathleen and Bryan.

The plot against Bryan is put into operation when an anonymous letter from Hycy sends the inspector to discover the illicit still at Ahadarra, on Bryan's farm. Faced with financial ruin and his family's loss of their leases, the young peasant does not know what to do. Because his own honesty keeps him from believing that Hycy is working against him in such a manner, Bryan even takes advice from the man who is bent on ruining him. A parliamentary election is taking place in which the M'Mahons' landlord is standing for a seat. The voting results in a tie until Bryan, angry with his landlord and following Hycy's advice, votes for his landlord's opponent. By doing so, he makes himself appear false in everyone's eyes, for his landlord is a liberal who favors the Irish peasantry and religious freedom, while the opponent is a conservative who works against the peasants and the Roman Catholic Church. By taking Hycy's advice, Bryan finds himself worse off than before.

When Hycy sends another letter and encloses in it a fifty-pound note, it looks as if Bryan has accepted a bribe for his vote. The evidence is so damning that even Kathleen, who loves Bryan sincerely, is forced to believe him guilty. Faced with calamity and disfavor in his community, Bryan and his family plan, like many unfortunate Irish at the time, to emigrate to America in order to start a new and more successful life.

Bryan's friends, however, go to work for him. Displeased at Hycy's treatment of her niece and the troubles facing Kathleen when she loses her beloved, Kate Hogan begins investigating Hycy's activities. She, Patrick O'Finigan, Nanny Peety's father, and others gather additional information about Hycy and present it to the magistrates with their demands for a hearing. At the hearing, it is proved that Hycy robbed his father, had been an accomplice of the whiskey smugglers, had placed the still at Ahadarra to incriminate Bryan, had plotted to make his victim appear to have taken a bribe, and had also become a counterfeiter. Confronted with the proof, Jemmy Burke gives his son two hundred pounds to leave the country and stay away. Hycy's accomplices are arrested, convicted, and transported as criminals from Ireland, thus becoming the "emigrants" of Ahadarra. Cleared of all charges, Bryan resumes his rightful place in the community and in the affections of Kathleen.

Critical Evaluation:

By the time he published *The Emigrants of Ahadarra* in 1848, William Carleton was considered the truest novelist of Ireland's "awfullest hours," and William Butler Yeats was to concede that the Irish novel began with Carleton. *The Emigrants of Ahadarra* was avowedly written not to amuse but to reform and inform. First published while Ireland's potato famine was raging, the work is informative and readable. Its folkloric value is enhanced by Carleton's exuberance and hyperbole, which are similar to the imaginative flights that created the ancient Celtic wonder tales.

The novel loftily defends virtue. Kathleen's simple dignity and virtue are not cloying but almost biblical and contrast with the paler virtues of other characters. Bridget M'Mahon, Bryan's mother, is also convincingly admirable and uniquely graces the story, which expounds human ideals. Landlords are near-ogres, members of secret societies, and Orangemen (although to a less prominent degree than in other of Carleton's works), but many individuals are tenderly etched. The novel is realistic, and in the Spain of the same era it would have been classified as *costumbrista* owing to its museum-like presentation of customs.

Modern scholars sometimes criticize *The Emigrants of Ahadarra* for allegedly sloppy construction, mushy sentiment, and—curiously enough—vagueness of purpose. Carleton is also accused of inserting excessive scenery and folklore for their own sake rather than to augment the novel's dramatic effect. Carleton did lack the benefit of proofreading by his publishers, but the novel accomplishes its obvious objective of dramatizing the life of the Irish country people of the time. Even its supposedly overdone rhetoric does not bore the reader.

It may be argued that readers have an accurate picture of the famine-ravaged Irish peasants from Carleton alone. Carleton was an enigmatic novelist who hated landlordism and the Penal Laws and who was a convert to Protestantism in a very Catholic land, but he scarcely owed loyalty only to his own pen, as some have asserted. Furthermore, some critics have conceded that they did not really know Irish life until they read *The Emigrants of Ahadarra*.

Carleton's fiction is best known for its realistic pictures of Irish peasant life during the nineteenth century, and *The Emigrants of Ahadarra* is one of his best novels in this respect. The most noteworthy sections are the chapters describing such things as a "kemp" (a spinning contest among the peasant women), a country funeral, an election, and the illegal distillation of whiskey. While Carleton's treatment of these matters is outstanding, the entire novel is filled with specific and colorful details of peasant life. The speech and character of the people, their homes, the farm routine, landlord-peasant relations, and whiskey smuggling—all are related with a view to giving the reader a true picture of rural Irish life in the nineteenth century.

Further Reading

Brand, Gordon, ed. *William Carleton: The Authentic Voice*. Illustrated by Sam Craig. Gerrards Cross, England: Colin Smythe, 2006. Compendium of materials about Carleton includes primary source documents, a chronology of the events of his life, a history of his publications, and detailed maps of the countryside that provided the settings for his works of fiction. Also reprints selected lectures about Carleton that were delivered at the William Carleton Summer School from 1992 through 2005, including discussions of Carleton's "embattled" place in Irish literature and his depictions of the peasantry, Ulster Catholics, Protestants, and Protestantism.

Flanagan, Thomas. *The Irish Novelists, 1800-1850*. 1959. Reprint. Westport, Conn.: Greenwood Press, 1976. Influential overview did much to reestablish Carleton in the context of nineteenth century Irish literature and culture. Devotes three chapters to Carleton's work, though treatment of the short fiction is more extensive than that of the novels. Emphasizes the content of the works rather than their form.

Kiely, Benedict. *Poor Scholar: A Study of the Works and Days of William Carleton, 1794-1869*. 1948. Reprint. Dublin: Wolfhound Press, 1997. Accessible and sympathetic introduction to the novelist's world draws on Carleton's autobiography. Emphasizes Carleton's peasant background, awareness of which is indispensable for an appreciation of his work. Offers commentary on his major novels, including *The Emigrants of Ahadarra*.

Krause, David. *Revisionary Views: Some Counter-statements About Irish Life and Literature*. Dublin: Maunsel, 2002. Collection of essays includes an analysis of Carleton's writing by a scholar who has sought to redeem his reputation.

_____. *William Carleton, the Novelist: His Carnival and Pastoral World of Tragicomedy*. Lanham, Md.: University Press of America, 2000. Argues that Carleton has been unfairly denigrated by academic critics and attempts to alter this situation by describing why at least six of Carleton's novels are major works of fiction. Devotes a chapter to analysis of *The Emigrants of Ahadarra*.

Sloan, Barry. *The Pioneers of Anglo-Irish Fiction, 1800-1850*. Gerrards Cross, England: Colin Smythe, 1986. Study of the woks of Irish writers of the early nineteenth century includes coverage of the various phases of Carleton's career as a novelist. Includes brief commentary on *The Emigrants of Ahadarra* that locates the novel in the appropriate phase and enables the reader to see connections between the novel's preoccupations and those of other Irish fiction of the time. Includes an elaborate chronology of the literary period in question.

Sullivan, Eileen. *William Carleton*. Boston: Twayne, 1983. Provides a critical introduction to Carleton's life and works. Discussion of *The Emigrants of Ahadarra* links it to Oliver Goldsmith's poem *The Deserted Village* (1770), and the significance of the novel's theme of reconciliation is briefly noted.

Wolff, Robert Lee. *William Carleton, Irish Peasant Novelist:*

A Preface to His Fiction. New York: Garland, 1980. Presents a brief general overview of Carleton's fiction. Discussion of *The Emigrants of Ahadarra* focuses on the way the novel treats the social aspects of emigration and outlines the novel's political context.

Émile
Or, Education

Author: Jean-Jacques Rousseau (1712-1778)
First published: Émile: Ou, Del'éducation, 1762
   (English translation, 1762-1763)
Type of work: Novel
Type of plot: Novel of ideas
Time of plot: Eighteenth century
Locale: France

Principal characters:
JEAN-JACQUES ROUSSEAU, a tutor
ÉMILE, a healthy and intelligent French orphan
SOPHIE, a wellborn, warmhearted young woman

Jean-Jacques Rousseau's treatise on education—a novel in name only—is addressed to mothers in the hope that, as a result of learning Rousseau's ideas on education, they will permit their children to develop naturally without letting them be crushed by social conditions. Children cannot be left to themselves from birth, because the world as it is would turn them into beasts. The problem is to educate a child in the midst of society in such a manner that society does not spoil her or him.

In *Émile*, Rousseau argues that education comes from nature, from other people, and from things. The education from other people and from things must be controlled, so that habits conformable to nature will develop. Children have natural tendencies that should be encouraged, for nature intends children to be adults; the aim of education, according to Rousseau, is to make a child an adult. However, by swaddling children, by turning them over to wet nurses, and by punishing them for not doing what is said to be their duty, parents turn children from natural ways of acting and spoil them for life.

Rousseau insists that the proper way to bring up a child is to begin by having the mother nurse the child and the father train the child. If substitutes must be found, however, a wet nurse of good disposition who was lately a mother should be selected, and a young tutor should be chosen, preferably one with the qualities of Rousseau.

In order to explain his theory of education, Rousseau refers to an imaginary pupil, Émile. The child should come from France, since inhabitants of temperate zones are more adaptable and more intelligent than those from other climates. The child should be from a wealthy family, since the poor are educated by life itself, and should be an orphan in order to allow Rousseau free range as tutor. Finally, the child should be healthy in body and mind.

Rousseau recommends a predominantly vegetable diet, particularly for the nurse, since the milk will be better if meat is not eaten. The tutor should see to it that the child is taken out to breathe the fresh air of the country, and, if possible, the family should live in the country: "Men are devoured by our towns."

The child should become accustomed to frequent baths but should not be softened by warm water or by other pampering that destroys natural vigor. The child should also not be allowed to fall into habits other than that of having no habits. Regular mealtimes and bedtimes should not be imposed, and, as far as possible, the child should be free to act as he or she chooses. Injuries or illness may result, but it is better for a child to learn how to live naturally than to become a weak and artificial adult.

"The natural man is interested in all new things," wrote Rousseau, and he urged that the child be introduced to new things in such a way that things that are not naturally fearful will not be feared. He offers, as an example of the proper kind of education in this respect, an account of what he would do to keep Émile from becoming afraid of masks. He would begin with a pleasant mask, proceed to less pleasing, and, finally, hideous ones, all the while laughing at each mask and trying it on different persons. Similarly, to accustom Émile to the sound of a gun, Rousseau would start with a small charge, so that Émile will be fascinated by the sudden flash, then proceed to greater charges, until Émile can tolerate even large explosions.

Rousseau maintained that cries and tears are the child's natural expression of needs. The child should not be thwarted, because there is no other way to learn to live in the world, and education begins with birth. On the other hand, the child should not be allowed to control the house, demanding obedience from the parents.

It was Rousseau's conviction that children must be given more liberty to do things for themselves so that they will demand less of others. A natural advantage of the child's limited strength is that a child cannot do much damage, even when using his or her power freely. A child will learn to speak correctly, to read and to write, when it is advantageous to do so; threats and coercion only hinder progress.

Speaking of a mode of education that burdens a child with restrictions and that is, at the same time, overprotective, Rousseau wrote,

> Even if I considered that education was wise in its aims, how could I view without indignation those poor wretches subjected to an intolerable slavery and condemned like galley-slaves to endless toil . . . ? The age of harmless mirth is spent in tears, punishments, threats, and slavery. You torment the poor thing for his good; you fail to see that you are calling Death to snatch him from these gloomy surroundings.

Instead of torturing children with excessive care, he argues, one should love them, laugh with them, send them out into the meadows, and play with them.

Rousseau continues: "When our natural tendencies have not been interfered with by human prejudice and human institutions, the happiness alike of children and men consists in the enjoyment of their liberty." Here, the principle behind Rousseau's theory of education becomes clear. The tutor or parent should educate the child in such a way that the child will learn through his or her own efforts to be as free as possible within society. A child who is educated by rules and threats becomes a slave and, once free, seeks to enslave others. The most satisfactory general rule of education, Rousseau argued, is to do exactly the opposite of what is usually done.

Since the child is supposed to learn through personal experience, misdeeds should be punished only by arranging matters so that the child comes to experience the natural consequences of what was done. If there is any rule that can be used as a moral injunction, it would be, "Never hurt anybody"; only trouble comes from urging children or adults to do good to others.

Rousseau rejected the use of tales and fables for children. An amusing analysis illustrates his conviction that even the simplest fable, such as "The Fox and the Crow," strikes the child as ridiculous and puzzling, and encourages the careless use of language and foolish behavior.

After the child reaches adolescence, intellectual education should begin. Prior to this time, the concern of the tutor is to give Émile the freedom to learn the natural limits of his powers. Now he teaches Émile by showing him the natural advantages of the use of the intellect. The tutor answers questions, but only enough to make the child curious. His explanations are always in language the child can understand, and he encourages the child to solve problems independently and to make his or her own investigations. Interest should lead the child to increase his or her experience and knowledge; it is a mistake to demand that the child learn. Jean-Jacques, as the tutor, shows Émile the value of astronomy by gently encouraging him to use the knowledge that he possesses in order to find his way out of the woods.

Rousseau's accounts of his efforts to teach Émile owe some of their charm to the author's willingness to show himself unsuccessful in some of his efforts. Nevertheless, the pupil never becomes a distinctive character: Émile is merely a child-symbol, just as Sophie, the author indicates, is a woman-symbol devised to enable Rousseau to discuss marriage problems.

By the time Émile is fifteen years of age, he gains a considerable amount of practical and scientific knowledge; he can handle tools of all sorts, and he knows he will have to find some trade as his life's work. In book 4 of *Émile*, Rousseau discusses the most difficult kind of education: moral education, the study of the self in relation to others.

Rousseau presents three maxims that sum up his ideas concerning human sympathy, the foundation of moral virtue:

> First Maxim.—It is not in human nature to put ourselves in the place of those who are happier than ourselves, but only in the place of those who can claim our pity.
> Second Maxim.—We never pity another's woes unless we know we may suffer in like manner ourselves.
> Third Maxim.—The pity we feel for others is proportionate, not to the amount of the evil, but to the feelings we attribute to the sufferers.

These maxims fortify the tutor, but they are not imparted to Émile. The youth is gradually made aware of the suffering of individuals; his experience is broadened; and he comes to know, through personal experience, the consequences of various kinds of acts. The important thing is to turn his affections to others.

Émile is given insight concerning religious matters by hearing a long discourse by "a Savoyard priest" who tells of the difficult passage from doubt to faith. He affirms humanity's natural goodness and the reliability of conscience when uncontaminated by philosophers or by mere convention.

Sophie, or "Woman," is introduced in book 5, since Émile must have a helpmate. Rousseau begins curiously by saying, "But for her sex, a woman is a man"; but when he considers her education, it is apparent that sex makes quite a difference. Woman need not be given as many reasons as man, and she can get along with less intellect, but she must have courage and virtue. Rousseau offers a great deal of advice, even concerning Sophie's refusal of Émile's first attempt to share her bed. After a charming digression on travel, the book closes with Émile's announcement that he is about to become a father and that he will undertake the education of his child, following the example of his beloved tutor.

As a literary work, *Émile* stands near the beginning of a tradition common in European fiction: the novel of ideas. Character and incident serve only as pretext for Rousseau's more important task: the explanation of his ideas about the kind of education proper for men and women if humankind is to free itself from the self-imposed chains of social and political custom that stifle individual happiness. Although dated in its precepts (Rousseau makes it clear that boys should receive significantly more elaborate and extensive education than girls), *Émile* espouses an attitude toward education that links its author with the great European Romantics who held that expression and imagination should take precedence over reason and socialization in human development. The hallmark of his plan for education is the liberation of the self from conformity to artificial social norms. For Rousseau, education should be a process of individualization, not socialization. Émile's tutor (a veiled portrait of the author) is little more than a conduit through whom Nature works her magic on the youngster, leading, rather than cajoling, him to appreciate both himself and the world around him.

In *Émile* and elsewhere, Rousseau attacks the conventional wisdom that elevates refined civilization as the greatest good toward which human society can aspire. He is especially vitriolic in castigating the intellectuals of his day who denigrate the simple life of country folk; in Rousseau's eyes, these people are promoting false values, especially in their praise for commercial and financial success. In this way, Rousseau is predecessor to two of the great figures of nineteenth century letters: William Wordsworth and Karl Marx. From Rousseau, Wordsworth takes up the cause of the rustic communities whose lifestyles seem to make people happier. His poetry celebrates the same qualities of natural inquisitiveness and appreciation for natural beauty that Rousseau recommends as the hallmarks of education. Marx's railings against the upper classes and his insistence on economic equality also have their roots in Rousseau's writings. Unlike the father of communism, however, Rousseau was not an advocate of revolution; instead, he stresses in *Émile* the necessity for gradual change as means for achieving desired social ends.

Revised by Laurence W. Mazzeno

Further Reading

Blanchard, William H. *Rousseau and the Spirit of Revolt: A Psychological Study.* Ann Arbor: University of Michigan Press, 1967. Explores the psychological motivation for the educational reforms developed in *Émile.* Describes the many contradictions in Rousseau's writings on education.

Bloch, Jean. *Rousseauism and Education in Eighteenth-Century France.* Oxford, England: Voltaire Foundation, 1995. Chronicles *Émile*'s reception in eighteenth century France, with particular attention to the reactions of the nation's revolutionaries.

Cranston, Maurice. *The Noble Savage: Jean-Jacques Rousseau, 1754-1762.* New York: Penguin Books, 1991. Explores Rousseau's aesthetic and literary evolution during this prolific period in his literary career. The chapter on *Émile* describes both practical and unreasonable recommendations by Rousseau for educational reform.

Crocker, Lester G. *The Prophetic Voice, 1758-1778.* Vol. 2 in *Jean-Jacques Rousseau.* New York: Macmillan, 1968. Analyzes the last twenty years of Rousseau's career. The lengthy chapter on *Émile* examines the conflict between Rousseau's praise of freedom and his desire for teachers to control their pupils' activities.

Damrosch, Leo. *Jean-Jacques Rousseau: Restless Genius.* Boston: Houghton Mifflin, 2005. This one-volume biography is a useful addition to Rousseau scholarship, providing an incisive, accessible account of Rousseau's life and contributions to philosophy and literature. Includes illustrations, time line, bibliography, and index.

Havens, George R. *Jean-Jacques Rousseau.* Boston: Twayne, 1978. Contains an excellent general introduction to Rousseau's life and career and an annotated bibliography of important critical studies on his work. The analysis of *Émile* stresses the positive elements in Rousseau's desire to sensitize parents and teachers to the emotional needs of children.

Novello, Mary K. *For All the Wrong Reasons: The Story Behind Government Schools*. Lanham, Md.: University Press of America, 1998. Begins with a brief discussion of Rousseau's philosophy of education, continuing to a more detailed examination of his influence on the nineteenth century progressive education movement and the creation of government-operated school systems.

Riley, Patrick, ed. *The Cambridge Companion to Rousseau*. New York: Cambridge University Press, 2001. Two of the essays analyze *Émile*: "*Émile*: Learning to Be Men, Women, and Citizens" by Geriant Parry and "*Émile*: Nature and the Education of Sophie" by Susan Meld Shell.

Wokler, Robert. *Rousseau*. New York: Oxford University Press, 1995. A thoughtful study of Rousseau's belief that successful educational reform will eventually make citizens unwilling to tolerate despotic governments. Describes well the many connections between *Émile* and Rousseau's *Du contrat social* (1762; *The Social Contract*, 1764).

Emilia Galotti

Author: Gotthold Ephraim Lessing (1729-1781)
First produced: 1772; first published, 1772 (English translation, 1786)
Type of work: Drama
Type of plot: Tragedy
Time of plot: Early eighteenth century
Locale: Guastalla and Sabionetta, Italy

Principal characters:
EMILIA GALOTTI, a beautiful, middle-class young woman
ODOARDO GALOTTI, her father
CLAUDIA GALOTTI, her mother
HETTORE GONZAGA, the prince of Sabionetta and Guastalla
COUNT APPIANI, betrothed to Emilia
THE MARQUIS MARINELLI, chamberlain to the prince
THE COUNTESS ORSINA, a mistress spurned by the prince

The Story:

Prince Hettore Gonzaga, once happily in love with and loved in return by Countess Orsina, falls in love with Emilia Galotti. She is the daughter of a soldier who resisted the conquest of Sabionetta by the prince, and she is betrothed to Count Appiani from the neighboring principality of Piedmont. This union of a nobleman and a beautiful, middle-class woman is the result of her mother's studied plan.

The treacherous Marquis Marinelli proposes that the prince retire to his palace at Dosalo after sending Count Appiani on a mission to the princess of Massa, to whom the prince affianced himself after leaving Countess Orsina. Once her betrothed is away, Emilia will be vulnerable to the prince's designs. The ruler eagerly agrees to this plan.

Odoardo Galotti readies his villa at Sabionetta in preparation for the wedding of his daughter and returns to his wife in Guastalla to accompany the bridal party. A young assassin gathers these facts from a family servant so that he can plan the abduction of Emilia. Count Appiani, disturbed by presentiments of evil, rejects the prince's proposal to send him off

on his wedding day. He is killed for his temerity when the bridal party is attacked. Closely guarded, Emilia is taken to the palace by the prince's people, under pretense that they are rescuing her from brigands. There the prince, playing the gallant, allays Emilia's fears by apologizing for his former behavior and promising to escort her to her mother. Claudia, in the meantime, is frantic at being separated from her daughter. Grieving over the death of Count Appiani, she accuses Marinelli of plotting this deed of treachery and violence.

The prince, beset by a furious mother and a swooning young woman whom he desperately desires, did not reckon with the wrath of a rejected mistress as well. The Countess Orsina, whose spies uncovered the prince's guilty secrets, arrive at the palace in Dosalo and, failing in an attempt to blackmail him, reveal Prince Hettore's guilt to Odoardo when he comes in haste and unarmed to the aid of his daughter and wife. The countess, determined to have revenge on her former lover, gives Odoardo the dagger she intended to use herself. Odoardo insists on his rights as a father to take his daughter to her home, but his petition is denied by the crafty Marinelli. Meanwhile, the prince, unaware of Odoardo's knowledge and purpose, tries to appear as a benefactor who will see justice done in the courts. Until that time, however, he will keep Emilia apart for security's sake. To this arrangement Odoardo pretends to agree, ironically commenting on each provision of treachery as it is proposed.

When the anxious father is finally allowed to see his daughter, she tells him that she fears her virtue might yield where force can never prevail, for the arts of seduction are brilliantly practiced in Prince Hettore's court. To protect her virtue, Odoardo stabs Emilia, presents her body to the lustful prince, throws the dagger at his feet, and goes off to give himself up to the authorities.

Critical Evaluation:

There has never been a simple interpretation of Gotthold Ephraim Lessing's *Emilia Galotti*. The tragedy portrays a father-daughter theme at the same time that it portrays the tensions between the bourgeoisie and the nobility in eighteenth century Germany. Setting the play in Italy at the court of Hettore Gonzaga, Lessing skillfully uses the Italian prince's character to criticize the nobility that rules its subjects according to whim and fancy. The prince gives his consent to a woman's request merely because her name is Emilia; because he is in a hurry, he carelessly pronounces a death sentence. The prince represents the corrupt and lascivious court where rulers who possess the weapon of gallantry indulge their romantic desires to the fullest and destroy women's lives without remorse. The prince's flaws become even more pronounced when Lessing introduces the character of Odoardo Galotti, Emilia Galotti's proud, upright father, who belongs to the middle class and remains purposefully aloof from the court because he regards it as a place of decadence. His contempt for the court is so strong that he has only unwillingly allowed his wife and his daughter to stay in the city in its vicinity for the sake of Emilia's education. He himself spends his retirement years on his country estate.

Despite portraying the prince as a man with great shortcomings, Lessing is successful in also making him a likable character. He is a young man who finds it hard to exercise control over his amorous leanings, prevaricates when he should be firm, and trusts his aides too much. Because he is diffident about making decisions, he depends on his chamberlain, Marinelli, who sets the various plots in motion. To some extent, Lessing directs his audience's wrath away from the prince toward his chamberlain, which may be interpreted as a softening of his stance toward the ruling class. The prince is thus presented as a victim of his circumstances who

is exploited through his vulnerability. At the conclusion of the play, the prince even bemoans the fact that to be a prince and a human being is tragic. A prince must be able to rule his emotions to rule effectively, but being a human being he finds it difficult to control his emotions. In the prince's exclamation: "Is it not enough, for the misery of the many, that princes are human? Must it also be that devils disguise themselves as their friends?" Lessing shifts the blame of Emilia's tragic death to Marinelli. The prince is reduced to a mere puppet in the hands of his corrupt court official.

Because Emilia knows that her father values chaste thoughts and conduct above everything else, she asks him to stab her so that her virtue may remain intact, crying out, "What we call brute force is nothing: seduction is the only true force.—I have blood pulsing in my veins, my father, blood that is as youthful, as warm as anyone's. And my senses are senses too. I vouch for nothing. I will be responsible for nothing." In his depiction of Odoardo's regard for virtue that exceeds his love for his daughter, Lessing draws attention to the emptiness of the concept of bourgeois morality. He forces the audience to ask whether this bourgeois concept of virtue must indeed be upheld at the cost of human life.

Lessing's characterization of the prince's previous mistress, Countess Orsina, provides yet another character type, a fiercely independent, active woman. The dagger she carries with her when she visits the prince in Dosalo shows that she is even ready to avenge her humiliation caused by the prince's rejection. In fact, she is indirectly responsible for Emilia's stabbing, because she provokes Odoardo by saying, "The bridegroom is dead: the bride—your daughter—worse than dead." Countess Orsina's characterization also reveals Lessing's concern about the strict imposition of gender roles during his time. Orsina correctly understands the limitations imposed on her sex. When the prince rejects her, she responds, "How can a man love a thing that wants to think in spite of him? A woman who thinks is as loathsome as a man who powders his nose." Lessing may have given these words to Orsina, who is on the verge of madness and an ambiguous character in the play, so as to disassociate himself from too obvious an endorsement of her views. Their mere expression, however, brings to the fore the subject of gender inequality and its tragic consequences.

"Critical Evaluation" by Vibha Bakshi Gokhale

Further Reading

Allison, Henry E. *Lessing and the Enlightenment.* Ann Arbor: University of Michigan Press, 1966. Excellent source for information on Lessing's philosophy of religion.

Brown, F. Andrew. *Gotthold Ephraim Lessing*. New York: Twayne, 1971. A good introduction to Lessing's life as a critic, dramatist, and theologian. Discusses Lessing's major works against the backdrop of eighteenth century German literature and culture.

Fischer, Barbara, and Thomas C. Fox, eds. *A Companion to the Works of Gotthold Ephraim Lessing*. Rochester, N.Y.: Camden House, 2005. Collection of essays, including discussions of Lessing's life and times, his place within the European Enlightenment, his theory of drama, and Lessing and philosophy, theology, and the Jews.

Graham, Ilse. *Goethe and Lessing: The Wellsprings of Creation*. New York: Barnes & Noble, 1973. Offers a new reading of *Emilia Galotti* by concentrating on the ideal image of the character and the failure of its realization. Discusses Lessing's and Johann Wolfgang von Goethe's different sources of creativity.

Lessing, Gotthold Ephraim. *Emilia Galotti*. Translated by Edward Dvoretzky. New York: Felix Ungar, 1962. Intro-

duction provides information about the source of this play and its reception in eighteenth century Germany. Translation has successfully retained the original flavor of the play by taking into account its rhetorical devices.

_____. *"Nathan the Wise," "Minna von Barnhelm," and Other Plays and Writings*. Edited by Peter Demetz. New York: Continuum, 1991. Includes a foreword by Hannah Arendt, which discusses Lessing's idea of friendship and fraternity and its political relevance in eighteenth century Germany. Provides translations of selections from Lessing's philosophical and theological writings.

Ottewell, Karen. *Lessing and the Sturm und Drang: A Reappraisal Revisited*. New York: Peter Lang, 2002. Analyzes Lessing's dramas within the context of the Sturm und Drang movement. Ottewell views Lessing as an important precursor of the movement, and she analyzes his attitudes toward and his impact upon writers associated with the movement, including Johann Gottfried Herder and Friedrich Schiller. Devotes a chapter to *Emilia Galotti*.

Eminent Victorians

Author: Lytton Strachey (1880-1932)
First published: 1918
Type of work: Biography

Principal personages:
HENRY EDWARD MANNING, a cardinal of the Roman Catholic Church
FLORENCE NIGHTINGALE, a nineteenth century reformer and educator
DR. THOMAS ARNOLD, an English educator
CHARLES GEORGE GORDON, a British general

Although they have been considered controversial, the biographical writings of Lytton Strachey are never dull. When he addresses himself to the Victorian period, those writings possess a special interest, for the biographer himself was a product of that period, and his feelings about it, while mixed, were far from vague or uncertain. The age of Victoria at once fascinated and repelled him. Its pretentiousness exasperated the artist in Strachey, but he could not help acknowledging its solidity and force and its many outstanding scientists and individuals.

Four such individuals are his subjects in *Eminent Victorians*. Not the greatest of their time, these four, superficially diverse in their activities, belong among the most appropriate representatives of the age. Strachey picked an ecclesiastic, a

woman of action, an educational authority, and a man of adventure to illustrate the multifaceted era in which they lived and worked. The quartet of portraits proved to be a critical and financial success, and it became the cornerstone of an increasingly solid career. After its publication, Strachey was no longer in need of assistance from family or friends. Nevertheless, his treatment of Cardinal Manning, Florence Nightingale, Arnold of Rugby, and General Gordon did not go unchallenged. He was accused of having been unduly severe with his subjects, of handling facts with carelessness, and of indulging in superficial judgments. Such indictments often came from partisans of one or more of the subjects of *Eminent Victorians*, but not infrequently they were joined by more objective critics as well.

Some of these critics overlooked the point that Strachey's biographical method aimed at verisimilitude, not photographic realism. His determination to rise above mere facts sometimes carried him too far—to outright and even outrageous caricature—but the writing remained brilliant and stimulating. The intelligent reader is more likely to be diverted than deceived by the author's prejudices and dislikes, for they are hardly disguised. Whatever charges may be brought against Strachey today, it is generally admitted that he brought to biographical writing good proportion, good style, and colorful realism.

Cardinal Manning provided ideal biographical material and, despite his distinction as a churchman, he does not escape a touch of the Strachey lash. This representative of ancient tradition and uncompromising faith is revealed as a survivor from the Middle Ages who forced the nineteenth century to accept him as he was. Practical ability, rather than saintliness or learning, was the key to his career. In the Middle Ages, says Strachey, he would have been neither a Francis nor an Aquinas, but he might have been an Innocent.

Very early in his life, Manning had fixed his hopes on a position of power and influence in the world. Upon leaving college he aspired to a political career, but its doors were abruptly closed to him by his father's bankruptcy. He tried the Church of England as an alternative, perhaps less promising, avenue to fulfillment. By 1851, already over forty, he had become an archdeacon, but this was not enough for him. For some time his glance had been straying to other pastures; finally, he made the break and became a convert to Roman Catholicism. In the process he lost a friend—a rather important one—named William Gladstone.

Thereafter his ecclesiastical career was an almost unbroken series of triumphs and advances. One important asset was his ability to make friends in the right places, especially in the Vatican. Manning became the supreme commander of the Roman Church in England, then a cardinal. His magnetism and vigor spread his influence beyond church boundaries, and at his death crowds of working people thronged the route of his funeral procession. At the end of a long and twisted road, his egoism, fierce ambition, and gift for intrigue had brought him desired as well as some unexpected rewards, not least among them the regard of the poor.

The second of Strachey's eminent Victorians is Florence Nightingale. In his treatment of one of the most remarkable women of any age, the biographer is conspicuously successful in resisting any urge to be gallant. What her friends called calm persuasiveness, he characterized as demoniac fury; it is clear that to him the "Lady with a Lamp" might have been

extremely capable but she was also tiresomely demanding and disagreeable. His account makes clear the almost miraculous energy and endurance that carried Nightingale past the many obstacles in her path.

For the sake of convenience, Strachey divides Nightingale's accomplishments into two phases. The first is her dramatic contribution to the welfare of the British wounded during the course of the Crimean campaign; the second deals with her unflagging efforts after the war to transform the Army Medical Department, revolutionize hospital services, and work much-needed reform in the War Office itself. These aims dominated her completely, and in their execution she drove her friends ruthlessly but used herself with even less mercy. Enduring to the age of ninety, she became a legend, though, ironically and cruelly, her last years brought senility and softness upon her. They also brought, after consciousness had dulled almost into insensibility, the Order of Merit.

Dr. Thomas Arnold, the father of the poet and critic Matthew Arnold, is generally considered to have been the founder of the British public school system. Strachey's bias against the doctor is obvious in *Eminent Victorians*, based largely on the fact that Dr. Arnold was determined to make good Christians, as well as good Englishmen, out of his public school boys. (Strachey had little patience with either Christianity or Christian institutions, a point of view that colors his attitude toward all his subjects in *Eminent Victorians*.) Strachey also disapproved of the prefectorial system Dr. Arnold instituted at Rugby, which Strachey credits with two dubious, if unexpected, effects on later English education: the worship of athletics and the worship of good form. Although to some Victorians, Dr. Arnold was one of the most influential pedagogues, Strachey considers him the apostle of harmful and absurd ideas.

It is with apparent relief that the biographer turns to his fourth and final portrait, which provides a strong contrast between the single-mindedness of the educator and the maddening inconsistencies of General Charles George Gordon. The general's personality is unveiled as a mass of contradictions that no biographer could ever hope completely to unravel. A mischievous, unpredictable boy, he developed into an undisciplined, unpredictable man, and a romantic legend wove itself about his early, swashbuckling exploits in China and Africa. His deeds were genuinely heroic—no one has ever questioned Gordon's bravery—but they combined oddly with his passion for religion. He was influenced strongly, and to an approximately equal degree, by brandy and the Bible. Inclined, on the whole, to be unsociable, he maintained an icy reserve, except for fits of ungovernable temper vented upon unlucky servants or trembling subordinates.

Gordon, in his fifties, was chosen by the English government for a delicate African mission. The mission, a military one requiring the utmost of a negotiator's self-control, tact, and skill, was the arrangement for the inglorious evacuation of British forces from the Sudan, a project for which Gordon was disqualified by his opinions, his character, and everything in his life. What followed was the tragedy at Khartoum, an episode seldom matched in military annals for the mystery and horror with which it enveloped the fate of the principal actor.

Thus the biographer's searching glance at four eminent Victorians ends on a dramatic note. Widely differing in background, vocation, and personality, the four individuals illustrate different phases of the England of the later nineteenth century. They are related to one another, however, by the possession of a restless, questing vitality and by the fact that each left a mark upon the age.

Further Reading

Altick, Richard. "Eminent Victorianism: What Lytton Strachey Hath Wrought." *American Scholar* 64, no. 1 (Winter, 1995): 81-89. Argues that Strachey's aim in *Eminent Victorians* was explicitly literary. Because he took such liberties with historical fact, it is Strachey's method that came to be discredited, rather than the Victorian ethos he attempted to subvert.

_____. "The Stracheyan Revolution." In *Lives and Letters: A History of Literary Biography in England and America.* New York: Alfred A. Knopf, 1966. An excellent summary of the pivotal role of *Eminent Victorians* in the development of biography as a genre. Surveys Strachey's iconoclastic strategies.

Holroyd, Michael. *Lytton Strachey: The New Biography.* New York: Farrar, Straus and Giroux, 1995. Provides a rich historical context for understanding the development of *Eminent Victorians*, including information regarding negotiations with Strachey's publisher. The first and fuller version of this biography, published in 1968, contains more literary criticism.

Monk, Ray. "This Fictitious Life: Virginia Woolf on Biography and Reality." *Philosophy and Literature* 31, no. 1 (April, 2007): 1-40. Examines Woolf's essay "The New Biography" (1927), which explored various ideas about the practice of writing biographies. Argues that Woolf erred in choosing Sidney Lee and Harold Nicolson as representative of the old and new styles, respectively; maintains that the "new style" was best exemplified by Strachey.

Powell, John. "Official Lives: Lytton Strachey, the Queen's Cabinet, and the Eminence of Aesthetics." *Nineteenth Century Prose* 22, no. 2 (Fall, 1995): 129-152. An analysis of Strachey's introductory indictment of so-called official lives. Argues that a preoccupation with aesthetic form obscured Strachey's concern for accurate biographical representation.

Stratford, Jenny. "Eminent Victorians." *British Museum Quarterly* (Spring, 1968): 93-96. Provides a full description of Strachey's four exercise books of notes and drafts, which are now in the British Library. Discusses the various influences on Strachey's writing.

Taddeo, Julie Anne. *Lytton Strachey and the Search for Modern Sexual Identity: The Last Eminent Victorian.* New York: Harrington Park Press, 2002. Chronicles Strachey's struggles as a gay and neurasthenic writer to defy Victorian ideology and create new forms of art and identity.

Emma

Author: Jane Austen (1775-1817)
First published: 1816
Type of work: Novel
Type of plot: Bildungsroman and domestic realism
Time of plot: Early nineteenth century
Locale: Highbury, England

Principal characters:
EMMA WOODHOUSE, the heiress of Hartfield
MR. WOODHOUSE, her father
HARRIET SMITH, Emma's protégé
MISS BATES, the village gossip
JANE FAIRFAX, her niece
GEORGE KNIGHTLEY, a landowner
MRS. WESTON, Emma's former governess
MR. WESTON, her husband
FRANK CHURCHILL, their stepson
PHILIP ELTON, a rector
AUGUSTA ELTON, his wife
ROBERT MARTIN, a farmer

The Story:

Emma Woodhouse, a rich, clever, and beautiful young woman, has just seen her friend, companion, and former governess, Miss Taylor, married to a neighboring widower, Mr. Weston. While the match is suitable in every way, Emma cannot help sighing over her loss, for now only she and her father are left at Hartfield. Mr. Woodhouse is too old and too fond of worrying about trivialities to be a sufficient companion for his daughter.

The Woodhouses are the great family in the village of Highbury. In their small circle of friends, there are enough middle-age ladies to make up card tables for Mr. Woodhouse, but there is no young lady to be a friend and confidant to Emma. Lonely for her beloved Miss Taylor, now Mrs. Weston, Emma takes under her wing Harriet Smith, the parlor boarder at a nearby boarding school. Although not in the least brilliant, Harriet is a pretty seventeen-year-old girl with pleasing, unassuming manners and a gratifying habit of looking up to Emma as a paragon.

Harriet is the natural daughter of some unknown person; Emma, believing that the girl might be of noble family, persuades her that the society in which she has moved is not good enough for her. She encourages Harriet to give up her acquaintance with the Martin family, respectable farmers of some substance though of no fashion. Instead of thinking of Robert Martin as a husband for Harriet, Emma influences the girl to aspire to the Reverend Philip Elton, the young rector.

Emma believes from Elton's manner that he is beginning to fall in love with Harriet, and she flatters herself on her matchmaking schemes. Her landowner neighbor George Knightley, the brother of a London lawyer married to Emma's older sister and one of the few people who can see Emma's faults, is concerned about her intimacy with Harriet. He warns her that no good can come of it for either Harriet or herself, and he is particularly upset when he learns that Emma has influenced Harriet to turn down Martin's proposal of marriage. Emma herself suffers from no such qualms, for she is certain that Elton is as much in love with Harriet as Harriet—through Emma's encouragement—is with him. Emma suffers a rude awakening when Elton, finding her alone, asks her to marry him. She suddenly realizes that what she had taken for gallantries to Harriet had been meant for herself. Elton has taken what Emma had intended as encouragement to his pursuit of Harriet as encouragement to aspire for her own hand. His presumption is bad enough, but the task of breaking the news to Harriet is much worse.

Another disappointment occurs in Emma's circle. Frank Churchill, who has promised for months to come to see his father and new stepmother, again puts off his visit. Frank, Mr. Weston's son by a first marriage, has taken the name of his mother's family. Knightley believes that the young man now feels superior to his father. Emma argues with Knightley, but she finds herself secretly agreeing with him. Although the Hartfield circle is denied Frank's company, it does acquire an addition in the person of Jane Fairfax, a niece of the garrulous Miss Bates. Jane rivals Emma in beauty and accomplishment; this is one reason why, as Knightley hints, Emma has never been friendly with her. Emma blames Jane's reserve for their somewhat cool relationship.

Soon after Jane's arrival, the Westons receive a letter from Frank that sets another date for his visit. This time he actually appears, and Emma finds him a handsome, well-bred young man. He frequently calls on the Woodhouses and also on the

Bates family, because of a prior acquaintance with Jane. Emma, rather than Jane, is the recipient of Frank's gallantries, however, and Emma can see that the Westons are hoping that the romance will prosper.

About this time, Jane receives the handsome but anonymous gift of a pianoforte. It is presumed to have come from wealthy friends with whom Jane, who is an orphan, has lived, but Jane seems embarrassed at the present and refuses to discuss it. After Mrs. Weston points out to Emma that Knightley seems to show great preference and concern for Jane, Emma begins to wonder if the gift has come from him. Emma cannot bear to think of Knightley's marrying Jane; after observing them together, she concludes to her own satisfaction that he is motivated by friendship, not love.

It is now time for Frank to end his visit, and he departs with seeming reluctance. During his last call at Hartfield, he appears desirous of telling Emma something of a serious nature; but she, believing him to be on the verge of a declaration of love, does not encourage him because in her daydreams she always sees herself refusing him and their love ending in quiet friendship.

Elton returns to the village with a hastily wooed and wedded bride, a lady of small fortune, extremely bad manners, and great pretensions to elegance. Harriet, who had been talked into love by Emma, cannot be so easily talked out of it. What Emma has failed to accomplish, however, Elton's marriage does, and Harriet at last begins to recover. Her recovery is aided by Elton's rudeness to her at a ball. When he refuses to dance with her, Knightley, who rarely dances, offers himself as a partner, and Harriet, without Emma's knowledge, begins to think of him instead of Elton. Emma has actually begun to think of Frank as a husband for Harriet, but she resolves to do nothing to promote the match. Through a series of misinterpretations, Emma thinks Harriet was praising Frank when she was really referring to Knightley.

The romantic entanglement is further complicated because Mrs. Weston continues to believe that Knightley is becoming attached to Jane. In his turn, Knightley sees signs of some secret agreement between Jane and Frank. His suspicions are finally justified when Frank confesses to Mr. and Mrs. Weston that he and Jane have been secretly engaged since October. The Westons' first thought is for Emma, for they fear that their stepson's attentions to her might have had their effect. Emma assures Mrs. Weston that she had at one time felt some slight attachment to Frank, but that time is now safely past. Her chief concerns now are that she has said things about Jane to Frank that she would not have said had she known of their engagement, and also that she has, as she believes, encouraged Harriet in another fruitless attachment.

When she goes to break the news of Frank's engagement gently to Harriet, however, Emma finds her quite unperturbed by it; after a few minutes of talking at cross-purposes, Emma learns that it is not Frank but Knightley upon whom Harriet has now bestowed her affections. When she tells Emma that she has reasons to believe that Knightley returns her sentiments, Emma suddenly realizes the state of her own heart; she herself loves Knightley. She now wishes she had never seen Harriet. Aside from wanting to marry Knightley herself, she knows a match between him and Harriet would be an unequal one, hardly likely to bring happiness to either.

Emma's worry over this state of affairs ends when Knightley asks her to marry him. Her complete happiness is marred only by her knowing that the marriage will upset her father, who dislikes change of any kind; she is also aware that she has unknowingly prepared Harriet for another disappointment. The first problem is solved when Emma and Knightley decide to reside at Hartfield with Mr. Woodhouse as long as he lives. Harriet's situation remains problematic; when Knightley was paying attention to her, he was really trying to determine the real state of her affections for his young farm tenant. Consequently, Knightley is able to announce one morning that Robert Martin has again offered himself to Harriet and has been accepted. Emma is overjoyed that Harriet's future is now assured. She can reflect that all parties concerned have married according to their stations, a prerequisite for their true happiness.

Critical Evaluation:

Jane Austen had passed her fortieth year when her fourth published novel, *Emma*, appeared in 1816, the year before her death. Although *Pride and Prejudice* (1813) has always been her most popular novel, *Emma* is generally regarded as her greatest. In this work of her maturity, she deals once more with the milieu she preferred: "3 or 4 Families in a Country Village is the very thing to work on."

Emma can be viewed as a bildungsroman, or coming-of-age novel, in which the main character grows in awareness of herself and others. Emma Woodhouse, pretty and clever, lives in a world no bigger than the village of Highbury and a few surrounding estates; in that small world, the Woodhouse family is the most important. As Austen states, the real dangers for Emma are "the power of having rather too much her own way, and a disposition to think a little too well of herself."

These dangers are unperceived by Emma. In the blind exercise of her power over Highbury, she involves herself in a series of ridiculous errors, mistakenly judging that the Reverend Philip Elton cares for Harriet Smith rather than for her;

Frank Churchill for her rather than for Jane Fairfax; Harriet for Frank rather than for George Knightley; and Knightley for Harriet rather than for her. It is the triumph of Austen's art that however absurd or obvious Emma's miscalculations, they are convincingly a part of Emma's charming egotism. Emma's vulnerability to error can in part be attributed to inexperience, since her life has been circumscribed by the boundaries of Highbury and its environs. She is further restricted by her valetudinarian father's gentle selfishness, which resists any kind of change and insists on a social life limited to his own small circle.

Emma is convinced that she has no equals in Highbury. Knightley well understands the underlying assumption of superiority in Emma's friendship for Harriet: "How can Emma imagine she has anything to learn herself, while Harriet is presenting such a delightful inferiority?" Emma fears superiority in others as a threat. Of the capable farmer Robert Martin, Harriet's wooer, she observes, "But a farmer can need none of my help, and is therefore in one sense as much above my notice as in every other way he is below it." Her resolution to like Jane is repeatedly shattered by the praise everybody else gives Jane's superior attractions.

Emma's task is to become undeceived and to break free of the limitations imposed by her pride, by her father's flattering tyranny, and by the limited views of Highbury. She must accomplish all this without abandoning her self-esteem and intelligence, her father, or society. The author prepares for the possibility of a resolution from the beginning, especially by establishing Knightley as the standard of maturity for which Emma must strive. Emma is always somewhat aware of his significance, and she often puts her folly to the test of his judgment. There are brief, important occasions when the two, united by instinctive understanding, work together to create or restore social harmony; however, it is not until Harriet presumes to think of herself as worthy of his love that Emma is shocked into recognizing that Knightley is superior to her as well as to Harriet. She is basically deficient in human sympathy, categorizing people as second or third rank in Highbury or analyzing them to display her own wit. She begins to develop a sensitivity, however, as she experiences her own humiliations. She regrets her rudeness to Miss Bates not only because Knightley is displeased but also because she herself perceives that she has been cruel.

Far more, however, than merely a coming-of-age novel, *Emma* also examines the larger themes of community and class. Austen's idea of community, while circumscribed by geography, ignores physical proximity as the sole determinant of neighborhood in favor of class discrimination. In Austen, the strictures of class determine both the community's membership and how it works in the lives of its members. For example, there is no community between the gentry and the servant classes, except that demanded of landowners by noblesse oblige. The Coles, while visited by the Westons, are not part of the Hartfield community until they rise in the world sufficiently to socialize with the Woodhouses. Those in the upper class may visit those of lower degree, but the less highborn must wait for an invitation to visit the homes of the rich, although they may associate with them in public places. Thus, Emma visits the homes of poor cottagers to bring soup and drops in on the Martin family as well as at the Bateses; however, these families do not come to Hartfield until invited. Emma herself has to do some soul-searching before determining whether she may properly accept the Coles's invitation: Are the Coles of high enough degree to be able to properly invite a Woodhouse to their premises?

Austen's community provides necessary functions for its members, weaving the social connections among them that are necessary for providing awareness of each person's welfare. We see the community sociality at work in *Emma* in the frequent visits Knightley makes to Hartfield to check on the Woodhouses and the Bateses, bringing occasional gifts of game or produce. As the vicar, Elton visits the members of his parish, a duty shared by his wife, Augusta. Other neighbors bring food to the Bateses when Jane is ill.

In addition to welfare, another important function of Austen's community is the dissemination of news and updates about neighbors and friends, seen as an expression of social and emotional caring and support. Weston is an indefatigable visitor and sharer of news and gossip, as he lets everyone know as soon as he receives letters from his son, Frank, and airs their contents as they pertain to mutual interests. Miss Bates, while tedious, is still trying to perform her duty to the community by talking upon small matters and letting people know every piece of news about her niece, Jane. Those who are derelict in this social duty, including Frank, are viewed with dissatisfaction; Frank deceives people about his affairs. Another derelict in social duty is Jane, who refuses to share her views or enter into the general interest in community relationships.

Manners are very important to the Highbury community. Visitors and new members are welcomed politely. Jane, Frank, and Mrs. Elton are treated warmly upon their arrival, despite private reservations such as those entertained by Emma and Mrs. Weston about Mrs. Elton. Faults and foibles of community members, like Miss Bates's garrulousness, Mr. Woodhouse's hypochondria, and Emma's snobbery, are tolerated with kindness. The general civility of the community is considered so important that when Emma ruptures it with her ill-natured insult of Miss Bates at Box Hill, Knightley takes steps to let her know of her gaffe, and she corrects it as soon as she can, aware of the necessity for courtesy and amity among neighbors. Knightley, the community watchdog, also points out to Emma that she is being insufficiently friendly to Jane. Other members of the community ignore insults to maintain good feeling, such as when the Martins continue to be kind to Harriet even following her Emma-instigated snobbery and her refusal of Robert.

Austen ridicules, punishes, and otherwise disparages characters in *Emma* who insufficiently carry out the obligations of neighborliness, just as much as she castigates characters who display flaws of moral character. Indeed, the two failings are often conflated in this novel, which does not contain dastardly villains so much as people who ignore or misread their responsibilities to the commonweal. The antagonists in *Emma* are Frank (non-frank) Churchill, who places his own interests in concealing his engagement above the community's interest in honest disclosure, and Jane (less than fair) Fairfax, who withholds her opinions and friendship from the community to keep a private agreement. The other antagonists are Elton, who feeds his own social and pecuniary ambitions by disparaging Harriet, a disadvantaged member of the community he has an obligation to foster; and his wife, Augusta, who attempts to further community goals in befriending Jane and in organizing socials, but who also unwisely ignores the tacit rules of class decorum that demand she submit to those above her in the social hierarchy. While these characters do not ruin anyone's life or fortune, they create potential rifts in the social fabric of Highbury. To Austen, these offenses that affect community sociality are more heinous than the external threats of poultry theft and outsider predation.

In *Emma*, social class is so prevalent that it is possible to read the novel as a primer on the proper observance of class distinctions and the obligations of the upper class. All the problems in the plot are caused by faulty perceptions of rank and its duties. When these errors are corrected and the characters assume their proper places in the social hierarchy, peace reigns. Emma, first in consequence in her sphere because she has a large income independent of labor, owns property, and possesses old and distinguished family connections, must learn how to act her part. High social rank demands superior manners, education, and appearance. As a Woodhouse and the mistress of Hartfield, Emma's only social peer is Knightley, proprietor of Donwell Abbey and the highest-ranking gentleman in the area. While Emma's behavior and ideas about the meaning of rank

are frequently erroneous, Knightley's opinions and actions can always be taken as a model for proper upper-class behavior.

Because Emma's former middle-class governess, Mrs. Weston, has recently risen into the upper class by marrying into a respectable family, Emma aspires to similarly raise her new friend Harriet to a higher class. Emma feels that to elevate Harriet into the gentry would detach her from bad acquaintance and introduce her into good society. Knightley, however, opposes Emma's friendship with, and plans for, Harriet because he feels nothing good can come from crossing class boundaries; that raising Harriet's expectations will make her unhappy with the situation in which her birth and circumstances have placed her. So it proves that under Emma's tutelage, Harriet loses her first suitor and raises her expectations for a husband beyond what is realistic.

Knightley, however, unlike Emma, is no blind snob: Emma rejects Harriet's suitor, Robert Martin, as being illiterate and coarse because he is a farmer, even though readers find that he reads, writes a good letter, and is polite and respectful. Knightley, by contrast, respects Robert and considers him a friend. Harriet, with Emma's encouragement, focuses her hopes upon Elton, who as a member of the clergy occupies a social position above that of a farmer. However, Elton, also hoping to advance himself socially, refuses to consider Harriet, deeming her beneath his level. Harriet then raises her sights to Knightley. When Emma realizes this, she sees the evil of raising expectations beyond one's class and considers that Harriet's unequal marriage to Knightley, while an amazing elevation on her side, would be a debasing folly for Knightley. Emma thus abandons Harriet as a confidant, whereupon Harriet returns to Robert and achieves happiness in the associations belonging to her own class, from which she should never have tried to rise.

Augusta Elton's behavior is another illustration of the impropriety of trying to rise in class. The Reverend Elton had married Augusta Hawkins because she had substantial wealth, yet this wealth was only recently earned through her father's business rather than through inheritance. Augusta tries to correct the taint of "new money" by continually flaunting her relationship to her sister's husband, who owns an estate. She also tries to insinuate herself into the same class as Knightley and Emma by calling them by familiar names, proposing social gatherings with them, and otherwise ignoring class distinctions. Making herself obnoxious with her egotistical pretensions and her insults to lower-class Harriet, Augusta shows her lack of refinement and manners, illustrating that true upper-class gentility cannot be acquired simply by having enough money. Elton's attempt to rise socially by marrying Augusta is properly punished by his ending up married to a woman whose attitudes and behavior will always display ignorance of true gentility.

The Bateses, by contrast, were born into upper-class gentility but have lost all their wealth. Truly high-class neighbors such as Knightley and the Woodhouses still associate with the Bateses, while trying to relieve their poverty with frequent gifts of goods and services. As the model of gentlemanly behavior, Knightley urges Emma to befriend the Bates's niece, Jane, rather than Harriet, because Jane, while equally needy, belongs to a higher class because of her birth, accomplishments, and refinement. He also castigates Emma for insulting Miss Bates at the Box Hill picnic, because as one who was born and bred into the upper class, Miss Bates deserves Emma's respect. Knightley also points out that as the highest-ranking young woman in the neighborhood, Emma has the obligation to set an example of courtesy and polite behavior, which she has failed to do.

Frank, adopted into wealth and given an upper-class education, is an example of one who can act convincingly gentlemanlike, yet because his adoptive family has no fair pretense to family or blood but only newly acquired riches, still betrays character flaws that show his inferiority to someone like Knightley. Although he has the good taste to fall in love with the refined Jane, Frank's willingness to form a secret engagement and deceive those around him show that he falls short of an ideal gentleman's honesty and integrity. Throughout the novel, Emma learns through her mistakes and through the tutelage of Knightley the true meaning of class. Initially, she looks down upon everyone in a lower economic sphere, such as Robert, and respects those, like Elton, who pretend to gentility. Later, however, she discovers Robert's respectability and learns that Elton is petty, self-serving, and shallow. She learns that the Coles family, whom she considered too lowborn to socialize with, are courteous and kind associates. She at first ridicules Miss Bates and Jane, but at last discovers them to be cordial and discerning friends. She criticizes Knightley for insufficiently displaying his rank by walking rather than riding around in his carriage and by associating with farmers like Robert. However, Emma finally learns that Knightley has such true gentility of mind and heart that he does not need to flaunt his superiority with surface pretensions.

Altogether, Austen is telling the reader that gradations in social strata contribute to the orderly workings of society, and that happiness and peace result from recognizing and accepting class boundaries. Furthermore, she shows that there is more to gentility than simply money, birth, and connections: that true gentility of mind includes personal moral

integrity, wise judgment, and respect for and kindness to everyone. At the novel's close, Emma has learned this lesson well enough to be the proper companion of the estimable Knightley, and she is well on her way to developing the superior character necessary to accord with her high position on the social ladder.

Later criticism has addressed the gender issues in *Emma*, examining, for example, Emma's defense of single and independent womanhood, which occurs early in the novel. The novel raises questions about the possibility of womanly fulfillment in a society focused on rank and wealth, about the social construction of womanhood, and about assumptions that women are merely extensions of the property of men. Furthermore, regarding class, other critics have viewed Knightley as an innovative, more egalitarian landlord for his acceptance and incorporation of the views of tenants like the Martins. *Emma*, a deserved classic, has a rich menu of themes and topics that continues to evolve with modern interests and concerns.

"Critical Evaluation" by Catherine E. Moore;
revised by Sally B. Palmer

Further Reading

Adams, Carol, Douglas Buchanan, and Kelly Gesch. *The Bedside, Bathtub, and Armchair Companion to Jane Austen.* New York: Continuum, 2008. A highly readable reference work providing biographical and literary information on Austen and all of her novels, including *Emma*.

Austen, Jane. *Emma: An Authoritative Text, Backgrounds, Reviews, and Criticism.* 3d ed. Edited by Stephen M. Parrish. New York: W. W. Norton, 2000. An excellent beginning for the student first reading *Emma*. Brings together the definitive text, the background materials that Austen may have used, and important critical articles. This third edition contains several features, including Austen's letters to her sister, Cassandra, and biographical sketches of Austen written by family members.

Copeland, Edward, and Juliet McMaster, eds. *The Cambridge Companion to Jane Austen.* New York: Cambridge University Press, 1997. One of the thirteen essays focuses on an analysis of *Emma, Mansfield Park* (1814), and *Persuasion* (1818), while other essays deal with broad issues, such as class consciousness, religion, and domestic economy in Austen's work. This excellent overview includes a chronology and concludes with an assessment of late twentieth century developments in Austen scholarship.

Folsom, Marcia McClintock, ed. *Approaches to Teaching Austen's "Emma."* New York: Modern Language Association of America, 2004. Designed to help instructors prepare lessons about the novel. Helpful to students as well. Includes discussions of politics, society, and everyday life in early nineteenth century England and advice for teaching about class, gender, language, and other aspects of the book.

Hecimovich, Gregg A. *Austen's "Emma."* New York: Continuum, 2008. A summary of plot, themes, and characters, along with a useful bibliography. Part of the Continuum Reader's Guides series.

Kirkham, Margaret. *Jane Austen, Feminism, and Fiction.* New York: Methuen, 1986. Kirkham asserts that Austen's viewpoint on such topics as the status of women, female education, marriage and authority, and women in literature is strikingly similar to that of eighteenth century English feminists. Includes a twenty-page chapter on *Emma.*

Lambdin, Laura Cooner, and Robert Thomas Lambdin, eds. *A Companion to Jane Austen Studies.* New York: Greenwood Press, 2000. A collection of twenty-two essays interpreting Austen's works. Two of the essays examine *Emma:* "Lampoon and Lampoonability: *Emma* and the Riddle of Popularity" and "'And Very Good Lists They Were': Select Critical Readings of Jane Austen's *Emma.*"

Stafford, Fiona, ed. *Jane Austen's "Emma": A Casebook.* New York: Oxford University Press, 2007. Collection of essays written between 1815 and 2000, in which writers, reviewers, and scholars offer numerous interpretations of the novel. Austen's own opinions of her novel, described in an essay published in 1816, are also included.

Tanner, Tony. *Jane Austen.* New York: Macmillan, 1986. An important book by one of the best-known Austen scholars, to which most subsequent criticism responds.

Todd, Janet M. *The Cambridge Introduction to Jane Austen.* New York: Cambridge University Press, 2006. Todd, an Austen scholar and editor of the author's work, provides an overview of Austen's life, novels, context, and reception. Includes a detailed discussion about each novel and provides a good starting point for the study of her major works.

Tomalin, Claire. *Jane Austen: A Life.* New York: Knopf, 1998. This compelling account of Austen's life is exceedingly well written and attempts to tell the story from the subject's own perspective. Proceeding in chronological order, the book concludes with a postscript on the fates of Austen's family members and two appendixes: a note on Austen's final illness and an excerpt from the diary of Austen's niece, Fanny.

The Emperor Jones

Author: Eugene O'Neill (1888-1953)
First produced: 1920; first published, 1921
Type of work: Drama
Type of plot: Expressionism
Time of plot: Early twentieth century
Locale: West Indies

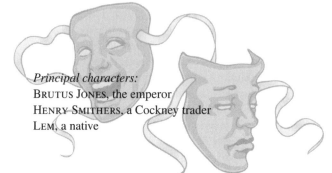

Principal characters:
BRUTUS JONES, the emperor
HENRY SMITHERS, a Cockney trader
LEM, a native

The Story:

Henry Smithers, a Cockney adventurer, learns from a woman that the followers of Brutus Jones, the self-styled emperor of a West Indian island, are about to desert their ruler. With Smithers's help, Jones, a former Pullman porter and escaped convict, duped the natives into believing that he is a magician. The superstitious natives make him emperor of the island. Smithers discloses to the emperor the disaffection of his subjects, who are taxed and cheated by the pair beyond human endurance. Jones judges that he has six more months of power before the natives catch on to his skullduggery. He

had a silver bullet cast as a good luck charm; it will be a useful tool if he is ever caught by his subjects.

At Smithers's suggestion, Jones rings a bell for his attendants; no one appears. Jones resigns his position as emperor on the spot and makes immediate plans to escape through the jungle to the coast. Drums begin to beat in the hills. The former emperor gives the palace to Smithers, takes up his white Panama hat, and walks boldly out the front door.

At the edge of the jungle, Jones searches unsuccessfully for the canned food he cached for such an emergency. The drums continue to beat, louder and more insistent. Night falls, and formless fears come out of the jungle to beset Jones. The moon rises. Jones comes into a clearing and there in the moonlight sees Jeff, a Pullman porter he killed in a razor duel. Jeff is throwing dice. When the kneeling figure refuses to answer him, Jones shoots at him. The phantom disappears. Drums still thud in the distance. Jones, now sick with fright, plunges into the inky jungle.

After a while, he comes upon a road and pauses to rest. A chain gang comes out of the forest. The guard of the gang motions to Jones to take his place in the gang and to get to work. When the guard whips him, Jones lifts his shovel to strike him, but he discovers that he has no shovel. In his rage of fear and frustration, he fires his revolver at the guard. The road, the guard, and the chain gang disappear; the jungle closes in. The louder beat of the tom-toms drives Jones on in frantic circles.

Now in tatters, the terrified Jones repents of the murders he committed and of the way he has cheated the islanders. He comes next upon a slave auction attended by white people dressed in the style of the 1850's. An auctioneer puts Jones on the auction block. Frightened, Jones shatters this apparition by firing one shot at the auctioneer and another at a planter. He dashes into the forest, mad with fear. The drums continue to beat.

At three o'clock, Jones comes to a part of the jungle that strangely resembles the hold of a slave ship. He finds himself one of a cargo of slaves who are swaying slowly with the motion of the ship. Jones and the other slaves moan with sorrow at being taken away from their homeland. With only the silver bullet left in his revolver, Jones saves it and dashes on again into the dark of the night.

Next he comes upon an altarlike arrangement of boulders near a great river. He sinks to his knees as if to worship. A Congo witch doctor appears from behind a large tree and begins a primitive dance. Jones is hypnotized by the ritual. The witch doctor indicates to Jones in pantomime that the former emperor must offer himself as a sacrifice in order to overcome the forces of evil. A great green-eyed crocodile emerges from the river; Jones fires the silver bullet at the monster, and the witch doctor disappears behind a tree, leaving Jones lying on the ground completely overcome by fear.

At dawn Lem, the leader of the rebels, comes with Smithers and a group of natives to the edge of the jungle, where Jones entered on the previous night. Lem was delayed in pursuing Jones because of the necessity of manufacturing silver bullets, which, Lem believes, are the only means of taking Jones's life. Several of Lem's men enter the jungle. They soon find the prostrate Jones, who was running in cir-

cles throughout the night. One of them shoots Jones through the chest with a silver bullet. Jones's body is brought back to Lem, who thinks that the silver bullet is what killed Jones. Smithers, however, looking at Jones's fear-contorted face, knows differently.

Critical Evaluation:

The production of *The Emperor Jones* by the Provincetown Players in 1920 was a turning point for Eugene O'Neill. The play, a huge success both in Provincetown, Massachusetts, and in New York, represented O'Neill's first foray into expressionism, the European movement influenced by the work of Sigmund Freud and Carl Jung that emphasized presenting psychological reality on stage. With this production, O'Neill earned a reputation as an important playwright both in the United States and in Europe.

The Emperor Jones is a long, tightly constructed, one-act play with eight scenes. The first and last scenes form a realistic frame, beginning with Smithers informing Jones that the natives are preparing to hunt him down to finish his two-year reign as emperor, and ending with the native leader, Lem, and Smithers discussing the death of Jones.

The middle scenes portray a journey into the jungle that is both physical and psychological, for when Jones fearfully plunges into the dark tangle of trees, he is also entering the troubled recesses of his mind. During this journey, he must face hunger and heat, repressed violent incidents from his own past, and his collective racial past—from slave auction to a face-to-face encounter with an African crocodile god. Jones's journey into racial memory demonstrates O'Neill's debt to Jung's concept of the collective unconscious.

O'Neill portrays Jones's psychological quest in striking stage images. The first scene features Jones's throne room, blindingly white except for accents of red and a huge rough throne dominating the stage. Jones enters in a red uniform, an imposing figure who clearly inspires fear in the cowardly Smithers, to whom he displays his pistol with its six bullets, the last one being silver, for Jones has convinced the natives that only a silver bullet can kill him.

When Jones leaves his palace and enters the jungle, he finds himself in an area of shadows and increasing darkness, the fading of the light paralleling Jones's movement into his own blackness. Sounds are also important. Before Jones leaves his palace, Lem's men start beating their drums at the tempo of a normal heartbeat, increasing this as Jones progresses, feeding his nervousness and the audience's tension. The pistol shots, which Jones uses to dispel his hallucinations, punctuate several scenes. The audience counts the shots (as Lem is surely doing as well), realizing that when the sixth shot, the silver bullet, is fired, Jones is defenseless—ready to become the sacrifice demanded by the crocodile god.

Another significant stage image is Jones's gradual loss of pieces of his uniform, a costume parody of white power and grandeur that Jones "has a way of carrying . . . off." When he is finally stripped to a remnant of clothing resembling a breechcloth, Jones has lost the overlay of white civilization and seems ready for his journey on a slave ship and a confrontation with the African culture of his ancestors.

The figure of Brutus Jones himself is a significant stage image. In 1920, American audiences were accustomed to the "stage Negro" stereotype, but O'Neill shatters expectations in two ways. The stereotype is a comic one. (On the rare occasions when African Americans were serious characters, they were portrayed as light-skinned, sometimes even "passing" as white.) The usual theatrical practice was also to cast white actors, who played black roles in blackface. Instead, O'Neill presented a black actor, Charles Gilpin, as a character who could be viewed as a tragic hero.

Jones displays a number of attributes of the Aristotelian hero. His status is elevated, and he is intelligent. He has learned the native language and has skillfully used the opportunities that have presented themselves. When a shot from a would-be assassin misses Jones, he quickly invents the myth of the silver bullet, keeping the natives under his control for a longer period of time. Jones also demonstrates the typical pride, and his hamartia, or tragic error in judgment, is clear. He has adopted the "garments" of the white civilization that had oppressed him in the United States, cutting himself off from his own culture.

Chief among these overlays are his greed and his emphasis on material gain for himself without consideration of the effect his rapacity will have on the native people for whom he should feel kinship. Instead, he contemptuously refers to them as "bush niggers" and "bleeds em dry," sending money to European bank accounts while planning his own escape. He tells Smithers he has learned his methods by listening to the "white quality" on the Pullman cars where he served as a porter. Another overlay of white society is the Christian religion. Although Jones "lays [his] Jesus on the shelf" as he exploits the natives, he expects "Lawd Jesus" will rescue him from the ghosts of his past. This does not happen, and he becomes the sacrifice demanded by the African god, slain by the natives he has exploited. They use a silver bullet made from melted money, an appropriate symbol for the fallen would-be capitalist.

O'Neill's use of dialect and of some stereotypical attributes has been seen as problematic, as is the fact that Jones's dialect becomes "blacker" as he progresses in his psychological journey, moving away from the trappings of "civilization" that he has assumed. Both Jones and the white Smithers are outsiders, speaking what is considered by insiders to be debased forms of the language. O'Neill's interest in sympathetically portraying outsiders is a consistent thread running through his plays, often attributed to his own experience with prejudice as part of the Irish minority in New England.

In addition to the theme of the outsider, O'Neill was concerned with the emphasis that American society places on materialism, which he viewed as a dangerously destructive force. Jones's fall becomes more tragic when one considers that, if Jones had resisted the values of white American society, he might have provided positive leadership for the natives on "his" island, thus advancing his people. From a historical perspective, it may be significant that O'Neill was inspired to create Jones in part by his knowledge of two Haitian dictators: President Sam, who spread the rumor that he could be killed only by a silver bullet, and Henri Christophe, who proclaimed himself emperor of part of Haiti, then later committed suicide.

The Emperor Jones marked the beginning of O'Neill's experimentation with expressionism and related theatrical devices. The success of this experimentation was mixed, but this play, with its interesting blend of realism and expressionism, is clearly a theatrical success.

"Critical Evaluation" by Elsie Galbreath Haley

Further Reading

Bloom, Harold, ed. *Eugene O'Neill*. Updated ed. New York: Bloom's Literary Criticism, 2007. Includes critical essays analyzing individual plays, as well as more general discussions about O'Neill's life and work.

Bloom, Steven F. *Student Companion to Eugene O'Neill*. Westport, Conn.: Greenwood Press, 2007. Includes a brief biographical sketch, a discussion of O'Neill's literary heritage, and a chapter providing critical analysis of *The Emperor Jones*.

Bogard, Travis. *Contour in Time: The Plays of Eugene O'Neill*. New York: Oxford University Press, 1972. Bogard's study of O'Neill's plays revolves around his assertion that O'Neill's experiments with theatrical devices were part of his attempt to create theater from his quest for identity. The section on *The Emperor Jones* compares the play to Henrik Ibsen's *Peer Gynt* (1867).

Falk, Doris V. *Eugene O'Neill and the Tragic Tension*. New Brunswick, N.J.: Rutgers University Press, 1958. A study of O'Neill's plays with emphasis on the psychoanalytic theories of depth psychology, noting the influence of Carl Jung's theory of the collective unconscious on *The Emperor Jones.*

Floyd, Virginia. *The Plays of Eugene O'Neill: A New Assessment.* New York: Frederick Ungar, 1985. This study for general readers features analyses of fifty plays, supplemented with information from O'Neill's notebooks. The section on *The Emperor Jones* discusses O'Neill's use of expressionism, noting similarities to August Strindberg's *A Dream Play* (1902). Floyd considers this a "landmark drama" for the American stage, with its first use of an African American actor in a leading role in New York theater.

Frenz, Horst. *Eugene O'Neill.* Translated by Helen Sebba. New York: Frederick Ungar, 1971. Provides an assessment of the man whose experiments transformed American drama. In his analysis of *The Emperor Jones* as one of O'Neill's expressionist experiments, Frenz compares the play to Georg Kaiser's *From Morn to Midnight* (1916).

Manheim, Michael, ed. *The Cambridge Companion to Eugene O'Neill.* New York: Cambridge University Press, 1998. Collection of essays about O'Neill's life and works, including discussions of the theater in his time; notable stage productions of his work; his depiction of female, African, and Irish American characters; and analyses of his plays written in his early, middle, and late periods.

Martine, James J., ed. *Critical Essays on Eugene O'Neill.* Boston: G. K. Hall, 1984. Two essays in this collection are of interest to students of *The Emperor Jones*: Frank R. Cunningham's "Romantic Elements in Early O'Neill" views Jones as one of O'Neill's failed romantics, and Lisa M. Swerdt's "Blueprint for the Future" examines the play as a seminal work, introducing themes that O'Neill would develop more fully in later plays.

Törnqvist, Egil. *Eugene O'Neill: A Playwright's Theatre.* Jefferson, N.C.: McFarland, 2004. Demonstrates how O'Neill was a controlling personality in the texts and performances of his plays. Describes his working conditions and the multiple audiences for his works. Examines the titles, settings in time and place, names and addresses, language, and allusions to other works in his dramas.

Empire Falls

Author: Richard Russo (1949-   )
First published: 2001
Type of work: Novel
Type of plot: Historical realism
Time of plot: Late 1990's
Locale: Empire Falls, Maine; Martha's Vineyard, Massachusetts

Principal characters:
MILES ROBY, the proprietor of the Empire Grill
JANINE ROBY, his estranged wife
CHRISTINA "TICK" ROBY, their daughter
MAX ROBY, Miles's father
GRACE ROBY, Miles's mother
DAVID ROBY, Miles's brother
CHARLENE GARDINER, a waitress at the Empire Grill
WALT COMEAU, Janine's lover
FRANCINE WHITING, wealthy owner of the Empire Grill
CHARLES BEAUMONT WHITING, Francine's late husband
CANDACE BURKE, Tick's friend
ZACK MINTY, Tick's former boyfriend
JOHN VOSS, Tick's classmate

The Story:

On a quiet afternoon at the Empire Grill diner, Miles Roby, the proprietor and fry cook, is looking out the window. His life has not been easy. His father rarely provided his mother Grace with any financial support for him and his brother David. Instead, Grace Roby worked long hours at the local shirt factory to pay the bills for her family. Miles had dreams of attending college, but those dreams were deferred when his mother discovered she had cancer and Miles came home to take care of her. Moreover, Miles's wife has recently left him. The one hope that remains to him is the promise that the owner of the Empire Grill, Francine Whiting, made to him twenty years ago: that when she dies, he will inherit the diner. Even this hope is fading. Owning the diner seemed like a good idea to the younger Miles, but the closed storefronts along his street suggest that the Grill may not be worth owning by the time he inherits it.

Miles's daughter Christina, nicknamed Tick, shortly arrives, burdened by her heavy bookbag, and solemnly greets her father and her uncle David. She pointedly ignores Walt Comeau, who comes to the Grill only to taunt Miles with the fact that Walt seduced Miles's wife Janine away from him. Tick is nearly as glum as her father, primarily because, having broken up with her abusive boyfriend Zack, she is no longer accepted by his friends and has to sit with other social rejects such as the emotionally disturbed John Voss. Her one friend, Candace, is shallow and oblivious to Tick's feelings. While Tick feels comfortable working at her father's diner, she wonders if she will ever feel positive about growing up in a town that seems to be dying.

Today is the day that Miles has to visit Francine Whiting and provide her with the Grill's financial details. For many years, his profit and loss statement has reflected far more loss than profit. As Miles walks to the Planning and Development Commission Office, he wonders why Mrs. Whiting has allowed him to remain open. Most of the businesses she has acquired over the years, including the shirt factory, the mills, and many others, have closed their doors after unsuccessfully struggling to realize a profit. This year's meeting, like the ones before, ends without any resolution: The Grill will remain open for another year. Miles thinks that he should be happy about keeping his job, but, in his sadness over his divorce and his anxiety over his daughter's growing distance from him, he feels trapped. He thinks about the history of Empire Falls and the factory's former owner, C. B. Whiting, who had planned such a bright future for the little town.

Miles is unaware of the full extent of C. B.'s influence on his life. His mother's boss, Whiting became attracted to Grace Roby just after Miles was born, and he sought for years to win her heart. C. B.'s marriage was unpleasant for the aging playboy, and Grace's prettiness was impossible for him to ignore. The summer that Miles was nine, Whiting took both Grace and her son to Martha's Vineyard for a week, hoping to persuade Grace to leave her husband and accompany Whiting to a new life in Mexico. Grace would have acquiesced and escaped her drunken husband Max had she not been pregnant with another child at the time. Whiting was willing to accept Miles, but two children would have been too many for him. When Grace and Miles returned home to

Empire Falls, Grace knew that she would never escape her life there.

Life in Empire Falls continues to move at a depressing, glacial pace. Janine's relationship with Walt proves to be even more difficult than the life she had with Miles, as she slowly discovers how extensively the so-called Silver Fox has lied to her. Although he claims to be fifty, Walt is actually sixty. Janine's affair inspired her to get in the best physical shape of her life and taught her how to enjoy sex for the first time, but she feels that she can no longer relate to Tick and worries that her daughter is disappointed in her.

Miles is informed that Mrs. Whiting's daughter Cindy has been allowed to leave the mental hospital in which she has been since she last tried to commit suicide. Cindy is coming back to Empire Falls for a while. As always, Miles has mixed feelings about Cindy. She has always had a serious crush on Miles, and romancing her would ensure his own financial future, but he simply cannot make himself feel anything besides pity for the crippled girl.

Tick, buoyed by a strange sense of inner peace, has decided to befriend the silent John Voss. She even offers him a job washing dishes at her father's diner. She does not know how deeply troubled her friend really is, however. John brings a pistol to school with him and murders Justin Dibble, the art teacher Mrs. Rodrigues, and the principal, Otto Meyer. Candace is seriously wounded in the attack. A background check on Voss reveals that he suffered severe child abuse at the hands of his parents and then lived in extreme poverty and humiliation with his grandmother. Eventually, he took revenge on both his grandmother and the family dog. The bullying he suffered at school triggered his final homicidal rage.

The murders at school convince Miles to leave Empire Falls. He had already informed Mrs. Whiting that he no longer wanted to work for her. Now, he packs his belongings and takes his sobbing daughter to Martha's Vineyard. Their flight proves not to solve their problems, however.

Six months later, Miles assesses his dwindling savings and decides to return to his hometown. He learns that Mrs. Whiting has died and that a romance is budding between his brother and Charlene Gardiner, a waitress at the Grill. After the loss of the Grill, David and Charlene decided to start their own restaurant by expanding one of the local bars to include a full menu. Since their building was one of the few not owned by Francine Whiting, they have been able to realize a small profit. Many of the storefronts and the empty factory were sold by Mrs. Whiting shortly before her death, and the new proprietors have big plans for revitalizing the little town. No longer feeling trapped by circumstances, Miles and Tick decide that going back home is finally a welcome prospect.

Critical Evaluation:

Empire Falls received extensive critical acclaim when it was published in 2001, winning the Pulitzer Prize in fiction the following year. Richard Russo's realist portrayals of the hardships and economic suffering faced by residents of northeastern working-class towns drew praise from reviewers and inspired a film adaptation by Home Box Office in May of 2005. As a result of the difficulty of translating to traditional cinema the intertwining plot threads that compose *Empire Falls*, Russo's screenplay made some artistic compromises that lessened the dramatic impact of the original text. Nevertheless, the film manages to express the inexorable power of fate, which shifts and twists despite humanity's feeble attempts to control it.

Unlike other works by Russo, *Empire Falls* is composed of many subplots that run alongside the main plot of Miles Roby's loss of the Empire Grill. Miles's father begs shamelessly and takes a trip to Key West, where he and others win thirty-two thousand dollars and he spends all of his share. Horace Weymouth goes to the home of John Voss's grandmother at night and sees the young boy torturing a dog. The threads of these stories all share a sense of despair and futility even in the best of situations. There is no truly optimistic character in *Empire Falls*—the closest approximation to an optimist is the feckless Max Roby, a drunk who claims little responsibility for anything in his life and readily abandons his family in pursuit of his own, selfish pleasure.

Russo has remarked that the characters of *Empire Falls* all feel as though they are trapped by their circumstances and have little or no ability to alter their fates. Miles's mother, Grace, falls in love with her boss at the factory in which she works. Charles Beaumont Whiting is one of the wealthiest men in Maine, but all his money cannot free him from his odious marriage to Francine. After discovering the affair, Mrs. Whiting banishes her husband to Mexico. Mrs. Whiting, afterward, continues to govern with an iron fist and lives, like a queen in state, as the dominant power in Empire Falls, but she herself is herself trapped. She is haunted by the knowledge that a common factory girl stole her husband's love from her and that her only child, far from being a beauty queen or towering intellect, is a depressed cripple who can barely manage to live from day to day without trying to hurt herself.

Miles plans on going to college and becoming a professor, but he regards it as his duty to take care of his mother in her final illness. His return to Empire Falls ends his formal schooling and prepares him for the decades of ignominy that he will face as one of Mrs. Whiting's tenants. Miles is mired in the myriad expectations of other people, and not even his daughter, Tick, has the strength to escape the leaden grasp of their hometown. The best they can do is to try to change the town from within—a prospect that, given its reliance on the influx of funding from newcomers from Massachusetts ("Massholes," as the locals refer to them)—is not entirely positive. A syndicate of commercial investors wants to turn the old factory into a commercial district, and the population of the town has increased. Hope is not quite dead, although the future is far from certain.

Even the name of the town, Empire Falls, suggests the aging decrepitude of Miles's surroundings. C. B. once tries to change the course of the Knox River to prevent a mountain of refuse from piling up on the river's edge within view of his mansion. He spends much money researching the problem and altering the banks of the dark waters. Ultimately, however, he is unsuccessful, and the return of the river to its original banks sweeps his wife, Francine, right off her gazebo to her death. No attempts to change one's destiny dramatically meet with success here. Like the settings of the novels of Charles Dickens and William Faulkner, Russo's bleak landscapes are detailed reflections of the inner lives of characters who struggle to find meaning in the random events of which their lives are composed.

Julia M. Meyers

Further Reading

Charles, Ron. "Grease Spots on the American Dream." *Christian Science Monitor*, May 10, 2001, pp. 18-19. Echoes the sentiments of many critics who have studied Russo's writings. Points out that the people of Empire Falls have the same blue-collar, impoverished mentality that Russo witnessed during his own childhood.

Gussow, Mel. "Writing a Novel in the Deli, Making Revisions in the Bar." *The New York Times*, August 29, 2001, p. E1. Provides biographical details on author Richard Russo and describes the circumstances in Russo's life surrounding his choice of setting for the novel.

Heinegg, Peter. "You Still Can't Get There from Here." *America* 187, no. 12 (October 21, 2002): 26. Admires Russo's unflinching realism in representing the problems faced by traditional, East Coast mill towns. Praises the novel for being honest about its limited horizons and stunted futures, because otherwise, it could provide no impetus for social change.

Roberts, Rex. Review of *Empire Falls*, by Richard Russo. *Insight on the News* 17, no. 30 (August 13, 2001): 25. Highly praises the novel, finding it to be an excellent example of tragicomedy—a tragedy that, despite its painful subject matter, manages to find comic elements inherent in suffering.

Smith, Wendy. "Richard Russo: The Novelist Again Explores the Crucial Impact of Place on Individual Destinies." *Publishers Weekly* 240, no. 23 (June 7, 1993): 43-44. Argues that the negative qualities of the town of Empire Falls define the fate of its citizens. Place seems to predetermine characters' destinies to be unsatisfying or even destructive. It is no surprise, then, that the town raises a boy capable of a massacre.

Empire of the Sun

Author: J. G. Ballard (1930-2009)
First published: 1984
Type of work: Novel
Type of plot: Bildungsroman
Time of plot: 1941-1945
Locale: Shanghai, China

Principal characters:
JIM GRAHAM, a British schoolboy
BASIE, an American merchant seaman
DR. RANSOME, a British physician
MR. MAXTED, father of Jim's best friend
PRIVATE KIMURA, a young Japanese prison-camp guard

The Story:

Jim Graham is an eleven-year-old schoolboy from a privileged expatriate family living in Shanghai, China, on the eve of the Japanese attack on Pearl Harbor. Jim is fascinated with the coming war; he loves airplanes and admires Japan's military strength. In early 1942, amid the chaos of the first days of Japanese attacks on the Americans and British living in Shanghai, Jim becomes separated from his parents.

Jim returns to his family's mansion to find his parents and the servants all gone. The Japanese occupying Shanghai have not yet restored order to the city, so Jim is able to live undetected for weeks in residences vacated by the Americans and British whom the Japanese army have arrested. When his food supplies become exhausted, Jim is forced onto the streets of Shanghai. With no friends or protectors, Jim finds his way to scuttled merchant ships in Shanghai's harbor. There, he chances on two American merchant seamen who, like Jim, are trying to avoid capture. Basie, a cabin steward on passenger ships, takes an interest in Jim.

Basie provides Jim with food and shelter. Jim hopes Basie will be a protector who helps find his family, but he soon realizes that Basie intends to sell him to the highest bidder. No Chinese want a young British boy, however, and Jim is told he is worthless.

Japanese soldiers come upon Jim and his companions and arrest them. Jim is glad to escape from Basie and feels safer with the Japanese. He is sent to a detention center in an open-air movie theater. During a three-week stay there, Jim sleeps under a concrete overhang and becomes ill with a fever. Jim

sees that the stronger detainees are being assigned to various prison camps, but he is always left behind with the older and weaker detainees. He thinks he will die there.

A severely beaten Basie arrives at the detention center, and Jim nurses him back to health. The Japanese guards prepare a truckload of detainees for a prison camp at Woosung, on Shanghai's northern outskirts. Basie is assigned to the truck but makes no effort to take Jim along. Jim realizes that he remains disposable, but at the last minute he manages find a place on the truck.

The Japanese driver fails to locate the Woosung camp. Lost, the truck wanders through Shanghai's outskirts for several days. Among the truck's prisoners is a young British physician, Dr. Ransome, who tries to get water for the other prisoners. The Japanese guarding the truck have no provisions for the prisoners, but Jim shows initiative by cadging both water and food for himself and the others. Dr. Ransome appreciates Jim's initiative and courage. Jim, who seemed worthless at the start of the trip, has shown he has value.

Some of the missionaries among the prisoners die of sickness and exposure, but Jim, Basie, and Dr. Ransome all survive. The truck finally ends up in Lunghua, on Shanghai's southern outskirts. The surviving detainees are placed in a new concentration camp located next to a Japanese air base.

In late 1943, Jim, Dr. Ransome, and Basie have all become accustomed to regular prison-camp life. Jim remains fascinated with the Japanese airplanes at the Lunghua field. He admires the Japanese pilots, and he is befriended by the

Japanese guards at the camp, especially Private Kimura. Jim teaches Kimura to speak English and plays with Kimura's martial-arts gear.

Jim serves on the camp's food-distribution detail with Mr. Maxted, the father of his old school friend; he obtains extra food through this job. He also continues his association with Basie, who controls a supply of food and other scarce items. Jim benefits from Basie's gifts, even though he realizes that Basie is self-serving and amoral. Dr. Ransome also helps Jim with food and school lessons, but he disapproves of his close association with Basie. Jim lives behind a rigged sheet in the corner of a small room with the Vincent family, a British father, mother, and a young boy. Their dislike of Jim reflects the unfriendly and unhelpful treatment Jim meets from most of the British in the camp.

Jim misses his parents, but he no longer remembers what they look like. Young and alone, he has acquired the necessary prison-camp survival skills. Some other prisoners see him as an opportunist, but Jim rationalizes his behavior as helping keep life going for his fellow prisoners. Jim comes to regard war, privation, and prison camp as normal. He wants to live but understands that he must expect to die.

By late 1944, as Americans begin raids on Shanghai, the Japanese military cannot find sufficient food even for itself, much less its prisoners. Life for the prisoners in Jim's camp grows ever more bleak. By the summer of 1945, rations have been cut repeatedly for both the guards and the prisoners. The sheen of power disappears from the Japanese military, and the prisoners' health declines as the American attacks on Shanghai increase. Throughout this traumatic period, Jim continues his fixation upon airplanes and war. His allegiances shift from the Japanese to the Americans.

In early August, 1945, most Japanese guards depart the camp, and order declines. Basie and other American prisoners escape, but most prisoners remain in the camp. Rumors of the war's end sweep through camp; food rations almost cease. Private Kimura is shot by an armed prisoner. In the war's final days, a small Japanese detachment marches most of the remaining Lunghua camp prisoners several miles to a stadium at Nantao. Exposed to the sun, weakened from lack of food, and often ill, many prisoners collapse along the way and die. Jim helps Mr. Maxted on the march, but Mr. Maxted dies after they reach the stadium.

Finally, the Japanese surrender after the nuclear attacks on Hiroshima and Nagasaki, and order in Shanghai and in the prison camp breaks down completely. Following the death march, Jim walks back to the Lunghua camp from Nantao only to be denied entrance by the British prisoners, who have taken over and refuse entrance to anyone not inside the barbed wire fences. American B-29 bombers are no longer spreading destruction; instead, they parachute huge metal containers of food and rescue supplies. The prisoners jealously hoard the Spam, chocolate, and other supplies, keeping them away from the remaining Japanese soldiers and the hoards of Chinese refugees in the city. New sources of violence appear from rivalries among Chinese Nationalist and Communist troops, while armed prisoners assault Chinese peasants. In this apocalypse of violence, criminal gangs prey on anyone weaker than themselves. Basie reappears in one of the gangs, and Jim joins him for a while. Jim believes that as World War II ends another war will break out.

Jim comes on the body of a young Japanese kamikaze pilot from the Lunghua airfield. Believing the pilot to be dead from bullet and bayonet wounds, Jim sits beside the corpse to eat a can of Spam. The pilot is not quite dead and sits up. Jim imagines that he has resurrected the pilot, and, for the first time since the war's outbreak, he takes hope in the future. Exhilarated, he runs back to the Lunghua camp to find Dr. Ransome, who has come to reunite Jim with his parents.

Jim returns briefly to his prewar life with his family in their Shanghai mansion surrounded by servants. Soon, though, Jim and his mother sail for home, an England he has never seen. His father remains in Shanghai to restart the cotton mill he managed before the war.

Critical Evaluation:

Empire of the Sun was J. G. Ballard's best received work from among his extensive oeuvre of science fiction, short stories, and novels. Ballard was raised in Shanghai and interned at the Lunghua camp from 1942 to 1945, so the novel is semiautobiographical. However, Ballard was not separated from his family while in captivity. The author also shared Jim's fascination with airplanes.

The second section of the novel ends with a chapter titled "Empire of the Sun," the same title as the book. Because the sun is the national symbol of Japan and the two characters for Japan mean "source of the sun," the book and chapter titles appear to refer to Japan. However, in this chapter a second meaning is suggested: Jim and other prisoners are blinded by a momentary flash of light as bright as the sun. They believe the flash came from the detonation of the atomic bomb over the Japanese city of Nagasaki, about five hundred miles east of Shanghai. Thus, the title refers both to Japan and to the United States, which has harnessed the power of the sun and created a new American empire.

Jim's easy accommodation of suffering and death fits into the recurrent themes of violence and nihilism in Ballard's writing. Years before *Empire of the Sun*, Ballard acquired a cult following of readers who found in his dystopian views of present and future human life a bold expression of an existentialist nihilism.

Ballard's writing in his earlier science fiction and novels, such as *The Atrocity Exhibition* (1969) and *Crash* (1973), goes far beyond the horrors of prison-camp life. In his cult classic *Crash*, Ballard's characters find eroticism in the pain and suffering caused by automobile accidents. Many of the themes of Ballard's earlier fiction appear in a more muted form in *Empire of the Sun*. *Empire of the Sun* depicts British expatriate life in prewar Shanghai as hedonistic and cold, the Japanese as unfeeling about the casual brutality of their armies, and the Americans as unaware of the dark consequences made possible by their wealth and nuclear weapons. Jim is fascinated by these things, without expressing much emotion concerning the trauma surrounding him. Still, Ballard suggests that Jim is deeply marked by these experiences.

In postwar Great Britain, Ballard attended medical school at Cambridge and undertook flight training in Canada. He completed neither course and wound up an advertising copywriter in London. He turned to writing science fiction and attracted attention for his dystopian portrayal of human life in the future, when violence and anomie have not been banished but rather have flowered in new ways fostered by technology and capitalism. In a 2006 British Broadcasting Corporation (BBC) interview, Ballard defended himself against criticism that his books were filled with depictions of suffering and human perversity with a characteristically avuncular

comment: "I think of myself as some sort of a weather forecaster. I see stormy weather, but most storms eventually pass. I just want to limit the damage."

David D. Buck

Further Reading

Ballard, J. G. *The Kindness of Women*. New York: Harper-Collins, 1991. This second autobiographical novel also follows the main outlines of Ballard's real life. The book begins with a retelling, from other viewpoints, of events in *Empire of the Sun*.

Gasiorek, Andrzej. *J. G. Ballard*. New York: Manchester University Press, 2005. Emphasizes the extent to which *Empire of the Sun* is less dark and disturbing than the stories and novels that made Ballard a cult figure. Characterizes Ballard's late novels as asserting that "pure violence is the only possible response to an absurd universe."

Goddard, James, and David Pringle. *J. G. Ballard: The First Twenty Years*. Middlesex, England: Bran's Head Books, 1976. This early appraisal of Ballard's science fiction characterizes him as seeing "twentieth century history as a disaster area, full of intimations of more terrible and wonderful things to come."

Wood, Frances. *The Lure of China: Writers from Marco Polo to J. G. Ballard*. Hong Kong: Joint, 2009. The curator of the British Museum's China collection places Ballard at the end of a long line of Western writers who have set their work in China.

Enamels and Cameos

Author: Théophile Gautier (1811-1872)
First published: *Émaux et camées*, 1852; enlarged
    edition, 1872 (English translation, 1903)
Type of work: Poetry

Théophile Gautier's poetry forms the transition between Romanticism and the Parnassus school in France. As a young man, Gautier was a prominent member of the group surrounding Victor Hugo in the battle of *Hernani* (1830), Hugo's play that resulted in open conflict between classicists and Romanticists. Later, however, though he did not formally renounce his support of Romanticism, his name was to become associated with the doctrine of Art for Art's sake, and it is espe-

cially in connection with his body of ideas that his name is remembered.

Gautier's earliest poetry was collected into a volume entitled, simply, *Poésies*, first published in 1830. A pronounced taste for the Middle Ages, a love of lonely places, an impression of alienation—all traditional sources of inspiration for the Romantic poets—find a place in this collection, which is not noted for its originality.

"Albertus, or the Soul and Sin," a long narrative poem describing a young painter's fatal infatuation with a witch, appeared in 1833. This work is little read today, but worthy of note, however, is Gautier's use of the stock-in-trade of the lesser Romantic writers: slugs and toads, phantoms and vampires.

"La Comédie de la mort" (*The Comedy of Death*), a long poem that came out in 1838, is in two parts. The first part, titled "Life in Death," involves a dialogue in a graveyard between a worm and a corpse. It is obviously the poet's intention to shock his reader. In the second part, "Death in Life," Gautier reveals the grotesque if superficial side of his Romanticism. The intensity with which the poet insists that death overshadows all of life seems to suggest in Gautier a deep-seated pessimism with which he has not always been credited. This impression is reinforced by several pieces in his *Poésies diverses*, a collection of poems that appeared in one volume with "La Comédie de la mort." Especially worthy of mention is a short piece called "La Caravane." Gautier develops beautifully the symbol of a caravan crossing the Sahara as suggestive of humankind making its way in the world. The only oasis, the only resting place, claims the poet, is the graveyard; this idea is evoked in the simplest of terms: "a wood of cypresses strewn with white stones."

Not all of the poems in this collection are pessimistic, however. "Chinoiserie" ("Chinese Fantasy") illustrates Gautier's taste for distant lands and things exotic. The poet affirms that his love goes out not to William Shakespeare's Juliet, Dante's Beatrice, or Petrarch's Laura. Rather, he loves a girl in China who lives in a tower of porcelain:

> The one I love, at present, is in China;
> She is living with her old parents,
> In a tower of fine porcelain,
> At the Yellow River, where the cormorants are.

Although not profound, "Chinoiserie" is a delightful piece, which was subsequently set to music. It is worth remarking that even at this relatively early stage in his development, Gautier could offer his dream vision in a precise, finely executed form.

In 1840, Gautier lived in Spain for six months. The first edition of *España* appeared in 1845; in it the reader gets the impression that the starkness and acute relief of the Spanish landscape and the paintings in the Spanish art galleries sharpened Gautier's eye.

In "Ribera" and "À Zurburan," two poems in *España* written in terza rima, Gautier reveals a remarkable talent for giving a life in verse to the paintings of the two Spanish masters. Moreover, in trying to understand José Ribera's love of ugliness, and the cruelty and violence of Francisco de Zurburán's studies of early Christian martyrs, Gautier makes his art criticism into a powerful art form in its own right. Elsewhere in this edition, Gautier's approach to his art is perhaps more characteristic of the plastic arts than of poetry. In "Le Pin des Landes," for example, it is the scene viewed that calls to mind the symbol, whereas more commonly a poet will seek out a symbol to illustrate an idea.

Gautier describes how in the Landes, an area of southwest France, the only tree to be seen is the pine, with a gash in its side, to allow its resin to drip into a bowl. He develops the symbolic value of the tree beautifully; the poet, standing upright and alone, is like the tree. For the poet is cut off from others by his superiority and their jealousy. When he is unhurt, he keeps his treasure, Gautier claims; he needs a deep wound in his heart to make him release his works, his golden tears:

> Without regretting its blood that flows drop by drop,
> The pine pours out its balsam and its frothing sap,
> And still it stands upright by the side of the road,
> Like a wounded soldier, who wishes to die on his feet.

> The poet is thus in the wastes of the world;
> While he is unwounded, he keeps his treasure.
> He must have a deep gash upon his heart
> To release his verses, these divine, golden tears!

"Dans la Sierra," also in *España*, involves a landscape as a symbol, too. Inspired by the arid mountains of Spain, Gautier insists that he prefers them to the fertile plains. The cult of beauty for its own sake, suggested in this poem, was crafted into a new poetic doctrine by Gautier.

The collection *Enamels and Cameos*, to which additions were made in the five editions between 1852 and 1872, marks a major development in Gautier's poetry; it is the collection for which he is best remembered and that which illustrates his doctrine of art for art's sake.

As early as 1832, in the preface to his *Poésies*, Gautier declared that the value of art lay in its beauty and not in its usefulness: It was not the artist's business to exercise an influence on the crowd. "In general," he wrote, "as soon as a thing becomes useful, it ceases to be beautiful." Art, he claimed, was a luxury, offered to a small, elite public capable of understanding it. In the preface to his novel *Mademoiselle de Maupin* (1835-1836), moreover, Gautier went on to say that only that which serves no purpose is beautiful. In an article in *L'Artiste* he insisted that the artist's sole aim was to capture beauty.

Gautier's poetic doctrine may have been influenced by two aspects of his life. The subordination of idea to form brings to mind the plastic arts, and Gautier did start his artistic career as a painter. In addition, he earned his living as a journalist, drama critic, and art critic at a time when the writer risked becoming a commodity, the prey of unscrupulous editors and publishers. He was only too aware of the difficulties a writer faced in trying to retain his integrity. On the other hand, Gautier was too much of a critic not to see that in trying to follow all the tenets of the Romantic movement, its adherents frequently sacrificed accuracy for effect.

Enamels and Cameos is Gautier's attempt to return to precision and clarity, even at the expense of subject matter. The title of the collection is significant; the poems grouped under it are highly polished, exquisitely crafted pieces. The tone of the edition is set by the preface. Here Gautier states that just as Johann Wolfgang von Goethe at Weimar cut himself off from the world to write, so he, Gautier, disregarding the storms lashing his windows, wrote *Enamels and Cameos*.

If Gautier's aim in poetry was now beauty, he tells how the poet might achieve this effect in a poem written in 1857 and added as a conclusion to *Enamels and Cameos*. In "L'Art," Gautier claims that, like painting or sculpture, poetry is both an art and a skill to be learned. The poet, a craftsman, must have a firm grip on all the resources of the language. If he succeeds in overcoming the problems of rhyme, syntax, and vocabulary, while creating no artificial obstacles, the work of art will resist the ravages of time as no other human creation can:

> All things pass on.—Robust art
> Alone possesses eternity;
> > The bust
> Survives the city.
> The very gods die,
> But verse, sovereign,
> > Remains
> Stronger than the sword

In this collection Gautier's extreme attachment to form results in carefully executed, sophisticated poetry, which is generally more impersonal than his previous work. On the other hand, the subject matter is often slight: "Study of Hands," "To a Red Gown," and "The Tea-Rose" are representative titles.

In *España*, especially, Gautier attempted artistic transpositions, trying to reproduce in verse the effect obtained by a work of art in another medium. In *Enamels and Cameos*, such attempts become more ambitious. In "Variations on

the Carnival of Venice," for example, the poet offers a series of four pieces in which the point of departure is a musical phrase from a Venetian song. In rhythmic, colorful verse, Gautier creates a picture of Venice as he imagines it once was.

In "Symphony in White Major," Gautier again attempts an artistic transformation, showing all the nuances and associations of white. This is a fine display of virtuosity, but there is little development within the poem.

The appeal of *Enamels and Cameos* is limited because, in trying to banish himself from his work, Gautier creates what might be considered "cold" poetry. By shutting himself off from the world, he severely restricts his choice of subjects. It might be argued, moreover, that Gautier's choice of art for its own sake is made at the expense of content—that beauty of form is not enough.

The "impersonal" poetry of the Parnassians owed much to Gautier, and his artistic transpositions were of great consequence for Charles Baudelaire and the Symbolists. Moreover, if Gautier's creative talents were limited, he did, nevertheless, by his respect for his calling and for the word, renew a tradition that began with François Malherbe. Baudelaire lavished perhaps excessive praise on Gautier, but in writing that Gautier was a poet for whom the inexpressible did not exist, he paid his compatriot a merited compliment.

Further Reading

Bénichou, Paul. *The Consecration of the Writer, 1750-1830*. Translated by Mark K. Jensen. Lincoln: University of Nebraska Press, 1999. This study of French Romantic literature focuses on the period after the French Revolution, when writers no longer represented political or religious powers and became spiritual authorities in their own right. Gautier and other poets from the 1830's are discussed in chapter 9, "1830 and the Jeune France."

Coward, David. *A History of French Literature: From Chanson de Geste to Cinema*. Malden, Mass.: Blackwell, 2002. Includes a section on nineteenth century poetry with information on Gautier and other poets. Places Gautier in a broader literary context.

Cutler, Maxine. *Evocations of the Eighteenth Century in French Poetry, 1800-1869*. Geneva: Librairie Droz, 1970. Examines ten of Gautier's poems to reveal how he relied on both the poetic tradition and a sense of the immediate past as stimuli for his work.

Dillingham, Louise. *The Creative Imagination of Théophile Gautier: A Study in Literary Psychology*. Princeton, N.J.: Princeton University Press, 1927. Provides a psychological explanation for the production of Gautier's works, including the poems. Useful for understanding the unconscious sources of the poet's imagination.

Grant, Richard B. *Théophile Gautier.* Boston: Twayne, 1975. Introductory study aimed at providing an understanding of Gautier's work to general readers. A chapter on *Enamels and Cameos* discusses Gautier's vision of art as he expressed it in these poems; it also comments on structure and theme.

Majewski, Henry F. "Painting into Text: Theophile Gautier's Artistic Screen." *Romance Quarterly* 47, no. 2 (Spring, 2000): 84. Examines the relationship of painting to Gautier's poetry, discussing how he describes artworks and the role of paintings in poems from *Enamels and*

Cameos and other collections. Excerpts from the poems are provided in French, without English translation.

Richardson, Joanna. *Théophile Gautier: His Life and Times.* London: Max Reinhardt, 1958. Comprehensive biography of the writer. Comments on the publication of *Enamels and Cameos* and discusses its place in Gautier's canon. Also explores the diversity of ideas expressed in the poems that make up the volume.

Tennant, P. E. *Théophile Gautier.* London: Athlone Press, 1975. General introduction to the writer's works. Devotes part of a chapter to a discussion of *Enamels and Cameos.* Praises the variety of the collection, calling it "the melting pot of so many literary and artistic trends."

Encheiridion

Author: Epictetus (c. 55-c. 135)
First published: c. 138 C.E. (English translation, 1567)
Type of work: Philosophy

The *Encheiridion*, or "manual," is a collection of short essays representing the principal teachings of the Greek philosopher Epictetus. Born as a slave in Phrygia (now Turkey), Epictetus was brought to Rome by his master, who was an influential freedman of the Roman emperor Nero. Epictetus was permitted to study under the famous philosopher Musonius Rufus. After he obtained his freedom, he began to lecture informally on philosophy at Rome, where, however, he found few followers. Later, when Greek philosophers were exiled from Rome by Emperor Domitian, Epictetus traveled to Nicopolis in Greece and established a school that attracted large numbers of students. Like Socrates, Epictetus wrote nothing himself, but a devoted student, Flavius Arrian, transcribed his brilliant lectures and gave them the title *Discourses*; a considerable portion of this work survives. Arrian made a short selection of these lectures and published them separately as the *Encheiridion*. These two works, the only surviving examples of academic teaching by a Stoic philosopher, had enormous influence on the later development of this school of philosophy. Moreover, the *Encheiridion*, with its convenient distillation of the philosopher's powerful ethical message, left its mark on the thought of a wide range of later readers who include Marcus Aurelius, Michel Eyquem de Montaigne, Matthew Arnold, and Adam Smith.

Epictetus propounded the philosophy of Stoicism, which is named for the stoa or portico in ancient Athens where the earliest representatives of this school congregated. A chief objective of Stoicism is to secure happiness by overcoming the confusion caused by the emotions and to demonstrate the liberating powers of reason. The earlier Stoics also frequently engaged in academic disputes about physics, logic, and epistemology. By contrast, Epictetus cultivated a kind of popular philosophical sermon called the diatribe. His message was directed primarily not at specialists but at students of philosophy, though in fact most of these students were, like Arrian, from aristocratic families. Accordingly, the *Encheiridion* in its fifty-three short chapters seeks to encourage, to exhort, even to convert readers to the philosopher's life. Some scholars have emphasized Epictetus's beginnings as a slave and the influence of that experience on his teaching. Indeed, while the *Encheiridion*'s emphasis on the liberating power of reason is consistent with the writings of other Stoics, the personal style of the diatribe frequently suggests that the author was familiar with the realities of enslavement. Another striking difference between Epictetus and earlier Stoics is the religious tone in his work. Because he viewed reason as an aspect of the universe and of the divine, Epictetus demands a virtual conversion to philosophy. He goes far beyond philosophical predecessors in expecting his readers not merely to study philosophy but to ensure that each step taken in life is in harmony with divine reason.

The *Encheiridion* opens with a discussion of this important theme of the liberating power of reason, which allows people to differentiate between those aspects of life that can and those that cannot be controlled. Human attitudes, choices, desires, and aversions can be controlled through the exercise of reason; possessions, bodies, and lives cannot. True happiness can be secured only by abandoning the frustrating pursuit of or flight from the uncontrollable things. Control of desire and of aversion is key to the philosophy of Epictetus. Reason will tell people, for example, that if a piece of pottery they admire breaks, that pottery was merely something subject to breakage. Similarly, if a beloved child or spouse dies, reason will remind individuals that the loved ones were mortal and were subject to death. People seek to avoid what they think is harmful, but reason reveals that this perception actually resides in the human being, not in the thing itself. Epictetus applies the same analysis to the petty annoyances of life as to the fear of death: Whatever cannot be controlled should not be seen as dreadful. A famous dictum of Epictetus offers a summation of his teaching: "It is not things that disturb human beings, but their attitudes toward things."

The *Encheiridion* cites numerous everyday examples—repetition was a characteristic technique of the philosophical diatribe—to reinforce its message. Reason dictates that to take pride in a fine stallion one owns is, in fact, to take pride in what is not truly one's own and can be taken away. Disease or a handicap may be impediments to the body, but they need not be impediments to moral choice or to the exercise of reason. In a memorable comparison, Epictetus stresses that all the pleasures of life should be seen as merely given on loan. On a sea voyage, if people wander away from the ship at a port of call, captivated by the attractions of the unfamiliar place, they must be prepared to abandon everything and return to the ship when the captain calls. It is so in life, where, when the time comes, people must be prepared to leave behind spouse and child and all material things. Accordingly, Epictetus advises people to say of something not, "I have lost it," but rather, "I have returned it." Whatever takes away what was possessed should be seen as the instrument by which the Giver takes back what is given.

With his primarily aristocratic audience in mind, Epictetus addresses himself to the concerns of youthful ambition. By not striving for wealth or fame, people may indeed end up with fewer external things than could have been possible, but through the exercise of reason and moral choice, they

will gain freedom and true happiness. The aspiring philosopher, attempting to maintain the proper attitude toward external things, may appear ridiculous and clumsy. (Epictetus's vivid depiction of the ridicule the aspirant can expect may reflect his own early experience of teaching at Rome.) Nevertheless, despite this opposition, the philosopher will know how to live properly. Just as when delicacies are passed around at a feast and polite guests wait patiently until the dish comes their way (or not, as the case may be), so the philosopher will accept with equanimity what is given (or not given) in life. Like Heracleitos or Diogenes, the true philosopher may even take less than is given, as he attaches less importance to externals than do others.

In some respects, the Stoic attitude toward strong human emotions may seem brutal or simplistic. Epictetus warns his readers not to be moved too much by the apparent misfortune of another who has lost property or a child, because this event is no more than that, an apparent misfortune. All the same, the philosopher does recommend the expression of sympathy in moderation. Superstitious fear caused by an evil omen will yield to reason, which says, "Every omen is favorable, if I wish it so." Envy and jealousy are similarly vanquished by a sense of proportion and an understanding of what is, and is not, under control. The philosopher will understand that anger and irritation arise not from events themselves but from the human attitude toward events. Epictetus subjects friendship and patriotism to the same analysis. To the objection that without power or wealth people must abandon their friends, Epictetus answers that friends who require others to have what they have risk losing their moral purpose and are not true friends. Stoicism found great favor among the Romans because it did not preach a withdrawal from politics as the Epicureans did. At the same time, Epictetus urges that such service should be undertaken only to the extent that it does not compromise an individual's moral purpose.

Another central idea that Epictetus weaves into his work is the Stoic command to "follow Nature," that is, to learn to accept whatever happens as part of the natural order and not as misfortune. When a slave breaks one of the host's drinking cups, remarks Epictetus, all the guests say, "It happens." All people should say the same when their own cup is broken or even when their child dies. Nature is not evil, and the philosopher's moral purpose must be brought into harmony with it. Epictetus even analyzes social relationships in this way. A son who complains of a bad father was, after all, just "given" this father by nature; he should consider not what the father does, but what he himself should do to bring his own life in harmony with nature. Living according to nature will even bring an individual into a proper relationship with the gods, for by accepting whatever happens that individual acknowledges his or her just and proper governance of the universe.

In later chapters, the *Encheiridion* moves from these lofty thoughts to seemingly more trivial ones, such as how the philosopher should speak and behave in company, what kinds of entertainment to avoid, and how food, drink, and sex fit into the philosopher's lifestyle. These admonitions, which form a sizable proportion of this short work, are intended to cover the range of roles that the individual, like an actor, may be compelled to play in life. The metaphor of acting is conscious. As in learning a role for the theater, preparation for the philosophical life can be arduous, as difficult as becoming a master of rhetoric or competing at Olympia. Rather than specify each and every human situation, Epictetus offers what could be viewed as a simple rule of thumb: In a moment of perplexity, the philosopher might ask, "What would Socrates or Zeno do in this circumstance?" Epictetus clearly assigns great importance to showing others how to act by example, not merely by lecturing them. He notes that Socrates was eager to be a philosopher, but not at all eager to be recognized as one.

The *Encheiridion* exercised an enormous influence over later thinkers. Intended by Arrian as a useful epitome of his master's teaching, for some the manual came to represent pagan philosophy generally. Freethinkers such as Baruch Spinoza eagerly embraced a moral system that depends only vaguely on divine sanction, whereas Christian thinkers detected fascinating intimations of divine revelation in the writings of this Greek slave. In fact, the *Encheiridion* had the distinction of being the only pagan work adopted by early Christianity as a religious text. Paraphrases were prepared for use by monastic orders, with only slight alteration of the text. Later readers saw other merits and defects in the work. Blaise Pascal fulminated against the arrogance of Epictetus. Frederick the Great slept with a copy of the *Encheiridion* under his pillow. Matthew Arnold saw in Epictetus and his spiritual descendant, Marcus Aurelius, "the great masters of morals." It is arguable that no single book, except the New Testament, has provided so many with spiritual sustenance, solace, and sanity as the *Encheiridion* of Epictetus.

John M. Lawless

Further Reading

Arnold, E. V. *Roman Stoicism*. New York: Cambridge University Press, 1991. A valuable work on the development of Stoicism during the Roman Empire. Notable for its careful choice of citations in recounting Epictetus's philosophy.

Epictetus. *The Discourses as Reported by Arrian, the Manual, and Fragments*. Edited and translated by W. S. Oldfather. 2 vols. Cambridge, Mass.: Harvard University Press, 1925-1928. Standard edition of the complete works with Greek text and facing translation. Translation is very literal and therefore useful to consult for difficult passages. Contains a somewhat dated but still important introduction, as well as extensive English indexes.

_____. *Epictetus' "Handbook" and the "Tablet of Cebes": Guides to Stoic Living*. Edited and translated by Keith Seddon. New York: Routledge, 2005. A new translation of *Encheiridion* with extensive commentary on the work, as well as a lengthy introduction providing information on Epictetus's life and writings, Stoicism, and the key concepts in his philosophy. Includes a glossary of key Greek and English terms.

Long, A. A. *Hellenistic Philosophy*. New York: Charles Scribner's Sons, 1974. Chapter 4 provides background absolutely essential to understanding the philosophy of Epictetus. Provides an accurate sketch of the main tenets of Greek Stoicism that were modified by Epictetus.

Scaltsas, Theodore, and Andrew S. Mason, eds. *The Philosophy of Epictetus*. New York: Oxford University Press, 2007. Collection of essays examining various aspects of Epictetus's philosophy, including his Stoicism and ideas about cynicism, the self, and morality.

Stadter, Philip A. *Arrian of Nicomedia*. Chapel Hill: University of North Carolina Press, 1980. An interesting study of Arrian, who edited Epictetus's works but was also a biographer of Alexander the Great. Deals with problems of the transcription of Epictetus's lectures and provides insights into the period in which he lived.

Stephens, William O. *Stoic Ethics: Epictetus and Happiness as Freedom*. London: Continuum, 2007. A study of Epictetus's moral philosophy, focusing on his conception of happiness.

The End of the Road

Author: John Barth (1930-   )
First published: 1958
Type of work: Novel
Type of plot: Existentialism
Time of plot: 1951-1955
Locale: Wicomico, Maryland

Principal characters:
JACOB HORNER, a teacher of English and the narrator
JOE MORGAN, a teacher of history
RENNIE MORGAN, his wife
PEGGY RANKIN, a teacher of English
THE DOCTOR, a doubtful M.D.

The Story:

The End of the Road begins with some doubt as to the existence of the narrator, Jacob Horner. He tells readers that he became a teacher of English at Wicomico State Teachers College on the advice of the Doctor, never given a name, who operates a Remobilization Farm for the treatment of functional paralysis. Between this doubtful beginning and the nonending, John Barth examines the problems of existence and identity that began with his first novel, *The Floating Opera* (1956). Read on a literal level, the story is a rather banal love triangle involving Jacob, Joe Morgan, and Joe's wife. Read on a serious abstract-ethical level, it becomes the setting for a duel of opposing points of view, both concerned with the problems of nihilism.

Jacob meets the Doctor in a railroad station, where he goes after finishing his oral examination for his master's degree. In trying to decide where to go for a vacation, he is overcome by paralysis. He is unable to make a choice. No one destination seems better than another; his will to do anything at all is paralyzed. The Doctor takes him to his Remobilization Farm near Wicomico and begins a series of therapy sessions designed to avoid situations involving complicated choices, the point being to make some choice, any choice, in order to keep moving, so that he will not fall into immobility again. Mythotherapy, based on the existentialist premises that existence precedes essence, and that people are free not only to choose their essence but also to change it at will, is the chief therapy prescribed for Jacob. It is a process of assigning a role to himself and carrying it out logically. It is essentially a mask to protect the ego.

At the college, Jacob becomes acquainted with Joe Morgan and his wife, Rennie. The relationship quickly develops into a love triangle, but one in which the moral responsibility is shared equally by all three. Here, as elsewhere, Barth gives readers no chance to make any judgments, to fasten onto any solid ethical ground. *The End of the Road* is a short novel with the characters sketched and filled in quickly, with very little background or examination of motivational processes.

Jacob's modus operandi is mythotherapy. Joe's is one of ethical positivism; he has a set of consistent, relative values that he is trying to impress on Rennie. It is on Rennie that the action centers. While teaching Jacob to ride horseback, she tells him of her meeting with Joe and their subsequent relationship and marriage. Until she met Joe, she had no philosophy of her own, and she willingly erased her own personality to adopt that of her husband. She is still unsure of herself and not quite at ease with her adopted role. Later on, she comes to see Jacob as Satan, tempting her to abandon her assumed personality. She sees him as inconsistent, as having nothing but ever-changing masks, donning one after the other as the situation demands. Following logically, she sees Joe as a god: consistent, moral, and logically right. Over the battleground of Rennie, Jacob and Joe fight out their opposing points of view: Jacob with the shifting inconsistencies and limited goals of existentialism, Joe with his relative ethical values that deny any absolutes.

Rennie and Jacob commit adultery, almost casually, while Joe is away. The seeds were planted for it when Jacob and Rennie, peeking in on Joe after one of their rides, watched him making faces at himself in the mirror and engaging in a series of disgusting sex activities. Rennie was shattered; her god had his inconsistencies, too.

Rennie tells Joe of her infidelity, and he confronts Jacob with it. Instead of behaving like an outraged husband, Joe tries to find the reasons behind the deed. All Jacob can say is that he does not know why it happened. Joe's search for causes goes so far beyond the point of believability that it is viewed in abstract terms. The action is exaggerated until it becomes parody.

Jacob's relationship with Peggy Rankin is a parody of Joe and Rennie's relationship. Both fail: Joe's because it is too intellectualized and Jacob's because it is too physical.

Upon Joe's urging, Rennie visits Jacob several more times. She tells him that she does not know whether she hates or loves Jacob, but she wants to find out. When both Rennie and Joe visit Jacob one evening, it is to tell him that Rennie is pregnant and that they do not know whose child it is. All she knows is that she will commit suicide if she cannot have an abortion. This situation drives Jacob to decision and action.

Through a series of lies, impersonations, and gall, he convinces one of the local doctors to give Rennie something to make her abort. When he tells Rennie what he did and that she must give a false name and story, she refuses. She would rather shoot herself than lie. Jacob, by his imperfect realization of his role and his readiness to assume all the responsibility, becomes fully involved, but his commitment is the very thing that the Doctor told him he must avoid. Joe fails in his personal absolutism by turning to Jacob for an answer.

In desperation, Jacob goes to the Doctor and asks him to perform an abortion. The Doctor finally agrees on the condition that Jacob will give him all his money and go with him to a new location in Pennsylvania. Jacob agrees and brings Rennie to the Remobilization Farm. While on the operating table, Rennie dies.

Jacob is afraid that Joe will inform the police. Several days later, he receives a telephone call from Joe, who tells him that he took care of everything. Joe and his convictions suffer a mortal blow. He is lost and desperate. He turns to Jacob for an explanation, but Jacob has nothing to offer. Both positions—moral nihilism and ethical positivism—are wrecked in their encounter with reality. Joe is left to reconstruct his life. Jacob returns to the Doctor because he is not yet ready to assume the responsibilities of life.

Critical Evaluation:

There is no real moral center for any of the major characters in John Barth's *The End of the Road*. Those who begin by believing that they are in secure possession of such an unshakable core of moral certitude—most notably, Joe Morgan and his wife, Rennie—are forced to accept that they have deluded themselves, first in claiming that their philosophy offers a coherent view and response to the world, and second when it is made clear that they do not, in fact, fully embrace their own philosophy. In effect, they are living a lie, and it turns out to be a lie that is not even a useful one. This realization destroys them. In the case of Rennie, she is literally destroyed.

For the Doctor and especially for his patient, Jacob Horner, there is not even the pretense of an overriding moral philosophy to guide their actions and shape their perceptions of the world. Things simply are, and the Doctor quotes, without attribution, the philosopher Ludwig Wittgenstein: "The world is everything that is the case." The world, including human existence, must be accepted as it is, in all its conflicting confusion. There is no way to fashion it into an understandable unity. In this sense, both the Doctor and Horner are existentialists, accepting the essential absurdity of their situation and dealing with it by fashioning their own interpretations and even identities—interpretations and identities that are arbitrary and frequently changed. In the end, however, the tactics and response of existentialism prove as impractical as the moral absolutism espoused by Joe Morgan.

Ultimately, *The End of the Road* is concerned with two basic questions of identity and meaning: Who am I? What am I to do? Neither question is answered, and Barth's unspoken but inescapable conclusion is that there are no answers. The novel introduces the theme of identity and meaning in its opening sentence: "In a sense, I am Jacob Horner," writes the narrator, and throughout *The End of the Road* the sense of Jacob's reality—indeed, the reality of all of the characters—constantly shifts and changes. Jacob is encouraged in his mutability by the Doctor's highly idiosyncratic cures, most notable of which is mythotherapy, which demands the creation of a series of outward personalities totally unrelated to any inner condition. The point is for Jacob to continue acting in order to avoid the state of paralysis in which the Doctor initially finds him. Choice is essential, even if it is meaningless. As the Doctor advises Jacob, "If the alternatives are side by side, choose the one on the left; if they're consecutive in time, choose the earlier. If neither of these applies, choose the alternative whose name begins with the earlier letter of the alphabet."

Just as there is no morality to the Doctor's precepts for selection, there is no morality for Jacob's actions. His emotionally brutal seduction of Peggy Rankin, the English teacher he picks up on the beach, and his adultery with Rennie are equally without emotion or purpose. Traditional human motives, such as passion or even simple lust, are not truly applicable. Horner is acting only to be acting, to assert his existence. That the results are terribly destructive in terms of human life and suffering is, in the end, to him a matter of indifference, perhaps of incomprehension.

As counterpoint to Jacob's frightening flexibility, Barth presents Joe's mental and moral rigidity. In place of conventional morality he has erected his own system of rigorous intellectual honesty: Every action, every word, even every thought, must be capable of being explained and defended to the utmost. He is scornful and contemptuous of those who do not measure up to this standard, which he pursues to its logical, if absurd, conclusion. When he learns that his wife, Rennie, has committed adultery with Jacob, Joe reacts not as an outraged and deceived husband, but as a philosopher whose central tenets have been improperly and carelessly challenged. His response is to force Rennie to continue seeing Jacob, perhaps even having sex with him, until she can logically explain her actions—and Jacob's—to Joe's satisfaction. Since Rennie's actions have an emotional rather than logical basis, and since Jacob's actions have no reason at all, this proves impossible. The contradiction not only destroys the Morgans' marriage but also ultimately proves the cause for Rennie's death on the operating table during a botched abortion performed by the Doctor. By refusing to accept the reality and power of irrationality, Joe reveals the emptiness of his own philosophy and his life based on it.

The End of the Road is a bitter commentary on the plight of humanity. Barth, in his examination of nihilism, has given no answers. There are no moments of high good humor, as in *The Sot-Weed Factor* (1960), only an unrelieved pessimism. On the surface, the novel is akin to the Theater of the Absurd in its insistence on telling only the observable actions of a story. Barth points out no morals and draws no conclusions. The actions of his characters show that nihilism, in its several guises, is not an end in itself.

To present this bleak and arbitrary world, Barth creates a plot that is simple, even banal in its events, and presents it in a style of scrupulous meanness. Events and actions are described flatly, unemotionally, in language that tends to keep the reader uninvolved with the characters and their fates. The clarity of the language, which presents outward activities clearly and precisely, underscores the ambiguity and arbitrary nature of the human motives for those actions. With only one exception, a flashback that describes the initial meeting between Jacob and the Doctor, the novel is recounted in strictly chronological terms that could be broadly paraphrased as "This happened and then this happened and then nothing else happened." Since no action has any more meaning than any other action, nothing is emphasized, and little is analyzed. The plot is presented, but the meanings of actions are not revealed; characters are described, but their personalities are not disclosed. The reason for this is quite simple: In the world Barth has fashioned for his novel, actions have no meaning, and there are no personalities. For those involved, it is indeed the end of the road.

"Critical Evaluation" by Michael Witkoski

Further Reading

Bowen, Zack. *A Reader's Guide to John Barth*. Westport, Conn.: Greenwood Press, 1994. An accessible and helpful survey of Barth's writings, with valuable insights into the underlying philosophical themes that are at the core of *The End of the Road*.

Clavier, Berndt. *John Barth and Postmodernism: Spatiality, Travel, Montage*. New York: Peter Lang, 2007. Clavier analyzes Barth's work from a perspective of postmodernism and metafiction, focusing on theories of space and subjectivity. He argues that the form of montage is a possible model for understanding Barth's fiction.

Fogel, Stanley. *Understanding John Barth*. Columbia: University of South Carolina Press, 1990. An excellent introductory account of Barth's fictions, including his early "ethical" novels, *The Floating Opera* and *The End of the Road*.

Harris, Charles. *Passionate Virtuosity: The Fiction of John Barth*. Champaign: University of Illinois Press, 1983. A scholarly discussion of Barth's fiction, ranging over philosophical and psychological sources.

Scott, Steven D. *The Gamefulness of American Postmodernism: John Barth and Louise Erdrich*. New York: Peter Lang, 2000. Scott applies postmodernist theories to analyze Barth's work. He theorizes on the motifs of play and game in American postmodernist fiction generally, eventually focusing on "gamefulness" in the writings of Barth and Louise Erdrich.

Thorpe, Jac. *John Barth: The Comic Sublimity of Paradox*. Carbondale: Southern Illinois University Press, 1974. Through his concentration on the philosophical content of Barth's works, Thorpe sheds light on the ethical and existential situations in *The End of the Road*.

Walkiewicz, E. P. *John Barth*. Boston: Twayne, 1986. This brief but informative book is undoubtedly one of the best places to start in a study of John Barth.

Endgame
A Play in One Act

Author: Samuel Beckett (1906-1989)
First produced: 1957, as *Fin de partie*; first published,
    1957 (English translation, 1958)
Type of work: Drama
Type of plot: Absurdist
Time of plot: Indeterminate
Locale: Unnamed

Principal characters:
HAMM, a blind and disabled man
CLOV, his attendant, possibly his son
NAGG and NELL, Hamm's legless parents

The Story:

The world is nearing its end when Clov begins another day. He carefully surveys his employer's unfurnished living space, then with the aid of a ladder looks out each window. With a single laugh, he seems to sum up what he sees. He then moves on to uncover two trash cans, one at a time, and looks inside each. With a brief laugh once again, he sums up what he sees within and then replaces the lids. He goes to remove the sheet that is covering the man he is caring for, Hamm, who sits in a makeshift wheelchair made of a wooden armchair on casters. Hamm is dressed in a housecoat, socks, a felt hat, and dark glasses to cover his sightless eyes.

Hamm awakens slowly and pulls off the bloodstained handkerchief that has been covering his face. Then, Clov says "it" is nearly finished. Hamm talks briefly to himself, ending his little monologue by saying that it is time to play the game. The two men talk about their daily routines, about each day being filled with the same questions and the same answers.

Clov, although able to stand and walk, is unable to sit down. Through habit, he has learned how to parry Hamm's orders and insults by talking back and by taking his time about doing as he is told. More than once, Clov threatens to leave Hamm for good, yet he continues the repartee with Hamm until interrupted by Hamm's father, Nagg, who lifts the lid on his trash can to beg for pap, food that is commonly given to the elderly or to infants.

Nagg pounds on the lid of the other can until his wife, Nell, pokes her head out. He asks her if she wants to make love, but because they are both in trash cans and have no legs, this is quite impossible. From their conversation, it becomes clear that Nagg and Nell lost their legs years earlier in a tandem accident and are now forced to live in the trash cans. Hamm, supposedly trying to sleep, tells his parents to be quiet, yet Nagg rambles on, regaling Nell with a long, involved joke that she has heard from him over and over again.

Tired of listening to them, Hamm orders Clov to "bottle them up." Clov closes the lids of the trash cans. Hamm then orders Clov to push him on a ride around the room. During the ride, Hamm hugs the walls of his domain. He orders Clov to put him back where he was before, then they argue about whether Hamm is now in the exact center of the room, where he is supposed to be.

Hamm then orders Clov to look out the window to see if anything has changed. Clov reports back that the weather is the same, "light black from pole to pole." However, a change seems imminent, as Clov feels a flea on his body. Fearing that humanity will start all over again, Hamm and Clov work desperately to kill the flea. Hamm then asks Clov if his dog is near. Like the makeshift wheelchair, the dog is actually a manufactured dog with only three legs. Again, as always, Hamm insists that Clov tell him about the dog's looks and color.

Nagg, reappearing from his trash can, begins to tell a story about Hamm's background as his son and how, for the most part, he and Nell ignored him just as Hamm is now doing to them. Hamm then begins to tell his own story, recalling how he was the lordship of a large estate, and how a beggar had come to him begging for food, and how the beggar gave his only son to Hamm. The question of the identity of Clov's actual father comes up, but without any resolution.

Nagg then raps on the lid of Nell's trash can and gets no answer. Clov checks on her and announces that she is dead. Nagg slides back down into his trash can and is covered by Clov.

Hamm lapses into a monologue, as Clov continues to keep busy about the room, still threatening to leave. Clov looks out the window again, and this time it seems there might be a change: A small boy may be visible in the distance. Clov delivers a monologue of his own before heading into the kitchen to pack his things. Meanwhile, Hamm settles down to sleep, or to die. Clov comes back into the room and watches silently as Hamm rambles on and on with more stories of his own.

Nagg apparently is still alive, although he remains closed up in his trash can. Hamm sits in his wheelchair, quietly waiting to die, and Clov, dressed and ready to leave, does not depart. Thus ends the game for the day.

Critical Evaluation:

Born in Dublin, Ireland, in 1906, Samuel Beckett lived in Paris during the 1920's and made his permanent residence there from 1937 until his death more than fifty years later. In the late 1940's, Beckett, who had published a few novels and some poetry in English, began writing in French, with almost immediately positive results. Beginning with *Molloy* (1951; English translation, 1955) Beckett achieved critical if not popular success, exploring the possibilities and limits of the novel. Ironically, however, it was as a playwright, composing originally in French, that Beckett achieved his full measure of fame and critical acclaim, initially with *En attendant Godot* (pb. 1952, pr. 1953; *Waiting for Godot*, 1954).

As with his novels, Beckett prepared his own English translations of the plays, achieving an originality of style that had eluded him when he wrote originally in English. *Endgame* was his second play to be performed and published, its fortunes closely rivaling those of the earlier, groundbreaking *Waiting for Godot*. With the early efforts of Eugène Ionesco and Jean Genet, Beckett's first two plays helped to define and illustrate the trend described, analyzed, and labeled by Martin Esslin in 1961: Theater of the Absurd. Although the three playwrights were, as Esslin points out in his study *The Theatre of the Absurd*, more different than similar, their combined works would redefine and reorient the "serious" Paris stage for the next two or three decades, with worldwide repercussions.

Endgame is interpreted by certain observers as a psychodrama portraying the fragmentation of the human personality. Much of the so-called stage business, prescribed in the written text, accounts for a fair share of the action: Clov folding sheets, moving or stepping on the stepladder, or wheeling Hamm around the room. Hamm, although stationary, utilizes gestures and poses that constitute stage business as well, such as his movement with his glasses, or his handkerchief or stuffed pet dog. Many of these moments of stage business help to instill a comic effect that is a counterpoint to the depressing aspects of the play, or "the game." Many of the lines in the play, in particular those of Hamm, reference the game, how it is proceeding, and how it ends.

The dialogue often deals with various elements of humanity. The aspect of aging is approached in the conversations between Hamm and his father, Nagg, who seems to return to his infancy by needing his pap and by feeling he is no longer needed or wanted; thus the reason for his living in an ash bin, or trash can. A constant game exists between Clov and Hamm: Clov wants to know if he is Hamm's son. A monologue by Hamm, which Clov does not hear, makes it clear that Clov is indeed his son, or is considered so by Hamm. The game comprises the continuous torture of the characters, whether by each other or by the desolate world around them. It is a game the characters are all forced, or choose, to play.

Endgame has four highly individuated and memorable characters, and their interactions are no less dramatic for the compression of dialogue and plot that often borders on the cryptic. The end of the world is at hand, and play, or playing, is all that is left to do. By the end of the play the audience is left with questions: Is this actually the final stage of the game, much like in chess, the endgame, or does the game continue to go on and on? Because the play ends with the characters in a tableau, only Beckett knows the answers.

If the desolate landscape of *Waiting for Godot* can be likened to that of war-torn, occupied France, the ravaged interior of *Endgame* seems to suggest the threat of a world laid to waste by nuclear war. In neither case, however, is the equation expressly stated. Interpretation is left to the director, actors, and spectators. Arguably, *Endgame* is addressed even more to the actor than to the spectator, as its greatest potential impact derives from participation in the play that is made central.

Following the success of *Endgame*, Beckett went on to write *Krapp's Last Tape* (pr., pb. 1958), an equally remarkable spectacle featuring a single actor and a tape recorder on which the character has attempted to keep track of time; the play also explores time's effects on his personality. Unlike most of Beckett's other mature work in any genre, *Krapp's Last Tape* was written first in English, then translated into French. Although Beckett continued to write for the theater well into the 1970's, none of his later pieces achieved quite the success or impact of his first three efforts for the theater. *Endgame* remains perhaps the most remarkable, rivaled only by *Waiting for Godot*.

David B. Parsell; revised by Carlos Perez

Further Reading

Chevigny, Bell Gale, ed. *Twentieth Century Interpretations of "Endgame."* Englewood Cliffs, N.J.: Prentice-Hall, 1969. Contains illuminating contributions by director Alan Schneider and critics Ross Chambers and Hugh

Kenner, among others. Also features an excerpt from Martin Esslin's landmark book *The Theatre of the Absurd*.

Fletcher, John. *Samuel Beckett: "Waiting for Godot," "Endgame," "Krapp's Last Tape."* London: Faber & Faber, 2000. A critical guide designed to introduce readers to the three plays. Contains analysis of the plays' language, structure, characters, and features of performance. Includes a select bibliography.

Gontarski, S. E., ed. *On Beckett: Essays and Criticism*. New York: Grove Press, 1986. Essays by various scholars, including Ruby Cohn's "Beckett Directs: *Endgame* and *Krapp's Last Tape*," which discusses Beckett's adeptness at staging.

Kalb, Jonathan. *Beckett in Performance*. New York: Cambridge University Press, 1989. An exhaustive and perceptive production study of Beckett's plays, primarily in Western Europe. Contains good information on productions of *Endgame*.

Kennedy, Andrew K. *Samuel Beckett*. New York: Cambridge University Press, 1989. Published shortly before Beckett's death, Kennedy's study provides a balanced view of all of his work. Offers a particularly stimulating analysis of Beckett's plays in general and *Endgame* in particular.

Knowlson, James. *Damned to Fame: The Life of Samuel Beckett*. New York: Simon & Schuster, 1996. Knowlson,

Beckett's chosen biographer, provides a meticulously detailed book, containing much new material, detailed notes, and a bibliography.

McDonald, Rónán. *The Cambridge Introduction to Samuel Beckett*. New York: Cambridge University Press, 2006. Chapter 3 of this concise overview of Beckett's life and work includes a discussion of *Endgame*.

McMillan, Dougald, and Martha Fehsenfeld. *From "Waiting for Godot" to "Krapp's Last Tape."* Vol. 1 in *Beckett in the Theatre*. London: Calder, 1988. Complements Jonathan Kalb's study of *Beckett in Performance*. Contains useful production notes and history on *Endgame*.

Popovic Karic, Pol. *Ironic Samuel Beckett: Samuel Beckett's Life and Drama—"Waiting for Godot," "Endgame," and "Happy Days."* Lanham, Md.: University Press of America, 2007. Analyzes the three plays from the perspective of irony, demonstrating how Beckett uses irony as a means of communication, catharsis, and freedom for characters living in a world of permanent chaos.

Worton, Michael. "*Waiting for Godot* and *Endgame*: Theatre as Text." In *The Cambridge Companion to Beckett*, edited by John Pilling. New York: Cambridge University Press, 1994. This analysis of the two plays, written by a professor of French language and literature at University College London, is included in a collection of essays examining Beckett's work.

Endymion
A Poetic Romance

Author: John Keats (1795-1821)
First published: 1818
Type of work: Poetry
Type of plot: Narrative
Time of plot: Ancient times
Locale: Mount Latmos, the Garden of Adonis, caverns, a place under the ocean, Neptune's palace, the sky, and the Cave of Quietude

Principal characters:
ENDYMION, a shepherd
PEONA, his sister
CYNTHIA, the Moon goddess
GLAUCUS, an ancient man condemned by Circe
INDIAN MAIDEN, an incarnation of Cynthia

The Poem:

The narrator begins the poem with the famous line "A thing of beauty is a joy for ever" and the brief argument that "All lovely tales that we have heard or read" bring happiness because they "Haunt us until they become a cheering light/ Unto our souls." The narrator then traces the story of Endymion, a young shepherd.

Endymion and his people gathered to worship the shepherd-god Pan at an altar on Mount Latmos. Endymion was not caught up in the mood of the festivities. Instead, he was depressed and dreamy. His sister, Peona, worried about him and pulled him aside to ask about the source of his sorrow. Endymion told her about the dream he had had. In the dream, he saw his idealized version of womanly perfection. He told Peona that he fell in love with the woman in his dream, and when he awoke to find himself alone, the world seemed repulsive and he felt heartbroken. Peona urged her brother not to waste away his life on a dream woman whom he would never find.

Endymion digressed and told his sister that there are various degrees of happiness, from the simplest to the loftiest. Peona asked her brother why he would pursue love over fame, and he replied that there are three sources of happiness. The first is sensual pleasure that comes from direct experience with nature, such as hearing the music the wind makes with an aeolian harp. The second is pleasure that comes from art, especially of old heroic stories. The third is the best source of happiness: relationships. Endymion spoke of the happiness of human "entanglements" that allow people to get beyond the self and the limits of a single existence. Endymion determined that friendship is a "steady splendor," but love is loftier—a "radiance" where two souls "interknit." Endymion explained that men who might have achieved deeds of heroism have chosen love instead, finding in it contentment because love makes the soul feel its immortality. Endymion suggested to Peona that love is worth more than fame. Endymion told Peona that since his dream, he saw the face of his dream lover in a well and heard her voice coming from a cave. Endymion resigned himself to a life of unrequited love and took Peona's hand and "stept into the boat, and launch'd from land."

Endymion began his search for his dream lover. He met a naiad who warned him that he must search in remote regions for the woman of his dreams if he wished to find consummation. When a voice urged him to descend, a despondent Endymion moved onward to the Garden of Adonis. He found Adonis, Venus's love, asleep. Venus arrived as Adonis awoke. Adonis beseeched Venus to have pity on Endymion. Venus and her minions vanished. Endymion wandered farther and found a giant eagle that flew him farther into caverns. With the "power to dream deliciously," Endymion found his dream lover. She told him that she loved him, but she could not bring him to Olympus. She did not reveal her name. (She was Cynthia, Moon goddess and the goddess of chastity.) After they made love, Endymion fell asleep and she left him. Endymion woke up in deeper despair. He came upon two streams, Alpheus and Arethusa—two streams who wanted to intermingle but could not because Cynthia would not allow it. Endymion pled his case to the "gentle Goddess of [his] pilgrimage" to "assuage" the lovers' pains of Alpheus and Arethusa. The vision of the rivers disappeared, and Endymion saw "the giant sea above his head."

At the bottom of the sea, Endymion met Glaucus, an ancient man who was condemned to sit at the bottom of the sea for a thousand years because he had witnessed Circe deform some of her lovers and turn others into beasts. Glaucus welcomed Endymion as his savior, the one who fulfilled the end of Circe's curse. Glaucus's curse had begun when he entered the sea. There, he had encountered his first love, Scylla, dead. Glaucus had placed Scylla's body in a crystal mausoleum. Many years passed before he encountered another being. A ship capsized and Glaucus found a dead man clenching a scroll. The scroll foretold that a youth would rescue Glaucus at the end of his thousand years of suffering. Until the rescue, it was Glaucus's responsibility to place all drowned lovers at each other's side in the crystal mausoleum.

Moved by Glaucus's tale, Endymion helped the old man regain his youth by performing rituals that reanimated the dead lovers in the crystal mausoleum. Rejoicing, the lovers went to Neptune's palace. During the festivities at Neptune's palace, Venus told Endymion that she had discovered the identity of his immortal lover. Endymion fainted and was carried upward by Nereids to a crystal bower. While unconscious, Endymion heard in his "inward senses" the voice of his beloved, who promised him that they would soon be together and bade him to awake.

Endymion awoke near a placid lake in a green forest and met a beautiful Indian Maiden. She longed desperately for love because she had been deserted by Bacchus. Despite his love for his dream lover, Endymion fell in love with the Indian Maiden (who was actually Cynthia). Endymion was torn between the two lovers. Two flying horses appeared to Endymion and the Indian Maiden. The lovers mounted the winged pair and flew upward. During the journey, they fell asleep. While asleep, Endymion learned that his dream lover and Cynthia were the same entity. Endymion was still also drawn to the Indian Maiden. When the Indian Maiden disappeared, Endymion entered the Cave of Quietude.

Endymion returned to Earth, still torn between his earthly love for the Indian Maiden and his divine love for Cynthia. Endymion encountered the Indian Maiden and told her their love was hopeless because of his love for Cynthia. Endymion decided to live out the rest of his life as a hermit. The Indian Maiden revealed that she was Cynthia. Peona watched as the two lovers disappeared together.

Critical Evaluation:

John Keats died at age twenty-five. He wrote at a feverish pace and left behind a body of work distinguished by its genius. His poetry ranks him among the greatest Romantic poets. Keats was deeply influenced by Edmund Spenser's *The*

Faerie Queene (1590, 1596) and the works of Leigh Hunt. This influence is especially evident in *Endymion: A Poetic Romance.*

Keats wanted to write a "long poem" that would be a "trial of invention." The poem became *Endymion*, an effort of some four thousand lines that he wrote in less than a year, the result of Keats's self-imposed poetic apprenticeship. In it, he appropriates (and often changes) Greek myth.

Keats was not satisfied with *Endymion*, aware of the extent and nature of the poem's shortcomings. In a letter to John Taylor, his publisher, Keats wrote, "I am anxious to get *Endymion* printed so that I may forget it." He thought of the poem as an exercise or tool in his growth as a poet. He put forth his negative thoughts on *Endymion* in the preface to the poem, where he spells out his regret that he made it public: "What manner I mean, will be quite clear to the reader, who must soon perceive great inexperience, immaturity, and every error denoting a feverish attempt, rather than a deed accomplished." Keats places himself somewhere between the healthy "imagination of a boy" and "mature imagination of a man"—a place where "the soul is in a ferment, the character undecided, the way of life uncertain. . . ." From such ferment derives what Keats called the "mawkishness" of *Endymion.*

The structure of *Endymion* follows what Jack Stillinger calls a "spatial conception of two realms in opposition and a mythlike set of actions involving characters shuttling back and forth between them." In book 1, Endymion and his sister occupy the actual world, although Endymion wants to move up to the realm of the ideal world—a place of higher reality. In books 2, 3, and 4, Endymion journeys on a quest for his dream lover, occupying realms of the fantastic. In book 4, Endymion briefly returns to the actual world but disappears back into the ideal world. The pain-pleasure dichotomy of life is addressed in *Endymion*—as in most of Keats's works—with the painful aspect existing in the actual world and the pleasure aspect existing in the idealized world. To make this dichotomy work, Keats, at his best, generally employs character pairings of mortals and immortals.

In *Endymion*, Keats freely borrows from Greek mythology, using the character of Endymion, a chieftain king, and his passion for the Moon goddess Cynthia (known in Greek mythology as Diana). Keats is very free in his interpretation of Cynthia, generally considered a goddess of chastity, the Moon being out of reach. The "pleasure thermometer" passage, so named from a letter Keats sent to his publisher, Taylor, sets the tone of the poem and allows the introduction of eroticism and sexual imagery. Endymion's encounters with his dream lover Cynthia occur in dreams, but they are any-

thing but chaste. Instead, they are very erotic; the lovers entwine, pant, sigh, faint, caress—the supposedly chaste Cynthia speaks of melting into Endymion. This eroticism is balanced by sexual imagery in the poem. The love between Adonis and Venus in the Garden of Adonis is presented as a sexual relationship that can never develop or mature. On the other hand, the relationship between Glaucus and Circe symbolizes the destructive nature of mature sexuality. The sexual relationship that Endymion seeks with Cynthia lies somewhere between that of Adonis and Venus and that of Glaucus and Circe—an idealized, mature sexual relationship that is emotionally fulfilling. By combining Endymion's dream lover into the earthly Indian Maiden and the spiritual Cynthia, Keats allows Endymion to attain the highest level of pleasure on the pleasure thermometer: an immortal love in which two souls "interknit."

Through the use of dream visions, Keats makes a statement about the growth of the human mind through the imagination—one of the principles of the Romantics. Although *Endymion* is an immature work, it is interesting in its approach to the inner workings of the mind involved in a young man's experience of erotic love, which seems to be the poem's central idea. Fluent and facile, *Endymion* gains its power from Endymion's search for self-fulfillment through beauty and sex. Given the poem's abrupt ending, it may well be that Keats discovered the full meaning of a young man's experience of erotic love after he finished writing *Endymion.*

Thomas D. Petitjean, Jr.

Further Reading

Blades, John. *John Keats: The Poems.* New York: Palgrave, 2002. Detailed textual analysis of the themes and techniques in Keats's poems, including a discussion of *Endymion* in chapter 2. Places Keats's poetry within the contexts of his life and of nineteenth century Romantic literature.

Bloom, Harold, ed. *John Keats.* Updated ed. New York: Chelsea House, 2007. Collection of essays providing various interpretations of Keats's poetry, including "Lisping Sedition: Poems, *Endymion*, and the Poetics of Dissent," by Nicholas Roe.

Mayhead, Robin. *John Keats.* New York: Cambridge University Press, 1967. Discusses *Endymion* in the context of Keats's entire body of works. This study serves as a basic introduction to Keats and his works.

Stillinger, Jack, ed. Introduction to *John Keats: Complete Poems.* Cambridge, Mass.: Belknap Press, 1982. Stillinger, the definitive Keats scholar, presents all of Keats's poems with a readable introduction that defines a basic critical approach.

Walsh, William. *Introduction to Keats*. New York: Methuen, 1981. Walsh uses the commentaries of a number of respected Keats scholars to place *Endymion* in the appropriate critical context and rank among Keats's other works.

Wolfson, Susan J. *The Cambridge Companion to Keats*. New York: Cambridge University Press, 2001. The book's essays discuss common characteristics of Keats's poetry, including the sources of his allusions, his use of language, and his representation of gender. "*Endymion*'s Beautiful Dreamers," by Karen Swann, analyzes this poem.

Endymion, the Man in the Moon

Author: John Lyly (c. 1554-1606)
First produced: 1588; first published, 1591
Type of work: Drama
Type of plot: Comedy
Time of plot: Antiquity
Locale: Ancient Greece

Principal characters:
ENDYMION, a courtier
CYNTHIA, the queen, loved by Endymion
TELLUS, in love with Endymion
EUMENIDES, Endymion's friend
SEMELE, loved by Eumenides
CORSITES, in love with Tellus
DIPSAS, an enchantress
GERON, her long-lost husband
SIR TOPHAS, a fop
FLOSCULA, Tellus's friend
DARES and SAMIAS, Eumenides' pages
BAGOA, a servant of Dipsas

The Story:

To his friend Eumenides, Endymion declares his love for Cynthia, goddess of the Moon. Eumenides chides Endymion, reminding him of the Moon's inconstancy, whereupon Endymion extols inconstancy and change as virtues, attributes of everything beautiful. Convinced that Endymion is bewitched, Eumenides prescribes sleep and rest for the lovesick swain, but Endymion rejects the advice and berates his friend.

In the hope of misleading his friends, Endymion has also professed love for Tellus, a goddess of the Earth. Enraged by his apparent perfidy, Tellus swears to take revenge. Because she still loves Endymion, Tellus is unwilling for him to die; therefore, she resolves to resort to magic and witchcraft in order to awaken his love for her. Her friend Floscula warns that love inspired by witchcraft will be bitter, but Tellus ignores the warning and leaves to consult Dipsas, an enchantress.

In contrast to Endymion and Tellus, Sir Tophas habitually scoffs at love and has dedicated his life to war—against blackbirds, mallards, and wrens. When mocked by Endymion's and Eumenides' pages, Dares and Samias, Sir Tophas swears to kill them, but he pardons them when they explain

that they have been speaking in Latin. Meanwhile, Tellus has found Dipsas, whom she consults about the possibility of killing Endymion's love for Cynthia and supplanting it by magic with love for the Earth goddess herself. Dipsas declares that since she is not a deity, she can only weaken love, never kill it. At Tellus's request, Dipsas agrees to enchant Endymion in such a way that his protestations of love for Cynthia will be doubted. Accompanied by Floscula and Dipsas, Tellus confronts Endymion in a garden and tries to make him confess his love for Cynthia. Although he admits that he honors Cynthia above all other women, he insists that he loves Tellus.

Later, the two pages, Dares and Samias, stroll in the gardens with their own ladyloves, whom they have shown Endymion and Eumenides in the act of mooning over their own loves. As a jest, Dares and Samias ask the two women to feign love for Sir Tophas, who, as usual, is playing at warfare in the gardens. The women comply, but Sir Tophas, ignoring them, reiterates his contempt for love and his passion for war.

Still later, Dipsas comes upon Endymion asleep in a grove. Assisted by Bagoa, her servant, Dipsas casts a spell on

Endymion to keep him in a sleep from which he will not awaken until he is old and gray. In a dream, three women appear to Endymion, and one of them starts to stab him. When asked by the third woman to stop, the first woman peers into a looking glass and throws down her knife. At this moment, an old man appears carrying a book that contains only three pages. Endymion refuses to read the book until the man has torn up two of the pages.

When informed of Endymion's mysterious slumber, Cynthia agrees with Eumenides that the sages of the world should be consulted about a remedy. Angered by the impertinence of Tellus, Cynthia makes her a prisoner in Corsites' palace, where she is to weave tapestries depicting stories of people who have been punished for their long tongues.

On the way to Thessaly, where Cynthia is sending him to seek a cure for Endymion, Eumenides meets Geron, an old hermit. Geron says that if Eumenides were a faithful lover, he could learn the cure from a magic fountain nearby. Since Eumenides has always been true to Semele, the fountain promises to grant any single wish he might make. Although tempted to wish that his love for Semele might be requited, he dutifully asks for a cure for his friend. The fountain answers that the cure is a kiss from Cynthia.

Tellus, slowly pining away in prison, promises Corsites, her jailer and suitor, that she will marry if he can perform the impossible task of bringing Endymion to a cave, where she might see him once more. Corsites undertakes this task but is put to sleep by fairies guarding Endymion's body.

Thus Cynthia finds two sleeping men when she arrives at the grove accompanied by wise men who she hoped will wake Endymion. The sages succeed in waking only Corsites, who freely confesses his love for Tellus and what that love has inspired him to do. At last, Eumenides returns and persuades Cynthia to attempt the cure. Upon her kiss, Endymion wakes, but his forty-year slumber has withered him: He is so senile that he cannot stand. At Cynthia's request, however, he relates his strange dream, explaining that, in the book that the old man gave him to read, he saw Cynthia being attacked by beasts of ingratitude, treachery, and envy. Cynthia promises to listen later to a fuller account of this vision.

A short time later, Bagoa discloses that Tellus and Dipsas were responsible for enchanting Endymion. For her pains, Bagoa is transformed into an aspen tree by Dipsas. Cynthia is more lenient than Dipsas. Learning that Tellus was motivated by unrequited love, Cynthia forgives her and gives her to Corsites as his wife. Dipsas, too, is pardoned, on condition that she will be reunited with Geron, her husband, whom she sent away many years ago. This reunion displeases Sir Tophas, who has discarded his armor out of love for Dipsas;

he is content, however, when Cynthia disenchants Bagoa and gives her to Tophas as his wife. To Eumenides, she promises Semele, but Semele objects on the grounds that Eumenides did not ask for her at the magic fountain. She is placated, however, when Geron explains that Eumenides would not have learned the fountain's secret had he not been faithful. Most important, Cynthia restores the youth of Endymion and tells him to persevere in his love.

Critical Evaluation:

Most famous for his novel *Euphues, the Anatomy of Wit* (1578), John Lyly was also a prolific playwright. He was the most fashionable English writer in the 1580's, praised as the creator of a "new English." Certainly *Endymion, the Man in the Moon* made possible such later plays as William Shakespeare's *A Midsummer Night's Dream* (pr. c. 1595-1596, pb. 1600) and *As You Like It* (pr. c. 1599-1600, pb. 1623). Lyly's comedies were a great advance over those of his predecessors. He possessed a unique skill in taking the Italian pastoral and Latin comedy of intrigue and adapting them to the English style by combining them with fanciful plot and mythological characters as well as characters from the lower levels of English life. The grace and charm of his witty dialogue and his analysis of love were not surpassed until Shakespeare's later comedies.

Lyly was chief dramatist for the company of boy players attached to St. Paul's Cathedral, the favorite entertainers of Queen Elizabeth's court. The structure and style of *Endymion* would have been appreciated by their educated audience. The play is filled with references and allusions directed especially to this audience. The division of *Endymion* into acts and scenes is molded on Latin precedent, and the stage directions are of the classical pattern also employed by Ben Jonson: At the head of each scene are listed the characters who take part in it. The stage setting, however, is romantic; places separated by vast distances (the lunary bank, castle in the desert, and fountain) were represented by sections of the same platform stage, and the journey was visualized by stepping across the stage. The treatment of time in the play was that of a fairy tale.

The story of Cynthia, the Moon goddess, and Endymion was probably borrowed from the Roman poet Lucian. Sir Tophas is a blend of Latin parasite and braggart soldier. To the Elizabethan court, the main interest in the play lay in its reference to contemporary personalities. Cynthia was associated with Queen Elizabeth, and Tellus—in her jealousy, her captivity in a desert castle, and her wiles—must have recalled Mary, queen of Scots, who was beheaded in 1586. Endymion must have suggested the earl of Leicester.

Endymion is undeniably an effete, even trivial play. The plot is inconsequential and artificial, the characters unreal, the dialogue pedantic. The work is significant historically in that Lyly was trying to make the English theater a high art. Writing for the court rather than the populace, Lyly replaced the earthiness and crudity of earlier English plays with refinement and polish, thereby setting new standards that later dramatists, including Shakespeare, emulated. Although today's audiences will likely find the play precious, it nevertheless possesses great charm and wit, as well as much beauty and humor, and has been unjustly neglected in the centuries since Lyly's death.

Further Reading

Braunmuller, A. R., and Michael Hattaway, eds. *The Cambridge Companion to English Renaissance Drama*. 2d ed. New York: Cambridge University Press, 2003. Although none of the essays in this collection deals specifically with Lyly, there are references to *Endymion* and some of his other plays listed in the index. These references help place his plays within the broader context of English Renaissance drama.

Hunter, G. K. *John Lyly: The Humanist as Courtier*. London: Routledge & Kegan Paul, 1962. The work against which subsequent criticism of Lyly is compared. Suggests that Lyly was motivated primarily by a desire to establish himself at Elizabeth I's court. Concentrates on *Endymion* more than any other play.

Knapp, Robert S. "The Monarchy of Love in Lyly's *Endimion*." *Modern Philology* 73 (May, 1976): 353-367. Argues that Lyly is intentionally enigmatic, mixing a wide range of possible interpretations under the general heading of love allegory.

Lenz, Carolyn Ruth Swift. "The Allegory of Wisdom in Lyly's *Endimion*." *Comparative Drama* 10, no. 3 (Fall, 1976): 235-257. Analyzes the play in terms of sixteenth century religious and philosophical thought, with special reference to Neoplatonic conceptions of love.

Pincombe, Michael, ed. *The Plays of John Lyly: Eros and Eliza*. New York: Manchester University Press, 1996. A study of Lyly's eight plays, including *Endymion*, with a separate chapter devoted to each. Focuses on the courtly aspects of his plays, the majority of which were written for court performance.

Saccio, Peter. *The Court Comedies of John Lyly: A Study in Allegorical Dramaturgy*. Princeton, N.J.: Princeton University Press, 1969. Suggests a complex dramaturgical structure involving both moral and political allegory. Includes an eighteen-page section on *Endymion* and many other references to the play.

Enemies
A Love Story

Author: Isaac Bashevis Singer (1904-1991)
First published: Sonim, de Geshichte fun a Liebe, 1966 (English translation, 1972)
Type of work: Novel
Type of plot: Domestic realism
Time of plot: Mid-twentieth century
Locale: New York City and upstate New York

Principal characters:
HERMAN BRODER, a young Jewish immigrant from Poland
TAMAR RACHEL BRODER, his first wife
YADWIGA PRACZ, his present wife
MASHA TORTSHINER, his mistress
SHIFRAH PUAH BLOCH, her mother
RABBI MILTON LAMPERT, Herman's wealthy employer

The Story:

On a summer morning, Herman Broder stirs from his troubled dreams, wondering if he is in Nazi-occupied Poland, perhaps in the hayloft where his parents' servant girl, Yadwiga, concealed him in order to save his life. Then, fully awake, he realizes that he is in the apartment in Brooklyn that he shares with Yadwiga, whom he marries after learning of the deaths of his wife and his children.

Herman tells Yadwiga that he must make another of his overnight train trips to sell books. Actually, he remains in New York City, spending the day in the office of Rabbi Milton Lampert, for whom Herman works as a ghostwriter, and the night at the apartment of his mistress, Masha Tortshiner, and her mother, Shifrah Puah Bloch, who are also Holocaust survivors. Although Masha knows that Herman is married, her mother does not. She is determined to have Masha get a divorce from her husband, Leon, so that she can marry Herman.

One day, Shifrah Puah calls Herman's attention to a notice in the newspaper asking him to telephone a certain number. When he makes the call, Herman finds himself speaking to the uncle of his first wife, Tamara, who, it seems, is alive and in New York. When Herman and Tamara are reunited, he is surprised to find her prettier than ever and considerably easier to get along with than she was in the past. Although Herman knows that he must choose between his two wives, he has to admit that he would like to keep them both, and the volatile Masha as well.

Herman's trips to see Tamara arouse Masha's suspicions, even though she does not guess that Herman's first wife has come back from the dead. Herman thinks he might be able to reassure Masha about his feelings for her during a vacation in the Adirondack Mountains that they are planning. At first, they do relax and enjoy themselves, but then Masha tells Herman that she is pregnant. Taken by surprise, Herman rashly promises to marry Masha.

Blithely ignoring the fact that Herman is already married, which, after all, involves only a mere Gentile, Masha works on getting a divorce. Meanwhile, Herman's other two relationships with women are becoming even more complicated. On an outing in the Catskill Mountains, he and Tamara, who were merely friends, find themselves making love and enjoying it. Then, Yadwiga decides that she can become closer to her husband if she converts to Judaism and gives him a Jewish child. Though he does not want to bring a child into a world so full of cruelty and suffering, Herman cannot refuse her.

Herman is still managing to keep the three women apart. However, he worries constantly about exposure, which he knows will cost him his job with the rabbi and might well lead to his being imprisoned or deported. He has a little time to decide about which of his present wives to keep, because he married Yadwiga in all innocence, believing Tamara to be dead. However, he will have no excuse, moral or legal, for acquiring a third wife.

Quite unexpectedly, Leon Tortshiner offers Herman a way out. He meets with Herman in order to warn him that Masha is a promiscuous, deceitful woman. Leon tells Herman that Masha was consistently unfaithful during their marriage and also that she betrayed Herman by sleeping with Leon as the price of obtaining her divorce. Herman's immediate response is to end the relationship with Masha; however, she manages to convince him that it is Leon who is lying, and the two are married after all.

By the time winter arrives, Herman is in serious financial trouble. Yadwiga is expecting a baby, which means more bills in Brooklyn, and, after Masha's pregnancy turns out to be purely psychological, she is too depressed to work, and so Herman has to provide all the support for the Bronx household as well. As a new convert to Judaism, Yadwiga is driving Herman crazy with her questions about a faith he no longer observes.

Finally, the inevitable happens. First, Tamara drops in at the Brooklyn apartment, and Yadwiga recognizes her. Then some neighbors bring a gossipy man named Nathan Pesheles to meet Mrs. Broder, and, though Tamara pretends to be Herman's cousin, Pesheles takes a good look at Yadwiga. When Rabbi Lampert finds out that Herman recently married, he visits Masha and invites the newlyweds to a party. One of the rabbi's guests is the observant Pesheles. He promptly informs Masha that he met a Tamara Broder at Herman's apartment in Brooklyn, thus tipping her off to the fact that the dead wife is not dead, and then goes on to tell everyone else, including the rabbi, that, in addition to Masha, Herman also has a pretty, pregnant wife named Yadwiga.

Before the evening ends, the kindly rabbi offers Masha a job and both Masha and her mother a place to live. Masha accepts, telling Herman that she never wants to see him again. Tamara comes to Herman's rescue, taking him in, giving him a job in her uncle's bookstore, and even helping Yadwiga in any way she can.

Then, just when things are going well, Masha comes back into Herman's life. Now she wants him again, and he agrees to run away with her. However, she is delayed, first by finding that her apartment is burglarized, then by her mother's death. Herman and Masha consider a double suicide, but finally Herman decides to leave not only Masha but also everyone else.

Masha kills herself. Yadwiga moves in with Tamara, who runs the bookstore while Yadwiga takes care of their place and of her baby girl, little Masha. No one ever knows what happens to Herman.

Critical Evaluation:

Generally considered the most important Yiddish writer of the twentieth century, Isaac Bashevis Singer won a Nobel Prize in Literature in 1978, in large part because of his recreation of a world that no longer exists. Singer often wrote about life in Polish-Jewish villages before they and their inhabitants were destroyed by the Nazis. *Enemies*, however, is set in the postwar, post-Holocaust period. Its subject is serious: the ways in which those who survived the Holocaust dealt with their memories and built new lives.

Appropriately, *Enemies* begins with Herman Broder's reliving the past. Even though he is now safe, Herman has been forever changed by his experiences. He has lost his faith in God and in human life. While he has married again, Herman hedges his bets by also keeping a mistress and remaining open to other possibilities. He is adamantly opposed to having more children, for it is clear that one cannot count on a beneficent God to preserve them. In fact, all that Herman now believes in are lust, which existed even in the death camps, and deceit, which he believes is the only way one can make it through the world.

Singer also shows how his four major women characters have responded to the Holocaust. Shifrah Puah wears black to keep alive the memories of those who died and feels guilty because she is alive. However, Shifrah still believes in God and observes the Jewish rituals.

Masha hates God as much as her mother loves him. Now, the central reality in her life is the Holocaust. Masha finds sexual stimulation in telling stories of those days while she and Herman are making love. Masha is enchanted with death, and, indeed, she does finally commit suicide.

In a sense, Tamara does die in the Holocaust, for she has become a new person: more unselfish, more considerate, and far wiser than she was before the war. After she and Herman are reunited, Tamara asks nothing for herself, not even that he return to her. Ironically, it is Tamara who now becomes Herman's only real friend and confidant. Even when he tells her that he is running off with Masha, Tamara accepts his decision with grace, and it is she who will fill Herman's place at the bookstore and care for his wife and his child.

It is also ironic that it is a Polish Catholic, Yadwiga, who replaces Herman within the Jewish community. What begins as her attempt to please her husband by observing his rituals ends with her wholeheartedly accepting the faith in which he no longer believes. Although Herman would blame his Holocaust experience for his actions, Singer points out that Herman's character was formed long before the Nazis came to power. It is appropriate that, at the end of the novel, the self-centered Herman, if not dead, is alone somewhere, while the generous Yadwiga is being cherished by her new community.

The tone of *Enemies* is not uniformly serious. Like the village storytellers from whom he drew his inspiration, Singer delights in the eccentricities of human behavior and in the capacity of human beings to make fools of themselves. Herman's adventures in *Enemies* are essentially farcical, and Herman himself, though appealing, is devoid of common sense. After he escapes from the Nazis by hiding from them and from God by denying him, Herman uses his new freedom to become the willing slave of lust, especially as it is embodied in the equally irrational Masha.

Of his three wives, Masha alone is as irrational and as self-destructive as Herman. While both Tamara and Yadwiga try to keep Herman out of trouble, Masha always encourages him to behave like a fool. She gets him to marry her at the risk of being imprisoned or deported, and eventually she causes him to lose his job. Then, after ending the relationship with him, she quits her job and persuades him to quit his so that they can run off together; she even agrees with him that, because of a slight hitch in their plans, they might as well commit suicide. Ironically, at that point Herman is saved by his own irrationality. When Masha confesses that she deceived him about sleeping with her husband, Herman fails to see the parallel with his lying about sleeping with his wife Tamara, and he decides not to kill himself after all. Like a thwarted child, he decides to quit the whole world.

As it is applied to Herman and Masha, Singer's subtitle, "A Love Story," points to the accuracy of the title "Enemies." Certainly these two lovers are each other's worst enemies. However, the epilogue suggests that love can be redemptive rather than destructive. Thus, after Herman has rejected their aid and turned his back on life, Yadwiga and Tamara find gratification in helping each other, in loving the child Herman left them, and in being a part of the community which, through this new Jewish child, will itself be renewed.

Rosemary M. Canfield Reisman

Further Reading

Alexander, Edward. *Isaac Bashevis Singer: A Study of the Short Fiction*. Boston: Twayne, 1980. A thorough and insightful work. The chapter devoted to *Enemies* emphasizes the importance of the Holocaust in the novel and in Jewish intellectual history.

Farrell, Grace, ed. *Critical Essays on Isaac Bashevis Singer*. New York: G. K. Hall, 1996. Collection of essays, including pieces by literary critics Irving Howe, Susan Sontag, Alfred Kazin, John Bayley, and Leslie Fielder, providing numerous interpretations of Singer's works. "Death by the Word: Victims of Language in *Enemies: A Love Story*" by Marilyn R. Chandler analyzes this novel.

_____. *Isaac Bashevis Singer: Conversations*. Jackson: University Press of Mississippi, 1992. A collection of interviews in which *Enemies* is frequently mentioned. Singer points out that he understands Herman Broder's lack of belief in God but does not share his attitude.

Friedman, Lawrence S. *Understanding Isaac Bashevis Singer*. Columbia: University of South Carolina Press, 1988.

Shows how the novel reflects its post-Holocaust setting. The Jews who survived and immigrated to America had to deal with religious doubt, along with their loss of a common language and of a sense of community.

Hadda, Janet. *Isaac Bashevis Singer: A Life*. New York: Oxford University Press, 1997. Focusing on both the forces of family and the social environment that influenced Singer, Hadda uncovers the public persona to reveal a more complex man than previously understood.

Kresh, Paul. *Isaac Bashevis Singer: The Magician of West Eighty-sixth Street*. New York: Dial Press, 1979. An insightful critical biography. The brief but useful discussion of *Enemies* argues that Singer himself was the model for Herman Broder.

Lee, Grace Farrell. *From Exile to Redemption: The Fiction of Isaac Bashevis Singer*. Carbondale: Southern Illinois University Press, 1987. Systematically traces the development of Singer's thought, classifying the late work *Enemies* as a story of redemption. Although Herman exiles himself from God, Yadwiga and Tamara affirm their faith by nurturing a Jewish child.

Noiville, Florence. *Isaac B. Singer: A Life*. Translated by Catherine Temerson. New York: Farrar, Straus and Giroux, 2006. An informative biography written in concise, easy-to-read language. Noiville gleans information from interviews with Singer's wife, son, friends, and colleagues, as well as from his autobiography, *In My Father's Court* (1966). She focuses on Singer's life struggles, his relationships with others, and the adversity he had to overcome as a Jewish writer.

Qiao, Guo Qiang. *The Jewishness of Isaac Bashevis Singer*. New York: Peter Lang, 2003. Analyzes the Jewishness in Singer's work, finding a unique place for the writer within American Jewish literature. Focuses on Singer's depiction of past and present Jewish assimilation in both Poland and the United States, examines Singer's narrative strategies, and compares the Jewish identity and Jewish historical consciousness in works by Singer, Saul Bellow, Bernard Malamud, and Philip Roth.

Wolitz, Seth L., ed. *The Hidden Isaac Bashevis Singer*. Austin: University of Texas Press, 2001. A collection of essays, including discussions of Singer's use of the Yiddish language and cultural experience, themes that persist throughout his writing, his interface with other times and cultures, his autobiographical work, and a translation of a previously unpublished "gangster" novel.

An Enemy of the People

Author: Henrik Ibsen (1828-1906)
First produced: En folkefiende, 1883; first published, 1882 (English translation, 1890)
Type of work: Drama
Type of plot: Social criticism
Time of plot: Late nineteenth century
Locale: Southern Norway

Principal characters:
DR. THOMAS STOCKMANN, a medical officer
MRS. STOCKMANN, his wife
PETRA, his daughter
PETER STOCKMANN, his brother, the mayor
MORTEN KIIL, Mrs. Stockmann's father
HOVSTAD, an editor
BILLING, a subeditor
ASLAKSEN, a printer
CAPTAIN HORSTER, Dr. Stockmann's friend

The Story:

All the citizens of the small Norwegian coastal town are very proud of the Baths, for the healing waters make the town famous and prosperous. Dr. Stockmann, the medical officer of the Baths, and his brother Peter, the mayor and chairman of the Baths committee, do not agree on many things, but they do agree that the Baths are the source of the town's good fortune. Hovstad, the editor of the *People's Messenger*, and his subeditor, Billing, are also loud in praise of the Baths.

Business is good, and the people are beginning to enjoy prosperity.

Then Dr. Stockmann receives from the university a report stating that the waters of the Baths are contaminated. Becoming suspicious when several visitors became ill after taking the Baths, he felt it his duty to investigate. Refuse from tanneries above the town is oozing into the pipes leading to the reservoir and infecting the waters. This means that the big pipes will have to be relaid, at a tremendous cost to the owners or to the town. When Hovstad and Billing hear this news, they ask the doctor to write an article for their paper about the terrible conditions. They even speak of having the town give Dr. Stockmann a testimonial to honor him for his great discovery.

Dr. Stockmann writes up his findings and sends the manuscript to his brother so that his report can be acted upon officially. Hovstad calls on the doctor again, urging him to write articles for the *People's Messenger*. It is Hovstad's opinion that the town fell into the hands of a few officials who do not care about the people's rights, and it is his intention to attack these men in his paper and urge the citizens to get rid of them in the next election.

Aslaksen, a printer who claims to have the compact majority under his control, also wants to join in the fight to get the Baths purified and the corrupt officials defeated. Dr. Stockmann cannot believe that his brother refuses to accept the report, but he soon learns that he is wrong. Peter goes to the doctor and insists that he keep his knowledge to himself because the income of the town will be lost if the report is made public. He says that the repairs will be too costly, that the owners of the Baths cannot stand the cost, and that the townspeople will never allow an increase in taxes to clean up the waters. He even insists that Dr. Stockmann write another report, stating that he was mistaken in his earlier judgment. He feels this action necessary when he learns that Hovstad and Billing know of the first report. When the doctor refuses to change his report or to withhold it, Peter threatens him with the loss of his position. Even the doctor's wife pleads with him not to cross his powerful brother; he is sustained in his determination to do right only by his daughter Petra.

Hovstad, Billing, and Aslaksen are eager to print the doctor's article so that the town can be aware of the falseness of the mayor and his officials. They think his words so clear and intelligible that all responsible citizens will revolt against the corrupt regime. Aslaksen does plead for moderation but promises to fight for what is right.

Peter Stockmann appears at the office of the *People's Messenger* and cleverly tells Aslaksen, Hovstad, and Billing that the tradespeople of the town will suffer if the doctor's report is made public. He says that they will have to stand the expense and that the Baths will be closed for two years while repairs are made. The two editors and the printer then turn against Dr. Stockmann and support Peter, believing that the majority would do so.

The doctor pleads with them to stand by the promises they gave him, but they are the slaves of the very majority opinion they claim to mold. When they refuse to print his article, the doctor calls a public meeting in the home of his friend, Captain Horster. Most of the citizens who attend already dislike him because the mayor and the newspaper editors spread the news that he wants to close the Baths and ruin the town. Aslaksen, nominated as chairman by the mayor, so controls the meeting that a discussion of the Baths is ruled out of order.

Nevertheless, Dr. Stockmann takes the floor and in ringing tones tells the citizens that it is the unbelievable stupidity of the authorities and the great multitude of the compact majority that causes all the evil and corruption in the world. He says that the majority destroys freedom and truth everywhere because the majority is ignorant and stupid. The majority is really in slavery to ideas that long outlived their truth and usefulness. He contends that ideas become outdated in eighteen or twenty years at the most, but that the foolish majority continues to cling to them and deny new truths brought to them by the intelligent minority. He challenges the citizens to deny that all great ideas and truths are first raised by the persecuted minority, those few who dare to stand out against the prevailing opinions of the many. He says that the real intellectuals can be distinguished as easily as can a thoroughbred animal from a crossbreed. Economic and social position has no bearing on the distinction. It is a man's soul and mind that separate him from the ignorant masses.

Dr. Stockmann's challenge goes unheard. As he knows, the majority cannot understand the meaning of his words. By vote they name him an enemy of the people. The next day they stone his house and send him threatening letters. His landlord orders him to move. He loses his position as medical director of the Baths, and his daughter Petra is dismissed from her teaching position. In each case the person responsible for the action states that it is public opinion that forced that action. No one has anything against him or his family, but no one will fight the opinion of the majority. Even Captain Horster, a friend who promised to take the Stockmanns to America on his next voyage, loses his ship because the owner is afraid to give a ship to the only man who stands by the radical Dr. Stockmann.

The doctor learns that his father-in-law bought up most of the now-undesirable Bath stock with the money that was to go to Mrs. Stockmann and the children. The townspeople accuse the doctor of attacking the Baths so that his family can buy the stock and make a profit, and his father-in-law accuses him of ruining his wife's inheritance if he persists in his stories about the uncleanliness of the Baths. Reviled and ridiculed on all sides, Dr. Stockmann determines to fight back by opening a school. Starting only with urchins he finds on the streets, he will teach the town and the world that he is stronger than the majority, and that he is strong because he has the courage to stand alone.

Critical Evaluation:

The Norwegian playwright Henrik Ibsen, considered by many to be one of the greatest dramatists of all time, is also called the founder of modern drama. In the mid-1870's, he created a new tradition of realistic prose drama that dealt boldly with contemporary social problems and individual psychology, offering an alternative to the melodrama that had dominated early nineteenth century theater. In the first twenty-five years of his career, Ibsen wrote romantic and historical dramas designed to glorify Norway and to wean Norwegian audiences from popular Danish plays. With his later, major works—twelve prose dramas of increasing complexity, beginning with *Samfundets støtter* (1877; *The Pillars of Society*, 1880) and ending with *Naar vi dø de vaagner* (1899; *When We Dead Awaken*, 1900)—Ibsen set a standard for realistic theater that would be emulated throughout the Western world. Ibsen's nineteenth century audiences were often shocked by the new and realistic subject matter of his plays. *Gengangere* (1881; *Ghosts*, 1885) openly referred to inherited venereal disease, and *Et dukkehjem* (1879; *A Doll's House*, 1880) displayed an astonishingly liberal attitude toward the emancipation of women. Both plays were attacked as "immoral" and banned from several cities in Europe.

An Enemy of the People, though somewhat less controversial, was revolutionary in its unflinching portrayal of the greed and self-interest in small-town politics. Ibsen spares almost no one as he examines the power of self-interest to shape human attitudes toward truth and civic responsibility. The townspeople are portrayed in act 4 as little more than an unthinking mob. In fact, Ibsen at times seems so critical of the power of the "compact majority" that some scholars interpret his play as an elitist attack on democracy. The extreme vacillation of the newspapermen, Hovstad and Billing, seems marked for special scorn. They enthusiastically support but then quickly abandon Dr. Stockmann as soon as they perceive their self-interest differently. Even Stockmann himself, heroic figure that he might be, is clearly motivated by self-interest. In the first act, his excitement over the discovery of pollution in the Baths is obviously motivated, at least in part, by extreme and petty competitiveness with his brother Peter. Stockmann is so absorbed in the singularity of his discovery that he naïvely ignores its obvious ramifications, hoping instead for rewards from the town. At the end of the play, Stockmann declares that "the strongest man in the world is he who stands alone," but he is ignoring his family,

who will have to stand and suffer along with him. With nearly everyone in the play motivated and blinded by self-interest, Ibsen seems to imply that this distorting power dominates nearly all human minds and thus all aspects of human life.

Only a minor character, Captain Horster, seems free from the motivations of self-interest. Horster offers his house for Stockmann's speech in act 4 when no one else in the town dares support him, and at the end of the play Horster offers his house to the Stockmanns permanently, even though he has been dismissed from his ship's command as a result of his support of Stockmann. Horster has nothing to gain from helping Stockmann and no particular interest in the political issues involved. He helps Stockmann simply because Stockmann is a friend in need.

Horster functions in this play as a kind of *raisonneur*, a type of character who usually appears as a minor figure somewhat detached from the action and who represents a calm, levelheaded, rational standard against which the usually more irrational behavior of other characters is contrasted and measured. Ibsen's use of this traditional kind of dramatic character is unusually subtle. Horster is almost a shadowy figure in the play, appearing infrequently and saying little, though his presence can be very powerful in a sensitive reading or state production of the play. In his entrance with Stockmann in the first scene, Horster's reluctance to take advantage of Stockmann's somewhat extravagant largess is very subtly contrasted with the gluttony of Billing, who greedily gobbles up Stockmann's roast beef. Though he says little, Horster's words are powerfully indicative of the rational standard that underlies the play. When Billing loudly asserts that "a community is like a ship; every one ought to be prepared to take the helm," Captain Horster responds to this easy platitude with one line of hard, common sense: "Maybe that is all very well on shore; but on board ship it wouldn't work."

Ibsen's realistic style inaugurated a new style of drama because the settings, characters, and issues of his plays comment directly and forcefully on the life of his audiences. Ibsen is also called the father of modern drama because his plays possess a rich, thematic complexity typical of twentieth century literature. In his later plays, an increasing use of symbolism generates an even more complex, dense, and poetic drama. Ibsen's technical brilliance in the service of thematic complexity is already clear in *An Enemy of the People*. In Stockmann's discovery of the polluted Baths, Ibsen presents a very modern situation—the genuine dilemma with no satisfactory solution. The Baths are obviously dangerous and must be closed, but the closing of the Baths will also destroy the town, and it is the unresolvable nature of this dilemma between social responsibility and business interests that dominates the play. The accumulation of incidents in the play makes that dilemma clearer until the audience must accept a dramatic situation with no satisfactory resolution. In the play's first two acts, all "right-thinking" people appear to agree that the Baths must be closed. In act 3, when Peter specifically outlines the economic devastation that will result from the closing of the Baths, nearly everyone in town shifts to Peter's point of view. Now Dr. Stockmann stands alone. In act 5, Ibsen adds a final twist to the situation. Stockmann's father-in-law, Morten Kiil, has used Mrs. Stockmann's inheritance to purchase the remaining stock in the Baths. Stockmann's persistence in closing the Baths now financially endangers his entire family and could destroy them as well as him. The price of idealism has been raised to an uncomfortable level. Thus, at the end of the play, Ibsen makes it impossible for the audience to choose sides comfortably. Stockmann can easily appear supercilious, even unbalanced, as he announces in the last scene that he will remain in town and start his own school, recruit "street urchins—regular ragamuffins," and "experiment with curs." Is Stockmann a hero, a fool, or both? The audience is unable to resolve their ambiguous attitudes toward Stockmann and the town that turned against him. They thus experience through Ibsen's play the radical uncertainty that typifies much of twentieth century literature and thought.

"Critical Evaluation" by Terry Nienhuis

Further Reading

Gray, Ronald D. "*An Enemy of the People*." In *Ibsen: A Dissenting View*. New York: Cambridge University Press, 1977. Gray develops in a interesting way the widely held theory that *An Enemy of the People* is an allegory on the hostile reception generally given Ibsen's previous play, *Ghosts*.

Haraldsson, Róbert. *Plotting Against a Lie: A Reading of Ibsen's "An Enemy of the People."* Reykjavík: University of Iceland Press, the Philosophical Institute, 2004. Argues that Dr. Stockmann is not a "mouthpiece" for Ibsen, although the playwright identifies with Stockmann's plight as well as with his ideas about truth and human nature.

Hornby, Richard. "The Validity of the Ironic Life: *An Enemy of the People*." In *Patterns in Ibsen's Middle Plays*. Lewisburg, Pa.: Bucknell University Press, 1981. An extremely thorough and convincing interpretation of the play as an ironic portrait of Dr. Stockmann, a "multifaceted" character "mixing noble and base impulses."

Knutson, Harold C. "*An Enemy of the People*: Ibsen's Reluctant Comedy." *Comparative Drama* 27 (Summer, 1993): 159-176. Analyzes the comic tone of the play. In Stockmann's inflated ego Ibsen is, to some extent, consciously parodying himself.

Ledger, Sally. *Henrik Ibsen*. 2d ed. Tavistock, England: Northcote House/British Council, 2008. Includes a close reading of *An Enemy of the People*, placing the play within its cultural, historical, and intellectual contexts.

McFarlane, James, ed. *The Cambridge Companion to Ibsen*. New York: Cambridge University Press, 1994. Collection of essays, including discussions of Ibsen's dramatic apprenticeship, historical drama, comedy, realistic problem drama, and working methods. The references to *An Enemy of the People* are listed in the index.

Robinson, Michael, ed. *Turning the Century: Centennial Essays on Ibsen*. Norwich, England: Norvik Press, 2006. Collection of the essays published in the journal *Scandinavica* during the past four decades, including discussions of Ibsen's style, his language, and the reception of his plays in England. One of the essays analyzes *An Enemy of the People*.

Shaw, George Bernard. "*An Enemy of the People*: 1882." In *The Quintessence of Ibsenism*. 1891. Reprint. New York: Hill and Wang, 1958. Shaw's book introduced Ibsen to England and helped make Ibsen's works popular worldwide. It remains an indispensable guide to the plays.

Templeton, Joan. *Ibsen's Women*. New York: Cambridge University Press, 1997. Templeton examines the women characters in Ibsen's plays and their relationship to the women in the playwright's life and career. Chapter 7 includes an analysis of *An Enemy of the People*.

Weigland, Hermann J. "*An Enemy of the People*." In *The Modern Ibsen: A Reconsideration*. New York: E. P. Dutton, 1960. Originally published in 1925, Weigland's essay is still one of the most thorough examinations of the play.

The English Patient

Author: Michael Ondaatje (1943-   )
First published: 1992
Type of work: Novel
Type of plot: Historical realism
Time of plot: 1930-1945
Locale: Tuscany, Italy; Cairo; Egyptian-Libyan desert

Principal characters:
LADISLAUS DE ALMÁSY, a Hungarian count, a desert explorer, and the badly burned "English" patient
HANA, his Canadian nurse
DAVID CARAVAGGIO, an Italian Canadian thief turned spy
KIRPAL "KIP" SINGH, an Indian who works for the British army's bomb disposal unit
GEOFFREY CLIFTON, an English pilot, adventurer, and spy
KATHARINE CLIFTON, Almásy's lover and Geoffrey's wife

The Story:

Near the end of World War II in 1945, the Villa San Girolamo in Tuscany, Italy—a former nunnery and German headquarters—has become a badly bombed out Allied military hospital. All the hospital staff and patients have moved on with the Allies, who are advancing across Europe. The only ones left behind are Hana, a twenty-year-old Canadian nurse from Toronto, and her badly burned and unidentifiable dying patient, who is believed to be English. Hana is joined at the villa by David Caravaggio—an Allied spy from Toronto who is a friend of her father—and Kirpal (Kip) Singh, a Punjabi Indian military engineer, or sapper, who works for the British army dismantling and defusing bombs. This motley foursome spends the summer of 1945 together in the villa.

All four characters have experienced losses due to the war. Hana's father, Patrick, and her lover have both been killed in action, and she miscarried the child she conceived with that lover. The English patient—Count Ladislaus de Almásy—was forced to abandon his injured former lover, Katharine Clifton, after her husband intentionally crashed an airplane in an attempt to kill all three of them; he was prevented from returning to her rescue by the outbreak of the war. Caravaggio, an Italian Canadian thief turned spy, lost his thumbs when he was captured and interrogated by the Germans. Kip left his home in Punjab to fight in the war in Europe and lost his mentor, Lord Suffolk, when a bomb that Suffolk had been trying to defuse exploded. The four main characters also experience a loss of home and identity in their war-torn setting: All are foreigners in Tuscany.

Over the course of the summer of 1945, Kip and Hana (who celebrates her twenty-first birthday that summer) become intimate but celibate friends, but celibate for only one month. Caravaggio, who has become addicted to morphine, takes it upon himself to uncover the identity of the "English" patient through the use of morphine, to which the patient is also addicted. Almásy's history is revealed nonchrono-

logically, in bits and pieces. Hana first learns of his journeys as a desert explorer from 1930 to 1936. After many years of searching, he and his companions finally found the lost oasis of Zerzura. Aided by morphine, he continues his story to Caravaggio. He met Geoffrey and Katharine Clifton in 1936. About a year and a half later, he and Katharine had a tempestuous and passionate affair that she initiated and eventually broke off after a year.

Although his wife's affair was over, Clifton—a pilot, adventurer, and spy for the British—became mad with jealousy at the knowledge of it. While flying with Katharine to pick up Almásy in September, 1939, Goeffrey attempted to kill all three of them by crashing the plane into Almásy with his wife still on board. The plane missed Almásy; Geoffrey died on impact, but Katharine lived. Almásy carried Katharine's badly injured body to a nearby cave, the Cave of Swimmers, and left on foot to get help. He walked seventy miles in three days, reaching the British military installation at El Taj, but the soldiers there did not believe Almásy's story. Instead of providing help to save Katharine, they imprisoned Almásy on suspicion of espionage.

Three years later, Almásy escaped, determined to return to the Cave of Swimmers to retrieve Katharine's body. To gain the necessary supplies, he agreed to guide the German spy Eppler across the desert to Cairo. When Almásy recounts this episode to Caravaggio, Caravaggio becomes certain of the patient's identity. He reveals to Almásy that British Intelligence officials had known about the affair between the English-educated Hungarian desert explorer and the wife of their agent, Clifton. They had suspected him of murdering Geoffrey, and they had planned to kill Almásy in the desert in 1942 but were unable to locate him.

Almásy reveals to Caravaggio how he evaded death. Almásy went to look for Katharine's body in the Cave of Swimmers. He brought a gasoline can with him and carried her body to a buried plane that once belonged to his partner in desert explorations, Madox. (Madox had returned to England in 1939 at the start of the war and had committed suicide in a church.) Almásy was able to uncover and start the plane, but it caught fire and crashed before he could reach his destination. Almásy was badly burned in the accident, but he was looked after by Bedouins in exchange for his knowledge of weaponry. The Bedouins eventually brought him to Siwa Oasis, and he was flown to Italy by the Allies.

In August, 1945, Kip hears on his radio that atomic bombs have been dropped on Hiroshima and Nagasaki. Upset by what he sees as yet another betrayal by the West of the East, he leaves on his motorcycle. Hana writes him letters that he never answers. Eventually, he becomes a doctor, marries, and has two children, but he still thinks frequently about Hana.

Critical Evaluation:

The English Patient, Michael Ondaatje's third novel, won the Booker Prize, the Canadian Governor General's Award, and the Trillium Award. It was in part a sequel to *In the Skin of a Lion* (1987), which featured Patrick, Hana, and Caravaggio. In 1996, *The English Patient* was adapted by Anthony Mighella into a very successful film that focused mainly on the love affair between Almásy and Katharine Clifton. The film won nine Academy Awards, including Best Picture, Best Director, Best Film Editing (Walter Murch), and Best Actress in a Supporting Role (Juliette Binoche). It also won three Golden Globe Awards, including Best Picture and Best Director, as well as five British Academy of Film and Television Arts Awards, including Best Film.

Ondaatje is both a poet and a novelist. *The English Patient* combines the best of both genres: It has a very powerful, elegiac, lyrical, imagistic, and romantic quality, and it also has a very strong sense of narrative setting (historical, geographical, artistic, and architectural) and plot (the mystery of the unidentifiable burned patient). In addition, Ondaatje skillfully weaves into his story an intertextuality that blurs genres and texts. He includes direct quotations from bomb manuals, historical sources, British Geographical Society meeting minutes, popular songs, poems, letters, and other novels—including Rudyard Kipling's *Kim* (1901), Stendhal's *La Chartreuse de Parme* (1839; *The Charterhouse of Parma*, 1895), and Leo Tolstoy's *Anna Karenina* (1875-1877; English translation, 1886). He also includes quotations from the biblical stories of David, Solomon, Jeremiah, and Isaiah; Tacitus's *Ab excessu divi Augusti* (c. 116; *Annals*, 1598), and—most of all—Herodotus's *Historiai Herodotou* (c. 424 B.C.E.; *The History*, 1709). Pushing the boundaries of genre and of text also allows Ondaatje to emphasize his theme of the blurring of personal and national identities in the theater of war.

Ondaatje is mainly concerned with the ways in which history and memory produce personal and national identity. In *The English Patient*, national identity is secondary to the personal identity that is formed through love. Almásy proclaims, "Erase nations!" Romantic love is transgressive, crossing and confusing boundaries. Almásy is primarily identified by his love for the desert and his love for Katharine, each of which crosses boundaries. He is an explorer and cartographer of a shifting and inhospitable landscape, and his love for Katharine is illicit. Both loves feature prominently in Almásy's bedraggled, annotated, and supplemented copy of Herodotus's *The History*, which becomes a symbol of his self and his life. The book becomes all that remains of him after his death.

As Almásy puts it, "Words . . . have a power." The mutilated and addicted Caravaggio, a man who is physically and spiritually fragmented, rediscovers his friend's daughter Hana and reestablishes his love for her, which is both paternal and erotic. She creates a necessary link to his personal past, but his future is indeterminate: Readers never discover what happens to Caravaggio after the war. Like Almásy's love for Katharine, Caravaggio's love for Hana is not clearly redemptive. The emotionally scarred Hana and the socially and culturally alienated Kip uncover a sacred and sensual love for each other based on mutual need (the war, her father's death, and his mother's death). Their relationship transcends nation, race, and culture. However, it is broken and betrayed by the atomic bombing of Hiroshima and Nagasaki, an attack of the West on the East. Once again, this relationship reflects a love that is temporarily satisfactory but ultimately unfulfilling.

The personal stories and identities of Ondaatje's characters intersect and clash with their national identities and the politics of war. These postcolonial conflicts are most clearly seen in Almásy (whose identity becomes central to the story's plot) and Kip (a Punjabi Indian who has been transplanted to Europe). In addition to its postcoloniality, *The English Patient* is marked by the postmodernity of its highly subjective, arbitrary, and associative treatment of history and memory and of its rampant intertextuality. This attitude is most clearly reflected in Almásy's copy of Herodotus's *The History*. In spite of the novel's engagement with postcoloniality and postmodernity, Ondaatje has very successfully created a story that is accessible, aesthetically pleasing, and appealing. His beautiful prose and powerful images carry the novel.

Lydia Forssander-Song

Further Reading

Friedman, Rachel D. "Deserts and Gardens: Herodotus and *The English Patient*." *Arion: A Journal of Humanities and the Classics* 15, no. 3 (Winter, 2008): 47-83. Discusses the use to which Ondaatje puts Herodotus's text in *The English Patient*.

Ganapathy-Doré, Geetha. "The Novel of the Nowhere Man: Michael Ondaatje's *The English Patient*." *Commonwealth Essays and Studies* 16, no. 2 (Spring, 1993): 96-100. Explores the representations of home and identity in *The English Patient*.

Jewinski, Ed. *Michael Ondaatje: Express Yourself Beautifully*. Toronto, Ont.: ECW Press, 1994. Biography of Ondaatje that examines the relationship between his life, aesthetics, and works.

Novak, Amy. "Textual Hauntings: Narrating History, Memory, and Silence in *The English Patient*." *Studies in the Novel* 36, no. 2 (Summer, 2004): 206-231. Explores the intertwining of memory, history, and narrative at the heart of *The English Patient*.

Ondaatje, Michael. "An Interview with Michael Ondaatje." Interview by Eleanor Wachtel. *Essays on Canadian Writing* 53 (Summer, 1999): 250-261. Ondaatje discusses the process of writing *The English Patient* and the reception of that work.

Scobie, Stephen. "The Reading Lesson: Michael Ondaatje and the Patients of Desire." *Essays on Canadian Writing* 53 (Summer, 1994): 92-106. Extended reading of the image of fire in *The English Patient* and its resonance throughout the text.

Shin, Andrew. "The English Patient's Desert Dream." *Lit: Literature Interpretation Theory* 18, no. 3 (July, 2007): 213-236. Treats both the intertextuality of the novel and the adaptation of the text to the big screen.

Simpson, D. Mark. "Minefield Readings: The Postcolonial English Patient." *Essays on Canadian Writing* 53 (Summer, 1994): 216-237. A postcolonial reading of *The English Patient*, examining the novel's relationship to the postcolonial literary tradition and to the extraliterary politics of postcoloniality.

Tötösy de Zepetnek, Steven, ed. *Comparative Cultural Studies and Michael Ondaatje's Writing*. West Lafayette, Ind.: Purdue University Press, 2005. One of the few books that is solely dedicated to Ondaatje's work. Contains at least four essays on *The English Patient*.

The Enneads

Author: Plotinus (205-270 C.E.)

First transcribed: c. 256-270 C.E., as *Enneas* (English translation, 1918)

Type of work: Philosophy

Plotinus's life and philosophical thought are known today mainly through the work of his fellow philosopher and his sometime student Porphyry, who wrote an important biography of Plotinus that forms the preface to Porphyry's compilation of Plotinus's philosophical discourses. In making his compilation, Porphyry was following thinkers such as Apollodorus of Athens, who collected the works of Epicharmus, and Andronicus of Rhodes, the Peripatetic, who organized the work of Aristotle and Theophrastus. Porphyry arranged the discourses by topic and separated the thinkers into six groups of nine. This organization gave rise to the title *The Enneads*, which comes from the Greek word *ennea*, the cardinal numeral nine.

In this work, Plotinus deals with a wide range of subjects and covers an array of questions concerning ethics, natural phenomena, the soul, the intellect, beauty, and the origin of evil. He does not, however, discuss politics. Constituting the earliest sources for Plotinus are Porphyry's collection, along with another edition (now lost) that was made by one of Plotinus's associates, a physician named Eustochius. Also, he used as a source brief comments made by Eusabius and Eunapius in the Suda, a tenth century Byzantine historical encyclopedia written in Greek.

Although Plotinus's name attests to a Roman ancestry, he was said by Eunapius to have been born in an Egyptian city located 200 miles south of Cairo on the Upper Nile River known as Asyut, also known as Siout. This ancient city founded in the time of the pharoahs was known as Lycopolis or Lyco during the period of Roman rule. Details of Plotinus's childhood and student life are not known, but according to Porphyry, in 232, Plotinus, in his twenties, decided to move north to Alexandria and was admitted to study with the philosopher Ammonius Saccas. After eleven years of study, Plotinus left Ammonius and headed east on an expedition against Persia that was led by the teenage Roman emperor Gordian III. Plotinus's goal was to carry out his own firsthand investigations into Persian and Indian thought. The expedition collapsed almost immediately; Gordian III was murdered, and Plotinus escaped through Syria to Rome, where he set up his own school in 244, the same year that Emperor Marcus Julius Philippus, also known as Philip the Arab, began his reign.

In Rome, Plotinus lived as the houseguest of a Roman woman and her daughter, both of whom were named Gemina. Plotinus's lectures, which were based for a decade or so on the precepts of his teacher Ammonius, attracted an influential group of men and women such as Amelius Gentilianus, a philosopher from Etruria and a prominent member of Plotinus's school; Paulinus, a physician from Scythopolis; Zoticus, a critic and man of letters; Amphiclea, the wife of Ariston; and the senators Sabinillus, Castricius Firmus, Marcellus Orantius, and Rogantianus. To follow Plotinus's precepts, Rogantianus had given up his extravagant lifestyle. As a result, he regained his health. Plotinus, known for his asceticism and his abstinence in matters of food and sleep, was said to have had a face that gleamed with intelligence and kindliness as he spoke. According to Porphyry, his powers of perception, psychological insight, and intellectual acuity were immense.

In the decade after 253, Plotinus began to put his lectures into written format. By the time Porphyry arrived in Rome in 263, Plotinus had already completed the writing of twenty-one treatises. In the five years between 263 and 268, he put another twenty-four of his lectures into writing, and in the last two years of his life he wrote down nine more, bringing the total to fifty-four, which remain extant. These treatises, first delivered as individual lectures to his students in the dialectic style of Socrates, are conversational and idiosyncratic. His style of argument, both written and oral, was sui generis. Furthermore, whether it was because of his poor eyesight or a fundamental distrust of the written word, he did not bother to make any changes to his texts, which left Porphyry the job of editing works filled with unusual orthography. As a result, A. Hilary Armstrong warns in the introduction to his twentieth century edition of Plotinus, it is "extremely dangerous to emend him according to any preconceived ideas of Greek."

Plotinus's reputation continued to grow. He corresponded with Greek rhetorician Cassius Longinus and attracted the interest of Emperor Gallienus and his wife, Salonina, to whom Plotinus had suggested the creation of a special enclave to be set up on the site of a derelict city in Campania. In this enclave, the inhabitants would live according to Plato's laws. For reasons unknown, the enclave, called Platonopolis, was never realized.

In 268, at Plotinus's suggestion, Porphyry left Rome for a rest cure in Sicily. Plotinus remained behind in the city, but his own health was breaking down. A degenerative disease thought to have been leprosy or tuberculosis so debilitated Plotinus that he withdrew into the isolation of a self-imposed quarantine on an estate in Campania that belonged to his friend, Zethos. Plotinus died there in 270.

Plotinus's style, both eclectic and often obscure, draws from earlier systems of thought, like those designed by the pre-Socratics, the Stoics, the Pythagoreans, the Epicureans, and Plato's teacher, Aristotle. Plotinus's treatises, as preserved by Porphyry, do not reveal a developing evolution of thought and are rightly called static because they are the culmination of decades of teaching and reflection. Plotinus saw himself as an interpreter of Plato, and he would not be comfortable with the terms "Neoplatonist" or "Neoplatonism," which are widely applied to him today. His work involves the clarification of Plato's ideas as he saw them and the application of these thoughts to his own era. In this way, he responds to and soothes the anxieties of an era that had not yet anchored itself in Christianity and was sinking into a mire of political, social, and economic problems, from which the Romans were unable to extricate themselves. In this way, Plotinus's interpretation of Plato's forms and of the soul's contemplative capacity, as well as his emphasis upon realizing the ideal, the One, and the Good, provides spiritual salvation by pointing to an eternal state underlying the visible world that brought joy to those who were able to achieve complete and supreme unity with it.

Considered of little consequence by many people during the nineteenth century, Plotinus has, since the start of the twentieth century, come into his own. He is widely hailed as the founder of Neoplatonism. His thought shaped the doctrines of the Eastern Orthodox Church and the traditions of medieval mysticism. The shadow of his influence has fallen over many, including Marius Victorinus, the African rhetorician, and the early church fathers. He also influenced thinkers such as Michael Psellus, Origen, Saint Augustine, Proclus, Gregory of Nyssa, Ambrose, Saint Thomas Aquinas, Marsilio

Ficino, and philosopher Leszek Kołakowski (1927-2009), who had traced the intellectual underpinnings of Marxist thought to Plotinus. Among the English writers Plotinus influenced are Samuel Taylor Coleridge and W. B. Yeats.

Plotinus's last words, uttered in true Plotinian style, were recorded by Eustochius and remain open to interpretation. By one translation, Plotinus avers that he has been "trying to return the divine part of myself to the divine in the universe." By another translation, he advises his followers to "return the divine aspect of yourself to the divine in the universe." Either statement provides summation of his life's work.

Michele Valerie Ronnick

Further Reading

Dufour, Richard. *Plotinus: A Bibliography, 1950-2000*. Boston: E. J. Brill, 2002. This bibliography is a necessary research tool for all serious students of Plotinus.

Gerson, Lloyd P., ed. *The Cambridge Companion to Plotinus*. New York: Cambridge University Press, 1996. This is a collection of sixteen essays edited by a leading expert on ancient philosophy. The essays cover a number of important questions about Plotinus and his work.

McGroarty, Kieran. *Plotinus on Eudaimonia: A Commentary on Ennead I.4*. New York: Oxford University Press, 2006. This work, which is based on McGroarty's doctoral dissertation, provides an excellent example of current Plotinian exegesis.

Plotinus. *Enneads*. Translated by A. Hilary Armstrong. 7 vols. Cambridge, Mass.: Harvard University Press, 1966-1984. In addition to providing an excellent introduction, Armstrong's work, as part of the Loeb Classical Library, is well known and well accepted.

Rist, John M. *Plotinus: The Road to Reality*. New York: Cambridge University Press, 1967. Rist's book is a standard point to begin studying Plotinus.

Stamatellos, Giannis. *Plotinus and the Presocratics: A Philosophical Study of Presocratic Influences in Plotinus' Enneads*. New York: State University of New York Press, 2007. This is an important new study setting forth the connections between Plotinus and the pre-Socratic philosophers.

The Enormous Room

Author: E. E. Cummings (1894-1962)
First published: 1922
Type of work: Autobiography
Type of plot: Autobiographical
Time of plot: 1917
Locale: France

Principal characters:
E. E. CUMMINGS, an American ambulance driver
W. S. B., his American friend
APOLLYON, the head of the French prison
ROCKYFELLER,
THE WANDERER,
ZOO-LOO,
SURPLICE, and
JEAN LE NÈGRE, other prisoners

The Story:

The poet E. E. Cummings and his friend W. S. B. are unhappy as members of the Norton-Harjes Ambulance Service, a unit sent by Americans to aid the French during World War I. One day they are arrested by French military police. From hints dropped during an investigation, Cummings gathers that W. S. B. wrote letters the censor found suspicious. Because they are good friends, both men are held for questioning. They never find out exactly what they are suspected of doing. On one occasion, Cummings is asked whether he hates the Germans. He replies that he does not, that he simply loves the French very much. The investigating official cannot understand how one can love the French and not hate the Germans. Finally, Cummings and W. S. B. are separated and sent to different prisons. Again and again Cummings is questioned and moved from one spot to another, always under strict guard.

Late one night, he is taken to a prison in the little provincial town of Macé. There he is thrown into a huge darkened room, given a straw mattress, and told to go to sleep. In the darkness, he counts at least thirty voices speaking eleven different languages. Early the next morning he meets W. S. B. in the room, who tells him that all the prisoners there are suspected of being spies, some only because they speak no French.

That morning, he learns the routine of the prison. The enormous room is lined with mattresses down each side, with a few windows to let in light at one end. It smells of stale tobacco and sweat. Some of the men in the room are insane, and most of the others are afraid they might become so. The dull routine begins at five thirty in the morning, when someone is sent down to the kitchen under guard to bring back a bucket of sour, cold coffee. After coffee, the prisoners draw lots to see who will clear the room, sweep the floors, and collect the trash. At seven thirty, they are allowed to walk for two hours in a small, walled-in courtyard. Then comes the first meal of the day, followed by another walk in the garden. At four, they are given supper. At eight, they are locked in the enormous room for the night.

There is little entertainment except fighting and conversation. Some of the men spend their time trying to catch sight of women, who are kept in another part of the prison. The poet begins to accustom himself to the enormous room and to make friends among the various inmates. One of the first of these is Count Bragard, a Belgian painter who specializes in portraits of horses. The count is a perfect gentleman, even in prison, and always looks neat and suave. He and Cummings discuss painting and the arts as if they are at a polite party. Before Cummings leaves, the count begins to act strangely and withdraw from his friends. He is losing his mind.

One day, Cummings is taken to see the head of the prison, a gross man he calls Apollyon. Apollyon has no interest in the prisoners as long as they make no trouble for him. He questions Cummings for a considerable time in an effort to learn why the American is there, a circumstance over which the American himself often puzzles.

When new inmates arrive in the room, everyone looks them over with anticipation, some to find a man with money he can lend, some to find a fellow countryman, and some to find a friend. One day, a very fat, rosy-cheeked man arrives. He was a successful manager of a disreputable house, and because he has a large sum of money with him, he is nicknamed Rockyfeller. He hires a strong man to act as his bodyguard. Nobody likes him, for he buys special privileges from the guards.

During his stay in the room, Cummings meets three men, very different from one another, whose personal qualities are such that they make life seem meaningful to him. He calls them the Delectable Mountains, after the mountains Christian found in John Bunyan's *The Pilgrim's Progress* (1678,

1684). The first is the Wanderer, whose wife and three little children are in the women's ward of the prison. He is a strong man and simple in his emotions and feelings; Cummings likes to talk with him about his problems. One of the Wanderer's children, a little boy, sometimes comes to the enormous room to visit his father. His pranks and games both bother and amuse the men. The Wanderer treats his son with love and the deepest kind of understanding. Until he is sent away, he remains Cummings's best friend.

The second Delectable Mountain is Zoo-loo, a Polish farmer who can speak neither French nor English but who can communicate by signs. In a short time, he and Cummings know all about each other. Zoo-loo has a knack for hiding money, and despite the fact that the head of the prison repeatedly has him and his belongings thoroughly searched, he always seems able to produce a twenty-franc note from his left ear or the back of his neck. His kindnesses to Cummings and W. S. B. are innumerable.

The third Delectable Mountain is a little man named Surplice. Everything astonishes him. When Cummings has some candy or cheese, Surplice is sure to come over to his cot and ask questions about it in a shy manner. His curiosity and friendly conversation make everything seem more important and interesting than it really is.

One morning, Jean Le Nègre is brought to the enormous room, a gigantic, simple-minded black man whom Cummings was to remember as the finest of his fellow prisoners. Jean is given to practical jokes and tall tales; he was arrested for impersonating an English officer and sent to the prison for psychopathic observation. The women prisoners call their approval and admiration of his powerful body when he walks in the courtyard. His favorite among the women is Lulu, who smuggles money and a lace handkerchief to him. When she is sent to another prison, Jean is disconsolate. When one of the prisoners pulls at Lulu's handkerchief, Jean fights back, and a scuffle follows. The guards come, and Jean is taken away for punishment. Calls from the women prisoners arouse him so that he attacks the guards and sends them flying until he is quieted and bound by a fellow prisoner whom he trusts. After that experience, Jean grows quiet and shy.

Just before Cummings is released, W. S. B. is sent away. Jean tries to cheer Cummings with his funny stories and exaggerated lies, but without much success. Although Cummings is afraid that W. S. B. might never be freed from the prisons of France, he later learns that W. S. B. was eventually released. Cummings himself leaves the enormous room knowing that in it he learned the degradation, the nobility, and the endurance of human nature.

Critical Evaluation:

When *The Enormous Room* was first published in 1922, it was viewed as a war book, a "realistic" story exposing the horrors of World War I, as one representative critic put it. The book is indeed about war, but it is also about other things—society, language, and art—and about E. E. Cummings himself. An examination and evaluation of the various aspects of *The Enormous Room* reveal its strength as an experimental autobiography and as a portrait of modern culture.

Although it is a book about war, Cummings's work is more a parody than a protest. The tone of the opening paragraph reveals this when the narrator pokes fun at the pompous rhetoric of "Our Great President" and contrasts it with the simple, honest language of a man such as E. E. Cummings, who is in a war started by the rhetoric of politicians. Cummings sustains this tone throughout the book as he contrasts those who are imprisoned with those who are their captors. The prisoners, particularly those whom Cummings calls the Delectable Mountains, are simple, innocent, and naïve victims, whereas the victimizers are ruthless, uncaring bureaucrats. Using Bunyan's book *The Pilgrim's Progress* as his organizing principle, Cummings shows how he, the pilgrim, progresses through the war. He experiences the brutality of such figures as the one he calls Apollyon (named after Bunyan's devil) and learns that in war innocent human beings battle against manipulative predators.

This context of war is actually a microcosm of society, another theme Cummings develops. The qualities that Cummings the poet pokes fun at and satirizes are the same ones he criticizes in *The Enormous Room*: the dehumanizing qualities of modern culture, its mechanization, and its substitution of thinking for feeling. Cummings rails against such institutions of culture as religion, education, and government, and he uses the individual prisoners in the French jail as reminders of the power of the self against society.

Cummings uses experimental language in describing the prisoners, showing that a new use of language can be a tool for understanding, and that language and art are means of celebrating individuals who successfully rebel against the old order of living, speaking, and writing. Cummings uses antirhetoric to contrast with the pompous language of politicians, and he shows that language can help people see things in a new way. He describes the reason for his linguistic manipulation at the end of the autobiography when he points out that "to create is first of all to destroy." Indeed, Cummings does destroy the predictable, ordinary, traditional ways of writing and speaking, and he creates his story through wrenched syntax, poetic descriptions, and shocking imagery.

In addition to war, society, language, and art, *The Enormous Room* is about E. E. Cummings himself. He paints a portrait of a brash Bostonian who goes off to war not because of any passionate commitment to a cause but for the adventure of it. The young man is elitist and overly sensitive to the smells and sights of the prison into which he is thrown; above all, he is a detached observer who, as he views his surroundings and fellow prisoners, believes that he occupies a privileged position. As this pilgrim progresses, he learns about himself through the lives of those with whom he shares his small space. He learns from Surplice the importance of being amusing and amused, and that this quality of being mocked while mocking the world is integral to the suffering inherent in the human condition. He learns from Zoo-loo the power of unwritten and unspoken language and discovers that he, a person who luxuriates in the written and spoken word, must remain connected to language that transcends those human tools. Finally, he learns the quiet strength of loyalty to others from the Wanderer, who is separated from his wife and children through the crass brutality of the "little, very little, *gouvernement français.*" These three Delectable Mountains, together with the other innocent prisoners, teach Cummings about his relationship with humanity. Thus the detached, isolated Cummings is transformed into an involved, connected one who emerges from his temporary confinement with a more mature sense of himself as a person and as an artist. When he writes a poem at the end of his narrative, it is with a maturity and serenity that he did not possess at the beginning of his captivity, when he simply was playing with language and poking fun at bureaucrats. In the concluding chapter, entitled "I Say Good-Bye to La Misère," Cummings bids farewell to his prison while greeting New York as a person whose liberation from his old self could only have occurred through his imprisonment.

It has been noted that *The Enormous Room* follows not only the pattern outlined in Bunyan's *Pilgrim's Progress* but also the classical pattern of the Dark Night of the Soul in which, as Cummings once wrote in a letter, "a spirit descends to ascend." The spirit in this autobiography does indeed descend into himself and into a confining yet expansive prison before ascending to assume a new identity and a new role in the postwar America to which he returns. An enormous room is thus also an enormous journey.

"Critical Evaluation" by Marjorie Smelstor

Further Reading

Blazek, William. "Artistry and Primitivism in *The Enormous Room*." In *The Literature of the Great War Reconsidered:*

Beyond Modern Memory, edited by Patrick J. Quinn and Steven Trout. New York: Palgrave, 2001. This explication of Cummings's book is included in a collection of essays that apply late twentieth century critical theories to analyze literature about World War I.

Cooperman, Stanley. *World War I and the American Novel.* Baltimore: Johns Hopkins University Press, 1967. Calls *The Enormous Room* "a carnival in a graveyard" and shows how Cummings avoids conventional rebellion by manipulating language to depict the prison as adding foolishness to tragedy.

Dougherty, James P. "E. E. Cummings: *The Enormous Room.*" In *Landmarks of American Writing*, edited by Hennig Cohen. New York: Basic Books, 1969. Maintains that in *The Enormous Room*, Cummings's intent was to expose the stupidity and cruelty of wartime governments. Victims are implicitly advised to undergo a process of "unlearning" previously accepted values.

Kennedy, Richard S. *E. E. Cummings Revisited.* New York: Twayne, 1994. An introductory critical biography that identifies factual bases of *The Enormous Room*, notes its three-part structure, and details its allusions and corre-

spondences to John Bunyan's *The Pilgrim's Progress.* Defines the work's antiwar and antiauthority themes and its comic-opera descriptions. Lauds Cummings's preference for feeling, nature, children, and ignorance.

Olsen, Taimi Anne. *Transcending Space: Architectural Places in Works by Henry David Thoreau, E. E. Cummings, and John Barth.* Lewisburg, Pa.: Bucknell University Press, 2000. Examines *The Enormous Room* and other literary works in which the authors find a sense of the infinite in unlikely places, altering readers' perceptions of physical and cultural space.

Russell, John. "E. E. Cummings, *The Enormous Room*: Jail Journals." In *Reciprocities in the Nonfiction Novel.* Athens: University of Georgia Press, 2000. Russell analyzes Cummings's book and ten other works that traditionally have not been considered nonfiction novels to create a new definition of the genre. He describes how nonfiction novels differ from works of journalism.

Sawyer-Lauçanno, Christopher. *E. E. Cummings: A Biography.* Naperville, Ill.: Sourcebooks, 2004. A comprehensive biography, in which Sawyer-Lauçanno devotes an entire chapter to *The Enormous Room.*

An Enquiry Concerning Human Understanding

Author: David Hume (1711-1776)
First published: 1748
Type of work: Philosophy

"Philosophical decisions," says David Hume toward the end of his *An Enquiry Concerning Human Understanding*, "are nothing but the reflections of common life, methodised and corrected." This simple, homely epigram conceals a great deal. For one thing, *An Enquiry Concerning Human Understanding* is actually a sort of popularized revision of ideas that were systematically developed in book 1 of his precocious *A Treatise of Human Nature* (1739-1740), which, although it was completed before the author was twenty-five, has been characterized as one of the most profound, thoroughly reasoned, and purely scientific works in the history of philosophy. Second, Hume's method for correcting the reflections of common life actually involves a thorough attack on the obscurities of metaphysical idealists.

Born in an age of reason, Hume at first shared the optimism of those who were certain that pure reason could un-

lock the secrets of nature, and as he read Francis Bacon, John Newton, Thomas Hobbes, and John Locke, he longed for fame equal to theirs. However, as he reported in a letter to Sir Gilbert Elliot, although he "began with an anxious search after arguments, to confirm the common opinion; doubts stole in, dissipated, returned; were again dissipated, returned again; and it was a perpetual struggle of restless imagination against inclination, perhaps against reason." That last, "perhaps against reason," is the crucial phrase, for no philosopher before Hume used reason so brilliantly in an attack against the certainties of reason. The twelve essays of *An Enquiry Concerning Human Understanding* reflect Hume's three principal attacks against rationalism: against the doctrine of innate ideas and faith in ontological reasoning and an ordered universe; against empiricism, both the kind that led to Lockean dualism and the kind that led to Berkeleyan idealism, on the ground that neither the physical nor the spiritual can be proved; and against deism, based on universal axioms and the law of causality. It is not surprising that religions since Hume have largely made their appeals to faith rather than to reason.

Considering what remains when such thoroughgoing skepticism rejects so much of the beliefs of rational human beings, Hume himself readily admitted (in the fourth essay, "Sceptical Doubts Concerning the Operations of the Understanding") that as a man he was quite satisfied with ordinary reasoning processes but that as a philosopher he had to be skeptical, for reasoning was not based on immediate sense experience. "The most lively thought is still inferior to the dullest sensation," he asserted in his second essay, "The Origin of Ideas." Unless the mind is "disordered by disease or madness," actual perceptions have the greatest "force and vivacity," and it is only on such matters of basic mental fact rather than on the abstract relations of ideas, as in mathematics, that human beings must depend for certainties about life. No amount of reasoning, for example, could have led Adam in the Garden of Eden to believe that fluid, transparent water would drown him or that bright, warm fire would burn him to ashes. "No object ever discovers, by the qualities which appear to the senses, either the causes which produced it, or the effects which arise from it." In dealing with this idea, Hume doggedly backs every argument into a corner, into some "dangerous dilemma." What is more, he enjoys himself immensely while doing it—"philosophers that gave themselves airs of superior wisdom and sufficiency, have a hard task when they encounter persons of inquisitive dispositions," he says. Concerning cause and effect, he argues that similar effects are expected from causes that appear similar, yet this relationship does not always exist and, even when observed, is not reasoned. Furthermore, it is merely an arbitrary assumption, an act of faith, that events that are remembered as having occurred sequentially in the past will continue to do so in the future. Causation thus was merely a belief, a belief he defined as a "lively idea related to or associated with a present impression."

This seemed to Hume not merely an impractical philosophical idea, but a momentous discovery of great consequence. Since causation was an a priori principle of both natural and moral philosophy, and since causation could not be reasonably demonstrated to be true, a tremendous revolution in human thought was in preparation. Only in the pure realm of ideas, logic, and mathematics, not contingent on the direct sense awareness of reality, could causation safely (because arbitrarily) be applied—all other sciences are reduced to probability. The concluding essay, "Of the Academical or Sceptical Philosophy," reaches grand heights of eloquence

when Hume argues that a priori reasoning can make anything appear to produce anything: "the falling of a pebble may, for aught we know, extinguish the sun; or the wish of a man control the planets in their orbits."

> When we run over libraries, persuaded of these principles, what havoc must we make? If we take in hand any volume; of divinity or school metaphysics, for instance; let us ask, Does it contain any abstract reasoning concerning quantity or number? No. Does it contain any experimental reasoning concerning matter of fact and existence? No. Commit it then to the flames: for it can contain nothing but sophistry and illusion.

The polemic vigor of the essays stems in large part from the bitter experiences Hume had in the years immediately preceding the publication of *An Enquiry Concerning Human Understanding.* In 1744, he had sought to fill a vacancy in the chair of ethics and pneumatical philosophy at Edinburgh University, but to his astonishment his *A Treatise of Human Nature* was invoked to prevent the appointment: "such a popular clamor has been raised against me in Edinburgh, on account of Scepticism, Heterodoxy, and other hard names . . . that my Friends find some Difficulty in working out the Point of my Professorship." Then he was dismissed without full salary as tutor to the mad son of the marquis of Annandale. These experiences played a part in sharpening the cutting edge of his thought and prose style.

After refining his conception of reason and its modes of function, Hume applies it to four crucial problems: "Liberty and Necessity," "Reason of Animals," "Miracles," and "Particular Providence and a Future State." Concerning the first, Hume argues that since the subject relates to common life and experience (unlike such topics as the origin of worlds or the region of spirits), only ambiguity of language keeps the dispute alive. For a clear definition, he suggests that it be consistent with plain matters of fact and with itself. Difficulty arises when philosophers approach the problem by examining the faculties of the soul rather than the operations of body and brute matter. In the latter, people assume that they perceive cause and effect, but in the functioning of their minds they feel no connection between motive and action. However, the doctrine of cause and effect cannot be invoked without, ultimately, tracing all actions—including evil ones—to the deity whom people refuse to accept as the author of guilt and moral turpitude in all creatures. As a matter of fact, freedom and necessity are matters of momentary emotional feeling "not to be controuled or altered by any philosophical theory or speculation whatsoever."

The reason of animals, according to Hume, consists—as it does in children, philosophers, and humankind in general—not so much in logical inferences as in experience of analogies and sequential actions. Observation and experience alone teach a horse the proper height that he can leap or a greyhound how to meet the hare in her tracks with the least expenditure of energy. Hume's learning theory here seems to be based on the pleasure-pain principle and forms the background for certain theories of twentieth century psychology. However, Hume ends this essay with a long qualification in which he cites the "Instincts," unlearned knowledge derived from the original hand of nature, and then adds this curious final comment: "The experimental reasoning itself, which we possess in common with beasts, and on which the whole conduct of life depends, is nothing but a species of instinct or mechanical power, that acts in us unknown to ourselves."

The essay on miracles is perhaps the most spirited of the entire collection, and it is the one that Hume expected, correctly, would stir the greatest opposition. Nevertheless, he was certain that his argument would be for the wise and the learned "an everlasting check to all kinds of superstitious delusion, and consequently . . . useful as long as the world endures." Events can be believed to happen only when they are observed, and all reports of events not directly observed must be believed only to the degree that they conform with probability, experimentally or experientially derived. A miracle is a violation of the laws of nature; therefore it violates all probability; therefore it is impossible. History gives no instance of any miracle observed by a sufficient number of unquestionably honest, educated, intelligent individuals. Despite the surprise, wonder, and other pleasant sensations attendant upon reports of novel experiences, all new discoveries that achieve credibility among people have always resembled in fundamentals those objects and events that have already been experienced. The most widespread belief in miracles exists among so-called primitive peoples. Finally, since there is no objective way of confirming miracles, believers have no just basis for rejecting those claimed by all religions. "So that, on the whole, we may conclude, that the Christian Religion not only was at first attended with miracles, but even at this day cannot be believed by any reasonable person without one. Mere reason is insufficient to convince us . . . to believe what is most contrary to custom and experience."

In the 1777 posthumous edition of *An Enquiry Concerning Human Understanding* appeared the announcement that these unsystematic essays should be regarded only as containing Hume's philosophical sentiments and principles. Although professional philosophers, especially the logical positivists, still prefer Hume's earlier *Treatise of Human Na-*ture, it is *An Enquiry Concerning Human Understanding*, with its livelier style and popular appeal, that stands as his personal testament. In it he said that he would be "happy if . . . we can undermine the foundations of an abstruse philosophy, which seems to have hitherto served only as a shelter to superstition, and a cover to absurdity and error." The irony is that he succeeded so well in undermining reason that he opened the door to the Romanticism of the late eighteenth and early nineteenth centuries. His voice has, however, outlasted that babel and his humanistic skepticism survives. "Be a philosopher," he cautioned himself, "but amidst all your philosophy, be still a man."

Further Reading

Bailey, Alan, and Daniel O'Brien. *Hume's "Enquiry Concerning Human Understanding": Reader's Guide.* London: Continuum, 2006. Introductory overview, aimed at undergraduate students and general readers. Discusses the philosophical background, key themes and concepts, critical reception, and influence of Hume's work.

Buckle, Stephen. *Hume's Enlightenment Tract: The Unity and Purpose of "An Enquiry Concerning Human Understanding."* New York: Oxford University Press, 2001. A commentary on *An Enquiry Concerning Human Understanding* by a leading Hume scholar. Buckle explicates Hume's arguments and places the work within its historical and intellectual context and its relationship to Enlightenment thought.

Noxon, James. *Hume's Philosophical Development.* Oxford, England: Clarendon Press, 1973. Compares Hume's *A Treatise of Human Nature* and *An Enquiry Concerning Human Understanding.*

Olshewsky, Thomas M. "The Classical Roots of Hume's Skepticism." *Journal of the History of Ideas* 52, no. 2 (April-June, 1991): 269-288. Interprets Hume's work through an analysis of skepticism on the basis of the Stoic philosophy of Sextus Empiricus.

Radcliffe, Elizabeth S., ed. *A Companion to Hume.* Malden, Mass.: Blackwell, 2008. Collection of twenty-eight essays interpreting the various aspects of Hume's philosophy. The numerous references to *An Enquiry Concerning Human Understanding* are listed in the index.

Read, Rupert, and Kenneth A. Richman, eds. *The New Hume Debate.* Rev. ed. New York: Routledge, 2007. The "debate" concerns Hume's ideas about the existence of causes and objects. Traditionally, scholars considered him to be a skeptic regarding these matters, but many modern critics now regard him as a "skeptical realist." This collection ofessays provides various interpretations of the "new

Hume," with numerous references to *An Enquiry Concerning Human Understanding*.

Stumpf, Samuel E. *Philosophy: History and Problems*. New York: McGraw-Hill, 1977. Stumpf's chapter on empiricism in Britain is one of the clearest explanations of the issues and responses that form the context of the philosophies of a trio of thinkers—John Locke, George Berkeley, and Hume. An understanding of the first two is essential to grasping the importance of Hume's *An Enquiry Concerning Human Understanding*.

An Enquiry Concerning Political Justice

Author: William Godwin (1756-1836)
First published: 1793, as *An Enquiry Concerning Political Justice, and Its Influence on General Virtue and Happiness*
Type of work: Politics

In 1793, William Godwin, the first philosopher of anarchism, published *An Enquiry Concerning Political Justice*. This three-volume work gives evidence of being strongly influenced by the ideas of the French Revolution and argues that the rational being, the human, must be given complete freedom to exercise pure reason. All forms of government, being founded on irrational assumptions, are tyrannical and eventually must be eliminated. Laws have been produced not by wisdom but by greed and fear, so they should be replaced by the products of reasonable people's ability to make decisions. Accumulated property is a means of exploitation and, consequently, must be abolished. This last point was, however, modified in a later edition. With its varying degrees of indebtedness to Aristippus, Plato, Jean-Jacques Rousseau, and Claude-Adrien Helvétius, and despite its equivocating alterations in the final revision, Godwin's book gave evidence of original thinking and provided generations of revolutionary thinkers with stimulation and guidance.

Godwin asserts that the general human objective is happiness; that politics, the promotion of individual good, is humanity's most important pursuit; and that the two traditional articles of political liberty have been, first, "security of our persons," and, second, "security of our property." Godwin asks, however, would not a good government "take away all restraints upon the enquiring mind"? The early chapters of the book develop Godwin's view that throughout history government has had a corrupting influence, but only because people have not lived up to their potential truthfulness and to their ability to see what is evil and what is good. The assumption is that if people will define clearly to themselves the genuinely good principles of life, government will improve.

Godwin surveys historically the destructiveness and futility of war, and to emphasize its irrational causes, he quotes at some length from the satire on war in book 2 of Jonathan Swift's *Gulliver's Travels* (1726). In the present condition, Godwin continues, punishment is the only means of repressing the violent revolt of the deprived masses. If government is a subject for discussion, however, then people might reasonably agree about it some day and see the advantages of freedom and equality.

From these premises Godwin proceeds to demonstrate that, of the three principal causes of moral improvement, both literature and education, though beneficial, have limitations, and that the third cause, political justice, is strong where the first two are weak. Political justice is strong in the extent of its operation. When political justice is equally addressed to all, it will impart virtue to all. Since error and injustice tend to destroy themselves, it is doubtful whether they could be perpetuated without governmental support, for government "reverses the genuine propensities of mind, and instead of suffering us to look forward, teaches us to look backward for perfection." To exemplify how political institutions have in the past militated against moral improvement, Godwin points out the destructive passions engendered by the inequality of property, the magnificence accorded to enormous wealth, and the insolence and usurpation of rich persons. Traditionally, both legislation and administration of the law have favored the rich and have repressed the freedom of the poor to resist the rich.

Godwin asserts strongly that humanity's most distinguished and most important characteristic is its perfectibility, by which he means not the capacity to become perfect but, rather, the capability to improve. Evidences of humanity's progressive nature are the development of language and the invention of alphabetical writing. Having asserted that all science and all art are capable of being further perfected, Godwin asks why the same should not be true of morals and social institutions. On the usefulness of history in this regard, he comments: "Let us look back, that we may profit by the experience of mankind; but let us not look back as if the wisdom of our ancestors was such as to leave no room for future improvements."

The true instruments of moral influence, in Godwin's opinion, are not direct physical causes such as climate but, rather, such concepts as desire and aversion or punishment and reward. Definitely restrictive to moral progress are the institutions or professions that always operate to produce a certain character or stereotype and thus suppress frankness of mind. The example cited by Godwin is the priesthood, which requires that all priests must be alike in their subservience. Godwin is certain that free people in any country will be "firm, vigorous and spirited in proportion to their freedom," as, conversely, slaves will be "ignorant, servile and unprincipled."

When the magic of the indoctrinated idea is dissolved and the great majority of any society seek true benefits, the struggle need not involve tumult or violence. Indeed, "the effort would be to resist reason, not to obey it." Just views must be infused into the liberally educated, but this process must come about gradually. Humanity's basic error in politics is the supposition that a change is impracticable, with the result that humanity does not look forward incessantly to the accomplishment of change. People, Godwin asserts, do not choose evil when they see it to be evil. Therefore, once having shaken off an injurious evil, a society will not permit its revival unless its conviction of truth becomes obliterated.

An Enquiry Concerning Political Justice develops a theme that is in close agreement with Thomas Paine's belief that society, being produced by human wants, is a blessing, but that government, necessitated by human wickedness, is at its best a necessary evil. Godwin defines the term "justice" as meaning that the individual should contribute everything in his or her power to the benefit of the whole, the whole being not the state but other individuals. The importance to the general weal must be the only standard, and a benefit conferred upon an individual to the detriment of the society is wrong. Even one's self-preservation must be based on the premise of one's good to the society—to all. An important theme in Godwin's book is the propriety of applying more justice in order to ascertain political truth.

Society is bound to do for its members everything that can contribute to their welfare. In Godwin's view, what most enlarges the mind—virtue and consciousness of independence—contributes most to this welfare. Individuals, for their part, must follow the best knowledge obtainable. Regarding the possibility that a wrong action may result even from the individual's best intention, Godwin says: "If the disposition by which a man is governed have a systematical tendency to the benefit of his species, he cannot fail to obtain our esteem, however mistaken he may be in his conduct." Virtue is essentially the incessant search for accurate knowledge about utility and right, in which search the exercise of private judgment and the dictates of individual conscience must be accorded primary importance. Since pleasure is to be desired and pain to be avoided, individuals should contribute to the pleasure and benefit of one another and should oppose the despot's power, which is based on indoctrination and is productive of pain.

Moral equality consists of "the propriety of applying one unalterable rule of justice to every case that may arise." Two persons cannot have opposite rights. Moreover, people really have no rights. Since rights can apply only to totally indifferent issues (where to sit and the like), and since an intelligent person immediately becomes a moral person with duties, rights and duties are absolutely exclusive of each other. Although society, composed of individuals, also has no rights, people must, under the present inadequate government, assert some "rights."

Godwin argues further that judgment is founded on evidence, so compulsion cannot bring people to uniformity of opinion. Government needs to be perfected away from the concept of compulsion; the insignificant individual must be made free to criticize the august senate. Countries in which decrees instead of arguments are what rule contain "mere phantoms of men," who give no indication of what they might be if they were entirely free to follow the dictates of conscience and to speak and to act as they think. Finally, individual justice—equality and freedom—must be the basis and goal of improvement in government.

Having set forth the underlying principles of his theory, Godwin proceeds to criticize existing society, develop his system of social ethics, and predict conditions of the future. His confidence in the power of reason gives the book an optimism which has frequently been criticized as unresponsive to the lessons of history. While it is true that his emphasis on necessity (cause and effect viewed as an invariable sequence) is inconsistent with his simultaneous assertion of the efficacy of education, Godwin has been unfairly criticized for maintaining that enlightened education could rectify the falsity and the ignorance of human judgment. Such a criticism cannot be fairly administered until after the society has made a concerted effort to educate itself as Godwin proposed.

Further Reading

Carlson, Julie A. *England's First Family of Writers: Mary Wollstonecraft, William Godwin, Mary Shelley.* Baltimore: Johns Hopkins University Press, 2007. Examines Godwin's work within the context of writings by his wife Mary Wollstonecraft and his daughter Mary Wollstonecraft Shelley, demonstrating how their works engage in a "dialogue" with each other.

Clark, John P. *The Philosophical Anarchism of William Godwin.* Princeton, N.J.: Princeton University Press, 1977. A major study of Godwin's vision of a fundamentally reformed society.

Esterhammer, Angela. "Godwin's Suspicion of Speech Acts." *Studies in Romanticism* 39, no. 4 (Winter, 2000): 553. Discusses how Godwin denounces promises in *An Enquiry Concerning Political Justice* and analyzes other aspects of his linguistic theory about the interpersonal functions of language. Explains his ideas about the relationship of language and truth as reflected in his writings of the 1790's.

Hodson, Jane. *Language and Revolution in Burke, Woll-*

stonecraft, Paine, and Godwin. Burlington, Vt.: Ashgate, 2007. Focuses on *An Enquiry Concerning Political Justice* and other works that engaged in the British and American debate about the French Revolution. Hodson demonstrates the role of language in Godwin's book and provides information about contemporary reviews and modern criticism of the work.

Kelly, Gary. *The English Jacobin Novel, 1780-1805.* New York: Oxford University Press, 1976. Discusses Godwin's novels as reflections of his political philosophy.

Monro, D. H. *Godwin's Moral Philosophy: An Interpretation of William Godwin.* New York: Oxford University Press, 1953. Emphasizes the closely related connections between Godwin's political thinking and his ethics.

Philp, Mark. *Godwin's "Political Justice."* Ithaca, N.Y.: Cornell University Press, 1986. An excellent starting point. Helpful commentary on Godwin's *An Enquiry Concerning Political Justice.*

St. Clair, William. *The Godwins and the Shelleys: The Biography of a Family.* New York: W. W. Norton, 1989. A biography with a unique point of view. William Godwin married Mary Wollstonecraft, the noted feminist, and their daughter, Mary, became the wife of Percy Bysshe Shelley.

Epicœne
Or, The Silent Woman

Author: Ben Jonson (1573-1637)
First produced: 1609; first published, 1616
Type of work: Drama
Type of plot: Comedy
Time of plot: Early seventeenth century
Locale: London

Principal characters:
MOROSE, a gentleman who loves no noise
SIR DAUPHINE EUGENIE, his nephew
NED CLERIMONT, one of Sir Dauphine's friends
TRUEWIT, another friend
SIR JOHN DAW, a ridiculous knight
SIR AMOROUS LA-FOOLE, another silly knight
CUTBEARD, a barber
CAPTAIN OTTER, a heavy drinker
MISTRESS OTTER, his wife
MISTRESS EPICŒNE, the supposed silent woman

The Story:

Clerimont and Truewit, young men-about-town, meet and discuss various matters, including the relative merits of natural beauty and the use of cosmetics. Shifting the topic to their friend Sir Dauphine Eugenie, they wonder how he is able to put up with his uncle Morose, an eccentric character

who can abide no noise except the sound of his own voice. Clerimont's page amuses them with accounts of various noisy pranks that have been played on the ridiculous old man. Sir Dauphine joins them and complains that his uncle blames all the pranks on him and his friends and that he threatens to marry and leave his fortune to his new wife instead of to his nephew. Morose has heard of a soft-voiced woman, extremely frugal of speech, and has negotiated with his silent barber, Cutbeard, to arrange a meeting, possibly even a marriage, with her.

Truewit, amazed at hearing of a silent barber and a silent woman, is struck with a sudden inspiration and excuses himself. After Truewit departs on his undisclosed mission, Sir Amorous La-Foole arrives to invite the gentlemen to a feast at the home of his kinswoman Mistress Otter. The guests are to include the silent Mistress Epicœne, Lady Haughty, Lady Centaur, Mistress Mavis, and Sir John Daw. Sir Dauphine and Clerimont identify Sir John and Sir Amorous as ridiculous targets for comedy.

Meanwhile, Morose is instructing his servant Mute to use only sign language or, in extreme emergencies, to speak through a tube when they are interrupted by a loud blast from a post horn. Mute goes to the door and returns followed by Truewit, who is carrying a post horn and a halter. Morose and Mute are overwhelmed by a volley of words from Truewit and intimidated by a dagger when they attempt to leave the room. Truewit suggests that Morose choose some way of self-destruction other than marriage and offers him the halter to hang himself. After another voluble outpouring Truewit leaves, but he adds the final torture of another blast from his horn. When Cutbeard arrives, he finds Morose in such a state that he has to be put to bed.

In the company of Mistress Epicœne, Sir Dauphine and Clerimont encourage the fantastic knight Sir John Daw to quote and explain his own poetry, to show off his copious but confused mass of knowledge, and to boast of his romantic prowess. They are interrupted by Truewit, returning with his horn. Sir Dauphine is greatly disturbed by Truewit's account of his prank, which Truewit assures him will break off the intended marriage. Sir Dauphine tells Truewit that the marriage was his own plot, abetted by his confederates, Cutbeard and Mistress Epicœne. Cutbeard hastens in to announce that Morose, furious with Truewit and certain that Sir Dauphine sent him to break off the match, has determined to marry immediately. Cutbeard conducts Mistress Epicœne away, and the young gentlemen comment on her apparent desertion of her gallant, Sir John. They encourage him to indulge his melancholy.

Morose welcomes Cutbeard and Mistress Epicœne, who speaks so softly that she can hardly be heard. Cutbeard does all his communicating through sign language only. Carried away with Mistress Epicœne's noiseless charm, Morose promises large rewards to the barber, reminding him to deliver his thanks silently, and sends him to find a soft-voiced

minister to perform the marriage ceremony. He gloats over his imminent marriage and his begetting of children to inherit his estate after he has cast out his impudent nephew.

When Cutbeard announces the results of Truewit's prank to Sir Dauphine and his friends, Truewit suggests that the whole of Sir Amorous's party be transported to Morose's house to celebrate the wedding with proper sound effects. The young men then join the crowd gathered at the Otters' house for the party. Clerimont and Sir Dauphine stir up trouble between Sir Amorous and Sir John Daw by making each believe that the other is putting a slight on him. They make it seem that Sir Amorous knows that Morose is taking Sir John's sweetheart from him and that Sir John is taking Sir Amorous's guests to the wedding feast. They suggest to Sir Amorous that he have his provisions carried to Morose's home, in the hope that the smell of the venison will attract some fiddlers and trumpeters on the way.

Morose has the wedding ceremony performed by a parson who can hardly be heard because of a bad cold. Morose rewards the parson handsomely, but then he is angered by the man's crashing cough and demands that part of the payment be returned. Cutbeard suggests that making change might be difficult for the parson, but that he can cough out the rest. This suggestion silences Morose, who dismisses the parson. Immediately following the ceremony, Mistress Epicœne exhibits her voice in an outburst of shrewish scolding. Reeling from the shock of this, Morose looks around to see Truewit entering with loud congratulations, shortly followed by the whole procession of noisy guests. The collegiate ladies invite Mistress Epicœne to join their circle. When they begin to whisper confidentially, Morose has a glimmer of hope, but this is immediately dashed by their loud criticisms of the lack of wedding festivities. Clerimont ushers in a host of musicians playing loudly, and Captain Otter follows with his drinking mugs and a group of drummers and trumpeters to sound for toasts. Morose flees, groaning, to lock himself in the attic with a nest of nightcaps pulled over his ears.

The party continues noisily, enlivened by a quarrel between Captain Otter and his wife; she beats him until he howls repentance. Morose returns with his sword to drive away the guests, but, overcome by their clamor, he flees again, followed by Sir Dauphine, who endeavors to console him, and Truewit, who reminds him of his warning about the dangers of marriage. Morose accepts Truewit's advice that he sue for a divorce.

Continuing their pranks on Sir John and Sir Amorous, the young men reduce them into such a state of terror that they hide from each other. At last each is persuaded to consent to be blindfolded and to accept indignities from his furious opponent. Sir John is to receive five kicks from Sir Amorous and to surrender his sword; Sir Amorous is to surrender his sword, receive a blow on the mouth, and have his nose tweaked. Sir Dauphine, impersonating each in turn, inflicts the indignities on the hoodwinked knights. On Morose's return, Truewit shows him the swords and says that the quarrel had arisen over the bride's amorous favors. Since Morose is unable to face the noise in the law courts, Truewit promises to find him legal help for the divorce proceedings. He departs, and, prodded by the young men, both Sir John and Sir Amorous boast of successful love affairs with Mistress Epicœne.

Truewit returns with Cutbeard disguised as a lawyer and Captain Otter disguised as a parson. These two engage in a noisy dispute on secular and canon law concerning divorce proceedings. During the dispute, which is exquisite torture to Morose, Mistress Epicœne and the ladies enter, screeching about her wrongs. Every effort of Morose to free himself from the marriage fails, even the accusation of adultery, for neither knight can claim intimacy after the marriage. Sir Dauphine proposes to his uncle that he will free him from his tormenting bride if Morose will reward him by restoring him as heir. Morose eagerly accepts the terms and signs an agreement, at which Sir Dauphine pulls off Mistress Epicœne's wig to disclose that the supposed silent woman is a boy. Sir John and Sir Amorous are discredited and discomfited, the collegiate ladies are covered with embarrassment at having exposed feminine mysteries to a member of the opposite sex, and Morose retires to welcome silence.

Critical Evaluation:

A landmark in English theatrical history, *Epicœne* was written by Ben Jonson, whose abilities have long been ranked alongside those of William Shakespeare. One of Jonson's four greatest comedies, following *Volpone: Or, The Fox* (pr. 1605) by four years, *Epicœne* was followed by *The Alchemist* (pr. 1610) and *Bartholomew Fair* (pr. 1614), Jonson's last prose comedy. Of his seventeen plays, *Epicœne* occupies the midpoint in Jonson's career. Its contemporary and continued popularity through the Restoration—William Congreve probably patterned Mirabell in his play *The Way of the World* (pr., pb. 1700) after Truewit and certainly patterned Heartwell in his play *The Old Bachelor* (pr., pb. 1693) after Morose—was due in part to its superbly constructed prose. Lauded at length by John Dryden, in his *Essay of Dramatic Poesy* (1668), as the most nearly perfect example of English drama, *Epicœne* offers a number of obstacles—quite surmountable obstacles, but obstacles nevertheless—for the modern-day reader.

Paradoxically, Jonson's expert use of the theatrical conventions of his time, such as boys playing women's parts and whole companies of boy actors, by whom *Epicœne* was first performed, now requires an agility of imagination to appreciate. Most crucially, no commentary or analysis can do justice to the force and vitality of Jonson's linguistic achievement, which can be savored only in Jonson's own words, whether read or heard, and its difference from Shakespeare's achievement is problematic to some audiences. Long witty speeches that do not provide motivation or create suspense are no longer valued in drama for their own sake. Furthermore, Jonsonians, such as Jonas A. Barish and John J. Enck, emphasize that of all Tudor and Stuart playwrights, only Jonson is condemned because he is not Shakespeare.

Barish points out that whereas Shakespeare deals in causality, Jonson does not. Consider, for example, Shakespeare's *Twelfth Night: Or, What You Will* (pr. c. 1600-1602, pb. 1623), from which Jonson most probably derived the idea for contriving a duel between Sir John Daw and Sir Amorous La-Foole. While in *Twelfth Night* the duel between Cesario, who is really Viola, and Sir Andrew Aguecheek ultimately redounds to no one's discredit because a woman and a clown are free not to enjoy physical combat, the fact that Sir John Daw and Sir Amorous La-Foole are so afraid of each other only reveals them as cowards. In Shakespeare, the audience learns how the characters are motivated and why they relate to one another as they do. Hence Shakespeare's Malvolio, victim of a hoax as is Jonson's Morose, causes confusion in the audience, which Morose never does. It is much easier to laugh at those we do not have to understand. In Jonson's dramatic world, motivation is not at issue, and while not all of Jonson's characters are types or humors, their reactions are not caused by the actions of others.

In *Epicœne*, Dauphine wants his inheritance; Morose hopes to beget an heir and keep Dauphine from inheriting anything; Clerimont and Truewit amuse themselves with their prank pulling, while assisting their friend Dauphine; and each character pursues his own course, colliding now and then with others. The audience is not told why Dauphine needs his uncle's money—unlike Bassanio in Shakespeare's *The Merchant of Venice* (pr. c. 1596-1597, pb. 1600), who needs money to win Portia as his wife—nor does the audience learn why Morose is pathologically unable to tolerate any sound around him. Possible reasons for Morose's intolerance of sound, such as childhood trauma, are irrelevant and would ruin the comedy.

The story plays with gender and gender expectations. The action, which consists of tricking Morose into making Dauphine his heir, involves "unmanly," cowardly men who are gossips and "unwomanly," promiscuous, deliberately barren women who fear the effects of aging. Different from the standard comedy that ends with everyone rightly married, *Epicœne* ends with the right couple divorced. Morose, who has been reduced to asserting that he is impotent, discovers that in marrying Epicœne he has wed a boy. Furthermore, silent Epicœne is neither male nor female, since speech is a virtue in a man but a vice in a woman.

In *Epicœne*, silence is associated with cold, impotence, and the country; noise is associated with animals, procreation, and the town. The play maintains a precarious balance between extremes. At one moment, Truewit maintains that women want men to take them by force; the next moment, he is maintaining that a man must adapt to a woman—hence, if a man wants a woman who loves wit, he must give her verses. *Epicœne* continues to offer a magnificent play on the ways men relate to men, women to women, and men to women; it provides a series of brilliant variations without pretending to resolve what must remain irresoluble.

"Critical Evaluation" by Carol Bishop

Further Reading

Barish, Jonas A. *Ben Jonson and the Language of Prose Comedy*. 1960. Reprint. New York: W. W. Norton, 1970. Influential work remains essential to any study of Jonson's comedies.

Brock, D. Heyward. *A Ben Jonson Companion*. Bloomington: Indiana University Press, 1983. Valuable resource provides information on Jonson's work, the events of his life, and the times in which he wrote.

Donaldson, Ian. *Jonson's Magic Houses: Essays in Interpretation*. New York: Oxford University Press, 1997. Offers new interpretations of Jonson's personality, his writings, and his literary legacy.

Enck, John J. *Jonson and the Comic Truth*. Madison: University of Wisconsin Press, 1966. Examination of Jonson's comedies is essential to any study of the dramatist's work. Barish's (cited above) and Enck's studies are in many ways complementary.

Harp, Richard, and Stanley Stewart, eds. *The Cambridge Companion to Ben Jonson*. New York: Cambridge University Press, 2000. Collection of essays provides information about Jonson's life and career, analyses of his comedies and late plays, and an evaluation of his critical heritage. Also presents a description of London and its theaters during Jonson's lifetime.

Loxley, James. *The Complete Critical Guide to Ben Jonson*. New York: Routledge, 2002. Introductory overview of Jonson's life and work is particularly useful for students. Provides biographical information and places Jonson's life and work within the context of his times before discussing several works, including *Epicœne*. Presents critical analysis of the themes in Jonson's plays, the style of his writing, and a comparison of his work to that of William Shakespeare.

McEvoy, Sean. *Ben Jonson, Renaissance Dramatist*. Edinburgh: Edinburgh University Press, 2008. Presents analyses of all of Jonson's plays and attributes their greatness to the playwright's commitment to the ideals of humanism during a time of authoritarianism and rampant capitalism in England. Chapter 5 focuses on *Epicœne*.

Noyes, Robert Gale. *Ben Jonson on the English Stage, 1660-1776*. 1935. Reprint. New York: Benjamin Blom, 1966. Classic work presents valuable information on early productions of Jonson's plays, as provided in contemporary records by such diverse notables as John Dryden, John Dennis, Samuel Pepys, Jeremy Collier, Thomas Shadwell, and William Congreve.

Epigrams

Author: Martial (Marcus Valerius Martialis; c. 38/41-
c. 103 C.E.)
First transcribed: Epigrammata, 86-98 C.E. (English
translation, 1860)
Type of work: Poetry

Martial was the foremost satirical poet of his day in Rome; he also remains one of the greatest satirists in the history of literature. He was born in modestly comfortable circumstances in the province of Spain, possibly on a farm near Tarraco, and also received his education there. He moved to Rome around 64 C.E. and, most likely, was sponsored by his countrymen, including Seneca the Younger and Lucan. Martial then spent most of his writing career under the patronage of other writers, patrician sponsors, and eventually emperors such as Titus, Domitian, Nerva, and Trajan. A friend of major Roman authors, including Quintilian, Martial was elevated to the equestrian order by Emperor Domitian, although he was not reluctant to satirize even some of his own imperial patrons after their deaths.

Widely considered the master of the short epigram as a literary form, he wrote approximately fifteen books and about fifteen hundred epigrams that were published in annual volumes beginning in 86 C.E. More than twelve hundred of his epigrams were written as couplets, the other three hundred extending to twice as many or more lines. His lively wit and flair for irony are noted in acerbic cheerful observations that marked him as obviously gifted for satire, making him popular in his day and into modern times for lampooning individuals and highlighting notable scandals in Rome in his biting commentary. Martial valued virtue above other human characteristics, where his mocking tone and often humorously salacious descriptions render a naughty side to his wit. Martial is still often perceived as hitting below the belt or even as raunchy as he probes the social life of urban Rome at the end of the first century C.E.

Although Martial sometimes took absences from Rome for a few years, he still composed epigrams and could never stay away from the city too long because Rome itself was his inspiration, supplying him with endless subjects of folly. His epigrams, whether long or short, are almost always set up for a matching final punch line.

Martial's first book of epigrams was written to commemorate the opening of Rome's Flavian Amphitheater, now called the Colosseum, in 80 C.E., although his state praise is anything but slavish. His subjects range across every type of social compass Rome contained. For example, the opening epigram from book 1, on public entertainment and the reactions of critics, states "The play you knew was of a risqué type/ nothing that a prude or saint could hype,/ so why come at all, your ringside seat receive/ if this quickly you would frown and leave?" Here, Martial suggests that if a critic could attend as a hypocrite and vent displeasure by abandoning the performance midway, it only made the critic look worse than the play he deliberately came to snub.

Another favorite topic of Martial's sniping was the bungling professional who only made things worse, some of whom were charlatans or cheats, others merely incompetent. In the following epigram, also from book 1, he says "There was a doctor who also as mortician troubled,/ sending his patients to the underworld, fee doubled."

As a farmer in Spain and having rural property in Italy, Martial could also deliver a tough verdict on reaping profit from fickle nature, as this epigram from book 1 relates: "No end to rain will cause your vines to swell,/ Perhaps it is not wine but water you should sell." Here a farmer's pragmatism and rough logic over commercial loss make this epigram humorous.

Martial also usually took great pains to expose injustice in the Rome of his day, believing that there was invariably some form of social retribution, as described in the following epigram from book 2 on vice and cruelty: "You thought your crime was safely silenced, not a soul to tell,/ by cutting out your slave's tongue, to everyone it magnified your hell." Thus, the dirty deed done in private was inevitably all the more public by its monstrosity of maiming the witness.

Many of Martial's epigrams are risque, written for shock value. They are about sexual foibles and posturing, and they make fun of gendered masquerades and peccadilloes, skewering Romans for their bawdy behavior. One lengthy epigram in book 3 is a good example of Martial's sharpness about sex and infidelity:

Your wealth is known both far and wide,
your gold and silver assets are diversified,
your real estate stretches beyond measure,
your library teems with every literary treasure,
but one item where you'll never have security
is perfect faith in your trophy wife's fidelity.

Thus, a man who has everything, including a trophy wife, really has nothing worth having. Martial is reminding his readers of the old adage that money cannot buy love.

One of Martial's favorite peeves is lost youth or pretended beauty, as in the following epigram from book 3:

When your face has gone to wrinkles
    you use lots of cream
thinking your lovers will be fooled as
    in a misty dream
but your wrinkles would be better left alone,
    less visible,
now so caked, standing out all the more
    they're risible.

Also as expected from one used to farming, Martial shows the irony in nature with an epigram from book 4 that is similar to others he composed: "Caught in a drop of amber was a bee/ who found his richer destiny,/ trading sap for honey he put on eternity." Trading on literary similitude, a device used by many, including his literary friend Quintilian, the consonance of honey and amber together makes a great image.

Martial also scorned misinterpreted popularity, as in this epigram from book 6: "You think at your banquet it is you they applaud,/ but they praise your generous table, otherwise, you're a clod." Martial also loved to poke fun at physical oddities, and while not necessarily cruel, he must have drawn a laugh from even the objects of his attention, as in this epigram from book 7: "This man had the fastest ever growing beard/ where first cheek regrew soon as the second was sheared."

Making fun of his contemporaries who could not age gracefully, Martial targets someone easily recognizable for vanity throughout all history in this epigram from book 12: "Your teeth and hair you falsify,/ unfortunate you could not find an eye." Ever the judge, Martial complains about poor value for money in this epigram about wine in book 13, a collection associated with the Roman festival of Saturnalia: "Better money on cheap wines with great taste/ than on snobby vintages without gusto waste."

While a bulk of Martial's epigrams are about sex, promis-

cuity, and mores, as in this epigram from book 14, also associated with Saturnalia, he values circumspection where even furniture can be voyeurs yet not betrayers of secrets: "Regardless how many lovers in my bed noisily camp/ observant but quiet you remain, my bedroom lamp." Thus, Martial's scope from folly to every possible vice in human behavior is peerless in his needling jabs. However, he also could be equally tender, as when lamenting a servant girl's early death in this longer epigram from book 5:

My parents in the Underworld, take care
of this my servant girl so unaware,
from fearful shadows her safely keep
that was too young o'er Death to leap.
In years she was not yet even six
who now must navigate darkest Styx.
Let her but play with children's toys
who was all innocent of lustful boys
and barely learned her master's name,
none of life's sins accruing to her shame.
Earth, you who now cover her with fresh dew
rest lightly on her as she walked light on you.

Martial's enormous influence in writing epigrams has had a lasting legacy in literature, with imitators and admirers all through the ages that include William Shakespeare, Alexander Pope, Samuel Butler, Mark Twain, and Oscar Wilde. That Rome felt the goad of his sharp wit and still preserved most of his epigrams is a sign of his genius. It was a surety that even his high-placed enemies or those lampooned by his barbs in patrician circles often learned, at their own expense, to laugh at themselves, thanks to Martial.

Patrick Hunt

Further Reading

Fitzgerald, William. *Martial: The World of the Epigram*. Chicago: University of Chicago Press, 2007. Argues that Martial is a major author who deserves attention from today's readers and critics. Provides an insightful tour of Martial's works. Includes a helpful bibliography.

Hunt, Patrick, ed. and trans. *Selected Martial Epigrams*. San Francisco: Peirene Press, 2010. This collection of selected Martial epigrams consists of loose verse translations. Includes editor commentary.

Shackleton Bailey, D. R., ed. and trans. *Martial: Epigrams*. Loeb Classical Library 480. Cambridge, Mass.: Harvard University Press, 1993. This translation is intended primarily for academic readers. While its accuracy is impeccable and magisterial, it can lack immediacy and pungency of wit at times.

Spisak, Art L. *Martial: A Social Guide*. London: Gerald Duckworth, 2007. In this brief work, Spisak argues that Martial, "through his poetry, played a serious and vital role in his community as a social guide or conscience."

Wills, Garry, ed. and trans. *Martial's "Epigrams": A Selection*. New York: Viking/Penguin, 2008. Although only a selection of Martial, this collection is rendered in verse like its original and is framed in language both accessible and picaresque with racy word choices.

Epigrams

Author: Meleager (c. 140-c. 70 B.C.E.)
First transcribed: First century B.C.E. (English translation, 1890)
Type of work: Poetry

Meleager is one of the few surviving voices in Greek literature from the early first century B.C.E. This century, so rich for Roman literature, was perhaps the scantiest of all the classical period for Greek literature. Our sense of dearth is intensified by the kind of literature that survived. Ancient Greek literature at no time produced seriously realistic writing, and when the mythical core vanished, the remains took the form of history, philosophy, or artificial styles such as New Comedy, Romance, and Epigram. Ironically, in this unsettled century, when the details of daily life would have been so fascinating, the chief creative writer transmitted some 130 epigrams consisting chiefly of picturesque variations on standard themes and topics of earlier epigrammatic love poets. The incongruity is made all the keener by the fact that Meleager's home until manhood was Gadara in Syria, the town in which Jesus was to cast devils into swine. The juxtaposition is startling.

Meleager's work might be taken for somewhat less the hothouse orchid if his earlier efforts were preserved. His earliest writings were satirical dialogues in prose, modeled on the writings of Menippus, the famous Cynic philosopher and teacher at Gadara. Something of their character may be sensed from the later dialogues of Lucian. The subject of one is reported as a comparison of pease porridge with lentil soup. These were lost, however, and Meleager's literary heritage now consists of the epigrams found in the great collection known as *The Greek Anthology* (c. 90-80 B.C.E.). His epigrams and those of others he imitated may be found in this volume.

The last of Meleager's literary productions was one of the early entries of that anthology: His *Stephanos* (usually translated as *Garland*, also c. 90-80 B.C.E.) is a collection of epigrams of some fifty poets, himself included, with a famous verse preface that compares each poet to that flower that most suggests his poetic character. Later anthologists included *Garland* in larger gatherings; the final collection (apart from the additions derived from Planudes) was made in the tenth century. The poetically significant sections of that collection are the love poems, dedicatory inscriptions, epitaphs, and declamatory, moralizing, convivial, and satiric epigrams. Only about twenty of Meleager's epigrams, however, are to be found outside the love poems.

There is a tendency in the anthology, even within the major sections, to arrange poems on the same theme in a sequence. This tendency provides the most important clue for the appreciation of Meleager. The innocent reader on first encounter is likely to ascribe to Meleager both a hectic variety of erotic liaisons and a continuous intensity of emotion reflected in the extravagant language, both of which in fact distract the reader from the true poetic center of most of the epigrams. The poems are best approached as exercises in various types, attempts at overbidding previous treatments of a topic—overbidding in wit, imagery, and rhetoric. To illustrate, here is an epigram by the earlier poet Asclepiades:

Let this that is left of my soul, whatever it be, let this at least, ye Loves, have rest for heaven's sake. Or else no longer shoot me with arrows but with thunderbolts, and make me utterly into ashes and cinders. Yea! yea! strike me, ye Loves; for withered away as I am by distress, I would have from you, If I may aught, this little gift.

Meleager takes up the notion of the incinerated lover and exploits it in various ways. For example:

> I am down; set thy foot on my neck, fierce demon. I know thee, yea by the gods, yea heavy art thou to bear: I know, too, thy fiery arrows. But if thou set thy torch to my heart, thou shalt no longer burn it; already it is all ash. If I perish, Cleobulus (for cast, nigh all of me, into the flame of lads' love, I lie, a burnt remnant, in the ashes), I pray thee make the urn drunk with wine ere thou lay it in earth, writing thereon, "Love's gift to Death."

The practice of poetry-as-one-upmanship comes all the more naturally to Meleager in that he was part of the wave of rhetorical fashion known as the Asianic. Meleager was a Syrian, but race or culture has nothing to do with Asianism, which is a name for a development within classical literature. The Asianic style sought for something like the Baroque: extravagance in diction and imagery, special tricks and effects in word arrangements. Most of this is hard to illustrate outside the original Greek, but the use of repetition and fancy compounds in the following may give some of the flavor: "Tears, the last gift of my love, even down through the earth I send to thee in Hades, Heliodora—tears ill to shed, and on thy much-wept tomb I pour them in memory of longing, in memory of affection." The witty side of Meleager's Asianism brings him close at times to the Metaphysicals' conceits: "Love-loving Asclepias, with her clear blue eyes, like summer seas, persuadeth all to make the love-voyage."

None of the foregoing is meant to deny the existence of genuine emotion in Meleager's poetry. The point is that, where emotion is found, it emerges from, launches, or sets on fire the already existing framework of artificial craft, and artifice is inseparable from the result. In various ways, of course, the same can be said of all poetry, but this pattern is so dominant in Meleager (and other epigrammatists) that it needs special emphasis as a defining characteristic.

There is a mystical, almost medieval strain in Meleager's love poetry. Meleager at times approaches a religious quality: More than the other epigrammatists, he expresses the total subjection, abasement, and humiliation of the lover, much as the courtly lover of the Middle Ages conceived himself as the abject servant of his lady. For example: "The goddess, queen of the Desires, gave me to thee, Theocles; Love, the soft-sandalled, laid me low for thee to tread on."

Along with the intermittent intensity of his passion, however, there is an element of coyness and sentimentality that pervades Meleager as well as most of the other love epigrammatists of *The Greek Anthology*. This element is absent from the love poetry of the great lyric age of Greece (c. 700-500 B.C.E.). Perhaps it is possible to account for the change by the fact that the great lyric age's love poetry was written when Eros was integrated within or demonically opposed to a genuine religious framework. For most educated people of Meleager's time there was no serious religion but rather philosophy.

One other notable feature of Meleager's love poetry, at least for contemporary readers, is the characteristic type of the beloved. Meleager's loved ones fall exclusively into two classes: *hetaerae* (professional female entertainers or courtesans) and boys in their early teens. Since these two classes account for practically all extant ancient Greek love poetry (Sappho is the exception), this phenomenon needs no special discussion in connection with Meleager.

One should not overemphasize Meleager as a love poet, nor should one be concerned with seeking out those poems that embody "genuine passion," as if these must necessarily be his best. Sheer flights of linguistic dexterity and brilliant variations of traditional themes can produce fine epigrams. Perhaps the most memorable characteristic of Meleager is an outgrowth of this side of his poetry; his bursts of wit often have an element of playfulness and tender humor. In one poem he sends forth a gnat on the dangerous Herculean mission of rousing Heliodora from the side of her current lover to bring her back: The reward will be Hercules' club and lion skin. In another he asks the dew-drunk cicada to strum in antiphon with Pan's piping at high noon and lull him to sleep. An epitaph he writes for himself makes fun of his own garrulity. In all this one can see a survival of the Meleager who wrote on pease porridge and lentil soup.

Meleager's oeuvre is a curious mixture of the complex and the trivial, the passionate and the sophisticated. Connoisseurs of the short lyric will be immensely rewarded by reading Meleager's epigrams.

Further Reading

Cameron, Alan. *The Greek Anthology from Meleager to Planudes*. New York: Oxford University Press, 1993. Superb analysis of the texts, composition, and sources of Meleager's poetry. Traces the literary history of the work as it has been preserved through the centuries.

Clack, Jerry. *Meleager: The Poems*. Wauconda, Ill.: Bolchazy-Carducci, 1992. An excellent introduction to the *Epigrams*. In addition to the poems themselves, Clack provides an introduction, a lengthy commentary, and an explanation about the sources for the epigrams.

Gow, A. S. F., and D. L. Page. *The Greek Anthology: Hellenistic Epigrams*. 2 vols. New York: Cambridge University Press, 1965. Comprehensive scholarly assessment of Meleager's work. An introduction provides information on dating, influences, and content, the arrangement of texts in *Garland*, and an analysis of several poems. The commentary section explicates individual works and includes extensive information on variants.

Gutzwiller, Kathryn J. *Poetic Garlands: Hellenistic Epigrams in Context*. Berkeley: University of California Press, 1998. Gutzwiller's study includes information about Meleager's anthology, and she devotes the final chapters to a reconstruction of that collection.

Jay, Peter. Introduction to *The Poems of Meleager*, by Meleager. Berkeley: University of California Press, 1975.

Brief sketch of the poet's life; concentrates on efforts to assemble the collection of epigrams that are included in *Garland*. Notes the influence of the philosophical movement of Cynicism on Meleager's poetry.

Webster, T. B. L. *Hellenistic Poetry and Art*. New York: Barnes & Noble, 1964. Discusses the love epigrams that Meleager included in *Garland*. Cites numerous examples of the poet's techniques for presenting amorous themes.

Wright, F. A. *A History of Later Greek Literature*. London: Routledge & Kegan Paul, 1951. Brief summary of the poet's literary achievements. Discusses the various women who inspired Meleager's work and the principles he employed in selecting works for inclusion in *Garland*.

Epistles

Author: Horace (65-8 B.C.E.)
First transcribed: Epistulae, book 1, c. 20 B.C.E.;
　　book 2, c. 15 B.C.E. (English translation, 1567)
Type of work: Poetry

The close and intimate life of the Greek city-state gave rise to most of the literary forms of ancient literature, the greater number of which were adopted and adapted by the Romans. However, the epistle, the letter in verse, was a Roman literary invention brought to perfection by Horace during the first days of the Roman imperial period. With Rome administering most of the known world, friends would often be separated in different parts of the empire for years; even those who remained in Italy would often, as did Horace, retire to their country estates. Letter writing in verse not only became a matter of occasional necessity but also was often the only means of communication. It was natural that poets and men of letters should turn the epistle into a literary form so that even at a distance friends could share both poetry and, in some measure, epistolary conversation.

Horace's epistles were published in two books: The first, containing twenty letters, or verse poems, appeared about 20 or 19 B.C.E. The second, containing two long letters, probably appeared in 13 B.C.E. Some scholars argue that the second book of epistles should contain the famous *Epistle to the Pisos*, the *Ars Poetica*. However, this work has traditionally been published separately.

In his first book, Horace is a moralist; in the second, he is a literary critic. The shorter epistles in the first book, some less

than fifteen lines long, are familiar and intimate; there is no doubt that they were written as letters first and poems second. In these shorter letters Horace, a man of forty-five, claims his days of writing lyric poetry are finished, expressing interest in the writing of the younger generation, inviting a friend to dinner, and the like. The longer epistles of the first book, however, are much more formal and tend to be didactic; they smack of the tour de force, and although they may well have been sent to the people to whom they are addressed, they read more like open letters to the poet's general audience. Typical of these longer letters, and setting the moral tone of the first book, is epistle 1, addressed to the poet's friend and patron, Maecenas. In it the poet bids farewell to poetry and states that in his declining years he will devote himself to philosophic inquiry. He will, however, be an eclectic, limiting his speculation to the precepts of no single school of philosophy, for his interest is to find what is ultimately and lastingly profitable for the achievement of virtue. The calm pursuit of wisdom, he states, is the highest good, not the frantic pursuit of things. Showing himself to be as much a Stoic as anything else, he claims that the secret of happiness is not to value anything too much. Other matters he speaks of in the first epistle are the need to control the passions so as not to ruin enjoyment, the need to train one's character, and the need to adapt oneself to both company and oneself alone. In conclusion, Horace's wish from life is enough books and enough food to keep him comfortable.

Thus setting the tone, Horace proceeds to write of the following matters in the successive epistles of the first book. Epistle 2, to Lollius, begins with the old doctrine that important moral lessons are to be learned from the study of Homer. Horace quickly turns to his real subject, however, which is the foolishness of putting off or not exerting the effort requisite for moral self-improvement. Epistle 3, to Julius Florus, was written to a friend who was abroad campaigning with Claudius; the poet inquires about other young friends on Claudius's staff. He is particularly interested in their literary activity. Epistle 4, to Tibullus, the poet, is a short note of warm friendship in which Horace gently recommends the Epicurean idea that one should live each day as if it were the last. Epistle 5, to Torquatus, is an invitation to a frugal but cheerful and friendly dinner party. Epistle 6, to Numicius, is a lay sermon on the famous Horatian phrase *Nil admirari* (wonder at nothing). The wise man should love nothing but virtue: Live, and be happy. Epistle 7, to Maecenas, is a note of appreciation for various favors. Horace apologizes for absenting himself from Rome for so long, and he uses the occasion to describe the ideal giver and, with some humor, the ideal receiver. Self-sufficiency, he claims, is preferable to all other blessings. Epistle 8, to Celsus Albinovanus, is a letter to a member of Tiberius's staff. The poet describes his own ill health and admonishes Celsus to bear up well under prosperity. Epistle 9, to Claudius Tiberius Nero, is a graceful letter of recommendation for Horace's friend Septimus. Epistle 10, to Aristius Fuscus, praises the superiority of country life as being more conducive to the contented mind and more favorable to liberty of spirit than the city life of Fuscus.

Epistle 11, to Bullatus, is an attempt to call this friend back to Rome from the East, where he retired because of his despair over the civil wars. Happiness, Horace says, is not in travel but in the mind and is to be achieved anywhere or nowhere. Epistle 12, to Iccius, ironically ridicules miserliness, introduces a friend, and gives news of recent events in the empire. Epistle 13, to Vinnius Asina, cautions Asina, Horace's emissary, to present certain of Horace's writings to Augustus at a propitious and proper moment and with due decorum. Epistle 14 chastises the caretaker of his farm, to whom the letter is written, for missing city life. Horace briefly reminisces about his wild younger years and then advises the wisdom of contentment. Epistle 15, to C. Numonius Vala, asks about the situation and conditions of the town of Velia, where Horace was advised by his physician to take a cure. Again he comments on country life. Epistle 16, to Quinctius, describes the situation and advantages of Horace's Sabine farm. His description is detailed enough that its position can be determined. The poet goes on to philosophize on the nature of true virtue and the self-sufficiency and freedom of the virtuous man. Epistle 17, to Scaeva, is a letter of advice to one who would seek advantage by frequenting the company of the great. The friendship of the great, the poet says, is a good thing, but one must always solicit favors from them with modesty and caution. Epistle 18, to Lollius, in a more elaborate way treats the same topic as the seventeenth. Horace discusses the tact and discretion a client of the great must have; he concludes with remarks concerning peace of mind, a quality difficult to achieve when one depends on the favor of the great. Epistle 19, to Maecenas, is a review of the poet's literary career; he decries the folly of slavish imitation, and he attacks his detractors. Epistle 20, addressed to his book, is developed as an argument between the poet and his now-completed first book of epistles. The book is addressed as if it were a young slave, a favorite of his master, who wants to be sold out of a quiet country household and into an exciting city house where he can seek advancement. Horace explains all the troubles and changes he must undergo. He ends the poem with remarks on what he expects from posterity. The tone of the nineteenth and twentieth epistles implies that the poet is finished now with his writing career.

The impression left is that middle-aged Horace is feeling old and in delicate health, and that he will write no more. Perhaps he really did believe he was through with poetry; however, he still had a few more poems to write, and among them were the two long discourses on literature (companion pieces, in effect, to the *Ars Poetica*) that make up the second volume of epistles.

The first of these two letters is to Augustus. After first paying the emperor the highest kind of compliments, Horace plunges into a consideration of the current state of literature. First he intervenes in the then raging Roman "battle of the ancients and the moderns." He acknowledges the greatness of the earlier Greek poets, but he wants to have the early Latin poets respected more than they usually are. Horace sketches out the history of Latin poetry from the beginnings up through the Greeks' "capture" of their captor, Rome, and then on to his own day. Looking at the present state of letters, Horace judges (and history shows him to have been quite correct) that the drama would not reach great heights in Rome: The taste of the people was for spectacle, mimes, and elaborate staging. Nondramatic poetry, he thinks, will do very well, for Augustus, whose taste is impeccable, will encourage poetry and will not be deceived by second-rate poets.

The second epistle of the last book is to Julius Florus, a friend of the poet who apparently wanted also to be a poet. This letter is much more personal in tone than the letter to Augustus and full of intimate detail. Horace begins by testifying that he is rather lazy and undependable now that he no longer must write poetry in order to stay alive, as he did when he was young. Moreover, poetry is one of the follies of the young and, now that he is growing old, he must give it up as he has his other youthful pastimes. How, he asks, can a man write real poetry amid the hustle and bustle and distractions of Rome? The real poet must live and write in the quiet countryside. The poets who stay in the city form worthless mutual admiration societies out of which come no true criticism. A good poet is a good critic, too, and he can take and use valid criticism of his own work. Bad poets hate criticism of any kind. Perhaps the happiest writer is the madman who writes very badly but who thinks he writes divinely. At any rate, Horace concludes, at his age it is proper to think of gaining happiness, which is found in calm and in contentment, not in wealth.

Further Reading

Armstrong, David. *Horace*. New Haven, Conn.: Yale University Press, 1989. A general introduction to Horace's works that covers the developing stages of his life and his relation to his changing society. Chapter 4 on the *Epistles*, which analyzes important themes in the poems, is especially good. Includes a useful index, notes, and a rewarding bibliography of primary and secondary sources. An excellent source for beginners.

Fraenkel, E. *Horace*. Oxford, England: Clarendon Press, 1957. An important analysis of the major aspects of Horace's life and the relationships among his works. Provides an introduction to issues of classical scholarship in the study of Horace.

Harrison, Stephen, ed. *The Cambridge Companion to Horace*. New York: Cambridge University Press, 2007. Critical overview of Horace's life and work. Some of the essays discuss Horace and ancient Greek and Hellenistic poetry, Horace and Roman literary history, and Horace and Augustus, while others explore the themes and style of his work. Chapter 9 is devoted to an examination of *Epistles*.

Hills, Philip D. *Horace*. London: Bristol Classical Press, 2005. An introductory overview of Horace's life, times, work, and literary influence. The two parts of *Epistles* are examined in chapters 5 and 7.

Kilpatrick, Ross. *The Poetry of Friendship*. Edmonton: University of Alberta Press, 1986. A detailed and scholarly discussion of Horace's first epistle and its thematic relation to other works in the ancient world.

Oliensis, Ellen. *Horace and the Rhetoric of Authority*. New York: Cambridge University Press, 1998. Examines how Horace created a public self-image in his work. Oliensis argues that Horace shaped his poetry so he could promote his authority and remain deferential to his patrons, while taking account of the jealousy of rival poets and the judgment of posterity. Chapter 4 focuses on *Epistles*.

Reckford, Kenneth J. *Horace*. New York: Twayne, 1969. An extremely accessible introduction to Horace that provides a solid overview of the important issues in his poetry. Includes an excellent section on the *Epistles* as well as a useful chronology of Horace's life, an index, and a rewarding bibliography of primary and secondary sources

Rudd, Niall. Introduction to *The Satires of Horace and Persius: A Verse Translation*. Harmondsworth, England: Penguin Books, 1973. A thoroughly enjoyable translation of Horace's *Epistles*. Provides useful notes and commentary to the text and translation and offers a sound introduction to the poems, life, and influence of Horace. An excellent source for beginners who seek both a lively translation and a solid basic introduction.

Epitaph of a Small Winner

Author: Joaquim Maria Machado de Assis (1839-1908)
First published: Memórias póstumas de Brás Cubas,
    1881 (*The Posthumous Memoirs of Brás Cubas,*
    1951; better known as *Epitaph of a Small Winner,*
    1952)
Type of work: Novel
Type of plot: Philosophical realism
Time of plot: 1805-1869
Locale: Rio de Janeiro

Principal characters:
BRAZ CUBAS, a wealthy, cultured Brazilian
MARCELLA, his first mistress
VIRGILIA, his fiancé and later his mistress
LOBO NEVES, Virgilia's husband
QUINCAS BORBA, a philosopher and pickpocket

The Story:

Braz Cubas, a wealthy Brazilian, dies of pneumonia in his sixty-fifth year. After his death, he decides to write his autobiography, to while away a part of eternity and to give humanity some record of his life. Braz was born in 1805. His childhood was an easy one, for his father was extremely wealthy and indulgent, only pretending to be severe with his child for the sake of appearances. One of the earliest experiences the boy remembered was the elation of the Brazilians over the defeat of Napoleon, an occasion marked in his memory by the gift of a small sword. The sword was the most important aspect of the occasion, and Braz remarked that each person has his own "sword" that makes occasions important.

As a child, Braz did not like school. In his seventeenth year, he had his first love affair with a courtesan named Marcella. Trying to please his mistress, Braz spent all the money he could borrow from his mother and then gave promissory notes to fall due on the day he inherited his father's estate. His father, learning of the affair, paid off his son's debts and shipped him off to a university in Spain. At first, Braz hoped to take Marcella with him. She refused to go.

Graduated from the university and awarded a degree, Braz admitted that he knew very little. He then took advantage of his father's liberality and wealth and spent several years traveling about Europe. Called back to Rio de Janeiro by news that his mother was dying of cancer, he arrived home in time to see her before she died. After her death, he went into retirement, remaining in seclusion until his father came to him with plans for a marriage and for a seat in the Brazilian legislative body. After some vacillation, Braz decided to obey his father's wishes. The reason for his hesitation was a love affair with a rather beautiful girl. His discovery that she was lame, however, turned him away from her. On his return to social life, he learned that the young woman his father had picked out for him, a girl named Virgilia, had position, wealth, and beauty. It was through her father's influence that

the elder Cubas expected his son to get ahead politically. Unfortunately for the schemes of both father and son, Virgilia met Lobo Neves, a young man with more ambition and greater prospects. She decided to marry him, a decision that ended, at least temporarily, prospects of a political career for Braz.

Disappointed and disgruntled with life, he accidentally met Marcella, his former mistress. He found her greatly changed, for smallpox destroyed her beauty. After losing her looks, she left her earlier profession to become the keeper of a small jewelry shop.

Disappointment over his son's failure to win Virgilia was too much for his father, who died shortly afterward. There was a great to-do after the father's death, for Braz's brother-in-law turned out to be an avaricious man who wanted his wife, Braz's sister, to have as much of the estate as possible. Braz accepted calmly the selfish and unfortunate aspect of human nature thus revealed and agreed, for his sister's sake, to be reconciled with his greedy brother-in-law.

Not very long after his father's death, Braz learned from Virgilia's brother that Virgilia and her husband were returning to Rio de Janeiro. Braz was pleased; he was still in love with her. A few days after the return of Virgilia and her husband, he met them at a ball. Virgilia and Braz danced several waltzes together and fell more deeply in love than they were while Braz was courting her. They continued to meet, and before long Virgilia became his mistress.

One day, Braz found a package in which were several bundles of banknotes. He kept the money and later used it to establish a trust fund for Dona Placida, a former servant of Virgilia's family, who maintained the house in which Virgilia and Braz kept their assignations. They managed for several years to keep their affair a secret, so that Braz could be a guest in Virgilia's home as well. In fact, he and Lobo Neves were good friends.

One day, Braz met Quincas Borba, an old schoolmate who was reduced to begging. The man took some money from Braz and, as he discovered later, also stole his watch. That night, Braz suggested to Virgilia that they run away. She refused to do so. They had a lovers' quarrel, followed by a tender scene of repentance.

A short time later, Lobo Neves was offered the governorship of a province, and he suggested that Braz accompany him as his secretary. The situation was inviting to the two lovers, but they knew that in the smaller provincial capital their secret could not long be hidden. Their problems were unexpectedly solved when superstitious Neves refused the government post because the document appointing him was dated on the thirteenth of the month.

The love affair continued until Virgilia became pregnant. Neither of the lovers doubted that Braz was the father of the child, and he acted very much like a husband who expected to be presented with his firstborn. The child, not carried the full term, died at birth, much to the sorrow of Virgilia and Braz, and of the husband as well, who thought the child was his.

One day, Braz received a letter from Quincas Borba, the begging schoolmate who stole his watch. Improving his finances, the beggar became a philosopher, a self-styled humanist. Borba's ideas fascinated Braz, who always fancied himself an intellectual and a literary man. He was also pleased when Borba sent him a watch as good as the one he stole. Braz spent a great deal of time with Borba, for Neves became suspicious of the relationship between his wife and her lover, and the two were discreet enough to stay away from each other for a time.

At last, Virgilia and her husband left Rio de Janeiro after Neves received another political appointment. For a time, Braz felt like a widower. Lonely, he turned to public life. Defeated for office, he then became the publisher of an opposition newspaper, but his venture was not successful. He also fell in love and finally decided to get married. Once more, he was disappointed, for his fiancé died during an epidemic.

The years passed rather uneventfully. Braz grew older and so did his friends. Not many weeks after the death of Quincas Borba, who became a close companion, Braz fell ill of pneumonia. One visitor during his last illness was Virgilia, whose husband died, but even her presence was not enough to keep Braz from slipping into delirium. In his dying moments, he cast up the accounts of his life and decided that in the game of life he was the winner by only a small margin, in that he brought no one else into the world to suffer the misery of life.

Critical Evaluation:

Joaquim Maria Machado de Assis is one of the most remarkable figures of Brazilian literature. He is often regarded as its central figure and has been compared with such giants of world literature as Henry James, Gustave Flaubert, and Jorge Luis Borges. Machado was a mestizo (a person of mixed racial descent) and was reared in poor circumstances. Nevertheless, he taught himself English, German, and French and read widely in American and European literature. He lived almost his entire life in his home city of Rio de Janeiro, where he worked as a journalist, dramatist, translator, government official, and theater critic. A sociable man, Machado de Assis moved easily among the intellectual circles of Brazilian society. An epileptic, he was often sick as a child, and his ill health continued into his adulthood. He began *Epitaph of a Small Winner*, which was a sharp departure from his earlier, more conventionally Romantic works, while taking a rest cure in Tijuca, outside Rio de Janeiro. Several chapters of this novel were dictated to his wife Carolina, as Machado de Assis's eyesight was too poor for him to be able to write them out himself.

Epitaph of a Small Winner is the first of what are sometimes called Machado de Assis's carioca novels, which refers to their focus on the society of Rio de Janeiro. These novels, including Machado de Assis's acknowledged masterpiece *Dom Casmurro* (1899; English translation, 1953), share many stylistic and thematic concerns. Some general themes include: problems of good and evil, the destructive nature of time, the dangers of the human ego, the unreliable nature of human judgment, the contrast between human longing for perfection and the frailty of human nature, the danger of totalizing scientific and philosophical systems, and the correlation between pleasure and disillusionment.

Many of these themes are readily apparent in *Epitaph of a Small Winner*. The humanism of Quincas Borba is the sort of explain-everything philosophy that Machado de Assis considers dangerous. Braz Cubas demonstrates the natural laziness of human nature; he is often all too willing to accept the easy answer. Braz accepts things as they happen to him; he reacts rather than acts. He yearns for great things, yet accepts his mundane life.

One of the most obvious features of *Epitaph of a Small Winner* is the remarkable narrator. The novel is told in the first person by a narrator who is already dead. The narrator's memories of past events are highly subjective, and Braz demonstrates himself to be egotistical, self-interested, and not particularly bright; in short, the reader is presented with an untrustworthy narrator. This narrator often pauses to address the reader, even going so far as to say that, if there is a flaw in the book, the reader is that flaw. The narrator is not only untrustworthy but also arrogant.

This feature affects the reader's response to the novel. The reader's role in the storytelling process is emphasized, for the reader cannot relax and let the story happen, since veracity of Braz's entire narrative is called into question. There are times when Braz seems to be trying to justify himself; he may be telling his story in such a way as to make himself look good. If a reader cannot trust the narrator of a novel, who can be trusted? The novel thus proposes questions regarding the reliability of language and, with that, a doubting of the nature of reality itself, as reality seems to change according to the words used to describe it. If Braz describes his life in a particular way, then that is what that life becomes, regardless of what actually happened, or how another character might tell the story.

Thus, the stylistic innovations of the story emphasize some of the thematic concerns, as the reader is called on to interact directly with a flawed human being in the form of the narrator. The reader must question not only Braz's judgment but also the reader's own. This demonstrates Machado de Assis's primary concern in his novels—the inner life of his characters. He attempts to examine problems of good and evil, not merely by describing human cruelty, violence, or injustice, but by demonstrating how easy it is for one individual to accept evil, not necessarily because evil is attractive but because it is easy to accept.

Despite the novel's somewhat pessimistic view of life, it is often admired for its satirical and ironic humor. Braz's pessimism is often mistakenly applied to Machado de Assis. It is true that Braz draws pessimistic conclusions about life, but attributing them to Machado de Assis may not be entirely appropriate, and not only because the author warned against biographical readings of his works. Braz's pessimism is not presented as an admirable thing; rather, it makes him appear ridiculous. It is clear that Machado de Assis was certainly aware of humanity's shortcomings; however, there would be no point in illustrating them so well if he did not at least hope, as every good satirist does, that they could be amended.

"Critical Evaluation" by Kelly C. Walter Carney

Further Reading

Caldwell, Helen. *Machado de Assis: The Brazilian Master and His Novels*. Berkeley: University of California Press, 1978. One of the primary translators of Machado de Assis's work into English focuses upon his novels, with special emphasis on *Epitaph of a Small Winner*.

Duarte, Eduardo de Assis. "Machado de Assis's African Descent." *Research in African Literatures* 38, no. 1 (Spring, 2007): 134-151. Focuses on how Machado de Assis's work expressed his African ancestry in regard to slavery and interracial relations in nineteenth century Brazil.

Fitz, Earl E. *Machado de Assis*. Boston: Twayne, 1989. An excellent general introduction to Machado de Assis's life and work. Discusses all of his novels as well as his plays, short stories, poetry, and journalism.

Kristal, Efraín, and José Luiz Passos. "Machado de Assis and the Question of Brazilian National Identity." In *Brazil in the Making: Facets of National Identity*, edited by Carmen Nava and Ludwig Lauerhass, Jr. Lanham, Md.: Rowman & Littlefield, 2006. This essay discussing Machado de Assis's impact on Brazilian identity is included in a collection examining the unique character of the country and the identity of its citizens.

Neto, José Raimundo Maia. *Machado de Assis, the Brazilian Pyrrhonian*. West Lafayette, Ind.: Purdue University Press, 1994. Part 2 concentrates on the second phase of Machado de Assis's career, the years from 1879 to 1908, with a separate chapter on *Epitaph of a Small Winner*. Includes detailed notes and bibliography.

Nunes, Maria Luisa. *The Craft of an Absolute Winner: Characterization and Narratology in the Novels of Machado de Assis*. Westport, Conn.: Greenwood Press, 1983. Focuses on the novels, paying particular attention to the characters and to Machado de Assis's ideas about time.

_____. "Story Tellers and Character: Point of View in Machado de Assis's Last Five Novels." *Latin American Literary Review* 7, no. 13 (1978): 52-63. Discusses how these novels, including *Epitaph of a Small Winner*, use their unusual narrators to involve the reader in the text. Discusses Machado de Assis's ironic humor.

Schwarz, Roberto. *A Master on the Periphery of Capitalism: Machado de Assis*. Translated by John Gledson. Durham, N.C.: Duke University Press, 2001. Schwarz, a Brazilian literary theorist, applies a Marxist interpretation to his literary and cultural analysis of *Epitaph of a Small Winner*, discussing the novel's style and structure as well as its views of nineteenth century Brazilian society.

Epithalamion

Author: Edmund Spenser (c. 1522-1599)
First published: 1595
Type of work: Poetry
Type of plot: Love
Time of plot: June 11, 1594
Locale: Southern Ireland

Principal characters:
THE POEM'S SPEAKER, a groom
THE SPEAKER'S BRIDE
VARIOUS CLASSICAL DEITIES AND SPIRITS

The Poem:

On the day of his wedding, the poem's speaker calls upon the muses. They have often inspired him with verse, he says, so he now asks them to assist him in singing the praises of his love and preparing for the wedding. It is not yet dawn when he asks the muses to wake his bride after gathering lilies, roses, and flowers of all kinds to prepare her bower and her path for the moment when she awakes. The poet then calls directly upon the nymphs who care for various facets of nature's beauty to come to help prepare his bride and to sing to her.

The groom next addresses his bride herself, urging her to awake. All nature is singing in affirmation, he tells her, of the day's joyous event. Asking why she still sleeps, he invokes various divine attendants to assist in preparation. He prays to Phoebus Apollo, father of the muses, asking that this particular day be given to the poet and promising to then praise Phoebus with loud singing.

The groom turns his description to his bride's procession and her beauty. Much music, singing, and dancing anticipates her coming forth. She appears, dressed in white that he says is so appropriate to her virginity that one might think she were an angel. The poet tells the daughters of merchants to consider his bride's beauty: her golden hair, her modest countenance, her eyes, cheeks, lips, breasts, neck, and figure, shining in perfect purity so that other virgins stand in amazement to look at her. Her inner beauty, he tells them, is even more glorious. The virtues of love, chastity, faith, respect, and modesty rule her heart and keep temptation far from her mind. If only they could see those invisible virtues, he says, they would be filled with wonder and song.

The groom then calls for the church to be opened for the bride's entrance to the ceremony itself. He instructs the attendant maidens to observe and learn from his bride's reverence. The bride is brought to the altar for the ceremony, as music plays in praise of the Lord. She blushes as the priest blesses her; even the angels attending the altar are distracted by the beauty of her face. The poet asks his bride why she so shyly takes his hand in oath.

Once the ceremony is complete, the celebration commences. The new husband cries to all those in attendance, telling them to rejoice, to let the feasting begin, to pour the wine, and to ring the bells. He laments that this day, midsummer's day, is the longest day and shortest night of the year; thus, the hours until they can consummate the marriage are passing too slowly. At last, the evening star appears, twinkling with gladness for their sakes.

The celebration concludes as darkness approaches. The groom calls for his bride to be escorted to the bower. He addresses the night, asking it to wrap the newlyweds together in peaceful darkness, free of fear or trouble or tears. He urges that nothing, whether whispers, dreams, evil spirits, birds, or frogs, make any disturbance, calling for complete silence as they spend their first night together. The groom next turns his song into a prayer for a blessing upon his bride's womb and their offspring, petitioning various deities overseeing marriage or procreation, including Juno, Genius, and Hymen. He closes the poem by addressing the song itself, commissioning it to serve as a decoration for and monument to his bride.

Critical Evaluation:

Edmund Spenser wrote *Epithalamion* for his wife, Elizabeth Boyle, whom he married on midsummer's day, 1594, the longest day of the year. (By the Julian calendar in use in England at that time, midsummer's day fell on June 11.) The poem's title comes from the Greek roots *epi* ("on") and *thalmos* ("bridal chamber"). Spenser joins a classical tradition of writers of epithalamia with this poem. He employs classical and Christian allusions and precise formal structure to create a masterpiece unique in English literature, simultaneously personal and universal, sexual and spiritual, temporal and eternal, as it celebrates the beauty of marriage and the marriage bed.

The poem was originally published with *Amoretti*, a collection of eighty-nine sonnets that express the speaker's love for his beloved and that are also believed to have been written for Elizabeth Boyle. *Epithalamion* documents the wedding day itself from start to finish, celebrating the long-awaited consummation of the love described in *Amoretti*.

In the tradition highly characteristic of early modern (Renaissance) literature, Spenser uses classical allusion heavily. His calling on deities and spirits such as Hymen, Juno, and the muses is an example of Christian neo-Platonism, in which classical figures are appropriated in the service of Christian spirituality. Thus, for example, the groom's prayer to "Phoebus, father of the Muse" to "let this day let this one day be myne/ . . . / then I thy soverayne praises loud will sing" would be understood as a prayer to God the Father. Spenser highlights the essentially Christian nature of their union by leaving all classical allusion out of stanzas 12-13, where he describes the wedding ceremony itself, the only stanzas in the poem employing exclusively Christian language. Other, less direct biblical allusions to the Song of Solomon, the Psalms, and the Book of Revelation highlight parallels between Spenser's earthly union and the anticipated wedding of Christ and the Church.

The formal structure of the poem also reflects the Christianized classical poetics and philosophy common in Renaissance literature. The first and second halves contain a symmetry that places the holy union at the center. Stanza 1 is a prologue; stanzas 2-11 prepare for the ceremony; stanzas 12-13, the center of the poem, describe the ceremony itself; stanzas 14-23 describe the postwedding celebration and consummation; stanza 24 is an envoi dedicating the poem. Other thematic parallels between stanzas in the first and second halves of the poem add to its overall sense of unity.

Spenser structured the poem using a unique astronomical pattern first documented in A. Kent Hieatt's study *A Short Time's Endless Monument*: The twenty-four stanzas correspond to the hours in a day, paralleling the progression of the poem through the speaker's wedding day. The 365 long lines (mostly iambic pentameter) correspond to the days of the year. Night falls at line 300, precisely sixteen stanzas into the poem, corresponding to the sixteen hours of daylight and eight hours of darkness that occur on the summer solstice at the latitude of the southern Irish locale of Spenser's wedding. The negatives introduced into each stanza's refrain beginning in stanza 17 underscore the poem's shift from light to darkness at this point. Spenser used this numerology to emphasize the relationship between particular and universal time and the eternal, spiritual quality of the marriage as a whole.

Christopher E. Crane

Further Reading

Greenlaw, Edwin, et al., eds. *The Works of Edmund Spenser—A Variorum Edition: The Minor Poems, Vol. II.* Baltimore: Johns Hopkins University Press, 1947. This significant critical edition of the poem (along with all of Spenser's works) offers detailed annotations with explanations, cross references, and analogues for key words in nearly every line of the poem. Appendixes provide excerpts from major critical and historical treatments of the poem, as well as its sources, poetics, and influence.

Hadfield, Andrew, ed. *The Cambridge Companion to Spenser.* New York: Cambridge University Press, 2001. Includes a wide range of essays covering Spenser's major poetry groupings, historical and cultural influences, biography, and influence. *Epithalamion* is discussed among the "shorter poems."

Hieatt, A. Kent. *Short Time's Endless Monument: The Symbolism of the Numbers in Edmund Spenser's "Epithalamion."* New York: Columbia University Press, 1960. A seminal study of specific numerical patterns in the poem as an essential elements of Spenser's primary meaning. Includes an annotated text of the poem.

Larsen, Kenneth J., ed. *Edmund Spenser's "Amoretti" and "Epithalamion": A Critical Edition.* Tempe, Ariz.: Medieval & Renaissance Texts & Studies, 1997. This critical edition of the poem provides a useful introduction and a thorough commentary with excellent glosses, cross references, and a detailed explication. An appendix provides a listing of scripture readings and lessons from *The Book of Common Prayer* for 1594 for the dates covered by the two poems.

Oram, William A. *Edmund Spenser.* New York: Simon & Schuster/Macmillan, 1997. Accessible for students and other nonspecialists, this chronological overview of Spenser's poetry offers a chapter on each major phase of Spenser's career, including one on the *Amoretti* and *Epithalamion* that details sources, major themes, and specifics of genre.

Van Es, Bart, ed. *A Critical Companion to Spenser Studies.* New York: Palgrave Macmillan, 2006. Collection of essays touching on various aspects of Spenser's life and poetry, including his representations of politics, religion, and women. An essay titled "Shorter Verse Published 1590-95" includes detailed discussion of *Epithalamion*. A final essay on resources for Spenser studies and an extensive bibliography make the volume a useful starting point for further research.

Equus
A Love Story

Author: Peter Shaffer (1926-   )
First produced: 1973; first published, 1973
Type of work: Drama
Type of plot: Psychological realism
Time of plot: Late twentieth century
Locale: Great Britain

Principal characters:
MARTIN DYSART, a child psychiatrist
ALAN STRANG, a disturbed boy of seventeen
FRANK STRANG, Alan's father
DORA STRANG, Alan's mother
HESTHER SALOMON, a magistrate
JILL MASON, a worker at the stables
HARRY DALTON, the owner of the stables

The Story:

Martin Dysart, a child psychiatrist, recognizes that his life is filled with emptiness and pain. He is confronted by this recognition through his treatment of Alan Strang, an adolescent who inexplicably blinds six horses with a horsepick. It is a crime that shocks and outrages the owner of the stables, who believes that Alan should be imprisoned. However, Hesther Salomon, the magistrate in charge of the case, recognizes a deep need in the boy, and she brings him to Dysart hoping that he can make the boy "normal." Dysart comes to recognize that he can, but at a terrible cost.

At first distrustful of Dysart, Alan sings jingles to block Dysart's overtures. Unperturbed, Dysart begins seeing Alan and then begins to make inquiries. He finds the Strang household to be absolutely normal superficially, but, beneath this appearance of normality, strange tensions vibrate. Mr. Strang is dictatorial and repressed; Mrs. Strang is filled with religious mania. Neither is able to deal in any real way with what happened.

Alan himself seems unable to deal with his actions, and Dysart works to find ways to allow Alan to tell him things that will help to explain the blinding of the horses. Using a small recorder, Alan tells Dysart of his first encounter with a horse on a beach when he was six years old. A rider took him up and down through the surf, Alan glorying in the ride until his enraged father pulled him down from the horse, claiming that the horse and rider were menaces to safety. For Alan, it was a moment of great passion; it began his sense of a godlike spirit in horses, a god he named Equus.

From Mr. Dalton, Dysart learns that Alan was introduced to the stable by Jill Mason, and at first he believed that he found a good worker, since Alan did much more than his share of grooming the horses and cleaning the stables. Oddly, however, Alan never rode the horses, though Mr. Dalton suspected that periodically they were ridden at night. Clearly, Alan was passionately fascinated by horses; in fact, he wor-

shiped the god Equus in them, something Mr. Strang discovered disconcertingly when he saw Alan chanting before a picture of a horse, putting a bit in his own mouth, and beating himself.

Dysart is more and more taken with Alan; he sees in him someone who is filled with a passion, whose life is filled with worship, and he envies Alan. His own life seems so safe and secure, so empty of energy and passion that he questions whether his treatment of Alan is anything less than a monstrous sacrifice to the normal.

Under hypnosis, Dysart takes Alan's mind back to one of the nights when he took a horse, Nugget, out riding. It was an evening of passionate devotion, of the worship of the god Equus. Alan led the horse gently out from the stables to a field, where he stripped and bowed to the god. He inserted a bit in his own mouth, and then, in complete worshipful ecstasy, he galloped around the field. Afterward, he stood beside the horse, fully devoted, fully alive. It was a sense of passion that Dysart never experienced.

Soon after, Mrs. Strang comes to visit Alan, and, in a terrible fight, he silently accuses her of some responsibility for his behavior. She refuses to accept the accusation, and, when Dysart intervenes, she claims that what Alan did is Alan's responsibility, not that of his parents. Nevertheless, she also blames the Devil and leaves without any real understanding of what is troubling her son.

Alan suggests obliquely to Dysart that he is waiting to be given a truth pill; Dysart picks up on the suggestion and, giving Alan a placebo, has him tell about the night he blinded the horses. Before he begins, Alan reveals that he knows that Dysart is in pain; Dysart is startled by Alan's perception but leads him back hypnotically to that night. It began on a date with Jill to see a pornographic film, at which they discovered Mr. Strang. After the initial shock and embarrassment, Alan suddenly recognized that his father, too, had a secret inner life, that everyone did. It was a freeing recognition for him.

When they walked back to the stables and Jill proposed that they make love, Alan sensed the confining and overpowering presence of his god, Equus, who would always be watching. He found himself impotent in the face of his god, and, after chasing Jill away, he blinded the horses so that Equus could not see him.

The crisis being reached, the episode being lived through again, Alan falls asleep, dreamless for the first time in a long time. Dysart recognizes that he is now beginning a recovery, but his recovery means that he will no longer be passionate, that he will no longer gallop with a god. Dysart recognizes that, in destroying this passion, he, too, stabs at faces with picks.

Critical Evaluation:

In many ways, *Equus* exhibits strong connections to classical drama, particularly Greek drama. Its solemn, stately, and ceremonial manner duplicates classical ceremonies. The strongest connection, however, is the presence of the chorus, which in Greek drama is meant to comment upon and explain the meaning of what is happening on the stage. Here, the chorus is played by a group of six actors who play the horses. The presence of the god is suggested by the Equus noise that they make in chorus, and it seems that they watch the action throughout; they see everything.

This "seeing" is an important part of Alan Strang's perception of his god. In one way, Equus is a god-slave, in that Alan can lead Equus out and control him, making him gallop in the field. In this sense, Equus recalls Christ in his chains being led to Calvary. In fact, Alan keeps a gruesome picture of Christ in chains until his father tears it down; he replaces it with a picture of a horse with enormous eyes.

However, in another way, Equus is a beloved. After the gallop, Alan and the horse stand neck to neck, and there is a wonderful intimacy that fills Alan with life and passion. In yet another way, Equus is completely demanding and compelling, taking on the role of the avenging God that Mrs. Strang can envision so vividly. "God sees you, Alan, he sees you," she insists, presenting God as always hovering, waiting to avenge. Thus, in the stable scene, Alan, though he has come to recognize that he is not the only one with a secret inner life, also senses that the god will always demand him completely, that he will never find passion elsewhere, that he is always within in the sight of Equus. It is this consuming sight against which he strikes.

Perhaps the central crisis of the play, though, is within Martin Dysart. In a dream, he imagines himself wearing a classical mask and being the chief priest at a sacrifice of five hundred children. He must go on with his task, but he cannot continue. This becomes for him a symbol of what he does to children through his psychiatry. He sacrifices essential parts of them that make them uniquely themselves. In fact, he sacrifices them to the god of the normal. When Hesther Salomon suggests that at the least he is able to take their pain away, Dysart realizes that even in doing this he has taken away something that is uniquely theirs, substituting only the safe and bland normal.

Equus is a play about passion and worship, and the strong suggestion of the dramatist is that modern society has lost its ability to worship anything, let alone worship it passionately. Dysart realizes that while he looks at books on classical Greece and travels there with all accommodations booked and all eventualities covered, out on a field a young boy is trying to become a centaur; he is galloping with a god. This worship is what Dysart longs for, this awareness of gods springing out at every turn. Instead, he lives in a dry, sterile flat, in a dry, sterile marriage, taking away passion from children.

Dysart is not the only one in this situation. Dora and Frank Strang lead proper, secure British lives; they will not let their son ride a horse on a beach. They have sublimated all passion in their own lives, Dora into a religious mania, Frank into prurient films which he goes to see secretly. Dora talks about her relatives indulging in "equitation": dressing in a stately manner and riding horses in a proper and sedate manner. Alan has a safe and secure job, working in an electrical shop and handling brands of merchandise. It is this proper and secure world that Alan fights when he rides, naked on a naked horse, filled with ecstasy. Only Dysart seems to recognize this and envy it. Only he seems to realize the consequences of taking this passion from Alan, consequences damaging to both Alan and himself.

The form of the play contributes to the focus upon Dysart and the dilemma of worship. The setting is minimal, with several benches and railings around a revolving set. All actors are present onstage throughout the performance, and the sense is that they are all witnesses, particularly Dysart, who is trying to discern the pattern in what he is seeing. The horses are noble and stately, but they are mimetic in that there is no attempt to reproduce them with any realism or to make them domestic and safe. They are the carriers of the god Equus, who, thus, is always on stage as well.

Though Alan is riveting, the central dilemma is Dysart's, and Peter Shaffer indicates this by beginning the play with a rambling statement of that dilemma, even before the audience is aware of the action that has led to it. The first act is in essence a long flashback, and it is composed of a series of vignettes, each of which contributes to Dysart's understanding. Many of these are reflections of Alan's sessions with Dysart, and they are played out simultaneously as Alan's spoken revelations to Dysart and as actions on the stage. Alan reacts with his parents as he is torn from the horse on the beach, but he also is answering—and sometimes not answering—Dysart's questions.

The result of this technique is to bridge the past and the present and to make them occur simultaneously. It is also to maintain a focus on Dysart, who is helping Alan relive these memories. This focus is particularly striking when Dysart slips away from the action and addresses the audience directly; this kind of address both opens and closes the play. In these addresses, Dysart struggles with his role and explicitly ponders the questions of worship, of passion, and of the normal. By the end of the play, he is unable to rescue the tensions between these or, to put it in his own words, to "account for Equus."

At the end of the play, the audience, too, is left to account for Equus, a complex and powerful symbol of all that seems to have been lost in a modern society driven to eradicate its own pain. In becoming normal, it has lost the sublime. In eradicating pain, it has lost the chance of utter delight. In creating a world superficially proper, it denies passions that must come to the surface. In all this, what is left to worship, to what to be utterly committed? Is it possible for modern humanity to gallop with gods? All these questions, spiritual at their center, are posed by *Equus*.

Gary D. Schmidt

Further Reading

Beckerman, Bernard. "The Dynamics of Peter Shaffer's Drama." In *The Play and Its Critic: Essays for Eric Bentley*, edited by Michael Bertin. Lanham, Md.: University Press of America, 1986. Examines Shaffer's stagecraft by analyzing the dramatic structure of several of his plays.

Gianakaris, C. J. "The Artistic Trajectory of Peter Shaffer." In *Modern Dramatists: A Casebook of Major British, Irish, and American Playwrights*, edited by Kimball King. New York: Routledge, 2001. Critical examination of Shaffer's career, providing information about his life and tracing the development of his dramatic techniques and themes. Characterizes Shaffer's plays as works of "trans-literalism," or a combination of literal realism and the "provocative, abstract pictorial."

_____. *Peter Shaffer.* New York: St. Martin's Press, 1992. Focuses on thematic issues in Shaffer's dramatic works, examining particularly the role of stagecraft in terms of the presentation of these themes.

Klein, Dennis A. "A Note on the Use of Dreams in Peter Shaffer's Major Plays." *Journal of Evolutionary Psychology* 9 (March, 1989): 25-32. Examination of Dysart and the role that dreams play in *Equus*, focusing both on the dreams of Alan and those of Dysart in terms of the progress of the play's meaning.

_____. *Peter Shaffer.* Rev. ed. New York: Twayne, 1993. An updated edition of the book originally published in 1979. Begins with a chapter of biography before it moves to a chronological handling of Shaffer's plays, providing basic background as well as major thematic concerns. Chapter 6 is devoted to an analysis of *Equus*.

_____. "Peter Shaffer's *Equus* as Modern Aristotelian Tragedy." *Studies in Iconography* 9 (1983): 175-181. After detailing Aristotle's vision of the nature of tragedy and how it is encapsulated in drama, Klein examines the ways in which *Equus* fits the patterns of tragic drama that Aristotle outlines.

MacMurraugh-Kavanagh, M. K. *Peter Shaffer: Theatre and Drama.* New York: St. Martin's Press, 1998. Critical study of all of Shaffer's plays to date, focusing on the thematic concerns of his dramas, such as alienation, dysfunction, and murdering divinities.

Mustazza, Leonard. "A Jealous God: Ritual and Judgement in Shaffer's *Equus*." *Papers on Language and Literature* 28 (1992): 174-184. Focusing on the treatment of Equus as the jealous, demanding god figure in Alan's life, this article examines the relationship of the play's meanings to the mythic figure of Dionysius.

Plunka, Gene A. *Peter Shaffer: Roles, Rites, and Rituals in the Theater.* Rutherford, N.J.: Fairleigh Dickinson University Press, 1988. Examines the uses to which Shaffer puts ritual and rite—particularly religious ritual and rite—in his theatrical productions and notes the effects of these rites, both in terms of the meaning of the dramas and in how the dramas are produced on stage.

Rosefeldt, Paul. "The Search for God, the Father: John Pielmeier's *Agnes of God*, Peter Shaffer's *Equus*." In *The Absent Father in Modern Drama*. New York: Peter Lang, 1995. Focuses on Alan's search for God, an absent father figure in the play. Another chapter in this book examines a similar search for God, the father, in Shaffer's play *Amadeus*.

Erec and Enide

Author: Chrétien de Troyes (c. 1150-c. 1190)
First transcribed: Erec et Enide, c. 1164 (English
    translation, 1913)
Type of work: Poetry
Type of plot: Arthurian romance
Time of plot: Sixth century
Locale: Arthurian England

Principal characters:
KING ARTHUR
QUEEN GUINEVERE
EREC, a knight of the Round Table and son of King Lac
ENIDE, his bride
GUIVRET THE LITTLE, Erec's friend and benefactor

The Poem:

One Easter season, while King Arthur holds his court in the royal town of Cardigan, he summons all of his knights to a hunt for the white stag. Sir Gawain, hearing of the king's wish, is displeased and says that no good will come of that ancient custom, for the law of the hunt decrees that the successful hunter must also kiss the lady whom he considers the most beautiful damsel of the court. As Sir Gawain notes, there is likely to be dissension among the assembled knights and each, believing his own true love as the loveliest and gentlest lady in the land, will be angered by the slight if she is not so considered by the others.

At daybreak, the hunters set out. After them rides Queen Guinevere, attended by Erec, a fair and brave knight, and one of the queen's damsels. While they wait by the wayside to hear the baying of the hounds or the call of a bugle, they see coming toward them a strange knight, his lady, and a dwarf who carries a knotted scourge. The queen sends her damsel to ask who the knight and his fair companion might be, but the dwarf, barring her way, strikes the damsel across the hand with his whip. Then Erec rides forward and the dwarf lashes him across the face and neck. Being unarmed, Erec makes no attempt to chastise the dwarf or his haughty master, but he vows that he will follow the strange knight until he can find arms to hire or to borrow that he might avenge the insult to the queen.

In the fair town to which the strange knight and his companions presently lead him, Erec finds lodgings with a vavasor, who tells him the reason for all the stir and bustle that Erec saw as he rode through the gates. On the next day, a fine sparrow hawk will be given to the knight who can defend against all comers the beauty and goodness of his lady. The haughty knight won the bird in two successive years and will be allowed to keep it if his challenge goes unanswered the next day. At the home of the vavasor, Erec meets his host's daughter, Enide, who is despite her tattered garments the most radiantly beautiful damsel Erec ever saw. With her as his lady and with arms borrowed from his host, Erec

challenges and defeats in single combat the arrogant knight, whose name is Yder. Then Erec dispatches the vanquished knight, along with his lady and his dwarf, to Queen Guinevere to do with as she pleases. He also sends word that he will return with his beautiful bride, the damsel Enide.

Erec promises Enide's father great riches and two towns to rule in his own land, but he refuses all offers to have Enide dressed in robes suitable to her new station: He wishes all in King Arthur's court to see that even in her humble garments she is the most beautiful lady who ever lived. So great is her beauty that King Arthur, who killed the White Stag, kisses her, and there is no demur from the assembled knights and ladies. The king also grants Eric the boon of a speedy marriage, so eager is the young knight for the love of his promised bride. The ceremony is performed by the archbishop of Canterbury at the time of the Pentecost before an assemblage of knights and ladies from every corner of the kingdom, and the celebration continues for a fortnight.

A month after Pentecost, a great tournament is held near Tenebroc, and in the lists there Erec shows himself the most valiant of all the knights assembled. On his return, he receives from the king permission to visit his own land, and he and Enide set out with an escort of sixty knights. On the fifth day, they arrive in Carnant, where King Lac welcomes his son and Enide with much honor. Erec finds so much pleasure in his wife's company that he has no thought for other pastimes. When tournaments are held in the region around, he sends his knights to the forays but he remains behind in dalliance with the fair Enide. At last people begin to gossip and say that he turned a craven in arms. These reports so distress Enide that one morning while they are still abed she begins to lament the way in which the brave and hardy knight changed because of his love for her. Hearing her words, Erec is moved to anger, and he tells her to rise and prepare herself at once to take the road with him on a journey of knight-errantry in search of whatever perils he might encounter by chance. At the beginning of the journey he gives orders that she is never to tell him of anything she might see, nor to speak to him unless he addresses her first.

As Enide rides ahead, forbidden to speak, she laments her disclosure and the sudden loss of the life she enjoyed with her loving husband. She disobeys him, however, when they are about to be attacked by three robber knights, and again when they are assailed by five recreants. Erec, overcoming all who oppose him, feels no gratitude for her wifely warnings and fears for his safety and speaks harshly to her because she disobeyed his command.

That night, since they know of no town or shelter nearby, they sleep in an open field. There, the squire of Count Galoin comes upon them the next day and conducts them to lodgings in the town where the count is master. That nobleman, going to pay his respects to the strange knight and his lovely lady, is much smitten with Enide's beauty, so much so that, going to the place where she sits apart, he expresses his pity for her obvious distress and offers to make her mistress of all his lands. When Enide refuses, he declares that he will take her by force. Fearing for her husband's life, Enide pretends to accede to his wishes. It is arranged that on the next day the count's knights are to overtake the travelers and seize Enide. Erec, coming to her rescue, will be killed, and she will be free to take the count as her lord. Once again, Enide disobeys her husband and tells him of Count Galoin's plan. Forewarned, Erec overcomes his assailants and knocks the count senseless from his steed. When Galoin's followers pursue Erec and Enide, the count restrains them, praising Enide's prudence and virtue and the bravery of her knight.

Departing from Count Galoin's lands, the travelers come to a castle from which the lord comes riding on a great steed to offer Erec combat at arms. Enide sees him coming but does not dare tell her husband for fear of his wrath. At last she does speak, however, and Erec realizes that it is her love for him that makes her disobedient to his commands. The knight who challenges Erec, Guivret the Little, is of small stature but stout heart, and both he and Erec are wounded in the fight. Though the courageous little knight loses, he puts up such a good fight that he and Erec become friends. Guivret invites Erec to have his wounds dressed and to rest at his castle, but Erec thanks him courteously and rides on with Enide.

At length, they arrive at a wood where King Arthur comes with a large hunting party. By then, Erec is so begrimed and bloodied that Sir Kay the seneschal does not recognize him. He would take the wounded knight to the king's camp, but Erec refuses and they fight until Sir Kay is unhorsed. Sir Gawain then rides out to encounter the strange knight, and he is able to bring Erec to the place where the king ordered tents set up in anticipation of their coming. There is great joy in

that meeting for the king and Queen Guinevere, but there is also distress at Erec's wounds. Although the king pleads with Erec to rest there until his hurts are healed, the knight refuses to be turned aside or delayed on his journey, and early the next morning he and Enide set out once more.

In a strange forest, they hear the cries of a lady in distress. Leaving Enide to await his return, Erec rides in the direction of the sound and finds a damsel weeping because two giants carried away her knight. Riding in pursuit, Erec kills the giants and rescues the knight, whose name is Cadoc of Tabriol. Later, he sends Cadoc and the damsel to King Arthur's camp, to tell the story of how he fares. Meanwhile, Erec's wounds reopen, and he loses so much blood that he falls from his horse in a swoon.

While Enide is weeping over his prostrate body, a count with his suite comes riding through the forest. The nobleman gives orders that the body is to be taken to Limors and prepared for burial. On their arrival at the palace, the count declares his intention of espousing Enide at once. Although she refuses to give her consent, the ceremony is performed in great haste and guests are summoned to a wedding banquet that night.

Erec, recovering from his deep swoon, awakens in time to see the count strike Enide across the face because in her great grief she can neither eat nor drink at her new husband's bidding. Springing from the funeral bier, he draws his sword and strikes the count on the head with such force that blood and brains gush out. While the other guests retreat in fear of the ghostly presence that so suddenly returns to life, Erec and Enide make their escape. Erec assures his wife that he is now convinced of her devotion and love.

Guivret the Little receives word that a mortally wounded knight was found in the forest and that the lord of Limors carried off the dead man's wife. Coming to see that the fallen knight receives proper burial and to aid his lady if she is in distress, the doughty little knight comes upon Erec, whom he fails to recognize in the murky moonlight, and strikes a blow that knocks Erec unconscious. Enide and Guivret remain by the stricken man all that night, and in the morning they proceed to Guivret's castle. There Erec is nursed back to health by Enide and Guivret's sisters. After his recovery, escorted by Guivret and burdened with gifts, the couple prepare to return to King Arthur's court.

Toward nightfall, the travelers see in the distance the towers of a great fortress. Guivret says that the town is named Brandigant and that there is a perilous passage called the "Joy of the Court." King Evrain welcomes the travelers with great courtesy, but that night, while they feast, he also warns Erec against attempting the mysterious feat that no knight thus far survived. Despite the disapproval of his friend and his host, Erec swears to attempt the passage.

The next morning he is conducted into a magic garden filled with all manner of fruits and flowers, past the heads and helmets of the unfortunate knights who braved danger to blow the magic horn whose blast would signify joy to King Evrain's land. At the end of a path he finds a beautiful damsel seated on a couch. While he stands looking at her, a knight appears to engage him in combat. They fight until the hour of noon passes; then the knight falls exhausted. He reveals that he was held in thrall in the garden by an oath given to his mistress, whose one wish is his eternal presence by her side. Erec then blows the horn and all the people rejoice to find him safe. There is great joy also when the knight of the garden is released from his bondage and the beautiful damsel identifies herself as the cousin of Enide.

Erec and Enide, accompanied by Guivret, continue their journey to the court of King Arthur, where they are received with gladness and honor. When his father dies, Erec returns to reign in his own land. There he and Enide are crowned in a ceremony of royal splendor in the presence of King Arthur and all the nobles of his realm.

Critical Evaluation:

Erec and Enide is the first of a collection of metrical romances by Chrétien de Troyes, a master tale teller of the medieval period about whom very little is otherwise known. The poem is the oldest romance on Arthurian materials extant in any language. It has sometimes been called the first novel because of its consistent plot. Written in eight-syllable rhyming couplets, the story provides the most idealized expression of the code of chivalry by a single writer of medieval times.

Like the author's *Yvain* (c. 1170), *Erec and Enide* deals among other things with the conflict between and the attempt to reconcile knightly and marital responsibilities. Apparently Chrétien himself thought much of the work: In the romance's first paragraph he states that "now I shall begin the tale which will be remembered so long as Christendom endures. This is Chrétien's boast."

His scarcely modest claim was well founded, for this romance of Arthurian England in the sixth century has outlived myriad other medieval romances. The poem offers various and contrasting riches, including a mélange of real and unreal incidents, exact and exaggerated statistics, logical and implausible motivation, and wildly supernatural events in close juxtaposition with homely, concrete ones. From this often unlikely material, Chrétien devised a well-constructed plot. Moreover, the author, in welding his diverse and sometimes incongruous elements together, had a serious purpose,

for he was interested in problems of individual conscience and in the choices individuals had to make in the face of conflicting loyalties and personal emotions. Chrétien was intrigued with how humans solve these problems as members of a social group. All the usual and contrived situations of medieval romance served Chrétien as a means of setting forth these problems and providing complicated webs to entrap the protagonists.

Although Erec, a king's son, married the daughter of a poor vavasor, or country squire, Chrétien takes care to make them equal in beauty and breeding. However, when because of excessive love of his wife, reports circulate that Erec has permitted himself to desert the tourneys and quests and fail to continue proofs of his knighthood, the story becomes the tale of married love subjected to the pressures of the man's other obligations and duties. It is also a story of a wife's patient endurance of her husband's eccentricities and abuse. In many respects, Chrétien intended *Erec and Enide*, for all its comic incidents and exaggerated postures, to be a straightforward narrative of love being testing. In this it is similar to Geoffrey Chaucer's late fourteenth century "Clerk's Tale" on the familiar theme of the patient Griselda.

It is characteristic of Chrétien that he focuses on the analysis of love, particularly as felt by his heroines. Such subtleties of thought are rare in medieval romance, but Chrétien's women in love verbalize their considerations in matters of the heart. Enide, for example, upbraids herself for false pride after she told Erec what others were saying about his valor, and in a soliloquy she tells herself it is right that she suffers: "One does not know what good fortune is until he has made trial of evil." Not until the fourteenth century, in Chaucer's Criseyde, is there a romance heroine engaged in such subtle love analysis.

Chrétien provides convincing characters, not merely stock figures. In *Erec and Enide*, he does not focus on battles or such farcical scenes as the one in which Enide must marry the Count against her will but rather on Erec's gradual realization of the great love his wife has for him. The plot development takes Erec to the point where at the end he says, "for I love you now more than ever I did before." He has learned the value of humility and faithfulness.

In a time when *fin amour*, or courtly love (in other words, adulterous love), was supposed to be the reigning material for poets and romance writers, Chrétien showed far more concern for love within the marriage bond. As a matter of fact, he stressed this kind of love as the ideal union. When he dealt with adulterous love as in his *Lancelot* (after 1164), he seems ill at ease and handles both plot and characterization with less finesse. Most critics as a result conclude that in this latter work he wrote on demand and not out of inclination. In both *Yvain* and *Erec and Enide*, however, he concentrates on the difficulties in marriage and on solutions of those difficulties.

Chrétien said at the beginning of his romance that "jongleurs were accustomed to garble and mutilate" the story, but that he himself had ordered his material into a unified, coherent whole. Chrétien not only successfully develops the plot but also shows progression in character development. He combines descriptions of lavishly ornamented watered silk, ivory, gold tapestries, and red armor; of the ragged garments of a peasant girl in a poor household; of the hardships of wayfaring on roads infested with evils of all sorts; and finally of a brilliant coronation ceremony and a happy ending for the reconciled Erec and Enide. With consummate artistry he makes his poem entertaining and at the same time poses comments on the problems of married love.

"Critical Evaluation" by Muriel B. Ingham

Further Reading

Buckbee, Edward J. "*Erec et Enide*." In *The Romances of Chrétien de Troyes: A Symposium*, edited by Douglas Kelly. Lexington, Ky.: French Forum, 1985. Buckbee argues that Erec and Enide are a perfect couple who fit the ideal of Arthur's elite society of knights and ladies, but he also notes that the characterization is ambiguous because Chrétien does not state their motives clearly.

Duggan, Joseph J. *The Romances of Chrétien de Troyes*. New Haven, Conn.: Yale University Press, 2001. Duggan's analysis focuses on the common characteristics of Chrétien's romances, such as the importance of kinship and genealogy, his art of narration, and his depiction of knighthood. Contains many references to *Erec and Enide* that are listed in the index.

Frappier, Jean. "Chrétien de Troyes." In *Arthurian Literature in the Middle Ages*, edited by R. S. Loomis. Oxford, England: Clarendon Press, 1959. Provides a good overview of Chrétien's work and deals primarily with his sources. An admirable starting point for new readers.

Lacy, Norris J., and Joan Tasker Grimbert, eds. *A Companion to Chrétien de Troyes*. New York: D. S. Brewer, 2005. Collection of essays, including discussions of Chrétien in history, his patrons, his literary background, the Arthurian legend before him, and the medieval reception and influence of his work. Also includes an analysis of *Erec and Enide*, "*Erec et Enide*: The First Arthurian Romance" by Donald Maddox and Sara Sturm-Maddox.

Loomis, Roger Sherman. *Arthurian Tradition and Chrétien de Troyes*. New York: Columbia University Press, 1949. Loomis shows how most episodes in Chrétien's romances have their parallels in other Irish, Welsh, and Breton stories. Some of Loomis's work has been questioned, but he remains an acknowledged authority in the field.

Luttrell, Claude. *The Creation of the First Arthurian Romance: A Quest*. Evanston, Ill.: Northwestern University Press, 1974. A study specifically of *Erec and Enide*, which focuses on Chrétien's sources and the meaning as revealed by the poem's structure. Also discusses romances that resemble *Erec and Enide*.

Murray, K. Sarah-Jane. *From Plato to Lancelot: A Preface to Chrétien de Troyes*. Syracuse, N.Y.: Syracuse University Press, 2008. Murray argues that there were two intersecting sources for Chrétien's work: the works of Plato, Ovid, and other Greco-Roman writers, and the Celtic myths and legends found in Irish monastic scholarship.

Noble, Peter S. *Love and Marriage in Chrétien de Troyes*. Cardiff: University of Wales Press, 1982. Examines the theme of love and marriage in all of Chrétien's romances. Concludes that *Erec and Enide* is a celebration of married rather than unmarried or premarital "courtly love."

Reichert, Michelle. *Between Courtly Literature and al-Andalus: Matière d'Orient and the Importance of Spain in the Romances of the Twelfth-Century Writer Chrétien de Troyes*. New York: Routledge, 2006. Reichert analyzes the references to Spain in Chrétien's romances, maintaining that these allusions occur at key moments and are often combined with linguistic "riddles" that suggest how the romances are to be read. Chapter 1 focuses on *Erec and Enide*.

Erewhon
Or, Over the Range

Author: Samuel Butler (1835-1902)
First published: 1872
Type of work: Novel
Type of plot: Utopian
Time of plot: 1870's
Locale: Erewhon and England

Principal characters:
HIGGS, a traveler in Erewhon
CHOWBOK, a native
NOSNIBOR, a citizen of Erewhon
AROWHENA, his daughter

The Story:

Higgs, a young man of twenty-two years, works on a sheep farm. From the plains, he looks often at the seemingly impassable mountain range that forms the edge of the sheep country and wonders about the land beyond those towering peaks. He learns from an old native named Chowbok that it is forbidden to visit that land. Chowbok assumes a strange pose when questioned further and utters unearthly cries. Curious, Higgs persuades Chowbok to go on a trip with him into the mountains.

They are unable to find a pass through the mountains. One day, Higgs comes upon a small valley and goes up it alone. He finds that it leads through the mountains. When he goes back to get Chowbok, he sees the old native fleeing toward the plains. He goes on alone. After climbing down treacherous cliffs and crossing a river on a reed raft, he finally comes to beautiful rolling plains. He passes by some strange man-like statues, which make terrifying noises as the wind circles about them. He recognizes in them the reason for Chowbok's performance.

Higgs awakens next morning to see two girls herding a flock of goats about him. When the girls see him, they run and bring some men to look at him. All of them are physically handsome. Convinced at last that Higgs is a human being, they take him to a small town close by. There his clothing is searched, and a watch he has with him is confiscated. The men seem to be especially interested in his health, and he is allowed to leave only after a strict medical examination. He wonders why there was such confusion over his watch until he is shown a museum in which is kept old pieces of machinery. Finally, he is put in jail.

In jail, he learns the language and some of the strange customs of the country, which is called Erewhon. The oddest custom is to consider disease a crime; anyone who is sick is tried and put in jail. On the other hand, people who commit robbery or murder are treated sympathetically and given hospital care. Shortly afterward, the jailor informs Higgs that

he is summoned to appear before the king and queen and that he is to be the guest of a man named Nosnibor. Nosnibor embezzled a large sum of money from a poor widow, but he is now recovering from his illness. The widow, Higgs learns, will be tried and sentenced for allowing herself to be imposed upon.

In the capital, Higgs stays with Nosnibor and his family and pays several visits to the court. He is well received because he has blond hair, a rarity among the Erewhonians. He learns a great deal about the past history of the country. Twenty-five hundred years before, a prophet preached that it was unlawful to eat meat, since man should not kill his fellow creatures. For several hundred years, the Erewhonians were vegetarians. Then another sage showed that animals were no more the fellow creatures of man than plants were; if man could not kill and eat animals, he should not kill and eat plants. The logic of his arguments overthrew the old philosophy. Two hundred years before, a great scientist presented the idea that machines had minds and feelings and that, if man were not careful, the machine would finally become the ruling creature on earth. Consequently, all machines were scrapped.

The economy of the country is unusual. There are two monetary systems—one worthless except for spiritual meaning, and one used in trade. The more respected system is the valueless one, and its work is carried on in Musical Banks where people exchange coins for music. The state religion is a worship of various qualities of godhead, such as love, fear, and wisdom, and the main goddess, Ydgrun, is at the same time an abstract concept and a silly, cruel woman. Higgs learns much of the religion from Arowhena, one of Nosnibor's daughters. She is a beautiful girl, and the two fall in love.

Because Nosnibor insists that his older daughter, Zulora, be married first, Higgs and his host have an argument, and Higgs finds lodgings elsewhere. Arowhena meets him often at the Musical Banks. Higgs visits the University of Unreason, where the young Erewhonian boys are taught to do anything except that which is practical. They study obsolete languages and hypothetical sciences. He sees a relationship between these schools and the mass-mind, which the educational system in England is producing. Higgs also learns that money is considered a symbol of duty; the more money a man has, the better man he is.

Nosnibor learns that Higgs is meeting Arowhena secretly. Then the king begins to worry over the fact that Higgs entered the country with a watch, and he fears that Higgs might try to bring machinery back into use. Planning an escape, Higgs proposes to the queen that he make a balloon trip to talk with the god of the air. The queen is delighted with the idea. The king hopes that Higgs will fall and kill himself.

Higgs smuggles Arowhena aboard the balloon with him. The couple soon find themselves high in the air and moving over the mountain range. When the balloon settles on the sea, Higgs and Arowhena are picked up by a passing ship. They are married in England, and Higgs tries to get up an expedition to go back to Erewhon. Only the missionaries listen to his story. Then Chowbok, Higgs's faithless native friend, shows up in England teaching religion, and his appearance convinces people that Erewhon actually does exist. Higgs hopes to return to the country soon to teach it Christianity.

Critical Evaluation:

Samuel Butler's utopian satire *Erewhon* is a series of essays written between 1860 and 1870 that anticipates the works of Aldous Huxley and George Orwell. Like these later utopian writers, Butler attempts to expose and deflate the hypocrisies that flawed the England of his day rather than to prophesy or to propose corrective measures. As a result, his novel is really dystopian in vision. It savages a society full of easy self-congratulation and at the same time remains pitiless toward misfortune. Butler's artistic versatility—he was an accomplished, though unappreciated, painter, musician, and essayist—enabled him to offer social commentary from a variety of perspectives. *Erewhon* also helped Butler sharpen social critiques that he voiced even more effectively in his great autobiographical novel, *The Way of All Flesh* (1903), published only after his death.

In his preface to *Erewhon*, Butler concedes that the book contains "hardly any story, and little attempt to give life and individuality to the characters." He tries throughout the work to keep readers at a critical distance from the usual distractions of the novel genre. As a satirist, Butler asks the readers to examine every issue with detachment and to register every distortion and shift in perspective. However, he makes his task treacherous with various techniques such as his use of anagrams—"Erewhon" is an anagram of "Nowhere." Just as the readers must untwist the title to assess its meaning, so they can never fully trust the novel's narration. In his unabashed desire both to exploit Erewhon and to convert its natives, the adventurer-narrator, Higgs, is clearly himself a target of Butler's satire. Nevertheless, despite his own hypocritical bent, Higgs also records and loudly decries Erewhonian foibles. Himself insensitive to irony, he provides readers access to duplicities Butler wishes to reveal.

In general, Erewhonian society, like its English counterpart, confuses individual responsibility with bad luck and moral choice with mischance. By punishing disease as criminal, for example, Erewhon reflects Victorian England's desire to maintain appearances; visible blemishes—the hapless sick or poor—mar society's self-image and are eradicated. Because they are living reminders of the costs of progress and industry, they must be treated severely by being hidden away in poorhouses or prisons. In a sort of moral anagram, crime in Erewhon becomes a disease; it is attended by solicitous "straighteners" and wins the sympathy of the "patient's" friends. Here, Butler takes aim at English society's willingness to ignore all sorts of moral failures in the name of order and profit. He tacitly implies that people admire those who thrive by immoral means, blaming instead those who are so weak and gullible as to be victimized by them. Thus, Nosnibor, Higgs's host, is treated for having embezzled and is allowed to keep his ill-gotten profits, while the widow he cheats is prosecuted.

Similarly, children in Erewhon, rather than their parents, are made responsible for their birth and upbringing. The unborn commit a "felony" in inflicting themselves upon the living, for which they must make "obedient and abject" amends throughout their lives. In return, truly exemplary parents spend great sums educating their offspring at the Colleges of Unreason, "in order to render their children as nearly useless as possible." In this tortured relationship, Butler rehearses the account of his own childhood, which he later provides in *The Way of All Flesh*. In accord with family tradition, and against his own inclination, Butler was educated for the ministry, though he failed to enter the church. Through the Erewhonian "birth formulae," he exposes the coercion, guilt, and estrangement that troubled his typically Victorian family. Butler mocks his expensive but irrelevant Cambridge education in the obsolete "hypothetical language" (that is, Latin) taught to Erewhonian students.

Butler also depicts Victorians as being confused about objects of worship. Erewhon's two systems of currency reflect a similar religious hypocrisy. Commercial interests supplant genuine religious feeling so that, finally, worship is expressed through commerce. Though publicly lauded, the "coin" of the Musical Banks is worthless, and the banks themselves are rarely visited. In the same way, Victorians went through the motions of religious observance, paying their tithes on Sunday, but their offerings remained worthless. They kneeled instead to the goddess Ydgrun, Butler's anagram for the Victorian "Mrs. Grundy," who enforces only a shallow social conformism.

Finally, in "The Book of the Machines," Butler ridicules the Victorians' misunderstanding and fear of Charles Darwin's theory of evolution, as well as their disproportionate faith in progress through industrialization. While the Erewhonians fear the "evolution" of machines (Higgs's watch is therefore regarded as dangerous), such an evolution was already at work in industrialized England. For the greedy Victorians, a factory possessed more life and potential than the workmen who operated it; machines—and the profit they sustain—threatened to become more real than the needs of colorless and expendable workers. At the same time, society fretted about the question of the descent of humanity and resented being linked to the animal world as strongly as the Erewhonians mistrusted the machine. Butler's twist neatly exposes the blindness of a society that neglects living, breathing individuals, all the while insisting upon humans' divine origin.

"Critical Evaluation" by Sarah A. Boris

Further Reading

Cannan, Gilbert. *Samuel Butler: A Critical Study*. Folcroft, Pa.: Folcroft Press, 1969. A sound, general introduction to Butler's literary work, diverse talents, and interests.

Greenacre, Phyllis. *The Quest for the Father: A Study of the Darwin-Butler Controversy*. New York: International Universities Press, 1963. A psychoanalytic account of Butler's connection with Darwin that sets "The Book of the Machines" into interpretative context.

Holt, Lee E. *Samuel Butler*. New York: Twayne, 1964. A solid introductory overview of Butler's life and work.

Muggeridge, Malcolm. *The Earnest Atheist: A Study of Samuel Butler*. London: Eyre and Spottiswode, 1936. A lively and insightful account of Butler's attitudes. Helps to explain the ferocity of his attack on religion in *Erewhon*.

Paradis, James G., ed. *Samuel Butler, Victorian Against the Grain: A Critical Overview*. Toronto, Ont.: University of Toronto Press, 2007. Collection of essays, including discussions of *Erewhon*, Butler's views on evolution, his bachelorhood, his travel writing, and his photography.

Parrinder, Patrick. "Entering Dystopia, Entering *Erewhon*." *Critical Survey* 17, no. 1 (2005): 6-21. Parrinder describes the characteristics of dystopian romances written in the late Victorian era, focusing on the representations of dystopia in *Erewhon* and W. H. Hudson's *A Crystal Age*.

Stillman, Clara G. *Samuel Butler: A Mid-Victorian Modern*. Port Washington, N.Y.: Kennikat Press, 1972. Offers a helpful chapter on *Erewhon*, analyzing Butler's satirical methods.

An Essay Concerning Human Understanding

Author: John Locke (1632-1704)
First published: 1690
Type of work: Philosophy

John Locke's purpose in *An Essay Concerning Human Understanding* is to inquire into the origin and extent of human knowledge. His conclusion—that all knowledge is derived from sense experience—became the principal tenet of empiricism, which has dominated Western philosophy ever since. Even George Berkeley, who rejected Locke's distinction between sense qualities independent of the mind and sense qualities dependent on the mind, produced his idealism in response to Locke's provocative philosophy and gave it an empirical cast that reflected Western culture's rejection of innate or transcendental knowledge.

An Essay Concerning Human Understanding is divided into four books: book 1, "Of Innate Notions"; book 2, "Of Ideas"; book 3, "Of Words"; and book 4, "Of Knowledge, Certain and Probable."

In preparation for his radical claim that all ideas are derived from experience, Locke begins his essay with a careful consideration of the thesis that there are innate ideas. Locke first examines the notion that there are ideas that are a necessary part of human understanding and are, therefore, common to all people. Locke's attack on this thesis is from two directions. He argues that many of the ideas that are supposed to be innate can be and have been derived naturally from sense experience, that not all people assent to those ideas that are supposed to be innate. Locke maintains that even if reason enables people to discover the truth of certain ideas, those ideas cannot be said to be innate, for reason is needed to discover their truth.

In book 2, "Of Ideas," Locke considers the origin of such ideas as those expressed by the words "whiteness," "hardness," "sweetness," "thinking," "motion," "man," and the like. The second section states his conclusion:

> Let us then suppose the mind to be, as we say, white paper void of all characters, without any ideas. How comes it to be furnished? . . . Whence has it all the materials of reason and knowledge? To this I answer, in one word, from experience. . . . Our observation, employed either about external sensible objects, or about the internal operations of our minds perceived and reflected on by ourselves, is that which supplies our understandings with all the materials of knowledge.

The two sources of ideas, according to Locke, are sensation and reflection. By the senses people come to have perceptions of things, thereby acquiring the ideas of yellow, white, or cold, for example. Then, by reflection, by consideration of the mind in operation, people acquire the ideas of thinking, doubting, believing, knowing, willing, and so on.

By sensation people acquire knowledge of external objects; by reflection people acquire knowledge of their own minds. Ideas that are derived from sensation are simple; that is, they present "one uniform appearance," even though a number of simple ideas may come together in the perception of an external object. The mind dwells on the simple ideas, comparing them to one another, combining them, but never inventing them. By a "simple idea" Locke means what some modern and contemporary philosophers have called a "sense-datum," a distinctive, entirely differentiated item of sense experience, such as the odor of some particular glue or the taste of coffee in a cup. He calls attention to the fact that people use sense experience to imagine what they have never perceived, but no operation of the mind can yield novel simple ideas.

By the quality of something, Locke means its power to produce an idea in someone sensing the thing. The word "quality" is used in the essay in much the same way the word "characteristic" or "property" has been used by other writers. Locke distinguishes between primary and secondary qualities. Primary qualities are those that matter has constantly, whatever its state. As primary qualities Locke names solidity, extension, figure, motion or rest, and number. By secondary qualities Locke means the power to produce various sensations that have nothing in common with the primary qualities of the external objects. Thus, the power to produce the taste experience of sweetness is a secondary quality of sugar, but there is no reason to suppose that the sugar itself possesses the distinctive quality of the sensation. Colors, tastes, sounds, and odors are secondary qualities of objects. Locke also refers to a third kind of quality or power, called simply "power," by which he means the capacity to affect or to be affected by other objects. Thus, fire can melt clay; the capacity to melt clay is one of fire's powers, and such a power is neither a primary nor a secondary quality.

Locke concludes that primary ideas resemble external objects, but secondary ideas do not. It is this particular claim that excited other professional philosophers, with Berkeley arguing that primary qualities can be understood only in terms of human sensations, so that whatever generalization can be made about secondary qualities would have to cover primary qualities as well, and with other philosophers arguing that Locke had no ground for maintaining that primary ideas "resemble" primary qualities, even if the distinction between primary and secondary qualities is allowed.

Complex ideas result from acts of the mind, and they fall into three classes: ideas of modes, of substances, and of relations. Modes are ideas that are considered to be incapable of independent existence since they are affections of substance, such as the ideas of triangle, gratitude, and murder. To think of substances is to think of "particular things subsisting by themselves," and to think in that manner involves supposing that there is a support, which cannot be understood, and that there are various qualities in combination which give various substances their distinguishing traits. Ideas of relations are the result of comparing ideas with each other.

After a consideration of the complex ideas of space, duration, number, the infinite, pleasure and pain, substance, relation, cause and effect, and of the distinctions between clear and obscure ideas and between true and false ideas, Locke proceeds to a discussion, in book 3, of words and essences. Words are signs of ideas by "arbitrary imposition," depending upon observed similarities that are taken as the basis for considering things in classes. Words are related to "nominal essences," that is, to obvious similarities found through observation, and not to "real essences," the actual qualities of things. Locke then discusses the imperfections and abuses of words.

In book 4, Locke defines knowledge as "the perception of the connection of and agreement, or disagreement and repugnancy, of any of our ideas." An example cited is one's knowledge that white is not black, Locke arguing that to know that white is not black is simply to perceive that the idea of white is not the idea of black.

Locke insists that knowledge cannot extend beyond the ideas one has, and that people determine whether ideas agree or disagree with each other either directly, by intuition, or indirectly, by reason or sensation. Truth is defined as "the joining or separating of signs, as the things signified by them do agree or disagree one with another." For example, the proposition "White is not black" involves the separation by "is not" of the signs "white" and "black," signifying the disagreement between the ideas of white and black; since the ideas are different, the proposition is true. Actually to have compared the ideas and to have noted their disagreement is to know the fact that the true proposition signifies.

Locke devotes the remaining chapters of book 4 to arguing that people have knowledge of their existence by intuition, of the existence of God by demonstration, and of other things by sensation. Here the influence of René Descartes is clearly evident. It is the empiricism of the earlier parts of the book that won for Locke the admiration of philosophers.

Further Reading

Ayers, Michael. *Locke*. New York: Routledge, 1999. An excellent biographical introduction to the thoughts of the philosopher, clearly presented and requiring no special background. Includes bibliography.

Brantley, Richard E. *Locke, Wesley, and the Method of English Romanticism*. Gainesville: University Press of Florida, 1984. Brantley argues that Locke influenced John Wesley, the founder of the Methodist Church, and that Wesley's work influenced the eighteenth century Romantic poets.

Chappell, Vere, ed. *John Locke: Theory of Knowledge*. New York: Garland, 1992. Contains thirty critical essays about Locke and his ideas concerning knowledge, reprinted from their original publications.

Kramer, Matthew H. *John Locke and the Origins of Private Property*. New York: Cambridge University Press, 1997. A detailed analysis of Locke's theories about the rewards of labor and the relationships between labor and ownership.

Lennon, Thomas M. *The Battle of the Gods and Giants*. Princeton, N.J.: Princeton University Press, 1993. Although this book is about René Descartes and Pierre Gassendi, a forty-page chapter and a few pages at the end of the book are devoted to Locke's inheritance from both philosophers.

Newman, Lex, ed. *The Cambridge Companion to Locke's "Essay Concerning Human Understanding."* New York: Cambridge University Press, 2007. Collection of essays analyzing the essay, including discussions of Locke's polemic against nativism; his ideas about power, substance, identity, and diversity; and language, meaning, and mind in the essay.

Schouls, Peter A. *Reasoned Freedom: John Locke and the Enlightenment*. Ithaca, N.Y.: Cornell University Press, 1992. Compares Locke to Descartes, then invites comparison to other philosophers, such as Michael Oakeshott, by presenting Locke's defense of reason and his explications of freedom, self-determination, and education.

Uzgalis, William. *Locke's "Essay Concerning Human Understanding": A Reader's Guide*. London: Continuum, 2007. Overview of the essay, designed for undergraduates. Includes discussions of the essay's philosophical background, key themes, reception, and influence, and provides analyses of key passages in the text.

Yolton, John W. *The Two Intellectual Worlds of John Locke: Man, Person, and Spirits in the "Essay."* Ithaca, N.Y.: Cornell University Press, 2004. Focuses on the religious and theological ideas in *An Essay Concerning Human Understanding*. Yolton maintains that Locke comprehends human understanding as a subset of a larger understanding of intelligent beings—angels, spirits, and an omniscient God.

An Essay on Criticism

Author: Alexander Pope (1688-1744)
First published: 1711
Type of work: Poetry

Published when Alexander Pope was twenty-two years of age, *An Essay on Criticism* remains one of the best known discussions of literary criticism, of its ends and means, in the English language. It is the source of numerous familiar epigrams known to the reading public. Pope was young when he wrote the work; existing evidence points to 1708 or 1709 as the probable period of composition. Pope wrote of its composition: "The things that I have written fastest, have always pleased the most. I wrote the *Essay on Criticism* fast; for I had digested all the matter in prose, before I began upon it in verse."

Although Pope may seem to rely too heavily upon the authority of the ancient authors as literary masters, he recognizes, as many readers fail to note, the "grace beyond the reach of art" that no model can teach. True genius and judgment are innate gifts of heaven, as Pope says, but many people possess the seeds of taste and judgment that, with proper training, may flourish. The genius of the ancients cannot be imitated, but their principles may be.

The poem is structured in three parts: the general qualities of a critic; the particular laws by which a critic judges a work; and the ideal character of a critic. Part 1 opens with Pope's indictment of the false critic. He remarks that as poets may be prejudiced about their own merits, so critics can be partial to their own judgment. Judgment, or "true taste," derives from nature, as does the poet's genius; nature provides everyone with some taste, which, if not perverted by a poor education or other defects, may enable the critic to judge properly. To be a critic, one's first job is to know oneself, one's own judgment, tastes, abilities; in short, to know one's personal limitations.

The second task of the critic is to know nature, which is the critic's standard as it is the poet's. Nature is defined ambiguously as

> Unerring Nature, still divinely bright,
> One clear, unchanged, and universal light,
> Life, force, and beauty, must to all impart,
> At once the source, and end, the test of Art.

Nature thus becomes a universal or cosmic force, an ideal sought by poet and critic alike in the general scheme, things universally approved throughout history by all persons. This ideal must be apprehended through the critic's judicious balance of wit and judgment, of imaginative invention and deliberative reason.

The rules of literary criticism may best be located in those works that have stood the test of time and universal approbation, the works of antiquity. From the ancient authors, critics have derived rules of art that are not self-imposed at the whim of the critic but are discovered justly operating in the writings of the best authors. Such rules are "Nature still, but Nature methodized."

Formerly, critics restricted themselves to discovering rules in classical literature; in Pope's time, however, critics had strayed from the principles of these earlier critics whose motive was solely to make art "more beloved," and prescribed their own rules, which are pedantic, unimaginative, and basely critical of literature. What was once a subordinate sister to creative art has replaced or turned against its superior, assuming a higher place in the order of things. Criticism, once destined to teach the "world . . . to admire" the poet's art, now presumes to be master.

The true critic must learn thoroughly the ancients, particularly Homer and Vergil, for "To copy nature is to copy them." There are beauties of art that cannot be taught by rules; these intangible beauties are the "nameless graces which no methods teach/ And which a master-hand alone can reach." Modern writers should avoid transcending, unless rarely, the rules of art first established by the great artists of the past.

Part 2 traces the causes hindering good judgment—that chief virtue of a true critic. Pope advises critics to avoid the dangers of blindness caused by pride, the greatest source of poor judgment, by learning their own defects and by profiting even from the strictures of their enemies. Inadequate learning is another reason a critic errs: "A little learning is a dangerous thing;/ Drink deep, or taste not the Pierian spring." A critic who looks too closely at the parts of a poem may come to prefer a poem dull as a whole yet perfect in parts to one imperfect in part but pleasing as a whole. It is the unity of the many small parts in one whole that affects readers: "'Tis not a lip, or eye, we beauty call,/ But the joint force and full result of all." Faultless art can never exist. Finally, a critic who condemns a work for failing to achieve that which its author never intended errs: One should "regard the writer's End,/ Since none can compass more than they intend."

As some critics deviate from nature in judging "by a love to parts," others confine their attention to conceits, images, or metaphors. Poets who dissimulate their want of art with a wild profusion of imagery have not learned to control their imagination; they overvalue mere decoration and paint, not "the naked nature and the living grace," but the external variables of nature. "True Wit," Pope says, "is Nature to advantage dressed,/ What oft was thought, but ne'er so well expressed."

Other critics too highly praise style and language without respect for content; true eloquence clarifies and improves the thought, revealing nature at her finest, but false eloquence imposes a veil upon the face of nature, obscuring with its finery the truths of nature. Proper expression, in addition, should fit with the content; the poet should never attempt to lend false dignity by archaic words. Proper diction is neither too old nor too modern.

Most false critics judge by meter, criticizing according to the roughness or smoothness of the verse. Overfondness for metrics results in the dull clichés of poetry, such as "the cooling western breeze," and the like. Pope avers that rough or smooth verse should not be the poet's ideal; the poet should aim rather to fit the sound to the sense:

> Soft is the strain when Zephyr gently blows,
> And the smooth stream in smoother numbers flows;
> But when loud surges lash the sounding shore,
> The hoarse, rough verse should like a torrent roar.

Lines 344-383 of the poem constitute a digression by Pope to illustrate "representative meter." The true critic generally abides by rules of tolerance and aloofness from extremes of fashion and personal taste. The critic who indulges in petty predilections for certain schools or kinds of poets sacrifices objectivity. Be a patron of no separate group, whether ancient or modern, foreign or native, Pope advises. The critic should be pledged to truth, not to passing cults. Nor should a critic fear to advance his or her own judgment merely because the public favors other poets and schools; no critic should echo fashion or be influenced by a writer's name. Especially reprehensible is that critic who derives opinions about literature from lords of quality.

The final pitfall of the false critic is subjectivity, measuring by personal preferences. Private or public envy may distort one's evaluation. The critic must put aside personal motives and praise according to less personal criteria. Nor

should the critic be led astray by self-love: "Good-nature and good-sense must ever join." A critic may justly attack more worthy targets, of which many exist in "these flagitious times." Obscenity, dullness, immodesty—all should concern the critic and be exposed. The vices of an age, however, should not infect a critic's judgment on other matters.

Part 3 outlines the ideal character of a critic. It lists rules for a critic's manners and contrasts the ideal critic with the "incorrigible poet" and "impertinent Critic," concluding with a brief summary of literary criticism and the character of the best critics. It is not enough for the critic to know, Pope writes; a critic must also share the qualities of a good person, worthy of respect not only for intellect but also for character. Integrity stands at the head of a list of good qualities for a critic. Modesty that forbids both unseemly outspokenness and rigid adherence to erroneous opinion, tact that supports truth without alienating by bluntness, and courage to pursue truth despite censure are important attributes for the true critic. As some dull and foolish poets are best not maligned for fear of provoking them to greater folly, so the critic full of pedantry and impertinence should be ignored. Nothing is too sacred for the learned fool, who rushes in "where Angels fear to tread." The true critic is one "Still pleased to teach, and yet not proud to know." Such a person has knowledge both "of books and human kind."

Having outlined the characteristics of true critics, Pope catalogs the most famous critics, "the happy few" of Greece and Rome: Aristotle, Horace, Dionysius, Quintilian, Longinus. Aristotle, "Who conquered Nature," respected by the poets as the lawgiver; Horace, who "still charms with graceful negligence"; Quintilian's "justest rules, and clearest method": such are the true critics who flourished along with the great empires of their nations.

With the fall of the empire came the fall of learning, enslavement of mind and body. Desiderius Erasmus stemmed the barbarian's reign of ignorance, and Nicolas Boileau of France signified the advancement of critical learning in Europe. England, however, almost entirely despises and remains untouched by the return to the "juster ancient cause."

Many later critics, following the lead of their nineteenth century predecessors, dismissed *An Essay on Criticism* as a mere collection of well-worn epigrams and dated restatements of literary commonplaces. Ironically, Pope might agree in part with that assessment. *An Essay on Criticism* is not radical, in the way Percy Bysshe Shelley's *A Defence of Poetry* (1840) is. It offers no clear statement of poetics that differs markedly from those of Pope's contemporaries; it is, in one sense, little more than an eighteenth century updating of the precepts espoused by the Latin poet Horace in

Ars poetica (c. 17 B.C.E.), a kind of handbook for writers and critics who might want to create art that pleases while it teaches.

Such a glib assessment, however, masks the major achievement of the poem. In *An Essay on Criticism*, Pope manages to use art as a means of commenting on it. Most significant, he provides a convincing, eloquent statement of what was then a new form of literary evaluation, a method that has been dubbed "the criticism of judgment." Modeling his argument on the premises outlined by philosopher John Locke, Pope argues that judgment gives critics an objective, external standard that permits them to escape the hegemony of authority—slavish adherence to the rules derived from the writings of the ancients—while not succumbing to the anarchy inherent in accepting the vagaries of taste. Pope's criteria for assessing the value of a literary work provide ways for critics to accept as great the works of writers as diverse as the French playwright Pierre Corneille and William Shakespeare.

Underlying Pope's discussion of the nature of criticism is the belief that the function of the critic is essentially evaluative. Pope is concerned with establishing the overall value of a literary production, as were other seventeenth and eighteenth century critics. Not surprisingly, therefore, interpretation is, for him, a secondary activity; the chief role of the discerning reader is to determine if a work of art deserves the accolade of greatness, or if it should be relegated to the ranks of the merely amusing—or worse, to the literary trash heap. In this role, he stands with John Dryden and Samuel Johnson as one of the chief arbiters of his age.

Revised by Laurence W. Mazzeno

Further Reading

Baines, Paul. *Alexander Pope: A Sourcebook*. New York: Routledge, 2000. Provides biographical information and historical and social context for Pope's life and work. Offers analysis of *An Essay on Criticism* and other works, with suggestions for further reading about each one. Contains critical comment on Pope's poetry, politics, and depiction of gender issues.

Barnard, John, ed. *Pope: The Critical Heritage*. London: Routledge & Kegan Paul, 1973. Contemporary reaction to *An Essay on Criticism* is showcased in six essays dating from 1711 to 1741; later responses to the whole of Pope's writings are represented by essays dating to 1782. Includes a brief bibliography with helpful annotations.

Goldsmith, Netta Murray. *Alexander Pope: The Evolution of a Poet*. Burlington, Vt.: Ashgate, 2002. Uses modern research on creativity to examine Pope's poetry in relation to his intellectual peers and to explain why he enjoyed spectacular success as a poet in his lifetime.

Hotch, Ripley. "Pope Surveys His Kingdom: *An Essay on Criticism*." In *Critical Essays on Alexander Pope*, edited by Wallace Jackson and R. Paul Yoder. New York: G. K. Hall, 1993. Reviews the structure and meaning of *An Essay on Criticism*. Argues that the work is less about criticism than about Pope himself; Pope offered the poem as a demonstration that he merits the throne of wit.

Isles, Duncan. "Pope and Criticism." In *Alexander Pope*, edited by Peter Dixon. Athens: Ohio University Press, 1972. Connects *An Essay on Criticism* to its predecessors and to Pope's later critical writings, following the development of Pope's critical ideas in his writings and conversations.

Mack, Maynard, ed. *Essential Articles for the Study of Alexander Pope*. Hamden, Conn.: Archon Books, 1964. Includes three important studies: "Pope on Wit: The *Essay on Criticism*" by Edward Niles Hooker, "Wit in the *Essay on Criticism*" by William Empson, and "The Unity of Pope's *Essay on Criticism*" by Arthur Fenner, Jr.

Morris, David B. *Alexander Pope: The Genius of Sense*. Cambridge, Mass.: Harvard University Press, 1984. Chapter 2 discusses the originality of Pope's critical thinking and delineates the components of Pope's critical theory.

Rogers, Pat, ed. *The Cambridge Companion to Alexander Pope*. New York: Cambridge University Press, 2007. Collection of critical essays on various aspects of Pope's life and work, including several pieces about his poetry, as well as discussions of Pope and gender, money, and the book trade. The references to *An Essay on Criticism* are listed in the index.

An Essay on Man

Author: Alexander Pope (1688-1744)
First published: 1733-1734
Type of work: Poetry

Alexander Pope's *An Essay on Man* stands as an intellectual landmark of the eighteenth century because it embodies the cosmological, theological, and ethical thought of its age. Heavily influenced by Pope's friend Lord Bolingbroke, whose philosophy was congenial to Pope, *An Essay on Man* actually sums up the leading principles of the time. Arthur Lovejoy's *The Great Chain of Being* (1936) provides the essential background for a thorough understanding of the traditions upon which Pope drew.

The central conception of this poem rests, however, upon the ideas of plenitude, gradation, and continuity. Plenitude, for Pope, means the overwhelming fullness of creation, of a universe inhabited by all possible essences created by God. The abundance and variety of creation are also marked by gradation, the notion that there exists a graduated chain or rank among creation, moving from the lowest created thing up to God. This chain implies, of course, subordination of lower creatures to higher because each step up the ladder marks a slight variation upon the preceding step. Thus man (given the poem's title, the use of this word, rather than "people" or "humanity," may be considered accurate) is superior by virtue of his reason to lower beings. The ordered harmony of the entire creation depends upon the proper ordering of parts. Continuity, this ordered continuum of creation, is for Pope the principle of social and divine love that ties together all forms of creation in measured rule.

Epistle 1 explains the relationship of man to the universe. Man's knowledge of the universe must be limited to this world only; however, because evil exists on earth, one should not question God's ways or his justice. It is enough to know that God, because of his infinite goodness, created a perfect system and that man is merely a small part of the gigantic whole. God created the universe in one vast chain; somewhere along this chain man's place may be found. The imperfections in his nature man pretends to find are not really imperfections, for God created man suited to his place and rank in creation. Our happiness here consists in two things: our ignorance of the future and our hope for better things in the future. "Hope springs eternal in the human breast:/ Man never Is, but always to be blest."

Man's chief error is his pride, which causes him to aspire to be better than he is, to question Providence about the fitness of things. Such pride inverts the real order since people are the judged, not the judges. Man must not presume to doubt the justice of God's dispensations. Another error is that man sees himself wrongly as the final cause of all creation, as though all nature exists to serve him alone.

Equally unjust is man's wish for the strength of wild beasts or the power of angels, because God made the earth and all its inhabitants in a graduated scale; at the bottom of this scale are the lowest of creatures, man stands in the middle, and above men are multitudes of angels and, finally, God:

> Vast chain of Being! which from God began,
> Natures ethereal, human, angel, man,
> Beast, bird, fish, insect, what no eye can see,
> No glass can reach; from Infinite to thee,
> From thee to Nothing.

Each animal is subordinated to the ranks above and superior to those below. Man, by virtue of his reason, rules all creation below, but he is not of ethereal substance, as an angel is, and does not possess angelic power. Therefore it is absurd to claim another's place since each is a part of the whole ordained by God. To break this vast chain at any point would destroy the whole and violate God's plan. Man should not view creation as imperfect because he can envision only a part of it. His middle place on the scale implies a limited perception of the complete plan, and what he sees as evil is actually from God's larger vision, partial evil contributing ultimately to his universal good.

> All partial Evil, universal Good:
> And, spite of Pride, in erring Reason's spite,
> One truth is clear, WHATEVER IS, IS RIGHT.

Epistle 2 discusses the nature and state of man as an individual whose tragic situation is that he is in this middle state, both god and beast, both spirit and body. In human nature two principles, self-love and reason, operate often at odds with each other. Neither is entirely good nor bad; when each does its function properly and works in conjunction with the other, good results occur. Pope compares these two principles to the mechanism of a watch; within men self-love is the spring, reason the balance wheel. Without one, man could not act;

without the other, action would be aimless. Without self-love men would vegetate; without reason men would consume themselves in lawless passion. Self-love motivates, inspires, while reason checks, advises. Self-love judges by present good and reason by future consequences. Reason through time acquires power to control impulsive self-love.

The passions are modes of self-love good as long as they conform to reason's dictates. One, the Ruling Passion, often dominates all others and determines the character of a man. No virtue arising from any passion can be wholly without value if subdued, as lust may be turned to gentle love, anger to zeal.

Although man contains both vice and virtue, Heaven compensates by converting individual defects into the strength of all. Our weaknesses motivate mutual reliance. Since each man is given his due portion of happiness and misery, no one should wish to exchange his state for another's. Each should rest content with his own lot.

Epistle 3 discusses the role of man in society. Pope sees the whole universe as one comprehensive society, a complex system of interrelations cementing all creation. Each part relates to others but rank in the chain of being confers power and control over inferior ranks. However, with rule comes responsibility, and man, the imperial race, must care for his underlings as God cares for him.

Whether ruled by animal instinct or human reason, each enjoys that power best suited to his place. Although God set the necessary bounds to each species, allotting to each its particular share of happiness, he designed to ensure the happiness of the whole rather than of the part. The happiness of all depends entirely upon maintaining the proper relations among the individuals; each should love itself and others.

In the primitive state of society, self-love and social love existed. Man's reason then learned useful rules from instinct. Reason observed principles of government from monarchical bees and republican ants. Man constructed his own cities and societies and soon common interest suggested the need for a ruler, who was chosen for his virtues in learning and arms. True religion and government were united in love. Superstition and tyranny arose to invert nature's order, but man's self-love taught him to protect his interests by erecting governments and laws, finding private good in public. Self-love directed to social love returned general social harmony. It is this charity that renders particular forms of government and religion unessential, for charity always seeks the happiness of all, linking self-love with social love, enlisting all ranks of creation into a harmonious order.

Epistle 4 views man in relation to happiness. Since God works by general laws, he intends all to be happy, not merely a few. Order is Heaven's first law, so there can be only one result: Some beings will be greater than others. However, if Heaven intended all to be equally happy, to be greater is not to be happier. True happiness is not located in external condition or possessions. God compensates those who lack them with hope for the future, those who have them fear the future.

Individual bliss on earth rests on three possessions: health, peace, and competence. To good or bad men fortune may bestow its blessings, but gifts of fortune dispose the individual as he obtains them to enjoy them less. In achieving bliss the virtuous man has most advantages. One must not impute injustice to God because the virtuous man often finds calamities his reward for virtue. Calamity occurs through fortune or natural law; God does not dispense with his laws merely to favor a special person. Virtue, moreover, is not rewarded with material gifts.

Virtue's reward is not earthly and external. Its reward resides in the peace and joy of the heart. Earthly recompense will either be disdained as unworthy or will destroy the very virtue that prompted it. No shame or honor arises from one's station in life. True honor comes from faithful employment of one's responsibility. It is character that distinguishes a person, not his or her worldly fortune or fame. History teaches that those who attain worldly prizes frequently pay dearly for them. What deeds make the hero often corrupt the person.

Only true virtue is happiness. It is the sole thing a man may possess without loss to himself. Heaven's bliss is bestowed on him who avoids the extremism of sect and who observes in the creation the presence of God and the divine chain that links all to God. Such a man knows that true happiness belongs not to the individual but to the whole creation, that the source of all faith, law, morality, and happiness is love of God and of man. Self-love, transcending self in pursuing social love and divine, showers blessings upon all things. Self-love awakens the virtuous mind, and like a pebble dropped into water, stirring ripples on the surface, ever embraces wider and wider spheres, from friend, to parent, to neighbor, until it encompasses all living creation.

Further Reading

Baines, Paul. *Alexander Pope: A Sourcebook.* New York: Routledge, 2000. Provides biographical information and historical and social context for Pope's life and work. Offers analysis of *An Essay on Man* and other works, with suggestions for further reading about each one. Contains critical comment on Pope's poetry, politics, and depiction of gender issues.

Cutting-Gray, Joanne, and James E. Swearingen. "System, the Divided Mind, and the *Essay on Man.*" *Studies in En-*

glish Literature, 1500-1900 32, no. 3 (Summer, 1992): 479-494. Considers the poem from philosophical and religious viewpoints, questioning whether Pope was merely compiling accepted truths or undermining the system that he claims to support.

Goldsmith, Netta Murray. *Alexander Pope: The Evolution of a Poet*. Burlington, Vt.: Ashgate, 2002. Uses modern research on creativity to examine Pope's poetry in relation to his intellectual peers and to explain why he enjoyed spectacular success as a poet in his lifetime.

Mack, Maynard. *Alexander Pope: A Life*. New Haven, Conn.: Yale University Press, 1985. Definitive biography of Pope, written by a great scholar. References to the poem appear throughout the book, but the major commentary is provided in chapter 21.

Nuttall, A. D. *Pope's Essay on Man*. Winchester, Mass.: Allen & Unwin, 1984. Addresses the poem as the major philosophical statement in eighteenth century English. Views the poem as including religious issues. Contains a section on public and critical reaction to the poem.

Piper, William Bowman. "Pope's Vindication." *Philological Quarterly* 67, no. 3 (Summer, 1988): 303-321. Confronts questions related to the poem's religious issues by comparing it to John Milton's *Paradise Lost*. Although traditional readings have disregarded this comparison, Piper asserts that Pope is more persuasive concerning the reality of God than Milton is.

Pope, Alexander. *An Essay on Man*. Edited by Maynard Mack. London: Methuen, 1964. Contains a detailed introduction that analyzes the structure and artistry of the poem, its philosophical context, and Pope's Roman Catholic background. The scholarly notes are not intrusive.

Rogers, Pat, ed. *The Cambridge Companion to Alexander Pope*. New York: Cambridge University Press, 2007. Collection of critical essays on various aspects of Pope's life and work, including several pieces about his poetry, as well as discussions of Pope and gender, money, and the book trade. The references to *An Essay on Man* are listed in the index.

Essays

Author: Francis Bacon (1561-1626)
First published: 1597; revised, 1612, 1625
Type of work: Essays

Francis Bacon had many accomplishments. He was a scientist, a philosopher, and a politician, and he was adept, too, at taking bribes; for this he had been imprisoned. It is, however, as a literary man that he is perhaps best remembered, a writer so competent with the pen that for decades there have been some persons willing to argue that Bacon wrote the plays attributed to William Shakespeare.

The essay form is rare in the modern age, although there are some faint signs of its revival. As Bacon used it, the essay is a carefully fashioned statement, both informative and expressive, by which a person comments on life and manners, on nature and its puzzles. The essay is not designed to win people to a particular cause or to communicate factual matter better put in scientific treatises. Perhaps that is one reason why it is not so popular in an age in which the truth of claims and their practical importance are always questioned.

The *Essays* first appeared, ten in number, in 1597. They were immediately popular because they were brief, lively, humane, and well-written. Perhaps they were effective in contrast to the rambling, florid prose written by most writers of the time. A considerable part of their charm lay in their civilized tone. In these essays, Bacon reveals himself as an inquisitive but also an appreciative man with wit enough to interest others. The first edition contained the following essays: "Of Studies," "Of Discourse," "Of Ceremonies and Respects," "Of Followers and Friends," "Of Suitors," "Of Expense," "Of Regiment of Health," "Of Honour and Reputation," "Of Faction," and "Of Negociating."

By 1612, the number of essays had been increased to thirty-eight, the earlier ones having been revised or rewritten. By the last edition, in 1625, the number was fifty-eight. Comparison of the earlier essays with those written later shows not only a critical mind at work but also a man made sadder and wiser, or at least different, by changes in fortune.

The essays concern themselves with such universal concepts as truth, death, love, goodness, friendship, fortune, and praise. They cover such controversial matters as religion, atheism, "the True Greatness of Kingdoms and Estates," custom and education, and usury, and they consider such intriguing matters as envy, cunning, innovations, suspicion, ambition, praise, vainglory, and the vicissitudes of things.

The *Essays or Counsels, Civil and Moral*, as they are called in the heading of the first essay, begins with an essay on truth entitled "Of Truth." The title formula is always the same, simply a naming of the matter to be discussed, as, for example, "Of Death," "Of Unity in Religion," "Of Adversity," "What is Truth? said jesting Pilate; and would not stay for an answer." One expects a sermon, and one is pleasantly surprised. Bacon uses his theme as a point of departure for a discussion of the charms of lying, trying to fathom the love of lying for its own sake. "A mixture of a lie doth ever add pleasure," he writes. This pleasure is ill-founded, however; it rests on error resulting from depraved judgment. Bacon reverses himself grandly: " . . . truth, which only doth judge itself, teacheth that the inquiry of truth, which is the lovemaking or wooing of it, the knowledge of truth, which is the presence of it, and the belief of truth, which is the enjoying of it, is the sovereign good of human nature."

When it comes to death, Bacon begins by admitting that tales of death increase humanity's natural fear of it, but he reminds the reader that death is not always painful. By references to Augustus Caesar, Tiberius, Vespasian, and others, Bacon shows that, even in their last moments, great men maintained their characters and composure. Death is natural, he concludes, and it has certain advantages: It opens the gate to good fame and puts an end to envy. The good man is in no fear of death because he has better things to do and think about, and, when he dies, he knows he has obtained "worthy ends and expectations."

The essay "Of Adversity" is particularly interesting since it reflects Bacon's own experience after imprisonment, the loss of friends and position, and enforced retirement. He writes, "Prosperity is the blessing of the Old Testament; Adversity is the blessing of the New; which carrieth the greater benediction, and the clearer revelation of God's favour." Adversity puts life's brighter moments into effective contrast, and it allows a person the chance to show his or her virtues.

Bacon is no casual essayist. One does not need the report of history to know that the essays as they are found are the product of numerous revisions. Sentences do not achieve a careful balance and rhythm accidentally, nor does a moment's reflection provide apt allusions, pertinent Latin phrases, and witty turns of thought. The essay "Of Beauty" begins with a well-fashioned, complex statement: "Virtue is like a rich stone, best plain set; and surely virtue is best in a body that is comely, though not of delicate features; and that

hath rather dignity of presence, than beauty of aspect." The essay continues by commenting on the sad fact that beauty and virtue are not always conjoined, but then Bacon remembers some noble spirits who were "the most beautiful men of their times"—Augustus Caesar, Titus Vespasianus, Philip le Bel of France, Edward the Fourth of England, Alcibiades of Athens, and Ismael the Sophy of Persia. Then he comes to a striking thought in a simple line: "There is no excellent beauty that hath not some strangeness in the proportion."

Although appreciative of beauty, Bacon is modern in his appreciation of use. "Houses are built to live in," he writes in the essay "Of Building," "therefore let use be preferred before uniformity, except where both may be had." He is aware of the importance of location; he warns the reader to be wary of an "ill seat" for his house and mentions in particular the discomfort that results from building a house in a hollow of ground surrounded by high hills. So aware is he of the mistakes that a builder can make that Bacon follows a catalog of dangers and difficulties with a charming and involved description of an ideal dwelling: a place for entertaining, a place for dwelling, and the whole a beautiful construction of rooms for various uses, courts, playing fountains—all of large, but proper dimensions, and built to take account of summer sun and winter cold.

Although there is a prevailing moral character to the essays so that, in retrospect, they seem to be a series of beautiful commands to erring spirits, there is enough of wisdom, education, humor, and common sense in them to save the author from the charge of moral arrogance. For example, Bacon does not begin his essay on anger by declaring how shameful anger is; he says instead, "To seek to extinguish Anger utterly is but a bravery of the Stoics." He then gives practical advice. To calm anger there is no other way but to consider the effects of anger, to remember what it has done in the past. To repress particular angry acts, Bacon advises the reader to let time pass in the belief that the opportunity for revenge will come later, and he particularly warns against the bitterness of words and the doing of any irrevocable act.

In writing of atheism, Bacon combines philosophical argument with moral persuasion and intensity of expression. If it seems strange that a scientist, the father of induction, should so easily accept the teachings of traditional Christianity, it is only because one tends to think of people as playing single roles and as living apart from their times. In any case, Bacon's philosophical skill was most at evidence in scientific matters, and there is no more reason to expect that he would be adept at philosophizing about religion than to expect that he should have anticipated Albert Einstein's reflections about science. The essay contains the famous line: "It is true, that a little philosophy inclineth man's mind to atheism; but depth in philosophy bringeth men's mind about to religion."

Although the essays naturally reflect a lifetime of experience, they do so in general, not in particular. One looks in vain for reports of adventures and misadventures at court—and Bacon had many of both. His ideas sound a bit like those of Niccolò Machiavelli in his essay on simulation and dissimulation, but there are no personal references to events in which he was involved and from which he acquired the knowledge imparted here. Nor would one suspect that Bacon was one of the leading scientific minds of his age; he discourses on friendship, parents and children, gardens, study, and the rest, as a gentle, humane scholar. One realizes that in the *Essays* Bacon gave up the roles that ambition made him play. In his contemplative moments, he sought to satisfy a twofold goal: to present the wisdom of his living, the wisdom that comes from experience and reflection on it, and to make this presentation by means of a style designed to be economical and ornamental at the same time.

Further Reading

Bowen, Catherine D. *Francis Bacon: The Temper of a Man.* Boston: Little, Brown, 1963. Although this work is basically a biography of Bacon, Bowen includes some discussion of the publishing history of the essays and an analysis of Bacon's style, concentrating particularly on his aphorisms and wit.

Bush, Douglas. *English Literature in the Earlier Seventeenth Century, 1600-1660.* 2d ed. rev. New York: Oxford University Press, 1979. Bush examines Bacon's essays in the light of his other prose writings, noting particularly the limitations of Bacon's understanding that led him to evaluate success in rather materialistic terms.

Matthews, Steven. *Theology and Science in the Thought of Francis Bacon.* Burlington, Vt.: Ashgate, 2008. Examines Bacon's religious beliefs and how his theological ideas influenced his program to reform learning and the natural sciences.

Patrick, John Max. *Francis Bacon.* London: Longmans, Green, 1966. This short work is a general introduction to Bacon's life and work. Patrick notes that the essays are not intended to be a personal expression and examines Bacon's fondness for balance, antithesis, three-item series, and aphorism.

Quinton, Anthony. *Francis Bacon.* Edited by Keith Thomas. New York: Hill and Wang, 1980. Quinton discusses the literary quality of the essays giving particular attention to their aphoristic style; he notes that their subjects range from public affairs to private life and frequently deal with abstractions such as truth or beauty. He also notes the cynical quality of Bacon's thought.

Sessions, William A. *Francis Bacon Revisited.* New York: Twayne, 1996. A critical and historical analysis of Bacon's writings, in which Sessions argues that Bacon's works are both "contemplative inscriptions" and "instruments for the remaking of history." Chapter 2, "The Essays: Reading Them as Dispersed Meditacions," provides a detailed interpretation of those writings.

Williamson, George. *The Senecan Amble: A Study in Prose from Bacon to Collier.* Chicago: University of Chicago Press, 1951. Williamson uses the essays, as well as the other prose, to examine Bacon's style in detail, noting that Bacon considered the function of rhetoric to be the joining of imagination and reason. He considers the relationship between Bacon and the classics.

The Essays

Author: Michel Eyquem de Montaigne (1533-1592)
First published: Essais, books 1-2, 1580; books 1-2, revised, 1582; books 1-3, 1588; books 1-3, revised, 1595 (English translation, 1603)
Type of work: Essays

Michel Eyquem de Montaigne began his essays as a stoical humanist, continued them as a skeptic, and concluded them as someone concerned with the condition of human beings.

This evolution, one substantially agreed upon by Montaigne scholars, is apparent in *The Essays.* The three volumes include writings such as "To Philosophize Is to Learn to Die," in which Montaigne considers how human beings should face pain and die; writings such as the famous "Apology for Raimond Sebond," in which the skeptical attack on dogmatism in philosophy and religion is most evident; and writings such as "The Education of Children," in which Montaigne makes a constructive effort to encourage humans to know themselves and to act naturally for the good of all.

Montaigne retired to his property when he was thirty-eight. Public life had not satisfied him, and he was wealthy enough to live withdrawn from active life and give himself to contemplation and the writing of essays. He did spend some time in travel a few years later, and he was made mayor of Bordeaux, but most of his effort went into the writing and revision of his writings, the attempt to essay, or test, his ideas.

An important essay in the first volume, "That the Taste for Good and Evil Depends in Good Part upon the Opinion We Have of Them," begins with a paraphrase of a quotation from Epictetus to the effect that humans are bothered more by opinions than by things. The belief that all human judgment is, after all, more a function of the person than of the things judged suggested to Montaigne that by a change of attitude human beings could alter the values of things. Even death can be valued, provided those who are about to die are of the proper disposition. Poverty and pain can also be good, provided a person of courageous temperament develops a taste for that. Montaigne concludes that "things are not so painful and difficult of themselves, but our weakness or cowardice makes them so. To judge of great and high matters requires a suitable soul."

This stoical relativity is further endorsed in the essay "To Philosophize Is to Learn to Die." Montaigne's preoccupation with the problem of facing pain and death was caused by the death of his best friend, Étienne de La Boétie, who died in 1563 at the age of thirty-three, and by the deaths of his father, his brother, and several of his children. Montaigne was also deeply disturbed by the Saint Bartholomew Day massacres. As a humanist, he was well educated in the literature and philosophy of the ancients, and from them he drew support of the stoical philosophy suggested to him by the courageous death of his friend La Boétie.

The title of the essay is a paraphrase of Cicero's remark "that to study philosophy is nothing but to prepare one's self to die." For some reason, perhaps because it did not suit his philosophic temperament at the time, perhaps because he had forgotten it, Montaigne does not allude to a similar expression attributed by Plato to Socrates, the point there being that the philosopher is interested in the eternal, the unchanging, and that life is a preoccupation with the temporal and the

variable. For Montaigne, however, the remark means either that the soul in contemplation removes itself from the body, or that philosophy is concerned to teach individuals how to face death. It is the second interpretation that interests him.

Asserting that all human beings strive for pleasure, even in virtue, Montaigne argues that the thought of death is naturally disturbing. He refers to the death of his brother, Captain St. Martin, who was killed when he was twenty-three by being struck behind the ear by a tennis ball. Other instances enforce his claim that death often comes unexpectedly to the young, for which reason the problem is urgent. With these examples, he writes, how can people "avoid fancying that death has us, every moment, by the throat?" The solution he recommends is to face death and fight it by becoming so familiar with the idea of death that individuals are no longer fearful. "The utility of living," he writes, "consists not in the length of days, but in the use of time." Death is natural, and what is important is not to waste life in the apprehension of death.

In the essay "Of Judging the Death of Another," Montaigne argues that people reveal their true character when they show how they face a death they know is coming. A "studied and digested" death may bring a kind of delight to a person of the proper spirit. Montaigne cites Socrates and Cato as examples of men who knew how to die.

Montaigne's most famous essay is his "Apology for Raimond Sebond," generally considered to be the most complete and effective of his skeptical essays. What Montaigne is skeptical of here is not religion, as many critics have asserted, but the pretensions of reason and dogmatic philosophers and theologians. When Montaigne asks, "Que sais-je?" (What do I know?), the expression becomes the motto of his skepticism, not because he thinks that people should give up the use of the intellect and imagination but because he thinks it wise to recognize the limits of these powers.

The essay is ostensibly in defense of the book titled *Theologia naturalis: sive Liber creaturarum magistri Raimondi de Sebonde*, the work of a philosopher and theologian of Toulouse, who wrote the book about 1430. Montaigne considers two principal objections to the book: the first, that Sebond is mistaken in the effort to support Christian belief on human reason; the second, that Sebond's arguments in support of Christian belief are so weak that they are easily confuted. Montaigne agrees that the truth of God can be known only through faith and with God's assistance, but he argues that Sebond is to be commended for his noble effort to use reason in the service of God. If one considers Sebond's arguments as an aid to faith, they may be viewed as useful guides. Montaigne's response to the second objection takes up most of the essay, and since the work is, in some editions, more than two hundred pages long, the length alone may be considered to reflect the intensity of Montaigne's conviction. Montaigne argues against those philosophers who suppose that by reason alone human beings can find truth and happiness. The rationalists who attack Sebond do not so much damage the theologian as show their own false faith in the value of reason. Montaigne considers "a man alone, without foreign assistance, armed only with his own proper arms, and unfurnished of the divine grace and wisdom," and he sets out to show that such a man is not only miserable and ridiculous but grievously mistaken in his presumption. Philosophers who attempt to reason without divine assistance gain nothing from their efforts except knowledge of their own weakness. That knowledge, however, has some value, for ignorance is then not absolute ignorance. Nor is it any solution for the philosopher to adopt the stoical attitude and try to rise above humanity, as Seneca suggests; the only way to rise is by abandoning human means and by suffering and causing oneself to be elevated by Christian faith.

In the essay "Of the Education of Children," Montaigne writes that the only objective he had in writing the essays was to discover himself. In his opinions, Montaigne shows how studying himself led him from the idea of philosophy as a study of what is "grim and formidable" to the idea of philosophy as the path to the health and cheerfulness of mind and body. He claims that the "most manifest sign of wisdom is a continual cheerfulness," and that "the height and value of true virtue consists in the facility, utility, and pleasure of its exercise." Philosophy is "that which instructs us to live." The aim of education is to lead children so that they will come to love nothing but the good, and the way to this objective is an education that takes advantage of youth's appetites and affections. Though his love of books led Montaigne to live in such a manner that he was accused of slothfulness and "want of mettle," he justifies his education by pointing out that this is the worst men can say of him.

Not all of Montaigne's essays reflect the major stages of his transformation from stoic and skeptic to a man of good will. Like Ernest Bacon, he found satisfaction in working out his ideas about the basic experiences of life. Thus he wrote of sadness, constancy, fear, friendship (with particular reference to La Boétie), moderation, solitude, sleep, names, and books. These essays are lively, imaginative, and informed with the knowledge of a gentleman well trained in the classics. He is most eloquent when he writes of pain and death, as when he refers to his own long struggle with kidney stones and to the deaths of those he loved, and when he writes of his need for faith and of the human need for self-knowledge. In

such essays, the great stylist, educated thinker, and struggling human being are one. It was in the essaying of himself that Montaigne became a great essayist.

Further Reading

Cave, Terence. *How to Read Montaigne*. London: Granta, 2007. Argues that *The Essays* are not expressions of Montaigne's philosophy but are "mappings of the mental landscape." Examines the importance of literary technique, including metaphor and sentence length, in these works.

Fontana, Biancamaria. *Montaigne's Politics: Authority and Governance in "The Essais."* Princeton, N.J.: Princeton University Press, 2008. Examines the political philosophy expressed in *The Essays* within the context of Montaigne's life and times. Describes his participation and interest in politics. Argues that *The Essays* were the first major critique of the ancien régime and a precursor of Enlightenment thought.

Frame, Donald Murdoch. *Montaigne in France, 1812-1852*. New York: Octagon Books, 1976. A book that sets the tone for all further criticism of Montaigne by one of the foremost English-speaking critics of the author and one of the best translators of his works. Examines nineteenth century criticism of Montaigne after his popularity had declined in previous centuries.

Langer, Ullrich, ed. *The Cambridge Companion to Montaigne*. New York: Cambridge University Press, 2005. Collection of essays, including discussions of Montaigne's political and religious context, his legacy, his skepticism, and his moral philosophy.

Regosin, Richard L. *The Matter of My Book: Montaigne's "Essais" as the Book of the Self*. Berkeley: University of California Press, 1977. A lucid work that analyzes the sense of self developed by Montaigne in *The Essays* by examining his reading, his friendships, and other external influences.

Sayce, R. A. *The Essays of Montaigne: A Critical Exploration*. London: Weidenfeld & Nicolson, 1972. An examination of the text and form of *The Essays*, with special attention to Montaigne's views on the human condition, movement and change, religion and skepticism, and politics and government. Considers his place in the history of Renaissance thought.

Starobinski, Jean. *Montaigne in Motion*. Translated by Arthur Goldhammer. Chicago: University of Chicago Press, 1985. Examines the impact on *The Essays* of Montaigne's travels, his friendships, and his interaction with the turbulent politics of his day. Shows the "honest dissimulation" that he practiced in order to protect and develop his true views.

Tetel, Marcel. *Montaigne.* New York: Twayne, 1974. One of the best books with which to begin a study of Montaigne.

Examines briefly his life, sources, and influences, as well as the process by which he rendered those influences into *The Essays.* Contains a useful bibliography for further reading.

Essays of Elia *and* Last Essays of Elia

Author: Charles Lamb (1775-1834)
First published: Essays of Elia, 1823; *Last Essays of Elia*, 1833
Type of work: Essays

The essays Charles Lamb wrote for *London Magazine* in the early 1820's, which were collected in the *Essays of Elia* and *Last Essays of Elia*, mark the acme of his literary achievement and are an enduring and loved contribution to English letters. Lamb had written familiar essays since 1802. After "The Londoner" appeared in the *Morning Post* (February 1, 1802), Thomas Manning wrote to him to express admiration for the piece, adding, "If you were to write a volume of essays in the same stile you might be sure of its succeeding." Although Lamb did not immediately take Manning's advice, he did over the next sixteen years produce other periodical essays, volumes of criticism, books for children, and a farce. In 1818, his collected works appeared in two volumes.

Then in 1820, John Scott, the editor of the newly established *London Magazine*, asked Lamb to contribute. Lamb's "Recollections of the South Sea House" appeared in the August issue, the first of the essays written under the pseudonym "Elia." Most of the fifty-three items collected in the two volumes of Elia essays were written for the *London Magazine* between 1820 and 1823, though the last piece in the second volume, "Popular Fallacies," appeared in the *New Monthly Magazine* in 1826 (January-June, September).

In the introduction to the *Last Essays of Elia*, ostensibly written by "a Friend of the Late Elia," Lamb accuses the essays of being "pranked in an affected array of antique models and phrases." The same accusation had been raised by Mary Lamb, the writer's sister and sometime coauthor of children's books, who criticized his fondness for outdated words. Lamb replied, "Damn the ages! I will write for antiquity!" This love for the past, which was, as Elia's "friend" conceded, natural to the author, surfaces in a variety of ways, particularly in literary debts, allusions, and subject matter. In

"Oxford in the Vacation," the second essay, Lamb observes that the reader of his previous piece might have taken the author for a clerk. Lamb adds, "I do agnize something of the sort." The word agnize, acknowledge, probably came to Lamb from William Shakespeare's *Othello, the Moor of Venice* (pr. 1604, pb. 1622); by 1820, it was no longer a common word. Lamb claims that the libraries of Oxford "most arride and solace" him; arride, to please, is an Elizabethan word that Lamb probably took from Ben Jonson's *Every Man out of His Humour* (1599). Similarly, his use of "perigesis" for journey is likely a borrowing from Jonson's *Underwoods* (1640) and is the first recorded use of the word in the *Oxford English Dictionary* since Jonson's nearly two hundred years earlier. "Visnomy" for physiognomy (in "The Two Races of Men"), "pretermitted" instead of overlooked and "reluct" for rebel against (in "New Year's Eve"), and "keck" for reject (in "Imperfect Sympathies") all derive from seventeenth century authors. In at least two instances—"obolary" (having little money) in "The Two Races of Men" and "raucid" for raucous in "To the Shade of Elliston"—Lamb imitated these earlier writers by inventing words; the *Oxford English Dictionary* credits Lamb as the origin of both.

Lamb knew many of the leading authors of the age, including William Wordsworth, Samuel Taylor Coleridge, John Keats, William Hazlitt, Thomas De Quincey, and William Godwin. However his shelves and mind admitted almost no modern literature. His 1808 *Specimens of English Dramatic Poets, Who Lived About the Time of Shakespeare with Notes* called attention to Elizabethan and Jacobean authors whom Lamb admired and whose influence is evident in his Elia essays. Although Lamb's formal education ended at the age of fourteen, he read extensively, as is evident from the more than 130 authors he quotes in his work. For example, the epigraph for "A Quaker Meeting" comes from a 1653 poem by Richard Fleckno; that of "Imperfect Sympathies" is taken from Sir Thomas Browne's *Religio Medici* (1642). "Christ's Hospital Five-and-Thirty Years Ago" presents the "wit-combats" between Coleridge and a fellow student in the same way that Thomas Fuller in his *History of the Worthies of England* (1662) describes the rivalry between Shakespeare and Jonson. The very term "wit-combats" comes from Fuller, whom Lamb called "the dear, fine, silly, old angel." "Popular Fallacies" is modeled on Browne's seventeenth century exploration of "vulgar errors." In "Detached Thoughts on Reading," Lamb lists some of his favorite authors, among them Christopher Marlowe, Michael Drayton, William Drummond, and Abraham Cowley; the youngest of them, Cowley, died in 1667.

This love for the past is evident in the very titles of the essays: "Christ's Hospital Five-and-Thirty Years Ago," "The Old Benchers of the Inner Temple," "On Some of the Old Actors," "On the Artificial Comedy of the Last Century," "The Old Margate Hoy," and "Old China." "Oxford in the Vacation" includes a paragraph-long paean to antiquity, a quality that endears the university to Elia. In "The Old and the New Schoolmaster" Lamb praises the life of the old schoolmaster as idyllic and contrasts it with the hectic existence of the new one. "The Old Benchers of the Inner Temple" laments the passing of the old familiar faces as well as the fashion for fountains and objects to the remodeling of the entrance to the Inner Temple. Elsewhere Lamb observes that "the gardens of Gray's Inn . . . were then far finer than they are now" ("On Some of the Old Actors"). "Dream Children: A Reverie" again criticizes the modern. Lamb here relates that Blakesware, a country house in Hertfordshire, contained an old chimney piece bearing the carved story of the Children in the Wood. The new owner removed this mantelpiece in favor of a sterile "marble one of modern invention . . . , with no story upon it." The title of "Barrenness of the Imaginative Faculty in the Production of Modern Art" summarizes Lamb's conviction; he here compares the skills of the great Renaissance masters with what he regards as the diminished achievement of more recent painters. "There is a cowardice in modern art," he maintains. The same falling off strikes him in the theater, where no one could any longer perform Shakespeare's *Twelfth Night: Or, What You Will* (pr. c. 1600-1602, pb. 1623) or Richard Brinsley Sheridan's *The School for Scandal* (1777) as they could in Lamb's youth, and where the delightful escapism of Restoration comedy had yielded to the "all-devouring drama of common life" ("On the Artificial Comedy of the Last Century").

In this love for the past Lamb is one with the Romantic

movement. Other Romantic traits that surface in the essays are the emphasis on the autobiographical and the dream state. Introspective, Lamb could have said with Michel Eyquem de Montaigne, "It is myself that I portray." The eighteenth century essays of Joseph Addison and Samuel Johnson adopted a familiar style and a persona—the Tatler, Mr. Spectator, the Rambler, the Idler—but they used this persona to separate writer and subject. The Elia pseudonym may be an anagram for "a lie" as well as for "Lamb." On August 16, 1820, just before the appearance of "Recollections of the South-Sea House," Lamb wrote to Barron Field, "You shall have soon a tissue of truth and fiction impossible to be extricated, the interlacing shall be so delicate, the partitions perfectly invisible, it shall puzzle you . . . , & I shall not explain it." Unlike his essayistic predecessors, however, Lamb used his persona to gain the freedom to get closer to, not further away from, the self. Though reality is thinly disguised, Lamb's life beats clearly just beneath the veiled surface of his work.

One method of camouflage is the change of names, beginning with Elia himself. Lamb's father appears as Lovel in "The Old Benchers of the Inner Temple." Lamb's brother John becomes his cousin James Elia, and his sister Mary appears as Cousin Bridget. Lamb's first love, Ann Simmons, is the Alice W—(n) of "Dream Children" and "New Year's Eve." Blakesware is translated to Blakesmoor. When Lamb describes his schooldays at Christ's Hospital, he writes as Elia writing as Samuel Taylor Coleridge; his own experiences are presented as those of a third person, L. Changing dates is another masking device. "The Superannuated Man" deals with Lamb's retirement but alters his last day at the East India House from March 29 to April 12, 1825. "Recollections of the South-Sea House" supposedly recounts events of 1780, when Lamb was only five years old.

The essential truth of Lamb's life, particularly his childhood, is, however, little altered. As he recounts in "Oxford in the Vacation," he was in fact "defrauded . . . of the sweet food of academic institution," and he enjoyed spending his limited free time at one or the other of the English universities. Coleridge's habit of borrowing, annotating, and sometimes returning Lamb's books is accurately depicted in "The Two Races of Men." Lamb enjoyed the quiet of a Quaker meeting; "My First Play" is a factual account of the beginning of his lifelong love affair with the theater. Even the fictional "A Dissertation upon Roast Pig" includes a recollection of a schoolboy incident in which he gave a beggar an entire plum cake.

"A Dissertation upon Roast Pig" is rightly regarded as one of the finest examples of Lamb's wit, which relies on exaggeration, word play, and absurdity. Lamb here relates that

Bo-bo accidentally burns down the family hut, and that in the conflagration nine suckling pigs perish. Horrified at first, Bo-bo and his father, Ho-ti, soon discover the excellent taste of roast pig (one of Lamb's favorite dishes). Ho-ti's cottages thereafter regularly burn down. Once others taste this delicacy, their houses also catch fire, until someone finds a way to cook a pig without consuming a house in the process. His essay also contains the story of the plum cake and so demonstrates how Lamb used humor to distance the tragedies and disappointments of his life. The burned house and the dead pigs transformed into a delicious food could serve as metaphors for the transformation of Lamb's sorrows into the delightful essays of Elia.

The dream also allows Lamb to get closer to his experience through seeming distance. "The Child Angel: A Dream" purports to recount a vision concerning Ge-Urania, an infant angel. In its imaginative portrayal it seems a tale that Coleridge might have written, and its concerns with childhood and reverie place it squarely within the Romantic sensibility. However, it is uniquely Lamb's in its nostalgic melancholy, just as the child angel itself is yet another avatar of Lamb, with his fear of hereditary madness and his limp: Ge-Urania "was to know weakness, and reliance, and the shadow of human imbecility, and it went with a lame gait." In the similarly titled and better-known "Dream Children: A Reverie," Lamb presents his youthful love for Simmons and his sometimes troubled relationship with his brother John in the guise of a reverie. The piece contains humor and expresses no bitterness, but a gentle sadness suffuses the writing, a sense of loss and regret for what might have been. Like many other Lamb pieces, it plays variations on the *ubi sunt* theme: Where are all the great actors, the great artists of the past, one's former friends and acquaintances, where is one's first love, one's youth?

Though most of the Elia essays are personal as well as familiar, occasionally they demonstrate Lamb's skill as a critic. "On the Artificial Comedy of the Last Century" explains that because Restoration comedy is not meant to be taken seriously, it should not be regarded as immoral. "Stage Illusion" extends this argument to comedy in general. Whereas Coleridge argued that at a play the audience engages in a willing suspension of disbelief, Lamb more persuasively maintains that the spectator can enjoy the representation of a coward or a miser only when the spectator recognizes that such a despicable character is being acted, not actually present on the stage. In his essay on the sonnets of Sir Philip Sidney, Lamb takes on another leading Romantic critic, William Hazlitt, to defend the Elizabethan poet. Like Romantic criticism generally, Lamb's is subjective. Still, his assessments, whether of William Hogarth or Sidney or his favorite actors, are invariably fascinating and usually correct.

Joseph Rosenblum

Further Reading

Aaron, Jane. *A Double Singleness: Gender and the Writings of Charles and Mary Lamb.* New York: Oxford University Press, 1991. A feminist reading. Aaron maintains that Charles Lamb's writings "encode his resistance to the cult of manliness prevalent during his period." The last chapter looks specifically at the Elia essays, but discussions of individual pieces are scattered throughout the book.

Barnett, George L. *Charles Lamb.* Boston: Twayne, 1976. A critical biography that devotes a long chapter to the Elia essays. Barnett argues that Lamb's essays resemble Romantic poetry in their emphasis on the dream state and the past. Also discusses Lamb's style and maintains that it is not an imitation of seventeenth century writing.

_____. *Charles Lamb: The Evolution of Elia.* Bloomington: Indiana University Press, 1964. Analyzes the development of Lamb's writing, especially that seen in his essays, and places him in the tradition of the familiar essay. Pays particular attention to the relationship between Lamb's private letters and his published work.

Burton, Sarah. *A Double Life: A Biography of Charles and Mary Lamb.* New York: Penguin Putnam, 2003. A dual biography of Charles Lamb and his sister Mary, focusing on their close bonds. The siblings were drawn together after Mary, in a fit of insanity, murdered their mother. Charles assumed responsibility for his sister, who continued to experience fits of madness, and he suffered severe depression and alcoholism.

James, Felicity. *Charles Lamb, Coleridge, and Wordsworth: Reading Friendship in the 1790's.* Basingstoke, England: Palgrave Macmillan, 2008. A reevaluation of Lamb's roles as reader, writer, and friend to the poets Samuel Taylor Coleridge and William Wordsworth. Analyzes works from the three writers to trace the creative dynamics of early English Romantic literature.

Lucas, E. V. *The Life of Charles Lamb.* 1905. Reprint. London: Methuen, 1921. In this standard biography, Lucas identifies 1821 as Lamb's "golden year," in which he wrote most of his best Elia essays. Discusses Lamb's activities while he was writing these essays and provides essential biographical background.

Monsman, Gerald. *Charles Lamb as the London Magazine's "Elia."* Lewiston, N.Y.: Edwin Mellen Press, 2003. Examines the essays Lamb wrote for *London Magazine,* which differ in form from the essays included in *Essays of Elia*. Focuses on the satiric elements in these essays, which Monsman describes as an "important component of Romantic emotional intensity." The essays critique Romantic poets, including Lamb's friends Samuel Taylor Coleridge and William Wordsworth.

_____. *Confessions of a Prosaic Dreamer: Charles Lamb's Art of Autobiography*. Durham, N.C.: Duke University Press, 1980. Examines Lamb's use of a persona in his essays, arguing that such a mask was necessary in dealing with the difficulties of his life. Monsman also considers the place of the Elia essays in the Romantic movement and concludes that Lamb "rejects the visionary and demonic poetry of the egotistical sublime and replaces it with a prose model of a safe and nourishing social reality."

Esther Waters

Author: George Moore (1852-1933)
First published: 1894
Type of work: Novel
Type of plot: Realism
Time of plot: Late nineteenth century
Locale: England

Principal characters:
ESTHER WATERS, a young servant
WILLIAM LATCH, her betrayer
JACKIE, their son
MRS. BARFIELD, Esther's mistress
SARAH TUCKER, Esther's enemy
FRED PARSONS, Esther's betrothed
MISS RICE, Esther's employer

The Story:

The first person Esther Waters meets when she arrives at Woodview is William Latch, the son of the cook under whose direction Esther is to work. William is the worry of his mother's life, for, like his dead father, he is a gambler. Mrs. Latch has hoped that William would become a delivery boy and leave Woodview, but William is determined to go into service for Mr. and Mrs. Barfield, the owners of Woodview, so that he can observe their racing stable.

The position as kitchen maid at Woodview is a godsend to Esther, for her stepfather, claiming that he has too many mouths to feed, has forced her to leave home. The workhouse might have been her only refuge if she had not secured a position with the Barfields. In spite of her efforts to do her work well, however, it is hard for her to get along with the other servants. Mrs. Latch seems to go out of her way to make life unpleasant for her, and the maids tease her because she is religious. William is at first her only champion among the servants, for which she is grateful to him. Then Esther finds an unexpected friend in her mistress, Mrs. Barfield, who is also deeply religious.

Learning that Esther cannot read, Mrs. Barfield tries to teach her. William continues to pay her special attention, to the anguish of Sarah Tucker, another of the maids. After a servants' ball in celebration of the victory of one of the Woodview horses, William takes Esther out to some wheat stacks and seduces her, telling her they will be married as soon as he has enough money. By the following morning, Esther has convinced herself that she had been betrayed, and she refuses to speak to William. Tiring at last of her sulking, he turns to Peggy Barfield, a cousin of his master, and after a few weeks elopes with her.

Three months later, Esther realizes that she is pregnant. Strangely, the servant girls who had been her former tormentors become kind and sympathetic, which only makes her feel more ashamed of her wickedness. Mrs. Barfield is sympathetic, too, but she has to send Esther away, for she has become a bad example for the other girls.

There is no place for Esther to go but to her home, where she finds that her mother is also pregnant. Her stepfather is crueler than ever, but he tolerates her as long as she pays rent and gives him money to buy beer. At last, realizing that she has to leave before all of her savings disappear and there is nothing left for her baby, Esther takes lodgings close to the hospital where she is to be confined. After her son is born, she is filled with a happiness she has never known, but her joy is lessened when she learns that her mother has died in childbirth, just a few days after Esther's Jackie was born. Soon afterward, Esther's stepfather and the other children go to Australia; Esther now feels entirely alone in the world.

The next few years are terrible ones for Esther. She has to work as much as seventeen or eighteen hours a day, and on one occasion is forced to go to the workhouse. Her greatest grief is the need to leave her child in the care of others while she works, for Jackie is her whole life. When her son is six years old, Esther finds work with Miss Rice, a writer whose home is a haven to Esther. Miss Rice knows Esther's story and tries to make the girl's life easier for her.

Esther meets Fred Parsons, a colorless but honest, dependable, and religious man. When Esther tells him her story, he readily forgives her. She takes Fred to see Jackie, and the man and the boy become fast friends from the first meeting. Esther and Fred plan to be married as soon as Miss Rice can get another servant, for Esther refuses to leave her mistress without someone to care for her. One evening, while on an errand for Miss Rice, Esther unexpectedly meets William Latch, who tells her that Peggy has left him. When he learns that Esther had his child, he pleads to come back to her and hints that it is her Christian duty to Jackie to give the boy his rightful father. Esther knows that she would be better off with Fred, as would Jackie, for William has become a tavernkeeper and a bookie. Jackie, however, meets his father and loves him instantly. For his sake, Esther and William are married.

At first, William makes money. Jackie is placed in a good school, and Esther has two servants to wait on her. Nevertheless, there are many days of anxious waiting to hear the results of a race. Often William has thousands of pounds to cover if the favorite wins. After a time, he begins to lose heavily. It is illegal to accept bets at the tavern, and William is in constant danger of being reported to the police. Fred Parsons comes to warn Esther to leave William, to tell her that the tavern is to be raided, but she refuses to desert her husband. Then Sarah Tucker comes to the tavern to ask for help after she had stolen a silver plate from her employer. The police find her there. After the tavern is raided, William is heavily fined. Business begins to dwindle, and Esther and William have lean times.

After William contracts tuberculosis, the dampness and fog of the racetracks only make him cough more, and at last he has to go to the hospital. There the doctors tell him that he must go to Egypt for his health. He and Esther gamble all of their money on a single race and lose. Esther tries to be cheerful for William's sake, but when he dies a few days later, she wishes that she too had died. She has no money and no place

to go. Her only blessing is that Jackie is old enough to take care of himself.

Esther goes back to Woodview. Only Mrs. Barfield is left, and she is poor. Most of the land has gone to pay racing debts. Esther, however, is ready to stay with Mrs. Barfield without wages, for she has never forgotten her old friend's kindness. Jackie enlists in the army and goes to Woodview say good-bye to his mother. With pride, she introduces him to Mrs. Barfield. She knows that her sin has been redeemed and that she will never have to be ashamed again. She has given her country a fine soldier. Few women could do more.

Critical Evaluation:

Nineteenth century fiction maintains a delicate balance between realism and Romanticism, often with a strong foundation of sentimentality. In England at the end of the century, George Moore led the way toward the kind of literary realism represented in France by Gustave Flaubert and Émile Zola, but he believed that the most carefully observed facts are insufficient unless seen through the glass of imagination and humanity. Marked by unprecedented frankness, *Esther Waters* was the first English novel to reveal the pilgrimage through life of a human being as a physical creature. The novel caused a scandal almost as great as that caused by Thomas Hardy's *Jude the Obscure* (1895) and was for a time banned from circulating libraries; it had a tremendous influence on the works of younger writers, among them W. Somerset Maugham, who was inspired to write his first novel, *Liza of Lambeth* (1897).

Moore deliberately took a mundane subject, wrote about it using circumstantial and realistic detail, and did so without melodrama; his simple prose style nonetheless establishes place and setting with surprising poetic impact. The novel presents a vivid picture of the life of a lower-class young woman from a large family, with a mother who has married a man who is not prepared to support his step-children. Blessed with little education, Esther Waters has few alternatives other than to become a servant, and Moore portrays in unflinching detail the lives of such girls in the nineteenth century in large country houses and lower-middle-class homes. At best, such work represents a temporary refuge, and servants live in fear of being cast out and thus being deprived of shelter. Often the only alternatives for a girl like Esther, once she becomes pregnant, are prostitution or suicide. For Esther, as a deeply religious young woman, such alternatives are untenable, depriving her of further means of survival.

While Esther is a woman of great principle, those same principles are limited and limiting. Functionally illiterate, despite her employer's efforts to teach her to read, Esther is also unable to read her life in emotional terms. Having led a sheltered existence, she is frequently unable to read the situations in which she finds herself. Although she has a well-developed sense of what is right and wrong, she is easily led by arguments that center on her religious belief. Thus, William Latch is able to persuade her to marry him by hinting that it is her Christian duty to do, even though she knows that she will be much happier with Fred Parsons, whose outlook is similar to her own. Thus, while Esther briefly enjoys the fruits of William's seeming success, elevated to the role of mistress with servants of her own, it is inevitable that the rise in her fortunes will be followed by a fall. It is enough that Esther has managed to educate her son, Jackie, during these prosperous years.

Esther has been absorbed by one central focus: her child. Her thoughts are on how to save him, how to raise him, and how to make him into a decent man. Her overwhelming concern for her son has led her to make heroic stands against social injustice. One thinks in particular of her refusal to pay for her newborn son to be murdered by the baby farmer and, similarly, of her rejection of a post as wet nurse to save her own son. When Esther suggests to Mrs. Rivers that she might like to nurse her own child and, thus, ensure the survival of two children, Esther's criticism of the wet-nurse system is unequivocal. Her speech, however, is directed purely by her care for her own child rather than by any awareness of social injustice. Her moral sense is powerful but limited because she cannot see beyond her own situation (she lacks even the opportunity to do so). This is her strength in terms of her ability to survive, but it is perceived as a weakness by early commentators because Esther cannot represent anyone but herself; middle-class heroines have a more universal appeal and an ability to speak.

Nonetheless, Esther's struggle, told in human terms, speaks powerfully to the reader. Regardless of how limited her viewpoint may be, she emerges as a heroine of majestic proportions, all the more magnificent because in her own eyes she is only a miserable creature doing the best she can with little hope and few expectations. Moore offers a powerful critique of the narrowness and hypocrisy of the middle-class households through which Esther passes, which by their very contrast illuminate the genuine goodness of Esther, Miss Rice, Mrs. Barfield, and a few others. He also provides a vivid portrait of the ways in which the lower classes struggle to survive. The various social scourges—drinking and gambling among them—are described in detail, but Moore provides a view that is as much sympathetic as it is critical. He also grants Esther a final respite when, having

lost her husband and her home, she is able to return to her original situation at Woodview, where she supports her newly debt-ridden former mistress. While this irony will not be lost on the reader, Esther herself remains content.

Similarly, Esther reveals her pride in her son, Jackie, when he visits to say good-bye before he goes to war. She is proud of having brought him up to serve the imperial project. The reader wonders whether Jackie will ever return. Esther has no long view to take, and for that reason she is content.

Revised by Maureen Kincaid Speller

Further Reading

Cave, Richard Allen. *A Study of the Novels of George Moore*. New York: Barnes & Noble, 1978. Discusses specific texts from Moore's oeuvre. Provides an overview of the works and the stylistic subheadings under which they may be categorized. Includes concise notes and references for further research.

Dorré, Gina M. "Reading and Riding: Late-Century Aesthetics and the Cultural Economy of the Turf in George Moore's *Esther Waters*." In *Victorian Fiction and the Cult of the Horse*. Burlington, Vt.: Ashgate, 2006. Dorré analyzes *Esther Waters* and other Victorian novels for their depiction of horses. Argues that the representation of horses symbolizes the attitudes of Victorian society during a period of massive technological, economic, and social changes.

Farrow, Anthony. *George Moore*. Boston: Twayne, 1978. Provides a chronology of the significant events of Moore's life and explores the influences and other factors to which he was exposed as a writer.

Federico, Annette. "Subjectivity and Story in George Moore's *Esther Waters*." In *English Literature in Transition, 1880-1920*. Greensboro: University of North Carolina Press, 1993. A study of the motivations that led Moore to write this socially provocative novel. Explores the cultural significance of the character of Esther.

Frazier, Adrian. *George Moore, 1852-1933*. New Haven, Conn.: Yale University Press, 2000. A thorough biography, drawing on much previously unpublished material and emphasizing Moore's historical and cultural contexts. Not a critical examination of his works but a narrative of his life, including his presence in Paris during the era of impressionism and in Dublin during the Irish literary renaissance.

Gray, Tony. *A Peculiar Man: A Life of George Moore*. London: Sinclair-Stevenson, 1996. A useful biography of Moore, which takes into account his different vocations, such as art critic and landowner. Includes a short bibliography and an index.

Pierse, Mary, ed. *George Moore: Artistic Visions and Literary Worlds.* Newcastle, England: Cambridge Scholars Press, 2006. A collection of papers delivered at a 2005 international conference on Moore. The papers analyze his works, discussing, among other topics, his literary innovations, avant-garde feminism, and his legacy in the realm of literature.

Swafford, Kevin. "Reification and Respectability in Thomas Hardy's *Tess of the D'Urbervilles* and George Moore's *Esther Waters.*" In *Class in Late-Victorian Britain: The Narrative Concern with Social Hierarchy and Its Representation.* Youngstown, N.Y.: Cambria Press, 2007. Swafford's study of how social class distinctions were depicted by late nineteenth century British authors includes this comparison of *Esther Waters* with Thomas Hardy's *Tess of the D'Urbervilles* (1891).

Ethan Frome

Author: Edith Wharton (1862-1937)
First published: 1911
Type of work: Novel
Type of plot: Psychological realism
Time of plot: Late nineteenth century
Locale: Starkfield, Massachusetts

Principal characters:
ETHAN FROME, a New England farmer
ZENOBIA "ZEENA" FROME, his wife
MATTIE SILVER, Zeena's cousin

The Story:

Ethan Frome is twenty-one years old when he marries Zenobia Pierce, a distant cousin who nursed his sick mother during her last illness. It is a wedding without love. Zenobia, called Zeena, has no home of her own, and Ethan is lonely, and so they are married. Zeena's talkativeness, which was pleasing to Ethan during his mother's illness, quickly subsides, and within a year of their marriage, Zeena develops the sickliness that is to plague her husband all her life. Ethan becomes increasingly dissatisfied with his life. He is an intelligent and ambitious young man who hoped to become an engineer or a chemist. He soon, however, finds himself stuck with a wife he detests and a farm he cannot sell.

The arrival of Mattie Silver brightens the gloomy house considerably. Mattie, Zeena's cousin, comes to Starkfield partly because she has no other place to go and partly because Zeena feels in need of a companion around the house. Ethan sees in Mattie's goodness and beauty every fine quality that Zeena lacks.

When Zeena suggests that Ethan help Mattie find a husband, he begins to realize how much he is attracted to the girl. When he goes to a church social to bring Mattie home and sees her dancing with the son of a rich Irish grocer, he realizes that he is jealous of this rival and in love with Mattie. On his way home with her, Ethan feels his love for Mattie more

than ever, for on that occasion, as on others, she flatters him by asking him questions on astronomy. His dreams of happiness are short-lived, however, for when he reaches home, Zeena is her nagging, sour self. The contrast between Zeena and Mattie impresses him more and more.

One day, Ethan returns from his morning's work to find Zeena dressed in her traveling clothes. She is going to visit a new doctor in nearby Bettsbridge. Ordinarily, Ethan would have objected to the journey because of the expensive remedies that Zeena is in the habit of buying on her trips to town. On this occasion, however, he is overjoyed at the news of Zeena's proposed departure, for he realizes that he and Mattie will have the house to themselves overnight.

With Zeena out of the way, Ethan again becomes a changed man. Later in the evening, before supper, Ethan and Mattie sit quietly before the fire, just as Ethan imagines happily married couples would do. During supper, the cat breaks Zeena's favorite pickle dish, which Mattie used to brighten up the table. In spite of the accident, they spend the rest of the evening happily. They talk about going sledding together, and Ethan tells Mattie shyly—and perhaps wistfully—that he saw Ruth Varnum and Ned Hale, a young engaged couple, stealing a kiss earlier in the evening.

In the morning Ethan is happy, but not because of anything out of the ordinary the night before. In fact, when he went to bed, he remembered sadly that he did not so much as touch Mattie's fingertips or look into her eyes. He is happy because he can imagine what a wonderful life he could have if he were married to Mattie. He gets glue to mend the pickle dish, but Zeena's unexpected return prevents him from repairing it. His spirits are further dampened when Zeena tells him that the Bettsbridge doctor considers her quite sick. He advised her to get a girl to relieve her of all household duties, a stronger girl than Mattie. She already engaged the new girl. Ethan is dumbfounded by this development. In her insistence that Mattie be sent away, Zeena gives the first real hint that she may be aware of gossip about her husband and Mattie.

When Ethan tells Mattie of Zeena's decision, the girl is as crestfallen as Ethan. Zeena interrupts their lamentations, however, by coming downstairs for something to eat. After supper, she requires stomach powders to relieve a case of heartburn. In getting the powders, which she hides in a spot supposedly unknown to Mattie, Zeena discovers the broken pickle dish, which was carefully reassembled. Detecting the deception and learning that Mattie is responsible for the broken dish, Zeena calls Mattie insulting names and shows plainly that the girl will be sent away at the earliest possible moment.

Faced with the certainty of Mattie's departure, Ethan thinks of running away with her. His poverty and his sense of responsibility to Zeena permit no solution to his problem, only greater despair. On the morning Mattie is to leave Starkfield, Ethan, against the wishes of his wife, insists on driving Mattie to the station. The thought of parting is unbearable to both. They decide to take the sleigh ride that Ethan promised Mattie the night before. Down the hill they go, narrowly missing a large elm tree at the bottom. Mattie, who told Ethan that she would rather die than leave him, begs until Ethan agrees to take her down the hill a second time and to run the sled into the elm at the bottom of the slope; but they fail to hit the tree with force sufficient to kill them. The death they seek becomes a living death, for in the accident Mattie suffers a permanent spine injury and Ethan an incurable lameness. The person who receives Mattie into her home, who waits on her, and who cooks for Ethan is Zeena.

Critical Evaluation:

Ethan Frome has enjoyed greater popularity than any other of Edith Wharton's twenty-two novels and novellas. It is also better known than any of her short stories, nonfiction, or poetry. Appearing first as a three-part serial in *Scribner's* magazine, the 1911 book got its start around 1907 when

Wharton developed aspects of the narrative as an exercise in writing French. The story appeared as a play in 1936. Moving away from depicting the manners of high society, Wharton treats, in *Ethan Frome*, poor, inarticulate people living in the countryside. Early critics complained that a New York sophisticate such as Wharton knew nothing about the lives of the kind of people depicted in *Ethan Frome*. The book's popularity argues otherwise.

Wharton frames her story. Prior to chapter 1, an engineer observes Ethan Frome coming to town and inquires about his history. Later, caught in a snowstorm, the engineer spends a night at the Frome house, and the engineer intuits events of long ago. An omniscient narrator relates nine chapters that conclude with the accident. In the epilogue the engineer comments on Ethan, Zeena, and Mattie living in the lonely farm house for twenty-four years.

The novel employs few symbols. Beside the emblematic landscape, the cat implies the witchlike influence of Zeena on Mattie and Ethan, and the family graveyard suggests that Ethan will never escape Zeena or the farm. In her foreword to a 1922 edition, Wharton writes that *Ethan Frome* intends to convey a sense of the harsh and beautiful New England countryside. Thus, Wharton adopts an austere realism, a tone in keeping with the hard landscape and with the shocking outcome.

This harsh tone informs the theme of Ethan's isolation. Wharton describes Ethan as like the landscape, mute and melancholic, as if he were one of the outcroppings of slate that push up through the snow. Ethan is "an incarnation of the land's frozen woe with all that was warm and sentient in him fast bound below the surface." The central narrative occurs in winter, but flashbacks contrast happy summer occasions. Ethan recalls to Mattie a picnic the previous summer at Shadow Pond where he found her locket; then he points to a tree trunk recalling that there they sat together in the summer evening. At the time he speaks the winter snow has nearly buried that tree trunk.

Isolation pervades the novel. When Ethan comes to town from his farm, he speaks to no one. Four or five years prior to the main action, Ethan had had one year of study at a technological college in Worcester, and he had been to Florida. The encounter with the greater world contrasts with Ethan's confinement to his rural farm. The isolation drives Ethan's mother crazy. The road past the house has lost its traffic and the mother can no longer see passersby. Once a talker, the mother grows silent and seldom speaks. Ethan, desperate in the long winter evenings for the sound of a voice, asks why she does not say something; his mother, insane, answers that she is listening to the people talking out in the storm. Then

Zeena—a distant relative—comes to nurse the mother. After his mother's funeral, fearful of being left alone, Ethan too quickly proposes marriage.

Ethan is trapped on the farm. A villager notes early that most of the smart people got away from the area, but Ethan had to care first for his father, then his mother, then his wife, and then Mattie. Ethan made some attempts to get away. When his mother dies, Ethan hopes to move to a town, but Zeena prefers notoriety as a sickly person in Starkfield to anonymity in a city. Ethan considers running off with Mattie; he even writes a note to Zeena explaining his desertion. He recalls that a man in the area did run off to the West and that he found happiness.

Ethan, however, cannot bring himself to abandon Zeena. She cannot support herself on the farm. Then his eye fastens on a newspaper advertisement offering train trips to the West at reduced rates. He has no money with which to buy train fare for himself and Mattie. The facts of poverty and his marital obligation act like prison guards to chain him, "a prisoner for life." The toboggan accident leaves him lame so that his every step seems checked by the jerk of a chain. Circumstances and his own conscience prohibit Ethan from ever leaving Starkfield.

Zeena counters her husband of seven years in all his desires. She speaks in a flat whine, keeps her hair tight with crimping pins, dresses always in dark calico, and complains constantly about imagined illness. She demands that the lovely Mattie be banished from the house and that a new girl come to wait on her. Zeena, witchlike, dominates Ethan. After the crash, Zeena creates a living hell for Mattie and for Ethan.

"Critical Evaluation" by Emmett H. Carroll

Further Reading

Bloom, Harold, ed. *Edith Wharton.* New York: Chelsea House, 1986. A collection of critical essays on the body of Wharton's work. "*Ethan Frome*: This Vision of His Story," by Cynthia Griffin Wolff, analyzes this novel, including a good discussion of the role of the narrator. Wolff implies that the narrator as character is on an equal footing with the other main characters and that the narrator's "vision" is a manipulation of reality and must be questioned.

Farwell, Tricia M. *Love and Death in Edith Wharton's Fiction.* New York: Peter Lang, 2006. An insightful look at Wharton's beliefs about the nature of love and the way they reflect her philosophical views, shaped by those of Plato and Charles Darwin. Wharton's own shifting feelings on the role of love in life are revealed in conjunction with the shifting role that love played for her fictional characters. Chapter 5 provides an examination of *Ethan Frome.*

Fournier, Suzanne J. *Edith Wharton's "Ethan Frome": A Reference Guide.* Westport, Conn.: Praeger, 2006. Provides a plot summary and discusses the novel's style, themes, and contexts, and the influences of Nathaniel Hawthorne and other writers upon Wharton. Surveys the critical response to the novel.

Howe, Irving, ed. *Edith Wharton: A Collection of Critical Essays.* Englewood Cliffs, N.J.: Prentice Hall, 1962. Two of the essays deal directly with *Ethan Frome*: Blake Nevius's "On *Ethan Frome*" disputes previous positive interpretations and posits the idea that the work demonstrates a "despair arising from the contemplation of spiritual waste." Lionel Trilling's influential essay "The Morality of Inertia" takes the position that Ethan, paralyzed by inaction, makes no moral decision, and this "inertia" characterizes a large part of humanity. Both essays are valuable in terms of understanding the traditional critical perspectives on this work.

Lee, Hermione. *Edith Wharton.* New York: Knopf, 2007. An exhaustive study of Wharton's life, offering valuable insights and pointing out interesting analogies between her life and her fiction.

Lewis, R. W. B. *Edith Wharton: A Biography.* New York: Harper & Row, 1975. Excellent presentation of Wharton's life. Discusses the relationship between *Ethan Frome* and Wharton's divorce from her husband Teddy.

McDowell, Margaret B. *Edith Wharton.* Rev. ed. Boston: Twayne, 1991. A succinct overview of Wharton's work, including a section entitled "The Harsh Artistry of *Ethan Frome.*"

Waid, Candace. *Edith Wharton's Letters from the Underworld: Fictions of Women and Writing.* Chapel Hill: University of North Carolina Press, 1991. A distinctively modern approach to Wharton, using the terminology and premises of postmodernist literary criticism. Chapter 2 analyzes *Ethan Frome* in terms of the theme of infertility inherent in Wharton's images.

Wolff, Cynthia Griffin. *A Feast of Words: The Triumph of Edith Wharton.* New York: Oxford University Press, 1977. Offers a psychological study of Wharton and of *Ethan Frome.*

Ethics

Author: Baruch Spinoza (1632-1677)
First published: Ethica ordine geometrico demonstrata,
    1677 (English translation, 1870)
Type of work: Philosophy

A geometric demonstration of ethics is a novelty in the history of thought, but Baruch Spinoza's *Ethics* is famous not because of, but in spite of, its novelty of method. The principal advantage of the method is that it reveals Spinoza's thought as clearly as possible. Although the demonstrations may not satisfy critics who concern themselves only with definitions and logical form, they are strongly persuasive for those who, already committed to the love of the good and of God, need clarity and structure in their thoughts.

Spinoza begins with definitions, proceeds to axioms (unproved but acceptable), and then moves to propositions and demonstrations. If one wishes to find fault with Spinoza's argument, any place is vulnerable: One can quarrel about the definitions, doubt the truth of the axioms, or question the validity of the demonstrations. To reject the book, however, one would need to question the integrity of Spinoza's spirit.

It has long been regarded an error in philosophy to attempt to deduce what people ought to do from a study of what people do, but what Spinoza attempts is a deduction of what people ought to do from a study of what must be, according to his definitions and axioms. The primary criticism of his method, then, is not that he errs—although most critics find errors in Spinoza—but that he tries to use logical means to derive ethical truths. The criticism depends on the assumption that ethical truths are either matters of fact, not of logic, or they are not truths at all but, for example, emotive expressions.

Spinoza begins *Ethics* with definitions of "cause," "finite," "substance," "attribute," "mode," "free," "eternity," and "God," the last term being defined to mean "Being absolutely infinite, that is to say, substance consisting of infinite attributes, each one of which expresses eternal and infinite essence." To understand this definition one must relate it to the definitions of the terms within it—such as "substance," "finite," and "attribute"—but one must also resist the temptation to identify the term, so defined, with any conventionally used term. Spinoza's God is quite different from other conceptions. The point of the definition is that what Spinoza means by "God" is whatever is "conceived through itself" (its substance), has no limit to its essential characteristics

(has infinite attributes), and maintains its character eternally. As one might suspect, the definition of "God" is crucial.

The axioms contain such logical and semantical truths as "I. Everything which is, is either in itself or in another"; "II. That which cannot be conceived through another must be conceived through itself"; "VI. A true idea must agree with that of which it is the idea"; and "VII. The essence of that thing which can be conceived as not existing does not involve existence." At first, the axioms may be puzzling, but they are not as extraordinary as they seem. Axiom number 7, for example, means only that anything that can be thought of as not existing does not, by its nature, have to exist.

The propositions begin as directly implied by the definitions: "I. Substance is by its nature prior to its modifications" follows from the definitions of "substance" and "mode," and "II. Two substances having different attributes have nothing in common with one another" is another consequence of the definition of "substance." As the propositions increase, the proofs become longer, making reference not only to definitions but also to previous propositions and their corollaries. For those interested in technical philosophy, the proofs are intriguing, even when they are unconvincing, but for others they are unnecessary; the important thing is to understand Spinoza's central idea.

Proposition 11 is important in preparing the way for Spinoza's main contention: "XI. God or substance consisting of infinite attributes, each one of which expresses eternal and infinite essence, necessarily exists." Although one may be tempted to seize upon this proposition as an instrument to use against atheists, it is necessary to remember that the term "God" is a technical term for Spinoza and has little, if anything, to do with the object of religious worship.

Proposition 14 makes the startling claim that "Besides God no substance can be nor can be conceived." A corollary of this proposition is the idea that God is one; that is, everything that exists, all of nature, is God. Individual things do not, by their natures, exist, but only through God's action, and God is not only the cause of their existence but also of their natures (24, 25). Readers might expect, consequently, that a great deal of the universe is contingent; that is, it depends upon something other than itself and need not be as it is. Spinoza argues in proposition 24 that "In Nature, there is nothing contingent, but all things are determined from the necessity of the divine nature to exist and act in a certain manner." Consequently, the human will is not free but necessary (32). This was one of the ideas that made Spinoza unpopular with both Jews and Christians.

Having used part 1 of *Ethics* to develop the conception of God, Spinoza goes on in part 2, after presenting further definitions and axioms, to explain the nature and the origin of mind. He concludes that "In the mind there is no absolute or free will." (48). In part 2, he also develops the idea that God is a thinking and extended being.

In part 3, "On the Origin and Nature of the Emotions," Spinoza argues that emotions are confused ideas. "Our mind acts at times and at times suffers," he contends in proposition 1 of part 3; "in so far as it has adequate ideas, it necessarily acts; and in so far as it has inadequate ideas, it necessarily suffers." One should note that Spinoza defines "emotion" as any modification of the body "by which the power of acting of the body itself is increased, diminished, helped, or hindered, together with the ideas of these modifications."

By this time, Spinoza creates the idea that God, as both thinking and extended substance, is such that all nature is both thinking and extended (since everything that is must be part of God). Another way of expressing this idea is that everything that exists does so both as body and as idea. Thus, the human being exists as both body and idea. If the human being, as idea, does not adequately comprehend the modifications of the human body, the mind suffers.

In part 4, "Of Human Bondage: Or, Of the Strength of the Emotions," Spinoza defines the good as "that which we certainly know is useful to us." In a series of propositions, he develops the ideas that each person necessarily desires what is considered to be good; that in striving to preserve his or her being, a person acquires virtue; and that the desire to be happy and to live well involves desiring to act, to live, "that is to say, actually to exist." In this attempt to relate freedom to one's will to act, and in the identification of the good with the striving toward existence, Spinoza anticipated much of the more significant work of the twentieth century existentialists.

In proposition 28 of part 4, Spinoza writes that "The highest good of the mind is the knowledge of God, and the highest virtue of the mind is to know God." This claim is prepared for by previous propositions relating the good to what is desired, the desire to action, action to being, and being to God. Because of the intricacy of Spinoza's argument, it becomes possible for him to argue that to seek being, to seek the good, to use reason, and to seek God are one and the same. To use rea-

son involves coming to have adequate ideas, having adequate ideas involves knowing the nature of things, knowing the nature of things involves knowing God.

It might appear that Spinoza's philosophy, for all its references to God, is egoistic, in that this crucial phase of his argument depends upon the claim that all people seek to preserve their own beings. A full examination of part 4, however, shows that Spinoza transcends the egoistic base of action by arguing that to serve the self best, one uses reason; but to use reason is to seek an adequate idea of God and, consequently, to seek what is good for all people. In fact, Spinoza specifically states that whatever causes people to live in harmony with one another is profitable and good, and that whatever brings discord is evil.

A person's highest happiness or blessedness, according to Spinoza, is "the peace of mind which springs from the intuitive knowledge of God." This conclusion is consistent with Spinoza's ideas that humanity's good consists in escaping from the human bondage of the passions, that to escape from the passions is to understand the causes that affect the self, that to understand the causes involves action, and that action leads to God.

When, through rational action, people come to determine themselves, they participate in the essence of all being; they become so at one with God that they possess an intellectual love of God, which is humanity's blessedness and virtue. The eternal is known only by the eternal; hence, in knowing God, one becomes eternal—not in a finite or individual way, but as part of God's being.

Spinoza is usually bracketed with René Descartes and Gottfried Wilhelm Leibniz as a rationalist philosopher. Eschewing the approach of the classic philosophers and the Scholastics alike, Spinoza relies almost exclusively on reason, devoid of any imaginative or theological superstructures, to develop his system of metaphysics. Like Descartes, he finds the method of the mathematician the best approach to philosophical inquiry: In identifying and developing the logical relationships between statements about the world, he is able to show how all things are related causally. Unlike Descartes, however, he does not hesitate to question traditional notions of God and construct a metaphysics that eliminates the need for a conventional deity.

The system Spinoza presents in all of his writings, but especially in *Ethics*, has been described alternatively as pantheistic and atheistic. Although he makes frequent references to God, Spinoza is not simply another in the line of Scholastic philosophers who, like St. Thomas Aquinas, devoted his life to proving the rationality of theological belief. Spinoza's God is not a personal, transcendent being on whom all creation depends; for Spinoza, "God" is equivalent to "Nature," an infinite substance in whom all finite substances reside. God and all that people generally consider "creation" are actually one. A similar monism characterizes Spinoza's view of "mind" and "body"; these two aspects of human nature, often described as dualistic components of humanity, are, for Spinoza, merely different modes of expressing the essential "oneness" of humanity—which, in turn, is simply an expression and extension of the infinite substance, which he calls God.

Within his highly structured mathematical approach, Spinoza devotes considerable attention to the notion of human desires and emotions. Reversing the traditional Aristotelian notion that people innately desire what is good, Spinoza argues that whatever one desires becomes viewed as a good. A large part of the central sections of *Ethics* is devoted to explaining how people may overcome emotions and desires to reach a genuine understanding of what is truly good, and come to some appreciation of the infinite.

This complicated and highly theoretical system of metaphysics was castigated by Spinoza's contemporaries, and, for more than a century after his death, his works were little more than footnotes in the history of philosophy. His insistence that God is simply a part of nature and not a distinct being worthy of reverence led to charges of atheism; his complex analysis of philosophical questions, organized in the form of geometric propositions, caused many in the seventeenth century to dismiss him as too obscure. Not until the rise of Romanticism did his ideas—with their overtones of pantheism and insistence on the essential unity of all reality—become popular with thinkers and writers. Then they were embraced enthusiastically by Gotthold Ephraim Lessing and Johann Wolfgang von Goethe in Germany and Samuel Taylor Coleridge in England. Since the eighteenth century, Spinoza has risen in stature to become one of the most revered thinkers in European philosophy. He has been linked with the Stoics, who also found little real freedom in human activities and believed that much of human behavior was determined by forces that people simply could not identify. He also has been described as a kind of Socrates, working diligently to uncover the truth despite the hardships he experienced in his own life.

Revised by Laurence W. Mazzeno

Further Reading

Chappell, Vere, ed. *Baruch de Spinoza.* New York: Garland, 1992. A brief biography of Spinoza accompanied by a series of essays explaining and discussing his ideas.

Cook, J. Thomas. *Spinoza's "Ethics": A Reader's Guide.* New York: Continuum, 2007. Provides an explanation of the philosophical concepts in *Ethics*, devoting a chapter to each of the work's five parts. Describes the philosophical background in which the book was written, as well as the reception and influence of the work.

Garrett, Don, ed. *The Cambridge Companion to Spinoza.* New York: Cambridge University Press, 1996. In the introduction, Garrett places Spinoza's work in the tradition of philosophy, and in the opening essay, W. N. A. Klever offers a biography of Spinoza and a general discussion of his works. What follows is a series of essays examining specific aspects of Spinoza's thought.

Gullan-Whur, Margaret. *Within Reason: A Life of Spinoza.* London: Jonathan Cape, 1998. A feminist account of Spinoza's life that contrasts his acceptance of male-dominated society with his egalitarian republican ideals. Contains a bibliography and an index.

Hampshire, Stuart. *Spinoza and Spinozism.* New York: Oxford University Press, 2005. An excellent source for understanding Spinoza's philosophy. Hampshire, a twentieth century British philosopher, was an acknowledged expert on Spinoza. This volume brings together all of his previous works on the seventeenth century philosopher, including *Spinoza: An Introduction to His Thought* (1951), one of the best introductions to Spinoza's ideas. The 1962 essay "Spinoza and the Idea of Freedom" and a later essay, "Spinoza and Spinozism," are also included.

Harris, Errol F. *Spinoza's Philosophy: An Outline.* Atlantic Highlands, N.J.: Humanities Press, 1992. A good book for beginners, discussing Spinoza's life and style, his principal works, and the means of understanding his methods and writings.

Hunter, Graeme, ed. *Spinoza: The Enduring Questions.* Toronto, Ont.: University of Toronto Press, 1994. Essays that attempt to settle Spinoza's place in the history of philosophy.

Lloyd, Genevieve. *Part of Nature: Self-Knowledge in Spinoza's "Ethics."* Ithaca, N.Y.: Cornell University Press, 1994. Illuminates the connection between Spinoza's metaphysics and ethics in relationship to the dilemma of alienation inherited with René Descartes's notion of self. Argues that Spinoza, in his strangeness, exposes Western philosophy's assumptions of individuality while offering an alternative understanding.

Nadler, Steven M. *Spinoza's "Ethics": An Introduction.* New York: Cambridge University Press, 2006. Explains the key philosophical concepts in *Ethics* and provides information on Spinoza's geometric method, his life, and his career. Discusses his philosophy in relation to that of his contemporaries, René Descartes and Thomas Hobbes, to the Stoics and other ancient philosophers, and to Judaic concepts.

Scruton, Roger. *Spinoza*. New York: Routledge, 1999. An excellent biographical introduction to the thoughts of the philosopher, clearly presented and requiring no special background. Includes bibliography.

Eugene Onegin

Author: Alexander Pushkin (1799-1837)
First published: Evgeny Onegin, 1825-1832, serial; 1833, book; revised, 1837 (English translation, 1881)
Type of work: Verse novel
Type of plot: Impressionistic
Time of plot: Nineteenth century
Locale: Russia

Principal characters:
EUGENE ONEGIN, a Russian dandy
VLADIMIR LENSKY, his friend
TATYANA LARIN, a woman in love with Eugene
OLGA, her sister

The Story:

Eugene Onegin is brought up in the aristocratic tradition. Although he has little classical background, he has a flashing wit, and he is well read in economics. He becomes an accomplished man of the world by the time he reaches young adulthood. In fact, he is so successful in love and so accustomed to the social life of Moscow that he habitually feels a supreme boredom with life. Even the ballet lately fails to hold his attention.

Eugene's father leads the usual life. He gives parties regularly and tries his best to keep up his social position by borrowing recklessly. Just as he declares bankruptcy, Eugene receives word that his uncle is dying. Since he is the heir, he leaves in haste to attend the dying man. Grumbling, meanwhile, at the call of duty, he is thankful to be coming into an inheritance.

His uncle, however, dies before he arrives. After the relatives depart, Eugene settles down to enjoy his uncle's handsome country estate. The cool woods and the fertile fields charm him at first, but after two days of country life his former boredom returns. He soon acquires a reputation as an eccentric. If neighbors call, Eugene finds himself obliged to leave on an urgent errand. After a while, the neighbors leave him to himself.

Vladimir Lensky, however, remains his friend. At eighteen, Vladimir is still romantic and filled with illusions of life and love. He was in Germany, where he was much influenced by the philosopher Immanuel Kant and the poet-dramatist Friedrich von Schiller; this more German temperament sets him apart. He and Eugene become more and more intimate.

The Larins have two daughters, Olga and Tatyana. Olga is pretty and popular, and although she is the younger, she is the leader in their group. Tatyana is reserved and withdrawn, but a discerning observer would see her real beauty. She makes no effort to join in the country life. Olga was long betrothed to Vladimir, but the family despairs of finding a husband for Tatyana.

On Vladimir's invitation, Eugene reluctantly agrees to pay a visit to the Larins. When the family hears that the two men are coming, they immediately think of Eugene as a suitor for Tatyana. Eugene, however, is greatly bored with his visit. The refreshments are too ample and too rustic, and the talk is heavy and dull. He pays little attention to Tatyana. After he leaves, Tatyana is much disturbed. Falling deeply in love with Eugene, she has no arts with which to attract him. After confiding in her dull-witted nurse, she writes Eugene a passionate, revealing love letter.

Eugene, stirred by her letter, pays another visit to the Larins and finds Tatyana in a secluded garden. He tells her the brutal truth. He is not a good man for a husband, for he had too much experience with women and too many disillusionments. Life with him would not be at all worthy of Tatyana. The girl, making no protest, suffers in silence.

On his lonely estate Eugene lives the life of an anchorite. He bathes every morning in a stream, reads, walks and rides in the countryside, and sleeps soundly. Only Vladimir calls occasionally.

That winter the Larins celebrate Tatyana's name-day. When Vladimir represents the gathering as only a small family affair, Eugene consents to go. He feels betrayed when he finds the guests numerous, the food heavy, and the ball obligatory. For revenge, he dances too much with Olga, preventing Vladimir from enjoying his fiancé's company. Vladimir becomes jealously angry and challenges Eugene to a duel. Eugene stubbornly accepts the challenge.

Before the duel, Vladimir goes to see Olga. His purpose is to reproach her for her behavior, but Olga, as cheerful and affectionate as ever, acts as if nothing happened. More lighthearted but somewhat puzzled, Vladimir prepares to meet Eugene on the dueling ground.

When the two friends meet, Eugene shoots Vladimir through the heart. Remorseful at last, Eugene leaves his estate to wander by himself. Olga soon marries an army man and leaves home. In spite of the scandal, Tatyana still loves Eugene. She visits his house and makes friends with his old housekeeper. She sits in his study reading his books and pondering his marginal notes. Eugene is especially fond of cynical works, and his notes reveal much about his selfishness and disillusionment. Tatyana, who read very little, learns much bitterness from his books and comes to know more of Eugene.

At home, Tatyana's mother does not know what to do. The girl seems to have no interest in suitors and refuses several proposals. On the advice of relatives, the lady decides to take Tatyana to Moscow, where there are more eligible men. They are to visit a cousin for a season in the hopes that Tatyana will become betrothed. From her younger cousins, Tatyana learns to do her hair stylishly and to act more urbanely in society. At a ball, a famous general, a prince, is attracted to Tatyana. In spite of the fact that he is unattractive, she accepts his proposal.

After more than two years of wandering, Eugene returns to Moscow. Still indifferent to life, he decides to attend a fashionable ball, simply to escape from boredom for a few hours. He is warmly greeted by his host, whom he knew well in former times. While the prince is reproaching him for his long absence, Eugene cannot keep from staring at a queenly woman who dominates the gathering. She looks familiar. When he asks the prince about her, he is astounded to learn that she is Tatyana, his host's wife.

The changed Tatyana shows no traces of the shy rustic girl who wrote so revealingly of her love. Eugene, much attracted to her, frequently goes to her house, but he never receives more than a cool reception and a distant hand to kiss. Finally, Eugene begins to write her letters in which he expresses his hopeless longing. Still, Tatyana gives no sign. All that winter Eugene keeps to his gloomy room, reading and musing. At last, in desperation, he calls on Tatyana unannounced and surprises her as she is reading his letters.

Tatyana refuses to give in to his importunate declarations. She does not understand why he scorned her when she was a country girl but pursues her now that she is a married woman. She would rather listen to his brutal rejection than to new pleadings. She once was in love with Eugene and would gladly have been his wife; perhaps she is still in love with him. Perhaps she was wrong in listening to her mother, who was insistent that she marry the prince. However, she is now married, and she will remain faithful to her husband until she dies.

Critical Evaluation:

Eugene Onegin is generally considered Alexander Pushkin's most outstanding and characteristic work. Written between 1823 and 1831, the verse novel reflects Pushkin's development as a poet and marks a transition to prose fiction, which occupied his later years. The time of the fictional action of the novel spans the years 1820 to 1825, ending with the period of the Decembrist uprising in a fragmentary tenth chapter. The eight full cantos, or chapters, as Pushkin called them, were published individually and as a complete edition in 1833.

The work is written in a highly ornate stanza form that is based on sonnet form and has been rarely attempted since. The plot is shaped by symmetrical refusals of love. First Onegin rejects Tatyana; then Tatyana dismisses Onegin. Although the form is highly polished, the plot is frequently overshadowed by the narrator's digressions, many of which explore the author's own biography and the process of writing the novel itself. Only about one-third of the novel concerns the plot, while the rest presents descriptions of life in St. Petersburg and the provinces and digressions on the theater, contemporary politics, amorous adventure, or literary craftsmanship. The work combines the pathos of a psychologically plausible affair with epigrammatic wit.

In spite of the strong French influence in his works, Pushkin expressed Russian life in lively Russian. The depth of his insight into Russian life led contemporary critics to call *Eugene Onegin* "an encyclopedia of Russian life," even though the novel ignores the concerns of the peasantry and the growing urban middle class. The novel depicts, however, a lively account of Russian customs and beliefs as well as a variety of contemporary portraits, interiors, and landscapes. *Eugene Onegin* brings together conflicting discourses and worldviews, including the hackneyed provincial taste of Tatyana's family, which lags several years behind that of fashionable society; the simple wisdom of peasant culture represented by the nanny; and the contemporary cosmopolitan lifestyle interpreted by the author-narrator, embodied in Eugene, and presented in Tatyana's salon at the end of the novel.

Eugene Onegin raises a series of problems concerning the relationship between literature and life. It also concerns the limits on social action and artistic expression imposed by the conventions and expectations of polite society. Life and literature repeatedly intersect. Pushkin inserts readers, both friends and foes, whom he addresses throughout the text. In this way, the audience also enters the fictional world of the novel. The author-narrator enters his created world to befriend Eugene. The narrator's muse merges with the novel's heroine, Tatyana. Tatyana, Lensky, and Eugene attempt to recreate the literature they have read while the author-narrator parodies these same works. Tatyana models herself on the sentimental heroines of Samuel Richardson and of Madame de Staël. Lensky acts out patterns of romantic verse, such as that written by Vasily Zhukovsky or André-Marie de Chénier. Eugene plays the role of the disillusioned hero, typically found in the works of Lord Byron, who abandons civilization. Both Eugene, a dandy, and Tatyana, host of a fashionable salon, ultimately play roles that unite social and aesthetic goals. At the same time, the author-narrator, as a published writer, counters the literary aspirations of the young poet, Lensky, and the Byronic hero, Eugene.

The main characters, including the author-narrator and the fictionalized readers, belong to the Westernized gentry of Russia and therefore acknowledge the same cultural conventions. During the course of the novel, the characters trace several stages of development, which occur at different rates but span youthful enchantment, a period of disenchantment, and then mature re-enchantment. The author-narrator develops from a child writing sentimental verse to the author of the novel itself. Tatyana, who begins as a young girl who sees people as literary stereotypes, learns that life's imitation of literature can be a parody and emerges as the host of a salon, which was the highest form of aesthetic creativity open to a woman at the time. Although Tatyana develops her ability to utilize cultural convention, Eugene finds himself trapped by a literary paradigm, while Lensky is never able to integrate life and art. All the characters live within a world from which there is no lasting retreat into the refuges of romantic imagination: nature, dream, and primitive society.

Although in the preface he refers to the novel as a satirical work, written "in the manner of Byron's *Don Juan*," Pushkin later diminished its satirical content. He did, however, admire the structure of Byronic poems. Like Byron, Pushkin shapes elliptical narratives with digressive asides and develops a stylistic link between the poet and his hero, who is also a product of contemporary society. Romantic irony, which presents the same ideas or events from conflicting points of view, colors the entire plot of Pushkin's narrative and is emphasized in a number of ways. Internal discrepancies are consciously inserted to allow for variations of meaning. Pushkin purposefully does not introduce a unifying scheme of images to enhance the impression of an open novel. In addition, the author-narrator frequently interrupts with comments on the text itself. He also parodies contemporary literary works and the sentimental moods of the characters. The tone alternates between frivolous and profound, derisive and sentimental.

Eugene Onegin does not, however, merely copy Byronic elements but evaluates and extends popular Byronic conventions. Although the narrator's point of view is frequently ironic, he, unlike Byron's narrators, mocks the romantic mood rather than poetry itself. Eugene's characters seem to exhibit the bitter rebelliousness, aristocratic arrogance, and passionate excess of one of Byron's heroes, yet the imitation is conscious on Eugene's part and parodic on the author-narrator's. By the end of the novel, the pose is considered outmoded in St. Petersburg society, unwittingly leaving Eugene in a state of truly Byronic alienation.

Pushkin's predilection for linguistic clarity, sparkling wit, and elegance is enhanced by a light touch, or the ability to make the complex configuration of plots, digressions, and intricate poetic arrangements appear easy. The loose structure of *Eugene Onegin* allows Pushkin to experiment with stylistic and generic convention while including a varied commentary on contemporary Russian life by way of the plot and the digressions from it. *Eugene Onegin* amply exemplifies Pushkin's powers of observation and insight into life and art.

"Critical Evaluation" by Pamela Pavliscak

Further Reading

Bethea, David M. *Realizing Metaphors: Alexander Pushkin and the Life of the Poet*. Madison: University of Wisconsin Press, 1998. Describes the relationship between Pushkin's life and his art and discusses why, more than two hundred years after his birth, his work remains relevant. Includes index and illustrations.

Binyon, T. J. *Pushkin: A Biography.* New York: Knopf, 2004. The winner of the Samuel Johnson prize for British non-fiction, this biography chronicles Pushkin's literary success alongside his personal failures. Binyon describes how the writer included small pieces of his life in *Eugene Onegin* and other works.

Driver, Sam. *Pushkin: Literature and Social Ideas.* New York: Columbia University Press, 1989. Considers Pushkin as an engaged social thinker rather than as an alienated Romantic poet. Traces the development of Pushkin's social ideas and his involvement in contemporary politics. The chapter devoted to dandyism offers an insightful discussion of *Eugene Onegin* in light of European fashion.

Hasty, Olga Peters. *Pushkin's Tatiana.* Madison: University of Wisconsin Press, 1999. Feminist focus on the character of Tatiana, demonstrating how she is able to overcome risk and constraint in order to realize her imaginative potential.

Hoisington, Sona S., trans. *Russian Views of Pushkin's "Eugene Onegin."* Bloomington: Indiana University Press, 1988. A varied collection of Russian considerations of Pushkin's work. Contains several famous essays by nineteenth and twentieth century writers and critics, including Fyodor Dostoevski, Yuri Lotman, and Mikhail Bakhtin. Includes a discussion of the social significance of *Eugene Onegin*, an elaboration of the novel as multiple-voice text, and an evaluation of the narrative structure.

Kahn, Andrew, ed. *The Cambridge Companion to Pushkin.* New York: Cambridge University Press, 2006. Collection of essays by Pushkin scholars discussing the writer's life and work in various genres; Pushkin and politics, history, and literary criticism; and Pushkin's position in Soviet and post-Soviet culture. Chapter 3 provides analysis of *Eugene Onegin.*

Nabokov, Vladimir. *Eugene Onegin: A Novel in Verse by Aleksandr Pushkin.* 4 vols. Rev. ed. Princeton, N.J.: Princeton University Press, 1975. Nabokov's translation of *Eugene Onegin* includes an extensive and thorough commentary on the style and content of Pushkin's novel. Although his gloss on *Eugene Onegin* is eclectic and often digressive, Nabokov's discussion is always interesting.

Ryfa, Juras T., ed. *Collected Essays in Honor of the Bicentennial of Alexander Pushkin's Birth.* Lewiston, N.Y.: Edwin Mellen Press, 2000. A selection of scholarly essays devoted to various works by Pushkin and his influence on his literary descendants. Some of the essays discuss *Eugene Onegin* and *The Captain's Daughter* and compare Pushkin to Russian writers Leo Tolstoy and Anton Chekhov.

Vickery, Walter. *Alexander Pushkin.* New York: Twayne, 1970. Provides extensive plot commentary and a detailed consideration of Pushkin's versification. The chapter on *Eugene Onegin* offers a good, basic introduction to the work.

Eugénie Grandet

Author: Honoré de Balzac (1799-1850)
First published: 1833 (English translation, 1859)
Type of work: Novel
Type of plot: Naturalism
Time of plot: Early nineteenth century
Locale: Saumur, France

Principal characters:
MONSIEUR GRANDET, a miser
EUGÉNIE, his daughter
CHARLES GRANDET, his nephew
NANON, his servant
MONSIEUR DE GRASSINS, a banker
MONSIEUR CRUCHOT, a notary

The Story:

In the French town of Saumur, old Grandet is a prominent personality, and the story of his rise to fortune is known throughout the district. He is a master cooper who marries the daughter of a prosperous wood merchant. When the new French Republic offers for sale the church property in Saumur, Grandet uses his savings and his wife's dowry to buy the old abbey, a fine vineyard, and several farms. Under the consulate, he becomes mayor and grows still more wealthy. In 1806, he inherits three additional fortunes from the deaths of his wife's mother, grandfather, and grandmother. By this time he owns the abbey, a hundred acres of vineyard, thirteen farms, and the house in which he lives. In 1811, he buys the nearby estate of an impoverished nobleman.

Grandet is known for his miserliness, but he is respected for the same reason. His manners are simple and his table is meager, but his speech and gestures are the law of the countryside. His household consists of his wife, his daughter, Eugénie, and a servant, Nanon. Old Grandet, who uses his wife as a screen for his devious financial dealings, reduces his wife almost to slavery. Nanon, who does all the housework, is gaunt and ugly but very strong. She is devoted to her master because he took her in after everyone else refused to hire her because of her appearance. On each birthday, Eugénie receives a gold piece from her father and a winter and a summer dress from her mother. Each New Year's Day, Grandet asks to see the coins and gloats over their yellow brightness.

Grandet begrudges his family everything except the bare necessities of life. Every day, he carefully measures and doles out the food for the household—a few lumps of sugar, several pieces of butter, and a loaf of bread. He forbids the lighting of fires in the rooms before the middle of November. His family, like his tenants, live under the austere circumstances he imposes.

The townspeople wonder whom Eugénie will marry. There are two rivals for her hand. One of them, Monsieur Cruchot, is the son of the local notary. The other, Monsieur de Grassins, is the son of the local banker. On Eugénie's birthday, in the year 1819, both call at the Grandet home. During the evening, there is an unexpected knock at the door, and in comes Charles Grandet, the miser's nephew. Charles's father amassed a fortune in Paris, and Charles himself, dressed in the most fashionable Parisian manner, exemplifies Parisian customs and habits and tries to impress these awkward, gawking provincials with his superior airs.

Eugénie outdoes herself in an effort to make the visitor welcome, even defying her father in the matter of heat, candlelight, and other luxuries for Charles. Grandet is polite enough to his nephew that evening. Charles brings a letter from his father, in which Grandet's brother announces that he lost his fortune, he is about to commit suicide, and he entrusts Charles to Grandet's care. The young man is quite unaware of what his father wrote, and when Grandet informs him next day that his father's business failed and he committed suicide, Charles bursts into tears and remains in his room for several days. Finally, he writes to a friend in Paris, asking him to dispose of his property and pay his debts. He gives little trinkets to Eugénie, her mother, and Nanon. Grandet looks at them greedily and says he will have them appraised.

He informs his wife and daughter that he intends to turn the young man out as soon as his father's affairs are settled.

Charles feels that there is a stain on his honor. Grandet feels so, too, especially since he and his late brother had the same family name. In consultation with the local banker, Monsieur de Grassins, he arranges a plan whereby he can save the family reputation without spending a penny. Monsieur de Grassins goes to Paris to act for Grandet, but instead of returning he enjoys a life of pleasure in the capital.

Eugénie falls in love with Charles. She sympathizes with his penniless state and gives him her hoard of coins so that he will be able to go to the Indies and make his fortune. After the two young people pledge everlasting love to each other, Charles leaves Saumur.

On the following New Year's Day, Grandet asks to see Eugénie's money. Her mother, who knows her daughter's secret, keeps silent. In spite of Eugénie's denials, Grandet guesses what she did with the gold. He orders her to stay in her room and announces that he will have nothing to do with either her or her mother. Rumors begin to circulate in town. The notary, Monsieur Cruchot, tells Grandet that if his wife were to die, Eugénie could insist on a division of the property. The village whispers that Madame Grandet is dying of a broken heart caused by her husband's treatment of her. Realizing that he might lose a part of his fortune, Grandet relents and forgives his wife and daughter. When his wife dies, he tricks Eugénie into signing over her share of the property to him.

Five years pass with no word from Charles to brighten Eugénie's drab existence. In 1827, when Grandet is eighty-two years old, he is stricken with paralysis. He dies urging Eugénie to take care of his money.

Eugénie continues to live with old Nanon and to wait for Charles to return. One day, a letter comes from Charles, in which he tells her that he no longer wishes to marry her. Instead, he hopes to marry the daughter of a titled nobleman and secure his father-in-law's title and coat of arms. Eugénie releases Charles from his promise, but Monsieur de Grassins hurries to Charles and tells him that his father's creditors are not satisfied. Until they are, his fiancé's family will not allow a marriage. When she learns of his predicament, Eugénie pays the debt, which enables Charles to marry.

Eugénie continues to live alone. Her routine is exactly what it was while Grandet lived. Suitors come to the house again. Young de Grassins is disgraced by his father's loose life in Paris, but Monsieur Cruchot, who rises to a high post in the provincial government, continues to press his suit. At last, Eugénie agrees to marry him, providing he does not demand the prerogatives of marriage; she will be his wife in name only. They are married only a short time before Monsieur Cruchot dies. To her own property, Eugénie thereupon adds his. Nanon marries, and she and her husband stay with Eugénie. Convinced that Nanon is her only friend, the young widow resigns herself to a lonely life. She lives as she always lived in the bare old house. She has great wealth but, lacking everything else in life, is indifferent to it.

Critical Evaluation:

Eugénie Grandet is part of Honoré de Balzac's grandly designed *La Comédie humaine* (1829-1848; *The Human Comedy*, 1895-1895, 1911). Rather late in his prolific writing career, Honoré de Balzac conceived the idea of arranging his novels, stories, and studies in a certain order. He first described his plan in *Avant-propos* (1842), claiming that the idea originated as early as 1833, and named the project *The Human Comedy*. Balzac was influenced in his idea by the naturalists Georges Louis Leclerc de Buffon, Étienne Geoffroy Saint-Hilaire, and Jean Lamarck, whose scientific principles—especially the taxonomic system—Balzac sought to apply to literature, particularly for the purpose of organizing information. Balzac firmly believed that "social species" could be classified just as zoological species were, and he retroactively attempted to classify his fifty-odd previous works as well as all future writings to fit his scheme. To accommodate his plan, he adopted eight major topic headings: "Scenes from Private Life," "Scenes from Provincial Life," "Scenes from Parisian Life," "Scenes from Political Life," "Scenes from Military Life," "Scenes from Rural Life," "Philosophical Studies," and "Analytical Studies." The works were arranged, rearranged, and arranged again. *Eugénie Grandet* finally came to be categorized with the "Scenes of Provincial Life." In line with this ambitious organizational plan, Balzac tailored his earlier output to the new standards, with some predictably disastrous results. The literary qualities of the novels, however—notably of *Eugénie Grandet*—are irrefutable testimony to the triumph of art over science.

Balzac realized his goal of presenting typical human species in spite of, not because of, his "scientific" system of taxonomy. As the unsurpassed historian of the French middle class during the first half of the nineteenth century, he incarnated the stereotypes that were new then but so well known today, among them the snob, the provincial, the prude, the miser, and the lecher. He did so on the strength of his artistic skill and not by virtue of scientific analysis, for Balzac was not a systematic philosopher or a scientist but an artist. His novels, though they are often marred by his insensitivity to language and his proclivity for excessive details, outlined the essential characteristics of the nineteenth century French

middle class more clearly than anyone else has ever done. Matching Juvenal and Martial, Balzac satirized avarice, ambition, lust, vanity, and hypocrisy. Greed, however, was his *bête noire*, and money is a pervasive theme in Balzac's novels. The figure of the greedy miser Monsieur Grandet epitomizes greed and furnishes Balzac with one of his best characters. Ironically, the novel reflects Balzac's own preoccupation with money and his desire to earn vast sums of it. Like many of his characters, he wanted wealth and social position. As a young man, he was poor and constantly in debt, but he never did learn how to manage money, even after his novels began earning him sizable sums. He was constantly in debt because he lived extravagantly and beyond his means. While writing, he lived like a monk, working furiously for long hours with virtually no time out even for eating. When the novel was completed, however, Balzac devoted that same energy to nonstop revelry. His feasts were legendary and his capacity for fine foods was gargantuan; he is said to have consumed one hundred oysters as an *hors d'oeuvre*, for example. His drinking and other debauches were no less excessive. He agreed with Monsieur Grandet that money is power and power is all that matters; therefore, money is the only important factor in life.

The difference between Balzac and his fictional characters, however, is that Balzac wanted money for what it would buy, whereas Grandet wanted money for its own sake. Balzac cultivated his Dionysian lifestyle with the same single-minded dedication with which Grandet cultivated abstemiousness. He enjoyed a grand style, in contrast to Grandet, who took pleasure from self-denial.

Though the novel is entitled *Eugénie Grandet*, it is Monsieur Grandet who dominates the novel just as he dominated his family. He is the force that determines his wife's destiny (who is ultimately killed by his penny-pinching vindictiveness) and that of his daughter (who is emotionally warped by his miserly indoctrination). Thus the novel is as much about Grandet as it is about Eugénie.

Monsieur Grandet is what literary critics call an undeveloped or a "flat" character. He undergoes no change in the course of the novel and experiences no enlightenment. From start to finish, he is venal and miserly. In fact, Eugénie is the only character who undergoes change, for she progresses from innocence to experience. The others remain as they are at the beginning.

Although Eugénie knows nothing of Grandet's machinations in accumulating his fortune, she is nevertheless shaped by her father's influence. Grandet thus exerts his wishes even beyond the grave, since his training of Eugénie—implicit and explicit—is reflected in her behavior long after he is dead. Although she is publicly charitable, she adopts his parsimonious living habits. Without effort, but presumably because she learns from her father, she increases her fortune. Eugénie would not be what she is without having grown up with such a father. The matrix of this relationship illustrates one of Balzac's major premises, which was to become a tenet of late nineteenth century literary naturalism: that the combined effects of genetics and environment cannot be surmounted. This phenomenon is labeled "determinism," more precisely, "mechanistic determinism," to distinguish it from its religious counterpart of predestination. Eugénie is born into a given social environment with a given genetic makeup. She is unable to change those factors, and they are the twin determinants of her fate. The novel traces her development up to the time when she accepts the fate that has been foreordained at the outset: She is very, very rich and very, very unhappy. The inescapable forces of determinism work through to their inevitable conclusion.

Eugénie Grandet is an unusually moving work, for the reader can hardly fail to sympathize with Eugénie while despising her father. It comes as something of a shock, then, to realize that Eugénie bears her father no malice. Even her response to Charles's betrayal is so subtle that it is untainted; Charles is oblivious to subtlety, and the reader does not begrudge Eugénie her one, lone exercise of financial power. Balzac's incredible prestidigitation is at work here, manipulating the readers so that they accept the novel's point of view without imposing extraneous judgments. *Eugénie Grandet* is a tribute to Balzac's craft and art.

"Critical Evaluation" by Joanne G. Kashdan

Further Reading

Bertault, Philippe. *Balzac and "The Human Comedy."* Translated by Richard Monges. New York: New York University Press, 1963. A general survey of Balzac's novels, offering little critical analysis of individual works but usefully locating them in relation to Balzac's major themes and interests. Includes a brief biographical sketch.

Bloom, Harold, ed. *Honoré de Balzac.* Philadelphia: Chelsea House, 2003. Collection of essays on some of Balzac's individual novels, including "Eugénie Grandet's Career as Heavenly Exile" by Alexander Fischler. Other essays discuss the creation of a fictional universe, use of narrative doubling, and allegories of energy in *The Human Comedy.*

Garval, Michael D. "Honoré de Balzac: Writing the Monument." In *"A Dream of Stone": Fame, Vision, and Monumentality in Nineteenth-Century French Literary Culture.* Newark: University of Delaware Press, 2004. Garval describes how France in the nineteenth century developed an ideal image of "great" writers, viewing these authors' work as immortal and portraying their literary successes in monumental terms. He traces the rise and fall of this literary development by focusing on Balzac, George Sand, and Victor Hugo.

Hemmings, F. W. J. *Balzac: An Interpretation of "La Comédie Humaine."* New York: Random House, 1967. Chapter 4, "The Cancer," presents a comparative analysis of *Eugénie Grandet, Cousin Bette,* and *Père Goriot* as a trilogy of works centering on a father whose private obsession jeopardizes his family.

Levin, Harry. *The Gates of Horn: A Study of Five French Realists.* New York: Oxford University Press, 1963. A study of literary realism in France. In chapter 4, Levin includes several specific references to *Eugénie Grandet.*

Madden, James. *Weaving Balzac's Web: Spinning Tales and Creating the Whole of "La Comédie humaine."* Birmingham, Ala.: Summa, 2003. Explores how Balzac structured his vast series of novels to create continuity both within and between the individual books. Madden describes how internal narration, in which characters tell each other stories about other characters, enables the recurring characters to provide layers of meaning that are evident throughout the series.

Maurois, André. *Prometheus: The Life of Balzac.* Translated by Norman Denny. Harmondsworth, England: Penguin Books, 1971. A thorough biography of Balzac, which provides detailed context for and some commentary on all of the major works, including *Eugénie Grandet.*

Robb, Graham. *Balzac: A Life.* New York: W. W. Norton, 1994. A detailed biographical account of Balzac's life and work. Robb describes Balzac's philosophical perspectives and speculates on the psychological motivations underlying his writing.

Schor, Naomi. *Breaking the Chain: Women, Theory, and French Realist Fiction.* New York: Columbia University Press, 1985. In chapter 5, *"Eugénie Grandet:* Mirrors and Melancholia," Schor presents a closely detailed feminist reading of the novel, relying on the insights provided by psychoanalytic theory.

The Eunuch

Author: Terence (c. 190-159 B.C.E.)
First produced: Eunuchus, 161 B.C.E. (English translation, 1598)
Type of work: Drama
Type of plot: Comedy
Time of plot: Fourth century B.C.E.
Locale: Athens

Principal characters:
PHAEDRIA, a young Athenian in love with Thais
THAIS, a courtesan
THRASO, a soldier and a rival of Phaedria
PARMENO, Phaedria's slave
CHAEREA, Phaedria's younger brother, in love with Pamphila
PAMPHILA, a slave
CHREMES, Pamphila's brother

The Story:

Phaedria, a young Athenian of good family, is disturbed because he was excluded from the house of Thais, a courtesan. He is also perturbed because of the love he feels for the woman. Phaedria's slave, anxious to help his master, advises that Phaedria retire to the country for a time and try to forget her. Parmeno, the slave, really believes the woman is wicked and that his master will be better off without her. As master and slave stand before Thais's house, which is next to Phaedria's father's residence, the courtesan herself comes out to explain why she refuses to admit the young man. She explains that Thraso, a warrior, purchased a slave who formerly belonged to her mother. Thais believes that the slave, a young woman, is actually a free citizen of Athens. In order to get a good name in Athens, to which city she recently came, Thais hopes to learn the woman's identity and restore her to her family. Thais has to humor the captain in order to get possession of the slave.

Phaedria believes Thais and promises to go away into the country for two days, so that she can work on the captain with her charms and get possession of the young slave woman. Before he leaves, Phaedria gives Parmeno orders to go into his father's house and get the two slaves whom he purchased for Thais. One of the slaves is an Ethiopian woman, the other is a eunuch. Thais wants a eunuch because royalty prefers them.

On his way to get the slaves for Thais, Parmeno meets Phaedria's younger brother, Chaerea, who saw the slave woman Thais wants and falls in love with her. Chaerea persuades Parmeno to introduce him into Thais's household in place of the eunuch, and the exchange is made. In the meantime Thraso's parasite brings the slave woman to Thais's house as a present to the courtesan from the warrior. He also bids Thais meet his master for dinner.

Thais and some of her maids go to Thraso's house as he

requests. While they are gone, Chaerea, in the person of the eunuch, is entrusted with the care of Pamphila, the slave woman. He sends her to be bathed by other slaves. When she returns, he is so overcome by her charms that he rapes her. Ashamed at what he has done, he flees.

While Thais is gone, Pamphila's brother, Chremes, comes to the house at the request of Thais. Told that she is not at home, he goes in search of her at Thraso's residence. Thraso, thinking Chremes a rival for Thais's affections, behaves boorishly. Disgusted, Thais takes her leave, after telling Chremes to meet her shortly thereafter at her own house.

Phaedria, in the meantime, leaves for the country, but, overcome by his affection for Thais, he turns back. Arriving at his father's house, he is met by one of Thais's maids, who tells him that the eunuch raped Pamphila. Phaedria, swearing that such things cannot happen, finds the eunuch, who is dressed in Phaedria's brother's clothing. The maid, upon seeing the eunuch, realizes that the guilty man is not the eunuch but Phaedria's brother. The brother, meanwhile, goes off to a dinner with some friends. He is both sorry and glad for his deed; most of all, he wants to marry the slave.

Thais returns, distressed and angry when she hears what has happened. Her anger is cut short by the arrival of Chremes, who thinks that Pamphila is his sister, stolen in infancy. To make sure, he goes off to get the nurse who was in charge of his sister. Before he leaves, however, he chases off Thraso, who arrives with a band of servants to reclaim the slave he gave to Thais.

Chaerea returns and confesses his actions to Thais. When she accuses him of doing the deed to spite her, a courtesan, he demurs, swearing that he raped the slave because he loved her overmuch. He still claims that he wants to marry her. Chremes returns with the nurse, who quickly identifies Pamphila as Chremes's long-lost sister, a free citizen of the city, a member of a good family, and a fine wife for Chaerea, if the lad can get his father's consent.

While they are conferring, Thais's maid resolves to have her own revenge on Parmeno, Phaedria's slave. She tells Parmeno that Chaerea was seized and that he is about to be mutilated, as is the customary treatment of rapists in ancient Athens. Parmeno runs to Laches, the father of Phaedria and Chaerea, to get the older man's help.

When Laches learns the true facts, he is quite willing to permit a marriage between his younger son and the woman he dishonored. More than that, the father becomes reconciled to his older son's love for the courtesan, since she proved herself in her efforts to restore the slave to freedom and her proper position in life. He agrees to look after the courtesan's welfare and to permit his older son to live with her. This plan makes Phaedria and Thais very happy, for they truly love each other.

When Thraso returns for one last attempt to regain the favor of the courtesan, Phaedria threatens to kill him if he appears in that street again. Thraso's parasite suggests to Phaedria and Thais that they keep the braggart for entertainment. The parasite points out that Thraso is very foolish, has a lot of money, and can be kept dangling a long time by the courtesan without ever receiving any of her favors. Phaedria, seeing the humor of the situation, agrees to the terms. The warrior, not realizing he is to be made a fool, is so happy with the arrangement that he promises to behave himself and to be more generous than ever with the parasite who got him into the silly situation.

Critical Evaluation:

Of the two major Roman comic playwrights (the other was Plautus), Terence has always been considered the more thoughtful. Like Menander, the Greek writer whose works he imitated, Terence used the genre not simply to amuse his audience but also to explore human psychology and moral issues. Because some characters and scenes seem to have been introduced into *The Eunuch* merely for their farcical value, however, it has been suggested that Terence may have written this play primarily to please his audience. *The Eunuch* is often called Terence's most Plautine work; certainly it is his most lighthearted. Nevertheless, there is evidence that even in *The Eunuch*, Terence meant to touch on a serious theme.

As is typical of a play by Terence, *The Eunuch* has a double plot. The first story involves the love of Phaedria for Thais, and the second story involves Chaerea's desire for Pamphila. In *The Eunuch*, however, Terence also adds an underplot to his play. His source for the characters of Thraso and Gnatho has not been determined, but they could have

been drawn from an ample supply of stereotypes available to Roman dramatists. The boastful soldier appears often in Roman comedy, as does the parasite, who makes his living by flattering wealthy dupes. The important question is why Terence introduced these characters into the play; some critics argue that their presence is gratuitous. Gnatho's description of his activities is, in itself, uproarious. Thraso is a variation of the stereotype he represents. As a soldier who, though stupid, is not brave, and, though boastful, is proud not of his military exploits but of his wit, Thraso adds color and humor to the play. His siege of Thais's house is one of the most humorous scenes in *The Eunuch*. Nevertheless, neither that scene nor the characters of Thraso and Gnatho can be considered essential to the two primary plotlines. Thraso does not need to be as fully developed a character as he is, nor does he need to be as involved in the action as he is.

It may be that even in this atypical play, Terence wished to challenge the comfortable assumptions of his audience. This argument is supported by the fact that the frequent derogatory comments about courtesans are contradicted by the actions of the courtesan-protagonist. Thais wishes to return Pamphila to her family because she wants to win the respect of the Roman nobility; however, she is also motivated by unselfish love. In fact, except for Thais's conscientious maid, Pythias, Thais is the least motivated by self-interest. At the end of the play, when Laches takes Thais under his protection and permits Phaedria to retain her as his mistress, Laches is more than just a perceptive father or even a wise elder citizen; he is also acting as an agent of poetic justice and as a spokesperson for the playwright.

None of the male characters in *The Eunuch* can be compared to its courtesan protagonist in terms of generosity, integrity, and courage. Like Thais, Gnatho must be self-sufficient. Unlike her, however, he is willing to be dishonest and self-centered in order to survive. The slave Parmeno is drawn more sympathetically, since, unlike the scheming slave in most Roman comedies, Parmeno does try to draw a moral line. He is shocked when Chaerea acts upon his idle comment about masquerading as a eunuch. More important, however, he fears that he will be blamed for Chaerea's misconduct. Terence holds Parmeno responsible, at least to some degree, for Chaerea's misconduct; Terence's feelings are evident in the punishment that he allows Pythias to mete out to Parmeno. It can also be argued that the fictional castration is meant to symbolize the punishment that Chaerea deserves.

In the first scene of *The Eunuch*, Parmeno defines love, which constitutes the subject of the play; its theme is self-interest. Love, Parmeno says, is a madness, subject to no rules, and once people are overtaken by love, their best hope is to pay as small a price as possible. Phaedria is willing to stay away from Thais for two days, not because he cares about her feelings, but because he hopes that, by obeying her now, he will have her favors in the future.

The love Chaerea professes for Pamphila is another example of self-interest. Not only does he deceive an innocent, but he also rapes her. The reason that Terence never brings Pamphila onstage, even to show her reinstated with her family and betrothed to Chaerea, may be that he thinks it best not to dispel the comic mood.

Another example of self-interest is represented by Thraso and Chremes. During the siege, both are concerned about themselves. While Thais courageously defends her home, Chremes cowers beside her, and Thraso hides behind his small army of servants. The siege scene may have been added in order to expose two more male characters.

If Terence means *The Eunuch* to be taken seriously, however, it is difficult to explain why Phaedria makes the accommodation he does at the end of the play. Though his love may be selfish, it seems to motivate everything he does. He wants to eliminate his rival and to have his mistress to himself. For financial reasons, however, he is willing to share her with Thraso. Either Terence has decided to end his play with a cynical comment on human nature, or he is primarily concerned with entertaining his audience. It is hardly surprising that critics continue to debate Terence's intentions in *The Eunuch*.

"Critical Evaluation" by Rosemary M. Canfield Reisman

Further Reading

Dutsch, Dorota M. *Feminine Discourse in Roman Comedy: On Echoes and Voices.* New York: Oxford University Press, 2008. Analyzes the dialogue of female characters in Terence's plays, noting its use of endearments, softness of speech, and emphasis on small problems. Questions if Roman women actually spoke that way.

Forehand, Walter E. *Terence.* Boston: Twayne, 1985. Exam-ines *The Eunuch* from the standpoint of plot, structure, and theme. Discusses the eight most important characters in the play. Includes extensive notes and an annotated bibliography.

Goldberg, Sander M. *Understanding Terence.* Princeton, N.J.: Princeton University Press, 1986. A study of the playwright. Includes an index to passages and an analysis of *The Eunuch* in the chapter titled "*Contaminatio.*" The bibliography contains numerous citations to foreign-language publications.

Hunter, R. L. *The New Comedy of Greece and Rome.* New York: Cambridge University Press, 1985. Sees the play as an exploration of male-female relationships; in a dramatic reversal, a woman protagonist attains power over men. The three primary male characters are also thematically important, however, since they represent various aspects of love.

Leigh, Matthew. *Comedy and the Rise of Rome.* New York: Oxford University Press, 2004. Analyzes the comedies of Plautus and Terence, placing them within the context of political and economic conditions in Rome during the third and second centuries B.C.E. Discusses how audiences of that time responded to these comedies.

Lowe, J. C. B. "The *Eunuchus*: Terence and Menander." *Classical Quarterly* 33, no. 2 (1983): 428-444. An attempt to resolve the question of Terence's intent by examining the ways in which he altered his source in Menander. Argues that an answer can be found in Terence's development of two key scenes.

Sandbach, F. H. *The Comic Theatre of Greece and Rome.* London: Chatto & Windus, 1977. Both the chapter on Menander and the chapter on Terence include observations about *The Eunuch*. Discusses Terence's alterations and additions to the works of Menander, his Greek source.

Segal, Erich, ed. *Oxford Readings in Menander, Plautus, and Terence.* New York: Oxford University Press, 2001. Includes essays on the originality of Terence and his Greek models and on the problems of adaptation in Terence's version of *The Eunuch*.

Euphues, the Anatomy of Wit

Author: John Lyly (c. 1554-1606)
First published: 1578
Type of work: Novel
Type of plot: Didactic
Time of plot: Sixteenth century
Locale: Naples and Athens

Principal characters:
EUPHUES, a young gentleman of Athens
PHILAUTUS, a nobleman of Naples and his friend
DON FERARDO, a governor of Naples
LUCILLA, his daughter and Philautus's fiancé
LIVIA, her friend
EUBULUS, an old gentleman of Naples

The Story:

Euphues, a young gentleman of Athens, is graced by nature with great personal beauty and by fortune with a large patrimony, but he uses his brilliant wit to enjoy the pleasures of wickedness rather than the honors of virtue. In his search for new experiences, the young man goes to Naples, a city famed for loose living. There he finds many people eager to encourage a waste of time and talent, but he is cautious, trusting no one and taking none for a friend. Thus, he escapes real harm from the company of idle youths with whom he associates.

One day, Eubulus, an elderly gentleman of Naples, approaches Euphues and admonishes the young man for his easy ways, warning him of the evil results that are sure to follow and urging him to be merry with modesty and reserve. In a witty reply, Euphues rebuffs the old man's counsel and tells him that his pious urgings only result from his withered old age. In spite of the sage warning, Euphues remains in Naples, and after two months there he meets a pleasing young man named Philautus, whom he determines to make his only and eternal friend. Impressed by the charm of Euphues, Philautus readily agrees to be his firm friend forever. Their friendship grows, and the two young men soon become inseparable.

Philautus long before earned the affection and trust of Don Ferardo, a prominent official of Naples, and he fell in love with his beautiful daughter Lucilla. While Don Ferardo is on a trip to Naples, Philautus takes his friend with him to visit Lucilla and a group of her friends. After dinner, Euphues is given the task of entertaining the company with an extemporaneous discourse on love. He declares that one should love another for his mind, not for his appearance. When the conversation turns to a discussion of constancy, Lucilla asserts that her sex is wholly fickle. Euphues begins to dispute her, but, suddenly struck by Lucilla's beauty and confused by his feelings, he breaks off his speech and quickly leaves.

Lucilla discovers that she is attracted to the young Athenian. After weighing the respective claims of Euphues and

Philautus on her affections, she convinces herself that it will not be wrong to abandon Philautus for Euphues; however, she decides to pretend to each that he is her only love. Euphues, meanwhile, persuades himself that Lucilla must be his in spite of Philautus: Friendship must give way before love. In order to deceive his friend, Euphues pretends to be in love with Livia, Lucilla's friend. Philautus is overjoyed and promises to help him win Livia.

The two young men go immediately to the house of Don Ferardo. While Philautus is attending the governor, who finally completes arrangements for his daughter's marriage to the young man, Euphues and Lucilla engage in a subtle debate about love and finally declare their passion for each other. When Don Ferardo tells his daughter of his plans for her marriage to Philautus, she tells him of her love for Euphues.

Philautus, betrayed at once by his friend and by his beloved, blames first one and then the other. He writes a scathing letter to Euphues, saying that they are friends no longer and that he hopes Euphues will soon be in his own unhappy situation; he warns that Lucilla, proving untrue, might be faithless again. Euphues replies in a taunting letter that deception in love is natural. He expresses confidence that Lucilla will be faithful to him forever.

After what happened, however, it is impossible for Euphues to visit Lucilla while her father is at home. During her lover's absence, she falls in love again, this time with Curio, a gentleman who possesses neither wealth nor wit. When Euphues at last goes to apologize for being away so long, Lucilla replies curtly that she hoped his absence would have been longer. Admitting that her new lover is inferior to both Philautus and Euphues, she supposes God is punishing her for her fickleness. Although she realizes that her life is likely to be unhappy, a fate she earned, she does not hesitate to scorn Euphues. Don Ferardo argues that it is her filial duty to give up the worthless Curio. When she refuses, her father dies of grief shortly thereafter.

Having renewed his friendship with Philautus before departing from Naples, Euphues leaves with his friend a written discourse against the folly of love. It states that love, although it starts with pleasure, ends in destruction and grief, and he urges his friend to forget passion and to turn his attention toward more serious pursuits.

After returning to Athens where he engages in long hours of study, Euphues writes a treatise on the proper way to rear a child. His own upbringing did not steer him away from the shoals of sloth and wickedness. With this weakness of upbringing in mind, he urges that a young man should be legitimately born and reared under the influence of three major forces: nature, reason, and use. In this manner, the young man will be educated in the ways of virtue as well as in the customs of use. Euphues writes many other letters and treatises: In one, he urges the gentlemen scholars of Athens to study with the laws of God in mind; in another, he debates with an atheist and converts him to godliness; a letter to Philautus encourages him to abandon his dissolute life in Naples; in a letter to Eubulus, Euphues thanks the old man for his good advice and tells him of his return to righteousness; another letter to Philautus expresses regret at the death of Lucilla and at the irreligious character of her life; two letters to a pair of young men tell them to accept their destiny and to live virtuously; in response to a letter in which Livia tells of her intention to be virtuous, Euphues praises her and tells her of Philautus's possible visit to Athens.

Critical Evaluation:

John Lyly's *Euphues, the Anatomy of Wit* is one of the most significant works in the development of English prose style. First published in 1578, the novel was one of the most popular fictions of the period, going through thirteen editions by 1613 and inspiring imitation among a number of contemporary writers, including Robert Greene, Thomas Lodge, and even, in a parodic tone, William Shakespeare. While the ornate, balanced, and highly artificial style that came to be known as euphuism did not originate with the novel, *Euphues* did make the style immensely popular and transformed the way in which English prose was written.

The essential hallmarks of euphuism are rhetorical; they undeniably emphasize sound over sense. Chief among these devices is balance, in the form of antithesis and in the form of parallelism, in which grammatical forms are kept carefully even. Alliteration and assonance, in which similarities in sound help tie phrases and sentences together, are also important to the style.

Antithesis, which comes form a Greek word meaning "opposition," combines and contrasts ideas in a balanced

rhetorical form that gives equal weight to both. Euphues's advice to Lucilla—"If you will be cherished when you be old, be courteous when you be young"—is an example of a balanced, antithetical statement. The second half of the sentence duplicates the grammatical structure of the first half, while the two parts of the sentence complement each other in form and meaning. "Cherished" is balanced against "courteous" and "old" against "young."

This balanced, antithetical pattern is the most characteristic feature of *Euphues*, and Lyly's obsessively regular use of it has caused some critics and scholars of the novel to remark on its metronomic rhythm and to complain that the work is all sound and no sense. The perception that Lyly is obsessed with sound at the total expense of sense is mistaken; in *Euphues*, antithesis is used to express Lyly's view of human life as a conflict between appearance and reality. Lyly uses his specific rhetorical devices to examine the paradox of human perceptions and feelings.

"Do we not commonly see that in painted pots is hidden the deadliest poison, that in the greenest grass is the greatest serpent, in the clearest water the ugliest toad?" Under the moralizing tone of this question from Euphues, and implicitly expressed in its rhetorical form, is the recognition that human life consists of a series of contradictions, all equally valid at their particular moment. Lyly's euphuistic prose is not merely a rhetorical performance; it is an analytic instrument for examining human feelings and emotions.

Parallelism, in which grammatical forms are kept carefully even, is another important part of Lyly's style. Carried to the extreme that Lyly achieves in *Euphues*, it attains a highly artificial level, but, as with balance and antithesis, with which parallelism is often associated in the novel, parallelism serves to reinforce the paradoxical nature of human existence.

A notable example, cited by Joseph Houppert in his study of Lyly, is the rebuke of the nominally good man Eubulus for his normal human distress over the loss of a loved one: "Thou weepest for the death of thy daughter, and I laugh at the folly of the father; greater vanity is there in the mind of the mourner, than bitterness in the death of the deceased." Here, the parallelism is obsessively exact, since "tears" and "laughter" contrast, while "death" and "daughter" alliteratively balance "folly" and "father," at the same time that the verb pattern is strictly maintained. However, as Houppert notes, the seeming paradox between death and life, and grief and joy, is resolved if one places this quotation in the context of the religious sentiment of Elizabethan England.

This quotation also illustrates a third major facet of Lyly's prose style, alliteration and assonance. Alliteration, the recurrence of initial consonant or vowel sounds, is clearly present in the passage: "Death" and "daughter," and "folly" and "father" are examples. Assonance, a similarity in sounds, is also present in this passage, as the sequence of vowels in "laugh," "folly" and "father" indicate. Lyly uses a sophisticated, even artificial rhetorical device to knit his narrative more closely together in terms of sense and content.

Euphues, the Anatomy of Wit is not an important landmark in English literature simply because of its style. The basic movement of the plot—Euphues's journey to ultimate wisdom after passing through the temptations and dangers of courtly society—is based to a large degree on the story of the prodigal son, as found in the New Testament. The novel's central theme, that life is a pilgrimage during which the truly wise person learns to disregard the appearance of the world, is a highly moral one. Lyly expresses this theme in a highly moralistic fashion. Quite consciously and deliberately, *Euphues* intends to teach its readers some important lessons.

Euphues contains a large number of dialogues, discourses, and letters in which the characters advise, admonish, and encourage one another in the pursuit of virtue and the avoidance of sin. Repeatedly, Lyly's highly structured prose style emphasizes the distance between what seems and what is. The Elizabethan Age was profoundly concerned with this topic and obsessively fearful of hypocrisy and dissimulation. Lyly's elaborate and ornate handling of it helps explain the considerable enthusiasm for the book.

In the end, however, it is the combination of theme, content, characters, and especially style that makes *Euphues* a singular element of English writing. The novel opened new and largely unparalleled avenues for English literature.

"Critical Evaluation" by Michael Witkoski

Further Reading

Croll, Morris. Introduction to *Euphues, the Anatomy of Wit*, by John Lyly. New York: Russell & Russell, 1964. Discusses the novel's themes and style. Perceptive and instructive.

Dolven, Jeffrey Andrew. *Scenes of Instruction in Renaissance Romance.* Chicago: University of Chicago Press, 2007. Examines *Euphues, the Anatomy of Wit* and *Euphues and His England* to describe how Lyly in these works combined the narrative romance with sixteenth century humanist pedagogy.

Houppert, Joseph W. *John Lyly.* Boston: Twayne, 1975. An excellent starting place for the student of Lyly who wishes to achieve a well-rounded sense of the political, cultural, and artistic setting in which he lived and wrote.

Hunter, G. K. *John Lyly: The Humanist as Courtier.* Cambridge, Mass.: Harvard University Press, 1962. Places Lyly within the context of his times and the social status to which he aspired. Interesting in its study of how Elizabeth I's court viewed—and used—language.

Maslen, R. W. "The Dissolution of Euphues." In *Elizabethan Fictions: Espionage, Counter-Espionage, and the Duplicity of Fiction in Early Elizabethan Prose Narratives.* New York: Oxford University Press, 1997. Study of works by Lyly and three other writers within the context of changing attitudes to fiction in Elizabethan England. These writers—and the censors—were aware that the new prose narratives could transform the nature of fiction and might threaten the security of the Elizabethan state. Maslen examines how these works mocked contemporary platitudes and conventions with a self-conscious style and subtlety and argues that they are precursors of Shakespearean comedies and works by Christopher Marlowe and Sir Philip Sidney.

Wilson, John Dover. *John Lyly.* New York: Haskell House, 1970. A reprint of the 1905 edition, this volume remains one of the best studies of Lyly's life and works, and is especially sensitive to the use of language in *Euphues, the Anatomy of Wit*.

Wilson, Katharine. *Fictions of Authorship in Late Elizabethan Narratives: Euphues in Arcadia.* New York: Oxford University Press, 2006. Examines Lyly's two Euphues books and other "sensational" narratives that established prose fiction as an independent genre in late sixteenth century England. Describes how these works created an alternative vernacular writing that combined elements of both high and low culture.

The Eustace Diamonds

Author: Anthony Trollope (1815-1882)
First published: 1871-1873, serial; 1873, book
Type of work: Novel
Type of plot: Social realism
Time of plot: Late nineteenth century
Locale: London and Scotland

Principal characters:
LIZZIE GREYSTOCK EUSTACE, a young, wealthy widow
FRANK GREYSTOCK, Lizzie's cousin, a lawyer and politician
LUCY MORRIS, a governess engaged to marry Frank

The Story:

Lizzie Greystock is the only child of old Admiral Greystock, a retired naval officer and widower who devotes his declining years to wine, whist, and wickedness. Raised without the usual parental guidance, Lizzie enters womanhood headstrong, independent, strikingly beautiful, and, within the constraints of Victorian society, a little immoral. Her father dies when she is nineteen; he leaves her penniless. She is taken in by her aunt, Lady Linlithgow, a truculent old dowager who is as rigid in her principles as she is poor. She and her niece, for the brief period they live together in genteel poverty, despise each other.

Lizzie manages to attract the attention of a wealthy young nobleman, Sir Florian Eustace. After a brief courtship, they are married. The marriage is also brief, but it is long enough to produce a male heir and for Sir Florian to become disillusioned with his bride, who is a liar and a spendthrift. Sir Florian, not a well man, dies within a year of his marriage. He leaves Lizzie a wealthy young widow, with four thousand pounds a year, a castle in Scotland, and a diamond necklace worth ten thousand pounds.

In the settling of the estate, Mr. Camperdown, the Eustace family lawyer, pressures Lizzie to place the necklace, which he declares a family heirloom, in a bank or some other place of security, but Lizzie claims the necklace as personal property, given to her expressly as a gift from Sir Florian. She refuses to comply with the lawyer's request. Determined to protect the family's interests, Mr. Camperdown begins a prolonged legal campaign to have the diamonds returned. As the lawyer begins his efforts, Lizzie is working her charms on Lord Fawn, a noble but impoverished member of Parliament for the Liberal Party. For the aspiring politician, marriage to the lovely and wealthy Lady Eustace seems, at first, a definite asset, but as the diamond necklace controversy becomes increasingly public, Fawn, a timid and self-centered man, begins to question the wisdom of his marriage proposal. Rather than face the formidable Lizzie, he simply neglects her. Lizzie turns for assistance to her cousin, Frank Greystock.

Frank is a Conservative member of Parliament and a political opponent of Fawn. As a matter of honor, Frank takes up the cause of his widowed cousin, accepting her story that Sir Florian gave her the diamonds as an outright gift, to do with as she pleased. The story, however, is another of Lizzie's many fabrications.

Fawn and Frank become personal, as well as political, enemies, and the issue is further complicated by the fact that Frank falls in love with Lucy Morris, a young woman with no fortune. She is the highly regarded governess for the Fawn family. Lucy is a great favorite of Fawn's unmarried sisters, and a particular favorite of Lady Fawn, their mother. Lucy enthusiastically returns Frank's affections, and she agrees to marry him at a time in the near future, when he will be able to provide for her. The match is opposed by everyone close to either of them. When Fawn, on a visit to his mother and sisters, speaks disparagingly of Frank, Lucy vigorously defends him. To the profound regret of Lady Fawn and her daughters, Lucy then feels that she must leave the Fawn family home, in order not to divide a family she loves. She finds a position as companion to Lady Linlithgow.

Lizzie then takes a particular interest in her handsome cousin, and she considers the possibility of marrying him instead of Fawn. To lure Frank away from Lucy, she begins a course of seduction, initiating it by repeatedly stressing to Frank that she is alone and friendless, besieged by Mr. Camperdown, who is determined to make her relinquish what she continues to assert is her personal property. To escape the pressure, she leaves London for a prolonged visit to Portray, her castle in Scotland. She invites Frank for a visit. At the castle, Frank is introduced to some of Lizzie's new and rather peculiar friends. There are Mrs. Carbuncle and her niece, Lucinda Roanoke; Lord George de Bruce Carruthers, an adventurer and soldier of fortune whom Lizzie considers another candidate for a second husband; Sir Griffin Tewett, an unpleasant, ill-tempered young nobleman intermittently in pursuit of Lucinda Roanoke; and Mr. Emilius, a preacher with a popular following and a suspicious character. Frank finds them all rather unsavory; he leaves at the earliest opportunity.

Fearful that Mr. Camperdown will use some legal means to seize the diamonds, Lizzie keeps them in an iron box, and she takes them with her on her travels. On the return trip to London, the entourage spends the night at a hotel in Carlisle. Lizzie's room is burglarized during the night, and the box is taken. During the investigation, she does not inform the police that the diamonds were not in the box at the time; instead, they are under her pillow. She is then, technically, guilty of perjury. In London, she becomes the guest of Mrs. Carbuncle, who tries to manipulate her titled guest to her best advantage. Mrs. Carbuncle's primary objective is to arrange a marriage between her niece, Lucinda Roanoke, and Sir Griffin. Sir Griffin has no real interest in Lucinda, but he is perversely determined to marry her because she so openly loathes him. In the meantime, there is a second burglary, and this time the diamond necklace is stolen. It is discovered that the burglary is a conspiracy between Lizzie's maid, Patience Crabstick, and Mr. Benjamin, a jeweler and money lender to whom Lizzie is in debt; she consulted him about the possibility of disposing of the necklace. The police soon apprehend the culprits, and Lizzie is advised, under threat of severe penalty, to tell the truth, which she does. The diamonds, however, were sold through foreign criminal channels; they are never recovered.

Pressured toward marriage with a man she despises, Lucinda has a nervous breakdown. Sir Griffin leaves the country; Lucinda and Mrs. Carbuncle also leave the country, the latter without paying Lizzie the money she had borrowed from her. Lord George is not interested in marriage, and Frank, thoroughly disillusioned with Lizzie's lying and duplicity, follows his heart and marries Lucy. Lizzie returns to Portray Castle, where she charms a Scottish doctor into giving her a medical certificate in order to prevent her from having to return to London for further legal proceedings. At that point, the fortune-hunting Mr. Emilius returns, and, seeing his main chance, he proposes marriage, and Lizzie accepts.

Critical Evaluation:

Anthony Trollope is noted for his penetrating analysis of Victorian society; he is particularly noted for the manner in which he treats the understated interaction between virtue and hypocrisy. The values that motivate this interaction are the primary themes of the novel: marriage and money. In *The Eustace Diamonds*, marriage, the sanctioned union between man and woman in love, is an ill-considered venture for the bachelor without a personal fortune. Love, although ostensibly revered and idealized, is a secondary concern. Lizzie Eustace, the protagonist of the novel, is very beautiful and engagingly clever, but it is quite clearly the income inherited from her deceased husband that attracts her suitors. Her counterpart and diametric opposite, in both values and outward appearance, is Lucy Morris, plain, virtuous, highly principled, and penniless. Characteristic of Victorian novels, both women are orphans who enter adulthood without money; however, Lizzie, motivated by material ambition, seduces and charms a wealthy young nobleman in order to alter this condition. Lucy, however, is fundamentally incapable of seduction and duplicity. Once Frank Greystock has proposed marriage (to take place at some future undetermined time) her fidelity is constant and unwavering. Even when she is close to believing the popular view that Frank's proposal has been hasty and impractical, and that the pressures of his fledgling political career may make it necessary for him to rescind his offer, she is quite willing to release him if that is his choice. She remains resolute and unvindictive in her belief in his goodness and integrity. Conversely, Lord Fawn's second thoughts regarding his proposal to Lizzie inspire Lizzie to thoughts of vengeance and humiliation. The reader is fully aware of the fact that Lizzie will feel no ethical impediment in exacting her revenge. Lucy is incapable of telling a lie; Lizzie is almost incapable of telling the truth.

In *The Eustace Diamonds*, Trollope creates the same literary paradox that makes John Milton's Satan a more compelling character than Christ in *Paradise Lost* (1667, 1674). Although Lucy is a paragon of Victorian womanhood, in her constancy she is relatively static. She lacks complexity, and she is eminently predictable. By contrast, Lizzie is by far the more interesting character, perhaps the most engaging bad woman in English literature since William Makepeace Thackeray created Becky Sharpe in *Vanity Fair* (1847-1848, serial; 1848, book). For readers removed by time from the social environment of Victorian England, Lizzie, compared to Lucy, is considered by some critics the more admirable of the two. Her pragmatism and ingenuity in a society dominated by men and masculine values reveal a commendable fortitude and, in an oblique way, a personal integrity. Pressured by the formidable legal establishment of conventional London to relinquish the diamond necklace to the Eustace estate as a protected heirloom, she has the temerity to resist. When Mr. Camperdown redoubles his efforts to intimidate her into compliance, she cleverly circumvents both coercion and persuasion, becoming in the process a *cause célèbre*, London's notorious woman.

The diamonds, however, and the burden of the money they represent remain a symbol of discord. Throughout the novel, money brings disruption rather than stability, discontent instead of tranquillity. The diamond necklace, which Lizzie seeks to appropriate from the holdings of the Eustace family, affords her no personal pleasure. She has the constant anxiety that it will be seized by Mr. Camperdown, whom she stubbornly, and often inexplicably, resists. Paradoxically, even as she wishes to be free of the necklace, she guards it constantly, trusting no one.

Unlike Lucy, Lizzie is a solitary figure. Other than her credulous and naïve cousin, Frank Greystock, Lizzie has no friends; she has only parasitic adherents such as Mrs. Carbuncle and Lucinda Roanoke. Money remains central to Lizzie's eligible suitors, and it is continually conflicting in its roles of lure and impediment. Frank and Lord Fawn recognize that their careers require a marriage that brings with it a significant financial advantage. Marriage to Lizzie is for both men a very genuine and promising option. Frank's marriage to Lucy, however, is Trollope's sentimental concession to his readers, in direct contradiction to the reality of the society in which Frank has made his way. As Lizzie's notoriety in the matter of the necklace threatens to be a full-blown scandal, Fawn realizes that his marriage for money may, conversely, prove to be prohibitively expensive to his career in other ways. Lord George de Bruce Carruthers, whom Lizzie realizes is a cynical fortune hunter—and, perversely, finds him more appealing because of it—concludes that the dangers outweigh the financial incentive. Mr. Emilius, the preacher (confidence) man who is far more cunning and deceptive than the roguish but straightforward Lord George, waits in the figurative shadows, making his advances to Lizzie only after the scandal of the diamonds is resolved, and there is no danger that those close to her will be drawn into it.

Although Trollope concludes the Lucy/Frank relationship with a conventional happy ending, *The Eustace Diamonds* reveals the degree to which Trollope sees nineteenth century British society as governed by what Thomas Carlyle termed the "cash nexus." It is a world in which the honored values of civilized society are inevitably subsumed by wealth and the social position that such wealth creates and sustains.

Richard Keenan

Further Reading

Bury, Laurent. *Seductive Strategies in the Novels of Anthony Trollope, 1815-1882.* Lewiston, N.Y.: Edwin Mellen Press, 2004. A study of seduction in all of Trollope's novels. Argues that seduction was a survival skill for both men and women in the Victorian era and demonstrates how Trollope depicted the era's sexual politics.

Cecil, David. *Victorian Novelists: Essays in Revaluation.* Chicago: University of Chicago Press, 1961. A classic work in Victorian studies. Still one of the best basic introductions to Trollope, it establishes the quality of his work in comparison to his literary contemporaries.

Felber, Lynette. *Gender and Genre in Novels Without End: The British Roman-Fleuve.* Gainesville: University Press of Florida, 1995. A study of multivolume novels written during three periods of history, including *The Eustace Diamonds* and the other novels in Trollope's Palliser series. Argues that the narratives of these novels inherently have "narrative features designated feminine."

Glendinning, Victoria. *Anthony Trollope.* New York: Alfred A. Knopf, 1993. A thorough biography particularly helpful in its treatment of the relationship between Trollope's attitude toward women in his personal life and the genesis of heroines, such as Lizzie Eustace.

Harvey, Geoffrey. *The Art of Anthony Trollope.* New York: St. Martin's Press, 1980. Excellent analysis of character and psychological motivation, particularly in the commentary on the fox hunting chapters as a metaphor for social forms of maneuvering and entrapment.

McMaster, Juliet. *Trollope's Palliser Novels: Theme and Pattern.* New York: Oxford University Press, 1978. A thorough analysis of Lizzie Eustace's penchant for lying and of her preoccupation with pseudoromanticism. Discusses the influence of other contemporary literary heroines, particularly William Makepeace Thackeray's Becky Sharp and Blanche Amory, in the development of Lizzie's amoral character.

Markwick, Margaret. *New Men in Trollope's Novels: Rewriting the Victorian Male.* Burlington, Vt.: Ashgate, 2007. Examines Trollope's novels, tracing the development of his ideas about masculinity. Argues that Trollope's male characters are not the conventional Victorian patriarchs and demonstrates how his works promoted a "startlingly modern model of manhood."

_____. *Trollope and Women.* London: Hambledon Press, 1997. Examines how Trollope could simultaneously accept the conventional Victorian ideas about women while also sympathizing with women's difficult situations. Demonstrates the individuality of his female characters. Discusses his depiction of both happy and unhappy marriages, male-female relationships, bigamy, and scandal.

Mullen, Richard, and James Munson. *The Penguin Companion to Trollope.* New York: Penguin, 1996. A comprehensive guide, describing all of Trollope's novels, short stories, travel books, and other works; discusses plot, characters, background, tone, allusions, and contemporary references and places the works in their historical context.

Tracy, Robert. *Trollope's Later Novels*. Berkeley: University of California Press, 1978. Examines the role of the recurring character in the later Palliser novels, particularly Lizzie Eustace's reappearance in *The Prime Minister*. Tracy draws an effective and helpful character analogy between Lizzie and Lady Glencora Palliser, whom Lizzie both admires and, to some degree, imitates.

Evangeline

Author: Henry Wadsworth Longfellow (1807-1882)
First published: 1847
Type of work: Poetry
Type of plot: Pastoral
Time of plot: Mid-eighteenth century
Locale: French Canada and the United States

Principal characters:
EVANGELINE BELLEFONTAINE, an exile
GABRIEL LAJEUNESSE, her betrothed
BASIL LAJEUNESSE, Gabriel's father
BENEDICT BELLEFONTAINE, Evangeline's father

The Poem:

In the Acadian province, in the village of Grand-Pré, live a peaceful farming people who are undisturbed by the wars between the French and British. In a land where there is enough for all, there is no covetousness and no envy, and all live at peace with their neighbors. Benedict Bellefontaine's farm is somewhat apart from the village. His daughter, Evangeline, directs her father's household. Although she has many suitors, she favors only one, Gabriel Lajeunesse, the son of Basil, the village blacksmith. Gabriel and Evangeline grew up together, and their fathers are friends.

One fall day, while Benedict rests by the fire and Evangeline sits at her spinning wheel, Basil brings word that the men of the village are to meet at the church the next day. They are to be told the plans of the English, whose ships are riding at anchor in the harbor. That night, Benedict and Basil sign the wedding contract that will unite their children. Then, while their fathers play checkers, Evangeline and Gabriel whisper in the darkening room until it is time to say good-night.

The next morning everyone, including the folk from the outlying districts, comes to the village to hear the announcement the English commander is to make. They wear holiday dress, as if the occasion is one for celebration. At the Bellefontaine farm there is special joy, for with a feast and dancing the family and their guests are celebrating the betrothal of Gabriel and Evangeline. In the afternoon the church bell rings, summoning the men to the church. When they file in, they are followed by the guard from the ship. Outside, the women stand, waiting.

The news the English commander has for the little community renders a crushing blow. By order of the king, their lands, houses, and cattle are forfeited to the British crown, and the entire population of Grand-Pré is to be transported. The men are to consider themselves the king's prisoners.

The tragic news spreads quickly through the village and to the farm where Evangeline is awaiting Benedict's return. At sunset she starts toward the church, on her way comforting the downcast women she meets. Outside the church where the men are imprisoned, she calls Gabriel's name, but there is no answer.

The men are held prisoner for five days. On the fifth day, the women bring their household goods to the shore to be loaded onto boats, and late that afternoon the men are led out of the church by their guards. Evangeline, standing at the side of the road, watches them coming toward her. She is able to comfort Gabriel with the assurance that their love will keep them from harm, but for her father she can do nothing. In five days he has aged greatly.

Basil and his son are put on separate ships, and Evangeline remains on the beach with Benedict. That night, the villagers of Grand-Pré watch their homes go up in flames and listen to their animals bellowing as the barns burn. Turning from the sight, Evangeline sees that her father has fallen dead. She drops in a swoon upon his chest and lies there until morning; then, with the aid of Father Felician, the village priest, the Acadians bury Benedict Bellefontaine by the shore. That day, Evangeline sails with the other exiles.

The scattered exiles from Grand-Pré wander far over the

face of North America in search of their friends and family members. Sometimes Evangeline lingers for a while in a town, but always she is driven on by her longing for Gabriel. Looking at unmarked graves, she imagines that one of them might contain her lover. Sometimes she hears rumors of Gabriel's whereabouts; sometimes she speaks with people who have actually seen and known him, but always long ago. The notary's son, Baptiste Leblanc, follows Evangeline faithfully and loyally through her years of searching, but she will have no one but Gabriel for a husband.

Finally, a band of exiles rows down the Mississippi River, bound for Louisiana, where they hope to find some of their kinsmen. Evangeline and Father Felician are among them, Evangeline heartened because she feels she is nearing Gabriel at last. Then in the heat of midday, the voyagers pull their craft to shore and lie down to sleep behind some bushes. While they slumber, Gabriel, in the company of hunters and trappers, passes the spot on his way to the West. That evening, when the exiles set out to explore the area, they are welcomed by a prosperous herdsman who turns out to be Basil. Evangeline learns that Gabriel left home that day, too troubled by thoughts of his love to endure the quiet life in his father's house.

For a time Basil helps Evangeline carry on her search. Leaving his peaceful home in the South, the herdsman and the young woman travel with some other companions to the base of the Ozark Mountains, guided by rumors of Gabriel's whereabouts. Sometimes, from a distance, they see, or think they see, his campfire, but when they reach the spot, he has already gone on ahead.

One evening a Shawnee Indian woman comes into their camp on her way back to her own people after her husband's murder by Comanches. In the night, after the others are asleep, she and Evangeline exchange stories. When Evangeline has finished hers, the woman tells the tale of Mowis, the bridegroom made of snow, and the Indian woman who married and followed him, only to see him dissolve and fade with the sunshine. She tells of Lilinau, who followed her phantom lover into the woods until she disappeared forever. Evangeline feels that she, too, is following a phantom.

The next day, Evangeline and her party travel to the Jesuit mission on the western side of the mountains, where they hope to hear some word of Gabriel. A priest tells them that Gabriel went to the north to hunt six days before. It seems certain that he will pass that way on his journey home in the fall, so Evangeline decides to wait at the mission. Basil and his companions return to their homes.

Autumn and winter pass and spring comes, with no news of Gabriel. Finally Evangeline hears that he is camping in the forests of Michigan on the Saginaw River. When she reaches his camp, however, it is deserted and in ruins.

For many years, Evangeline wanders over the country in search of her lover, but always she meets with disappointment. At last, grown gray, her beauty gone, she becomes a Sister of Mercy in Philadelphia, where she has gone because the soft-spoken Quakers remind her of her own people. When pestilence strikes the town, she visits the almshouse to nurse the destitute. One Sunday morning, she sees on the pallet before her a dying old man. It is Gabriel. In his last moments he dreams of Evangeline and Grand-Pré. Trying to utter her name, he dies. Evangeline murmurs a prayer of thanks as she presses her lover to her.

After Evangeline's death, the lovers lie side by side in nameless graves in Philadelphia. Although they are far from their old home in the north, a few peasants who wander back from exile still keep their story alive.

Critical Evaluation:

It is difficult in an unsentimental age to appreciate and understand the enormous appeal that *Evangeline* had for readers in Henry Wadsworth Longfellow's time. It was hailed from the beginning as a truly "American" poem, and its success was virtually unlimited. This pastoral romance relates an odyssey of sorts and dwells on the ideas of searching, wandering, and Evangeline's constancy.

Longfellow sought to imbue the poem with a classical flavor within the framework of the American landscape. It is enriched with elaborate descriptions of the historic American drive toward the West and the South. The rivers, forests, and prairies about which Longfellow wrote were the imaginative product of his reading and research, for most of the places the poem mentions he had never seen.

The basic story of *Evangeline* revolves around the cruel displacement of the Acadians by the British. Longfellow does not elaborate on the inequities of the British mandate to drive people from their homes; he is more interested in achieving a melancholy emotional tone by concentrating on the reality of exile and the frustration of searching. The mood is a tranquil one. Longfellow looks at his two lovers from a distance, creating a hazy image of things far away; much of the poem's action takes place at night, or by moonlight.

There is no doubt that the constancy and patience of Evangeline were appealing to Longfellow and his readers. Evangeline's loyalty and fidelity play a major role in the structuring of this romance. While Evangeline is the embodiment of feminine virtue, tenderness, and chastity, she does not have the dimension of a heroic figure. The poem suggests minor poetic form, certainly not epic grandeur. Evangeline and Gabriel are not realistic lovers but exponents of the romanticism of the times.

Longfellow felt that the English world was not sufficiently awakened to the beauty of the classical hexameter, so he decided from the beginning to employ this meter in *Evangeline*. There are difficulties with the use of this meter in English, and Longfellow was aware of them, yet he painstakingly sought to adhere to this classical measure. The meter does add an intrinsic charm that is appropriate to the tale, despite the sometimes monotonous quality of the lines. Longfellow's use of hexameter triggered a new interest in the meter and inspired much critical evaluation of its use and value.

Further Reading

Arvin, Newton. *Longfellow, His Life and Work*. 1963. Reprint. Westport, Conn.: Greenwood Press, 1977. Benchmark study discusses Longfellow as a man and as a writer. Devotes a full chapter to an articulate and insightful exploration of *Evangeline*, including the work's narrative structure, characters, settings, symbols, themes, and verse form. Places the poem squarely in the idyllic tradition.

Calhoun, Charles C. *Longfellow: A Rediscovered Life*. Boston: Beacon Press, 2004. Comprehensive and sympathetic biography seeks to rehabilitate Longfellow's reputation and document his contributions to American culture and literature.

Chevalier, Jacques M. *Semiotics, Romanticism, and the Scriptures*. Berlin: Walter de Gruyter, 1990. Book-length evaluation of *Evangeline* offers a sophisticated line-by-line analysis of the prologue and the first canto of book 1. Concentrates on the poem's scriptural and romantic elements in light of the work's role as a variation on the myth of the lost paradise.

Gale, Robert L. *A Henry Wadsworth Longfellow Companion*. Westport, Conn.: Greenwood Press, 2003. Informative resource contains several hundred alphabetically arranged entries about Wadsworth's individual poems, other writings, family members, associates, and other aspects of his life and work. Includes an introductory essay and a chronology of the events of Longfellow's life.

Hirsh, Edward L. *Henry Wadsworth Longfellow*. Minneapolis: University of Minnesota Press, 1964. Analyzes *Evangeline* in the context of Longfellow's other long narrative poems, especially *The Song of Hiawatha* (1855) and *The Courtship of Miles Standish* (1858). Emphasizes Longfellow's tendency to mythologize his subjects and his preference for pastoral coloring.

Lyons, Rosemary. *A Comparison of the Works of Antonine Maillet of the Acadian Tradition of New Brunswick, Canada, and Louise Erdrich of the Ojibwe of North America with the Poems of Longfellow*. Lewiston, N.Y.: Edwin Mellen Press, 2002. Compares Longfellow's poems about Native Americans, including *Evangeline*, with the writings of Acadian Canadian and Native American authors.

Wagenknecht, Edward. *Henry Wadsworth Longfellow: His Poetry and Prose*. New York: Frederick Ungar, 1986. Offers focused analyses of Longfellow's major works, including a full chapter on *Evangeline*. Especially informative in its treatment of Longfellow's original authorial intentions and his alterations to and expansion of the text.

Williams, Cecil B. *Henry Wadsworth Longfellow*. Boston: Twayne, 1964. Contains one chapter on Longfellow's verse narratives, including *Evangeline*. Provides an introductory treatment of Longfellow's sources and influences and discusses the poem's meter, plot, and critical reception. Argues that *Evangeline* provides a sentimental journey that even a cynical modern reader may find attractive.

The Eve of St. Agnes

Author: John Keats (1795-1821)
First published: 1820
Type of work: Poetry
Type of plot: Romance
Time of plot: Middle Ages
Locale: A castle

Principal characters:
MADELINE, a young woman
PORPHYRO, her lover
ANGELA, an old nurse

The Poem:

It is a cold St. Agnes's Eve—so cold that the owl with all its feathers shivers, so cold that the old Beadsman's fingers are numb as he tells his rosary and says his prayers. Passing by the sculptured figures of the dead, he feels sorry for them in their icy graves. As he walks through the chapel door, he can hear the sound of music coming from the castle hall. He sadly turns again to his prayers. The great hall of the castle is a scene of feasting and revelry, but one among the merry throng is scarcely aware of her surroundings. The lovely Madeline's thoughts are on the legend of St. Agnes's Eve, which tells that a maiden, if she follows the ceremonies carefully and goes supperless to bed, might there meet her lover in a dream.

Meanwhile, across the moonlit moors comes Porphyro. He enters the castle and hides behind a pillar, aware that his presence means danger, because his family is an enemy of Madeline's house. Soon the aged crone, Angela, comes by and offers to hide him, lest his enemies find him there and kill him. He follows her along dark arched passageways, out of sight of the revelers. When they stop, Porphyro begs Angela to let him have one glimpse of Madeline. He promises on oath that if he so much as disturbs a lock of her hair, he will give himself up to the foes who wait below. He seems in such sorrow that the poor woman gives in to him. She takes Porphyro to the maiden's chamber and there hides him in a closet, where is stored a variety of sweetmeats and confections brought from the feast downstairs. Angela then hobbles away, and soon the breathless Madeline appears.

She comes in with her candle, which blows out, and kneeling before her high arched casement window, she begins to pray. Watching her kneel there, her head a halo of moonlight, Porphyro grows faint at the sight of her beauty. Soon she disrobes and creeps into bed, where she lies entranced until sleep comes over her.

Porphyro steals from the closet and gazes at her in awe as she sleeps. For an instant a door opens far away, and the noises of another world, boisterous and festive, break in; but soon the sounds fade away again. In the silence he brings dainty foods from the closet—quinces, plums, jellies, candies, syrups, and spices that perfume the chilly room. Madeline sleeps on, and Porphyro begins to play a soft melody on a lute. Madeline opens her eyes and thinks her lover a vision of St. Agnes's Eve. Porphyro, not daring to speak, sinks upon his knees until she speaks, begging him never to leave her or she will die.

St. Agnes's moon goes down. Outside the casements, sleet and ice begin to dash against the windowpanes. Porphyro tells her that they must flee before the house awakens. Madeline, afraid and trembling, follows her lover down the cold, gloomy corridors, through the wide deserted hall and past the porter, asleep on his watch. They flee—into the wintry dawn.

Critical Evaluation:

John Keats wrote "The Eve of St. Agnes" in January and February of 1819, the first of an astonishing spate of masterpieces that came one after another, despite his failing health and emotional turmoil. "La Belle Dame Sans Merci," "Lamia," and six great odes were all written before October of that year. The circumstance of his death shortly afterward seems to throw into a kind of relief the luscious descriptions of physical beauty in this and other poems. More striking still is the poet's refusal to take comfort in the simplistic assurances of any religious or philosophical system that denied either the complexity of mind or the reality and importance of sense. "The Eve of St. Agnes" manifests Keats's characteristic concern with the opposition and subtle connection of the sensual world to the interior life. He shared this preoccupation with other Romantic poets, notably Samuel Taylor Coleridge and William Wordsworth, taking as his subject the web of an antithesis at the heart of human experience; like them, he cloaked his meditations in sensuous imagery.

In this and other ways, Keats and all the Romantics abandoned the poetic theory of the century before. Eighteenth century poetry was formal, didactic, and objective in stance. Its chief aim was to show to humanity a picture of itself for its own improvement and edification. Its chief ornament was wit: puns, wordplay, satiric description, and so forth. In short, what eighteenth century poets saw as virtue in poetry was logic and rigid metrics. Nineteenth century poets wrote from a radically different philosophical base, due in part to the cataclysmic political changes surrounding the American and French Revolutions. Before these upheavals occurred, a belief in order and in measure extended into all facets of life, from social relations to literature; extremes were shunned in all things as unnatural, dangerous, and perhaps blasphemous.

After 1789, when the social order in France turned upside down, an expectation of the millennium arose in England, especially in liberal intellectual circles; the old rules of poetry were thrown off with the outworn social strictures, and a new aesthetic bloomed in their place. Its ruling faculty was imagination. The world seemed made new, and poetry released from bondage. Romantic poets frequently stated that poems ought to be composed on the inspiration of the moment, thereby faithfully to record the purity of the emotion. In fact, Keats and his contemporaries labored hard over their creations; they exerted themselves not to smoothness of meter but to preserving the grace of spontaneity while achieving precision in observation of natural and psychological phenomena. Poets saw themselves as charting hitherto unexplored reaches of human experience, extremes of joy and dejection, guilt and redemption, pride and degradation. They wrote meditations, confessions, and conversations, in which natural things were seen to abet internal states, and they wrote ballads and narratives, such as "The Eve of St. Agnes," set in the past or in distant parts of the world and using archaic language and rhythms to make the events related seem even more strange and wonderful. Over and over they described epiphanous moments when the human consciousness becomes one with nature, when all is made new, when divinity animates the inanimate, and the lowest creature seems wondrous. This way of seeing was thought to be a return to an earlier consciousness lost in early childhood and is the theme of Wordsworth's seminal *Ode*.

In "The Eve of St. Agnes," Keats attempts, among other things, to maintain this elevated state of mind throughout the narrative. He sets the story in medieval times, so that the familiar fairytale characters take on charm from their quaint surroundings and from the archaic language in which they speak and are described. Its verse form is the smooth, supremely difficult-to-write Spenserian stanza, with its slightly asymmetric rhyme scheme that avoids the monotony of couplet or quatrain, and the piquant extension of the ninth line that gives to the whole an irregularity echoing ordinary

speech. The first five stanzas contrast the Beadsman, coldly at his prayers, with the "argent revelry" of the great hall. This imagery of cold and warmth, of silver and scarlet, of chastity and sensuality continues throughout the poem, a comment on the plot.

That the poem is named for a virgin martyr yet tells the story of an elopement is likewise significant; the point of the poem, on the one hand, is that piety and passion are opposing but inseparable drives. Each without the other has no point of reference. Porphyro without Madeline becomes the gross Lord Maurice, the savage Hildebrand; Madeline without Porphyro becomes the Beadsman with his deathlike abrogation of sense. Instead, Porphyro is made to faint at the celestial beauty of Madeline at her prayers, Madeline to be wooed by songs and colors and delicacies. The passage describing the array of food that Porphyro set out is understandably famous; these are not mere groceries but rather the glowing essence of fruitfulness, tribute to a love match of the meditative and emotional faculties that, when accomplished in one individual, fulfills the whole human potential.

The other theme, or perhaps the other face of the same theme, is the relentless press of quotidian misery on the poetic personality, another favorite arena of reflection among the Romantics, and one that was poignantly near Keats's heart, menaced by tuberculosis as he was, and his younger brother dying of the disease the previous winter. The lovers are shown, unearthly fair, escaping from a house where wrath and drunkenness hold sway, bound for a dream-vision of happiness. Significantly, the poet does not follow them to their southern sanctuary. Instead he relates the wretched end of Angela, who dies "palsy-twitched" in her sleep; the cold sleep of the Beadsman among the ashes; the drunken nightmares of the Baron and his guests. The ending, in short, is not unreservedly happy but partakes of that bittersweet emotion which in the midst of joy acknowledges wretchedness, the mark of a mind that strives for aesthetic detachment while believing in its duty to the rest of humankind.

"Critical Evaluation" by Edward E. Foster

Further Reading

Blades, John. *John Keats: The Poems*. New York: Palgrave, 2002. Detailed textual analysis of the themes and techniques in Keats's poems, including a discussion of *The Eve of St. Agnes* in chapter 5. Places Keats's poetry within the contexts of his life and of nineteenth century Romantic literature.

Bloom, Harold, ed. *John Keats*. Updated ed. New York: Chelsea House, 2007. Collection of essays providing various interpretations of Keats's poetry, including an analysis of *The Eve of St. Agnes* by Andrew Bennett.

Danzig, Allan, ed. *Twentieth Century Interpretations of "The Eve of St. Agnes."* Englewood Cliffs, N.J.: Prentice-Hall, 1971. Excellent source for beginning discussion of Keats's poem. Contains seven essays exploring such topics as narrative structure, contrary states of imagination, musical and pictorial settings, techniques of composition, literary influences, and the darker side of seduction.

Stillinger, Jack. Introduction to "The Eve of St. Agnes," by John Keats. In *John Keats: Complete Poems.* Cambridge, Mass.: Belknap Press, 1982. Excellent edition of the poem by a definitive Keats scholar. Includes commentary on the chronology of composition, Keats's subsequent revisions, textual sources, and an extensive bibliography.

_____. *Reading "The Eve of St. Agnes": The Multiples of Complex Literary Transaction.* New York: Oxford University Press, 1999. Explicates the multiple meanings of the poem and discusses the circumstances of its composition, revision, and publication. Assesses Keats's place within English poetry and describes why his work is considered canonical and continues to be read and studied.

Talbot, Norman. "Porphyro's Enemies." *Essays in Criticism* 38 (1988): 215-231. Argues that Madeline, Angela, and the Beadsman offer only minor resistance to the exploits of Porphyro. Dramatic tension centers on the male protagonist, who fluctuates between romantic hero, hot-blooded opportunist, and religious devotee.

Wolfson, Susan J. *The Cambridge Companion to Keats.* New York: Cambridge University Press, 2001. The book's essays discuss common characteristics of Keats's poetry, including the sources of his allusions, his use of language, and his representation of gender. "*Lamia, Isabella,* and *The Eve of St. Agnes*" by Jeffrey N. Cox analyzes these three poems.

Evelina
Or, The History of a Young Lady's Entrance into the World

Author: Fanny Burney (1752-1840)
First published: 1778
Type of work: Novel
Type of plot: Sentimental
Time of plot: Eighteenth century
Locale: England

Principal characters:
SIR JOHN BELMONT, an English nobleman
EVELINA, Sir John's unacknowledged daughter
THE REVEREND MR. ARTHUR VILLARS, Evelina's guardian
MADAME DUVAL, Evelina's grandmother
LORD ORVILLE, Evelina's husband
SIR CLEMENT WILLOUGHBY, a gentleman of fashion
MRS. MIRVAN, Evelina's patron

The Story:

Abandoned by her father and her maternal grandmother upon the death of her mother, Evelina is for many years the ward of the Reverend Mr. Arthur Villars, an English clergyman. At last, her grandmother, Madame Duval, writes from France to say that she will take charge of Evelina, providing proper proof of the child's relationship is forthcoming. Mr. Villars, however, refuses to send Evelina to France. He also objects to the invitation of Mrs. Mirvan, who wants Evelina to join her family in London. He thinks that Evelina, brought up carefully at Berry Hill in Dorsetshire, should not be exposed to London society life, particularly so since her own father, Sir John Belmont, will not admit his parentage and

she is without enough income to permit her to live as the Mirvans do.

After some urging, he finally allows Evelina to visit Lady Howard, Mrs. Mirvan's mother, at Howard Grove. A short time later, Mrs. Mirvan and her daughter, who are delighted with Evelina, secure permission to have her accompany them to London.

Almost at once, she is swept into fashionable London life. Having grown up in the provinces, Evalina finds the city is a constant joy. She soon meets Lord Orville, and they are attracted to each other. On several occasions, her lack of London manners causes her embarrassment, and she expresses a desire to return to Dorsetshire. Sir Clement Willoughby is her chief tormentor.

By chance, she meets her odious grandmother, the vulgar and presumptuous Madame Duval. On an outing, the French-woman becomes the subject of ridicule when she is pitched into a mudhole. Evelina meets some of her other relations and finds them no better than her grandmother.

Madame Duval, attaching herself to the Mirvans, succeeds in making Evelina very unhappy. Evelina goes reluctantly to the opera with her relatives and is made miserable by their crudeness. Hoping to escape them, she joins Sir Clement but is only further embarrassed when Sir Clement intentionally delays his coach while escorting her to her lodging. Evelina is severely scolded by her guardian for the escapade. In a letter to her, he indicates that he lives in daily fear for her honor. He is relieved when he hears that the Mirvans are at last returning with her to Howard Grove.

Lady Howard, urged on by Madame Duval, puts forth the plan of forcing Sir John Belmont to acknowledge Evelina as his daughter. Mr. Villars does not approve of this action; he promised Evelina's mother that the young woman would never know her cruel and "unnatural" father.

At Howard Grove, Evelina unknowingly participates in a cruel joke planned by Captain Mirvan and Sir Clement. Again made a laughingstock, Madame Duval takes to her bed after she is sent upon a fool's errand and loses her false curls. When Sir John Belmont refuses to admit that Evelina is his daughter, Madame Duval plans to take Evelina to confront Sir John in person and to demand his recognition. Mr. Villars will not listen to her proposal. He does agree, however, to let Evelina spend a month with her grandmother in London. Evelina is unhappy under Madame Duval's chaperonage because her vulgar relations attempt to use her to ingratiate themselves with her fashionable friends. Sir Clement visits Evelina while she is staying with her grandmother, but Madame Duval embarrasses everyone by her uncivil remarks to him. She remembers the joke played on her at Howard Grove.

In her London lodgings, Evelina is instrumental in preventing the suicide of Mr. Macartney, an impoverished Scottish poet. Out of pity for his plight, she relieves his need with money from her own purse. At a fireworks display, Evelina is again chagrined, being discovered by Lord Orville while she is in vulgar company.

Madame Duval announces that she hopes to marry Evelina to the boorish young son of Mr. Branghton, a silver-smith. Mr. Branghton is Madame Duval's nephew. Evelina is much distressed, the more so when her grandmother's friends attach themselves to Lord Orville in a familiar man-

ner. When Mr. Branghton asks his lordship's custom for any silver the nobleman might want to buy, Evelina feels ruined forever in Lord Orville's eyes.

In her distress, Evelina writes to Mr. Villars, who orders her to return immediately to Berry Hill. From there, she writes about her London adventures to her friend, Miss Mirvan. A most painful surprise to her is a letter she receives from Lord Orville, to whom she wrote to disclaim responsibility for her relatives' crudeness. His reply is so insulting that she becomes ill and has to be sent to a rest home at Bristol Hot Wells, where she goes in the company of Mrs. Selwyn, a neighbor.

At the watering place, Evelina meets many of her fashionable London friends, among them Lord Orville. He is so courteous that she forgives him for his impolite letter. As Evelina is beginning to feel at home once more among people of wealth and position, Mr. Macartney appears and embarrasses her with his importunities.

A new arrival at the baths is Miss Belmont, an heiress reputed to be Sir John Belmont's daughter. Mrs. Selwyn, hearing of the young woman's identity, decides to learn more about Miss Belmont. Mrs. Selwyn is convinced that Evelina is the true daughter of Sir John.

Mr. Macartney is trying to return the money Evelina gave him, but she does not want her friends to learn that she ever knew him. She fears that they will suspect her of having an affair with him. Lord Orville, however, encourages her to see the unfortunate young poet. From Mr. Macartney, Evelina learns that he believes himself to be an unacknowledged son of Sir John Belmont. Evelina, realizing that she must be the sister of Mr. Macartney, does not reveal her knowledge.

When Sir John Belmont returns to England, Mr. Villars is finally stirred to action against him; for by introducing to society the woman who poses as his daughter, Sir John is indicating that Evelina is an impostor. Determined that Evelina have her rights, Mr. Villars prepares to force Sir John to acknowledge Evelina as his daughter.

Through the good offices of Mrs. Selwyn and others, the affair is at last untangled. The supposed daughter of Sir John proves to be the daughter of a penniless nurse, who substituted her own child for Lady Belmont's infant. Evelina, delighted to learn that Sir John's attitude is the result of error and not neglect, is happily reconciled with her father, who receives her warmly. The impostor is treated with great kindness by all concerned as she herself is innocent of the design. She marries Mr. Macartney, who is also acknowledged by Sir John. As Sir John's daughter, Evelina is sought after by Lord Orville, to whom she gladly gives her hand in marriage.

Critical Evaluation:

Evelina is Fanny Burney's first and most successful novel. When it was published in 1778, the book's appeal was attributed to its sentimental value, but it has held lasting interest because of the realistic portrayal of eighteenth century English life. In *Evelina*, Burney's attentiveness to the manners and pretentiousness of socialites enabled her to show a culture its foibles. *Evelina* is particularly descriptive of the social position of women.

Sensitively reared by the Reverend Mr. Villars, the heroine, Evelina, has become a kind, compassionate young woman. As she steps into the social life of London, her unblemished perception of society affords both delight at its marvels and disdain for its unscrupulousness and frivolity. Her letters to Mr. Villars convey clear images of London high society.

Evelina first writes with some amazement that London life begins so late that people spend the morning in bed. She adjusts, however, to the nightlife and enjoys the opera, plays, and other events with which she and her company are entertained almost nightly. She is annoyed by audiences who are so talkative throughout the events that the artists cannot be heard, and she quickly realizes that the purpose of the events is more for socializing than for the merit of the performances themselves.

Burney places her heroine with various guardians in a variety of situations in city and country. Evelina's first awkward fortnight in London with the kind Mirvan ladies abruptly contrasts with her second visit in London in the company of Madame Duval and her relatives, the Branghtons. Crude and ill-mannered, they cause Evelina embarrassment by her forced association with them. In her third venture away from her benefactor Mr. Villars, Evelina is again in cultured company under the guardianship of the aggressive Mrs. Selwyn.

In each group, regardless of its social position, Evelina finds individuals of sincerity and those who are masters of divisiveness and deception. Mrs. Mirvan and Maria are sincere and well-mannered. Although uncouth, cruel, and contemptuous, Captain Mirvan is, nevertheless, sincere. He is his own person, honest in his brutal way. Madame Duval shares with her tormentor, Captain Mirvan, the quality of being her own person, disagreeable as she, too, may be.

Evelina readily acknowledges the honorable qualities of Lord Orville and Mr. Macartney. She also quickly perceives the duplicity of Sir Clement, Mr. Lovel, Lord Merton, the Branghtons, Lady Louisa, and Mr. Smith. In lady or silversmith, airs and presumptuousness repel Evelina. Evelina is shocked at the insincerity of those for whom honor and good manners directly relate to dress, immediate company, and situation. Lord Merton ignores Evelina while Lady Louisa is present yet lavishes her with attention at Lady Louisa's absence. Sir Clement is a chameleon whose attention to Evelina is gained at any expense. Lady Louisa acts out roles constantly, purposely ignoring Evelina until she learns that Evelina is to become her brother's wife.

Evelina detects affectation and shows it as being ridiculous. She describes for Mr. Villars an episode from her first dance at which a young man approached her with comically stilted mannerisms and speech. "Allow me, Madam . . . the honour and happiness—if I am not so unhappy as to address you too late—to have the happiness and honour." She confesses that she had to turn away to conceal her laughter.

Evelina is bewildered by the social etiquette that she has had no opportunity to learn at Berry Hill, but her sense of propriety causes her to suffer for her ignorance. She is always aware of her dependent position and constantly relies on her protectors, benefactors, and guardians.

Burney does not intend that Evelina's dependence be read negatively. On the contrary, Evelina is idyllic in her feminine compliance and sensibility. She is a model lady for the times. It is interesting to note, however, how vastly the roles and rights of men and women in the novel differ. Mr. Lovel says, "I have an insuperable aversion to strength, either in body or mind, in a female." Lord Merton echoes a similar view—"for a woman wants nothing to recommend her but beauty and good nature; in everything else she is either impertinent or unnatural."

Burney comments on women's sensibility through her characters. Lady Louisa, whose feigned delicate nature corresponds with her posturing, seems to be the extreme of insincere sensibility. Mrs. Selwyn represents another extreme. She is powerful and aggressive and is disliked by both men and women for her outspokenness. Evelina wishes that Mrs. Selwyn were more sensitive to her needs in awkward situations and finds her lacking in femininity. Evelina writes, "I have never been personally hurt by her want of gentleness, a virtue which nevertheless seems so essential a part of the female character." Lord Orville, the ideal male in the novel, is described by Evelina as "feminine," a compliment to his gentle character. Evelina's description of Mrs. Selwyn as "masculine," however, is definitely a negative criticism.

Given the impropriety of acting independently, Evelina and all gentlewomen must rely upon others for advice. Unfortunately, those counselors are likely to take advantage of women's dependency. Fortunately, Evelina's good sense alerts her to unreliable protectors, but her situation clearly indicates the powerless situation of women who are perpetually rescued or victimized.

Perhaps Mr. Villars's response to Evelina's interference in the attempted suicide of Mr. Macartney best expresses Burney's attitude toward women. "Though gentleness and modesty are the peculiar attributes of your sex, yet fortitude and firmness, when occasion demands them, are virtues as noble and as becoming in women as in men."

Evelina was first published without the name of the author and was generally assumed to have been written by a man. Burney was as dependent as her Evelina in getting the book into publication; a male secret agent smuggled the manuscript to the publisher.

"Critical Evaluation" by Mary Peace Finley

Further Reading

Bloom, Harold, ed. *Fanny Burney's "Evelina."* New York: Chelsea House, 1988. Includes previously published material, plus Julia L. Epstein's "Evelina's Deceptions: The Letter and the Spirit" and Jennifer A. Wagner's "Privacy and Anonymity in *Evelina*."

Doody, Margaret Anne. *Frances Burney: The Life in the Works*. New Brunswick, N.J.: Rutgers University Press, 1988. Examines all of Burney's novels not only as a reflection of but also an indictment of Burney's society's perversities of structure, function, and belief. Discusses Burney's insight into her society's comical and obsessive traits.

Harman, Claire. *Fanny Burney: A Biography.* New York: Alfred A. Knopf, 2001. An accessible and authoritative biography. Harman points out inconsistencies in Burney's memoirs, providing a more accurate account of the author's life and placing Burney within the broader context of her times.

Newton, Judith Lowder. *Women, Power, and Subversion: Social Strategies in British Fiction, 1778-1860.* Athens: University of Georgia Press, 1981. Newton devotes an entire chapter to *Evelina*, finding in Burney's novel an unresolved conflict between Burney's desire for artistic freedom and the demands of patriarchal authority.

Sabor, Peter, ed. *The Cambridge Companion to Frances Burney.* New York: Cambridge University Press, 2007. Collection of essays covering Burney's life and work, including an essay discussing both *Cecilia* and *Evelina*. Other essays survey her critical reputation, political views, and Burney and gender issues.

Spencer, Jane. *The Rise of the Woman Novelist: From Aphra Behn to Jane Austen.* 1986. Reprint. New York: Blackwell, 1993. A compelling study of the emergence of the woman writer in England in the period from the late seventeenth to the early nineteenth centuries.

Spender, Dale. *Mothers of the Novel: One Hundred Good Women Writers Before Jane Austen.* London: Pandora, 1986. Spender's purpose in this important treatment of women writers from the seventeenth and eighteenth centuries is to challenge and ultimately to overthrow the traditional view that the novel was "fathered" by a handful of male writers. She devotes a chapter to Burney and her contemporary Maria Edgeworth.

Straub, Kristina. *Divided Fictions: Fanny Burney and Feminine Strategy.* Lexington: University Press of Kentucky, 1987. Straub's is one of the best sustained critical examinations of Burney's work. The chapters on *Evelina* are excellent.

Thaddeus, Janice Farrar. *Frances Burney: A Literary Life.* New York: St. Martin's Press, 2000. Scholarly account of Burney's life and career that greatly expands the reader's understanding of the novelist. Includes discussion of her four novels, as well as a genealogical table, notes, and index.

Zonitch, Barbara. *Familiar Violence: Gender and Social Upheaval in the Novels of Frances Burney.* Newark: University of Delaware Press, 1997. Devotes individual chapters to analysis of *Evelina* and Burney's other novels. Zonitch's introduction, "Social Transformations: The Crisis of the Aristocracy and the Status of Women," is especially useful to understanding Burney's place within eighteenth century English society.

Every Man in His Humour

Author: Ben Jonson (1573-1637)

First produced: 1598; first published, 1601; revised, 1605, 1616

Type of work: Drama

Type of plot: Comedy

Time of plot: Late sixteenth century

Locale: London

Principal characters:

KNOWELL, an old gentleman

EDWARD KNOWELL, his son

BRAINWORM, Knowell's servant

DOWNRIGHT, a plain man

WELLBRED, his half brother

KITELY, a merchant

CAPTAIN BOBADILL, a cowardly braggart

DAME KITELY, Kitely's wife

COB, a water carrier

TIB, Cob's wife

The Story:

In Hogsden, a conservative suburb north of London's wall, Edward Knowell, a dignified, practical citizen, is somewhat concerned over his son Edward's interest in poetry. Old Knowell is further alarmed that his nephew Stephen, a country simpleton, shows interest in the gentle art of falconry. Old Knowell wishes to have his son and his nephew engaged in more practical arts.

One day he is handed a letter meant for his son. The letter, signed by Wellbred, a London gallant, is an invitation to young Knowell to renew his association with a group of young madcaps. Old Knowell, reading the letter and convinced that his son is up to no good, has his servant, Brainworm, deliver the letter to the youth in his study, with the directions not to reveal that the letter was opened. Contrary to orders, Brainworm tells his young master that old Knowell read the letter. The young man, delighted with the prospect of fun in the city, gives little thought to what his father might do.

Meanwhile, in the city, Matthew, an urban fool, calls on Captain Bobadill, a spurious cavalier who rooms in the low-class lodgings of Cob, a water carrier. Matthew, his taste questioned by Downright, a plain-spoken man, asks for and receives instructions in dueling from the braggart, swaggering Bobadill.

In his house nearby, Kitely, a merchant, discusses with Downright the dissolute ways of his brother-in-law, Wellbred, who rooms with the Kitelys. Wellbred becomes the leader of a group of scoffers, young men who apparently have no respect for anyone or anything; their greatest sport is to discover fools and make sport of them. Kitely fears that his relation to this sporting crew might endanger his business reputation. In addition, he is jealous of his wife. When Matthew and Bobadill call for Wellbred, Bobadill insults Down-

right on Matthew's behalf. Kitely restrains Downright from avenging his honor on the spot.

Brainworm, young Knowell's ally, appears in Moorfields disguised as a disabled veteran for the purpose of intercepting old Knowell, who he knows will follow young Knowell into the city to spy on him. Brainworm encounters the old gentleman, who, out of pity, hires Brainworm, who styles himself Fitz-Sword, as a personal servant.

Inside the city wall, young Knowell reveals to Wellbred that old Knowell read Wellbred's letter; the pair agree to make a joke of the situation. Stephen, Matthew, and Bobadill provide rare fun for young Knowell and Wellbred. Stephen assumes a ridiculous air of melancholy, which he thinks befits a lovesick poet; Matthew, a poetaster, reflects this melancholy in what he thinks is the urban manner. Bobadill provides entertainment with preposterous lies about his military experiences and with oaths that especially impress rustic Stephen. Brainworm joins the group, reveals his true identity, and reports to young Knowell that old Knowell came to the city and is stopping at the house of Justice Clement.

Kitely, meanwhile, obsessed with a growing fear that his wife might be unfaithful to him, decides to forgo a profitable business transaction in another part of the city. Later he changes his mind, but before he leaves home he orders his servant, Thomas Cash, to report immediately the coming to the house of Wellbred and his companions, or of any stranger. The young gallants come to the house shortly afterward. Cash, in desperation, enlists Cob to carry the message to Kitely. Receiving the message at the house of Justice Clement, where he is doing business, Kitely hurries home, plagued by the imagination of a jealous husband.

In Kitely's house, Downright reproaches his sister, Mistress Kitely, for permitting their brother, Wellbred, to use her house as a meeting place for his mad company. Matthew, to the amusement of young Knowell and Wellbred, reads bits of stolen verse to Bridget, Kitely's maiden sister. When Downright asks Wellbred and his followers to leave, rapiers are drawn. After Cash and the other servants separate the antagonists, Bobadill makes brave gestures. As Wellbred and his companions leave, Kitely enters excitedly and begins a search for young Knowell, whose virtues are being praised by Mistress Kitely and Bridget. He fears the women hid the young man in the house.

Armed with a warrant and aroused by Kitely's husbandly apprehensions, Cob goes by his house to see that all is well with his wife Tib. He advises her to remain indoors and not to admit anyone. Meanwhile Brainworm, as the disabled veteran, returns, at the direction of young Knowell, to inform old Knowell that his son can be apprehended at Cob's house, where an assignation is to take place.

Downright arrives in Moorfields while Bobadill entertains young Knowell, Matthew, and Stephen with unbelievable accounts of his prowess as a swordsman. After Downright disarms Bobadill easily and thrashes him, Matthew, frightened, runs back to the city. Stephen claims the russet cloak that Downright leaves at the scene of the fight.

Back in town, Kitely continues to be tortured by his jealousy. Brainworm, now disguised as Justice Clement's man, Formal, enters and tells Kitely that Justice Clement wishes to see him immediately. While Kitely again admonishes Cash to guard the house against all interlopers, Wellbred conspires with Brainworm for the marriage of young Knowell and Bridget. Wellbred, ever seeking amusement at the expense of others, suggests to Mistress Kitely that perhaps her husband is a philanderer. At this, Mistress Kitely departs to spy on the activities of her husband. Kitely returns to find his wife absent, and when he is told that she went to Cob's house he follows, fearful that he is cuckolded. Wellbred takes the opportunity, while neither of the Kitelys is home, to take Bridget to the church.

After their shameful conduct in Moorfields, Bobadill and Matthew meet in the city; Bobadill rationalizes their cowardice. They encounter Brainworm, still disguised as Formal, and give him jewelry and clothing to pawn for the price of a warrant to arrest Downright, who they say wears a russet cloak.

The tricks played by Brainworm, young Knowell, and Wellbred begin to rebound on the knavish threesome. Old Knowell goes to Cob's house, where he is told by the indignant Tib that she knows no Edward Knowell. At the same time, Mistress Kitely appears and is suspected by old Knowell of being young Knowell's mistress. Kitely arrives next. He and his wife exchange bitter words of mistrust, for

Kitely suspects old Knowell of being his wife's paramour, Mistress Kitely accuses her husband of dalliance with Tib. Cob appears and thrashes his wife for not obeying him. As a result of misunderstandings all around, Kitely insists that all concerned present themselves before Justice Clement.

In the meantime, Brainworm, assuming the disguise of a constable, and accompanied by Matthew and Bobadill, arrests Stephen, who is wearing Downright's russet cloak. Brainworm's mistake is quickly recognized, but when Downright himself approaches, Matthew and Bobadill depart in haste. Downright, although Stephen surrenders the cloak, insists that the matter be explained to Justice Clement.

Practically all of the principals gathering in the hall of his house, Justice Clement holds an investigation of the misunderstandings that took place. Brainworm throws off his disguise and explains his part in the confusion of the day. He is forgiven by his master, old Knowell. Young Knowell and Bridget, now husband and wife, enter with Wellbred. Kitely and Mistress Kitely, as well as Cob and Tib, are reconciled after explanations are made. Justice Clement, seeing peace and trust reestablished, dedicates the ensuing evening to celebration and conviviality.

Critical Evaluation:

Ben Jonson substantially revised *Every Man in His Humour* for his 1616 folio publication and added a famous prologue that defends his sort of comedy. He changed the setting of the play from exotic Italy to everyday London, renamed the characters, eliminated extraneous speeches, and particularized general and high-flown speeches of several characters. He writes in the prologue that the play will not utilize the marvelous or the mechanistic such as thunder machines, "But deeds and language such as men do use." He also explains that his comedy will "sport with human follies, not with crimes." *Every Man in His Humour* is thus a lighthearted portrayal of human stupidity, and the medieval theory of the four humors is not very important to the play. For Jonson, the humors were simply the exaggerated and often caricatured manners of people, so that the comedy of humors is really a comedy of manners.

Perhaps more than any other comedy by Jonson, *Every Man in His Humour* is a comedy of noninteraction—in structure and plot, in character and language. By contrast, Shakespearean comedy thrives on close consequence; for example, the resolution of subplot and main plot always results in the plotlines crossing. What resolution there is at the end of *Every Man in His Humour* is artificial, imposed by Justice Clement, and not strongly felt by the audience to be genuine. The traditional concluding symbols of judgment, marriage, and banquet are arbitrarily imposed on an ending that would otherwise seem hopelessly fragmentary.

Structurally, noninteraction is here very apparent, because the subplots that serve to make up plot seem to be accidental rather than mutually necessary. Meetings between members of different subplots are coincidental and suggest disorder rather than resolution; the meetings in Moorfields and outside Cob's house are good examples. In addition, Jonson's characters are each extremely individualistic, almost solipsistic in their belief in the importance of their own existence. This subjectivism produces mazes of misapprehension and nonunderstanding when characters try to communicate. This condition is compounded by the disguises of Brainworm, who casts himself as manipulator of much of the action.

Most of the characters seem unable to practice directness; they resort to communication through go-betweens, thus increasing the possibilities of mistakes and misperceptions. Knowell deals with Edward through Brainworm, who also mediates for Edward with his father. Wellbred conducts Edward's courtship; Kitely tells Cash of his fears about his wife, and Cash then sends Cob with the message to Kitely. Bobadill insults Downright for Matthew, and Justice Clement even relates to a client who is standing before him by means of his assistant. A desire to avoid encounters motivates much of the action: Kitely and Dame Kitely do not speak their minds to each other; Knowell is worried about Edward's and Wellbred's friendship; Brainworm tries to keep apart those he is manipulating. Direct, emotion-filled conversation usually does not occur. Bridget and Edward utter not a single word to each other either before or after marriage, nor does Knowell congratulate Edward. Kitely's feeble remarks to his wife after their reconciliation suggest their essential estrangement. The only place for protestations of real feeling is in soliloquy. The characters are incapable of genuine dialogue.

Noninteraction comes to its logical conclusion in the events that take place before Cob's house (act 4). Instead of creating a recognition and discovery scene, the characters misunderstand the action and one another because they refuse to go beyond their ossified solipsisms. Thus, Knowell "recognizes" Dame Kitely as Edward's lover; Kitely believes Knowell to be his wife's lover; and Knowell mistakes Kitely for Edward. Justice Clement's plea for reconciliation is not met by any real change in the characters.

In this early Jonson comedy, the debate about poetry that frames the play (Knowell's opening speech and Clement's closing one) does not provide the unity that similar debates do in later Jonson works. The ideal of poetry seems unlikely here to do more than achieve an arbitrary connection with the unity dictated by Clement. Although the characters often speak about poetry, they do not seem to be particularly concerned with it.

As in most Jonsonian comedy, characters' names—be they serious, satiric, or comic—disclose ideas about personality. Justice Clement, as his name suggests, tempers his justice with mercy, but Knowell usually acts the opposite of a knowledgeable father. Some of the characters are recognizable types deriving from Roman comedy, especially that of Plautus: Brainworm, the witty servant; Kitely, the jealous husband; Knowell, the strict father; Wellbred, the man-about-town; Bobadill, the *miles gloriosus*, or braggart soldier. Although Jonson borrows these typed characters, he makes them thoroughly English and assimilates them to his ideas of human follies.

The characters are often connected by contrasts, so that those who appear similar are shown to be different, while those who seem opposed are linked. Thus Matthew, the town gull, supposedly different from Stephen, the country gull, is actually the same sort of person. Both ape fashions in sport (rapier dueling or hawking) and praise a particular fashion in dress; the difference is that the town gull is in style and the country gull is out of style. Similarly, Edward is shown to be essentially different from his friend Wellbred—the one serious and temperate, the other frivolous and extreme. There are also sets of characters that seem to parody each other's behavior: Cob's jealousy burlesques Kitely's, and both reflect Knowell's spying on his son; the relationship of Edward to Wellbred is mimicked by that of Matthew to Bobadill. These contrasts and distorted mirrors help to give a structural balance to the play but do not change its nonrelational quality. Each character is set on a particular course by his personality, a course that is not altered by any collision with another person.

Every Man in His Humour portrays a multiplicity of human aberrations, although here they are more lighthearted follies. Jonson's favorite satiric targets can be found—illusions about education, love, poetry, social place—as a group of characters reiterates each issue. Justice Clement's plea "to put off all discontent" marks the necessary illusion of change and unity at the end. Only the later Ben Jonson (of *Bartholomew Fair*, 1614) can accept these follies and aberrations as part of human nature.

"Critical Evaluation" by Margaret McFadden-Gerber

Further Reading

Barton, Anne. *Ben Jonson, Dramatist*. New York: Cambridge University Press, 1984. Compares Jonson's and

William Shakespeare's treatment of the country and the city as settings. Indicates that, contrary to Elizabethan convention, Jonson would not allow sudden conversions in character. Analyzes Jonson's revisions in a later version of the work.

Brock, D. Heyward. *A Ben Jonson Companion.* Bloomington: Indiana University Press, 1983. A valuable resource. Defines key terms; identifies both real people who were important in Jonson's world and characters who appear in the plays. Selected bibliography.

Donaldson, Ian. *Jonson's Magic Houses: Essays in Interpretation.* New York: Oxford University Press, 1997. Donaldson, a Jonson scholar, provides new interpretations of Jonson's personality, work, and literary legacy.

Dutton, Richard. *Ben Jonson: To the First Folio.* New York: Cambridge University Press, 1983. A chapter on the early plays shows how Jonson had to educate his audience to appreciate a kind of comedy different from Shakespeare's because Jonson's comedy relies heavily on neoclassical principles.

Harp, Richard, and Stanley Stewart, eds. *The Cambridge Companion to Ben Jonson.* New York: Cambridge University Press, 2000. Collection of essays about Jonson's life and career, including analyses of his comedies and late plays, a description of London and its theaters during Jonson's lifetime, and an evaluation of his critical heritage.

Loxley, James. *A Sourcebook.* New York: Routledge, 2002. An introductory overview of Jonson's life and work, particularly useful for students. Part 1 provides biographical information and places Jonson's life and work within the context of his times; part 2 discusses several works, including *Every Man in his Humour*; part 3 offers critical analysis of the themes in his plays, the style of his writing, and a comparison of his work to that of William Shakespeare.

McEvoy, Sean. *Ben Jonson, Renaissance Dramatist.* Edinburgh: Edinburgh University Press, 2008. McEvoy analyzes all of Jonson's plays, attributing their greatness to the playwright's commitment to the ideals of humanism during a time of authoritarianism and rampant capitalism in England. *Every Man in His Humour* is discussed in chapter 2, with other references listed in the index.

Riggs, David. *Ben Jonson: A Life.* Cambridge, Mass.: Harvard University Press, 1989. A chapter on the comedy of humors discusses the theory and the origins of that genre and explains how Jonson's theory of satire differed from Shakespeare's.

Watson, Robert N. *Ben Jonson's Parodic Strategies: Literary Imperialism in the Comedies.* Cambridge, Mass.: Harvard University Press, 1987. The chapter on *Every Man in His Humour*, "The Purging of Monstrous Conventions," shows how "wits supersede the fools," and how satire supersedes the usual plot patterns.

Every Man out of His Humour

Author: Ben Jonson (1573-1637)
First produced: 1599; first published, 1600
Type of work: Drama
Type of plot: Comedy
Time of plot: Early seventeenth century
Locale: Probably London

Principal characters:
MACILENTE, a malcontent
CARLO BUFFONE, a scoffer
SOGLIARDO, a wealthy country fool
SORDIDO, a rural miser
FUNGOSO, his son
PUNTARVOLO, a fantastic knight
FASTIDIOUS BRISK, a courtier
SAVIOLINA, a lady of the court

The Story:

Macilente, disgusted by the injustices of society, flees to the country. As he lies idly under a tree he overhears a conversation between the wealthy young farmer, Sogliardo, and Carlo Buffone, a railing cynic whom the rustic bumpkin chooses as his guide in becoming a gentleman. Macilente winces at Sogliardo's presumption and at Buffone's callous instructions to the foolish Sogliardo. Buffone, seeing Macilente and knowing him to be a malcontent, hurries away with Sogliardo, but in departing he tells Macilente that they are going to Puntarvolo's house.

Still musing under the tree, Macilente next listens while Sordido, a miserly farmer, consults his almanac and hopes for rainy weather in order that his hoarded grain might soar in value. A farmhand delivers to Sordido a note, an official order for him to bring his grain to market. Sordido scorns the order and swears that he will hide his surplus harvest.

In front of Puntarvolo's house, Buffone and Sogliardo talk with the braggart courtier, Sir Fastidious Brisk. The three watch with amazement Puntarvolo's return from the hunt. Puntarvolo, an old-fashioned fantastic knight, is given to extravagances in the form of little homecoming plays which he writes himself. Assuming the role of a strange knight, Puntarvolo approaches his house, inquires about the owner, and hears his virtues praised by his indulgent wife and her women. In another part of the play Puntarvolo woos his wife in the manner of a knight-errant. Sordido and his son, Fungoso, a law student in the city, appear. Fungoso is so impressed with the stylish cut of Brisk's clothes that he asks his uncle, Sogliardo, to get him money from Sordido, ostensibly for law books but actually for a suit of clothes in the latest style. All the while hoping for rain, Sordido reluctantly gives his son money, but not enough.

Reaction varies to Puntarvolo's announcement that he wagered five thousand pounds at five-to-one odds that he and his wife and their dog can travel to Constantinople and back without a fatal mishap. Buffone sees in this venture material for a colossal joke, while Brisk is interested in investing a hundred pounds in the venture. Fungoso, meanwhile, taken with Brisk's courtly manner and dress, is pleased to learn that his brother-in-law, Deliro, is Brisk's merchant.

The next day Macilente advises his friend Deliro to exercise some control in his doting love for his wife, since this dotage causes the wife, Fallace, to react petulantly to Deliro's affections. Fungoso, wearing a new suit, goes to Deliro's house and borrows money from his sister, Fallace, in order to complete his costume. No sooner does he receive the money than Brisk enters in a new suit. Fungoso, frustrated by this new development, writes his father for more money. Brisk, meanwhile, brags of his actually nonexistent triumphs at court; he also makes arrangements with Deliro for mortgaging his land in the country. Fallace, impatient with her workaday husband, admires Brisk's courtliness and dreams of becoming a court lady.

Buffone, accompanied by Puntarvolo, tries to find two retainers for his newly arrived gentleman, Sogliardo. Puntarvolo, who has with him a dog and a cat, explains that his wife withdrew from the Constantinople venture and that the cat will go in her place.

Brisk promises to take the hopeful Macilente to court if Macilente will purchase himself a fitting suit of clothes. Actually, it is Macilente's purpose to discover Brisk's true standing at the court. Fungoso and his tailor, ever in pursuit of the latest fashion, studies Brisk's clothes as the knight talks to his companions. Sogliardo, who desires to have every gentlemanly attainment, retains a braggart down-at-heels rascal, Shift.

The good weather that prevails in the country becomes the despair of Sordido. In desperation, he attempts to hang himself, but he is rescued from that folly by the neighboring farmers, who will save him despite his despicable miserliness. The revelation to him of his evil nature causes him to have a change of heart; he vows to be a kind and generous neighbor henceforward.

Dressing themselves in new clothes, Brisk and Macilente appear at the court, Macilente to observe court life and Brisk's deportment. Macilente marvels at the inane discourse between Brisk and Saviolina, a court lady, and he is amused when Saviolina puts Brisk out of countenance for his abominable habit of smoking.

Fallace, meanwhile, dreams of the virtues of courtier Fastidious Brisk and pays no attention to Deliro's efforts to please her. When Macilente tells them of Brisk's folly at court, Deliro is determined to foreclose on the knight. Fallace, shocked at Macilente's disloyalty and eager to help Brisk, sends Fungoso, whom she gives money to buy himself a new suit, to warn Brisk of her husband's intentions.

Brisk fails to keep an appointment at the notary's, where he is to contribute a hundred pounds to Puntarvolo's venture. Not finding Brisk immediately, Deliro has time to reconsider his plan. He decides not to foreclose on Brisk and he renounces Macilente's friendship because Macilente, he feels, unreasonably urged him to be more realistic in his attitude toward his wife. Sogliardo, meanwhile, is delighted with his man Shift, who pretends to be a former highwayman, but who is, in reality, a shiftless, cowardly indigent. Brisk makes his belated appearance at the notary's, with the explanation that he was detained by ladies of the court. Fungoso, gone to see his tailor, fails in his mission to intercept Brisk.

Puntarvolo prepares for his journey to Constantinople with his dog and cat. Sogliardo, persuaded by Buffone and Brisk that the time finally comes, decides to become a courtier. All of his acquaintances conspire to make a fool of him. Fungoso, dressed in what he thinks is the latest fashion, discovers Brisk to be wearing a new suit and is unhappy.

At the palace foolish old Puntarvolo puts his dog in the care of a surly groom. Macilente privately obtains the dog from the groom and poisons it. Brisk and Puntarvolo tell Saviolina that they are presenting to her an incomparable courtier, Sogliardo, and that this courtier enjoys playing the part of a country boor. Confronted by clownish Sogliardo, Saviolina insists that she can detect the gentleman in him; she is appalled to discover that Sogliardo, who is not aware of the joke, is a rude peasant. When Puntarvolo misses his dog, he accuses Shift of doing away with the animal and threatens to beat the man. Shift, frightened, confesses, to the disenchantment of Sogliardo, that he never had the courage to commit even one of the crimes of which he boasted.

At the Mitre Tavern, Buffone, who cannot endure the follies and affectations of court life, greets his companions. Puntarvolo, dejected by the loss of his dog and the loss of his wager, is teased by Buffone. In a rage, Puntarvolo seals Buffone's lips with sealing wax. When the police arrive, everyone tries to flee. Brisk is seized. Fungoso, hiding under a table, is discovered and held to pay the reckoning for all the company ate and drank.

Macilente, seeing in the situation a chance to rid Deliro and Fallace of their humors, sends Deliro to rescue Fungoso at the tavern and Fallace to the jail to comfort Brisk. Deliro pays the bill at the Mitre Tavern. Fungoso declares that he is through with fashion forever. Macilente then sends Deliro to the jail to obtain Brisk's release, after telling him that by so doing Deliro will be reconciled to his wife. At the jail Deliro, seeing Fallace's interest in Brisk, is suddenly awakened from his misperceptions. Brisk is doomed to serve a term for his debts. Thus the air is cleared and all who were taken with a folly are cured.

Critical Evaluation:

With *Every Man in His Humour* (1598) having been a tremendous success, Ben Jonson—possibly urged on by his fellow investors in the theater—wrote *Every Man out of His Humour* as a companion piece to his earlier play. In this play, produced the following year, Jonson overreaches himself: There are too many characters and the plot seems to ramble pointlessly. One explanation for the comparative weakness of the play lies in the fact that at the time of its composition Jonson was actively engaged in the so-called war of the theaters, a controversy in which rival playwrights employed the stage to satirize each other and to ridicule actors of the rival companies. As a play, *Every Man out of His Humour* is a hodgepodge that manages somehow to work out; as personal satire it no longer holds meaning for the modern audience. Its subject and treatment, however, make it a work of particular interest to historians of literature.

Although intended as a battle in the war of the theaters, particularly as an attack upon Thomas Dekker and John Marston, *Every Man out of His Humour* is more than that.

Jonson's comedy of humors conceived of stage personalities on the basis of a ruling trait or passion, much as Charles Dickens later gave his fictional characters certain dominant traits or characteristics. By placing these typified traits in juxtaposition, the spark of comedy is struck in their conflict and contrast. The result, in *Every Man out of His Humour*, is often funny. Jonson possessed an arrogant, self-righteous personality and he smarted under the satire of his competitors, seeking to get back at them with this play. The satirical picture of contemporary manners, vivid caricatures, and the witty dialogue carry the play beyond any mere personal attacks. *Every Man out of His Humour* not only satirizes individuals but also levels a general attack upon corruptions.

Jonson could not resist lampooning his enemies, and he raised dramatic lampooning to an art. Marston probably was intended as the character Carlo Buffone, that "public, scurrilous, and profane jester." Asper is undoubtedly meant to be a comic idealization of Jonson himself—wholly admirable and just, "an ingenious and free spirit" and "one whom no servile hope of gain or frosty apprehension of danger, can make to be a parasite."

While John Lyly and others were perfecting the filigree of their prose for courtly audiences, another kind of prose was beginning to be heard in the popular theater, a rough-and-tumble language based on the vernacular. Jonson was among the writers adopting a more abrupt, staccato language, truer to life than the oratorical speeches of most of his contemporaries. The speeches of Carlo and some of the other characters in *Every Man out of His Humour* simulate the real language of Jonson's time much more closely than had been done before. Carlo's spiteful disposition is chiefly revealed in his penchant for coining scurrilous likenesses, and he leaps in a single speech from the figure of a starved dog to that of scalding oil and fire to that of gunpowder, all to describe Macilente. His speech rhythms trip, stumble, and flicker back and forth between metaphoric and literal abuse.

The characters in this play remain isolated, blocked off from one another, immobilized in their humors. The plot is a kaleidoscopic series of characteristic poses adopted by the personalities; each individual pursues his or her humor, oblivious of everything else. For example, Fungoso, eyes greedily fastened on Fastidious Brisk's suit, makes half-answers to his uncle, while privately calculating how much it will cost him to duplicate the suit. Sogliardo, at the same time, is too engrossed by the prospect of vulgar pleasures in London to notice Fungoso's inattention. Sordido, scarcely aware of the others, gazes into the sky for signs of rain that will raise the value of his wheat.

Jonson's characters rail at one another in a scorching indictment of folly, but they are not mere mouthpieces for their author. Even during the war of the theaters, Jonson was too much of an artist to use the satiric speeches of his characters merely as clubs. Falling victim to their own imbalance of humors and distempered view of the world, they nevertheless always have their place in a larger design.

Further Reading

Beaurline, L. A. *Jonson and Elizabethan Comedy: Essays in Dramatic Rhetoric.* San Marino, Calif.: Huntington Library, 1978. Analyzes the rhetorical devices Jonson uses to satirize literary pretensions. The intent of *Every Man out of His Humour* is more "corrective" than its predecessors, *Every Man in His Humour*, and its occasional roughness derives from its being an experiment.

Brock, D. Heyward. *A Ben Jonson Companion.* Bloomington: Indiana University Press, 1983. A guide to Jonson's life and works and to the literary milieu in which Jonson flourished. Summarizes his plays, identifies characters in the works and people in Jonson's life, and defines literary terms. Includes bibliography.

Dessen, Alan C. *Jonson's Moral Comedy.* Evanston, Ill.: Northwestern University Press, 1971. Sees Jonson as converting the materials of nondramatic verse satire to the stage in *Every Man out of His Humour*. The characters Macilente and Carlo Buffone replace the satirist of the nondramatic tradition. Dessen maintains that *Every Man out of His Humour* reveals much about Jonson's aims as a satirist.

Donaldson, Ian. *Jonson's Magic Houses: Essays in Interpretation.* New York: Oxford University Press, 1997. Donaldson, a Jonson scholar, provides new interpretations of Jonson's personality, work, and literary legacy.

Enck, John J. *Jonson and the Comic Truth.* Madison: University of Wisconsin Press, 1957. Useful discussion of the background to the theory of humors and an analysis of Jonson's adaptation of it. Identifies Desiderius Erasmus's *Moriæ Encomium* (1511; *The Praise of Folly*, 1549) as a source of inspiration.

Harp, Richard, and Stanley Stewart, eds. *The Cambridge Companion to Ben Jonson.* New York: Cambridge University Press, 2000. Collection of essays about Jonson's life and career, including analyses of his comedies and late plays, a description of London and its theaters during Jonson's lifetime, and an evaluation of his critical heritage.

Loxley, James. *The Complete Critical Guide to Ben Jonson.* New York: Routledge, 2002. An introductory overview of Jonson's life and work, particularly useful for students. Part 1 provides biographical information and places Jonson's life and work within the context of his times; part 2 discusses several works, including *Every Man out of His Humour*; part 3 offers critical analysis of the themes in his plays, the style of his writing, and a comparison of his work to that of William Shakespeare.

McEvoy, Sean. *Ben Jonson, Renaissance Dramatist.* Edinburgh: Edinburgh University Press, 2008. McEvoy analyzes all of Jonson's plays, attributing their greatness to the playwright's commitment to the ideals of humanism during a time of authoritarianism and rampant capitalism in England. *Every Man out of His Humour* is discussed in chapter 2, with other references listed in the index.

Watson, Robert N. *Ben Jonson's Parodic Strategy: Literary Imperialism in the Comedies.* Cambridge, Mass.: Harvard University Press, 1987. Stresses three features of *Every Man out of His Humour*: the indifference to unity in plot and tone, the treatment of literary characters, and the attention to audience attitudes.

Everyman

Author: Unknown
First published: 1508, first extant version
Type of work: Drama
Type of plot: Morality
Time of plot: Indeterminate
Locale: Unnamed

Principal characters:
GOD
DEATH
EVERYMAN
GOOD-DEEDS

The Story:

One day a Messenger appears to announce that in the beginning of life, human beings should look to the ending, for they shall see how all earthly possessions avail little in the final reckoning. Sin may look sweet at first, but in the end it causes the soul to weep in pain.

Then God speaks. All living creatures are unkind to him. They live with no spiritual thought in their worldly possessions. The crucifixion is a lesson they forget. Human beings turn to the seven deadly sins, and every year their state grows worse. Therefore, God decides to have a reckoning, lest humankind become more brutish than the beasts.

At an imperative summons, Death comes to receive his instructions. He is ordered to search out all human beings and tell them that they have to make a pilgrimage to their final reckoning. Death promises to be cruel in his search for everyone who lives outside God's law.

Spying Everyman walking unconcernedly about his business, his mind on fleshly lust and treasure, Death bids him stand still and asks him if he forgot his maker. Death announces that God dispatched him in all haste to warn Everyman. Everyman is to make a long journey, and he is to take with him his full book of accounts. He is to be very careful, for he did many bad deeds and only a few good ones. In Paradise, he will soon be forced to account for his life.

Everyman protests that Death cannot be further from his thoughts. Death, who sets no store by worldly goods or rank, is adamant; whom he summons must obey. Everyman cries in vain for respite. Then he asks if he must go on the long journey alone. Death assures him that he can take any companions who will make the journey with him. Reminding him that his life is only his on loan, Death says he will return very shortly, after allowing Everyman an opportunity to find companions for his journey.

Weeping for his plight and wishing he was never born, Everyman thinks of Fellowship, with whom he spent so many agreeable days in sport and play. Fortunately, he sees Fellowship and speaks to him. Seeing Everyman's sad countenance, Fellowship asks his trouble. Everyman tells him he

is in deep sorrow because he has to make a journey. Fellowship reminds him of their past friendship and vows that he will go anywhere with him, even to Hell. Greatly heartened, Everyman tells him of Death's appearance and his urgent summons. Fellowship thinks of the long trip from which there will be no return and decides against accompanying Everyman. He will go with him in sport and play, he declares, or to seek lusty women, but he definitely refuses to go on that pilgrimage.

Cast down by this setback, Everyman thinks of Kindred. Surely the ties of blood are strong. His Kindred swear that they will help him in any way they can, but when they hear that Everyman has to account for his every deed, good or bad, they know at once the last journey he has in mind. They refuse unanimously to go with him. Everyman appeals directly to his favorite cousin, who says he would go willingly were it not for a cramp in his toe.

Everyman think of turning to Goods. All his life he loved Goods. Goods hears his plea and offers to help him, but when asked to go on the journey to the highest judge of all, Goods promptly refuses. Everyman reminds him that money is supposed to right all wrongs. Goods disagrees with him. Anyway, if Everyman takes Goods with him he will be the worse off for it, for worldly goods are not given, only lent.

Everyman becomes ashamed of having sought unworthy companions. Calling aloud to Good-Deeds, he asks again for help. Good-Deeds answers feebly, for he is lying on the cold ground, bound by sins. Good-Deeds already knows of the projected journey and wants to go along, but he is too weak to stir. Everyman learns that Good-Deeds has a sister, Knowledge, who will stay with him until Good-Deeds can regain strength.

Knowledge promptly offers to go with him and guide him in his great need. Knowledge led him to Confession, who lived in the house of salvation, to ask for strength for Good-Deeds. Confession in pity gives penance to Everyman to shrive his soul. Accepting penance joyfully, Everyman scourges his flesh and afterward Knowledge bequeaths him to his Savior. Thankfully Good-Deeds rises from the ground, delivered from sickness and woe. Declaring himself fit for the journey, Good-Deeds promises to help Everyman count his good works before the judgment throne. With a smile of sympathy, Knowledge tells Everyman to be glad and merry, for Good-Deeds will be his true companion. Knowledge gives a garment to Everyman to wear, a garment of sorrow that will deliver him from pain.

Asking Good-Deeds if his accounts are ready, Everyman prepares to start his pilgrimage. Good-Deeds reminds him that three other companions will go part of the way: Discretion, Strength, and Beauty. Knowledge proposes also the Five Wits, who will be his counselors. After Knowledge calls the new companions together, Everyman, now well fortified, sets out on his last journey.

Knowledge says that their first stop must be to see the priest, who will give Everyman unction and ointment, for priests perform the seven unctions as intermediaries of God. Surely priests are human beings' best hope on earth, in spite of the many weak and venal people who are often invested with Holy Orders.

After receiving the last rites from the priest, Everyman prepares to meet Death. Again he is troubled, however, for one by one his companions leave him. Even Knowledge refuses to go with him into the presence of his maker. Only Good-Deeds stays with Everyman until the end. Thus it is with everyone who must die. Knowledge, Strength, Beauty—all the other companions are a help in the journey, but only Good-Deeds can face Death.

The Angel greets Everyman as an elected spouse of Jesus. Taking him on high, he announces that Everyman is thus exalted by reason of his singular virtue. When Everyman's soul is taken from his body, his reckoning is crystal clear. Thus shall it be with everyone who lives well before the end.

Finally a Doctor appears to remind all human beings that on the last journey, Beauty, Strength, Discretion, and the Five Wits forsake everyone at the end; only Good-Deeds avail at the final judgment.

Critical Evaluation:

The morality play, of which *Everyman* is the best extant example, and the mystery play are the two principal kinds of medieval drama. The mystery play is a dramatic re-creation of a story from the Bible, its aim being the elucidation of the revelation therein. The morality play, by contrast, is an allegorical form, peopled by personified abstractions such as Beauty, Justice, and Fortitude and types such as Everyman, Priest, and King. Here the subject matter is admonitory, particularly concerning death. As Albert Baugh pointed out, it is

difficult to discover precise sources for the subject matter or the dramatic method. There are, however, certain parallels with medieval sermons, which often bolstered moral exhortations with allegorical examples. Indeed, allegory is pervasive in medieval literature, as is, for that matter, concern for a happy death. It is not known, however, how these evolved into the particular form of the morality play.

Few morality plays have survived, and only *Everyman* remained sufficiently well regarded in later times to be dignified with performance. One reason for the unpopularity of the genre is the limitation of dramatic complication resulting from the static nature of the personifications. The characters are of necessity simple, and there is no possibility of change except perhaps in a central protagonist like Everyman. As a result, there can be little psychological insight and little diverse movement that invigorate earlier and later drama.

Like all forms of allegory, the method is essentially intellectual. The active involvement of the spectator is not through emotion so much as it is in the discovery of the meanings of characters and the significance of the configurations in which they are arranged. Allegory engages the mind and *Everyman* succeeds well in representing a complex, highly specific, theological system at the same time that it generates, by juxtaposition and order, sufficient immediacy to give force to the moral exhortation. The structure is elegant and compact. There is no attempt to catalog the deficiencies of Everyman's past life; rather, the play focuses on the poignant hour of death and implies what Everyman is and what he ought to be at that critical moment.

Because of the allegorical method, it is easy to trivialize the significance of the play by reducing it to the identification of the personifications. To do so would be to miss the power of its abstractions and the complex view of life that is represented. A play about the reaction to imminent death, *Everyman* with its configurations of characters implies much about how life should be lived. God initiates the action with the premise that all human beings are to be called to give an account of their actions. As the plot develops, it would perhaps be more accurate to refer to the central character as Anyman, but the use of the name Everyman implies that the experience is not random, not what might happen, but paradigmatic of what will happen and how people ought to respond.

Everyman turns to his valued, habitual companions for comfort on his difficult and dangerous journey, but the play does not present a pageant of specific sins. Instead, Fellowship, Kindred, and Goods are summary abstractions, which are not particular sins in themselves but rather examples of the distractions that divert people away from positive direction toward God and salvation. Thus Everyman's failures are represented not by a static series of vices but by the vital enticements that took too much of his attention. The conception is a Dantescan analysis of sin as a turning away from God.

In the theology of the play, salvation obviously cannot come by faith alone, since it is imperative that Everyman be accompanied to judgment by Good-Deeds. However, Good-Deeds is so infirm because of Everyman's prior misdirection that a prior step is necessary: Everyman is entrusted to Knowledge for guidance. The implication is that knowledge of the institutional Church and its remedies is necessary for the successful living of the good life. Knowledge first directs Everyman to Confession, one of the tangible means of repentance and regeneration. Once Confession takes place, Good-Deeds begins to revive, as contrition and amendment free the accumulated merits of past virtuous actions.

Knowledge also summons other attainments, which can travel at least part way with Everyman. Beauty, Strength, Discretion, and Five Wits are all auxiliary human accomplishments that can help and comfort human beings along their way, though none can persevere to the final moment of judgment. As they fall away, one by one, the play presents the process of death. Beauty is obviously the first to depart in this telescoped version of an individual's demise. Strength follows as life ebbs. The last of the attainments to leave is Five Wits, the sensual means through which human beings acquire whatever understanding they gain in life.

In the end, even Knowledge, the representative of the human intellect, which builds on sense and is a higher power than sense, cannot go the whole distance with Everyman. The respect for Knowledge in the play's implied theological system is enormous: Knowledge plays the pivotal role in informing Everyman of the way to salvation. However, in the final analysis, only Good-Deeds can descend into the grave with Everyman because it is only the efficacious result of knowledge in right living that merits eternal reward.

An examination of the abstractions and their arrangement in *Everyman* reveals the complex shape of medieval Christianity. The play suggests a means to salvation everywhere consistent with the prescriptions of the medieval Church: There is an ultimate accountability, but human beings have the capacity, through faith and reason, to direct themselves toward God by using the institution of the Church, which enables them to do the good required of all.

"Critical Evaluation" by Edward E. Foster

Further Reading

Gilman, Donald, ed. *"Everyman" and Company: Essays on the Theme and Structure of the European Moral Play*. New York: AMS Press, 1988. The essays place the play within a European context, relating it to other medieval morality plays from France, Italy, Spain, Germany, England, and Holland.

Kaula, David. "Time and the Timeless in *Everyman* and *Dr. Faustus*." *College English* 22 (October, 1960): 9-14. Kaula compares the two morality plays and the kinds of time represented in them. In *Everyman*, astronomical time is finally replaced by moral time with its attendant freedom, in which human beings can control their destiny.

King, Pamela. "Morality Plays." In *The Cambridge Companion to Medieval English Theatre*, edited by Richard Beadle and Alan J. Fletcher. 2d ed. New York: Cambridge University Press, 2008. King's examination of morality plays includes a discussion of *Everyman*.

Kinghorn, A. M. *Mediaeval Drama*. London: Evans Brothers, 1968. Examines the plot and themes of the play and its place in the tradition of the morality play.

Kolve, V. A. "*Everyman* and the Parable of the Talents." In *Medieval English Drama: Essays Critical and Contextual*, edited by Jerome Taylor and Alan H. Nelson. Chicago: University of Chicago Press, 1972. Examines the parable as a possible source for the play and includes a close reading of the play and its themes.

Potter, Robert. "The Unity of Medieval Drama: European Contexts for Early English Dramatic Traditions." In *Contexts for Early English Drama*, edited by Marianne G. Briscoe and John C. Coldewey. Bloomington: Indiana University Press, 1989. Examines the relationship between *Everyman* and its Dutch analogues to argue the importance of seeing the larger contexts for early English drama.

Sikorska, Liliana. *In a Manner of Morall Playe: Social Ideologies in English Moralities and Interludes, 1350-1517*. New York: Peter Lang, 2002. Sikorska analyzes the linguistic and ideological content of medieval English morality plays, such as *Everyman*, describing how these plays sought to create a morally sound society.

Van Laan, Thomas F. "*Everyman*: A Structural Analysis." *PMLA* 78, no. 5 (December, 1963): 465-475. Argues that the play's popularity arises from a structure that accentuates its dramatic qualities. In the first half, there is a falling toward damnation; in the second, there is a rising toward God.

Everything Is Illuminated

Author: Jonathan Safran Foer (1977-   )
First published: 2002
Type of work: Novel
Type of plot: Magical Realism
Time of plot: 1791-1969 and 1997-1998
Locale: Odessa, Lvov, Lutsk, and Trachimbrod, Ukraine

Principal characters:

JONATHAN SAFRAN FOER, an American Jew looking for Augustine
ALEXANDER PERCHIV, Foer's Ukranian translator
GRANDFATHER, Alexander's grandfather
SAMMY DAVIS, JUNIOR, JUNIOR, Grandfather's dog
AUGUSTINE, the woman who supposedly saved Jonathan's father
BROD, Jonathan's great-great-great-great-great-grandmother
YANKEL D, foster father of Brod
KOLKER, Brod's husband and Jonathan's great-great-great-great-great-grandfather
SAFRAN, Jonathan's grandfather

The Story:

Jonathan Safran Foer travels to Ukraine to find the woman who may or may not have saved his father from the Nazis in Trachimbrod—his family shtetl, or village. He hires as his personal translator Alexander Perchiv, a young Ukrainian man, to help him in this quest. Alex is accompanied by his grumpy grandfather, who is officially the driver for the trip, and his dog, Sammy Davis, Junior, Junior, whose temper is rather unpredictable.

Alex's father asks him to help the American Jew in his search because doing so will enable the wayward young Ukrainian to earn some money. In addition, Alex is the only one in the family who can be of help because he has been studying English at the university. He speaks a peculiar form of broken English, and his narrative sounds as though it has been pieced together with the help of a thesaurus. Parts of his story represent the letters he sends to Jonathan in America.

At the same time, Jonathan's letters to Alex narrate a quasi-magical history of his family in Trachimbrod. These tales are part of a novel that Jonathan plans to write. They begin with the story of the 1791 drowning of Trachim, Jonathan's great-great-great-great-great-great-grandfather. Trachim's daughter, Brod, is the only one to survive the accident, and the citizens of the shtetl must find a foster family to raise her. The choice is made in a lottery, and Yankel D, who has lost his own wife and children, becomes Brod's foster father.

Armed with a picture of Augustine (the woman who may have saved his father), Jonathan begins his trip with Alex, Grandfather, and Sammy Davis, Junior, Junior, by going to Lvov, where the group spends the first night. From there,

they travel to Lutsk and the area where the shtetl is supposed to be. They ask random people on the way for directions, but nobody has heard of Trachimbrod or Sofiowka, the previous name of the village. In the end, they come across a woman who initially denies knowing anything about Trachimbrod. However, after she sees the picture of Augustine and the suspicious Alex has tortured her with his questioning, the woman eventually breaks into tears, admitting that she knows something about Trachimbrod. The woman invites them for lunch at her house, where they discover a multitude of boxes whose labels indicate that they are full of artifacts and memories from Trachimbrod.

Jonathan and Alex firmly believe that the woman is Augustine, the one they are looking for, although she persistently denies it. As she shows them pictures from the shtetl, it suddenly becomes clear that Alex's grandfather has a connection with the past of Jonathan's family. He appears to have been one of the few who fled Trachimbrod, managing to escape by betraying his best friend. Jonathan, Alex, and Grandfather ask the woman to take them to Trachimbrod. She insists that there is nothing left of the shtetl, but they are convinced only after they go there and see for themselves that the place where Trachnimbrod used to be is nothing but a bare field.

The woman, whom they think of as Augustine, tells them the story of how the Nazis liquidated the shtetl of Jonathan's family. Alex's grandfather listens to her version, occasionally disagreeing with parts of her narrative. Then, the woman tells Jonathan that his grandfather, Safran, was the first boy she ever kissed. Before the group leaves her house, the woman gives Jonathan one of the boxes containing memorabilia from Trachimbrod, as well as a wedding ring that used to belong to one of the shtetl's women, Rivka.

In the past, Brod was the most beautiful girl in the shtetl. By her twelfth birthday, she has already received at least one proposal of marriage from every citizen of the village. However, she does not care for anyone besides her foster father, Yankel, who asks her not to marry before his death. On the day of the most important event in the village, the annual Trachimday festival, many things happen that change Brod's life. She is raped, her father dies, and Kolker makes her agree to marry him. In return, Brod asks Kolker to kill her rapist.

Brod and Kolker live happily for several years until one day Kolker gets into an accident at the mill where he works. A disk-saw blade from the chaff splitter carves vertically right in the middle of his head. The blade does not kill him, but the accident dramatically changes his and Brod's life. Kolker's personality splits in two: The loving husband of Brod now shares the same body with a man overcome by malicious eruptions. Initially, Brod continues to live with her transformed husband, patiently trying to overlook his insults, curses, and beatings. Kolker's state, however, quickly worsens, leaving the couple only one possibility for continuing to live together—separated in different rooms, communicating through a hole in the wall. Their third son is conceived through that hole and is born on the day when Kolker dies. This young boy, who, like his brothers, is named Yankel, will become the great-great-great-great-grandfather of Jonathan Safran Foer.

Jonathan's grandfather, Safran, becomes sexually active in 1924, at the age of ten. He has an affair with a widow whose house he is cleaning on behalf of the Sloucher congregation. The encounter begins a long series of affairs, and he eventually has 132 mistresses, most of them widows for whom he works. He has long-term relationships with several women, including a Gypsy girl, and in 1941 he marries into the richest family in the village. The wedding reception is Trachimbrod's event of the year.

After Jonathan, Alex, and Grandfather leave Augustine, the two Ukrainians convince Jonathan to open the box she has given him, which is labeled "IN CASE." Among other items, they find within a pearl necklace, an old map of the world, a history book of Tranchimbrod, and a photograph of a boy that looks just like Alex. The picture prompts Alex's grandfather to reveal that he lived in the same shtetl at the same time and even knew Jonathan's grandmother. The old man tells him all he knows about her, while Jonathan carefully takes notes that he will use in his future novel.

Critical Evaluation:

Jonathan Safran Foer's debut novel received immediate acclaim in the literary circles after its publication in 2002. Critics applauded its narrative strategy, language, and style. The dual narrative of *Everything Is Illuminated* unfolds in several temporal levels and has two separate narrators. The story is divided by chapters, and the tales of the two narrators are separated into disjointed sections that readers must assemble into a linear sequence. There are two concurrent narrative threads: A Jewish Magical Realist epic, told in high literary English, intertwines with the broken language of Alex's narration. Alex tells the story of Jonathan's trip to Ukraine, while the epic incorporates a series of legends and mythical tales that shape the history of Jonathan's family in Trachimbrod (an invented name for the real village of Trochenbrod). The language of the sections narrated by Alex breaks linguistic conventions, creating a unique and humorous style for the text.

Everything Is Illuminated received recognition from distinguished authors including John Updike, Joyce Carol Oates, Salman Rushdie, and Isabel Allende. The novel's success led to the production of a film adaptation in 2005, directed by Liev Schreiber and starring Elijah Woods and Eugene Hutz.

Critics of *Everything Is Illuminated* place the text within the postmodernist canon. Foer's narrative incorporates some of the main features often associated with postmodern texts: fantastic elements (such as the saw-blade perched in the middle of Kolker's head), the coexistence of multiple worlds (both the eighteenth century and the twentieth century stories have traces of Russian and American reality), and reconciliation of different languages (the mythical and magical language of the Jewish epic combined with the thesaurus-based English of Alex). Some researchers of World War II history have tried to match the places and characters portrayed in *Everything Is Illuminated* with those found in real historical documents, thus effacing the postmodern literary nature of Foer's text. However, reviewers who seek similarities between the historical Holocaust in Ukraine and the events described in the text stumble upon obvious problems regarding the story's authenticity that reestablish the place of the novel in the postmodern literary canon.

A postmodern novel, *Everything Is Illuminated* masterfully combines a realist or a quasi-realist narrative about Jonathan's quest for family roots with a mythical epic story about Trachimbrod's citizens that begins in the eighteenth century. The latter narrative exemplifies features characteristic of Magical Realism, a genre established in the 1960's by Latin American authors such as Gabriel García Márquez. Foer successfully uses motifs and themes associated with archetypal symbolism—the drowning of Trachim as a beginning of the epic serves as a good example—and this symbolism inscribes his text in the aesthetic tradition of the Magical Realists.

The experimental arrangement of the sections of the book disrupts the linear presentation of events—a strategy that facilitates the gradual disclosure of traumas of the past. The events related to the Holocaust, Jonathan's father, and Alex's family slowly become part of a larger picture encompassing individual and collective traumas. A reader's experience of piecing together the story bit by bit into a linear narrative corresponds to the structure of trauma as a disruption of history and temporality.

The characters of Foer's novel are children and grandchildren of Holocaust survivors and perpetrators. They resemble one another in their approaches to memory and post-Holocaust reconciliation. The relationship between the two main characters of the novel, Jonathan and Alex, reflects their different attitudes toward memory—one seeing it as tragic and the other as comic. Alex tries to win Jonathan's friendship throughout the novel in an attempt to reconcile with the past, while, by resisting Alex's friendship, Jonathan refuses to adopt a comical approach to memory and attain full reconciliation with the past.

Elitza Kotzeva

Further Reading

Collado-Rodriguez, Francisco. "Ethics in the Second Degree: Trauma and Dual Narratives in Jonathan Safran Foer's *Everything Is Illuminated.*" *Journal of Modern Literature* 32, no. 1 (Spring, 2009): 54-68. Examines Foer's structural strategies in *Everything Is Illuminated* and the implications they have for an ethical reading of the text.

Feuer, Menachem. "Almost Friends: Post-Holocaust Comedy, Tragedy, and Friendship in Jonathan Safran Foer's *Everything Is Illuminated.*" *Shofar: An Interdisciplinary Journal of Jewish Studies* 25, no. 2 (Winter, 2007): 24-48. Studies the relationship between two grandchildren of Holocaust survivors and perpetrators and how they gain post-Holocaust reconciliation.

Gessen, Keith. "Horror Tour." *New York Review of Books* 52, no. 14 (September 22, 2005): 68-72. Reviews two books by Jonathan Safran Foer–*Everything Is Illuminated* and *Extremely Loud and Incredibly Close.*

Kohn, Robert E. "Foer's *Everything Is Illuminated.*" *Explicator* 65, no. 4 (Summer, 2007): 245-247. Provides an overview of the elements of the novel that classify it as postmodern fiction.

Spies, Marion. "Recent Directions in Holocaust Writing." *Religion and the Arts* 8, no. 2 (June, 2004): 244-259. Reviews several books about Holocaust studies.

The Executioner's Song

Author: Norman Mailer (1923-2007)
First published: 1979
Type of work: New Journalism
Type of plot: Narrative
Time of plot: April, 1976, to January, 1977
Locale: Marion, Illinois; Orem, Salt Lake City, and Provo, Utah

Principal characters:
GARY GILMORE, a career criminal and murderer
BRENDA NICOL, his cousin
RIKKI BAKER, Gary's sometime drinking buddy
NICOLE BAKER, Rikki's sister, who becomes Gary's girlfriend
MONT COURT, Gary's parole officer

The Story:

Long-time felon Gary Gilmore, an intelligent man with artistic talents, a sense of pride, and little common sense, has spent nearly two-thirds of his thirty-five years of life in various penal institutions. He is being released early from the federal maximum-security penitentiary in Marion, Illinois, after a term for robbery in Oregon. He writes his cousin Brenda Nicol, with whom he has maintained a sporadic correspondence since they grew up together, to ask if she would serve as his sponsor once he regains his freedom. Brenda, who is in Utah, agrees.

Soon after Gary arrives in Provo, Utah, he moves in with his aunt and uncle, Vern and Ida Damico. Gary begins working at low pay as a shoe repairman in Vern's shoe store and tries to become acclimated to his freedom. He clumsily dates a few women, plays cards with new acquaintances who quickly take a disliking to him, drops in without warning on area relatives and their families, and often drinks too much. He is a restless loner, is awkward with other people—his quick temper and talk of prison and violence makes others nervous—and has difficulty adjusting to life out of prison.

Gary violates his parole by hitchhiking to Idaho, and he is arrested there for driving without a license and for beating up a man; the charges, however, are dropped. Gary's parole officer, Mont Court, a devout Mormon, does not report Gary to prison authorities in Oregon, where Gary's parole originated. Though he takes a better paying but menial job at a thriving insulation shop, Gary's frustration escalates. He performs acts of vandalism and petty theft, and stays inebriated much of the time. He invites new drinking buddy Rikki Baker to help him rob a bank, but Rikki refuses. Gary becomes more confrontational with those around him, and more out of control.

Despite his antisocial behavior, Gary acquires a car and a beautiful, sexually adventurous young girlfriend, Nicole Baker, Rikki's nineteen-year-old, several-times-married-and-divorced sister. Nicole, her young children Sunny and Jeremy, and Gary move in together. Their relationship becomes uneasy, fraught with tension because of money worries, Nicole's infidelity, and Gary's drinking and emotional instability. Gary obtains a cache of guns through theft and leaves Nicole, who is afraid of him because of his wild mood swings.

Gary trades his Ford Mustang for a pickup truck. One night, with nothing better to do and no real plan in mind, he holds up a gas station in Orem, Utah. Though the attendant cooperates fully, Gary kills him, execution-style. The following night, Gary robs a motel in Provo and murders the front-desk clerk without remorse. Gary is particularly sloppy with the second killing, almost as though he has an unspoken wish to be caught. A passerby witnesses the crime. Gary accidentally shoots himself in the hand while attempting to hide the murder weapon and leaves a bloody trail. He sets himself up for betrayal (by cousin Brenda, who tells the police where to find him), and shortly afterward is captured without incident. He is held in jail and later confined to a psychiatric institution for examination.

Gary reestablishes contact with Nicole, and the two pledge undying love for one another through torrid correspondence and brief face-to-face visits. With no hope for mitigation because he is considered legally sane, Gary is finally put on trial, and with no defense for his crimes, he is quickly convicted and sentenced to death. He stoically accepts the verdict and asks for the sentence to be carried out on schedule.

A media frenzy erupts after Gary insists on being allowed to die without appeal, an action contrary to that of most persons on death row. Several judicial delays follow. Gary is executed by firing squad on January 17, 1977, just two months after the original date of his scheduled demise and only nine months following his parole from the prison in Illinois. Before his execution, he had requested that his corneas and other viable body parts be donated for transplantation; donors are soon found. After a graphically described autopsy, his remains are cremated and scattered in Utah. The survivors return to interrupted lives, sadder but no wiser for their experiences with Gary.

Critical Evaluation:

The Executioner's Song, like all memorable literature, is a good story well told. The plot revolves around a multitude of large issues, matters such as good and evil, sacred and profane, nature versus nurture, acceptance and rejection, and life and death. Characters are complex persons sharply defined by their speech and behavior. Action, particularly in the first half of this "true-life novel," is crisp and clear. Suspense rises to a satisfying conclusion. The implications of the story resonate in the readers' minds long after the book has been finished. Norman Mailer's genius in this best-selling, Pulitzer Prize-winning work lies not in the story itself but in its presentation. Because the story is based on real-life people and events that transpired—and were played out by media—not long before Mailer's book was published, the typical reader knows in advance how the story ends.

Mailer takes advantage of his journalist's eye: He offers small, telling details gleaned from exhaustive research and hours of interviews with many of the principals and dozens of minor figures in the case. Mailer gives information from a nonjudgmental, unobtrusive, omniscient perspective, an unusual position for Mailer, who in one form or another is often a significant presence in his work.

Mailer employs a cinematic approach as a refinement of the reportorial methods of such "nonfiction novels" as Truman Capote's *In Cold Blood* (1966). These novels comprise the genre called New Journalism. In *The Executioner's Song*, Mailer cuts from scene to scene. He zooms in for extreme close-ups or pulls back for long panoramic shots. He uses a multitude of viewpoints and filters everything through his own consciousness. Despite its length (more than one thousand pages), *The Executioner's Song* seldom drags, though it sometimes digresses to the point that the main narrative thrust, that the wages of sin is death, is lost.

Like a modern illustration of Leo Tolstoy's maxim at the beginning of his novel *Anna Karenina* (1875-1877; English translation, 1886)—"every unhappy family is unhappy in its own way"—*The Executioner's Song* provides a realistic and compelling examination of a specific life, showing the twisted path that led inevitably to a particular fate: An extended version of the popular idea of "suicide by cop." Along the way the book demonstrates the mundane nature of evil and the senselessness of murder, especially random murder committed by a relatively ordinary, flawed person who might have succeeded in life under different circumstances.

Gary Gilmore, an intelligent man with hidden talents who never found an appropriate way to put his latent creativity to good use, is a subject worthy of Mailer's study. Gilmore had been a bundle of contradictions, the product of his heredity and upbringing. He was charming and loving one minute and irrational and angry and destructive the next, providing Mailer with the opportunity to touch upon many of the topics that typically drive his fiction: existentialism, sex, relationships, religion, politics, and violence. Furthermore, because Gilmore had been the first convicted person to be executed after a long nationwide moratorium on capital punishment, had been one of the first to demand he be put to death without appeal or delay, and had chosen to die by firing squad, his story is unique in the annals of crime.

The structure of this work is key in understanding Mailer's vision and intent and in appreciating his ability to reduce abstract concepts to their component parts. *The Executioner's Song* is divided almost exactly in half. The first half, "Western Voices," tells Gilmore's story, in his own recreated speeches and in remembered impressions of him, all related in the plain, simple words of the generally down-to-earth, hard-working people who knew or interacted with him. Together, the words offer jigsaw pieces that collectively produce as complete a portrait as possible of someone who is ultimately unknowable. The first part encompasses everything from Gilmore's birth to the murders, trial, conviction, incarceration, and pending execution. "Western Voices" reflects the wide-open, stark landscape of the West. Sentences are straightforward and direct, and there is little embellishment of language. Metaphors, such as the ironic distinction between unlawful murder by firearm as committed by Gilmore and legal murder as carried out by the state, are as broad and sweeping as the bleak terrain.

The latter half of this work, "Eastern Voices," symbolically shows the disruptive, after-the-fact effects of outsiders' interference upon criminal proceedings. Paragraphs seem denser, more crowded, like East Coast metropolitan areas. Sentences grow more complicated, and the vocabulary becomes more formal, less colloquial. While the main characters from the first part of the narration are allowed to speak,

they are almost crowded off the stage by a whole army of newcomers who seem more like parasites than participants and who have agendas unrelated to the idea of justice. The story line, with more threads to follow, becomes fragmented. The language, including excerpts from newspaper reports and verbatim passages from protracted legal arguments that repeatedly traverse the same ground, grows complex. It is difficult for the reader to maintain focus on the crux of the matter: A man has committed two senseless murders, for which he had been judged, and has accepted his punishment without argument. The media attention made Gilmore seem larger-than-life, more heroic and more sympathetic than someone in his position should be.

It is almost a relief when, fifty pages from the end, the execution is finally carried out and the narrative—a masterly if lengthy example of creative journalism that always insists on impartially showing rather than telling—can glide to its poignant conclusion.

Jack Ewing

Further Reading

Algeo, Ann M. *The Courtroom as Forum: Homicide Trials by Dreiser, Wright, Capote, and Mailer*. New York: Peter Lang, 1996. A comparative study of the fictional works of four twentieth century American novelists whose books present actual crimes and punishments while addressing important social issues of the times in which they were written.

Bloom, Harold, ed. *Norman Mailer*. Philadelphia: Chelsea House, 2003. This collection features essays by many of Mailer's most perceptive critics. Includes an informative editor's introduction, bibliographic references, and an index.

Cotkin, George. *Existential America*. Baltimore: Johns Hopkins University Press, 2002. An examination of the European philosophical movement—characterized by a sense of alienation and the absurd—as expressed in the works of such writers as Mailer, Herman Melville, Emily Dickinson, William James, Richard Wright, and Ralph Ellison.

Dearborn, Mary. *Mailer: A Biography*. Boston: Houghton Mifflin, 1999. An astute, full-scale biography that presents penetrating discussion of Mailer's life and work as well as important interviews with his family and friends.

Leeds, Barry H. *The Enduring Vision of Norman Mailer*. Bainbridge Island, Wash.: Pleasure Boat Studio, 2002. This overview focuses on several themes—particularly women, politics, and violence—that run through much of

Mailer's work, showing how such threads bind large ideas to the story lines and give them substance.

Lehtimäki, Markku. *The Poetics of Norman Mailer's Nonfiction: Self-Reflexivity, Literary Form, and the Rhetoric of Narrative.* Tampere, Finland: Tampere University Press, 2005. Originally written as a dissertation, this English-language study explores the literary style and rhetorical techniques found in Mailer's nonfiction works, with particular attention to *The Executioner's Song.*

Lennon, J. Michael. *Critical Essays on Norman Mailer.* Boston: G. K. Hall, 1986. Lennon, Mailer's friend and authorized biographer, presents his essays on the two-time Pulitzer-Prize winner that were first published in *The New Yorker, Paris Review, Playboy,* and other periodicals.

Exiles

Author: James Joyce (1882-1941)
First produced: 1919, in German; 1925, in English; first published, 1918
Type of work: Drama
Type of plot: Naturalism
Time of plot: 1912
Locale: Dublin

Principal characters:
RICHARD ROWAN, an Irish writer
BERTHA, his common-law wife
ARCHIE, their son
ROBERT HAND, a newspaper editor
BEATRICE JUSTICE, Robert's cousin, a music teacher

The Story:

Richard Rowan and Bertha, unmarried lovers, return from Italy with their eight-year-old son Archie to Dublin, where, although physically at home, they are in spiritual exile. The two people most involved in their return are Robert and Beatrice, first cousins once engaged to be married. Robert, however, was always dominated by Richard's ideas and was tenuously in love with Bertha. When he recognized Bertha's love for Richard, he was gradually drawn to Beatrice, who was in love with him. She, too, was always fascinated by Richard and found that, without him, charming but weak Robert became a mere cipher. Finally, her engagement to Robert broke off—a situation from which Beatrice, as she tells Richard, is still in emotional recovery.

Richard thus was a dominant force behind at least three sensitive and intelligent people in their youth. In maturity, his physical passions and his commitment to people still complement his ideals of freedom and integrity. This fact is demonstrated in a conversation with Robert who, while explaining his eagerness to promote Richard's academic career, declares that he finds in Richard the same faith that a disciple has in his master. Richard answers cryptically that his is a master's faith in the disciple who will eventually betray him. In this fashion he is trying to indicate to Robert, who uneasily becomes the editor of a conventional Dublin newspaper, his desire to avoid influencing those he loves while remaining wholly loyal to them.

In somewhat the same fashion Richard desires to be united with Bertha, but not to be bound or to bind, even in love. In Italy, Richard was absorbed in his writing and Bertha was often sad and lonely. She remained devoted to him but understood neither his aesthetic standards nor his ethics. In marked contrast is his relationship with Beatrice. She always understands what he writes and is fascinated by his unique courage. Through his exile they corresponded about his writing, and on his return Beatrice comes to his house to give piano lessons to Archie. Upon renewed contact, Richard finds that there is much in Beatrice's character that he can use in his current novel. This is the most vital bond between them.

Through the perversity of passion Bertha identifies herself with Richard and thus sees his relationship with Beatrice as a love affair. Her concern causes her to crystallize her feeling of loss toward him, and she turns to Robert, whom she always liked because he, too, looks up to Richard. She subsequently explores Robert's feelings for her and for a time passively accepts his wooing. Once, when Robert visits the house, he brings Bertha roses, a gesture of courtship that confuses and moves her. At that meeting they kiss, and Bertha agrees that they must meet somewhere alone and talk together freely. She half promises to meet Robert at his house that evening.

When Richard questions Bertha about Robert, she answers willingly. At that time he is distressed neither by her involvement nor by Robert's love for her, but he is angered to learn that she is to meet Robert at the same hour as he, at Robert's arrangement, is to meet the vice chancellor of the university, where Richard is being considered for the chair of romance literature. He feels that this plan is a betrayal of everything that each of them stands for and that Robert is both a fool and a thief. Richard decides to see Robert himself. His intention infuriates Bertha, who feels that he will simply rob her of their friend's love and respect.

Having expected Bertha, Robert is discountenanced by Richard's arrival, but when Richard explains why he came, Robert is most eager to talk to him. While they talk, Richard reveals his own fears and doubts. He feels that by refusing to advise Bertha or to ask anything of her he neglected her, as she accused him. The conflict between personal integrity and love for another person is very real to Richard; he realizes that it is an inevitable one, yet he feels that his guilt destroyed Bertha's innocence. He expresses to Robert his willingness to let her go if Robert feels that she will find fulfillment with him. Faced with this need to accept moral responsibility, Robert falters. Richard fears that he will ultimately desert Bertha as he did other women in the past.

Richard admits that he desires some kind of betrayal that will enable him to redeem, through the rebuilding of his soul, his guilt and shame. In answer Robert wildly suggests a duel, but it would be a duel between the ghost of fidelity on one side, of friendship on the other. Richard declares wearily that such was the language of his youth, expressing emotions of which he is no longer capable. Completely disoriented by Richard's rejection of his heroic pose, and distracted by his emotions, Robert flees when Bertha arrives.

The talk between Richard and Bertha in Robert's cottage leads to a partial resolution of their conflict. Bertha is overwhelmed by Richard's apparent lack of faith in her, while he is angry that she is using Robert's love without herself loving him. For the last time she begs Richard to guide her; he merely repeats his statement of faith in her and leaves the house. When Robert returns, Bertha is uneasy with him and maintains against all persuasion that she can never betray Richard.

Surviving her crisis with Robert, Bertha is repossessed by the problem of Beatrice and Richard. After a sleepless night she tells Richard that she wishes she could meet her lover freely. Only later in conversation with Robert, who plans to leave Ireland, does Richard realize what Bertha means, that she wishes she could freely revive her former relationship with him. Out of this desire she is able to accept Richard's account of his relationship with Beatrice. Thus they arrive at a point at which they can stay together while continuing to live as independent individuals, self-exiled from the passions and the romantic notions of their youth.

Critical Evaluation:

James Joyce's themes include Irish mores, art, sexuality, and aesthetic integrity. Within this pattern *Exiles* can be considered a part of the continuing development of his genius. The play's importance lies in the fact that it is Joyce's last portrait of the artist. *Exiles* marks a turning point in Joyce's career.

Exiles is also generally regarded as Joyce's least successful work. It never managed to succeed on the stage, and it attracted little critical or popular support. Critics found the play to be inert and dramatically static. One of the problems is the overly diagrammatic portrayal of the characters. Each of them clearly represents an intellectual position, and they are pitted against each other until they come to dramatically unsatisfying resolution.

Joyce described the dramatic form to be the highest to which the artist can aspire. It is to be achieved after passing through the lesser stages of lyric and epic. Joyce, however, does not seem at home in this form; it lacks the narrative voice that he uses with such effect in his fictional works. Without that voice, readers are left with the dogmatic and undramatic dialogue of Richard Rowan and other characters.

The play does have a model, however; it is a version of a problem play by Henrik Ibsen, who was Joyce's earliest master. The play investigates the difficulty of having a relationship between man and woman while preserving the freedom of each. The protagonist, Richard, does not wish to abrogate the freedom of his wife, Bertha. He insists that she be free to accept an invitation to an assignation, even free to have an affair with one of his former friends. Indeed, Richard seems to feel that this betrayal is desirable. As Stephen Dedalus claims in *Ulysses* (1922): "There can be no reconciliation without a sundering." Thus betrayal is a prelude to a reconciliation and a deeper and closer relationship.

The characters are clearly symbolic; Richard and Beatrice represent the spiritual, and Robert and Bertha represent the physical or material. Richard was close to Beatrice for years, and their union becomes closer; she will become the inspiration for his art as Beatrice was for Dante Alighieri. Robert tries to instigate a love affair with Bertha. Joyce sees the necessity of contraries coming together for a true relationship. The union of Richard and Beatrice would be sterile and that of Robert and Bertha debased. The play ends with Richard's victory in Bertha's affirmation of her love for him; however, he has doubts about her fidelity, a "wound" that debilitates him. These doubts, like the betrayal, paradoxically enhance rather than diminish the relationship, as Joyce's own doubts about the fidelity of his wife, Nora Barnacle, increased his passion for her.

The play also has an important design in its imagery. Joyce uses images of water, stone, and roses to define the characters' nature. Robert and Bertha are closely associated with water. When Robert meets Bertha at the cottage, he is drenched in the rain, and Bertha spends time swimming in the nearby sea. This image would seem to be a positive one. It is the hydrophobe Richard, however, who seems to have the better of it. He does not sink "like a stone" in water as Robert does but rises up, as Joyce suggests in the notes to the play. The "stone" in the play is brought in by Bertha and admired by Robert. They both are closely connected to the lower elements, while Richard is associated with the soaring aspiration of the artist. The "roses" that Robert brings for Bertha are "blown" and corrupted, which identifies both of them with the corruptions of the flesh. Robert is a debased sensualist with no spiritual sense at all.

Freedom is clearly one of the most important thematic elements in the play. Individual freedom, even in marriage, is insisted upon by Richard for Bertha. Bertha seems quite willing to do without that freedom and to re-create her earlier surrender to Richard. Another aspect of freedom is, of course, the freedom of the artist. It is the essential state for any meaningful creation. Stephen Dedalus speaks of flying over the "nets" hindering his freedom to create, and Richard refuses to be tied down to a conventional position of professor that the tempter Robert is offering. In the play, however, what the audience sees is Richard's freedom from things, not his freedom to do anything such as to love or to create. It seems more of a negative virtue, a refusal. The audience hears of Richard's book, and he is constantly writing something offstage. However, the nature of that work and his status as a creator are unclear.

Another theme is that of exile. Joyce defined himself as an exile, and that condition gave him the perspective to analyze the Ireland that he left behind. Richard returns from exile—as Joyce did in 1912—but it is uncertain if he will settle in Dublin. Robert writes a newspaper article on Richard that describes him as an exile who left Ireland "in her time of need" and now comes back to reap rewards. If Richard remains in Dublin he will become a character similar to Gabriel Conroy in "The Dead," a short story in *Dubliners* (1914) that describes a similar situation. Conroy is a fussy and sterile professor who learns about an earlier love of his wife, Gretta. This revelation destroys him; he cannot build upon the "betrayal" as Richard apparently can. Both characters suffer from the paralysis of Dublin.

Although the play did not meet with much critical approval, it does have some interesting connections to Joyce's other works. There are parallels between the play and "A

Painful Case," another story in *Dubliners*. Stephen Dedalus, who appears in *A Portrait of the Artist as a Young Man* (1914-1915) and *Ulysses*, is an exile and a character who insists on his freedom from family, church, and state. He sees it as the necessary condition for the artist. Leopold Bloom, in *Ulysses*, has an unfaithful wife whose infidelity may lead to a reconciliation and resumption of their sexual relationship. He shares some of the masochistic pleasures in betrayal that Richard does. *Exiles* has, therefore, an important place in the canon of Joyce's works.

"Critical Evaluation" by James Sullivan

Further Reading

Bowen, Zack R., and James F. Carens, eds. *A Companion to Joyce Studies*. Westport, Conn.: Greenwood Press, 1984. Devotes an essay to *Exiles*. Includes a textual history.

Brown, Richard, ed. *A Companion to James Joyce*. Malden, Mass.: Blackwell, 2008. Collection of essays, many of which focus on the worldwide influence of Joyce's work, with specific analyses of his impact on the literature of Ireland, Germany, Japan, India, New Zealand, and France. The influence of Joyce's drama is explored in Mark Taylor-Batty's essay "Joyce's Bridge to Late Twentieth Century British Theater: Harold Pinter's Dialogue with *Exiles*."

Bulson, Eric. *The Cambridge Introduction to James Joyce*. New York: Cambridge University Press, 2006. Introductory overview of Joyce's life and work, placing them within the context of Joyce as a modernist, journalist, translator, lecturer, and lover. Chapter 3 analyzes five of Joyce's works, including *Exiles*, while chapter 4 chronicles his works' critical reception from 1914 through 2005.

Deming, Robert H., ed. *James Joyce: The Critical Heritage*. 2 vols. London: Routledge & Kegan Paul, 1970. Volume 1 contains reviews of *Exiles* by such writers as George Bernard Shaw and Padraic Colum. Useful for tracing the beginnings of critical opinion on the play.

Ellmann, Richard. *James Joyce*. 1959. Rev. ed. New York: Oxford University Press, 1982. Contains references to *Exiles* throughout. Annotations and biographical information provide background on Joyce's artistic intentions in *Exiles*.

Tysdahl, B. J. *Joyce and Ibsen: A Study in Literary Influence*. Atlantic Highlands, N.J.: Humanities Press, 1968. Tysdahl argues that Joyce's well-known debt to Henrik Ibsen can mislead readers into reading *Exiles* as entirely a work of Ibsenesque realism.

Exodus

Author: Leon Uris (1924-2003)
First published: 1958
Type of work: Novel
Type of plot: Historical
Time of plot: 1946-1948
Locale: Cyprus and Israel

Principal characters:
ARI BEN CANAAN, Israeli independence leader
BARAK BEN CANAAN, father of Ari
AKIVA, Barak's brother
KATHERINE "KITTY" FREEMONT, an American nurse
DOV LANDAU, a Holocaust survivor and member of the Maccabees
KAREN HANSEN CLEMENT, a Holocaust survivor
MARK PARKER, an American journalist
BILL FRY, a Jewish American sea captain
TAHA, an Arab brought up with Ari

The Story:

It is 1946, and World War II is over. Throughout Europe, Jewish refugees from the Nazi death camps are trying to get to Palestine. The British have blockaded Palestine and interned many of the refugees in camps on Cyprus, where many of them continue to make plans in hopes of reaching Palestine. Ari Ben Canaan works for Mossad Aliyah Bet, the Organization for Illegal Immigration; he has a plan to lead an escape of three hundred Jewish children on a ship renamed *Exodus*. Ari convinces Kitty Freemont, a slightly anti-Semitic American nurse, and Mark Porter, an American journalist, to help with his plan.

During the war, Kitty's husband was killed, and her only child died shortly afterward. At first, Kitty is very determined not to help Ari. She tours the refugee camps and meets Karen Clement, a young refugee from Germany who spent the war years hidden as a Christian with a Danish family named Hansen. While in Denmark, she adopted Hansen as her last name, and she has kept it as her middle name. Through her interaction with Karen and especially through hearing the story of Karen's survival, Kitty learns to love Karen and decides to adopt her. She begins to overcome her anti-Semitism and starts working with Ari, who leads the successful escape. When the children are onboard *Exodus*, however, the British will not let them sail. The children go on a hunger strike. When the strike fails to convince the British to let them sail, the people onboard *Exodus* announce that ten volunteers will commit suicide daily until the ship is permitted to leave port. Thanks mainly to articles Mark publishes in American newspapers, world opinion forces the British to allow the ship to sail. Ari and Kitty sail with the children. The people on the ship recall events from their past that exemplify the history of the Middle East and of European Jewry.

In the early twentieth century, Jossi and Yakov Rabinsky walk from Western Russia to Palestine, witnessing and recalling generations of Russian anti-Semitism, including pogroms (organized riots, usually directed against Jews) in which whole Jewish populations are massacred. When they reach Palestine, Jossi changes his name to Barak Ben Canaan. He becomes the father of Ari. Barak works with the Haganah, a Jewish paramilitary organization that later becomes part of the Israeli Defense Forces. Yakov changes his name to Akiva. He helps form the Maccabees, a group intent on extracting vengeance from the English for all atrocities they have committed. The two brothers become estranged.

Just as Germany begins to persecute the Jews before World War II, the British produce a white paper that ends Jewish migration to Palestine. Even though Palestinian Jewish forces fight for Britain in World War II and many Arab nations side with the Nazis, after the war, the British side with the Arabs in Palestine because of the Arab nations' oil and refuse to allow Jews to leave Europe and come to Palestine. In response, the Maccabees blow up the King David Hotel in Jerusalem, where the British have their headquarters. The *Exodus* arrives in Palestine on the second day of Hanukkah, a holiday that celebrates, among other things, the Maccabbees' winning independence from King Antiochus and his successor and the establishment of Judea.

Ari loves a fellow Haganah soldier, Dafna, who is raped and killed by Arabs when she is seventeen. As Ari shows Kitty through Palestine, he finds himself drawn to her, and she is drawn to him. As British rule of Palestine becomes more brutal, the Maccabees and the Haganah, with whom Ari sides, work together to attack the British. Ari's Uncle Akiva and Dov Landau, a young survivor of the Warsaw Ghetto and the Auschwitz concentration camp whom Ari got into Palestine on the *Exodus*, work for the Maccabees. The British capture them and try them in secret. When Ari's father asks Ari to free the prisoners, Ari leads a successful attack on the prison, but during the escape Akiva is killed and Ari is badly wounded. He goes to a Druse village, where Kitty helps him recover. The Druse are a group of Middle Eastern Muslims, many of whom support Israeli independence. Kitty and Ari fall in love, but Kitty says that she will not endure Ari's determination to fight for his people first and love her second.

The United Nations votes to partition Palestine into Jewish and Arab homelands, but the Arab nations refuse to accept the partitioning, wanting to take the whole of Palestine for themselves. Neither the British nor the United Nations do anything to stop Arab riots and Arab killing of Jews. When the British withdraw from Palestine, they leave the Arabs in control of most of the strategic parts of the land. A war breaks out between Israel and the Arabs, a war that the Israelis eventually win. After the successful War for Israeli Independence, Barak dies and is buried next to Akiva. Karen is killed by the Arabs. Kitty realizes that she loves Ari enough to remain with him even though she knows that, for him, Israel will come first. Immigrants continue to come to Israel from Europe and from Arab nations.

The main surviving characters of the story meet in Jerusalem. They celebrate Passover, a holiday that involves retelling the story of the biblical book of Exodus, which recounts the Jews' liberation from bondage in Egypt.

Critical Evaluation:

Leon Uris performed extensive background research when writing all of his historical novels, and *Exodus* is no exception. He traveled all over Israel, covering about 12,000 miles, interviewed more than a thousand people, and read about three hundred books in preparation for writing the novel.

Exodus became a very popular work, selling great numbers of copies year after year. It was translated into dozens of languages, and although it was banned in the Soviet Union, it enjoyed great underground popularity there. Some early reviewers praised the work. Others called it a fabric of oversimplifications full of stereotypes. It has even been labeled a melodrama—that is, an unrealistic work with no ambiguity and no depth of characterization, in which the world is divided between characters who are exaggeratedly good and those who are exaggeratedly evil. Many critics especially criticize what they see as Uris's portrayal of Israelis as good and Arabs as bad.

For all of its oversimplifications, *Exodus* rejects the idea that Jews are the only ones who can be depended on to help the Jews. Uris writes of non-Jews from America, France, and Cyprus helping the Jews in their successful attempt to estab-

lish a Jewish state. He also recognizes the contribution of many of the Druse in helping the Israelis. Early in the book, Ari repeatedly says that Americans have consciences, so it is not surprising that he asks Americans for help. Mark Parker is instrumental in gaining British permission for *Exodus* to sail, and Kitty helps the Jews throughout the book, in spite of her early anti-Semitic belief that all Jews are arrogant and aggressive like the Jewish doctors she worked with in America and in spite of the discomfort she initially feels in the presence of Jews. Kitty is a dynamic character who changes markedly over the course of the book.

In *Exodus*, Uris tries to create a novel of epic scope incorporating the history of the Jews and focusing on the founding of the state of Israel. His title indicates one of the main organizing principles of the book. Uris explicitly bases his story on the book of Exodus's narrative of the escape of the Hebrews from bondage in Egypt and their travel to the Holy Land, where they established Israel. In Uris's tale, Europe under Nazi rule and later Cyprus under British rule become Egypt, and the Jews escape to form the modern state of Israel. The fact that the name of the ship on which the children escape is itself *Exodus* is highly symbolic.

Uris's central characters are larger than life. Barak and Ari are giants of men. Many of Uris's novels contain male characters of this sort. They are morally upright, handsome, clever, intelligent, large heroes who accomplish things other people cannot. In most of his works, these heroes are Jewish.

Bill Fry captains the first boat that takes Karen to Israel. The British catch Bill and Karen, and Karen is sent to Cyprus. When Karen asks Bill why he helps the Haganah, he asserts that he wants to help counter the stereotype that all Jews are cowards. He says that he works for the Palmach, the army of the Haganah, because they present the world with a picture of Jews who are courageous fighters. Here, Fry arguably speaks for Uris himself. However, Uris works in the tradition of another stereotype of Jews in American literature, that of the tough Jew or Jewish athlete. This stereotype is based in part on historic figures like the boxer Slapsie Maxie Rosenbloom and the baseball player Hank Greenberg. It also incorporates such fictional characters as Robert Cohn, the Jewish boxer portrayed in Ernest Hemingway's *The Sun Also Rises* (1926), and the gangsters portrayed in Michael Gold's *Jews Without Money* (1930) and Daniel Fuchs's *Summer in Williamsburg* (1934). These are large, brave, virile men with tremendous physical and emotional energy.

In 1960, Uris's best-selling novel was adapted into a very successful film starring Paul Newman and Eva Marie Saint. Uris was dissatisfied with the film because, among other things, he felt that it was less Zionist than the book. The film presents the British and Arabs in a more favorable light than the book does, even omitting some of the Arab and British atrocities that Uris treats. It conveys the idea that the conflicts between the British and Arabs on one hand and the Jews on the other hand were purely political, and it seems to emphasize a message of peace, especially when it ends, not with a Passover Seder but instead with Ari's Arab childhood friend Taha and Karen Clement being buried together.

Richard Tuerk

Further Reading

Breines, Paul. *Tough Jews: Political Fantasies and the Moral Dilemma of American Jewry.* New York: Basic Books, 1990. Sees Ari Ben Canaan as a forerunner of other "tough Jews" in American literature.

Cain, Kathleen Shine. *Leon Uris: A Critical Companion.* Westport, Conn.: Greenwood Press, 1998. A book-length study of Uris. Chapter 5 treats *Exodus* at length, examining its plot, characters, and themes and ending with a Marxist reading of the book.

Furman, Andrew. *Israel Through the Jewish-American Imagination: A Survey of Jewish-American Literature on Israel, 1928-1995.* Albany: State University of New York Press, 1997. Chapter 3, "Embattled Uris: A Look Back at *Exodus*," examines Uris's book at length, looking especially at the controversies involving the book's use of stereotypes.

Gonshak, Henry. "'Rambowitz' Versus the 'Schlemiel' in Leon Uris's *Exodus*." *Journal of American Culture* 22, no. 1 (1999): 9-16. Compares the figure of the larger-than-life Jewish action hero reminiscent of Jewish versions of Sylvester Stallone's Rambo film character with the weak and cowardly Jewish stereotype of the schlemiel. Gonshak treats his own ambivalence concerning the tough Jew of the sort Uris creates.

Lehmann-Haupt, Christopher. "Leon Uris, 78, Dies; Wrote Sweeping Novels Like *Exodus*." *The New York Times*, June 25, 2003. An obituary that includes a summary of Uris's life and works. Reviews the research that went into the writing of *Exodus*.

Uris, Leon. *"Exodus" Revisited.* Photography by Dimitrios Harissiadis. New York: Doubleday, 1960. A photographic treatment of Israel based on many of the events and places portrayed in *Exodus*.

Weissbrod, Rachel. "*Exodus* as a Zionist Melodrama." *Israel Studies* 4 (1999): 129-152. Treats both Uris's book and the movie based on it as melodramas.

The Expedition of Humphry Clinker

Author: Tobias Smollett (1721-1771)
First published: 1771
Type of work: Novel
Type of plot: Satire
Time of plot: Mid-eighteenth century
Locale: England, Scotland, and Wales

Principal characters:
MATTHEW BRAMBLE, a Welsh squire
MISS TABITHA BRAMBLE, his sister
LYDIA MELFORD, his niece
JERRY MELFORD, his nephew
WINIFRED JENKINS, a maid
HUMPHRY CLINKER, a servant, discovered to be
    Mr. Bramble's natural son
LIEUTENANT OBADIAH LISMAHAGO, an adventurer and
    sportsman
MR. DENNISON, a country gentleman
GEORGE DENNISON, his son and an actor known as Wilson

The Story:

Squire Matthew Bramble, who owns large estates in Wales, is an eccentric and skeptical gentleman. With him lives his sister, Miss Tabitha Bramble, a middle-aged woman with matrimonial hopes that exceed probability. Painfully afflicted with gout, the squire sets out for Bath, England, to try the waters, but he has few hopes of their healing properties. His sister goes with him, as does her servant, Winifred Jenkins, the squire's manservant, and, at the last minute, his orphaned niece and nephew, Lydia and Jerry Melford.

The young Melfords are Squire Bramble's wards. Lydia

has been in boarding school, where she unfortunately fell in love with an actor named George Wilson, a circumstance Squire Bramble hopes she will soon forget among the bright and fashionable gatherings at Bath. Her brother, who just finished his studies at Oxford, hopes to fight a duel with the actor, but no opportunity to defend his sister's honor yet presents itself to his satisfaction.

On the way to Bath, George Wilson makes his way into Squire Bramble's lodgings on the pretext of being a Jewish peddler selling glasses. When in a whisper he makes himself known to Lydia, she orders Winifred Jenkins to follow him and talk with him. The maid comes back in a great flurry. The actor told her that Wilson is not his real name, that he is a gentleman, and that he intends to sue for Lydia's hand in his proper character. In her excitement, however, the maid forgets Wilson's real name. There is nothing for poor Lydia to do but to conjecture and to daydream as the party continues on toward Bath.

Arriving at Bath without further incident, the party enters the festivities there with various degrees of pleasure. Tabitha tries to get proposals of marriage out of every eligible man she meets. The Squire becomes disgusted with the supposed curative powers of the waters that are drunk and bathed in by people with all sorts of infirmities trying to regain their health. Lydia is still pining for Wilson, and Jerry enjoys the absurdity of the social gatherings. Hoping to raise his niece's spirits, Squire Bramble decides to go on to London.

They travel only a short distance toward London when the coach overturns. In the excitement, Miss Tabitha's lapdog bites the Squire's servant. Miss Tabitha makes such loud complaint when the servant kicks her dog in return that the Squire is forced to discharge the man on the spot. He also needs another postilion, since Miss Tabitha declares herself unwilling to drive another foot behind the clumsy fellow who overturned the coach. The Squire hires a ragged country fellow named Humphry Clinker to take the place of the unfortunate postilion, and the party goes on to the next village.

Miss Tabitha is shocked by what she calls Humphry's nakedness, for he wears no shirt. The maid adds to the chorus of outraged modesty. Yielding to these female clamors, the Squire asks about Humphry's circumstances, listens to the story of his life, gruffly reads him a lecture on the crimes of poverty and sickness, and gives him a guinea for a new suit of clothes. In gratitude, Humphry refuses to be parted from his new benefactor and goes on with the party to London.

In London, they are well entertained by a visit to Vauxhall Gardens as well as by several public and private parties. Squire Bramble is disconcerted to learn that Humphry is a preacher by inclination and that he is giving sermons in the manner of the Methodists. Miss Tabitha and her maid are already among Humphry's followers. The Squire attempts to stop what he considers either hypocrisy or madness on Humphry's part. Miss Tabitha, disgusted with her brother's action, begs him to allow Humphry to continue his sermons.

The family is shocked to learn one day that Humphry was arrested as a highway robber and is in jail. When the Squire arrives to investigate the case, he discovers that Humphry is obviously innocent of the charge against him; he learns that the charge was placed by a former convict who makes money by turning in criminals to the government. Humphry makes a fine impression on the jailer and his family, and he converts several of his fellow prisoners. The Squire finds the man who supposedly was robbed and gets him to testify that Humphry is not the man who committed the robbery. In the meantime, Humphry preaches so eloquently that he keeps the prison taproom empty of customers. No sooner does this become evident than he is hurriedly released. Squire Bramble promises to allow him to preach his sermons unmolested.

Leaving London, the travelers continue north, stopping in Scarborough, where they go bathing. Squire Bramble undresses in a little cart that can be rolled down into the sea, so that he is able to bathe nude with the greatest propriety. When he enters the water, he finds it much colder than he expected and gives several shouts as he swims away. Hearing these calls from the Squire, Humphry thinks his good master is drowning and rushes fully clothed into the sea to rescue him. He pulls the Squire to shore, almost twists off his master's ear, and leaves the modest man shamefaced and naked in full view upon the beach. Humphry is forgiven, however, because he meant well.

At an inn in Durham, the travelers make the acquaintance of Lieutenant Lismahago, who seems somewhat like Don Quixote. The Lieutenant, regaling the company with tales of his adventures among the Indians of North America, captures the heart of Miss Tabitha. Squire Bramble is also charmed with the conversation of the crusty retired soldier and makes plans to meet him later on in their journey. The group, especially Winifred, become more and more fond of Humphry as time goes on. After a short and frivolous flirtation with Jerry's part-time valet, she settles down to win Humphry as a husband.

The trip continues through Scotland. In Edinburgh, Lydia faints when she sees a man who looks like Wilson, which shows her uncle that she did not yet forget her actor. After visiting several parts of Scotland and enjoying the most gracious hospitality everywhere, the party continues by coach back to England. Lieutenant Lismahago rejoins the party, and Miss Tabitha renews her designs on him.

Just outside Dumfries, the coach overturns in the middle of a stream. Jerry and Lismahago succeed in getting the women out of the water and Humphry stages a heroic rescue of the Squire, who is caught in the bottom of the coach. They find lodgings at a nearby inn until the coach can be repaired. While all are gathered in the parlor of a tavern, Squire Bramble is accosted by an old college friend named Dennison, a successful farmer of that county. Mr. Dennison knows the Squire only as Matthew Lloyd, a name he took for a while to fulfill the terms of a will. When Humphry hears his master called Lloyd, he rushes up in a flutter of excitement and presents the Squire with certain papers he always carries with him. These papers prove that Humphry is the Squire's natural son. Squire Bramble graciously welcomes his offspring and presents him to the rest of his family. Humphry is overcome with pleasure and shyness. Winifred is afraid that his parentage will spoil her matrimonial plans, but Humphry continues to be the mild religious man he was before.

The Squire also learns that the actor who calls himself Wilson is really Dennison's son, a fine, proper young man who ran away from school and became an actor only to escape a marriage his father planned for him. He tells his father about his love for Lydia, but Dennison does not realize that the Mr. Bramble mentioned as her uncle is his old friend Matthew Lloyd. The two young lovers are reunited.

Lieutenant Lismahago asks for Miss Tabitha's hand in marriage, and both the Squire and Miss Tabitha eagerly accept his offer. The whole party goes to stay at Mr. Dennison's house while preparations are underway for the marriage of Lydia and George. The coming marriages prompt Humphry to ask Winifred for her hand, and she, too, says yes. The three weddings are planned for the same day.

George and Lydia are an attractive couple. The Lieutenant and Tabitha seem to be more pleasant than ever before. Humphry and Winifred both thank God for the pleasures he sees fit to give them. The Squire plans to return home to the tranquillity of Brambleton Hall and the friendship of his invaluable doctor there.

Critical Evaluation:

The Expedition of Humphry Clinker has often been called the greatest of the epistolary novels, a genre very popular during this time, and an outstanding example of English humor. The novel is also considered by many critics to be the best of Tobias Smollett's works. First published in the year of the author's death, the lively novel was written while Smollett, like his character Matthew Bramble, was in retirement and seeking help for his failing health. Despite the novel's artful treatment of the effect of an individual's health on character and mentality, *The Expedition of Humphry Clinker* caters delightfully to the tastes of its eighteenth century audience. Eighteenth century readers thrived on novels of the exotic, and Smollett focuses primarily on travel, distant societies, and manners. At the same time, however, he lends that same exotic excitement to the travels of Bramble and his party through England, Scotland, and Wales. Smollett combines his audience's thirst for the remote with their increasing desire to learn more about history and social structure, particularly their own.

The structure of *The Expedition of Humphry Clinker* is at first glance deceptively simple. As an epistolary novel, it lends itself readily to a straightforward, chronological structure. Dates and locations are given with every letter; even directions are given about where the author will be to receive an answer by return mail. Nevertheless, it is not the passing of time that is important: Nothing really changes over time; no one's opinions change; Lydia continues to love Wilson; Jerry continues to despise him; Tabitha continues to hope for masculine attention; Clinker continues to devote himself to a humble way of life; and Matthew Bramble continues to reaffirm his sense of distinct social divisions. Instead, action is of prime importance. Although the conclusion of the novel seems to imply a tremendous change of orientation toward life, this is deceptive. The social structure had been tampered with by chance, but now it has been rectified and all continue to love and despise as before; only the outer semblance of the objects has changed in having been returned to what it should have been in the first place.

The novel also has picaresque aspects in being episodic and treating various levels of society, but the reader is led to ask, who is the picaro? He is not the titular hero, who actually appears long after the novel is under way. It is Bramble, a type of picaro who appeared often in the eighteenth century. He is neither a criminal with loose morals nor a sympathetic antihero but rather a reflection of the author himself. In his character of Bramble, Smollett is a moralizer, which allows Smollett to unify the novel through humor. Beyond that, however, Smollett-Bramble is that special kind of moralizer, an idealist. According to Bramble's view of humanity, society is to be separated into strict social classes that give society order; with order, humans are essentially safe from the many bothersome problems that would otherwise prevent them from pursuing the style of life to which they feel entitled. Such is the latent subject of the majority of Bramble's letters to his dear Dr. Lewis; but the ironic and humorous vehicle for the moralistic treatises is the description of his encounters with the odd assortment of "originals." While these figures for the most part concur with Bramble's views on society, socially they are not what they seem. Sons of refined blood appear to be lowly; people of adequate means satisfy the richest of tastes; worthy gentlemen are treated ill by life and reduced to impoverished, nearly inescapable circumstances. Most of Bramble's acquaintances are eccentrics and thus "humorous" in the true sense of the word. Each has a master passion that he fervently pursues, often to the point of ludicrousness. Bramble, in his effort to comprehend them magnanimously, creates an equally humorous effect—his endearing desire to help everybody is obviously his own master passion—and the conflict between his head and his heart is never resolved.

In *The Expedition of Humphry Clinker*, humor eventually leads to satire. Smollett is at least partially successful here, though he tends to direct his satire against personal enemies with allusions too obscure to be easily appreciated, One device by which he executes satire more accessibly is by setting up opposites—town versus country, for example, or commoner versus gentleman—where one at first appears clearly preferable to the other. The reader soon sees, however, that Smollett does not present logical alternatives when opposites are in conflict. By their actions and their verbalized reactions, the characters seem to hold common views on propriety, but when the reader tries to reconstruct what these views are, the result is elusive. Although readers know that propriety depends on good favor, a good name, and money, Smollett refuses to spell out what it is these commodities then bring.

The success of *The Expedition of Humphry Clinker* is based on Smollett's reaffirmation of the genuine emotional response. Bramble is presented as someone with sensitivity toward his physical and social surroundings and experiences. He is tempted, for example, to believe that Scotland as he sees it during his trip could provide that ideal way of life he has been searching for and proselytizing; he senses, however, that modernization threatens Scotland with the same laziness and complacency that are seen in England. Smollett also emphasizes how character is shaped by experiences and emotional responses. Bramble's solitary reflections imply that the most intense and meaningful emotions are those an individual does not feel constrained to share in words. In this way, the emotions of Smollett's characters are safe from both the reader's pity and his ridicule.

"Critical Evaluation" by Bonnie Fraser

Further Reading

Beasley, Jerry C. *Tobias Smollett: Novelist*. Athens: University of Georgia Press, 1998. An analysis of Smollett's five novels, which Beasley interprets as "exercises in the visual imagination," written by an author who believed the private, interior life could be defined by the externally visible. Chapter 5 focuses on *The Expedition of Humphry Clinker*.

Bouce, Paul-Gabriel. *The Novels of Tobias Smollett*. London: Longman, 1976. One of the best studies of the totality of Smollett's fiction. The author, a distinguished French scholar, shows how all of the novelist's interests converge in this last novel. Discusses the formal, thematic, and historical aspects of each of Smollett's novels.

Brack, O. M., Jr., ed. *Tobias Smollett, Scotland's First Novelist: New Essays in Memory of Paul-Gabriel Bouce*. Newark: University of Delaware Press, 2007. Collection of essays on Smollett's fiction and nonfiction, including a comparison of his work with that of Henry Fielding, an examination of his contributions to the gothic novel, and "On the External Uses of Water in *The Expedition of Humphrey Clinker*" by Robert A. Erickson.

Gibson, William. *Art and Money in the Writings of Tobias Smollett*. Lewisburg, Pa.: Bucknell University Press, 2007. Analyzes some of Smollett's novels and nonfiction writing, focusing on issues of aesthetics, commercialism, luxury, and taste in order to describe how these works provide insights into the eighteenth century art world.

Lewis, Jeremy. *Tobias Smollett*. London: Jonathan Cape, 2003. An appreciative look at Smollett's life, written by an acclaimed biographer. Includes bibliography and index.

Price, John Valdimir. *Tobias Smollett: "The Expedition of Humphry Clinker."* London: Edward Arnold, 1973. A brief and intelligent interpretation of the novel. Discusses many of its elements from a variety of critical approaches, all in a clear, concise manner.

Senora, John. *Luxury: The Concept in Western Thought, Eden to Smollett*. Baltimore: Johns Hopkins University Press, 1977. An exhaustive book-length study of *The Expedition of Humphry Clinker*, arguing that its politics, history, structure, and characters are informed by the important idea of luxury. Regards the book as "the most successful conservative attack upon luxury written in any genre during the 1750's and 1760's, a pearl in a generation of sand."

Smollett, Tobias. *The Expedition of Humphry Clinker*. Edited by Thomas R. Preston. Athens: University of Georgia Press, 1990. The authoritative source for all levels of students. Provides a definitive text, valuable period illustrations, an elaborate introduction, and exhaustive annotations.

Explosion in a Cathedral

Author: Alejo Carpentier (1904-1980)
First published: El siglo de las luces, 1962 (English
    translation, 1963)
Type of work: Novel
Type of plot: Social realism
Time of plot: 1789-1809
Locale: Caribbean islands and Europe

Principal characters:
CARLOS, the son of a Cuban merchant
SOFÍA, Carlos's sister
ESTEBAN, Carlos's and Sofía's cousin
VICTOR HUGUES, a father figure to Carlos and Sofía
OGÉ, a Haitian doctor and revolutionary

The Story:

A wealthy Cuban merchant dies in Havana, leaving behind an orphaned son and daughter, Carlos and Sofía, and a nephew, Esteban, also an orphan who grew up with Carlos and Sofía. In the absence of paternal authority, the three adolescents are free to pass the time as they wish. They eat and sleep at odd hours and transform the family mansion into a house of "perpetual games," a disorderly labyrinth of unpacked shipping crates. Their harmonious existence in the midst of external chaos is brought to an abrupt end, however, when Victor Hugues, a cosmopolitan businessman from Port-au-Prince, Haiti, arrives one stormy Easter Sunday. Victor, executor of their father's will, restores order to the house and assumes the role of surrogate father. He restores the old values of their deceased father and introduces both Esteban and Sofía into the world of adulthood. He also introduces the young people to the liberal ideas of the Enlightenment and the French Revolution. When Victor, a Freemason, is threatened with arrest by the colonial authorities because of his subversive ideas, Sofía offers the family's country home as a refuge to him and his friend, Ogé, a mulatto doctor from San Domingo. Sofía and Esteban accompany the two men to the estate. There they become fascinated by heated political discussions about revolution, class war, liberty, and equality.

Although Victor and Ogé use the same language in their discussions about the necessity for social change, Victor, though he upholds the egalitarian principles of the Declaration of the Rights of Man, is primarily concerned with business. For him, the advanced ideas of the New Age are important because they challenge the colonial monopoly of trade in the Americas. He is one of several Creole merchants who set up a contraband organization to circumvent specifically the Spanish monopoly. His mission in Havana is to contact local merchants sympathetic to Freemasonry and to form a secret organization to combat the economic tyranny of Spain, but he finds little active interest in social issues among the Cubans.

In contrast to Victor, Ogé, though a man of science, espouses a form of revolutionary mysticism that aims at bringing about change by awakening the transcendental powers of the human spirit. Sofía and Esteban are more attracted to Victor's scientific views of human progress and most of all to his powerful personality as an energetic man of action. When Victor and Ogé are forced to escape the island, they invite Sofía and Esteban to accompany them on a trip to Port-au-Prince. Esteban eagerly joins in the revolutionary adventure that he hopes would be his initiation into manhood. During the sea voyage, Sofía yields to Victor's sexual advances.

Shortly after their ship docks at Santiago de Cuba, Victor, Ogé, and Esteban leave Sofía in that city and proceed on to Port-au-Prince. There, they find the city in flames and Victor's business establishment burned to the ground. Despite the destruction of his property, Victor feels a sense of freedom, of being on the threshold of a new life. The uprising puts an end to his friendship with Ogé, however, whose younger brother was executed by white settlers in Cap Français. Ogé becomes bitter toward all whites and warns Victor to leave before he is killed by the black insurgents. Victor and Esteban decide to sail for revolutionary France. In Paris, Victor quickly aligns himself with the new government and begins to rise to power as agent of the Revolution of the Americas. Though infected in Paris by the fervor of the early days of the Revolution, Esteban is content to witness rather than to participate in the struggle. He perceives it in terms of a stage in the spiritual human progress toward domination over more selfish and violent instincts. After witnessing the Terror, he begins to see the contradictions of the revolutionary process and the threat it poses to those who dare to dissent. Esteban grows increasingly disillusioned and returns to Havana.

After her husband dies in an epidemic, Sofía seeks out Victor and joins him in Cayenne. Sofía's hope of lending herself to an epic struggle that will give meaning to her life fails even more quickly than Esteban's did in France. Victor is transformed from a libertarian to a ruthless tyrant as he leads a catastrophic campaign against the rebellious black population in Cayenne. Abandoning Victor, Sofía sails for Spain. There she secures release for Esteban, who was deported from Cuba to Spain for concealing subversive propaganda and who now engages once more in the revolutionary struggle. Victor dies defending the interests of the new bourgeoisie in Cayenne; Esteban and Sofía join the first revolution to challenge those values and die anonymously in the streets of Madrid fighting Napoleon's troops.

At the end of the novel, Carlos, who remained in Havana tending to his deceased father's businesses, reconstructs the last day of Esteban and Sofía in Madrid. He begins to carry on what Sofía and Esteban began. Wealthy, but with the liberal ideas acquired through his contact with the revolution, he will be the one to bring about the wars of independence in Cuba.

Critical Evaluation:

In seeking to write about a twentieth century Caribbean culture liberated from both the European conquerors and their allies, the plantation class, Caribbean writers such as Alejo Carpentier selected the drama of history as the terrain of cultural resistance. What is most significant in the Caribbean narrative of history is the form and design of the chronicle and the nature of its subject. In the prologue to his novel *El reino de este mundo* (1949; *The Kingdom of This World*, 1957), Carpentier comments that the American language has yet to exhaust its "mythological mine." He views the history of the Americas as a "chronicle of magic realism." At the heart of Carpentier's notion of magic realism (he originated the term, which was later applied to various writers in the Caribbean and Latin America) is the belief that the West Indian language offers literary forms that resist the rationality and chronology embedded in colonial doctrines of modernism.

In *Explosion in a Cathedral*, the dominant European worldview is transplanted into the Caribbean islands, but its central doctrine, the Enlightenment, is systematically destroyed. The Caribbean intellectual Esteban is placed in the European "circus of civilization," the French Revolution, to test its claim to have ushered society into a previously unknown period of freedom and happiness. He returns home, however, disillusioned with European notions of progress and the idea of modernity itself. As a result, the Caribbean man is forced to turn inward and to search for an American way of interpreting America.

Carpentier's novel focuses on the discontinuity and retardation of European history in the Caribbean and its eventual collapse in the Antilles. The degeneration of European history is here proposed as a precondition for a new Caribbean way of life: At the moment when European models collapse, the colonized writer can rewrite American realities anew.

History is the main topic of Carpentier's fiction, and the history he deals with is that of beginnings. He represents two spiritually contradictory worlds of the Caribbean at the turn of the eighteenth century. Carpentier's narrative subverts the premise that reason liberates the individual and enriches everyday social life. What the Enlightenment casts as a totality of culture is exposed as a fragment suspended in a temporal void somewhere between Europe and the Caribbean.

While most of the monumental changes affecting the Caribbean in the eighteenth century—the French Revolution, the Haitian Revolution, and the Counter-Revolution—are dramatized in the novel, on a deeper level things remain the same. What is important in this context is that both past and future are cast in a new light.

Carpentier's thematic concern with the colonization of the Caribbean is illustrated through the figure of Victor, who functions in the novel as the modern hero. In whatever role he is encountered, whether as liberator, revolutionary, or reactionary, Victor is a constant reminder that the central problem of Caribbean culture is the imposition of meanings by the European other. The contradictions that define Victor's relationship with his age are both a reflection of the consciousness of the plantation bourgeoisie as it enters the new age and an indication of the worldview of the eighteenth century. Described as a man of "indeterminate age," Victor is a man who rationalizes nature and attempts to impose a new system of thought in which the conflicting ideologies of the age are formalized into a rational system.

The universalism Victor exhibits throughout the novel is matched only by his desire to secure power over others and to legitimize his image as the new rational man. Victor is also a contradiction in terms, however: Although he owns slaves in Guadeloupe, it is he who introduces the notion of equality of races into the Cuban merchant's house. He also sets out to usurp the position of the dead family patriarch. As the narrative unfolds, Victor's claim to originality is seen to be suspect, his blind revolutionary zeal is exposed as counterfeit, and his actions cast doubt on his integrity.

Victor also draws the reader's attention to the problem encountered by European systems of thought as soon as they are transplanted into the New World economic system. In the novel, there is poignant tension between shattered old beliefs and the new individual who needs to order things to "know" them. Throughout the novel, the shattering of the old is dramatized by the French Revolution, which masquerades as a unique historical event. The shattering gesture has actually already been foreshadowed by the painting "Explosion in a Cathedral," which dominates the text. The painting is variously described as the "apocalyptic immobilization of a catastrophe" and as the "illustration of the End of Time." Nevertheless, the people who herald the nineteenth century strive to rationalize, to reorder things, so that they can establish their uniqueness in the precariousness of things.

Ultimately, Victor's belief that revolution restores authority to the individual is questioned rigorously by a narrative voice that constantly contests the hero's revolutionary words and their authority. While Victor and Ogé introduce revolution as a natural and inevitable phenomenon, even Esteban already knows that a gap exists between this "authorized" view of revolution and revolution itself. Esteban joins the revolution to become part of what is regarded as a natural and inevitable process, but he returns merely as a man laden with stories.

The novel underscores the notion that the corruption of the French Revolution actually enables the Haitian Revolution, which recenters Caribbean history. A basic irony, however, is that the revolution is not transferred to the Caribbean to restore freedom to the slaves but to establish a new system of regulation and exchange.

Genevieve Slomski

Further Reading

Gikandi, Simon. *Writing in Limbo*. Ithaca, N.Y.: Cornell University Press, 1992. An insightful study that discusses the work of Carpentier in the context of twentieth century modernism and Caribbean literature.

Gilkes, Michael. *The West Indian Novel*. Boston: Twayne, 1981. Carpentier's work is analyzed within the larger context of the historical and cultural environment of West Indian literature. Includes a chronology and bibliography.

Gonzalez Echevarria, Roberto. *Alejo Carpentier: The Pilgrim at Home*. Ithaca, N.Y.: Cornell University Press, 1977. Asserts that the core of Carpentier's fiction lies in the dilemma of what constitutes American history and how to narrate it. Includes a bibliography.

King, Bruce, ed. *West Indian Literature*. Hamden, Conn.: Archon Books, 1979. Excellent overview of the major figures of West Indian literature. Compares and contrasts Carpentier's work with that of other prominent novelists. Includes a bibliography.

Unruh, Vicky. "The Performing Spectator in Alejo Carpentier's Fictional World." *Hispanic Review* 66 (Winter, 1998): 57-77. Argues that Carpentier uses the concept of performance to explore subjectivity and identity; asserts he is fascinated by performance because of his interest in switching identities; claims his theater activity is a key to understanding his fictional world, in which spectatorship is an important way of experiencing the world.

Wakefield, Steve. *Carpentier's Baroque Fiction: Returning Medusa's Gaze*. Rochester, N.Y.: Tamesis, 2004. Traces the origins of Carpentier's literary style to his interest in Spanish baroque architecture and the Spanish Golden Age. Wakefield explains how Carpentier's historical fiction sought to create the ambience of this period through descriptions of architecture and the visual arts and parodies of Spanish Golden Age writers. Chapter 6 is devoted to an analysis of *Explosion in a Cathedral*.

Webb, Barbara J. *Myth and History in Caribbean Fiction*. Amherst: University of Massachusetts Press, 1992. An excellent examination of the use of myth and history in the works of Carpentier, Wilson Harris, and Edouard Glissant. Includes an extensive bibliography.

F

A Fable

Author: William Faulkner (1897-1962)
First published: 1954
Type of work: Novel
Type of plot: Allegory
Time of plot: 1918
Locale: Western front in France

Principal characters:
THE CORPORAL, a Christ figure
THE MARSHAL, commander-in-chief of the Allied armies
   in France
GENERAL GRAGNON, the French division commander
THE QUARTERMASTER GENERAL, the Marshal's former
   fellow student
THE RUNNER, a former officer, in sympathy with the
   Corporal's aims
THE REVEREND TOBE SUTTERFIELD, a black American
   preacher
MARTHE, the Corporal's younger half sister
MARYA, the Corporal's feebleminded half sister
DAVID LEVINE, a British flight officer
POLCHEK, a soldier in the Corporal's squad
PIERRE BOUC, another soldier in the Corporal's squad
BUCHWALD, a U.S. soldier

The Story:

On a Monday in May, 1918, a most unusual event takes place on a battlefield in France. French and German troops face one another after four years of trench warfare. At dawn, the regiment under the command of General Gragnon refuses to attack. Another unbelievable event occurs when the Germans, who are expected to take advantage of the mutiny, do not move either. At noon, the whole sector of the front stops firing and soon the rest of the front comes to a standstill. Division Commander Gragnon requests execution of all three thousand mutineers; he also demands his own arrest.

On Wednesday, the trucks carrying the mutinous regiment arrive at headquarters in Chaulnesmont, where the dishonor brought on the town arouses the people to noisy demonstration. Relatives and friends of the mutineers know that a corporal and his squad of twelve, moving in a mysterious way behind the lines, succeeded in spreading their ideas about peace on earth among the troops. Four of the thirteen men are not Frenchmen by birth; among those only the Corporal speaks French, and he is the object of the crowd's fury.

This situation creates uncertainty among the Allied generals because a war ended by mutiny is not reconcilable with military principles. To clarify the confusion, a conference takes place to which a German general is invited, and an agreement is reached for continuation of the war. To young Flight Officer David Levine, the unsuspected pause in war means tragedy. Determined to find glory in battle but realizing that he might miss his opportunity, he commits suicide. To another soldier, the Runner, the truce at the front is a welcome sign. A former officer, he rejected submissive principles and abuse of authority by superiors, and he was returned to the ranks. Having heard about the Corporal from the Reverend Tobe Sutterfield, an American black preacher who arrived under unexplainable circumstances in France, the Runner tries to show once again the power of the Corporal's ideas. He forces a sentry, who profiteered by collecting fees for life insurance among the soldiers, to leave the trenches and join a British battalion in a peaceful walk toward the German line. When they show their empty hands, the Germans also come unarmed to meet the French. A sudden artillery barrage by French and German guns kills the sentry and cripples the Runner.

The man to decide the fate of the mutineers is the Commander-in-Chief of the Allied armies, an aged French Marshal. The orphaned son of a prominent family, he attended the French military school, St. Cyr. There his unselfish attitude combined with his devotion to studies made him an outstanding and beloved student. Especially devoted to him is the man who is now his Quartermaster General. After leaving school, the Marshal was stationed in the Sahara, where he incurred blood guilt by sacrificing a brutal legionnaire to tribal justice. Later, he spent several years in a Tibetan monastery. In the Middle East, he met a married woman with two daughters. The affair resulted in the birth of a son in a stable at Christmas. The mother died in childbirth, and Marthe, one of the daughters, cared for the boy. When World War I broke out, the Marshal became the Allied commander and the hope of France.

The mutinous troops are kept in a former factory building while awaiting trial. The Marshal, not surprised by the court proceedings, seems to anticipate all answers. Marthe and Marya, the Corporal's half sisters, and his wife arrive in Chaulnesmont and, in an interview with the Marshal, reveal that the Corporal is his son. Marthe married a French farmer, Dumont, and the boy grew up on her farm. Soon after the outbreak of war, he enlisted in the army and received a medal for bravery in action. He married a former prostitute from Marseilles. Again, the old Marshal is not surprised and seems to know every detail.

On Thursday, a meal is served to the squad during which it becomes known that soldier Polchek betrayed the Corporal. Another soldier, Pierre Bouc, denies the Corporal three times. After the meal, the Corporal is called away to meet the Marshal. On a hill overlooking the town, the Marshal tries to explain the futility of his son's martyrdom. When he promises a secret ocean passage to escape the death penalty, the Corporal refuses the offer. Later the Marshal makes a last attempt to influence his son with the help of an army priest. Recognizing his own unworthiness before the humble Corporal, the priest commits suicide. On the same evening, General Gragnon is executed by an American soldier named Buchwald.

On Friday, the Corporal is tied to a post between two criminals. Shot, he falls into a coil of barbed wire that lacerates his head. The Corporal's body and his medal are buried on the Dumont farm near St. Mihiel. After the burial, a sudden artillery barrage plows the earth, leaving no trace of the Corporal's grave.

After the war, a unit is sent to reclaim a body to be placed in the Unknown Soldier's tomb under the Arc de Triomphe in Paris. As a reward, they are promised brandy. Near Verdun, they obtain the body and then drink the brandy. While they are guarding the coffin, an old woman approaches. Having

lost her mind because her son did not return from the war, she sold her farm in order to search for him. Knowing about the mission of the soldiers, she wants to look at the body. Convinced that the dead soldier is her son, she offers all her money for the corpse; the soldiers accept and buy more brandy with the money. They secure another body from a field adjoining the Dumont farm. Thus, the body of the Corporal reaches Paris. Four years later, the Runner visits the Dumont farm and picks up the medal.

Six years later, the Marshal's body is carried to the Arc de Triomphe, with dignitaries following the coffin on foot to pay their respects to the dead leader. As soon as the eulogy starts, a cripple makes his way through the crowd. It is the Runner, who throws the Corporal's medal at the caisson before an angry mob closes in and attacks him. Rescued by the police, he is dragged into a side street, where a few curious onlookers gather around the injured cripple. While he lies in the gutter, a man resembling the old Quartermaster General steps forward to comfort the Runner, who declares that he will never die.

Critical Evaluation:

A Fable is probably the most ambitious, although not the most successful, work of one of the twentieth century's most ambitious novelists. By juxtaposing elements of the Passion of Christ against a story of trench mutiny in World War I, William Faulkner attempts to combine two very different types of narrative: an allegorical "fable" and a realistic narrative of war, politics, and personal relationships.

Most of the similarities to Christ's life and death are clear. The Corporal, who was born in a stable and is thirty-three years old, leads a mutinous group of twelve followers, and the events surrounding his capture and execution suggest the Passion: One disciple betrays him for money, another denies him three times; the followers have a "Last Supper"; the Corporal is executed between two thieves in a manner that suggests Christ's crucifixion; he acquires a crown of thorns; he is mourned by women who resemble Mary Magdalene and Mary; and his body vanishes three days after burial. It is necessary, however, to remember that *A Fable* is not the Passion retold in modern dress. Faulkner does not simply update or interpret Christian myth: He alters it. Therefore, any attempt to come to terms with *A Fable* must consider the unique, personal vision that Faulkner presents in his book.

Some critics have faulted the novel on the grounds that the Corporal's personality is insufficiently developed. It is true that he is not strongly individualized, but to present the character in greater detail would risk either the creation of a purely symbolic figure or one too humanized to maintain the

Christ parallel. Instead, the Corporal remains a silent, mysterious embodiment of humankind's spiritual side; the concrete presentation of his significance is entrusted to other characters. The most important thing is that, for all the biblical allusions, the Corporal is not the chosen Son of God but is definitely a son of man—specifically of the Marshal—and the thematic center of the novel is dramatized in the conflict between the Corporal and his father-Marshal antagonist. In the novel's most powerful and important scene, the final confrontation is between the two men, who represent two inimical conditions.

Thus, *A Fable* is not really about one's relationship to God, or to society, but to oneself. Each character stands for one aspect of the human personality, and the conflict between them can be seen in several ways: child versus father, youth versus age, idealist versus realist, common person versus authority, heart versus mind. In short, the major conflict of the book is, in the words of Faulkner's Nobel Prize speech, "the human heart in conflict with itself"—the basic human dualism, which is the major theme of Faulkner's late fiction.

The Corporal is the shadowy incarnation of humanity's spiritual side, but the Marshal, both in his symbolic and his realistic functions, is a much more vivid and complicated character. On the literal level, he is the supreme commander of the Allied armies in France. He masterminds the Allies' successful military counterstrategy. Symbolically, he is the primary representative of secular power; the Marshal represents everything in human society that denies personal autonomy and spiritual freedom. Any attempt to pin down the Marshal's symbolic import more precisely is very difficult. At times he suggests Satan, at times Pilate or Caesar, or simply military authority, but in the central confrontation scene, his role seems to most closely resemble that of the "Grand Inquisitor," who appears in the greatest of earlier "Second Coming" fictions, Ivan Karamazov's parable in Fyodor Dostoevski's *Bratya Karamazovy* (1879-1880; *The Brothers Karamazov*, 1912).

Like the Grand Inquisitor, the Marshal faces a Christ surrogate who poses a threat to the established order. Likewise, the Marshal makes an offer to his antagonist of life and freedom in return for betrayal, which he knows in advance will be refused. The Marshal's background also resembles the Inquisitor's in that he, too, began life with a spiritual quest by renouncing the world in favor of the desert and the mountains. Like the Inquisitor—and Christ—the Marshal was tempted and, like the Inquisitor—but unlike Christ—he accepted the temptations and the view of life they represented in return for temporal power.

Thus, although he knows and understands human duality, the Marshal rejects the spiritual and creative side of humanity and accepts the individual only as a mundane, earthbound creature who needs security and control rather than individual freedom and spiritual fulfillment. Further, on the practical level, the Marshal commits himself to the human institution that fixes and formalizes this view of humanity. As does the Inquisitor, the Marshal justifies his actions on the grounds that they are what humanity needs and wants. He taunts his opponent with the notion that he, not the Corporal, is the true believer: "after the last ding dong of doom has rung and died there will still be one sound more; his voice, planning still to build something higher and faster and louder . . . . I don't fear man, I do better: I respect and admire him . . . . Because man and his folly—they will prevail."

These words echo the Nobel Prize speech but differ in one important respect from the novelist's own; in the address, Faulkner went on to add, "He is immortal, not because he alone among creatures has an inexhaustible voice, but because he has a soul, a spirit capable of compassion and sacrifice and endurance." This statement defines the essence of the conflict between the Marshal and the Corporal and their visions.

If the Marshal's view of humankind is correct, then the military hierarchy, the rituals and institutions it supports, and the war itself are things the human race creates for itself and needs for survival. The Corporal's mutiny is, therefore, not only foolish, but even destructive to humanity's well-being. On the other hand, if the Corporal's vision is true, such things are artificial, malevolent restraints on human potential. The mutiny in this context becomes a necessary act in the struggle to cast off the life-denying lies and organizations imposed on him and to fulfill his own human and spiritual capacities by taking control of his own destiny. The immediate secular power belongs to the Marshal, so the earthbound view seems to win, but the question Faulkner raises is whether the impact of the Corporal's actions and martyrdom does not postulate the ultimate triumph of the spiritual vision.

To answer that question, Faulkner attempts to work out the implications of the Corporal's ethic in the actions of several other characters and especially in the attempt of the English Runner to foment a second and wider mutiny. Here lies the primary critical problem of the book: Do these secondary actions establish and elaborate the novel's main thrust, or do they obscure and finally bury it?

Although Faulkner borrows Christian symbolism, he is clearly not presenting a conventionally religious message. He affirms the human spirit, but his attitude toward its ultimate fate is ambiguous. If the Corporal dies a heroic martyr, the other witnesses to the human spirit—the English Runner, the Sentry, the Reverend Sutterfield, the Quartermaster General—suffer dubious or ignominious fates and even the Corporal's death has no clear effect beyond stimulating the Runner's quixotic gestures. Faulkner postulates hope and faith as vital elements in human fulfillment, but they are presented as ends in themselves; it is unclear as to what humanity should hope for or have faith in.

It seems likely that Faulkner began to write *A Fable* with a number of abstract concepts in mind rather than a special set of human experiences. In his best works, however, the meanings grow out of the concrete situations; in *A Fable*, he tries to impose his meanings on his characters' actions. Consequently, the novel is not completely satisfying on either the realistic or the symbolic level. Nevertheless, even with these problems, *A Fable* is a powerful reading experience. If it fails to fulfill completely Faulkner's most ambitious intentions, it does present separate characters and scenes that are powerful and memorable. If all of Faulkner's concepts are not completely clear, his dramatization of human duality is stimulating and provocative.

"Critical Evaluation" by Keith Neilson

Further Reading

Brooks, Cleanth. *William Faulkner: Toward Yoknapatawpha and Beyond.* New Haven, Conn.: Yale University Press, 1978. Critiques the five Faulkner novels that take place outside Yoknapatawpha County. Brooks finds *A Fable* to be less realistic than other Faulkner novels and therefore weaker.

Butterworth, Keen. *A Critical and Textual Study of Faulkner's "A Fable."* Ann Arbor: University of Michigan Press, 1983. Compares *A Fable* to Faulkner's great novels, then explains the events of the novels and elaborates on the characters and their significance.

Dowling, David. *William Faulkner.* New York: St. Martin's Press, 1989. Includes a chronology and sections outlining the major works completed during different periods in Faulkner's life. Gives considerable criticism of *A Fable* and finds it to be the last great novel written by Faulkner.

Leary, Lewis. *William Faulkner of Yoknapatawpha County.* New York: Thomas Y. Crowell, 1973. A good general guide and introduction to the life of Faulkner. Traces his biography and work with some reference to *A Fable.*

Reed, Joseph W., Jr. *Faulkner's Narrative.* New Haven, Conn.: Yale University Press, 1973. A view of Faulkner's writing technique, form, and thematic devices. Examines his voice and narrative style and the impact of that style on other writers. Useful references to *A Fable.*

Towner, Theresa M. *The Cambridge Introduction to William Faulkner.* New York: Cambridge University Press, 2008. An accessible book aimed at students and general readers. Focusing on Faulkner's work, the book provides detailed analyses of his nineteen novels, discussion of his other works, and information about the critical reception for his fiction.

A Fable for Critics

Author: James Russell Lowell (1819-1891)
First published: 1848
Type of work: Poetry

James Russell Lowell's *A Fable for Critics* appeared in 1848, three years after Edgar Allan Poe's "The Raven" and three years before Herman Melville's *Moby Dick*. Born the same year as Melville and Walt Whitman, Lowell was twenty-nine years old and had already gained something of a reputation as poet and antislavery essayist.

Writing in the age of Ralph Waldo Emerson and Nathaniel Hawthorne, Lowell believed that native American literature had come of age. He argues this in a section of *A Fable for Critics*, echoing Emerson's "The American Scholar" address of eleven years earlier and looking ahead to Whitman's famous preface to the 1855 edition of *Leaves of Grass*. "Forget Europe wholly," he advised the American writer.

Eventually, *A Fable for Critics* has come to be read—though rarely all the way through—for its satire. The author flippantly exhibits his contemporaries: Emerson, Henry Wadsworth Longfellow, John Greenleaf Whittier, Richard

Henry Dana, Sr., and many lesser-known writers. With his young man's irreverence and capacity for industry, Lowell produced in this 2,100-line poem a number of choice verbal thrusts that have always delighted readers: "There comes Poe, with his raven, like Barnaby Rudge,/ Three-fifths of him genius and two-fifths sheer fudge." Of James Fenimore Cooper he wrote, "the women he draws from one model don't vary,/ All sappy as maples and flat as a prairie."

Lowell often makes acute judgments, as in the quotations above, but the poem has serious defects. It is no systematized essay in verse in the manner of Alexander Pope but, rather, a rambling and digressive caricature. Unfortunately, too, many of the objects of Lowell's satire have so declined in reputation that the point of the satire is lost. Lowell's clattering anapestic tetrameter and his sometimes embarrassing rhymes (as in "philosopher" and "loss of her") prove hard to endure, even in a poem intentionally comic.

The structure of the poem is also problematic. Lowell chose the long way around to get at his satire. Ostensibly the poem merely describes various American writers parading past the not too interested personage of Phoebus Apollo. The writers are in the form of cackling fowls led by "Tityrus Griswold" (Rufus W. Griswold, an influential anthologist of the day). This rather mechanical scheme offers little excitement or sense of direction.

Lowell had precedents for this sort of lampooning. Literary ancestors of *A Fable for Critics* are such works as Pope's *The Dunciad* (1728-1743), Lord Byron's *English Bards and Scotch Reviewers* (1809), and Leigh Hunt's *The Feast of the Poets* (1814), to which it bears the greatest resemblance. Lowell's work itself served as model when a related Lowell, the poet Amy Lowell, decided to produce her own *Critical Fable* in 1922.

Lowell wrote his satire "con amore," to use his term. His high spirits are immediately evident in the title page and the introduction. The elaborate title page, ostensibly no more than an imitation of wordy, old-fashioned book format, is actually the beginning of the rhymed couplets: "Reader! walk up at once (it will soon be too late), and buy at a perfectly ruinous rate *A Fable for Critics*."

In the rhymed introduction that follows, a candid Lowell limits his purpose and forestalls possible censures. The poem, he avers, is a mere "trifle," full of digressions and written in "neither good verse nor bad prose." It is a jeu d'esprit whose verbal portraits are both cynical and faithful. Lowell attached a considerably longer essay in rhyme to the second edition. Here, in the spirit of exuberance that pervades the work from beginning to end, he remarks on the mixed critical reception of the first edition.

Lowell himself narrates the poem throughout, but the first personage encountered is Phoebus Apollo from Greek mythology. Lowell, of course, here uses a favorite device of the fabulist, using setting and characters of other times and other places to add ludicrousness and perspective to his satire on people of his own day.

Apollo, sitting under a laurel tree, has been reading recent poetry and bemoans its mediocrity. Feeling the need to write something himself—to mourn his Daphne—he decides that a lily is needed to set his faculties to work. One of his sycophants, a pedantic bore ("The defect in his brain was just absence of mind"), hastens to fetch it. Apollo meanwhile is "killing the time" when the first of Lowell's real people walks up to him. This is Evert Augustus Duyckinck, editor and critic, who is pictured as a small, muttering, reputation-conscious individual. While he and Apollo exchange barbs, the procession of American authors, which makes up the bulk of the poem, commences with the appearance of Ralph Waldo Emerson, who by 1848 had published his two famous series of essays. It is Apollo who describes the procession, and all descriptions are from his mouth. Lowell's use of the fable device thus allows him to satirize without using his own voice. Emerson has "a Greek head on right Yankee shoulders"; the Transcendentalist " . . . sits in mystery calm and intense/ And looks coolly around him with sharp common sense." Two writers who "trod in Emerson's track" then appear: William Ellery Channing, poet and Concord litterateur, and Henry David Thoreau. Both are inferior to Emerson; all they do is pick up the "windfalls" from Emerson's tree.

Fourth and fifth in the procession are Bronson Alcott and Orestes Brownson. Alcott, the Platonic idealist and mystic, avoids the mundane, has "never a fact to perplex him or bore him." Brownson is the New England individualist who turned from Presbyterian to Universalist to Roman Catholic. Amid the satire, Lowell-Apollo speaks commendation: Alcott is a magnificent talker; Brownson writes "transparent and forcible prose." These two vignettes typify Lowell's willingness to laugh as well as to compliment, if compliments are deserved.

Fifty lines characterize the now-forgotten Nathaniel Parker Willis as a foppish and shallow yet delightful and witty poet and playwright. Theodore Parker, Unitarian clergyman and writer, comes next, his doctrinal radicalism satirized as well as his erudite sermons. William Cullen Bryant, the poet of nature, is no William Wordsworth, says Apollo, but perhaps he is a James Thomson or a William Cowper. In any case, he is quiet and cool and as dignified as an iceberg. John Greenleaf Whittier is a pacifist Quaker engaged in militant wars for human rights. In his poetry, there is a major defect: "torrent of verse bursts the dams of reflection." Whittier's human qualities lead Apollo into a general panegyric on all poets who ever "spoke out for the dumb and the down-trodden."

Two lesser-known writers—Richard Henry Dana, Sr., and John Neal, a journalist and novelist—continue the procession, followed by Nathaniel Hawthorne, one of the few writers on parade who receives unqualified approval. He is strong, earnest, graceful, good-tempered—"fully and perfectly man." James Fenimore Cooper fares less well in twice as many lines. According to Apollo, he has created one character, the woodsman Natty Bumppo, and has done nothing but copy him ever since. Cooper's virtue is boldness of utterance; he speaks his mind whether people like it or not.

The admirable way in which Cooper "lectures his countrymen gratis" reminds Apollo of several "truths you Americans need to be told," the main one being that they should refuse to be intimidated by England. Americans brag of their New World but do not really quite believe in it and keep looking to England for ideas and literature. Instead, they should reflect their own land and their own century.

After a quick jab at slavery from Apollo, the conversation is interrupted by Miranda (Margaret Fuller), a rather obnoxious egoist "with an I-turn-the-crank-of-the-Universe air." She inspires Apollo to give a digression on bores. Congress is full of them. The parade resumes with a description of the novelist Charles Frederick Briggs, who is amiable, if self-contradictory, followed by the famous vignette of Poe, "who has written some things quite the best of their kind,/ But the heart somehow seems all squeezed out by the mind." This description is interrupted by a spirited defense of Longfellow.

Lydia Maria Child, another forgotten novelist to whom Lowell devotes more than one hundred lines, is succeeded by Washington Irving, who is presented as a man of "warm heart and fine brain." Praise for Irving yields to recognition of Sylvester Judd, a novelist of New England.

At this point Lowell himself enters the poem again, for the purpose of a digressive paean to the state of Massachusetts, the home of workers and industry where the rough new continent was tamed. Here Lowell raises the theme of great art and literature.

Apollo then resumes his commentary on the parade. The vigor, fancy, and fun of Oliver Wendell Holmes receive acclaim, and then comes none other than Lowell himself, "striving Parnassus to climb." After him appears Fitz-Greene Halleck, a minor versifier, followed by figures even more insignificant. Apollo amuses himself by laughing at their self-importance.

Apollo's lily-searchers, who had disappeared at the beginning of the poem, now reenter to lead matters to a conclu-

sion. Before ending, however, Apollo makes some pointed remarks about literary criticism. In the good old days when poets were visionary, free, and prophetic, there were no critics, but now the domain of art is overrun by pedantic and carping critics: "He who would write and can't write can surely review." No sooner has Apollo worked himself into a furious rage, however, than loquacious Miranda intrudes her opinion. Thereupon, Apollo flees, as does Lowell, and the burlesque comes to an abrupt end.

Further Reading

Arms, George. *The Fields Were Green: A New View of Bryant, Whittier, Holmes, Lowell, and Longfellow, with a Selection of Their Poems*. Stanford, Calif.: Stanford University Press, 1948. Places Lowell and his production in the context of the best popular poetry of the times. Approaches *A Fable for Critics* as a series of verse essays that only incidentally contain shrewd critical judgments of Lowell's contemporary authors.

Broaddus, Dorothy C. *Genteel Rhetoric: Writing High Culture in Nineteenth-Century Boston*. Columbia: University of South Carolina Press, 1999. Lowell and other writers living in Boston in the mid-nineteenth century shared a belief that an American writer should be moral, educated, appreciative of fine art and literature, and conduct himself with genteel bearing and good manners. Broaddus discusses the life and work of these writers and describes how this vision of gentility was altered by the reality of the abolitionist movement and the Civil War.

Butler, Leslie. *Critical Americans: Victorian Intellectuals and Transatlantic Liberal Reform*. Chapel Hill: University of North Carolina Press, 2007. Recounts how Lowell and three of his friends—writers George William Curtis, Thomas Wentworth Higginson, and Charles Eliot Norton—worked with British intellectuals to promote progressive and cosmopolitan reform in the decades between the 1850's and 1890's.

Duberman, Martin. *James Russell Lowell*. Boston: Houghton Mifflin, 1966. Includes a discussion of *A Fable for Critics* that points out the work's weaknesses, especially its hasty composition, forced puns, and digressions. Also emphasizes its many strengths and, notably, its still valid critical judgments.

Heymann, C. David. *American Aristocracy: The Lives and Times of James Russell, Amy Lowell, and Robert Lowell*. New York: Dodd, Mead, 1980. Sketches early responses to *A Fable for Critics* and compares relevant aspects of the work to Amy Lowell's somewhat similar *A Critical Fable* (1922).

McGlinchee, Claire. *James Russell Lowell*. New York: Twayne, 1967. Analyzes *A Fable for Critics* as a demonstration of Lowell's critical acumen and his ability to make dispassionate and lasting judgments about his contemporaries. In particular, praises his perceptive comments on Ralph Waldo Emerson and Edgar Allan Poe.

Smith, Herbert F., ed. *Literary Criticism of James Russell Lowell*. Lincoln: University of Nebraska Press, 1969. Reprints *A Fable for Critics*, accompanied by a detailed introduction and extensive annotations of all persons named, non-English quotations, and difficult literary references and allusions.

The Fables

Author: Jean de La Fontaine (1621-1695)
First published: Books 1-6, 1668; books 7-11, 1673-1679; book 12, 1694, as *Fables choisies, mises en vers* (English translation, 1735)
Type of work: Poetry

While one may be tempted by tradition to think of Jean de La Fontaine's *The Fables* as children's stories, such a notion does a disservice to La Fontaine's elegant poetry and down-to-earth, sometimes bitter philosophy and view of life. A point to keep in mind in reading *The Fables* is that they were written over a period of more than twenty-five years. The first six books of fables were published in 1668, five more books appeared in 1673-1679, and the twelfth and final book was published in 1694. As such, *The Fables* reflect the changes in point of view of a writer who matured and perhaps mellowed as he wrote and published his fable-poems.

To a certain degree, La Fontaine's ideas also reflect social and political problems and philosophical styles in France during the reign of Louis XIV (1643-1715). Many of the early fables seem to comment on specific injustices of Louis XIV's regime, especially as they affected the common people, while the fables from La Fontaine's later years mainly express a spiritual withdrawal that resembles stoicism in certain respects.

As the literary heir of ancient fabulists such as Aesop, Bidpai, and Phaedrus, La Fontaine makes use of a form that was familiar to his readers. Most of his fables feature a story and a moral, the latter often separated from the text of the tale. La Fontaine's verse form varies; he uses eight-syllable lines as a basic structure, but he often exploits the dignified twelve-syllable Alexandrine form, the verse form identified with seventeenth century French tragedy, when he wishes to express exceptional drama and seriousness.

As for the fables' casts of characters, most of the fables present, as usual, familiar characters from the animal kingdom. "I use animals to teach men," says La Fontaine in the poem that serves as a preface to *The Fables*. Some of the fables do, however, feature humans of various social classes and nationalities. In the case of his animal characters, La Fontaine often endows certain creatures with what would be considered traditionally symbolic traits. His lion, therefore, is always a character that represents royalty and the caprice of absolute power; La Fontaine's wolf is always vicious and violent; the lamb is weak and timid; the fox is clever and insinuating, and so on.

Usually, also, the first fable of each book is especially important because it sets the tone for the fables that follow in that book; similarly, the last fable of each book often sums up or punctuates the themes of the entire book. Indeed, many of the most famous and familiar fables are to be found in book 1. "The Grasshopper and the Ant," which opens book 1 and serves as a passageway to all the fables, is typical of La Fontaine's style. This short fable expresses a peasant or bourgeois wisdom, a practicality that may strike some modern readers as cruel. There are only two characters in this poem, the grasshopper and the ant of the fable's title. The first of these is carefree, a poet or a singer who wastes her time singing in the summer when she should prepare for the winter to come. As fall approaches, seeing that she will be short of supplies, the grasshopper beseeches her neighbor, the ant, for a loan. The ant, however, is quite unsympathetic, dismissing the grasshopper's airy appeal with curtness. Similarly, the last fable in book 1, "The Oak and the Reed," tells yet another tale of the downfall of the proud and complacent. In this case, the mighty oak tree who mocks the weakness of the reed at the fable's beginning is laid low by a storm at the story's end. The moral of this story is that it is not always best to be strong and rigid; sometimes, being able to bend with prevailing winds is an asset.

"The Fox and the Crow," the second fable in book 1, presents a wily fox who outwits a vain crow. The following fable, "The Frog Who Would Be an Ox," pokes fun at those who want to be something they are not. In this poem, La Fontaine adds a moral that applies what the fable teaches to the world of seventeenth century humans, pointing out that all bourgeois want to be great nobles (in an era when the titles of hereditary nobility could be bought by affluent middle-class people), all petty princes want to have their own ambassadors, and all minor noblemen want to have their own servants. A bit later, "The Wolf and the Dog" suggests that a life of freedom is much better than the life at court, which requires the sacrifice of one's dignity. "The Wolf and the Lamb" illustrates the lesson that force gets the best of any argument, regardless of any question of abstract justice.

By the time readers arrive at the seventeenth fable of the first book, they are well conditioned to the author's rather negative outlook on life and its lessons. This poem, "Death and the Woodman," offers a broad comment on what one ought to do when one discovers that life is not as easy as one would like. The woodman of the fable's title arrives at a point in his existence when he considers that death might offer a good way out of what proves to be a difficult life of poverty, hard work, and fiscal burdens placed on him by Louis XIV's regime. Once the woodman summons Death, however, he reconsiders quickly. The lesson here, says La Fontaine, is that, all things considered, people will usually choose to suffer rather than to die. This expresses one of La Fontaine's fundamental positions, a point he defends in various forms throughout *The Fables:* One ought not to complain too much, one should know that things could always be worse, and one should understand that some things can never change.

Even though La Fontaine elaborates and modifies certain perspectives in the latter books of *The Fables,* these central texts of the first book set the stage for what he would tell his readers in succeeding books in the years to come. Politics, for example, surfaces again in "The Frogs Asked for a King" (book 3), "The Gardener and the Squire" (book 4), and perhaps most notably in "The Animals Sick of the Plague" (book 7). In the first of these, the race of frogs is so stupid that it grows weary of democracy. Creatures that make decisions precipitously and without justification are always targets of La Fontaine's ridicule, and here, the frogs that ask Jupiter for a king are devoured in short order by a rapacious crane. Self-interested and uncaring nobles appear in "The Gardener and the Squire," where it is again shown that the best recourse in misfortune is to not complain too loudly. The moral of "The Animals Sick of the Plague" is that justice is determined by one's social status rather than by true objectivity. In this fable, the lion-king presides over a sham trial, a search for a scapegoat in a time of trouble. The victim turns out to be the ass, an animal that is not really guilty but that is too dimwitted and weak to offer an effective self-defense.

The tone of withdrawal from society and from a life of involvement in the world found in the last two books of fables, published when the author was in his early seventies, is well represented by "The Mogul's Dream" (book 11) and by the last of the fables, "The Judge, the Hospitaler, and the Hermit." The title character of "The Mogul's Dream" dreams of a vizier (a government minister) who finds limitless pleasure in heaven. In contrast, in the same dream, the mogul sees a hermit who, oddly enough, is tortured by eternal fire. The mogul is confused and seeks out a wise man who interprets his dream by pointing out that in life the minister longed for solitude while the so-called hermit spent his time seeking favor at court. In the fable's extended moral, the narrator says directly that he would like to inspire his reader with a love of peace, quiet, and reflection. If one follows his advice, he suggests, one will escape the contingencies of human passion and caprice. "The Judge, the Hospitaler, and the Hermit" focuses on three saints trying to find salvation in different ways. The first saint, moved by the trials and tribulations he sees in courts of law, decides to be a judge and to try cases equitably and free of charge. The second saint chooses to care for others in a hospital. Both, however, regret their decisions, soon getting their fill of human complaints and discontent. The two saints turn for advice to a third. The last tells his friends that the greatest obligation in life is to know oneself, which requires leaving society and taking refuge in tranquil places. In the fable's moral, the narrator expands on what happens in the fable. Since people do go to courts of law and hospitals, the narrator tells the reader, lawyers, judges, and doctors are needed. He adds, however, that one forgets oneself when involved in public pursuits and becomes the plaything of the chance, the misfortune, and the corruption that mere worldly happiness brings.

With this recommendation, La Fontaine ends his *Fables,* saying in the last words of the collection that he hopes this encouragement to withdraw into oneself and away from society is a lesson that future centuries will learn. He presents this lesson, he continues, to kings and to wise men alike. "Where better end my work than here?" is the final, rhetorical question of *The Fables*.

Ultimately, readers of La Fontaine's *The Fables* learn about the author's awareness of life's misfortunes, including problems that can be traced specifically to abuses of Louis XIV's political and social system. The poor and socially disadvantaged seem to receive La Fontaine's sympathy up to a point. They are overtaxed and unjustly so; they are the victims of the petty humor of the bourgeoisie, of the nobility, and of the legal system; and they suffer the ills common to all men and women: sickness, pain, and death. However, La Fontaine never advises revolt against the political and social abuses that he knows exist. While he sympathizes with human suffering, it is clear that he believes one to be responsible for one's own difficulties. Complaining about life is of no use, the author says, primarily because one can change very little in one's social and political environments. Times change, kings die and are replaced by new kings, but human nature remains essentially the same: a mixture of virtue, vice, flawed values, and vain desires.

Growing older, La Fontaine expressed that the best way to survive life's travails is to take responsibility only for what can be controlled: one's state of mind. In making this suggestion, La Fontaine follows the example of such ancient philosophers as Marcus Aurelius Antoninus and Epictetus, who encourage looking to oneself, reflecting on one's own identity, and narrowing one's focus of activity. Only in this way can one attain real peace of mind, removed from the transitory nature of life in the world.

Gordon Walters

Further Reading

Birberick, Anne L. *Reading Undercover: Audience and Authority in Jean de La Fontaine.* Lewisburg, N.J.: Bucknell University Press, 1998. Examines *The Fables* and some of La Fontaine's other works, demonstrating how he used techniques of both concealment and disclosure to please an unconventional audience while simultaneously ingratiating himself with his more conventional patrons.

Brereton, Geoffrey. *A Short History of French Literature.* New York: Penguin Books, 1960. An analysis of *The Fables*, placing both the work and La Fontaine within the broader context of French literature.

Cruickshank, John, ed. *French Literature and Its Background.* Vol. 2. New York: Oxford University Press, 1969. Contains essays on French seventeenth century literature as well as a fine study of *The Fables* by Margaret McGowan, in which she examines both La Fontaine's philosophy and its relevance to his milieu.

Fumaroli, Marc. *The Poet and the King: Jean de La Fontaine and His Century.* Translated by Jane Marie Todd. Notre Dame, Ind.: University of Notre Dame Press, 2002. Recounts La Fontaine's life and career within the context of political and cultural developments in seventeenth century France, describing how he sought to maintain his artistic integrity against the oppressive regime of Louis XIV.

Hollier, Dennis, ed. *A New History of French Literature.* Cambridge, Mass.: Harvard University Press, 1994. This massive volume, challenging in its unusual perspectives, contains an interesting chapter by Georges Van Den Abbeele on La Fontaine and two other seventeenth century French moralists, Jean de La Bruyère and François de La Rochefoucauld. The chapter's emphasis is on ideas.

La Fontaine, Jean de. *"The Fables" of La Fontaine.* Translated by Marianne Moore. New York: Viking Press, 1952. An indispensable translation of La Fontaine's *The Fables*, rendered by one of America's great poets. Moore's translation preserves the style, point of view, voice, and sense of *The Fables* without straining for rhyme and rhythm at the expense of meaning.

Runyon, Randolph Paul. *In La Fontaine's Labyrinth: A Thread Through "The Fables."* Charlottesville, Va.: Rookwood Press, 2000. Traces the connections between each fable and the succeeding one, locating a common unity throughout the work.

Slater, Maya. *The Craft of La Fontaine.* London: Athlone Press, 2001. A detailed explication of *The Fables*, including analyses of their humor, depiction of animals, literary qualities, and moralistic core.

The Faerie Queene

Author: Edmund Spenser (c. 1552-1599)
First published: Books 1-3, 1590; books 4-6, 1596
Type of work: Poetry
Type of plot: Allegory
Time of plot: Arthurian Age
Locale: England

Principal characters:
GLORIANA, the Faerie Queene, representing Queen
  Elizabeth
THE RED CROSS KNIGHT, representing Holiness
UNA, representing Religion
ARCHIMAGO, a magician
DUESSA, representing Roman Catholicism
BRITOMART, representing Chastity
GUYON, representing Temperance
ARTEGALL, representing Justice
PRINCE ARTHUR, legendary English king

The Poem:

Gloriana, the Faerie Queene, is holding her annual twelve-day feast. As is the custom, anyone in trouble can appear before the court and ask for a champion. The fair lady Una comes riding on a white ass, accompanied by a dwarf. She complains that her father and mother are shut up in a castle by a dragon. The Red Cross Knight offers to help her, and the party sets out to rescue Una's parents. In a cave the Red Cross Knight encounters a horrible creature, half serpent, half woman. Although the foul stench nearly overpowers him, the knight slays the monster. After the battle, the Red Cross Knight and Una lose their way. A friendly stranger who offers them shelter is really Archimago, the wicked magician. By making the Red Cross Knight dream that Una is a harlot, Archimago separates Una from her champion.

Una goes on her way alone. Archimago quickly assumes the form of the Red Cross Knight and follows her to do her harm. Meanwhile the Red Cross Knight falls into the company of Duessa, an evil enchantress. They meet the great giant Orgoglio, who overcomes the Red Cross Knight and makes Duessa his mistress. Prince Arthur, touched by Una's misfortunes, rescues the Red Cross Knight from Orgoglio and leads him to Una. Once again Una and her champion ride on their mission.

At last they come to Una's kingdom, and the dragon that imprisoned her parents comes out to do battle. After two days of fighting, the Red Cross Knight overthrows the dragon. After the parents are freed, the Red Cross Knight and Una are betrothed. Still hoping to harm the Red Cross Knight, Archimago tells Sir Guyon that the Red Cross Knight despoiled a virgin of her honor. Shocked, Guyon sets out to right the wrong. The cunning Archimago disguises Duessa as a young girl and places her on the road, where she tells a piteous tale of wrong done by the Red Cross Knight and

urges Guyon to avenge her. When Guyon and the Red Cross Knight meet, they lower their lances and begin to fight. Fortunately the signs of the Virgin Mary on the armor of each recall them to their senses, and Guyon is ashamed that he was tricked by the magician.

In his travels Guyon falls in with Prince Arthur, and the two visit the Castle of Alma, the stronghold of Temperance. The most powerful enemy of Temperance is the demon Maleger. In a savage battle Prince Arthur vanquishes Maleger. Guyon goes on to the Bower of Bliss, where his archenemy Acrasy lives. With stout heart Guyon overthrows Acrasy and destroys the last enemy of Temperance. After sending Acrasy back to the fairy court under guard, Guyon and Prince Arthur go on their way until on an open plain they see a knight arming for battle. With Prince Arthur's permission, Guyon rides against the strange knight, and in the meeting Guyon is unhorsed by the strong lance of his opponent. Ashamed of his fall, Guyon snatches his sword and continues the fight on foot.

The palmer, attending Guyon, sees that the champion cannot prevail against the stranger, for the strange knight is enchanted. When he stops the fight, the truth is revealed: The strange knight is really the lovely Britomart, a chaste and pure damsel, who saw the image of her lover, Artegall, in Venus's looking-glass and sets out in search of him. With the situation explained, Britomart joins Guyon, Prince Arthur, and Arthur's squire, Timias, and the four continue their quest.

In a strange wood they travel for days, seeing no one, but everywhere they meet bears, lions, and bulls. Suddenly a beautiful lady on a white palfrey gallops out of the brush. She is Florimell, pursued by a lustful forester who spurs his steed cruelly in an attempt to catch her. The three men join the chase, but out of modesty Britomart stays behind. She waits a long time; then, despairing of ever finding her companions again, she goes on alone.

As she approaches Castle Joyous she sees six knights attacking one. She rides into the fight and demands to know why they are fighting in such cowardly fashion. She learns that any knight passing has to love the lady of Castle Joyous or fight six knights. Britomart denounces the rule and with her magic lance unhorses four of the knights. She enters Castle Joyous as a conqueror. After meeting the Red Cross Knight in the castle, Britomart resolves to go on as a knight errant. She hears from Merlin, whom she visits, that she and Artegall are destined to have illustrious descendants.

Meanwhile Timias is wounded while pursuing the lustful forester. Belphoebe, the wondrous beauty of the Garden of Adonis, rescues him and heals his wounds. Timias falls in love with Belphoebe. Amoret, the fair one, is held prisoner by a young knight who attempts to defile her. For months she resists his advances. Then Britomart, hearing of her sad plight, overcomes the two knights who guard Amoret's prison and free her. Greatly attracted to her brave rescuer, Amoret sets out with Britomart.

At a strange castle a knight claims Amoret as his love. Britomart jousts with him to save Amoret, and after winning the tourney Britomart is forced to take off her helmet. With her identity revealed, Britomart and Amoret set off together in search of their true loves.

Artegall, in search of adventure, joins Scudamour, knight errant. They meet Amoret and Britomart, who is still disguised as a knight. Britomart and Artegall fight an indecisive battle during which Artegall is surprised to discover that his opponent is his lost love, Britomart. The two lovers are reunited at last, but in the confusion Amoret is abducted by Lust. With the help of Prince Arthur, Scudamour rescues Amoret from her loathsome captor. He woos Amoret in the Temple of Love, where they find shelter.

Artegall, champion of true justice, is brought up and well trained by Astraea. When Artegall is of age, Astraea gives him a trusty groom, and the new knight sets out on his adventures. Talus, the groom, is an iron man who carries an iron flail to thresh out falsehood. Irene, who asks at the fairy court for a champion against the wicked Grantorto, sets out with Artegall and Talus to regain her heritage. With dispatch Artegall and Talus overcome Grantorto and restore Irene to her throne.

Later Artegall enters the lists against a strange knight who is really the disguised Amazon, Radigund. Artegall wounds Radigund, but when he sees that his prostrate foe is a comely woman, he throws away his weapons. The wounded Amazon

then rushes on the defenseless Artegall and takes him prisoner. Artegall is kept in shameful confinement until at last Talus informs Britomart of his fate. Britomart goes to her lover's rescue and slays Radigund.

Continuing his quest, Artegall meets two hags, Envy and Detraction, who defame his character and set the Blatant Beast barking at his heels. Artegall forbids Talus to beat the hags and returns to the fairy court. The Blatant Beast, defamer of knightly character and the last remaining enemy of the fairy court, finally meets his match. The courteous Calidore, the gentlest of all the knights, conquers the beast and leads him, tamed, back to the court of the Fairie Queene.

Critical Evaluation:

The Faerie Queene was the first sustained poetic creation after that of Geoffrey Chaucer, and its beauty and power made for it a secure place in English literature as soon as it was given to the world. At present it is generally accorded a high place in the history of English literary art. Combined with Edmund Spenser's poetic power was his high moral purpose.

Only six books of the twelve planned by Spenser were completed. The fragmentary seventh book was published in 1609, ten years after his death. What he did finish is so great that *The Faerie Queene* is, sad to say, generally more honored than read. The grand conception and execution of the poem reflect both the life of the poet and his participation in the life and ideals of his age. Spenser was committed to public service in the expansive period of Elizabethan efflorescence. A gentleman poet and friend of the great, Spenser never received the preferment he hoped for, but he remained devoted to Elizabeth, to England, and to late sixteenth century optimism. Even during his lifetime, Spenser was honored as a poet by the court and by other men of letters. Spenser's allegorical imagination and his masterful control of language have earned him a reputation as "the poet's poet."

Like other Elizabethan poets, Spenser produced eclogues and a sonnet sequence, but *The Faerie Queene* is his great accomplishment. In a famous letter to Sir Walter Ralegh, Spenser explained the ambitious structure and purpose of his poem. It was to be composed of twelve books, each treating one of Aristotle's moral virtues as represented in the figure of a knight. The whole was to be a consistent moral allegory, and the twelve books taken together would describe the circumscribing Aristotelian virtue of magnanimity, which Spenser called Magnificence.

At some point Spenser apparently decided to modify this plan. By the fourth book the simple representation of one virtue in one hero has broken down, though each book still does define a dominant virtue. More significantly, virtues are included that are not in Aristotle. Spenser is true to Aristotle, however, in consistently viewing virtue as a mean between extremes, as a moderate path between many aberrations of excess and defect.

The poem owes many debts to other antecedents. It is filled with references to and echoes of the Bible and the Greek and Latin classics. It is suffused with the spirit and much of the idealized landscape and atmosphere of medieval romance. However, its greatest debts are to the writers of the Continental Renaissance, particularly Ludovico Ariosto. Ariosto's loosely plotted *Orlando furioso* (1516, 1521, 1532; English translation, 1591) was the most influential single model, and Spenser borrows freely, but where Ariosto was ironic or skeptical, Spenser transforms the same material into a serious medium for his high ethical purposes. Moreover, while allegory is a dimension added to Ariosto by his critics, Spenser's allegorical purpose is unmistakable. In this aim, he is within the Renaissance tradition of writing courtesy books, such as Baldassare Castiglione's *Il libro del cortegiano* (1528; *The Book of the Courtier*, 1561), guides to conduct for the gentleman who would seek excellence in behavior and demeanor. *The Faerie Queene* is a courtesy book turned to the highest of purposes—the moral formation of the ideal Christian gentleman.

Book 1, the story of Red Cross Knight, the Knight of Holiness, is the truest to the original structure intention. Red Cross is assigned to Una to relieve her kingdom of a menacing dragon. Through the book Red Cross's chivalric exploits gradually develop in him the virtue he represents, so that he can ultimately kill the dragon. Book 2 also makes its demonstration in a relatively straightforward way. Sir Guyon, the Knight of Temperance, despite temporary setbacks and failures, eventually gains the knowledge of what true temperance is by seeing how it is violated by excess, by defect, by self-indulgence, and by inhuman austerity. Ultimately Guyon can reject the opulent pleasures of the sensuous Bower of Bliss.

In book 3 the allegorical method begins to change, probably because the virtues represented are more sophisticated in concept and more difficult to define. This complexity is mirrored in plot as earlier characters reappear and subsequent characters make brief entries. The result is an elaborate suspense and an intricate definition of virtues by means of examples, comparisons, and contrasts.

Book 3 deals with Chastity, book 4 with Friendship; both incorporate Renaissance platonic notions of love. Chastity is infinitely more than sexual abstinence, because by the perception of beauty and experience of love a person moves closer to divine perfection. The concept of mutuality is emphasized in book 3 by the fact that Scudamour cannot accomplish his quest without Britomart's contribution to his development. Book 4 further explores platonic love by defining true friendship through a series of examples and counter examples that culminate in the noblest kind of friendship: that between a man and a woman.

In book 5, the adventures of Artegall, Spenser develops a summary statement of his political philosophy. Justice is relentless and inexorable; it is not only a matter of abstract principle but also of wise governing. After the stringency of the Book of Justice, book 6 is a softer, more pastoral treatment of the chivalric ideal of Courtesy in the person of Sir Calidore.

Spenser's allegory is enlivened by the meanderings of plot as well as by the fullness and appeal of his personifications. In addition to the well-wrought moral allegory, there is sporadic political allegory, as Elizabeth occasionally becomes visible in Una or Britomart or Belphoebe, or as contemporary events are evoked by the plot. At every point Spenser's style is equal to his noble intentions. The verse form, the Spenserian stanza, is an ingenious modification of the rhyme royal stanza, in which the last line breaks the decasyllabic monotony with a rhythmically flexible Alexandrine. The diction has often been called archaic, but it is perhaps more a capitalizing on all the resources of Elizabethan English, even the obsolescent, in the service of the beauty of sound. Alliteration and assonance also contribute to a consummate aural beauty that not only reinforces sense but also provides a pervasive harmony that is distinctly Spenserian.

"Critical Evaluation" by Edward E. Foster

Further Reading

Alpers, Paul J. *The Poetry of "The Faerie Queene."* Princeton: N.J.: Princeton University Press, 1967. Describes the language of *The Faerie Queene* and discusses the nature of Spenser's poetry.

Freeman, Rosemary. *"The Faerie Queene": A Companion for Readers.* Berkeley: University of California Press, 1970. Displays a keen appreciation of Spenser's poetry and the peculiarity of his epic. Part one discusses the poem's origin, structure, and allegory; part two provides a book-by-book thematic analysis.

Hadfield, Andrew, ed. *The Cambridge Companion to Spenser.* New York: Cambridge University Press, 2001. Collection of essays providing an overview of Spenser's life and work. Some of the essays discuss the relevance of Spenser, his life and career, the historical contexts of his work, his use of language, and his literary influence. Susanne L. Wofford examines books 1-3 of *The Faerie Queene*, while Andrew Hadfield analyzes books 4-7.

Hough, Graham. *A Preface to "The Faerie Queene."* New York: W. W. Norton, 1962. A seminal work of Spenser criticism. Relates *The Faerie Queene* to the tradition of the romantic epic. Provides a book-by-book commentary and considers the poem as a whole.

King, Andrew. *The "Faerie Queene" and the Middle English Romance: The Matter of Just Memory.* New York: Oxford University Press, 2000. Emphasizes the importance of regionalism on Middle English writers, especially Spenser. Explores the thematic role of exiled youth and his counterpart, the outcast virgin.

Lethbridge, J. B., ed. *Edmund Spenser: New and Renewed Directions.* Madison, N.J.: Fairleigh Dickinson University Press, 2006. Reprints a collection of papers originally delivered at a conference about Spenser. Includes discussions of the Spenserian stanza, Spenser's relationship to Ireland, and the trend toward a new historical criticism of his work. Several of the essays examine *The Faerie Queene*, including "'Well Grounded, Finely Framed, and Strongly Trussed up Together': The 'Medieval' Structure of *The Faerie Queene*" by Andrew King, "Acrasia and Bondage: Guyon's Perversion of the Ovidian Erotic in Book II of *The Faerie Queene*" by Syrithe Pugh, and "Ralegh, Spenser, and Elizabeth: Acts of Friendship in *The Faerie Queene*, Book IV" by Graham Atkin.

McCabe, Richard A. *Spenser's Monstrous Regiment: Elizabethan Ireland and the Poetics of Difference.* New York: Oxford University Press, 2002. Analyzes how Spenser's experiences of living and writing in Ireland challenged his ideas about English nationhood. Assesses the influence of colonialism on the themes, imagery, language, and structure of his poetry. Several of the chapters focus on *The Faerie Queene*.

Sale, Roger. *Reading Spenser: An Introduction to "The Faerie Queene."* New York: Random House, 1968. Speculates that Spenser's transformation from a medieval to a modern poet prevented him from finishing his epic. Argues that the poem is intentionally "undramatic."

Suttie, Paul. *Self-Interpretation in "The Faerie Queene."* Rochester, N.Y.: D. S. Brewer, 2006. Reexamines Spenser's use of allegory. Argues that his heroes are poised between rival codes of morality, uncertain which is the true code of right and wrong. Describes how the poem reflects the conflict in England between proponents of feudalism and absolute monarchy and the country's religious divisions.

Woodcock, Matthew. *Fairy in "The Faerie Queene": Renaissance Elf-Fashioning and Elizabethan Myth-Making.* Burlington, Vt.: Ashgate, 2004. Examines Spenser's use of fairy mythology in the poem, arguing that its identification of the Faerie Queene with Elizabeth I is more ambiguous than previously recognized. Maintains that Spenser was not only creating a mythological persona for Elizabeth, but also was using the poem to draw attention to his own role as a mythmaker.

Fahrenheit 451

Author: Ray Bradbury (1920-   )
First published: 1953 (expanded version of "The Fireman," 1951)
Type of work: Novel
Type of plot: Science fiction
Time of plot: The future
Locale: North America

Principal characters:
GUY MONTAG, a fireman
CLARISSE MCCLELLAN, his young neighbor
MILDRED MONTAG, Guy's wife
CAPTAIN BEATTY, the fire chief
FABER, a retired English teacher
GRANGER, leader of the "book people"

The Story:

Like all firemen in the future society of the novel, Montag burns books, which are entirely prohibited. One day, while returning home from work, Montag meets Clarisse, his mysterious young neighbor. Her probing questions cause him to reflect critically on the purpose of his job. When he enters his house, he finds that his wife has taken an overdose of sleeping pills. Montag calls the emergency hospital to have her stomach pumped.

The next day, however, Mildred fails to recollect the event and returns to her usual life of watching mindless television shows. After talking again to Clarisse, Montag returns to the firehouse. There the Mechanical Hound, a dangerous robotic creature used to track suspects, starts acting aggressively toward him. During the following weeks Montag meets Clarisse every day, and they discuss the moral and spiritual emptiness of their society, caused by its obsession with frantic consumption and shallow entertainment. One day, however, Clarisse is suddenly gone. Montag now begins to ask his colleagues questions concerning the historical origins of book-burning. During the next book-burning raid on an old woman's home, he secretly takes a book. The old woman, rather than submitting to be arrested, sets fire to herself and her books.

At home, Montag feels increasingly alienated from Mildred. While Mildred is watching her favorite shows on the television screens that cover three entire walls, she casually mentions that Clarisse was run over by a car. Montag goes to bed imagining he can hear the Mechanical Hound outside his house.

The next day, Montag feels sick and stays home from work. Shortly afterward, Montag's boss, Captain Beatty, the fire chief, arrives at his house and starts to explain to him how firemen became book-burners. According to Beatty, the increasing population pressure caused all entertainment to be leveled down to the lowest common denominator. Furthermore, books were censored in order to avoid offending any particular group in society. In the end, the majority of people preferred happiness to critical awareness, and books were entirely banned.

After Beatty leaves the house, Montag confesses his doubts to Mildred and brings out several books he hid in the house. He begins to read to her, but Mildred simply cannot understand his fascination with the printed word. Montag therefore visits Faber, a retired English teacher whom he once caught reading a book. Faber explains to Montag that books offer a rich texture of life, leisurely enjoyment, and freedom to act on one's ideas—all values despised by the materialistic society around them. Faber believes that the imminent atomic war will soon destroy society. He gives Montag a pair of earphone-transmitters, so that they can stay in permanent radio contact. That night, Mildred's friends arrive to watch television. Montag shatters their complacency by reading a Matthew Arnold poem, "Dover Beach," to them and eventually drives them out of the house.

Montag then returns to the firehouse, where Beatty tries to prove the insignificance of books by citing contradictory passages from world literature. The alarm bell rings, and Montag sets off with the team, only to find that Mildred denounced him and the firemen are going to his own house. After Montag uses the flamethrower to burn the hidden books, he accidentally loses the miniature transmitters Faber gave him. When Beatty threatens to trace the owner, Montag kills him with a blast of the flamethrower. He also manages to incinerate the Mechanical Hound, but not before he is injured by it.

While Montag is running for his life, he hears that war is declared. He is almost killed by teenagers in a speeding car but manages to escape and even hide a book in another fireman's house and call in an alarm in order to distract his pursuers. Finally, he reaches Faber's apartment. Faber tells him to flee toward the open country, where teachers and writers are living as tramps. After changing his clothes to distract the new Mechanical Hound brought in by the police, Montag makes a final dash for the river.

After floating down the river, Montag meets a group of social outcasts who keep books alive by memorizing them word for word. The book ends with the destruction of the cities by atomic bombs and the hope that civilization, like the mythical Phoenix, will rise again from its ashes. In the meantime, Montag and his newfound friends will remain "living books."

Critical Evaluation:

Fahrenheit 451 was Ray Bradbury's first major novel. His earlier book-length work, *The Martian Chronicles* (1950), was a loosely connected cycle of short stories. In the opinion of many critics, *Fahrenheit 451* remains his only really impressive novel. Appropriately enough for a writer who has generally been considered a master of short fiction, this novel grew out of a story, titled "The Fireman," which Bradbury had published in 1951. *Fahrenheit 451* reached a wide audience through François Truffaut's film adaptation of 1966, which starred Julie Christie as both Mildred and Clarisse and Oscar Werner as Guy Montag.

Bradbury's novel is a classic example of dystopian fiction, a subgenre of utopian literature. Literary utopias, such as Thomas More's *De Optimo Reipublicae Statu, deque Nova Insula Utopia* (1516; *Utopia*, 1551), after which the entire genre was named, present fictional depictions of societies that are clearly superior to the one in which the author lives. The societies described in such seventeenth century works as Francis Bacon's *New Atlantis* (1627) and Tommaso Campanella's *Civitas Solis* (1623; *The City of the Sun*, 1885) are highly structured and static. Utopian novels of the nineteenth and early twentieth centuries (most notably Edward Bellamy's immensely popular *Looking Backward: 2000-*

1887, 1888) added the concept of progress, situating their utopian communities in the future rather than in a remote place. Utopian books of that time exhibit a strong belief in the social benefits of advancing technology.

After World War I, however, there was a vehement backlash against the very idea of utopianism, which took the form of dystopian novels. Dystopian novels show that any attempt at establishing utopia will only make matters much worse. The great works of this tradition, such as Yevgeny Zamyatin's *My* (1920-1921; *We*, 1924), Aldous Huxley's *Brave New World* (1932), and George Orwell's *Nineteen Eighty-Four* (1949), establish a pattern that is clearly reflected in Bradbury's *Fahrenheit 451*.

The set of characters in Bradbury's novel closely follows established genre traditions. Like the protagonists of many other dystopian novels, Montag starts out as a loyal member of the future society and only gradually shows signs of disaffection. His progress toward rebellion is aided by a female companion (Clarisse) and an older mentor figure (Faber, and to some extent Beatty) who provide alternate sets of values.

The most crucial element in the dystopian hero's process of initiation, however, is the discovery of books that help explain the existence of the dystopian society and offer means to overcome it. This is a stock scene in dystopian literature, and it is found in such diverse works as Huxley's *Brave New World*, Orwell's *Nineteen Eighty-Four*, and Ira Levin's *This Perfect Day* (1970). Bradbury developed this standard motif into a spirited defense of literature itself. In Montag's world of state-sponsored book-burning, books are not simply carriers of potentially subversive messages—their very physical existence evokes a rich cultural tradition antithetical to the leveling tendencies of the mass media. Furthermore, Montag, as a lone reader engrossed in a book, symbolizes the ideal of individualism in a society intent on standardizing every aspect of people's lives. Thus, *Fahrenheit 451* takes the genre of dystopia to its logical conclusion by enthusiastically proclaiming the power of the written word against any kind of oppression.

Bradbury's imagery is both vivid and highly ambiguous. The very first paragraph depicts Montag's flamethrower as a "great python spitting its venomous kerosene upon the world." This sets the pattern for a complex juxtaposition of natural and mechanical images that dominates the novel and reflects its central tensions between the country and the city, or culture and technology. Many elements of this future society are portrayed as perverted versions of natural objects: the "beetle" cars used for joy riding, the "seashell" radios that keep people awash in sound, the "cobra-like" stomach pump used on Mildred after her suicide attempt, and, most

significantly, the merciless killer robot called the Mechanical Hound. This contrast between the natural and the artificial is also employed in relation to Clarisse and Mildred (both of whom were played by Christie in Truffaut's film version of *Fahrenheit 451*). While Clarisse is associated with trees and the change of the seasons, Mildred is depicted as cold and mechanical.

As the novel progresses, however, Bradbury transcends the static opposition of the natural and the technological and focuses on the ambiguity of his central symbol, fire. Montag is initially fascinated by fire, and this fascination persists, even as his repulsion against the act of book-burning grows. He once compares Clarisse's luminous face to the light of a candle, an image that brings up a nostalgic childhood memory. The first of the many literary quotes that draw Montag inexorably toward forbidden books describes a martyr's death as the lighting of a candle.

The destructive aspect of fire is embodied by Beatty, a true pyromaniac who is constantly playing with fire. For Beatty, fire is the ultimate weapon that allows him to cleanse and to purify society by literally incinerating any dissenting voices. When Montag turns the flamethrower on Beatty after having torched his own house, Montag momentarily switches roles with this devil's advocate, and he briefly muses afterward whether Beatty might not have wanted him to do this.

The ambiguity of fire reaches its climax at the end of the novel, when the cities are destroyed in a nuclear war. Strangely, this scene employs no fire imagery at all and lyrically describes the destroyed cities as briefly floating in the air before they disintegrate. Out of the ashes of the cities, as Granger hopes, the Phoenix of a new civilization will arise, yet the bird Phoenix is also the emblem of the book-burning firemen. Thus, *Fahrenheit 451* at least partially disassociates the reader from the optimism of its protagonists and remains poised between dystopian despair and a utopian belief in the inevitability of the triumph of reason.

Frank Dietz

Further Reading

Bloom, Harold, ed. *Ray Bradbury's "Fahrenheit 451."* New York: Chelsea House, 2007. Collection of essays providing various interpretations of the novel, including an introductory essay by Bloom. Includes bibliography.

Bradbury, Ray. *Match to Flame: The Fictional Paths to "Fahrenheit 451."* Edited by Donn Albright and Jon Eller. Colorado Springs, Colo.: Gauntlet, 2006. Between 1944 and the publication of *Fahrenheit 451* in 1953, Bradbury wrote nine short stories and novellas about book-burning that he later described as antecedents to his novel. This book contains those stories, including "The Fireman" (1951), the novella he later expanded into *Fahrenheit 451*, tracing the development of Bradbury's writing and the genesis of the novel.

Greenberg, Martin Henry, and Joseph D. Olander, eds. *Ray Bradbury*. New York: Taplinger, 1980. This collection contains several essays discussing various aspects of *Fahrenheit 451*. Extensive bibliography.

Johnson, Wayne L. *Ray Bradbury*. New York: Frederick Ungar, 1980. Deals with central themes related to science fiction and fantasy in Bradbury's works.

Mogen, David. *Ray Bradbury*. Boston: Twayne, 1986. Provides biographical background as well as analyses of major works. Sees *Fahrenheit 451* as a satire of 1950's McCarthyism, as well as a general attack on totalitarianism.

Reid, Robin Anne. *Ray Bradbury: A Critical Companion*. Westport, Conn.: Greenwood Press, 2000. Designed for high school and college students. Provides a brief biography, discusses Bradbury's place in the science-fiction genre, and devotes separate chapters to analyses of *Fahrenheit 451* and other novels. The analyses include discussions of plot, themes, character development, and setting.

Touponce, William F. *Ray Bradbury and the Poetics of Reverie: Fantasy, Science Fiction, and the Reader*. Ann Arbor: University of Michigan Press, 1984. Applies reader-response theories to Bradbury's works. Focuses on *Fahrenheit 451* as a critique of technological rationalism and the contemporary culture industry.

Weller, Sam. *The Bradbury Chronicles: The Life of Ray Bradbury*. New York: William Morrow, 2005. Biography focusing on Bradbury's private life and the successes and difficulties of his professional career.

Fail-Safe

Authors: Eugene Burdick (1918-1965) and
   Harvey Wheeler (1918-2004)
First published: 1962
Type of work: Novel
Type of plot: Political realism
Time of plot: 1967
Locale: Washington, D.C.; New York City; Omaha,
   Nebraska; Moscow

Principal characters:
PETER BUCK, a Russian translator
PRESIDENT OF THE UNITED STATES, unnamed but most
   likely John F. Kennedy
NIKITA KHRUSHCHEV, the Soviet premier
LIEUTENANT GENERAL GRANT LEE BOGAN, commander
   of the Strategic Air Command's war room
COLONEL CASCIO, General Bogan's deputy, a former
   classmate of Groteschele
MR. RASKOB, U.S. representative from New York
GORDON KNAPP, president of Universal Electronics
BRIGADIER GENERAL WARREN ABRAHAM BLACK, a
   Pentagon official and former classmate of the president
SWENSON, U.S. secretary of defense
WALTER GROTESCHELE, a professor of political science
LIEUTENANT COLONEL GRADY, head of Vindicator
   Bomber Group Six
MARSHAL NEVSKY, commander of Soviet Air Defense
   Command, Ziev
GENERAL KONIEV, Nevsky's deputy

The Story:

   Peter Buck goes to work at his office at the White House. It is an ordinary day until the red phone, which has never rung before, rings. The president is on the phone, requesting Buck's immediate presence at the White House bomb shelter.

   Meanwhile, at the Strategic Air Command (SAC) war room, General Bogan and Colonel Cascio are giving a tour to Congressman Raskob and Mr. Gordon Knapp. Bogan explains to his visitors how the room works, including explaining the Big Board, which projects large maps indicating the movements of submarines, ships, and airplanes. Suddenly, the war room goes to Condition Blue: An unidentified flying object (UFO) is heading toward the United States from the Soviet Union. Six squadrons of six Vindicator nuclear bombers each are ordered to their fail-safe positions.

Bogan explains the fail-safe system to Raskob: It is meant to ensure that retaliatory measures will be taken against a Soviet first strike, even if the strike destroys all U.S. command and control capabilities. Raskob worries about mistakes triggering a war, but Cascio reassures him the system is foolproof. However, in a neighboring room, a small capacitor in Fail-Safe Activating Mechanism number six blows out unnoticed. The UFO turns out to be an off-course commercial jet with engine trouble, and the alert is cancelled. Five of the Vindicator squadrons turn back from their fail-safe positions. Because of the capacitor malfunction, Vindicator Group Six continues to fly toward Moscow.

Buck leaves his office and joins the president and his staff in the White House bomb shelter. In Omaha, Bogan and Cascio place the war room at Condition Red. At various U.S. bases, bombers, fighter jets, and ballistic missiles are prepared for action.

In New York City, General Black awakes from a recurring nightmare in which he is a bull being flayed alive. He flies to Washington to attend a briefing at the Pentagon with the secretary of defense and Professor Groteschele. During the flight, he recalls a cocktail party the night before where Professor Groteschele argued to Emmett Foster, editor of *Liberal Magazine*, that a nuclear war could be winnable. Foster countered that peace is the only way for humanity to survive. Black thinks nuclear war is inevitable.

In Bomber Group Six, Colonel Grady receives the fail-safe signal. He unseals the group's orders and learns that their target is Moscow. He attempts to verify the fail-safe signal with Omaha, but finds that their communications are being jammed. This causes Grady to believe that the Soviets are attacking.

Black enters the Pentagon's big board room for the scheduled briefing. They discuss the fail-safe system and different nuclear attack scenarios. Groteschele worries that the Soviets may be able to move their missiles into space, which could reduce the reaction time to a Soviet attack to a level impossible for humans to achieve. However, everyone in the room ignores him, because the big board is indicating Condition Blue. Shocked, they watch as a U.S. bomber group flies past its fail-safe point. The president calls Omaha and orders Skyscraper fighter planes to go after the bombers. Unfortunately, the fighters had turned back after the all-clear was

given and may now be too far from the Vindicators to overtake them. The president orders Bogan to tell the Skyscrapers to use their afterburners—effectively ordering them on a suicide mission, since the fighters will burn up all their fuel reaching the bombers, leaving them unable to return to their base.

Cascio is uncomfortable with the president's decision and argues with Bogan, wasting valuable seconds. Meanwhile, the president calls the Pentagon and asks Swenson and his group to figure out what should be done if the fighters cannot shoot down the bombers. They set up a conference call with Omaha. Cascio feels the situation is a Soviet trick, despite the fact that surveillance can find no evidence of aggressive action by the Soviets. Groteschele thinks the Soviets, having more to lose in a war, would surrender if attacked because they know that the United States has a system of Doomsday tapes that will allow U.S. missiles to retaliate against them even if everyone in the United States is killed.

The big board displays the action as the Skyscraper fighters shoot at the bombers, fail to bring them down, and then—their fuel spent—crash into the sea. Raskob knows Khrushchev will have no choice but to retaliate from a nuclear attack. Swenson tells the president that they are sure that two of the Vindicators will be able to make it through all Soviet defenses.

The president then calls Premier Khrushchev. He tries to convince the premier that the attacking bombers are not following his orders. Some of the premier's advisers think the president's call is a trick and that they should retaliate. Both sides agree to set up a second conference line between SAC and its Russian counterpart.

With conflicting feelings, the Americans watch seventy Soviet fighters try to intercept Group Six. The Russians shoot down two Vindicators but lose sixty-five of their fighters. Khrushchev calls, and again the president tries to convince the premier of his sincerity. Khrushchev tells the president he will call again, once he is a safe distance from Moscow. The president then calls General Black, asking him if he remembers the story of Abraham. He orders Black to Andrews Air Force Base.

The president, the premier's personal staff, Bogan, Nevsky, the American ambassador to Moscow, and the Soviet delegate to the United Nations join a conference call. The president orders Bogan to communicate with Marshal Nevsky to coordinate efforts in shooting down the remaining Vindicators. The president hangs up. Cascio refuses to answer Nevsky's questions. Cascio still does not trust the Soviets and argues that the military command should override the president. The president calls back and asks if the remaining

Vindicators will break radio silence as they near their target. Bogan says that they will.

Nevsky asks for the position of the three remaining planes. Just as Bogan begins to answer him, Cascio strikes him with a heavy ashtray. Cascio takes command of the war room. At the same time, Grady breaks radio silence. The president orders Grady to abort the mission. Grady ignores him, thinking it is a trick. Cascio's mutinous command is short lived, as two Air Force guards take him into custody. Bogan gives the Vindicator positions to Nevsky, but valuable time has been lost.

Bogan tells Nevsky to ignore Vindicator Six, as it is a defensive plane carrying no bombs. Nevsky ignores the advice. Through a last-ditch diversionary move, Vindicator Six sacrificially draws off the Soviet fighters, while the other two remaining bombers fly as close to the ground as possible. Realizing the bombers will now make it through to Moscow, Nevsky collapses and Koniev takes over. Koniev decides to fire nuclear missiles at the Vindicators, hoping to take them out before they can reach Moscow. Grady launches his remaining air-to-air missiles straight up as decoys. The ruse works, as the Soviet missiles strike the American missiles instead of the bombers. However, the crew is fatally irradiated by the nearby explosions. Since they cannot survive long anyway, the bomber's crewmen decide the best way to assure the success of their mission is to fly low and detonate their bombs inside their planes.

Back at the White House bomb shelter, a conference line is set up between the president, Khrushchev, the American ambassador to Moscow, and the Soviet delegate to the United Nations. The president proposes to Khrushchev that to prevent all-out war, as soon as the ambassador's phone shrieks—indicating that it has melted in a nuclear blast—he will order a SAC squadron to drop the same number of nuclear bombs on New York City that were dropped on Moscow. Each country will have lost an important city, but each country will survive. Khrushchev is shocked but accepts the plan. The Vindicators make it to Moscow and detonate their bombs. The president orders Black to bomb New York City, where Black's family lives and the president's wife is visiting. Black tells his crew that he will handle the bombing alone. After dropping the bombs, he kills himself with his suicide kit.

Critical Evaluation:

Fail-Safe reads as a journalistic piece. However, Eugene Burdick and Harvey Wheeler state in their preface that the work is not an exposé. Their main purpose in writing it, they say, was to confront head-on the lack of public awareness of military activity in nuclear defense and the all-too-real possi-

bility of accidental nuclear war, even when some of the information is declassified and discussed in technical journals.

The authors masterfully weave together accounts of actions in several places. They do this through several devices, including reminders of time, parallel big boards, and the red phone. The novel uses an omniscient point of view to allow readers to understand the motivations behind characters' actions. Flashbacks recall the familial and military backgrounds of the primary characters. From these, readers learn that the characters are all very intelligent, capable men. This helps drive home the theme that, even with the best intentions of the most intelligent people, no human oversight is failsafe.

A related theme is that no complex technical system is foolproof. The fail-safe system ironically fails to be fail-safe. As Knapp argues at one point in the novel, the more complex a system is, the more prone to accidents and breakdowns it becomes. Such systems can also operate too fast for human oversight to correct.

The novel portrays humans as becoming prisoners of technology, as well as losing their humanness. Many of the military characters are described with computerlike terms: "methodical," "automatic," "under control," and "preprogrammed." In the human-computer military systems, people are biological machines, trained to be automatic cogs. Members of Vindicator crews rotate so they will not form close bonds with one another. Instead, they become identical biological cogs bonding with the Vindicators. In the planes, they are largely encased by machinery—only their eyes are left uncovered. The president and the premier, as they await the destruction of Moscow, lament that they have become prisoners of technology. Khrushchev suggests that, instead of allowing computers to control people's lives, they should instead adopt the philosophy "The computer proposes; man disposes."

A final theme in the novel is sacrifice. The Skyscraper fighter pilots sacrifice themselves trying to stop the Vindicators. Vindicator Six sacrifices itself so the remaining bombers can make it to Moscow. Grady detonates his bombs within his plane, sacrificing himself and his crew to ensure a successful mission. The president sacrifices New York City and his wife, and Black sacrifices his family, to prevent all-out thermonuclear war. Black sacrifices himself to help alleviate some of the blame from his crew. Black's middle name, Abraham, echoes the sacrifice of the biblical Abraham in the Old Testament—except that God does not step in at the last minute to prevent his sacrifice.

David Michael Merchant

Further Reading

Hook, Sidney. *The Fail-Safe Fallacy*. New York: Stein & Day, 1963. Criticizes the plot and arguments of Burdick and Wheeler's novel.

Lipschutz, Ronnie D. *Cold War Fantasies: Film, Fiction, and Foreign Policy*. Lanham, Md.: Rowman & Littlefield, 2001. Discusses dominant Cold War literary and cinematic conventions and narratives, as well as the foreign policy of the period.

Piette, Adam. *The Literary Cold War, 1945-Vietnam: Sacrificial Logic and Paranoid Plotlines*. Edinburgh: Edinburgh University Press, 2009. Survey of the subgenre of Cold War fiction, placing *Fail-Safe*'s thematic interests in both sacrifice and paranoia in their cultural and historical context.

Seed, David. "Military Machines and Nuclear Accident: Burdick and Wheeler's *Fail-Safe*." *War, Literature, and the Arts* 6, no. 1 (March, 1994): 21-40. Excellent beginner's source for discussion of *Fail-Safe*. Places the novel within the political context of the time. Examines literary influences on the novel. Analyzes structure and themes.

The Fair Maid of Perth

Author: Sir Walter Scott (1771-1832)
First published: 1828
Type of work: Novel
Type of plot: Historical
Time of plot: 1396
Locale: Scotland

Principal characters:
HENRY GOW, the smith and armorer of Perth
CATHARINE GLOVER, his sweetheart, the fair maid of Perth
SIMON GLOVER, her father
CONACHAR, Simon's apprentice and heir to the chief of Clan Quhele
THE DUKE OF ROTHSAY, son of King Robert III and heir to the Scottish throne
SIR JOHN RAMORNY, his master of horse
ROBERT III, king of Scotland
THE DUKE OF ALBANY, his brother
THE EARL OF DOUGLAS, the "Black Douglas"
OLIVER PROUDFUTE, a Perth burgher and a friend of Henry Gow
HENBANE DWINING, Ramorny's physician and a Perth apothecary
SIR PATRICK CHARTERIS, the provost of Perth

The Story:

As Catharine Glover and her father, Simon, walk to church, an unidentified young nobleman, muffled in a cloak, joins them and asks the young woman's permission to come to her window the next morning to take part in the traditional Valentine's Day ritual. When she sensibly refuses to make any alliance above her social standing, he leaves in anger. A welcome guest, Henry Gow, appears at the Glovers' home that evening; he has just returned from a trip on which he sold armor throughout Scotland. Although Simon approves heartily of Henry's suit for Catharine's hand, she is disturbed by the young man's propensity for quarreling. Henry's fiery spirit leads him to rise up vigorously that evening against Conachar, Simon's Highlander apprentice, who jealously pours a tankard of beer on the armorer and then tries to stab him.

Henry's martial bent is put to better use the next morning, when, coming to present himself to Catharine as her valentine, he discovers a group of men attempting to climb through her bedroom window. While he and Simon are fighting them off, Henry severs the hand of one assailant. Again, a mysterious nobleman is involved. When Simon hears his voice, he sends Henry into his house and frees the other man.

In gratitude for Henry's protection, Catharine agrees to be his valentine, but she will not promise to marry him. She assures him that she is not in love with Conachar, who has just returned to his Highlands home, or any other man.

While King Robert is discussing the rising power of the earl of Douglas with his confessor, the earl arrives at the castle just in time to see his son-in-law, the duke of Rothsay, kiss a traveling entertainer. The "Black Douglas" is infuriated and threatens to kill both the prince and the innocent young woman. The duke of Albany, King Robert's brother James, and another nobleman calm the two men. Rothsay commits the entertainer to the care of Henry, who has just entered the courtyard while engaged in a scuffle with some of Douglas's men. Although he is reluctant to accept such a charge, especially on the day he has become Catharine's valentine, he takes the young woman home with him and then sends her on to Dundee the next morning.

The meeting of the king's council that follows Rothsay's foolish flirtation reveals the tensions surrounding the weak and easily influenced king. After King Robert prevents a duel between the archrivals the earls of March and Douglas, March stalks out to join the English. Albany and the prince, too, are struggling for control over king and country. As these personal conflicts smolder, the men discuss the enmity between the clans Quhele and Chattan and decide to settle the clans' differences by setting the bravest men from each clan against one another in a combat to be fought before the king. After Douglas leaves, the king and Albany question the prince about the early-morning disturbance at Simon's house, reported to them by Sir Patrick Charteris, the provost of Perth. Confronted with a ring found at Simon's house, Rothsay confesses that he was present; the ring belongs to Sir John Ramorny, his master of horse. Rothsay agrees to dismiss Ramorny, whom both older men regard as an evil influence over the young prince.

Conachar comes back to Perth briefly when Catharine requests that he give refuge to Father Clement, her confessor, who has been accused of heresy. The Highlander tells her that he is the son of the chief of Clan Quhele and that his real name is Eachin (Hector) MacIan. As he promises protection for Father Clement, he also hints at his love for Catharine.

Ramorny, whose hand was cut off in Perth, plans vengeance on his assailant with Henbane Dwining, an apothecary who is jealous of Henry's power and influence. Having gained only a mild revenge by spreading the tale of Henry's association with the itinerant young woman entertainer, he is eager to help Ramorny plot Henry's assassination. That night, as Shrovetide revelers mill about Perth, Oliver Proudfute, a well-meaning but tactless burgher, assures Si-

mon that Henry is not hiding the young woman; he saw Henry send her to Dundee. Then, fearing that he has made matters worse, Proudfute escapes from a group of taunting masquers and goes to Henry to apologize. Proudfute, who likes to think of himself as a hero but is really a timid soul, avoids the subject of his visit as long as possible. His belated and sheepish confession serves only to deepen Henry's depression over his relationship with Catharine; Henry orders his friend out, but not until he has granted the burgher's request that he be allowed to wear Henry's helmet and jacket to frighten away assailants. Ironically, these garments cause Proudfute's death: As he walks down the street imitating Henry's swagger, he is struck down from behind and killed.

Rothsay, who has been among the masquers, goes to find Ramorny to invite him to join the fun. Rothsay is horrified to learn of the loss of Ramorny's hand, and the prince suspects that Ramorny is planning revenge when he notices the surly murderer Bonthron in the room. Ramorny's suggestion that they "allow" Albany to die and force King Robert to abdicate shocks Rothsay further. He leaves immediately, vowing to see Ramorny no more and arousing the bitter hatred of his former friend.

The discovery of Proudfute's body the next morning sets off a rumor that Henry is dead, and Catharine flies disheveled through the streets to see whether he is safe. Henry's joy at this evidence of her affection is marred by the news of the murder and his realization that he must ignore Catharine's feelings and declare himself the champion of Proudfute's widow.

After a brief investigation, the provost suspects that Proudfute's death was the result of the enmity aroused during the Valentine's Day encounter between Henry and Ramorny. The council decides to determine the identity of the murderer by using an ancient test, the bier-right, which is based on the superstition that a murdered person's body bleeds in the presence of the killer. The members of Ramorny's household are later marched past Proudfute's body, with no result until Bonthron refuses the test and chooses the alternative, trial by combat. Henry defeats the murderer, who, in his confession, follows the instructions of Ramorny and Dwining and lays the principal blame on Rothsay. Albany immediately puts the prince in the hands of the high constable to protect him and keep him out of further trouble.

Sir Patrick Charteris arrives to tell Simon and Catharine that they are to be arrested for heresy. Simon plans to seek asylum with his old friend, Conachar's father, in the Highlands; however, knowing his former apprentice's feelings, he is relieved when the provost offers to take Catharine to Lady Marjory, duchess of Rothsay.

When Simon reaches his destination, he learns that his friend has died, but he is received courteously by the young chief of the clan. Conachar confesses to him that he fears the coming combat with Clan Chattan, and a coward is not a fit leader for a brave clan. He begs Simon to let him marry Catharine, for he feels that her love would strengthen him. Simon refuses to break his word to Henry, however.

Meanwhile, Ramorny has enticed Rothsay to flee to the former residence of his duchess by telling him that Catharine is coming there. When Catharine arrives, thinking Lady Marjory is still there, the prince at first tries to seduce her, but later he gives in to her appeal to his honor. He entrusts her to Louise, the itinerant entertainer he was earlier seen kissing, whom he encountered again by chance.

Ramorny and Dwining starve the prince to death while spreading arumor that he is ill. Louise and Catharine discover what is happening, and Louise escapes to bring Douglas to the rescue while Catharine tries to get food to Rothsay. Douglas arrives in time to force Ramorny's surrender and to save Catharine's life, but not in time to save the prince; Dwining poisons himself to avoid his confederate's fate of death by hanging.

Douglas and Albany decide to keep Rothsay's death secret until after the clan combat on Palm Sunday. That morning, Henry volunteers to take the place of a missing Chattan warrior and fights valiantly in order to have a chance to meet Conachar, whom he believes is a rival about to wed Catharine. Conachar's foster father sacrifices his eight sons and himself in an attempt to protect Conachar, but their efforts are useless. When the young leader faces Henry at last, the Highlander flees across the River Tay. Later that day, he goes to Catharine to tell her of his cowardice before he plunges to his death in the river.

Catharine and Henry are married a few months later. Although she is reconciled to her husband's warring impulses, he vows to take up arms again only in behalf of his country. Their first son has as godparents the earl of Douglas, Lady Marjory, and Sir Patrick Charteris.

King Robert dies soon afterward, brokenhearted by the death of one son and the capture by the English of the other, later James I of Scotland, whom Robert was sending away to protect him from Albany's power. Albany, acquitted by Parliament of the charge that he was responsible for Rothsay's death, nevertheless does penance for his guilt. His son, who inherited the regency, pays for his father's sins on the scaffold when James I comes to the throne years later.

Critical Evaluation:

Sir Walter Scott was one of the greatest novelists of the nineteenth century. His popularity and influence were not limited to Scotland or to the British Isles—he was admired and widely read throughout Europe and the United States. His novels are sweeping historical romances, but underneath the swordplay and the grandeur lies a firm moral underpinning.

Scott was born in Edinburgh, but, when he was less than two years of age, a childhood illness forced the family to send him to live with his grandparents at their home, Sandy Knowe, thirty miles southeast of the city. He remained there until he was seven or eight years of age. This was border country, a region filled with visual historic landmarks of the Scots' long and bloody conflicts with the English. Scott himself was descended from ancient chieftains as well as from the first laird of Raeburn. To keep the young Scott entertained, both of his grandparents recounted the oral history of the region and of his own family. He grew up immersed in the romance and tragedy of the Jacobite rebellion and the endless skirmishes in which the Scots fought to keep themselves free from British dominion.

Scott retained his childhood fascination with both the history and the landscape of Scotland, and these constitute the settings of almost all of his novels. Indeed, one of Scott's crowning achievements as a novelist is his ability to make history and landscapes breathe with life. Almost all of Scotland's history is presented in one or another of his novels. *The Fair Maid of Perth*, which portrays medieval Scotland, provides an excellent example of this. In its preface, Scott informs the reader of his fascination with the story of the battle between members of two prominent Highland clans that took place in Perth in 1396, in front of the court of King Robert III. Using this incident as a starting point, Scott gives a clear and accurate picture of the period and those who lived then. His portrayal of the weak and ineffectual King Robert, who is dominated by his treacherous brother, the duke of Albany, puts a human face on history. Robert's relationship with his son, Rothsay, is recounted in all of its tragedy. History itself proves melodramatic. Two other historical figures play key roles in the story. Conachar is based on a Highlands chief who fled the conflict, and Henry Gow on a townsman named Henry Wynd, who took part in the battle. All of the novel's historic characters are developed clearly and effectively.

Scott provides many rich characterizations, in contrast to a formulaic romance novel. All three of the suitors for Catharine's hand are unique. Conachar's character is extremely complex. In the city, where he works as an apprentice to Simon Glover, he appears arrogant, feisty, often unlikable. In the Highlands, however, a new side of Conachar is introduced. He has inherited his father's leadership of Clan

Quhele. Behind his flamboyant appearance, however, he has been forced to face the fact that he is a coward. In dealing with this, he becomes a far more compelling figure than a stock warrior. He may not be a totally sympathetic figure, but he is extremely human.

The novel's hero, Henry Gow, also varies from type. His physical appearance is not that of the handsome hero. His moral character, too, falls short of tradition. He has a hot temper and often indulges in battle for the sheer sake of fighting and excitement. He is not completely virtuous; only the love of Catharine restrains him from his sometimes destructive behavior.

Scott also creates a vivid picture of the growing merchant and artisan class that was beginning to have influence in Scotland. In his novel the city of Perth teems with bourgeois life. Little more than a century before, Scotland was ruled under a feudal system. In this tale, Scott shows how members of the growing merchant class are beginning to exert their power to challenge the nobility.

Not just history but also the landscape of Scotland unfolds before the reader in *The Fair Maid of Perth*. Chapter 1 lovingly describes Perth, noting its importance as far back as the days of the Roman occupation of the land. The chapter even opens with a quote comparing the Tiber with the Tay, the river that will figure so prominently at the novel's end.

The theme of *The Fair Maid of Perth* involves contrasts. The main conflict lies between violence and pacifism. From the beginning of the novel, Catharine decries the violence and bloodshed in the world around her. While she admires Henry, she is also repelled by his attraction to battle. Henry, the armorer, by trade and by inclination finds fighting both noble and necessary. By the novel's end, however, both Catharine and Henry come to accommodate each other. Catharine has realized that it is not always possible to avoid fighting in a violent world, and Henry has had his fill of bloodshed. When the Black Douglas invites Henry to join his army and become a knight, the young man refuses, noting, "I have shed blood enough already."

Other conflicts also play key roles in the novel. The townspeople are determined to establish their rights and no longer be victimized by the arrogant actions of the nobility. The burghers meet and voice their claims successfully. The traditional enmities appear: between Highlands and Lowlands, between Scotland and England. Scott develops his theme using symbolism, a characteristic that does not occur in many of his novels. Simon is a glover, and from the novel's opening, emphasis is placed on the importance of the hand and the head. *The Fair Maid of Perth*, one of the darkest and most violent of Scott's novels, is also one of the best of his later works.

"Critical Evaluation" by Mary Mahony

Further Reading

Hart, Francis. *Scott's Novels: The Plotting of Historic Survival*. Charlottesville: University Press of Virginia, 1966. Includes discussion of *The Fair Maid of Perth* that analyzes the novel's characterization, noting that Henry is a nontraditional hero and that both major and minor characters display mythical qualities. Also discusses theme and symbolism in the novel.

Irvine, Robert P. "The State, the Domestic, and National Culture in the Waverley Novels." In *Enlightenment and Romance: Gender and Agency in Smollett and Scott*. New York: Peter Lang, 2000. Chapter devoted to the depiction of Scottish culture in Scott's Waverley novels, of which *The Fair Maid of Perth* is one, is part of an analysis of the fiction of Scott and Tobias Smollett within the context of the emergence of social sciences and the dominance of novels written by female writers in the eighteenth century. Describes how the authors adapted the feminine romance and the domestic novel to assert control over the narrative structure of their novels.

Johnson, Edgar. *Sir Walter Scott: The Great Unknown*. 2 vols. New York: Macmillan, 1970. Extensively researched biography explores Scott both as a man and as a writer. Argues that the struggle between courage and cowardice depicted in *The Fair Maid of Perth* becomes a philosophical discussion of the difficulty of being nonviolent in a violent world. Evaluates the novel's characterization and style, paying particular attention to Scott's imagery. An excellent introductory source.

McMaster, Graham. *Scott and Society*. New York: Cambridge University Press, 1981. Includes discussion of *The Fair Maid of Perth* that focuses on the disillusionment with many aspects of society that are revealed in the ironic portrayals of some characters. Analyzes the novel's characterization, style, and theme.

Shaw, Harry E., ed. *Critical Essays on Sir Walter Scott: The Waverley Novels*. New York: G. K. Hall, 1996. Collection of essays published between 1858 and 1996 discusses Scott's series of novels. Includes journalist Walter Bagehot's 1858 article about the Waverley novels and discussions of such topics as Scott's rationalism, storytelling and subversion of the literary form in Scott's fiction, and what Scott's work meant to Victorian readers.

Sutherland, John. *The Life of Walter Scott: A Critical Biography.* New York: Blackwell, 1995. Discusses Scott's use, in *The Fair Maid of Perth*, of a fourteenth century story to mirror the political situation in his own time, providing a detailed chronology. Asserts that the novel centers on weak sons who betray their strong father figures.

Wagenknecht, Edward. *Sir Walter Scott.* New York: Continuum, 1991. Describes *The Fair Maid of Perth* as Scott's darkest and most violent novel, with its savage contrasting of the differences between the Highlands and the Lowlands, war and peace, and the burghers and the ruling class. Notes that Henry Gow is a wild, at times licentious, hero, often out of control, and asserts that Catharine is the most saintly of Scott's heroines.

The Faithful Shepherdess

Author: John Fletcher (1579-1625)
First produced: c. 1608-1609; first published, 1629
Type of work: Drama
Type of plot: Tragicomedy
Time of plot: Antiquity
Locale: Thessaly

Principal characters:
PERIGOT, a shepherd, in love with Amoret
THENOT, a shepherd, in love with Clorin
DAPHNIS, a modest shepherd, in love with Cloe
ALEXIS, a wanton shepherd, in love with Cloe
THE SULLEN SHEPHERD
AMORET, a shepherdess, in love with Perigot
CLORIN, a hermit, the faithful shepherdess
AMARILLIS, a shepherd, in love with Perigot
CLOE, a wanton shepherd

The Story:

Clorin, who buries her sweetheart in a woodland arbor, vows to forsake all of the pleasures of a shepherd's life and devote herself to chaste vigil over his grave, relinquishing it only to cure sick people and beasts through her knowledge of the secret virtues of herbs. So great is the power of her virginity that nothing in the woodland can harm her; her mere presence tames a rough and brutish satyr, who becomes her servant. Among the other shepherds and shepherdesses, however, love affairs of various kinds are progressing. The beautiful Amoret agrees to meet her sweetheart Perigot that night in the wood so that they can plight their troth beside a sacred well. Amarillis, a rejected admirer of Perigot, also has plans for the evening. Hoping that Perigot might accept her if he can only be parted from Amoret, she promises the Sullen Shepherd her love if he will break up the meeting. The Sullen Shepherd, who wants only to satisfy his lust, agrees to carry out any plan she might propose.

Cloe is also seeking a partner for the evening. First she approaches Thenot, but he declines her advances because he is in love with the unattainable Clorin. Daphnis, whom she next meets, agrees to meet her in the wood, but his modest bearing promises so little that Cloe also makes an engagement with Alexis, a youth who is much livelier.

After nightfall, Amarillis and the Sullen Shepherd prepare to deceive Perigot. Following a magical formula, the Sullen Shepherd lowers Amarillis into the sacred well, and when he draws her out again she takes on the form of Amoret. In this shape, she meets Perigot and attempts to seduce him, but he is so offended by her conduct that he attempts to kill her. Seeing her danger, the Sullen Shepherd uses another charm to change her back into her true appearance. Perigot rushes off into the dark wood to find and kill the supposedly lustful Amoret.

Cloe, meanwhile, meets Daphnis and finds his intentions to be purer than she hoped. Making an appointment to meet him later at a certain hollow tree, she goes in search of Alexis. This swain's desires are in perfect accord with hers, but their embraces are interrupted by the Sullen Shepherd, who attacks and wounds Alexis. Undoubtedly, Alexis would have been killed but for the arrival of Clorin's satyr, who frightens both Cloe and the Sullen Shepherd away and bears Alexis off to his mistress to be healed. Perigot during this time finds the true Amoret, stabs her, and leaves her for dead. She is discovered by the Sullen Shepherd who, wishing to make sure of his bargain with Amarillis, throws her into the sacred well to drown. From this fate she is saved by the river god, who also heals her wounds.

Perigot, thinking Amoret dead, is about to take his own life when Amarillis, seeing that things have gone much too far, attempts to explain her deception. In order to convince him, she asks only an hour in which to reappear in Amoret's shape. She hardly leaves him, however, when she comes upon the true Amoret. Realizing that virtuous love cannot be frustrated, she directs the unfortunate shepherdess to the place where Perigot waits; but when Amoret arrives, her sweetheart takes her to be Amarillis transformed and, wishing to be revenged, he again stabs her. Once more the satyr arrives opportunely. As the frightened Perigot flees, the satyr bears Amoret off to Clorin's arbor.

There Clorin nearly effects Alexis's cure by purging him of lust, but her treatment of Amoret is interrupted because of intemperate influences in the atmosphere. Seeking them out, the satyr finds Daphnis and Cloe in the hollow tree. Being innocent of lechery, the young man is dismissed, but Cloe fails the test of chastity to which she is put and is kept for Clorin's ministrations. Perigot, meanwhile, arrives to be cleared of the blood he shed and to his astonishment finds Amoret alive and well. The two are happily reunited. Alexis and Cloe, purged of lust, also swear a chaste love to each other.

Critical Evaluation:

John Fletcher's first complete play, *The Faithful Shepherdess*, was available in an undated quarto probably in 1609, although it may have been performed by a company of boy actors as early as 1608. In his dedicatory verse to Sir Walter Aston, Fletcher acknowledges the failure of the drama on stage, but he defends its virtues as a poetic "interlude"; in his introduction to the reader, he remarks upon the originality of its concept. A "pastoral tragicomedy," the play is, according to the author's famous definition of the new type, "not so called in respect of mirth and killing, but in respect it wants deaths." Although the play comes close to tragedy, "which is enough to make it no comedy," its conclusion for the characters concerned is sober but not dreadful. As a model of tragicomedy, *The Faithful Shepherdess* is the first in a line of Jacobean dramas that became popular after Francis Beaumont and Fletcher's *Philaster* (c. 1609) and William Shakespeare's *Cymbeline* (pr. c. 1609-1610, pb. 1623).

From a historical point of view, *The Faithful Shepherdess* is interesting as a forerunner of the courtly masque during the period of Caroline (Cavalier) verse drama, 1625-1642. Unlike the more robust Elizabethan masques, notable for their lavish entertainments, rambling forms, and splendid pageantry, Fletcher's play established a more nearly classical model, formally elegant, artificial, and finely structured. Based on Giambattista Guarini's *Pastor Fido* (1589) and

Giambattista Giraldi Cinthio's *Egle* (1545), *The Faithful Shepherdess* reduces many of the complicated subplots from the sources to a symmetry of design: the conflict between chaste love and lust.

Fletcher's elaborate presentation of this conflict may appear strained to later audiences. The play celebrates the chief virtue of virginity, and the characters, either virtuous or lewd, become stereotypes either of sexual restraint or of license. Clorin, who has renounced love to preserve her chastity, acts as the agent of redemption for the wanton Cloe and Amarillis, heals Amoret's wounds, teaches Perigot to recognize Amoret's fidelity, and pronounces sentence upon the unrepentant, lascivious Sullen Shepherd. She even tames the satyr, and he becomes her servant in the cause of sexual continence.

Fletcher's emphasis on the theme of virginity as a test of moral conduct may be explained as a retrospective nod to the cult of Queen Elizabeth's chastity, or it may be understood historically as a defense against mounting Puritan attacks on the lechery of the theater. Another and more satisfactory explanation is that the subject is treated with such exaggeration that it is intended, for sophisticated patrons of the stage, as a satire. As Helen C. Gilde ably demonstrated in her studies on Elizabethan erotic verse romances, a tradition of that genre is, at least partly, satiric and comic. Read in this light, *The Faithful Shepherdess* is an elegant, static, but witty play that explores with sly delicacy the comedy of sexual pursuit.

Further Reading

Appleton, William W. *Beaumont and Fletcher: A Critical Study*. London: George Allen & Unwin, 1956. Appleton equivocates about the merits of *The Faithful Shepherdess*, but he shows that this play and other tragicomedies, although they are hybrids and reflect a decadent age, are important forerunners of Restoration heroic drama.

Edwards, Philip. "The Danger Not the Death: The Art of John Fletcher." In *Jacobean Theatre*, edited by John Russell Brown and Bernard Harris. New York: Capricorn Books, 1967. Edwards analyzes what he considers the key elements in Fletcher's plays: improbable, elaborately complicated plots, prurience, strong scenes, mystification and disguise, and disputation and persuasion.

Ellis-Fermor, Una. *The Jacobean Drama: An Interpretation*. New York: Vintage Books, 1964. In the chapter on Fletcher and his collaborator Francis Beaumont, Ellis-Fermor treats the tragicomic genre in detail and discusses the strengths and weaknesses of the form in various plays, including *The Faithful Shepherdess*. Declares that this play has a weak plot but some fine poetry.

Finkelpearl, Philip J. *Court and Country Politics in the Plays of Beaumont and Fletcher.* Princeton, N.J.: Princeton University Press, 1990. Looking at the plays as dramatic criticism of the court and monarch, Finkelpearl links Clorin and Pan in *The Faithful Shepherdess*, which he says is the prototypical Fletcher tragicomedy, with Elizabeth I and James I.

Foster, Verna A. "Sexuality and Tragicomic Genre in the Plays of Fletcher." In *The Name and Nature of Tragicomedy.* Burlington, Vt.: Ashgate, 2004. This analysis of Fletcher's tragicomic plays includes a discussion of *The Faithful Shepherdess*. Foster analyzes tragicomedies from the Renaissance and twentieth century, describing the characteristics and perceptions that differentiate these plays from comedies and dramas.

Leech, Clifford. *The John Fletcher Plays.* London: Chatto & Windus, 1962. Analyzes the pastoral form, language, and poetry of *The Faithful Shepherdess* that distinguish it from other Fletcher plays. Shows that Fletcher's attitude toward human behavior first emerges in this early work. Also discusses similarities between *The Faithful Shepherdess* and William Shakespeare's *The Tempest* (pr. 1611, pb. 1623).

Wells, Stanley W. "The Move to Tragicomedy: John Fletcher and Others." In *Shakespeare and Co.: Christopher Marlowe, Thomas Dekker, Ben Jonson, Thomas Middleton, John Fletcher, and the Other Players in His Story.* New York: Penguin Books, 2007. Wells examines the plays of William Shakespeare by placing them within the broader context of Elizabethan theater, discussing Fletcher and other playwrights of the period, the work of acting companies, and the staging of theatrical productions. The chapter on Fletcher includes a discussion of *The Faithful Shepherdess*.

The Fake Astrologer

Author: Pedro Calderón de la Barca (1600-1681)
First produced: c. 1624, as *El astrólogo fingido*; first published, 1633 (English translation, 1668)
Type of work: Drama
Type of plot: Farce
Time of plot: Seventeenth century
Locale: Madrid

Principal characters:
MARÍA, a girl of Madrid
JUAN DE MEDRANO, an impoverished young nobleman
DON CARLOS, his friend
DON DIEGO, a wealthy nobleman in love with María
MORÓN, his servant
BEATRIZ, María's servant
LEONARDO, María's father
DOÑA VIOLANTE, a woman in love with Juan

The Story:

Looking from the balcony of her Madrid home, María watches Juan de Medrano ride by, courting her from a distance as he did for two years, and she is moved to confess to her servant Beatriz that she much prefers him to the more aggressive Don Diego. Juan is at last tired of seeing María only at a distance. That afternoon he comes to call, with the excuse that next day he is leaving for the wars in Flanders. María postpones their farewells until that night, when Beatriz will bring Juan to her.

Don Diego, too, decides on direct action. He arrives with a highly rhetorical demand for her affections. Claiming that she is unable to understand his proposal, María turns him down in the same kind of jargon. Angered, Don Diego directs his servant Morón to try to learn from Beatriz how María might be approached. Though the gift of a gold chain does not open her mouth, Morón knows that Beatriz will in time tell him everything.

Juan wants his friend Don Carlos to spread the story of his departure for the army, while actually he plans to stay in lodgings in Madrid. As a first step, he sends his farewells to Doña Violante, an errand that Don Carlos performs gladly because, with Juan away, he thinks he can win the lady for himself.

The next morning, as she sneaks Juan out of María's house, materialistic Beatriz reflects on how silly aristocratic ladies are. They will not be seen talking to a man on the street for fear of gossip, but they are prepared to entertain him secretly in their rooms. This time, however, the assignation does not remain a secret. Morón worms out of Beatriz all the details of Juan's visit and runs with them to his master. Don Diego elaborates on the event as he passes it on to his friend Antonio, and the story grows further as Antonio tries to elicit the true facts. Exasperated and resentful, Don Diego decides to confront María.

When Don Diego mentions Juan's nocturnal visit, María is sure that her servant gossiped. To protect Beatriz, whom he loves, Morón explains that Don Diego is an astrologer who can summon up demons and who knows the past and the future. Don Diego does not deny this claim. In fact, when María's father, Leonardo, comes up to them, he predicts an impoverished husband for her. The father, who had experiences with magicians, does not believe in them, and he would have unmasked Don Diego had Morón not cleverly saved his master from disclosure.

Don Diego's friends, passing on the story, convince Doña Violante of Don Diego's powers, and she begs him to materialize the absent Juan. To his protest that his power cannot cross water, she replies that, according to a letter just delivered by Don Carlos, he is in Zaragoza. At Don Diego's prompting, Doña Violante writes Juan a letter inviting him to visit her. The note, mysteriously delivered by Don Carlos, brings Juan to her house. There he frightens her and he becomes thoroughly confused, since he knows nothing about the pretended astrologer.

Juan is more eager than ever to see María. Since Leonardo does not know him, he presents himself as a friend of Leonardo's brother, just arrived from Zaragoza. María gives him a ribbon with a costly pin and tells him to sell it in order to provide himself with spending money. Then, scheming to bring him back to her, she tells her father that the pin was stolen. Leonardo hurries to consult Don Diego. Since Beatriz already babbled the new developments to Morón, Don Diego appears to have miraculous powers, and Leonardo goes in search of Juan. When he is discovered, Juan, fearing for María's reputation, confesses to the theft. Angered, Leonardo refuses Juan's request to marry María.

His supposed magic prowess brings Don Diego nothing but trouble. Even his servant claims a share in his strange powers and tries to send another servant on an aerial journey to his home town. Then Don Diego angers Doña Violante by refusing to give her a spell with which to kill Juan and María. He is, moreover, no further advanced in his own courtship. The conflicting prophecies he gives, hoping that some might come true, cause everyone to turn against him. Finally, when Beatriz explains how he secured his information, the mock astrologer renounces all claims to magic powers, but not before he accomplishes one good deed. When he reveals the whole truth about the jewel robbery, María and Juan are reunited.

Critical Evaluation:

If Lope de Vega wrote plays at an early age, Pedro Calderón de la Barca was no less precocious. When his *Death, the Best Friend* was published in 1657, it was announced as the work of a nine-year-old boy. In his letter of 1680 to his friend the duke of Veragua, he stated that *Cart of Heaven* was completed when he was thirteen. Very likely he was practicing the art of playwriting before he graduated from the University of Salamanca in 1619, certainly immediately afterward. One critic dated *The Fake Astrologer* before 1622 because of its mingling of Tirso de Molina and Lope de Vega, and all critics put it before 1625, when Calderón went into military service. Because of the many pirated copies by publishers and actors, it quickly appeared in several authorized versions before being included, with additional scenes, in part 2 of his *Collected Plays* in 1637, a volume reissued posthumously in 1682 by Calderón's friend Juan de Vera Tassis.

In *The Fake Astrologer*, a satire on grifters and impostors, there is no deep philosophy and little beyond a fast-moving farce. The first scene of act 2 provides a good sample of the belabored language of Gongorism as Diego pleads his love in baroque style and María replies in language no less flowery and figurative. It takes the servant to bring the speakers down to earth. There is no moral lesson, unless it is Morón's insistence that one cannot trust a woman with a secret.

The Fake Astrologer also satirizes astrology, which had adherents even in devout Catholic Spain of the Golden Age. Calderón, like other literary greats of the time in Spain and Portugal, did not take astrology seriously but sometimes felt compelled to bludgeon it as a pseudoscience that had an unfortunate hold on gullible people. The pretensions of Don Diego to extrasensory talent were typical of the astrological plague that afflicted Europe sporadically for centuries, despite the opposition of Christianity. As a playwright steeped in Christian theology, Calderón was aware of the biblical injunction against a misuse of astrology and sought to expose the folly of this practice to Spain's dramatic public. Consequently, he lampoons the crude machinations of Don Diego as well as the simplemindedness of anyone naïve enough to place faith in such deception. The play's basic plot is simple, and Calderón adds various complications, especially the paralysis of action through a pretense.

The evasion of reality in *The Fake Astrologer*, and Calderón's poetic handling of this flight, has a baroque quality to it. The law of contrast attains maximum effect through the contrast of Don Diego's supposed magic prowess with the empty reality of his true incapacity. Deception governs Don Diego's behavior as he flutters between the two lives of truly being and only potentially being. Typical also of Calderón's dramatic craft is the largeness of Don Diego's role as an antagonist, which symbolizes negation and evil. As protagonist, Don Juan symbolizes the positive and good. Calderón also uses continued contrast, movement, and flight to enhance the mocking of reality; the word *burla* (mockery) and its synonyms are used seventy times in the play.

Some critics feel that Calderón avoided a deep study of his play's personalities because he had an instinctive, baroque aversion to empty and undecorated space and inner emptiness. *The Fake Astrologer* portrays external shapes through its lyric poetry and erudition, which are apparently used deliberately to expose the appearance of learnedness in such personalities as Don Diego, who hollowly crave knowledge without studying.

Even the play's apparently brisk action is more pretense than reality, since decisive action is paralyzed by the dreamy, fictional pretenses of both Don Diego and Juan de Medrano, including the latter's suspended-action courting of Doña María from a distance for two years. Calderón here emphasizes the clash between the world of reality and the world of fiction, and he implies—in a manner so typically Calderónian—that all in this life is truth and that all is a lie.

Further Reading

Benabu, Isaac. *Reading for the Stage: Calderón and His Contemporaries.* Rochester, N.Y.: Tamesis, 2003. Analyzes playtexts for works by Calderón and contemporary playwrights. A playtext is usually read by the theater company at the beginning of a play's production and provides the playwright's directions for staging his or her work. Benabu's examination of playtexts discusses the religiosity of Spanish theater in the Golden Age, Calderón's devotional comedies, and the character of Pedro Crespo in *The Mayor of Zalamea.*

Calderón de la Barca, Pedro. *The Fake Astrologer.* Translated by Max Oppenheimer. Lawrence, Kans.: Coronado Press, 1976. An accessible English edition of the work, with the Spanish and English versions on facing pages. Contains bibliographical references.

Cohen, Walter. *Drama of a Nation: Public Theater in Renaissance England and Spain.* Ithaca, N.Y.: Cornell University Press, 1985. Good analysis of the differences and similarities between the national theaters of both countries. Discusses the borrowing of plots and characters, which in the case of *The Fake Astrologer* is between Calderón and John Dryden by way of Pierre Corneille.

Heigl, Michaela. *Theorizing Gender, Sexuality, and the Body in Calderonian Theater.* New Orleans, La.: University Press of the South, 2001. Focuses on the transvestites, scolds, sodomites, monsters, and other "deviant" characters in Calderón's plays, demonstrating how they embody the idea of excess and subvert the boundaries between the sexes and between different social classes. Heigl maintains that these characters represent the inherent corruption and perversion in society.

Nicoll, Allardyce. *A History of Restoration Drama, 1660-1700.* 3d rev. ed. Cambridge, England: Cambridge University Press, 1940. Traces the links between Spanish and British theater. Notes that Charles II was interested in Calderónian theater.

Rodríguez Cuadros, Evangelina. "Pedro Calderón de la Barca." In *The Cambridge History of Spanish Literature,* edited by David T. Gies. New York: Cambridge University Press, 2004. An overview of Calderón's life and work, placing his work within the broader context of Spanish literature.

Thacker, Jonathan. *A Companion to Golden Age Theatre.* Rochester, N.Y.: Tamesis, 2007. An introductory overview of Spanish Golden Age theater. In addition to a chapter on Calderón, the book examines the work of other playwrights, describes the different types of plays produced in this era, and traces the growth and maturation of Spanish theater.

Wardropper, B. W. "Calderón's Comedy and His Serious Sense of Life." In *Hispanic Studies in Honor of Nicholson B. Adams,* edited by John Esten Keller and Karl-Ludwig Selig. Chapel Hill: University of North Carolina Press, 1966. A study by one of the foremost scholars of Calderónian theater that discusses the playwright's serious purpose lurking behind such comic scenes as the "clavileño" episode of *The Fake Astrologer.*

Wilson, Margaret. *Spanish Drama of the Golden Age.* Oxford, England: Pergamon Press, 1969. A good starting point for any discussion of Spanish Golden Age theater. Includes detailed footnotes and a list of English translations.

Falconer

Author: John Cheever (1912-1982)
First published: 1977
Type of work: Novel
Type of plot: Psychological realism
Time of plot: Early 1970's
Locale: New York

Principal characters:
EZEKIEL "ZEKE" FARRAGUT, a college professor and
    heroin addict jailed for murdering his brother
MARCIA FARRAGUT, his wife
CHICKEN NUMBER TWO, an older career felon who
    befriends Farragut
JODY, an inmate, a hustler, and Farragut's lover

The Story:

When Ezekiel Farragut is escorted, shackled to nine other prisoners, into the grim edifice of Falconer State Correctional Facility to begin serving a twelve-year sentence, he is certain that he will die there. Farragut has been convicted of beating his brother to death with a fireplace poker while high on heroin. A forty-eight-year-old university humanities professor who has struggled throughout his adult life with heroin addiction, Farragut sees incarceration as a long-shot chance for penance and redemption. His life of affluence and privilege now seems distant—he is haunted by dreams of beautiful women on exotic island beaches—and when his wife, Marcia, visits him early on, her chilling distance reminds him that that world is now irrevocably lost to him.

Farragut is on a court-mandated methadone program to ease him off heroin, and his initial days in the prison center on getting his fix. His addiction began in the South Pacific jungles when he was a rifleman during World War II. He would drink entire glasses of codeine cough syrup before going into battle. As a college professor, he would shoot up heroin with his colleagues before classes. Farragut describes his generation as a generation of addicts who, facing the cataclysmic implications of atomic holocaust, opted for either alcohol or drugs as avenues to touch a desperate transcendence. Thus, when two spoons hidden in Farragut's cell by another inmate are discovered during routine inspection and Farragut faces six days of revoked privileges, his greatest worry is over getting his fix, as he will be unable to go to the infirmary. Far from being sympathetic toward his plight, the guards anticipate watching the withdrawal "show"—indeed, Farragut goes into convulsions, beats his head against the floor, and tries to hang himself. When a guard intervenes and cuts him down, Farragut makes a break for the infirmary, only to have a chair smashed over his head. Recovering, he considers suing the state for denying him his methadone. He uses his bed sheet to write three elaborate letters on his own behalf, one to the governor, one to his bishop, and one to a fantasy lover.

Farragut then meets Jody in the prison showers. Jody, a mortgage banker jailed for robbery, is much younger than the professor. The two become lovers, although both inmates and guards warn Farragut that Jody is a conman who uses people. Predictably, Jody abruptly abandons Farragut to pursue another inmate who secures him the chance to escape. When the archbishop of New York comes to the prison to say Mass and confer degrees on eight inmates who have completed a pilot program in banking, Jody disguises himself as an altar server and simply departs with the bishop's entourage in a state-provided helicopter. Farragut is devastated to be left alone and realizes the deep impress of love (the alternative is The Valley, an old bathroom in the prison where the inmates go to masturbate with each other).

When a riot in a nearby prison causes Falconer to go under a lockdown, with radio and television privileges denied, Farragut, desperate for connection to the outside world, sets about unsuccessfully to build his own radio receiver. To mollify the inmates and provide a distraction to prevent them from rioting themselves, the facility arranges with the help of a local philanthropist to stage Christmas photos for inmates to send to their families. In the stifling August heat, the prisoners are escorted to an old prison classroom, where, next to a brightly lit Christmas tree and stacks of empty boxes wrapped like gifts, they have their photos taken. After the commotion of the lockdown, Farragut realizes that he no longer needs his methadone fix: He is now "clean."

An older inmate referred to as Chicken Number Two is dying, but the infirmary is filled with flu patients, so he is moved into Farragut's cell. Farragut at last shares an account of his crime with his new cell mate. He tells the dying inmate about his brother, a callous man who, even as he busied himself doing philanthropic work through a foundation, ignored significant problems with his wife and his own children. One night, after a particularly brutal dinner, Farragut's brother, in a moment of vodka-induced anger, told Farragut that their father had tried to convince their mother to abort Farragut. Provoked and high, Farragut struck his brother more than twenty times with a fireplace iron.

After he has shared his story with Chicken Number Two, Farragut comforts the old prisoner while he dies. When the infirmary guards leave the burial bag in the cell until morning, Farragut removes the corpse, places it in his cot, and, grabbing a razor, zippers himself into the bag in its place. Attendants carry him out and, in a stroke of unanticipated luck (the hearse has been delayed while it gets an oil change), Farragut cuts himself out of the bag with the razor, substitutes rocks to mimic his weight, and simply walks away from Falconer. He walks into the nearest city, where he chances upon a stranger at a bus stop. The stranger, who has just been evicted from his apartment and is on his way to live with his sister, takes an interest in Farragut, pays his bus fare, gives him his phone number, and invites him to share an apartment. As Farragut gets off the bus, walking now in a cleansing rain, he feels for the first time the splendid release of joy.

Critical Evaluation:

The most immediate achievement of *Falconer* was its impact on the career and reputation of John Cheever. Regarded as one of the preeminent short-story writers of the post-World War II generation, Cheever was known for stories that explored with Chekhovian irony and a poetic sense of language the unhappy lives of upper-crust suburbia. By the 1970's, however, Cheever had edged into obscurity. His brand of traditional psychological realism had fallen out of fashion in an era that emphasized highly experimental narratives. *Falconer* changed that. It exhibited a darker, grittier Cheever, far from the quiet streets and elegant homes of his fictional suburbia. In *Falconer*, for the first time in his long career, Cheever confronted in fiction the demons of his private life—his struggle with addiction (to alcohol), his estrangement from his own family (the abortion episode in the novel was apparently autobiographical), and, most significant, his torment over his bisexuality. The intensely personal nature of the subject matter gave the narrative a harrowing immediacy.

Long thought of as "just" a short-story writer, Cheever produced a novel that was lauded for the tight, parable structure it imparted to Farragut's movement toward redemption, which drew so richly on the moral allegories of Fyodor Dostoevski's prison narratives. Some criticized Cheever for avoiding the harsher realities of prison homosexuality and guard brutality and for incorporating patently implausible prison escapes so prominently into the narrative. Critics also pointed out that Farragut never expresses remorse or explains in any depth why he killed his brother. Nevertheless, the novel was a best seller. *Newsweek*, in a cover story, called it a great American novel, and in 2005 *Time* listed the novel as one of the one hundred best English-language novels writ-

ten since 1923. His reputation revived, Cheever published his collected stories the following year and was awarded the Pulitzer Prize in fiction. Until his death three years later from cancer, Cheever once again enjoyed a reputation as a major American writer.

Thematically, *Falconer*—more than any of Cheever's earlier works—reflects his fascination with the dynamic of the Christian fall and redemption, the tension between flesh and spirit, and the movement from suffering to joy. Himself a lifelong Episcopalian, Cheever had often cast a wary eye on his suburbia, where people unable to tap into the promise of Christian love were savaged by disappointment, carnal indulgences, and alcoholic escape. *Falconer*, by contrast, follows a decidedly ascendant moral arc. Initially, Farragut battles intense alienation as he adjusts to the brutal environment of the prison. To represent this environment, Cheever drew on his own experiences when he taught creative writing at New York's notorious Sing Sing Penitentiary. He also, however, transformed the prison environment, investing his story with a sense of transcendent possibility. The novel is weighted with religious imagery, and it portrays Farragut doing more than serving time for killing his brother, and kicking his drug addiction. It portrays him redeeming his soul.

Farragut begins by discovering the difficult dynamic of love; his wife, a frustrated painter who prides herself on her beauty and her independence, has never given him the closeness of intimacy. The sexual relationship Farragut finds with the inmate Jody gives him insight into the depths of love with its attendant needs, anticipations, hungers, and consolations. The failure of his love to last leads Farragut inevitably to a higher kind of love, one that taps into the spiritual rather than the physical. In confronting his difficult relationships with his father, his mother, his son, and ultimately the brother he killed (a brother who once shoved Farragut through an open window), Farragut performs the Christian obligation of self-scrutiny. It is a difficult struggle; midway through the narrative, Farragut, incensed over the guards' treatment of him, writes the three extended (and overwrought) letters of complaint that reveal the depth of his egocentricity and his stubborn pride. Farragut's evident sensual appetite—he misses the woods and the mountains, he hankers after his fix, he relishes the release of orgasm—further reminds readers how far Farragut has to go to reclaim his soul.

Cheever's use of Christmas imagery throughout the narrative helps prepare readers for Farragut's reformation, his turn toward higher love, which is demonstrated most dramatically in his ministering to the dying Chicken Number Two. The old inmate—entirely abandoned by the world, his own real name long forgotten—gives up, sells his guitar, and simply wills himself to die. Cheever juxtaposes that surrender with Farragut's contrapuntal movement toward freedom, his determination that suffering lead to joy. The novel closes with the angelic stranger promising Farragut help, even as Cheever employs images of cleansing: Farragut lingers before a laundromat and later walks in the sweet wash of a light rain.

The novel's pat closing may be read as increasing the work's complexity. It depicts a salvation earned by a character who has never really suffered in prison (he spends only a few months there), has never really atoned for his crime, has never actually confronted the dark demons that drove him to murder his own brother, and has never whispered remorse. Thus, perhaps the most intriguing achievement of *Falconer* is that Cheever undercuts his own hero's easy (and too deliberate) movement toward redemption. The novel may be intended to underscore just how difficult it is to achieve authentic redemption by showing a character whose glib assurance of his own redemption Cheever rejects with the scathing satire that often marked his best short stories.

Farragut whines rather than suffers; he dwells in fantasies and dreams; he privileges the flesh; he is judgmental; he is secretive; and he is a schemer who rationalizes his actions. He never suffers the dark night of the soul typically necessary for moral redemption. Thus, the novel may evoke caution in readers who are unconvinced by Farragut's improbable escape, amused by the "angel" who happens to be waiting at the bus stop for the escaped convict, and doubtful of Farragut's too easy embrace of joy that closes the text. Cheever, himself at the close of a long and often tormented life that had taught him that redemption was anything but easy, perhaps fashions an intricately ironic parable, a complex parody of Dostoevski's narratives of redemption.

Joseph Dewey

Further Reading

Bailey, Blake. *Cheever: A Life*. New York: Alfred A. Knopf, 2009. Landmark biography that includes accounts of Cheever's experiences at Sing Sing and of *Falconer*'s reception.

Batey, Robert. "*Falconer*: John Cheever's Prison Novel." *Legal Studies Forum* 25, nos. 3/4 (2001). Indispensable, thorough analysis of the novel's use of the imagery of jurisprudence and the concept of punishment to explore the inhumanity of imprisonment and to encourage sympathy for the incarcerated.

Bosha, Francis J. *The Critical Response to John Cheever*. Westport, Conn.: Greenwood Press, 1993. An illuminating record of Cheever's career-long love-hate relationship with the critical press. Includes six reviews of *Falconer*.

Clemons, Walter. "Cheever's Triumph." *Newsweek*, March 14, 1977, pp. 61-71. Cover story that examines how *Falconer* significantly altered the perception of Cheever as a writer. Includes a fascinating interview that explores ties between Farragut and Cheever.

Johnson, Glen M. "The Moral Structure of Cheever's *Falconer*." *Studies in American Fiction* 9 (1981): 21-31. An excellent starting point for approaching the novel. Stresses the evolution of Farragut toward spiritual rejuvenation, sees the prison as a purgatorial environment wherein Farragut works through alienation to genuine communion.

Meanor, Patrick. *John Cheever Revisited*. New York: Twayne-Macmillan, 1995. Important introduction to Cheever's fiction, written after Cheever's death, that sees *Falconer* within the context of Cheever's own development and argues that Cheever, at career's end, was freeing himself from his own private demons by portraying Farragut's salvation.

The Fall

Author: Albert Camus (1913-1960)
First published: La Chute, 1956 (English translation, 1957)
Type of work: Novel
Type of plot: Psychological realism
Time of plot: 1950's
Locale: Amsterdam and Paris

Principal characters:
JEAN-BAPTISTE CLAMENCE, formerly a lawyer and presently a judge-penitent
AN UNIDENTIFIED LISTENER
THE PROPRIETOR, owner of an Amsterdam bar called Mexico City

The Story:

In an Amsterdam bar called Mexico City, Jean-Baptiste Clamence is involved in a strange dialogue, strange because he addresses an unidentified silent listener who never answers his questions or comments on his remarks. Clamence, in his forties, talks daily for five consecutive days with the stranger whom he meets in Mexico City bar. The subject of this one-sided dialogue is Clamence, specifically his fall from innocence to sin.

The judge-penitent illuminates his past experiences, clarifies the inner motives behind his actions, and imposes his feigned friendliness, his humorous sarcasm, his false humility, his black bitterness, and the cruelty of his lucidity on his listener. Clamence relates that at one time he had to feel superior in order to make his life bearable. To relinquish his seat to someone else in the bus, to help a blind person across the street, or to give up his theater seat so that a couple can sit together—all of these incidents created in him a feeling of superiority, resulting in his regarding himself as a type of superman. His sense of superiority kept him in harmony with people around him, with life in general. He attained a certain state of happiness as a mechanical human being who could anticipate what was expected from him and live up to the pleasant image other people had of him. He lived on the surface of a life of words and gestures, but he never touched reality through the people he knew, the books he read, the places he visited, the women he possessed briefly. As a lawyer, he realized that the monotony of modern life turned human beings into puppets and made them completely anonymous. Disgusted with their anonymity, they committed crimes, their only means of attracting attention.

Then one evening at the Pont des Arts in Paris, Clamence heard laughter behind him; he turned around but nobody was there. It was Clamence laughing at himself, a sarcastic and triumphant laughter that chilled his existence. Something broke in him; his image of himself was shattered, and he became aware of his double face. He went home to escape from the laughter, but he could still hear it under his window. His existence as he knew it received a dangerous blow. The same evening, he watched his reflection in the mirror, and it seemed to him that his smile became double. This laughter started Clamence's fall from innocence to sin. Somehow his usual confidence in himself and his actions was shattered. The nonexistent sarcastic laughter suddenly made his mind lucid, a lucidity that showed him the absurdity of his own existence. The recognition of his lucidity, powerful and convincing, channeled his thinking into a different direction. He gave up his position as lawyer. Human beings pretend to be equal and innocent, but nothing was more natural in them, he concluded, than a constant desire to judge: It makes them feel above others. Clamence left his position as lawyer because he saw the fraud in concepts of innocence and guilt. He soon realized, however, that he was still playing the same game and changed only his part. Clamence, who formerly felt in harmony with life and superior to others, fell to the other extreme: He constantly accused himself, insisted on his self-accusations, which elevated him to a new level of superior feeling. He achieved the same satisfaction as before, only from a different, perhaps more cowardly, personal position.

Clamence practiced a kind of Pascalian diversion and self-deception. He used the power of his mind not to get to know himself but to drift away constantly from his authentic self. His desire to maintain a feeling of superiority turned into an existential necessity. Diversion carried him through the recognition of his own absurdity and provided him with moments of ephemeral satisfaction.

Clamence's diabolic laughter menaced his existence. Occasionally, it would creep up behind him and threaten him. Not only the laughter but also the memory of the woman who drowned herself lurked like a lion in the back of his mind. One night in November, two or three years before he heard the laughter, Clamence was crossing a bridge in Paris shortly after midnight and saw the slim figure of a woman bent over the railing. When he crossed the bridge, he heard a loud splash followed by several cries. He did not return to the bridge, informed nobody about the incident, and avoided the newspapers for several days afterward. In this case again, as always, Clamence avoided the existential decision. He closed his ears to the immediate choice and walked home that evening the same way he always went. Clamence had only one weapon to overcome those moments of despair and failure in the past: the power to forget.

Critical Evaluation:

Albert Camus's death in 1960, at the early age of forty-six, was completely unexpected; it was a great shock to those who followed his literary and philosophical development from *Le Mythe de Sisyphe* (1942; *The Myth of Sisyphus*; 1955) and *L'Étranger* (1942; *The Stranger*, 1946). Camus broke with tradition, engaged himself in a new direction, and had showed vital and promising concepts of his new vision. His sudden death left his oeuvre unfinished. He bequeathed to the world finished works with an unfinished vision. The spiritual wasteland of the modern world was his obsession. He traced the dilemma of modern life back to its absurd roots but offered no new alternative. He died before he could express such an alternative.

Camus intended to incorporate *The Fall* into a collection of short stories. The story soon outgrew its planned length, however, and was published as a separate novel in 1956.

In *The Fall*, Camus recalls *The Stranger*. Jean-Baptiste Clamence is an intensified Meursault. The themes of *The Stranger* are treated with greater lucidity and bitterness in *The Fall*. The idea of death, the problem of indifference and anonymity in modern life, the notion of guilt and innocence in the individual, the awareness of the absurdity of human actions, and the ambiguous relativity of all traditional values haunt both novels.

In form, *The Fall* is a confession, a philosophical confession of a former lawyer by the name of Clamence, who becomes a judge-penitent. His confession differs in tone and attitude, however, from those of Saint Augustine and Jean-Jacques Rousseau; there are no sentimental outflows, no softness of language, and, above all, no pity. Clamence makes his confession, reconstructs the past with all of its small incidents, and intertwines it with the present; however, his confession goes beyond the personal realm and assumes the dimensions of a general confession of the modern world, a cruel and dehumanized world where empty words replace life.

Amsterdam represents the stage of this modern world; impersonal and indifferent human beings play their role as lifeless puppets in the narrow-minded, suffocating bourgeois world. Camus even ventures to compare the concentric canals of this city to Dante's circles of hell. Amsterdam and all modern cities turn into a bourgeois hell. The ugliness and forlornness of the modern city build the framework for Camus's novel.

The reader is kept in a constant state of suspense. The reader participates actively in the development of Clamence's thinking and is stimulated to conjecture on the listener's unexpressed responses. Camus reverses the Proustian concept of remembrance. Marcel Proust aims to reconstruct and revive the past: It imparts richness and happiness to the present moment. Clamence fears the past: It becomes a danger to the present. He remembers those moments in which he failed to make the existential choice, and he lives with the awareness that he will always miss his moment of choice. The novel ends with his expressed realization that he will always be too late—fortunately—to choose.

Attacking the monotony and indifference of modern life, Camus questions all the usually accepted values and shows their ambiguous and often absurd nature. He revives the concept that nothing can exist without its reverse. Good and evil, innocence and sin exist side by side. Clamence must live with his own duplicity; he must accept the paradox that in trying not to fool himself, he fools himself. With *The Fall*, Camus opened the way to what came to be known as the New Novel by showing the relativity of traditionally accepted objective values. From Camus, it is only one step to the novels of Alain Robbe-Grillet and Nathalie Sarraute, who destroy the standard notions of what a novel and, by extension, what the world are supposed to be like.

Further Reading

Bloom, Harold, ed. *Albert Camus*. New York: Chelsea House, 1989. Collection of critical essays on the writer's career. An article on *The Fall* provides a close analysis of Camus's complex narrative method and reveals the author's concerns about the modern condition of humanity.

Bree, Germaine, ed. *Camus: A Collection of Critical Essays*. Englewood Cliffs, N.J.: Prentice-Hall, 1962. Essays by eminent scholars give an overview of Camus's accomplishments as a novelist and philosopher. One entry focuses on the later novels, including *The Fall*, which is seen as a personal statement by the novelist against the readers who failed to appreciate his earlier work.

Carroll, David. *Albert Camus, the Algerian: Colonialism, Terrorism, Justice*. New York: Columbia University Press, 2007. Analyzes Camus's novels, short stories, and political essays within the context of the author's complicated relationship with his Algerian background. Carroll concludes that Camus's work reflects his understanding of both the injustice of colonialism and the tragic nature of Algeria's struggle for independence. Includes bibliography and index.

Ellison, David R. *Understanding Albert Camus*. Columbia: University of South Carolina Press, 1990. Study of the major works. Includes a detailed discussion of *The Fall*, concentrating on its setting, its structure, and its narrative techniques and commenting on Camus's handling of religion.

Hughes, Edward J., ed. *The Cambridge Companion to Camus*. New York: Cambridge University Press, 2007. Collection of essays, including "Withheld Identity in *La Chute*" by David R. Ellison, interpreting Camus's work. Other essays discuss his life and times, his formative influences, his relationship with Jean-Paul Sartre, Camus and the theater, and social justice, violence, and ethics in his work.

Longstaffe, Moya. *The Fiction of Albert Camus: A Complex Simplicity*. New York: Peter Lang, 2007. Examines Camus's novels and short stories, discussing the coherent themes and philosophy expressed in these works. Longstaffe also describes the origins of Camus's philosophy and the narrative techniques of his fiction.

Sprintzen, David. *Camus: A Critical Examination*. Philadelphia: Temple University Press, 1988. Critical analysis of Camus's major works, from a philosophical perspective. A chapter on *The Fall* examines the work as a study of modern anxiety and compares it to other novels by the author.

Thody, Philip. *Albert Camus*. London: Macmillan, 1989. General survey of Camus's novels, examining common themes and focusing on his rejection of Christianity in favor of an existential position. A chapter on *The Fall* concentrates on the author's satiric portrait of lawyers as a scourge of modern society.

Todd, Olivier. *Albert Camus: A Life*. Translated by Benjamin Ivry. New York: Alfred A. Knopf, 1997. Utilizing material such as unpublished letters made available after the death of Camus's widow, this detailed biography reveals much about Camus's love affairs and his many important friendships.

The Fall of the House of Usher

Author: Edgar Allan Poe (1809-1849)
First published: 1839
Type of work: Short fiction
Type of plot: Gothic
Time of plot: Nineteenth century
Locale: House of Usher

Principal characters:
RODERICK USHER, a madman
MADELINE, his sister
THE NARRATOR, a visitor

The Story:

As the visitor approaches the House of Usher, he is forewarned by the appearance of the old mansion. The fall weather is dull and dreary, the countryside is shady and gloomy, and the old house seems to fit perfectly into the desolate surroundings. The windows look like vacant eyes staring out over the bleak landscape. The visitor comes to the House of Usher in response to a written plea from his boyhood friend, Roderick Usher. The letter tells of an illness of body and mind suffered by the last heir in the ancient line of Usher, and although the letter strangely fills him with dread, the visitor feels that he must go to his former friend. The Usher family, unlike most, left only a direct line of descent, and perhaps it is for this reason that the family itself and the house became one—the House of Usher. As the visitor gets closer, the house appears even more formidable. The stone is discolored and covered with fungi. The building gives the impression of decay, yet the masonry did not fall. A barely discernible crack extends in a zigzag line from the roof to the foundation, but otherwise there are no visible breaks in the structure.

The visitor enters the house, gives his things to a servant, and proceeds through several dark passages to the study of the master. There he is stunned at the appearance of his old friend. In Usher's cadaverous face, eyes are liquid and lips are pallid. His weblike hair is untrimmed and floats over his brow. All in all, he is a depressing figure. In manner, he is even more morbid. He is afflicted with great sensitivity and strange fear. There are only a few sounds, a few odors, a few foods, and a few textures in clothing that do not fill him with terror. In fact, he is haunted incessantly by unnamed fears.

Even more strangely, he is imbued with the thought that the house itself exerts great influence over his morale and that it influences his spirit. Usher's moodiness is heightened by the approaching death of his sister, Lady Madeline. His only living relative, she is wasting away from a strange malady that baffles the doctors. Often the disease reveals its cataleptic (muscular rigidity marked by a lack of response to external stimuli) nature. The visitor sees her only once, on the night of his arrival. She passed through the room without speaking, and her appearance filled him with awe and foreboding.

For several days, the visitor attempts to cheer the sick master of Usher and restore him to health, but it seems, rather, that the hypochondria suffered by Usher affects his friend. More and more, the morbid surroundings and the ramblings of Usher's sick mind prey upon his visitor. More and more, Usher holds that the house itself molded his spirit and that of his ancestors. The visitor is helpless to dispel this morbid fear and is in danger of subscribing to it himself, so powerful is the influence of the gloomy old mansion.

One day, Usher informs his friend that Madeline is no more. It is Usher's intention to bury her in one of the vaults under the house for a period of two weeks. The strangeness of her malady, he says, demands the precaution of not placing her immediately in the exposed family burial plot. The two men take the encoffined body into the burial vault beneath the house and deposit it upon a trestle. Turning back the lid of the coffin, they take one last look at the lady, and the visitor remarks on the similarity of appearance between her and her brother. Then Usher tells him that they are twins and that their natures were singularly alike. The man then closes the lid, screws it down securely, and ascends to the upper rooms.

A noticeable change now takes possession of Usher. He paces the floors with unusual vigor. He becomes more pallid, while his eyes glow with even greater wildness. His voice is little more than a quaver, and his words are utterances of extreme fear. He seems to have a ghastly secret that he cannot share. More and more, the visitor feels that Usher's superstitious beliefs about the malignant influence of the house are true. He cannot sleep, and his body begins to tremble almost as unreasonably as Usher's.

One night, during a severe storm, the visitor hears low and unrecognizable sounds that fill him with terror. Dressing, he paces the floor of his apartment until he hears a soft knock at his door. Usher enters, carrying a lamp. His manner is hysterical and his eyes those of a madman. When he throws the window open to the storm, they are lifted almost off their feet by the intensity of the wind. Usher seems to see something horrible in the night, and the visitor picks up the first book that comes to hand and tries to calm his friend by reading. The story is that of Ethelred and Sir Launcelot, and as he reads, the visitor seems to hear the echo of a cracking and ripping sound described in the story. Later, he hears a rasping and grating, of what he knows not. Usher sits facing the door, as if in a trance. His head and his body rock from side to side in a gentle motion. He murmurs some sort of gibberish, as if he is not aware of his friend's presence.

At last, his ravings become intelligible. He mutters at first but speaks louder and louder until he reaches a scream. Madeline is alive. He buried Madeline alive. For days, he heard her feebly trying to lift the coffin lid. Now she has escaped her tomb and is coming in search of him. At that pronouncement, the door of the room swings back and on the threshold stands the shrouded Lady Madeline of Usher. There is blood on her clothing and evidence of superhuman struggle. She runs to her terrified brother, and the two fall to the floor in death.

The visitor flees the house in terror. He gazes back as he runs and sees the house of horror split asunder in a zigzag manner, down the line of the crack he saw as he first looked upon the old mansion. There is a loud noise, like the sound of many waters, and the pond at its base receives all that is left of the ruined House of Usher.

Critical Evaluation:

Edgar Allan Poe probably remains, both in his life and in his work, America's most controversial writer. Numerous biographical and critical studies did not succeed in rectifying the initially distorted "myth" of Poe, promulgated by his hostile first biographer, as a self-destructive, alcoholic, almost demoniac creature. Even today, after much serious research and analysis, the true Poe remains enigmatic and elusive. The same is true of his works. Experts as important and varied as D. H. Lawrence, Henry James, T. S. Eliot, Charles Baudelaire, and Aldous Huxley differed greatly in assessing his works' merits, with opinions ranging from extravagant eulogy to total dismissal. No work of his excited more diverse opinion or earned more conflicting analyses than his short story "The Fall of the House of Usher."

The problem is that there are many completely different, yet seemingly valid, interpretations of the tale; contradictory readings can explain all of the story's numerous ambiguities. However, clearly, as one prominent Poe critic lamented, the contradictory readings "cannot all be right." Is there any way of choosing among these views or of synthesizing the best of them into a single one? Perhaps the task is not impossible if two important facts about the author are remembered: He was an adroit, conscious craftsman and critic who worked out his ideas with mathematical precision, and yet he was essentially a lyric poet.

These diverse readings can be divided roughly into three primary types: natural or psychological, supernatural, and symbolic. In the first approach, the analysis focuses on the "unreliable" narrator as he chronicles Roderick Usher's descent into madness. As an artist, intellectual, and introvert, Usher becomes so lopsided that his prolonged isolation, coupled with the sickness of his sister, drives him to the edge of madness; along with the narrator, the reader sees him go over the edge. Another possibility is that the tale is simply a detective story minus a detective; Usher manipulates the narrator into helping him murder Madeline and then goes insane from the emotional strain. The crucial "fantastic" elements in the story—Madeline's return from the tomb and the collapse of the house into the tarn—are "logically" explained in terms of the narrator's mounting hysteria, the resulting hallucination, and the natural destructiveness of the storm.

According to the second general view, the actions of the characters can be explained only by postulating a supernatural agency: The Usher curse is working itself out; the house is possessed and is destroying the occupants; Roderick is a demon drawing vitality from his sister until, as a nemesis figure, she returns to punish him; Madeline is a vampire claiming her victim.

In the third view, the story is seen as an allegory: Roderick as intellect is suppressing sensuality (Madeline) until it revolts; Madeline is a mother figure who returns from the grave to punish Usher-Poe for deserting her and for having incestuous desires; Roderick is the artist who must destroy himself in order to create; the entire story is a symbolic enactment of the Apocalypse according to Poe.

Both as a critic and a writer, Poe was thoroughly aware of the machinery of the gothic, and "The Fall of the House of Usher" is a veritable catalog of devices from the genre—the haunted mansion, the artistic hero-villain, the twins motif, suggestions of vampirism, the dark crypts, the violent electrical storms. It does not follow, however, that because Poe utilizes the conventions of the form, he is also holding himself to the substance of them. It is precisely because he does not commit himself exclusively to a rational, supernatural, or symbolic reading of the tale that he is able to provoke emotional reactions by indirection and implication that would be impossible if he fixed his meaning more precisely. The technique is essentially that of the lyric poet who uses the power of image, atmosphere, and suggestion to evoke emotions and to produce exactly one emotional, not rational, effect on the reader—which was Poe's stated aim as a short-story writer.

"I feel that the period will sooner or later arrive," says Roderick Usher, "when I must abandon life and reason together, in some struggle with the grim phantasm, FEAR." Thus, Poe underscores "fear" as the central emotion he wishes to provoke, and the story can best be discussed in terms of how he develops this response.

The tale divides into five distinct parts: first, the description of the house and the background of the narrator's relationship to Usher; second, his meeting with Usher that ends with his glimpse of Lady Madeline; third, the survey of Usher's art, that is, music, painting, the recitation of the poem "The Haunted Palace," Roderick's theory of "sentience," and the description of the library; fourth, Madeline's "death" and entombment; and, fifth, her return from the crypt counterpointed against the narrator's reading of "The Mad Trist" story that culminates in the death of the twins, the narrator's flight, and the collapse of the house into the tarn. Each of these phases not only furthers the plot line but also intensifies the emotions provoked in the reader by means of the narrator's progressive hysteria and the growing distortion of the atmosphere.

The narrator is quickly characterized as a skeptic, who attempts to explain everything rationally but who is, at the same time, quite susceptible to unexplained anxieties and undefined premonitions. His first glimpse of the Usher mansion provokes "a sense of unsufferable gloom." As he describes it, the house resembles a giant face or skull with "eye-like windows" and hairlike "minute fungi" that almost seem to hold the decayed building together and has a "barely perceptible fissure" that threatens to rip it apart. He is even more horrified when he looks into the tarn (a small, stagnant lake in front of the house) and sees the house's inverted reflection in the black water. Thus, in the first paragraph of the tale, readers are introduced to three crucial elements: the subjective reactions of the narrator, which begin with this furtive, general uneasiness and will end in complete hysteria; the central image of a huge, dead, decaying object that is, paradoxically, very alive; and the first of many reflections or doubles that reinforce and intensify the atmosphere and implications of the story.

When the narrator meets his old friend Usher, the other side of the death-life paradox is suggested. Whereas the dead objects seem "alive," the "live" things seem dead. All the peripheral characters—the two servants, the doctor, the "living" Madeline—are shadows. Usher, with his "cadaverous" complexion, "large, liquid and luminous eyes," "thin and very pallid" lips, and "hair of more than web-like softness," seems more zombie than human. Moreover, his description mirrors that of the house's exterior: His eyes are like the windows; his hair resembles the fungi.

Usher does, however, have a definable personality. For all of the spectral hints, Poe never abandons the possibility that Usher's character and fate can be explained naturally. Although Usher's behavior is violent and erratic, perhaps manic-depressive by modern clinical standards, tenuous rationalizations are provided for everything he does. Nor does Usher's role as an artist resolve the questions about his character. The extended catalog of his artistic activities may seem digressive in terms of Poe's strict single-effect theory, but it is, in fact, the necessary preparation for the story's harrowing finale. Each of Usher's artistic ventures conforms to both his realistic personality and the otherworldliness of the situation; they can either signal his descent into psychosis or his ineffectual attempts to understand and withstand the incursion of supernatural forces. His dirges suggest death; his abstract painting of a vaultlike structure previews Madeline's interment. When he recites "The Haunted Palace" poem, he is either metaphorically recounting his own fall into madness, or he is, literally, talking about "haunting." Usher's statements about the sentience of all vegetable things—that is, the conscious life in all inanimate matter—brings a notion that previously was latent in the reader's mind to the surface. Finally, Usher's exotic library, made up almost entirely of books about supernatural journeys, suggests either a perversely narrow and bizarre taste or an attempt to acquire the knowledge needed to defend against demoniac intruders.

Nevertheless, for all of the mounting intensity of suggestion and of atmosphere, the actual story does not begin until almost two-thirds of the narrative has been completed. When Usher announces that Lady Madeline "is no more," the story quickens. It is at this point that the narrator notices the "striking similitude between the brother and sister" and so emphasizes the "twin theme," the most important reflection or double in the tale. As they entomb her, the narrator takes note of the "mockery of a faint blush upon the bosom and the face." Does this suggest a trace of life and implicate Usher, consciously or unconsciously, in her murder? Or, does it hint at an "undead" specter who, knowing that she will return from the grave, mocks the attempt to inter her?

Nowhere is the value of indirection in the maximizing of suspense more evident than in the last sequence of the story. Having established the literary context of the narrative, Poe then counterpoints the reading of a rather trite medieval romance against Madeline's actual return from the crypt. At the simplest level, "The Mad Trist" tale is a suspense-building device that magnifies the reader's excitement as the reader awaits Madeline's certain reappearance. Thematically, it suggests a parallel—either straight or ironic, depending on the reader's interpretation—between the knight Ethelred's quest and Madeline's return from the tomb. Reinforced by the violent storm, the narrator's frenzy, and Usher's violence, Madeline's return, her mutually fatal embrace of her brother, the narrator's flight, and the disintegration of the house itself fuse into a shattering final effect, which is all that Poe claimed he wanted, and a provocative insight into—what? The collapse of a sick mind? The inevitable self-destruction of the hyperintroverted artistic temperament? The final end of aristocratic inbreeding? Or incest? Or vampirism? Or the end of the world?

Although the meaning of "The Fall of the House of Usher" remains elusive, the experience of the story is powerful, disturbing, and lasting. In the final analysis, the experience of the story is where its greatness lies and why it must be considered one of the finest short stories of its kind ever written.

"Critical Evaluation" by Keith Neilson

Further Reading

Ackroyd, Peter. *Poe: A Life Cut Short*. London: Chatto & Windus, 2008. Ackroyd, a novelist, provides a concise chronicle of Poe's brief, unhappy life.

Beebe, Maurice. "The Universe of Roderick Usher." In *Poe: A Collection of Critical Essays*, edited by Robert Regan. Englewood Cliffs, N.J.: Prentice-Hall, 1967. Discusses the cosmological theory that underlies "The Fall of the House of Usher." Claims that an understanding of Poe's *Eureka* helps the reader understand the story as symbolic drama.

Brennan, Matthew C. "An American Case: Edgar Allan Poe's 'The Fall of the House of Usher.'" In *The Gothic Psyche: Disintegration and Growth in Nineteenth-Century English Literature*. Columbia, S.C.: Camden House, 1997. Applies Jungian psychoanalytic theories to analyze Poe's story.

Fisher, Benjamin F. *The Cambridge Introduction to Edgar Allan Poe*. New York: Cambridge University Press, 2008. Overview of Poe's literary career and writings. Describes how Poe's fiction advanced from gothic fantasy to more sophisticated explorations of human psychology. The references to "The Fall of the House of Usher" are listed in the index.

Hayes, Kevin J., ed. *The Cambridge Companion to Edgar Allan Poe*. New York: Cambridge University Press, 2002. Collection of essays, including discussions of Poe's aesthetic theory, humor, feminine ideal, Poe and the gothic tradition, and Poe, sensationalism, and slavery. Scott Peeples's essay, "Poe's 'Constructiveness' and 'The Fall of the House of Usher,'" analyzes this work.

Hoffman, Daniel. *Poe Poe Poe Poe Poe Poe Poe*. Garden City, N.Y.: Doubleday, 1972. A personal study of the mind of Poe, containing an extensive discussion of doubling and desire in "The Fall of the House of Usher." Argues that the story is a catalog of all of Poe's obsessional themes.

May, Charles E. *Edgar Allan Poe: A Study of the Short Fiction*. Boston: Twayne, 1991. A study of Poe's development of the short story as a genre. Discusses "The Fall of the House of Usher" as an aesthetic, self-reflexive fable of the basic dilemma of the artist. Includes an essay with a reader-response approach to the story by Ronald Bieganowski.

Robinson, E. Arthur. "Order and Sentience in 'The Fall of the House of Usher.'" *PMLA* 76 (1961): 68-81. One of the most extensive studies of the story, focusing on its underlying pattern of thought and thematic structure.

Thompson, G. R., and Virgil L. Lokke, eds. *Ruined Eden of the Present*. West Lafayette, Ind.: Purdue University Press, 1981. Contains a debate between G. R. Thompson and Patrick F. Quinn about the psychic state of the narrator in the story.

The Family at Gilje

Author: Jonas Lie (1833-1908)
First published: Familjen paa Gilje, 1883 (English
    translation, 1920)
Type of work: Novel
Type of plot: Domestic realism
Time of plot: Nineteenth century
Locale: Norway

Principal characters:
CAPTAIN JÄGER, an army officer
JORGEN, his son
INGER-JOHANNA, his daughter
THINKA, another daughter
MRS. JÄGER, his wife
CAPTAIN RÖNNOW, another officer
ARENT GRIP, a student
GULCKE, the sheriff

The Story:

It is obvious that Inger-Johanna is her father's favorite. He is an army captain, in charge at Gilje. When a fellow officer, Captain Rönnow, stops at the house, Captain Jäger is delighted because the guest seems so charmed by Inger-Johanna. Mrs. Jäger is a sister of the governor, and Captain Rönnow tells the Jägers that he will petition the governor's wife, with whom he is in favor, to take Inger-Johanna into their home for a year, so that she can learn the ways of society in the city. Gilje is a deserted mountain post and not at all suitable for a young lady of Inger-Johanna's obvious charms.

Captain Jäger wants his beloved daughter to visit her aunt, but when he learns the cost of the new clothing required, he storms at his poor wife and cannot be quieted. Perhaps his blustering is caused by sorrow at losing his favorite daughter, although he is happy that she will have such a fine opportunity.

Before Inger-Johanna leaves, she meets a student named Arent Grip, the son of an old friend of her father. In spite of his radical ideas, the girl finds him interesting and is glad that he, too, will be in the city.

After the departure of his oldest daughter, the captain's house is desolate, for Thinka, another daughter, goes to work for a judge in Ryfylke. Poor Jorgen, the only son, and a younger daughter are put through hours of lessons to ease their father's loneliness.

Each letter from Inger-Johanna is read again and again. After her initial shyness wears off, she loves her life in the city. Parties and balls delight her. Both Captain Rönnow and Grip are present at many of the functions, her aunt having secured a place for Grip in her husband's office. The aunt also writes to confide that she secretly hopes a match will develop between the girl and Captain Rönnow, who is advancing rapidly and will be a good catch. The aunt is not fond of Grip; she finds him too spirited and unrestrained in expressing his unpopular ideas. Inger-Johanna, however, completely wins

over her aunt, who insists that the girl return home for a visit and then come back to the city for another season.

During his daughter's visit, Captain Jäger is in a delighted mood. Grip calls on the family again and arranges to spend time alone with Inger-Johanna. They take a surveying trip into the mountains with her father and Jorgen, and Grip finds Jorgen a bright lad who deserves a better education. In his talks with Inger-Johanna, Grip claims that fundamentals are all that matter in life, not the external symbols of success. He wants people to be themselves, not influenced by worldly values.

Inger-Johanna returns to the city before Thinka comes home for a visit. The younger daughter fell in love with a young clerk in her uncle's office, but when her relative learned of the affair, he fired the clerk, who is poor and without prospects. Thinka often thinks of him after her return home, although her parents urge her to forget him.

Sheriff Gulcke calls at Gilje and finds Thinka attractive. Because his wife died only three months before, he can say nothing so soon after his loss; but during his stay, he often casts an appreciative eye toward Thinka. In the meantime, Thinka writes long letters to her sister, to tell of her love for the poor clerk, for whom she promised to wait. Inger-Johanna, tiring of balls and city life, writes that she remains only to please her aunt. Grip changed her way of thinking and made her see the uselessness of such a life.

Jorgen goes to the city to school. Grip tutors him but says that Jorgen should be sent to England or to America to learn a mechanic's trade, because that is the field in which he has great talent. Later Jorgen sails for England and then to America, a fact that Captain Jäger forever holds against Grip.

Thinka is right in her fear that she will never be allowed to marry her clerk. Sheriff Gulcke asks for her hand, and because she is without will to deny her father's wishes, she accepts the older man. After the marriage, she is a good and faithful wife, acting almost as a nurse to her husband. He is kind to her and consents to her every desire, but her heart is sad. Inger-Johanna is dismayed that her sister has no will of her own, and she refuses to accept the idea that women are to bend to the will of their fathers and husbands.

Inger-Johanna is soon to be tested. Captain Rönnow writes her father for her hand. It is the proudest moment of Captain Jäger's life. At first, Inger-Johanna accepts, for Grip makes no proposal and she knows that Captain Rönnow is the man her father desires for her. Before the wedding, however, she returns suddenly from the city. She admits to herself and to her family that she can love no one but Grip and cannot marry Captain Rönnow. Although her father is bitterly disappointed, he cannot force his favorite daughter to marry against her will. Sorrowfully, he writes his old friend his decision.

From that day on, Captain Jäger's health rapidly fails. He suffers dizziness and weakness. He is forced to take a leave of absence from his military duties. One day his carriage does not return home. When the servant goes to look for him, he finds the horse standing at the foot of Gilje hill, the reins loose on the ground. The captain of Gilje is dead.

Twenty years pass. Mrs. Jäger is dead, and Jorgen is doing well in America. Inger-Johanna, a schoolteacher, teaches the children the ideas and ideals she learned from Grip. Meanwhile, he wanders over the land, a drunkard and an ascetic by turn. He carefully avoids Inger-Johanna but constantly seeks news of her. Finally he goes to her school and stands by the window to hear the sound of her voice. He sees her face again as she looks out into the night. He leaves then, sick with pneumonia. When word of his illness reaches Inger-Johanna, she goes to him and nurses him until his death. Often he is irrational; at times he is completely lucid. After his death, she knows that he gave her her only reason for living, her spirit for truth and freedom.

Critical Evaluation:

The Family at Gilje is often considered only a minor Scandinavian classic. It is accorded little significance outside Scandinavian literary history. The novel nevertheless reflects many of the major themes of mainstream European literature of the nineteenth century. One of the most striking commonalities is the theme of the conflict between the individual and various social codes. Very often, this is expressed in terms of romantic love as a metaphor for individual choice. Inger-Johanna Jäger is obliged to chose between submission to what her society wants for her and her own desires.

In raising Inger-Johanna, the Captain and Mrs. Jäger are faced with a paradox. As members of the relatively prosper-

ous landholding class, they are at the top of the social pyramid, as far as Gilje is concerned, but in the eyes of the wider world they are rural, backward, and, most importantly, culturally impoverished. In sending Inger-Johanna to the city, they try to gain entry for their daughter into social circles that they have not themselves penetrated. The parents find, however, that once the process of Inger-Johanna's acculturation is under way, it cannot be controlled. The reader senses before it happens that Inger-Johanna will find the charms of the conventional Captain Rönnow lacking and prefer the earnest student Arent Grip. One of Grip's charms is that Inger-Johanna's aunt and her parents find him an unattractive candidate for her hand in marriage. As often happens in the nineteenth century European novel, the choice of a spouse is used as a metaphor for self-discovery and the exploration of various philosophical alternatives. Inger-Johanna is exposed to various potential directions in life, and she is encouraged to have the appearance of exploring all her options, but she finds that ultimately her family tries to constrain her freedom.

Although the Jägers are frustrated by Inger-Johanna's willful and headstrong ways, they nevertheless prefer her to the more earthbound Thinka, whose ordinariness illuminates by contrast Inger-Johanna's intellectual and spiritual curiosity. Jorgen is more like his oldest sister in his ambition and drive. He eventually finds his energies cannot be contained by provincial Norway and ends up immigrating to America, where the traits that threaten to make his life unfulfilled at home assist him in achieving considerable success in America. Being a woman, Inger-Johanna does not really have the option of emigrating alone in the society of her day.

The plot of *The Family at Gilje* surprises by its relative unconventionality. Throughout the first half of the book, the reader is led to think either that Inger-Johanna will elope with Grip and be spiritually and emotionally fulfilled, or that she will marry Captain Rönnow and have her energy and impulsiveness co-opted and reintegrated into the existing structure of social manners and mores. She ends up marrying neither man. Looking beyond the superficial plot contrivance by which Jonas Lie secures this outcome, the reader sees that Inger-Johanna's disappointment and renunciation of her once-cherished personal goals provide, for all their depressing limitation, an opportunity for the fulfillment of her spiritual potential. This outcome stands in vivid contrast to that of Thinka, who does not have the backbone to resist the imposition of an unwanted husband by her family. Inger-Johanna is aging, alone, and disappointed at the end of the book. However, unlike Thinka, she has not only kept her freedom but also maintained her personal and moral integrity.

The crucial force in the book's unexpected plot is Grip. Grip is a character type familiar to the nineteenth century novel. He is the idealist who rebels against ingrained social expectations and who advertises vague, radical ideas while also exerting a sort of romantic charisma—a figure highly familiar to European readers of the day. Most of these figures turn out to be either hopelessly shallow and unrealistic or ultimately slack and self-serving, but Grip is different. He has deep beliefs to which he faithfully adheres and by which he lives his life. More important, he is a good man. He is not only intelligent and engaging but also genuinely charitable, wanting unselfishly to help others. The crude and backward Norway of his day cannot comprehend these traits, so his life seems a waste. His life is not wasted, however, because he provides Inger-Johanna with the vision of how life should be, how it should have meaning. Even though they see each other only briefly in the twenty years between the time of their failed courtship and that of Grip's death, and although their relationship is never consummated, their relationship has, in spiritual terms, a positive ending. Grip enables Inger-Johanna to glimpse the full beauty of life, even if she never fully experiences it.

Lie's novel thus turns from being a rather conventional chronicle of bourgeois family life to being a portrait of the imaginative triumphs that the framework of family life cannot fully succeed in containing. Lie is not hostile to bourgeois society; he recognizes its necessity and its achievements. The Jäger family is a genuinely happy one, and without the kindness of her parents Inger-Johanna could never achieve her own unusual and winning personality. In a way, Lie argues, all Inger-Johanna is trying to do is take her childhood happiness and reproduce it on a higher, more spiritual plane by marrying Grip; it is only the constraints of society that prevent Inger-Johanna from fulfilling herself within the bounds of family life.

After this book, Lie's interest turned much more toward the mystical and the spiritual, toward strange sea tales and ghost stories. *The Family at Gilje*, being his most mainstream work, is the only book of Lie's to have any recognized place in world literature. It holds that status because of the depth of its characters and the importance of its themes.

"Critical Evaluation" by Nicholas Birns

Further Reading

Gustafson, Alrik. "Impressionistic Realism: Jonas Lie." In *Six Scandinavian Novelists*. Minneapolis: University of Minnesota Press, 1966. Places Lie within contemporary developments in European fiction. Argues that the scrupulous realism of *The Family at Gilje* does not preclude formal experiments with tone, character, and symbolism. Examines Lie's stance toward his own characters, especially Captain Jäger.

Larsen, Hanna. "Jonas Lie, 1833-1909." *American-Scandinavian Review* 21 (1993): 461-471. Demonstrates the centrality of *The Family at Gilje* to Lie's career and argues that the rest of his achievement was a falling-off from the clarity achieved in the novel. Examines the role of the town of Gilje and the surrounding landscape in the thematic and symbolic architecture of the novel.

Lyngstad, Sverre. *Jonas Lie*. Boston: Twayne, 1977. A comprehensive discussion of Lie's work in English. Sees the novel as presenting Norwegian cultural history within the frame of the story of the Jäger family. Examines the differences between Inger-Jonhanna and her sisters and the issues at play between Inger-Johanna and Grip. Comments extensively on the symbolism and values of the book.

_____. "The Vortex and Related Imagery in Jonas Lie's Fiction." *Scandinavian Studies* 51 (Summer, 1979): 211-248. Explores Lie's achievement with a closely textured analysis of his work, focusing on the meaning and integration provided to the novel through its symbols.

McFarlane, James W. "Jonas Lie." In *Ibsen and the Temper of Norwegian Literature*. London: Harrap, 1960. Compares Lie to later innovators in Norwegian literature such as Ibsen; finds considerable importance in Lie's depictions of bourgeois lifestyles.

_____. "Realism and Naturalism." In *A History of Norwegian Literature*, edited by Harald S. Naess. Lincoln: University of Nebraska Press in cooperation with the American-Scandinavian Foundation, 1993. McFarlane's overview of Norwegian literature from 1860 until 1910 includes a six-page discussion of Lie's life and works, including *The Family at Gilje*. McFarlane describes Lie as being the "founder of the Norwegian novel and Norway's first great practitioner in the field of fiction."

The Family of Pascual Duarte

Author: Camilo José Cela (1916-2002)
First published: La familia de Pascual Duarte, 1942
   (English translation, 1946)
Type of work: Novel
Type of plot: Social realism
Time of plot: Early twentieth century
Locale: Extremadura, Spain

Principal characters:
PASCUAL DUARTE, a convict
PASCUAL'S MOTHER
MARIO, his brother
ROSARIO, his sister
LOLA, his first wife
EL ESTIRAO, Rosario and Lola's lover

The Story:

Sentenced to death, Pascual Duarte decides to write a history of his life to serve as a warning to others, or so he implies. Pascual was born to a poor Extremaduran peasant family and raised in an atmosphere of hate and resentment. Both parents were abusive drunkards, and his younger brother Mario was mentally disabled, unable even to walk. The only saving grace of the family was Rosario, his sister, but she left home to better her situation by becoming a prostitute. She returned home once, ill with fever, but left as soon as she was well. Fifteen years after Rosario, Mario was born. Two days before his birth, Pascual's father, Esteban, was bitten by a rabid dog. The family, afraid of being attacked, locked Esteban in an armoire, where he died on the day of Mario's birth, screaming, driven mad by the disease.

Mario, scorned by everyone except Rosario, crawled and lived on the floor with the pigs and dogs. One day, the pigs ate his ears, and, from then on, it was hard for the family even to look at him. Generally unresponsive, Mario would go into shrieking fits at the sight of pigs. During one of these episodes, Don Rafael, who may have been the boy's father, kicked the child into unconsciousness, blood gushing from the boy's ear cavity. Pascual's mother laughed, but although Pascual, fearing to be called soft, also did nothing, from that day forward, his active hatred of his mother grew. Shortly afterward, Mario was found drowned in a vat of oil, perhaps murdered by Rafael.

Pascual fell in love with, and raped, Lola. On discovering that she was pregnant, he married her. On their wedding day, their horse injured an old woman, a bad omen that presaged Lola's fall from that same horse on the day they returned from their honeymoon. The fall caused a miscarriage. Pascual was not with her. He was celebrating with friends in a bar, on a drinking spree that ended in Pascual's seriously wounding a friend who taunted him.

Pascual was always given to violence. When he learned of his wife's miscarriage, he blamed the horse and stabbed the

animal to death. One day, while sitting in his favorite spot with his only friend, his dog, nearby, he seemed to read reproach in the animal's eyes and repeatedly shot the dog to rid himself of that look. Pascual also was tormented by premonitions of ill fortune. When his first child (his wife's second pregnancy) was born, although the baby seemed healthy, he could not rid himself of a sense of foreboding, and the child died of illness in early infancy. After the baby's death, Pascual could not endure the atmosphere in his home and fled to Madrid. From Madrid, he traveled to La Coruña, hoping to set sail for America. The trip was too costly, however, and after two years of working at odd jobs, Pascual returned home, only to find his wife pregnant with another man's—El Estirao's—child.

El Estirao was the abusive pimp and lover of Rosario who always delighted in taunting Pascual. His seduction of Pascual's wife maddened the peasant, and, after the effort of confessing the truth to him, Lola suddenly died in Pascual's arms. When El Estirao returned, looking for Rosario, Pascual killed him, crushing his spine. For this crime he was sent to prison but was released for good behavior after only serving two years.

When he returned home after his imprisonment, he found no one there to welcome him. Rosario was gone again, and his mother's conduct toward him worsened. He married again, this time to the timid daughter of the local midwife, who secretly cared for him. His mother's treatment of Esperanza, however, was terrible, and Pascual, now certain that his mother was still the source of all of his trouble, decided he must kill her to survive. Full of loathing, he carefully planned the crime, but at the last moment he was unable to strike. He stood paralyzed by her bed until she awoke. After a fierce struggle, he finally subdued and killed her. Earlier, Pascual might have been responsible for the assassination of the village patriarch, Don Jesús, during an uprising at the start of the civil war. Pascual was captured and is waiting to be hanged, but whether for the death of his mother or Don Jesús is uncertain.

Pascual, in his memoirs, professes to have come to terms with his fate, but, at the end, he is led kicking and screaming to the scaffold. He does not describe this episode, as one might expect, in his memoirs. Other witnesses report his shameful end.

Critical Evaluation:

It is now a commonplace to state that Camilo José Cela, who won the 1989 Nobel Prize in Literature, is one of the foremost writers in the Spanish language. In 1942, the publication by a then-unknown writer of the violent *The Family of Pascual Duarte* caused a sensation. Its appearance marked the start of the contemporary Spanish novel, and critics and public were shocked by its theme and by the apparent lack of censorship in a Spain where many writers and intellectuals were dead, exiled, or still incarcerated in Franco's prisons.

Narrated in first person, the novel purports to be the life history of an Extremaduran peasant, awaiting execution, who is mired in a black destiny of heredity and environment. The core of the novel is the question of responsibility. How much influence did Pascual Duarte have on the course of his own life? The bleak answer seems to be: none. Although Duarte states that he is recounting his life so that others may flee from his example and choose other paths, it is evident that Duarte himself believes that his life is predestined, a fate that he was born into. There are ambiguities and ironies in the text, however, that allow for many interpretations, moral and otherwise.

Duarte's history, after all, is the truth according to Duarte. All the characters are seen through the filter of Duarte's vision of the world. For instance, it becomes clear that Duarte is in some way responsible for the premeditated assassination of Don Jesús, the rich man of the village, but Duarte only hints at this. He wants to be viewed as only the victim of his circumstances and his actions to be viewed as the product of spontaneous and understandable rage. In addition, parts of the story are told in unchronological flashbacks so that the motivations that trigger Duarte's responses are often vague and imprecise.

Duarte's defense in a hostile environment is to strike out with violence. It is a measure of the brutishness of the human characters that his attacks on his nonhuman victims— his dog, for example—are more appalling than his actions against his fellow human beings. The tenuous line between bestiality and humanity is symbolized by Mario, his pathetic little brother, who lives in filth on the floor and who is treated worse than the pigs that live with him. Duarte's violence ac-

celerates until his hatred centers on the one person he always hated and blames for everything and who is never even given a personal name. His mother's death is a symbol to him of freedom, and his first words after her murder are "I could breathe."

This sense of suffocation by society and family is one of the basic themes of the novel. Its images change from the cramped shack in which Pascual lives, to the black circle of grieving women belittling and badgering him after the death of his child, to the graveyard with its high walls, and to Duarte awaiting death in another cramped box.

The shocking murder of his mother is one extreme act in a life characterized by extreme violence. *The Family of Pascual Duarte* is representative of *tremendismo*, a literary movement of the early 1940's that described its protagonists as trapped in an encircling vise of poverty, ignorance, and oppression from which the only escape is violent rebellion. The desired effect is one of shock at the "tremendous" nature of the actions depicted and their resultant consequences.

Nevertheless, although the definition of *tremendismo* can serve equally well as a description of the life of Duarte, the success of the work and perhaps its lack of censorship were due to its being very much within the Spanish narrative tradition. Realism has always been the hallmark of the Spanish novel. Spanish naturalistic writers never shied away from violence, and Duarte can be seen as a modern-day, although much more negative, successor to the famous *picaro* of the sixteenth and seventeenth centuries. Another tribute to the past is Cela's use of the Spanish literary device of a neutral transcriber who just happens to have found the pages of a curious manuscript.

What is purely Cela and sets the novel apart is the intense blending of environment and atmosphere. The harshness of Extremadura (the name joins the words "extreme" and "hard" or "harsh") becomes a character just as real as the people. The grim presence of a brutish superstitious land is in Duarte's description of his village and hovel, of the unpaved roads that all seem to lead to the cemetery, and of the black landscape dimly seen through a dirty train window. It is significant that whenever Duarte leaves Extremadura, he is treated relatively well. He enjoys his life in Madrid and makes friends; he finds work in La Coruña. Even in prison his jailers see some good in him, and he gains early release, but he returns to Extremadura. His fate seems to be calling him back (he says so in his narrative), and it seems inevitable that it will crush him, just as the death of his mother seems inevitable. His past is always his future.

Charlene E. Suscavage

Further Reading

Busette, Cedric. *"La familia de Pascual Duarte" and "El Tánel": Correspondences and Divergencies in the Exercise of Craft*. Lanham, Md.: University Press of America, 1994. Busette compares and contrasts the debut novels of Cela and Ernesto Sábato, analyzing their narrative purposes, language, protagonists, and other elements of the two books.

Charlebois, Lucile C. *Understanding Camilo José Cela*. Columbia: University of South Carolina Press, 1998. A thorough if progressively difficult study of Cela's equally difficult novels. Each chapter focuses on one of the novels, beginning with *The Family of Pascual Duarte* through *La cruz de San Andrés*. Includes chronology and select bibliography.

Foster, David W. *Forms of the Novel in the Work of Camilo José Cela*. Columbia: University of Missouri Press, 1967. Analyzes Cela's constant tinkering with the narrative structure and intent of his novels and his seeming lack of satisfaction with previous efforts.

Hoyle, Alan. *Cela: "La familia de Pascual Duarte."* London: Grant & Cutler, 1994. A concise introductory overview and critical interpretation of the novel. Written in English with Spanish quotations.

Kirsner, Robert. *The Novels and Travels of Camilo José Cela*. Chapel Hill: University of North Carolina Press, 1963. Discusses the narrative techniques used in Cela's novels and travelogues, in which the line between the two genres is often blurred. A good analysis of the treatment of landscape in *The Family of Pascual Duarte*.

McPheeters, D. W. *Camilo José Cela*. Boston: Twayne, 1969. One of the best and easiest introductions to the early work of Cela, with special emphasis on *The Family of Pascual Duarte*.

Peréz, Janet. *Camilo José Cela Revisited: The Later Novels*. New York: Twayne, 2000. Peréz updates and expands McPheeters's overview. Analyzes Cela's novels and provides biographical material, an index, and an annotated bibliography for further study.

Spires, Robert C. *Mode of Existence and the Concept of Morality in "La familia de Pascual Duarte."* Ames, Iowa: Orrin Frank, 1968. Analyzes the moral climate of the time as well as that of the novel. Good discussion of how Pascual sees the world and how the world sees him.

Turner, Harriet, and Adelaida López de Martínez, eds. *The Cambridge Companion to the Spanish Novel: From 1600 to the Present*. New York: Cambridge University Press, 2003. Cela's work is discussed in several places, particularly in chapter 11, "The Testimonial Novel and the Novel of Memory." Places Cela's work within the broader context of the Spanish novel.

The Family Reunion

Author: T. S. Eliot (1888-1965)
First produced: 1939; first published, 1939
Type of work: Drama
Type of plot: Symbolic realism
Time of plot: Twentieth century
Locale: England

Principal characters:
AMY, LADY MONCHENSEY, an old lady
HARRY, her son
AGATHA, her sister
DOWNING, Harry's servant
MARY, Amy's ward

The Story:

Amy, Lady Monchensey, is reluctant to have the lights turned on. She has to sit in the house from October until June, for in winter the sun rarely warms the cold earth of northern England. Since all she can do is measure time, she hardly wants to make night come too soon.

The whole family, except her three sons, gathers to celebrate her birthday, and the sons are expected that evening. The conversation while they wait out the time is tasteless.

Gerald and Charles, Amy's brothers-in-law, feel that the younger generation does not accept its responsibilities. Ivy and Violet, her younger sisters, agree that youth is becoming decadent. When they ask Mary her opinion, as a representative of the new generation, Amy's ward is nettled. Nearing thirty, she was always poor and remains unmarried; she thinks she belongs to no generation.

Amy lives only to keep Wishwood, the family estate, together. Since her husband's death, she has been head of the house. She knows her family, settled in its ways, is getting older; soon death will come as a surprise for them all. Only Agatha, her older sister, seems to find a meaning in death. Harry, the oldest son, was gone eight years. Amy hopes he can drop back into the old routine at the family home, but Agatha is doubtful. The past is over; the future can be built only on the present. When Harry comes back he cannot take up life where he left off, because he would be a new Harry.

The others begin speculating. They do not like Harry's wife, a demanding woman who persuaded him to take her away from Wishwood. On their travels she was lost at sea, apparently swept overboard in a storm. Amy says they must feel no remorse for her death.

Harry surprises them by being the first of the sons to arrive. When he seems upset because the blinds are not drawn, the others remind him that in the country there is no one to look in. Nevertheless, Harry keeps staring at the window. He can see the Eumenides, the vengeful spirits. They were with him a long time, but only at Wishwood can he see them. He greets the assembled company with an effort.

Harry becomes impatient when the relatives begin talking of all the old things waiting at home for him. Nothing ever happens to them; they go through life half asleep. Harry, however, is doing some soul searching. In mid-Atlantic he pushed his wife overboard. Now the Furies are always with him.

Only Agatha seems to understand him. The others think him overtired and urge him to go lie down for a while. When he leaves, they decide to invite Dr. Warburton for dinner so that the family doctor can have a look at him.

Charles and Gerald call in Downing, Harry's servant, to question him. Violet and Ivy object because they fear scandal. Agatha, however, makes no objection, because questioning Downing is as irrelevant as calling in Dr. Warburton. Downing seems to be frank. He hardly thinks Harry's wife had the courage to commit suicide, and while he is a little distrait, Harry always appears normal. The only thing amiss that Downing noticed was that Harry was always too much with his wife.

Mary appeals to Agatha for help in getting away from Wishwood. She knows that Amy wants her to stay on and marry Harry; in that way Amy will have a tame daughter-in-law for a companion. Agatha, however, refuses help. Mary should have had the courage to leave earlier; since Harry returned she cannot run away.

When Harry talks with Mary about his fears and doubts, she tries to understand his feeling that change is inevitable. They reminisce about the hollow tree in which they played as

children and about their regret when Amy had it cut down. Harry sees the Furies again in the window embrasure. Startled by his manner, Mary pulls back the curtains to show that nothing is there.

Dr. Warburton comes early for dinner to have a confidential talk with Harry. He tries to attack Harry's disturbance indirectly by warning him that Amy's health is very poor and that Harry must take the burden of Wishwood off her shoulders. Harry recalls the unpleasantness of his boyhood when being good meant pleasing Amy. Abruptly, he demands to know something of his father. The old doctor assures him that there was no scandal. His father and mother just agreed to separate, and his father went abroad to die.

A police sergeant comes to tell the family that John, having suffered a slight concussion in an auto accident, cannot be there for the birthday dinner. Although the family buzzes with the news, Harry shocks them with his statement that it hardly matters because his brother John is unconscious all the time anyway.

A long-distance call comes from Arthur, the other brother. He was in an accident, too, and his license has been suspended for drunken driving. Still troubled about his father, Harry presses Agatha for more details. Agatha remembers his father's feelings, but his mother complemented his weaknesses. Then Agatha loses her inhibitions and tells the truth. While Amy was pregnant with Harry, her husband plotted to kill her. Agatha talked him out of his scheme; she could not bear to think of destroying the new life Amy was carrying.

At that news Harry feels a great release, for the curse of the house seems clearer. When the Eumenides appear again, Harry is no longer frightened. He knows at last that the Furies are not pursuing him; he is following them. Harry decides to leave Wishwood.

Amy, furious at the news that Harry is going away, blames Agatha, the younger sister who stole her husband thirty-five years ago and now is taking her son. Mary pleads with Agatha to stop Harry's departure, but to no avail; Harry has crossed the frontier of reality. Then Mary asks her help in getting a situation, perhaps a fellowship, so she can leave, too. As the two women become more confidential, they reveal to each other that they have also seen the Eumenides. That knowledge is a bond uniting them outside the stifling confines of Wishwood. When they talk with Downing, he confesses he sees the Furies but he pays little attention to them; they are Harry's ghosts. Just before she dies, Amy begins to understand what is happening at Wishwood. Agatha and Mary bring in the birthday cake and blow out the candles as they circle around it. The rest of the family begins talking about the will.

Critical Evaluation:

The Family Reunion, T. S. Eliot's second full-length play, is a significant contribution to the world of verse drama. After *Murder in the Cathedral* (1935), Eliot declined all invitations to write more religious, historical dramas. He chose instead to attempt a synthesis of religious and secular drama on a contemporary theme. *The Family Reunion* was his first effort in that direction.

As in most of Eliot's plays, the characters in *The Family Reunion* represent four basic role types: pilgrims or martyrs, witnesses, watchers, and tempters. Harry Monchensey, the play's pilgrim, is the only character to experience growth or at least a turning point. Harry learns to take the way of self-denial to discover redemption for himself and his community; he learns that he must perfect his will and deny himself the comfortable life of Wishwood, which would prevent him from reaching his spiritual potential. Harry functions as the center of a concentric pattern representing the integration of spiritual values with temporal ones. Harry is surrounded by four witnesses—Agatha, Mary, Downing, and Dr. Warburton—who in various ways aid and reveal Harry's progress. These four characters function like points on the face of a clock on which Harry is the pivotal point, a clock that symbolizes the new order of time he ushers into Wishwood. The walk Mary and Agatha take around the birthday cake at the end of the play portrays this new order.

In contrast to the witnesses, the watchers—Ivy, Violet, Gerald, and Charles—see much on the surface but choose to ignore the inklings of spiritual insight they encounter. They form a second concentric pattern around Amy Monchensey, who represents frozen, lifeless time. In her effort to persuade Harry to sacrifice his life to maintain her illusory world at Wishwood, Amy is the tempter. When the aunts and uncles stand around at the end of the play after Amy's death, they betray their incapacity to move beyond old patterns of merely doing "the right thing."

The characters in Eliot's second full-length drama resemble those in his first, but their pattern of distribution is different. Eliot's most important innovation in characterization is his employment of the Eumenides, or Furies, to function in the double role of haunting the Harry who tries to evade the truth and leading the Harry who seeks enlightenment. Although the Eumenides at first seem like tempters (as in Aeschylus's *Oresteia* of 458 B.C.E., the Greek model for this play), in the end they appear as "bright angels" leading to the "single eye above the desert" where Harry the pilgrim can at last work out his salvation.

The verse in *The Family Reunion* sometimes suffers from artificiality. The choral passages and the lyric duets are particularly difficult to make believable because both types of verse are spoken in a kind of trance during moments broken off from the action of the play. These passages tell rather than show what is happening. The choral passage spoken by the aunts and uncles at the end of the first act illustrates this point well. This passage has poetic qualities but it is encumbered with a self-conscious tone that breaks with the tone employed by the characters in the rest of the play. As Eliot noted in his 1953 lecture "The Three Voices of Poetry," in such instances the poet is speaking rather than the characters. Ideally, the characters should use what Eliot calls the "third voice," which emanates from the persona or character instead of from the writer.

The Family Reunion uses several images from the Christian liturgy and it is indebted to the Eucharistic worship service for its pattern of action. As the title suggests, the play focuses on the reuniting of a family for a special dinner, an activity symbolically similar to the "love feast" of the liturgy. The gathering to which Amy calls her relatives, however, involves little love and even less feasting; the meals take place off stage in a cold and formal ritual. The only visible sharing of food occurs in the opening scene, when the aunts and uncles stand around and complain about the bad habits of the younger generation, including habits of smoking and drinking in which the uncles themselves indulge freely. This unawareness of their own actions illustrates their unawareness of life, as Harry later points out. Because they have never wakened to life, they cannot draw any meaningful pleasure from it or participate in any feast, least of all the Eucharist. Their lives consist of empty rituals.

The drama revolves around a fundamental tension between the empty rituals promoted by Amy's Wishwood and the purposeful rituals sponsored by those who accept a spiritual order of time surpassing that of Wishwood. This tension between rituals is depicted in several varieties of sacrifice, including fruitless sacrifices that result from loveless or self-centered motives. Harry's wife dies at sea because of the lovelessness, selfishness, and malice of her husband and relations. Amy experiences a tragic end because she is so intent on preserving her illusory Wishwood that she rejects a spiritual life. In contrast, Agatha sacrifices her life for Harry's sake, and Harry sacrifices his life for the benefit of his family. These sacrifices are motivated by love and produce something positive. Although some critics find Harry's quest a cold and selfish one, others point out that his quest is to discover the irreplaceable qualities of love that make of a family more than an association of isolated people joined solely by the accidents of heredity.

"Critical Evaluation" by Daven M. Kari

Further Reading

Ackroyd, Peter. *T. S. Eliot: A Life*. New York: Simon & Schuster, 1984. A useful biography that includes a discussion of *The Family Reunion*, its genesis, mixed critical reception, and importance to Eliot's early career as a playwright. Ackroyd considers the play to be Eliot's most powerful work because of its use of symbolism.

Däumer, Elisabeth. "Vipers, Viragos, and Spiritual Rebels: Women in T. S. Eliot's Christian Society Plays." In *Gender, Desire, and Sexuality in T. S. Eliot*, edited by Cassandra Laity and Nancy K. Gish. New York: Cambridge University Press, 2004. Däumer analyzes Eliot's depiction of women in *The Family Reunion* and several other plays.

Evans, Giles. *Wishwood Revisited: A New Interpretation of T. S. Eliot's "The Family Reunion."* Lewes, England: Book Guild, 1991. A subtle analysis of the play, with references to the work of critics and biographers. The author recognizes that the play develops the Christian sympathies and philosophical concerns of earlier works, and he regards it as Eliot's best drama.

Gordon, Lyndall. *T. S. Eliot: An Imperfect Life*. New York: W. W. Norton, 1999. An authoritative, thoroughly researched biography that concedes Eliot's many personal flaws as well as describes his poetic genius.

Kari, Daven M. *T. S. Eliot's Dramatic Pilgrimage: A Progress in Craft as an Expression of Christian Perspective*. Lewiston, N.Y.: Edwin Mellen Press, 1990. Considers the play to offer an important experiment in religious verse drama. Examines Eliot's use of characterization, verse techniques, and stagecraft.

Moody, A. David, ed. *The Cambridge Companion to T. S. Eliot*. New York: Cambridge University Press, 1994. Collection of essays, including discussions of Eliot's life; Eliot as a philosopher, a social critic, and a product of America; and religion, literature, and society in Eliot's work. Also features the essay "Pereira and After: The Cures of Eliot's Theater" by Robin Grove.

Raine, Craig. *T. S. Eliot*. New York: Oxford University Press, 2006. In this examination of Eliot's work, Raine maintains that "the buried life," or the failure of feeling, is a consistent theme in the poetry and plays. Chapter 5 focuses on Eliot's plays.

Spanos, William V. *The Christian Tradition in Modern British Verse Drama: The Poetics of Sacramental Time*. New Brunswick, N.J.: Rutgers University Press, 1967. One of the most eloquent and insightful treatments of how Christian beliefs have been expressed through modern British verse drama. Excellent discussion of *The Family Reunion* in chapter 6.

The Far Field

Author: Theodore Roethke (1908-1963)
First published: 1964
Type of work: Poetry

"The Far Field" is the fifth poem in "North American Sequence," which contains six long poems in all and opens Theodore Roethke's last book, *The Far Field* (1964). Therefore, although "The Far Field" is a distinct poem, it must be viewed in the larger poetic context to appreciate its significance. The six poems of this sequence are written in free verse. Roethke expands and contracts the lengths of the lines as though on a journey that requires quick turns, frequent pauses, and long and short strides. The central theme of the work—the individual's quest for spiritual fulfillment—is reflected in the poem's rhythms and structures. The lines lengthen to coincide with the poet's desire to flow like water and to move with a flurry of leaves. The natural world the poet explores and whose center he seeks is portrayed in catalogs of images that depict experiences whose "deep center" becomes his ultimate goal. The poet journeys in search of a self that is at one with the natural world.

In "The Longing," the first poem in the sequence, the poet finds himself in a world that paralyzes the soul and reduces the individual to a creature who stares through empty eyes. This world fills the poet's soul with disgust, even despair. He longs to escape it at the same time that aspects of nature offer him a felicity that sets his soul in motion. The first of his revelations comes to him: "The rose exceeds, the rose exceeds us all." His quest commences: He wants to become like the rose, freed from the emptiness in which the spirit is mired. To do so, he must retreat from the stifling miasma of civilization and rediscover the fresh, vigorous joy of childhood and the expansive energy of the natural world, which is symbolized by flowers in bloom.

He does not wish to escape from the world of the senses. Rather, he longs to escape into it, for the senses are the means by which he can be part of the natural world. Nature is both an experience of the senses and a place where the spiritual and the physical intersect. This initial poem ends on the poet's deliberate commitment to go on a journey. He will take on the nature of the Native American, become an explorer: "Old men should be explorers?/ I'll be an Indian./ Iroquois." Ironically, the movement forward begins with an imaginative retreat into the past.

The second poem in the sequence, "Meditation at Oyster River," finds the poet on a rock by a river. The sounds, the sights of undulant waves, dew, salt-soaked wood, fish, snake, bird—he would be with them all. There, flesh and spirit merge, and he discovers a spiritual repose. His experience is that of one just born, yet he has not lost his fear. In sleep he is afraid, and he sees Death's face rise. The river, symbol of the birth of experience and of the onward flow of his exploration, envelops him with the rhythms of the newborn. The rhythms of morning and of a world that is the "cradle of all that is" bring him a peace otherwise unattainable. As night comes on and the moon rises, he discovers the pervasive nature of light, how it illuminates all within and without.

The title of the third poem in the sequence, "Journey to the Interior," tells where the poet is heading both geographically and psychologically. The opening line ironically speaks of that journey as a journey out of oneself. He must leave some aspect of himself behind as he journeys inward.

He remembers racing along a gravel road, stopping at an old bridge, and discovering that the world all around him is filled with debris, death, and decay. The vision blurs into an awareness of a larger journey, that of the spirit that takes him out of time. In the final section of this poem, the soul observes, the world flows, and in the suspended moment, the poet's senses take on a keenness that enables him to know the heart of the sun and to hear a song in the leaves. He joins the birds, and the spirit of wrath is transformed into the spirit of blessing: "And the dead begin from their dark to sing in my sleep." His journey to the interior has brought him a measure of peace, even bliss.

Where he would be, dreams would no longer bring frightful figures out of the past. One can see how far the poet has come if one recalls what the poet said in the poem's opening lines, that sleep brings no balm. Even now, he feels the weight of his sensual self. In "The Long Waters," the fourth poem in the sequence, the poet returns to the sea. All he sees enriches his spirit, and the place, filled with life forms, continues to refine his powers of sensuous understanding. His body "shimmers with a light flame," and he is transported out of time and place, becoming "another thing." He loses himself and finds himself. In his newly found largeness, he can embrace the world. Throughout the journey, the poet's relation to the world expands and contracts. At one moment, he is among the stones and leaves; in another moment, he is a river that circles the world or a spirit that embraces it.

Contraction, expansion, ebb and flow, retreating and advancing, going forward and back, finding light in the darkness, a wakeful dream out of a dreaming sleep—these are the rhythms that the poet's journey brings. These elements all come together in "The Far Field," which begins with the poet dreaming of journeys. These journeys, however, are those of the physical man, the untransformed mortal whose car stalls at the end of a road, its wheels spinning futilely. Mired in this physical universe, the poet has reached the end of his journey. His attention turns to the birds, emblems of nature's capacity to rise above the slag-heaps and the effluvia of the degraded city. Throughout his journey, he has admired and felt a spiritual kinship with the birds. They represent nature's ability to confer flight, and the poet wants to be one of them. He imagines himself returned to earth as a bird. Birds are the voices of the land, incarnations of nature's prolific diversity.

The poet's journey to the edge of the city and of his own spiritual perimeters has brought him a triumph over the darkness and has taught him not to fear what lies beyond—death, eternity. He envisions how natural objects rejuvenate themselves and triumph over time and change: "The river turns on itself,/ The tree retreats into its own shadow." The journey inward and outward is a circle that brings the poet back to where he began, only now his discoveries have taken him out of time. He has gained a new insight, a peace with the natural process. Death no longer frightens him. In fact, he is renewed by it, and though he may not yet have found the "deep center," he has come to realize that all he loves is around him, in the earth and air. He has not retreated into a spiritual world. Rather, he has found a spiritual kinship with the world by letting it engulf him and by experiencing it with all of his senses. He sees confluence throughout the natural world and feels a part of it.

The final poem in the sequence, "The Rose," continues the metaphor of the poet's blending with natural objects and events, going beyond himself. The white and red roses the poet remembers seeing in his father's greenhouse beckoned him out of himself even then. They may have been early intimations of his spiritual mission, for he has become something other. He has come out of the whale and into the world, has journeyed to the edge of the field; he has seen the far field and has learned to accept death, not to fear infinity, and to realize that all he desires is here and now, within and without. He has become like the rose, which "Stays in its true place,/ Flowering out of the dark."

The poet, like the rose, has discovered his true place, among the rocks, the places where nature surrounds him and infuses his spirit. In a grove of madronas and half-dead trees, near the rose, the poet finds a culmination of his journey, and an acceptance:

> I came upon a true ease of myself,
> As if another man appeared out of the depths
>   of my being,
> And I stood outside myself,
> Beyond becoming and perishing,
> A something wholly other,
> As if I swayed out on the wildest wave alive,
> And yet was still.
> And I rejoiced in being what I was.

In that revelation—and elevation—the lost man and the final man discover each other, see that they are separate yet of the same spirit. He realizes the spirit unites what before was viewed as irreconcilable opposites. Finally, the poet sees that the lost, wandering man is not lost if he is in his true place, and the final man is not finite man or the last man. Rather, the final man is the culmination of man, even as "the far field" is the culmination of his earthly journey. Language grounds the poet in what he feels and sees; it blends the abstract with the concrete and in that way symbolizes the poet himself. The final man is the final word.

Bernard E. Morris

Further Reading

Barillas, William David. "Theodore Roethke." In *The Midwestern Pastoral: Place and Landscape in Literature of the American Heartland*. Athens: Ohio University Press, 2006. Analyzes *The Far Field* and some of Roethke's other work, focusing on the work's relationship to his local geography. Examines how the work of Roethke and other midwestern writers reflects a practical and mystical attachment to the land.

Heyen, William, ed. *Profile of Theodore Roethke*. Westerville, Ohio: Charles E. Merrill, 1971. Includes eight major studies of Roethke's work.

Hickman, Trenton. "Theodore Roethke and the Poetics of Place." In *Reading the Middle Generation Anew: Culture, Community, and Form in Twentieth-Century American Poetry*, edited by Eric Haralson. Iowa City: University of Iowa Press, 2006. Roethke is one of the poets whose work is reassessed and whose legacy is reexamined in this study of American poetry published from the 1940's through the 1960's.

Kalaidjian, Walter B. *Understanding Theodore Roethke*. Columbia: University of South Carolina Press, 1987. All the major collections of Roethke's poems are discussed in this book, which begins with an overview and ends with two chapters devoted to *The Far Field*. Includes an excellent bibliography.

Malkoff, Karl. *Theodore Roethke: An Introduction to the Poetry*. New York: Columbia University Press, 1966. Discusses the major themes in Roethke's poetry and the influences of T. S. Eliot, William Butler Yeats, and others, tracing Roethke's poetic development to its conclusion in *The Far Field*.

Sharpe, Peter. *The Ground of Our Beseeching: Metaphor and the Poetics of Meditation*. Selinsgrove, Pa.: Susquehanna University Press, 2004. Analyzes and compares the meditative poetry of T. S. Eliot, Wallace Stevens, and Roethke, with special emphasis on their use of metaphor. Argues that the poets created metaphorical language in order to fulfill their spiritual yearning.

Sullivan, Rosemary. *Theodore Roethke: The Garden Master*. Seattle: University of Washington Press, 1975. Sheds light on the relation of Roethke's personal life to his poetry. The discussion of "North American Sequence" illuminates the symbols and images of that work.

Far from the Madding Crowd

Author: Thomas Hardy (1840-1928)
First published: 1874
Type of work: Novel
Type of plot: Psychological realism
Time of plot: 1869-1873
Locale: Wessex, England

Principal characters:
GABRIEL OAK, a shepherd
BATHSHEBA EVERDENE, the mistress of Weatherbury Farm
SERGEANT TROY, her first husband
WILLIAM BOLDWOOD, her suitor and a farmer and neighbor
FANNY ROBIN, a woman betrayed by Troy

The Story:

Gabriel Oak is a small-scale farmer, but his honesty, integrity, and ability win him the respect of all of his neighbors. When he hears that a young woman named Bathsheba Everdene has moved into the neighborhood, he goes out of his way to see her and falls immediately in love. Gabriel is the kind of man who looks only once to know that he has found the right woman. After seeing her only a few times, he goes to her aunt, for whom Bathsheba works, and asks for the girl's hand in marriage. Although he is refused, he feels that it is the relative, not Bathsheba, who denies him.

A short time later, Gabriel's sheepdog becomes excited and chases his flock of sheep over a cliff, killing them all. Ruined, Gabriel gives up his farm and goes elsewhere to find work. On his way across the country, he passes a burning barn and runs to aid the men fighting the flames. After the fire is put out, the owner of Weatherbury Farm arrives, and it is suggested that Gabriel be hired as shepherd in return for the fine work he did. To his surprise, the owner of the farm is Bathsheba, who recently inherited the place from her uncle. Gabriel becomes her shepherd. He is struck by the change in their positions in such a short while. Now Bathsheba is the landowner, and Gabriel is the servant.

On his way to his new quarters, Gabriel meets a girl standing in the woods. She speaks to him and asks him not to say that he saw her, and he promises to keep silent. The next morning while working at his new job, he hears that Fanny Robin, one of Bathsheba's maids, disappeared, and he rightly guesses that Fanny is the girl he met. It is suspected that she went off to meet a soldier who was stationed in the area a short time before. This suspicion is correct. Fanny went to find Sergeant Troy at his new station, for he promised to marry her if she came to him. A date is set for the wedding, but Fanny goes to the wrong church. When she finally finds Troy, he refuses to make arrangements for a marriage a second time.

Bathsheba is a good manager, and Weatherbury Farm prospers; but she has her caprices. One of these is to send an anonymous valentine to William Boldwood, a conservative, serious man who is her neighbor. Boldwood is upset by the valentine, especially after he learns that Gabriel recognized Bathsheba's handwriting. The more Boldwood sees of Bathsheba, however, the more deeply he falls in love with her. One day during the sheep washing, he asks her to marry him, but she refuses his proposal. Nevertheless, Gabriel and the rest of the workers feel sure that she will eventually marry Boldwood.

About that time, Sergeant Troy returns to the neighborhood. Bathsheba is attracted to him at once. Gabriel knows enough of Troy's character to know that he is not the man for Bathsheba, and he tells her so. Not knowing the story of Fanny, Bathsheba is furious at Gabriel's presumption. She and Troy are married soon afterward, and the former Sergeant becomes the master of Weatherbury Farm. With Troy running the farm, things do not go well. Gabriel is forced to do most of the work of overseeing, and often he is compelled to correct the mistakes Troy makes. Troy gambles and drinks and causes Bathsheba much unhappiness. Gabriel and Bathsheba are alternately friendly and unfriendly. One day Troy and Bathsheba, riding in a horse cart, pass a young woman walking down the road. Troy stops the cart and goes to talk to her. The woman is Fanny, who is feeble and ill. Troy tells her to go on to the next town and wait there for him to come and give her money. As soon as they arrive home, Troy asks Bathsheba for some money. She gives it to him after a quarrel.

Fanny goes on to Casterbridge, but she is so weak and ill when she arrives there that she dies shortly afterward. When news of her death reaches Weatherbury Farm, Bathsheba, unaware that Troy was the girl's lover, sends a cart to bring the body to the farm for burial. When the body arrives, Gabriel sees scrawled on the coffin lid a message that both Fanny and a child are inside. He erases the last words in his fear that the real relationship of Fanny and Troy might reach Bathsheba's ears; but Bathsheba, suspecting that the coffin conceals some secret, opens the casket late that night. At the same moment, Troy enters the room and learns of Fanny's death and of the death of his child. Torn with grief, he tells Bathsheba that she means nothing to him, that Fanny was the only woman he ever loved, and that he married Bathsheba only for her looks and for her money. Bathsheba shuts herself up in an attic room.

Troy has a beautiful tombstone put up over Fanny's grave, which he covers with roses and lilies. During a heavy storm that night, water pours from the church roof through the mouth of a gargoyle, splashes on the grave, and ruins all of his work. Troy disappears from Casterbridge. News comes shortly afterward that he was caught in a dangerous current while swimming in the ocean and drowned. Bathsheba does not believe that Troy is really dead; Boldwood, convinced of Troy's death, does his best to get Bathsheba to promise to marry him if Troy does not reappear within seven years, at the end of which time he will be legally declared dead. At a party Boldwood gives for her one night, Bathsheba yields to his protestations of love and says that after the time passes, she will marry him. As she is leaving the party, Troy enters. He was rescued at sea and wandered slowly back to Casterbridge in the character of a strolling player.

At his entrance, Bathsheba faints and falls to the floor. Everyone is so concerned for her and surprised by Troy's appearance that they do not see Boldwood when he takes down a gun from the wall. Boldwood aims at Troy and shoots him in the chest. Troy dies immediately. Boldwood is tried for the murder, but because his mind has given way, he is committed to an institution. Gabriel, who makes every effort to save Boldwood from hanging, becomes a leader in the neighborhood. As Bathsheba's bailiff, he manages her farm and that of Boldwood as well. Of her three lovers, he is the only one left.

One day, Gabriel goes to Bathsheba and tells her that he is planning to leave her service. Bathsheba listens quietly and agrees with all he says. Later that night, however, she goes to his cottage and there tells him, by gesture more than by word, that he is the only person left to her now and that she needs both his help and his love. The farmers of the district are all delighted when Bathsheba becomes Mrs. Oak, and Gabriel becomes the master of Weatherbury Farm.

Critical Evaluation:

As the title indicates, Thomas Hardy's first major novel has an isolated setting: rural, remote from the world, and mainly centered upon Upper Weatherbury Farm in Wessex. Unlike that in *Under the Greenwood Tree* (1872), however, this secluded environment at times gives way to the town:

the busy corn exchange in Casterbridge, the King's Arms Hotel, the Casterbridge workhouse, the cities of Bath and Budmouth, and the lively Buck's Head Inn on the Casterbridge Road.

Nevertheless, the setting has a timeless quality, accentuated by the round of seasonal activities and the continuity of agricultural life. Major scenes in the novel focus around the sheep shearing, saving of hayricks in the storm, spring sheep washing, and the autumn sheep fair at Greenhill. Nature here, however, is not merely background or a constant factor informing characters' actions and proclivities; it is more powerful, a force vast and indifferent to man's thoughts and actions. This is the nature that in Hardy's later novels evolves into inexorable fate, before which the individual is helpless and in opposing which he or she comes to destruction. The main characters in this novel who survive are those who succeed in adjusting themselves to nature's laws and often hostile dominance: Gabriel Oak and Bathsheba Everdene.

Far from the Madding Crowd exhibits confident power throughout in its fully developed characters, the imperceptible movements in the various conflicts involving Bathsheba and her three lovers, and in the way these conflicts evolve from their varied personalities. The combination of the four personalities furnishes the most explosive potential for melodramatic situation: Bathsheba's capriciousness and attractiveness to men; Oak's stolid, patient, unswerving loyalty and love for her; Boldwood's composite character with its "enormous antagonistic forces" and "wild capabilities"; Sergeant Troy's impulsiveness, his living only for the present moment, dashing but totally irresponsible; and the simple nature of Fanny, unaffected and victimized. Interactions of these intimately associated characters, in an almost closed environment, engender passionate and at times almost unbelievable conflicts.

Further complicating the clashes and intricate relationships among these four are the unforeseen, relentless accidents of nature: the initial loss of Oak's sheep, the heavy storm with water that ruins Troy's flowers on Fanny's grave and that precipitates his disappearance, the loss of Boldwood's hayricks in a second storm. The novel progresses in turns, driven headlong by Bathsheba's careless whim of sending Boldwood an anonymous valentine and again by Troy's determination to possess her in spite of all odds. Even Oak and Fanny, the two who outwardly seem driven by the impulsive actions of others, unconsciously complicate the plot by their very quiet and uncomplaining natures. Fanny, betrayed by Sergeant Troy, goes down before forces she has no means to combat, although she has a macabre revenge in the scene in which Bathsheba opens her coffin to find Troy's child dead with its mother.

Oak, of stronger stuff, endures—like the nature he is so close to and of which he seems an integral part. Although he feels Bathsheba rules his life and the reader may be swept into this illusion, it is the earth and all of its creatures to which he is bound. Only when Bathsheba comes full circle through her marriage to the dissolute, unstable Troy, her half acceptance of Boldwood's position and estate, back to an understanding of the land and its enduring qualities as embodied in Oak, can their marriage be possible. What Gabriel holds to in Bathsheba and what she herself does not recognize is the same elemental belonging to the land and its eternal strength.

The language of the novel is bound to the earth; the best example of this is the rural chorus, which is to figure in Hardy's later novels and which provides much of the humor. The habitués of Warren's Malthouse on the Casterbridge Road are intimately involved in the action and contribute to domestic scenes and rural atmosphere. They not only serve to comment on the various episodes but also reinforce the setting, for they, too, belong to the earth. In fact, they form part of the novel's foundation; it is of importance that Oak is at home with them and shares their social outlook. When the Malthouse crowd appears at the end of the book to serenade the newly married Gabriel and Bathsheba with their "venerable worm-eaten instruments," Gabriel invites them: "Come in, souls, and have something to eat and drink wi' me and my wife."

In this novel, the reader finds the emerging role of nature, the typical romantic, dramatic situations that will even intensify in later novels, and devices such as the village chorus and rural activities to mark the continuity and coherence of human existence. Apparent also are the chance encounters, series of coincidences, unforeseen accidents, overheard conversations, and secretly observed actions—all of which make up the fabric of a typical Hardy narrative. His plots, because of these devices, share an improbability and sense of the miraculous found in folklore. The coffin scene where Bathsheba finds Fanny and Troy's child is the stuff of which ballads are made. The scene in which Troy woos Bathsheba with a sword exercise, in its bold sexual symbolism, also foreshadows such scenes as the fight between Henchard and Farfrae in *The Mayor of Casterbridge* and the entwined couples at the hay-trusser's dance in *Tess of the D'Urbervilles* (1891).

Although not as carefully structured as his later novels, this work shows Hardy's ability to convey the mental life of his characters, especially that of a complicated woman. He boldly draws his theatrical scenes, exploits his evocative ru-

ral settings, and for the first time in his career as a novelist dares give his work amplitude and passion. Not yet, however, does the reader find in this book the intense sense of gloom over a vanishing way of life—a depression that marked much of Hardy's later writing; nor does the story embody humanity's defeat and tragedy that increasingly became Hardy's preoccupation.

"Critical Evaluation" by Muriel B. Ingham

Further Reading

Buckler, William. *The Victorian Imagination: Essays in Aesthetic Exploration.* New York: New York University Press, 1980. Explores the politics and society of Victorian England as they affect the formal elements (plot, character construction, imagery) and the political and social aspects (gender, class, rural/urban relations) of Hardy's work; specifically addresses *Far from the Madding Crowd.*

Bullen, J. B. *The Expressive Eye: Fiction and Perception in the Work of Thomas Hardy.* New York: Oxford University Press, 1987. Distinguishes Hardy from other writers of the period by examining his painterly eye and visual accuracy. Discusses Hardy's descriptions of landscapes.

Daleski, H. M. *Thomas Hardy and Paradoxes of Love.* Columbia: University of Missouri Press, 1997. Daleski reevaluates the treatment of gender in Hardy's novels, defending the author from charges of sexism and maintaining that some of Hardy's female characters are depicted sympathetically. Daleski argues that Hardy is the premodern precursor of sexual failures and catastrophic ends.

Kramer, Dale, ed. *The Cambridge Companion to Thomas Hardy.* New York: Cambridge University Press, 1999. An introduction and general overview of all Hardy's work and specific demonstrations of Hardy's ideas and literary skills. Individual essays explore Hardy's biography, aesthetics, and the impact on his work of developments in science, religion, and philosophy in the late nineteenth century. The volume also contains a detailed chronology of Hardy's life and Penny Boumelha's essay "The Patriarchy of Class: *Under the Greenwood Tree, Far from the Madding Crowd, The Woodlanders.*"

Mallett, Phillip, ed. *The Achievement of Thomas Hardy.* New York: St. Martin's Press, 2000. A collection of essays that analyze some of the novels and other works and discuss Hardy and nature, the architecture of Hardy, and the presence of the poet in his novels, among other topics. Includes bibliography and index.

Millgate, Michael. *Thomas Hardy: A Biography Revisited.* New York: Oxford University Press, 2004. This biography enhances and replaces Millgate's 1982 biography, considered to be one of the best and most scholarly Hardy biographies available. Includes bibliography and index.

Page, Norman, ed. *Oxford Reader's Companion to Hardy.* New York: Oxford University Press, 2000. An encyclopedia containing three hundred alphabetically arranged entries examining Hardy's work and discussing his family and friends, important places in his life and work, his influences, critical approaches to his writings, and a history of his works' publication. Also includes a chronology of his life, lists of places and characters in his fiction, a glossary, and a bibliography.

Shires, Linda M. "Narrative, Gender, and Power in *Far from the Madding Crowd.*" *Novel* 24, no. 2 (Winter, 1991):

162-178. Examines the character of Bathsheba Everdene and her feminine power over Oak, Boldwood, and Troy. A feminist analysis that points out Hardy's portrayal of Bathsheba is unusual, in contrast to other heroines such as Eustacia Vye and Tess Durbeyfield.

Swann, Charles. "*Far from the Madding Crowd*: How Good a Shepherd Is Gabriel Oak?" *Notes and Queries* 39, no. 2 (June, 1992): 189-201. Analyzes Gabriel Oak as a character and as a prototype of a Wessex shepherd; addresses Hardy's interpretation of the rural world.

Tomalin, Claire. *Thomas Hardy.* New York: Penguin, 2007. This thorough and finely written biography by a respected Hardy scholar illuminates the novelist's efforts to indict the malice, neglect, and ignorance of his fellow human beings. Tomalin also discusses aspects of his life that are apparent in his literary works.

Far Tortuga

Author: Peter Matthiessen (1927-   )
First published: 1975
Type of work: Novel
Type of plot: Adventure
Time of plot: 1968
Locale: Cayman Islands, Honduras, Nicaragua, and the Caribbean

Principal characters:
RAIB AVERS, captain of the *Lillias Eden*
JIM EDEN "BUDDY" AVERS, his son
WILL PARCHMENT, the mate of the *Lillias Eden*
VEMON DILBERT EVERS,
BYRUM POWERY WATLER,
WODIE GREAVES, and
JUNIOR "SPEEDY" BODDEN, turtlers
MIGUEL MORENO SMITH, the boat's engineer
ATHENS EBANKS, the boat's cook
ANDREW AVERS, Raib's father, also a turtle-boat captain
DESMOND EDEN, another captain

The Story:

Raib Avers is captain of the *Lillias Eden*, a schooner that travels the West Indian turtle banks between the Cayman Islands and the coast of Central America, primarily Honduras and Nicaragua, capturing green sea turtles. Son of another turtle-boat captain, Andrew Avers, Raib tries to round up a suitable number of turtles with the help of and often despite his sometimes quarrelsome crewmen. Raib needs to catch as many turtles as possible before they move south to lay eggs.

Raib has tried to modernize the *Lillias Eden*, converting it from a wind schooner to an engine-driven vessel, but the ship is a ramshackle mess, replete with defects such as a bent

engine shaft. The captain cannot afford the additional modifications to make his craft truly seaworthy. There are complaints that Raib relies too much on the wind, preferring to zigzag instead of going straight. Some of the crew also object to how inferior their vessel is to competing ships, but generally they have faith in any ship built in the Caymans because of the superiority of the wood there.

The crewmen of the *Lillias Eden* talk about all manner of topics, from the navigating skills of the green turtle to ghosts, often revealing their prejudices, especially when intoxicated. Vemon Dilbert Evers, the most outspoken and colorful of the men, is not alone in denigrating Spanish-speaking countries, claiming that the people of Honduras and Nicaragua do not care about life. The turtlers, as the crewmen are called, are proud to be from the Caymans, where ethnic background is of little concern. They are suspicious of the boat's engineer, Miguel Moreno Smith, who calls himself Brown because he is Spanish and seems unstable. Raib teases the men for spreading rumors that turtler Wodie Greaves is wanted for murder.

The men also suspect the motives of the United States, always referred to as the place of the Yankees, for trying to tell the rest of the world how to behave. They ridicule the Bay of Pigs disaster. Vemon hates communists and wants to bomb Cuba. Raib keeps everything going by making allowances for his crew, realizing that Speedy only pretends to be a fool so that others will not expect too much of him. He is disappointed, however, in his son, Buddy, for lacking spirit.

Raib becomes annoyed at the mention of a rival captain, Desmond Eden, who claims to be Raib's illegitimate half-brother. Byrum also hates Desmond, who was once caught smuggling guns on a Nicaraguan fruit boat; Byrum was fired along with him. The *Lillias Eden* eventually encounters Desmond's ship, the *Davy Jones*, and Raib is angered to discover his elderly father, Andrew, aboard. Because Andrew has had a stroke and cannot speak, Raib takes him aboard the *Lillias Eden*, assigning Buddy to look after his grandfather. The men accuse Desmond of taking every last cent from naïve immigrants for smuggling them to Florida and Texas and of killing a man in Honduras.

Desmond's appearance is seen as a bad omen and is soon followed by signs of a potential hurricane. The increasing winds make the crewmen nervous. Raib calls the howling wind the sound of hell. The turtlers then start to consider Wodie a Jonah. Will Parchment recalls swearing he would never go turtling again after surviving a hurricane. Despite the looming dangers, Buddy realizes he wants to be a turtler.

The inadequacies of the *Lillias Eden* become more obvious when its crew encounters the more modern *Alice H. Adams*, which is carrying 450 turtles compared to the seventeen on Raib's ship. Andrew Avers is found dead, and his body is being gnawed by a rat. Another ominous sign leads to several of the crew abandoning the ship. Before leaving, Athens Ebanks, the cook, complains that only three men do any work, as dissension and drinking increase. Raib resents the departure of Vemon, whom he has known for forty years. Brown leaves after threatening Raib with a knife. Adding to uncertainties about the future are rumors that Nicaragua will close off its turtle banks to vessels from the Caymans.

In the ensuing storm, the *Lillias Eden* strikes a reef and begins sinking. Raib, Buddy, and Will are killed. Byrum and Woodie soon die, leaving Speedy the only survivor.

Critical Evaluation:

In *Far Tortuga*, Peter Matthiessen contrasts the naturalness of the sea, where the wind and waves can be saviors or enemies, with intrusions into the natural order. As the crew of the *Lillias Eden* points out derisively, American tourists in their boats befoul the Caribbean just as the United States as a country pollutes the sea with debris from atomic-bomb testing. To the crew, the rules of the sea must be respected, and violators run the risk of nature's displeasure. The turtlers find comfort in routine, and they dislike changes in the ways they have performed their jobs. Making adjustments for the volatility of nature is just another routine.

Environmental concerns are central to most of Matthiessen's fiction and nonfiction, and *Far Tortuga* can be seen as an environmental parable. The crew of the *Lillias Eden* frequently express their admiration, even love, for the green turtle. The turtlers abide in nature, but it is hardly benign, with storms coming out of nowhere to make their tasks more difficult and even threaten their lives.

After the deaths of his shipmates, Speedy releases a turtle he had planned to eat, a respectful gesture seemingly offered to redress an imbalance in nature.

The island from which *Far Tortuga* takes its name is presented as the ultimate goal to be reached by the *Lillias Eden*. The island is an unspoiled paradise comparable to Eden, and it offers the best possible turtling grounds. Arriving there is an achievement in itself. The island of Far Tortuga slowly takes on mythic proportions over the course of the novel, and it appears that the turtlers will go there instead of to heaven when they die—in a sense, they do. After the ship hits the reef and sinks, Far Tortuga can be glimpsed shimmering in the sunrise.

Matthiessen looks at the consequences of physical and emotional isolation. The nature of the Caribbean as a collection of small islands spread out over 2,500 miles isolates the crewmembers. Within this context the Caymans are especially small. The novel, which grew out of "To the Miskito Bank," a 1967 article Matthiessen wrote for *The New Yorker* about a trip on a turtle boat, is both an exploration of the mundane and a look at how even the humblest interactions between people and nature have mythological aspects. Raib and his men are testing themselves against each other, against the sea, and against their very natures. Matthiessen's characters are far from naïve innocents and seem unreflective only on the surface. Within each person is a tempest of contradictory emotions. They are in conflict as much with themselves as with nature.

The biggest enemy for the crew is change, which threatens their way of life. Raib repeatedly reminds the men that the times are changing and only hard work can help them survive. Speedy asserts that modern times are frightening because it lacks a place to hide. A sense of foreboding permeates *Far Tortuga*, as Matthiessen presents the gravestone of Will Parchment early in the novel. Raib tells Speedy that he is just going through the motions—life has passed him by.

The characters also seem to drift through life. Vemon says the world is full of such people as Brown, with no permanent name or home, merely existing. Their fortunes are always shifting up or down, mostly the latter, as with Vemon, who once owned six miles of beach. The crew's sad state is exemplified by the ship's radio, which receives messages but cannot send them. One crewman wishes he could speak better so that he could express the complex emotions he is feeling. Communication is frequently tentative or impossible.

Raib is the closest Matthiessen comes to creating a central character. All the actions of the others are eventually filtered through him, as he struggles to maintain control of his crew and ship. Without articulating it, Raib seems to realize that all aboard the *Lillias Eden* are carrying on an antiquated livelihood threatened by changing times, a major enemy of rugged individuality.

Storytelling, too, is a central theme of *Far Tortuga*, as Matthiessen alternates a narrative of daily life on the *Lillias Eden* with the yarns the men spin. The tellers of these tales strive to elevate their own status to reflect their past lives and fortunes; and they tell their stories to keep alive the recent glorious past, when turtling was a better way of life. Raib enjoys recounting the adventures of Captain Steadman because he was a rare turtler who could do anything. The stories combat boredom and mitigate the chaos that can, and does, arrive at any moment.

The most notable aspect of *Far Tortuga* is its style. The novel is written in simple, unembellished prose with little figurative language. Likewise, the characters are grittily realistic, painted in a few broad strokes. More dramatically, Matthiessen presents his narrative almost as a poem. There are no quotation marks for the dialogue, and it is sometimes difficult to determine who is speaking. The dialogue constitutes most of the text; the remainder comprises short descriptive passages. The text is broken into brief paragraphs, some with only a single word, and even includes stage directions, as in a play or screenplay. Chapter breaks are indicated by primitively drawn circles, indicating the stages of the sun and moon. Other images appear as well, such as an annotated drawing of the *Lillias Eden*. The overall effective is impressionistic, creating an almost stream-of-consciousness narrative. This technique leads *Far Tortuga* to be slowly erased, and to recede into the past.

Michael Adams

Further Reading

Bender, Bert. "*Far Tortuga* and American Sea Fiction Since *Moby-Dick*." *American Literature* 56, no. 2 (May, 1984): 227-248. Analyzes Raib Avers as an Everyman sea captain.

Cooley, John R. "Matthiessen's Voyages on the River Styx: Deathly Waters, Endangered Peoples." In *Earthly Words: Essays on Contemporary American Nature and Environmental Writers*, edited by John R. Cooley. Ann Arbor: University of Michigan Press, 1994. Examines how Matthiessen's characters are caught between environmental and societal change. Part of a larger study of nature and environmental writers and writing.

_____. "Waves of Change: Peter Matthiessen's Caribbean." *Environmental Review* 11, no. 3 (Autumn, 1987): 223-230. A study of the ways in which *Far Tortuga* reflects Caribbean cultural issues of the 1960's.

Dowie, William. *Peter Matthiessen*. Boston: Twayne, 1991. Provides a good introduction to Matthiessen for the beginning student of his fiction. Includes bibliographical references and an index.

Grove, James P. "Pastoralism and Anti-Pastoralism in Peter Matthiessen's *Far Tortuga*." *Critique* 21, no. 2 (1979): 15-29. A look at how Matthiessen's impressionistic style in *Far Tortuga* helps convey his themes.

Patteson, Richard F. "Holistic Vision and Fictional Form in Peter Matthiessen's *Far Tortuga*." *Rocky Mountain Review of Language and Literature* 37, nos. 1/2 (1983): 70-81. Discusses the influence of Zen Buddhism on Matthiessen's environmental themes as they manifest in *Far Tortuga*.

Raglon, Rebecca. "Fact and Fiction: The Development of Ecological Form in Peter Matthiessen's *Far Tortuga*." Critique 35, no. 4 (1994): 245-259. Looks at Matthiessen's work, *Far Tortuga* especially, as a criticism of the dualistic view of nature and humanity. Argues that Matthiessen sees no separation between nature and humanity and writes instead of their necessary interrelatedness.

Roberson, William. *Peter Matthiessen: An Annotated Bibliography*. Jefferson, N.C.: McFarland, 2001. This useful guide to resources on Matthiessen's work provides listings of primary and secondary source literature.

Tredinnick, Mark. "The Long Coastline: Peter Matthiessen." In *The Land's Wild Music: Encounters with Barry Lopez,*

Peter Matthiessen, Terry Tempest Williams, and James Galvin. San Antonio, Tex.: Trinity University Press, 2005. Presents a profile of Matthiessen and reflections on his writings, interwoven with an extended interview conducted as Matthiessen guides Tredinnick through his home landscape.

Yamashiro, Shin. "Seascapes as a Critical Framework in American Sea Literature." *Tamkang Review* 37, no. 1 (Autumn, 2006): 99-120. Compares the sea storm in *Far Tortuga* to that presented in *Two Years Before the Mast* by Richard Henry Dana, Jr.

A Farewell to Arms

Author: Ernest Hemingway (1899-1961)
First published: 1929
Type of work: Novel
Type of plot: Impressionistic realism
Time of plot: World War I
Locale: Northern Italy and Switzerland

Principal characters:
FREDERIC HENRY, an American serving with an Italian ambulance unit
CATHERINE BARKLEY, an English nurse

The Story:

Lieutenant Frederic Henry is a young American attached to an Italian ambulance unit on the Italian front. An offensive is soon to begin, and when Henry returns to the front from leave, he learns from his friend, Lieutenant Rinaldi, that a group of British nurses arrived in his absence to set up a British hospital unit. Rinaldi introduces him to Nurse Catherine Barkley. Between ambulance trips to evacuation posts at the front, Henry calls on Miss Barkley. He likes the frank young English girl in a casual sort of way, but he is not in love with her. Before he leaves for the front to stand by for an attack, she gives him a St. Anthony medal.

At the front, as Henry and some Italian ambulance drivers are eating in a dugout, an Austrian projectile explodes over them. Henry, badly wounded in the legs, is taken to a field hospital. Later, he is moved to a hospital in Milan. Before the doctor is able to see Henry in Milan, the nurse prohibits his drinking wine, but he bribes a porter to bring him a supply that he keeps hidden behind his bed. Catherine comes to the hospital, and Henry knows that he is in love with her. The doctors tell Henry that he will have to lie in bed six months before they can operate on his knee. Henry insists on seeing another doctor, who says that the operation can be performed the next day. Meanwhile, Catherine manages to be with Henry constantly.

After his operation, Henry convalesces in Milan with Catherine as his attendant. Together they dine in out-of-the-way restaurants, and together they ride about the countryside in a carriage. Henry is restless and lonely at nights and

Catherine often comes to his hospital room. Summer passes into autumn. Henry's wound heals, and he is due to take convalescent leave in October. He and Catherine plan to spend the leave together, but he comes down with jaundice before he can leave the hospital. The head nurse accuses him of bringing on the jaundice by drink, in order to avoid being sent back to the front. Before he leaves for the front, Henry and Catherine stay together in a hotel room; already she has disclosed to him that she is pregnant. Henry returns to the front with orders to load his three ambulances with hospital equipment and go south into the Po valley. Morale is at a low ebb. Rinaldi admires the job that has been done on the knee and observes that Henry acts like a married man. War weariness is all-pervasive. At the front, the Italians, learning that German divisions have reinforced the Austrians, begin their terrible retreat from Caporetto. Henry drives one of the ambulances loaded with hospital supplies. During the retreat south, the ambulance is held up several times by wagons, guns, and trucks, which extend in stalled lines for miles. Henry picks up two straggling Italian sergeants. During the night, the retreat is halted in the rain for hours.

At daybreak, Henry cuts out of the long line and drives across country in an attempt to reach Udine by side roads. The ambulance gets stuck in a muddy side road. The sergeants decide to leave, but Henry asks them to help dislodge the car from the mud. They refuse and run. Henry shoots and wounds one; the other escapes across the fields. An Italian ambulance corpsman with Henry shoots the wounded sergeant through the back of the head. Henry and his three comrades strike out on foot for Udine. On a bridge, Henry sees a German staff car with German bicycle troops crossing another bridge over the same stream. Within sight of Udine, one of Henry's group is killed by an Italian sniper. The others hide in a barn until it seems safe to circle around Udine and join the mainstream of the retreat toward the Tagliamento River.

By that time, the Italian army is nothing but a frantic mob. Soldiers are throwing down their arms and officers are cutting insignia of rank from their sleeves. At the end of a long wooden bridge across the Tagliamento, military carabiniere are seizing all officers, giving them drumhead trials and executing them by the riverbank. Henry is detained, but in the dark of night he breaks free, plunges into the river, and escapes on a log. He crosses the Venetian plain on foot, then jumps aboard a freight train and rides to Milan, where he goes to the hospital in which he was a patient. There he learns that the English nurses went to Stresa.

During the retreat from Caporetto, Henry made his farewell to arms. He borrows civilian clothes from an American friend in Milan and goes by train to Stresa, where he meets Catherine, who is on leave. The bartender of the hotel in which Henry is staying warns Henry that authorities plan to arrest him for desertion the next morning; he offers his boat by means of which Henry and Catherine can escape to Switzerland. Henry rows all night. By morning, his hands are so raw that he can barely stand to touch the oars. Over his protests, Catherine takes a turn at the rowing. They reach Switzerland safely and are arrested. Henry tells the police that he is a sportsman who enjoys rowing and that he comes to Switzerland for the winter sports. The valid passports and the ample funds that Henry and Catherine possess save them from serious trouble with the authorities.

During the rest of the fall and winter, the couple stay at an inn outside Montreux. They discuss marriage, but Catherine will not be married while she is pregnant. They hike, read, and talk about what they will do together after the war. When the time for Catherine's confinement approaches, she and Henry go to Lausanne to be near a hospital. They plan to return to Montreux in the spring. At the hospital, Catherine's pains cause the doctor to use an anesthetic on her. After hours of suffering, she delivers a dead baby. The nurse sends Henry out to get something to eat. When he gets back to the hospital, he learns that Catherine had a hemorrhage. He goes into the room and stays with her until she dies. There is nothing he can do, no one he can talk to, no place he can go. Catherine is dead. He leaves the hospital and walks back to his hotel in the dark. It is raining.

Critical Evaluation:

Ernest Hemingway once referred to *A Farewell to Arms* as his version of William Shakespeare's *Romeo and Juliet* (pr. c. 1595-1596, pb. 1597). Several parallels exist. Both works are about star-crossed lovers; both show erotic flirtations that rapidly develop into serious, intense love affairs; and both describe the romances against a backdrop of social and political turmoil. Whether *A Farewell to Arms* finally qualifies as tragic is a matter of personal opinion, but it certainly represents, for Hemingway, an attempt to broaden his concerns from the aimless tragicomic problems of the expatriates in *The Sun Also Rises* (1926) to the fundamental question of life's meaning in the face of human mortality.

Frederic Henry begins the affair as a routine wartime seduction, "a game, like bridge, in which you said things instead of playing cards." He feels mildly guilty, especially after learning about Catherine's vulnerability because of the loss of her lover in combat, but he still foresees no complications from the temporary arrangement. It is not until he is wounded and sent to her hospital in Milan that their affair deepens into love—and from that point on, they struggle to free themselves in order to realize it. However, they are constantly thwarted, first by the impersonal bureaucracy of the military effort, then by the physical separation imposed by the war itself, and, finally, by the biological "accident" that kills Catherine at the point where their "separate peace" at last seems possible.

As Henry's love for Catherine grows, his disillusionment with the war also increases. From the beginning of the book, Henry views the military efforts with ironic detachment, but there is no suggestion that, prior to his meeting with her, he has had any deep reservations about his involvement. Hemingway's attitude toward war was always an ambiguous one. He questioned the rationales for fighting them and the slogans offered in their defense. Like Henry, he felt that "abstract words such as glory, honor, courage, or hallow were obscene." For the individual, however, war could be the necessary test. Facing imminent death in combat, one either demonstrated "grace under pressure" and did the "one right thing" or one did not; one either emerged from the experience as a whole person with self-knowledge and control, or one came out of it lost and broken.

There is little heroism in this war as Henry describes it. The hero's disengagement from the fighting is made most vivid in the extended "retreat from Caporetto," generally considered one of the great sequences in modern fiction. The retreat begins in an orderly, disciplined, military manner. As it progresses, however, authority breaks down, emotions of self-preservation supersede loyalties, and the neat military procession gradually turns into a panicking mob. Henry is caught up in the momentum and carried along with the group in spite of his attempts to keep personal control and fidelity to the small band of survivors he travels with. Upon reaching the Tagliamento River, Henry is seized, along with all other identifiable officers, and held for execution. After he escapes by leaping into the river—an act of ritual purification as well as physical survival—he feels that his trial has freed him from any and all further loyalty to the Allied cause.

Henry then rejoins Catherine, and they complete the escape together. In Switzerland, they seem lucky and free at last. Up in the mountains, they hike, ski, make love, prepare for the baby, and plan for their postwar life together. Even in their most idyllic times, however, there are ominous hints; they worry about the baby; Catherine jokes about her narrow hips; she becomes frightened by a dream of herself "dead in the rain." Throughout the novel, Hemingway associates the plains and rain with death, disease, and sorrow; the mountains and the snow with life, health, and happiness. Catherine and Henry are safe and happy in the mountains, but it is impossible to remain there indefinitely. Eventually everyone must return to the plains. When Catherine and Henry descend to the city, it is, in fact, raining, and she does, in fact, die.

Like that of Romeo and Juliet, the love between Catherine and Henry is not destroyed by any moral defect in their own characters. Henry muses that Catherine's fate is the price paid for the good nights in Milan, but such a price is absurdly excessive. Nor, strictly speaking, is the war responsible for their fate, any more than the Montague-Capulet feud directly provokes the deaths of Shakespeare's lovers. Nevertheless, the war and the feud provide the backdrop of violence and the accumulation of pressures that coerce the lovers into actions that contribute to their doom. In the final analysis, both couples are defeated by bad luck—the illness that prevents the friar from delivering Juliet's note to Romeo, the accident of Catherine's anatomy that prevents normal childbearing. Thus, both couples are star-crossed. If a "purpose" can be vaguely ascertained in Shakespeare's version—the feud is ended by the tragedy—there is no metaphysical justification for Catherine's death; it is, in her own words, "a dirty trick," and nothing more.

Hemingway does not insist that the old religious meanings are completely invalid but only that they do not work for his characters. Henry would like to visit with the priest in his mountain village, but he cannot bring himself to do it. His friend Rinaldi, a combat surgeon, proclaims atheism, hedonism, and work as the only available meanings. Count Greffi, an old billiard player Henry meets in Switzerland, offers

good taste, cynicism, and the fact of a long, pleasant life. Catherine and Henry have each other: "You are my religion," she tells him.

All of these things fail in the end. Religion is only for others, patriotism is a sham, hedonism becomes boring, culture is a temporary distraction, work finally fails (the operation on Catherine was "successful"), and even love cannot last. Catherine dies; they both know, although they will not admit it, that the memory of it will fade.

All that remains is a stoic acceptance of the above facts with dignity and without bitterness. Life, like war, is absurd. Henry survives because he is lucky; Catherine dies because she is unlucky. There is no guarantee that the luck ever balances out and, since everyone ultimately dies, it probably does not matter. What does matter is the courage, dignity, and style with which one accepts these facts as a basis for life, and, more important, in the face of death.

"Critical Evaluation" by Keith Neilson

Further Reading

Berman, Ronald. *Fitzgerald, Hemingway, and the Twenties*. Tuscaloosa: University of Alabama Press, 2001. Berman examines the novels and short stories that Hemingway and F. Scott Fitzgerald wrote during the 1920's within the context of the decade's intellectual history, philosophy, and popular culture. Includes analysis of *A Farewell to Arms*.

Beversluis, John. "Dispelling the Romantic Myth: A Study of *A Farewell to Arms*." *Hemingway Review* 9, no. 1 (Fall, 1989): 18-25. Part of a special issue on *A Farewell to Arms*. Rejecting the common romantic interpretation, Beversluis asserts that this novel explores the problem of self-knowledge. His reading of the character of Catherine is especially interesting.

Bloom, Harold, ed. *Ernest Hemingway's "A Farewell to Arms."* New York: Chelsea House, 1987. Offers a representative selection of some of the best scholarship available on the novel. Includes Bloom's introduction, chronology, bibliography, and index.

Donaldson, Scott, ed. *New Essays on "A Farewell to Arms."* New York: Cambridge University Press, 1990. Appropriate for specialists and nonspecialists. The introduction discusses the novel's composition, publication, and reception, as well as its major critical readings from publication to 1990.

Fantina, Richard. *Ernest Hemingway: Machismo and Masochism*. New York: Palgrave Macmillan, 2005. Focuses on Hemingway's heroes. Fantina argues that Hemingway's male protagonists are "profoundly submissive" and display a "masochistic posture toward women." References to *A Farewell to Arms* are listed in the index.

Gajdusek, Robert E. *Hemingway in His Own Country*. Notre Dame, Ind.: University of Notre Dame Press, 2002. A collection of essays that interpret Hemingway's works from a wide variety of perspectives. Some of the essays compare the work of Hemingway with that of James Joyce and F. Scott Fizgerald, discuss Hemingway's representation of women and androgynous elements in his fiction, and analyze *A Farewell to Arms*.

Lewis, Robert W. *"A Farewell to Arms": The War of the Words*. Boston: Twayne, 1992. Comprehensive resource. Concludes that the novel is about language—particularly the language by which truth and falsehood are revealed.

Trogdon, Robert W., ed. *Ernest Hemingway: A Literary Reference*. New York: Carroll & Graf, 2002. A compendium of information about Hemingway, including photographs, letters, interviews, essays, speeches, book reviews, copies of some of his manuscripts-in-process, and his comments about his own work and the work of other writers.

Wagner-Martin, Linda. *Ernest Hemingway: A Literary Life*. New York: Palgrave Macmillan, 2007. Examines Hemingway's life, especially his troubled relationship with his parents. Wagner-Martin makes insightful connections between his personal life, his emotions, and his writing.

_____. *Ernest Hemingway's "A Farewell to Arms": A Reference Guide*. Westport, Conn.: Greenwood Press, 2003. Describes the novel's genesis, plot, background, themes, style, and critical reception.

Farewell to Manzanar
A True Story of Japanese American Experience During and After the World War II Internment

Authors: Jeanne Wakatsuki Houston (1934-   ) and James D. Houston (1933-2009)
First published: 1973
Type of work: Memoir
Type of plot: Historical
Time of plot: 1941-early 1970's
Locale: Owens Valley and Los Angeles, California

Principal personages:
JEANNE WAKATSUKI, the narrator
KO WAKATSUKI, her father
RIKU WAKATSUKI, her mother
WOODY WAKATSUKI, her older brother

The Story:

Seven-year-old Jeanne Wakatsuki stands with her mother, Riku Wakatsuki, and sisters-in-law on a wharf in Long Beach, California, waving good-bye to her father as his fishing boat sails out with the sardine fleet. At the farthest point in sight, the boats turn around and sail back to the harbor. Jeanne's life is about to change irretrievably. The fishermen bring news that Pearl Harbor in Hawaii has been bombed by the Japanese.

That night, Ko Wakatsuki burns his heirloom Japanese flag and the documents he had brought to the United States when he moved from Japan thirty-five years ago. Two weeks later, two federal agents take him away. The family moves several times in subsequent weeks. In April, 1942, they are ordered to report to a Buddhist temple as a pickup point for what they have been told is resettlement. The bus ride that takes them into the California desert takes all day. Jeanne has never been out of the Los Angeles area before, and she finds the trip a grand adventure. Her older brothers and sisters are relieved to be away from the hostility directed at them by whites.

The family arrives at a camp of black barracks, hastily constructed in a desert wasteland north of Los Angeles, in the Owens Valley along the eastern Sierra Nevada. Sand is everywhere in and around the camp, Manzanar. Unlike many other Japanese American "evacuees," the Wakatsukis have at least managed to stay together as a family. They are assigned two units in Block 16—two 16 by 20 foot spaces to hold twelve people. They immediately partition the rooms with blankets, giving the two young couples some privacy, and try to sleep despite the howling wind that drives sand through every crack. In the morning, Woody, in his father's absence the de facto family head, puts his brothers to work nailing can lids over holes in the floor and turning waste paper into impromptu weather stripping.

As the youngest child, Jeanne is protected by her older siblings, who care for her as best they can. Jeanne gets to sleep next to her mother. No one can protect her, though, from diarrhea caused by spoiled food, from latrines that do not work, and from many other indignities of forced group life under semiprimitive conditions.

Children, however, are resilient. Despite the initial lack of basic services, such as a school, Jeanne explores the camp, discovering interesting things to do. During her time at Manzanar, she frequents the Maryknoll sisters' chapel, listening to their stories of saints and martyrs. She joins the recreation program that takes children outside the barbed wire fences for cookouts and hikes. She even samples a lesson from an old geisha in the traditional *odori* dance, but the performance seems so weird that Jeanne never returns. Her favorite activity is the baton-twirling lessons, which she loves.

As time goes on, life at Manzanar improves in some ways. A hospital and schools open. The worst construction defects are remedied, and barracks become a bit more comfortable and homelike. Jeanne's father, Ko, returns to his family after nine months spent at Fort Lincoln. The experience has changed and aged him drastically—not so much from physical privation as from the stigma of disloyalty and loss of dignity that it represents. For months after Ko's arrival he huddles in the family's unit, making homemade wine in an improvised still and having outbursts of explosive anger.

Halfway through World War II, some restrictions keeping Japanese Americans in the camps are lifted. Nisei (second-generation Japanese Americans who are U.S. citizens by birth) are allowed to leave and move elsewhere, if they have a job lined up. Nisei men are also declared eligible for the military draft. Jeanne's brother Woody argues with his father over the draft, but when the time comes, the whole family proudly sees Woody off with his unit.

When the camp closes and Jeanne moves back to Los Angeles with her parents, she wants most of all to be a normal American girl. Things do not quite work out this way, however. She cannot join some groups, like the Girl Scouts, because of her Japanese ancestry. She does have some ego-boosting achievements, though: being a drum majorette for a Boy Scout band, and, in her senior year, being elected by her classmates as carnival queen. Still, she always feels branded by being different, and the shame of the internment years is hidden so deep that she can hardly speak of them.

Many years later, Jeanne begins to recall her Manzanar experiences and starts writing about them. A visit to the site stirs many memories, but it also gives her the ability to deal with them. Now the place that had shaped her life is being reshaped into desert by the inexorable forces of nature.

Critical Evaluation:

Farewell to Manzanar is notably unpretentious and even-tempered in tone, at the same time that it portrays one of the more shameful episodes of twentieth century American history. The memoir, written by Jeanne Wakatsuki Houston and James D. Houston, who were married, is both a factual account of life under the restrictions of a World War II relocation camp and the story of a young woman's quest for her real identity. The latter effort is made more complicated by her Japanese heritage and by other people's distrust of that heritage. The memoir remains a popular text for secondary school students.

The story is told mostly in chronological order, in the narrator's first-person voice. The exceptions are three chapters interspersed with the rest of the text, relating events that occurred to other family members: One, "Fort Lincoln: An Interview," is a dialogue of Ko's interrogation by a young military officer who is trying to classify the older man as a security risk. Two, "The Reservoir Shack," tells of an encounter between a guard unit made up of detainees—led by Jeanne's brother-in-law, Kaz—and an excitable group of military police officers. Fortunately, no one comes to blows in the standoff. The third, "Ka-ke, Near Hiroshima, April 1946," describes Woody's meeting with his great-aunt, a meeting that gives him new insights into Japanese culture and his father's past. These episodes deepen and enrich the main narrative.

Although *Farewell to Manzanar* is primarily Jeanne's story, in some ways it is Ko's story, too. The author says that while Manzanar is where her life began, her father's life, in effect, had ended there. Actually, Ko lived for quite a few years after Manzanar, but the internment destroyed his self-esteem and his zest for life. Ko is a bigger-than-life person, full of swagger and enthusiasm and with unusual skills and strong opinions. He also has a strong entrepreneurial spirit. In the book, he becomes an unforgettable character.

The themes of injustice, prejudice, and fear of the "other" subtly underlie the whole experience, although the authors never editorialize on these subjects. The poor living conditions at Manzanar become obvious, and are a logical outcome of hasty, ill-considered measures enacted in the first panic after the air attack on Pearl Harbor. The theme of intergenerational tension is made more poignant by camp features that weaken family life, like the lack of individual kitchens. Above all, the internees' courage in returning to re-build their lives, without help and after losing property, jobs, and dignity, is a testimony to their strength of spirit. Altogether, the book brought back to life and illuminated an important slice of American history that most had forgotten and even deliberately ignored. The memoir played a vital role in prodding the American conscience about this "lapse" in American ideals.

Farewell to Manzanar is Jeanne Wakatsuki Houston's first published book, written with her husband, James D. Houston, who already had several novels in print. The Houstons also collaborated on a television-film script of the book. Jeanne Houston wrote several other books and essays about the internment experience.

Emily Alward

Further Reading

Bryant, Dorothy. "The School Yearbook with the Barbed-Wire Design." *Nation* 219, no. 15 (November 9, 1974): 469. A brief but incisive article about *Farewell to Man-zanar* and the difficulties of teaching about the Japanese American internment experience of World War II.

Houston, James D. *In the Ring of Fire: A Pacific Basin Journey.* San Francisco: Mercury House, 1997. Account of a journey of discovery by the Houstons to the island nations of the Pacific Rim, seeking the cultural ties they share.

Houston, Jeanne Wakatsuki. *The Legend of Fire Horse Woman.* New York: Kensington, 2003. Houston's novel that draws on the camp experience to show three generations of women discovering their strengths while interned.

McGovern, Edythe M. "Jeanne Wakatsuki Houston." *Cyclopedia of World Authors.* 4th rev. ed. Pasadena, Calif.: Salem Press, 2004. A biographical essay on Houston that briefly covers *Farewell to Manzanar.* Good for background on Houston.

Tateishi, John, comp. *And Justice for All: An Oral History of the Japanese American Detention Camps.* Seattle: University of Washington Press, 1999. Thirty former camp residents speak about the internment experience and its effect on their lives.

The Farming of Bones

Author: Edwidge Danticat (1969-   )
First published: 1998
Type of work: Novel
Type of plot: Historical fiction
Time of plot: 1937 to c. 1957
Locale: Dominican Republic and Haiti

Principal characters:
AMABELLE DÉSIR, the narrator, a Haitian migrant and domestic worker in the Dominican Republic
SEBASTIEN ONIUS, Amabelle's lover, a cane worker
MIMI, Sebastien's sister, a domestic servant for Doña Eva
YVES, a cane worker
JOËL RAYMOND LORIER, a cane worker
KONGO, Joël's father, a cane worker
SEÑORA VALENCIA, Amabelle's Spanish Dominican mistress, whom she has served all her life
DON IGNACIO (PAPI), Señora Valencia's father, an immigrant to the Dominican Republic from Spain
SEÑOR PICO DUARTE, Señora Valencia's husband, a military officer
DOCTOR JAVIER, son of Doña Eva, another Spanish immigrant to the Dominican Republic
FATHER ROMAIN, a Haitian priest
MAN RAPADOU, Yves's mother
GENERALISSIMO RAFAEL LEONIDAS TRUJILLO MOLINA, dictator of the Dominican Republic

The Story:

The Massacre River runs along the border between Haiti and the Dominican Republic; it is named for a conflict that took place between France and Spain when they were the colonial powers on Hispaniola. Amabelle is an orphan whose parents accidentally drowned in the river when she was very young. She was found by Señora Valencia of Alegría and her father, Don Ignacio (Papi). She has grown up with the Valencias, working as their servant. Amabelle's lover Sebastien, a Haitian cane worker, came to Alegría, Dominican Republic, with his sister Mimi after their father died in a hurricane.

Amabelle acts as a midwife for Señora Valencia in the birth of her first children. They are fraternal twins: a boy and girl. Rosalinda Teresa is born with a caul over her face and is darker than her brother, Rafael (Rafi), who is very fair. Señora Valencia notes this difference, hoping that her daughter will not be mistaken for one of Amabelle's people. The Valencias' doctor, the Dominican Doctor Javier, runs a clinic at the Haitian border. He later offers Amabelle a position there.

One day, Señor Pico Duarte, Señora Valencia's husband, is going home to see his children. He drives too fast and hits one of three cane workers walking in the road. The man hit, Joël Lorier, is the son of Kongo, the most senior cane worker in the Haitian community. Joël lands in a ravine and dies. Papi desires to meet with Kongo and pay for Joël's funeral. Amabelle gives Sebastien cedar planks from Papi's store of wood to give to Kongo for a coffin, but Kongo carries Joël off and buries him in the earth. Three days later, Rafi dies suddenly, an event that some consider a return for Joël's death.

Rumors circulate that Generalissimo Rafael Trujillo, the Dominican dictator for whom Rafi was named, is speaking against Haitians and desiring to force Haitians to leave the Dominican Republic or even to kill them. Amabelle and others agree that Haitians in the Dominican Republic are not respected as fellow people, even those whose families have lived there for generations, but they dismiss these rumors.

Sebastien and Amabelle make plans to marry. Hearing that General Trujillo has ordered Haitians to be removed from the country, Amabelle, Sebastien, and Mimi become convinced of the urgency of leaving. They plan to meet at a church where Doctor Javier has told Amabelle that he and Father Romain will drive a group across the border. They arrive late, and Amabelle hears that all those who were there on time were taken to a border prison.

Amabelle and Yves travel to the border, encountering many dead and injured along the way. In Dajabón, the prison border town, Yves, Amabelle, and others fail a test designed to separate Dominicans from Haitians: Unable to pronounce the Spanish word for parsley, *perejil*, they are made to eat handful after handful of parsley and severely beaten or killed. Amabelle, Yves, and another couple, Wilner and Odette, cross the river back to Haiti, but Wilner is shot and Amabelle accidentally drowns Odette while trying to silence her.

After slowly recovering at a border clinic, and receiving no word of Sebastien or Mimi, Yves and Amabelle go to Cap Haïtien, where Yves's mother, Man Rapadou, houses them. Amabelle keeps trying to find word of Sebastien and Mimi. She and others who have survived the massacre try to find ways to tell their stories and to have them recorded. They hear that General Trujillo is giving compensation to those who record their story with the justice of the peace, but soon the money is gone and no more stories will be recorded.

In the meantime, Yves begins planting his father's land. Amabelle continues to live with Yves and his mother, sewing for anyone for whatever they will pay or trade. Time passes, and Amabelle and Yves grow older. Neither finds a partner, either in each other or in another. Neither returns to a "normal" life again, always missing those they lost in the massacre.

Amabelle returns to Alegría, trying to find a waterfall she and Sebastien treasured. She sees Señora Valencia, who has another Haitian servant. She also hears a story about General Trujillo's experience as a guard in cane fields: Upon hearing a Haitian cane worker mispronounce *perejil*, the general said that he had found a way to identify Haitians, as their pronunciation would always give them away.

Returning, Amabelle takes off her clothes and lies in the river, face up, only partially submerged. The river is very shallow and warm at this time of year—October, the same month as the massacre that took place decades earlier. She thinks of all those who have been lost in the river and on either side of it. A "crazy" man affected by the massacre watches her lying in the water and then walks away, as Amabelle floats in the water and in her dreams.

Critical Evaluation:

The Farming of Bones depicts a historical event—an ethnic cleansing massacre that occurred in the Dominican Republic in 1937—as well as the event's aftermath. The massacre was a horrible, defining moment in Haitian and Dominican history.

Born in Haiti in 1969, Edwidge Danticat moved to New York when she was twelve years old to rejoin her parents, who had immigrated to the United States earlier to find work.

One of a limited number of Haitian, or even of Caribbean, writers, particularly women, whose work is published and available in the United States and Western countries, Danticat's experiences as a Haitian immigrant to the United States inform her writing, teaching, and work advocating for immigrant and human rights. Her works explore current and historical relationships between Haiti, the United States, and individuals whose lives are affected by these places. She is also interested in those who are affected by living near a political border, such as that between Haiti and the Dominican Republic in *The Farming of Bones*.

Danticat grew up speaking Kreyol, the creole language of Haiti, and French, the language used in Haitian schools, learning English after coming to the United States. The title, *The Farming of Bones*, is a translation of a Kreyol phrase describing work in the cane fields, *travay te pou zo*, as the cane stalks at harvest resemble bones. The phrase takes on a different meaning as well, referring to Trujillo's order to kill, or cut down, thousands of Haitian migrants working in the cane fields, as domestic servants, and in other lower levels of employment in the Dominican Republic. The novel includes other uses of Kreyol and of Spanish (the language of the Dominican Republic), demonstrating the linguistic mélange of transnational communities—whether they are historically or recently combined.

Danticat's writing, including *The Farming of Bones*, demonstrates a use of modern and contemporary narrative techniques and visual presentations of text (changes in font type and style, for example) that serve to emphasize a background of oral storytelling traditions. Visible changes in the text also often highlight the presence in Haitian and other communities of multiple languages. Danticat's emphasis on oral storytelling and oral history, an important aspect of expression in Haitian communities, is significant, even while her printed, published books and story collections also represent a turn toward written work, written communication, and engagement of audiences in many different countries and communities.

The Farming of Bones narrates events similar to those that occurred during the 1937 massacre and produces a sort of written history from a counter-nationalist viewpoint. The narratorial style of storytelling, meanwhile, emphasizes the names, birthplaces, and events of "regular" individuals' lives, placing importance on the living memories of these events and the need for such memories to be passed on. Although it is a work of fiction, the book represents the recovery and recording of oral history, a history of individuals whose stories are often not recorded in official histories, whether in books or historical records.

Along with this plurality of individual voices, Danticat also addresses, although less comprehensively, larger contexts of Haiti and the Dominican Republic. She alludes to previous conflicts within and between the countries, as well as those involving the European and U.S. colonial occupations. In several cases, Danticat suggests that inequities exist within migrant communities, and she points to the complicity of the Haitian national government in failing to respond significantly to the massacre of thousands of Haitians. The impossibility of maintaining total separation of the countries and those within them is also demonstrated in the border crossings that continue even after stronger physical and military barriers are placed along the river.

Critics have noted the importance of physical imagery to memory and history within Danticat's works, including *The Farming of Bones*. Critics April Shemak and Heather Hewett have examined ways in which the bodies of characters in the novel are sites of memory and evidence of trauma as well. Further expansion of memory and history in criticism of this work takes into account gendered aspects of history and collective memory, as discussed by critic Kelli Johnson.

The Farming of Bones approaches the often repetitive nature of human history in a broader sense as well: The novel's epigraph is a biblical quotation referencing a conflict that occurred long before the 1937 massacre. Just as in 1937, one group of people was massacred by another, and those killed often were identified through their mispronunciation of a word from the aggressor group's language. *The Farming of Bones*'s recurring imagery of birth, rebirth, and death also emphasizes recurring cycles and themes within the novel's stories and the recurrent tendencies within history in general.

Virginia Pannabecker

Further Reading

Danticat, Edwidge. "An Interview with Edwidge Danticat." Interview by Bonnie Lyons. *Contemporary Literature* 44, no. 2 (Summer, 2003): 183-198. Substantial interview about Danticat's personal background, her works, her motivation, and her views on Haiti and related social issues.

Fulani, Ifeona. "Caribbean Women Writers and the Politics of Style: A Case for Literary Anancyism." *Small Axe* 9, no. 1 (March, 2005): 64-79. Discusses the difficulty Caribbean writers of literature, especially women, have in publishing their works in the United States and elsewhere. Examines Danticat and Jamaica Kincaid's success as writers and explores aspects of each author's writing and life to understand the reception of their works by U.S. and Western audiences.

Hewett, Heather. "At the Crossroads: Disability and Trauma in *The Farming of Bones*." *MELUS* 31, no. 3 (Fall, 2006): 123-145. Focuses on the novel's representation of disability and its relationship to trauma, memory, and experience. Some discussion of Haitian and African diasporic folklore as well.

Johnson, Kelli. "Both Sides of the Massacre: Collective Memory and Narrative on Hispaniola." *Mosaic: A Journal for the Interdisciplinary Study of Literature* 36, no. 2 (June, 2003): 75-91. Discusses Danticat's *The Farming of Bones* and Julia Alvarez's *In the Time of the Butterflies* (1994). Focuses on how these works represent collective memory as counters to institutional memory and recorded histories. Includes information about the authors' research and emphasizes gendered aspects of memory and history.

Shemak, April. "Re-membering Hispaniola: Edwidge Danticat's *The Farming of Bones*." *MFS: Modern Fiction Studies* 48, no. 1 (Spring, 2002): 83-112. Focuses on

methods of remembering, including physical representations of memory in bodies marked by labor and the massacre. Describes *The Farming of Bones* not as a testimonial but as a collective testimony. Explores the concepts of border and borderlands, considering Gloria Anzaldúa's work but suggesting that Danticat expands upon or redefines the meanings of these terms.

Smartt Bell, Madison. "A Hidden Haitian World." *The New York Review of Books* 55, no. 12 (October 26, 1997): 40-42. Overview article that discusses Danticat's works, including *The Farming of Bones*, within the context of Haitian history and literature.

Wucker, Michele. "Edwidge Danticat: A Voice for the Voiceless." *Américas* 52, no. 3 (May, 2000): 40-45. Incorporates an interview and a general profile of Danticat, as well as some commentary on her writing, including *The Farming of Bones*. Emphasis on how Danticat's writing and other work contribute to a life focused on engagement and dialogue with others to address immigrant and human rights.

Fateless

Author: Imre Kertész (1929-   )

First published: Sorstalanság, 1975 (English translation, 1992; also as *Fatelessness*, 2004)

Type of work: Novel

Type of plot: Psychological realism

Time of plot: 1944-1945

Locale: Budapest; Auschwitz, German-occupied Poland; Buchenwald and Zeitz, Germany

Principal characters:

GEORGE KÖVES, a fifteen-year-old Hungarian Jew

BANDI CITROM, a fellow prisoner

UNCLE LAJOS, his uncle

UNCLE STEINER and UNCLE FLEISCHMANN, old family friends

The Story:

Although his perspective is cool and calm, the story George Köves tells of his arrest and incarceration by the Nazis builds to a harrowing vision of evil. His ordeal begins in his home in Hungary, where things are already unraveling. George's parents have divorced, and his father, because he is a Jew, has been forced to relinquish his successful business and work instead in a German labor camp. Although George's Uncle Lajos tells him that he must accept what is happening and understand that such persecution is the Jewish fate, George does not agree. Similarly, he resists his little girlfriend's suggestion that his Jewish identity is fated by biology. George upsets his uncle and his playmate when he

refuses to accept the premise that his life is somehow in the hands of a predetermined collective destiny. Nevertheless, it is as a Jew rather than for any more personal reason that George is first forced to labor at an oil refinery outside Budapest and then sent to the Auschwitz concentration camp in Poland. His identity is made even more impersonal and abstract when his name is taken from him in the camps and he is known only as #64,921.

Along with the other boys with whom he was arrested, George has claimed to be one year older than he really is because he has been told that as an older boy he is more likely to be put to work rather than slaughtered in the gas chambers. After a short time at Auschwitz and then Buchen-wald, George is transferred to Zeitz, a work camp where he labors in a quarry. He begins to understand that, despite everything, he and his fellow prisoners are still not completely under the rule of the Nazis; they are free to dissent from the Nazi perspective and to resist its perverse logic.

George describes this resistance to himself as stubbornness. His own detached perspective is one instance of this stubbornness; another is the way the prisoners help one another rather than descending to the law of the jungle as the Nazis expect them to do. For instance, a fellow prisoner makes sure that the young George's food ration is not purloined. Even more important, a fellow Hungarian, a resourceful twenty-year-old man named Bandi Citrom, befriends George. Bandi gives him numerous tips that will help him survive the hardships of his circumstances.

Bandi's belief in the value of an ordered, ethical daily life rescues George from confusion and despair and represents another way to dissent from the demoralizing, dehumanizing world of the camps. Another form of resistance is George's imagination: Even though he is captive, his imagination is still free, and he can travel backward in his mind to memories of safety and comfort, as well as imagining hopeful future scenarios. The idea of the future is crucial to George's ability to resist the Nazi regime. An important aspect of his developing philosophy of life is that he understands that the future can always bring change, new possibilities, and alternatives unforeseen in the present.

At Zeitz, the young boys with whom George was originally arrested have been dispersed. Having lost the sense of adventure with which they began their imprisonment, the youths have either died or become old before their time. In another sign that things are changing for the worse, food becomes more closely rationed, enfeebling and emaciating George. Already weakened by a leg wounded while working at the quarry, George's health fails to such an extent that he hovers near death. Although he is dying, however, he knows that the Nazis cannot deprive him of his will to live or of his appreciation of life itself, which, even in the concentration camp, he finds beautiful. Just when George is at his lowest ebb, things take an unexpected turn when, instead of being delivered to the crematorium, George is brought to the infirmary, where he is nursed back to health and given extra food by two compassionate attendants. On top of this almost miraculous change in his fortunes is the surprising and sudden collapse of the seemingly invincible Nazi system. The war ends, American soldiers liberate the camp, and George is sent home to Hungary.

Embittered by his experience and further upset by the distinct possibility that his friend Bandi has not survived, George finds he must endure what he feels are absurd questions from a journalist. George refuses to cooperate with the journalist's wish for an inspiring article, instead telling him that, far from feeling safe back in civilization, what he feels is implacable hatred for everyone and everything in the outside world. His repeated use of the word "naturally" when the journalist asks about his experience further suggests that the camps were the natural outcome of a larger social system in which the journalist himself lives and that the journalist has failed to question.

In Budapest, George confronts Uncle Steiner and Uncle Fleischmann, old family friends who managed to avoid arrest and deportation to the camps and who fail to understand the suffering George has endured. As with the journalist, George informs them that the concentration camps are one aspect of a larger European social disorder, a continuation of a system to which they all belonged. This conversation demonstrates the alienation George feels from his family and his old world, which he does not perceive as an exception from the system that produced the camps. Instead, he remembers the times within the camps, where, George feels, the reality of European modernity had to be recognized for what it was.

This recognition of the corruption of modernity, paradoxically, was what allowed George to secure an independence from it. In the camps, George understood that he could transcend the circumstances dictated by the camp, affirming the beauty and importance of life itself. It is this philosophy that will sustain him in the postwar world of Hungary, still shadowed as it is by totalitarianism even after the fall of the Nazis. It is understood that George has come of age; he is no longer a child and will think for himself. He will not give in to despair but will continue to live with that sense of inner freedom that sustained him throughout his time in the Nazi concentration camps.

Critical Evaluation:

Although *Fateless* is narrated from the first-person point of view of a teenage boy, a more sophisticated philosophical consciousness develops as the boy puts together all the details of his experience to build a larger and more comprehensive meaning. He understands that everything that happens in the camps is the result of remote executive decisions, as on a corporate board. He begins to realize that his arrest and imprisonment go according to a plan and are the natural outcome of a totalitarian power structure, which requires efficiency and compliance. None of this is accidental or deviant. On the contrary, the brutality and degradation of the camps are part of the normal workings of dictatorship. George's deployment of the words "of course" and "naturally" point to the way in which what happens to him is a natural consequence of an entire social system; death camps and work camps, in fact, will always emerge as a consequence of a modern totalitarian system. The camps are then the natural outcome of a deep disturbance in European civilization that must be recognized and mended.

In order to explain the existence of the camps to himself, George uses the analogy of a group getting together to play a practical joke; for the joke to work, everything has to be taken into consideration, everything must be perfectly planned. This attention to administration produces a nearly mechanistic efficiency, so the imposition of order masks its lethal purposes. The power of this system is such that individuals are manipulated into acceptance and cooperation, losing the will to question or resist, as if the system had created the equivalent of fate. This means that what happens to George is not a consequence of some mystical and mysterious destiny. The title of George's story, *Fateless*, underlines Imre Kertész's conclusion, namely that Jews are not metaphysically fated to become victims. George and his parents, for instance, saw themselves before the war as assimilated Hungarians; it was the Nazis who informed them otherwise.

Coming from a family of nonbelievers, George does not speak Yiddish or Hebrew and knows no prayers. He does not get along with the religious Jews in the camps. Although being a Jew means little to him, however, he is assigned that identity and is systematically persecuted by the Nazis as a Jew. His fate then becomes one indicated by his concentration camp number, #64,921, which utterly depersonalizes him, depriving him of a sense of personal destiny and instead substituting a future dictated by a perverse ideology. George ultimately concludes that it is not the Nazis who have the power to determine who he is, but only he himself who can choose to be a Jew. Even as he becomes simply a number in the camps, his identity as a Jew becomes paradoxically paramount. It is his developing realization that he is, despite the Nazis, free to do otherwise that allows him to choose to identify himself as a Jew.

Similarly, despite his imprisonment, George affirms that he is free to discard the punitive fate imposed on him by the Nazis. He concludes that nothing has to be the way it is, that life does not follow a fated pattern but will always bring surprising changes. The novel's conclusion, in which a seemingly unassailable authoritarian government utterly collapses, is a profound example of George's intuitive recognition that every step he takes may lead to something unexpected and emancipatory. Ironically, the lack of freedom in the camps leads him to make freedom itself the basis of his own view of the world and his own identity. In his refusal to give up, in the free play of his imagination, in his curiosity and love of life under circumstances calculated to encourage him to give up the will to live, George retains a sense of inner freedom. Additionally, he and the other prisoners retain a moral compass that helps them resist the criminality and injustice of the system that has imprisoned them.

Returning to Budapest with this perspective, George confronts those who remained behind, suggesting that they fell into the error of assuming that the Nazi dictatorship must simply be accepted as a historical necessity. He returns from the camps to reject the idea that the Nazi persecution was an instance of a larger spiritual fate associated with being a Jew. He also returns to suggest to the Hungarians who were not imprisoned that their failure to question authority led them to accept the system that sent George to the camps and that they could have done otherwise. George, on the other hand, himself resisted on a psychological level the fate assigned to him by the Nazis, becoming "fateless." This is a perspective that is not specific to George as a Jew but affirms George's conviction that personal liberty and personal responsibility will allow all individuals the ability to resist political repression and social conformity.

Margaret Boe Birns

Further Reading

Adelman, Gary. "Getting Started with Imre Kertész." *New England Review: Middlebury Series* 25, nos. 1/2 (2004): 261-278. Discusses *Fateless* as a redemptive novel in which the mental clarity of the conclusion promises a successful future.

Bachmann, Michael. "Life, Writing, and Problems of Genre in Elie Wiesel and Imre Kertész." *Rocky Mountain Review* 63, no. 1 (Spring, 2009): 79-88. Compares and contrasts the works of Kertész and Elie Wiesel in terms of their status as "witness literature." Examines Kertész as keeping his work alive in a zone somewhere between testimony and fiction.

Kertész, Imre. "Eureka! The 2002 Nobel Lecture." *World Literature Today* 77, no. 1 (April-June, 2003): 4-8. Kertész's Nobel Prize lecture discusses the Holocaust as a trauma of European civilization, but affirms liberty as the greatest European value.

Nádas, Péter. "Imre Kertész's Work and His Subject." *Hungarian Quarterly* 43, no. 168 (Winter, 2002): 38-40. Discusses the impact of the Holocaust on Kertész's work and the connections Kertész makes between Nazi and Communist dictatorships

Sicher, Efraim. *The Holocaust Novel*. New York: Routledge, 2005. Discusses Kertész's work in the context of Holocaust literature as a major postwar literary genre—and in terms not only of fiction but also of history and autobiography. Chronology and annotated bibliography.

Vasvári, Louise O., and Steven Tötösy de Zepetnek, eds. *Imre Kertész and Holocaust Literature*. West Lafayette, Ind.: Purdue University Press, 2005. This important study of Kertész features essays by scholars from various countries; discusses narrative techniques, film treatment, the Holocaust, and Jewish identity. Includes a bibliography.

The Father

Author: August Strindberg (1849-1912)
First produced: 1887; first published, 1887 as *Fadren* (English translation, 1899)
Type of work: Drama
Type of plot: Psychological realism
Time of plot: Mid-nineteenth century
Locale: Sweden

Principal characters:
THE CAPTAIN, an officer and amateur scientist
LAURA, his wife
BERTHA, their daughter
DR. ÖSTERMARK, the village physician
THE PASTOR, Laura's brother
MARGARET, an old nurse
NÖJD, a soldier

The Story:

When Nöjd gets a servant girl named Emma in trouble, the captain sends an orderly to bring Nöjd to face the pastor. The culprit is vague about his affair and hints that the paternity of the child is uncertain and that it is possible that Ludwig is the real father. The pastor tells Nöjd that he will have to support the child, but the soldier claims that Ludwig should contribute also. The captain declares angrily that the case will go to court. After Nöjd leaves, the captain, who is married to the pastor's sister Laura, berates the pastor for his gentleness. The pastor says he thinks it a pity to saddle Nöjd with the support of a child if he is not the real father.

In his house, complains the captain, there are too many women: his mother-in-law, a governess, old nurse Margaret, and his daughter Bertha. The captain, worried about his daughter's education, which is being influenced in all different directions by the people around her, deplores the incessant struggle between men and women.

After the pastor leaves, Laura enters to collect her household money. Because his affairs are near bankruptcy, the captain asks her to keep an account of the money she spends. Laura asks what he has decided about Bertha's education. Laura objects when he announces his intention to send her to town to board with Auditor Safberg, a freethinker, but the captain reminds her that a father has the sole control of his children. When Laura brings up the subject of Nöjd's affair, the captain admits that the paternity will be difficult to determine.

Laura scoffingly claims that if such were the case, even the child of a married woman could be any other man's offspring.

Laura confides to Dr. Östermark, the new village doctor, her suspicion that her husband is mentally ill. He buys books he never reads, and he tries to fathom events on other planets by peering through a microscope. He has become a man who cannot stand by his decisions, although he is vehement when he first utters one. The captain, speaking confidentially with his old nurse, expresses his fear that his family is plotting against him and that something evil is about to happen.

The family quarrel is clearly outlined when Bertha complains to her father that her grandmother is trying to teach her spiritualism and has even told the girl that the captain, who is a meteorologist by profession, is a charlatan. Bertha agrees with her father that she ought to go away to study, but Laura boasts that she will be able to persuade Bertha to stay home. She hints again that she can prove the captain is not Bertha's father.

Dr. Östermark explains to Laura that she is mistaken about her husband; he used a spectroscope, not a microscope, to examine the elements on other planets. Still, the doctor says, he will watch the captain for any other signs of insanity. Laura also tells the doctor that the captain fears he is not Bertha's father, an idea that Laura planted in her husband's mind. When he begins to worry over his daughter's paternity, old Margaret tries to reassure him.

The captain tries to stop his wife's continued persecution of him. She intercepts some of his mail, thwarting him in the progress of his scientific ventures. He further accuses her of spreading among his friends the idea that he is insane. Afraid that under such provocation he might lose his reason, he appeals to his wife's selfishness. It will be in her best interests for him to remain sane, he says, since insanity might lead to his suicide, which would invalidate her right to collect his life insurance. She can assure his sanity by confessing that Bertha is not his child, a suspicion that is undermining his sanity.

When she refuses to admit a sin of which she is not guilty, he reminds her that in doing so she will gain sole control of Bertha's future. The tables are turned. Now the captain begins to believe that Bertha is not his child and Laura begins to insist that she is. The captain, recalling the circumstances of Bertha's birth, recollects how a solicitor told Laura that she has no right of inheritance without a child. At that time the captain was ill. When he recovered, Bertha was born.

The captain understands the power his wife holds over him. At first he loved her as he would love a mother; she loathed him after he became her lover. Laura shows him a letter she forged, in which he confesses his insanity, and tells him that she sent the letter to court. Boasting that she employed him only as a breadwinner, she declares that she will use his pension for Bertha's education. In anger, the captain hurls a lamp at her.

Laura succeeds in locking her husband in another room while she examines his private papers. Although the pastor sees through her scheme, she dares him to accuse her. The doctor arrives with a straitjacket shortly before the captain, armed with literary evidence of cases in which a child's paternity was questioned, bursts into the room. His talk is so erratic and his raving about conjugal fidelity so wild that when the doctor tells him he is insane, the captain acknowledges his own madness.

Bertha, accusing him of a deliberate attempt to injure her mother, announces that he is not her father if he behaves so badly. The captain, in reply, tells her that her soul is in two parts; one is a reflection of his own, and to preserve it he intends to destroy the part that is not his. He seizes a revolver but finds it empty. Bertha runs out screaming.

Old Margaret soothes the raving man by talking softly to him of his childhood, and when he is off guard she slips the straitjacket on him. Seeing him seated on the sofa, helpless and dejected, Laura nearly repents the course she took as the captain piteously describes his life of torment with mother, wife, and child, all of whom rejected him. After she assures him that Bertha is his own child, the captain, calling to old Margaret for comfort, suffers a stroke. As he lies uncon-

scious, Bertha runs to her mother, who caresses her and calls the girl her own daughter.

Critical Evaluation:

The plays of August Strindberg have exerted a powerful and pervasive influence on modern drama in both Europe and America. His insights into naturalism, in such early plays as *The Father* and *Fröken Julie* (1888; *Miss Julie*, 1912), were central in the shaping of that dramatic movement, while his later experiments with expressionism, in such works as *Spöksonaten* (1907; *The Ghost Sonata*, 1916), *Ett drömspel* (1902; *A Dream Play*, 1912), and the *Till Damaskus* trilogy(1898-1904; *To Damascus*, 1913), have profoundly effected nonrealistic approaches to the modern stage. It is virtually impossible to separate Strindberg's life from his works, and this is particularly true in the case of *The Father*. Even Strindberg recognized the close alliance between the two when on November 12, 1887, he wrote to Axel Lundegard: "It is to me as if I were walking in my sleep—as if creation and life were mingled. I do not know whether *The Father* is a creative work, or whether that was my real life."

The relationship between Strindberg's reality and his writing becomes apparent in an examination of *Le Plaidoyer d'un fou* (1893; *A Madman's Defense*, 1912), an autobiographical novel that contains many references essential to an understanding of *The Father*. Written between 1887 and 1888, it chronicles fourteen years of Strindberg's life, including his fateful meeting and marriage to Siri Von Essen. Strindberg intended the work as an exposé of Siri's attempts to confine him for mental treatment, but in reality it presents a clear picture of developing paranoia and acute mental instability.

Strindberg's first-person narrator names his wife Maria and portrays her as suspicious of her husband's sanity from the beginning of their marriage. (Indeed, in 1886 Siri consulted a Swiss doctor about Strindberg's instability, confirming his suspicion that she suspected mental imbalance in him all along and desired to obtain his insurance money or marry again.) Based on her conviction, Maria attempts to provoke behavior from the narrator that can be used as evidence to justify confinement. When she sides with the critics of her husband's book, he calls her a traitor who is responsible for starting rumors about his sanity. When he escapes to Paris to seek comradeship with friends, she follows him and insists on a retreat in Switzerland. Once there, she convinces the doctor, guests, proprietor, and servants that he is, indeed, insane.

Beginning to doubt his own sanity and feeling a persecution mania, the narrator turns his suspicions and hostility on his wife. He studies her behavior and comes to believe that she is an adulteress trying to cover her wrongdoings and gain his insurance money and writings by proving him mentally incompetent. He looks for evidence to prove his theory by rifling through her letters and subjecting her to strenuous cross-examinations. Neither her denials nor the confessions he believes he extracts provide him with convincing answers, but they intensify his agitation and instability. The reader of *A Madman's Defense* cannot help but see the parallels between this autobiographical account and the basic plot of *The Father*, as well as the similarity between the narrator in the novel and the captain in the play. *The Father* becomes almost an adaptation of *A Madman's Defense*.

Along with the fictionalization of the growing paranoia in *A Madman's Defense*, Strindberg's account closely parallels the events that surrounded the publication and subsequent blasphemy trial of *Giftas I* (1884), the first volume of his *Getting Married* (1973). This collection of short stories deals with the relationship between husbands and wives, drawing for some of the material on Strindberg's early married life and *The Father*. The most important contribution from that collection to *The Father* is in the portrayal of women. Strindberg is scornful toward the "emancipated" woman in marriage, feeling that such a woman wants not equality with her mate but domination over him. The ideal role for the woman, Strindberg believes, is that of wife and mother—anything else can only be destructive.

This view of women had its origins in Strindberg's own background, for he had cause to believe in the evil nature of his mother. Having been unwanted at birth and rejected as a child, Strindberg grew up a stranger in his own home. What Strindberg sought in a mate (he went through three stormy marriages) was not only a wife but also a substitute mother, a confusion of roles that greatly exacerbated his experiences of marriage. Strindberg describes Siri after first meeting her as "a deliciously girlish mother." Even during their trial separation, Strindberg stated that he felt "like an embryo prematurely detached from the umbilical cord." This attitude is echoed by the characters in *The Father*, when Laura tells the captain: "I loved you as if you were my child. But you know, you must have felt it, when your sexual desires were aroused, and you came forward as my lover, I was reluctant, and the joy I felt in your embrace was followed by such revulsion that my very blood knew shame. The son became the lover—oh!"

Strindberg's confusion and disillusion led him naturally into bitter antifeminism, although he was hardly unusual in this respect. His philosophy paralleled that of many contemporaries, particularly those in France—a country he frequented during his exile periods—where the literary atmo-

sphere in the 1870's was extremely misogynistic. The theater had become particularly receptive to the movement, as is especially evident in the character of the femme fatale as popularized by such actors as Sarah Bernhardt. It was felt at the time that people of talent and intellect—particularly men, since they were the more imaginative and talented sex— were being exploited. The female was seen as a parasitic being who lived off the productivity of the male. As Laura states to the captain: "The mother was your friend, look you, but the woman was your enemy,—for sexual love is strife; and don't imagine that I gave myself; I gave nothing, I only took—what I meant to have."

The source for the question of paternity that is so central to *The Father* is provided by yet another biographical reference. When Strindberg married Siri she was pregnant and had, not long before their marriage, shared the company of her first husband, Baron Wrangel. After Strindberg became actively paranoid, his remembrance of that situation provoked him to harbor active doubts about the paternity of his children. That the suspicion was in his mind was confirmed by his reaction to Henrik Ibsen's play *Vildanden* (1884; *The Wild Duck*, 1891). After its appearance, Strindberg considered suing Ibsen for slander on the grounds that Ibsen had used him as a model for Hjalmar Ekdal, the central character of the play, who doubts the paternity of his child. Strindberg and Siri were also at odds about the future occupations of their two daughters. Siri wished them to become actors, while Strindberg wanted them to be trained as midwives. These two personal conflicts became central issues in *The Father*.

Although Strindberg's own experiences provided the major inspiration for *The Father*, he was also deeply influenced by the literary and cultural milieu of his time. The novels of the Goncourt brothers, with their emphasis on the physiological and psychological approach in human character analysis, and particularly *Chérie* (1884), which was Edmond de Goncourt's last novel, may have directly affected the play. A naturalistic play with the same analytical emphasis, Émile Zola's *Thérèse Raquin* (1873), may also have provided Strindberg with some insight. Before he began writing *The Father*, he studied popular contemporary theories in psychiatric and hypnotic literature, and after finishing *The Father*, he articulated the results of these researches in an essay series entitled *Vivisektioner* (1887, *Vivisections*). From their titles alone, two of the essays reveal their influence on *The Father*: "The Battle of the Brains" and "Psychic Murder."

These influences, coupled with "the battle of the brains" and the "psychic murder," connect *The Father* with the school of naturalism. The battle of the brains between Laura and the captain is actually a Darwinian struggle for power, with survival going to the fittest—a central concept in the naturalist school of thought. The captain states that the battle with his wife is "to eat or to be eaten." At one point, the discussion becomes overtly Darwinistic:

CAPTAIN: I feel in this battle one of us must succumb.
LAURA: Who?
CAPTAIN: The weaker, of course.
LAURA: And the stronger is right?
CAPTAIN: He is always right because he has the power.
LAURA: Then I am right.

The amorality of action—with the end justifying the means— the detached scientific tone, the emphasis on the psychological, and the playwright's objectivity strengthen the play's naturalist tendencies.

It was Zola, however, the founder of naturalism in the novel, who saw the yet undeveloped aspect of Strindberg's attempt to bring naturalism into the drama. Despite his extremely adequate psychological emphasis and scientific attitude, Strindberg, as Zola pointed out, failed to give the play a "social setting"—that is, he had failed to emphasize the importance of heredity and environment in his characterization. Although attributing the captain's weakness to his feelings of being unwanted when born and to the upbringing given him by a "bad" mother, Strindberg went no further in demonstrating the power of environmental influences on his characters. Despite this weakness, Zola apparently saw Strindberg as his potential dramatic counterpart and encouraged him in his pursuits. After his crucial beginning in *The Father*, Strindberg presented perhaps the first important naturalist drama with his next play, *Miss Julie*. The vital naturalist factors of heredity and milieu are even more explicitly emphasized in this powerful play, which dramatizes the destruction of a willful aristocratic female by her father's brazen valet.

At the time he wrote *The Father*, Strindberg was a man of mental and emotional complexity who stood on the brink of developing one of the most important movements in modern dramatic literature—naturalism. In the third section of his autobiography, covering the period around 1886, Strindberg expresses an awareness of his position in the development of the modern drama. He saw himself as spanning the gap between romanticism and naturalism and being "like the blindworm, which retains rudimentary lizard feet inside its skin." This dependence on his background and his "rudimentary lizard feet" was, however, no detriment to his dramatic career.

Rather than holding him back, these autobiographical reliances controlled, polished, and became the driving force in his naturalistic writings and, in a different way, were to become the substance of his later experiments with expressionism. His influence was felt throughout Europe as well as in the United States, and he was noted by Eugene O'Neill in his acceptance speech for the Nobel Prize in Literature as one of O'Neill's foremost literary inspirations. Certainly since that time, Strindberg has been generally regarded, along with Henrik Ibsen and Anton Chekhov, as one of the three giants most responsible for the shape, direction, and power of twentieth century theater.

"Critical Evaluation" by Phyllis E. Allran

Further Reading

Brustein, Robert. "Male and Female in August Strindberg." In *Modern Drama: Essays in Criticism*, edited by Travis Bogard. New York: Oxford University Press, 1965. Focuses on Strindberg's paradoxical view of masculine and feminine as reflected in several of his major plays, including *The Father*. Discusses Strindberg's early misogynist views and his recurring fascination with the so-called war between the sexes. Includes explanatory notes.

House, Poul, Sven Hakon Rossel, and Göran Stockenström, eds. *August Strindberg and the Other: New Critical Approaches*. Amsterdam: Rodopi, 2002. Collection of papers delivered at a 2000 conference, "Strindberg at the Millennium—Strindberg and the Other," interpreting the motif of "the other" and "otherness" in Strindberg's work.

Lagercrantz, Olof. *August Strindberg*. Translated by Anselm Hollo. New York: Farrar, Straus & Giroux, 1984. Discusses relevant biographical information concerning many of Strindberg's major plays, including *The Father*. Useful in understanding and interpreting Strindberg's work, which many critics assert is largely autobiographical.

Lyons, Charles R. "The Archetypal Action of Male Submission in Strindberg's *The Father*." *Scandinavian Studies* 36, no. 3 (August, 1964): 218-232. Argues that the models for male submission within *The Father* might be found in such ancient myths as those of Adam and Eve, and Samson and Delilah.

Robinson, Michael, ed. *The Cambridge Companion to August Strindberg*. New York: Cambridge University Press, 2009. Collection of essays analyzing Strindberg's work, placing it within the context of his life and times. Includes bibliography and index.

Shideler, Ross. "Strindberg's Struggle." In *Questioning the*

Father: From Darwin to Zola, Ibsen, Strindberg, and Hardy. Stanford, Calif.: Stanford University Press, 1999. Examines how Strindberg adapted late nineteenth century Darwinian ideas and the women's rights movement to create family dramas and novels in which he questioned the role of the father. Argues *The Father* is one of three Strindberg plays that best exemplify the confronta-tion between a Darwinian-centered bioworld and the Scandinavian patriarchal family.

Valency, Maurice. *The Flower and the Castle: An Introduction to Modern Drama.* New York: Macmillan, 1963. A comprehensive discussion of Strindberg's major plays and his contribution to modern theater. Includes subject index and selected bibliography.

Father and Son
A Study of Two Temperaments

Author: Edmund Gosse (1849-1928)
First published: 1907
Type of work: Autobiography

In chapter 1, Edmund Gosse depicts himself as a small child in a staunchly Puritan, middle-class household where stringent worship takes place daily. As he grew, Gosse enjoyed great freedom during the day, and in the evenings he was lovingly included as an equal third party in his parents' eager, mutually enjoyable discussions of Puritan doctrine.

In chapter 2, Gosse records his life from earliest memory through age six. He emphasizes the dichotomous experience of having loving parents who had no sense of the despairing oppressiveness their religious zeal had on their small son. Some escape from the oppressive worship came when, at age six, Gosse discovered a private duality that brought a "consciousness of self, as a force and as a companion," one with whom he secretly conversed during worship.

In chapters 3 and 4, Gosse presents events of his seventh year, chief among them his mother's death. On her deathbed, she extracted from Gosse's father, Philip, a promise to see that their son Edmund would dedicate himself to their Puritanism. That dedication was to remain an intolerable burden. Adjusting to his mother's death, Gosse realized that the pain it brought finally allowed his emotions, not merely his intellect, to be stimulated; he felt, for the first time, in touch with his own humanity. His father continued indoctrinating him into Puritan beliefs, leaving no gaps "for nature to fill."

In chapters 5 and 6, Gosse reviews his eighth and ninth years. On his eighth birthday, he and his father, with a new governess, moved to Devonshire. There, his father became a preacher in a Wesleyan church of Cornish people who retained, intact, the traditions of the eighteenth century. His father saw the new scientific works of Charles Lyell, Charles Darwin, Thomas Huxley, and others as attacks on those traditions. A renowned naturalist himself, Philip determined to write a book that would reconcile the account in Genesis of a six-day creation with the new scientific accounts of a slower evolution, thus making compatible his religion and natural science. The book failed. Philip assumed an even stricter faith, an even narrower mind. Pondering this, Gosse believed that his father habitually "mistook fear for love."

In chapters 7 through 9, Gosse relates experiences from his ninth, tenth, and eleventh years, which bring even greater distance between his and his father's spiritual beliefs. Paradoxically, during this period, his father introduced Gosse to Vergil's classical works. At ten, Gosse suddenly wanted to be all his father expected, and, for diametrically opposed reasons, the father and son successfully instigated the unprecedented inclusion of a child in the adult affairs of a church. Philip wanted his son "saved" before puberty could assail him; Gosse wanted the power and prestige of being a child prodigy.

"Conversion" brought increased religious accountability to Gosse: He was expected to witness daily and to reject all boyish behavior. Despairingly, Gosse was forced to realize that his father expected him to enter the ministry. He saw himself, inevitably, imprisoned for life in the Puritan system. Nevertheless, he clung to a "hard nut of individuality," to the duality that allowed him to speak in himself to himself in "inviolable secrecy." Reading more widely, he realized that, unlike his father's "saving" faith, his own had intellectual roots.

At eleven, because of his son's interest in geography, Gosse's father gave him a novel about the sea that he had enjoyed as a boy. This gift marked a turning point in Gosse's life, as it opened his imagination and taught him the power of words and books. He attributed the continuing "fortitude" of his individuality to his reading of that book.

In chapters 10 and 11, Gosse covers the events of his eleventh through thirteenth years, including his father's marriage to Eliza Brightwen and her positive influence upon his life.

In chapter 12, Gosse presents an account of boarding-school years during his fourteenth through seventeenth years. The very bleakness of his school experience allowed the pursuit of his own "moral and mental development," which taught him to dream, to speculate, and to think for himself. During these years, his father took him to London to an evangelism conference, where a speaker said that William Shakespeare was suffering in hell. Gosse was devastated, for he loved Shakespeare's works but now would not read them if the writer were "lost." After the meeting, his father said he thought the man wrong to so judge Shakespeare, who may well have made a profession of faith before he died. This unexpected observation swept a relieved Gosse with love for his father.

At sixteen, however, while home from school, he confronted the narrow views of his father's faith and his own inability to conceive such a "rigid conception" of God's mercy. He found incongruous his tenderhearted father's belief that God would punish human beings forever because of an intellectual error of comprehension.

He still believed, however, in the apocalyptic return of Christ to the earth, which his father preached. In what he calls the "highest moment" of his religious experience, Gosse stood alone in his room at school, praying expectantly that Jesus would return right then and take him to Paradise. When Jesus did not, Gosse knew Christ was not coming and would never come. Then he felt an initial crumbling of the "artificial faith" he had constructed. He knew his and his father's beliefs would take opposite paths, the "world between [them]."

In the epilogue, Gosse writes of events from his seventeenth through twenty-first years, when he lives on his own in London. His father demanded a constant account of his most private thoughts, rejecting all Gosse's pleas for some small portion of private soul. On a visit home, a final confrontation with his father ended with Gosse's denying that his father was responsible for his "secret, most intimate convictions." Back in London, he received a letter of ultimatum from his father saying that he could make all well between them by repenting and becoming again submissive to his father's will in matters of faith and thought; otherwise, their fellowship would remain broken. Thus challenged, at twenty-one years of age, Gosse says his conscience rejected his father's yoke

and took a man's privilege to design his "inner life for himself."

Three central themes weave their way through the tapestry of Gosse's spiritual autobiography: dualism, the passing of Victorianism, and the faltering faith that heralded modernity. The tapestry itself is what the writer calls, in his preface, an anecdotal documentary. Dualism, the doctrine of a paradoxically divided nature, runs through the pages. Gosse's early dualism separated him into companionable halves that would keep each other company, enabling him mentally to escape long hours of religious study and prayer. His father's dual nature, evidenced variously, is nowhere more significantly shown than by his evident willingness, despite his strict faith, to share forbidden fiction with his son. This sharing introduced Gosse to what became a life's work in literature. This encouragement of his son's literary interests, at significant moments of need, ultimately resulted in the divergence of their respective beliefs.

With his focus on the experience of having the fading religious concepts and practices of Puritanism thrown against his own spiritual development, Gosse reveals himself to be a true child of that transitional, Western age wherein faith went awry as the nineteenth century became the twentieth. Sweeping new scientific "truths" stunned those who were comfortable with the old doctrines. Indeed, Gosse (symbolic of the growing Victorian tendency to embrace modernity) paralleled his developing, differing insights with the self-satisfied confidence his father (symbolic of the traditions from which modernity broke) held toward Puritan dogma.

Of all that lay buried in the passing of the Victorian age, religious faith proved the most traumatic loss. That loss is keenly analyzed in Gosse's autobiography through the schism that grew between father and son as their respective faiths diverged. This schism reflects the rushing changes of modernity that swamped people's long-held spiritual belief in absolute, unchanging truths. In this time of the scientific investigations of Charles Lyell and Charles Darwin, the socio-philosophical revolutions of Georg Hegel and Karl Marx, and the psychological insights of Carl Jung and Sigmund Freud, intellectual advancements challenged and frightened those whose understanding was built on an uninvestigated faith of fear.

Unhappily, it was also the period when traditional faith, failing the challenge, gave way in many people's minds—not from new truths but because the old faith was based on a narrow human perspective, fraught with human pride, and could not maintain its limited understanding against those truths. In this, the father proves the son's suspicion that, in spite of his tenderness, his faith in Divine Providence is built on fear, not love. As Gosse (and modernity) said, such fearful faith cannot say, simply, "I don't know," although biblical text confirms that the only answer faith can give to unanswerable paradoxes is exactly that. The faith based on fear falls apart in the face of these paradoxes.

Late twentieth century critics challenged the validity of Gosse's masterpiece, saying perhaps his father had reason to fear his son's lifestyle in London, since he evidently went to parties with young women. Gosse, however, states in the 1907 autobiography that his father never concerned himself with the son's physical actions or attitudes, trusting him implicitly in those areas. Rather, his father was concerned with the matter of "insidious infidelity," which Gosse is careful to connect with his father's fear that new intellectual views that reached fruition in the modern age would lead him astray. His father's worst fears were right, but his son, too, was right: Every person and every generation have the right to grapple with new beliefs, weighing them against the old verities and truths.

Gosse's autobiography is an important work, particularly so for generations at the crossroads of a new century—or a new millennium. The postmodern writer Robert Coover, for example, said that late twentieth century Fundamentalism's inflexible dogma is the cause of "about 90 percent" of society's "unnecessary pain," because it demands rigid acceptance of its dogma as society's only truth. Such demands were not a new phenomena, even in Gosse's age; the Jews of the first century, likewise, rejected new ideas that did not conform to their rigid interpretation of Scripture.

Having access to all necessary truth, the Jews, the Victorians, and the Fundamentalists evidence the same "congenital lack" of what Gosse called "that highest modesty," which enables people to admit, "I do not know," when confronted by the wideness of God's many truths of grace. Such inability robs people of imagination and thereby erases the hope of a silencing awe. Such awe alone affirms the possibility of the "impossible." As Gosse pointed out, his father could not countenance the potential of truth to have "two forms, each of them indisputable, yet each antagonistic to the other." Such, of course, is the supreme dualism that begs the age-old, paradoxical question of faith: How can a holy God dwell in human flesh? A saving faith, which must wait to see, really has only one answer: "I don't know." Certainly, as Gosse concludes, each person has the right to a mind—and a faith—of his or her own. As his life proves, to deny that right robs a person of what Scripture calls "the substance of things hoped for," which is faith itself.

Jo Culbertson Davis

Further Reading

Amigoni, David. "Edmund Gosse's Cultural Evolution: Sympathetic Magic, Imitation, and Contagious Literature." In *Colonies, Cults, and Evolution: Literature, Science, and Culture in Nineteenth-Century Writing*. New York: Cambridge University Press, 2007. Amigoni's analysis of *Father and Son* and other works of nineteenth century literature demonstrates how these works were influenced by the evolutionary writings of Charles Darwin and other scientists.

Mattheisen, Paul F., and Michael Millgate, eds. *Transalantic Dialogue: Selected American Correspondence of Edmund Gosse*. Austin: University of Texas Press, 1965. The introduction gives insight into Gosse's relationship with American writers. Contains assorted references to *Father and Son*, including America's favorable response. Includes an extensive index with almost seven pages of autobiographical references.

O'Gorman, Francis. "Romance and Victorian Autobiography: Margaret Oliphant, Edmund Gosse, and John Ruskin's 'Needle to the North.'" In *A Companion to Romance: From Classical to Contemporary*, edited by Corinne Saunders. Malden, Mass.: Blackwell, 2004. This history of romance literature includes an analysis of the influence of this genre on *Father and Son*.

Porter, Roger J. "Conflict and Incorporation: Edmund Gosse's *Father and Son*." In *Self-Same Songs: Autobiographical Performances and Reflections*. Lincoln: University of Nebraska Press, 2002. Examines a range of autobiographical literature, including *Father and Son*, analyzing the various techniques used to create these books and the authors' motivations for writing them. Porter demonstrates how writing an autobiography allows authors not only to discover their self-identities but also to change their lives.

Thwaite, Ann. *Edmund Gosse: A Literary Landscape, 1849-1928*. 1984. Reprint. Stroud, England: Tempest, 2007. Provides a balanced study of the pros and cons of Gosse's life and work. Thwaite began the work to discover what happened after Gosse's twenty-first year, when *Father and Son* ended. She covers Churton Collins's notorious attacks on Gosse's literary criticism, and she emphasizes Gosse's far-reaching influence in England.

Woolf, James D. *Sir Edmund Gosse*. New York: Twayne, 1972. An introductory overview of Gosse, providing an array of Gosse's criticism. Emphasizes Gosse's views on Christianity relative to his religious focus in the early part of *Father and Son*. Provides extensive editorial notes to the text.

The Fathers

Author: Allen Tate (1899-1979)
First published: 1938
Type of work: Novel
Type of plot: Historical realism
Time of plot: 1860-1861
Locale: Virginia; Georgetown, Washington, D.C.

Principal characters:
LACY GORE BUCHAN, the narrator
MAJOR LEWIS BUCHAN, his father
SEMMES BUCHAN, Lacy's older brother, killed by George Posey
SUSAN BUCHAN POSEY, Lacy's sister
GEORGE POSEY, Lacy's brother-in-law
JANE POSEY, George's sister, who is loved by Lacy and Semmes
JOHN LANGTON, George's rival
YELLOW JIM, George's mulatto half brother, a slave George sells to buy a horse

The Story:

Lacy Buchan, a sixty-year-old bachelor, thinks back over the year 1860, when he was fifteen and his mother died. That April, family and friends gathered at Pleasant Hill in Fairfax County, Virginia, for the funeral, the last time they were all together. Among those present were the Poseys, Lacy's sister Susan's in-laws. Susan's husband, George Posey, rode his horse away from the funeral, causing much gossip.

Young Lacy recalled memories of George, his brother Semmes's friend. During a visit two years before, George gave Lacy a gun. The next day, Lacy went to a jousting tournament and stayed with his father's slave, Coriolanus, who talked to some slaves who had just been sold. One was called Yellow Jim; George sold him and bought a mare.

Riders in the tournament had five tries to take rings from hooks with lances. George and John Langton succeeded each time, and George was awarded the prize for his superior form. When the drunken Langton protested, George threw him to the ground. The victor shared his reward with Lacy's sister, Susan. Langton challenged George to a duel; George shot at a target, then discarded his pistol and punched Langton. Lacy admired his new friend very much.

At the funeral, Lacy's sister-in-law Lucy gave Lacy violets to put in his mother's hands. As he moved from the coffin, Jane, George's sister, took his hand. They left the room, and Lacy kissed Jane. Afterward, Lacy held a garment belonging to his mother and thought of Jane and of his mother at the same time.

After marrying Susan, George began managing the Buchans' business affairs. Once he sold a family of slaves that Major Buchan had asked him to free, applying the money to one of the major's debts. George was a practical man, not a principled one like Major Buchan.

During the winter of 1860-1861, the Buchans stayed in Alexandria at the home of Lacy's cousin, John Semmes, who went to Washington. Lacy's brother, Charles, and his sister-in-law, Lucy, moved in with the Buchan family. South Carolina seceded from the Union, and other Southern states followed. Lacy's father was a Unionist, but his cousin John favored secession. The Buchans discussed civilly which side they would take in the war, but could not agree. Charles, who was in the United States Army, drilled with the National Rifles, from which the Unionists withdrew. George supplied the company with firearms. Charles resigned his commission with the U.S. Army because he knew Abraham Lincoln would send troops to South Carolina. George told Major Buchan that he sympathized with Unionists, but his loyalty was with Virginia; Colonel Robert E. Lee made the same decision several days later. Langton became captain of the National Rifles.

Lacy went to stay with the Poseys in Georgetown because his sister sent for him. Her husband, George, was often mysteriously away. In the Posey household were Susan and her daughter, little Jane; George's sister Jane; and Jane and George's mother, uncle, and aunt. Each resident lived in seclusion, and only Susan, Jane, and Lacy dined together.

Northern soldiers kept Washington, D.C., under martial law, and John Semmes was arrested for secessionist activity. When Lacy's brother Semmes became a Confederate, Major Buchan disclaimed the young man.

One night, Lacy heard a noise and went downstairs. The slave Blind Joe (who was not really blind) took him to Yellow Jim, who explained that he ran away and came home. No one was there to send him back to his new owner, so Jim resumed his duties as butler. Jim, who was also George and Jane's half brother, had been Jane's caretaker, but during his three years away, she grew up and did not need him anymore. In fact, she feared him. Lacy understood her fear, having once seen Jim beat a horse who bit him—the very mare George sold him to buy.

Lacy's brother Semmes proposed to Jane, whom Lacy loved. When Semmes asked Lacy if he loved Jane, Lacy lied. The night after Semmes proposed to Jane, he left. Lacy heard a scream, then a door slam. He ran upstairs and found Jim crouching in the hall. Susan came from the mother's room and said that the woman died of fright. Susan and Lacy deduced that the scream had come from Jane, whom they discovered supine on her bedroom floor. They inferred that Jim raped Jane. Lacy locked him in the basement and sent Blind Joe for George.

The next day, nuns took Jane to a convent. Susan, whose hair turned white overnight, begged Jim to run away, but he refused. Semmes and George returned and took Jim out to the river; Lacy accompanied them. To avenge Jane, Semmes shot Jim; in reflex, George shot Semmes. Lacy ran ten miles back to the city. He saw that the Confederate flag was no longer flying over Arlington, and Union soldiers told him that the first fatalities of the war had occurred. Lacy, exhausted, headed toward home. By the time he got there, he was ill and delirious. After six weeks, he recovered to learn that his father knew the whole story. The major forbade him to avenge Semmes's death and accepted some blame for the incident, feeling that he injured Semmes's pride by denying him.

Lacy's sister, Susan, went mad and came home. George came to get her, but she did not seem to recognize him. George donned a Confederate uniform, and he and Lacy left to find General Longstreet's brigade.

They later learned that Union soldiers came to Pleasant Hill and told Major Buchan to get out. He did not tell them that he was a Unionist; instead, he hanged himself. The soldiers burned the house to the ground. Lacy became a Confederate soldier.

Critical Evaluation:

Allen Tate had the misfortune to have *The Fathers* published two years after Margaret Mitchell's *Gone with the Wind* (1936) appeared, with the result that his novel soon became a dinghy bobbing in the wake of Mitchell's overwhelming popular success. The reappearance of Tate's book in a slightly revised version twenty-two years later was an event of considerable importance. *The Fathers*, as *Gone with the Wind* does not, provides an occasion for defining the idea of the South and for critical reflection on the moral significance Tate was able to extract from his social scene and his

historical perspective. That the novel failed to evoke any such critical response is shown by the reviews written at the time.

Reading these reviews is an illuminating experience, as much for what they do not say as for what they do. The critics were, on the whole, sympathetic toward the book and generous in their comments, but one takes away the impression that many had not read it carefully and almost none understood the writer's intention. Many readers saw it only as a moving story of one family's tragic collapse during the Civil War; certainly this reading testifies to the richness of the narrative if to nothing else. Others thought that Tate was dramatizing within a family unit the fatal clash of two social orders—that of the traditional society of the South, symbolized by Major Buchan, and that of the industrial society of the North, represented by George Posey, the major's son-in-law. This conflict was viewed in all its dramatic tensions and implications, but with a feeling on the part of the reviewers that Tate had failed to prove the superiority of the Buchans' ancestral code over George's antitraditional conduct. It is possible to read *The Fathers* in this way, as one can read much of William Faulkner's works in a similar fashion, but to do so is to miss the point, so to speak, of a novel remarkable for its realistic detail, thematic extensions of symbolic reference, moral intensity, and passionate historical sense.

The Fathers presents a philosophical view of society and history within a framework of particular events. It is only natural that these events should center upon the Civil War, for to the Southern writer concerned with the life or culture of his region, the war is central. It is no longer enough to know what happened in that conflict; it is also necessary to know what the conflict meant. For this purpose, the Civil War provides a vast controlling image that gives meaning to the facts of the regional experience, not only to the structure of Southern society but also to the code of morality on which it was based.

Before *The Fathers* appeared, Tate had already defined his position on the South in a series of essays written between 1930 and 1936. In one of these, "Religion and the Old South," he outlines his theory of history in terms of the long view and the short view. Within the perspective of the latter, all history reduces to a variety and confusion of images out of which it is possible for readers to make choices in reconstructing the scene or the period. The long view sees history as idea or concept, not as an account of the particular lives of particular people in a setting that often bewildered them, but as a record of events without accident, contingency, or personal involvement. Tate's own choice between these two ways of historical vision and thinking is as apparent in his fiction as in his poetry. The reviewers who found no real meaning in his novel were looking at history as an abstract concept of principles and causes. *The Fathers* incorporates the short view.

The novel is spacious in outline, as any work must be that attempts to contain within its limits the picture of a whole society. It is beautifully selective in attention to the detail with which people and places are described, habits of speech and manners are recorded, and the impressions made by events upon the mind of the narrator are carefully noted. Tate achieves his organizational effect, the configuration of theme and structure, by his skillful management of a special point of view. The person telling the story is Lacy Buchan, who as an old man is looking back on events that had happened almost a half century before. As a story retrieved in memory, the novel moves simultaneously on two levels: one, the plane of action conveying with all immediacy the impact of events upon the consciousness of a young boy whose reactions to experience are direct and sensuous; the other, the plane of reflection on which the man, now old, looks back on those happenings and contemplates meanings unperceived at the time of his boyhood. The ease with which Tate moves from past to present and back, setting up a relevant interplay between some event and its significance in retrospect, all the while causing the narrative to expand, its values to join and grow into one another, becomes one of the major triumphs of the novel. What is presented is a deep concern with historical processes and moral issues, but it is all done simply, without resort to the self-conscious or the portentous in association or image. The older Lacy reflects that only in memory and symbol can knowledge of the past be preserved, never in the feelings of the time.

Through all of Lacy Buchan's reflections runs the question of evil; problems of sin, responsibility, and guilt remain shadowy and unresolved. He wonders why life cannot change without entangling many lives; why the innocent, for example, lose their innocence and become violent or evil, thus causing change. He reflects that as people need to recognize the innate aspect of evil in human nature, there is also need to face that evil.

The image at the center of *The Fathers* is the family, the social unit that, with all its widespread connections of kinship, was the foundation of Southern society. The story tells how the Buchan family of Fairfax County, Virginia, is weakened and disrupted by the fierce energies of George, the son-in-law for whom all life—because he cannot recognize, or submit to, the authority that tradition imposes—becomes impulse and motion. In later years, Lacy always thinks of him as a horseman galloping over an abyss, a man of courage and generosity and charm, but doomed because his reckless and irresponsible deeds menaced himself as well as family unity and social order.

Lacy reflects that the Poseys possessed more refinement than the Buchans but were less civilized. This difference is emphasized at the beginning of the novel when Major Buchan, at the time of his wife's funeral, plays the role of the gracious host and not the bereaved husband; he is merely upholding the accepted code of good manners. In much the same way, he leaves his place in his wife's funeral procession to take the hand of Mrs. Buchan's black maid and draw her, immediately behind the coffin, into the line of mourners. George, on the other hand, orders his horse saddled and rides away, unable to face the idea of death. Another trait that he displays is a heartless disregard for others, as when he sells his mulatto half brother in order to buy a blood mare, an act that involves the Buchans and Poseys in a family catastrophe even more devastating than the disunion caused by the Civil War. Before the end of the novel, he has destroyed the Buchans' agrarian economy, killed his brother-in-law Semmes, driven his wife mad, brought about his sister's ruin, and caused his father-in-law's death.

It is important to note that George is neither a villain by nature nor a symbol of Northern capitalism assaulting Southern tradition. He stands for that element in Southern life that was wild and undisciplined from the beginning, just as Semmes Buchan's weakness and John Langton's violence were a part of the tradition as well. In Tate's view, apparently, the old order was already corrupted from within before the Civil War destroyed it from without. (This is Faulkner's belief as well.) Whether that way of life truly satisfied the needs of those who created it is a matter of relative unimportance. What is important is the fact that the traditional order established sanctions and defined virtues and obligations by which, for a time, people could assume social and moral responsibilities; it set up a concept of truth that made the human effort seem worthwhile. Major Buchan recognizes these sanctions and obligations and acts accordingly, but George does not; therefore, he corrupts or destroys all who come in contact with him.

This is the meaning of the episode in which Lacy, semi-delirious with fever, imagines that he and his dead grandfather are sitting on a pile of fence rails while the old man retells the myth of Jason and Medea. The scene is poetically conceived and morally instructive. Jason's fate, the old man says, was to secure the Golden Fleece or attempt some impossible feat, at the same time becoming involved with the humanity of others whom, in the end, he betrayed not through his intention but through his nature. The old man says that George never really intends to commit evil; his flaw is the lack of will to do good. Thus the only future possible for him is loneliness and the grave.

The Fathers is a novel in which the private life of the family and the public life of action converge upon a decisive moment in history, the outbreak of the Civil War. Its importance as fiction is its power to illuminate, through realistic detail and symbolic extension, the meaning of the past and the shape of the future.

"Critical Evaluation" by M. Katherine Grimes

Further Reading

Benson, Melanie. "The Fetish of Surplus Value: Reconstructing the White Elite in Allen Tate, William Alexander Percy, William Faulkner, and Thomas Wolfe." In *Disturbing Calculations: The Economics of Identity in Postcolonial Southern Literature, 1912-2002*. Athens: University of Georgia Press, 2008. Argues that mathematical calculations play a major role in twentieth century southern literature, demonstrating how writers use numbers to determine individual worth and identity, and social and racial classifications. The chapter about Tate includes discussion of *The Father*.

Carpenter, Lynette. "The Battle Within: The Beleaguered Consciousness in Allen Tate's *The Fathers*." *Southern Literary Journal* 8, no. 2 (Spring, 1976): 3-23. Argues that Lacy Buchan is the central character in Tate's novel, and that his confused narration is representative of the book's theme: the ambiguity of experience and memory.

Holman, C. Hugh. "*The Fathers* and the Historical Imagination." In *Literary Romanticism in America*, edited by William L. Andrews. Baton Rouge: Louisiana State University Press, 1981. Provides a useful review of earlier criticism of *The Fathers*. Discusses the work as a bildungsroman that examines a family's events through a historical viewpoint.

Law, Richard. "'Active Faith' and Ritual in *The Fathers*." *American Literature* 55 (October, 1983): 345-366. Posits that part of the novel's greatness lies in its questioning its own thesis: the value of tradition and community. Asserts that it is not a tract, although it represents Agrarianism.

Montgomery, Marion. *John Crowe Ransom and Allen Tate: At Odds About the Ends of History and the Mystery of Nature*. Jefferson, N.C.: McFarland, 2003. Tate and Ransom were members of the Fugitives, a literary group organized at Vanderbilt University in the 1920's; the two later became southern poets with different philosophies. Montgomery examines their Fugitive-Agrarian concepts of nature, history, science, industry, personhood, family, and community.

Underwood, Thomas A. *Allen Tate: Orphan of the South*. Princeton, N.J.: Princeton University Press, 2000. Biography recounting Tate's difficult childhood, in which his parents burdened him with the myth of the embattled South, and the later conflict between his artistic vocation and his reactionary politics. Describes how he eventually attained the self-knowledge needed to write *The Fathers*, in which he examined the restrictions imposed by the South's cultural contradictions.

Young, Thomas Daniel. "Allen Tate's Double Focus: The Past in the Present." *Mississippi Quarterly* 30 (Fall, 1977): 517-525. Asserts that *The Fathers* shows the likelihood that the antebellum South would have destroyed itself even if the Civil War had not occurred. Quotes Tate extensively.

Fathers and Sons

Author: Ivan Turgenev (1818-1883)
First published: Ottsy i deti, 1862 (English translation, 1867)
Type of work: Novel
Type of plot: Social realism
Time of plot: 1859
Locale: Russia

Principal characters:
KIRSANOV, a Russian gentleman
PAVEL, his older brother
ARKADY, his son
FENICHKA, Kirsanov's mistress
BAZAROV, Arkady's friend
VASILY, Bazarov's father
MADAME ODINTZOV, a widow
KATYA, her younger sister

The Story:

At a provincial posting station, Kirsanov waits impatiently for his son, Arkady, who has completed his education at the university in St. Petersburg. Kirsanov reflects that Arkady probably has changed, but he hopes his son has not grown away from him entirely. Arkady's mother is dead, and the widower is strongly attached to his son.

At last the coach appears, rolling along the dusty road. Arkady jumps out, but he is not alone. Lounging superciliously behind is a stranger whom Arkady introduces as Bazarov, a fellow student. Something in Arkady's manner tells Kirsanov that here is a special attachment. In a low aside, Arkady begs his father to be gracious to his guest.

Feeling some qualms about his unexpected guest, Kirsanov is troubled during the trip home. He is hesitant about his own news but finally tells Arkady that he took a mistress, Fenichka, and installed her in his house. To his great relief, Arkady takes the news calmly and even congratulates his father on the step. Later, Arkady is pleased to learn that he even has a little half brother.

Kirsanov soon finds he has good reason to distrust Bazarov, who is a doctor and a clever biologist. Arkady seems too much under his influence. Worse, Bazarov is a nihilist. At the university the liberal thinkers consciously decided to defy or ignore all authority—state, church, home, pan-Russianism. Bazarov is irritating to talk to, Kirsanov decides, because he knows so much and has such a sarcastic tongue.

Pavel, Kirsanov's older brother, is especially irritated by Bazarov. Pavel is a real aristocrat, bound by tradition, who comes to live in retirement with his younger brother after a disappointing career as an army officer and the lover of a famous beauty, the Princess R——. With his background and stiff notions of propriety, Pavel often disagrees with Bazarov.

Luckily, Bazarov keeps busy most of the time. He collects frogs and infusoria and is always dissecting and peering into a microscope. He would be an ideal guest, except for his calmly superior air of belonging to a generation far surpassing Pavel's. Kirsanov, loving his son so much, does his best to keep peace, but all the while he regrets the nihilism that so greatly affects Arkady.

Kirsanov is harassed by other troubles. Soon, by law, the serfs will be freed. Kirsanov strongly approves of this change and anticipates the new order by dividing his farm into smaller plots that the peasants rent on a sharecropping basis. With their new independence, however, the peasants cheat him more than ever and are slow in paying their rent.

Arkady and Bazarov, growing bored with quiet farm life, go to visit in the provincial capital, where they have introduc-

tions to the governor. In town, they run into Sitnikov, a kind of polished jackal who feels important because he is one of the nihilist circle. Sitnikov introduces them into provincial society.

At a ball, the two friends meet and are greatly taken by a young widow, Madame Odintzov. Arkady does not dance, but he sits out a mazurka with her. They become friends at once, especially when she finds that Arkady's mother was an intimate friend of her own mother. After the ball, Madame Odintzov invites the two men to visit her estate.

Arkady and Bazarov accept the invitation promptly. In a few days, they settle down to the easy routine of favored guests in a wealthy household. Katya, Madame Odintzov's young sister, is especially attracted to Arkady. Bazarov, older and more worldly, becomes the good friend of the widow. Although Bazarov, as a good nihilist, despises home and family life, he makes a real effort to overcome his scruples. However, when he finally begins to talk of love and marriage to Madame Odintzov, he is politely refused. Chagrined at his rejection, he induces Arkady to leave with him at once. The two friends then go on to Bazarov's home.

Vasily, Bazarov's father, is glad to see his son, whom he both fears and admires. He and his wife do all they can to make the young men comfortable. At length Arkady and Bazarov quarrel, chiefly because they are so bored. Abruptly they leave and impulsively call again on Madame Odintzov. She receives them coolly. Feeling that they are unwelcome, they go back to the Kirsanov estate.

Because Bazarov is convinced that Arkady is also in love with Madame Odintzov, his friendship with Arkady becomes greatly strained. Arkady, thinking constantly of Katya, returns by himself to the Odintzov estate to press his suit of the younger sister. At the Kirsanov home, Bazarov becomes friendly with Fenichka. He prescribes for her sick baby and even for her. Out of friendship, Fenichka spends much of her time with Bazarov. One morning, as they sit in a garden, Bazarov kisses her unexpectedly, to her distress and confusion. Pavel witnesses the scene by accident and becomes increasingly incensed at the strange nihilist.

Although Pavel does not consider Bazarov a gentleman, he challenges him to a duel with pistols. In the encounter, Pavel is wounded in the leg, and Bazarov leaves the house in haste, never to return. Pavel recovers from his wound, but he feels a never-ending shame at being wounded by a low nihilist. He urges Kirsanov to marry Fenichka, and he returns to his old life. He spends the rest of his days as an aging dandy in Dresden.

Bazarov stops briefly at the Odintzov home. Still convinced that Arkady is in love with Madame Odintzov, he attempts to help his friend in his suit. Madame Odintzov ridicules him, however, when Arkady makes his request for the hand of Katya. With a sense of futility, Bazarov takes his leave and rejoins his own family. Vasily is the local doctor, and he eagerly welcomes his son as a colleague. For a time, Bazarov leads a successful life, helping to cure the ailments of the peasants and pursuing his research at the same time. When one of his patients contracts typhus, he accidentally scratches himself with a scalpel he used. Although Vasily cauterizes the wound as well as he can, Bazarov becomes ill with a fever. Sure that he will die, he summons Madame Odintzov to his side. She comes gladly and helps to ease him before his death.

Madame Odintzov eventually makes a good marriage with a lawyer. Arkady is happy managing his father's farm and playing with the son born to him and Katya. Kirsanov becomes a magistrate and spends most of his life settling disputes brought about by the liberation of the serfs. Fenichka, at last a respected wife and mother, finds great happiness in her daughter-in-law, Katya.

Critical Evaluation:

In *Fathers and Sons*, Ivan Turgenev attempted to examine the forces for change operating, for the most part in isolation and frustration, in mid-nineteenth century Russia. The storm of protest and outrage produced from the moment the novel appeared indicates that he had indeed touched a sensitive nerve in Russian society. In fact, Turgenev never really got over the abuse heaped upon him; his periods of exile in Germany, France, and Italy were all the more frequent and of longer duration after the publication of the novel. One wonders at the excitement occasioned by *Fathers and Sons*, for a cooler reading undertaken more than a hundred years later indicates that Turgenev clearly attempted and achieved a balanced portrait of conservative and revolutionary Russia—a triumphant achievement in political fiction, where the passions of the moment so often damage the artistic effort.

The subtlety and rightness of Turgenev's technique are most clearly seen in the central character Bazarov. Bazarov is a pragmatist, a scientist, and a revolutionary idealist. He is put into a relationship with every important character, and it is from these relationships that the reader gets to know him and to understand more about him than he understands about himself. A master of literary impressionism, Turgenev liked to do an "atmospheric" treatment of his characters, vividly rendering visual, auditory, and other sense impressions in a nicely selected setting. This technique admits all sorts of lively and contradictory details and prevents the novel—and

Bazarov—from falling into mere ideological rhetoric and political polemic. Most of all, for all of his roughness and bearishness, Turgenev really liked Bazarov and sympathized with him ("with the exception of [his] views on art, I share almost all his convictions," he wrote).

Bazarov's chief conflict is with Pavel Kirsanov, a middle-aged bachelor with refined continental tastes and a highly developed sense of honor. Pavel stands for everything Bazarov despises: an Old World emphasis upon culture, manners, and refinement, and an aristocratic and elitist view of life. He represents the traditions that Bazarov vainly struggles to destroy in his efforts to bring a democratic, scientific, and utilitarian plan of action into widespread use. For Bazarov, "a good chemist is more useful than a score of poets," because the chemist attacks the central problem of poverty, disease, and ignorance. The old humanism represented by Pavel is, for him, a manifestation of ignorance that perpetrates and countenances needless suffering, particularly for the lower classes. His rude and sneering treatment of Pavel is undercut by his participation in the duel, which is an absurd custom of the upper classes he despises. Bazarov is the loser in the duel and he knows it. His passion, which he tries to cover up with a cold, clinical attitude, leads him into it.

His relationship with Madame Odintzov shows that Bazarov is at heart a romantic, though he would hardly admit it. This cool and cultured widow provokes the most ardent response from him—despite his contention that women are mere instruments of amusement and pleasure. With Madame Odintzov, however, Bazarov has unfortunately chosen an inadequate object for his passion. She is lovely but cold and detached and is unable to respond to him.

Bazarov's romanticism, however, is chiefly frustrated in social and political matters. He deeply believes that conditions can be changed and that he and others can work together to that end. When readers look at these "others," they see how painful and tragic his situation is. Arkady, his schoolmate and friend, is a kindly fellow who imitates Bazarov's revolutionary attitudes. He is in awe of his friend's rough manner, but he does not understand that Bazarov really intends to follow his ideas to the end. Rather, Arkady is not even dimly aware at first that he is incapable of supporting Bazarov all the way. Like most men, Arkady is conventional and conforming out of natural adaptability. His marriage to Katya is a model of bourgeois comfort and serves to underline Bazarov's loneliness and ineffectuality. Like his father before him, Arkady chooses domestic satisfactions and a life of small compromises over the absurd "heroism" of his schoolfellow. The Kirsanov homestead remains, on the whole, ill-managed and unimproved. No revolution in land management has occurred even though the peasants are about to be freed. Life goes on in a muddle despite the passionate efforts of one or two enlightened persons to reform it.

Bazarov's curious and potentially violent behavior to Arkady when they are lying in a haystack suggests that he knows that Arkady cannot follow him. Furthermore, this scene reveals that Bazarov is full of violent distaste for those who pretend to be reformers. He cannot spare them ridicule, and his frustrated energies burst forth in threatening gestures. He is a leader without followers, a general without an army. Nevertheless, he loves his parents, two kindly old representatives of the traditional way of life, for they do not pretend to be anything they are not.

Bazarov's death is a form of suicide. His willingness to take no immediate steps to prevent the spread of infection after he has carelessly cut himself suggests that he has seen the absurdity of his position and, to some extent at least, given in to it. In his delirium, he states that Russia needs a cobbler, a tailor, a butcher more than she needs him. Nevertheless, for Turgenev, Bazarov was "the real hero of our time."

"Critical Evaluation" by Benjamin Nyce

Further Reading

Andrew, Joe, Derek Offord, and Robert Reid, eds. *Turgenev and Russian Culture: Essays to Honour Richard Peace.* Amsterdam: Rodopi, 2008. Some of the essays discuss the uses of poetry in Turgenev's prose, the dark side of the writer, and Turgenev and Russian culture, while others analyze individual works.

Bloom, Harold, ed. *Ivan Turgenev.* Philadelphia: Chelsea House, 2003. Collection of critical essays about Turgenev's work. Several essays discuss *Fathers and Sons,* while others compare Turgenev's works to those of Ernest Hemingway, Willa Cather, and Sherwood Anderson.

Costlow, Jane T. *Worlds Within Worlds: The Novels of Ivan Turgenev.* Princeton, N.J.: Princeton University Press, 1990. Argues that Turgenev's fourth novel focuses on the structures of human lives, especially on the sense of place. Maintains that *Fathers and Sons* is also an ideological work dealing with the years before the 1861 emancipation of the Russian serfs; Turgenev's social resolve is bolstered by his psychological perceptions.

Dessaix, Robert. *Twilight of Love: Travels with Turgenev.* London: Scribner, 2005. Dessaix, an Australian writer and a scholar of Russian literature, traveled to Turgenev's homes and conducted research at the Moscow Library to locate the "soul" of the Russian writer. The resulting memoir provides insights into Turgenev's life, particularly the writer's experience of love.

Freeborn, Richard. *Turgenev: The Novelist's Novelist.* New York: Oxford University Press, 1960. Chapter 5, "Four Great Novels," explores how Turgenev assimilated the short story form into the novel. The figure of the hero unifies the novel and establishes the tradition of organic form in Russian literature.

Knowles, A. V. *Ivan Turgenev.* Boston: Twayne, 1988. Argues that *Fathers and Sons* reflects Turgenev's keen interest in politics and his abhorrence of violence. Studies the time frame and construction of this novel, emphasizing its logical progress and sense of inevitability. Explores character development and theme.

Lowe, David A., ed. *Critical Essays on Ivan Turgenev.* Boston: G. K. Hall, 1989. Lowe's "Comedy and Tragedy in *Fathers and Sons*" suggests the novel's structure is determined by a sequence of trips and a set of confrontations that contribute to its dualism—two parallel but contrasting patterns of tragedy and comedy. Some discussion of other critical readings of the novel are included.

Orwin, Donna Tussing. *Consequences of Consciousness: Turgenev, Dostoevsky, and Tolstoy.* Stanford, Calif.: Stanford University Press, 2007. A psychological analysis of the work of Turgenev and two other great Russian realist novelists, examining how these writers depicted their characters' subjectivity. The references to *Fathers and Sons* are listed in the index.

Ripp, Victor. *Turgenev's Russia: From "Notes of a Hunter" to "Fathers and Sons."* Ithaca, N.Y.: Cornell University Press, 1980. Discusses the novel in light of the Emancipation Act, the contemporary reaction to Turgenev's treatment of his hero, and his impact on his successors. Maintains that Bazarov absorbs politics into psychology, and that the novel develops the theme of a home away from the corrupt world.

Valentino, Russell Scott. *Vicissitudes of Genre in the Russian Novel: Turgenev's "Fathers and Sons," Chernyshevsky's "What Is to Be Done?," Dostoevsky's "Demons," Gorky's "Mother."* New York: Peter Lang, 2001. Compares Turgenev's use of characterization and gender in *Fathers and Sons* with works of other Russian novelists.

Faultline

Author: Sheila Ortiz Taylor (1939-   )
First published: 1982
Type of work: Novel
Type of plot: Social realism
Time of plot: 1980's
Locale: Los Angeles

Principal characters:
ARDEN BENBOW, a mother of six
VIOLET GROOT, Arden's high-spirited Aunt Vi
WHITNEY MALTHUS, Arden's former husband
WILSON TOPAZ, a gay man who moves in with Arden and
    Alice as a babysitter for the children
ALICE WICKS, Arden's lover who lives with her

The Story:

Arden Benbow is caught releasing domestic rabbits into a wilderness area outside Los Angeles. She says that owning three hundred rabbits makes her look eccentric. She received a pair of rabbits that multiplied rapidly, so she decided to set them free.

Arden was born on the San Andreas Fault in Southern California, and she says that the minor earthquakes she experienced as a child developed her maternal instincts and made her determined to have a large family to counteract her fears of extinction. Arden tells the story of her life as an explanation of her present, and other people give their views of her suitability as a mother.

Arden was an English major in college, and, after her graduation in 1959, she met Whitney Malthus, whom everyone called Malthus. He looked like the actor William Holden and liked to talk about science and how everything worked. Arden was married to him for twelve years, during which time they had six children. She came to see Malthus as dull, egotistical, and unfair to women. Malthus gives his view that Arden humiliated him by becoming a lesbian. The mother of his children should not behave in such a way. Mothers should uphold the social standards; lesbians, Malthus believes, are social deviants. He claims that he should have custody of their children.

Ben Griffin gave Arden the original pair of rabbits and sold her feed for them. He says Arden is a smart woman who pays her bills, and that she deserves to raise her children. A man who works with Malthus says that Malthus treated Arden badly when she fell in love with a woman. A neighbor, Jim Muncey, likes Arden and says she is a dependable person. A receptionist at a veterinarian's office says she got a crank call from a lady asking about birth control for rabbits, so she hung up the phone.

Wilson Topaz identifies himself as a dancer who cannot get many dancing jobs because he is six feet tall, black, and gay. He saw the advertisement to work as a babysitter for a lesbian mother, met Arden and her lover, Alice, and the chil-

dren, and decided to join their energetic and happy household. He became part of Operation Bunnylift and was there when the police arrived just as the last of the rabbits disappeared into the wilderness.

The assistant registrar at Arden's college gives a negative character reference, complaining that Arden changed her surname from Malthus to Benbow, her grandmother's name, and further annoyed him because she hired Wilson, whom the assistant registrar considered a problem when Wilson was a student. The assistant registrar claims that none of this has to do with homosexuality or race.

Comments are made that Arden abducted her aunt, Violet Groot, from a hospital in 1959. Aunt Vi's oppressive husband had placed her there. Aunt Vi arranged a trip to Mexico with the help of an orderly, Maurio Carbonara. His real name was Homer Rice, but Aunt Vi fired his imagination and said he needed a better name. They escaped the institution one night and traveled with Arden in a blue van through Mexico, spending most of their time at Ruby's campground and trailer park. Ruby previously had worked as a stripper in a bar in San Francisco and then moved to Mexico to create and run the campground. She liked the trio of visitors and was energized and rejuvenated by Vi and her laughing ways.

Vi's husband hired a detective, Michael Raven, to find his missing wife. Vi decided to let him find and follow her, and Michael became enchanted with the lively group. They continued vacationing in Mexico together, and Michael fell in love with Maurio. Aunt Vi was delighted with their happiness, and as they celebrated with a party, another private investigator showed up, saying Mr. Groot had hired him to find them. Aunt Vi died that night. She enjoyed the last weeks of her life and nearly finished writing a gothic romance novel. Arden wrote the last few pages, pondering Aunt Vi's belief that life may end in marriage but never in death. The book became a best seller; Mr. Groot made all the money. Arden had married Malthus because he was persistent, but she came to understand her aunt's statement that marriages can be stifling, killing the spirit in a way that death does not.

A dozen years later, after Arden and Malthus had divorced, Allison Honey speaks up for Arden, saying that Arden fixed her car for her and found her a job at the catering service Maurio and Michael started in San Francisco. Alice Wicks explains that she met Arden three years earlier. She too was married. They became friends, fell in love, and started living together permanently. Malthus had hired a detective to spy on Arden, and started the child custody dispute. Winnifred Hooper, a social worker, had to be convinced that Arden is a fit mother. Winnifred was prepared to dislike her. Arden remembered Aunt Vi's way of taking in the enemy, and she made friends with her.

Ruby is invited to a big party Arden planned, and she is excited about seeing Arden and Maurio and Michael again. She goes to San Francisco to visit her old bar and then on to Los Angeles for the party, which turns out to be a double wedding ceremony: Arden and Alice, Michael and Mario. It is also a celebration of the thirteenth anniversary of Vi's death, and of the happy conclusion of the custody trial. Arden also invited Jim Muncey; she learns that Jim was engaged to Winnifred but that she ran off with another man. The man is gone now, and Jim wants Winnifred back. Arden makes it clear to Winnifred that she knows something of her past, but rather than blackmail her, she wins her over with happy domesticity. Winnifred agrees to preside at the "weddings" as well as to support Arden's right to child custody. Jim is happy to see Winnifred, and she is happy to see him.

Critical Evaluation:

Faultline is a comic novel with a serious message conveyed by example and implication rather than by preaching. Sheila Ortiz Taylor creates a shining cast of characters who speak about their relationships to Arden Benbow as Arden battles her former husband Malthus for custody of their six children. Malthus has never considered women equal to men, and his male ego is hurt when Arden prefers living with a woman to staying with him in their dull marriage. He provides the prime example of a person who cannot accept individual differences or see that others have a right to their own lives.

The theme of acceptance of individual differences runs throughout the novel. Malthus is a repeat of Arden's uncle, Mr. Groot, who tries to control his wife in every way. Aunt Vi, however, will not be stifled. She is full of energy and believes that life should be fun and joyful. Mr. Groot has a mistress, and he immediately puts Vi in a hospital when she has a mild stroke. Aunt Vi refuses to end her days in the confining

institution. She breaks free and takes Arden to Mexico with her, as much for Arden's sake as for her own.

Arden, however, falls into the same marriage trap her aunt did. For example, Malthus refuses to let her go to graduate school; his wife should stay home with the children. It is not until she and Alice Wicks fall in love that Arden can see what her aunt meant about freeing oneself to live fully and to develop the creative spirit within oneself. Alice too had married because that is what society expected of her, but she learns that she must be herself and follow her own spirit.

The "faultline" of the title refers to the actual geography of the setting in Southern California, but it is also a metaphor for unpredictability and the need for adaptability and acceptance of reality. One chapter is conveyed through the words of a professor of geophysics who specializes in plate tectonics, the study of the faultlines where earthquakes happen. "Earthquakes remind us," he says. They are dynamic reactions to changes in the earth's crust that remind people of their mortality and the need to live with enthusiasm. People should not waste their time being prejudiced against others who have their own lives to live. Although he is a scientist, the professor knows—as Malthus does not—that there is more to life than "facts."

The theme of celebrating differences instead of controlling others is shown throughout the novel by characterization. Aunt Vi and Wilson Topaz, for example, have learned to make the most of life despite people who would deny them social opportunities and human rights. Arden and Alice become finer people when they acknowledge their love for each other instead of suffering in socially approved but oppressive marriages. Michael Raven and Maurio Carbonara celebrate their love instead of being dragged down by hostile societal attitudes and proscriptions against gay love.

These characters all open their hearts to others and accept them and the changes that occur throughout the years. The characters who are rigid and domineering are shown to be unhappy, whatever material wealth they may have. Malthus will not accept Arden's love for a woman, and thus turns his own children against him; they do not want to live with an angry and spiteful father who does not even provide his share of child support. Mr. Groot made money from his late wife's novel, but he never shared Aunt Vi's vitality and sense of play. The pretentious and self-important assistant registrar from the college who speaks against Arden is revealed as a sour, unhappy man with no sense of humor and no love for anyone but himself. He cannot accept Arden as a lesbian or Wilson as an African American gay man; he lives in a prison that cuts him off from reality and from the acceptance of difference.

Faultline emphasizes the need for people to celebrate life rather than to oppress others. Arden is, after all, not only a fit mother, but an outstanding one who brings to her children and to all around her a sense of fairness and decency and, especially, a joy in living and loving.

Lois A. Marchino

Further Reading

Aldama, Frederick Luis. "Ana Castillo's and Sheila Ortiz Taylor's Bent Chicana Textualities." In *Brown on Brown: Chicano/a Representations of Gender, Sexuality, and Ethnicity.* Austin: University of Texas Press, 2005. Examines works by the two Chicana writers, focusing on their depiction of ethnic and sexual issues.

Bann, Stephen. "Plots." *London Review of Books*, November 17, 1982. Considers *Faultline* a picaresque novel with an improbable plot. The satire is carefully calculated as part of an almost didactic tone of advocacy. The faultline promises eventual chaos and the rabbits suggest a family run wild, but Arden shows a new type of family in which various people live together happily in a kind of modulated chaos.

Christian, Karen. "Invisible Chicanos: Gay and Lesbian Identities in the Fiction of Sheila Ortiz Taylor and John Rechy." In *Show and Tell: Identity as Performance in U.S. Latina/o Fiction.* Albuquerque: University of New Mexico Press, 1997. Analyzes how depictions of homosexuality in *Faultline* and other works by Taylor highlight the multifaceted and changing character of identity.

Faust

Author: Johann Wolfgang von Goethe (1749-1832)
First produced: 1829-1854; includes *Faust: Eine Tragödie,* 1829 (first published, 1808; *The Tragedy of Faust,* 1823); *Faust: Eine Tragödie, zweiter Teil,* 1854 (first published, 1833; *The Tragedy of Faust, Part Two,* 1838)
First published: Faust: Ein Fragment, 1790 (English translation, *Faust: A Fragment,* 1980)
Type of work: Drama
Type of plot: Philosophical
Time of plot: Indeterminate
Locale: The world

Principal characters:
FAUST, a student of all knowledge
GRETCHEN, a young woman
MEPHISTOPHELES, the devil
WAGNER, Faust's servant
HELEN OF TROY
HOMUNCULUS, a spirit

The Story:

While three archangels sing in praise of God's lofty works, Mephistopheles appears and says that he thinks conditions on earth to be bad. The Lord tacitly agrees that human beings have their weaknesses but points out that His servant Faust cannot be swayed from the path of righteousness. Mephistopheles makes a wager with the Lord that Faust can be tempted from his faithful service. The Lord is convinced that he can rely on the righteous integrity of Faust, but he knows that Mephistopheles can lead Faust downward if he is able to lay hold of Faust's soul. Mephistopheles considers Faust a likely victim because Faust is trying to obtain the unobtainable.

Faust is not satisfied with all the knowledge he acquires. He realizes the limits of human knowledge and sees his own insignificance in the great macrocosm. In this mood, he goes for a walk with his servant, Wagner, among people who are not troubled by thoughts of a philosophical nature. Faust finds this atmosphere refreshing, and he is able to feel free and to think clearly. Faust tells Wagner of his two souls, one clinging to earthly things, the other striving toward suprasensual things that can never be attained as long as his soul resides in his body. Limited in his daily life and desiring to learn the meaning of existence, Faust is ready to accept anything that offers him a new kind of life.

Mephistopheles recognizes that Faust is vulnerable to attack. In the form of a dog, Mephistopheles follows Faust when the scholar returns home. After studying the Bible, Faust concludes that human ability should be used to produce something useful. Witnessing Faust's struggle with his ideas, Mephistopheles steps forth in his true identity, but Faust remains unmoved by the arguments of his tempter.

The next time Mephistopheles comes, he finds Faust much more receptive. Faust decides that, although his struggles are divine, he produces nothing to show for them. Faust is interested in life on this earth. At Mephistopheles' suggestion that he can enjoy a sensual existence, Faust declares that if ever he could steep himself in sloth and be at peace with himself, or if ever Mephistopheles could so rule him with flattery that he becomes self-satisfied, then that should be his end. Because Faust renounces all things that make life worthwhile to most people, he further contracts with Mephistopheles that if ever he finds experience so profound that he wishes it to endure, then he would cease to be. This is to be a wager, not the selling of a soul.

Mephistopheles fails to tempt Faust in two trials of debauchery. The next offering he presents is love for a woman. He brings Faust to the Witch's Kitchen, where his youth is restored. Then a pure maiden, Gretchen, is presented to him, but when he sees her in her innocent home, he vows not to harm her. When, however, Mephistopheles woos the girl with caskets of jewels that she thinks come from Faust, Faust is tempted to return to Gretchen. She surrenders herself to him in fulfillment of her pure love.

Gretchen's brother convinces her that her behavior is shameful in the eyes of society. Troubled by her grief, Faust kills her brother, whereupon Gretchen at last feels the full burden of her sin. Mephistopheles shows Faust more scenes of debauchery, but Faust's spirit is elevated by contact with Gretchen and he is able to overcome the devil's evil influence. Mephistopheles hopes that Faust will desire the moment of his fulfillment of love to endure, but Faust knows that enduring human love cannot satisfy his craving. He regrets Gretchen's misery and returns to her, but she kills their child and does not let her lover save her from the death to which she is condemned.

Mephistopheles brings Faust to the emperor, who asks Faust to show him the most beautiful man and woman who ever existed—Paris and Helen of Troy. Faust produces the images of these mythological characters; at the sight of Helen, his desire to possess her is so strong that he faints, and during his swoon Mephistopheles, unable to comprehend Faust's desire for the ideal beauty that Helen represents, brings him back to his own laboratory.

With the help of Wagner, Mephistopheles creates a formless spirit of learning, Homunculus, who can see what is going on in Faust's mind. Homunculus, Mephistopheles, and Faust go to Greece, where Mephistopheles borrows from the fantastic images of classical mythology one of their grotesque forms. With Mephistopheles' intervention, a living Helen is brought to Faust. It seems to Mephistopheles that now, with the supreme joy of having attained Helen's beauty, Faust will ask for the moment to endure. Faust realizes, however, that the enjoyment of transient beauty is no more satisfying than his other experiences were.

Faust returns to his native land with a new understanding of himself. Achievement now becomes his goal, as he reaffirms his earlier pledge that his power should be used to produce something useful. He acquires a large strip of swamp land and restores it to productivity.

Many years pass. Now old and blind, Faust realizes he created a vast territory of land occupied by people who will always be active in making something useful for themselves. Having participated in this achievement, Faust beholds himself standing among free and active people as one of them. At the moment he realizes what he created, he cries out, wishing that fair moment to remain. Faust realizes that life can be worth living, but in that moment of perception he loses his wager to Mephistopheles. The devil claims Faust's soul, but in reality he, too, loses the wager. God is right. Although Faust makes mistakes in his life, he always remains aware of goodness and truth.

Seeing his own defeat, Mephistopheles attempts to prevent the ascension of Faust's soul to God. Angels appear to help Faust, however, and he is carried to a place in heaven where all is active creation—exactly the kind of afterlife that Faust would have chosen.

Critical Evaluation:

Faust, Johann Wolfgang von Goethe's masterwork of dramatic poetry, summarizes his entire career, stretching from the passionate storm and stress of his youth through the classical phase of his middle years to his mature, philosophical style. Composition of the work occupied him from the time of his first works in the 1770's until his death in 1832, and each of its various sections reveals new interests and preoccupations as well as different stylistic approaches. Nevertheless, the work possesses a unity that testifies to the continuing centrality of the Faust subject in Goethe's mind.

The first scenes that were composed, those of Faust in his study and of Gretchen, reflect the twenty-three-year-old Goethe still preoccupied with university parodies based on his student experiences but at the same time increasingly interested in titanic projects. In his desire to pursue knowledge and surpass previous limitations, he was typical of other young writers of this period. In fact, *Faust* was originally one of a planned series of dramas about heroic figures who transgress society's rules—among them Julius Caesar, Prometheus, and Götz von Berlichingen.

Goethe stresses the tragedy of the scholar whose emotional life is not fulfilled and who seeks for limitless knowledge, only to find himself frustrated by mortal limitations. The scenes with Gretchen provide emotional release but leave Faust with a sense of guilt for the destruction of purity. The theme of the unwed mother, a popular one among young poets of this period, represents a revolt against traditional bourgeois values, giving occasion for much social criticism. In the Gretchen scenes, Goethe, who as a student had romances with young village women, evokes great sympathy for Gretchen, who acts always out of sincere emotion and desires only the good. His theme of the corruption of all human questing, because of the inherent imperfections of human knowledge and of will, receives here its first expression, though with no philosophical elaboration. Neither Faust nor Gretchen wills evil, yet evil comes by way of Mephistopheles. The devil, in every utterance the cynic opposed to Faust's idealistic hopes, exposes the coarse reality that in his view is the sole aspect of human life on earth.

Faust was first published in 1790 as a compilation of fragments that dated back to the 1770's. Between 1797 and 1806, with Friedrich Schiller's encouragement, Goethe returned to the work and created the prologue in heaven and the pact with Mephistopheles, both of which are crucial to the philosophical aspect of the work. Mephistopheles, no longer the absolute opponent of God, is included in the divine framework; he is a necessary force in creation, a gadfly. The action in the work now becomes a wager between God and Mephistopheles, which God must win. The old blood contract between Faust and Mephistopheles is converted into a wager: Mephistopheles must make Faust deny his very nature by giving up his quest for ever higher satisfactions in a moment of absolute fulfillment. Damnation, for Goethe, is the cessation of human striving toward the absolute, and this striving is good, no matter what mistakes human beings make in their limited understanding. He makes this clear in the prologue: God recognizes that human beings will err as long as they strive, but He states that only by seeking after the absolute, however confusedly, can they fulfill their nature. Mephistopheles sees only the confusion and futility of the results as well as the coarseness of human life. He is blind to the visionary, poetic quality of Faust that animates his quest. This relationship, established in the first part, continues until the end of the play. In each episode, Faust begins with an idealistic vision of what he seeks, but he never attains it. Seen externally, Mephistopheles is always right—it is internally that Faust's quest has meaning.

In the original Faust story, Faust meets Helen of Troy, an episode that occupied Goethe in the period of his fascination with the classical world. The third act of part 2 is the union of Faust, the northern, modern, Romantic quester, with Helen, who represents classical harmony and ideal beauty. In this act, Goethe, after imitating the style of Greek tragedy, brings Faust and Helen together in an idyllic realm of fantasy filled with music. This music—Goethe actually wanted an operatic interlude—underlines the purely aesthetic nature of the experience. Helen cannot be the end of Faust's seeking; their relationship can exist only in the mythical Arcadia, where reality, symbolized perhaps by Helen's husband, Menelaus, cannot intrude. The act was subtitled "Classic-Romantic Phantasmagoria," and Goethe followed it immediately with a scene in which Faust sees visions of both Helen and Gretchen and is drawn toward the latter in spite of Helen's ideal perfection. Gretchen, however tragic, is real.

The final sections of *Faust* were composed between 1825 and 1831. In them, Faust's appearances at court are developed and the final scenes of Faust's redemption return to the framework established in the prologue. Faust's last days are still unsatisfied and his quest is as violent as ever; his merchant ships turn to piracy, and a gentle old couple is killed to make room for his palace. His final vision, however, is that of all humanity, which strives to turn chaos to order and seeks a dimly imagined goal represented in the final scene by an endless stairway. Here, on the path toward the divine, Faust continues to strive. His life is redeemed by a divine love represented by Gretchen, who in spite of her crimes is also there, a penitent who prays for Faust. On Earth all is transitory and insufficient. Only from the point of view of the divine does all the confused striving attain a meaning that was, in fact, implicit in the stanzas that the three archangels sing at the opening of the play, twelve thousand lines earlier.

"Critical Evaluation" by Steven C. Schaber

Further Reading

Armstrong, John. *Love, Life, Goethe: Lessons of the Imagination from the Great German Poet*. New York: Farrar, Straus and Giroux, 2007. Goethe's works are analyzed and his life examined in this comprehensive volume. Armstrong discusses a wide range of Goethe's writings, including his lesser known works, and gives a close study of his personal life. Knowing German and English, he provides translations of several key passages, while keeping his writing style plain and clear. This volume offers readers a better understanding of Goethe's writing and of the circumstances that inspired it.

Atkins, Stuart. *Goethe's "Faust": A Literary Analysis.* Cambridge, Mass.: Harvard University Press, 1958. Evaluates *Faust* first and foremost as a drama, showing each section's dramatic as well as symbolic function, and seeks to demonstrate the organic unity of the work. Highly recommended.

Bishop, Paul, ed. *A Companion to Goethe's Faust: Parts I and II.* Rochester, N.Y.: Camden House, 2001. Collection of essays analyzing numerous aspects of the play, including the characters of Faust and Mephistopheles, the function of the feminine characters, philosophical issues and scientific themes in the work, and the play in production.

Fairley, Barker. *Goethe's "Faust": Six Essays.* Oxford, England: Clarendon Press, 1953. A knowledgeable and well-written set of studies by a preeminent Goethe scholar. Recommended.

Gillies, Alexander. *Goethe's "Faust": An Interpretation.* Oxford, England: Basil Blackwell, 1957. An important and detailed analysis, with lucid, helpful comments. Recommended for the more advanced student.

Goethe, Johann Wolfgang von. *Faust: A Tragedy.* Translated by Walter Arndt and edited by Cyrus Hamlin. New York: W. W. Norton, 1976. Contains introductory essays by both the translator and the editor, as well as substantial interpretive notes. Offers sections on primary sources for *Faust*, Goethe's outlines and correspondence, reactions by contemporaries, twelve essays by modern critics covering different aspects of the work, and a select bibliography. Useful for all levels.

Gray, Ronald. *Goethe: A Critical Introduction.* New York: Cambridge University Press, 1967. A discussion of Goethe's life and works, highly useful as an introduction to *Faust*. Chapters 7 and 8 discuss *Faust* in detail. Gray also compares the value of *Faust* as literature to Goethe's lesser works. Includes a table of biographical dates, an index, and a select bibliography.

Sharpe, Lesley, ed. *The Cambridge Companion to Goethe.* New York: Cambridge University Press, 2002. Collection of newly commissioned essays analyzing Goethe's prose fiction, drama, and poetry; Goethe and gender, philosophy, and religion; and Goethe's critical reception, among other topics. Chapter 5 is devoted to an analysis of *Faust*

Swales, Martin, and Erika Swales. *Reading Goethe: A Critical Introduction to the Literary Work.* Rochester, N.Y.: Camden House, 2002. A comprehensive critical analysis of Goethe's literary output, which argues that the writer is an essential figure in German modernity. Chapter 5 is devoted to an analysis of Faust. Includes bibliography and index.

Van der Laan, J. M. *Seeking Meaning in Goethe's "Faust."* New York: Continuum, 2007. Demonstrates how the play continues to have significance for twenty-first century audiences because it explores timeless questions about order and chaos, rebellion, suffering, faith and its loss, technology, and human improvement.

Fear and Loathing in Las Vegas
A Savage Journey to the Heart of the American Dream

Author: Hunter S. Thompson (1937-2005)
First published: 1972
Type of work: Novel
Type of plot: Roman à clef
Time of plot: 1971
Locale: Las Vegas, Nevada; Los Angeles

Principal characters:
RAOUL DUKE, a journalist
DR. GONZO, an attorney

The Story:

Raoul Duke is behind the wheel of a convertible, realizing that the drugs he took earlier have just kicked in. Sitting beside him is his three-hundred-pound traveling companion Dr. Gonzo, an attorney. The two have just left Los Angeles and are headed for Las Vegas. Duke, who is a journalist, is set to cover a desert motorcycle race called the Mint 400 for a sports publication on the East Coast. He had been in Los Angeles at the time of the assignment and did not ask questions about the job. He had decided to take the job and go.

Once in Las Vegas, Duke and Dr. Gonzo check in to their hotel but find it difficult to do so because they are so high on drugs. They soon meet the photographer who is assigned to accompany Duke at the Mint 400. However, the journalists do not spend much time at the race. Turns out that Duke and Dr. Gonzo would rather visit casinos and drive their rented Cadillac about town. Still high on drugs, Duke begins to reflect both on the city of Las Vegas and what he hopes is the American Dream.

Dr. Gonzo leaves Las Vegas for an appointment, and Duke is left to escape from the hotel room the two of them destroyed. They also tallied a massive room-service bill. As Duke begins to leave the hotel, he receives a telegram and hurriedly reads it. He finally leaves Las Vegas, heads back to California, and encounters a police officer. He then stops in the small town of Baker—where he calls Dr. Gonzo, who reminds him that he needs to return to Las Vegas to attend a professional conference. The telegram had instructed him and Dr. Gonzo to attend the National District Attorneys Association's Conference on Narcotics and Dangerous Drugs. Duke returns to Las Vegas and faces the difficult task of trying to check in to the hotel with a briefcase full of drugs in the middle of countless law-enforcement officials.

Dr. Gonzo arrives at the hotel with a young woman he has picked up. Soon, however, Duke and Dr. Gonzo are facing another round of problems, such as taking care of the young woman, another destroyed hotel room, and the drugs in their systems. Still, the two somehow are able to attend one of the conference seminars. They snicker at the ignorance of the seminar presenters, who are discussing drugs.

Before leaving Las Vegas, Dr. Gonzo insults a waitress at a sleazy diner and then pulls a knife on her, and Duke sits awestruck. The next morning, Duke drops his friend off at the airport and then returns to the casinos. Soon, however, Duke is on a plane as well, thinking about the meaning of his trip to Las Vegas.

Critical Evaluation:

Hunter S. Thompson's *Fear and Loathing in Las Vegas* is an attempt at gonzo journalism. Thompson is the forerunner of this concept, in which the author becomes part of the story that is being covered. Gonzo journalism brought a radical change to how stories and events could be reported and to how accurate they had to be as pieces of creative nonfiction.

Fear and Loathing in Las Vegas was first published in two parts in *Rolling Stone*, which was a counterculture publication at the time. The work was a fitting piece for such a magazine, and Thompson's story received a generally warm reception from readers. The first reviews of the book version, however, ranged from tepid to highly negative. Some reviewers found the book to be almost incoherent, while others thought that the text—awash in drug usage and illegal acts combined with a rambling narrative—did not make for a worthwhile read. The reviewer from *The New Republic* believed that the book was nothing more than surface text, that Thompson often failed to go into any depth with the material he was covering and attempted to overcome this shortcoming with overwrought descriptions. Another criticism of the novel was that *Fear and Loathing in Las Vegas* seemed to exist in a loveless world, as Thompson is never able to generate emotion or a deeper sense of humankind. *The New York Times* printed an initial review instructing readers not to even bother with the novel because of the depravity that it portrayed. Nevertheless, the reviewer recognized a certain positive element to the book: The rapid-fire prose could be considered almost poetic at times.

As the book grew in popularity, however, many people were encouraged to give it closer examination. In contrast to its original assessment, *The New York Times* published a second review of the novel that proclaimed it "a desperate and important book, a wired nightmare, the funniest piece of American prose since *Naked Lunch*," William S. Burroughs's 1959 novel. This second review saw Thompson's book as the best piece of literature to emerge from the 1960's, even though it was written in late 1971.

One of the most remarked upon aspects of the book is what is often called "the wave speech"; whenever Thompson was asked to read from the work, it is the passage that he consistently selected. This bittersweet portion of the novel reflects on the changes of the 1960's and depicts how hippie culture and its movements had swelled, crested, and then receded, having run its course.

Fear and Loathing in Las Vegas continues to receive favorable critical reception. The book is now often taught in English literature courses in universities throughout the United States, and scholars are discovering new ways to assess the novel. Many now place Thompson's work alongside Jack Kerouac's *On the Road* (1957) and Tom Wolfe's *Electric Kool-Aid Acid Test* (1968). These books share the common element of being what are considered road novels, displaying a sense of adventure based on traveling the American highways. All these books also exhibit a sense of being almost autobiographical or biographical, adding to their parallelism. Scholars have also examined themes of the novel such as the impact of friendship.

P. Huston Ladner

Further Reading
Carroll, E. Jean. *Hunter: The Strange and Savage Life of Hunter S. Thompson*. New York: Hyperion Books, 1993.

Written by one of Thompson's compatriots, this book is filled with interviews and stories of his life and relayed in first person by the author.

Cowan, Jay. *Hunter S. Thompson: An Insider's View of Deranged, Depraved, Drugged Out Brilliance.* Guilford, Conn.: Lyons Press, 2009. Cowan, who lived on Thompson's compound in Colorado, is able to provide an indepth and intimate portrayal of the man.

McKeen, William. *Outlaw Journalist: The Life and Times of Hunter S. Thompson.* New York: W. W. Norton, 2008. This biography is considered one of the most comprehensive. Provides an unfaltering portrait of Thompson.

Perry, Paul. *Fear and Loathing: The Strange and Terrible Saga of Hunter S. Thompson.* New York: Thunder's Mouth Press, 1993. Perry, a former editor at *Rolling Stone*, offers a critical assessment of Thompson's life, from his poor upbringing through his drug usage to his later endeavors in life.

Stiles, S., and R. Harris. "Keeping Curious Company: Wayne C. Booth's Friendship Model of Criticism and the Work of Hunter S. Thompson." *College English* 71, no. 4 (March, 2009): 313-337. Stiles and Harris examine the role that friendship has in Thompson's works and how it is an integral element in *Fear and Loathing in Las Vegas*.

Whitmer, Peter O. *When the Going Gets Weird: The Twisted Life and Times of Hunter S. Thompson—A Very Unauthorized Biography.* New York: Hyperion Books, 1993. Whitmer's biography is the first well-researched and fact-filled work on Thompson. Still stands as a worthwhile read.

Fear and Trembling
A Dialectical Lyric

Author: Søren Kierkegaard (1813-1855)
First published: Frygt og Bæven: Dialektisk lyrik, 1843 (English translation, 1939)
Type of work: Philosophy

Fear and Trembling is Søren Kierkegaard's meditation on the meaning of one father's sacrifice of his own son, a story told in the book of Genesis. Specifically, Kierkegaard examines how Abraham, patriarch of the Israelites and generally regarded as the spiritual ancestor of Judaism, Christianity, and Islam, could sacrifice his son, Isaac. In the passages of the biblical story, God tells Abraham to sacrifice Isaac on Mount Moriah, and Abraham immediately accepts God's command. He takes Isaac to the mountain and binds the boy to an altar. As he is about to kill his son, he is stopped by an angel. A ram appears, and Abraham follows God's commandment to substitute the animal for his son.

From a modern moral perspective, the narrative of Abraham and Isaac poses difficult problems. God, the source of all ethical and moral values, has ordered his servant, Abraham, to kill an innocent boy, Isaac. Abraham accepts the command to commit murder. Kierkegaard does not attempt to solve this problem; he does, however, look at the story from several angles to demonstrate the fundamentally irrational and experiential nature of faith.

Kierkegaard, who published many of his works under pseudonyms, published *Fear and Trembling* as Johannes de Silentio, or John of Silence. As de Silentio, he begins the book with a preface that offers a criticism of the philosophy of his own time. He compares events in the world of ideas to a clearance sale, where everything is to be had at a cut rate. Thoughts, he suggests, have gathered into a market of answers to questions that fail to consider the mystery of faith. Kierkegaard is especially critical of the systematic philosophy of Georg Wilhelm Friedrich Hegel and his followers, who had attempted to bring all questions into a comprehensive order of reasoning. At the same time, Kierkegaard's preface is critical of the Cartesian process of doubting and questioning everything; this system—developed by René Descartes—in a sense puts all thoughts and ideas up for sale. Faith, Kierkegaard argues, happens outside the system and outside doubt.

In a prelude, Kierkegaard gives four accounts of Abraham's departing in the morning with Isaac, leaving his home without his wife, and Isaac's mother, Sarah. In each of these accounts, Kierkegaard emphasizes the humanity of Abraham's family members, their relations with each other, and the thoughts that might have gone through their minds during this day. Nevertheless, the prelude ends with a proclamation of the greatness and incomprehensibility of Abraham. By beginning his meditation in this way, Kierkegaard seems to be reminding the reader that there are different ways of seeing this biblical story, that this story is about ordinary human life. In telling something about the mystery in the ordinary, the story is relating the extraordinary.

Kierkegaard next presents a panegyric, or speech, in praise of Abraham. He is praised for his greatness in following God without doubt and for the difficulty of doing so. Kierkegaard exclaims that if there were no eternal consciousness in the human mind, and if everything were just a bottomless void of change, then life would be nothing more than say, leaves in a forest, growing and falling; life would be empty and without comfort. Heroes, such as Abraham, exist to refute this emptiness.

Kierkegaard moves his discussion to the problems posed by the story of Abraham and Isaac. The author begins by considering the ethical problem of Abraham as the intended murderer of his son. Abraham is characterized not by his infinite resignation—his acceptance of the command to kill his son—but by his faith: Abraham believes that by following God's order to sacrifice, he will sacrifice nothing. According to Kierkegaard, this makes Abraham a knight of faith, in contrast to a knight of infinite resignation.

Next, Kierkegaard addresses three specific problems posed by the biblical story. The first problem is whether there is such a thing as a teleological suspension of the ethical, a problem that goes beyond the question of whether the end justifies the means. The ethical is the universal, that which applies to everyone. Sin or unethical behavior consists in asserting one's particularity against the universal. Abraham acts against the universal obligation not to commit murder, but he does this on the grounds of the absolute, God. In faith, the particular or individual becomes higher than the universal. Faith moves beyond ethics to the ultimate end, or teleology.

The second problem is whether there is such a thing as an absolute duty toward God, that is, whether God is beyond the universal realm of the ethical. Kierkegaard maintains that in faith, the individual must transcend the universal and stand in an absolute relation to the absolute.

The third problem is whether Abraham can be ethically defended for hiding his intention to kill Isaac from his mother, Sarah, and from Isaac himself. This dilemma leads Kierkegaard to consider two things: the idea of concealment and the question of which ethical considerations require concealment. Again, the requirement to reveal one's intentions derives from the universal nature of ethical behavior; when a person conceals, that person is in sin. Concealment can be understood only within individual circumstances. Abraham's conduct would be indefensible if his case were not considered unique, as a situation in which the individual is higher than the universal and in direct relation to the absolute.

Kierkegaard is not an easy author to read or understand. As a philosopher, he does not present arguments in the form of a series of propositions. Instead, he approaches his concerns through examples, anecdotes, and sometimes unresolvable contradictions. This is because he does not see the most important matters of human life as logical puzzles that can be solved through reason. Human beings, in his view, live through faith and faith is ultimately paradoxical; it resides in the absurd. The goal of *Fear and Trembling*, and many of Kierkegaard's other works, is to illuminate the paradoxes and to thereby lead readers into an appreciation of the irreducible nature of faith and life.

Readers might note that Kierkegaard does not solve any of the problems he discusses. He does not answer the question of whether a person who acts as Abraham had acted would be considered ethical. Abraham apparently was acting ethically because he stood in a unique and particular relation to God and was, therefore, above the universal commandments of ethics. This rationale would not serve as a good guide for ethical decision making, for anyone could claim to be beyond the ethical. Providing a guide to behavior, however, is not Kierkegaard's aim. His goal is to awaken readers to the irreducible and illogical basis of religious existence.

Carl L. Bankston III

Further Reading

Carlisle, Clare. *Kierkegaard: A Guide for the Perplexed.* New York: Continuum, 2006. This helpful book discusses Kierkegaard as one of the founders of the philosophy of existentialism and lays out his thinking on ethics, religion, and other topics.

Ferreira, M. Jamie. *Kierkegaard.* Malden, Mass.: Wiley-Blackwell, 2009. Part of the Blackwell Great Minds series, this book offers a comprehensive introduction to all of Kierkegaard's work and helps make this difficult writer more approachable. Chapter 3 includes a discussion of *Fear and Trembling*.

Hannay, Alistair. *Kierkegaard: A Biography.* New York: Cambridge University Press, 2001. One of the best modern biographies of Kierkegaard. This book sets the philosopher's work in the context of his life.

Lippitt, John. *Routledge Philosophy Guidebook to Kierkegaard and "Fear and Trembling."* New York: Routledge, 2003. A good reference for those new to *Fear and Trembling*. Lippitt looks at Kierkegaard's life and the background to the text, outlining its main ideas.

Pons, Jolita. *Stealing a Gift: Kierkegaard's Pseudonyms and the Bible.* New York: Fordham University Press, 2004.

Studies the use of biblical quotations in Kierkegaard's pseudonymous works and argues that Kierkegaard was acting as a kind of sacred "plagiarist," stealing divine words to give them to his readers.

Walsh, Sylvia. *Kierkegaard: Thinking Christianly in an Existential Mode.* New York: Oxford University Press, 2009. Walsh looks at Kierkegaard as a Christian thinker and discusses his presentation of Christianity as a way of existence, rather than as an abstract doctrine.

Fear of Flying

Author: Erica Jong (1942-   )
First published: 1973
Type of work: Novel
Type of plot: Autobiographical
Time of plot: Mid-twentieth century
Locale: Vienna, Paris, and New York City

Principal characters:
ISADORA WING, a young Jewish poet
BENNETT WING, Isadora's husband, a child psychiatrist
ADRIAN GOODLOVE, Isadora's lover, an English psychoanalyst
JUDITH STOLOFF WHITE, Isadora's mother
BRIAN STOLLERMAN, Isadora's first husband, a schizophrenic
DR. SCHRIFT, Isadora's New York psychiatrist

The Story:

Isadora Wing, a young Jewish poet living in New York, accompanies her psychiatrist husband, Bennett Wing, to a psychoanalysts' conference in Vienna and then goes off with a lover she meets there. En route to the conference, she confesses that she is frightened of flying (a metaphor for her fear of independence and of taking risks) even though she had been treated by several of the psychiatrists on the flight to the conference.

In Vienna, Isadora meets Adrian Goodlove, an English psychoanalyst. She is strongly attracted to him (and he to her, apparently), and they flirt outrageously, go out together, and sleep together; turns out that he is better as a sexual fantasy than as an actual sexual partner because he is often impotent.

Adrian taunts Isadora about being trapped in the safe role of bourgeois wife and dares her to join him on a jaunt across Europe, saying she needs to learn to take risks and that he can give her an experience that will really change her. Isadora feels pulled in two directions: toward the security of life with Bennett, whom she feels loves her, and the urge to break out of a confining situation. She decides to return to New York with her husband but then suddenly changes her mind at Adrian's urging, and the two set out in his Triumph sports car.

Adrian lectures her to not be afraid of what is inside her and insists that he will be her teacher.

Drinking, arguing, and making love, they make their way to Paris. However, what is supposed to be a completely spontaneous and existential quest turns out to be a rather grim odyssey from grubby campsite to cheap hostel. To crown Isadora's disappointment, Adrian tells her that he will leave her in Paris because he has arranged to meet his wife and children. Isadora is furious, but she has already become disillusioned with him. She goes to a hotel, reads her diaries and notebooks, and concludes that she must look to herself for meaning in life. She decides to go back to New York to join her husband, but she is determined not to "grovel."

In a series of flashbacks, Isadora tells about growing up as an aspiring artist, about her two marriages, and about her youthful sexual adventures and affairs. She endures all the frustrations of growing up female in the 1950's. Her mother, Judith, an artist who had given up painting for marriage, tells Isadora again and again that the worst thing in the world is to be "ordinary." She also burdens her daughter with the dictum that it is impossible to be both an artist and a mother. Dr. Schrift, Isadora's psychiatrist, counsels Isadora to accept her femininity. Isadora laments in the story that in the years growing up, she had to learn about being a woman from men. In her case, she learned this, mostly, from writer D. H. Lawrence. To Isadora, however, the men do not tell the whole story.

After graduation, Isadora marries the brilliant Brian Stollerman, who soon has a mental breakdown—insisting that he is Jesus Christ and can walk on the surface of the lake in Central Park—and is institutionalized. Isadora then marries Bennett, thinking he will provide the security lacking in her life. She accompanies him to Heidelberg, West Germany, when he is drafted as a U.S. Army psychiatrist during the Vietnam War. There she confronts her Jewishness and writes journalism and poetry.

Critical Evaluation:

Fear of Flying is one of the first novels identified with the women's liberation movement, as the women's movement was known in the early 1970's. Erica Jong became famous (or infamous) as the author of fiction about sexuality, written from a woman's perspective. She had previously published poetry that had attracted attention for its sexual themes.

Fear of Flying, published in 1973, was widely reviewed. Some critics considered the novel tasteless and even mildly pornographic, a brazen affront to a more genteel female literary tradition. Other reviewers, largely feminist women but including many men, welcomed her honest and realistic portrayals. Some reviewers even said her work taught them much about female sexuality. Jong became a celebrity, and her book became an international best seller.

Much had been written at the time the novel was released about Jong's frank sexual vocabulary, a vocabulary that underlines her contention that women are sexual beings and are far from being sexless childlike figures. Jong was a pioneering voice in what came to be known as a women's sexual revolution. Some have claimed that *Fear of Flying* is a parody of the language used by "bad-boy" writers, including Henry Miller.

In this novel, Jong introduces the phrase "zipless fu—" (a phrase that has followed her through her career and which, she has joked, may well appear on her tombstone). In this ultimate sexual experience, Jong explains, two strangers enjoy a spontaneous sexual encounter. The pleasure and excitement is mutual and beyond the realm of the "power game" that usually accompanies sex. In itself the concept is a comment on the oppressive social conditions that surround sex in society. However, the protagonist, Isadora Wing, knows that such an encounter is merely a fantasy and that a meaningful and enduring love relationship is something else entirely. Indeed

the concept is mocked and undercut by the disappointments of the affair with Adrian Goodlove. Isadora is in touch with her own sexual nature, one of the aspirations of women in the feminist revolution of the time, and she is candid about her attraction to men and her enjoyment of sex. Isadora remarks that her readers (of her poetry) in New York expect her to act out their fantasies and give voice to their goals and dreams.

Isadora's relationship with Bennett has become routine and predictable, and she hears the echo of her "hunger thump," the voice inside that reminds her to demand more from life. Her hunger thump registers her dissatisfaction with marriage as a mid-twentieth century patriarchal institution and with the roles society has prescribed for women.

Common readers and feminist critics praised Jong for her insights. Like other young women of the time, Isadora has been bombarded with commercial messages telling her that if she learns the lesson presented by cosmetics advertisers and if she conforms to gender roles, she will find romantic fulfillment and personal happiness. It is not surprising that Isadora, like most women of her time, is drawn in two directions, toward independence and self-direction and also toward love and self-surrender. Isadora complains that in her relationships with men, she quickly becomes a kind of toady and relinquishes too much of herself.

Isadora, though, is seeking more than sexual fulfillment. Sexual freedom in itself is not enough to give meaning to life. Isadora's hunger thump includes her ambitions as a writer, and the novel is her coming-of-age story. Jong's act in the final chapter of the novel brings together her own personal and professional aspirations as she resolves to be her own woman and look inward for direction.

Jong has often been accused of telling her own story in her fiction. Indeed, there is a resemblance between Jong's life story and that of Isadora in *Fear of Flying*. Both the author and her protagonist are Jewish poets from New York's upper West Side. Both endure a first marriage to someone who becomes mentally ill, and both marry a Chinese American psychiatrist. However, like other successful writers, Jong transforms the factual material into artistic material. One way she does so is through comedy.

Fear of Flying is thoroughly comic and belongs in the category of mild or Horatian satire. Jong's characters are caricatures. Bennett, for example, is defined by his role as a psychiatrist and even insists that before he and Isadora can make any marital decisions, they should discuss them with their respective analysts. He spouts Freudian theory ad nauseam, not surprisingly insisting that freedom is an illusion. Adrian is a recognizable comic type: the person who preaches one thing but does another. Jong's sisters project a variety of comic voices. Sister Randy has a large brood of offspring and insists that Isadora will never be happy until she follows her example.

Feminist reviewers often commented on Jong's comedy while those with more traditional views failed to see the humor. Jong's comic gift, along with the resonance of her themes, has assured the novel a place on the list of notable books of the twentieth century.

Charlotte Templin

Further Reading

Haskell, Molly. Review of *Fear of Flying*, by Erica Jong. *Village Voice Literary Supplement*, November 22, 1973. Haskell's review illustrates the enthusiasm feminists had for Jong's telling, controversial novel.

Hogeland, Lisa Maria. *Feminism and Its Fictions: The Consciousness-Raising Novel and the Women's Liberation Movement*. Philadelphia: University of Pennsylvania Press, 1998. Jong's novel figures in chapter 3 of this study of feminist fiction. The chapter discusses the various discourses of sexuality that appeared in women's fiction in the era of *Fear of Flying*.

Templin, Charlotte. *Feminism and the Politics of Literary Reception: The Example of Erica Jong*. Lawrence: University Press of Kansas, 1995. This book presents a detailed account of the reception and influence of Jong's novel in the context of the social and cultural controversies surrounding feminism and the women's movement at the time *Fear of Flying* was published.

_____, ed. *Conversations with Erica Jong*. Jackson: University Press of Mississippi, 2002. This edited volume contains interviews with Jong conducted between 1973 and 2001. The talks reveal Jong's insightful, humorous, and articulate voice as she expounds on craft, culture, sexuality, and women's place in society. Contains many comments on the content and reception of *Fear of Flying*.

Updike, John. "Jong Love." In *Picked-up Pieces*. 1975. New ed. New York: Ballantine Books, 1986. Updike's rave review, reprinted from *The New Yorker* magazine, compares Jong to Geoffrey Chaucer's Wife of Bath. Updike argues that Jong invented a new form of female prose, and he praises her comic gift. The review gave a boost to the novel's reputation and was often quoted by subsequent reviewers.

The Federalist

Authors: Alexander Hamilton (1755-1804), James
  Madison (1751-1836), and John Jay (1745-1829)
First published: 1787-1788, serial; 1788, book
Type of work: Essays

The American Revolution was a product and a symbol of the Age of Reason, a period in which Western philosophical and political thought focused on the so-called rights of man. For the Americans, however, winning their freedom on the battlefield brought the even more complex task of using that freedom to unite thirteen former colonies under a legitimate form of government that would open the road for a new nation with new political goals. While the war brought about a necessary unity among the new states, it also hid a number of disagreements that flared up once the hostilities ended.

The Continental Congress that convened in November of 1777 adopted the Articles of Confederation, codifying a government for the thirteen states. This first attempt at a government proved insufficient, however. It embodied a mode of separatism that prevented the states from taking advantage of their geography, their natural resources, or their growth in population—or from satisfying their need for security. The states needed to be molded into a cohesive and loyal nation. Realizing that the Articles of Confederation created a national government that lacked the authority the new nation needed, the Congress appointed a Constitutional Convention to create a new document that would be the basis of a new government. When the Congress received the completed Constitution on September 20, 1787, another kind of battle was engaged, this one between the Federalists, who favored the Constitution as it was written, and the Anti-Federalists, who thought the document provided for an overly strong central government. This battle virtually consumed the states during the following year, as each side struggled to get the votes of nine states needed for victory.

Heavily involved in this struggle were three of the younger Founding Fathers: Alexander Hamilton, thirty years old; James Madison, thirty-six years old; and John Jay, forty-two years old. Because the Federalists in his home state of New York were facing an uphill battle, Hamilton convinced Madison and Jay to join him in carrying out a propagandistic strategy to support the new Constitution. Central to this strategy was a series of papers signed by the pseudonym Publius. Eventually numbering eighty-five in all, these papers first appeared in New York newspapers. In 1788, they were published in book form, titled *The Federalist*. In later years, the collection became known as *The Federalist Papers*. Although there is some question regarding the specific writer of a few of the papers, it is generally believed that Hamilton wrote fifty-two, Madison wrote twenty-eight, and Jay wrote five.

The first paper, written by Hamilton and appearing on October 27, 1787, sets the tone for the papers to come. Strongly supporting the new Constitution, it clearly lays out the basic problems of the new nation. Noting that politicians in their self-aggrandizement often make difficult situations even more difficult, Hamilton pleads for moderation to guard against narrow-minded bigotry and distrust. He warns, too, against letting zeal for the rights of the common people work against a firm and efficient central government.

In the ensuing days, Jay followed Hamilton, writing four of the five papers he was to contribute to *The Federalist*. In these contributions, Jay celebrates the necessity of a unified government and notes that the thirteen states' economic and political strengths lie in their abilities to bring together abundant natural resources and geographic blessings under a unified government. He also underscores the necessity for the new nation to achieve security, a security that can come only with unification of the states. To have thirteen states battling with one another militarily, economically, or socially, he asserts, would bring disaster. Such a situation would encourage England, France, and Spain to seek inroads in the New World, for without unity, the states would be easy targets for external powers.

In *Federalist* 6, 7, and 8, Hamilton emphasizes the likely results of wars that would without question plague a disunited group of states, particularly wars among themselves. Using examples of conflicts that occurred among the states when they were still British colonies, Hamilton grimly predicts a free-for-all among the states as each tries to strengthen itself at the expense of others. Internecine wars would be predatory and marked by plunder and devastation. He also points out the disagreements that would result from the debt of the public union. Reflected in these essays and in many of those written by Hamilton is his lack of trust of the individual states or, for that matter, of people in general.

Federalist 10, written by Madison, is considered by many scholars to be the most significant of the papers, addressing as it does the question of the factions and passions that would be common threats to the community. Madison sees two possible responses to such a faction: remove its causes or control its effects. Two methods of removing a faction's causes are to destroy the liberty that allows it to exist or to give every citizen the same opinions and passions regarding it. The first option, he notes, is unwise, and the second is impractical. As long as people are free to use their reason and as long as that reason is related to self-love, opinions and passions will influence each other. In short, factionalism for Madison is part of the very nature of humanity.

Madison agrees with Hamilton that the most common source of factions is the unequal distribution of property, and he notes that civilized nations need property owners, manufacturers, merchants, and bankers, all of whom need regulation. Factions and their regulation, then, are part of the operation of government. Madison goes on to say that pure democracy would magnify the violent effects of factions and that a republican, representational form of government is therefore the answer. He points out that republics, because they encompass a variety of parties and interests, can accommodate greater numbers of citizens than can democracies. Thus, the larger the republic, the more effective it can be in controlling factions. Madison concludes that a large union properly structured can provide a remedy for the most common diseases that might spring up in a republican government.

The early *Federalist* papers, then, exemplify the mastery of logic and its presentation that characterize all eighty-five of the papers. They reflect, moreover, the writers' desire to overwhelm readers by bombarding them with arguments that clearly show how and why the new Constitution would mold the individual states into a unified government that could function effectively in the New World. Other papers treat the importance of union; a strong central government with an energetic executive; equality among the states; the power of taxation; a strong banking system; the value of property; a balance of powers among the executive, legislative, and judicial branches; and commercial regulations. Some of the more popular papers among legal and political scholars include numbers 39, 51, 70, 78, and 84.

The Federalist, then, is meant to provide its readers with both a practical and a theoretical picture of the principles of free government and where they meet, not only in the political arena, but also in everyday life. To be sure, the papers and the Constitution they defend do not expect to reach either a perfect government or a more perfect government. They do expect to reach conditions more conducive for a more perfect government. Because each paper provides its own focus on a given aspect of the overall question of how a government should be run, it is not necessary for an average reader to read all of the papers. Indeed, one can choose at random any of the papers and find a detailed, scholarly, and partisan analysis of the Constitution. The papers will mean more to an average reader if they are accompanied by a reading of the Constitution itself, as well as one or more scholarly studies.

As an explicit glimpse into the thought processes informing the creation and adoption of the U.S. Constitution, *The Federalist* represents a classic document in American legal history. It is a commentary rather than a formal legal document, so it has no legal force. However, Supreme Court decisions involving fundamental constitutional issues often cite *The Federalist* to bolster their arguments as to the meaning and scope of the Constitution. Ranging from Hamilton's desire for a proper balance of powers incorporating strong executive authority, to Madison's caution that theoretical reasoning must be qualified by the lessons of practice, to Jay's emphasis on security for the new nation, these papers have become keys to understanding the characteristics of a republican form of government buttressed by democratic laws.

Both Madison and Jay lived into their mid-eighties. Hamilton, on the other hand, died at forty-seven as a result of a feud with Aaron Burr. In addition to their accomplishments with the pen, all three men held key positions in the new nation. Hamilton was the first secretary of the Treasury; Jay was the first chief justice; and Madison was the nations's fourth president. Moreover, Publius still lives in the pages of *The Federalist*.

Wilton Eckley

Further Reading

Allen, W. B., with Kevin A. Cloonan. *"The Federalist Papers": A Commentary—"The Baton Rouge Lectures."* New York: Peter Lang, 2000. This study of *The Federalist* and its place in constitutional history includes an extremely useful appendix listing the Supreme Court decisions that have cited the document.

Carey, George. *The Federalist Design for a Constitutional Republic.* Urbana: University of Illinois Press, 1995. An overview of *The Federalist* and the role it played in forming a republican government.

Epstein, David. *The Political Theory of "The Federalist."* Chicago: University of Chicago Press, 1988. A guide to the fundamental principles of American government as they were understood by the framers of the Constitution.

Kessler, Charles, ed. *Saving the Revolution: "The Federalist Papers" and the American Founding.* New York: Free Press, 1987. Includes an introduction and fourteen very informative essays on *The Federalist*.

Meyerson, Michael I. *Liberty's Blueprint: How Madison and Hamilton Wrote "The Federalist Papers," Defined the Constitution, and Made Democracy Safe for the World.* New York: Basic Books, 2008. Divided into two sections, "Writing *The Federalist*" and "Reading *The Federalist*," this study explores both the historical context that brought the papers into being and the meaning of those papers not only to history but also to modern constitutional law.

Monk, Linda. *Words We Live By: Your Annotated Guide to the Constitution.* Hyperion, N.Y.: Stonesong Press, 2000. Good source of commentary on aspects of the Constitution that relate to *The Federalist*.

Wills, Gary. *Explaining America: "The Federalist."* Reprint. New York: Penguin Books, 2001. Both examines and participates in the project of using *The Federalist* to define and develop the American system of government.

Felix Holt, the Radical

Author: George Eliot (1819-1880)
First published: 1866
Type of work: Novel
Type of plot: Social realism
Time of plot: 1831-1833
Locale: Rural Midland England

Principal characters:
FELIX HOLT, the Radical, an educated artisan
HAROLD TRANSOME, the heir to Transome Court and a
    Radical candidate for Parliament
MRS. TRANSOME, his mother
ESTHER LYON, a refined young woman
RUFUS LYON, her father and a dissenting minister
MATTHEW JERMYN, a lawyer
MR. JOHNSON, another lawyer hired by Jermyn
PHILIP DEBARRY, a Tory candidate for Parliament
SIR MAXIMUS DEBARRY, his father and the owner of Treby
    Manor
THE REVEREND AUGUSTUS DEBARRY, his brother
THE REVEREND JOHN LINGON, Mrs. Transome's brother
HENRY SCADDON (alias MAURICE CHRISTIAN BYCLIFFE), a
    servant in the Debarry household

The Story:

Mrs. Transome, who long held Transome Court together in spite of financial and legal difficulties and an incompetent husband, eagerly awaits the return of Harold, her younger son. Harold, who was building up a fortune in Smyrna for the preceding fifteen years, is called home to take his place as heir to Transome Court after the death of his weak older brother, Durfey. Harold, whose wife is dead, also brings with him a young son.

Mrs. Transome is soon disappointed by Harold. Although he is generous with money and renovates the shabby mansion, he is not willing to respect Mrs. Transome's wishes for a genteel country life, particularly when he announces that he intends to run for Parliament as a Radical candidate. To his mother, he seems to show a surprising knowledge and shrewdness about contemporary English life. In his campaign, he receives the support of his family's lawyer, Matthew Jermyn, and his uncle, the Reverend John Lingon. Neither had thought of deserting the Tory colors before his arrival.

More understandably committed to the Radical cause is Rufus Lyon, the local dissenting minister. One day he receives a visit from Mrs. Holt, one of his parishioners, who complains that her son deliberately stopped the business in patent medicines that she and her late husband painstakingly established. Her son, Felix, claims that the business is fraudulent; Mrs. Holt, on the other hand, is convinced that God would not allow a fraudulent business to prosper. The minister later sends for young Felix, whom he finds highly intelli-

gent, energetic, honest, and independent. Although well educated, Felix is working as a watchmaker in order to feel close to the people. The two men soon became close friends. At the Lyons' home, Felix also meets Rufus's daughter Esther, a slight, refined girl educated abroad, who is now teaching the daughters of the rich and reading Lord Byron's poems. The energetic and socially conscious Felix rails at Esther's refinement and at her reading of romantic fantasies, but as time passes, a strange attraction between the two begins to grow. Esther, although she does not know it at the time, is not the daughter of Rufus Lyon. Her mother was a Frenchwoman, alone and destitute, whom Rufus found wandering the English streets. Her soldier husband sent for her, but he died before she could find him. With her child, she is befriended by Rufus, who gives up a successful post in order to continue to be with her and who later marries her.

Harold, beginning his election campaign, leaves the organizing to his lawyer, Matthew Jermyn. Jermyn hires another lawyer, Mr. Johnson, to go to a workers' pub and stir the men into active support of the Radical candidate. Felix is in the pub at the time. Although a Radical, he objects strongly to the rabble-rousing technique used by Johnson and carries his protest directly to Harold. Although sympathetic to Felix's point of view, Harold feels somewhat indebted to Jermyn, who helped his mother retain her property through difficult years and an earlier lawsuit. While walking home through the woods, Felix finds a purse belonging to Christian, one of the Debarry servants; as a practical joke, the purse was stolen from his pocket and tossed away while Christian was asleep in the woods. Along with the purse are some papers belonging to Philip Debarry, the Conservative candidate for Parliament.

When Felix takes the papers to Rufus, his friend is amazed to discover evidence that Christian is the first husband of Rufus's French wife and the father of Esther. Through Jermyn, however, Rufus learns that Christian is really a scoundrel named Henry Scaddon who, in order to save himself, exchanged identities with Maurice Christian Bycliffe, Esther's real father, just before Bycliffe's death. Jermyn also knows that the Bycliffe line established Esther as the real heiress of Transome Court, should an old and senile Transome, who moved to Treby, die. Although Jermyn keeps his information for possible use against the Transome family, Rufus tells his daughter of her origins. Meanwhile, Harold continues campaigning, and the friendship between Esther and Felix grows.

As Felix fears, the workers riot on the day of the election. Felix, hoping to quell the riot, heads it for a time in a futile effort to lead the workers away from the town. Unsuccessful in his purpose, he is charged with killing a constable. The old Transome is also trampled in the riot. Esther is legally the heiress of Transome Court. Harold, who loses the election, now turns his attention to Transome Court. Discovering that Jermyn and Johnson, Jermyn's henchman, were cheating the estate for years, he decides to get rid of Jermyn at once and sue him. Jermyn tries to avoid the suit by telling Harold that the estate really belongs to Esther but that Jermyn will remain silent if Harold drops proceedings against him. Harold refuses the bribe. Later, he and his mother invite Esther to live with them at Transome Court. Both are charmed with Esther, and Harold courts her, partly to regain the estate through marriage.

Meanwhile, Felix's case is announced for trial. Rufus, Harold, and Esther testify to Felix's attempts to quell the riot, but he killed a man, although inadvertently, and so he is sentenced to an imprisonment of four years. Esther's plea is so powerful that it moves even the arch-Tory, Sir Maximus Debarry, who helps petition Parliament to grant Felix a pardon. Felix is soon released. In the meantime, Mrs. Transome is unhappy that Harold rejected Jermyn thoroughly and is attempting to sue him. Harold, claiming that Jermyn is a thief, intends to carry out the suit. In a final burst of fury, Jermyn tells Harold the truth: He is Harold's father and, during his long affair with Mrs. Transome, saved the estate during several difficult times. Harold is crushed, and only Esther is able to reconcile him to his unhappy mother. Feeling his illegitimacy keenly, Harold tells Esther that he cannot, as he intended, ask for her hand. This declaration saves Esther much

embarrassment, for she already acknowledged her love for Felix. To solve problems for all concerned, Esther signs over her rights to Transome Court to Harold, returns to her father's house, and soon marries Felix.

Critical Evaluation:

Written amid the hopes and fears of political upheaval before the second major Reform Bill passed in 1867, George Eliot's novel representing conditions accompanying the Reform Bill of 1832 suggests that authentic reform must come by much more than parliamentary legislation. Real reform requires, the novel implies, the slow cultivation of informed minds, class-bridging sympathies, courage, and clear-sighted rejection of personal and class-based delusions. Faithful to her artistic creed of realism—the true-to-life portrayal of human beings, including believably slow development of individuals and the relationships among them—Eliot represents evils that unquestionably urge reform, but she implies that some of these evils derive from human frailties. It is therefore a moral radicalism that would serve the nation best, one that would convert self-serving egotism to altruistic efforts and materialistic obsession to spontaneously creative living.

In a backward-looking introduction, Eliot directs her readers to view social change as a slow process. She returns, after the exotic settings of *Romola* (1862-1863) to the Midland England of her childhood and to the slower-paced life of 1831. Then, as in 1866, the elderly and established feared the rapidity of technological progress and resulting social changes, while progressives attacked blatant social evils. Eliot refers to the social evils of the 1830's as "departed," but the reference is ironic because many of the evils remained in 1866. She argues implicitly for continued reform. She reassures conservative readers of the 1860's that the nation had survived reforming changes and would survive more reform. She also addresses the disappointments of progressives who had hoped too much from the earlier bill. Legislation alone could not instantaneously replace feudalism with democratic capitalism, as if the nation could be "shot, like a bullet" from Winchester to Newcastle, an image that recalls England's long development from its ninth century political center, Winchester, still sleepily agrarian after ten centuries, to the new industrial railway center, Newcastle. Innovation was both inevitable and desirable, however, and Eliot's jabs at those who feared it in 1831 suggest that the author was attempting to quell similar fears in 1866.

Eliot's frequent irony and realistic characterization—her people are neither always heroic nor completely villainous—have obscured for some readers her sympathizing with the reform movement. She saw, however, that expanding the electorate to include hundreds of thousands among the uneducated might lead only to replacing the abuses of a self-interested propertied class with other abuses caused by the short-sighted gullibility and impassioned disorder of the lower classes that she represents in the novel. It is Esther Lyon's personal revolution, beginning with her fantasizing about luxurious vanities, continuing with her awakening to the emptiness of her silken-cushioned despair at Transome Court, and ending with her assertion of freedom to continue growing, that embodies Eliot's vision of authentic reform. Felix Holt, too, grows with new awareness of his limits after he fails to control the riotous mob—and fails to control himself—and inadvertently causes a death. Felix and Esther prepare to invest their energies in educating others toward the responsibilities of an extended franchise. Ample evidence for this need appears in the rioting miners, in Mrs. Holt's application of divine will to her personal economic plight, and in such corrupt practices as vote-buying, identity-exchanging, and embezzling. All suggest the need for moral, not merely political, reform among all classes.

Eliot was also reforming the fantasy-based fiction popular at the time. She reverses the stereotypical plot of a foundling later identified as gentry and rewarded with wealth and privilege. Instead, Esther, like Eppie Marner, returns to the simpler life of her adoptive father, rejecting the entrapment of Transome Court and affirming the values of useful work and personal freedom. She insists on the freedom to define herself and not be forced into roles governed by outworn feudal property laws or into a subservient relationship with a controlling husband who sees a woman as a means of acquiring and managing property. Eliot also reverses character stereotypes in fiction and political discourse. Mrs. Transome, the privileged, enviable lady, is bereft of power, influence, love, and respect. Her tragedy, cast in the imagery of Dante's underworld of retribution, is the outcome of her having chosen everything Esther rejects. Mrs. Transome's marriage for station and property, touted in popular fiction and practiced in the social world, is revealed as a hellish prison. Mrs. Transome is an object lesson to young woman readers as well as to Esther. Harold Transome—good-looking, competent manager of property and people, "radical" in politics but paternalistic, manipulative, and imperious—is the outward stereotype of a desirable husband. His former wife, however, was a Greek slave that he had bought. Her situation is the parallel of the sexual slavery of English wives. His unthinking, blatant egotism leaves no breathing room for his mother or for Esther. His ego collapses when he discovers his illegitimate birth, suggesting that social status without character is an insubstantial prop.

Eliot's portrayal of Mrs. Transome's powerless despair is a negative example on behalf of the nineteenth century feminist argument that women should be empowered politically and economically. That Mrs. Transome's malaise derives largely from dashed hopes based on her role as a mother is Eliot's pointed reply to a world that prescribed motherhood as the panacea for all female discontents. More broadly, the intricate plot, based on laws of inheritance, is Eliot's argument that generations-old property arrangements prevent national revitalization, just as ties to property preclude vital, spontaneous interpersonal bonds such as those between Esther and Felix. The open, generous nature of Rufus Lyon, who renounces a successful career to save Esther's mother and who can part unselfishly with his much-loved daughter when a better life appears for her, is Eliot's moral ideal, expressed also in Felix's wish to "make life less bitter for a few."

"Critical Evaluation" by Carolyn F. Dickinson

Further Reading

Carroll, David R. "*Felix Holt*: Society as Protagonist." In *George Eliot: A Collection of Critical Essays*, edited by George R. Creeger. Englewood Cliffs, N.J.: Prentice-Hall, 1970. Develops variations on the theme of rebellion among the characters. Characters move from a condition of illusion to a clearer understanding of reality. Distinguishes vision from illusion and justifies the novel's plot complexity as necessary to its theme.

Coveney, Peter. Introduction to *Felix Holt, the Radical*, by George Eliot. New York: Penguin Books, 1972. Offers a full historical background for the political context of the novel, including legal complexities, parliamentary activities, and many topical allusions.

DeCicco, Lynne Marie. *Women and Lawyers in the Mid-Nineteenth Century English Novel: Uneasy Alliances and Narrative Misrepresentation.* Lewiston, N.Y.: Edwin Mellen Press, 1996. An analysis of *Felix Holt, the Radical* and two other Victorian novels that prominently depict the public's suspicion of lawyers and lawyers' hostility toward women.

Hardy, Barbara. *George Eliot: A Critic's Biography.* New York: Continuum, 2006. An examination of Eliot's life combined with an analysis of her works, which will prove useful to readers with some prior knowledge of her writings. Includes an outline of her works and the events in her life.

_____, ed. *Critical Essays on George Eliot.* New York: Barnes & Noble, 1970. This collection, edited by a pioneer in Eliot studies, helped interest critics in feminist analyses of her work. One of the essays is devoted to an analysis of *Felix Holt, the Radical.*

Horsman, Alan. "George Eliot." In *The Victorian Novel.* New York: Oxford University Press, 1990. Gives voluminous details that enlighten Eliot's political views and artistic craft; places *Felix Holt, the Radical* in context with Eliot's other works. Includes bibliography.

Karl, Fred. *George Eliot: Voice of a Century.* New York: Norton, 1995. Karl's biography draws on valuable new archival material and feminist criticism, depicting Eliot as an author whose work symbolized "the ambiguities, the anguish, and divisiveness of the Victorian era."

Levine, George, ed. *The Cambridge Companion to George Eliot.* New York: Cambridge University Press, 2001. Collection of essays analyzing Eliot's work from various perspectives, including discussions of her early and late novels and of Eliot and realism, philosophy, science, politics, religion, and gender.

Rignall, John, ed. *Oxford Reader's Companion to George Eliot.* New York: Oxford University Press, 2000. An encyclopedic volume with entries that cover everything about the novelist, including her pets and homes, as well as her themes and various contexts in which to place her works.

Uglow, Jennifer. *George Eliot.* New York: Pantheon Books, 1987. Chapter 11 analyzes the dialectics, figurative language, mythic allusions, connotative imagery, and ironic narrative voice in the novel. Uglow particularly focuses on gender definitions and interaction. Includes bibliography.

The Fellowship of the Ring

Author: J. R. R. Tolkien (1892-1973)
First published: 1954
Type of work: Novel
Type of plot: Epic
Time of plot: The Third Age in a remote legendary past
Locale: Middle-earth between the Northern Waste and Sutherland

Principal characters:
BILBO BAGGINS, the finder of the One Ring and a famous hobbit of the Shire
FRODO BAGGINS, his young kinsman and heir and the chosen Ringbearer
MERIADOC BRANDYBUCK (MERRY), Frodo's cousin from Buckland
PEREGRIN TOOK (PIPPIN), another of Frodo's cousins
SAMWISE GAMGEE (SAM), Frodo's loyal servant and also a hobbit
GANDALF THE GREY (MITHRANDIR), a venerable wizard
ARAGORN (STRIDER), a ranger and the descendant of kings
BOROMIR, the son of Denethor of Gondor and a heroic warrior
GIMLI, the son of Glóin and a warlike dwarf
LEGOLAS, a wood elf and son of King Thranduil of Mirkwood
ELROND HALFELVEN, the ruler of Rivendell
GALADRIEL, the Elf Queen of Lothlorien
SAURON, the Dark Lord, maker of the One Ring, and the supreme agent of evil in Middle-earth

The Story:

Bilbo Baggins, the most adventurous hobbit of the Shire, plans to celebrate his 111th birthday. His old friend Gandalf the Grey, a wizard with special control over fire, tries to restrain him from using his magic ring to vanish at the end of the party. Gandalf is disturbed, for he suspects the ring of being the One Ring forged by Sauron, the Dark Lord, in the volcanic fires of Mount Doom. This ring gives long life but corrupts its user. Even Bilbo, who gained it without losing pity, begins to show signs of its evil influence. On his departure, however, after his spectacular vanishing, he leaves his property, reluctantly including the ring, to his nephew Frodo. Gandalf warns Frodo of its dangers and advises that he take it from the Shire.

Frodo leaves the Shire, accompanied by his loyal servant Sam Gamgee and two of his cousins, Merry and Pippin. Pursued by fearful Black Riders, they narrowly escape destruction in the Old Forest, and they are rescued by jovial, earthy Tom Bombadil, who proves to be immune to the ring's power. He sends them on their way refreshed.

At Bree, they meet a mysterious ranger called Strider and find a letter from Gandalf urging them to go to Rivendell with Strider, whose real name is Aragorn. On their fourth night out of Bree, they are attacked by Black Riders. In terror, Frodo puts on the ring and becomes invisible to his friends but visible and vulnerable to the Riders, Sauron's Ringwraiths, whose leader stabs Frodo with a weapon that breaks off in the wound and melts. Aragorn drives them off with torches, and the company hastens toward Rivendell. Glorfindel, an elf, meets them and puts Frodo on his horse. At the Ford near Rivendell, the Black Riders try to intercept him but are thwarted by a flood.

Frodo recovers consciousness to find Gandalf with him and to learn that Elrond of Rivendell was treating his fearful wound for days. In Rivendell, Frodo finds Bilbo and meets Elrond, his daughter Arwen Evenstar, and others, including Glóin, an elderly dwarf who formerly accompanied Bilbo. Elrond calls a council to discuss the ring. At the council are Elrond's elven subjects as well as a wood elf named Legolas, Glóin and his son Gimli, Gandalf, the five hobbits, Aragorn, and a noble gray-eyed warrior named Boromir of Gondor. Elrond recounts the history of the Rings of Power, which was made by elvensmiths in the Second Age, and of Sauron's secret forging of a ring to rule and bind all the rest. In that age, Sauron was overthrown by an alliance of human beings and elves, and Isildur cut off the Dark Lord's finger and took the ring, but it slipped from his finger and betrayed him to the orcs. Years later, it was found in the river by Deagol, a hobbit whose kinsman Smeagol murdered him for it and fled underground, becoming the repulsive Gollum. Bilbo found it underground. Pitying the murderous Gollum, he did not kill him but merely used the ring to escape. Sauron, though defeated, was not destroyed. He gathers an evil host in Mordor and seeks the ring to make himself ruler of the world. Gandalf tells of the treachery of Saruman the White, leader of the wizards, who imprisoned him. Gandalf escaped with the help of Gwaihir, the king of the Eagles.

The council decides to send the ring to Mordor to unmake it in the fires of Mount Doom, the only heat that can destroy it. Frodo reluctantly volunteers to remain the Ringbearer.

Eight others are chosen to complete the Fellowship of the Ring: Gandalf, Aragorn, Boromir, Gimli, Legolas, Sam, Merry, and Pippin. Aragorn's broken sword, Anduril, is reforged by the elves. Bilbo gives Frodo his elven sword Sting and a coat of mail made of mithril, a precious light metal harder than steel. Frodo wears it under his weather-stained clothes.

The travelers pass through cold, barren country and try to cross over the Misty Mountains, but a blizzard drives them back, and they are attacked by wolves. Gandalf drives away the wolves with magic fire and leads the company into the Caverns of Moria, the ancient dwarf kingdom. He tells them of Durin, the dwarf king, and his people who delved so deeply for mithril that they roused a terrible being that destroyed them. Bilbo's old companion Balin led a company of dwarfs from the Lonely Mountains to retake Moria. The travelers find Balin's tomb, signs of a terrible battle, and a blood-stained, tattered book from which Gandalf is able to reconstruct the fortunes of Balin's people to the time when their last battle began.

A drum far below signals an attack by orcs and trolls. The fellowship repels the first attack, and Frodo is struck down by a spear thrust, but his mithril coat saves him. When they are forced to retreat, Gandalf remains to hold a stone door. Something opposes his will fiercely, and the door shatters. They hasten to a narrow stone bridge across an abyss. A monstrous fire demon appears. Gandalf opposes him and destroys the bridge but is dragged into the cleft with the monster. Heavy-hearted, the others follow Aragorn to Lothlorien, home of high elves.

Lothlorien is a haven more wonderful than Rivendell. The ageless beauty of Queen Galadriel charms them all, especially Gimli, in spite of the ancient enmity between elves and dwarfs. Boromir alone is uneasy in her presence. On their departure, she gives them precious gifts, and the elves supply them with boats and provisions to continue their journey by water down the Anduin River. They soon learn they are being followed by Gollum, once owner of the ring and now apparently Sauron's spy. They are again attacked by orcs, led by a Ringwraith on a flying mount like a pterodactyl. Legolas gains respite for them by killing the mount with an arrow. After this escape, the evil of the ring corrupts Boromir, who attempts to take it from Frodo. To escape him, Frodo puts on the ring and vanishes. Boromir returns to the company in a penitent mood. They scatter to look for Frodo.

Alone and invisible, Frodo tries to decide on the right course of action. Suddenly he is aware of an evil eye searching for him, and he is paralyzed with terror; then an inner voice commands him to take off the ring. He regains control of himself and removes it. A groping shadow seems to pass over the mountain and to fade away. Frodo decides to take an elven boat and continue his perilous journey alone, but Sam anticipates his decision, discovers him, and begs to be allowed to go along. Frodo accepts Sam's loyal company, and they set out together for Mordor. The Fellowship of the Ring is broken.

Critical Evaluation:

Samuel Johnson is credited with saying that "A book should teach us to enjoy life or to endure it." J. R. R. Tolkien's trilogy *The Lord of the Rings* teaches both. It also fits the dictum of another writer, Robert Louis Stevenson, who said, "And this is the particular triumph of the artist—not to be true merely, but to be lovable; not simply to convince, but to enchant." Tolkien has been compared to Lodovico Ariosto and to Edmund Spenser. Indeed, he belongs to the tradition of writers of epic and romance going back to the days of Homer. His work is deeply rooted in the great literature of the past and seems likely itself to be a hardy survivor resistant to time. In *The Fellowship of the Ring*, the first volume of *The Lord of the Rings*, Celeborn the Elf King (no doubt speaking for his author) warns against despising the lore that has survived from distant years, for old wives' tales may be the repositories of needful wisdom.

Although *The Lord of the Rings* is a trilogy, each volume of which bears a different title, it is really a single, continuous tale. The author is in complete control of his copious material. He creates a consistent world with a sharply realized geography that includes maps; he works out a many-centuried time scheme and summarizes the chronology in an appendix to the third volume, *The Return of the King* (1955). With fertile inventiveness, Tolkien launches an amazing number of well-drawn, believable characters, places, and events. If there are any loose ends in the three volumes, they are so minor as to be negligible. The book has been pronounced an allegory; with equal certainty it has been pronounced not an allegory. At any rate, it is a gigantic myth of the struggle between good and evil.

The author first presents his invented creatures, the hobbits or halflings, in an early book, *The Hobbit*, to which *The Lord of the Rings* is a sequel, but a sequel with significant differences. Hobbits are small, furry-footed humanoids with a delight in simple pleasures and a dislike of the uncomfortable responsibilities of heroism. They share the world with human beings, wizards, elves, dwarfs, trolls, orcs, and other creatures. Although many of these creatures are not the usual figures of the contemporary novel, thoughtful readers can find applications to inhabitants and events of their world,

which has its share of traitors, malice-driven demidevils, and time-servers, yet is not completely destitute of heroes and individuals of goodwill. Of the three volumes, *The Fellowship of the Ring* has the widest variation in tone: After beginning with comedy and domestic comfort, it moves into high adventure, peril, and sorrow. Occasional verses appear in the pages, but Tolkien's poetry resides in both his prose and his verse.

The Fellowship of the Ring introduces two tales that run side by side throughout the trilogy. One tale is that of the destruction of Sauron and the return of King Elessar to the throne of his fathers; the other is the story of the journey of the hobbits from jolly complacency to unexpected heights of self-knowledge and self-sacrifice. The former gives the work its quality of ancient romance, for the characters are larger than life and speak to one another in elevated language; natural descriptions and expressions of emotion tend to be more formal and ceremonious than realistic. The second tale contains elements of realism; the most realistic, homey, and familiar characters are from Tolkien's invented race, the hobbits.

The major figure in Tolkien's high saga is Aragorn, later King Elessar. He is certainly the most heroic of the characters in the classical sense, but the very elevation of his character has led some critics to see him as inhuman, lifeless, or too good to be true. Actually, however, he is a character of considerable subtlety and complexity; he earns his credentials as a hero honestly. Initially, in his disguise as Strider, Aragorn must use guile and indirection to win the confidence of the hobbits. They understand neither the implications of their situation nor their own personal danger. Aragorn, on the other hand, realizes that he is as frightening to them as any of Sauron's agents. Therefore, he uses their apprehensions toward him to stimulate their sense of danger, after which he ingratiates himself by his wit and finally by Gandalf's letter of identification. When asked why he did not identify himself earlier, he replies that he wants to be accepted for himself. Once the quest begins, Aragorn proves his mettle and worthiness for kingship, not primarily by brute strength or heroic posturing but by his adroit handling of the others and his subtle strategies. A special poignancy and humanity are further given to him by his prolonged and tender love affair with Lady Arwen. Readers may never feel close to Aragorn, but they can understand and feel for him as a human being and admire him as a heroic figure.

Although Aragorn leads the troops to victory in battle, the primary task of the epic falls not to the most heroic of the men but to the mildest of the hobbits, Frodo Baggins. The name of this little race suggests a hob, hobnobbing, a dobbin;

it calls up visions of fireside comforts, companionship, patient steadfastness, and good sense. Descriptions of hobbits and hobbit life in the prologue outline the prototype: a steady, plain little person, none too clever.

This impression, however, is belied in the story by the characters of Samwise and Frodo; in developing the character of Sam, Tolkien begins with a collection of those homely virtues that most nations arrogate to their own peasant class and then adds, without loss of credibility, a quirky intelligence that outstrips shrewdness and a fancy for elfish lore. In Frodo, he marries the homely world of the Shire with the high deeds of the Dunedain. In Frodo are combined the best things of both worlds: He is the wisest and most noble of the hobbits and the bravest of the heroes because he is the smallest and most afraid.

It is primarily because of Frodo's unpretentiousness that he is "chosen" for the crucial task of casting the ring into the fire of Mordor. The "large" heroes of the book, Aragorn and Gandalf, refuse the task, not from fear of external dangers but from the knowledge that they would not be able to resist the ring's effect on them—they are too worldly and versed in the ways of power to be immune to the awful temptation to use it. Only Frodo is sufficiently small and humble to withstand its corrupting influence right up to the edge of the fire—where even he weakens and the ring is finally destroyed by powers beyond his control.

Further Reading

Clark, George, and Daniel Timmons, eds. *J. R. R. Tolkien and His Literary Resonances: Views of Middle Earth.* Westport, Conn.: Greenwood Press, 2000. A collection of fourteen essays devoted to Tolkien's Middle-earth works, including examinations of his images of evil and use of medieval allegory, and comparisons of his work to that of John Milton and C. S. Lewis.

Curry, Patrick. *Defending Middle-earth: Tolkien, Myth, and Modernity.* New York: HarperCollins, 1997. Reprint. Boston: Houghton Mifflin, 2004. Examines the relevance of Tolkien's mythological world for modern readers. Focuses on three aspects of Tolkien's depiction of Middle-earth: its social and political structure, its nature and ecology, and its spirituality and ethics.

Dickerson, Matthew T., and Jonathan Evans. *Ents, Elves, and Eriador: The Environmental Vision of J. R. R. Tolkien.* Lexington: University Press of Kentucky, 2006. A discussion of Tolkien's view of the natural world and environmental responsibility, in which the authors argue that the lifestyles of his fictional characters anticipate many of the tenets of modern environmentalism and agrarianism.

Drout, Michael D. C., ed. *J. R. R. Tolkien Encyclopedia: Scholarship and Critical Assessment.* New York: Routledge, 2007. A comprehensive reference containing five hundred entries on a wide range of subjects, including Tolkien's biography, characters, influence, critical reception, scholarship about the writer, his individual works, and adaptations of his writing to the screen and other media.

Giddings, Robert, ed. *J. R. R. Tolkien: This Far Land.* London: Vision Press, 1983. A collection of ten essays that discuss Tolkien's world and examine subjects ranging from narrative form and the use of humor to the construction of female sexuality.

Kocher, Paul H. *Master of Middle-earth.* Boston: Houghton Mifflin, 1972. A critical examination of Tolkien's major fictional works. Focuses on the creation and development of Middle-earth and provides perspective on the different qualities of the races inhabiting the realm. Offers critical insight on Tolkien's notions of choice within a Christian framework.

Lee, Stuart D., and Elizabeth Solopova. *The Keys of Middle-earth.* New York: Palgrave Macmillan, 2005. A handy portal into Tolkien's medieval sources, featuring modern translations of the original texts.

Lobdell, Jared. *The Rise of Tolkienian Fantasy.* Chicago: Open Court, 2005. Examines Tolkien's fantasy fiction, discussing the writers who influenced him, the elements of his fantasy literature, and his literary heirs, including writers Ursula K. Le Guin, Stephen King, and J. K. Rowling.

Penn, Anne C. *One Ring to Bind Them All: Tolkien's Mythology.* Tuscaloosa: University of Alabama Press, 1979. A critical examination of Tolkien's process of mythmaking, moving beyond traditional literary analysis to employ perspectives derived from linguistics, folklore, psychology, and folklore studies.

Rosebury, Brian. *Tolkien: A Cultural Phenomenon.* 2d ed. New York: Palgrave Macmillan, 2003. Traces the development of Tolkien's writing over several decades, devoting a lengthy analysis to *The Lord of the Rings.* The revised and expanded edition provides additional information on Tolkien scholarship and discusses director Peter Jackson's film adaptation of *The Lord of the Rings.*

Tolkien, J. R. R. *The History of Middle-earth.* Edited by Christopher Tolkien. 12 vols. Boston: Houghton Mifflin, 1988. Edited and fully annotated by Tolkien's son, this series documents the creation of Middle-earth and its mythology in chronological fashion. Volume six, *The Return of the Shadow*, contains the initial drafts of *The Fellowship of the Ring* and demonstrates the painstaking creation of the story in fascinating detail.

The Female Quixote
Or, The Adventures of Arabella

Author: Charlotte Lennox (c. 1729-1804)
First published: 1752
Type of work: Novel
Type of plot: Quixotic
Time of plot: 1740's-1750's
Locale: London, Bath, and the English countryside

Principal characters:
ARABELLA, the heroine
THE MARQUIS, her father
CHARLES GLANVILLE, her cousin and love interest
SIR CHARLES GLANVILLE, her uncle and guardian
CHARLOTTE GLANVILLE, her cousin
SIR GEORGE BELLMOUR, Arabella's suitor
MR. HERVEY, a man from London
EDWARD, a neighbor's gardener
THE COUNTESS OF ——, an esteemed acquaintance of Arabella

The Story:

The marquis, Arabella's father, had retreated to the English countryside and married a much younger wife who read romances for entertainment. Their daughter, Arabella, had been born a year after the wedding, but the marchioness, Arabella's mother, had died in childbirth.

Older now, Arabella finds her mother's romance books and reads them obsessively. She believes them to be truthful accounts of proper conduct between men and women. No one disobliges her of this notion.

At church, Arabella sees Mr. Hervey, a gentleman from London, and believes that he wants to kidnap her to rape her. She later meets Edward, an attractive and well-spoken gardener on a neighboring estate, and believes he is disguising his true aristocratic identity to be near her. Her cousin, Charles Glanville, arrives and falls in love with her. He soon realizes that Arabella is acting a role and submits because he loves her. Arabella falls in love with Charles but will not admit it.

Arabella's father dies. Sir Charles Glanville, Arabella's uncle and (now) guardian, arrives and is confounded by Arabella's incessant discussion of romance books. He tells his son, Charles, that Arabella will not make him happy unless she changes her ways. Arabella then befriends Miss Groves and interrogates the woman's servant about her lady's adventures. The servant divulges the scandalous history of Miss Groves. Miss Groves admonishes Arabella for her rudeness and leaves. Arabella is perplexed.

Charles and his sister come for a visit, and Arabella is overjoyed to meet her cousin, Charlotte. They all go to the races, where they meet Sir George Bellmour.

Later, Arabella fears that Edward now intends to kidnap her. She flees her house, sprains her ankle, and faints. Lucy,

her maidservant, runs to find help, and Arabella asks assistance from a stranger. Charles arrives, as does Edward, and Arabella accuses Edward of trying to kidnap her. Edward denies it. She banishes him and then commands Charles to kill him. Charles loves Arabella but is embarrassed by her inability to distinguish reality from fantasy.

Sir George is interested in Arabella, more for her property than her person, and quickly realizes that she is taken with romance books. He resolves to use his vast knowledge of romances to seduce her.

Charles falls dangerously ill. Assuming it is because of his love of her, Arabella commands Charles to live and waits for his immediate recovery. When he does recover, she instructs him in the tenets of romance. While Arabella is later alone with Sir George, he speaks to her in romance terms and she is pleased. When Arabella later speaks this way in front of Sir Charles, Charles is embarrassed and tries to change the subject.

Arabella sees Mr. Hervey and wants Charles to defend her honor, as she thinks Hervey is there to kidnap her. The men fight, but for another reason, and no one is hurt. Later, Sir George speaks in romance terms to Arabella in front of Charles and Charlotte, which incites Charles to chastise George for indulging Arabella's inappropriate behavior. George vows to quit by degrees but also gives his history, which involves intrigues with many ladies, and Arabella calls him inconstant. Arabella believes that her Uncle Charles has fallen in love with her but she learns from Charles that he was only trying to press his son's suit with her and that all is resolved.

In Bath, the group befriends Mr. Selvin and Mr. Tinsel. Arabella believes that both men are in love with her and finds, to her disappointment, that this is not the case. Tinsel, in fact, believes her to be mad. The Countess of —— befriends Arabella in Bath and tries to speak sense to her. While Arabella is respectful of the countess's views and does consider them, she continues in her peculiar ways. The group leaves Bath for London. At Vaux Hall, Arabella vows protection for a woman who is a prostitute. Charles chastises Arabella for her carelessness.

Arabella moves to Richmond, where she befriends a woman named Cynecia, princess of Gaul, who tells Arabella that she is miserable for love of her absent lover, Arimenes. Cynecia then claims that Charles is actually Arimenes. A heartbroken Arabella banishes Charles; he is bewildered but realizes that Sir George is behind the accusation.

Convinced that four men on horseback are going to kidnap her, Arabella jumps into the River Thames. She is rescued but is unconscious.

Charles sees Sir George and also a woman in a veil. Enraged and believing the woman to be Arabella, Charles wounds Sir George with his sword. The woman is Charlotte, and not Arabella, and Charles immediately repents. George asks Charles's forgiveness for the Cynecia business.

Fearful of her mental state because he just had a strange conversation with her, Arabella's doctor tells Charles that she might still be delirious. Charles explains Arabella's obsession with romances and asks the doctor to speak to her. The doctor tells Arabella that romances are untrue, ridiculous, and criminal. Ashamed, Arabella quits romance books forever, asks Charles's forgiveness for her foibles, and consents to be his wife, if he will have her. They are married in a joint ceremony with Sir George and Charlotte. Both couples enjoy happy marriages.

Critical Evaluation:

Born around 1729, Charlotte Lennox spent her formative years in Gibraltar and America until her father died in 1743; her family then returned to England. There, Lennox enjoyed the patronage of Lady Cecilia Isabella Finch and the countess of Rockingham, thus enabling her to dedicate her time to writing poetry. She published *Poems on Several Occasions* in 1747 and married Alexander Lennox the same year. Charlotte Lennox enjoyed the friendships of such notables as writers Samuel Richardson, Henry Fielding, and Samuel Johnson. Although she continued to write for the rest of her life, nothing equaled the success of *The Female Quixote*. Lennox died a pauper in 1804.

By the time Lennox wrote and published *The Female Quixote* in 1752, the heyday of reading romances was over, but the genre was still in fashion. At that time, romances in-

cluded tales of chivalry, knighthood, history, and courtly love. *The Female Quixote* bridges a time in literary history when the primacy of poetry as the serious literary genre was soon to be rivaled by prose, particularly with the popularity of such novels as Richardson's *Pamela, Or Virtue Rewarded* (1740) and *Clarissa: Or, The History of a Young Lady* (1747-1748). Richardson actually advised Lennox in her writing of *The Female Quixote* and is believed to have written the dedication to the earl of Middlesex. *The Female Quixote* is instrumental in the history of the novel for its discussion of the unequal position of women in society and the problems they face because of their powerlessness. Equally important is the treatment of women by other women. Arabella, however, is the model of sentimentality at its finest. So influential was this novel that many authors noted its significance, the most famous writer being perhaps Jane Austen, who cited *The Female Quixote* as inspiration for her novel *Northanger Abbey* (1817).

Central to *The Female Quixote* is the tenet of quixotism, a foolish, impractical, and idealized notion of the world; the idea was first demonstrated in Miguel de Cervantes' novel *Don Quixote de la Mancha* (1605, 1615). Quixotism was a popular plot line in Cervantes' and Lennox's times, but it was Lennox's novel that was the most popular and that remained in continual publication for one hundred years. At the heart of the story is Arabella's misguided education, which leads her to believe that romance books are factual guides for her adult life. Because of the boredom of her stifling and isolated life, Arabella takes to romances and finally finds a place where she can be powerful and noticed.

Romances are famous for their antiquated subject matter, including the courtly romance and the love stories of lesser known historical figures. More important to the political economy of *The Female Quixote* is Arabella's inherent understanding of the primacy of women in these romances. The women have supreme power over their adoring subjects and even, it seems, hold the balance between life and death. Because Arabella has no mother or any female acquaintances or relatives to explain to her what a woman's life is actually like, or to instruct her in the realities of what to expect in modern society, she is in for a terrible shock. In fact, the running joke among the characters is how long it will take her to acquiesce to the proposals of her cousin, Charles Glanville, for Arabella does not understand that she is regarded as chattel—first the property of her father and then the property of her husband upon marriage.

Although Charles cannot demand that she marry him—the only real right that women enjoyed in English society at this time was the right of refusal—it is assumed that she will do so because it had been the dying wish of her adored father. Arabella's power over Charles is illusory, and Charles frequently comments that he is embarrassed by her whims and that he wishes she would come to her senses. Because Arabella is a model of sentimentality, she sees reason at the end so that she can enjoy a happy marriage with Charles. Had she remained true to her vision, Arabella ran the risk of falling prey to men like Sir George or, worse, being a spinster in a world that believed that an unmarried woman was useless.

While her society is sexist, and this includes women's own sexism against other women, Arabella, to the contrary, refuses to denigrate her gender. She is loyal to all of the women she meets, from the unfortunate Miss Groves and her two illegitimate children to the prostitute at Vaux Hall; she does not even register the snide remarks intended for her by jealous women. While romances give her convoluted notions of the appropriate relationships between men and women, they also give her an understanding of the importance of the bond of loyalty between women, and the need for honesty and unity among them.

Upon publication, *The Female Quixote* was lauded as an important book for its excellent quixotic plot, its refined language, and its moving, sentimental portrait of Arabella. It is heralded today as highly significant in the history of the novel for its clear commentary on the roles of women and the tradition of sexism in English society in the eighteenth century.

Valerie Murrenus Pilmaier

Further Reading

Armstrong, Nancy. *Desire and Domestic Fiction: A Political History of the Novel*. New York: Oxford University Press, 1987. Armstrong argues that women novelists were instrumental to the rise of the middle-class ethos in English society because of their preoccupations with domestic subjects, domesticity, and sentimentality. Arabella, Armstrong argues, is the epitome of sentimentality and the "tamed" woman.

Doody, Margaret Anne. *The True Story of the Novel*. New Brunswick, N.J.: Rutgers University Press, 1996. A provocative look at the political issues surrounding the rise of the novel. Examines why there existed such a push to distinguish between romances and the novel in English society, even though, Doody argues, there had been a symbiotic relationship between the two.

Gallagher, Catherine. *Nobody's Story: The Vanishing Acts of Women Writers in the Marketplace, 1670-1820*. Berkeley: University of California Press, 1994. This book is essential to any study of Lennox. Gallagher devotes one chapter to Lennox's place in the history of the woman novelist between the late seventeenth and early nineteenth centuries.

Small, Miriam Rossiter. *Charlotte Ramsay Lennox: An Eighteenth Century Lady of Letters*. 1935. Reprint. New Haven, Conn.: Yale University Press, 1969. This is considered the best biography of Lennox and is widely cited in scholarly articles. Part of the Yale Studies in English series.

Spencer, Jane. *The Rise of the Woman Novelist from Aphra Behn to Jane Austen*. New York: Blackwell, 1986. Spencer demonstrates a demarcation in style and theme between women writers of the early eighteenth century—whose themes involved sexuality and power dynamics—and those women writers of the later century—who helped to fashion the new definition of "modest" or "acceptable" femininity in English society. Lennox falls into the latter category.

Todd, Janet. *The Sign of Angellica: Women, Writing, and Fiction, 1660-1800*. New York: Columbia University Press, 1989. This book discusses the precipitating factors that created the stigma attached to the English female novelist: finances, patriarchy, and a rapidly growing reading public.

The Feminine Mystique

Author: Betty Friedan (1921-2006)
First published: 1963
Type of work: Social criticism

In *The Feminine Mystique*, Betty Friedan addresses what she terms "the problem that has no name," questioning the aims of post-World War II American society and, especially, the roles of women. Born in Peoria, Illinois, and a graduate of Smith College, Friedan worked as a writer and researcher for women's magazines before writing her groundbreaking book. During her research work, she discovered and interviewed a generation of women who identified themselves with the phrase "occupation: housewife." Many of these "housewives" were college-educated women and were the daughters of college-educated women who became cultural pioneers in the 1920's and 1930's, working as teachers, nurses, doctors, lawyers, engineers, and other professionals.

With the triumph of woman's suffrage still fresh in the national conscience, pre-World War II women, despite an economic depression and a war raging in Europe and Asia, saw a limitless future for both their sons and their daughters. Circumstances, however, intervened, and the mood changed. The daughters of Rosie the Riveter and the granddaughters of Jazz Age flappers found a different America. World War II ended, and men came home to reclaim their jobs. The world saw the dawning of the nuclear age, the surging of the U.S. economy, a rise in marriages, and an increasing birthrate. As new houses were built and filled with wondrous new time-saving appliances, such as the dishwasher, the washing machine and clothes dryer, and the self-cleaning oven, the modern American woman became the mythical domestic goddess.

Writers of popular women's magazines, who were mostly men, touted the new norm of easy home living. At the center of this blissful picture was the wife and mother, doting on her children, attentive to her husband, glorying in her beautifully decorated home. She lived through her children and her husband, not worrying herself about the larger issues of the day. More than just the myth, these were the commonly held expectations for women in the United States after the war.

In an effort to justify the gap between their reality and the ideal expectations, housewives turned to a number of diversions: alcoholism, psychiatry, prescription drugs, sexual conquests, and a fierce denial of their feelings, which often served as a springboard to feelings of inadequacy. All of these diversions sought to answer the often-stated question,

Is this all there is? Many women, after raising their children, keeping their house spotless for years, encouraging their husbands—in short, serving as the bedrock of support for the family unit—looked around to ponder their accomplishments. What did they have to show for their efforts? What differences had they made in the world?

Beneath this seemingly serene surface, Friedan found layers of angst, dissatisfaction, and regret. Society viewed unsatisfied housewives as hysterical women who were victims of too much education and too many unrealistic expectations. Intelligent writers of the period attributed women's unhappiness to penis envy. Indeed, decades earlier, Sigmund Freud argued that a woman more than anything else desires to have a penis and is never truly fulfilled in life until she gives birth to a son of her own. To other intelligent people, women's unhappiness was merely a matter of biology; women are born to nurture. Anthropologist Margaret Mead, too, encouraged women to embrace their femininity, which apparently meant sacrificing any chance for self-actualization. A woman's role in American society was presented in the popular media of the day as a clear choice: career versus home.

After the war, education for women was revamped. Courses focused on home economics, child rearing, and other practical approaches to everyday domestic problems. Women were not interested, so the argument had gone, in learning for the sake of learning. A deeper understanding of science and mathematics, for example, was unnecessary because women needed to learn only enough to support their families and help with tasks such as balancing the family budget, planning meals, and decorating for the holidays.

The housewife trap, as Friedan calls it in *The Feminine Mystique*, is "a comfortable concentration camp." Years of this existence have turned women into zombielike creatures without sparkles in their eyes or cheerful notes in their voices. To break this spell, Friedan recommends education, a renewed emphasis on teaching and retraining women who long to return to the workforce but fear it may be too late. By Friedan's argument, women have been sold on a false premise: Women can have the best of both worlds, family and career. Working women with adequate education, Friedan argues (and presents evidence for), have a happier life, better sex, better marriages, and better-adjusted children.

One has to consider *The Feminine Mystique* within the context of its time. What may seem like common sense in the early twenty-first century appears obvious only through the lens of experience. Friedan published her work in 1963; the research was impressive though perhaps deliberately slanted and presented to bolster the author's biases. What persists without question, however, is the social and cultural impact of *The Feminine Mystique*. However, would the same book have had similar effects in the United States if published a few years later, in 1969 or 1973?

The Feminine Mystique represents the opening volley in what has become known as the second wave of the women's movement in the United States. The book was published on the cusp of great social and cultural changes, just before the assassination of U.S. president John F. Kennedy, the height of the Civil Rights movement, "Beatlemania," the escalation of the war in Vietnam, the Moon landing, Woodstock, and Watergate. Could these staggering events, all occurring within ten years of the book's publication and all shaping America's mood and attitude, have overshadowed *The Feminine Mystique*, lessening its impact? *The Feminine Mystique* was perhaps an answer, a criticism, and a warning for a previous generation, but its continued relevance and significance cannot be denied. Women now are major political-party candidates for president of the United States, serve on the U.S. Supreme Court, serve in the military, and fill more than half the seats in college and university classrooms.

Frustrating barriers to equality remain, including the realities of the two-income family (in which women still do most of the housework and child rearing), a lack of adequate child care for working women, the perspective of husbands who still see the world in terms of men's work and women's work, the biases of employers who offer little sympathy to women dealing with young children and aging parents, the glass ceiling, and lower pay for equal work. The United States that Friedan influenced had developed in unanticipated ways, and the role of the housewife still exists as an option, but not, in large part because of *The Feminine Mystique*, as an expectation.

After publishing *The Feminine Mystique*, Friedan went on to write the statement of purpose of the then-new National Organization for Women (NOW), serving as one of its founders and its first president in 1966. She published other books, including *It Changed My Life: Writings on the Women's Movement* (1976), *The Second Stage* (1981), *The Fountain of Age* (1993), and *Life So Far* (2000), her autobiography.

Randy L. Abbott

Further Reading

Hennessee, Judith. *Betty Friedan: Her Life*. New York: Random House, 1999. This book examines the contradictions of Friedan's life. She was a celebrated feminist leader and also a flawed woman whose own life missed the mark as measured by her own standards.

Horowitz, Daniel. *Betty Friedan and the Making of "The Feminine Mystique": The American Left, the Cold War, and Modern Feminism*. Amherst: University of Massachusetts Press, 1998. This biography explores Friedan's methods in presenting herself in *The Feminine Mystique* as something other than a left-leaning, prolabor unionist, which had been Friedan's background.

Miller, Meredith. "*The Feminine Mystique*: Sexual Excess and the Pre-Political Housewife." *Women: A Cultural Review* 16, no. 1 (Spring, 2005): 1-17. This article puts Friedan's book into the context of the history of feminist thought and activism in the mid-twentieth century.

Oliver, Susan. *Betty Friedan: The Personal Is Political*. New York: Pearson Longman, 2008. A biography that examines Friedan's life and work, which included nearly fifty years of political activism and leadership, journalistic writings, scholarship, speaking, and teaching. Part of the Library of American Biography series.

Seligman, Dan. "The Friedan Mystique." *Commentary* 121, no. 4 (April, 2006): 42-46. This article explores the effect of Friedan's book on feminism in the United States, investigating her assertion that being a housewife is the same as being denied personhood.

Wolfe, Alan. "The Mystique of Betty Friedan." *Atlantic Monthly* 284, no. 3 (September, 1999): 98-105. Wolfe takes a critical look at the sources Friedan used in researching her book.

Fences

Author: August Wilson (1945-2005)
First produced: 1985; first published, 1985
Type of work: Drama
Type of plot: Domestic realism
Time of plot: 1957-1965
Locale: An industrial city in the United States

Principal characters:
TROY MAXSON, a garbage collector
JIM BONO, his friend of thirty years
ROSE, Troy's wife of eighteen years
LYONS, Troy's married son
GABRIEL, Troy's younger brother
CORY, Troy and Rose's teenage son
ALBERTA, Troy's lover
RAYNELL, the daughter of Troy and Alberta

The Story:

Longtime friends Troy Maxson and Jim Bono are participating in their Friday (payday) night ritual of drinking and talking on Troy's porch. They discuss a complaint Troy had filed about working conditions that deny black garbage workers the opportunity to drive garbage trucks. Jim shifts the conversation to the subject of Alberta, for whom he believes Troy has more than a passing interest, but Troy denies the accusation.

Rose, Troy's wife, joins Troy and Jim on the porch. Troy explains to Jim about how he and Rose first met; Rose corrects his version of what happened. Troy and Rose disagree about shopping at the local black grocery store versus shopping at the A&P supermarket. Their difference of opinion continues when they discuss their teenage son, Cory, and his plans to play college football. Troy tells a story about how he had wrestled Death and won. Lyons, Troy's son by an earlier marriage, stops by. Troy anticipates that he wants to borrow money. Lyons rejects Troy's offer to get him a job because it is his music that gives his life meaning. Troy directs his son to get ten dollars from Rose, because she is the one who gets her husband's paycheck every Friday.

The next morning, Rose sings while she hangs up the laundry, and Troy considers her playing the numbers as a waste of money. Gabriel, Troy's younger brother, visits. He suffers from a World War II brain injury, which has left him mentally deficient. He carries with him a basket of discarded fruits and vegetables as well as an old trumpet tied around his waist. Gabe, as he is called, is concerned that Troy is angry with him for moving out of their house. After Gabe leaves, Rose expresses concern that her brother-in-law may not be eating properly at his new boardinghouse, and she and Troy discuss the possibility of having him hospitalized again. Troy feels that no one wants to be locked up. He recalls that if it had not been for Gabe's injury, he would have the same condition, too. Rose expects her husband to work on the fence, but he says that he is going down to Taylor's.

Cory wants to know from his father why the family does not have a television. Troy responds by instructing his son on the importance of not going into debt. They discuss Troy's baseball days and current baseball players. Troy wants his son to work, not to play football. Troy's opposition prompts Cory to ask why his father does not like him. Troy responds by talking about responsibility. Cory is his son and he is obligated to take care of him, but he does not have to like him. Rose overhears their conversation and tells Troy that he is more than forty years old and too old to play in the major leagues. She says that the world is changing around him.

Two weeks later, Cory leaves the house carrying his football equipment, and Troy and Jim celebrate Troy's promotion to garbage-truck driver. When Lyons returns the ten dollars he had borrowed, he reminds his father that Cory is nearly grown up. Troy, however, is upset that Cory has pretended to be keeping his job at the A&P when he is really sneaking off to football practice without telling his father. Troy confides to his older son that he had been abused by his own father, abuse that had caused him to leave home for good when he was fourteen years old. He reminisces, too, about meeting Rose, meeting Jim, and learning to play baseball. Lyons invites his father to hear him play at the Grill, but Troy turns down the invitation. Cory comes home upset because he had learned that his father had told his coach that he could no longer play on the high school football team.

The next morning, Rose informs Cory that the police have picked up Uncle Gabe for disturbing the peace. Troy bails Gabe out of jail and then begins to work on the fence with Jim. The fence is important to Rose, who sees it as a symbol of keeping her family consolidated and secure within the warm circle of the household. As Jim points out to Troy, "Rose wants to hold on to you all. She loves you." Jim urges Troy not to do wrong by Rose and to get his life in order so that Rose will not have to find out about Troy's love affair with another woman. Troy reminds Jim to do right by his own wife and to buy her the refrigerator for which she has been asking. Jim agrees to buy the refrigerator after Troy finishes the fence for Rose.

Jim leaves, and Troy has an important conversation with Rose, revealing that another woman is pregnant with his child. During their conversation, Gabe visits, and Rose, though she is trying to process what Troy is disclosing to her, directs Gabe to get some watermelon. Rose is baffled by Troy's unfaithfulness at this point in their marriage of eighteen years. Troy's defense is that he thought he could be a new man with Alberta, who had taken him away from the pressures and problems of his life. To Troy's revelation that he felt trapped, Rose retorts that she had been right there standing beside him, willingly giving up whatever hopes and dreams that she could have nurtured to provide a home for him. Her discovery that he is not the finest man in the world only makes her hold on to him in love more tightly. At this point, Troy grabs Rose's arm too tightly, and Cory comes to her defense. Troy threateningly declares that Cory now has two strikes against him, and he had better not "strike out."

Six months later, Alberta is in the hospital about to give birth. Rose informs Troy, who cannot read, that a paper he had signed in front of a judge had committed Gabe to an institution, with half of his money earmarked to the hospital and the remaining half to Troy. A phone call from the hospital interrupts them with the news that Alberta had died giving birth to a healthy baby girl.

Three days later, Troy brings his baby home from the hospital, begging Rose for help. Rose agrees that the child is innocent and should not be punished for the sins of her father, but her agreement carries a consequence for Troy: "Okay, Troy . . . I'll take care of your baby for you . . . this child got a mother. But you a womanless man."

Two months later, Rose is baking cakes for a church bake sale and Troy is sitting on the porch alone drinking and singing a song about a dog named Blue. Jim visits Troy and tells him that since Troy's promotion to become a truck driver, he has not seen him. Troy informs him that driving up front is lonely with no one to talk to. Jim declines Troy's invitation to stay longer. Troy informs him that Lucille had told Rose about getting the refrigerator, and Jim notes that Rose had told Lucille that Troy had completed the fence. Cory comes home and tries to get by his father, who is sitting in the middle of the steps. They have a confrontation, and Troy kicks his son out of the house. Cory tells his mother that he will be back for his belongings; Troy, hearing this, says he is going to put his son's things on the other side of the fence.

Seven years later, Cory, a corporal in the U.S. Marine Corps, returns home; his father has died. Jim compliments Cory on his achievements and tells him, "Your daddy knew you had it in you." Lyons, who has been in prison, had received permission to attend his father's funeral. Still bitter, however, Cory informs his mother that he does not plan to attend the funeral. Rose reminds him that Troy was his father. Cory and his half sister, Raynell, strike up a conversation and begin to sing Troy's childhood song about Old Blue, prompting Cory to change his mind and attend his father's funeral. Gabe, who is still institutionalized, also had received permission to attend his brother's funeral. Gabe sees this as a momentous time: He takes out his trumpet and prepares to signal Saint Peter to open the gates of Heaven for Troy.

"The Story" by Jill B. Gidmark; revised by Barbara M. Whitehead

Critical Evaluation:

August Wilson ranks as one of the most significant voices in contemporary American theater. His plays, which reveal a remarkable talent to particularize the African American experience, simultaneously create a universal appeal. The centerpiece of his prolific writing career is a ten-play cycle in which he chronicles the lives of African Americans living in different decades of the twentieth century. Wilson's plays reflect his rhetorical aims to use art to change the relationship between blacks and society and to make clear that the culture of black America "exists and that it is capable of offering sustenance."

Fences, the second contribution to his ten-play cycle, earned Wilson a Pulitzer Prize in drama in 1987, as well as other awards. This two-act drama, conventionally structured, focuses on the lives of the Troy Maxson family, endeavoring to survive in a northern urban setting that is inhospitable and impoverishing. Not unlike the southern environment from which they came, this new setting is exploitive and is poised to wreak havoc on their aspirations and identities. The playwright's tragic sense about the influence of environment on the human spirit is most evident in the characterization of the protagonist, Troy, who falls from grace in the eyes of his wife, sons, and best friend. However, Troy's characterization is developed sympathetically to advance the play's concern regarding the interrelationship of responsibility, family, and personal fulfillment.

As with Wilson's other plays, poetry influences the style of *Fences*. Wilson relies on the metaphor to give his plays direction. Metaphors of the blues, baseball, and the past are interwoven into the development of plot—the refusal to cave under the adverse circumstances of life, life as a game in which one may land safely on base as well as strike out, and the relationship of ancestors, especially black fathers, to current generations. Still, the metaphor meeting the playwright's criterion of driving the play forward appears as the play's title: *Fences*.

Wilson uses the fence metaphor to interweave the themes of protection and barriers. In act 1, scene 2, Rose sings the chorus to "Jesus, Be a Fence Around Me," which is a petition for her protection. In act 2, scene 1, both Cory and Troy wonder why Rose wants the fence built. Jim explains that a fence may have a double function: To keep others out, or in. He concludes that Rose is trying to hold on to her loved ones. In spite of Rose's effort to be secure, Troy's extramarital affair with Alberta renders her unprotected with the realization that her husband of eighteen years betrayed her. To survive this broken trust, she seeks protection in the church and seeks fulfillment in her role as a mother.

While a barrier between husband and wife gives poignancy to *Fences*, the walls between fathers and sons foster the major conflicts between generations. Wilson's treatment of problems between father and son shows that their conflicts emanate frequently from barriers in society. Troy's father, for example, can never work hard enough to avoid being in debt because his work ethic is insufficient to combat the injustice of the sharecropping system. The barrier erected to disallow Troy's father to earn a just wage contributes to his hostile relationship with Troy and other family members. In turn, once Troy migrates to a northern setting, he encounters racial barriers that prohibit blacks from playing baseball in the major leagues. Relegated to a job as a garbage collector, he observes and eventually protests the lack of opportunity for blacks to be drivers.

Intolerant of any sport as a career for his son Cory, Troy creates a barrier in the father-son relationship when he denies Cory the opportunity to pursue his dream to attend college on a football scholarship. In contrast, the occasional barrier between Lyons and Troy emanates from Troy's incarceration, which had prevented him from being with Lyons during Lyons's formative years. In turn, Troy frowns on Lyons's upbringing and on Lyons's desire to be a jazz musician, a career that does not enable him to be the financial and, thereby, responsible head of his household.

While the play centers on Troy, the characterization of Gabe, his younger brother, reflects complexity and significance. He is the only one of eleven children with whom Troy is in touch. Like his brother Troy, who engages in fiction making through storytelling and modifying the truth, Gabe's world is etched by fantasy. His fantasies, however, are more serious; he is trapped in a world of illusion. Wilson links three important symbols to Gabe's characterization—wound, key, and trumpet. These three symbols are integral to the play's meaning regarding survival, responsibility, flexibility, decision making, and the family unit.

Gabe, a brain-damaged veteran of World War II, has a metal plate in his head. Misunderstood and perceived as threatening by outsiders, he is eventually placed in a mental institution. His war wound symbolizes the experiences of others in the play who have been wounded by rejection, injustice, misunderstanding, or neglect. His wound, however, does not obviate his need to maintain a semblance of personal worth. He delights in having a key to his two rooms at Miss Pearl's. The key represents freedom and the desire to maintain dignity in challenging circumstances, even when it involves selling damaged produce. His decision to leave Troy's home to live independently places Troy in financial difficulty, but Gabe has learned the same lessons about manhood and responsibility that Troy has learned from their father.

Gabe, named after the angel Gabriel, is characterized through biblical imagery and symbolism. He is convinced that his role is to blow his trumpet, signaling Saint Peter to open the gates of Heaven. During the last scene of the play, in which all family members are gathered for Troy's funeral, Gabe attempts to blow his trumpet. After much effort, he is unable to produce a sound. Undaunted, he begins to dance and sing, a song that sounds like howling. When he finishes, the gates of Heaven open and his brother enters. With Troy's redemption, the play comes full circle, for Wilson's epitaph—the conscious decision to forgive and to move forward—provides a clue about black culture and humanity in general.

"Critical Evaluation" by Barbara M. Whitehead

Further Reading

Awkward, Michael. "'The Crookeds with the Straights': *Fences*, Race, and the Politics of Adaptation." In *May All Your Fences Have Gates*, edited by Alan Nadel. Iowa City: University of Iowa Press, 1994. Discusses what happens when a play such as *Fences* is adapted into film. Includes Wilson's suggestions concerning directorial qualifications, as well as his claim of ownership over language production and representations of blackness.

Berkowitz, Gerald M. "August Wilson." In *American Drama of the Twentieth Century*. London: Longman, 1992. Maintains that Troy's tragedy is that, although he represents the first generation of black Americans to progress into the middle class through pride and determination, his instinct is to preserve and consolidate what he has.

Bigsby, Christopher, ed. *The Cambridge Companion to August Wilson*. New York: Cambridge University Press,

2007. A collection of essays providing interpretations of Wilson's oeuvre as well as critiques of individual plays. Matthew Roudané's essay, "Safe at Home? August Wilson's *Fences*," analyzes this play. Includes an interview with Wilson.

Bogumil, Mary L. *Understanding August Wilson*. Columbia: University of South Carolina Press, 1999. A comprehensive examination of Wilson's plays, analyzing their thematic structures, place within American drama, and depiction of African American experiences. Devotes a chapter to a discussion of *Fences*.

Clark, Keith. *Black Manhood in James Baldwin, Ernest J. Gaines, and August Wilson*. Urbana: University of Illinois Press, 2002. Describes how the three writers reject the image of African American men found in earlier literature by depicting black men whose lives are grounded in community, camaraderie, and intimacy. Chapter 4 focuses on Wilson's work.

Elkins, Marilyn, ed. *August Wilson: A Casebook*. New York: Garland, 1994. Includes two perceptive essays about *Fences*: One interprets *Fences* by emphasizing its universal qualities, and the other examines how *Fences* highlights the metaphoric relationship between black American history and the black body.

Harrison, Paul Carter. "August Wilson's Blues Poetics." In *Three Plays*, by August Wilson. Pittsburgh, Pa.: University of Pittsburgh Press, 1991. Maintains that unlike Willy Loman in Arthur Miller's *Death of a Salesman* (1949), Troy has no respect for the limitations imposed on him by a hostile world. Argues that Troy's declarations of patriarchal authority resonate in the hearts and minds of most African Americans.

Menson-Furr, Ladrica. *August Wilson's "Fences."* New York: Continuum, 2008. An introductory overview of the play, analyzing its structure, style, and characters and placing it within the context of African American history of the 1950's. Chronicles the play's production history.

Reed, Ishmael. "August Wilson: The Dramatist as Bearer of Tradition." In *Writin' Is Fightin': Thirty-seven Years of Boxing on Paper*. New York: Atheneum, 1988. Argues that *Fences* is informed by Wilson's belief that a man should have responsibility for his family.

Wilson, August. *Conversations with August Wilson*. Edited by Jackson R. Bryer and Mary C. Hartig. Jackson: University Press of Mississippi, 2006. Reprints interviews conducted from 1984 through 2004 in which Wilson discusses his background, his plays, his views on the assimilation of African Americans into white society, and his major influences.

Wolfe, Peter. "The House of Maxson." In *August Wilson*. New York: Twayne, 1999. Provides details about Wilson's references to baseball and explores a multifaceted characterization of Troy through discussions of allusions, entrapment, self-destruction, authoritarianism, treachery, and salvation. Useful insights into the play's characters, conflicts, and themes.

Ferdydurke

Author: Witold Gombrowicz (1904-1969)
First published: 1937 (English translation, 1961)
Type of work: Novel
Type of plot: Farce
Time of plot: 1930's
Locale: Poland

Principal characters:
JOHNNIE KOWALSKI, a thirty-year-old writer
T. PIMKO, a professor
MIENTUS, a seventeen-year-old schoolboy
MR. YOUTHFUL, an engineer
MRS. YOUTHFUL, his wife
ZUTKA, their daughter
AUNT HURLECKA, Kowalski's mother's sister
EDWARD, her husband
ISABEL and ALFRED, their children

The Story:

Johnnie Kowalski awakens one morning from a nightmare in which he reverted to adolescence: The adult in him was mocking the youth and vice versa, and all the ill-fitting parts of his adolescent body were jeering at one another in rude and raucous fashion. The dream brings back uncomfortable memories of his literary debut and his sense of being doubly trapped, by his own childhood and by the childishness in others' perception of him, "the caricature of myself which existed in their minds." At the moment he sat down to make a new start, to write a new book that would, this time, be truly identical with himself, the distinguished professor T. Pimko appeared on his doorstep. As the diminutive but terrible Pimko quizzed him on King Ladislas and Latin grammar, Kowalski felt himself shrinking to schoolboy size. His adult mind knew that the situation was absurd, but his body seemed paralyzed, and when Pimko dragged him off to enroll in school, Kowalski did not resist.

Neither the boys nor the schoolmasters seemed to notice anything odd or unusual, and Kowalski found himself conforming to schoolboy behavior in spite of himself. Like the others, he languished in stultifying classroom sessions where the masters taught that Juliusz Słowacki's poetry was great because Słowacki was a great poet; like the others, he smeared ink on his hands and picked his nose. Only one boy, Kopeida, seemed unaffected by any of this. Kowalski was drawn into a "duel of grimaces" between Siphon, the honorable, innocent Adolescent, and Mientus, the champion of crass, foulmouthed Boyhood. Mientus, on the verge of losing, simply called on his cronies to attack Siphon, and they held him down while Mientus poured all the obscenities he knew into Siphon's ear.

At the very climax of this "violation by the ear," Pimko reappeared and dragged Kowalski away again, this time to the home of the Youthful family, where he was to rent a room. The family consisted of Mr. and Mrs. Youthful (both educated and both earnestly progressive) and their daughter Zutka, who was the embodiment of the modern girl—athletic, unaffected, and absolutely invulnerable. At this point Kowalski became not only unable but also unwilling to reveal his true, thirty-year-old self: All he cared about was what Zutka thought of him. He tried to gain the psychological advantage by annoying her, but drunken Mientus, boasting of his exploits with the housemaid and rambling on about running away to the country to fraternize with honest stable lads, burst in and ruined the moment.

All Johnnie could do was continue his assault on Zutka's perfect, unreflective indifference by playing the fool and knave. He disgusted the Youthfuls with his table manners and invaded their orderly bathroom, where he danced a disorderly dance; he paid a beggar to stand in front of Zutka's window with a green twig in his mouth; and he spied on Zutka through the keyhole and rifled through her desk. There he found love letters from schoolboys, lawyers, doctors, landlords, and even Professor Pimko himself. Johnnie decided to lay low both Pimko and the Youthfuls with one stroke: Imitating Zutka's hand, he wrote notes inviting both Pimko and Kopeida to a rendezvous.

At first all went as planned. After Kopeida climbed through the girl's window, to Zutka's delight, followed by Pimko, to Zutka's consternation, he raised the alarm. The Youthfuls, however, were charmed by their daughter's lack of prudishness—yet another proof that she was thoroughly modern. Pimko, on the other hand, responded less calmly to the situation, and soon the entire group was nothing more than a rolling, punching, kicking, and biting heap on the floor.

As Kowalski made his escape from the house, Mientus popped up again and announced that he raped the maid, and he suggested that he and Johnnie make for the countryside, where the real people lived. They trudged through one deserted village after another. Puzzled, they knocked on a door and were greeted by furious barking; they soon discovered that the peasants turned themselves into dogs. Suspicious of city folk, bureaucrats, and "stitizens wi'eir intentions," the snarling pack of villagers set upon Mientus and Johnnie. Suddenly a car drove right into their midst; it was Kowalski's aunt on her way home to the country estate where he was raised. Clucking and chiding, she whisked both "boys" into the car. On the way, she tallied up events and birthdays to come up with Kowalski's true age, but it didn't matter. For her he would always be ten years old.

At the estate lived Uncle Edward, cousins Isabel and Alfred, many servants, and a multitude of hunting dogs. The masters sleepily ate, played cards, and discussed the various family ailments and their cures. Mientus discovered his ideal of a stable boy in the person of Bert, a young servant. The family therefore assumed he was either a homosexual or a communist, but they were not disturbed until Mientus resolved to show his solidarity with the common folk by goading Bert into hitting him in the face. Servants and masters alike were scandalized. Kowalski felt the atmosphere growing thick and poisonous, and once again plotted his escape, resigning himself to taking Bert at least part of the way because Mientus refused to leave without him. It occurred to Kowalski that abducting his cousin Isabel would be more logical than abducting a stable boy, but he discarded the idea.

The boys were discovered, and Uncle Edward's attempt to reestablish his feudal prerogatives by beating Bert into submission backfired. Bert hit back, and soon Bert, Mientus, Alfred, Edward, and the aunt were engaged in the fray. Johnnie left the pile of wriggling bodies and made for the gates, where cousin Isabel found him. Rather than explain the whole absurd situation to Isabel or some later audience, Kowalski declared his passion for the girl; she eagerly fell in with all the conventional expectations about runaway lovers and elopements.

As Isabel clung to him, the sun, the "arch-bum," rose over the forest, and Johnnie, knowing flight was useless, fled.

Critical Evaluation:

Many a Polish writer has ended up in exile, but the ironies of Witold Gombrowicz's situation are nearly as fantastic as some of his plots. In the summer of 1939, he set out on what was to be a leisurely transatlantic cruise to South America and back. By the time the ship docked in Argentina, Nazi Germany and Soviet Russia had invaded Poland and World War II had begun. Gombrowicz spent the next ten years contending with poverty and isolation, clerking by day and writing by night, until translations into Spanish and publications abroad again brought him some renown. Belligerently apolitical, Gombrowicz maintained ties with both the émigré press and the press in Poland, and he refused to take part in any ideological exercises. In his homeland, however, his earlier works were not reprinted, nor were his newer ones published until "the Polish October" of 1956-1958, a period of relative liberalization. The 1957 edition of *Ferdydurke* sold out in a matter of days, Gombrowicz's plays were staged, his correspondence was published, and he stood at the very center of debate on Polish literary and cultural life. His absolute rebellion against all fixed expectations of behavior, however, whether social, cultural, ideological, or national, made him too volatile an element in an atmosphere of forced stability and stale dogma. In 1958, his name and works virtually disappeared from print again, but he continued to exert a tremendous influence on Polish writing and thought.

Gombrowicz was a provocateur in life and in letters; it was his method of confronting reality, his style of existence. Paradox lies at the foundation of his work, in which he aimed to provoke, amuse, confound, and finally leave the reader nose to nose with some highly unpleasant psychological and philosophical truths. *Ferdydurke*, with its three acts and two intermezzos, resembles theater more than it does the traditional novel, and its characters are more puppet than human. Its language is playful and inventive, and its very title is a fantastic, meaningless word. In fact, Gombrowicz claimed to be bored by readers' constant questions about "meaning," and he wrote in his diary: "Come, come, be more sensuous, less cerebral, start dancing with the book instead of asking for meanings. Why take so much interest in the skeleton if it's got a body? See rather whether it is capable of pleasing and is not devoid of grace and passion."

Grace and passion might not be the reader's first impression of *Ferdydurke*, but the body can hardly be missed. Beginning with Kowalski's dream and ending with his futile flight from "the arch-bum," Gombrowicz's imagery grows out of the human form. The narrator-hero's "childish, idiotic little behind" is what glues him to his chair as Pimko talks, and he sees that everyone around him is ruled by "the tyranny of the backside." Kowalski cannot run from the classroom because he has stuck his finger into his shoe. Zutka's calves stand for an entire generation. The conflict between masters and servants comes down to the collision of faces and fists. "Philifor Honeycombed with Childishness," one of the two nonsensical fables with which Gombrowicz punctuates Kowalski's story, begins with a philosophical dispute and ends with a hail of gunfire and flying body parts, and each stage of Kowalski's own adventures ends with a welter of bodies writhing on the floor.

For Gombrowicz, observes fellow Polish writer Czesław Miłosz, these heaps may be an image of the only authentic form of human contact. All other contact, all other behavior is shaped by convention—by groups, not individuals. Ultimately there may be no such thing as an individual self, and when Kowalski sits down to write his new book, his new self, he takes on an impossible task. He wants to escape his own "greenness," his own inferiority, but the alternatives are even worse. Pimko, himself a collection of clichés, imposes his notion of boyhood on Kowalski; the schoolboys are also ruled by the expectation that "boys will be boys"; the Youthfuls' supposed frankness and liberality is merely another fixed form, as are Mientus's romantic notion of the rustic stable boy, the family relationships so dear to Kowalski's aunt, and the feudal ones so dear to his uncle. Underlying all of this is a fixed notion of what it is to be Polish. Every attempt at escaping one pattern simply leads to another, and the only thing that seems to break the form, at least temporarily, is a ridiculous or violent gesture—a green twig in a beggar's mouth or a bite just below the knee.

Jane Ann Miller

Further Reading

Berressem, Hanjo. *Lines of Desire: Reading Gombrowicz's Fiction with Lacan*. Evanston, Ill.: Northwestern University Press, 1999. Berressem interprets *Ferdydurke* and Gombrowicz's other novels from the perspective of contemporary literary theory and psychoanalysis, focusing on the psychoanalytic concepts of Jacques Lacan.

Gombrowicz, Witold. "Excerpts from *Diary*." In *Polish Writers on Writing*, edited by Adam Zagajewski. San Antonio, Tex.: Trinity University Press, 2007. This excerpt from Gombrowicz's diary is included in an English-language anthology of works in which Polish authors describe what it means to be a writer.

_____. *Ferdydurke*. Translated from the Polish by Danuta Borchardt. New Haven, Conn.: Yale University Press, 2000. This English-language translation of the novel contains a useful foreword by literary critic Susan Sontag, who calls the novel "extravagant, brilliant, disturbing, brave, funny, [and] wonderful."

Gőmőrn Language Review 73 (January, 1978): 119-129. A brief but essential introduction to Gombrowicz's major themes, with special attention to *Ferdydurke*, and emphasis on his use of paradox.

Holmgren, Beth. "Witold Gombrowicz in the United States." *Polish Review* 33, no. 4 (1988): 409-418. Gombrowicz has remained a rather obscure figure in the United States, and this article addresses some of the reasons why. Also gives a thorough overview of English-language writing on Gombrowicz.

Longinovic, Tomislav. *Borderline Culture: The Politics of Identity in Four Twentieth-Century Slavic Novels.* Fayetteville: University of Arkansas Press, 1993. Discusses the conflict of identity and ideology in *Ferdydurke*, and argues that it is a parody of the entire Western metaphysical tradition.

Thompson, Ewa. *Witold Gombrowicz.* Boston: Twayne, 1979. An excellent introduction to Gombrowicz, a straightforward discussion of his life and works. Includes a bibliography.

Ziarek, Ewa Plonowska, ed. *Gombrowicz's Grimaces: Modernism, Gender, Nationality.* Albany: State University of New York Press, 1998. A collection of essays, some of which explore physical and psychic aberrations in Gombrowicz's novels, his aesthetics, and his critical reception in the United States

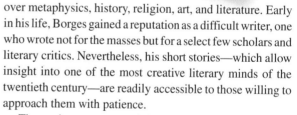

Ficciones, 1935-1944

Author: Jorge Luis Borges (1899-1986)
First published: 1944 (English translation, 1962)
Type of work: Short fiction

One of the most innovative Latin American writers in the twentieth century, Jorge Luis Borges is considered by many to have exerted a powerful force in reforming the Spanish language. His prose is precise, compact, and direct; it is at times deceptively simple yet abounds in psychological and philosophical subtlety. The author of essays and poetry, Borges is known primarily for two volumes of short stories, *Ficciones* (1944) and *El Aleph* (1949, 1952). *Ficciones* is an anthology of short stories in two parts entitled "The Garden of the Forking Paths" and "Artifices." Whereas part 1 was published separately several years earlier in Buenos Aires, part 2 contains a number of stories published for the first time.

Throughout his long career, Borges remained interested in a number of topics. He had a lifelong love of things Argentine, including a fascination with the country's great stark plains, the Pampa, and their violent and elemental cowboys, called gauchos. His broader attraction to Argentine life and literature found its focus in Buenos Aires, a city he loved and knew intimately and where he spent much of his life. Borges's second enduring interest can be classified as philosophical, though his thought and knowledge range widely over metaphysics, history, religion, art, and literature. Early in his life, Borges gained a reputation as a difficult writer, one who wrote not for the masses but for a select few scholars and literary critics. Nevertheless, his short stories—which allow insight into one of the most creative literary minds of the twentieth century—are readily accessible to those willing to approach them with patience.

The stories center around themes (destiny, time, infinity) that recur throughout the entire corpus of his work. Borges avoids, however, merely clothing ideas in literary form; rather, he carefully constructs plots that flow relentlessly to their conclusion. His elegant integration of complex philosophical concerns and the striking artistic unity of his stories are testimony to his skill as a writer.

In "Tlōn Uqbar, Orbis Tertius," Borges envisions the possibility of a world constructed according to the idealist tenets of the English philosopher Bishop Berkeley. Although Borges often insisted that he was not a philosopher in the traditional sense, he had a tendency to favor idealism, the proposition that thought is primary to matter. "Tlōn, Uqbar, Orbis Tertius" begins with the narrator, Borges himself, stating that he owes "the discovery of Uqbar to the conjunction of a mirror and an encyclopedia," an opening that hints more at a detective tale than a metaphysical one. Borges's friend and dinner companion, Bioy Casares, responds that the mirror is abominable, as is copulation, "since both multiply the numbers of man," a quote not from Casares himself but from an article on the country of Uqbar in the *Anglo-American Encyclopedia*. Narrator Borges and Casares are puzzled, however, to find that they are able to locate the article on Uqbar in only one set of the *Anglo-American Encyclopedia*, a fact made even more inexplicable by the mysterious inclusion of several additional pages in the volume containing the article. The story plays out in detective fashion. The narrator later accidentally discovers volume 11 of *A First Encyclopedia of Tlön*, a source of information about an imaginary land in the literature of the imaginary country Uqbar. Oddly enough, the nations of Tlön are "congenitally idealist"; their language, religion, literature, and metaphysics all reject any suggestion of materialism. There are, for example, no nouns in the language of Tlön but only sentences constructed of verbs and other parts of speech, which validates the idealist basis of life on Tlön. The seemingly impossible takes place when certain thinkers on Tlön attempt to demonstrate the validity of materialism, an undertaking that causes considerable unease.

Borges's fascination with idealism and its implications plays out in the final third of the story when, first inexplicably, then ominously, objects from Tlön begin to appear in the world of the narrator. The story, a finely crafted philosophical tale, may be a parable of the effects of thought on the formation of the world. Tlön, an imaginary planet in the literature of an imaginary country, which is itself created by a mysterious brotherhood, slowly permeates and dissolves the world and replaces it with Tlön itself. "The world," according to Borges, "will be Tlön."

As in "Tlön, Uqbar, Orbis Tertius," the central premise of "The Circular Ruins" revolves around the notion that "all is mind" and that the construction of a world in accordance with this tenet must conform to certain idealist strictures. In this story, a ragged wizard is instructed by an unknown god to dream a disciple, only to discover that he, too, the dreamer, is the dream of another. "The Circular Ruins," shorter than "Tlön, Uqbar, Orbis Tertius," is compact in structure and dense with possible meanings. The story is set in a thick jungle, in an imaginary land of Borges's invention made eerily familiar by the mention of Greek, which had not "contaminated" the Zend language. As in many of his other tales, Borges places a mystery at the core of his narrative whose solution provides the reader an epiphany or moment of realization in which certain aspects of reality can be examined. In

"The Circular Ruins," the ending suggests that the reader may be the fiction or dream of another being.

"The Garden of the Forking Paths" is perhaps the best example of Borges's artful blending of the detective story and the philosophical tale. In "The Garden of the Forking Paths," one of his most complex, detailed, and thought-provoking stories, Borges incorporates notions of time, infinity, and destiny. The tale is narrated by Yu Tsun, a German spy and great-grandson of Ts'ui Pên, the governor of Yunnan and author of the mysterious novel *The Garden of the Forking Paths*. The plot of the detective story revolves around Yu Tsun's efforts to relay a message to his superiors in Berlin, whom he despises. Borges weaves a parallel tale of Tsun's enigmatic ancestor, who set out to write a novel "with more characters than there are in the *Hung Lou Mêng*, and to create a maze in which all men could lose themselves." Tsun later discovers that the maze and the novel are one and the same. A hunted man, Tsun momentarily forgets his destiny—that he is to be tried and executed as a spy—as he meditates on his ancestor's curious project. Oddly, yet inexorably, Tsun is drawn toward a destiny that somehow merges with that of his ancestor of the labyrinthine novel. Ts'ui Pên's novel, which splits in time and creates multiple possibilities for the future, allows for a dizzying proliferation of scenarios. In one future, a man may be murdered by an assassin, while in another he himself may be the murderer of that man. In still a third, the two men may be friends. *The Garden of the Forking Paths*, writes Borges, "is an enormous guessing game, or parable, in which the subject is time," and it is in time, or in its bifurcation, that all men exist and find their destiny. It is Tsun's destiny to be hanged as a spy, which he accepts with resignation, sadness, and even joy.

Borges's fascination with time and destiny also forms the core of "The Secret Miracle," which takes place in Prague, in 1939, during the German occupation. In this tale, Jaromir Hladík, author of an unfinished tragedy *The Enemies, a Vindication of Eternity*, and "an inquiry into the indirect Jewish sources of Jakob Boehme," falls into the hands of the Germans, who promptly sentence him to death. Although his life is filled with creative activity, Hladík nevertheless considers his life wasted because he never wrote anything of lasting value, nothing that would justify him in the face of eternity or in the eyes of God. In "The Secret Miracle," as in other stories of Borges, a man's destiny depends on one task he must complete before his death. Often this is an action that in some way involves the protagonist in death itself. Moments before he is cut down by a German firing squad, his wish seems to have been granted, for the awesome machinery of time grinds to a halt. As a drop of rain grazes one of Hladík's temples and rolls down his cheek, he is catapulted into a timeless, productive limbo where he works to complete his unfinished tragedy.

Hladík cannot escape his destiny. He dies by firing squad exactly one year (in his mind) after standing before the German soldiers. The reader understands that nothing appears to be out of the ordinary and that to an observer a mere second passes. However, for Hladík, as for Borges perhaps, the enigmas of time and death leave room for the unexpected. Hladík, in making peace with himself and God in the moment before his death, apparently achieves a measure of liberty in the face of an irrevocable and ironclad destiny.

"The South," Borges's final story in *Ficciones*, explores the destiny of a man dying of septicemia in a hospital bed, who dreams a destiny for himself not unlike that of his soldier grandfather. Here Borges skirts the shadowy borders of dream and reality, where it is not clear what is actual and what is not. The protagonist's destiny cannot be revoked or even truly changed, yet Borges suggests that the perception of that destiny may be all. Juan Dahlmann, secretary of a municipal library in Buenos Aires and grandson of a German immigrant and a native Argentine who died defending Buenos Aires from Indians, chooses to die the honorable death of his grandfather. To avoid a shameful, perhaps meaningless death in a hospital, Dahlmann's delirium carries him to the South, into the brutal, elemental world of the Pampa. Though Dahlmann's apparent recovery from his illness and trip to the South are presented in realistic fashion, Borges injects subtle hints that Dahlmann is actually dying in his bed, a fact that may be less important than Dahlmann's choice of a death that embraces his romantic vision of his own destiny.

With the publication of *Ficciones*, Borges attracted the attention of critics and general readers alike in the Spanish- and non-Spanish-speaking worlds. His work has been translated into many languages. Always thought-provoking, his juxtaposition of the familiar and the unusual makes reality itself seem strange, a strangeness that causes the reader to perceive the familiar in new ways. Through his complex and subtle art, Borges aims both to entertain and to motivate readers to question the world and themselves. The pages of his tales become the impetus to complete the journey he started.

Howard Giskin

Further Reading

Alazraki, Jaime, ed. *Critical Essays on Jorge Luis Borges.* Boston: G. K. Hall, 1987. A collection of articles and reviews by literary critics and writers that aims at a contemporary assessment of the range and scope of Borges's work.

Barrenechea, Ana María. *Borges: The Labyrinth Maker.* Translated and edited by Robert Lima. New York: New York University Press, 1965. A thorough treatment of Borges's philosophy, covering such topics as his use of infinity, pantheism, and time.

Bell-Villada, Gene H. *Borges and His Fiction: A Guide to His Mind and Art.* Chapel Hill: University of North Carolina Press, 1981. Focuses on Borges's stories and essays and provides detailed discussion of a number of works. Part 1 includes introductory chapters that examine Borges's place in Argentine and world literature. In part 2, Bell-Villada classifies Borges's works according to theme and topic.

Di Giovanni, Norman Thomas. *The Lesson of the Master: On Borges and His Work.* New York: Continuum, 2003. Includes Di Giovanni's memoir of the 1970's, when he translated Borges's work and spent time with the writer. Also contains seven essays discussing, among other subjects, Borges at play, Borges and his interpreters, and Borges and autobiography.

Frisch, Mark F. *You Might Be Able to Get There from Here: Reconsidering Borges and the Postmodern.* Madison, N.J.: Fairleigh Dickinson University Press, 2004. Frisch reexamines the symbolism, literary technique, parody, irony, and ambiguity in Borges's works to demonstrate how he challenges a singular vision, affirming instead the varied and mysterious nature of the world. Assesses Borges's influence on twentieth century literature and philosophy.

Gracia, Jorge J. E., Carolyn Korsmeyer, and Rodolphe Gasché, eds. *Literary Philosophers: Borges, Calvino, Eco.* New York: Routledge, 2002. An analysis of the philosophical views of writers Borges, Italo Calvino, and Umberto Eco.

Rodriguez Monegal, Emir. *Jorge Luis Borges: A Literary Biography.* New York: E. P. Dutton, 1978. A detailed account of the evolution of Borges the man and his art. Draws extensively on interviews with Borges.

Stabb, Martin S. *Jorge Luis Borges.* New York: Twayne, 1970. A useful introductory treatment of Borges the poet, essayist, and writer of fiction. Chapter 1 is a biographical sketch that focuses on the development of Borges's art.

Williamson, Edwin. *Borges, a Life.* New York: Viking Press, 2004. A psychoanalytic biography. Williamson places Borges's life within the context of his works and of Argentine history.

The Field of Vision

Author: Wright Morris (1910-1998)
First published: 1956
Type of work: Novel
Type of plot: Psychological realism
Time of plot: Mid-twentieth century
Locale: Mexico

Principal characters:
WALTER McKEE, a middle-aged American
LOIS McKEE, his wife
GORDON McKEE, their son
GORDON BOYD, a failed playwright
DR. LEOPOLD LEHMANN, a psychiatrist
TOM SCANLON, Lois McKee's father

The Story:

Vacationing in Mexico in the 1950's, Walter McKee runs into his best friend, Gordon Boyd, whom he had not seen for fifteen years. Without any introduction, Boyd says, "How's the little woman?" McKee replies that he and his wife could not be happier, which irritates Boyd, who, instead of settling down like his friend McKee, spent his life on the road, wandering wherever fate took him. McKee made money and became a success, although years earlier he stood on his fiancé's front porch while Boyd gave Lois her first kiss.

At a bullfight to which they all go, Lois is busy supervising her elderly father and her young grandson. Both wear coonskin caps reminiscent of Davy Crockett and of the old man's solitary life on the midwestern plains. Mrs. McKee is alarmed when she hears that her husband met Boyd—for she wishes to conceal from the world that Boyd is the only man who ever excited her. Afraid of the desire he aroused in her that day on the porch, she instead married the steady but boring McKee, who annoys her with his overbearing manner and his habit of chewing such things as burned matches, cigars, and even things he picks up in the street. Above all, she dislikes the fact that her husband worships Boyd. Running into Boyd when they are on vacation strikes her as bad luck.

Boyd suggests to McKee that they all go to a bullfight together, explaining that he will also bring his psychiatrist, Dr. Lehmann, who is treating him for depression. None of Boyd's youthful dreams is fulfilled. Instead of becoming a successful playwright, he ends up eking out an existence in New York. His namesake and McKee's son, Gordon, is dissuaded from pursuing a career in the theater when he sees Gordon's dingy apartment and lonely life.

Lois does not like the idea of a bullfight, but since Boyd invites them and clearly expects her to decline, she decides to attend. As for her grandson, Boyd assures her that children like blood. McKee pretends to look forward to the bullfight until Dr. Lehmann informs him that more than one bull will be killed. To comfort herself, Lois reads a book entitled *Toros Without Tears*.

After they take their seats on the shady side of the bullring, where it is cold, making them wish they had seats in the sun, the first bull enters. McKee thinks he looks small. Up to his old clowning days, Boyd calls the bull over to the edge of the ring, shakes up a bottle of soda pop, and squirts the little bull in the face. The bull licks it off and the crowd laughs. Boyd takes a bow and McKee is thrilled, but his wife is embarrassed. Boyd still has not grown up, and it appears he never will. She is reminded of the time he tore the pocket of baseball legend Ty Cobb's pants as he rounded third at an exhibition game; in all the years that went by, that dirty piece of cloth is the only thing Boyd manages to keep. Much to her amazement, Lois saw it in Boyd's apartment in New York.

McKee tries to explain to his wife that Boyd is special, that once he even tried to walk on water at a sand pit where he nearly drowned, but Lois remains unconvinced. Boyd is an interesting and aging con man and nothing else. She admits, however, that she still finds him exciting.

Only Dr. Lehmann is not fooled. During the bullfight he catches Boyd's eye while Boyd is fooling around, to show him that as his physician he understands why Boyd is acting up. Dr. Lehmann forces his patient to confront the truth about himself: that his life did not work and that he even failed at failure.

At the end of the bullfight, Boyd throws Gordon McKee's coonskin cap into the ring. When the boy chases after it, Boyd mutters, "touch bottom," and feels himself push off against it. At that moment, he realizes that he must transform himself or perish. Reaching down, he rescues the boy and retrieves the cap. Then Boyd silently vows to renew his quest for truth and beauty and to turn his back on deterioration and failure.

Critical Evaluation:

Wright Morris worked in a variety of literary genres, including novels, short stories, and essays, and he was also a photographer. His award-winning novels focus on the interpersonal relationships between men and women, the effect of the past on people's lives, the pursuit of wealth and the American Dream, and the quest for an authentic identity. Many of Morris's characters come from the Midwest, an endless plain that forms the backdrop for the emotional lives of his ordinary men and women. For revealing them in their quests for meaning and love and for the humor and originality of his technique, Morris gained far-reaching critical success, but his popular acclaim remained comparatively small. The reason for his relative obscurity may lie in the fact that he does not use a traditional, linear plot. This accounts for certain difficulties in his works, yet their complexity is tempered by vivid characterization, country charm, and wit. Morris writes in the vernacular, playing off the peculiar rhythms and hidden meanings that infuse everyday speech. It is actually the author's colloquial jokes and startling images that form the texture of the novel.

In terms of structure, Morris's technique is sophisticated, if not avant-garde. As its title suggests, *The Field of Vision* is about point of view. More specifically, the novel poses the question, How do people know what they know? The answer is that all truth is subjective. At the bullfight, for example, there are as many bullfights as there are spectators. Nobody sees the same bullfight, because every individual's experience of the present is colored and shaped by memory of the past. Personal history is the lens through which each individual views the world. The form of Morris's novel reflects its content: Each chapter bears the name of the character whose perceptions filter the events of the narrative and act as channels for the reader.

Each character sees things differently. Consequently, the real bullfight disappears and the reader is left with contrasting impressions of the same event. After the moment when Boyd shakes up his soda pop and squirts it into the bull's face, Boyd sees himself as the clowning hero, the show-stealer, and life of the party. His friend McKee sees him as the same old joker, as the man who says he can walk on water and who persuades McKee to believe him. Lois sees Boyd as the foolish braggart who once stole her heart but idiotically refuses to grow up. Her father, Tom Scanlon, simply sees him as a ridiculous figure, and Boyd's psychiatrist, Dr. Lehmann, views him as a brilliant visionary who does not even come close to touching the rock bottom he mistakenly believes himself to have encountered.

Central to *The Field of Vision* is the problem of charisma, hero worship in general, and, specifically, the domination of one personality over another. Boyd is a charmer, a lady's man with the gift of gab. Lois cannot forget that Boyd was the first man to kiss her, and she is haunted by a sensual memory of

youth and happiness even while she despises her husband for catering to Boyd's vanity. Boyd is always in need of an audience; he has to be center stage, and this need has different effects on different people.

McKee has been enamored of Boyd ever since they were boys, and he sees nothing wrong with his infatuation; indeed, he is hardly conscious of it, going so far as to allow his own son to be named for Boyd. Symbolically, then, he relinquishes his paternity and masculinity just as he did when he allowed Boyd to kiss his fiancé. At the close of the novel, though, McKee undergoes the transformative experience that is central to Morris's work. When Boyd lowers McKee's grandson into the bullring, McKee finally stands up to him: "'If something should happen to that boy—' said McKee, but it left him speechless, just to think of it. 'Gordon—' he said, waving his arm, 'you get in there and get that boy.'" Thus McKee regains his identity and reasserts himself as a patriarch, the solid family man in contrast to the single, childless, and unhappy loner. McKee no longer wants Boyd in his life and realizes that this man is no friend. He does, however, accept that Boyd's hold over him—that is, Boyd's charisma—will never entirely disappear. The author poses the question whether the power of charisma is to be desired or feared, whether its effects are constructive or destructive. The McKees, for example, expose themselves to extreme psychological states when they encounter the likes of Boyd, but that may be precisely why they do it—to feel something, even if it is pain, that enlivens the ordinariness of their lives.

Boyd's charisma causes pain to himself as well. Indeed, thinking Boyd is just another bum on a park bench feeding his last crust of bread to a squirrel, a photographer takes a picture that ends up in a national magazine. Boyd is unable even to fail at failure. However, for Morris, Boyd remains a kind of hero: He acts with dash and audacity; he refuses to accept the harsh precepts of society and would rather make his own way, even if that way is more difficult. His individualism is of the self-reliant but of rebellious variety. Boyd is just clever enough to get by, without really joining society. Morris raises the question whether that is enough, and what an individual is to do with some, but not sufficient, talent.

The answer lies in the potential of transformation of character. Although an individual's field of vision may be limited to a particular perspective, this does not imply paralysis. On the contrary, even as Boyd believes himself to be hitting rock bottom, he is rebounding. As Dr. Lehmann points out, rock bottom lies a lot further down than Boyd ever reached. Indeed, it is Dr. Lehmann who becomes the scientific, rationalistic, and good-hearted conscience of the novel. Without becoming sweetly sentimental or subscribing to established religious dogma, Dr. Lehmann speaks for the author when he offers a way out: "He saw it take place. Before his eyes, the commonplace miracle of everyday life. You can begin with a will, a way, and you end up with something else. The human thing to do was transform something, especially yourself."

David Johansson

Further Reading

Hicks, Granville. Introduction to *Wright Morris: A Reader*, by Wright Morris. New York: Harper & Row, 1970. Discusses recurrent themes in Morris's work, such as setting and its effect on identity. Examines his place in American literary history. Includes an overview of the reasons for Morris's popular and critical neglect.

Knoll, Robert, ed. *Conversations with Wright Morris: Critical Views and Responses*. Lincoln: University of Nebraska Press, 1977. Covers a wide range of critical evaluation, including New Criticism and structuralism. Examines the author's postmodern use of point of view and investigates the absence of a traditional narrative structure.

Pollak, Oliver B. "Wright Morris and the Jews." *Shofar: An Interdisciplinary Journal of Jewish Studies* 20, no. 4 (Summer, 2002): 18. Focuses on what Pollak calls the "Jewish motif" in Morris's works, delineating the Jewish issues in selected books, including *The Field of Vision*.

Updike, John. "Wright on Writing." *The New Yorker*, April 14, 1975. Examines the characters and regions that are most prevalent in Morris's novels. The landscape of the Midwest is discussed in terms of its effect on character development.

Wilson, J. C. "Wright Morris and the Search for the 'Still Point.'" *Prairie Schooner* 49, no. 2 (Summer, 1975): 154-163. Examines the motif of the quest for identity in Morris's fiction and the pressure of past events on characters' present-day lives.

Wydeven, Joseph J. *Wright Morris Revisited*. New York: Twayne, 1998. Argues that Morris's works are about American dreamers who viewed the West as the place where they could fulfill their desires. Includes a portfolio of Morris's photographs

Yardley, Jonathan. "The Achievement of Wright Morris." *Book World—The Washington Post*, February 3, 1985. Examines the arc of Morris's literary career. Includes a discussion of his work in various genres, including photography, journalism, and autobiography.

Fiesta in November

Author: Eduardo Mallea (1903-1982)
First published: Fiesta en noviembre, 1938 (English translation, 1942)
Type of work: Novel
Type of plot: Social realism
Time of plot: Mid-1930's
Locale: Buenos Aires, Argentina

Principal characters:
EUGENIA RAGUE, a society leader born in England
GEORGE RAGUE, her wealthy husband
MARTA, their bored daughter
BRENDA, their younger daughter
SEÑOR RAÍCES, an Argentine financier
LINTAS, an artist
A POET, a political victim

The Story:

A young poet is writing a poem on love on a scrap of paper. The time is eleven o'clock at night. Suddenly a violent, protracted rapping sounds on the door. As he goes to answer, he takes with him a piece of bread. Opening the door, he is confronted by the leader of a patrol of armed men in dirty uniforms. The leader states that they have come for him.

At eight o'clock on a warm springlike evening in November, Eugenia Rague comes down the stairs for a final inspection of the setting for her fiesta. English by birth but Argen-

tine by adoption, she dominates her aristocratic surroundings as Cardinal Wolsey, whose portrait adorns her salon, dominated his. There passes through her head the memory of the lack of respect shown her by Lord Burglay and Lady Gower during her visit to London. However, she has to concentrate on her guests about to arrive.

Others in the house react differently to the hot evening. In another room, her husband, George, tries to concentrate on acquiring culture through a phonograph record, but he keeps thinking of how he could persuade Señor Raíces, after dinner, to sign a profitable stock purchase. Should delays result, he might lose everything. Intruding into these thoughts are those of his treadmill life, his wife's incessant pressure, and his own desire to relax and perhaps to dream. The arrival of the butler with the afternoon mail interrupts and infuriates him. Then it is time for him to prepare for the party. Marta, the older daughter, lies naked on her bed, wondering why she spurned a highborn lover.

At nine, the lights are turned on, the orchestra tunes up, and the first guests arrive, the elite of Argentine society. Their conversation is frivolous: the latest scandalous behavior of some politician, the proposal to exterminate the unimportant lower class. The reception, with its empty conversation and the borrowed phrases from the world of ideas, reveals the waste of these people's lives.

Meanwhile, Marta makes her entrance, prepared for a boring and perhaps detestable evening among unexciting people she fully comprehended years earlier. Several young men bring her drinks, and her father welcomes her assistance in his social duties. When Raíces appears, Rague gives the signal to proceed to the dining room. In perplexity, the poet questions the armed men, asking what they could possibly want with him.

At the reception the painter Lintas rushes in, late as usual, but in time for the chilled consommé. As he drinks it, he becomes attracted to Marta. Her sudden smile shows her reaction to him, but a pseudophilosophic discussion prevents any words. Lintas notices her distraught expression when her mother mentions the fact that Brenda is not there. Only Marta knows of the appeal from Brenda to come immediately to give her assistance. While dismissing her curiosity about the identity of the man across the table from her, she tries to imagine what help her sister could need. The characters become involved in their own thoughts.

After the meal, dancing begins in the garden. Lintas finds himself dancing with Marta as though they are enemies. Later, more friendly, they discuss some of his paintings. Then she remembers Brenda, and without a word of explanation she leaves. Meanwhile, the leader of the patrol begins to lose patience. His men glare at the young man who is wasting their time. They prepare to march their prisoner away.

Marta's flight takes her to a shabby house and into a stench-filled room, where she finds Brenda recovering from an abortion. Brenda needs her sister's help to conceal her situation from her parents and to supply additional money for the operation, which cost more than the previous one. Marta leaves the house and heads for home.

At the fiesta, no one notices Marta's absence. Rague and Raíces are discussing stock, and Raíces is trying to explain why he does not want to rush into the transaction. Eugenia Rague maneuvers Lintas into visiting her art gallery to pass judgment on some new purchases. Amid a group of interested guests, he pronounces them fakes. Lintas knows that he creates a conflict because Eugenia would prefer a comfortable lie to the unpleasant truth. Marta, returning as Lintas is leaving the fiesta, offers to take him home.

Through the door, the poet sees a fighting cock belonging to a neighbor. He tries to imagine what is going to happen to him. He is suddenly frightened.

In the car, Marta feels impelled to talk. She protests against the sterility of the civilized universe and the difficulty people find in trying to communicate. When they reach Lintas's home, he invites her in. The screams of a neighboring woman start him on the story of his life. Poverty engendered in him a hatred for people like her. He tells her of a gang of ruffians who beat up an old bookseller because he was foreign and was selling "subversive books." It is his widow who screamed. This atrocity, making him feel for the first time involved in humanity, increases his loathing for the governing class that permits such crimes to go unpunished. They continue their discussion during a walk at dawn through the woods. As she leaves, they realize that neither has convinced the other of his or her beliefs.

The prisoner asks for permission to get his hat. What he really wants is time.

Marta hates to go home. Brenda will be in a troubled sleep; her father will be snoring, and her mother will be sneaking down to the kitchen for a snack. Marta knows that in other parts of the world vigils more painful than hers are going on. She now realizes that her trouble is a hatred of herself because of an unsatisfied yearning for something. Suddenly, the thought comes to her that she, who is always served, ought to serve others. She pauses at a church, but it offers no promise of relief. She stops next at a coffee shop. Though sensing herself out of place among the customers, eventually she begins to feel a comprehension of them and a oneness with them all. She goes home. In her room, she takes stock of herself. She feels a resemblance to her country with its variety and abundance. Before she falls asleep, she decides that a true change from the horrors of life must come from the tormented people themselves.

The poet's cousin was already arrested and shot, and his family was denied permission to bury him. The poet joins the patrol, protesting, but the only reply is rifle butts in his face. When they reach a deserted house and an open space, he tries to run. The patrol fires after him. He falls to the ground and blood soaks the piece of bread he drops. One of the men turns over the body to make sure the poet is dead. The patrol, leaving him lying on the ground, walks away, loathing one another.

Critical Evaluation:

In a graceful style, rich with vivid, precise images, neither pretentious nor overly decorated, Eduardo Mallea tells the moving story of two people struggling to communicate with each other while lost in the midst of a shallow, violent world. Although the painter Lintas and Marta Rague are the two most sympathetic characters in this short novel, both are held back by their pride from the honesty and openness that would liberate them and enable them to achieve an authentic relationship. They are the only individuals in *Fiesta in November* who even care about moral concerns, except for the poet, unnamed and doomed, whose brief story alternates like an almost subliminal theme with the main body of the story, illuminating and commenting upon it.

The two fiestas, one social, the other of blood, are linked thematically by Lintas's account to Marta of the fatal beating of a Jewish bookseller in Buenos Aires by a group of Argentine fascists. An undercurrent of violence also lies behind the conversation and actions of the guests in the house of Marta's mother, Eugenia Rague. The fragments of the condemned poet's story are in italics, a sign of emphasis, suggesting that in spite of its shorter length, this narrative is the more important of the two.

The opening arrest of the poet could be that of Joseph K. in *Der Prozess* (1925; *The Trial*, 1937). There are more than casual similarities between the work of Kafka and this novel. The contrast between the scene with the poet and the luxurious setting of Eugenia's home is shocking. Eugenia is a vain, acquisitive character. Her only passions are for her collection of objects from the past and for power. "Power is power," she thinks, "and damn all the rest." She detests sentiment and everything connected with it, so it is not surprising that she is completely alienated from her two daughters. Her husband George, despite his wealth, feels no fulfillment or peace.

A sultry, perfumed lushness pervades the novel, the heat of summer and passion—and of violence. Objects seem to have lives of their own. The opening picture of the dinner party is a devastating glimpse of empty lives and futile social ritual. The characters are struggling with an inner tyranny, a psychic trap more terrible than the cruelty of society, if they only realized it. "All art," thinks Lintas, "is a great and terrible demand for response." Indeed, this unusual novel demands a response from the reader.

Lintas appears on the scene like a breath of fresh air in the stale world of the Rague mansion. Mr. and Mrs. Rague and their guests would be lost without their ceremonies, but Lintas deliberately walks over their carefully plotted maneuvers. Marta and Lintas recognize each other from the beginning as two of a kind—exiles in a world they detest. Marta, at the age of twenty-seven, still is filled with a passionate curiosity, still is eager to experience life. Human beings, she reflects, only seek their own private ends, only hope to satisfy their appetites. Marta hates the pretense of society, the constant betrayal of her own nature. A dream—unknown but tragic—burns in the depths of her spirit, stifled by daily compromises.

Mirrors, windows, and polished surfaces constantly reflect faces, oblique views of people, and staring eyes. The reflected images seem more real than many of the actual figures and faces. Mallea seems to be asking, what is the reality and what is false?

Brenda Rague, Marta's sister, is having an abortion while her mother's fiesta is in progress. This revelation causes Marta to think in a new way about their lives, and her meeting with Lintas continues to stimulate her chain of thoughts. Lintas himself was made suddenly aware by the episode of the brutal beating of the bookseller. Are there social castes, they ask, or only moral castes? Where is the moral answer? The word "serve" appears to Marta as she walks down the empty city streets before dawn. What does it mean? Could it be the answer for her? She realizes that each individual must be heroic and walk alone, bravely and honestly, toward fate.

The inner dramas of the novel are not resolved. They move from climax to climax, cumulatively, charged with great lyric tension. Seemingly insignificant individual lives are transformed by Mallea into the essence of the human condition. *Fiesta in November* is an extraordinary novel by a great author. It is a book that haunts the reader, as Mallea intended, for the questions that it raises are not easily answered.

Mallea's view of life is religious and moral. His works often suggest the European existentialists, although most of his writing anticipated their novels and dramas. He was descended from an old Creole family and attended an English school in Bahia Blanca, where the majority of his classmates were the sons of immigrants. (He never lost sight of the fact that Argentina is a melting pot.) At the age of thirteen, he moved to Buenos Aires with his family. The city was a revelation for the withdrawn adolescent. His first published stories won immediate attention, and he eventually became an acclaimed public figure. In the 1930's and 1940's, he was director of some of the most influential literary publications in Latin America. He was a steadfast opponent of the Juan Perón regime. After the revolution that overthrew the

Perón dictatorship, he was named ambassador to the United Nations Educational, Scientific, and Cultural Organization (UNESCO) in Paris. Subsequently, he returned to private life to devote himself exclusively to writing and lecturing in Europe and the United States. *Fiesta in November* and other novels and stories established Mallea as one of Latin America's greatest writers and one of the outstanding prose stylists in the world.

"Critical Evaluation" by Bruce D. Reeves

Further Reading

Belloni, Manuel. "The Inner Silence of Eduardo Mallea." *Américas* 19 (October, 1967): 20-27. Discusses Mallea's technique and theme of reaching the essential by means of describing the nonessential.

Flint, J. M. "The Expression of Isolation: Notes on Mallea's Stylistic Techniques." *Bulletin of Hispanic Studies* 44 (1967): 203-209. Another discussion of Mallea's masterful style.

Foster, David William, and Virginia Ramos Foster. "Mallea, Eduardo." In *Modern Latin American Literature*, edited by David William Foster and Virginia Ramos Foster. New York: Frederick Ungar, 1975. Surveys Mallea's production by providing excerpts from critical studies written by various critics. A good introduction to Mallea's most famous works.

Gertel, Zunilda. "Mallea's Novel: An Inquiry into Argentine Character." In *Retrospect: Essays on Latin American Literature*, edited by Elizabeth Rogers and Timothy Rogers. York, S.C.: Spanish Literature, 1987. A short analysis that concentrates on Mallea's oeuvre and indicates his contribution to the formation of contemporary Argentine society. Focuses on Mallea's literary and political importance.

Levine, Suzanne Jill. "The Latin American Novel in English Translation." In *The Cambridge Companion to the Latin American Novel*, edited by Efraín Kristal. New York: Cambridge University Press, 2005. Levine includes three of Mallea's novels—*The Bay of Silence*, *Fiesta in November*, and *All Green Shall Perish*—in her discussion of Latin American novels that have been translated into English.

Lewald, H. Ernest. *Eduardo Mallea*. Boston: Twayne, 1977. A good starting place in the study of Mallea and his work. Includes bibliography.

Lichtblau, Myron I. *The Argentine Novel: An Annotated Bibliography—Supplement*. Lanham, Md.: Scarecrow Press, 2002. Lichtblau, who has critiqued and translated Mallea's work, has compiled bibliographies of all editions, reprintings, and translations of Argentine novels published from 1788 through the end of the twentieth century. The book also includes critical commentary about the novels that originally appeared in American and Argentine newspapers and journals. This supplement expands the original 1997 edition.

The Fifth Child

Author: Doris Lessing (1919-   )
First published: 1988
Type of work: Novel
Type of plot: Allegory
Time of plot: 1960's to 1986
Locale: Suburbs of London

Principal characters:
HARRIET LOVATT, a mother of five children
DAVID LOVATT, her husband
LUKE,
HELEN,
JANE,
PAUL, and
BEN, the Lovatt children
DOROTHY, Harriet's mother

The Story:

Harriet and David meet at an office party. In no time, they find that they both want to start a family. Harriet is a virgin, despite her friends' sexual promiscuity, and David has had only one long relationship with another woman. Harriet and David decide to marry. Then they purchase a large Victorian-style home in the suburbs of London, planning to have many children. On the day they take ownership of the house, David and Harriet have sex in a bed left by the previous owners.

Harriet becomes pregnant and is now a stay-at-home wife. David continues his work as an architect.

David's mother, Molly; his stepfather, Frederick; his father, James; and his stepmother, Jessica, visit the couple's new home. James, a wealthy shipbuilder, agrees to pay the mortgage. Harriet's mother, Dorothy, also visits and agrees to stay and help Harriet through the pregnancy and to help raise the child. Luke is born in 1966. Three months after Harriet gives birth to Luke, she again becomes pregnant.

Meanwhile, Harriet and David's extended families visit and stay at their large house over Christmas and Easter holidays. Harriet's sister, Sarah, and her husband, William, struggle through marital problems, and Sarah gives birth to a baby with Down syndrome. Harriet has her second child, Helen, and soon thereafter her third, Jane. Despite Dorothy's protests that Harriet is having too many children too quickly, the Lovatts think of themselves as a perfect family that deserves its happiness. Harriet believes that Sarah and William had a child with Down syndrome because of their quarreling.

Harriet gives birth to a fourth child, Paul. David's parents and Dorothy continue to protest the number of children the Lovatts are having and question how they will afford to send them all to school. After Dorothy leaves to take care of Sarah's children, Harriet gets pregnant again and soon realizes the pregnancy will be exceptionally difficult. The fetus kicks early in the pregnancy, and Harriet becomes convinced that it is trying to tear out of her womb. Dorothy returns and chastises the couple again for being irresponsible.

The couple's marriage begins to deteriorate as Harriet becomes increasingly upset by the painful pregnancy and secretly takes tranquilizers. She begins to think of the fetus as a monster and, after giving birth, calls the baby a troll, goblin, and alien. Ben, the newest child, repulses the entire family with his abnormal strength, troll-like looks, and lack of affection. Harriet thinks she is a criminal for having given birth to a monster. Years later, the family suspects that Ben is guilty of killing pets that relatives bring over during holidays. The other children attempt to teach Ben some manners. He copies their behavior, but the children become afraid of him and lock their doors at night.

After seeing Ben's unruliness and Harriet's fatigue, relatives stop spending their holidays with the Lovatts. The other children, especially Paul, begin to feel neglected as Harriet, in spite of her repulsion for Ben, spends most of her time taking care of him. Under the advice and financial help of friends, Harriet and David send Ben to an institution, where "freak" children will eventually die under extensive drugging. Harriet feels guilty for sending Ben away. Against the wishes of David, she visits Ben at the institution. She discovers that he has been strapped in a straitjacket, drugged, and left to sit in his own excrement. By this time, Ben has lost all knowledge of social behavior and must be drugged to stop screaming. Upset by how the doctors have been treating Ben, Harriet takes him home and spends all her time rehabilitating him.

Harriet becomes increasingly distanced from her other children. They choose to attend boarding school and decide to spend their holidays with David's parents and stepparents. Paul becomes withdrawn and resentful of the attention given to Ben. After school, Paul spends his time watching television. The Lovatts send him to a psychologist, and he spends time with the psychologist's family instead of his own.

Meanwhile, Harriet asks the errand boy, John, and his friends to take care of Ben after school. Ben emulates John and his friends and, for the first time, seems to belong to a group. After John leaves for vocational school and Ben starts school, Ben becomes the leader of his own gang. His teachers tell Harriet that he is a slow learner but that he tries to learn. Harriet is content as long as Ben gets along with other students. Ben and his gang start joining in riots across England, and Harriet suspects that he and his friends are responsible for local robberies and a rape. Ben is eleven years old.

Harriet and David decide to sell the house now that all five children no longer spend much time there. Harriet gives Ben their new address, but he leaves it behind and disappears with his gang. Harriet reflects on the loss of her family through the years and wonders if Ben finds his own kind. She imagines that he meets members of his own "alien" race underground.

Critical Evaluation:

One of the most prominent contemporary writers, Doris Lessing won the Nobel Prize in Literature in 2007. Her best-known novel, *The Golden Notebook* (1962), experiments with narrative form to look at the interior lives of women. Lessing was born in Persia (now Iran), grew up in Southern Rhodesia (present-day Zimbabwe), and moved to London in 1949. Her outsider status as part of a minority in the former British colonies, and as a woman and a communist after she moved to England, helps her write poignantly about social and political issues. In her fiction, she frequently employs elements of myth, fable, science fiction, and mysticism, but other novels, such as *The Diaries of Jane Somers* (1984) and *The Good Terrorist* (1985), maintain a strictly realistic mode.

In *The Fifth Child*, Lessing begins with a seemingly realistic 1960's setting but integrates elements of science fiction into the narrative with the birth of the odd Ben, the Lovatt's "alien," "monster," or "Neanderthal" child. *The Fifth Child* remains a minor work in comparison to her masterpiece, *The Golden Notebook*, but it is innovative in playing with the boundary between social realism and science fiction to address mid-twentieth century anxieties about gender and motherhood. In 2000, Lessing published a sequel to the novel, *Ben, in the World*, which follows Ben's travels and recounts the hostility that he faces.

In *The Fifth Child*, Lessing uses a third-person limited narration that sticks closely to Harriet Lovatt's actions and reveals her happiness in being able to live in her dream home and her anguish after conceiving Ben. The novel rarely delves into the emotions of her husband or other characters—who ritualistically appear at every holiday until Ben's birth—nor does the novel give the reader a window into Ben's thoughts. The novel sets up a stark contrast between Harriet, whose complex emotions toward Ben are understandable, and Ben, who remains utterly alien. The novel never explains what Ben is—alien, monster, Neanderthal, or deformed child.

The absence of chapter breaks in the novel contributes to the way in which the story quickly and fluidly builds up to Harriet's horror toward Ben, her isolation from the rest of the family, and her resulting fear of motherhood in general. Read as an allegory or fable, the novel seems to warn against the idolization of domesticity and motherhood by the Lovatts. In the first half of the novel, the Lovatts fervently believe that they deserve the happiness they have found by purchasing a large home in the suburbs and deciding to have many children. The birth of Ben and his inexplicable monsterlike qualities, however, challenge and ultimately destroy their self-assurance and faith in family as a panacea.

Ben and the destruction of the Lovatt family function as critiques of common midcentury attitudes toward motherhood, the novel's major theme. Being a mother is always Harriet's first duty, and it defines her identity. Thus, when she cannot love Ben and struggles to care for all her children, David and her relatives consider her diseased. Also, despite Harriet's conviction that the fetus (later, Ben) inside her is trying to kill her, her fears are dismissed as mere hysteria by her doctor, husband, and relatives. To them, and to Harriet herself, motherhood is supposed to be instinctual; Harriet's repulsion toward Ben, therefore, is unnatural.

Harriet calls herself a criminal several times in the novel, and David stops wanting to sleep with her after Ben's birth. The novel's depiction of Harriet's guilt throws into relief that she never realizes her commonality with Ben as an "other"; both Ben, a biological oddity and possibly an atavistic "prim-

itive," and Harriet, a woman and mother, are objects of speculation, ridicule, curiosity, and racialization in the eyes of society.

Alice Chuang

Further Reading

Bloom, Harold, ed. *Doris Lessing.* New York: Chelsea House, 1986. A collection of essays examining gender in Lessing's novels. Considers gender in terms of Lessing's relationship to her African past, to women's authorship, to psychoanalysis, and to the British feminist tradition.

Greene, Gayle. *Doris Lessing: The Poetics of Change.* Ann Arbor: University of Michigan Press, 1997. Provides a concise biography of Lessing as well as excerpts from her radio interviews. Looks at Lessing's fiction through the lens of contemporary social issues and her conflicted politics.

Kaplan, Carey, and Ellen Cronan Rose, eds. *Doris Lessing: The Alchemy of Survival.* Athens: Ohio University Press, 1988. A collection of essays discussing Lessing's representation of radical ideology (for example, communism) and examining her subversive rejection of a single coherent definition of humanism and her documentation of British imperialism and social change.

Klein, Carole. *Doris Lessing: A Biography.* New York: Carroll & Graf, 2000. An unauthorized biography (Lessing specifically refused to cooperate with Klein) that nonetheless draws on interviews with Lessing's acquaintances and makes connections between events in Lessing's life and episodes in her novels.

Pifer, Ellen. "New Versions of the Idyll: Lessing's *The Fifth Child* and Kundera's Infantocracy." In *Demon or Doll: Images of the Child in Contemporary Writing and Culture.* Charlottesville: University Press of Virginia, 2000. A unique study examining Lessing's *The Fifth Child* as a story about the failed promises of domesticity, bliss, family, motherhood, and childhood. Part of a larger study on the complex depiction of children and childhood in modern culture and literature.

Rubenstein, Roberta. *The Novelistic Vision of Doris Lessing: Breaking the Forms of Consciousness.* Urbana: University of Illinois Press, 1979. Looks at Lessing's development of a theory of consciousness in her novels. A focused, detailed consideration of both form and thematic development.

Sage, Lorna. *Doris Lessing.* London: Methuen, 1983. A concise biography, accessible to students and general readers, which focuses on the development of her fiction.

St. Andrews, Bonnie. *Forbidden Fruit: On the Relationship Between Women and Knowledge in Doris Lessing, Selma Lagerlöf, Kate Chopin, Margaret Atwood.* Troy, N.Y.: Whitston, 1986. Places Lessing in context with other writers who use myth and the fairy tale form to explore gender and the feminist implications of women's knowledge.

Saxton, Ruth, and Jean Tobin, eds. *Woolf and Lessing: Breaking the Mold.* New York: St. Martin's Press, 1994. Useful collection of essays for students of canonical literature. Compares Virginia Woolf's and Lessing's use of multiple voices in their novels, their representation of subjectivity, and the importance of place and gender in their novels.

The Fifth Horseman

Author: José Antonio Villarreal (1924-   )
First published: 1974
Type of work: Novel
Type of plot: Historical realism
Time of plot: 1893-1915
Locale: The north of Mexico

Principal characters:
HERACLIO INÉS, a horseman and a revolutionary
DAVID CONTRERAS, his boyhood friend turned mortal enemy
CARMEN BECERRA, the patrón's daughter
PANCHO VILLA, a bandit turned rebel leader
MARCELINA ORTIZ, Heraclio's devoted wife
XÓCHITL SALAMANCA, Heraclio's mistress

The Story:

After Heraclio Inés's mother dies while giving birth to him and his father dies while attempting to tame a wild stallion five years later, he is sent to be a lowly shepherd on the Hacienda de la Flor, even though his family enjoys the protection of the patrón, Don Aurelio Becerra, who is also his godfather. Heraclio leaves behind his fellow pastor, the young but already embittered David Contreras, Don Aurelio's illegitimate son by María Contreras, who is thought to be a witch. Heraclio's brothers treat him cruelly in his new home, forcing him to break horses as they once did and to be brave beyond his years. Under the threat of a lashing should he return home on foot, the brothers leave Heraclio, the proud and diffident fifth horseman, to tame a wild stallion thirty kilometers away from the hacienda.

When Heraclio is rude to the patrón's children, Crispín and Carmen Becerra, Don Aurelio does not rebuke him because Don Aurelio is inordinately fond of his godson and asks only that he provide the two with riding lessons. For the haughty Carmen, these occasions soon turn into opportunities for sexual encounters that all would frown upon for their scandalous violation of the church's moral teachings as well as for their violation of society's strict class boundaries. Heraclio's discovery of their irreconcilable worldviews concerning the future of Mexico leads him to tell Carmen about her father's sexual exploitation of the native women living on the Hacienda de la Flor; he discloses this before she and her brother leave to attend the university in Seattle. In their absence, Carmen's dissolute cousin from Spain, Domingo Arguiú, arrives to fulfill a contract to unite in marriage the Becerra fortune with the noble name of his family. Heraclio takes an immediate dislike to his dandified elitism but perversely thinks that Domingo might make a suitable husband for Carmen.

Some time later, the patrón organizes a fiesta to welcome home his children from the United States. Carmen, more eager than Heraclio to continue their illicit relationship, eventually discloses the situation to her parents. The knowledge prompts Don Aurelio to plan a hasty marriage for the boy. Meanwhile, Crispín vows never to succeed his father as patrón in such an oppressive social order, and he goes to the United States with his American wife. After the Inés brothers dominate the hacienda's equestrian competition, winning and sharing prizes in every category of horsemanship, Heraclio kills the patrón's contador, Juan Vásquez, who came upon him making love to Carmen. He thereupon flees to the hills, where he joins a bandit group that includes his childhood friend David Contreras.

The aged Ysabel Pulido, leader of the thieves who redistribute their booty among the rural poor, is taking his men to join forces with the emerging rebel hero, Pancho Villa, when he dies suddenly in his sleep. Though he is still a teenager, Heraclio declares himself the new leader of this rebel band, much to the envy of David and to the amusement of Villa. David tries to shoot Heraclio in the back at Juárez. Upon his return to the hacienda during a lull in the fighting, Heraclio marries the saddlemaker's daughter, Marcelina Ortiz, and spends the night with María Contreras. David's robbery and murder of a merchant seals his fate as an outlaw. Soon, though, Heraclio is called to rejoin the ever more powerful and seemingly unstoppable Villa, who is celebrating victories in Jiménez and Chihuahua. Villa sets up his revolutionary headquarters in Chihuahua, and he passes the virginal Indian circus performer Xóchitl Salamanca on to Heraclio to be his mistress; she has innocently declared that she would prefer to be violated by the more handsome of the two men. Decisive rebel victories follow at Torreón and Zacatecas, where the foolish Domingo perishes during a bandit attack; Domingo goes against Heraclio's advice not to surrender.

After a variola plague in Zacatecas kills off the devoted Xóchitl, Heraclio loses his revolutionary fervor and returns to resume his family life on the Hacienda de la Flor, where he expresses his condolences to the widowed Carmen. In a brutal attack that seethed inside him since the night his revered Ysabel Pulido died, David kills Heraclio's baby daughter and rapes Marcelina, who also dies. This forces Heraclio to murder David in revenge. Heraclio refuses Carmen's suggestion that he marry her and become patrón. Instead, he travels a great distance by train to kill the traitorous General Celestino Gámez. He decides against wedding his brother Concepción's widow, Otilia, for whom he always felt a great affection, and flees into California to begin a life in exile. Villa's decimated Division of the North heads for sure defeat.

Critical Evaluation:

The Fifth Horseman is the second of José Antonio Villarreal's three influential novels about the Mexican American experience that helped define the parameters of Chicano literature. Although particularly notable for its stark depiction of the social inequalities leading up to the Mexican Revolution (1910-1920), this work ends promisingly with the protagonist's flight into the United States as one of a wave of refugees who were the first to embody the problematics of Chicano identity that lie at the core of all subsequent Mexican American works. Villarreal's *Pocho* (1959), by contrast, treats the coming of age of Richard Rubio, whose conflicts with his Old World parents in the more progressive social milieu of the United States lead him to join the military in

World War II to fight for his adopted country, thus forging for himself a coherent sense of cultural belonging. *Clemente Chacón* (1984) presents a similar American Dream saga, this time of a successful Mexican immigrant who feels no need to deny either his heritage or his newfound nationality; he proudly declares himself a Chicano.

An amalgam of two literary genres, *The Fifth Horseman* displays the influences both of American historical novels and of Mexican novels of the revolution, including Mariano Azuela's *Los de abajo* (1915, serial; 1916, book; *The Underdogs*, 1929), Agustín Yáñez's *Al filo del agua* (1947; *The Edge of the Storm*, 1963), and Juan Rulfo's *Pedro Páramo* (1955, 1959, 1964, 1980; English translation, 1959, 1994). Villarreal largely eschews the more technically innovative styles of later novels of this type, such as Carlos Fuentes's *La muerte de Artemio Cruz* (1962; *The Death of Artemio Cruz*, 1964), and employs instead a realistic mode of narration. He describes the oppression and abuses of the prerevolutionary system of the hacienda, where native Mexican peons lived at the mercy of their patróns' whims, forever in their debt because of the inflated prices of provisions at their supply stores.

Villarreal's seamless blending of fact and fiction depicts Heraclio's developing political tendencies against the backdrop of the period's turbulent history. There were no less than ten changes in Mexican leadership over a span of twenty years. Villarreal also portrays the unique cultural flavor of the northern Mexican countryside, indulging in a spirited *costumbrismo* that includes the upper-class social world of the hacienda as well as the contests of daring horsemanship native to the region. The novel includes descriptions of the lavish ball thrown to welcome home the patrón's children and of the brothers Inés as they engage in the so-called ride of death. In keeping with his naturalist bent, Villarreal throughout the novel uses an English style characterized by Spanish syntactical structures. It is as if he is reminding his readers at every turn of the linguistic crossroads at the heart of the Chicano experience.

Heraclio's escape into California in the novel's conclusion, an apparent abandonment of his past revolutionary goals, aptly reflects the uncertainty of his motivations and involvement in the conflict. Does he embody as an individual the momentous change in historical consciousness that rejected the autocratic oppression of the hacienda system and occasioned the inevitable bloodletting of the revolution for the sake of a greater social equality, or can his rebelliousness be more simply and readily explained by his naturally arrogant disposition? After all, from a young age, Heraclio openly flouts his brothers' authority, and he decides that he will do only occasional work on the hacienda and shows little inclination to bow to the authority of the patrón or his family. Heraclio's determination to uphold the ideals of the revolution stands in stark contrast to the fatalistic belief in destiny that so many other characters in the novel hold. Whereas a number of *The Fifth Horseman*'s ruling-class Mexicans and peons see no possibility of or express scant sympathy for significant political change in their country, Heraclio takes history into his own hands and risks his life for what he believes will be a more socially just existence for all Mexicans.

However, disillusionment with the course of the conflict gripping the nation gnaws at Heraclio. He has trouble deciding whether the plundering rapist and murderer Pancho Villa is really anything more than the marauding fugitive he was at the start, or whether this master strategist and tactician perhaps represents the revolution's high-minded quest for greater social equality. Time after time, Heraclio heeds the call to return to battle from civilian life; on each occasion he reports dutifully to Villa, whom he considers the only true nationalist among the revolution's bickering generals and politicians. It is telling of the nebulous duality to his actions and motives, though, that Heraclio's loss of faith in the bloody, hard-fought campaign ultimately follows upon Villa's decision to isolate in Zacatecas those unfortunates afflicted by the variola plague—the order essentially seals the fate of the stricken Xóchitl Salamanca, who dies from lack of medical attention. Heraclio's behavior seems at least partially contingent on personal factors—the disaffection with Villa's callousness and the disheartening blow of his mistress's death—and not sheer political partisanship. With seemingly little left to fight for, Heraclio leaves his life as a ranch worker in order to kill a general who has been disloyal to Villa: He risks his life one last time for the revolution's elusive ideals before fleeing into California and permanently renouncing the fighting and its muddled objectives.

Gregary J. Racz

Further Reading

Bratcher, James T. "José Villarreal, Evil Eye, and a Cultural Strangehold." *Journal of the West* 45, no. 4 (Fall, 2006): 3-6. Provides history and criticism of Villarreal's work, focusing on his novels *The Fifth Horseman*, *Pocho*, and *Clemente Chacón*. Describes how these novels contain themes of ethnic identity, revolutionaries, culture, and the evil eye.

Jiménez, Francisco, ed. *The Identification and Analysis of Chicano Literature*. New York: Bilingual Press, 1979. A comprehensive collection of scholarly essays that chronicle the history of the rise of Chicano literature, with an emphasis on current critical approaches to Chicano literary texts. Provides detailed analysis of important trends, the role of women, and the issue of Mexican American identity.

Parotti, Phillip. "Heroic Conventions in Jose Antonio Villareal's *The Fifth Horseman*." *Bilingual Review* 17, no. 3 (September-December, 1992): 237. An analysis of the novel, discussing its epic structure, its literary technique, and other characteristics.

Rocard, Marcienne. *The Children of the Sun: Mexican-Americans in the Literature of the United States*. Translated by Edward G. Brown, Jr. Tucson: University of Arizona Press, 1989. Examines the forging of Chicano identity from both the Anglo and the Hispanic perspective. The work is notable for its careful tracing of the progression of Chicano cultural attitudes and their influence on self-representation.

Shirley, Carl R., and Paula W. Shirley. *Understanding Chicano Literature*. Columbia: University of South Carolina Press, 1988. Considers the canon of Chicano literature largely along generic lines and contains a separate section on *literatura chicanesca*, works about Chicanos by non-Chicano authors. Provides thumbnail sketches of Villarreal's three novels.

Sommers, Joseph, and Tomás Ybarra-Frausto, eds. *Modern Chicano Writers: A Collection of Critical Essays*. Englewood Cliffs, N.J.: Prentice-Hall, 1979. An excellent volume of diverse essays exploring the historical and cultural influences on contemporary Chicano literature, from indigenous folkloric traditions to the impact of the Mexican-American War. A narrative section focuses on Tomás Rivera.

Tatum, Charles. *Chicano Literature*. Boston: Twayne, 1982. Places Villarreal among the pioneer novelists of Chicano literature. While critical of the author's black-and-white portrayal of good versus evil, the study praises his evocative depiction of Mexico's exploitative prerevolutionary social order centered on the hacienda.

The Filostrato

Author: Giovanni Boccaccio (1313-1375)
First published: Il Filostrato, c. 1335 (English
    translation, 1873)
Type of work: Poetry
Type of plot: Romance
Time of plot: c. 1200 B.C.E.
Locale: Ancient Troy

Principal characters:
PRIAMO, king of Troy
TROILO and HECTOR, his sons
PANDARO, Troilo's friend
GRISEIDA, his cousin
CALCHAS, her father
DIOMEDE, a Greek commander

The Poem:

When Troy is besieged by Greeks who come to avenge
the abduction and rape of Queen Helen by Paris, son of
Priamo, Calchas, a Trojan priest, foresees the fall of Troy and
flees to the Greeks, leaving behind his widowed daughter,
Griseida. When the Trojan people hear of Calchas's treachery, they assemble to burn her house, but they are stopped by
Hector, who says she can remain in Troy.

Some days later Troilo happens to see Griseida at a religious festival and, overcome with her exquisite beauty, he
immediately falls in love with her. In order to keep his love
secret, however, he makes remarks about the stupidity of
love. In private he praises Griseida's beauty and declares
his love for her. Soon he begins to fight fiercely against
the Greeks in the hope that his feats will be pleasing to her,
but she shows no signs of recognizing his love. With each
day his pining for her grows worse until he cannot eat or sleep
but spends his time imploring Love to tell Griseida of his
pain.

Pandaro finds Troilo in this condition and asks what
causes his grief. Pledging Pandaro to secrecy, Troilo tells of
his unrequited love for Griseida. Pandaro, agreeing that
Griseida is worthy of such love, assures Troilo that he will,
with his cunning, find a way to win the girl for him.

Pandaro leaves Troilo and goes immediately to Griseida's
house to tell her that she is greatly loved by a noble and virtuous man of Troy. After considerable teasing Pandaro reveals
Troilo's name to her. Though she considers Troilo worthy,
Griseida still grieves for her dead husband, and she tells
Pandaro that Troilo's love will pass. Pandaro persists in telling
her of Troilo's miserable state, and at last she is convinced.

After Pandaro accomplishes his mission, he returns to
Troilo and tells him of his success. Troilo is overcome with
joy. After praising Venus, he goes with Pandaro to behold
Griseida's beauty.

For a time Troilo is satisfied with the knowledge that
Griseida acknowledges his love, but as his passion increases
he desires more than brief glimpses of her. His grief soon re-

turns. When he tells Pandaro of his frustration, his friend suggests that he write a letter that Pandaro will take to Griseida.

The heartrending letter is written and carried to Griseida.
Again she is hesitant, fearing that if she answers the letter she
will appear immodest. Again Pandaro convinces her, and she
writes a letter telling Troilo that she desires to meet him; once
more her better judgment restrains her. Pandaro returns to
Griseida after delivering the response and tells her that mere
words are not sufficient. After some argument he assures
her that her reputation will not be injured, as the matter will
be kept secret.

When Griseida consents to meet Troilo in a secret room in
her house, Pandaro cautions Troilo to be prudent. The young
lover goes to Griseida's house. Upon meeting, the two lovers
embrace and, after a few words, go to her bed chamber where
they pass the evening in physical delight.

A few days later the two lovers have another opportunity
to be together. Troilo again meets her in the secret chamber,
and once more they make love. They curse the morning
that ends their meeting and plan to meet again when they
can. The consummation of his love completely changes
Troilo. He becomes even more fierce as a soldier, and he
continually praises Love and the happy state of those who
share its bounties.

Meanwhile, after some savage fighting, the Greeks take
many of the best Trojan warriors as prisoners. Priamo is
granted a truce, however, and an exchange of prisoners takes
place. Calchas, hearing of this exchange, asks the Greeks to
give him one of the Trojan warriors to exchange for his
daughter Griseida. He is given the mighty Antenor.

During the negotiations Troilo hears that Griseida will be
exchanged, and, heartbroken that he might lose her, he
swoons. When he recovers, without revealing the cause of his
consternation, he returns to his palace. There he remains,
desolate and sick, reviling Fortune for permitting such a loss
to occur. Eventually he summons Pandaro, who consoles
him by saying that Griseida is not the only beautiful woman

in Troy and that a new love will drive away the memories of the old one. Troilo, failing to respond to Pandaro's words, wishes only for death. At last Pandaro suggests that Troilo abduct his love from the Greeks, a plan to which Troilo agrees, provided Griseida will consent.

That night Troilo visits Griseida, and the two bemoan their fate. Griseida suggests that the war might end soon and she can return, or, at the least, they can see each other during the truces. Troilo, not convinced, suggests that they run away. Fearing the loss of her honor, Griseida rejects this proposal. She tells Troilo to wait patiently for her return, which she will arrange within ten days.

After a tearful farewell, Griseida is delivered to Diomede in exchange for Antenor. Troilo passes the following days lamenting his loss until, at the suggestion of Pandaro, he goes with his friend to a feast in order to make the time pass more quickly.

In the Greek camp, meanwhile, Diomede discovers Griseida weeping. Upon learning the cause of her sorrow, he convinces her that Troy will fall and her love for Troilo is unwise. Eventually Griseida is overcome by his arguments and his suit of love, and her feeling for Troilo lessens.

On the tenth day Troilo and Pandaro go to the city gate. There they wait expectantly for Griseida's return, but she does not appear. For the next six days Troilo waits with hope at the gate. Soon he begins to lose his strength and to become sickly. Then, in a dream, he sees Griseida being ravished by a wild boar that he believes represents Diomede. Overcome by the vision, Troilo attempts to kill himself, but he is stopped by Pandaro, who tells him to verify the dream by writing to his love. He writes as Pandaro suggests, requesting that she return or quell his fears, but he receives no answer.

For a time he vents his anger in battle. Then he receives an answer from Griseida, reaffirming her love. Troilo, still believing that she is being held in the Greek camp against her will, sends numerous messages to which she responds favorably. During a battle, however, a Trojan soldier wounds Diomede and takes from him a brooch that Troilo identifies as a gift he gave Griseida. Feeling now that his suspicion is true, he seeks out Diomede in battle and the two fight fiercely, but neither is able to overcome the other. One day, after Troilo kills many Greeks, Achille slays Troilo and thus ends the ill-conceived love between Troilo and Griseida.

Critical Evaluation:

Giovanni Boccaccio took a minor incident in the story of the Trojan War and made it the center of his story. Geoffrey Chaucer is indebted to Boccaccio for Chaucer's *Troilus and Criseyde* (c. 1382). Though *The Filostrato* contains none of the psychological portraiture of Chaucer's work, it has great literary merit and is probably superior to Chaucer's work in its directness and passionate intensity.

The Filostrato, from a word coined by Boccaccio meaning "the one who is vanquished by love," contains many of the traditional courtly love elements found in medieval romance, but it also develops a worldview based upon moral standards that are new to the genre. It can thus be seen as a transitional work, bridging the medieval and Renaissance periods.

One factor distinguishing Boccaccio from earlier writers of medieval romance is that he represents the bourgeois class that was a decisive force in the dissolution of the Middle Ages. His attitude toward courtly love is thus quite different from the mystical orientation of such writers as Dante Alighieri or the aristocratic tradition of the writers of French romances such as Chrétien de Troyes.

An indication of the new manner in which Boccaccio approaches courtly love can be found in the particular way in which he transforms the tale of Troilus (Troilo) and Cressida (Griseida) as originally found in the *Roman de Troie* of Benoît de Saint-Maure, who lived during the twelfth century. The story as narrated by Benoît was within the tradition of the medieval epic and represents a masculine and military orientation in which the prowess of arms plays the primary role. Women and love, if they appear at all, are of only secondary importance. When Benoît describes love, his emphasis is on Troilus and Diomede, and not on Cressida. Indeed, his story appears to be that of Diomede rather than of Troilus (Troilo). Boccaccio took the basic plot of Benoît and transformed it for his own purpose.

This purpose is related in the poem to *The Filostrato*, in which Boccaccio indicates that he will narrate the suffering of Troilo so that the lady to whom the poem is addressed will understand that Boccaccio himself is suffering as Troilo suffered. This lady is generally acknowledged to have been Maria d'Aquino, the natural daughter of the king of Naples, who absented herself from Naples, where Boccaccio was then residing. *The Filostrato* was designed to function as a love letter. This may have been an extraliterary reason for Boccaccio's amplification of the role of Pandarus (Pandaro). The purpose of the work was to seduce Maria (and cause her to return to Naples) as Pandarus helps to seduce Cressida.

Superficially, *The Filostrato* appears to be a conventional tale of courtly love, and many familiar conceits associated with the tradition of courtly love are in evidence. The work opens in a courtly setting with the presentation of questions in a court of love. Love enters through the eyes in "the fair season." Griseida is described as being "so fair and so like an angel." Troilo is depicted as being ennobled by love; he becomes a more fierce and vigorous fighter against the Greeks because of the love bestowed upon him by Griseida. Troilo suffers—he is pale, lacks appetite, loses sleep, and becomes weak.

Boccaccio places particular emphasis on the courtly love doctrine of nobility as residing not in noble birth but in a noble heart. Since Boccaccio was a member of the bourgeoisie and was attempting to make his way in the royal court of Naples, this view was of personal interest. Nobility is depicted as based upon virtue, not power. Although of a lower social rank than Troilo, Griseida is considered worthy of his love because of her "proud and noble bearing . . . high worth and courtly speech . . . manner more courteous than those of other ladies."

Despite the presence of these traditional courtly love elements, other aspects of the tradition are contradicted within the poem. For example, the purpose of love is not ennoblement but satisfaction of Troilo's "hot desire." Griseida understands (as Boccaccio hoped Maria would understand) the true purpose of the courtship. She is outside the courtly love tradition, not because of her later betrayal but because of her easy seduction. The danger and barriers that confound the lover in a typical medieval romance are missing. Troilo, unlike the heroes of the medieval romances of Chrétien de Troyes, does not have to prove himself by submitting himself to constant danger. His love is unearned and too easily won. Troilo recognizes this when he states that "what I crave has not been earned by my service."

Boccaccio is not concerned with ennobling Troilo, however, but with telling of his passion. He wishes Maria to understand from the tale "how great and of what sort my desires are, what is their goal, and what beyond all else they crave." Like Troilo, Boccaccio is concerned with making his love known to his lady and drawing her to him. If his lady should fail to understand, he addresses her directly in the invocation to canto 3 and requests that she "refuse not my high desire; graciously grant that which I ask."

The noble purpose of courtly love is lacking, and so is the moral lesson. Boccaccio makes no distinction between earthly love and heavenly love. Boccaccio's salvation will come from his lady and not from heaven. The song of Troilo, dedicated to Venus, reinforces the recognition that Boccaccio is not conflating earthly and heavenly love. He is not rejecting religious values; they merely have no place within the context of his work.

The lack of a palinode in *The Filostrato* is thus not surprising. The palinode is the recantation of earthly love and the reassertion of the supreme value of heavenly love found at the conclusion of many traditional medieval romances. Its purpose is to remind the reader that although courtly love may be supreme on this earth, heavenly love is always preferable. Courtly love is, therefore, generally placed within a framework of religious values. Since Boccaccio's narrative is based solely upon worldly values, there is no need to recant. Boccaccio's only warning to the reader is presented not as a moral lesson but as a practical lesson, in keeping with the practical tone of his poem. He advises young men to place their love in ladies of true nobility, that is, ladies who will not betray them.

Although Boccaccio in *The Filostrato* utilizes the conventions of courtly love for a purely sensual end, this should not suggest that he could not write tales completely within a courtly tradition. One has only to turn to the fifth day of *Decameron* (1349-1351; *The Decameron*, 1620) to realize with what seriousness Boccaccio could write of courtly love. In *The Filostrato*, however, Boccaccio can be seen as a transitional figure, already drawing away from the values of the Middle Ages but not completely caught within the values of the Renaissance.

"Critical Evaluation" by Phyllis Mael

Further Reading

Bergin, Thomas G. *Boccaccio*. New York: Viking Penguin, 1981. Devotes a chapter to *The Filostrato*, summarizing the plot, examining the work's literary origins, and analyzing its themes. Notes the importance of the work to Geoffrey Chaucer's *Troilus and Criseyde*.

Boccaccio, Giovanni. *Il Filostrato*. Translated by Robert P. apRoberts and Anna Bruni-Seldis. Edited by Vincenzo Pernicone. New York: Garland, 1986. In a comprehensive introduction, the translators trace the history of the Troilus story, examine the autobiographical elements (including the now-discarded identifications of the woman to whom Boccaccio supposedly wrote his work), review Boccaccio's ideas about courtly love, and recount the appearance of the story in English literature.

Gittes, Tobias Foster. *Boccaccio's Naked Muse: Eros, Culture, and the Mythopoeic Imagination*. Toronto, Ont.: University of Toronto Press, 2008. Examines all of Boccaccio's works, including *The Filostrato*, to demonstrate how he used an innovative and coherent system of mythology in order to express his cultural experience and to address the needs of his readers.

Kearney, Milo, and Mimosa Schraer. "The Flaw in Troilus." *Chaucer Review* 22, no. 3 (1988): 185-191. Compares Chaucer's work to Boccaccio's, examining the scene in which Pandarus encourages Troilus to find other women if he cannot have Criseyde. Troilus's failure to defend his love exemplifies several situations in which Chaucer makes his hero more passive than Boccaccio's.

Serafini-Sauli, Judith Powers. *Giovanni Boccaccio*. Boston: Twayne, 1982. Examines *The Filostrato* with reference to its use of courtly love, character development, and Griseida's betrayal of her lover.

Stillinger, Thomas C. *The Song of Troilus: Lyric Authority in the Medieval Book*. Philadelphia: University of Pennsylvania Press, 1992. Stillinger analyzes three narrative books that are in some way constructed around lyric poems: Boccaccio's *The Filostrato*, Chaucer's *Troilus and Criseyde*, and Dante's *Vita Nuova* (c. 1292). He maintains that these books attempt to achieve an unprecedented "lyric authority" that combines the subjectivity of courtly love poetry with the objective authority of biblical commentary.

Final Payments

Author: Mary Gordon (1949-   )
First published: 1978
Type of work: Novel
Type of plot: Domestic realism
Time of plot: Early 1970's
Locale: New York

Principal characters:
ISABEL MOORE, a thirty-year-old woman
JOSEPH MOORE, Isabel's father and a devout Catholic
ELEANOR, Isabel's best friend
LIZ, Isabel's close friend
MARGARET CASEY, the former housekeeper for Isabel and her father
HUGH SLADE, Isabel's lover

The Story:

Isabel devotedly cares for her father, Joseph Moore, for eleven years until he dies, believing it her penance for having betrayed him. When she was nineteen, he found her in bed with his student, David Lowe. Three weeks later, he suffered his first stroke. Many years earlier, the housekeeper, Margaret Casey, wanted to marry Joseph. Isabel, then thirteen years old, jealously despised Margaret and did what neither her authoritarian father nor their loyal parish priest, Father Mulcahy, would do—she fired Margaret. When Isabel sees Margaret at her father's funeral, she feels the same revulsion she felt sixteen years earlier.

Isabel and her two childhood friends, Eleanor and Liz, maintain their friendships. All three women give up Catholicism. With her newfound freedom and the support of her friends, Isabel rapidly begins to change her life. She buys stylish, comfortable clothes with Eleanor, and she spends a weekend in Ringkill with Liz, Liz's glamorous but oafish husband, John, and her children. Liz introduces Isabel to her beautiful young lover, Erica. John, whom everyone, including his wife, knows to be a womanizer, offers Isabel her first job, a six-month pilot program involving home care for the aged. She gratefully accepts.

Isabel returns to Queens, sells her father's house, endures the painful insertion of an IUD, and moves upstate. She finds her own apartment and begins her job. At the first social gathering with her young colleagues, Isabel, out of anxiety, drinks too much; after the party, she allows John to have sex with her. Isabel craves affection, but this leaves her feeling dirty and out of control. Liz is angry with Isabel for allowing John to seduce her, and out of spite and curiosity she introduces Isabel to another married man, Hugh Slade, a cool rationalist who describes Isabel's Catholic upbringing as "barbarous." Isabel decides that she will be Hugh's lover, although John continues to pursue her.

It is Isabel's job to visit private homes where elderly people receive care and to judge the caretakers and the living conditions. She is often deeply moved by the individual stories she hears as she visits the homes, but they confirm her belief that there is no way to control what makes people happy.

One day, on a hike with Hugh, Erica, and Liz, Isabel is quick to tire and becomes infuriated with the patronizing tolerance with which the others treat her. When she finally reaches the end of the climb and Hugh tells her for the first time that he loves her, she feels both the richness of the moment and the first foreboding that what she values now is impossible to guarantee.

John continues to pursue her. When Isabel fends off his advances by punching him in the eye, he leaves her alone, but not without threatening to pay her back. When Hugh comes to eat a dinner she lovingly prepares, he scolds her for living in filth when he finds a moldy coffee cup in her living room. His words make Isabel realize that he cannot be trusted with her new and shaky womanhood.

Some weeks later, Hugh tells her he is considering leaving his wife, Cynthia. At a party Cynthia verbally accosts Isabel, calling her "the little bitch." John maliciously tells Cynthia a great deal about Isabel, and on the basis of that knowledge Cynthia knows exactly what to say to hurt Isabel, telling her that she is selfish and perverted and that she was impatient for her father to die. Cynthia's words crumble Isabel's illusions and all semblance of equilibrium. Completely distraught, she withdraws, believing she is utterly alone and inexorably guilty. She breaks off her relationship with Hugh, telling him to return to Cynthia.

Out of an irrational need to stop causing others pain, to do penance, and to cast her life back in the role that is safe, Isabel goes to take care of Margaret. Margaret treats her hatefully, but Isabel perseveres. As she cooks and cleans, she eats and gains weight, with her dress size increasing from ten to sixteen. When Margaret insists, she has her long, lovely hair cut into a "bubble." Father Mulcahy's visit gives her an evening of respite, but when Margaret insults him, Isabel finally sees that what she is doing in this ugly house with a mean-spirited woman is trying to give up all that she loves so as never to have to lose it.

Realizing this, Isabel can write to Hugh and ask him to wait for her while she heals and call Eleanor to come for her. To free herself from Margaret, she makes her final payment: She gives her all the money she possesses, the twenty thousand dollars she received from the sale of her father's house. Eleanor and Liz come to get her late that night and, exhilarated and free, they drive off into the dawn.

Critical Evaluation:

Isabel's new life is an absolute transformation from the one in which her father and her father's bed had served as her center. She emerges as if from a cocoon after her years of all-consuming caregiving. She lived on the perimeter of a decade, and her marginality makes her feel like a blundering outsider. Always defining herself as her father's devoted daughter, it is impossible for her to be an adult as long as he is alive. With his death, Isabel no longer has his authoritarian certitude of right and wrong, nor does she know how to define herself. She therefore continues to look to others for self-definition and self-confirmation, a dependency that leaves her especially vulnerable.

Although Liz tries to persuade Isabel that her past has nothing to do with her new life, she knows that it has a great deal to do with it. Even though it may seem that she is starting fresh, Isabel brings demons with her, especially her ineradicable feelings of guilt and self-condemnation. Her sexuality, on hold for eleven years, once again proves unsettling. She long believed that her father's first stroke was caused by his discovery of David Lowe and her having sex. Although her sexual encounters with John are unsatisfactory, her body wants to be satisfied. Caught in a web of desire and of guilt, she luxuriates in her passionate affair with Hugh but believes his wife Cynthia's accusation that Isabel is selfish and sick. Isabel sees her sexual desire as a disease, and the only way she can protect herself against it is to bury herself in Margaret's house and overeat until she hides her beauty.

Isabel's inability to keep a clean, orderly house is another source of irrational guilt. When at thirteen she fires Margaret, she is completely unequipped to take on the responsibilities of housekeeping, and she never truly learns. When Hugh cruelly insists that he could never live with a woman "who could live in such filth," Isabel accepts his criticism as confirmation of her unwomanliness. She feels so much shame that she compares it to discovering the beginnings of a beard on her face. Overwhelmed, she is unable to control either the demands of her body or those of her home and to find order beneath the chaotic surface of everyday life.

Through her work and sifting through her past, Isabel comes to the conclusion that what everybody wants is "to be loved alone" but that most do not get that. When Hugh tells her that he loves her, she becomes aware not only of the impoverishment of her previous life but also of the danger of loss that love brings with it. As she waits for him to leave his wife, she realizes she again makes herself subject to a man's power: Her happiness depends on Hugh, just as it once depended on her father.

When confronted with Cynthia's condemnation, Isabel is powerless to offer an alternative interpretation. Instead, she is wrenched from the sanctuary that being the "good daughter" had offered. When Cynthia suggests Isabel could not wait for her father to die, she agrees and even goes so far as to hold herself accountable for his death. After that, it is only by devoting herself to Margaret that she can return to the safety offered her in the self-sacrificing role of caretaker, believing she will "get more, far more, by giving up life than by embracing it."

Nevertheless, in her despair and in the isolation of Margaret's home, Isabel begins to heal and to think that by giving reasonably of herself she might be able to enjoy love, work, and friends. When she can accept that the greatest love also carries with it the greatest danger, she is no longer defeated; instead, she sees ways she might be able to flourish despite the danger of loss. She sees that Margaret, an exhausted and frightened old woman, can be helped by Isabel's money. With self-understanding, a newfound courage and faith in human beings, and the nurturing and unselfish loyalty of Liz and Eleanor, Isabel can enter the miraculous though risky world of real life.

Janet Mason Ellerby

Further Reading

Becker, Brenda L. "Virgin Martyrs." *American Spectator*, August, 1981. This acerbic analysis notes that many of Gordon's religious themes are hackneyed relics of James Joyce and many feminist writers. However, Becker praises the quality of Gordon's detailed observation and her ability to characterize the Catholic Church both in its repressive qualities and in its triumphs.

Bennett, Alma. *Mary Gordon*. New York: Twayne, 1996. Introductory overview, with brief biography and chapters devoted to an analysis of each of Gordon's books published during the first twenty years of her career.

Gordon, Mary. *Conversations with Mary Gordon*. Edited by Alma Bennett. Jackson: University Press of Mississippi, 2002. Reprints previously published and broadcast interviews with Gordon, in which she discusses her life and work.

_____. "More Catholic than the Pope: Archbishop Lefebvre and a Romance of the One True Church." *Harper's*, July, 1978. Gordon discusses her own Catholic upbringing and her visit to the Society of St. Pius X, radically conservative followers of Archbishop Lefebvre. She writes of having sought "miracle, mystery, and authority" but of finally being disillusioned.

Gray, Francine du Plessix. "A Religious Romance." *The New York Times Book Review*, February 15, 1981. Gray gives primary attention to religious themes in *Final Payments* and in *The Company of Women* (1981) and notes Gordon's conclusion in both novels that friendship is the prime ingredient in human happiness.

Lodge, David. "The Arms of the Church." *Times Literary Supplement*, September 1, 1978. Lodge analyzes the character of the narrator, praising Gordon's portrayal but noting that other characters are less well drawn. He also looks at the novel's picture of the Catholic Church and sees Isabel's father as a metaphor for the church's power.

Neary, John M. "Mary Gordon's *Final Payments:* A Romance of the One True Language." *Essays in Literature* 17 (Spring, 1990): 94-110. Neary focuses on Isabel's central crisis, which he sees as a realization that human existence cannot provide an absolute presence of God, of a parent, or of an ordered world.

Sheldon, Barbara H. "Pretending No Mo(o)re: Mary Gordon's *Final Payments*." In *Daughters and Fathers in Feminist Novels*. New York: Peter Lang, 1997. Focuses on the father-daughter relationship in *Final Payments* and other feminist novels in which daughters defy their fathers' expectations of socially acceptable behavior.

Ward, Susan. "In Search of 'Ordinary Human Happiness': Rebellion and Affirmation in Mary Gordon's Novels." In *Faith of a (Woman) Writer*, edited by Alice Kessler-Harris and William McBrien. New York: Greenwood Press, 1988. Ward addresses three themes that run through Gordon's work: Self-assertive, intelligent young women must rebel against any code they were raised to obey unthinkingly; fathers are often dominant influences and growing up must involve replacement and reconciliation with the father; and patriarchal institutions offer little hope to modern women.

Wolcott, James. "More Catholic than the Pope." *Esquire*, March, 1981. Wolcott discusses Gordon's second novel, *The Company of Women*, comparing it to *Final Payments*. He faults both novels for inadequate characterization and overly refined writing.

The Financier

Author: Theodore Dreiser (1871-1945)
First published: 1912; revised, 1927
Type of work: Novel
Type of plot: Naturalism
Time of plot: c. 1850-1874
Locale: Philadelphia

Principal characters:
FRANK A. COWPERWOOD, a financier
LILLIAN SEMPLE COWPERWOOD, his wife
EDWARD BUTLER, a contractor and politician
AILEEN BUTLER, his daughter
HENRY COWPERWOOD, Frank's father

The Story:

At a young age, Frank Cowperwood becomes interested in only one thing—making money. When he is still in his teens, he makes his first successful business transaction: Passing by an auction sale, he successfully bids for a lot of Java coffee, which he sells to a grocer at a profit of 100 percent. His family marvels at Frank's ability, and his wealthy uncle, Seneca Davis, encourages him to go into business as soon as possible. Through several well-paying positions and shrewd speculation, Frank acquires enough money to open his own brokerage house. Within a short time, he is one of the most enterprising and successful young financiers in Philadelphia.

One day he meets Lillian Semple, the wife of a business associate. About a year later, her husband dies, and Frank marries the widow. By that time, he had accumulated a large fortune, and he is familiar with local and state politicians, among them Edward Butler, who rose from garbage collector to a leading position in local politics. Through Butler, Frank meets many other influential people, and his business and popularity increase.

Frank and Lillian have several children, but the youngsters do not particularly interest him, for his sole interest remains his business. When his father, Henry Cowperwood, finally becomes president of the bank in which he is employed, both Cowperwoods build expensive houses and furnish them luxuriously. Frank buys fine paintings and rare objects of art.

His home life is not satisfactory, since Lillian is older and more passive than he is; moreover, her beauty has almost disappeared. By contrast, Edward's daughter Aileen is young, beautiful, and high-spirited. Frank falls in love with her, and she, in spite of her strong religious training, becomes his mistress. He rents a house where they meet and furnishes it with his paintings and statues.

Because Frank is one of the financial powers in Philadelphia, he plans and schemes continually in order to thwart more powerful monopolists. He manages to acquire large sums from the state treasury through local politicians. The city treasurer, Stener, proves amenable in many ways, and he and Frank become involved in many shady transactions. Frank buys shares in railroads and local streetcar properties. After the great Chicago fire, some of Frank's investments are in a perilous state. He goes to friends and associates and urges them to stand together in order to avoid losses. So widespread are the effects of the fire, however, that the manipulations of the city politicians are certain to be discovered on the eve of an election. Something has to be done to satisfy indignant reform groups who are sure to demand action when they discover what occurred.

In the meantime, someone sends an anonymous note to Edward, telling him that Frank and Aileen are living together. When Frank goes to Edward and the contractor refuses to help him, Frank knows that he must have discovered his relationship with Aileen. Edward becomes his enemy and urges the other politicians to make Frank the scapegoat for everyone's dishonest dealings.

As a result, Frank and Stener, the city treasurer, are indicted on charges of embezzlement and grand larceny, and Frank is ruined financially. He pleads not guilty, but the jury convicts both him and Stener. He appeals and posts bail to avoid jail, but the appeal is denied, although the judges are not united in their decision. As soon as the appeal is denied, the sheriff is supposed to take Frank to jail until sentencing, but Frank bribes the sheriff and has a few more days of freedom. His property is sold to pay his debts, and his father resigns his position at the bank.

Frank and Aileen give up the house where they used to meet. Their meetings now take place at a house in another part of town. Determined to put an end to the affair, Butler and Pinkerton detectives enter the house and confront the couple. Edward tries various schemes to make Aileen leave Philadelphia, but he is unsuccessful once Aileen learns that he hired detectives to trail her.

Frank is sentenced to four years and nine months in the penitentiary. Aileen remains faithful to him. When Lillian goes to visit him, Frank asks her for a divorce, but she refuses.

After Edward dies, Frank's friends manage to get him a parole. At the end of thirteen months in jail, in March, 1873, he is freed. Through Wingate, a friend and business associate, he succeeds in rebuilding his business, and he keeps a bachelor apartment where Aileen visits him. Though he is ostensibly still living with his wife, everyone long ago learned of his relationship with Aileen.

In September, 1873, there is a panic. Frank, who bought stocks cheaply, makes a fortune. Several months later, he goes with Aileen to Chicago, where he plans to reestablish himself. Lillian gets a divorce but remains friendly with the Cowperwood family. She lives luxuriously, since Frank, to buy his own freedom, provides handsomely for her and the children.

Critical Evaluation:

Two symbolic passages concerning sea predators, one early in the novel and one at the conclusion, provide important clues to understanding Theodore Dreiser's theme in *The Financier*. As a boy, Frank Cowperwood stoically observes an unequal contest in a large fish tank between a lobster and a squid. The lobster, certain of victory, bides his time and slowly devours the defenseless squid. In the context of Dreiser's social metaphor, the strong destroy the weak, whether with sudden terrible force or gradually and relentlessly, like the lobster. The final symbolic passage, crudely added as an epilogue to the novel, treats the *Mycteroperca bonaci* (or black grouper), which, chameleonlike, changes its colors to avoid danger or to strike out at a weaker adversary. From Dreiser's point of view, the black grouper represents an element of "subtlety, chicanery, trickery" that is also part of the human condition. The fish is no more responsible, in a Godless universe, for its trickery than humans are morally responsible for using deception as a means of power. In *The Titan* (1914), Dreiser continued the theme embodied in Frank's rise to wealth and influence, an ascent that is determined by what the author understands as the laws of social Darwinism, as well as the theme of his socially conditioned fall from power. In *The Financier*, Dreiser details, with a naturalistic concern for inductive evidence, the causes both for Frank's success and his eventual failure, just as a scientist might describe the behavior of a fish in an aquarium.

However, unlike a true scientist who observes phenomena objectively and dispassionately, Dreiser views the activities of his hero from the vantage point of his socialist philosophy. With that bias, the ruthless financier Frank ought to serve as an object lesson on the corruption of the capitalistic system. Despite the Marxist determinism at the center of his economic philosophy, however, Dreiser obviously admires

Frank as a man, if not as a social creature. He sympathizes with his hero's single-minded ambition to succeed, his contempt for intellectual inferiors, his violent sexual passions, and his stubborn, egoistical will. Although Dreiser's early view of Frank may have been satirical, he treats him ultimately as a Nietzschean superman, advanced beyond the conventional feelings of petty morality, beyond remorse, pity, or loyalty for anyone but Aileen Butler, whose iron will and courage match his own. Even in Frank's love for Aileen, there is, however, a measure of selfishness, for, quite simply, she satisfies his needs. Unlike many of the protagonists of Dreiser's other novels—among them Carrie Meeber, Jennie Gerhardt, Clyde Griffiths, and Eugene Witla—Frank is a strong, magnetic, self-assured character, more the predatory lobster than the pitiful squid. Because Dreiser's attitude toward Frank is ambivalent—he admires the man but is contemptuous of his capitalistic endeavors—the message of the novel is correspondingly ambiguous.

The Financier has other weaknesses, including a sometimes careless use of language. In the major scenes, however, Dreiser sustains a powerful, honest sense of realism. The author is at his best in analyzing Cowperwood's tangled love affair with Aileen. The trial scene is masterly, as are the prison scenes. Without sentimentality, Dreiser touches life. In spite of its ambiguous theme and some stylistic weaknesses, *The Financier* is a novel of massive integrity that continues to move readers.

Further Reading

Cassuto, Leonard, and Clare Virginia Eby, eds. *The Cambridge Companion to Theodore Dreiser*. New York: Cambridge University Press, 2004. A collection of twelve essays focusing on the novelist's examination of American conflicts between materialistic longings and traditional values. Includes essays on Dreiser's style and on Dreiser and women, as well as Bruce Robbins's article "Can There Be Loyalty in *The Financier*? Dreiser and Upward Mobility."

Dreiser, Theodore. *The Financier*. New York: New American Library, 1967. After publishing *The Financier* in 1912, Dreiser in 1927 published a revised, shortened version, to which Larzer Ziff wrote a new afterword.

Gerber, Philip L. *Theodore Dreiser Revisited*. New York: Twayne, 1992. This revised reference work contains background on Dreiser's life and novels. Includes a chapter on Dreiser's "trilogy of desire," of which *The Financier* is the first volume.

Gogol, Miriam, ed. *Theodore Dreiser: Beyond Naturalism*. New York: New York University Press, 1995. Ten essays interpret Dreiser from the perspectives of new historicism, poststructuralism, psychoanalysis, feminism, and other points of view. Gogol's introduction advances the argument that Dreiser was much more than a naturalist and deserves to be treated as a major author.

Juras, Uwe. *Pleasing to the "I": The Culture of Personality and Its Representations in Theodore Dreiser and F. Scott Fitzgerald*. New York: Peter Lang, 2006. Juras examines how the two authors depicted the newly emerging concept of personality, defined as the outward presentation of self, in their work. Includes a discussion of *The Financier.*

Lingeman, Richard R. *An American Journey, 1908-1945.* Vol. 2 in *Theodore Dreiser*. New York: Putnam, 1986-1990. Provides biographical information and analyzes Dreiser's fiction. Includes bibliographical references and indexes.

Loving, Jerome. *The Last Titan: A Life of Theodore Dreiser.* Berkeley: University of California Press, 2005. This engrossing survey of the author's life and work is a welcome addition to Dreiser scholarship. Focuses on Dreiser's work, including his journalism, discussing the writers who influenced him and his place within American literature.

Michaels, Walter Benn. *The Gold Standard and the Logic of Naturalism: American Literature at the Turn of the Century*. Berkeley: University of California Press, 1987. In a chapter titled "Dreiser's *Financier*: The Man of Business as a Man of Letters," Michaels argues that instead of attacking the excesses of the marketplace, as most critics have claimed, Dreiser and *The Financier* participate in and promote consumer capitalism.

Pizer, Donald. *The Novels of Theodore Dreiser: A Critical Study.* Minneapolis: University of Minnesota Press, 1976. Pizer, a recognized authority on Dreiser and naturalism, offers both a solid reading of *The Financier* and important background information on the novel.

Finn Cycle

Author: Unknown
First transcribed: Possibly eleventh century
Type of work: Poetry
Type of plot: Folklore
Time of plot: Third century
Locale: Ireland

Principal characters:
FINN, the leader of the Fianna Erinn
OISIN, Finn's son
OSCAR, Oisin's son
GOLL MAC MORNA,
DERMOT,
KEELTA, and
CONAN THE BALD, Finn's men
NIAM, Oisin's fairy mistress
GRANIA, King Cormac's daughter

The Poem:

Long ago in Ireland, Cumhal is the leader of the Fianna Erinn, the king's warriors. A rival clan in this group grows envious of Cumhal, takes up arms against him, and slays him at the battle of Castleknock. Cumhal's wife, Murna, gives birth to a boy shortly thereafter. Fearing for the child's life now that Goll Mac Morna is in power, she gives him to two wise women to rear.

Under these two women, the child grows to be a handsome lad. He learns to run faster than the rabbit, to kill deer without hounds, and to bring down birds with his sling. One day, while roaming in the fields, he finds a group of boys playing. He joins them, and it is soon obvious that he is a match for all of them. In envy, the boys try to kill him, but he overcomes seven of them and chases the rest home. From that day, he is called Finn, meaning the fair. His two nurses feel that because the warriors of the Morna clan will kill him if they find him, he must start off on his own.

Finn gathers a group of youths about him and begins to seek adventure. His first exploit is to avenge a woman whose son was killed by the lord of Luachar. Finn and his companions storm the ramparts of the chieftain's castle, recover jewels Cumhal lost in battle, and slay the lord of Luachar and his men. Finn then returns the jewels to the old men who fought with his dead father in battle.

Finn sets out to learn wisdom and the art of poetry from the sage Finegas. While he is with the sage, he catches the salmon of wisdom and accidentally tastes it. Learning wisdom and the art of poetry, Finn composes a song in praise of May and then sets out to become the leader of the Fianna Erinn.

At that time, Conn is the ruler of Ireland. He holds an annual banquet at which peace is declared among the various clans. When Finn enters the banquet hall, Conn asks him who he is. The king accepts him immediately because he is the son of an old friend. Soon Finn inquires whether he would become captain of the Fianna Erinn if he would rid the royal town of the goblin that now haunts it. The king agrees, and Finn sets out with a magic spear to slay the goblin. The goblin appears with his magic harp and enchants Finn with the music, but with the aid of his spear, Finn slays the spirit and returns victorious. Conn keeps his word, and Finn is made captain of the Fianna Erinn. Faced with the choice of serving his clan enemy or leaving Ireland, Goll Mac Morna chooses to serve Finn, and the rest of his men follow him.

Finn is a strong, generous, and wise captain who draws the best poets and warriors of Ireland around him. Oisin is his gallant son, one of the finest fighters and poets; Oscar, Oisin's son, is the fiercest fighter of the group; Goll Mac Morna is strong and loyal; Dermot of the Love Spot is the fair ladies' man of great endurance and agility; Keelta is another strong warrior and fine poet; Conan the Bald is full of trickery, gluttony, and sloth; and there is also Mac Luga, whom Finn instructs in the art of courtesy, and many other brave warriors. Finn is generous to all. It is necessary to pass extremely rigorous tests of strength, skill, poise, and poetic ability to enter the Fianna Erinn.

One day, Finn and his companions give chase to a doe. The doe far outstrips everyone but Finn and his two hounds. When Finn reaches the doe, he finds his two hounds playing with her, and he gives orders that no one should hurt her. That night, Finn awakens to find a beautiful woman standing by his bed. She informs him that she was changed into a deer by the Dark Druid because she refused to give him her love and that Finn restored her to her original form. Finn takes her to live with him as his wife. After a few months of happiness, Finn is called away to fight the Northmen. Returning victorious, he finds his new wife gone; the Dark Druid came for her in the shape of Finn, and when she rushed to greet him he took her away. For three days, Finn mourns before returning to his band. Seven years later, Finn finds a brave young man fighting off a pack of hounds. On calling off the dogs and questioning the boy, Finn learns that this is the son he had by his wife before the Dark Druid came again and took her

away forever. Finn takes his son and trains him to be a great warrior-poet.

Finn and his men are hunting one day when the giant Vivionn comes seeking Finn's protection from a lover she scorned. While she is talking, her lover appears and thrusts his spear into her breast. Finn and Goll stay by the dying giant, and the rest of the company sets out after the giant. They chase him over hill and plain to the sea, where he escapes after they gained his sword and shield. Returning, they find the giant dead. They bury her and mourn her death.

Once when Finn and his companions are hunting, they see an ugly, clumsy giant coming toward them with an equally ugly old nag. In an unmannerly way, the giant tells Finn that he wants to join his band, and Finn reluctantly agrees. Finn's companions turn the giant's horse out to pasture with the other horses, but it immediately begins injuring them. Finn tells one of his men to ride the nag to death. When the animal refuses to move, thirteen men get on its back in jest. Seeing that they are making fun of him, the giant runs off in fury, and his nag follows with thirteen of Finn's men on its back. Finn and the rest of his men give chase, but they are outdistanced when the giant and his nag cross the ocean.

Finn thereupon outfits himself and his men with a ship, food, and gold and sets out across the sea in search of his missing men. At last, they come to a huge, slippery cliff. Because Dermot is the ablest, he is sent to investigate the land. Before long, Dermot comes to a woodland pool where for three days he fights an armed warrior. On the third night, he dives into the pool with the warrior and finds himself in a land of wonders. He is beaten by the men of this land and left for dead. Eventually, Dermot is awakened by a man who leads him into a friendlier kingdom. There he is welcomed by the king, who himself served in the Fianna Erinn under Finn. Meanwhile, Finn and his men enter the underground kingdom by another route, and he and his warriors are reunited. They learn that they were brought there to fight in the service of the underground king against the king of the Well and his allies. In battle, Finn and his men prove matchless. After winning the enemy king's daughter, Finn defeats the foe and restores peace to the land. Finn asks for no reward from the king, but when Conan makes a jest, the king transports the band back to the Irish hills in the space of a second. The whole adventure seems like a dream.

One day the old feud between Finn's clan and Goll's clan begins again over a dispute about booty. A battle starts in the hall, and blood is shed until Fergus, the minstrel, awakens and reminds them with his music of the dangers they shared. Peace is restored.

For many years, Finn and his men pass their lives in adventures, hunts, and enchantments. There comes a time, however, when the Fianna Erinn begins to disintegrate, when Finn's men become dishonest and unruly, and when Finn loses his honor through treachery.

When Finn is an old man, he plans to marry Grania, daughter of the king of Ireland. Grania falls in love with Dermot, the ladies' man, however, and begs him to run away with her. Dermot is extremely reluctant to do so, but Grania binds him by the laws of Fian chivalry, and he is forced to abduct her on her wedding night. Finn jealously chases the pair over Ireland. At length, Dermot makes peace with Finn. While Finn and Dermot are hunting one day, a boar fatally wounds Dermot. The only way to save Dermot is for Finn to bring him water. Remembering his hurt pride, Finn lets the water fall, and Dermot dies. The king of Ireland then orders the Fianna Erinn to disband forever. The final blow to the company comes at the battle of Gabhra, in which Oscar, Finn's grandson, is killed and the Fenians are all but wiped out.

Niam, a fairy princess, then comes to take Oisin to an enchanted land where all wishes come true. She sings a magic song to him, and he bids farewell to his companions forever. In this land, Oisin can love, hunt, and fight without growing old. The time comes, however, when he longs to return to Ireland to see his old companions. Niam tearfully lets him go but warns him not to set foot on the soil. On returning to Ireland, he finds a degenerate race that is both smaller and weaker than the lowliest men of his time. Impetuously, Oisin dismounts his horse to help the weaklings move a stone, whereupon he immediately becomes an old man. He soon learns that his companions were dead for three hundred years. Oisin is taken to Saint Patrick. At first, there is strong distrust between the two men, but gradually the saint grows to love Oisin's tales of the Fianna Erinn and he records them. Oisin, for his part, is baptized into the Church.

Critical Evaluation:

The Finn Cycle, also known as the Fenian Cycle, is a series of ballad tales celebrating the deeds of Finn, a third century Irish hero, and his band of warriors. Their organization, known as the Fianna Erinn, fought and hunted under service to the king of Ireland, and the warriors enjoyed privilege and wealth. The tone of these ballad stories is romantic, and the stories show a delight in sensuous details and a deep feeling for the Irish countryside and glen. Finn himself stands out as a strong, courageous leader who inspires devotion in his men, but he is not without a touch of cunning and treachery. In many respects, he is like Robin Hood and King Arthur—a bold hero, capable leader, and tender lover. Like them, he

witnesses the passing of his strength, the dissolution of his band, and the waning of a heroic era.

The audience for whom the Finn Cycle was composed was naïve, socially young, and intellectually credulous, although it had a definite protocol and a certain dignified etiquette. This audience demanded stirring words as well as a stimulating imagination from the storyteller. Although these tales were very popular in the eleventh and twelfth centuries, the stories of Finn, Oisin, and the others existed among the people for many centuries. A note of nostalgia for a past glory and a longing for a heroic period exist in the stories. There is perhaps a contrast between the old hierarchical society of the legends and the society telling them, a society facing a rapidly changing and hostile world. The old ballad system was breaking down by this time, and these tales were the beginnings of a new, popular literature in Ireland and Scotland. As the literature passed into the hands of the people, the versification became easier and the meters drastically simplified.

Most, although not all, of the ballads and prose of this period are concerned with Finn, the hero, and his war band, or fian (hence, the word "Fenian"). The original meaning of the word "fian" was "a driving, pursuing, hunting," but eventually it came to mean a band of warriors on the warpath. In a stricter sense, fian meant a band of roving warriors who had joined together for the purpose of making war. They were not, however, mere robbers or marauders. They were often men who were expelled from their clan, landless men, the sons of kings who quarreled with their fathers, or men who seized this way of avenging some private wrong. They were the only professional soldiers in Ireland in the old times, apart from mercenaries, who were often foreigners. For this reason the word fian was often used, especially in poetry, to refer to any war band. The various fianna were held together by discipline and had their own organization and customs; as is shown in the Finn Cycle, men who wished to join the ranks had to pass a test of skill or bravery. The various fianna took their names from their leaders. From their roving life, adventures, and exploits, the various fianna and their chiefs naturally evolved into the early subjects of storytelling. Many such stories and ballads probably were lost.

In later times, the word "fianna" came to be used exclusively for the war band headed by Finn, or Mac Cumhal, as he came to be called, for the development of this legend overshadowed all the others. Even as late as the tenth century, however, Finn and his fianna were only one among several well-known similar bands. In popular imagination, the figure of Finn overpowered other heroes and attracted to itself, from century to century, exploits originally attributed to others. The Finn Cycle absorbed much of the legendary lore of the older cycles, until all of Ireland held up Finn as the supreme heroic leader.

The popular imagination blended the tales and made them into the kind of legend the people needed and wanted. People were close to the earth and nature, and this is reflected in the tales of Finn, which refer to a time when wild woods were giving way to pasture and tillage and people no longer had reason to consider every wild cry of the night, to ponder each call of the birds and beasts. For Finn, the battles were only interruptions in the life of hunting. The ballads speak of his delight in the cackling of ducks, the bellowing of the oxen, and the whistle of the eagle. Many metaphors and allusions in the tales draw upon nature and animals, as when the women, sorrowing, feel sympathy for the wild birds and beasts that are like themselves.

Finn himself seems to transcend the world of which he is a part; certainly he is larger than his moment in history. When the Fianna broke up at last, after hundreds of years of hunting and fighting, it hardly seems that he dies. More likely, he comes back repeatedly in different shapes, and his son, Oisin, is made king over a divine country. In these tales, Finn is not so much an individual man as he is a force of nature, a part of the universe like the clouds or the gods that shape and reshape the clouds. Seer and poet, king and druid, Finn was a mortal who became immortal. He was a better fighter and hunter and infinitely wiser than any other mortal. Quiet in peace, the ballads say, but angry in battle, Finn was the perfect leader.

The men in the stories are warriors, men of action rather than thought. Their existence is devoted to love and companionship, and they can imagine no higher consideration. There is none of the philosophical worrying of Arthur and Merlin in these ballads. The men here do not speculate on eternity; they are sure of their simple values and fight to defend them. The brotherhood of the warrior is all. It is based on their hard and vigorous way of life and on their few necessary belongings. Running through the ballads is a strong sense of material possession, of the things that people use to live. A feeling of the matter-of-factness of life colors the ballads and the attitudes of the characters.

The structure of the Finn Cycle is loose and rambling, and it lacks the tightly woven pattern of the great epics. The many incidents that compose the cycle are a succession of detached episodes rather than a continuing story, such as that of the *Iliad* (c. 750 B.C.E.; English translation, 1611) or the legends of King Arthur. The people who imagined the cycle did not comprehend a large, encompassing design. Their stories wander without aim, each adventure independent of the previous one and the one that will follow. Cumulatively, however, the ballads of the cycle tell vividly of the heroic life, of the strength necessary to survive in a young and hard world, and of the codes of honor and companionship that make survival worthwhile.

"Critical Evaluation" by Bruce D. Reeves

Further Reading

Gregory, Isabella Augusta. *Gods and Fighting Men*. 2d ed. Gerrard Cross, England: Colin Smythe, 1976. A reprint of Lady Gregory's 1904 retelling of Irish legends. Includes an introduction to the influence of Irish myth by William Butler Yeats and a preface. Most of the book represents stories from the Finn Cycle with some explanation. Includes interesting notes.

Mac Cana, Proinsias. *Celtic Mythology*. New York: Peter Bedrick Books, 1985. An excellent introduction to Celtic mythology and the Finn Cycle. A perfect source for beginners. Includes index.

McCullogh, David Willis, ed. *Wars of the Irish Kings: A Thousand Years of Struggle from the Age of Myth Through the Reign of Queen Elizabeth I*. New York: Crown, 2000. McCullogh combines myth and historical events to recount tales of Irish heroes, such as Finn MacCool, who battled a succession of invaders.

Matthews, John. *Celtic Battle Heroes: Cuchulainn, Boadicea, Fionn MacCumhail, Macbeth*. Poole, England: Firebird, 1988. An informative and accessible supplement that provides information on all essential elements of the Finn Cycle. Examines the legend's thematic relation to contemporary ideas.

Ó hÓgáin, Dáithí. *Fionn MacCumhaill, Images of the Gaelic Hero*. Dublin: Gill and Macmillan, 1988. Ó hÓgáin, a professor of Irish folklore, provides a detailed examination of the legendary character.

Rolleston, T. W. *Celtic Myths and Legends*. 1911. Reprint. New York: Dover, 1990. An exhaustive study of Irish and Welsh myths within a historical, literary, and religious setting. A solid, often enjoyable retelling of the stories. Includes drawings, a copious index, and glossary.

Sutcliff, Rosemary. *The High Deeds of Finn Mac Cool*. New York: Dutton, 1967. An enjoyable retelling of the legends surrounding the Finn Cycle. Drawings enhance the text. Includes an interesting introduction to the project.

Finnegans Wake

Author: James Joyce (1882-1941)
First published: 1939
Type of work: Novel
Type of plot: Fantasy
Time of plot: Early twentieth century
Locale: Chapelizod, Dublin, Ireland

Principal characters:
HUMPHREY CHIMPDEN EARWICKER, an innkeeper
ANNA LIVIA PLURABELLE, his wife
SHEM, their artistic son
SHAUN, his philistine brother
ISSY, their sister

The Story:

Finnegans Wake is an expression of the dreaming collective psyche as it relives the major conflicts of myth and history. This psyche is divided into the two sexual principles, the major representations of which are Humphrey Chimpden Earwicker (HCE) and Anna Livia Plurabelle (ALP). As the archetypal husband-father, HCE (Haveth Childers Everywhere/Here Comes Everybody) is burdened with guilt over an indiscretion in Dublin's Phoenix Park. This obscure event is central to the entire dream. A lone man encounters two girls and performs an obscure offense, an incident witnessed by three soldiers or boys, and news of it spreads by the gossipy Four Old Men. The retellings through rumor, gossip, and popular song render everything about this Original Sin unreliable, except that it happened. Protesting his innocence, HCE goes to sleep. In his dreams, however, he encounters previous versions of his crime, which, encrusted with sexual and scatological innuendo, further cloud the precise nature of the offense.

News of this sin is carried throughout the dreambook of history through rumors and documents, lectures and arguments, accusations and recriminations. Interrogators appear in fours, accompanied by twelve bystanders: variously jurymen, apostles, mourners, and drinkers. As HCE is identified with the Dublin landscape—from Chapelizod to "Howth Castle and Environs"—his wife is the personification of the River Liffey (Livia) flowing through that landscape. She is the universal wife-mother and, like all the rivers of the world, constantly in flux.

The three soldiers and their familial equivalents, Shem and Shaun, represent the younger generation taking advantage of HCE's and ALP's age to displace them. Even while so doing, however, Shem and Shaun, the contrary twins, in their various manifestations, represent the contention between opposite character types: introvert and extrovert, artist and man of affairs, relativist and dogmatist. While Shem is an irresponsible bohemian and exile, Shaun is a dull, bourgeois hypocrite. Their sister Issy is the divisive ingenue of *Finnegans Wake*, in contrast with her mother, whose influence is unitive.

Finnegans Wake progresses through four books, following the structure of human history according to Giambattista Vico's theory in *Principi di scienza nuova d'intorno alla comune natura delle nazioni* (1744; *The New Science*, 1948), the four phases of theocratic, aristocratic, democratic, and anarchic, and thence through a *ricorso* to a new cycle. In the course of the nighttime of *Finnegans Wake*, the five principal "characters" undergo a series of metamorphoses as they pass through these four phases of history, representing the totality of individual and collective development. Through a vast exfoliation of such metamorphoses, James Joyce structures and populates his universe.

Thus while HCE the Protestant innkeeper is a current manifestation of the collective unconscious, the principle he represents appears in many other forms in the course of the night: Jarl van Hoother, Festy King, the Norwegian Captain, the Russian General, Persse O'Reilly, and Mr. Porter. As opposite aspects of Earwicker's personality, Shem and Shaun are sometimes identified (as Butt and Taff) but are usually at odds: as the Mookse and the Gripes, Chuff and Glugg, Kev and Dolph, the Ondt and the Gracehoper, Jaun and Dave, or Kevin and Jerry. In sum, these characters represent major thematic and structural principles, as, for example, in the argument between St. Patrick and the Archdruid Berkeley: whether reality is best described as white light (unity) or the spectrum of colors (diversity).

In broad outline, the first book, composed of eight chapters, corresponds to Vico's divine age. Dominated by the two parental figures, it represents the male and female cycles. First, the mythic Finnegan falls and is replaced by Earwicker. His primal transgression is enacted in the trial of Festy King. Meanwhile, following Earwicker's death, ALP enters the universe through the resurrection of her letter, and her sons Shem and Shaun engage in a duel of wits. Sharing the responsibility for her husband's sins, ALP makes her exit as the River Liffey dilutes in Dublin Bay.

In book 2 the children replace their parents, both in their heroic quest for knowledge and in their usurpation of their authority; they then reenact their transgressions. Thus, while ostensibly studying grammar, history, and mathematics, they are actually investigating their parents' identities and their relationships with them. Earwicker, having closed up the bar, falls asleep on the floor and in a dream concedes to his children under various personas: the Norwegian Captain, the Russian General, Fionn Mac Cool, and Roderic O'Conor. This disintegration of his psyche takes the form of the disagreement between the Four Old Men about the departing loveship of Tristram and Iseult.

The four chapters of book 3 represent the future, civil age, and center on Shaun, Earwicker's heir. With HCE and ALP in bed at midnight, Shaun the Postman enters the dreamer's vision. Having heard the fable of the Ondt and the Gracehoper, Shaun attacks it and, claiming equal literary ability with Shem, denounces his father and vilifies his brother. Under a succession of personae (Jaun, Juan, Yawn), he degenerates until, tumbling into a barrel, he rolls backward down the river. Issy and all of Ireland mourn him, but his return is assured.

Book 4, a recapitulation of the whole book, takes place in an instant between death and resurrection. As dawn approaches, the sleep of the Porter family (another manifestation of the archetypal family) is interrupted by the child Jerry's cry. As the new era begins, the newspapers tell of HCE's indiscretion, St. Kevin is seen meditating in his bathtub-altar, Muta and Juva watch the encounter between St. Patrick and the Archdruid, and ALP's letter is in the morning mail. Finally, Anna Livia soliloquizes resignedly as she flows out to sea.

Critical Evaluation:

Finnegans Wake sets out to render the collective unconscious in appropriate form and language. Thus, it encompasses all of human experience through the millennia in a cycle or recurring forms through a universal language, the language of dreams. To this end, it employs a language with simultaneous references to multiple tongues, expressing the major theme of the cyclical nature of history.

Thus, *Finnegans Wake* is not a novel with characters and plot, nor is it a narrative with mythic overtones. Earwicker and his family are perhaps best understood as contemporary, local instances of a great allegory. In reading *Finnegans Wake* readers confront the anxiety and confusion of their own dreams. No character exists as an independent, stable personality. Similarly, perspectives are continuously shifting between various aspects of the collective unconscious. Thus Earwicker is a kind of Everyman. He can be identified with all the characters to some extent, but whereas he can be called

Adam in the biblical system, the Finn Mac Cool of Irish myth, the Tim Finnegan of popular song, or a concession to the bias of his living readers, his identity is most easily comprehended as the Chapelizod pubkeeper Earwicker.

The major themes of *Finnegans Wake* are death and resurrection, the Fall, guilt, family relations, generational conflict, sexual identity and desire—all marshaled under a quasi-Jungian concept of collective identity. Similarly, following Vico, Joyce presumes that all aspects of a culture—its government, religion, language, and other institutions—are related to one another and that all have a profound impact on the way that individuals within that culture view themselves and their world, since Joyce planned to portray his hero, Earwicker, as inseparable from the cultural matrix of his society. All the figures in this dream-vision are fluid composites involving an unconfined blur of myths and fictitious characters as well as nonhuman elements. This vision is structured in cyclic form, establishing intricate parallels between the broad patterns of historical development and the events and conflicts in the life of an ordinary Irish family. In *Finnegans Wake*, imagination subsumes the events it describes, radically destabilizing language, identity, and narrative. In these ways it constitutes a clear break with the mainstream of English literature.

Decades of attempts to explicate *Finnegans Wake* appear to confirm Joyce's prediction that the work would keep the professors busy for centuries. A general opinion among those who take the work seriously is that as a dreambook and a leading expression of the twentieth century worldview, it is indeterminate, untranslatable, and irreducible. It is a work in which every single element has a function; it contains no nonsense yet is finally beyond explication. Critical analyses of *Finnegans Wake* have been either macrocosmic or microcosmic, emphasizing its overall design (by reference to Vico, dream theory, and other systems) or attempting to gloss particular passages (the Pranquean episode or the Encounter with the Cad, for example). Thus while *Finnegans Wake* is generally well understood, specialized studies from either of these perspectives continue to appear.

The apparent impenetrability of *Finnegans Wake* is an essential aspect of its intention: to give adequate shape to the sleeping experience. Thus although it stands up to literal scrutiny, it should not be read in a literal-minded way. Wordplay in *Finnegans Wake* is multilingual, etymological, associative, and acoustic. Therefore it is best read aloud, and in an open-minded way, the inferences shared and sifted among a group of simultaneous readers. This helps each reader best appreciate the "collideorscape" of its language, figures, moods, and themes, preventing any single reading from becoming unduly dominant.

Finnegans Wake is a virtuoso production: Drawing on more than thirty languages, it has a cast of hundreds from every phase of world history and digests an encyclopedia of information. It is a book of many moods, of many degrees of opacity, a book of many exits and entrances. Some sections are relatively clear set pieces, such as the portrait of Shem or the fable of the Ondt and the Gracehoper—immediately delightful to the new reader. Others, such as the opening chapter, are extremely dense and daunting to first-time readers. Others, however, are poetic prose of supreme beauty, notably ALP's departure, which was made available in an audio recording of its author's own voice.

Finnegans Wake is Joyce's most ambitious literary endeavor. Within the narrow confines of immediate family relations he aims to encompass all human experience, mythic and historical. Drawing on the traditions of intellectual and popular culture, he forges a literary language that is both high-minded and lowbrow. He anticipated, yet underestimated, the difficulties his readers would encounter and was disappointed that so many of those who acclaimed *A Portrait of the Artist as a Young Man* (1914-1915, serial; 1916, book) and *Ulysses* (1922) as supreme expressions of modernity were unprepared to pursue his explorations to the limits of language in *Finnegans Wake*.

Cóilín D. Owens

Further Reading

Beckman, Richard. *Joyce's Rare View: The Nature of Things in "Finnegans Wake."* Gainesville: University Press of Florida, 2007. Beckman demonstrates how the novel reflects Joyce's oblique perception of the world as unstable and dreamlike, comprehensible only by glimpses and guesses. This perception, Beckman argues, is the source of the novel's satire.

Bishop, John. *Joyce's Book of the Dark: "Finnegans Wake."* Madison: University of Wisconsin Press, 1986. Argues that Joyce's determination to represent nocturnal experience accounts for the form, shape, direction, and language of *Finnegans Wake*. Relates *Finnegans Wake* to dream theory and interpretation, thanatology, optics and phonetics, embryology and gender, and sexuality and power.

Bulson, Eric. *The Cambridge Introduction to James Joyce.* New York: Cambridge University Press, 2006. Introductory overview of Joyce's life and work, placing them within the context of Joyce as a modernist, journalist, translator, lecturer, and lover. Chapter 3 analyzes five of Joyce's works, including *Finnegans Wake*, while chapter 4 chronicles his works' critical reception from 1914 through 2005.

Ellmann, Richard. *James Joyce.* Rev. ed. New York: Oxford University Press, 1982. Elegant and authoritative biography providing valuable information on the writing of *Finnegans Wake*, Joyce's intentions, his methods, and the difficulties he encountered.

Fordham, Finn. *Lots of Fun at "Finnegans Wake": Unravelling Universals.* New York: Oxford University Press, 2007. Surveys the critical, scholarly, and theoretical approaches to interpreting the novel and offers detailed analyses of key passages.

Kitcher, Philip. *Joyce's Kaleidoscope: An Invitation to "Finnegans Wake."* New York: Oxford University Press, 2007. Kitcher maintains that the novel's theme revolves around a central question: What makes life worth living? He describes how Joyce answers that question from the perspective of the novel's aging dreamer, who feels his long life is now ending.

McCarthy, Patrick A., ed. *Critical Essays on James Joyce's "Finnegans Wake."* New York: G. K. Hall, 1992. Contains twenty essays surveying past criticism and broad concerns, including studies of structure, voice, narration, language, and interpretation; analyses of important themes; and readings of passages in ways that pose crucial questions about *Finnegans Wake* as a whole. Shows how enjoyable an experience reading *Finnegans Wake* is.

McHugh, Roland. *Annotations to "Finnegans Wake."* Rev. ed. Baltimore: Johns Hopkins University Press, 1991. A line-by-line explication of the novel's foreign words, English overtones, place names, personal names, phrases parodied, song titles and quotations, literary sources, and historical events. A basic reference tool, designed to be consulted in tandem with a reading of *Finnegans Wake*.

Pierce, David. *Reading Joyce.* New York: Pearson Longman, 2008. Pierce, who has taught and written about Joyce for forty years, provides a framework to enable the general reader to understand Joyce's work. He devotes a chapter to an explication of *Finnegans Wake*.

Rose, Danis, and John O'Hanlon. *Understanding "Finnegans Wake": A Guide to the Narrative of James Joyce's Masterpiece.* New York: Garland, 1982. A section-by-section synopsis of *Finnegans Wake*. A very useful companion for the beginning reader, it clarifies the main techniques and themes in the form of a running commentary.

The Fire Next Time

Author: James Baldwin (1924-1987)
First published: 1963
Type of work: Essays

James Baldwin's *The Fire Next Time*, according to writer William Styron, is "one of the great documents of the twentieth century." It articulates the anger, frustration, and hope felt by African Americans during the 1960's. The two essays composing this work were published in 1963, selling more than one million copies, making Baldwin—according to *The New York Times*—the widest read African American writer of his time. The book is Baldwin's response to the social and racial injustice he witnessed in America. Having lived in Europe for almost twenty years, Baldwin felt compelled to return to America to participate in the Civil Rights movement. He offered *The Fire Next Time* as "a kind of plea" because "we, the black and the white, deeply need each other here if we are really to become a nation."

The first short essay, "My Dungeon Shook: Letter to My Nephew on the One Hundredth Anniversary of the Emancipation," is Baldwin's diagnosis of America's racism as well as his prescription for his young nephew's survival in such a diseased society. As a man who has seen America at its worst, Baldwin warns his nephew of the dangers threatening a young black man. He also offers him a challenge: to be a catalyst of change. Baldwin contends that the fates of black and white Americans are inextricably intertwined, that for America to fulfill its promise, both must acknowledge the need for the other. White America holds fast to ideals that are not actually practiced. This failure to practice its ideals is proven in its steadfast denial of the value of black lives. Baldwin tells his nephew that American society has narrowly circumscribed his world so that his dreams will never move beyond the street corner of the Harlem ghetto.

Baldwin offers hope to all African Americans, but it comes with great responsibility. He maintains that because white America insists on its innocence, on the ideal image it has created of itself, it cannot initiate change. Baldwin observes that "these innocent people have no other hope. They are, in effect, still trapped in a history which they do not understand; and until they understand it, they cannot be released from it." African Americans must force white America to examine itself. African Americans, Baldwin predicts, "can make America what America must become." Neither white America nor black America, however, can find free-dom or justice apart from each other. Their fates are necessarily and inextricably connected.

The second, much longer and more substantial essay, "Down at the Cross: Letter from a Region in My Mind," can be divided into three sections. The first discusses Baldwin's growing up in the Harlem ghetto and the influences that led to his involvement in the church. The second is a reflection on the black nationalism (advocated by the Black Muslims) occasioned by Baldwin's meeting with Elijah Muhammad of the Nation of Islam. The third part proposes as much of a solution to the racial conflict existing in America as Baldwin can offer.

Baldwin tells the story of his childhood in his autobiographical novel, *Go Tell It on the Mountain* (1953), and in his famous essay, "Notes of a Native Son" (1955). The additional account in *The Fire Next Time* proves an argumentative point—that the racism experienced daily by African Americans is overwhelming and devastating. Baldwin describes the overwhelming fear that permeated his life from his earliest memory, a fear affecting every aspect of his life. He reports that every black child is raised not only to fear his parents' punishment, but also white people's judging his every word and action. He sees the terror in his parents' eyes lest he should say or do something in the presence of white people that could lead to his demise. Baldwin's own dreams of finishing high school and becoming a writer drew down the wrath of his father. Better to beat such dangerous aspirations from the child early than to have him beaten or killed in the hostile white world.

In the ghetto, a child had to have a gimmick, Baldwin claims, a method that would save him from the constant humiliation that was his life. The street's alcohol, drugs, and sex offered one kind of escape—a carnal seduction. The church held out to him a "spiritual seduction." The woman minister who led him to his salvation asked fourteen-year-old Baldwin, "Whose little boy are you?" It was a question asked of him every day on the street by pimps, pushers, and prostitutes. He wanted to be someone's little boy; he wanted to escape the sense of alienation and self-hatred that had been a condition of his life from his earliest memory. The church spoke to that state. For three years, Baldwin was a boy preacher. He soon became disillusioned. The church was a human institution, and he came to recognize its flaws. He saw the church as theater and himself as a mere performer able to work the congregation for an emotional or financial response. His "redemption" did not alleviate his sense of self-loathing. Christ could not change the color of his skin.

His experience in the church, however, led Baldwin to further revelation: Despite its claims of love, hope, and charity, the church's fundamental principles were "Blindness, Loneliness, and Terror." After a year in the pulpit, Baldwin realized that he was preaching a gospel written by white men and that their revelation could not change the basic fact of his life and the cause of his sense of worthlessness and alienation: his blackness. He also came to see that "there was no love in the church. It was a mask for hatred and self-hatred and despair." The loving kindness of Christ's words, it seemed, applied only to those who believed as the church members did and to white people not at all. Baldwin came to question his salvation and the love of God if it did not permit him to love others, including white people. He concludes the first section of this essay with the observation, "If the concept of God has any validity or any use, it can only be to make us larger, freer, and more loving. If God cannot do this, then it is time we get rid of Him." Baldwin left the church. In the 1960's, many African Americans sought answers from another source—the Nation of Islam.

The second part of "Down at the Cross" examines the appeal for African Americans of the Nation of Islam. Baldwin himself was never attracted to Muslim teaching. Police inaction in protecting black people and the radical life changes in the followers of Islam, however, prompted Baldwin's curiosity. He found in Elijah Muhammad a quiet but confident man who offered his young followers an explanation for and an alternative to the society that rejected them. Baldwin asserts that the times were ripe for the Muslim message. World War II convinced African Americans that white Christian culture had nothing to offer them. The Third Reich, emblematic of white Christian "civilization," may have shocked the world, but it did not surprise African Americans, who had long known the cruelty and the inhumanity of which white Christians are capable. Germany's actions only confirmed what they had experienced, in the United States and elsewhere, for hundreds of years. Returning "home" after risking their lives in defense of their country, black soldiers faced a segregated society that had treated German prisoners of war with more respect than it did its own black citizens. They found in foreign countries more acceptance than they did in their own homeland. A white God and Christianity were proven void; Allah and Islam provided another alternative.

Baldwin identifies some key ideas promoted by the Nation of Islam. First, Elijah Muhammad claims that all white men are devils, that they are the results of experiments by black scientists thousands of years ago, and that their period of dominance is now over. There is simply "no virtue in white people." Second, he offers an explanation of black people and culture that obviates white culture altogether. Third, Elijah Muhammad gives African Americans hope in proposing a separate black American nation with its own economy that is independent of white sources of wealth and in which black people will own land. Finally, Islam replaces the white God with a black one. Baldwin writes, "The white God has not delivered them; perhaps the Black God will."

Baldwin's critique of the Nation of Islam is uncompromising: just as white America cannot change until it acknowledges and embraces black America, black America cannot change until it acknowledges the fact that it has been shaped and formed by white America. Both black and white Americans, Baldwin insists, need each other if they are ever to come to terms with themselves. Baldwin states that Black Muslims have invented a past that helps them to explain the suffering and the humiliation African Americans have had to endure at the hands of the white people. Conversely, white Americans have held on to their notions of "innocence" and their American Dream, neither of which accurately describes real life. African Americans must face the fact that their identities have been formed in America, not Africa. They must accept their true past, he insists, not invent a more favorable one.

In the final section of the essay, Baldwin proffers an answer to the radical conflict dividing America. Literary critic Nick Aaron Ford has remarked that *The Fire Next Time* "offers no new solutions to the problem of race relations in America. Indeed, its basic solution is as old as the Holy Bible and as simple as the Sermon on the Mount." Baldwin insists that there will be no progress in this nation without radical social and political change. In his now famous conclusion, he prescribes what must be done to heal the racial rift in the country:

If we—and now I mean the relatively conscious whites and the relatively conscious blacks, who must, like lovers, insist on, or create, the consciousness of the others—do not falter in our duty now, we may be able, handful that we are, to end the racial nightmare, and achieve our country, and change the history of the world. If we do not now dare everything, the fulfillment of that prophecy, re-created from the Bible in song by a slave, is upon us: *God gave Noah the rainbow sign, No more water, the fire next time!*

With the publication of this book, Baldwin became—as African American literary critic Henry Louis Gates, Jr., states—"exalted as *the* voice of black America. . . . Perhaps not since Booker T. Washington had one man been taken to embody the voice of 'the Negro.'" It was a voice heeded by both black and white America. *The Fire Next Time* was the text to which America listened.

Laura Weiss Zlogar

Further Reading

Baraka, Amiri. "Jimmy! (Eulogy for James Baldwin, 1987)." In *The LeRoi Jones/Amiri Baraka Reader*, edited by William J. Harris. New York: Thunder's Mouth Press, 1991. Delivered on December 8, 1987, Baraka's eulogy praises Baldwin's contributions to the Civil Rights movement and to African American aesthetics.

Bloom, Harold, ed. *James Baldwin*. New York: Chelsea House, 1986. Bloom's introduction pays tribute to the prophetic intensity of *The Fire Next Time*, exactly the quality that F. W. Dupee attacks in his analysis, which is included here. Dupee argues that by substituting rhetoric for criticism, Baldwin weakens his cultural analysis. Overall, the criticism here is eager to dismiss *The Fire Next Time* as a minor work by a major writer.

_____. *James Baldwin*. Updated ed. New York: Chelsea House, 2007. This updated edition includes essays by Henry Louis Gates, Jr., Mario Puzo, and Irving Howe, and two essays focusing on *The Fire Next Time*: "Africa and *The Fire Next Time*" by David Lemming and *"The Fire Next Time* This Time" by Mel Watkins.

Campbell, James. *Talking at the Gates: A Life of James Baldwin*. New York: Viking Press, 1991. Campbell considers the essay "Down at the Cross" as Baldwin's masterwork, most successfully merging the creative work with advocacy of the black struggle. In the context of literary biography, Campbell records the range of reactions to the book. Includes thorough notes and a chronological bibliography.

Gates, Henry Louis, Jr. "The Fire Last Time." *The New Republic*, June, 1992. An insightful reflection on the career and reputation of Baldwin, the important role he played during the 1950's and 1960's as spokesperson of the Civil Rights movement, and the critical disfavor he experienced during the 1970's and 1980's.

Gibson, Donald B., ed. *Five Black Writers: Essays on Wright, Ellison, Baldwin, Hughes, and LeRoi Jones*. New York: New York University Press, 1970. Includes four essays on the works of Baldwin.

McBride, Dwight A., ed. *James Baldwin Now*. New York: New York University Press, 1999. Collection of diverse essays that seek to reevaluate Baldwin's works and interpret them from new perspectives. Part 1, "Baldwin and Race," contains three essays that discuss the author's treatment of racial identity and racial consciousness and his critique of white liberalism.

Porter, Horace A. *Stealing the Fire: The Art and Protest of James Baldwin*. Middletown, Conn.: Wesleyan University Press, 1989. The thesis narrows points of reference for Baldwin's art, particularly the works of Richard Wright, Harriet Beecher Stowe, and Henry James. In an extended discussion, *The Fire Next Time* is compared to *Uncle Tom's Cabin: Or, Life Among the Lowly* (1851-1852, serial; 1852, book) in the relationship both books strike with the reader, wanting the audience to "feel right" on race issues. The good of the artist, for both Stowe and Baldwin, is to humanize the reader.

Pratt, Louis H. *James Baldwin*. Boston: Twayne, 1978. Pratt centers discussion on religious issues. He sees the context of Baldwin's rejection of his youthful ministry as a statement on "Black Culture," dismissing Christianity as a white religion. Pratt's logic connects Baldwin's concerns to those of playwrights Ed Bullins and Amiri Baraka.

Standley, Fred L., and Nancy V. Burt. *Critical Essays on James Baldwin*. Boston: G. K. Hall, 1988. A collection of essays on the major works of Baldwin. Included are a review of *The Fire Next Time* and an essay on Baldwin and the 1960's.

Thorsen, Karen, dir. *James Baldwin: The Price of the Ticket*. San Francisco: California Newsreel, 1989. An excellent videotape on the life and career of James Baldwin. Included are interviews with family members, friends, writers, and critics. Provides a thorough understanding of Baldwin's literary and political contributions.

Troupe, Quincy, ed. *James Baldwin: The Legacy*. New York: Simon & Schuster, 1989. A tribute collection that sets out to acknowledge the breadth of Baldwin's social and literary contributions. Budd Schulberg's interview clarifies themes of nationalism versus integrationism in *The Fire Next Time*. Contains a useful bibliography.

The Firebugs
A Learning-Play Without a Lesson

Author: Max Frisch (1911-1991)

First produced: Biedermann und die Brandstifter, 1953 (radio play); 1958 (stage play); first published, 1958 (English translation, 1959)

Type of work: Drama

Type of plot: Absurdist

Time of plot: Post-World War II

Locale: Germany

Principal characters:

GOTTLIEB BIEDERMANN, a manufacturer of hair tonic

BABETTE, his wife

ANNA, their maidservant

SEPP SCHMITZ, a wrestler

WILLI EISENRING, a waiter

MRS. KNECHTLING, widow to Biedermann's former employee

PH.D., a professor

POLICEMAN

CHORUS OF FIREMEN

The Story:

Gottlieb Biedermann, a businessman, while on his way home, lights a cigar and witnesses the Chorus of Firemen setting their watch. Afterward, at home, seated in his living room, reading the newspaper, Biedermann vents his disgust with the arsonists plaguing his city, convinced that they should all be hanged. He is interrupted by Anna, his servant, who informs him that a peddler waits to see him. Biedermann tells her to get rid of the man, but the intruder enters unbidden, identifying himself as Sepp Schmitz, a circus wrestler. The astonished Biedermann, nonplussed by the stranger's sudden appearance, invites the ingratiating Schmitz to have some bread, which the visitor manages to parlay into a substantial snack through flattery and self-deprecation mixed with quiet but insistent demands. Their discussion is briefly interrupted when Herr Knechtling, a former employee released by Biedermann, comes to the door seeking an audience. His request outrages Biedermann, who directs Anna to send him away. He then takes Sepp to his attic, where the visitor is invited to stay on the condition that he swears that he is not an arsonist—one of the firebugs. Sepp only laughs, but Biedermann, satisfied, permits Schmitz to stay.

The next morning, after Biedermann's wife, Babette, spends a troubled night, fearful that there might be a firebug in the attic, Biedermann introduces her to Schmitz before leaving for work. Although Babette is determined to send the wrestler away, she feeds him breakfast while searching for a tactful way of doing so. Sepp plays on her kindness, preparing her to receive the next suspicious guest, Willi Eisenring, an unemployed waiter. The next day, Biedermann, set on throwing both men out, goes to his attic, where Schmitz and Eisenring just finish stacking up some large drums. Biedermann's anger is soothed by Willi, who admonishes Sepp for his lack of manners and insensitivity to Biedermann's feelings. Biedermann spots the drums and becomes alarmed. The labels clearly reveal their contents: gasoline. He then threatens to call the police, but a policeman already arrives to tell Biedermann that Herr Knechtling committed suicide the previous night. Oddly, when the policeman asks what is in the drums, Biedermann tells him it is only Hormotone, the hair tonic made by Biedermann's firm. After justifying his behavior to the Chorus of Firemen, arguing that one has to maintain trust in people, Biedermann explains to Babette that even if the two men are firebugs, it is best to treat them as friends. He then tells her to include them for dinner.

Somewhat later, in the attic, Eisenring explains to the increasingly officious Biedermann that Sepp is out on an errand, looking for sawdust to help spread the fire. He also explains that he is a former prisoner and tells Biedermann that he is looking for a detonator cap. Biedermann takes these bald admissions as a joke, and Eisenring confirms that a joke is a good camouflage but that the truth is even better. He then tactfully advises Biedermann to extinguish his cigar and asks him to help wire the detonator and fuse. Unshaken, Biedermann reveals that he comes to invite Eisenring and Schmitz to dinner. After Biedermann leaves, Eisenring tells the professor, a Ph.D., to come out from the pile of gasoline drums, to keep guard while he and Sepp go to the dinner. The professor tries to warn Babette about the arsonists, but Babette, who accepts Biedermann's idea that they should not offend Eisenring and Schmitz, does nothing.

Before the dinner, Biedermann directs Anna to remove the table finery she puts out. Then, after a funerary wreath is delivered that mistakenly identifies Biedermann rather than Knechtling as the deceased, Biedermann leaves the room with instructions to Anna that she should also dress simply and not serve in a formal fashion. When Eisenring and Schmitz enter, Anna leaves the two men alone. In their talk, they realize that, after dinner, they will have to ask Biedermann for matches. The dinner proves a disaster. It begins in laughter, with Biedermann explaining Willi's "joke" that oil waste is a better incendiary than sawdust and upbraiding Babette for her lack of humor. As the fine food and excessive quantities of good wine are consumed, Eisenring and Schmitz admit that they have a taste for expensive things, despite their humble backgrounds. They even mention specific items, such as damask tablecloths, good crystal, finger bowls, and knife rests. Biedermann then orders Anna to bring back the elegant tableware that he earlier ordered her to remove, including the damask tablecloth and a silver candelabrum. Eisenring next tells how the restaurant where he worked burned to the ground and how he met Schmitz at the station where the police took him after his arrest. Schmitz then explains that he was briefly an actor, specializing in ghosts, and begins acting out a parody of the morality play *Everyman*, drawing Biedermann into the title role. The spoof abruptly ends when Schmitz identifies his part as the ghost of Knechtling, causing Babette to scream. Seemingly drunk, the two men start singing and are joined by Biedermann, who also hands out cigars. Then, while fire sirens wail in the distance, the two men confess that they are firebugs and that they have to leave. Biedermann, still unwilling to face the truth, tries to mollify the pair with a final toast to their friendship. They beg matches of him, then leave.

As the sky begins turning an ominous red, the professor enters to tell the Biedermanns that although he knew what the firebugs were up to in the attic, he did not know that they were doing it simply for fun. He then exits, and Babette asks Biedermann what he gave Schmitz and Eisenring. He admits that he gave them matches, then attempts to allay her concern with the argument that if they were firebugs, they surely would have had their own. At the end, the Chorus of Firemen laments the burning of the gas works as the sounds of explosions and crashing buildings announce the imminent destruction of the whole city.

Critical Evaluation:

Biedermann und die Brandstifter, variously translated from the German as *Biedermann and the Firebugs*, *Biedermann and the Fire Raisers*, or simply *The Firebugs*, bears the subtitle *A Learning-Play Without a Lesson*. It is easy to interpret as a modern allegory or parable, with a lesson. In a general sense, it seems aimed at people's irredeemable folly, their perverse tendency to act contrary to what is clearly in their own best interest. Barbara Tuchman has shown in *The March of Folly* (1984) that history offers plenty of examples of incredible wrongheadedness; people do not seem able to learn from past mistakes. For Max Frisch, the political appeasements that led to the pre-World War II rise of Nazism and postwar takeover of Czechoslovakia by communists were the specific political analogues, but his allegory, a secular morality play, is really timeless.

The long one-act play utilizes techniques that help convey a sense of that timelessness. Although the setting is modern, the action is not localized to any specific time or place. As with many absurdist plays, there is only a metaphysical present, a now, as opposed to a past or future. The details about things mentioned or used in the play are all generic, found everywhere, and, therefore, nowhere in particular. Biedermann is himself a kind of Everyman, with whom, during the play, he is specifically identified. He exhibits, too, the "empty good-naturedness" that, according to Martin Esslin, prevents the absurd antihero from distinguishing what is of value from what is not. His decency is tragically misplaced.

Frisch, who denounced the absurdist playwrights as purveyors of nonsense, is not interested in metaphysical conundrums. Unlike most of the plays of absurdist playwrights (those of Samuel Beckett and Eugène Ionesco, for example), *The Firebugs* is very transparent and logical. Biedermann's kind and deferential treatment of Schmitz and Eisenring can be interpreted as displaced guilt, a kind of compensation for his wretched treatment of his former, loyal employee, Herr Knechtling. His guilt is clearly what the firebugs trade on, as Eisenring confirms when, in scene 4, he and Schmitz stack up the cans of gasoline. He tells Schmitz, worried that Biedermann might call the police, not to fear, for "above a certain income every citizen is guilty one way or another." Thus, as obtuse as Biedermann seems to be, his behavior is psychologically validated.

The Firebugs has a causal pattern and logic of structure that most classic examples of absurdist drama deliberately lack. When there is such a pattern, as in Ionesco's *Rhinocéros* (1959; English translation, 1959), the work, like *The Firebugs*, usually lends itself to interpretation as an existential parable. The focus may be on some personal choice the protagonist has to make in a world devoid of moral certainty or purpose. In Frisch's play, the firebugs triumph over the shallow and shortsighted decency of Biedermann not so much because he lacks a moral rudder as because they lack all principle. As the professor explains, they are anarchists for fun, and their violence against the city is gratuitous and wholly senseless.

If not purely absurdist, *The Firebugs* is also a far cry from realism. It uses devices atypical of problem plays written from Henrik Ibsen forward. For example, it employs a chorus, whose lyrics, like the choric odes of Greek tragedy, have antiphonal exchanges between the leader and the rest of the chorus, in this case the firemen. In scene 7, Frisch has Biedermann address the audience directly, asking its advice as to how he should proceed. That is, of course, a common device used to shatter the conventional, invisible fourth wall of realistic theater.

Finally, *The Firebugs* has the pronounced tragicomic, farcical tone of much absurdist drama. There is, for example, the grimly comic appearance of the memorial wreath, sent to the Biedermanns' house, with Biedermann's name on it, identified as the deceased. There is also a sense of angst, of apprehension, and of a skewing of common sense. In general, too, the characters' speeches have some of the inane and mechanical features of Ionesco's dialogue. Language proves ineffectual, vacuous, pointless. Thus, given the anarchistic and insane world of the firebugs, language, reason, and human decency are completely inadequate tools of survival. That is a terrible, darkly comic conclusion that Frisch and the absurdists seem to share.

John W. Fiero

Further Reading

Butler, Michael. *The Plays of Max Frisch*. New York: St. Martin's Press, 1985. Most readable and succinct English introduction to Frisch's plays, recommended for further study. Discusses *The Firebugs* as a parable play and analyzes its language, using translated passages in German.

Köpke, Wulf. *Understanding Max Frisch*. Columbia: University of South Carolina Press, 1991. Explores the structure, themes, characters, and style of Frisch's plays and other works, as well as their social and political background. Includes bibliography and index.

Pickar, Gertrud B. *The Dramatic Works of Max Frisch*. Frankfurt: Peter Lang, 1977. The most comprehensive and insightful English-language study of Frisch's dramatic canon.

Probst, Gerhard F., and Jay E. Bodine, eds. *Perspectives on Max Frisch*. Lexington: University Press of Kentucky, 1982. A sampling of critical articles, including "The Drama of Frisch" by Manfred Jurgensen. Includes an extensive international bibliography.

Subiotto, Arrigo. "The Swiss Contribution." In *The German Theatre: A Symposium*, edited by Ronald Hayman. New York: Barnes & Noble, 1975. Relates the dramatic works of Frisch and Friedrich Dürrenmatt to the larger framework of modern German theater and post-World War II European politics.

Weisstein, Ulrich. *Max Frisch*. New York: Twayne, 1967. A useful critical biography with a chronology and guide to selected sources. Contrasts *The Firebugs* with absurdist drama.

White, Alfred D. *Max Frisch: The Reluctant Modernist*. Lewiston, N.Y.: Edwin Mellen Press, 1995. A chronological examination of Frisch's life and works, in which White argues that Frisch was a conservative regarding aesthetic and political issues. Includes an index of persons, places, concepts, and works by Frisch and a bibliography.

The First Circle

Author: Aleksandr Solzhenitsyn (1918-2008)
First published: V kruge pervom, 1968 (English translation, 1968)
Type of work: Novel
Type of plot: Political realism
Time of plot: December 24-27, 1949
Locale: Moscow

The Story:

On Christmas Eve, 1949, a young Soviet diplomat, Innokenty Volodin, tries to warn professor Dobroumov how provocative and dangerous it can be to give anything to for-

Principal characters:
GLEB NERZHIN, a prison inmate
LEV RUBIN, a prisoner
INNOKENTY VOLODIN, a diplomat
DMITRI SOLOGDIN, a prisoner serving his second term
NADYA, Nerzhin's wife
SERAFIMA (SIMOCHKA), a member of the secret police in prison

eigners because on a recent trip to Paris the professor had promised a French colleague some medicine. Gleb Nerzhin is a prisoner in Mavrino, a ward on the outskirts of Moscow.

He was a captain in the Soviet army but was caught blaming Soviet leader Joseph Stalin in a private letter for the defeats and losses of the war. For this "crime," he was sentenced to ten years in prison, where he works as a mathematician. He has befriended a fellow prisoner, philologist Lev Rubin, who teaches Russian to German prisoners. Rubin was imprisoned because he expressed doubts about Marxism, in which he idealistically believed. In one of many sarcastic statements, Rubin compares Mavrino to the hell portrayed by Dante in *La divina commedia* (c. 1320; *The Divine Comedy*, 1802). Dante's hell consists of nine progressively worse circles; the first circle contains the souls of everyone who was born before Christ and therefore necessarily died unredeemed by the Savior.

The prisoners, also known as "zeks," are working in the acoustics laboratory on phonoscopy—creating voice prints on cryptic telephones to provide a secure means of telephonic communication for Stalin. Nerzhin is working as a cryptographer in Laboratory Number Seven, which is responsible for the phonoscopy project. All free employees at Mavrino are secret police officers, including Simochka, whose assignment is to keep an eye on Nerzhin. She and Nerzhin have an affair while the cryptographer's wife Nadya is living somewhere in Moscow.

Nerzhin has been offered the chance to have his sentence commuted if his work is successful. However, in a heated discussion with Yakonov, the chief of operations at the Mavrino Institute, Nerzhin refuses the offer. He says, "Let them admit first that it's not right to put people in prison for their way of thinking, and then we will decide whether we will forgive *them*." Nerzhin has maintained a proud and defiant attitude throughout his incarceration. His outburst provokes Yakonov to issue the order "Nerzhin to be sent away."

Soviet officials at Mavrino—Abakumov, Yakonov, Pryanchikov, Bobynin, Poskrebyshev, and others, known to their critics as apparatchiks—demonstrate a subservient relationship to Stalin and are arrogant in their treatment of the prisoners. Nerzhin and Rubin, unafraid of further punishment, do not hesitate to condemn the apparatchiks with caustic remarks expressing the inmates' strong character and moral indignation. In answer to Stalin's questions about the unrest among the people, minister of state security Abakumov defends his work but begs Stalin to reinstate capital punishment. Stalin half-jokingly asks him whether he should be the first to be shot. This frightening conversation leads Abakumov to apply pressure on the lower apparatchiks, as each of them feels the threat of death lurks behind every corner.

Nerzhin is finally allowed to see his faithful wife Nadya, who has been trying constantly to find out where he is imprisoned. At the meeting, kissing and hand clasping is forbidden. Nerzhin, with four years of war behind him and at least ten years of imprisonment ahead, had written his wife a note asking her to give up hope of ever seeing him again. Despite the letter, Nadya has refused to abandon hope. To protect herself, however, she has ceased wearing her wedding ring and she always writes "unmarried" on official documents because Soviet wives are punished for the "sins" of their husbands. The couple parts with a kiss, and the watchman separates them forcefully, canceling all further meetings. After seeing Nerzhin, Nadya experiences miserable days and refuses to see anyone, even a young captain who offers her a drink "to the resurrection of the dead."

Back at Mavrino, Nerzhin meets another zek, who is ordered to paint pleasant pictures of the prisoners at work. He produces a painting titled *The Maimed Oak*, portraying a tree on a cliff, battered by storms but surviving. To Nerzhin, it represents the prisoners' struggle to survive. The painter also paints *The Castle of the Holy Grail*, a symbol of undying hope. Another young prisoner agrees to become a double agent, but only to report those whose punishment will benefit the rest of the prisoners. The zeks amuse themselves by staging a comedy, allegedly written by Rimsky and Korsakov (an allusion to composer Nikolay Rimsky-Korsakov). The comedy, based on an old opera, is adapted to their present, imprisoned circumstances. They also stage a parody of the visit of a Mrs. R. (an allusion to Eleanor Roosevelt).

Innokenty's connection with the professor is discovered through a trap set by the secret police, and he is arrested before he can go to Paris. He reminisces about necessary conditions for Soviet diplomats: a high level of ideological orientation, deep loyalty to the cause, deep devotion to Stalin, and unwavering obedience to instructions from Moscow. In Mavrino, Rubin and Sologdin carry on endless arguments about philosophical and political questions. Rubin accuses Sologdin of employing high-flown, empty verbiage, and Sologdin accuses Rubin of clinging to fanatical Marxist beliefs that are not confirmed by facts, as proven by Rubin's being in prison. Nerzhin, meanwhile, converses with Spiridon, an uneducated peasant who is extremely wise in practical matters. Another prisoner, Gerasimovich, is offered early discharge if he can build microphones into park benches, but he refuses, saying it is not his field.

After his wife's visit, Nerzhin must explain to the crying Simochka that they cannot continue their relationship. He realizes that by alienating the secret police agent, he may be condemning himself to be sent to another prison in Siberia, where he may die, but he feels that he has no choice, saying

"If you know when you die that you haven't been a complete bastard, that's at least some satisfaction." High morality in Nerzhin prevails, contracting sharply with the corruption of the authorities.

The novel ends with another reference to *The Divine Comedy*: "Abandon all hope, ye who enter here." Because of their failure successfully to complete the cryptographic telephone project, several prisoners, including Nerzhin, are sent to another camp. Looking through the van window, Nerzhin can see printed on the van the word "Meat" in four languages; the vans have been disguised so that onlookers will not know they carry prisoners.

Critical Evaluation:

In writing *The First Circle*, Aleksandr Solzhenitsyn included some important autobiographical elements. Like Nerzhin, Solzhenitsyn was a captain in the Soviet army, was arrested for making derogatory remarks about Stalin in a private letter, and was sentenced to eight years in prison. Solzhenitsyn incorporated his personal experiences when creating fictitious characters. At the same time, autobiography was not his primary intent in writing the novel. He used it to draw a bleak picture of the Communist system under Stalin, as he had done in almost all his works.

The Russian, German, and other prisoners at Mavrino are scientists and intellectuals doing research on various projects useful to the state, including those on radio and telephone technology. The novel tells the story of the interrelationships of people in prison whose fate is caused by external political circumstances. Since Solzhenitsyn employs a realist approach, the novel describes documentarily and historically happenings in the Soviet Union in the late 1940's. Soviet society is understandably depicted through the prisoners' discussions as bleak. Solzhenitsyn goes beyond the realist description of the prisoners' conditions. His characters question several premises of their society: the right of one man to rule over others by force, the moral justification of a state built by forced labor, the discrepancy between ideal and reality, the use of technology in the service of an unjust power or state, and the need for good people, even in prisons. The most important theme is the relationship between the individual and society. Thus, Mavrino becomes a microcosm of the Soviet Union.

Soviet society is portrayed as replete with conflicts that are reflected by the novel's characters. First, there is the conflict between the guards and the prisoners. There are also conflicts among idealistic prisoners and informants, as well as among the authorities themselves. Finally, there are conflicts within individual prisoners, as in the case of Rubin, who still believes in Marxist ideals but questions the guilt assigned to him by a nominally Marxist state.

Solzhenitsyn is at his best when creating multifaceted characters, especially the protagonist Gleb Nerzhin. Even though Solzhenitsyn is completely on the side of such characters, he reveals their weaknesses as well as their strengths. Thus, Nerzhin not only displays kindness and understanding when he deals with fellow prisoners but also demonstrates weakness when he has an affair with Simochka. He strikes a firm relationship with Rubin, who still believes in the Marxism that Nerzhin despises. Nerzhin is steadfast in his refusal to submit to his enslavers without being unpleasant about it. Rubin is also presented as a multifaceted character despite his fanaticism. He is intelligent, good-humored, and courageous in dealing with his predicament. Innokenty, whose name alludes to innocence, is also courageous and versatile. Many other characters are well-rounded, and some are unforgettable.

When *The First Circle* was published, in Russian and many other languages, the author was already the focus of interest not only in the literary world but in the political world as well. Some literary historians have relegated the novel to a particular moment in time, suggesting that it has not transcended its historical situation enough to remain relevant after the collapse of the Soviet Union. Despite this claim, *The First Circle* remains relevant. The acts of inhumanity and cruelty depicted in the novel are examples of human behaviors that have always existed and will always exist. By depicting such behavior in a compelling fashion, the novel achieves universal significance and literary greatness.

Vasa D. Mihailovich

Further Reading

Dunlop, John B., Richard Hauch, and Alexis Klimoff, eds. *Aleksandr Solzhenitsyn: Critical Essays and Documentary Materials*. 2d ed. New York: Collier Books, 1975. A comprehensive collection of forty-nine essays on Solzhenitsyn's life and works, written by leading literary critics from many countries.

Feifer, Georg, and David Burg. *Solzhenitsyn*. New York: Stein & Day, 1972. A trustworthy, lively, and readable biography.

Feuer, Kathryn, ed. *Solzhenitsyn: A Collection of Critical Essays*. Englewood Cliffs, N.J.: Prentice Hall, 1976. A collection of thirteen essays on Solzhenitsyn by renowned critics; includes discussions of *The First Circle*.

Fiene, Donald M. *Alexander Solzhenitsyn: An International Bibliography of Writings by and About Him*. Ann Arbor,

Mich.: Ardis, 1973. A bibliography containing a list of 2,465 critical works about Solzhenitsyn in thirty-eight languages.

Labedz, Leopold, ed. *Solzhenitsyn: A Documentary Record.* New York: Penguin Books, 1974. Compiles documents from Solzhenitsyn's life to reconstruct his biography; pays special attention to his struggle against the Soviet regime.

Moody, Christopher. *Solzhenitsyn.* New York: Barnes & Noble, 1973. A solid analysis in depth of Solzhenitsyn's main works, with two chapters of biography.

Pontuso, James F. *Solzhenitsyn's Political Thought.* Charlottesville: University Press of Virginia, 1990. A study of political matters in Solzhenitsyn's works, including *The First Circle.*

Scammell, Michael. *Solzhenitsyn.* New York: W. W. Norton, 1989. Extensive biography dealing adequately with Solzhenitsyn's life and works, with a valuable introduction for general readers.

Un-Chol Shin. "Conscience, Lie, and Suffering in Solzhenitsyn's *The First Circle.*" *Modern Age* 29, no. 4 (1985): 344-352. Discusses Solzhenitsyn's representation in *The First Circle* of the psychological features and reactions of characters experiencing particularly difficult circumstances.

First Poetic Works *and* New Poetic Works

Author: Alfred de Musset (1810-1857)
First published: Poésies nouvelles, 1840; *Premières poésies*, 1840; definitive edition, 1852 (English translation, 1905)
Type of work: Poetry

In 1852, the whole body of Alfred de Musset's poetry was gathered into two volumes and published as the *First Poetic Works* and *New Poetic Works.* The first volume is made up of *Romances of Spain and Italy* (1829) and *A Show from an Easy Chair* (1833). The second collection contains pieces written after 1833. It is worth recalling that by 1840, when the poet was thirty years old, Musset's creative talents were virtually exhausted. A complete explanation of this premature exhaustion should not be sought in the character of Musset's poetic doctrine. However, in the light of Musset's stated belief that the greatness of verse was commensurate with the magnitude of the poet's suffering and the intensity of his emotion, it will be readily understood that his creative talent was likely to fade relatively early.

Only a handful of people turned up for Musset's funeral in 1857. This seems remarkable now, in the light of Musset's continuing popular appeal both as poet and as dramatist. It is all the more remarkable in view of the enthusiastic welcome given him by the members of the Romantic *Cénacle* when he first joined the group in 1828. His precocious poetic talent and dazzling wit could not, and did not, fail to impress its members.

Musset's *Romances of Spain and Italy* was written after the first collected works of Victor Hugo were available. Just as it is of little moment that Hugo's *Les Orientales* (1829; *Les Orientales: Or, Eastern Lyrics*, 1879) was inspired by his watching the sun set over Paris, so it matters little that when Musset's collection first appeared, he was not familiar with either Spain or Italy. The brightness and color of these countries, remembered or imagined, appealed to the young Romantics seeking a vivid contrast with the drabness of France in their day; Spain and Italy provided a rich backcloth in front of which intense passion could be appropriately represented.

The poems for which Musset is best known are the series of four "Nights": "The Night of May," "The Night of December," "The Night of August," and "The Night of October." All four relate directly to his turbulent, unhappy love affair with the novelist George Sand. Although it is easy to exaggerate the effect of this liaison on Musset, it does seem certain that he was deeply marked by it and that subsequent affairs even served to remind him of it.

The four "Nights" contain some of the finest lyrical passages that may be found in French verse. They take the dramatic form of dialogues between the poet and his Muse, with the latter acting as a confidant who listens, advises, and consoles.

In "The Night of May," the Spring Muse vainly begs the poet to give form to his suffering in a work of art; by so doing, he will participate in the rites of creation and eternal renewal taking place around him. At first, the poet thinks he is only imagining the voice of the Muse, but little by little it grows louder and more urgent, and he clearly makes out the words "Poet, take thy lute." The Muse despairs of banishing the poet's indolence, after insisting, however, that his very unhappiness would have been a guarantee of the beauty of his verse: "The most desperate songs are the most beautiful;/ I know some immortal ones that are pure sobs." The poet breaks his silence to claim that the weight of his grief is such that no form of expression can bear it: "But I have suffered a hard martyrdom/ And the least I might say about it,/ Were I to try it on my lute,/ Would break it like a reed."

"The Night of December" presents, beside the poet, a mysterious companion who follows him through all the stages of his life. This brother reveals himself to be the image of loneliness. In "The Night of August" a happier note is struck, for the work is a hymn of praise to the forces of life that allow human beings to recover from the setbacks in life. However, "The Night of October" contains a return to anguish for the poet. He knows once more wrath and despair; he realizes that he did not in fact recover from his unhappy love affair.

In his series of "Nights," Musset seems to have moved away from the mainstream of the nineteenth century Romantic movement. However, in doing so, he renews contact with some of the resources of Romanticism in its ageless aspects. For here the poet places himself at the center of his poetic meditation and, in representing himself as sincerely and directly as possible, admits the reader to a position of privileged intimacy. The reader feels in sympathy with the poet. Musset's sincere, lyrical laying bare of the emotions in the form of confidential poetry was to be imitated frequently in the course of the nineteenth century.

The emotion that recurs most frequently in Musset's verse is love, which is generally associated with suffering and a form of regret. A partial explanation of Musset's considerable popularity may doubtless be sought in the lucidity with which he was able to analyze his sufferings and their causes. It is this lucidity and the regret that it provokes that make Musset's unhappiness especially poignant. One of the most moving illustrations of this sincere self-analysis, from which all trace of oratory or rhetoric is excluded, may be found in the short piece entitled "Sadness." This sonnet, collected in the *New Poetic Works*, was written in June, 1840. It is a confession of failure in life: a loss of pride, a wasting of energy, and a sense of shame about the whole situation: "I

have wasted my strength and my life,/ I have lost my friends, my gaiety;/ I have even lost my pride/ Which gave confidence in my genius." The simplicity of the language, its power to suggest the repentance of the sinner, reminds the reader of similar confessions by François Villon four hundred years earlier.

In Musset, the dramatist often coexists with the poet, and it is difficult to separate the two. This is readily evident in the dramatic dialogue employed in the "Nights." Regrettably, it also shows up in oratorical aspects of these poems. The double role of poet and dramatist seems part of a greater dualism and even dichotomy in Musset. On one hand, he was truly a child of his century, containing within himself many of its contradictions and much of its anguish. On the other hand, he was an admirer of the great French classics, too aware of the tradition of French letters ever to subscribe completely to the doctrines of the Romantic *Cénacle*. Some of the distrust with which he came to be viewed by members of the group may be explained by his mischievously parodying some of their excesses. If it is valid to talk of Musset as a poet aiming at a free transfer of emotion from himself to his reader, it is yet necessary to remark that irony and whimsical, critical detachment are also components of Musset's poetic repertory.

"A Wasted Evening," about an evening at the theater, is one of Musset's finest poems. It has the tone of a conversation. Whereas in other pieces by Musset one might regret the absence of those elements of density and surprise often held to be essential to a poem, here they are much in evidence. The poem is related to a precise circumstance in his life: a performance of Molière's *Le Misanthrope* (1666; *The Misanthrope*, 1709) in Paris in 1840. Musset proceeds from an ironic, effective treatment of current tastes in the theater: "I was alone, the other evening, at the Théâtre-Français,/ Or almost alone; the author had but little success./ Of course, it was just Molière." Then, in masterly fashion, he weaves in a new theme: The glimpse of a girl in the theater brings to mind a phrase from the poet André Chénier. This is enough to distract the poet from the task he set himself: to rehabilitate and to imitate the talent of the seventeenth century dramatist. Musset succeeds admirably here in calling to life an atmosphere and in making a concise, critical commentary on the tastes of men of his day. Moreover, he shows up strikingly the problem of his personal, artistic indolence.

That flippancy and irony were studied techniques becomes obvious in a piece such as "Upon Three Steps of Marble," a poem composed in 1849. The title refers to the stairs of the terrace of the *Orangerie* at Versailles. The beginning of the poem is a disrespectful description of the palace and park of Versailles:

I do not believe that there is on earth a place

. . . .

More described, more lauded, more sung
Than the boring park of Versailles.

The flippant beginning, with its implicit criticism of descriptive poetry, gives way, however, to a magnificent evocation of the century of Louis XIV, with which Musset patently feels considerable spiritual affinity.

When Musset's name is mentioned, regret is often expressed. It is felt by many readers that with a more sustained effort, he could have accomplished far more than he did, that his life of dissipation must be deplored. Some have the impression that Musset's emotional development never moved far beyond adolescence. The poet himself hints at this possibility in an address to the reader in the *First Poetic Works*: "My first poems are those of a child/ The second of an adolescent/ The last scarcely of a man." Even if this is true, and it seems possible, it is to be remembered that Musset is in good company. It could perhaps be shown that many great poets, although they did not write during their actual adolescence, frequently referred to it, consciously or unconsciously, as their primary source of inspiration.

Further Reading

Barine, Arvède. *The Life of Alfred de Musset.* Translated by Charles Conner Hayden. New York: Edwin C. Hill, 1906. Important early work on the writer, still highly useful for scholars and general readers. Describes the young Musset's growing awareness of his poetic talents and discusses the production of works that would be included in his two collections.

Brookner, Anita. "Alfred de Musset: Enfant du siècle." In *Romanticism and Its Discontents.* New York: Farrar, Straus and Giroux, 2000. Examines the works of Musset and other French Romantic writers and artists. Argues that the Romantics created an imaginary world in order to attain fulfillment in the aftermath of the French Revolution and Napoleon I's defeat at Waterloo.

Denomme, Robert T. "Alfred de Musset and the Poetry of Experience." In *Nineteenth-Century French Romantic Poets.* Carbondale: Southern Illinois University Press, 1969. Discusses the significance of human love as an informing principle in Musset's poetry. Focuses on the poet's attempts to capture the intensity of experience in his art.

Grant, Elliott M. *French Poetry of the Nineteenth Century.* 2d ed. New York: Macmillan, 1967. Briefly outlines the composition process for poems included in these volumes. Reproduces selected poems and explicates them for general readers, focusing on technical and thematic issues.

Haldane, Charlotte. *Alfred: The Passionate Life of Alfred de Musset.* New York: Roy, 1961. Offers perceptive commentary on Musset's poetry. Explains the genesis for many of his poems and interprets a number of them in detail.

Sedgwick, Henry Dwight. *Alfred de Musset, 1810-1857.* Indianapolis, Ind.: Bobbs-Merrill, 1931. A detailed study of the writer's life that interweaves commentary on the poems into the biographical narrative. Explains the source of Musset's inspiration for a number of the works included in his collections.

Wakefield, David. *The French Romantics: Literature and the Visual Arts, 1800-1840.* London: Chaucer, 2007. Wakefield's study of the French Romantic movement devotes a chapter to Musset, discussing his ideas about literature and art and his influence on painting.

The Fisher Maiden

Author: Bjørnstjerne Bjørnson (1832-1910)
First published: Fiskerjenten, 1868 (English translation, 1869)
Type of work: Novella
Type of plot: Pastoral
Time of plot: Early nineteenth century
Locale: Norway

Principal characters:
PETRA, the fisher maiden
GUNLAUG, her mother
PEDRO, her father
HANS ODEGAARD, the pastor's son

The Story:

Pedro Ohlsen, the son of Peter Ohlsen and the grandson of old Per Ohlsen, is not like either his father or his grandfather. They tended to their businesses like shrewd, practical men. Pedro, in contrast, is a dreamer. Scolded from morning to night by his father and his schoolfellows, he begins to seek out the poor children in the community for companions, among them a spritelike girl named Gunlaug, whom people call the fisher maiden.

When Peter dies, he leaves enough money for his widow and Pedro to live simply without working. Pedro devotes his time to flute playing. He and the fisher maiden separate after a quarrel; she thinks him a weakling and leaves the town. Nine years later, she returns with a child, Petra, a little girl who also becomes known as the fisher maiden.

One day Petra, who is as audacious as her mother was, steals apples from a tree belonging to Pedro. He catches her and identifies her as the child of his lost love. When Petra escapes, she tells her mother of the encounter. Gunlaug tells her never again to speak to Pedro.

Hans Odegaard, the pastor's son, asks permission to teach Petra to read, and she learns rapidly under his guidance. A tragedy befalls Hans's best friend, and, in his grief, Hans cannot be persuaded to take up his career. His indifference is a bitter thing for his father, the old pastor. Petra weeps when Hans leaves the village.

Young men come to woo Petra, among them Gunnar, the sailor, and a stranger who keeps his name from her and mystifies her with strange songs and tales. Finally, he gives her a gold chain and tells her his name is Yngve Vold. Unlike Gunnar, who is poor, Yngve owns his own ship. Both go suddenly to sea. When Yngve returns, he tells her that he intends to marry her. He is the richest man in the town, which frightens Petra, for she knows that many of the townspeople will not approve of the wealthy shipowner marrying the fisher maiden.

Gunnar, too, sends her a ring and a love letter. Before she

can decide between her two suitors, however, Hans returns, and she realizes that he is the man she loves best. The next day, Hans beats Yngve with his cane for announcing his plan to marry Petra. Hans then tells Petra that his life is ruined, for she betrayed him. Gunnar returns, and he, too, beats Yngve. The whole town buzzes with the gossip that Petra has three men engaged to her, all at the same time. A mob goes to Gunlaug's house and throws stones through Petra's window. Gunlaug helps her daughter to escape from the town by dressing her as a sailor, and Pedro rows her out to a boat that will take her to Bergen, where she is unknown.

In Bergen, Petra is greatly humiliated. The theater attracts her, but because she is awkward and unlettered, no theater manager will hire her. At last, she leaves Bergen and makes her home among shepherds to the north. A pastor takes her in for a time, and when he learns that Petra knows Hans, he permits her to stay in his household. There, for the next three years, she studies the great plays under the pastor and his daughter Signe. Eventually, however, the pastor becomes suspicious of Petra and suspects that she is artfully concealing secret admirers. Suddenly, Hans arrives. Signe wrote him, gently explaining how much Petra suffers.

He forgives Petra for the harm she did him and encourages her to go on the stage. When Pedro dies, he leaves Petra enough money to begin her career. Drawing on her experience of suffering and her knowledge of life, Petra follows her greatest desire, happy at the same time to know that Signe is going to marry Hans.

Critical Evaluation:

Much of Bjørnstjerne Bjørnson's writing is characterized by a Whitmanesque expansiveness and a generosity of spirit as notable for its elemental energy as for its moral fearlessness. Bjørnson was concerned with the issues underlying the fundamental connection between love and power. In *The Fisher Maiden*, he provides fascinating insights into some of the key elements involved in the genesis of the Scandinavian feminist movement. This movement flourished because of the social criticism and remarkable insights of such contemporaries as Camilla Collett, Alexander Kielland, Jonas Lie, Henrik Ibsen, and Bjørnson himself.

The Fisher Maiden is more than a novella and something less than a complete novel. It describes in both idyllic and Darwinistic terms the experiences of a young heroine, Petra, who is compelled to move from the country to the city, where her ambitions are realized in the theater. Petra is a woman of considerable genius, and she becomes entangled in a series of capricious affairs involving a succession of lovers who are utterly enchanted by her reveries. However, Petra is not truly in love with any of her suitors, and any relationship beyond the fanciful and the theatrical can serve only as a prop for her romantic genius and her artistic nature. Thus Bjørnson presents an elemental crisis that pits career against nuptial fulfillment. In Petra's case, the nuptial element is subordinated to the dramatic and creative. The result is a nineteenth century portrait that questions a woman's place at the hearth and the role of marriage as the mainstay of her fulfillment or salvation.

Bjørnson recognized an unbroken connection of his time to the beliefs, courage, and values of the Viking past, which all Norwegians cherished. At the same time, he was concerned with the problems of human estrangement and reconciliation, particularly in the relationship of the sexes. Throughout his literary career, Bjørnson advocated women's emancipation with oratorical fervor, and much of his work serves as a profound commentary on the degradation of women living in a society dominated by men. In *The Fisher Maiden*, he makes it clear that happiness and productivity are not necessarily attained only through marriage and that an immoral marriage involving abuse and subordination must be terminated. Bjørnson also felt that love is only one of many strands woven into the fabric of life, and he advocated that women's equality be founded on the dissolution of the double standard.

For Petra, no amount of saintly condemnation by the village bigots who will not countenance music and dancing can destroy her spirit; nor can that condemnation force her to seek refuge in marriage. Indeed, she has very little regard for the village ideas regarding the ethic of courtship, and she is not so overwhelmed by the supposed anguish of her suitors as to be overcome with pity. She refuses to be, like her mother, compelled to live in contempt and fervent regret because of an unfortunate affair or a momentary weakness. Petra feels destined to become an actress, and she does so despite the pressures and moral indignation of a society that would have her choose otherwise.

Bjørnson felt nothing but contempt for innocence predicated on ignorance and superstition. He believed that growth could not be manifested in the miraculous and the supernatural; rather, its fundamental tenet was based on reason, law, and political and social evolution. In many ways, Bjørnson presented the moral, spiritual, religious, and political crisis of orthodox Christianity in its support of traditional sociopolitical beliefs regarding women. As an aggressive radical, he believed that life must supersede religion, most especially when the two conflicted. As the pastor says to the village saints: "Spiritual life thrives but poorly in your mountain home, and partakes of the gloom of the surrounding vegetation. Prejudice, like the cliffs themselves, overhangs your life and casts a shadow upon it."

For Petra, as for so many of Bjørnson's fictional characters, guilt serves as a driving force of human motivation. It underlies much of the struggle for power, it is the primary consideration in the struggle for control, and in matters of personal fulfillment it has an extraordinary potential for confusing and undermining the relationships between the sexes.

Petra ultimately gains courage and wisdom from her suffering and from the betrayals, duplicity, and chicanery of the society that has driven her from her home. That wisdom is sufficient to support her in her dedication to the theater. Bjørnson questions whether it is reasonable to impose blame for certain forms of behavior or feeling without regard for the extent of provocation.

Indeed, he suggests the possibility of mutual culpability in certain situations involving attraction and seduction, and it seems that he also insists on some element of feminine responsibility. He poses difficult moral questions in *The Fisher Maiden* and appears to permit no easy answers.

The Fisher Maiden is a novel of remarkable lyric power, implicit optimism, and visionary fervor. By establishing a series of polarities and contrasts in the characters of Petra, Gunlaug, Hans, and Pedro, Bjørnson entertains and educates the reader with a story that is supported by a curious blend of mysticism and rationalism. That blend serves as an extraordinary means for revealing the fundamental egalitarianism of the Norwegian character.

"Critical Evaluation" by Matts Djos

Further Reading

Brandes, Georg. "Bjørnstjerne Bjørnson." In *Henrik Ibsen: A Critical Study—with a Forty-two Page Essay on Bjørnstjerne Bjørnson*. 1899. Reprint. New York: Benjamin Bloom, 1964. A firsthand biographical and critical portrait of Bjørnson's literary and political career. Brandes notes that Bjørnson's daring apostasy of the Norwegian cause was implicitly optimistic, idyllic, and distinctively feminist.

Kepos, Paula, et al., eds. "Bjørnstjerne Bjørnson." In *Twentieth-Century Literary Criticism*. Detroit, Mich.: Gale Research, 1991. An excellent biographical and critical overview of the author's work. Includes a comprehensive bibliography of his principal works and reprints of critical reviews of the author, including those of Max Beerbohm, William Payne, and Edwin Bjørkman, and an excellent contemporary analysis of *The Fisher Maiden* by William Dean Howells.

McFarlane, James Walter. "Bjørnstjerne Bjørnson." In *Ibsen and the Temper of Norwegian Literature*. New York: Octagon Books, 1979. A general survey of the work of this poet, dramatist, novelist, and national hero. Describes his talents in theater and as a writer and critiques his role as a public figure and passionate advocate of women's rights.

_____. "Bjørnstjerne Bjørnson." In *A History of Norwegian Literature*, edited by Harald S. Naess. Lincoln: University of Nebraska Press in cooperation with the American-Scandinavian Foundation, 1993. McFarlane's overview of Norwegian literature from 1860 until 1910 includes a ten-page discussion of Bjørnson's life, works, and significance in Norwegian literature and history.

Woertendyke, Ruis D. "Bjornstjerne Bjornson: In the Shadow of Ibsen." In *Nordic Experiences: Exploration of Scandinavian Cultures*, edited by Berit I. Brown. Westport, Conn.: Greenwood Press, 1997. Woertendyke's analysis of Bjørnson is included in this collection of conference papers that examine literature, art, music, folklore, and other aspects of culture in Norway, Denmark, Finland, Iceland, and Sweden.

Five Women Who Loved Love

Author: Ihara Saikaku (1642-1693)
First published: Kōshoku gonin onna, 1686 (English translation, 1956)
Type of work: Short fiction
Type of plot: Love
Time of plot: Seventeenth century
Locale: Japan

Principal characters:
SEIJŪRŌ, an apprentice
ONATSU, his master's younger sister
OSEN, a young wife
THE COOPER, her husband
CHŌZAEMON, a yeast maker
CHŌZAEMON'S WIFE
OSAN, a merchant's wife
RIN, her maid
MOEMON, the merchant's clerk
OSHICHI, a young woman
HER MOTHER
ONOGAWA KICHISABURŌ, a young samurai
GENGOBEI, a Buddhist monk, formerly a pederast
HACHIJŪRŌ, Gengobei's former lover
OMAN, a young girl

The Stories:

The First Story. Seijūrō, a handsome, gallant young man disowned by his wealthy father for his profligacies, apprentices himself to a shopkeeper and proves hardworking and reliable. When Onatsu, his master's younger sister, falls in love with him, he, after some reluctance, at last fully returns her affection. As an apprentice, he is far from an eligible suitor, and so the lovers are forced to elope. Seven hundred gold pieces disappear at the same time. When the lovers are discovered, Seijūrō, condemned for theft as well as for seduction, is executed. The gold is later found where it was mislaid. Onatsu goes mad for a time. Later, she enters a nunnery.

The Second Story. Osen, a country woman, is married happily to a cooper. When Chōzaemon, the yeast maker, is planning to celebrate the fiftieth anniversary of his father's death, Osen offers to help in the preparations. While she is arranging sweetmeats, Chōzaemon accidentally drops a bowl on her head, disarranging her hair. Chōzaemon's suspicious, jealous wife accuses Osen of adultery. Because she is unjustly accused, Osen impulsively decides to revenge herself on the wife by truly making love to Chōzaemon, although she cares nothing for him. When her husband, the cooper, discovers the lovers, Osen commits suicide and Chōzaemon is executed.

The Third Story. Osan's husband goes to Edo on business. Her maid, Rin, is in love with Moemon, a clerk. Moemon, however, feels coldly toward Rin and only reluctantly agrees to visit her bed. Together, Rin and Osan decide to punish him, and Osan takes Rin's place in the bed. The trick has other results, however, when Osan and Moemon find themselves hopelessly in love. After pretending to commit suicide together, they hide in a faraway village for a time. Eventually, they are discovered and executed.

The Fourth Story. Oshichi, an innocent young woman, is taken by her mother to find refuge in a temple after their house burns down. There she meets and falls in love with Onogawa Kichisaburō, a young samurai. When Oshichi and her mother return to their home, the lovers are not able to meet in secret. Oshichi, remembering how she first met her lover, decides to start another fire, but she is discovered, arrested, exposed to shame, and burned at the stake. Kichisaburō, who was ill, does not know of her death until he accidentally sees her gravestone. At first, he plans to commit suicide, but he is persuaded to delay his plan until after a talk with his mentor and sworn brother. As the result of his friend's advice, Kichisaburō decides to become a monk.

The Fifth Story. Gengobei, a pederast, takes priestly vows after the death of Hachijūrō, his lover. Later, he falls in love with another boy who returns from the dead to see him again. In his grief, Gengobei retires to a mountain hut. Meanwhile, a girl, Oman, sees and falls in love with Gengobei. Determined to win him, she disguises herself as a boy and visits his retreat. There she succeeds in winning Gengobei's love, even after her sex is revealed. Gengobei leaves the priesthood, and the lovers live in great poverty together until Oman's parents finally find her. Rejoicing at her recovery, her parents decide to have the two lovers marry and then give their family fortune to Gengobei. Oman's love story, therefore, comes to a happy ending.

Critical Evaluation:

The Japanese writer Ihara (sometimes Ibara) Saikaku was both a poet who wrote a prodigious number of seventeen-syllable *haiku* and the leading novelist of the Genroku Period

(1600-1868) in Japan. The subjects of his fiction fall chronologically into three distinct types: those dealing with matters of love and the pleasure quarter, those dealing with life among the warrior class, and those dealing with the lives of the merchant class. *Five Women Who Loved Love* belongs to the first group, and all five of the short novels of this work are based on actual happenings. The work was first published in 1686.

In order to appreciate fully the prose fiction of Ihara, it is necessary to understand the nature of Japanese society during the latter half of the seventeenth century. Although Edo (Tokyo) was still the feudal capital (the residence of the shōgun and the source of the real power), and Kyoto was still the residence of the mikado (the nominal ruler), Osaka witnessed the rise of a merchant class; but because of the rigid class distinctions and feudal laws maintained by the shōgun and samurai, the merchants were unable to convert their economic power into political or social power. The official religion was Confucianism, and the ensuing laws ensured the maintenance of a rigidly stratified society with a hierarchy of classes, making it punishable by death to attempt to move from one class to another. The merchants thus sought an outlet for the frustration of their thwarted power and for their money in the *ukiyo* (floating world).

Ukiyo originally had a Buddhist meaning of the transitory life, death, and decay, and the works of Ihara always retained some of this original meaning. In the seventeenth century, however, the *ukiyo* became the term for the diverting quarters of town or the theater. The new heroes of this society were the actors and courtesans; the new values were love and money.

The five stories of *Five Women Who Loved Love* are linked by a common theme: the transgression of the social code for love. Each tale is divided into five parts or chapters, perhaps because of the five-act division of the drama, and the third part depicts a journey (also borrowed from drama). The plots are simple and, with one exception, tragic. The strength of the work lies in its evocation of character and subject. Each tale is linked to a particular locale, three to the major cities of Edo, Kyoto, and Osaka, and two to outlying provinces. In the first four tales, the transgression of the feudal law leads to death; in the fifth tale, however, the lovers live because they are both of the same social class. The five heroines are not languishing, leisurely ladies but rather women of character who have a part in creating their tragedies instead of being helplessly fated. Only Oman, the heroine of the last story, is allowed to live happily ever after, and she, in her charming determination to win her love, resembles in some respects William Shakespeare's Rosalind. Throughout the work, Ihara seems to imply that there should be no conflict between love and society, especially one made along class lines. The conflict exists, however; the heroines choose love and accept the consequences without despair.

Further Reading

Kato, Shuichi. *The Years of Isolation*. Vol. 2 in *A History of Japanese Literature*. New York: Kodansha International, 1983. Pages 104-112 deal primarily with the third story in the collection, relating it to Chikamatsu Monzaemon's dramatic version of the same episode.

Keene, Donald. *World Within Walls: Japanese Literature of the Pre-modern Era, 1600-1867*. New York: Holt, Rinehart and Winston, 1976. Reprint. New York: Columbia University Press, 1999. Chapter 8 discusses *Five Women Who Loved Love* in relation to Ihara's other works, particularly *Life of an Amorous Man* and *Life of an Amorous Woman*. The 1999 edition contains a new preface by Keene.

Kirkwood, Kenneth P. *Renaissance in Japan: A Cultural Survey of the Seventeenth Century*. Rutland, Vt.: Charles E. Tuttle, 1970. Pages 192-223 provide a general biographical sketch of Ihara, including his work as a poet, playwright, and fiction writer. It comments particularly on the Osaka cultural milieu.

Morris, Ivan. *Life of an Amorous Woman, and Other Writings*. New York: New Directions, 1963. Pages 3-51 deal with Ihara and his cultural and historical context. Comments on elements of literary style and illustrations.

Richie, Donald. *Japanese Literature Reviewed*. New York: ICG Muse, 2003. Richie's survey of Japanese literature includes a chapter on Ihara.

Rimer, J. Thomas. *A Reader's Guide to Japanese Literature from the Eighth Century to the Present*. New York: Kodansha International, 1988. Pages 66-69 contain a brief discussion of one of the five stories in the collection. Also comments on Ihara's literary background.

The Fixer

Author: Bernard Malamud (1914-1986)
First published: 1966
Type of work: Novel
Type of plot: Historical realism
Time of plot: Shortly before World War I
Locale: Around Kiev, Ukraine, Russia

Principal characters:
YAKOV BOK, a handyman, the fixer
BIBIKOV, the investigating magistrate
NIKOLAI MAXIMOVITCH LEBEDEV, a brick factory owner
ZINAIDA NIKOLAEVNA, his daughter
SHMUEL RABINOVITCH, father-in-law of Yakov Bok
RAISL BOK, wife of Yakov, daughter of Shmuel

The Story:

Yakov Bok, a fixer, decides in his thirties to leave his native village and go to the big city of Kiev, in search of a better life. His father-in-law, Shmuel, comes to see him off. They talk, a bit gingerly, about the fact that his wife, Raisl, daughter of Shmuel, left him a couple of months earlier and ran off with a stranger. Yakov feels humiliated by this, because he is the laughingstock of the village. Yakov reminds Shmuel that his daughter is also barren, for in the nearly six years they lived together she failed to give him a child. Yakov is also pessimistic about the village's economic future; he is finding it harder and harder to make a living there as a fixer and fears there will likely soon be pogroms in the area.

Shmuel gives Yakov his horse and wagon in exchange for Yakov's cow, which he hopes will prove more profitable. His parting advice to his son-in-law is to recall that it is illegal for Jews to live in Kiev, except in specified Jewish districts, and to advise him to settle in the Jewish district near the synagogue, because without spiritual support a Jew will be vulnerable in a hostile world. Soon after Yakov sets out, his wagon fails him. A wheel breaks, and even the fixer cannot repair it. He continues on horseback as far as the sickly horse can take him, then sells the horse as meat and completes his journey on foot. He settles in the Jewish district but finds no adequate housing there, and too little work as a handyman. He concludes that he ought to try other district and ventures into the larger city in search of better luck. Winter comes. One cold evening he encounters an elderly man lying face down in the snow. The man, who appears drunk, wears a button with the two-headed eagle of the Black Hundreds, a notorious anti-Semitic group. Nevertheless, Yakov feels obligated to help the man. He is joined by a young woman with a crippled leg, who says the man is her father. Yakov helps her carry the man to their nearby house, and as Yakov is leaving, the young woman urges him to return the next morning so that her father, Nikolai Maximovitch Lebedev, can thank him properly.

Yakov worries about going back to the home of an anti-Semite, but, hoping for a reward for his good deed, he goes anyway. The result is that Yakov is offered the job of manager of the brick factory the old man owns. With the job comes living quarters right in the factory. Yakov gives a false name, realizing it would be illegal for him to live in an area forbidden to Jews. Noting that the old man does not ask for his passport, Yakov decides to take the job and risk the consequences. To complicate his situation even more, Zinaida Nikolaevna, the old man's daughter, invites him to dinner, then tries to seduce him. He refuses, for fear of the discovery that would result, more than anything else, and knows that he made an enemy of her.

Through the winter and early spring, Yakov works as a manager, overseeing the making and shipping of bricks and trying to prevent theft by his workmen. One day, he reads in the newspaper that a twelve-year-old boy was found dead in a cave near the brick factory. It says the boy had dozens of stab wounds all over his body, which bled white. The newspaper article hints at ritual murder. Yakov anxiously watches the boy's funeral from a distance and sees that anti-Semitic pamphlets are distributed, blaming the boy's death on the Jews. He decides it is time to flee, since a pogrom is brewing, but as he gathers his belongings, he is arrested.

Yakov is first interrogated in the courthouse and held there in a cell. After many weeks, he is sent to a prison, where relentless interrogation continues, and he is kept in solitary confinement for eighteen more months. The one glimmer of light for Yakov is his frequent sessions with the investigating magistrate, whose name is Bibikov, who proves to be a man of integrity and compassion. Bibikov and Yakov even have one long discussion about Spinoza (whose autobiography Yakov read, in a volume he found in a junk shop). In his simple way, Yakov, untrained in philosophy, understands that Spinoza's main concern is how a man may be free, and Bibikov, impressed, helps Yakov understand a bit more by explaining some of Spinoza's complex ideas to him. Bibikov is the only person in authority who treats Yakov humanely during all the nearly two years Yakov is in custody. One day, Yakov has the horrible experience of passing a jail cell in which a man hanged himself with his belt. The man is Bibikov.

During Yakov's long travail in prison, he is abused every day by humiliating body searches and even served poisoned food. The purpose of the cruelty is to force him to confess to the murder, since the prosecutors are unable to obtain any positive proof against him. Yakov has no way to prove his innocence, either, since the evidence against him is vague and circumstantial. While in prison he has two especially painful visits. One is from Shmuel, who shows great sympathy but makes the empty promise to try to get him some help. The other is from his wife, Raisl, who wants him to sign a paper acknowledging her illegitimate child as his, so the boy will not be stigmatized as a bastard. Yakov wearily agrees. It is announced that Yakov is formally indicted, and he is led out of the prison and marched through the crowd-lined streets. Much shouting, some hostile, some friendly, accompanies him on his way to the courthouse to be tried for ritual murder.

Critical Evaluation:

Bernard Malamud readily acknowledged that *The Fixer* is a fictionalized adaptation of a notorious historical event. Jewish brick factory manager Mendel Beilis was accused of murdering a twelve-year-old Christian boy and of draining the boy's blood for use in making matzos for Passover. The arrest took place in 1911 in Kiev, and for two years afterward, while the Russian authorities strove to manufacture a believable case against Beilis, the accused languished in jail. A public outcry arose, both inside and outside Russia, at the spectacle of a state system of justice relying, for its case against a Jew, on an absurdly superstitious legend, circulated by anti-Semites, that Jews practiced ritual murder. When Beilis was finally brought to trial in 1913, the court returned a verdict of not guilty.

Malamud takes several significant liberties with the historical truth. For example, Malamud's victim is a handyman, unlike Beilis, and the owner of the brick factory where Yakov Bok is employed is a Christian anti-Semite, rather than a Jew, as was Beilis's boss. It is far more important to note how closely Malamud adheres to the main facts of the historical case. One of the finest achievements of the novel is the care and accuracy with which it evokes the atmosphere of czarist Russia in the years before World War I, including the restricted life imposed upon Jews and the horrors of its inhumane prisons and system of justice. As literature *The Fixer* is, more than anything else, a vivid exercise in historical realism. About three-fourths of the novel focuses on detailed description of what Yakov Bok endures at the hands of prosecutors and prison officials.

An essential feature of the novel is that, while the novel is a third-person narrative, Malamud has contrived to filter all of the novel's action through the consciousness of Yakov

Bok, giving the novel the effect of a first-person narrative. The point of view in the novel is steadily and unequivocally that of the protagonist. As a result, the reader sees the world as Yakov sees it, and that perspective is extremely pessimistic and cynical. Yakov always expects the worst to happen because his life has been an unbroken series of hard blows, beginning with the death of his father in a pogrom when Yakov was an infant. The death of his mother comes soon after, which forces him to spend his lonely childhood and youth in an orphanage. The humiliating disaster of his marriage and the hapless journey to Kiev in which everything goes wrong force from Yakov's mouth the phrase, "Who invented my life?" This is Yakov's veiled attack on the God he cannot quite believe in but worships anyway.

Malamud chose the name Bok for his protagonist because it defines his role perfectly. In Yiddish and in German *Bok* means a he-goat, the traditional image of the outcast and surrogate victim. Yakov Bok is a scapegoat, a born victim, to be blamed for whatever evils befall society and to be cast out of society, taking those evils with him, so society can be cleansed. It is a universal type that Malamud has in mind, to be found in every society, big or small, and in every age. That is why Yakov is a handyman, familiar to everyone yet living on the margins of society, an outsider who is easy to blame for bad times. Malamud seems to have intended Yakov to be an itinerant Everyman, a stranger everywhere, always viewed with suspicion, whose destiny is to bear the burdens of suffering for everyone else when trouble comes. The novel may be read as a protest against society's tendency to victimize the poor and helpless.

This universal scapegoating impulse, which Malamud saw as the essence of the Beilis case, may explain why Malamud chose to end his novel just as the trial of Yakov is about to begin. Critics have accused Malamud of a failure of nerve in refusing to conclude his novel with the exoneration of the intended victim. Surely Malamud wished to make the point that eventual exoneration, however welcome, cannot cancel the victim's suffering. By stopping his novel before the trial begins, Malamud forces his reader to focus on the real injustice against which he is protesting, namely the scapegoating itself, and does not allow the reader the false comfort of one isolated happy ending.

Murray Sachs

Further Reading

Avery, Evelyn, ed. *The Magic Worlds of Bernard Malamud.* Albany: State University of New York Press, 2001. A wide-ranging collection of essays on Malamud and his writings, including personal memoirs by members of his family and friends and analyses of some of his works.

Bloom, Harold, ed. *Bernard Malamud.* New York: Chelsea House, 2000. A collection of essays assessing the entire spectrum of Malamud's works. Includes a chronology of his life and a bibliography.

Cappell, Ezra. "Reflecting the World: Bernard Malamud's Post-Holocaust Judaism." In *American Talmud: The Cultural Work of Jewish American Fiction.* Albany: State University of New York Press, 2007. Cappell analyzes the fiction of Malamud and other American Jewish writers to examine how this fiction is linked to religious texts and traditions. He argues that these writers can be viewed as creating a new form of Jewish rabbinic scripture. The chapter on Malamud includes information on *The Fixer.*

Codde, Philippe. *The Jewish American Novel.* West Lafayette, Ind.: Purdue University Press, 2007. Malamud's novels are among those considered in this study of American Jewish novels that enjoyed unprecedented success in the post-World War II period, with Codde describing the reasons for this success.

Davis, Philip. *Bernard Malamud: A Writer's Life.* New York: Oxford University Press, 2007. The first full-length biography of Malamud. Davis chronicles the events of Malamud's life, describes his writing methods, and connects the events of his life to his work. He also provides literary analysis of Malamud's novels and other fiction. References to *The Fixer* are listed in the index.

Ducharme, Robert. *Art and Idea in the Novels of Bernard Malamud: Toward the Fixer.* The Hague, the Netherlands: Mouton, 1974. Argues that the theme of the tension between suffering and responsibility runs through all Malamud's work and provides a key to *The Fixer.*

Field, Leslie A., and Joyce W. Field, eds. *Bernard Malamud: A Collection of Critical Essays.* Englewood Cliffs, N.J.: Prentice-Hall, 1975. Excellent choice of essays, prefaced by a revealing interview with Malamud.

Hershinow, Sheldon J. *Bernard Malamud.* New York: Frederick Ungar, 1980. Good general study of Malamud's work, identifying his main themes.

A Flag for Sunrise

Author: Robert Stone (1937-   )
First published: 1981
Type of work: Novel
Type of plot: Political realism
Time of plot: 1976
Locale: New York City, American Gulf coast, and
   Central America

Principal characters:
FRANK HOLLIWELL, an American anthropologist
SISTER JUSTIN FEENEY, a nun and nurse
FATHER CHARLES EGAN, a priest
PABLO TABOR, a U.S. Coast Guard deserter
FATHER GODOY, a Tecanecan priest
LIEUTENANT CAMPOS, a member of Tecan's Guardia
   Nacional
OSCAR OCAMPO, an anthropologist in Compostela
TOM ZECCA, an American military attaché in Tecan
MARIE ZECCA, his wife
JACK CALLAHAN, a shady American
DEEDEE CALLAHAN, his lustful wife
FREDDY NEGUS, captain of the Callahans' boat
BOB COLE, an American journalist and possible spy
RALPH HEATH, a British expatriate
NAFTALI, a Holocaust survivor and a criminal
DON SEBASTIÁN AGUIRRE, a Tecanecan revolutionary
EMILIO ORTEGA CURTIS, a leader of the revolution
MARTY NOLAN, a U.S. federal agent
SISTER MARY JOSEPH, a nun

The Story:

Father Charles Egan has been in the fictional Central American country of Tecan, which resembles Nicaragua, for ten years. Though the Canadian priest has been ordered to close his mission, he intends to stay. His only companion is Sister Justin Feeney, a young American nurse more idealistic than he is. Lieutenant Campos of the Guardia Nacional is suspicious of Justin's political sympathies. After six years in Tecan, the nurse wants to see political and social change. When the Guardia kills a young American woman, Campos forces Father Egan to dispose of the body.

Frank Holliwell, an anthropology professor, drives to New York City to catch a flight to Central America. In Brooklyn, he has lunch with Marty Nolan, a CIA agent and friend with whom he worked during the Vietnam War. Nolan has heard from their mutual friend Oscar Ocampo, an anthropologist in Compostela, that Holliwell is scheduled to deliver a lecture there. Nolan wants any information Holliwell can provide about Tecan, which borders on Compostela.

Sister Mary Joseph, who works in Tecan's mountains, visits Father Egan and Justin, whom she sees as too good to be true, to try to talk some sense into them. Father Godoy, a Tecanecan priest, says both he and Justin have failed because

the country itself is a failure. Godoy is friendly with rebels who are based in the mountains.

Pablo Tabor feels he is wasting his life in the U.S. Coast Guard. He shoots his hunting dogs, threatens to kill his wife, and runs away to Central America. In Compostela, Pablo meets Jack and Deedee Callahan, drunken Americans who want to hire him to work on their boat. Pablo is suspicious about what they may be up to.

Holliwell's lecture at Compostela's House of the Study of Mankind is a disaster. A bit intoxicated, he drifts into an anti-American rant that leaves his audience hissing. Attending the lecture are Tom Zecca, a military attaché to the American embassy in Tecan, and his wife, Marie, a former social worker. Both have also spent time in Vietnam. They volunteer to drive Holliwell to Tecan. Holliwell receives a series of telephone calls threatening his life because of the lecture.

Justin and Father Egan are ordered to report to Metairie, Louisiana. Their mission is to be sold to the conglomerate that owns the International Fruit and Vegetable company. Produce is the only Tecanecan resource of value to the United States.

In fear for his life in Compostela, Holliwell asks the Zeccas to drive him to Tecan. Accompanying them is Bob

Cole, another Vietnam veteran, who plans to contact the Tecanecan rebels. Cole and Tom explain to Holliwell how Tecan has been exploited by U.S. interests. Tom warns Cole that visiting the rebels is too risky. As they arrive in Tecan, Holliwell sees ten thousand people living in a park near the presidential palace. They have been thrown off their land after copper was discovered on it.

Freddy Negus, captain of the Callahans' boat, the *Cloud*, is instantly distrustful of Pablo. The *Cloud* is ostensibly a shrimp boat, but Pablo recognizes it as being designed to smuggle contraband. There is considerable sexual tension between Pablo and the fortyish Deedee. Negus and the Callahans plan to kill Pablo after he has served his purpose.

Venturing into the interior of Tecan, Holliwell finds the Indian villages there as despairing as the capital. At the ironically named hotel the Paradise, Holliwell meets the British expatriate Ralph Heath, who views Tecan and its inhabitants with great cynicism.

Don Sebastián Aguirre, a friend of Ocampo, meets with the leaders of the coming revolution. He sees Emilio Ortega Curtis, an art professor, as Tecan's destined leader. Ortega reports that Cole, who claimed to be a journalist, has been executed as a spy. He wants something done about Father Godoy, whom he also mistrusts.

Holliwell goes diving with tourists, a family of five Cuban Americans from Miami, and swims dangerously deep. He meets Father Egan, and Justin comes to his aid when he steps on a sea urchin. She considers Holliwell absurd.

Pablo realizes the Callahans and Negus consider him a fool. He will have to take chances to prove his worth to them. He leaves the boat to confront Naftali, the gangster backing the Callahans' operation. Pablo finds the aging Holocaust survivor contemplating suicide and waxing philosophical: He says that he knows the value of everything because he has stolen and sold everything. Naftali gives Pablo a large diamond because he has never given anyone anything. Pablo suffocates the old man.

A conversation with Father Godoy leads Justin to the conclusion that her nursing is not enough for her, and she commits herself to the rebellion. Her conflicted emotions about her work, religion, Tecan, Father Godoy, and Father Egan leave her confused. She believes that working for the revolution will serve as penance for her. She realizes the mission can be a tactical location in the coming struggle. Visiting Justin again, Holliwell finds he is falling in love with her.

Unaware of Naftali's death, his men load the *Cloud* with weapons. Pablo intercepts a message for Negus reporting that he has murdered Naftali. His life in danger, Pablo prays for guidance. Deedee seduces Pablo, the thought that he will

soon be dead adding spice to the sex for her. To save himself, Pablo kills Deedee, Jack, and Negus, but he is wounded in the gunfight. After criminals remove the weapons from the *Cloud*, Pablo decides to join the rebels.

Holliwell wants to confess his connections to Nolan and Ocampo to Justin. She tells him she plans to leave the church. Tom ignores Holliwell's plea to help protect the mission. Pablo makes his way to the mission, where Justin tends his leg wound. Pablo thinks destiny has led him to the mission.

Holliwell tells Justin he loves her, and they consummate their relationship. He realizes that by seducing her he has lost her. He confesses that he was supposed to report on what he has seen in Tecan but never intended to do so. Justin condemns him for his despair.

Ocampo is dead. Heath accuses Holliwell of being a double agent, of knowing about the revolution but not reporting it. Heath, who works for a corporate security firm, promises Holliwell he will protect Justin. The Guardia is ambushed on its way to arrest Justin, who accuses Holliwell of betraying her. Holliwell and Pablo escape in the mission's boat.

Justin is arrested. Campos tortures her, then kills her. Terrified of Pablo, Holliwell kills him. When Father Egan refuses to hear Campos's confession, the priest is shot. Holliwell finds a fishing boat to begin his journey home.

Critical Evaluation:

As he had in *Dog Soldiers* (1974), Robert Stone in *A Flag for Sunrise* mingled philosophy, religion, politics, war, and crime to examine how his characters discover and maintain their identities in an ever-changing global society fraught with greed, corruption, violence, and conflicting interests. Holliwell, Justin, Egan, and Pablo are all alone in different ways, each struggling to find meaning in his or her life. Despite the various connections each makes, all remain essentially estranged from those around them, understanding themselves almost as little as they do others. Just before killing Pablo, Holliwell offers what he calls the abridgment of hope, the state in which all of Stone's protagonists find themselves.

Stone has acknowledged the influence of Joseph Conrad's *Nostromo: A Tale of the Seaboard* (1904), which also presents the interlaced fates of disparate characters in a fictional Latin American country. Conrad assembled similar characters, isolated in cultures they do not fully understand, in novels such as *Victory: An Island Tale* (1915), a philosophical work that Stone has called one of his favorite novels. Stone's characters also recall the burnt-out protagonists of such Graham Greene novels as *The Power and the Glory* (1940), *The Quiet American* (1955), and *A Burnt-Out Case*

(1961). Stone was influenced by the treatment of religiosity by Greene, who favored rum-soaked priests similar to Father Egan who have struggled with their faith.

Out of touch with his turbulent times, Father Egan conducts arguments with himself to justify his belief. Egan's faith seems moribund, yet he hopes it can somehow be rekindled. Another Greene influence can be seen in Holliwell's disastrous Compostela speech, which recalls the performance of the naive American pulp writer in *The Third Man* (1950) who is asked to discuss literature with a group of Viennese intellectuals. *A Flag for Sunrise* mentions B. Traven, whose novels, such as *The Treasure of the Sierra Madre* (1927), focus on Americans seeking wealth and possibly salvation in Latin America. Stone is constantly aware of his literary antecedents.

When Holliwell hesitates about agreeing to spy for Nolan, his friend reminds him that he lives in a world where it is impossible to take sides. *A Flag for Sunrise* is about the difficulty of making choices in a highly charged political world and of living with the consequences. Holliwell flees the revolution but has to kill Pablo to survive. Holliwell's realization that he is without belief or hope makes him reach out to Justin, but he remains totally alone. There are no easy answers or means of reconciliation in the modern world, Stone seems to be saying. Holliwell loses his identity through his failure to act.

The Vietnam War haunts several of the novel's characters, especially Holliwell. Although he remains vague about his intelligence work during the conflict, the experience seems to have resulted in extreme behavior that continues to affect his thoughts and actions. Holliwell considers his past dead and his present doing poorly. Heath's philosophical bent suggests to Holliwell that Heath, too, may be tainted by Vietnam. Tom Zecca calls Cole a Vietnam burnout, a condition leaving him in an endless search for a righteous cause. Scarred by Vietnam, Tom and Holliwell agree that the best they can say for themselves is that they are capable of honor.

As in Vietnam, Americans in Tecan are condescending toward the country's inhabitants. Jack Callahan ironically tells Pablo that the locals lack the spiritual values people have back in the United States and that Central American countries without democracy are breeding grounds for corruption and violence. Callahan reminisces about the old days, when he was the biggest villain around. Now, he is comparatively innocent.

Holliwell's character encompasses most of the themes of *A Flag for Sunrise*. His work both as an anthropologist, hovering around societies without penetrating them, and as a spy have isolated him from his family and the comforts of every-

day life. His life as husband, father, and teacher has value, but it is not enough for him. He is not testing his honor or exploring his true self. He feels like a visitor from another planet whose nature is to seek war. Pablo represents Holliwell's more violent alter ego. Holliwell believes in love, but Justin cannot return his affection, leaving his ethical rebirth stillborn.

The title of *A Flag for Sunrise* comes from Emily Dickinson's poem "A Wife—at Daybreak I Shall Be," which Justin quotes despairingly after her night of tepid passion with Holliwell. The line "sunrise—Hast thou a Flag for me?" captures her need for a cause she can believe in, the dilemma and hope of all the novel's protagonists. *A Flag for Sunrise* ends with Holliwell contemplating the meaning of the line. Stone offers only a pessimistic vision of the sunrise sought by his characters.

Michael Adams

Further Reading

Bull, Jeoffrey S. "'What About a Problem That Doesn't Have a Solution?' Stone's *A Flag for Sunrise*, DeLillo's *Mao II*, and the Politics of Political Fiction." *Critique* 40, no. 3 (Spring, 1999): 215-229. Discusses the novel's blending of philosophy, religion, politics, and adventure. Analyzes Holliwell's use of language.

Merullo, Roland. "America's Secret Culture." *Chronicle of Higher Education* 48, no. 25 (March 1, 2002): B7-B9. Considers Holliwell as representative of American political contradictions.

Parks, John G. "Unfit Survivors: The Failed and Lost Pilgrims in the Fiction of Robert Stone." *CEA Critic* 53, no. 1 (1990): 52-57. Looks at the pessimism of *A Flag for Sunrise* and the extent to which the text is haunted by the Vietnam War.

Solotaroff, Robert. *Robert Stone*. New York: Twayne, 1994. Analyzes Stone's use of religion, Gnosticism, and Vietnam.

Stephenson, Gregory. *Understanding Robert Stone*. Columbia: University of South Carolina Press, 2002. Discusses philosophical and political themes, similarities between Holliwell and Pablo, and the significance of images related to animals, jewels, flags, and light and dark.

Stone, Robert. "Robert Stone: The Art of Fiction XC." Interview by William Crawford Woods. *Paris Review* 98 (Winter, 1985): 24-57. Stone discusses individual scenes in *A Flag for Sunrise*, the significance of the title, the American influence on Central America, and his Catholicism.

Flaubert's Parrot

Author: Julian Barnes (1946-   )
First published: 1984
Type of work: Novel
Type of plot: Philosophical and metafictional
Time of plot: Mid-twentieth century to 1982
Locale: Rouen, France; London

Principal characters:
GEOFFREY BRAITHWAITE, an amateur biographer
ELLEN BRAITHWAITE, his wife
ED WINTERTON, an American academic
GUSTAVE FLAUBERT, a renowned French writer
LOUISE COLET, Flaubert's mistress
JULIET HERBERT, an English governess
ENID STARKIE, a literary critic
LOULOU, Flaubert's parrot

The Story:

Geoffrey Braithwaite, an amateur biographer, is at the statue of writer Gustave Flaubert in Rouen, France. Braithwaite's project, it seems, is to get to know as much as he can about Flaubert so that he can connect with him. He especially needs to establish which of two stuffed parrots at two rival museums is Loulou, the one who inspired Flaubert to write his short story "Un Cœur simple" (1877; "A Simple Heart," 1903). Braithwaite notes that Flaubert had disapproved of seeking out information about authors beyond what is found in their works, but Braithwaite pursues his quest nonetheless.

Braithwaite meets Ed Winterton, an American academic, at a book fair. Winterton acquires a book they both had wanted to buy. He later writes to Braithwaite to say that he has discovered some fascinating material related to Flaubert's life. This news intrigues Braithwaite, who imagines that based on this material he will be able publish a groundbreaking study about a hitherto unknown love affair between Flaubert and his niece's governess, Juliet Herbert.

Braithwaite meets Winterton to discuss the discovery. Winterton tells him that the material did indeed reveal that Flaubert had an affair with Juliet, but he also tells him the material also includes a letter in which Flaubert asks that the material be burned—Winterton has done that, and Braithwaite is furious.

Flaubert had compared himself to various animals, from lizards and camels to bears. Apparently, he most liked to compare himself to a polar bear, living far from civilization. There also had been many real parrots in his life. One contemporary newspaper story told of one man's parrot obsession, which may have been the inspiration for Flaubert's short story "Un Cœur simple." Talk of a parrot's empty perch in Flaubert's novel *L'Éducation sentimentale* (1869; *A Sentimental Education*, 1898) leads Braithwaite to discuss the way people approach the past; he also discusses

a number of dogs that had appeared in Flaubert's life and works.

Braithwaite expresses his dislike of coincidences but follows this with an account of what may or may not have been a coincidental discovery by Flaubert: that of a business card belonging to someone from his home town of Rouen, a card that turns up at the Great Pyramid in Egypt. Braithwaite then denounces literary critics for their tendency to point out authors' errors. He especially focuses on the work of French literature specialist Enid Starkie, who comments on the color of Emma Bovary's eyes in the famous novel by Flaubert, *Madame Bovary* (1857).

Braithwaite is on a ferry crossing the English Channel, commenting on seagulls, bilingual trash-can signs, misspellings of Flaubert's name, the seasons preferred by older people, the different look of the light in France, various French customs, and Flaubert's disdain for the notion of progress. He also notes that he has a true story he could tell about his own wife, Ellen, but instead talks more about Flaubert and then about himself, revealing that he is a doctor in his sixties who has never killed a patient; nor had he killed his wife, he says. He also muses about what books he would ban if he were literary dictator, and about the difficulty of knowing the past. He also says he finds it difficult to talk directly about himself.

Braithwaite talks about the role of trains in Flaubert's life and works; he also talks about the books Flaubert had planned but never wrote and about the life plans he never carried out. He next defends Flaubert against a variety of charges by critics and suggests that serious admirers of authors, though they may seek to know their vices, will also seek to defend them, more so than husbands or wives will defend their spouses.

After mentioning in passing that Flaubert's mistress, Louise Colet, had been something of a pest in her demands on Flaubert, Braithwaite muses that this may simply be because Flaubert's version of events is all that remains. Braithwaite then imagines Colet's version of her affair with Flaubert. He finally tells the story of his own wife, who, it turns out, was an adulterer who committed suicide. He then muses on loneliness and grief and expresses an inability to explain his wife's adultery or her suicide. He also notes that, technically, he did kill her, because she died only after he "pulled the plug" on her in the hospital.

Finally, Braithwaite discusses the mystery of the stuffed parrots. He revisits the two museums, consults a Flaubert scholar, and goes to see the bird collection at the Museum of Natural History. The result of his searches is inconclusive.

Critical Evaluation:

Julian Barnes published four works of fiction, including two detective novels under the pseudonym Dan Kavanagh, before *Flaubert's Parrot*, but he had the most success with the latter. The novel has remained his best-known and most admired work. From the beginning, however, debates have ensued about what sort of work it is. Some early reviewers had said it is not a novel at all, but "the antithesis of a novel," and it is certainly an unconventional novel, containing such things as chronologies of the life of writer Gustave Flaubert, an examination paper based on Flaubert's life and works, and catalogs of animals, trains, and commonly held ideas related to Flaubert. The novel also contains a denunciation of literary critics, but it also includes some sensitive literary criticism about Flaubert's writing, especially of the story "Un coeur simple," in which Flaubert's parrot appears.

The parrot loosely unifies the novel, but only loosely. The book's dislocations and mixing of genres, along with its emphasis on the difficulty of knowing the past, have led several commentators to classify it as a postmodernist novel, a view disputed by Merritt Moseley. He argues that while postmodernism posits a universe in which nothing can be known and in which all questions are undecidable, Barnes's novel merely suggests that it is difficult, not impossible, to know things. Moseley notes, too, that the character in the novel who comes closest to the postmodernist view, and who states that "every so often we are tempted to throw up our hands and declare that history is merely another literary genre," is not Barnes but Geoffrey Braithwaite. Braithwaite is a character whose slowly revealed story shows him to be someone who might have a special reason for saying the past cannot be understood.

There are actually two competing stories in the novel, or one story hidden beneath a series of philosophical explorations and conjectures. In the early parts of the novel,

Braithwaite, who is so hidden that he does not reveal his name until the third chapter, muses about such issues as whether the past can be known, why an author's admirers seek out relics from an author's life rather than being content with his or her books, whether writers are like parrots, and why it is easier to feel close to a dead author than to one's own friends. He also provides an odd assortment of information and analyses about the life and writings of Flaubert.

The philosophical or critical side of the novel helps to make it quite unconventional, though perhaps in line with such philosophical works of fiction as Leo Tolstoy's *Voyna i mir* (1865-1869; *War and Peace*, 1886) or Thomas Mann's *Der Zauberberg* (1924; *The Magic Mountain*, 1927). What gradually emerges, however, is the second side of the novel, the more conventional story, in which Braithwaite haltingly discusses himself and especially his relationship with his late wife, who was a serial adulterer who killed herself.

In one early chapter, chapter 3, the story side predominates. Braithwaite describes American academic Ed Winterton as having an air of failure about him. The notable thing about their interactions is that Winterton is the one who always triumphs in the end. Both Winterton and Braithwaite want to buy a book by Russian writer Ivan Turgenev, and it is Winterton who gets it, leaving Braithwaite to comment later that Winterton has his copy of Turgenev.

Later, Winterton manages to frustrate Braithwaite completely, tantalizing him with information about a cache of letters that Braithwaite is sure can be turned into a monumental discovery about Flaubert, only to tell him that he has burned the letters because that is what Flaubert said should be done with them. In addition, all the interesting information he conveys to Braithwaite about what was in the letters may be a lie because one of the letters had indicated that if anyone asks what is in them, those who ask should be told whatever they want to hear.

It is this frustrated, unhappy man Braithwaite, deprived of his chance at fame through a Flaubert discovery and left to brood over the actions of his unfaithful and suicidal wife, who produces the philosophical maxims sprinkled throughout the book. Braithwaite does not understand the past, and he suggests that the past cannot be understood. He is angry and full of frustrations. He denounces literary critics and presents a list of types of books that should be banned. He is melancholy, and he dismisses all the activities of ferry passengers, and perhaps the whole human race, as stupid and pointless.

Still, the philosophical musings in the novel are usually interesting, and they may even reflect the views of Barnes; or they may not. Like so much in this novel, it is difficult to tell what his views are. One of the points of the book—though again, one has to ask, is the point that of Barnes or of Braithwaite?—is that everything can look different when viewed from a different perspective: hence, the chapter giving Louise Colet's view of her affair with Flaubert to counter the more generally received view; and the competing chronologies in chapter 2, one of which suggests that Flaubert had a highly successful life while the other suggests he was an abject failure.

Braithwaite quotes Flaubert as discovering that life is mixed; life is not a simple choice between kings and pigs, fulfillment and failure. To the contrary, for example, there are "swinish kings and regal hogs." So, too, is this novel mixed. It is both a collection of thought-provoking maxims and the tale of the sad man who produces them. Readers may take the maxims seriously or may dismiss them as the work of a crank. Perhaps Barnes would have wanted his readers to do both.

Sheldon Goldfarb

Further Reading

Guignery, Vanessa. *The Fiction of Julian Barnes.* New York: Palgrave Macmillan, 2006. Provides an excellent assessment of Barnes's literary works, including *Flaubert's Parrot*, and presents a compilation of the interpretation of Barnes's works by other critics. Describes *Flaubert's Parrot* as a postmodernist experiment.

Holmes, Frederick M. *Julian Barnes.* New York: Palgrave Macmillan, 2009. Sees *Flaubert's Parrot* as an autumnal novel about loss and displacement and also as a metafictional work about itself.

Moseley, Merritt. "Julian Barnes's *Flaubert's Parrot.*" In *A Companion to the British and Irish Novel, 1945-2000*, edited by Brian W. Shaffer. New York: Blackwell, 2005. Argues that the novel is not postmodernist. Traces its reception, including the discussions of whether it is a novel at all, and explores what Barnes is doing in this book.

_____. *Understanding Julian Barnes.* Columbia: University of South Carolina Press, 1997. Provides background on Barnes, noting his longtime interest in France and Flaubert, and discusses various aspects of the novel.

Pateman, Matthew. *Julian Barnes.* Tavistock, England: Northcote House/British Council, 2002. Discusses the significance of the parrot quest in *Flaubert's Parrot*, relating that quest to the detective genre Barnes also writes in. Sees Barnes's novel as a narrative unifier. Also analyzes the narrator's character.

Rubinson, Gregory J. *The Fiction of Rushdie, Barnes, Winterson, and Carter: Breaking Cultural and Literary Boundaries in the Work of Four Postmodernists.* Jefferson, N.C.: McFarland, 2005. Considers *Flaubert's Parrot* a postmodernist work of mockery, genre mixing, and intertextual references. Argues that the narrator is an ineffectual cuckold, in contrast to the stereotypical hard-boiled detective.

The Flies

Author: Mariano Azuela (1873-1952)
First published: Las moscas, 1918 (English translation, 1956)
Type of work: Novel
Type of plot: Historical realism
Time of plot: Early twentieth century
Locale: Mexico

Principal characters:
MARTA REYES TÉLLEZ, a widow in her sixties
RUBÉN,
ROSITA, and
MATILDE, her son and daughters
DONACIANO RÍOS, a government officer
GENERAL MALACARA, an army officer opposing the revolutionary leader
VENUSTIANO CARRANZA, a revolutionist and military leader
SEÑOR DOCTOR, the town physician
RODOLFO BOCANEGRA, a lawyer
DON SINFOROSO, a former lieutenant in the federalist army

The Story:

In his struggle to wrest the Mexican presidency from Victoriano Huerta, Venustiano Carranza lays siege to Querétaro, a town to the north of Mexico City. Querétaro is in chaos. People flee to the train station, hoping to escape Carranza's squadrons. Among those thousands, Marta, her two daughters, and her son seek space on the train; however, their efforts are fruitless. The crowd separates them until Rosita's voice catches Marta's and Matilde's attention. Rosita and Rubén manage to convince a doctor to allow them to travel in the medical car. The doctor opposes Marta's and Matilde's traveling with them, but Matilde declares that she has permission from General Malacara, an officer in charge.

Marta and her family tell her fellow passengers about the siege by Carranza's army. The army took over the best houses, schools, and even the churches for military use. The cathedral was stripped of all valuables and turned into a hospital. Everyone agrees that greed is the worst enemy of the revolution—and the reason for its failure. The conversation is interrupted by the arrival of General Malacara, who, to Rosita's surprise, comes with two women. General Malacara was flirting with Rosita; she feels that his attentions are serious.

The train travels all night with no problems, but almost everyone fears an attack by Carranza's forces. Marta and her daughters prepare breakfast for the doctor; they believe that he is an important man, or at least one with money. The men continue their political discussion. The train suddenly stops near Irapuato, a town southwest of Mexico City. During an attempt to learn why the train stopped, Don Sinforoso insults a soldier, who threatens the old man with a rifle. Don Sinforoso's friends take him away from the soldier.

Rosita flirts with the doctor, who, surprised by her friendliness, confronts her with the rumor that General Malacara courted her. Malacara assures Marta that his young women companions are distant relatives. Their conversation is interrupted by news about reasons for the delay: The northbound trains were derailed by a blockade, and hundreds of boilers are burning. General Malacara invites Marta and her daughters to an automobile ride around town. To his surprise, Marta declines the invitation, claiming that the doctor already invited the women.

The doctor does not own a car; instead, he owns a horse cart. The women display their displeasure. They climb up into the cart only when they are sure that General Malacara cannot see them. At Irapuato, people are evacuating the town because they fear that Pancho Villa lost the battle to Carranza. Rubén leaves to find Quiñones, a friend connected to Obregón, Carranza's strongman. The women buy food with the doctor's money, and they promise to pay him back when Rubén returns from looking for his friend. They also make him pay for boots for Rosita. When Matilde also wants boots, the doctor shows them his empty wallet. Marta takes that action as an insult, and she leaves the doctor behind, with a promise that they will pay him later.

They see General Malacara's car approaching. Rosita again flirts with Malacara, denying any sentimental interest in the doctor. The women want Malacara to introduce them to Villa, who has a reputation for kindness. They plan to ask Villa for money, food, and passes to Juarez City. If Villa loses power, the women will have spent the money, while Rubén, aided by Quiñones, will be working on Carranza's side. Malacara promises to arrange an interview with Villa, and he takes them to buy shoes. While they are in the store, Rubén arrives with good news: Rubén saw Quiñones, and Quiñones can help them. Rubén claims that he left his wallet behind, so Malacara also buys shoes for Rubén. On their way back to the train, Marta asks Malacara to take them to the governor's personal car, claiming that the doctor flirted with Rosita.

Dissension among the supporters of Villa takes place. Men who swore loyalty to Villa decide to stay in Irapuato, so that the people from the town will think that they belong to the Carranza forces, and the Carranza men, when they come, will think that they are local citizens.

Marta and children arrive at the train station in search of Malacara. They are accompanied by Quiñones, who makes loud comments against Villa. A soldier overhears them and, by mistake, arrests Rubén, who is released when the women show proof that they are Villa followers; the proof is passes and Villa currency, presumably given to them by Villa. After the incident, they cannot find Malacara, but they find the doctor and again pretend friendship. Once in the hospital car, it is decided that Rubén should stay in the town in order to proceed with their plans. As the train rolls away from the town, military police suddenly climb into the wagons, as if escaping.

Critical Evaluation:

Considered the initiator of the literary movement known as the Novel of the Mexican Revolution, Mariano Azuela offers in his works an eyewitness account of historical incidents in the Revolution of 1910. A revolutionary ideologue, Azuela was an army surgeon in Francisco (Pancho) Villa's guerrilla forces from 1910 to 1920. His writing depicts his experiences as a doctor and as a revolutionary. In 1941, Azuela received a national award for his literary craft. His active participation in the political arena won for him a reputation as a founding father of modern Mexican society. He was buried with other heroes of the revolution in an official ceremony in Mexico City.

Azuela's novel of the Mexican Revolution belongs to the literary trend of realism, which sometimes offers a photographic depiction. Azuela presents the revolution's struggle against oppression by the former power structure. His simple, direct literary style documents the revolution as the first Latin American armed movement of the twentieth century. Aware of the fact that the revolution produced radical changes in the social core of Mexican life, Azuela presents the movement in a positive light. His characters are representative of those involved in the political reorganization that leads to a new group in power as the economic center shifts from millionaire landowners to the peasant class.

The new literature of writers such as Azuela incorporates the political themes reflected in the motto "land for all." These writers propose an examination of the new ruling class's role in the shaping of contemporary Mexican society. Their works also offer harsh criticisms of the revolution, and they constantly monitor the movement, praising its successes but also denouncing its irregularities.

Azuela assumes the tasks of documenting, acclaiming, or censuring the revolutionary events that he has witnessed. His analysis differs from that of other writers, however, as he is clearly inspired by socialist political theories of justice for the working masses. With the rational precision of a scientist, Azuela conducts a detailed observation of the characters involved in the reshaping of Mexican society, as promoted by the revolution. Azuela documents these changes, which are diverse and controversial, especially those related to landowners' loss of power (political and economic). Azuela accomplishes this by becoming a newspaper reporter. His numerous articles published in Mexican and Spanish newspapers in the United States are the work of an eyewitness.

Azuela is not, however, a historian. His training as a reporter provides him with material for documentation of scenes of the revolution in a literary form known as *costumbrismo*, an early genre of realist literature that reproduces everyday customs and incidents of historical relevance that create the spirit of an age. By means of careful reproduction of revolutionary times, Azuela aims to achieve a twofold purpose: to explore the significance of the revolution as a historical occurrence of worldwide importance, and to bring in fresh literary material that offers a metaphorical exploration of human behavior.

The Flies brings together a collection of stories at the moment when Francisco Villa and Venustiano Carranza, two legendary revolutionary leaders, were fighting for political power. Although these men do not appear in the text, their presence is strongly portrayed by characters who represent their leaders' political platforms. For instance, characters who take advantage of others (such as Marta and her children) reflect Carranza's ruthless ambitions for the Mexican presidency—in clear disregard of Villa's and other revolutionary leaders' services in deposing the brutal Victoriano Huerta.

The plot, although simple, reflects the strong personalities involved in the revolutionary fighting. *The Flies* exposes those who oppose the revolution solely because of their loss of wealth and social prestige. By contrast, the lower classes, in search of a better life, illustrate Francisco Villa's strong ethical values. Although the characters of the lower classes are scarce in *The Flies*, they are true heroes because they stand for positive moral values. On the other hand, the upperclass protagonists are parasites and opportunists. These formerly respected individuals are compared to flies, hanging together in a desperate attempt to survive by means of their old tricks.

Azuela's characters are not, however, caricatures. They are clearly Mexicans bound to a particular historical movement who, by their relation to that movement, would help or hinder the creation of a new society. His well-researched literary works promote the revolution as a key movement in the shaping of the modern Mexican psyche.

Rafael Ocasio

Further Reading

Dean, James Seay. "Extreme Unction for Past Power and Glory: Four Fictions on the Mexican Revolution." *Revista de Estudios Hispánicos* 17, no. 1 (January, 1983): 89-106. A comparative study of Azuela's novels and of novels by Malcolm Lowry, Luis Martín Guzmán, and Graham Greene, all of whose works are deeply influenced by historical events surrounding the Mexican Revolution.

Herbst, Gerhard R. *Mexican Society as Seen by Mariano Azuela.* New York: Abra Ediciones, 1977. Azuela's novels of the Mexican Revolution are studied for historical, eyewitness accuracy. Focuses on Azuela's use of realist techniques in his descriptions of key historical incidents of the revolution.

Leal, Luis. *Mariano Azuela.* New York: Twayne, 1971. An excellent introduction to Azuela's life and works. Offers an analysis of his works and a strong biographical and historical background.

Martínez, Eliud. *The Art of Mariano Azuela: Modernism in "La malhora," "El desquite," "La luciérnaga."* Pittsburgh, Pa.: Latin American Literary Review Press, 1980. Azuela is considered a precursor of Latin American modernism, one of the first literary movements of the twentieth century. This modernist analysis of three representative novels focuses on Azuela's interest in the Mexican Revolution.

Schedler, Christopher. "Mariano Azuela: Migratory Modernism." In *Border Modernism: Intercultural Readings in American Literary Modernism*. New York: Routledge, 2002. Schedler compares the works of Mexican, Native American, and Chicano modernists with their European and Anglo-American counterparts. He concludes that Azuela and other writers who worked in the borderlands of Mexico and the United States produced a new type of literature that sought to modernize the indigenous literary traditions of the Americas.

The Flies

Author: Jean-Paul Sartre (1905-1980)
First produced: Les Mouches, 1943; first published, 1943 (English translation, 1946)
Type of work: Drama
Type of plot: Existentialism
Time of plot: Antiquity
Locale: Argos, Greece

Principal characters:
ORESTES, Agamemnon's son and heir to the throne of Argos
ELECTRA, his sister
CLYTEMNESTRA, his mother
AEGISTHEUS, the ruler of Argos after Agamemnon's death
THE PEDAGOGUE, Orestes' tutor
ZEUS, the king of the gods
THE ERINYES, the Furies

The Story:

Fifteen years pass since the slaying of Agamemnon. Orestes, Agamemnon's son, arrives in Argos with his tutor. He travels under another name, for Aegistheus, who has ruled in Argos since killing Agamemnon, ordered him killed while he was still a child. Orestes, however, was saved and reared by wealthy Athenians. Orestes is eager to visit Argos, for his mother, Clytemnestra, now shares the throne with Aegistheus. His sister Electra is also still in Argos. Orestes arrives, not as one seeking vengeance but as a tourist. Young, rich, handsome, and well educated, he is free of obligations and commitments, light as air, and apparently reasonably happy to be so. He finds a city in which the atmosphere is leaden and oppressive. He receives no answer to his requests for directions, and the first person to address a word to him is an idiot. It is as though a conspiracy exists to exclude him from the affairs of the city.

The truth is that the people of Argos are so involved with their own problem that they are quite incapable of seeing beyond it. The problem from which they suffer is that they assumed a burden of collective guilt. Fifteen years before, they did nothing to prevent Agamemnon's death; instead of admitting their responsibility, they wrapped themselves up in remorse. This uniform pattern of behavior suits the god Zeus, since it holds Aegistheus's subjects in check and leaves little scope for personal initiative. Another sinister, persistent presence is swarms of flies, sent by the gods to plague the populace as a constant reminder of their guilt. Death seems to be curiously intermingled with life in this city of frightened people. Repentance is even institutionalized. Once a year, on the anniversary of Agamemnon's death, the "day of the dead" is announced.

One person in Argos, however, remains independent and defiant. Electra, though treated as a slave by her mother and Aegistheus, is rebellious. Contemptuous of the general fear and superstition, she lets it be known to Orestes, who did not yet reveal his true identity, that she lives only for the day when her brother will come to seek vengeance. At the same time, however, Electra is pathetic and occasionally childlike. While she vilifies Zeus with all her might, she also betrays her longing for warmth and affection in her questions about other cities of Greece. When Orestes asks her if she ever thinks of fleeing, she answers that she lacks the courage to do so because she will be afraid on the roads by herself. Electra, however, also has a fixed attitude. She feels a thirst for vengeance that does not ring true or confident when set alongside her gentleness in other matters. As is foreseeable, Orestes becomes sufficiently curious about the city, or sufficiently interested in the plight of his sister, to decide to remain a little longer in Argos.

At the beginning of the second act, the scene changes from Argos to a mountain slope outside the city. The people are gathered for the rites of the "day of the dead" and for the release of the dead from the underworld, for it is made known that a rock on the mountainside conceals the entrance to the underworld. Once a year, this rock is rolled back, and dead acquaintances of the people of Argos come back to torture the city's conscience. On this occasion, Aegistheus arrives late for the ceremonies, which he himself instituted. The solid, impenetrable fear of the crowd begins to give way to blind panic, as they feel quite helpless without some leadership when facing the presence of the dead. After Aegistheus appears and the stone is rolled back, the crowd—men, women, and even children—beg for pity and ask forgiveness for being alive.

Into this uncanny, grotesque, hysterical atmosphere steps Electra. Fired by what Orestes describes to her as happy, sunny towns elsewhere in Greece, she tells the crowd to throw off its burden of guilt. For a brief time, the assembled people listen hopefully. She, however, is no match for Zeus. Displaying his divine powers, he sends the stone that was supposed to bar the entrance to the underworld crashing against the steps of the temple built on the mountainside. Awed, the crowd turns against Electra.

In this sclerotic society, whose organization for fifteen years was hardened from above, no change from inside seems possible. Through contact with Orestes, Electra becomes enterprising enough to attempt a change. Electra's only weapon, however, is words, and her effort, though noble, is inevitably futile. It is to a considerable extent through Electra that Orestes becomes fully involved in the affairs of Argos and commits himself to a course of action. He reveals his identity to her. Electra, bewildered by the disproportion between her expectations and the Orestes she sees before her, cannot conceal her disappointment. The change is not sudden, but, more than ever, Orestes is conscious of his meaninglessness in Argos and elsewhere. Bitterly regretful, he says that he barely exists, for he is ignorant of the deep passions of living men and women.

He affirms that he wants to belong fully to the town and that he wishes to draw it to him. Still unsure of himself, however, he tries to appeal to a higher authority. Zeus, lurking in the background, is only too glad to suggest that Orestes continue in the path of humility. At this, Orestes rebels; he real-

izes that he must commit himself, that it is he who must make a decision. He decides that, in the circumstances, there is only one course that can be followed. He plans and executes the killing of Aegistheus and Clytemnestra.

In the end, in a speech to the people of Argos, Orestes claims that he killed for their sake, to free them. He proclaims that he assumes their guilt and that they need no longer be afraid. Taking the burden of guilt from the city, Orestes flees Argos. Electra, however, does not have the strength to follow Orestes. It is as though, in slaying Clytemnestra and Aegistheus, Orestes took away her one reason for living: her desire for vengeance. Zeus did not have much trouble in winning her over to the side of those who spend their lives in atonement. At the end of the play, Electra becomes credulous, tractable, repentant. No explanation is offered of where Orestes flees or of what happens to Argos.

Critical Evaluation:

The Flies, the first play by Jean-Paul Sartre to be presented to the public, was well received when it was staged in occupied Paris. If one bears in mind that the play is concerned with the problem of liberty, and that many of its references must have been pointedly topical in 1943, the interest it aroused is scarcely surprising. On the other hand, although *The Flies* has lost some of the immediacy of its appeal, the problem of liberty is not, of course, exclusive to any particular time period, and this play is still popular and frequently staged.

For Sartre, it is nonsense to speak of a universal human nature; only the situations in which human beings may find themselves can be universal. Indeed, all of his theater involves a character moving toward a choice or decision in relation or in opposition to a given situation. The success of Sartre's theater resides, at least in part, in his leaving his principal character or characters a considerable amount of freedom to develop in the course of the action. Moreover, he has successfully created situations that audiences often find familiar.

If his philosophical writings, such as *L'Être et le néant* (1943; *Being and Nothingness*, 1956), are difficult to understand, Sartre was nevertheless able to bring a wide audience to espouse the philosophical theory of existentialism. He accomplished this through striking statements and illustrations of his philosophy in both fiction, as seen in *La Nausée* (1938; *Nausea*, 1949), and theater. *The Flies* contends, through the hero's own discoveries, that existence and freedom, along with the need to act, constitute the existence of an individual.

The story of Orestes and Electra has been told many times in the theater, from different points of view. The Homeric myth of Orestes, driven by the Delphic oracle and by his sister, Electra, to avenge the murder of their father by killing their mother and her lover, is found in stylized form in the Greek tragedies of Aeschylus, Sophocles, and Euripides. Sartre, like other modern dramatists, draws variously on all three by freely adapting the myth to suit his purposes.

The Flies represents a moment of crisis and decision, since the central conflict consists of different ethical positions. In view of the fact that an existentialist situation must offer individuals the opportunity to make meaningful choices that will determine their acts, the problem of action is not merely the problem of what happens and why it happens, but the problem of commitment to a choice.

In the original myth, Orestes' actions are divinely ordered or forbidden, hence his dilemma as a thinking man confronted by religious power and arbitrariness as he tries to reconcile his relationship with the gods and to arrive at a possible meaning for human existence. The atheist Sartre, however, transforms these plays of fatality into a drama of choice that negates Judeo-Christian beliefs. No oracle is present to predict destiny, and no divine hand guides human events.

Before returning to Argos, Orestes led a life devoid of interest, devoid of purpose. Existentialism, however, posits that one's past has no influence on one's future because there is no cosmic time. The present is important, since it is a time of anguish and of choice—what Sartre calls respectively "nausea" and "commitment." When Orestes understands that he is free, he must act, but the act must represent the man he is committed to being. He performs a heinous crime, real, bloody, and horrible. The author provides his protagonist with a motive (to avenge his murdered father), but the real reason he kills is to validate his freedom. If, instead, he kills out of vengeance, he will have acted in bad faith and will find himself even more imprisoned.

Zeus appears in Argos to drive Orestes out of the city before he becomes aware of his true freedom to act, for Zeus knows that freedom destroys the power of the gods over humans. To Orestes, now liberated from social, moral, religious, and political barriers, Zeus can show his power only on objects. By transferring justice to earth, Sartre makes the myth more human, even humanistic, when Orestes asserts that Zeus is "not the king of man."

In the beginning of the story, Orestes is a stranger in his own country. However, through his willed double murder and his assumption of responsibility for it, not only does he show supreme love for the citizens of Argos by giving them freedom and by voluntarily offering himself to be punished in their place, but his metaphysical exile also disappears. He understands at last that his acts are his and only his, since

human beings are what they make of themselves. Furthermore, because they are irreversible, such acts are foreign to the traditional notions of good and evil.

It is significant that Sartre does not explore the dramatic potential of a confrontation between Orestes and Aegistheus, the murderer of his father. Instead, Sartre concentrates on the commitment Orestes makes in his decision to kill Aegistheus and Clytemnestra. This decision presents one of the main points of Sartre's philosophical theory. In choosing an action, Orestes defines himself. Existence, to Sartre, is the sum of one's actions, and Orestes begins to exist only when he involves himself in action. Being the only person responsible for his action and its consequences, Orestes cannot appeal to any higher authority for a justification or an excuse for the murders.

By means of a scene in which Jupiter warns Aegistheus of the danger to his life, Sartre also lays bare the workings of Aegistheus's mind. Aegistheus, though a ruler, is a victim of the image he has created for himself. Motivated by a love of order, all his actions have tended in that direction. Now, old and weary, prey to some of the fears and superstitions for which he is himself responsible, he looks forward gladly to death. The thought, however, that Orestes knows himself to be free can rouse Aegistheus to indignation, for this freedom constitutes a threat to order.

Set against this backdrop is Electra, Orestes' loyal and devoted sister. At first, she is passionately against her stepfather's reign and even suggests to Orestes the possibility of making a choice of action, but not an existentialist choice, since the choice of which she speaks is only one between retreat and vengeance. Understandably, after Aegistheus's death, she denies her participation in the assassination and accepts remorse and divine retribution: "I will be your creature and your slave. . . . I repent, Zeus, I bitterly repent." In this way, her conduct shows the worst example of bad faith.

The citizens are also not authentic in the existentialist way. While Electra wrongly believes that she was misled by Orestes, the citizens play at public confessions in blind conformity to collective remorse and in superstitious fear of words. They are told, but refuse to admit, that the plague is in fact no more than the imposition of responsibility on themselves from the outside, from the gods or from Aegistheus, and that they have the power to reject this allegedly superior order in recognition of humanity as the one and only value.

Besides a literary exposition of Sartre's philosophical ideas, *The Flies* can also be interpreted as a reference to the situation in France during the Nazi era. In this context, the flies represent the German occupiers; Zeus, as their leader trying to enforce his arbitrary rule on the French citizens through Aegistheus, obviously portrays Marshal Philippe Pétain, France's main collaborator with Adolf Hitler. That the French are willing to tolerate abuse and moral shame to survive is evident by their acceptance of the political status quo. Only Orestes and Electra are eager to resist the new order, although Electra is ultimately unable to withstand the physical and mental torture inherent in such a regime. For his part, Orestes proves by his actions that people are free and that dictators remain in power solely when no one rises to question their authority. In posing the central question of commitment, this drama foreshadows much of Sartre's postwar fiction.

"Critical Evaluation" by Pierre L. Horn

Further Reading

Champigny, Robert. *Sartre and Drama*. Birmingham, Ala.: French Literature Publications, 1982. After first developing a critical discussion based on Sartre's dramatic theories, this brief and well-argued monograph shows, by examining individual plays, that Sartre did not always put his theories into practice in his plays.

Contat, Michel, and Michel Rybalka, eds. *Sartre on Theater*. Translated by Frank Jellinek. New York: Pantheon Books, 1976. A handy anthology of various documents written by Sartre about the theater. Includes the jacket copy for the French publication of *The Flies* in book form, as well as excerpts of press interviews and articles pointing out the political content of this play.

McCall, Dorothy. *The Theatre of Jean-Paul Sartre*. New York: Columbia University Press, 1969. An excellent overview of Sartre's dramatic works with special emphasis on their philosophical, literary, psychological, and sociological ideas and values. Includes a useful bibliography.

O'Donohoe, Benedict. "Myth-Making: *Bariona: Ou, Le Fils du tonnerre, Les Mouches, Huis clos*." In *Sartre's Theatre: Acts for Life*. New York: Peter Lang, 2005. Reappraises Sartre's plays, including *The Flies*, drawing on his writings about philosophy, literature, and criticism. Situates each play in relation to Sartre's intellectual evolution and its broader historical context. Provides a survey of the journalistic and academic reception for each play.

Rickman, H. P. "The Death of God: Nietzsche's Influence on Sartre's *The Flies*." In *Philosophy in Literature*. Madison, N.J.: Fairleigh Dickinson University Press, 1996. Focuses on the philosophical ideas in the play.

Rowley, Hazel. *Tête-à-Tête: Simone de Beauvoir and Jean-Paul Sartre*. New York: HarperCollins, 2005. Rowley chronicles the relationship between the two French writers, discussing their writing, their politics, their philosophical legacy, and their commitment to each other. Includes bibliography and index.

Schilpp, Paul A., ed. *The Philosophy of Jean-Paul Sartre*. La Salle, Ill.: Open Court, 1981. Intelligent and scholarly presentation of the different aspects of Sartrean philosophy. Of particular interest to readers of *The Flies* are the chapters concerned with bad faith, authenticity, freedom, essence, and commitment.

Spoerri, Theophil. "The Structure of Existence: *The Flies*." In *Sartre: A Collection of Critical Essays*, edited by Edith Kern. Englewood Cliffs, N.J.: Prentice-Hall, 1962. An imaginative and penetrating interpretation exploring not only the play's main themes and characters but also the difficult obstacle of reconciling Orestes' ethical revolt with his love for his people.

The Floating Opera

Author: John Barth (1930-   )
First published: 1956; revised, 1967
Type of work: Novel
Type of plot: Psychological realism
Time of plot: 1930's
Locale: Maryland's eastern shore

Principal characters:
TODD ANDREWS, narrator of the novel and a lawyer in the town of Cambridge, Maryland
HARRISON MACK, Todd's friend
JANE MACK, Harrison's wife and Todd's mistress
JEANNINE MACK, the Macks' child and possibly Todd's daughter
CAPTAIN OSBORN JONES and MISTER HAECKER, roomers at the hotel where Todd lives

The Story:

Todd Andrews, the narrator, begins in 1954 to write the story of one important day in his life, June 21 or 22, 1937 (he cannot remember exactly which), the day he finally decided not to kill himself. *The Floating Opera* is not only the name of Todd's account of that day but also an important part of the narrative and a metaphor for the organization of the book. Todd imagines a kind of showboat that drifts up and down a waterway, moved by the currents and the tide. The boat carries actors who put on a show for the people along the shore. The boat is moving, so people see and hear only pieces of the show. Todd writes that life is like that, and so is his book. Such a showboat, also called *The Floating Opera*, figures in the climax of the book, for Todd originally plans to blow up himself and all the people on the boat during a performance.

Todd is a lawyer who lives in a hotel, where he sometimes has visits from his lover, Jane Mack, the wife of one of his friends and clients, Harrison Mack. The affair began some years earlier when Harrison and Jane wanted to prove that they had a liberal marriage by coercing Todd into sleeping with Jane. After the affair began, Harrison found that he did not feel as casual about sharing his wife with another man as he thought he would, and Jane also felt guilty, but the relationship between Todd and Jane continued in a haphazard manner for years. Jane has a daughter, Jeannine, who may be Todd's daughter; no one is sure. On the morning of Todd's important day, Jane visited him in his room.

After visiting with two other roomers in the hotel, Captain Osborn Jones and Mister Haecker, Todd paid his rent for one day at the hotel desk as he always did. Todd lived at the hotel for years, so there was no apparent reason for paying his rent one day at a time, but Todd did so to remind himself each day that it might be his last. There would be no point in paying for more than one day. In fact, Todd had much evidence in his life that death could overtake him at any time. He remembered his father chopping the head off a chicken and then handing the carcass to Todd to help prepare for supper. Todd was in World War I and shared a frightening night in a foxhole with a German soldier. As morning approached, although Todd felt a renewed sense of humanity from his contact with the German, Todd killed the other soldier. During a service physical Todd found that he had a weak heart that might fail at any moment.

The most stunning reminder of the closeness of death was the suicide of Todd's father, who was despondent over his business failures. Todd's attempt to make sense of his father's death was the purpose of the manuscript on which Todd labored at night, the *Inquiry*. Although the *Inquiry* was supposed to be an explanation of the reasons behind Todd's father's suicide, it expanded to cover a number of related topics and filled several large containers in Todd's room. Todd also worked from time to time on a boat that he was as likely to finish as the *Inquiry*. He considered his work on the boat and on the *Inquiry* to be as hopeful as his paying his rent one day at a time was not; his life might end at any time, but it also might go on for a long time. No one can know which.

On Todd's important day, he decided that after years of living and thinking, he could find no reason why any course of action was better or worse than any other. Therefore, there was no reason to live, so he resolved in the morning to live the day ahead as he would any other and then to kill himself at its conclusion. This action was gratuitous, but Todd had a history of gratuitous behavior. Besides the killing of the German soldier, which might make some sense because both men were participants in a war, Todd also gave five thousand dollars to wealthy Colonel Morton, an action so unusual that it bedeviled the colonel. To vary his regular activities would suggest that there was some reason for his suicide, so Todd continued to conduct the business of his law firm.

At the end of the day, there was a performance on *The Floating Opera* at the harbor, which Todd and the Macks attended. Todd arranged his suicide by turning on the gas jets in a cabin on the boat and waiting for the explosion that would kill him and everyone else on board. After a time, during which there should have been an explosion but nothing happened, Todd gave up and left the boat, along with the rest of the audience. Someone perhaps came along and closed the gas jets; Todd never found out why the boat did not blow up. The event made him rethink his reasons for choosing suicide. If there was no reason to do anything, there was no reason to kill oneself. One may as well go on living.

Critical Evaluation:

The Floating Opera is simultaneously funny, with a laugh on every page, and depressing, with a somber background that is difficult to dismiss even in the novel's most comic moments. Its narrator is a man who at one point in his life decides that he does not want to live and acts to kill himself. The day is shadowed over with dread as he moves toward that tragic conclusion. The dread is felt by the reader, not by Todd Andrews, who carries on as if the day were like any other. The reader knows that Todd does not kill himself, because he survives to write his narrative. Furthermore, Todd announces early in his story that the key day is really the day that he decides not to kill himself, although the day begins with the decision to commit suicide. Throughout the book Todd presents his reasons for self-destruction, yet the reader is held in psychological suspension, knowing that all the reasons Todd advances, with the attention to detail characteristic of a lawyer, will somehow be swept away. There is hope in the despair and laughter in the tears.

One of the literary antecedents of *The Floating Opera* is Laurence Sterne's novel *The Life and Opinions of Tristram Shandy, Gent.* (1759-1767), in which a first-person narrator, Tristram Shandy, sets out to tell the story of one day in his life—the day he was born. As Tristram begins to describe his mother, his father, and his uncle in order to explain the circumstances of his birth, he digresses to incidents before his birth and during his life to fill out the history of these other characters. After several hundred pages, in the course of which the reader finds out what kind of a person Tristram is, he is still no closer to his announced purpose than when he started. The general effect and most of the digressions are comic, but the novel makes a serious point about time, which is that time is not outside but inside. Each human being contains all the moments of his or her life. Many of the moments of one's past may have more impact on one's life than what is occurring in the present. *The Floating Opera* uses the same rambling, digression-filled approach to make the same point.

A profound moment for Todd is his father's suicide. Todd finds his father's blackened, bulgy-eyed hanged body, cuts it down, and carries it to a bedroom. Although Todd presents these details with the same kind of control that characterizes his handling of the rest of the novel, this event obviously has had a powerful impact upon him. It is an example of the past's dominance over the present. One's first source of love and assurance is one's parents, and when a parent commits suicide, a child feels the ultimate withdrawal of love and experiences the worst act of rejection. Todd had, even before his father's death, come to think of sex as little consolation. While making love for the first time with his high school friend Betty June Gunter, Todd looks in a mirror, sees how ridiculous the two of them look, and begins laughing.

Sex does not distract Todd; friendship and love do not help deter Todd from his goal of suicide either. When Jane Mack breaks off their affair, this disruption causes Todd no particular grief, and he resumes their relationship with the same indifference. He shows no special regard for Jeannine, the little girl whose father he might be. This point marks an important difference between the first version of the novel and the second. In the second version, Todd arranges not only for his own death but almost takes seven hundred people with him. The original publishers thought that readers would reject a mass murderer, so they had Barth change the ending to one in which Todd plans to destroy only the part of the boat that he is in. Moreover, he is interrupted by a crew member

who finds him and turns off the gas jets, giving Todd the news that Jeannine has become ill. Thus, Todd, prior to his attempted suicide, is concerned about the lives of others and is brought back from the brink of death by ordinary human concern for his possible daughter. Some of the reviewers of the first version of *The Floating Opera* thought that ending to be sentimental, unconvincing, and inconsistent with Todd's character.

The ending that Barth preferred all along and that he used in the second version fits Todd better. He is interested not in people and emotions, but in ideas. If nothing has any ultimate meaning, then there is no reason for Todd to try to preserve the lives of the hundreds of people on the boat, any more than there is a reason for him to preserve his own. The absence of the explosion in both versions gives Todd a chance to make a further observation: If nothing has any ultimate meaning or value, there is no point in choosing a course of action based on negativity, be is asceticism, cynicism, or suicide. To choose such a course of action would be to impute ultimate meaning to the theory that there is no ultimate meaning. It is reasonable, even logical, to go on living in the midst of the mystery of life.

Jim Baird

Further Reading

Bowen, Zack. *A Reader's Guide to John Barth.* Westport, Conn.: Greenwood Press, 1994. Contains a chapter on *The Floating Opera* with emphasis on the book's relationship to twentieth century philosophical and artistic concerns.

Clavier, Berndt. *John Barth and Postmodernism: Spatiality, Travel, Montage.* New York: Peter Lang, 2007. Clavier analyzes Barth's work from a perspective of postmodernism and metafiction, focusing on theories of space and subjectivity. He argues that the form of montage is a possible model for understanding Barth's fiction.

LeClair, Thomas. "John Barth's *The Floating Opera*: Death and the Craft of Fiction." *Texas Studies in Literature and Language* 14, no. 4 (Winter, 1973): 711-730. Focuses on Todd Andrews as narrator of his story and how his storytelling ultimately helps to save him from suicide.

Morrell, David. *John Barth: An Introduction.* University Park: Pennsylvania State University Press, 1976. The chapter on *The Floating Opera* notes carefully the differences between the two versions and comments on the philosophical values expressed in the novel.

Schickel, Richard. "*The Floating Opera.*" *Critique* 6, no. 2 (Fall, 1963): 53-67. This essay appeared before the second version of the novel, and it assesses the weaknesses of the first version, which the second version corrects.

Scott, Steven D. *The Gamefulness of American Postmodernism: John Barth and Louise Erdrich.* New York: Peter Lang, 2000. Scott applies postmodernist theories to analyze Barth's work. He theorizes on the motifs of play and

game in American postmodernist fiction generally, eventually focusing on "gamefulness" in the writings of Barth and Louise Erdrich.

Walkiewicz, E. P. *John Barth.* Boston: Twayne, 1986. A brief introduction to all of Barth's work, with sections on *The Floating Opera.*

The Floating World

Author: Cynthia Kadohata (1956-   )
First published: 1989
Type of work: Novel
Type of plot: Psychological realism
Time of plot: 1950's to 1960's
Locale: Arkansas and the West Coast of the United States

Principal characters:
OLIVIA ANN "LIVVIE" OSAKA, the teenage protagonist
OBĀSAN, Livvie's maternal grandmother
LAURA OSAKA, Livvie's young mother
CHARLIE-O (CHARLES OSAKA), Livvie's stepfather
BEN, WALKER, and PETER OSAKA, Livvie's younger brothers
JACK, Livvie's birth father
TAN (DAVID TANIZAKI), Livvie's first boyfriend
SHANE (TARO NAGASAKI), the lover of Livvie's mother
ANDY CHIN, Livvie's boyfriend
ROGER, Chin's criminal boss

The Story:

Olivia Ann Osaka, or Livvie, says that she did not like her maternal grandmother, Hisae Fujiitano, who had died in a motel bathroom when Livvie was twelve years old. While remembering her grandmother's life, Livvie also reflects on how the names in her own family reflect assimilation in the United States through the generations. When her grandmother had emigrated from Japan to America, her father had chosen a new last name—Fujiitano—for good luck. During World War II, all the children got American first names in addition to their Japanese ones. Livvie's mother's name, Mariko, for example, was changed to Laura. Livvie herself does not have a Japanese first name, but she always uses the formal Japanese term *obāsan* ("grandmother") when referring to the formidable old woman tormenting her, even after death.

Obāsan uses the term *ukiyo*, Japanese for "floating world," when referring to the world of Livvie and her parents and three younger brothers. Originally, the term had applied to the pleasure quarters of old Japanese cities. For Livvie, the floating world means life on the road in the Western United States, as her family travels from menial job to menial job in

many small towns, and the highway is her constant companion. Livvie believes that her family is steady, and the world floats around them.

Livvie has an ambiguous relationship with Obāsan. The seventy-six-year-old, cigar-smoking woman had had three husbands and seven lovers; the last one died just three years ago. Obāsan requires chores of Livvie and boxes her ears if she is slow at those chores, but when a strange man threatens Livvie in a town, Obāsan chases him off with a stick that is so hard, her palm gets bruised, showing her love for Livvie.

Livvie is out in the field with her eight-year-old brother, Ben, the outgoing one, and her six-year-old brother, Walker, the silent one, all accompanied by Obāsan; two-year-old Peter stays at home. The grandmother scolds the kids for being bullied into buying apples from a white farmer. She also pinches Livvie's wrist.

Later at night, Livvie discovers her grandmother huddled on the bathroom floor of the motel room where the family is staying. Obāsan repeatedly pleads with Livvie to get her mother. Livvie knows her grandmother is dying, but she ignores her pleas and goes back to sleep. In the morning,

Obāsan is dead, and Livvie feels guilty. None of the four grandchildren cries at Obāsan's funeral. Livvie feels a ghostly presence departing, yet much like her grandmother's diaries, which Livvie inherits, Obāsan continues to be a presence in Livvie's life.

Livvie's stepfather, Charles Osaka, or Charlie-O, decides to move the family to a small town in Arkansas, where he and a fellow Japanese American have bought a car-repair shop. The family embarks on the long road trip. It is obvious that Charlie-O and his young wife, Livvie's thirty-year-old mother, Laura, have problems in their relationship. From Obāsan, Livvie had earlier found out that Charlie-O had married her mother when she was seven months pregnant with Livvie, but she had been pregnant by another man, who was married.

After witnessing a roadside accident involving a woman passerby and a bus, the Osakas finally arrive in Gibson, Arkansas. There, the family is visited by Laura's lover from Oregon, Shane, whose real name is Taro Nagasaki. Thirteen-year-old Livvie considers him the enemy, and on one occasion throws his shoe in the incinerator in their garden as he comes to visit; he then fades out of the family's life.

As Livvie grows up with a circle of teenage friends, she learns more about the profession of the majority of the Japanese Americans working in the town nearby. They are experts in determining the sex of newborn chickens at the state's industrial-size hatcheries. This task requires dexterity, concentration, and a determination to work long, taxing hours. Hatcheries use either male or female chickens, but not both; the opposite sex is drowned as useless.

At the age of sixteen, Livvie gets her first job at the hatchery, inoculating chicks. She also falls in love with Tan (David Tanizaki), who works odd jobs at the hatchery, where his father is a professional "chicken sexer." Livvie and Tan decide to make love, their first time, and do so in Tan's parents' bedroom while the adults are away. They continue their love affair until Tan's father loses his job and Tan moves with his family to Indiana, floating out of Livvie's life.

After graduating from high school and after an emotional farewell party thrown by her parents, Livvie moves to Los Angeles to establish California residency for college there. However, she gets sidetracked by her job selling lamps and by falling in love with Andy Chin. Andy, a Chinese American, wrecks cars for a living. He is a small-time criminal employed by a white boss, Roger, who takes on assignments damaging cars in staged accidents for insurance fraud or for revenge. While Livvie loves Andy, she does not approve of his job. A visit by her brother Walker, who had been involved

with a failed suicide plot at home, brings on memories of their early life spent on the road.

When Livvie is twenty-one years old, she learns that her birth father, whom she calls Jack, has died. She agrees to run his vending-machine route until his widow can sell it. Initially, Livvie is joined by her stepfather, Charlie-O, who bonds again with Livvie, wishing her to be happy. Charlie-O smiles when Livvie assures him of her happiness; he then says farewell halfway into checking on the vending-machine route.

At one of the most remote locations on the route, Livvie sees the ghost of her father Jack as a young man servicing his route. The ghost does not speak, but Livvie does, telling him of her impending separation from Andy. Livvie feels she has made peace with her father, and his image fades away.

Critical Evaluation:

Cynthia Kadohata's first novel, *The Floating World*, is a straightforward, unsentimental look at a Japanese American family's unusual passage along the back roads of 1950's rural America, brought to life by the twelve-year-old protagonist's eye for telling details. The novel was influential immediately upon being published in 1989, the same year of Amy Tan's best-selling novel *The Joy Luck Club*. Both novels promised readers a fascinating look at the Asian American experience.

Teenage protagonist Livvie provides a rich picture of the quirkiness of her odd and mean grandmother. Through her remembrance of family stories, Livvie also indirectly provides the larger historical context of Japanese immigration to the United States and the issues faced by Japanese immigrants. Here, the reader quickly realizes that the cantankerous grandmother must have been a strong woman rebelling against equally strong societal conventions. The point is brought home by Livvie when the grandmother's rough and even abusive exterior is contrasted with her proven deep love for her grandchildren.

With *The Floating World*, Kadohata effectively combines a road novel with a coming-of-age narrative. There are powerful, vivid images of life on the road; for example, a motel's neon lights suddenly switch to no vacancy as its last room is rented out for the night. One of the most remarkable aspects of the novel is that Livvie appears to be most happy when the family is moving about, when it passes through a nighttime rural America that the sleeping mainstream society hardly acknowledges. She relishes being on the road to some destination that is not as important as the journey itself.

Personal pain, too, inhabits Livvie's life and the lives of members of her family. Whereas, for example, the strong Obāsan emerges as a woman who confronts life as it is, her daughter, Laura, lives a life fraught with much more pain and ambiguity. Pregnant at the age of seventeen by the married Japanese American small-business operator for whom she works as a maid, she has to forget her ambitions. Obāsan saves her daughter from social ruin (in 1950's America) by finding a man for her to marry.

The Floating World achieves a sense of closure, despite its episodic nature and its somewhat disjointed and emotionally detached narration, which some critics have linked to a postmodernist style. At the end of a nine-year journey, from the age of nine to age twenty-one, Livvie tells of a meeting with the ghost of her dead birth father, Jack. With this finality, Livvie makes some kind of peace. The novel opens with the foretold death of Livvie's grandmother and ends with her meeting her late father.

Most criticism of *The Floating World* was enthusiastically positive, but Kadohata was hurt most deeply by one Asian American critic who accused her of painting a misleading picture of Japanese American grandmothers. Kadohata was thrown into a controversy over the politically correct "duties" of an Asian American author. She reacted vehemently by asserting her freedom to create a unique character of her own who did not have to stand in for a whole ethnic group. Kadohata deliberately set her next novel, *In the Heart of the Valley of Love* (1992), in an unconvincing future Los Angeles of 2052, and even moved into fantasy with *The Glass Mountains* (1995), all in an attempt to free herself creatively. Her move backfired, leading to poor sales for the fantasy novel. Kadohata's fortunes revived only when her young adult novel *Kira-Kira* (2004) won the Newbery Medal in 2005, reviving Kadohata's early literary fame with *The Floating World* and helping to establish her as an influential contemporary American author.

R. C. Lutz

Further Reading

Cutter, Martha. "Finding a 'Home' in Translation: John Okada's *No-No Boy* and Cynthia Kadohata's *The Floating World*." In *Lost and Found in Translation: Contemporary Ethnic American Writing and the Politics of Language Diversity*. Chapel Hill: University of North Carolina Press, 2005. Cutter's academic analysis argues that Kadohata uses postmodern narrative techniques to give Livvie a means for survival in a hostile mainstream world. Examines the themes of family and home as they are presented in the two novels.

Kadohata, Cynthia. "Interview with Cynthia Kadohata." Interview by Hsiu-chuan Lee. *MELUS* 32, no. 2 (Summer, 2007): 165-186. In an extensive interview, Kadohata relates her perception of her identity as an Asian American and how her Japanese ancestry has shaped her writing. Good coverage of *The Floating World*. Focuses on Kadohata's views of Livvie and Obāsan as well as the novel's central issues. An excellent bibliography lists major reviews of the book.

Kafka, Phillipa. "Cynthia Kadohata, *The Floating World*: 'I Like the Diabolical Quality, the Clarity of Admitting I Want.'" In *(Un)doing the Missionary Position: Gender Asymmetry in Contemporary Asian American Women's Writing*. Westport, Conn.: Greenwood Press, 1997. Focuses on the family dynamics, cultural attitudes, and social roles in *The Floating World*.

Nyman, Jopi. "The Hybridity of the Asian American Subject in Cynthia Kadohata's *The Floating World*." In *Reconstructing Hybridity*, edited by Joel Kuortti and Jopi Nyman. Amsterdam: Rodopi Press, 2007. Nyman's scholarly essay discusses the role of ghosts in the novel. Also claims that the lack of a "home" in the novel indicates life in a broken, dangerous, and traumatic world.

Pearlman, Mickey. "Cynthia Kadohata." In *Listen to Their Voices: Twenty Interviews with Women Who Write*. New York: Norton, 1993. A sympathetic, perceptive interview conducted a few years after publication of *The Floating World*. A good, accessible discussion of the novel and its development.

Wong, Sau-ling Cynthia. "The Politics of Mobility." In *Reading Asian American Literature*. Princeton, N.J.: Princeton University Press, 1993. Contains straightforward analysis of Kadohata's novel. Scholarly but generally accessible. Places the novel in the context of Asian American literature of its time.

Woo, Celestine. "Bicultural World Creation: Laurence Yep, Cynthia Kadohata, and Asian American Fantasy." In *Literary Gestures: The Aesthetic in Asian American Writing*, edited by Rocío G. Davis and Sue-Im Lee. Philadelphia: Temple University Press, 2006. Analyzes literary techniques that Kadohata uses to depict characters whose travels immerse them in diverse cultures. Also looks at characters' responses to being marginalized.

Flowers for Algernon

Author: Daniel Keyes (1927-   )
First published: 1966 (expanded from a 1959 novelette)
Type of work: Novel
Type of plot: Science fiction
Time of plot: 1950's to early 1960's
Locale: New York City and Chicago

Principal characters:
CHARLIE GORDON, a mentally challenged man
ALGERNON, a white lab mouse
ALICE KINNIAN, an instructor at Beekman College Center for Retarded Adults
HAROLD NEMUR, director of the college's Psychology Department, who is in charge of an experiment to increase intelligence
DR. STRAUSS, a psychiatrist and neurosurgeon who performs an operation on Algernon
UNCLE HERMAN, Charlie's uncle and caretaker
NORMA GORDON, Charlie's younger sister
ROSE GORDON, Charlie's mother
GIMPY, Charlie's coworker
FANNY BIRDEN, a coworker and true friend of Charlie who sticks up for him at the bakery
FAY LILLMAN, Charlie's neighbor and postsurgery girlfriend

The Story:

Charlie Gordon is a gentle, happy, thirty-two-year-old with an intelligence quotient (IQ) of 68. For seventeen years, he has worked at Donner's Bakery, a job his Uncle Herman found for him. He also attends evening classes at the Beekman College Center for Retarded Adults to learn to read and write. His teacher, Alice Kinnian, recommends him for a research experiment on intelligence conducted by Dr. Strauss and Professor Nemur. This experiment, funded by the Welberg Foundation, has already been successful on a white lab mouse named Algernon, so the researchers are ready for a human participant.

Professor Nemur tells Charlie to keep a journal in the form of progress reports for the experiment. The first such "progris riport," dated in early March, documents Charlie's illiteracy and strong hope to be selected for the "operashun." Charlie worries that he will fail the personality and intelligence tests, especially after Algernon beats him when they compete in solving puzzles. He also describes, in a childlike manner, his desire to increase his intelligence to participate fully in discussions and make more friends.

Despite Professor Nemur's reservations, Charlie is selected to undergo neurosurgery along with enzyme and hormone treatments intended to triple his intelligence. He is nervous about the operation and brings a rabbit's foot and other superstitious objects with him to the hospital. After the suc-

cessful operation, he is disappointed that he is not instantly smarter.

Charlie is allowed to return to his job at Donner's Bakery. In the evenings, Miss Kinnian tutors him, and soon he is beating Algernon in maze races and has learned to read. His intelligence increases rapidly. He is promoted to dough mixer at work and slowly realizes that the people he thought of as friends have been making fun of him. They notice changes in him and become suspicious. Around the time he suggests a few improvements at the bakery, he also catches Gimpy stealing from Mr. Donner. After he confronts Gimpy, the employees band together to have Charlie fired. Only Fanny Birden stands on his side, but while saying goodbye she suggests that something unnatural is happening to Charlie.

Charlie throws himself into reading and spends time at Beekman University pretending to be a student. He also begins remembering childhood events and meets regularly with Dr. Strauss for therapy sessions. In the middle of June, Charlie and Algernon are put on display at the annual psychological association convention in Chicago. His intelligence has surpassed that of both Dr. Strauss and Professor Nemur, and he realizes there is a flaw in their research. This, combined with Nemur's continual references to Charlie as having been engineered into a human, so upsets Charlie that he releases Algernon, causing chaos. During the distraction, he and Algernon return to New York.

Charlie's disillusionment leads to self-reflection, and his memories lead him to understand his desire to become more intelligent and his struggle to develop a relationship with Alice Kinnian, to whom he is attracted. Both desires stem from his childhood, when his mother denied that Charlie's intelligence was low and developed schemes to boost it. Once his sister Norma was born, his mother's efforts shifted toward getting Charlie institutionalized. He works on finding his parents and sister to attempt reconnecting with them.

Charlie befriends a neighbor, Fay, who helps socialize him. They drink and go dancing. During this time, when memories surface, Charlie recognizes a sort of disassociation, as if a switch has been flipped: At such times, he seems either to watch his own behavior through the eyes of a frightened man with the intelligence of a six-year-old or to watch a developmentally disabled and confused young man through the eyes of a thirty-two-year-old genius.

By late July, Charlie has reached his intellectual peak, and the decline that Algernon is exhibiting begins to show itself in Charlie's behavior as well. A race begins, as he feverishly works to find the flaw in the experiment before he can no longer comprehend the science involved. By September, Algernon is dead. Charlie reacts violently to his progressive loss of knowledge and rejects Alice, with whom he had finally connected. By mid-November, he asks for his old job back at Donner's Bakery. He has come full circle. When he accidentally shows up at the Beekman Center and upsets Alice, he decides to leave for the Warren State Home, where he will not have to face anyone who remembers that he was a genius for almost eight months.

Critical Evaluation:

Flowers for Algernon originally appeared as a novelette in the April, 1959, issue of *The Magazine of Fantasy and Science Fiction*. It received the 1960 Hugo Award for best science-fiction novelette of the year. The story then appeared in numerous anthologies and was made into a television drama, *The Two Worlds of Charlie Gordon*, in 1961. From 1962 to 1965, Daniel Keyes reworked the story, expanding it into a full-length novel that was published in 1966. The novel won the Nebula Award for the best novel of 1966 from the Science Fiction Writers of America. A film adaptation, *Charly*, was released in 1968.

Keyes's idea of physical enhancement to boost intelligence was not new to the field of science fiction, but the brief duration of the result and the structure used to tell the story create a powerful narrative. The story is structured in journal format, heightening both characterization and story development. Readers know only what Charlie records in the "progris riports" he is told to keep for the experiment. Use of the journal, or progress reports, limits the viewpoint of the narrative solely to that of the main character. This limitation presents a challenge on two levels: Keyes must convey the narrative through the lens of Charlie's low intellect and illiteracy, as well as presenting information only through Charlie's limited perspective. Keyes superbly meets these challenges, fully plunging readers into Charlie's inner struggle.

Through Charlie's progress reports, readers become aware of truths that the character himself does not at first comprehend, such as that the coworkers he thinks of as friends are really playing cruel jokes on him. As Charlie develops intellectually, the emotional impact of that development is heightened once Charlie finally realizes these "friends" have been using him. Tension builds as Charlie races against the clock to try to solve the flaw in the experiment and save himself, if not Algernon. Once Charlie regresses, reader identification heightens the story's pathos, especially as Charlie feels helpless while his knowledge slips away. In the end, Charlie's expressions of his thoughts, once again riddled with misspellings, reflect what both he and a reader know: The experience he has undergone will prevent him from ever regaining his former contentment in his simple life, because a shadow remains in his memory of what he once knew, even as he realizes that that knowledge is now forever out of his grasp.

Charlie's progress reports symbolize one of the themes in the story: the role of science in moving society forward. They raise the question of whether or not scientific progress was achieved through the experiment that Charlie underwent. While Charlie demonstrates immense physical change in the development of mental ability, that development only creates social and emotions challenges for him.

Flowers for Algernon explores the assumption that science can fix society's woes. It is a result of science—the operation—in which readers are interested. The novelette follows Charlie's life through the course of the experiment, from his initial state to the peak of intelligence to his decline. The novel delves deeper into Charlie's personality and the emotional conflict arising from such a rapid increase in intelligence. The emotional consequences of the experiment make a statement against the progress of science. It is the emotional fallout of Charlie's increased intelligence that causes his greatest trials. Through knowledge comes awareness. For better or worse, memories surface that provide Charlie with understanding about his childhood and explain his intense need to improve his intellect.

Charlie's insights allow readers to journey with him and experience his evolution from an illiterate simpleton to a lonely, superior intellect who is devastated to realize the mental giants he had looked up to prior to the operation are now worlds beneath him. Readers are caught in the urgency of Charlie's race to correct the flaw in the experiment and, once that race proves futile, agonize over the knowledge that slips through Charlie's fingers as quickly as he acquired it. In the end, science has progressed Charlie no further; he comes full circle, returning to the same circumstances as before the operation.

Keyes uses Charlie's tale to explore the mistreatment of one person by another. Charlie's own mother cannot accept him for who he is; her desire to make him like other children is the driving force behind Charlie's need to be smarter, which leads him to the Beekman Center and the experiment. When he later reconnects with his sister, his mother's senility drives him away but reveals her fear of the old Charlie.

At the Beekman science lab, Charlie is angered from the onset that Algernon is motivated by food. He eats only if he solves ever-changing puzzles and mazes, the solutions to which unlock his food. Before the operation, Charlie sees this as cruel. Later in the novel, he creates mazes for Algernon that provide the mouse with the mere satisfaction of solving them.

Though he cannot express how insulted he feels prior to the operation, Charlie seems to understand that Professor Nemur thinks of him as subhuman and intends to "re-create" Charlie into a true human being. After the operation, Professor Nemur's continual inferences that Charlie is now a human or that he has been created by the experiment create a tension throughout the novel that culminates at the psychological convention, where Charlie feels both he and Algernon are on display. Charlie creates a diversion and leaves. Eventually, he confronts Nemur, only to realize that he has also succumbed to arrogance and superiority over those who have provided the opportunity for his intellectual development.

Charlie's progress reports also reflect the need to feel superior to others. This is initially evident when he becomes ashamed at realizing his coworkers were using him as the butt of their jokes. The realization causes tension, as Charlie

understands that what he mistook for friendship was really teasing. Later in the novel, the situation comes full circle. As he is struggling over other emotional hurdles, Charlie stops at a diner and witnesses a busboy accidentally drop and shatter dishes. As the busboy is increasingly heckled for his error, Charlie angrily defends the boy and leaves, but he admits that he was actually angry with himself for momentarily forgetting what it was like to be that boy and laughing along with the others. Charlie sees the human need to feel superior, however, and finally understands that intelligence does not guarantee love or happiness, nor does it necessarily improve humankind.

Lisa A. Wroble

Further Reading

Broderick, Damien. "New Wave and Backwash: 1960-1980." In *The Cambridge Companion to Science Fiction*, edited by Edward James and Farah Mendelsohn. Boston: Cambridge University Press, 2003. Discusses emerging approaches in science fiction over a twenty-year period; examines both of Keyes's versions of *Flowers for Algernon*.

Brown, Charles N. "Daniel Keyes: Forty Years of *Algernon*." *Locus Magazine* 38, no. 6 (June, 1997). Describes the history of the story in its various forms, from short story to film, and its impact on the science-fiction genre.

Keyes, Daniel. *Algernon, Charlie, and I: A Writer's Journey.* Boca Raton, Fla.: Challenge Press, 2000. Partially autobiographical insight on how the story evolved and developed, along with more general thoughts on the creative process. Includes the complete original novelette.

Scholes, Robert. *Structural Fabulation: An Essay on Fiction of the Future.* Chicago: University of Notre Dame Press, 1975. Discusses the science-fiction elements of *Flowers for Algernon* and the impact of the impermanence of Charlie's operation on the story's long popularity.

Small, Robert, Jr. "*Flowers for Algernon*." In *Censored Books: Critical Viewpoints*, edited by Nicholas J. Karolides, Lee Burress, and John M. Kean. New York: Scarecrow Press, 1993. Discusses the evolution of the story through each prose and film version.

Flowers of Evil

Author: Charles Baudelaire (1821-1867)
First published: Les Fleurs du mal, 1857; revised, 1861;
    definitive edition, 1868 (English translation, 1931)
Type of work: Poetry

Flowers of Evil, Charles Baudelaire's most famous work, is classical in its clarity, discipline, and form, yet Romantic in its subjectivity, spirit of revolt, and macabre elements. Baudelaire's collection contains none of the historical or narrative poems typical of contemporaneous poetic works. The poems of *Flowers of Evil* were written at various dates, but their grouping and emotional tenor lend coherence and heighten intertextual relation. In the enlarged second edition, the book opens with "Benediction," describing the poet's birth, and closes with a vision of death and promise of rebirth in "The Voyage." The punning title suggests the poems are products of "evil" and "illness" (both meanings of the French word *mal*). At the same time, they adorn evil. True poetry, like a flower, beautifies whatever it touches.

In the first and largest section, *Spleen and Ideal*, the poet discards previous criteria of ideal beauty and instead finds poetry in the hideous realities of everyday life. Although entitled *Spleen and Ideal*, the cycle tends more toward the ideal. The first twenty-one poems are all related to the problems facing the artist and to the nature of beauty. Within these poems, there are two subcycles: One considers the grandeur, the misery, and the ideal of beauty; the other considers the three women important to Baudelaire and different permutations of love.

"Benediction" depicts the poet persecuted by society and redeemed by posthumous fame. "The Albatross," one of the most famous poems of the collection, treats the Romantic theme of the poet's isolation. The poem builds the traditional antithesis between the genius of the poet and his inability to adapt to an indifferent society. "Correspondences" evokes Platonic correspondences between visible forms and higher reality, as well as those between the senses. "Beacons" delineates the work of eight writers and artists as proof of humankind's dignity. "A Former Life" revels in the sensuous pleasure of exotic beauty. "Beauty" suggests true beauty is passionless, while passion is animal. "The Ideal" and "The Giant" reveal that beauty is always strange and monumental. In "Hymn to Beauty," art results from attraction to good and evil simultaneously. In the end, beauty's chief value is its power to satisfy a longing for the infinite and an escape from the misery of the human condition.

The love poems in *Spleen and Ideal* divide into three groups, each devoted to a particular woman and the type of beauty she represents. Memory is both Baudelaire's theme and method in the love poems. His emotions reveal a mingling of love and hate, loathing of his own weakness and of his mistress's cruelty. The poems celebrating Jeanne Duval evoke physical passion and despair aroused by a woman incapable of appreciating his art or love. The sensuality of "The Jewels" is both cerebral and aesthetic. "Exotic Perfume" and "Her Hair" are both inspired by scent, which offers an exotic escape from reality. Baudelaire sees himself as a victim of desire in "The Vampire" and compares his tormentor to a cold, aloof feline in "The Cat." "The Balcony," however, traces feelings of nostalgia and anticipates a reconciliation. Madame Sabatier's cycle of poems parallels the sequence of experiences in the cycle devoted to Jeanne. The poems begin with a celebration of the blonde Venus's grace and end with contradictory emotions of love and hate. In "Evening Harmony," the poet's ecstasy is expressed in terms of religious adoration. The cycle of Marie Daubrun associates her beauty with autumn's misty skies. "The Invitation to a Voyage," another of Baudelaire's famed verses, returns to a lost Eden that he shares with his beloved. The cycle of Marie ends with a baroque poem, "To a Madonna," that combines love, hate, jealousy, and revenge in a rich, ornate style.

The rest of the poems in *Spleen and Ideal* first adopt a lighter tone before yielding to a somber mood, enhancing the irony that Baudelaire felt was fundamental to literary creation. Spleen is a metaphysical malady, a paralysis of emotions, a feeling of isolation, a lack of desire. Nature reflects his fear in "Obsession." "The Thirst for Nothingness," one of the better-known *Spleen and Ideal* poems, reflects the utter despair of the poet by images of absence. The most sadistic of the poems, "The Self-Torturer," seems an ironic commentary on his lover's deception but also seems to refer to his own self-deception.

In the next section, *Parisian Scenes*, Baudelaire finds inspiration in the streets of Paris, lingering in the mystical acuity of sensation. He added the Parisian poems in 1861 to create a cityscape. In "Landscape," which opens the new section, Baudelaire combines personal impression with realistic description. "The Swan" expresses the feelings of exile that he shares with other city dwellers. "The Blind," like the poet himself, wander through the city in bewilderment and despair. The poet, however, has no hope, while the blind, eyes heavenward, have faith. In "To a Passerby," the poet encounters a woman who, as she disappears from sight, brings a realization of a love that might have been. In "Parisian Dream," Baudelaire envisions a futuristic city without nature, sound, or light. The dream he recounts, induced by drugs, marks a preference for the artificial. In "Twilight" and "Dawn," he celebrates the city rather than nature. Baudelaire endows the cityscape with mystery and tragedy.

In the sections *Wine* and *Flowers of Evil*, the poet turns to wine and sadism as an artificial paradise. In the 1861 edition, wine and narcotics symbolize vices that ultimately lead to humanity's destruction. There are only five poems in the section *Wine*, and these are among the least successful in the collection. In *Flowers of Evil*, he indulges in sadistic dreams of torture and violence to stimulate his senses and enliven dead emotions. The opening poem, "Destruction," depicts a struggle between extreme sensuality and spiritual longing. Throughout the cycle, Baudelaire emphasizes the deceptive charm of evil and its disastrous consequences. In "A Martyr," the beauty of an ornate room redolent with decaying flowers frames the sight of a woman's decapitated body, rendering the horrible beautiful. "The Damned Women," which was banned in the 1861 edition, evokes compassion for those who ignore custom and law. Baudelaire, in the poems on lesbianism, pities those who suffer torment from pleasure. "Lesbos" looks back nostalgically to Sappho's time. "A Voyage to Cythera," one of the finest poems in the collection, is an ironic allegory of idealized love.

In *Revolt*, the poet rejects his illusions and revolts against an imperfect world. While admitting Christ's divinity and remembering his suffering, he reproaches his failure to seek reform through positive action. "The Denial of Saint Peter" encourages human struggle against pain and evil. "Abel and Cain" focuses on Cain, who rejects society and an unjust God, whereas Abel is smugly content. "The Litanies of Satan" are based on the Catholic liturgy. The prayers are directed to the Romantic Satan, who was a symbol of revolt and heroic energy. Since God is evil and Christ has failed, Satan comforts by offering revolt against the injustice of social order.

In the cycle entitled *Death*, the poet longs for the discovery of another world. Death is welcomed as the only hope in "The Death of the Poor." In "The Death of Artists," death brings fruition to their dreams. "The Voyage" brings the collection to a logical conclusion by reintroducing the taste for

the infinite, the desire to escape, the quest for the unknown, the prevalence of sin, and a disbelief in progress. The dramatic use of monologue and dialogue, the change of tone from casual to sweeping, alternations in mood from ironic to exalted, and inventive imagery mark the culmination of Baudelaire's poetic creation.

The conflicts between good and evil, spleen and ideal, and dream and reality unify the six sections. Obsessed with a belief in Original Sin and the duality of human nature, Baudelaire examines the spiritual problems of his age with a brutal self-analysis that distinguishes him from his predecessors. The poems are morally neutral, recording obsessions, fantasies, delinquency, inertia, and despair in a claustrophobic atmosphere. His sympathies for his fellow beings are selective, but he champions those on the margins of society, both meek victims and defiant rebels. Descriptions of nature are virtually absent from his poetry; instead, the city is invoked as a concentrated arena of human distress and of vitality.

Among Baudelaire's chief innovations are correspondences on a transcendental level between the visible and invisible worlds, and between exterior nature and inner thoughts and feelings. He finds symbols in exterior reality that correspond to his inner thoughts and feelings. Human beauty is a terrestrial experience, which finds its double in transcendent experience. This type of symbol not only gives concrete form to abstraction but also helps Baudelaire to achieve an indispensable obscurity that allows the reader's participation. Baudelaire also introduces correspondences between the senses in a synesthetic mixture of sounds, colors, and perfumes. Perfumes, colors, and sounds, in turn, suggest feelings and moods.

Baudelaire prefers analysis to pure exoticism. His poetry introduces the crude or prosaic image in the midst of highly poetic style and treats sordid reality without losing poetic elevation. Allegorical personifications dominate his poetry. Emotional and intellectual states are featured as characters, such as Pleasure and Bitterness, and recall baroque poetry. Irony, including puns, paradox, and antithesis, is the most common feature of expression. Images of infinity contrast with those of immobility throughout the collection. The very ideal of Beauty is absolute immobility. For all of Baudelaire's innovation in poetic expression, he does not experiment with prosody. The structure of his lines and stanzas is firmly entrenched in the classical French tradition.

Flowers of Evil spiritualizes both memory and sensuous fulfillment. The majority of the poems are marked by recollection. Baudelaire was among the first poets to explore the full potential of olfactory images and their association with memory. Memory heightens the contradiction between desire for the infinite and for the sensual and concrete. The love poems also turn to a past more strongly desired than the present. Love poems, which serve as tributes to the physical and moral attributes of women, examine psychological as well as physical moments of intimacy. The relationships move from passion to tenderness to disenchantment. As the poet moves from past to present, love evolves into obsession mingled with contempt, degradation, and torment.

Baudelaire was well aware that he risked prosecution for blasphemy and offenses against public morality on the publication of *Flowers of Evil*. The defense offered at the trial claimed that book should be taken as a whole. Blasphemous or obscene poems must be set against others of spiritual beauty and platonic love. His Satanism and rebelliousness reflect Romantic developments, while his subject matter resembles that of the realists, and his love poetry revives Renaissance traditions of gallantry. His exploration of the associative powers of language also anticipates Surrealism. Baudelaire not only synthesized traditions but also created innovative verse through the intensity and detail of his self-analysis, the emotional ambivalence that confuses hate and love, and an eye for the teeming pathos and mystery of city life.

Pamela Pavliscak

Further Reading

Benjamin, Walter. *The Writer on Modern Life: Essays on Charles Baudelaire*. Translated by Howard Eiland et al., edited by Michael W. Jennings. Cambridge, Mass.: Harvard University Press, 2006. A collection of essays that Benjamin, a German literary critic, wrote in the 1930's. He takes exception to critics who viewed Baudelaire as a late Romantic dreamer, contending that the French poet was a modern writer who struggled with alienation and criticized the industrialization and advent of materialist culture in nineteenth century Paris.

Houston, John Porter. *French Symbolism and the Modernist Movement: A Study of Poetic Structures*. Baton Rouge: Louisiana State University Press, 1980. Presents *Flowers of Evil* as the foundation of French Symbolism and European modernism. Houston focuses on the self-reflexive quality of Baudelaire's poetry and his demoniac persona.

Hyslop, Lois Boe. *Charles Baudelaire Revisited*. New York: Twayne, 1992. Excellent overview of the poet's life and works. The chapter devoted to *Flowers of Evil* examines the poems in their respective groupings, followed by a consideration of overarching themes. Suggests its continuity with Baudelaire's other works.

Leakey, F. W. *Baudelaire: "Les Fleurs du mal."* New York: Cambridge University Press, 1992. Extensive evaluation of each edition of *Flowers of Evil*. Analyzes the differences between the different editions; elaborates on the coherence of each section and the collection as a whole; discusses the main themes and stylistic features of the verse.

Lloyd, Rosemary. *Baudelaire's World*. Ithaca, N.Y.: Cornell University Press, 2002. Lloyd analyzes all of Baudelaire's writing, including the poetry, placing it within the contexts of Baudelaire's life and of historical and cultural developments in mid-nineteenth century Paris. She demonstrates how his writing depicts recurrent themes of childhood, women, reading, the city, dreams, art, nature, and death.

_____, ed. *The Cambridge Companion to Baudelaire*. New York: Cambridge University Press, 2005. Collection of essays, including discussions of Baudelaire's life, politics, ethics, use of intoxicants, and place in literary and cultural history. Chapter 3 provides an analysis of *Flowers of Evil*.

Peyre, Henri, ed. *Baudelaire: A Collection of Critical Essays*. Englewood Cliffs, N.J.: Prentice-Hall, 1962. Eleven important articles written by eminent Baudelaire scholars. Spans a wide range of topics, including an exploration of imagery, the poet's persona, public reaction, and Baudelaire's influence on contemporaries.

Porter, Laurence M., ed. *Approaches to Teaching Baudelaire's "Flowers of Evil."* New York: Modern Language Association of America, 2000. This guide contains suggestions for how to teach the work to advanced high school, advanced-placement French, and church-related-university students. Other chapters provide information about the narrative structure, meter, rhyme, and other aspects of *Flowers of Evil*; lists of English and French editions of the book; suggestions for readings and audiovisual materials that can be incorporated with lessons; and discussions of some of the problems associated with teaching the work.

F.O.B.

Author: David Henry Hwang (1957-   )
First produced: 1979; first published, 1979
Type of work: Drama
Type of plot: Social criticism
Time of plot: 1980
Locale: Torrance, California

Principal characters:
DALE, a second-generation Chinese American man in his twenties
GRACE, Dale's cousin
STEVE, a newly arrived Chinese immigrant to the United States

The Story:

A second-generation Chinese American, Dale stands at a blackboard dressed in preppie clothes and lectures "like a university professor" about the meaning of the initials F.O.B. He explains that the initials stand for "fresh off the boat," referring to a newly arrived immigrant, especially of Asian descent. Such F.O.B.'s, he asserts, are clumsy in appearance and dress and represent an embarrassment to an "A.B.C.": an American-born Chinese.

Steve enters through the back door of a small Chinese restaurant that is not yet open for the day. There, he meets Grace, a waitress in her family's restaurant who is also a student at the University of California, Los Angeles (UCLA). Grace is in a bad temper because she is having difficulty taping a package closed and is being forced to deal with obnoxious customers. Over the course of the scene, Steve's identity shifts: At first he and Grace are strangers, and he is a poor immigrant attempting to enter the United States; later, he takes on the identities of the Chinese god Gwan Gung and of the son of a wealthy Shanghai and Hong Kong family who has come to the United States to attend college. In the latter identity, he and Grace have already met each other at a Chinese American dance.

Steve insistently asks Grace whether the restaurant serves *bing*, a type of Chinese pancake, while Grace hostilely tells Steve that the restaurant is closed and that he should scrutinize a menu for the answer to his question. The hostility escalates to physicality, as Grace sticks the ill-working tape to Steve's forehead, Steve grabs the package, Grace picks up a telephone to call the police, and Steve slams the telephone down. Thereafter, their contention modulates into an argument about Steve's assertion that he is Gwan Gung, god of warriors, writers, and prostitutes. The two discuss Gwan Gung's actions and reputation in China and the contemporary United States, as well as the level of knowledge of the god among Chinese Americans. Grace asserts that the only Chinese Americans who know about Gwan Gung are those few who are enrolled as students in Chinese ethnic studies

classes at universities such as UCLA. She challenges Steve to test this assertion, and he leaves.

Grace metamorphoses into Fa Mu Lan, a mythical woman warrior better known as Hua Mulan, or simply Mulan. In this woman warrior identity, she has no difficulty with the package she has been trying to wrap. She then shifts back to her identity as Grace and telephones her cousin Dale to invite him to a last-minute dinner and movie with friends. In the conversation, she receives news that Frank, a rejected romantic admirer of Grace and a friend of Dale, is going to engage in the melodramatic gesture of lying down on railroad tracks.

Steve returns from confirming Grace's assertions about Gwan Gung's reputation among Chinese Americans. He discovers that Grace is a journalism major and thus comes under his supposed divine jurisdiction as god of writers. He asks Grace out on a date, but she replies that dinner and a movie must include her cousin Dale. Sulkily, Steve returns to his query about *bing*, is handed a menu by Grace, and exits. Grace again metamorphoses into Fa Mu Lan, now at the site of a massacre of the kind boasted of by Steve as Gwan Gung, and when Dale enters and taps her on the shoulder she knocks him to the ground.

Grace apologizes to Dale for her violence, for not having the friends available for the last-minute date, and for including Steve in their outing. She says she met Steve at a Chinese dance at UCLA. After a brief, humorous interchange about the hapless Frank, Dale strokes Grace's hair, and they freeze as Steve enters. Steve metamorphoses into a poor Chinese pleading before an American immigration panel in 1914.

Once that interlude is completed, discussion ensues about the date, with Steve revealing he has made reservations at a downtown Los Angeles French restaurant, including transportation by chauffeured Cadillac limousine. An argument ensues from Dale about whether to use his X-1/9 (a two-seat Fiat sports car) rather than the Cadillac, as well as where to eat. Dale and Steve, the latter still asking about *bing*, accept

Grace's proposal that they help set up and then prepare their own meal at her father's Chinese restaurant, prior to its official opening. After Grace leaves, Dale ridicules F.O.B.'s, detailing how the parents of an F.O.B. make money, why they send the F.O.B. to America, and how the F.O.B. will eventually betray them by not returning to China. In response, Steve, with pithy sarcasm, notes that Dale's parents might exemplify Dale's criticisms.

As the three eat their dinner in the restaurant that evening, Steve asks Grace if she would like to go dancing, which irritates Dale since he would be left out. Dale's renewed reference to the F.O.B. concept leads to a brief discussion of the differing pasts of Dale's father and Grace's mother when they immigrated. Rivalry and hostility between Dale and Steve lead to a contest between the two to see who consumes more hot sauce with their food. Meanwhile, Grace—in an audience aside—reveals her difficulties in adjusting to America after arriving from Taiwan when she was ten.

Act 2 opens with a monologue by Dale asserting his complete assimilation in America: He claims to be a human being rather than being "caged up" with "Chinese-ness." Dale then attempts to transform the appearance and behavior of Steve to make him a fashionable model American in the mold of John Travolta. Failing, Dale begins to help clean up and aggressively demands that Steve help as well, though Steve resists. Meanwhile, Grace has brought out the box she was wrapping earlier. Steve unsuccessfully tries to steal it but then rejects it when offered as a present by Grace.

After a brief discussion between Dale and Grace about whether she is an F.O.B., the two again freeze with Dale stroking Grace's hair. Steve metamorphoses into a poor Chinese of the nineteenth century, explaining to his parents what Caucasian recruiters in China, "white ghosts," have promised to convince Chinese people to emigrate to America as workers. Dale and Steve struggle over the box. Dale makes more derogatory comments about F.O.B.'s, and Steve repeatedly asks if Dale knows who Steve really is, meaning Gwan Gung. Steve demands that Grace reveal his identity to Dale.

In response to Grace's question about going out, Steve declares that the limousine they sent away earlier has returned at this very instant. When Dale exits to investigate, Steve and Grace discuss the possibility of Gwan Gung ever being vulnerable, and Steve becomes polite and begins stroking Grace's hair. Dale returns, mystified by the reappearance of the limousine and upset by the hair-stroking. He reluctantly agrees to Grace's suggestion of playing "Group Story," wearing a blindfold made by Grace out of Steve's necktie.

In the story formulated by Dale, Steve, and Grace, the baby bear of a family of three travels from America to China to find a cure for a fatal illness afflicting the bears. Grace, as Fa Mu Lan, intercedes with Steve, as Gwan Gung, about showing mercy to the American bear, though no such mercy was shown to Chinese when they journeyed to America. Fa Mu Lan's presentation of two pieces of cloth to Gwan Gung leads to the transformation of Steve into a child resisting his parents' demand that he emigrate to America for their needs. They then return to the group story, as the conflict between Fa Mu Lan and Gwan Gung culminates in a sword fight. Fa Mu Lan wins her second victory over Gwan Gung. Following the group story's conclusion, Steve transforms into a nineteenth century Chinese immigrant, his contracted labor over, begging for food from an American housewife and offering to do work she could really use—the "woman's work" of clothes cleaning.

Grace again presents Steve with the wrapped box, which contains *bing*, and with Grace's encouragement, Steve devours the food. Grace and Steve compare their beautiful hands, and they agree that these are the hands of warriors, not gods, since warriors travel and gods do not. After Grace accepts Steve's renewed offer to go dancing, Dale reluctantly agrees to let them go out together, says he may respond to Grace's concern about Frank lying on the railroad tracks, and marvels that Steve has picked up English faster than anyone else in Dale's experience. After saying their good-byes, Grace and Steve exit, leaving Dale behind. Dale examines the swords, the tablecloth, and the box, and then returns to his lecture on F.O.B.'s.

Critical Evaluation:

In *F.O.B.*, the subject of identity is subdivided into immigrants' identity in the new land, their identity in their native land (partly related to their identity in the new land), and the connection between gender and identity. The play's characters represent a range of immigrant identities, from newly arrived (Steve), to foreign born with ten years' experience (Grace), to second-generation American born (Dale), while their American first names all suggest the desire for assimilation. The facets and range of identity are well represented in the repeated fluctuations and metamorphoses of Steve: At various times during the play, he is a child sent to America for the sake of his parents, a nineteenth century recruit from China, a starving nineteenth century worker with a finished contract, a 1914 hopeful being reviewed by the immigration board, a newly arrived wealthy F.O.B., and the warrior and god Gwan Gung. The *bing* that Steve devours at the play's end suggests that the hungry Chinese immigrants from the 1800's through the 1940's he has represented over the course of the play are finally being fed. They are also an assertion of

Chinese identity embodied in a preference for a Chinese dish. Gwan Gung (originally named Guan Yu), like Fa Mu Lan, was a real warrior who was gradually deified and whose warrior identity suggests the necessity of struggle in the process of settling into a new country.

Grace's metamorphosis into Fa Mu Lan suggests her personal struggles after arriving in the United States at the age of ten and finding herself somewhat at odds with both Caucasian society and the American-born Chinese students in her elementary and high schools. Fa Mu Lan contends with patriarchy in China, as well as among male Chinese immigrants to America—one point implied in the dialogue between Grace and Dale contrasting the history of Dale's father with that of Grace's mother in the new country. The fine cloth blindfold donned by Gwan Gung when going out to wreak indiscriminate slaughter in the countryside suggests the disregard for common people, including women, by the superior male and the upper class. Fa Mu Lan finds her mother dismembered and her sister raped among the slaughter. The blindfold is represented by Steve's necktie as part of Fa Mu Lan's war in quest of equal consideration for women and the lower classes, both in China and in the United States. The tablecloth from the restaurant becomes the tablecloth on the banquet table of sins of oppression unknowingly consumed by Gwan Gung, as well as the symbol of oppression of children by parents sending them to a new country for selfish reasons. Grace and Fa Mu Lan teach Steve and Gwan Gung that the way to get *bing* is by waiting for it to be freely offered, not by taking it by force.

Dale metamorphoses much less than the other two characters, befitting his attempt at a settled though compromised identity. Both romantically attracted to and protective of his cousin Grace, Dale constantly competes with Steve. Dale does not know the name of "those burrito things" ("mooshoo," says Grace), while Steve repeatedly asks for *bing*. Dale engages in a sort of war of hot sauce with Steve, as each male attempts to prove his manliness and connection with the Chinese homeland. Dale has chosen an X-1/9 Fiat, a compromise between the lower-class Ford Pinto he despises and the Porsche driven by one of his rich friends. Dale's X-1/9 is no match for Steve's magical Fleetwood Cadillac limousine, which—with its chauffeur—appears or disappears almost supernaturally, suggesting that perhaps Steve really is the supernatural Gwan Gung. Dale's monologue at the beginning of act 2 reveals that he has not achieved connections in the new country, only the potential for them, and that in his suppression of his Chinese roots he has become less of a human being than he could be. Ironically, as shown in the play, Dale

is guilty of the same stereotyping of Chinese as is Caucasian American society, as when Caucasians fail to learn the specifics of China and of the Chinese in America.

F.O.B. incorporates the main subjects of David Henry Hwang's *The Dance and the Railroad* (pr. 1981, pb. 1983) and of his most famous play, *M. Butterfly* (pr., pb. 1988). The play is masterful in its use of symbolic props, plays within the play, direct address or reference to the audience, details of modern American life, and, above all, language. The range of identities of the characters is artfully embodied in and expressed by the range of language deployed throughout the play, including Chinese, English obscenities, colloquial English, standard English, and the broken or nonstandard English of nonnative speakers of English. *F.O.B.* is a major work of Hwang's dramatic corpus.

Norman Prinsky

Further Reading

Cooperman, Robert. "New Theatrical Statements: Asian-Western Mergers in the Early Plays of David Henry Hwang." In *Staging Difference: Cultural Pluralism in American Theatre and Drama*, edited by Marc Maufort. New York: Peter Lang, 1995. Includes a brief analysis of *F.O.B.* concentrating on aspects of staging, including the performance history of the play, blocking, and props.

Jew, Kimberly M. "Dismantling the Realist Character in Velina Hasu Houston's *Tea* and David Henry Hwang's *F.O.B.*" In *Literary Gestures: The Aesthetic in Asian American Writing*, edited by Rocio Davis and Sue-Im Lee. Philadelphia: Temple University Press, 2006. Treats *F.O.B.* along with Houston's play in the context of "nonrealistic aesthetics" in Asian American writing—especially the shifting of character in Steve and Grace.

Lee, Josephine. *Performing Asian America: Race and Ethnicity on the Contemporary Stage*. Philadelphia: Temple University Press, 1997. Extensive analysis of the play's symbolism, especially with reference to the American socioeconomic system.

Street, Douglas. *David Henry Hwang*. Boise, Idaho: Boise State University Press, 1989. Provides a history of first productions, summary, and brief identification of the play's main subjects.

Wong, Sau-ling Cynthia. *Reading Asian American Literature: From Necessity to Extravagance*. Princeton, N.J.: Princeton University Press, 1993. Analysis of the play in terms of the concept of the doppelgänger, or double, especially what Wong calls the "racial shadow."

The Folks

Author: Ruth Suckow (1892-1960)
First published: 1934
Type of work: Novel
Type of plot: Domestic realism
Time of plot: Early twentieth century
Locale: Iowa

Principal characters:
FRED FERGUSON, a husband and father
ANNIE FERGUSON, his wife
CARL WILLIAM FERGUSON, their older son
MARGARET "MARGOT" FERGUSON, their older daughter
DOROTHY FERGUSON, their younger daughter
BUNNY FERGUSON, a son, their youngest child

The Story:

On a beautiful September morning, Fred Ferguson gets up early and strolls around his yard. Although he is proud of his comfortable home and his position in the small town of Belmond, Iowa, where he lives, Fred feels burdened by his responsibilities. So many people seem to depend on Fred: his family, his coworkers at the bank, his fellow Presbyterians, in fact, the whole community. When Fred's wife, Annie, gets up, she thinks briefly about her dead parents and the inevitability of change. Then she begins her day's work. At breakfast, their daughter Margaret is generally nasty, causing Annie to wonder why this middle child is so different. As usual, Fred is obtuse; as usual, Annie tries to please him. After everyone leaves, she broods about how tired she is of pretending and how much she resents having to placate Fred's hypercritical mother and sister.

Life goes on. Margaret disobeys her mother and has to be punished. The Fergusons go out to dinner. The Monday Club meets with Annie, and for the first time the frugal Fred lets his wife hire someone to help her. That night, Annie amazes Fred by telling him of her feelings about the family. Although he assures her of his love, he still does not understand.

The children are growing up. Still playing his part as the good son, Carl is a star football player and a student leader of his high school. He is admired by everyone, especially his little brother, Bunny, and his girlfriend, Lillian White. At the Presbyterian college he attends, Carl is fascinated by livelier girls, but after graduation he marries Lillian. They have two sons. Carl becomes a school principal, then a superintendent. Bored by his work and frustrated by Lillian's sexual passiveness, Carl seeks the company of more vivacious women. The crisis comes when he tells Lillian that they are moving to Philadelphia, where one of his women friends finds him a new position. Upset about her pregnancy and certain that her husband does not love her, Lillian tries to kill herself, but Carl stops her in the nick of time. Turning down the Philadelphia offer, Carl becomes superintendent of schools in a town near Belmond. Although Lillian loses her baby, she is now

secure in their marriage. Carl, however, loses his faith in himself. He now knows that he is nothing special after all.

On Dorothy's wedding day, everything seems perfect. Her handsome fiancé, Jesse Woodward, likes her family and her little town. He has even been nice about going with her to be introduced to old family friends. Dorothy and Jesse have a shiny new roadster, their wedding gift from Jesse's wealthy grandfather. Almost before she knows it, Dorothy is putting on her bridal dress and hearing the familiar words. Suddenly the ceremony is over, and the two young people drive off to start their life together.

Margaret helps a friend elope and so is expelled from college and sent home, where she proceeds to inflict her own unhappiness on everyone around her. She can foresee spending her life working at the Belmond public library, but it is her library job that enables her to escape. Fred permits Margaret to go to New York in order to take a library course. Once there, Margaret quits school and leaves the family with whom her father deposited her. Encouraged by her artistic new friends, Margaret renames herself Margot, cuts her hair, and moves into a Greenwich Village apartment, supporting herself by working as a waitress.

When she meets Bruce Williams, an older, married man, Margot abandons the bohemian life. She always dreamed of a grand passion, and she is sure that this is it. When she sets off on a long trip to the West with Bruce, Margot could not have been happier. Bruce keeps thinking about his wife and his children, however, and eventually he returns home. Devastated, Margot goes back to Belmond, only to find that she is now regarded as a temptress. Determined to make a career for herself, Margot goes back to New York. Then Bruce telephones, and Margot takes him back on her own terms.

Just when Annie is thinking that at least she still has Bunny, he comes home with a wife. The former Charlotte Bukowksa does not like her new family any more than they like her. Annie thinks her rude and sullen. Charlotte, who is a Marxist, classifies the Fergusons as hopelessly bourgeois.

When the couple leave Belmond for Chicago, it does not seem likely that they will be back soon.

When Fred retires, he agrees to take Annie on the trip she always dreamed about, and the two set off for California. When they get to San Diego, they find that Dorothy and Jesse are so hard-pressed financially that they rent out their big home and are camping out in a tiny house with no room for guests. Living in a small apartment they rent, Fred and Annie cannot help wishing they were back home. On their way home, they stop at the luxurious home of Annie's sister Louise, but Annie finds that she and her sister lost their old closeness.

Back in Belmond, at first Fred and Annie feel displaced. Fred's church closes, and his bank is in difficulty. Fred soon finds that there are people who need his help, and once again he has a reason for living. As for Annie, now that she finally had her trip, she begins to feel her old tenderness toward Fred. Whatever the future holds, they both realize, they can face it together.

Critical Evaluation:

When it was published, *The Folks* was hailed as, if not the great American novel, at least the best novel about the Midwest that had ever been written. Unlike contemporaries such as Sinclair Lewis, who in *Main Street* (1920) and later novels pictured midwestern small towns as stifling, their inhabitants as pretentious and hypocritical, Ruth Suckow produced a book that critics called truly realistic. Although to outsiders Belmond may seem serene and even dull, its people have their share of inner conflicts and of uncertainty about the future.

In *The Folks*, the Ferguson home place represents the agrarian life and traditional values. At the beginning of the novel, Fred's aging parents still live in the old family home, which is appropriately called the rock house. Just across the road is the new house, built by Fred's sister and her husband, who works the farm. When they are young, all of Fred's children like to go out to the home place. As adults, however, Margaret finds her place in the city and Dorothy finds her place in the suburbs. Even for Carl, living on the farm is never a real option. During his midlife crisis, Carl daydreams about becoming a farmer, but he lacks the will to make any drastic change in his life. Perhaps what Carl really wants is not a new vocation but a return to his youth.

By the time Bunny takes his new wife out to the home place, his grandparents are dead, the rock house is deserted, and the farm is being worked by renters. Bunny speaks about spending a summer in the rock house; however, Charlotte feels a revulsion toward any land that is privately owned. Her aim is to move to Russia and work in an agricultural commune.

In *The Folks*, Americans are shown to be losing a system of values, along with their ties to the land. Annie may be correct in blaming Fred's frugality on his Scottish ancestry, but his sense of obligation to his church and to the less fortunate in his community reflects the ethical and religious standards of an earlier time, not of a particular national background. Fred always tries to do what is right, not what is convenient, but none of his children possesses the father's sense of moral certainty. Dorothy drifts along with Jesse, and Bunny, troubled by social injustice, meanders toward Marxism. The rebellious Margaret easily discards her parents' standards of sexual morality and embarks on her own pursuit of happiness. One might think that Carl, at least, is impelled by principle when he renews his commitment to Lillian. In fact, Carl is only too aware that his remaining with his wife is the result of his weakness rather than of any moral strength. Carl is not, like Fred, a man of conviction; he is simply a conformist, still trying to fit into the role of the good son that he assumed in childhood.

Despite Fred's goodness, he is too much a man of his time to comprehend the frustrations of his own wife. Annie loves Fred and wants to be a good wife to him; however, society defines that role as one of total submission. It is not just that Fred buys the cars and decides when the house should be remodeled, or even that he assumes Annie will attend his church. Even her smallest decision is designed to avoid criticism from him or from his family. When she runs out of eggs and needs to do some baking, Annie cannot just get what she needs from the store, for her thrifty husband will want her to wait for the free eggs from the farm. Even her treasured time alone, after everyone finishes breakfast and leaves the house, is cut short because someone from Fred's family might stop by, see that the dishes are not yet washed, and report Annie's slothfulness to her husband.

Annie blames Fred and his obtuseness for her occasional unhappiness. Like most of the women of Belmond, Annie has no idea that society can be structured other than as a patriarchal system. Suckow sees change coming even in the area of gender roles; ever the realist, she does not see the new independence of women as an unmixed blessing. Thus Margaret, who scorns docile women such as her mother and her sister, in fact gives up her freedom, as well as her future, when she agrees to be the mistress of a married man. Ironically, the most independent woman in the novel, Charlotte, is also one of the most unpleasant.

At the end of *The Folks*, even Fred sees that his era is over and that his children will lead lives much different from his. With her characteristic honesty, Suckow stops there. The future, she implies, must speak for itself.

Rosemary M. Canfield Reisman

Further Reading

Herron, Ima Honaker. *The Small Town in American Literature*. New York: Haskell House, 1971. Classifies Suckow as a fair, dispassionate, and accurate observer of small-town life in the Midwest. *The Folks* is also the story of rapidly changing times and a changing American society.

Kissane, Leedice McAnelly. *Ruth Suckow*. New York: Twayne, 1969. Major study of the author. In a lengthy analysis of *The Folks*, which she considers Suckow's best work, Kissane considers style, theme, and characterization. Includes chronology, extensive notes, and annotated bibliography.

Omrcanin, Margaret Stewart. *Ruth Suckow: A Critical Study of Her Fiction*. Philadelphia: Dorrance, 1972. A topical analysis of Suckow's works. References to *The Folks* are scattered throughout the chapters on setting, social significance, and universal themes. The appendixes contain a chronological bibliography of Suckow's writings and a comprehensive list of secondary sources.

Tomkinson, Grace. "Cycle of Iowa." *Canadian Forum* 15 (December, 1934): 119-120. Praises Suckow's skill, her honesty, her penetrating characterization, and her gentle satire. Argues that although *The Folks* is called the great midwestern novel, it has a universal appeal.

Van Doren, Dorothy. "Real People." *The Nation*, October 17, 1934. An interesting contemporary review. Argues that the novel is about the failure of an old order and the birth of a new, "as inevitable as it is unsatisfying." Despite some technical imperfections, *The Folks* is "warm with the breath of life."

Foma Gordeyev

Author: Maxim Gorky (1868-1936)
First published: 1899 (English translation, 1901)
Type of work: Novel
Type of plot: Psychological realism
Time of plot: Late nineteenth century
Locale: Russia

Principal characters:
FOMA GORDEYEV, a young man of the merchant class
IGNAT, his father
ANFISA, his aunt
MAYAKIN, his godfather
EZHOFF, a brilliant youth
LIUBOFF, Mayakin's daughter

The Story:

Ignat begins as a water pumper, but, by the time he is forty years old, he is a rich owner of barges and tugs and a determined and a ruthless trader. At times, however, he is subject to fits of depression, and he carouses with the dregs of the city; sometimes, he exults fiercely when one of his barges burns. He is a huge man with boundless energy. His greatest disappointment is that he has no son; his wife bears only daughters who die in infancy. When he is forty-three years old, his wife suddenly dies, and, within six months, he finds a young bride. Natalya is tall and handsome, dutiful but mysterious. Although ordinarily submissive, she has strength of character that makes boisterous Ignat afraid to beat her. She dies after the birth of Foma, Ignat's long-desired son.

Until he is six years old, Foma is reared in his godfather Mayakin's house. Under the watchful, stupid eye of a female relative, he plays unimaginatively with Liuboff, Mayakin's daughter. Ignat then takes back his son, and Foma's Aunt Anfisa looks after him. Anfisa tells him many fanciful tales that whet the young boy's imagination.

At the age of eight, Foma discusses the family business with Ignat and is disappointed that his father is only a river merchant instead of a pirate. To clear up his misapprehensions, Ignat takes the boy on a business trip down the river. Foma gets along well with the peasants until he tells his father how one worker was uncomplimentary to the capitalistic class. Ignat strikes the worker. This incident always seems brutal to the boy.

At school, Foma makes two friends: Smolin, a fat, rich boy, and Ezhoff, a quick-thinking poor boy. Foma progresses well in his classes because Ezhoff helps him study and prompts him during recitations. In and out of school pranks, Foma is a daring leader. His courage is due in part to his father's wealth, but he is also truly honest and fearless. As he grows up, Liuboff is the only girl he knows. Mayakin hopes that they will marry and unite the two family fortunes.

When Foma is not yet twenty, Ignat puts him in charge of a trading expedition and tells the tug captain to keep an eye on the young man. Foma quickly establishes his superiority over the older captain and takes complete command. He does quite well, except that he is often too generous in giving grain to the peasants. He notices on deck one night a peasant woman with attractive eyes. Although she is older than he, Foma desires to meet her, and the captain arranges to have her come to Foma's cabin at night. The woman is thirty years old, delightfully mature to the naïve Foma. He leaves her with regret when Mayakin sends a message requiring him to come home as soon as possible.

Mayakin tells Foma that his father is in the clutches of a conniving woman who already got large sums of money from him. At first, Foma is afraid that Ignat took a mistress. To Mayakin, the situation seems even worse; Madame Medynsky induced Ignat to give liberally to charity. Mayakin has no use for charity. The merchant class, he thinks, should use its money to make more money. For a time, Foma helps his father and faithfully attends to business. It is hard work for him, although he is far from stupid. He can see no point in trading, no excuse for amassing a fortune. Liuboff confuses him when he talks with her. She reads books, to Foma a foolish pastime, for in them he finds no answers to his questions. Foma never reads much; in polite society, he is always ill at ease.

When Ignat dies, Foma feels more insecure. Attending a public gathering to dedicate a building to which his father contributed, he leaves before the ceremony is over. Nevertheless, he is greatly interested in Madame Medynsky, the moving spirit in his father's philanthropies. He visits her often, and she is very gracious to him, for he is handsome as well as rich. All the while, however, Foma feels troubled, for she seems to play with his affections. When Foma hears she is an abandoned woman, he refuses to believe the tales. In fact, one night he soundly thrashes an official who speaks slightingly of her chastity.

When Mayakin tries to quiet the affair and to set Foma back on the path of commercial rectitude, Foma rebels. He goes on a spree with several others and finally winds up on a raft in company with coldly attractive Sasha. Drunk enough to be affected greatly by Sasha's duets with her sister, he cuts the mooring lines. As the raft floats away, Sasha swims to shore. She and Foma laugh immoderately as the others in the party float helplessly down the river.

After some days, he and Sasha come upon one of his barges, and Foma forces the captain to let him take command. He promptly steers the barge into a collision, and the craft sinks. It is an expensive and scandalous business to raise it. In the midst of their liaison, Sasha leaves Foma. She cannot stand his continual questioning as to the purpose of life. When Mayakin hears what happened to the barge,

he takes a power of attorney and leaves Foma to his own devices.

By chance, Foma encounters Ezhoff, now a brilliant, satirical journalist. Fascinated by his former schoolmate, he is puzzled because Ezhoff had so little worldly success. Once he goes with Ezhoff when the journalist makes a revolutionary speech to a gathering of printers, but mostly the two drink together. At last, Foma goes home, soberer but scarcely wiser. There he learns Liuboff is engaged to Smolin, who turned into an unctuous, polished trader. Mayakin, still hoping to redeem Foma, takes him to a ship launching. As he listens to the laudatory speeches and hears the blatant congratulations to the owner, Foma loses control of himself. He compels the rich businessmen to listen as he probes beneath their smug shells of respectability. One man barely escapes trial for seducing a little girl, another falsely accuses his mistress and has her sent to prison, a third turns out his nephews to starve, and still another owns a brothel. As Foma bawls out his terrible accusations, the men fall on him and bind him. His godfather has him confined in an asylum. Years later, he can be seen in the streets of the town, shabby, half-witted, and intoxicated. He lives in a little wing off Liuboff's courtyard.

Critical Evaluation:

Foma Gordeyev is Maxim Gorky's first novel. Some see in it the ebullience of a young writer flexing his wings, exhibiting shortcomings typical of a novice; others see it as his best novel. Interestingly, this early work harbors both Gorky's favorite themes and the main characteristics of his style. It can be said that the changes in Gorky's artistic style after this work were only a matter of degree.

From the outset, Gorky was preoccupied with social themes. At the end of the nineteenth century, Russia found itself in the throes of a rapid rise of the merchant class and of industry, while the huge peasant and working masses sank deeper and deeper into poverty and despair. This development led straight to the revolution of 1917 and to Communist rule for seven decades. Intellectuals played a significant role in this, and Gorky was one of the leading writers with revolutionary and Marxist leanings. He was determined to help right the wrongs and to bring about a better life for all people, especially the downtrodden. He chose the pen name Gorky ("bitter") to underscore the intensity of his feelings. He was basically an idealist, a humanitarian who wanted to achieve his altruistic goals with love and kindness, not with fire and sword. His moderate attitude often brought him into conflict with the less forgiving revolutionaries, although he remained a supporter of the revolution to the end.

All this was to come later in his life. In 1899, his revolutionary development had just begun. For that reason, *Foma Gordeyev* lacks the purposefulness of his later works, yet the contours of his ideological profile are discernible already. The novel deals with the rise of the merchant class, embodied in Ignat Gordeyev and his son, Foma. The two will eventually evolve into opposing poles. Ignat, an owner of boats and barges on the Volga River, is a powerful, ruthless, volcanic man whose brutal strength and merciless treatment of people under him enable him to amass great wealth. Even a seven-year-old Foma seems to understand his father's true nature when he asks, "But you are a robber, aren't you, father?" Although Foma admires his father's success, he also feels sorry for him because success does not bring him happiness.

Foma develops into the opposite type of person. He grows into a reserved, taciturn young man, self-confident, upright, with a fine sense for justice. After his father's death, he gradually brings on a demise of the family fortunes, despite the efforts of his godfather, Mayakin, to steer him in the "right" direction. Foma's greatest obstacle toward success is his idealization of the working class and his tendency to look for compassion in people. The end result is Foma's failure in the eyes of the merchant society and his descent into the limbo of a displaced, superfluous man who is declared insane and who spends the rest of his life roaming the streets in rags. In some ways, Foma echoes Gorky's own thoughts and desires, especially his hope that life can be changed for the better with love and understanding.

Gorky tells his tale in the fashion that would become his trademark: straightforward realism, buoyed by warmth and concern for every human being. He creates credible scenes, in which characters unburden themselves of their concerns freely. Gorky's proverbial gift of observation, seen perhaps at its best in his recollections of Leo Tolstoy and Anton Chekhov, enlivens the descriptions and dialogues. On the debit side, the novel is burdened by some of the notorious weaknesses of Gorky's writing habits. His characters philosophize too much, talk profusely, and state the obvious repeatedly. Even his realism sometimes slides into romanticism and sentimentality. The characters are frequently so concerned with their own thoughts that they seem to lose touch with others. Unlike the economy of words in his short stories, the descriptive profusion in Gorky's novels dilutes the overall striking effects that abound in the novel.

Despite these shortcomings, *Foma Gordeyev* is a colorful novel, with powerful characterization and with a vivid picture of the life in Russia at the turn of the century and of the merchant class that was the backbone of the Russian society just before the revolution. Some chapters offer the best pages

Gorky has written and a few characters, such as Foma, his father Ignat, his godsister Liuboff, his aunt Anfisa, and the firebrand intellectual Ezhoff, are indeed unforgettable.

"Critical Evaluation" by Vasa D. Mihailovich

Further Reading

Borras, F. M. *Maxim Gorky the Writer: An Interpretation.* Oxford, England: Clarendon Press, 1967. One of the more astute interpretations of Gorky's works, especially his novels and plays. Unlike many other books that concentrate on either biography or political issues, Borras emphasizes Gorky's artistic achievements. *Foma Gordeyev* is discussed in passing.

Clark, Katerina. *The Soviet Novel: History as Ritual.* 3d ed. Bloomington: Indiana University Press, 2000. Clark's chronicle of the development of the Socialist Realist novel includes information about Gorky and his pronouncements on fiction.

Cornwell, Neil, ed. *The Routledge Companion to Russian Literature.* New York: Routledge, 2001. Chapters 15 and 16 provide information about Gorky's contributions to the Russian novel.

Hare, Richard. *Maxim Gorky: Romantic Realist and Conservative Revolutionary.* New York: Oxford University Press, 1962. A substantial study of Gorky, including some interesting observations obtained from people who knew Gorky well. *Foma Gordeyev* is also discussed.

Levin, Dan. *Stormy Petrel: The Life and Work of Maxim Gorky.* New York: Appleton-Century-Crofts, 1965. A general biography, covering Gorky's entire life and written in a lively manner. *Foma Gordeyev* is discussed.

Muchnic, Helen. "Maxim Gorky." In *From Gorky to Pasternak.* New York: Random House, 1961. An extensive study of Gorky the man and the writer. Discusses his works, including *Foma Gordeyev.*

Weil, Irwin. *Gorky: His Literary Development and Influence on Soviet Intellectual Life.* New York: Random House, 1966. A scholarly book on Gorky in English, skillfully combining biography with critical analysis, including *Foma Gordeyev.* Especially valuable for the discussion of Soviet literary life and Gorky's connection with, and influence on, younger Soviet writers.

Yedlin, Tova. *Maxim Gorky: A Political Biography.* Westport, Conn.: Praeger, 1999. Yedlin's biography focuses on Gorky's political and social views and his participation in the political and cultural life of his country. Includes bibliography and index.

Fontamara

Author: Ignazio Silone (1900-1978)

First published: German edition, 1930; Italian edition, 1933; revised, 1958 (English translation, 1934, 1960)

Type of work: Novel

Type of plot: Social realism

Time of plot: Early 1930's

Locale: Abruzzi region, southern Italy

Principal characters:

BERARDO VIOLA, the strongest Fontamaran peasant

GIOVÀ (also GIUVÀ), a peasant

MATALÈ, his wife

THEIR SON

THE CONTRACTOR, a wealthy landowner

DON CIRCONSTANZA, a lawyer

DON ABBACCHIO, a priest

THE MYSTERY MAN, a revolutionary

The Story:

The hillside town of Fontamara is without electricity. While several *cafoni* (a common term for southern Italian peasants) are seated in front of Marietta Sorcanera's bar, a government bureaucrat named Pelino arrives on the scene with blank papers that the *cafoni* are asked to sign. The peasants balk at the idea, but they acquiesce when they are assured that no new taxes are involved. The official leaves with the signatures, some authentic, some forged; he threatens the peasants for having cursed the Church and the state. Perplexed, the Fontamarans return home in the dark. On the way, Giovà passes Berardo, who is intent on breaking the electric lamps no longer of use.

The next morning, a crew of roadmen begins to divert the stream that irrigates the peasants' soil. It is decided that the women will go to the town and complain to the mayor. At the town hall, the women are told that there is no longer a mayor, but, instead, there is a new *podestà* (a term for mayor, used during the Fascist period). The police escort the women to the home of the *podestà*, where, to their surprise, they learn that he is the rich and powerful Contractor, a newcomer who "discovered America" in southern Italy.

The women try in vain to speak to the Contractor. Out of desperation they turn to Don Circonstanza, a lawyer and self-proclaimed "Friend of the People" who is dining at the Contractor's house. Don Circonstanza solves the problem: The Contractor will receive three-quarters of the stream's water, and the Fontamarans will receive three-quarters of the remaining water. Confused, the women sign a hurriedly produced paper, once they are assured that there will be nothing to pay.

The next day, the digging continues as the quarrels among the peasants become more frequent and more furious. Don Abbacchio, the town priest, arrives in Fontamara and urges the peasants not to oppose the Contractor, who, he says, is the devil incarnate. The peasants notice, however, that Don Abbacchio arrived in a coach owned by the Contractor.

The Fontamarans are later summoned to Avezzano, where they will learn the decisions made by the new government concerning the redivision of the fertile Fucino plain. The *cafoni* are herded into a large square and are ordered to stand and cheer on cue as local administrators parade past amid myriad black flags marked with skulls and crossbones. Fortunately, the peasants do not allow themselves to be influenced by a police informant who tries to incite them to violence and then have them arrested.

A wooden fence is soon built around the community grazing ground in Fontamara. The Contractor apparently appropriated the land that was common property for thousands of years. After the fence is burned, rebuilt, and then burned a second time, several trucks arrive in the village while the men are in the fields. Gunshots from the trucks break the church windows. Two hundred armed men descend upon the homes of the peasants and destroy everything in their path; they also rape the women. The ringing of the church bells causes the violence to cease. The frightened men, departing hastily, do not see the tree trunks placed across the road, and many of them are injured.

In the meantime, Berardo, returning to the village from the fields, learns that Elvira fainted atop the bell tower. He picks her up in his arms and carries her to her home. The next day, it is rumored that Berardo and Elvira will marry. Berardo, who owns no land, has to find work. Don Circonstanza tricks him into working for a pittance, and Berardo's only consolation is a letter of recommendation that the lawyer sends to a friend in Rome.

The Contractor returns to Fontamara—this time with a hundred policemen—in order to resolve the issue of the diverted stream. Again Don Circonstanza comes to the aid of his "beloved" Fontamarans by proposing that the three-quarters of the water would belong to the Contractor for only ten lusters rather than for fifty years. The uneducated peasants, unaware that ten lusters is fifty years, accept his proposal.

The ensuing shortage of water causes the peasants great hardship. The crops are not growing, and the peasants face a terrible winter. Disillusioned with Don Circonstanza's help, the men talk of taking matters into their own hands. Berardo, however, will not hear of the revolt. He is going to Rome, where the lawyer's letter of reference will enable him to find work.

That next morning, accompanied by Giovà's son, Berardo takes the train to Rome. The two men stay in a modest inn where they meet Don Achille Pazienza, a lawyer who extorts money from them by promising to find them work. Thrown out of the inn because they cannot pay their bill, Berardo and Giovà's son run into the stranger from Avezzano; the stranger buys them something to eat. Shortly thereafter, the three men are arrested for allegedly leaving in the café a parcel of clandestine newspapers that attack the Fascist regime.

At that time, the police are looking for a suspect called the Mystery Man, who is responsible for spreading anti-Fascist literature in the city. While he is being interrogated at the police station, Berardo declares that he is the Mystery Man. The real Mystery Man is released while Berardo is subjected to numerous tortures. As he is about to inform on his friend, Berardo finds a newspaper that reports Elvira's death. He changes his mind. Berardo soon dies in prison after repeated beatings. His death is reported in the newspapers as a suicide.

Giovà's son is released from prison after he signs a statement attesting Berardo's "suicidal tendencies." He returns to Fontamara, where the Mystery Man already told the true story of Berardo's death and left a duplicating machine. The peasants are busy selecting a title for their newspaper.

Shortly after the first edition of the newspaper is distributed, gunfire breaks out in Fontamara. Most of the peasants are killed. Among the few survivors are Giovà, Matalè, and their son, who, with the help of the Mystery Man, are able to flee to Switzerland.

Critical Evaluation:

Ignazio Silone was born in Pescina, a small town in the Abruzzi region of southern Italy; the town served as a model for Fontamara. Silone was the son of small landowners and spent much of his youth among the impoverished peasants of the area. He witnessed the social injustices and economic hardships to which the *cafoni* were subjected.

It was Silone's sympathy for the peasants that led him to turn to political action as a vehicle for social and political change. He envisioned a society founded on the socialist concepts of solidarity and equality and the Christian virtue of charity. As a young activist, Silone joined the Socialist Youth League, and in 1921, he helped to found the Italian Communist Party. In 1930, sought by the Fascist police for his involvement in the underground movement against Mussolini's regime, he was forced to flee from Italy.

Fontamara was written while Silone was in exile in Davos, Switzerland. In the novel, he has three refugees from Fontamara—Giovà, Matalè, and their son—visit him in exile in order to relate the tragic story of their hometown. Giovà is the first to narrate, and within the narration, the other *cafoni* speak for themselves. This technique creates the impression of a choral narrative and appropriately so, for *Fontamara* is the story of all suffering peasants and oppressed people in the world.

Within Giovà's narration, one of the *cafoni*, Michele Zompa, relates a dream he had concerning the lice that plague the townspeople. In the dream, Christ tells the Pope that he wishes to celebrate the Concordat of 1929 between the Church and the Fascist state by granting the *cafoni* a favor such as a gift of land, an exemption from taxes, or an abundant harvest. The Pope rejects Christ's proposals because such favors, he argues, would damage the interests of rich landowners and government officials. The Pope chooses as a gift for the peasants a new and vicious strain of lice that will cause them to scratch fiercely, thus distracting them from their misery. The fable-like quality of the dream stands in sharp contrast to the biting realism of its implications—the Church's complicity with the oppressive Fascist government and the Church's blatant insensitivity to the plight of the peasants—recurrent themes in the novel, which are personified by the figure of a corrupt priest, Don Abbacchio.

Forsaken by the Church, the *cafoni* remain the helpless victims of Fascist oppressors; they are mercilessly burdened by government taxes, and they are repeatedly swindled by the Contractor and by Don Circonstanza. As Matalè relates in the second chapter, however, such treatment is to be expected, for the *cafoni* are looked upon by the rich and the middle class as "flesh used to suffering." Since time immemorial, the peasants of Fontamara have been resigned to the economic deprivation and the social injustices perpetuated by government officials.

Only Berardo Viola's anarchic acts of violence offer some resistance to government oppression. Berardo destroys the electric lamps, burns the Contractor's fences, and places a tree trunk in the path of the fleeing Fascist henchmen. Ironically, the *cafoni* are driven by desperation to active revolt against the state at the time when Berardo decides to conform—to work and to set aside a small sum of money—so that he can marry Elvira.

Elvira's death transforms Berardo's social consciousness so deeply that he emerges as a Christ figure. Giovà's son narrates the most poignant part of the novel, in which Berardo sacrifices himself for the love of his fellow men—for their socioeconomic redemption. His confession will enable the Mystery Man to go to Fontamara and incite the *cafoni* to revolt.

The novel ends as the three narrators ask, "What are we to do?" This question echoes the title of the clandestine newspaper that caused the destruction of Fontamara and its inhabitants. The novel ends on a positive note, however, and this note is consistent with Silone's faith in socialist ideals. Berardo, the first peasant to die for the love of his fellows, has pointed the way to the establishment of a society rooted in Christian brotherhood and charity, a society in which freedom, social justice, and equality will prevail.

Lucille Izzo Pallotta

Further Reading

Brown, Robert McAfee. "Ignazio Silone and the Pseudonyms of God." In *The Shapeless God: Essays on Modern Fiction*, edited by Harry J. Mooney, Jr., and Thomas F. Staley. Pittsburgh, Pa.: University of Pittsburgh Press, 1968. A study of Silone's novels as a quest for a "shapeless God" seen in such forces as socialism, revolution, and brotherly love. Discusses the salient events in Silone's life that influenced his writing.

Hanne, Michael. "Silone's *Fontamara*: Polyvalence and Power." *MLN* 107 (January, 1992): 132-159. A well-documented study of *Fontamara* based on Hanne's premise that the novel is not a historically accurate account of Fascist oppression and peasant resistance in southern Italy, but rather a text of universal significance.

Leake, Elizabeth. *The Reinvention of Ignazio Silone.* Toronto, Ont.: University of Toronto Press, 2003. In 1996, it was revealed that Silone, a hero among Italian liberals and a onetime high-ranking member of the Communist Party, had secretly supported the Italian Fascists. Leake reevaluates Silone's fiction from a psychoanalytic perspective, demonstrating how his novels reflect his struggles with this duplicity. *Fontamara* is discussed in chapter 3.

Lewis, R. W. B. "Ignazio Silone: The Politics of Charity." In *The Picaresque Saint.* Philadelphia: J. B. Lippincott, 1959. A detailed account of the author's life precedes this study of *Fontamara*, which is viewed as the first stage in Silone's "conversion from politics to love." Includes a discussion of the language, the humor, and the narrative devices in the novel.

Paynter, Maria Nicolai. *Ignazio Silone: Beyond the Tragic Vision.* Buffalo, N.Y.: University of Toronto Press, 2000. Critical study focusing on the controversies surrounding Silone and his writing. Analyzes his intellectual and political convictions and assesses his development as a writer. Includes bibliography and index.

Pugliese, Stanislao G. *Bitter Spring: A Life of Ignazio Silone.* New York: Farrar, Straus and Giroux, 2009. A comprehensive and detailed account of Silone's life and work that addresses many of the misconceptions about Silone's political involvement. Describes how Silone's personal faith defied political and religious orthodoxies and was reflected in his fiction.

Scott, Nathan A. "Ignazio Silone: Novelist of the Revolutionary Sensibility." In *Rehearsals of Decomposure.* New York: King's Crown Press, 1952. Sees *Fontamara* as the initial statement of major themes developed in Silone's later novels; these themes include corruption in government and the dichotomy between the middle class and the proletariat.

Sipe, A. W. Richard. "Will the Real Priest Please Stand Up: Ignazio Silone." In *The Serpent and the Dove: Celibacy in Literature and Life.* Westport, Conn.: Praeger, 2007. A study of religious celibacy, focusing on historic figures who were celibate, such as Mahatma Gandhi, and on literary accounts of celibacy, including the writings of Silone.

Fool for Love

Author: Sam Shepard (1943-)
First produced: 1983; first published, 1983
Type of work: Drama
Type of plot: Hyperrealism
Time of plot: Late twentieth century
Locale: Mojave Desert, California

Principal characters:
MAY, a young woman
EDDIE, a young man
MARTIN, May's date
THE OLD MAN, a presence in the motel room

The Story:

The shabby old man sits in a rocking chair drinking whiskey. He exists only in the minds of Eddie and May. May sits on the edge of the bed, staring at the floor. Eddie sits at the table facing May, working resin into his bucking glove. He tosses the glove on the table and insists to May that he is not leaving. She will not look at him. He moves closer to stroke her hair. She squeezes his legs, then pushes him away. May says he smells like he was with another woman. Eddie says it was the horses.

Eddie leaves, disgusted. May screams for him not to go, grabs a pillow, and throws herself on the bed, moaning and moving around on it. Eddie returns, slamming the door. May backs herself into a corner and says she will kill the countess he was with, and then she will kill Eddie. Eddie tells her how many miles he rode to see her. He lowers his eyes and says he misses her neck. Eddied insists he has it all figured out this time, but May does not want to hear it. She says she has her own job and life now. When Eddie seems ready to accept that May wants him to leave, they come together for a long, tender kiss. Then May knees him in the groin. Eddie doubles over and drops to the floor. May goes into the bathroom and slams the door. The old man points to a picture of Barbara Mandrell and claims he is married to her in his mind, and it is important that Eddie understand the difference between being married in his mind and being married in real life.

May comes out of the bathroom carrying a sleek red dress and heels. As she changes into the sexy clothes she says numbly that she hates Eddie. Eddie says he will go. May says he better, since someone is coming over to see her. Eddie wants to know how long this was going on, and then he leaves suddenly. May yells after him and then grabs a suitcase from under the bed and starts packing. When she hears Eddie returning, she shoves it back under the bed and begins brushing her hair. Eddie returns with a shotgun and a bottle of tequila. He takes a long drink from the bottle. May asks Eddie why he always messes her up like this. Eddie says nothing will ever separate them, and May tells him to get out. Eddie goes out the door carrying the shotgun.

May throws herself against the door and weeps. The old man tells a story about when May was a baby and would not stop crying. May crawls slowly to the bed, grabs a pillow, and rocks herself. Suddenly she stops grieving, sits at the table, and takes a long drink of tequila. Eddie returns with steer ropes. They ignore each other. Eddie loops the bedposts and says he does not believe there is any guy coming over.

May says there is no point in trying to impress her because it is all over. She tries to leave, but Eddie drags her, kicking and screaming, back into the room. Headlights shine through the window. May opens the door and sees a woman in a Mercedes-Benz. Just as Eddie slams the door shut and pushes May out of the way, a pistol shot rips through glass outside. May is furious, and she struggles to get away from Eddie, but he rolls on top of her to keep her down on the floor.

The countess blows the windshield out of Eddie's truck. He wants to keep the lights off or leave, but May will not do either. The old man says he cannot see himself in either one of them, and that it is a good thing that he got out when he did. Eddie insists May will never get rid of him, and May wants to know why she should believe this time is any different from the others. She opens the door and challenges the countess. Instead, her date, Martin, comes crashing in and tackles Eddie, believing he is trying to hurt May. May tells him it is okay since Eddie is her cousin. Eddie says May is lying. May goes into the bathroom.

Eddie tells Martin he and May are half brother and sister. Their father, the old man, fell in love twice but neither family knew about the other until May and Eddie had already met in high school and fallen in love. The old man drinks with Eddie and Martin during the story and comments occasionally on what Eddie is saying. Eddie describes going on a long walk one night with his father that ended up at the house where May and her mother lived. Eddie then realized his father had two lives, and that May was his sister.

May returns to the room, saying she heard every word. May claims Eddie is not telling the whole truth and insists on going to the movies, but Eddie will not let them leave, so May decides to tell Martin the rest of the story. She says she and her mother tracked her missing father down and discovered him eating dinner with his other family, Eddie and his mother. After that incident, the old man disappeared forever. Her mother grieved terribly. May said she was so much in love with Eddie at the time that they were both sick when they could not be together. Her mother begged them not to see each other anymore. She went to Eddie's mother with the truth. Eddie's mother shot herself in the head as a result.

The old man protests this version could not possibly happen, but Eddie calmly tells him that his own shotgun is the one his mother used to kill herself. May and Eddie meet and lock gazes. The old man tries to part them, but Eddie and May ignore him. They embrace tenderly. A loud explosion and the sound of shattering glass are heard outside. A gasoline fire burns, and horses scream and gallop away. Martin tells Eddie his horses are loose. Eddie decides to go check on them and tells May he will be back in a minute. May stares at the door as Eddie goes through it, then turns to get the suitcase. Martin asks her if she is going with Eddie. May straightens herself up and stares at Martin. She tells him Eddie already went, and then she leaves the room herself, suitcase in hand, without closing the door. The old man points to an imaginary picture, claiming it is the woman of his dreams and begins to rock slowly in his chair.

Critical Evaluation:

Sam Shepard began writing plays in the 1960's and had many of them produced in New York before he reached the age of thirty. *Fool for Love* shares the one-act structure and relentless pace of earlier plays such as or *Operation Sidewinder* (1970) or *Cowboy Mouth* (1971), but it was written after Shepard's longer "family plays," such as *Curse of the Starving Class* (1976) and *Buried Child* (1978), which won the Pulitzer Prize in drama 1979. It combines the wild urgency of some earlier plays with more complex character development. The most significant innovation in *Fool for Love* is that many critics consider it the first Shepard play in which a woman's character, May, is as fully and interestingly drawn as a man's.

The term "realistic," however, is not an accurate way to describe Shepard's rendering of May, or any other of his characters, if by "realistic" one means objectively consistent. May's character is not "absurd" in the traditional sense of that term, since the motivation for her actions is uncovered in the course of the play. Shepard's style of drama is hard to define according to existing, traditional formulas. A director who worked with Shepard makes an interesting case for labeling Shepard's work "hyperrealism." What makes Shepard's characters "hyperreal" is their awareness of what others consider "realistic" at the same time they have abandoned attempts to project an objective presentation of themselves. The audience meets all of them at a place well beyond the breakdown of objective pretense as a façade. All that the characters say and do comments on the discrepancy between the audience's conventional concept of how they should behave and the way their own obsessions motivate them.

May's character is an example of this dynamic. She is a pragmatist, a scathing foil to Eddie's stock Shepard-style male caricature, whose occupation is that of a cowboy, "who dreams things up." Unlike the women in earlier plays, May talks openly and frankly about her own emotional landscape and all its contradictory passions. The audience quickly learns that Eddie's attempt to pacify her with fantasy during his long absences (a pile of fashion magazines) sends her packing in search of her own life. The play's imperative to dramatize her reality is seen most strikingly when she tells Martin the rest of the story about her and Eddie, and, against the old man's protests, Eddie quietly corroborates her version as the truth.

Another significant way in which Shepard plays with dramatic conventions in *Fool for Love* is his usual attention to dramatization of images rather than ideas. Often the most significant, climactic moments are underscored by stage images rather than by dialogue. Dialogue is part of the image being performed and is used for emphasis of these images. There are many examples of this in *Fool for Love*, among them the long, motionless opening position of May on the bed, unresponsive to Eddie's coaxing, and the way Eddie and May physically back themselves up against and slam against the walls of the motel room as they argue. In this way stage directions place the dialogue in the visual context of the play more than the speeches themselves direct the action.

Although some contend the monologues in this play are prosaic by comparison to those in Shepard's other plays, the images they evoke are still memorable. The presence of animal instinct as an overriding motivator, for example, is present in the old man's speech about how he got May to stop crying one night by taking her unawares out into a herd of cattle neither of them could see. In other places, the clipped conversational style of the speeches emphasizes the physical settings each interaction dramatizes. Shepard uses words like paints or musical notes rather than as carriers of ideas. In *Fool for Love*, the fiery, tortured image of Eddie and May in the grips of incestuous love exhibits the contradictory way the American myth of masculinity defines love and the effect it has on American women.

Maria Theresa Maggi

Further Reading

Bottoms, Stephen J. *The Theatre of Sam Shepard: States of Crisis*. New York: Cambridge University Press, 1998. Traces the development of Shepard's playwriting from his experimental one-act dramas of the 1960's through his work in the mid-1990's. Chapter 6 contains an analysis of *Fool for Love*.

Hart, Lynda. *Sam Shepard's Metaphorical Stages*. Westport, Conn.: Greenwood Press, 1987. In the section of her book about Shepard's brand of realism, "Realism Revisited," Hart devotes several pages of discussion to the staging of *Fool for Love*.

Londre, Felicia Hardison. "A Motel of the Mind: *Fool for Love* and *A Lie of the Mind*." In *Rereading Shepard*, edited by Leonard Wilcox. New York: St. Martin's Press, 1993. An interesting discussion of motels as metaphors for states of mind and heart in Shepard's plays.

Marranca, Bonnie, ed. *American Dreams: The Imagination of Sam Shepard*. New York: Performing Arts Journal Publications, 1981. Compilation of analytical essays, reviews, and interviews with actors, directors, and Shepard himself.

Rosen, Carol. *Sam Shepard: A "Poetic Rodeo."* New York: Palgrave Macmillan, 2004. Provides analyses of all of Shepard's plays, discussing his experiments with dramatic structure, character, and the rhythms of performance. Includes a lengthy interview with Shepard.

Roudané, Matthew, ed. *The Cambridge Companion to Sam Shepard*. New York: Cambridge University Press, 2002. Includes an interview with Shepard, a production overview, a bibliographic essay, and essays discussing Shepard's ideas about writing, the classic Western and Shepard's family plays, and Shepard as a musical experimenter. The numerous references to *Fool for Love* are listed in the index.

Shewey, Don. *Sam Shepard*. Updated ed. New York: Da Capo Press, 1997. A biography examining Shepard's life and works, describing his ability to be both a serious artist and a pop culture figure.

Tucker, Martin. *Sam Shepard*. New York: Continuum Press, 1992. Contains an interesting discussion of *Fool for Love* that speculates about possible autobiographical links to the romantic and family dynamics explored in the play.

Wetzsetson, Ross. Introduction to *Fool for Love, and Other Plays* by Sam Shepard. New York: Bantam Books, 1984. An insightful and readable description of Shepard's dramatic sensibility, with special attention to *Fool for Love*.

The Fool of Quality
Or, The History of Henry, Earl of Moreland

Author: Henry Brooke (c. 1703-1783)
First published: 1765-1770
Type of work: Novel
Type of plot: Didactic
Time of plot: Eighteenth century
Locale: England

Principal characters:
HENRY CLINTON, earl of Moreland
MR. FENTON, his foster father
NED, Henry's friend
FANNY GOODALL, Mr. Fenton's cousin
ABENAIDE, princess of Morocco

The Story:

Put out to nurse when he was a baby, Henry Clinton, second son of the earl of Moreland, sees little of his noble parents and their favorite older son. At the age of five and a half, young Harry, as he is called, makes the acquaintance of Mr. Fenton, an old man of the neighborhood. The old gentleman is so impressed by the innate goodness of Harry's nature that he steals the boy away from his nurse, after leaving a note for the parents telling them that he will one day return their son. It is Mr. Fenton's purpose to train young Harry to become the most accomplished and perfect of men. The parents grieve for a short time but soon forget the boy in favor of his older brother.

Mr. Fenton takes Harry to a mansion at Hampstead. With them they take Ned, a beggar lad whom Harry befriends. There, Harry's education begins. Mr. Fenton, a very wealthy man, gives Harry large sums of money and hundreds of garments to distribute to the deserving poor. It is Harry's task to learn to distinguish the deserving from the rascals. At the same time, the boys are instructed in academic subjects, bodybuilding, and other suitable lessons. Ned has irrepressible spirits, and he constantly torments his teachers. Sometimes Harry joins in the fun, but he is such a good boy that he immediately performs a favor for anyone who may suffer because of Ned or himself.

Harry is so tenderhearted that he frequently brings whole families to live at the mansion and gives them money, clothing, and work. Mr. Fenton is highly pleased with the boy, who has purity of heart and a willingness to be instructed in all phases of life. The old gentleman teaches him theology, principles of government, moral rules, and many other forms of philosophy.

Harry becomes the champion of all those who are tormented by bullies, even though the ruffians are often larger and stronger than he. He soundly thrashes many boys and men and then immediately helps them to their feet and becomes their friend. Once he trounces the son of a nobleman. The mother, not knowing Harry is also an earl's son, would have him severely punished, but the father sees Harry's good character and defends the lad. Most of the people Harry thrashes become his devoted servants, seeing and loving the nobility of character he possesses.

One day, Mr. Fenton calls on a lady who has issued several invitations to him. He is delighted to learn that the woman, now Lady Maitland, is his cousin Fanny Goodall. In their youth they loved each other, but he was many years older than Fanny. Recognizing Mr. Fenton, Fanny now calls him Harry Clinton. He is the brother of young Harry's father, the earl of Moreland; thus, he is Harry's uncle. Cast out with a small inheritance as was the custom with younger sons, he made his fortune as a merchant, married a wealthy woman, and prospered still more, but his beloved wife, his children, and his dear father-in-law all died, leaving him bereft of any emotion but sorrow. Although he gained a great fortune on the death of his father-in-law, he considers himself the poorest of men. Fanny is also a widow, and the two friends comfort each other as they talk of their sad lives. Mr. Fenton sees that Fanny is almost overcome with grief and promises to tell her the rest of his story later, but the good lady is called away before she can hear more.

Harry's education continues. Mr. Fenton, as he is known to all but Fanny, sends him to the prisons to pay the debts of deserving persons and to secure their release. He continues to take unfortunates home with him, much to the joy of Mr. Fenton. Ned, too, is improving, although he still does not have the nobility of character that Harry possesses. One day, Ned's parents are found. Harry helped some people who suffered an accident nearby, and these people became friends of the household. By a scar that his old nurse recognizes, Ned is known to her and then to his parents. The boy was stolen in

infancy. It is with great joy that the parents greet their son. Although Ned is saddened to leave Mr. Fenton and his beloved friend Harry, he goes joyfully with his rightful parents.

Countless numbers of people become Harry's friends because of his concern for their well-being. Mr. Fenton sends him and his tutor, one of Harry's charities, to London to learn the ways of the city and the court. Even the king is impressed by the lad. Harry retains his modesty through all the adulation he receives, a fact that adds to his popularity. The queen and other noble ladies seek his company, but he eludes them all, making them better, however, for having known him.

When Mr. Fenton learns of the death of Harry's mother and brother, he returns the boy to his father, the earl of Moreland, who is overjoyed at finding his lost son. When he learns that the child's abductor was his own brother, thought dead, the earl is filled with remorse for having treated his brother so badly many years before. The brothers are united publicly, and everyone learns that Mr. Fenton is in reality the second son of the house of Moreland. The earl is grateful to his brother for stealing the boy and making a perfect man of him.

Mr. Clinton, as Mr. Fenton is called from then on, tells the rest of the story of his life. After the death of his loved ones, he lived in sorrow for many years. Then he married again after almost losing his life in his suit of the girl he loved, Louisa d'Aubigny. They had a lovely daughter named Eloisa. Sorrow, however, again haunted Mr. Clinton, for Louisa died from a fall and Eloisa was washed from a ship and seen no more. The bereaved man lived in solitude and misery until he met and abducted Harry.

Not long after learning his brother's story, Harry's father dies, and the boy becomes the earl of Moreland. He now has a huge fortune to spend for charity, and he spends wisely so that those who receive will profit from the money in all ways.

Before long, Mr. Clinton learns from his dead wife's brother that he is coming to England, accompanied by Fanny Goodall. Fanny married Louisa's brother and thus is Mr. Clinton's sister-in-law. The old friends rejoice at their reunion. Fanny is accompanied by a dark Moorish page to whom Harry is instantly attracted. The boy tells Harry that he has a sister Abenaide, as fair as he himself is dark. She will soon accompany their father, the emperor, who is coming to England with his wife. The boy was sent ahead as a page to be trained in genteel conduct. When the girl arrives, Mr. Clinton finds her to be the daughter of his own supposedly dead Eloisa. Saved from the sea, Eloisa married the emperor of Morocco. To Harry's extreme surprise, the Moorish princess is the same page whom he loves so dearly. She was in disguise to escape an unwanted royal lover and continued the deception in order to tease Harry. Princess Abenaide and

Harry marry, and their wedding is blessed with the prayers of the hundreds the perfect young man had befriended.

Critical Evaluation:

With a text that exceeds three hundred thousand words, about five times as long as an average modern novel, *The Fool of Quality* was originally published by installment in five volumes. Although it achieved success in its original form, the book became better known through a single-volume abridgment by John Wesley. It is a didactic work that does not readily fit any traditional category. It most nearly resembles the sentimental novel, a form pioneered in English by such writers as Samuel Richardson, Laurence Sterne, and Henry Mackenzie. On the other hand, its loosely knit, episodic plot, its sporadic exotic adventures, and its idealistic theme of constantly righting wrongs link it with the picaresque tradition, specifically with Miguel de Cervantes' *El ingenioso hidalgo don Quixote de la Mancha* (1605, 1615; *Don Quixote de la Mancha*; 1612-1620).

The preface establishes a tone of satire; Brooke assails his society for its self-indulgence, luxury, and greed and denounces these vices as threats to the nation. Although the novel includes little direct satire, occasional character names such as Lord Freelove, Mr. Sneer, Lady Cribbage, and Miss Trinket suggest satire against the vanity and superficiality of the upper class. Despite the novel's profession of egalitarianism, however, most of the commoners turn out to be gentle folk whose true identities have been either lost or concealed. In the end Brooke has his protagonist marry a Moroccan princess who, he has just learned, is his cousin.

In a general sense, the account of the hero's education follows the course laid down by Jean-Jacques Rousseau in *Émile: Ou, De l'éducation* (1762; *Émile: Or, Education*, 1911). Unschooled in the vanity and hypocrisy that pervade aristocratic society, Henry Clinton receives the ironic epithet "fool." As the second son of an earl, Henry is a man of quality, yet his father expects that he will have no aristocratic responsibility. He is thus sent from home to be reared in a modest rural setting by the family of his nurse. The simplicity and beauty of nature plus the kind treatment by his foster family lay the foundation for his education in right conduct. Removed by his uncle, Mr. Fenton, Henry gains further advantage through continuing his education by acquiring sound moral principles. Mr. Fenton's seemingly unlimited wealth enables Henry to learn the importance of compassion and charity in dealing with those less fortunate. An underlying theme, illustrated in the story of the wealthy Mr. Fenton, is that virtue is the road to wealth and power. The middle portion of his education—by the kindly Mr. Clement, a tutor

hired by Mr. Fenton—guides the youth in charitable activities.

Mr. Fenton himself directly educates Henry in matters of government, clarifying the English constitution in a lengthy lesson. In addition to a conservative, straightforward account of political entities, the lesson incorporates Rousseau's principles of popular sovereignty and consent of the governed. With the further assistance of a clergyman, Mr. Meekly, Mr. Fenton educates the young man in religion, their discourse upholding the rational Christianity widely accepted in eighteenth century England. Relying heavily on biblical passages, the account endorses the providential view of history. The unexpected death of Henry's brother ensures that Henry inherits the title and becomes able to apply all his lessons in virtue and practical power. Henry's coming to maturity thus portrays Rousseau's educational philosophy as beneficial and feasible.

As a sentimental novel, the work employs a narrative technique that makes it somewhat less successful than its predecessors. It offers an abundance of emotion, with mature characters fainting, blushing, bursting into tears, or freely embracing—reactions that serve to reinforce Rousseau's message that emotion is good. The most poignant parts of the narrative, however, are presented from the point of view of a character relating his or her past. Typically, these tales feature pitiable details of suffering, but the reader does not see the wretchedness at first hand through the narrator's eyes—as happens, for example, in Sterne's *A Sentimental Journey Through France and Italy* (1768), in which the plight of Maria is indelibly impressed on the memory. Brooke's method of narration distances the most moving events from the reader and thus reduces their emotional impact. Another narrative technique results in a further disruption of the already slow narrative pace. At the end of most chapters, Brooke includes a dialogue between the Author and Friend, who usually questions the author about the narrative and its themes.

In support of the theme of charity, the plot incorporates astounding coincidence and extravagant improbabilities. Long-lost relatives are recognized and reunited with family members, people live for years under assumed names until their true identity can be revealed, characters disguise themselves to take part in unlikely adventures, and astounding escapes are brought about. For example, as Mr. Fenton is narrating his life to Fanny Goodall, he includes the story of his wealthy servant John. Approaching his death without any living relatives, John resolved to leave his fortune to the next needy person who came to Mr. Fenton's door. The next arrival was a woman who asked for charity, and a small initial promise elicited her story. Her misfortune came about because her husband, in a fit of jealousy, had mistaken her long-lost brother for a lover and, after stabbing him, had fled. It was learned that the dying John was the husband, formerly Barnaby Tirrell, and the reunion was appropriately tearful. When another recipient of Mr. Fenton's bounty, Homely, narrates his unfortunate life, it is discovered he had saved Fenton from drowning twenty years earlier.

Its length, heavy didacticism, and departures from realism make *The Fool of Quality* an unlikely candidate for popular revival. From the standpoint of literary history, however, the work remains significant for its standing as a novel of sentiment, a precursor of the novel of reform.

"Critical Evaluation" by Stanley Archer

Further Reading

Baker, Ernest A. *The Novel of Sentiment and Gothic Romance*. Vol. 5 in *The History of the English Novel*. 10 vols. New York: Barnes & Noble, 1924-1939. Classifies the novel as sentimental and devotes discussion to its literary allusions and inset stories. Praises the work as the first novel that presents a full and sympathetic account of a boy growing to maturity.

Bellamy, Liz. *Commerce, Morality, and the Eighteenth-Century Novel*. New York: Cambridge University Press, 1998. Bellamy's examination of the eighteenth century novel contains several references to *The Fool of Quality* that are listed in the index. A two-page discussion of the novel is included in chapter 6, "The Sentimental Novel."

Foster, James R. *History of the Pre-Romantic Novel in England*. New York: Modern Language Association of America, 1949. Summarizes portions of the novel and points out incongruities in Brooke's narrative. An unsympathetic analysis draws attention to the book's exaggerations.

Probyn, Clive T. *English Fiction of the Eighteenth Century, 1700-1789*. London: Longman, 1987. Suggests that Brooke drew upon Henry Fielding's *Joseph Andrews* (1742) and *Tom Jones* (1749). Argues that the excesses of sentimentalism and idealism mar Brooke's didactic purpose.

Scurr, Helen Margaret. *Henry Brooke*. Minneapolis: University of Minnesota Press, 1927. Comprehensive and detailed examination of Brooke's life and career. The chapter on his novels centers on *The Fool of Quality*, treating it as a flawed narrative that exerted a measurable influence on subsequent fiction.

Shroff, Homai J. *The Eighteenth Century Novel: The Idea of the Gentleman*. London: Edward Arnold, 1983. Links Brooke with Henry Mackenzie, demonstrating how both differed from Jean-Jacques Rousseau's ideas about the essentials of education for the gentleman. Points out that despite its seeming egalitarianism, the novel usually portrays worthy characters as members of the gentry.

Spacks, Patricia Meyer. "The Novel of Sentiment." In *Novel Beginnings: Experiments in Eighteenth-Century English Fiction*. New Haven, Conn.: Yale University Press, 2006. Spacks's examination of the eighteenth century English novel includes a discussion of *The Fool of Quality* as a work of sentimental fiction.

Fools Crow

Author: James Welch (1940-2003)
First published: 1986
Type of work: Novel
Type of plot: Historical realism
Time of plot: 1868-1870
Locale: Montana Territory

Principal characters:
FOOLS CROW (formerly WHITE MAN'S DOG), a Pikuni Blackfeet youth
RIDES-AT-THE-DOOR, his father
FAST HORSE, Fools Crow's boastful friend
YELLOW KIDNEY, a respected warrior
RUNNING FISHER, Fools Crow's younger brother
FEATHER WOMAN, a legendary Pikuni woman

The Story:

White Man's Dog, an unlucky youth of the Lone Eaters band of Pikuni Blackfeet, is invited by his friend Fast Horse to join a winter horse-riding party on the Crow camp, to be led by the wise warrior Yellow Kidney. Most of the men are young and inexperienced; Yellow Kidney watches Fast Horse carefully, believing him to be too boastful and reckless.

Once at the great Crow camp of Bull Shield, White Man's Dog and three others are able to separate more than a hundred horses from the large herd and safely escape with them. Only

Yellow Kidney, who with Fast Horse went into the camp to steal the powerful horses of the Crow chiefs, fails to return. Fast Horse reports that he last saw Yellow Kidney in the camp, and they fear he is dead.

After a period of mourning, Yellow Kidney's wife requests that she be allowed to be the Sacred Vow Woman for the next Sun Dance ceremony. She offers this sacrifice to ensure the safe return of her husband. Meanwhile, White Man's Dog, gaining courage and power with the help of the healer Mik-api, supplies her family with meat and prepares to marry her daughter.

Months later, a weak and mutilated Yellow Kidney returns to the Lone Eaters camp. He relates how the Crows captured him after being alerted by the loud, foolish boasts of Fast Horse. Bull Shield cut off Yellow Kidney's fingers, a humiliation that will prevent him from hunting and providing for his family ever again. Then he was tied to a horse and sent into the snow. He was found and cared for by the Spotted Horse (Cheyenne) people. When the Lone Eaters council hears Yellow Kidney's story, they agree to banish Fast Horse for his lies and for causing harm to come to this brave warrior. Fast Horse flees to a renegade band of Pikuni raiders headed by Owl Child.

The Pikunis mass to send a war party of three hundred to avenge the mutilation of Yellow Kidney and punish Bull Shield. White Man's Dog has the honor of striking the enemy first on behalf of his father-in-law Yellow Kidney, and he manages to kill and scalp Bull Shield. His exploits earn him a new name, Fools Crow. His brother Running Fisher, on the other hand, loses courage and spirit.

A wounded Fast Horse returns to the Lone Eaters camp, gut-shot by a white settler he attacked. Fast Horse's father urges Fools Crow to speak with him, and when a sullen Fast Horse leaves the camp again, Fools Crow is sent after his friend to convince him to return. Fools Crow knows his attempt will be useless because Fast Horse refuses to accept responsibility for his betrayal of Yellow Kidney. Meanwhile, Yellow Kidney, who sees himself now as a nothing-man, determines to leave the camp and return to the Spotted Horse people. While he rests in an empty war lodge, he is found and killed by a vengeful white man in retaliation for the murders committed by Owl Child and his raiders.

A scout arrives at the Lone Eaters camp to call the chiefs to a council with the seizer (United States Army) chiefs. Most of the Pikuni chiefs refuse to attend. Only the peace chief Heavy Runner, a good man but too trusting, and three others agree to go, along with Fools Crow's father, Rides-at-the-door, who understands English and is asked to speak for the Lone Eaters. The seizer general is not pleased that so few

come to this council, and he makes demands that the chiefs know they cannot meet. Heavy Runner agrees not to make war upon the whites, but when the men's societies' chiefs meet afterward, they are unable to decide what to do.

Fools Crow fears that his people are helpless. Nitsokan, Dream Helper, tells him to journey for three days and three nights without stopping, in a quest for answers. When he comes to a strange valley between sky and earth, he finds Feather Woman, a figure from Pikuni legend. Her marriage to Morning Star, the child of Sun and Moon, resulted in the birth of her son Scarface, who brought the Sun Dance ceremony to the Pikunis. Feather Woman dug a sacred turnip out of the sky, creating a hole, so she was banished to this place, where she mourns for her lost husband and son.

For Fools Crow, she paints prophetic scenes upon a yellow skin—visions of the fate of his people. Feather Woman tells him that he can aid them best by preparing them for the hard times to come. When he returns, the dreaded white-scabs (smallpox) invades the Lone Eaters camp, and he struggles to help the sick.

After two weeks, those men who are still healthy ride out in search of meat. They meet eight wounded Pikunis, survivors of Heavy Runner's peaceful band, which was attacked by the seizers. Fools Crow goes on alone to the massacred camp to witness the horribly burned bodies. This becomes his role, knowing that, like Feather Woman, he is "burdened with the knowledge of his people." He also knows from his visions that his people will ultimately survive.

Critical Evaluation:

Combining history, fiction, and legend, *Fools Crow* received the Pacific Northwest Booksellers Association Book Award in 1987. Perhaps the novel's outstanding achievement is its evocation of the daily life and worldview of the Pikuni Blackfeet people. James Welch, who is of Blackfeet, Gros Ventre, and Irish ancestry, researched details of custom and ceremony. He translates names and idioms literally to suggest the flavor of Pikuni speech. For example, the moon is called Night Red Light, Fools Crow's power animal is Skunk-bear (wolverine), and the white soldiers become the seizers.

The novel culminates in the historic Marias River Massacre of January 23, 1870, in which 173 Blackfeet, mostly old people, women, and children, were attacked and killed by United States troops. The dead were members of the Pikuni band led by Heavy Runner, a chief friendly to the whites, who was given written assurance of safe conduct by General Alfred H. Sully. Welch's own great-grandmother, Red Paint Woman, was a survivor of this terrible event. This massacre of peaceful civilians has been ignored or forgotten in the annals of American history. The "massacre" six years later of General George Armstrong Custer's 210 armed troops, who were making war on the Indians, by a much larger force of Sioux and Cheyennes, however, has not been. Welch brings a different perspective, that of the Native American, to United States history.

In the world of *Fools Crow*, there is a blurring of the line between the truth of everyday reality and the truth of dream and legend. A dream may serve as a source of power; a myth offers an alternate perception of the world. Welch's characters readily accept both. Fools Crow's repeated dream of the white-faced girl who beckons to him makes him uneasy. He is horrified when he realizes that he has dreamed of the white-scabs death lodge into which Yellow Kidney later stumbles, and he feels guilty that he did not warn Yellow Kidney of his dream. At the same time another youth has dreamed of a blind white pony with streaks of blood across its back—a death horse and an omen. Dreams are even shared: Both Fools Crow and his father's young third wife dream simultaneously of consummating their guilty passion beside a white, unknown river.

The novel's loose structure lends itself to digression. Action slows in order to introduce a legend, such as that of Feather Woman, the Pikuni woman who married Morning Star and lived with him in the sky. She brought to her people the sacred medicine bonnet and digging stick. Her son Scarface taught the Pikunis the Sun Dance so that they could honor his grandfather.

Magical Realism, an element in the literature of Latin America, is also integral to Native American literature. When the young Fools Crow seeks his power animal in the mountains, he follows a raven. When they come to a clearing, the bird speaks: "It surprises you that I speak the language of the two-leggeds. It's easy." Raven helps him to find his power animal.

The last part of the novel involves the final quest that Fools Crow undertakes, wearing the painted face of death and riding through the snow to help his people. He must go as a supplicant, without weapons or belongings, to find his vision. When he arrives at the mysterious valley, it is summer. A woman in a white doeskin dress approaches him. At first she seems old but appears younger as she comes closer, wearing the short hair of one in mourning. Feather Woman tells Fools Crow that she has brought misery on her people, but that one day she will be allowed to return to her husband and son, and then the Pikunis will be happy.

Feather Woman paints for him the terrible visions on the yellow skin. He sees the Pikunis dying from the white-scabs. He sees hundreds of seizers riding out from their fort, heading north to Pikuni country. He sees starving people and a prairie barren of game. Nitsokan chooses him to see what is to come, and he is afraid. Then he hears children laughing and sees Indian children at a government school, and he is comforted. Somehow, the Pikunis will survive. For Fools Crow, dreams are real, animals speak, and one can see the future.

Joanne McCarthy

Further Reading

Barry, Nora. "'A Myth to Be Alive': James Welch's *Fools Crow*." *MELUS* 17, no. 1 (Spring, 1991-1992): 3-20. An examination of Fools Crow's role as character and mythic hero. Links him to the legend of Scarface, the unpromising hero, contrasted with the failed heroes Fast Horse and Running Fisher.

Gish, Robert F. "Word Medicine: Storytelling and Magic Realism in James Welch's *Fools Crow*." *American Indian Quarterly* 14, no. 4 (Fall, 1990): 349-354. An excellent discussion of the multiple levels of storytelling and language, and dreams and Magical Realism, present in the novel. Suggests that Native American literature establishes a crucial link between primitive and modern worldviews.

Lupton, Mary Jane. *James Welch: A Critical Companion*. Westport, Conn.: Greenwood Press, 2004. Includes a chapter on *Fools Crow* that discusses the novel's plot and character development, depiction of characters and animals, narrative point of view, structure, genre, setting, theme, and use of Magical Realism.

McFarland, Ronald E. *Understanding James Welch*. Columbia: University of South Carolina Press, 2000. Provides analysis and critical commentary on Welch's work. Argues that each of Welch's novels is written from a different perspective, with *Fools Crow* featuring characteristics of the epic.

Murphree, Bruce. "Welch's *Fools Crow*." *Explicator* 52, no. 3 (Spring, 1994): 186-187. Applies the legend of Seco-mo-muckon and the firehorn to the relationship between Fast Horse and Yellow Kidney during the horse-stealing raid on the Crow camp. Underscores the importance of tribal unity apparent in both legend and novel.

Ramsey, Jarold. "*Fools Crow*." *Parabola* 12, no. 1 (February, 1987): 108, 110-112. Praises the novel as a "magnificent" blending of historical accuracy and tribal myth, at the forefront of Native American literature.

Schorcht, Blanca. *Storied Voices in Native American Texts: Harry Robinson, Thomas King, James Welch, and Leslie Marmon Silko*. New York: Routledge, 2003. Examines the work of Welch and three other Native American writers, demonstrating how their writing has roots in the Native American storytelling tradition.

for colored girls who have considered suicide/ when the rainbow is enuf
A Choreopoem

Author: Ntozake Shange (1948-   )
First produced: 1975; first published, 1975
Type of work: Drama
Type of plot: Social realism
Time of plot: Twentieth century
Locale: Outside the cities of Chicago, Detroit, Houston, Baltimore, San Francisco, New York, and St. Louis

Principal characters:
LADY IN BROWN, pays the drama's only positive tribute to a black man
LADY IN RED, describes the methods she uses to get a man to love her
LADY IN YELLOW, summarizes the predicament of black women
LADY IN PURPLE, chooses companions who cannot comprehend her as a means of avoiding hurt
LADY IN GREEN, squanders her love on an indifferent man
LADY IN BLUE, a victim of emotional and physical abuse
LADY IN ORANGE, tries to use music to cure her pain

The Story:

All the ladies come onto the stage and freeze in positions of distress. The lady in brown calls upon the others to sing a black girl's song, to give her words and to bring her out of herself. Each lady declares her origins—the lady in brown outside Chicago, the lady in yellow outside Detroit, the lady in purple outside Houston, the lady in red outside Baltimore, the lady in green outside San Francisco, the lady in blue outside Manhattan, and the lady in orange outside St. Louis. Then they begin to sing songs of infancy and childhood: "Mama's Little Baby Likes Shortnin' Bread" and "Little Sally Walker."

The lady in yellow tells the story of graduation night when she was the only virgin in the crowd. She drank and danced and went out to the parking lot with Bobby, where she made love to him in the back seat of a Buick. The lady in blue then relates how, pretending she was Puerto Rican, she ran away at sixteen to the South Bronx to dance with Willie Colón, the famous salsa musician. When he did not show up at the dance hall, she got mad, refused to dance with anyone, and started yelling in English. Later she was possessed by the subtle blues of Archie Shepp, and she recited her poem as a thank-you for music that she loved "more than poem."

The lady in red recites a note attached to a plant she gave to her lover when she ended the affair. She loved him for eight months, two weeks, and a day; was stood up four times; left him presents, poems, and plants; drove miles to see him before work; and finally decided that her experiment of debasing herself to gain love was a failure. All of the ladies then dance to Willie Colón's "Che Che Cole"—they dance to keep from crying and to keep from dying.

A sudden light change stops the dancing, and the ladies in green, yellow, orange, and brown leave the stage. The ladies in red, blue, and purple discuss how difficult it is to press rape charges against someone you know, someone who took you out to dinner or made dinner for you and then beat you and betrayed you. The nature of rape changed; it haunts the places and people where companionship is sought. When the light again changes, the ladies are hit by an imaginary slap. The ladies in red and purple exit. The lady in blue reveals her experience of a lonely abortion. She went alone because she did not want anyone to see her or to know that she was pregnant and ashamed. After her monologue, she exits the stage.

Soft, deep music is heard and voices call "Sechita." The lady in purple enters and describes the quadroon balls in St. Louis and the gambling boats on the Mississippi. She narrates the story of Sechita, as the lady in green dances her life. Sechita dances in a creole carnival after the wrestlers finish their match; she dances the dance of Nefertiti, of the Egyptian goddess of love and creativity, of the rituals of the second millennium, and then she leaves the stage. Portraying an eight-year-old girl in St. Louis, the lady in brown explains how she was disqualified from a library reading contest because she reported on a book from the Adult Reading Room. The book, a biography of Toussaint L'Ouverture, the liberator of Haiti, introduced her to her first black hero, and she fell in love with him and decided to run away to Haiti. When she got down to the docks, she met a little boy whose name was Toussaint Jones, and she decided that they might be able to move some of their own spirits down by the river in St. Louis, 1955.

The lady in red follows with the tale of a dazzling coquette who lured men to her bed and made divine love to them. At four-thirty in the morning she arose, bathed, and became herself, an ordinary brown-braided woman who chased the men from her bed, wrote accounts of her exploits in a journal, and cried herself to sleep.

The lady in blue explains how she used to live in the world until she moved to Harlem, and that she felt her universe constricted to six blocks and a tunnel with a train. The ladies in purple, yellow, and orange enter and represent the strangers that the lady in blue feared. In another tone, the lady in purple tells the story of three friends all attracted to the same man, who dated one and flirted with the other two. When the first romance waned, he sought out one of the others, who told her friend that he claimed the relationship was over. The two found him with another woman, and the friends comforted each other.

A quartet of the ladies—in blue, purple, yellow, and orange—sing of their lost loves and pain until they are joined by the ladies in red, green, and brown, who chant with them an affirmation of their love, dancing until they are full of life and togetherness. The lady in green then celebrates the recovery of all of her stuff that "somebody almost walked off wid." After the ladies recite the excuses and apologies men gave them, the lady in blue asserts her right to be angry and to accept no more apologies.

The last story of Crystal and Beau Willie is told by the lady in red. Beau Willie, a Vietnam veteran, came home "crazy as hell" from the war. When he tried to go to school, he was put into remedial classes because he could not read, so he drove a gypsy cab that kept breaking down. His girlfriend Crystal had a baby while he was in Vietnam that he was not sure was his; she got pregnant again when he returned, so Beau Willie had two children, a girl and a boy. When Crystal refused to marry him, he got drunk and started swinging chairs at her, including the high chair with his son. Having almost died, Crystal got a court order to keep Beau Willie away. He went to Crystal's to try to convince her to marry him; when she would not open the door, he broke it down. He coaxed the children into his arms. When Crystal again refused to marry him, he held the children out of the fifth-story window and dropped them. The ladies come out and chant how each misses a "layin' on of hands" until "i found god in myself & i loved her/ i loved her fiercely" arises as a song of joy to each other and to the audience.

Critical Evaluation:

Ntozake Shange calls *for colored girls who have considered suicide/ when the rainbow is enuf* a choreopoem; it is a performance piece made up of twenty-three poems that are chanted, sung, and danced to musical accompaniment by seven women. Originally performed in improvisational style in Berkeley, California, in 1974, the play was picked up in an expanded form by the New York Shakespeare Festival, which first presented it in an Obie Award-winning production in 1976 at the Henry Street Play House and then moved it to the Booth Theatre on Broadway, where it had a long, successful run.

Shange is considered a pioneer both for the collage-like techniques of her drama and for her subject matter: the anger of African American women at their double subjugation at the hands of white America and black men. While some critics were disturbed at what they saw as her generally negative depiction of black males and her disconnection from traditional black political concerns, others saw in *for colored girls who have considered suicide/ when the rainbow is enuf* an attempt to find new solutions to the reality of the lives of African American women. Shange's work may be considered, along with that of Margaret Walker, Toni Morrison, and Alice Walker, a harbinger of the African American cultural renaissance that began in the early 1980's.

This emergence of African American culture into the mainstream of American life signifies the culture's transition from being an attack on the obstacles of black self-realization to what has been called "the moment of becoming." The possibilities of what that moment of change may mean open up numerous potential paths, some traditional, some not. Shange, in interviews, has identified herself not only with the North American black community but also with women's culture and with the culture of the developing world. She sees herself as a "child of the new world," who must help forge a new language in order to function fully and to express the experience of that new world. Fluent in French, Spanish, and Portuguese, Shange has been able to cross communication boundaries in American, African, and European cultures. Brought up as a Presbyterian, Congregationalist, and Unitarian, she practices Methodist Episcopalianism and Santería. Raised in the jazz culture and race politics of the 1950's, educated at Barnard and the University of Southern California (USC), she participated in the Civil Rights movement of the 1960's and in the communal feminism of the 1970's. While a graduate student at USC, she adopted the names ntozake, "she who comes with her own things," and shange, "she who walks like a lion."

In *for colored girls who have considered suicide/ when*

the rainbow is enuf, this complex of influences reveals itself. Praised for its faithful replication of black women's speech and movement that transcended stereotypes, the piece reflects the call-and-response pattern of the African American church in its use of monologue against a chorus of voices. Its incantatory use of music, language, and dance is a reflection of *candomblé* and Santería. The language in the play ignores standard grammar and punctuation in an effort to re-create the music of African American storytelling. Shange attempts both to confront the issues of black women's sexuality and exploitation and to transcend that exploitation in an exploration of the possibilities of re-creation of the self that is grounded in the life-giving forces of nature and sisterhood.

Jane Anderson Jones

Further Reading

Brown-Guillory, Elizabeth. *Their Place on the Stage: Black Women Playwrights in America*. New York: Greenwood Press, 1988. Assesses the contributions of Shange, Alice Childress, and Lorraine Hansberry to American and African American theater. Provides a particularly insightful analysis of *for colored girls*.

Christ, Carol P. "'I Found God in Myself . . . & I Loved Her Fiercely': Ntozake Shange." In *Diving Deep and Surfacing: Women Writers on Spiritual Quest*. Boston: Beacon Press, 1980. Describes how the women in the play come to an affirmation of themselves by envisioning a new image that acknowledges their history and moves beyond it to "the ends of their own rainbows."

Clarke, Cheryl. "Black Feminist Communalism: Ntozake Shange's *for colored girls who have considered suicide/ when the rainbow is enuf*." In *"After Mecca": Women Poets and the Black Arts Movement*. New Brunswick, N.J.: Rutgers University Press, 2005. Examines the influences of the Black Arts Movement and the lesbian rights and feminist movements in Shange's work.

DeShazer, Mary K. "Rejecting Necrophilia: Ntosake Shange and the Warrior Re-visioned." In *Making a Spectacle*, edited by Lynda Hart. Ann Arbor: University of Michigan Press, 1989. Presents Shange as a warrior-woman, reinventing the term "warrior" from a feminist perspective. A good study of the feminist politics in Shange's plays.

Effiong, Philip Uko. *In Search of a Model for African-American Drama: A Study of Selected Plays by Lorraine Hansberry, Amiri Baraka, and Ntozake Shange*. Lanham, Md.: University Press of America, 2000. Describes how Shange creates a new model of drama to address the concerns of African Americans. Demonstrates how the political ideals expressed in her plays are grounded in feminism and pan-African consciousness.

Fisher, James. "'Boogie Woogie Landscapes': The Dramatic/Poetic Collage of Ntozake Shange." In *Contemporary African American Women Playwrights: A Casebook*, edited by Philip C. Kolin. New York: Routledge, 2007. Describes how Shange in *for colored girls* created a new dramatic form, the "dramatic/poetic collage," or a mixture of character, poetry, song, and dance. Assesses this play's influence as "far reaching."

Keyssar, Helene. "Rites and Responsibilities: The Drama of Black American Women." In *Feminine Focus*, edited by Enoch Brater. New York: Oxford University Press, 1989. Keyssar tackles the problematic issue of "double-voicedness" in the plays of African American women. Her commentary on Shange illustrates the complex challenges inherent in Shange's works that seek to address both feminist issues and race issues. A useful contextualization of Shange's work with the plays of other important African American women playwrights.

Lester, Neal A. *Ntozake Shange: A Critical Study of the Plays*. New York: Garland, 1995. Provides a critical analysis of five of Shange's plays; argues she is a writer "enraged by and committed to writing about the injustices suffered by oppressed peoples of color, women and children."

Mitchell, Carolyn. "'A Laying on of Hands': Transcending the City in Ntozake Shange's *for colored girls. . . .*" In *Women Writers and the City*, edited by Susan Merrill Squier. Knoxville: University of Tennessee Press, 1984. Explores the spiritual and political implications of cleansing and healing in the play.

Vandergrift, Kay E. "And Bid Her Sing: A White Feminist Reads African-American Female Poets." In *African-American Voices: Tradition, Transition, Transformation*, edited by Karen Patricia Smith. Metuchen, N.J.: Scarecrow Press, 1994. Emphasizes the power of the song elements in the play, showing how bebop and jazz rhythms combine with literary, sociopolitical, and popular culture references in the poems.

For the Union Dead

Author: Robert Lowell (1917-1977)
First published: 1960; collected in *For the Union Dead,* 1964
Type of work: Poetry

Born to a prominent New England family noted for its contributions to American literature, Robert Lowell blends personal and cultural histories in his work. By the time the thirty-five poems of *For the Union Dead* appeared, Lowell was at the height of his powers, having won the Pulitzer Prize in poetry for *Lord Weary's Castle* in 1947 and the National Book Award for *Life Studies* in 1959. Most readers consider *Life Studies*, which includes a lengthy prose memoir of his dysfunctional family, to be his best book.

In 1949, Lowell was institutionalized for a nervous breakdown, and he suffered attacks of manic-depressive disorder for the rest of his life. In 1948, he divorced his first wife, novelist Jean Stafford, and the next year he married Elizabeth Hardwick, from whom he was divorced in 1972. "Old Flame," the second poem in the collection, concerns his first wife; the first poem, "Water," is a reminiscence of his relationship with the poet Elizabeth Bishop, whom he met in 1946 and who was to remain a lifelong friend.

Lowell is widely recognized as the "father" of the confessional movement in post-World War II American poetry, having taught both Sylvia Plath and Anne Sexton while at Boston University in the late 1950's. In general, the confessional poets, many of whom went through psychoanalysis, place themselves, and often their parents, at the center of their work, as Lowell does in "Middle Age," the third poem in this book, where, at forty-five, he claims to have met his father (who died in 1950) on the "chewed-up streets" of New York and asked him to "forgive me/ my injuries,/ as I forgive/ those I/ have injured!" The religious echo is common in Lowell's poems.

Typically, confessional poets work through pain and anger, even outrage, sometimes appearing self-analytical and harsh in their judgments on themselves, sometimes self-pitying and morbid. The self or ego is so prevalent in Lowell's poems that when the third person appears, as in "The Mouth of the Hudson," the reader may accept the third person as an alter-ego or another side of Lowell. In that poem, the man is isolated in an industrial wasteland, and he has "trouble with his balance" (both mental and physical). The poem ends with an image referring to "the sulphur-yellow sun/ of the unforgivable landscape." It is a curiosity, if not a symptom, of confessional poetry that the confessions rarely lead to a sense of healing forgiveness.

The title of the opening poem is "Water," and water is a conventional symbol of life or purification, but the lovers discover at the end that "the water was too cold for us." In "Eye and Tooth," which echoes the biblical "eye for eye, tooth for tooth," the myopic poet (Lowell's vision had been bad since boyhood) sees the cycle of life during a "summer rain" as "a simmer of rot and renewal." (The sound play between "summer" and "simmer" and the alliterative "r" sounds typify Lowell's acute ear.) At the end of that poem he declares, "I am tired. Everyone's tired of my turmoil."

One way of looking at *For the Union Dead* is that the poems show Lowell struggling against the limitations of his own subjectivity, not by rejecting the potential of the inner self, but by forcing the self out of its shell and into contact with the outer world of time and history. In "Fall 1961," for example, he confronts time, which he portrays as "the orange, bland, ambassadorial/ face of the moon/ on the grandfather clock." The talk of nuclear war during that time of the Cuban Missile Crisis created an apocalyptic anxiety, in which the speaker feels like a fish in an aquarium: "I swim like a minnow/ behind my studio window." Similarly, the state seems helpless, like "a diver under a glass bell." As "Our end drifts nearer,/ the moon lifts,/ radiant with terror," so that the symbol of romance is transformed into one of fear. Note Lowell's rhyming of "drifts" and "lifts" and his slant rhyming of "nearer" with "terror."

The father who appears in "Fall 1961" is not his own "dinosaur" father of "Middle Age," but himself: "A father's no shield/ to his child." Lowell's daughter was then four years old. In a simile that may reach back to a sermon entitled "Sinners in the Hands of an Angry God," by the eighteenth century Calvinist minister Jonathan Edwards (himself the subject of a poem later in the book), Lowell writes: "We are like a lot of wild/ spiders crying together,/ but without tears." At the conclusion of the poem, as the clock ticks tediously, the speaker retreats to his "one point of rest," which is an oriole's nest. He remains unready to face the threatening external world.

The references to fish, dinosaurs, birds, and spiders and to other nonhuman forms of life accumulate throughout this book, sometimes, as with the spiders, identified with humans, and sometimes depicted as victims of what humans are making of the world. In "The Public Garden," even in its title an effort to reach out from the self and into the world of current realities, the speaker first declares that "all's alive" as he watches children "crowding home from school at five." Then he sees that the swanboats are a "jaded flock" and the park is drying up so that "the heads of four stone lions stare/ and suck on empty faucets." The moon appears again as a perverse symbol, "always a stranger!" At the end the speaker remembers summer but sees people as "drowned in Eden," and in the closing lines, heavy with alliterative *f* sounds, he sees no spark of life or inspiration: "The fountain's failing waters flash around/ the garden. Nothing catches fire."

Near the center of the collection, however, in the poem entitled "Returning," even though the speaker sees the outer world as "rather a dead town," the poem may hold out some promise for reconciliation. The speaker remembers the world's "former fertility,/ how everything came out clearly/ in the hour of credulity/ and young summer." Religious overtones in this poem suggest that Lowell is looking back wistfully at his conversion to Roman Catholicism in 1940, but the "venerable elm" (the Church, presumably), now sick, "gave too much shelter."

In "The Drinker," Lowell, who had a serious drinking problem himself, resorts to the objectifying distance of the third person. The man in the first line is "killing time." Despite some ugly images ("the cheese wilts in the rat-trap"), the poem closes on a positive note, reversing the initial assertion into a question: "Is he killing time?" Lowell follows with an image of "two cops on horseback" in the April rain checking parking meters, "their oilskins yellow as forsythia."

The next two poems, in which Lowell reflects on historical personages (the nineteenth century American writer Nathaniel Hawthorne and Jonathan Edwards), concern cultural history. In "The Neo-Classical Urn" the speaker compares himself to the turtles that he caught as a boy, but which died in captivity. Lowell may intend the reader to think of English poet John Keats's "Ode on a Grecian Urn," but if so, the relationship between the poems is ironic, for Keats sees the urn as representative of timelessness and immortality, whereas the turtles die. Lowell's vision at the end is complex. As a man he can see that turtles have no mind or will; they are "nothings." When he rubs his head, he describes it as "that turtle shell," and he breathes in their "dying smell"; that is, he identifies himself with their mortality and with their place in "history," at least with his personal history.

The following poem, "Caligula," refers to the tyrannical Roman emperor whose name was the source of Lowell's nickname from prep school days, Cal. So, in that poem, too, he continues to expand from the confined self into the outer world. "Beyond the Alps," in fact, opens up both historically and geographically, and the next several poems continue that expansion: "July in Washington," "Buenos Aires," "Dropping South: Brazil," "Soft Wood" (in which the speaker, in Maine, regards his cousin dying in Washington, D.C.).

The compelling title poem, which concludes the book, moves from at least two historical vantage points (one personal and the other cultural) to make perhaps the most powerful political statement Lowell had made to date. (A critic of the war in Vietnam, Lowell was much involved with writers' protests after 1965.) The poem, in quatrains of varying line lengths, begins with Lowell's memory of himself as a boy at the South Boston Aquarium, now boarded up. Once his "hand tingled/ to burst the bubbles" of the "cowed, compliant fish," but now he draws back and yearns for "the dark downward and vegetating kingdom/ of the fish and reptile." He emerges from this reverse evolution, however, into the historical present of "one morning last March."

In the world at hand, he finds that the dinosaurs, in the form of steam shovels, still exist, gouging an "underworld garage." The "heart of Boston" is being crowded by luxuries in the form of parking spaces, and the Puritan legacy of the "tingling Statehouse" shakes with the "earthquake" caused by the construction. (Several words and images, such as tingled/tingling and bubbles, echo throughout the poem.) Lowell moves from the personal past to the cultural present in the third quatrain, but with the sixth stanza, which introduces the statue of Colonel Robert Shaw and the 44th Massachusetts Negro regiment, he moves into the cultural past. (The regiment's disastrous assault on Fort Wagner in 1863 is dramatized in the film *Glory*, 1989.)

Lowell examines the impact of the cultural past on the present, which involves the Civil Rights movement. South Boston was notorious for its racism in the early 1960's. "Their monument sticks like a fishbone/ in the city's throat." Unlike Lowell, the colonel is "out of bounds now," free of time and change. The heroism of Colonel Shaw is implicit in his choice of "life and death," which the churches of New England at least appear to commemorate. Shaw's choice of life and death constitutes the ultimate triumph of free human will.

In the thirteenth quatrain, Lowell says Shaw's father wanted no such monument. He was content with the "ditch," or mass grave, in which his son and his men were buried. (Lowell's mention of the word "niggers" in this stanza should not be ascribed to Shaw's father, but to racists generally, in

1863 and 1960.) In the last four stanzas, Lowell returns to the present: "The ditch is nearer." He concludes with a warning against nuclear war and racism, depicting Shaw "riding on his bubble" and waiting for it to pop, and in the last quatrain he indicts the society that he sees as greedy in its desire for luxury cars and insensitive to the value of such an institution as the city aquarium: "The Aquarium is gone. Everywhere,/ giant finned cars nose forward like fish;/ a savage servility/ slides by on grease." The phrase "savage servility," an oxymoron, encapsulates Lowell's condemnation of a materialistic culture, servile as, for example, a salesman, and savage in its war and racism (which a salesman would also support and participate in).

Out of its own dark turmoil, the troubled self detects a frightening and vicious world given over to greed and violence. It should be no wonder that when such poets move to a political voice, its tones will be apocalyptic.

Ron McFarland

Further Reading

Axelrod, Steven Gould. *Robert Lowell: Life and Art*. Princeton, N.J.: Princeton University Press, 1978. Comments on the movement between past and present in the collection; explores the poems as a sequence. Offers valuable contexts for the title poem.

_____, ed. *The Critical Response to Robert Lowell*. Westport, Conn.: Greenwood Press, 1999. A collection of representative criticism of Lowell's work. Two of the essays focus on the title poem and collection *For the Union Dead*: "'For the Union Dead'" by Axelrod and "A Poetry of Memory: *For the Union Dead*" by Katharine Wallingford. There are many other references to both the poem and collection that are listed in the index.

Doreski, William. *Robert Lowell's Shifting Colors: The Poetics of the Public and the Personal*. Athens: Ohio University Press, 1999. Doreski argues that Lowell's primary goal as a poet was to shape different voices into a single entity in which public and private concerns combine.

Fein, Richard J. *Robert Lowell*. 2d ed. Boston: Twayne, 1979. Surveys poems and remarks on animal imagery. Provides a close reading of the title poem.

James, Stephen. *Shades of Authority: The Poetry of Lowell, Hill, and Heaney*. Liverpool, England: Liverpool University Press, 2007. Examines the relationship between poetry and authority by examining how Lowell, Geoffrey Hill, and Seamus Heaney respond to political and cultural issues in their work.

Mariani, Paul L. *Lost Puritan: A Life of Robert Lowell*. New York: W. W. Norton, 1994. Biography focusing on the events in the complex life of the manic-depressive Lowell. Provides a detailed depiction of Lowell as a brilliant but tragic figure.

Mazzaro, Jerome. *The Poetic Themes of Robert Lowell*. Ann Arbor: University of Michigan Press, 1965. Reflects on solipsism and narcissism in the poems; argues that Lowell often slips into self-pity.

Rudman, Mark. *Robert Lowell: An Introduction to the Poetry*. New York: Columbia University Press, 1983. Maintains that the poems "progressively" darken and that the subject of the collection is "pain."

Tillinghast, Richard. *Robert Lowell's Life and Work: Damaged Grandeur*. Ann Arbor: University of Michigan Press, 1995. Tillinghast, a poet who was a friend and student of Lowell, offers a critical memoir. He reexamines Lowell's poetic career, describing how Lowell's talent for the "grand gesture" was interwoven with his manic-depression; he argues that Lowell should be restored to a preeminent place in the American literary canon.

Yenser, Stephen. *Circle to Circle: The Poetry of Robert Lowell*. Berkeley: University of California Press, 1975. Finds Lowell's poems sometimes "excruciatingly introspective." Comments on most of the poems in *For the Union Dead*.

For Whom the Bell Tolls

Author: Ernest Hemingway (1899-1961)
First published: 1940
Type of work: Novel
Type of plot: Impressionistic realism
Time of plot: 1937
Locale: Spain

Principal characters:
ROBERT JORDAN, an American fighting with the Spanish Loyalists
PABLO, a guerrilla leader
PILAR, his wife
MARIA, the beloved of Jordan
ANSELMO, another guerrilla

The Story:

At first, the only important thing is the bridge. Robert Jordan is a young American teacher who is in Spain fighting with the Loyalist guerrillas. His present and most important mission is to blow up a bridge that will be of great strategic importance during an offensive three days hence. Jordan is behind the Fascist lines, with orders to make contact with Pablo, the leader of a guerrilla band, and with his wife, Pilar, who is the strongest figure among the partisans. Pablo is a weak and drunken braggart, but Pilar is strong and trustworthy. A swarthy, raw-boned woman, vulgar and outspoken, she is so fiercely devoted to the Loyalist cause that Jordan knows she will carry out her part of the mission regardless of danger to herself.

The plan is that Jordan will study the bridge from all angles and then finalize the plans for its destruction at the proper moment. Jordan has blown up many bridges and three trains, but this is the first time everything has to be done on a split-second schedule. Pablo and Pilar are to assist Jordan in any way they can, even in rounding up other bands of guerrillas if Jordan needs them to accomplish his mission.

At the cave hideout of Pablo and Pilar, Jordan meets a beautiful young girl named Maria, who escaped from the Fascists. Maria was subjected to every possible indignity, being starved, tortured, and raped, and she feels unclean. At the camp, Jordan also meets Anselmo, a loyal old man who will follow orders regardless of his personal safety. Anselmo hates having to kill but will do so if necessary.

Jordan loves the brutal, shrewd, desperate, loyal guerrillas, for he knows that their cruelties against the Fascists stem from poverty and ignorance. The Fascists' cruelty, however, he abhors, for the Fascists come largely from the wealthy, ambitious class. The story of Maria's suffering fills him with such hatred that he could kill a thousand of them, even though he, like Anselmo, hates to kill.

The first night he spends at the guerrilla camp destroys his cold approach to the mission before him, for he falls deeply in love with Maria. She comes to his sleeping bag that night, and although they talk little, he knows after she leaves that he is no longer ready to die. He tells Maria that one day they will be married, but he is afraid of the future, and fear is dangerous for a man on an important mission.

Jordan makes many sketches of the bridge and lays his plans carefully, but the night before the bridge is to be blown up his work is almost ruined by Pablo, who deserts after stealing and destroying the explosives and the detonators hidden in Jordan's pack. Pablo returns repentant on the morning of the mission, but the loss of the detonators and explosives means that Jordan and his helper will have to blow up the bridge with hand grenades, a much more dangerous method. Pablo tries to redeem himself by bringing another small guerrilla band and their horses with him. Although Jordan despises Pablo by that time, he forgives him, as does Pilar.

At the bridge, Jordan works quickly and carefully. Each person has a specific job to do, and each does his work well. First Jordan and Anselmo kill the sentries, then Pablo and his guerrillas attack the Fascist lines approaching the bridge, so as to prevent their crossing before the bridge is demolished. Jordan is ordered to blow up the bridge at the beginning of a Loyalist bombing attack over the Fascist lines. When he hears the thudding explosions of the bombs, he pulls the pins and the bridge shoots high into the air. Jordan gets to cover safely, but Anselmo is killed by a steel fragment from the bridge. As Jordan looks at the old man and realizes that he might be alive if Pablo had not stolen the detonators, he wants to kill Pablo. However, he knows his duty, and he runs to the designated meeting place of the fugitive guerrillas.

There he finds Pablo, Pilar, Maria, and the two remaining Gypsy partisans. Pablo, herding the extra horses, says that all the other guerrillas were killed. Jordan knows, however, that Pablo killed the men so that he could get their horses. When he confronts him, Pablo admits the slaughter, but shrugs his great shoulders and says that the men were not of his band.

The next problem before them is to cross a road that could be swept by Fascist gunfire. Jordan knows that the first two people will have the best chance, since they will probably be able to cross before the Fascists are alerted. Because Pablo knows the road to safety, Jordan puts him on the first horse. Maria is second, for Jordan is determined that she should be saved before the others. Pilar is to go next, then the two remaining guerrillas, and, last of all, Jordan. The first four cross safely, but Jordan's horse, wounded by Fascist bullets, falls on his leg. The others drag him across the road and out of the line of fire, but he knows that he cannot go on and is too badly injured to ride a horse. Pablo and Pilar understand, but Maria begs to stay with him. Jordan tells Pilar to take Maria away when he gives the signal; then he talks to the girl, telling her that she must go on, that as long as she lives, he lives also. When the time comes, she has to be put on her horse and led away.

Jordan, settling down to wait for the approaching Fascist troops, props himself against a tree, with his submachine gun across his knees. As he waits, he thinks over the events that brought him to this place. He knows that what he did was right, but that his side might not win for many years. He knows, too, that if the common people keep trying, they will eventually win. He hopes they will be prepared when that day comes, that they will no longer want to kill and torture but will struggle for peace and good as they are now struggling for freedom. He feels that his own part in the struggle was not in vain. As he sees the first Fascist officer approaching, Jordan smiles. He is ready.

Critical Evaluation:

In 1940, Ernest Hemingway published *For Whom the Bell Tolls* to wide critical and public acclaim. The novel became an immediate best seller, erasing his somewhat flawed performance in *To Have and Have Not* (1937). During the 1930's, a time when Hemingway enjoyed great publicity, he went on the African safari that produced *Green Hills of Africa* (1935) and his column in *Esquire* (1933-1936). In 1940, he was divorced by his second wife, Pauline Pfeiffer, and married Martha Gellhorn. He set fishing records at Bimini in marlin tournaments, hunted in Wyoming, and fished at Key West, Florida, where he bought a home. In 1937, when the Spanish Civil War broke out, Hemingway went to Spain as a correspondent with a passionate devotion to the Spain of his early years. Not content merely to report the war, he became actively involved with the Loyalist army in its fight against Franco and the generals. He wrote the script for the propaganda film *The Spanish Earth* (1937), which was shown at the White House at a presidential dinner. The proceeds of the film were used to buy ambulances for the Loyalists. In 1939, with the war a lost cause and just as World War II was beginning its course of destruction, Hemingway wrote *For Whom the Bell Tolls*.

To understand Hemingway's motive in writing the book, it is helpful to study the quotation from John Donne, from which Hemingway took his theme, "any mans death diminishes me, because I am involved in Mankinde; And therefore never send to know for whom the bell tolls; It tolls for thee." Hemingway wanted his readers to feel that what happened to the Loyalists in Spain in 1937 was a part of a world crisis in which everyone shared.

Even more than in *A Farewell to Arms* (1929), Hemingway in *For Whom the Bell Tolls* focuses the conflict of war in the experiences of a single man. Like Frederic Henry, Robert Jordan is an American in a European country fighting for a cause that is not his by birth. Henry just happens to be in Italy when World War I breaks out; he has no ideological commitment to the war. Jordan, however, comes to Spain because he believes in the Loyalist cause. He believes in the land and the people, a belief that ultimately costs him his life. Jordan's death, however, is an affirmation, and the novel is a clear political statement of what a human being must do under pressure.

For Whom the Bell Tolls is a circular novel. It begins with Jordan in a pine forest in Spain, observing a bridge he has been assigned to destroy, and it ends with him in snow that covers the pine needles, carefully sighting on an enemy officer approaching on horseback. Between the opening and closing paragraphs is a time period of only seventy hours, and at the center of all the action and meditation is the bridge, the focal point of the conflict to which the reader and the characters are repeatedly drawn.

In what was at that point his longest novel, Hemingway forges a tightly unified plot, with a single place, a single action, and a brief time—the old Greek unities. Jordan's military action takes on other epic qualities associated with the Greeks. His sacrifice is not unlike that of Leonidas at the crucial pass of Thermopylae, during the Persian Wars. There, too, heroic action was required to defend an entry point, and there, too, the leader died in an action that proved futile in military terms but became a standard measure of courage and commitment.

Abandoning somewhat the terse, clipped style of his earlier novels, Hemingway makes effective use of flashbacks to delineate the major characters. Earlier central characters seemed to exist without a past. However, if Jordan's death is to "diminish mankind," then the reader has to know more about him. This character development takes place almost within suspended time, and Jordan and Maria try to condense an entire life into those seventy hours. The reader is never allowed to forget time altogether, for the days move, light changes, meals are eaten, and snow falls. Everything moves toward the time when the bridge must be blown up, and life, love, and death are compressed into those seventy hours. The novel becomes a compact cycle suspended in time.

In the Gypsy camp, each person becomes important. Pilar is often cited as one of Hemingway's better female characters, just as Maria is often criticized as being unbelievable. Nevertheless, Maria's psychological scars are carefully developed. She is just as mentally unstable as are Brett Ashley and Catherine Barkley. Jordan, too, is a wounded man. He lives with the suicide of his father and the killing of his fellow dynamiter. The love that Jordan and Maria share makes them both temporarily whole again.

The destruction of the bridge is meaningless in military terms. Seen in the larger political context, Jordan's courage and death are wasted. However, the bridge is important for its effect on the group, giving them a purpose and a focal point and forging them into a unity, a whole. They can take pride in their accomplishment despite its cost. Life is ultimately a defeat no matter how it is lived; what gives defeat meaning is the courage that a human being is capable of forging in the face of death's certainty. One man's death does diminish the group, for they are involved together, but Jordan's loss is balanced by the purpose he has given to the group.

Just as the mountains are no longer a place safe from the Fascists with their airplanes, Hemingway seems to be saying that no person and no place are any longer safe. It is no longer possible to make a separate peace as Henry did with his war. When Fascist violence is loose in the world, people must take a stand. Jordan does not believe in the Communist ideology that supports the Loyalists, but he does believe in the earth and its people. He is essentially the nonpolitical man caught in a political conflict that he cannot avoid, and he does the best he can with the weapons available to him.

Michael S. Reynolds

Further Reading

Bloom, Harold, ed. *Ernest Hemingway.* New York: Chelsea House, 1985. Although no essay in this collection deals exclusively with *For Whom the Bell Tolls*, the novel is mentioned in many of them. Of particular interest may be Robert Penn Warren's discussion of irony in *For Whom the Bell Tolls.* Includes a good index.

Gajdusek, Robert E. *Hemingway in His Own Country.* Notre Dame, Ind.: University of Notre Dame Press, 2002. A collection of essays that interpret Hemingway's works from a wide variety of perspectives. Some of the essays compare the work of Hemingway with that of James Joyce and F. Scott Fitzgerald, discuss Hemingway's representation of women and androgynous elements in his fiction, and analyze *For Whom the Bell Tolls.*

Josephs, Allen. *"For Whom the Bell Tolls": Ernest Hemingway's Undiscovered Country.* New York: Twayne, 1994. Considers the literary and historical context for the novel and gives a detailed reading. An interesting and accessible discussion. Includes an excellent annotated bibliography.

Reynolds, Michael. "Ringing the Changes: Hemingway's Bell Tolls Fifty." *Virginia Quarterly Review* 67 (Winter, 1991): 1-18. In this good general reference, Reynolds presents the novel in historical context and suggests ways in which it can be seen to transcend its own time.

Rovit, Earl, and Gerry Brenner. *Ernest Hemingway.* Rev. ed. Boston: Twayne, 1986. Focuses on the totality of Hemingway's fiction rather than on individual works. A useful and accessible source, with fairly detailed explication of *For Whom the Bell Tolls.* Includes an index.

Sanderson, Rena, ed. *Blowing the Bridge: Essays on Hemingway and "For Whom the Bell Tolls."* New York: Greenwood Press, 1992. Twelve essays that take a fresh look at Hemingway and his most neglected major novel. The introduction gives an overview of the novel's composition and critical reception and offers a reassessment fifty years after publication.

Trogdon, Robert W., ed. *Ernest Hemingway: A Literary Reference.* New York: Carroll & Graf, 2002. A compendium of information about Hemingway, including photographs, letters, interviews, essays, speeches, book reviews, copies of some of his manuscripts-in-process, and his comments about his own work and the work of other writers.

Wagner-Martin, Linda. *Ernest Hemingway: A Literary Life.* New York: Palgrave Macmillan, 2007. Examines Hemingway's life, especially his troubled relationship with his parents. Wagner-Martin makes insightful connections between his personal life, his emotions, and his writing.

Foreign Affairs

Author: Alison Lurie (1926-   )
First published: 1984
Type of work: Novel
Type of plot: Comedy of manners
Time of plot: Early 1980's
Locale: London

Principal characters:
VIRGINIA "VINNIE" MINER, a professor of children's
   literature
CHARLES "CHUCK" MUMPSON, a sanitation engineer
FRED TURNER, an assistant professor of British literature
LADY ROSEMARY RADLEY, a British television actor

The Story:

Virginia Miner is an unmarried fifty-four-year-old professor of children's literature at Corinth University, a major Ivy League college. She is flying to London for a six-month stay on a grant to study British schoolyard rhymes, her field of expertise. Her work has been criticized, most notably by fellow academic L. D. Zimmern, for being slight and inconsequential.

Miner is, by her own admission, unattractive (she is prone to self-pity and has an imaginary dog named Fido who appears whenever she feels sorry for herself). Although married briefly, she has been content with the series of prosaic, if passionate, affairs that she has had over the years, certain that she will never find love.

During the long transatlantic flight, Chuck Mumpson, a married waste-disposal engineer from Tulsa, Oklahoma, beginning a bargain package tour of England, engages Vinnie in rambling conversation, although Vinnie finds him unpleasant and coarse. He is overweight and is a sloppy drinker and a smoker. Desperate to distract him and to curtail their conversation, Vinnie gives him a copy of the British children's classic *Little Lord Fauntleroy*, a story about a poor Brooklyn schoolboy who finds out he is in fact a British aristocrat and the heir to a fortune. Vinnie and Chuck arrive at Heathrow Airport. Vinnie is unable to find a taxi, so Chuck invites her to ride with him on his tour bus to her hotel.

Meanwhile, Fred Turner, a strikingly handsome assistant professor of literature, also at Corinth, is in London on a five-month sabbatical to research a book on playwright John Gay. After a tempestuous argument with his wife, Ruth, a successful and controversial photographer (her current exhibition features photos of three penises, only one of which is Fred's, making him disquietingly jealous), Fred faces the possibility that his marriage to the free-spirited and independent Roo, as he calls Ruth, may be over. Not willing to offend a colleague who will have a considerable say in his upcoming tenure review, Fred attends a dinner party hosted by Vinnie. There he meets Lady Rosemary Radley, an older British television and cinema icon whose fawning temperament and needful affec-

tion is the very opposite of Roo's. He falls immediately under her spell.

Over the next several weeks, Lady Radley helps Fred circulate in the highest reaches of London's exclusive, glitzy social world. (Fred, a low-echelon academic, is acutely aware of his own pecuniary difficulties.) Fred embraces the tonic experience and moves in with the actor (and ignores his research project). It is an odd sort of affair—Lady Radley tells him little of herself and is even reticent to make love naked. Fred is falling in love. He is concerned, however, because he knows that he must return to Corinth soon to resume his work. When he tries to explain this to Lady Radley, she becomes furious and breaks off their affair.

Meanwhile, Vinnie is surprised to run into Chuck at a department store. He is depressed. He has been laid off and has consequently extended his stay in England, in part because, after reading *Little Lord Fauntleroy*, he has become interested in tracing his own roots, particularly an eccentric (and wealthy) lord who, centuries earlier, had reportedly become a recluse and then lived in a cave. Over tea, Vinnie offers advice on how to investigate his genealogy. Over the next several weeks, Vinnie begins to find herself attracted to Chuck. He confides in Vinnie about his own difficult childhood and loveless marriage, and, most pointedly, about the night he killed a sixteen-year-old while driving drunk. The two become lovers. Chuck, despite the overwhelming sorrows of his life, relishes the emotional energy of their relationship, and Vinnie begins to suspect this might be love.

Fred's wife (who is, coincidently, the daughter of Vinnie's academic nemesis, Zimmern) calls Vinnie unexpectedly and asks her to help contact Fred about reconciling. Vinnie, momentarily nursing the impulse to quash the message as a way to hurt Zimmern even indirectly, suddenly feels the generosity and openness of Chuck and personally delivers the message. Fred, preparing to return to New York, stops at Lady Radley's mansion to gather a few belongings, only to find the house a mess and the actor quite drunk, dressed as a Cockney maid and evidently in a role she is playing. Unable to fathom the depth of his former lover's psychosis, Fred determines to forget her, return to the United States, and work on his marriage.

Vinnie is becoming increasingly distressed. Chuck has stopped calling or visiting her. She begins to feel self-pity and fears another lover has left her. She is devastated, however, by a phone call from Chuck's daughter and the news that Chuck had died some days earlier from a heart attack while climbing a flight of stairs in the summer heat. The following day, Chuck's daughter drops off a beautiful framed drawing of Chuck's ancient eccentric ancestor—the hermit of South Leigh. It is an uneasy reminder of Vinnie's own position, now that she is so suddenly without her lover. Vinnie, certain now that Chuck was her last best chance at love, returns to her lonely scholarly endeavors. Not entirely surprisingly, she finds that her imaginary dog, Fido, has returned and that despite her evident academic accomplishments, Chuck's death has left her painfully incomplete.

Critical Evaluation:

Foreign Affairs tests characters under the influence of enormous (and often unexpected) emotional stress involving the opposite sex, much like the wry drawing-room comedies of Jane Austen and the international novels of Henry James. In *Foreign Affairs*, as is often the case in Alison Lurie's fiction, adultery is that emotional stress.

Like the characters in the novels of John Updike, a contemporary to whom Lurie is often compared, *Foreign Affairs*'s characters find in their experiences of illicit passion insights into the integrity of their emotional lives. Very much a product of the liberal counterculture sensibility of the late 1960's, Lurie does not see adultery as strictly right or strictly wrong. In this novel, adultery teaches, leads to insight, and reshapes self-perceptions; fulfillment in marriage is illusory, its passion played out inevitably into routine and disappointment.

Given that both Vinnie and Fred are accomplished academics (as is Lurie), Lurie could easily draw them as stereotypes and be content to satirize the emotional liaisons of the hyperintelligent. Lurie could have satirized their clumsy attempts at escaping their egghead status quo and instead express passion, but she resists simplistic caricatures. When readers first meet Vinnie, she is a staid and self-involved academic, judgmental and aloof, prim and fussy, and above all, self-sufficient. The relationship between her and Chuck Mumpson is delightfully improbable. That the affair becomes for Vinnie her most satisfying experience of love gives *Foreign Affairs* a profound poignancy. Vinnie understands, in the wake of Chuck's sudden death (from heart failure, ironically), that she is now most likely going to die alone.

Lurie's deft narrative has Vinnie accept her loneliness just as Fred returns to his marriage. Fred, disillusioned by the pretense and shallowness of British society and perplexed by the erratic behavior of Lady Radley, comes to believe he must revive his marriage and reconnect with his wife's potent sexuality and defiant free spirit. Such a storyline, with its use of casual sex, threatens to become little more than a glorified soap opera. Indeed, the novel was made into such a film for television. For Lurie, however, cheating is, ironically, the only way for both Vinnie and Fred Turner to see themselves honestly.

The novel displays an authorial sensibility that juxtaposes American and British lifestyles, giving *Foreign Affairs* its engaging sense of culture shock that recalls the international novels of Henry James. Lurie maintains a careful voice-over distance (the narrative is told in documentary-style present tense). If Lurie refuses to mock her characters' earnest (if disastrous) struggles to love, she relishes every opportunity to hold British culture and British mores, its pretensions and its smugness, to wry (although never mean-spirited) critique. She is a sharp-eyed observer of British society and captures the rich comedy of the collisions between American and British manners and customs (the charade game that Fred plays during a long weekend at a country house is a hilarious send-up of the British laid-back temperament). There is little doubt that the gregarious and rotund Chuck, who is the character least comfortable in London and most out of his milieu there, emerges as Lurie's most sympathetic character. Tested by great trials, he is authentic, willing to be exactly who he is; he maintains a simple goodness that cannot conceive of duplicity and meanness in others, a sincerity and honesty even in adultery and an uncomplicated up-front friendliness.

However, if the novel's engrossing sexual contretemps and its savvy satire of genteel and cultured British city life may account for its enormous sales, *Foreign Affairs* also enjoyed significant critical praise and, in fact, was awarded the 1985 Pulitzer Prize for fiction. The novel is a satire; as such, there lurks beneath it all an abiding discontent that gives the novel a gravitas typical of the most accomplished works of serious fiction. That Chuck dies measures the depth of Lurie's pessimism. Despite a narrative that is often riotously funny in its mordant observations about academics and artists, and despite a narrative rich in liberating sexual energy and the improbable wonder of mismatched people becoming lovers, *Foreign Affairs* ultimately qualifies its own apparent breeziness.

In the end, neither Vinnie nor Fred establishes a reliable connection, a sincere bond of love. Vinnie never tells Chuck of the depth of her affection, never shares even the word "love" with him. It is only his death, abrupt and jarring, that confirms to Vinnie that all she will know of love now is how to live without it. Fred's return to his fiercely independent wife represents no significant evolution in his character or his capacity to maintain that relationship—indeed, he appears more in retreat, uneasy of the implications of his affair with the psychotic actor and ready now to return to the familiar and, readers fear, a spiral inevitably toward future liaisons.

Vinnie is left only with the solace of her self-pity; Fred resubmits himself to a damaged relationship and the illusion that this time he can make it work. It is an unsettling close, and one that gives Lurie's keen-edged and highly readable comedy of middle-class morality its rich and suggestive texture.

Joseph Dewey

Further Reading

Costa, Richard Hauer. *Alison Lurie and the Critics*. New York: Twayne, 1992. An important assessment of Lurie's status among American writers that addresses her tendency to recycle plots about sexual intrigues and rely on the same character types, specifically middle-age women.

Levy, Barbara. *Ladies Laughing: Wit as Control in Contemporary American Women Writers*. New York: Routledge, 1997. Examines Lurie's cultural satire, her dry wit, and her contribution to the comedy of manners tradition.

Rogers, Katharine M. "Alison Lurie: The Uses of Adultery." In *American Women Writing Fiction: Memory, Identity, Family, Space*, edited by Mickey Pearlman. Philadelphia: University of Pennsylvania Press, 2009. Defends Lurie's repeated use of adultery as a way to explore the emotional pain of frustrated wives and the expectation that marriage and children will bring appropriate fulfillment.

Showalter, Elaine. *Faculty Towers: The Academic Novel and Its Discontents*. Philadelphia: University of Pennsylvania Press, 2009. A fascinating study of the strategies of the evolution of the academic novel and the university itself as an environment of power, frustration, elitism, and hypocrisy. Includes discussion of Lurie and her work.

Wright, Charlott. *The Rise of the Ugly Woman in Contemporary American Fiction*. New York: Routledge, 2000. Uses Lurie's fiction to define a significant new genre of late twentieth century postfeminist fiction: narratives of the emotional lives of unattractive woman torn between the freedom of the solitary life and the hunger for companionship.

The Foreign Girl

Author: Florencio Sánchez (1875-1910)
First produced: La gringa, 1904; first published, 1910
    (English translation, 1942)
Type of work: Drama
Type of plot: Comedy
Time of plot: Early twentieth century
Locale: Pampas, near Santa Fe, Argentina

Principal characters:
DON NICOLA, an ambitious Italian immigrant farmer
MARÍA, his wife
VICTORIA, their daughter
HORACIO, their son
DON CANTALICIO, an easygoing, native-born farmer
PRÓSPERO, his son, who is in love with Victoria

The Story:

Don Nicola is an immigrant landowner who works hard on his farm and expects his laborers to do the same. Privately, his workmen and less ambitious neighbors criticize him because he makes his wife and children get up at two o'clock in the morning to begin their daily chores.

One of his neighbors is Don Cantalicio, an easygoing creole farmer deeply in Nicola's debt. Próspero, his son, works for Nicola and casts many lingering glances in the direction of Victoria, his employer's pretty daughter. Early

one morning, coming to breakfast with the other laborers, Próspero finds Victoria at her work and seizes the chance to kiss her. She offers little resistance to his embrace. Later, one of the boys reports that he saw the Italian's white ox in old Cantalicio's pasture. Próspero is forced to defend his father against a charge of thievery.

With a payment of a loan of forty-five hundred pesos about to fall due, Cantalicio begs his neighbor for a year's extension of credit. Nicola says that he intends to foreclose on

Cantalicio's property because his son Horacio, studying in Buenos Aires, wants the land for a farm. Cantalicio is unable to pay the debt, but he refuses to give up the property. When Próspero comments that his father should have planted wheat instead of trying to pasture cattle, Cantalicio turns on his son and accuses him of becoming a gringo—a despised foreigner.

Not long afterward María, Nicola's wife, discovers Próspero hugging her daughter. When she tells her husband, he discharges the young man. It does no good for Próspero to ask for Victoria's hand. Nicola tells him that he is not making money for a creole son-in-law to squander.

A few days later, the customers in a nearby tavern are drinking and teasing the waitress when a call comes for the doctor to attend a sick but penniless peon. The doctor refuses to leave until some of the loiterers offer to pay his fee. Into the tavern to gossip with the manager's wife come María and Victoria, who are shopping in town while Nicola is with his lawyer discussing the confiscation of Cantalicio's property. Próspero also arrives, about to leave Santa Fe. He will not listen when Victoria pleads with him to stay. He quarrels again with his father, who again accuses him of taking the side of foreigners against those of good Argentineans.

Once Cantalicio loses the lawsuit he brought in an attempt to keep his property, he, too, prepares to leave the district. He complains bitterly that the immigrants are taking over all the land. When Nicola appears at the tavern to pay him the cash difference between the amount of the debt and the value of the farm, Cantalicio refuses to accept a note for a part of the settlement, even though the priest promises to see that the note is made good. The ruined Creole trusts no one, and he weeps as he declares that everyone is against him.

Two years later, many changes can be seen on the farm that Nicola took over. To make room for a new building, he plans to have the workmen chop down the ancient ombu tree, symbol of the old-time Argentine gaucho. Horacio, who settles on the farm, is explaining to his father the use of gravity in connection with a new reservoir when Victoria appears. She is listless and shows no interest in anything, not even in plans for her own room in the new house.

Old Cantalicio turns up unexpectedly. He is now working for others and driving oxen to a nearby town, and he stops to see what his old home looks like. Every change saddens him, but he reacts most strongly to the cutting down of the ombu. Nicola has no right to touch the tree, he asserts; it belongs to the land.

Victoria keeps trying to tell him something, but all she can bring herself to say is that she was in Rosario for several months. There she saw Próspero, who misses his father. She

lets slip the fact that she is receiving letters from him. Horacio reports that Mr. Daples, an agent for farm machinery in Rosario, regards Cantalicio's son as his most valued employee. The brother and sister offer to take the old man around the farm. Still resentful, he refuses and hurriedly mounts his horse.

At that moment, the automobile of the man who is building the new house chugs over the hill. That symbol of modern progress frightens Cantalicio's horse, who bolts and throws his rider in front of the car. Refusing the aid of everyone except Victoria, the hurt man begs her to help him to the ombu; he wants to die when it falls. He curses Nicola, calling him a gringo.

Several weeks later, everything is going well on the renovated farm. Buyers are offering bonuses to get Nicola's clean wheat as soon as the thresher arrives to harvest it. Nicola tells Horacio that the contractor wants to marry Victoria and asked for an answer before he leaves that night. The father is anxious to consult her as to her choice, but she is spending most of her time looking after Cantalicio, who lost his right arm through his accident. Some people in the household think that he will be better off in a hospital.

Overhearing their discussion, Cantalicio announces that he will leave the farm at once, on foot if they will not lend him a wagon. Victoria refuses to hear of his leaving, however. Breaking down, she insists that she needs him, for she is carrying Próspero's child.

Mr. Daples sends Próspero to the farm to run the threshing machine. Great is María's dismay when she again catches him embracing her daughter. When she calls for her husband to come and drive Próspero off the place once and for all, Nicola remarks on the young man's industry and calculates that if the boy marries into the family they can get their threshing done for nothing. Even Cantalicio becomes reconciled to the gringos—at least to one of them—and lets drop the announcement of his expected grandchild. All are excited. Nicola, however, is never one to waste time, even for such a reason. He declares that Próspero can wed Victoria, but meanwhile there is the threshing to be done. Grandchild or no grandchild, work must come first.

Critical Evaluation:

Born in Montevideo, Uruguay, to Argentine exiles, Florencio Sánchez was brought up in a poverty that made him closely acquainted with an emerging working class that flooded such major Latin American cities as Montevideo and Buenos Aires before World War I. Himself the child of immigrants, Sánchez showed a marked interest in the migration of thousands of foreigners to the cities. In *The Foreign Girl*, he shows the animosity and discomfort of the local population, especially the local peasant class, who felt displaced by an aggressive foreign working class.

The Foreign Girl also raises another important issue: What local traditions should be preserved despite the tremendous changes experienced in the area as the result of worldwide technological advances? Sánchez answers this question in the various types of characters he uses to define the social groups involved in the controversy.

As a newspaper reporter, Sánchez became an indefatigable traveler, which allowed him to witness local traditions representing the Argentine identity. Since much of that local folklore belonged to the lower social groups, he also got to know intimately the problems faced by those marginalized classes. Sánchez's characters represent genuine types of people, and his play *The Foreign Girl* is a realistic portrayal of life at the turn of the century. In fact, Sánchez's total production could be labeled a reliable reproduction of rural life in the outskirts of Southern Cone urban centers.

The Foreign Girl's main character, Victoria, represents the new Argentine of the twentieth century: a first-generation country girl of Italian parents. Her derogatory nickname, Gringa, reflects local animosity against foreigners. In the play, Victoria has the positive, sympathetic role of a hardworking young woman, who is well liked in the neighborhood because of her kindness and consideration toward all around her, including her Argentine neighbors. She considers herself an Argentine and displays deeply rooted attachment to the land.

Her father, Don Nicola, is her opposite: an abusive father and husband who forces his daughter and wife to do long hours of heavy farm labor. This strong Italian man has no connection to the land, from which he tries to force optimal productivity, showing no concern for environmental damage. Nicola keeps himself apart from the Argentine community, a fact that brings further resentment from the local inhabitants.

Sánchez achieves dramatic tension by contrasting Nicola's desire for quick wealth with the local people's more relaxed work ethic. A neighbor, Don Cantalicio, is typical of the native Argentine farmer, who takes time away from work to enjoy nature. Cantalicio loses his farm because he owes money to Nicola, which leads to a confrontation between these two strong-willed men.

Sánchez's social views rescue the play from being inflammatory antiforeigner propaganda. His stand is clear: The conflict between Nicola and Cantalicio is not due to one man's being more hardworking than the other, but to Nicola's exploitation of the land and his lack of attachment to the

country. Such lack of connection to the host country is not shared by the first generation born in Argentina, represented in the play by Victoria and Horacio, Nicola's son. Horacio, a university-trained land surveyor, instructs his father on more efficient ways to cultivate the land and warns him about the dangers of overworking the land. Some of this advice had already been offered by Cantalicio to Nicola.

In a dramatic turn of events, Cantalicio is also taught a lesson by his son, Próspero, who blames his father for losing his farm to Nicola because Cantalicio had not rotated his crops to revitalize the aging soil. Having fallen in love with Victoria, Próspero sets out to prove to her that he is a worthy, hardworking, intelligent man. He transforms a nearby farm into one of the most productive in the area. Final recognition of Próspero's knowledge of agricultural matters comes from Horacio, who seeks Próspero's advice for his father's farm, of which Horacio is now overseer.

The Foreign Girl's happy ending—Victoria and Próspero getting married with their parents' permission—reflects Latin American society's positive attitude at the time toward the twentieth century. Sánchez expresses a widespread belief that Latin America's entrance into the twentieth century began when its people accepted foreign help in the shaping of their society. Sánchez recognizes, however, that native values are in jeopardy, and he urges that modern Latin American society observe a balance between the ancient, local South American customs and the ideas of European industrialism.

Sánchez's contribution to Latin American theater lies in his concrete expression of social ideas. His characters, presented in photographic detail, prove that rural life with its many problems and joys is material worthy of the drama. Sánchez's aim to educate by means of simple plots and real characters makes him a precursor of the popular theater.

"Critical Evaluation" by Rafael Ocasio

Further Reading

Dorn, Georgette M. "Florencio Sánchez." In *Latin American Writers*, edited by Carlos A. Solé and María Isabel Abreu. Vol. 2. New York: Charles Scribner's Sons, 1989. Presents an overview of Sánchez's literary production. An ideal introduction to Sánchez's best known works.

Foster, David William. "Ideological Shift in the Rural Images in Florencio Sánchez's Theater." *Hispanic Journal* 11, no. 1 (Spring, 1990): 97-106. A detailed study of Argentina's rural life at the end of the nineteenth and beginning of the twentieth century. Compares two plays, *The Foreign Girl* and *Down the Gully* (1905), and emphasizes Sánchez's treatment of European immigration to Argentina.

Foster, David William, and Virginia Ramos Foster. "Sánchez, Florencio." In *Modern Latin American Literature*. New York: Frederick Ungar, 1975. Offers a survey of Sánchez's production by providing excerpts from critical studies by various critics.

Muñoz, Vladimiro. *Florencio Sánchez: A Chronology*. Trans-
lated by W. Scott Johnson. New York: Gordon Press, 1979. Traces Sánchez's life and places his works within the context of his many trips and political confrontations.

Richardson, Ruth. *Florencio Sánchez and the Argentine Theater*. New York: Instituto de las Españas en los Estados Unidos, 1933. Traces Sánchez's contributions as a founding father of contemporary Argentine theater and discusses the status of the national theater.

The Forsyte Saga

Author: John Galsworthy (1867-1933)
First published: 1922; includes *The Man of Property*, 1906; "Indian Summer of a Forsyte," 1918; "Awakening," 1920; *In Chancery*, 1920; *To Let*, 1921
Type of work: Novels
Type of plot: Family
Time of plot: 1886-1920
Locale: England

Principal characters:
SOAMES FORSYTE, a man of property
IRENE, his wife
OLD JOLYON FORSYTE, his uncle
YOUNG JOLYON, Old Jolyon's son
JUNE, Young Jolyon's daughter
PHILIP BOSINNEY, an architect engaged to June
ANNETTE LAMOTTE FORSYTE, Soames's second wife
FLEUR, their daughter
JON, Irene and Young Jolyon's son
WINIFRED DARTIE, Soames's sister

The Story:

The Man of Property. It is 1886, and all the Forsytes are gathered at Old Jolyon Forsyte's house to celebrate the engagement of his granddaughter, June, to Philip Bosinney, a young architect. Young Jolyon Forsyte, June's father, is estranged from his family because he ran away with a governess, whom he later married after June's mother's death. Because of the ensuing scandal, June has grown up in the home of her grandfather.

Old Jolyon complains that since June became engaged he has seen little of her. Because he is lonely, he calls on Young Jolyon, whom he has not seen in many years. He finds his son painting watercolors and also working as an underwriter for Lloyd's. Young Jolyon has two children, Holly and Jolly, by his second wife, and Old Jolyon comes to dote upon them. Old Jolyon, who has the tenderest heart among the six Forsyte brothers (there are ten siblings in all) realizes that he wishes for a complete reconciliation with his son.

The family knows that Soames, son of Old Jolyon's brother James, has been having trouble with his lovely wife, Irene. She has developed a profound aversion for her husband and has recently reminded him of her premarital stipu-
lation that she should have her freedom if the marriage were not a success. Desperate to please her, Soames plans to build a large country place at Robin Hill and hires June's fiancé to design and build the house.

When Soames suggests alterations to the plans, Bosinney appears offended, and in the end, the plans remain as they were drawn. As work on the house proceeds, the two men argue over the costs, which are exceeding the original estimate. One day, Soames's uncle, Swithin Forsyte, takes Irene to see the house, where she meets Bosinney. While Swithin dozes, the architect and Irene talk and fall deeply in love with each other. From this point on, Irene's already unbearable life with Soames becomes impossible. She asks for a separate room.

Problems over the house continue. Bosinney has agreed to decorate it but only if he can have a free hand, to which Soames finally agrees. Irene and Bosinney begin to meet secretly. As their affair progresses, June becomes more unhappy, and as her suspicions grow, her deep friendship with Irene is strained. Finally, Old Jolyon takes June away for a holiday. He writes to Young Jolyon, asking him to see Bosinney and learn his intentions toward June. Young Jolyon talks to Bosinney, but the report he makes to his father is vague.

When the house is completed, Soames sues Bosinney for exceeding his highest estimate. Irene refuses to move to Robin Hill. When the lawsuit over the house comes to trial, Soames wins his case without difficulty. This same night, Bosinney, after spending the afternoon with Irene and learning that Soames has forced himself on her, is accidentally run over and killed. There is a lingering suspicion that his death may have been a suicide. Irene leaves her husband on the day of the trial, but that night she returns to his house because there is nowhere else for her to go.

"Indian Summer of a Forsyte." June persuades her grandfather to buy Robin Hill for Jolyon's family. A short time after Bosinney's death, Irene leaves Soames permanently; she settles in a small flat and starts giving music lessons to support herself. Several years later, Irene visits Robin Hill secretly and meets Old Jolyon. She wins him over with her gentleness and charm, and during that summer, she makes his days happy. Each of her visits is a joy to the old man. Late in the summer, he dies quietly while waiting for her to come to him again.

In Chancery. After his separation from Irene, Soames devotes himself to making money. Then, still hoping to have an heir, he begins to court a young French woman, Annette Lamotte. His sister, Winifred Dartie, is facing difficulties. Soon, her profligate husband, Monty Dartie, steals her pearls and runs away to South America with a Spanish dancer. When Soames decides to marry Annette, he goes to Irene to see if she will provide grounds for a divorce. He finds that she has lived a very quiet, model life. Soames realizes that he still loves her and tries to persuade her to come back to him. When she refuses, he hires a detective to get evidence with which to divorce her.

Old Jolyon has left a legacy to Irene in his will, and Young Jolyon, now a widower, has been appointed trustee. Soames approaches Irene, who appeals to Young Jolyon for protection. She goes to Paris to avoid Soames; shortly afterward, Young Jolyon joins her. Their visit is cut short by Jolly, who announces that he has joined the yeomanry to fight in the Boer War. Holly has, in the meantime, fallen in love with Val Dartie, her cousin. When Val proposes to Holly, he is overheard by Jolly, who dares Val, whom he dislikes intensely, to join the yeomanry with him. Val accepts. June then decides to become a Red Cross nurse, and Holly goes with her. Monty reappears unexpectedly. To avoid further scandal, Winifred decides to allow him to come back.

Soames goes to Paris in a last effort to persuade Irene. Frightened, Irene returns to Young Jolyon. Before they be-

come lovers, they are presented with papers by Soames's lawyer. They decide to go abroad together. Before their departure, Young Jolyon receives word that Jolly has died of enteric fever during the African campaign. Later, Soames secures his divorce and marries Annette. To the discomfiture of both branches of the family, Val marries Holly.

Irene and Jolyon have a son, Jon. When Annette is about to give birth to a child, Soames has to choose between saving the mother or the child. Wishing an heir, Soames chooses to save the child. Fortunately, both Annette and the baby, Fleur, live. Little Jon grows up under the adoring eyes of his parents, and Fleur grows up spoiled by her doting father.

"Awakening." It is the summer of 1909, and Jon is eight years old. He is an imaginative boy, who vividly reenacts every story that he knows. He awakens to a sense of beauty, especially to the beauty of his mother's face and form and charm and tranquil spirit. From this moment forward, he worships her. Jon also shows signs of one day becoming an artist, not a painter like his father, but a poet.

To Let. Years have passed. Monty is dead. Val and Holly are training racehorses. One day in a picture gallery, Soames impulsively invites a young man, Michael Mont, to see his collection of pictures. That same afternoon, he sees Irene and her son, Jon, for the first time in twenty years. Fleur and Jon meet by chance. Having decided that he wants to try farming, Jon goes to stay with Val. Fleur also appears, to spend the week with Holly. Jon and Fleur fall deeply in love.

Only vague ideas exist regarding the cause of the feud between Jon and Fleur's respective branches of the family. Later, Fleur learns all the details from Prosper Profond, a cynical Belgian with whom Annette is having an affair, and from Winifred Dartie. She is still determined to marry Jon. Michael Mont has received Soames's permission to court Fleur. When Soames hears of the affair between Annette and Prosper, she does not deny it but promises there will be no scandal.

Fleur tries to persuade Jon to have a hasty marriage. She fails because Young Jolyon reluctantly gives his son a letter revealing the story of Soames and Irene. After reading the letter, Jon realizes that he can never marry Fleur. His decision becomes irrevocable when his father dies. He leaves England at once and goes to British Columbia, Canada, where Irene joins him. Fleur, disappointed, marries Michael. Timothy, Soames's uncle, is the last of the old Forsyte brothers; when he dies, Soames realizes that the Forsyte age has passed. Its way of life is like an empty house that is to let. He feels lonely and old.

"The Story" revised by Patrick Adcock

Critical Evaluation:

The Forsyte Saga led to John Galsworthy's Nobel Prize in Literature in 1932. The novel's initial immense popularity subsided for a time but was revived again in the 1970's, partly as a result of a televised dramatization by the British Broadcasting Corporation in 1969. The three novels that make up the trilogy—*The Man of Property*, *In Chancery*, and *To Let*—are sequences in the history of a wealthy, middle-class English family, the Forsytes, who are conscious of their social position and eager to keep it. Their pettiness in matters of decorum is typical of the wealthy bourgeoisie of the times.

The central conflict tying the three novels and two short stories—"Indian Summer of a Forsyte" and "Awakening"—together is between the sense of beauty and the acquisitive instinct, the desire to own, both property and people. Soames believes he owns Irene, yet he loses her twice—to men who, by his lights, are immoral and have no right to her. Fleur, her father's daughter, loves Jon desperately, but she is desperate that she may lose him, that she may not possess him. Soames becomes a perceptive collector of paintings, but in his mind, he can never really separate their artistic value from the prices they may bring. He always knows which artists are up, which down. He spends hours alone in his picture room, luxuriating in the collection he owns.

The differences among the various members of the Forsyte clan are to a great extent due to generational misunderstanding. The older members of the family, such as Uncle Swithin and Old Jolyon, lived in a different world, both chronologically and psychologically, from that of such young Forsytes as Fleur and Jon. Those two worlds are straddled by Soames and Winifred, products of the tranquil Victorian period but now faced with disturbing societal changes that make them cling to the old familiar ways and fear acceptance of new ideas and new people. The transition from the old world into the new is one of the major strengths of the novel, and Galsworthy draws readers into the lives of the Forsytes in such a way that they feel they are actually living through this time of change.

Perhaps the greatest merit of *The Forsyte Saga* is that while its overall aim is one of social criticism, the characters are not sacrificed to this end but used to illuminate the commentary. Although critics have claimed that most of the characters are incomplete, the mystery in each of the main characters, especially Irene and Bosinney, proves immensely engrossing.

With her striking combination of golden hair, warm brown eyes, and pale skin, Irene is the embodiment of earthly beauty. She is often likened to a goddess, to Venus, but she is a Venus who remains chaste during the twelve years between her two love affairs. Her loveliness of face and figure, her carriage, her skill at the piano, her awareness, her self-possession—all effortlessly cast an almost mystical spell over everyone in the novels, even those who are disposed to judge her. Soames never stops loving her. When others are drawn to her and her second husband (Young Jolyon has a very engaging personality), Soames is bitterly resentful. Each of them has been involved in two scandals within the family, while he considers himself blameless. Bosinney, the architect who cares only for Irene and his work, is like a character from writer Ayn Rand—although Galsworthy wrote several decades before Rand. Bosinney is an artist with complete faith in his own vision and his talent. He will design and decorate Soames's house according to that vision or not at all—no compromises. Soames's instructions to cut costs here, eliminate features there, deter him not at all. The readers can see why he appeals to Irene.

The novel is a period piece, but it can be appreciated by readers not primarily interested in that historical age because the turns of fortune in the lives of the main characters address universal human concerns. The first episode of the story, the festive occasion of a party celebrating the engagement of young June to Bosinney, is a case in point. The setting is that of a large family gathering intended to evaluate the worthiness of a prospective new member of the family. The conversation may at times have a uniquely Victorian flavor, but the setting and mood are ageless.

The complications among the characters are likewise ageless. Irene hopes to help June obtain family acceptance for Bosinney, but she falls in love with him herself. Soames tries to gain Irene's love by building a beautiful house for her, but he only succeeds in forcing her to leave him, which in turn makes him even more the distasteful man of property than he had been. This hardening of Soames's character makes him more a tragic character than a bad one.

Using an episodic structure in the novels, Galsworthy succeeds in portraying the thoughts and actions of an age in transition from the staid and superficially tranquil Victorian age to the bustling, confused early twentieth century. By using a large family as the base of the novel, he is able to introduce a representative variety of events and individuals. He uses many types of personality, among them Soames, the lonely businessman; Young Jolyon, the man who renounces his family to pursue a career as an artist; Fleur, the archetypal flapper of the post-World War I era. These and other characters play important roles in the progress of the story, but beyond that they are representative of the times.

The narrative has a circular quality. Fleur marries a man whom she does not love, just as Soames married Annette, whom he did not love, and Irene married Soames, whom she did not love. The readers are invited to speculate on Fleur's chances for a happier marriage than those that preceded hers. The family cycle ends with the death of Timothy, Soames's uncle. He has lived for more than a century, through the entire Victorian and Edwardian periods. At the end, he is an infant once again, cared for by his faithful housekeeper and cook, themselves remnants of an age that has passed. It is for these qualities and for the overall view of the period that this trilogy will retain its position in literature.

"Critical Evaluation" by Patricia Ann King;
revised by Patrick Adcock

Further Reading

Furst, Lilian R. "'The Ironic Little Dark Chasms of Life': Narrative Strategies in John Galsworthy's *Forsyte Saga* and Thomas Mann's *Buddenbrooks*." *Literature Interpretation Theory* 17, no. 2 (April-June, 2006): 157-177. Compares the narrative strategies in the two novels, particularly their treatment of the passage of time. Furst argues that both authors were writing about a social class and a way of life with which they had intimate knowledge.

Gindin, James. "Ethical Structures in John Galsworthy, Elizabeth Bowen, and Iris Murdoch." In *Forms of Modern British Fiction*, edited by Alan Warren Friedman. Austin: University of Texas Press, 1975. Concludes that the central concern of the Galsworthy trilogy is ethical and that it explores what people do to themselves and to others. The main struggle is often between property and beauty.

Kaye, Peter. "Dostoevsky and the Gentleman-Writers: E. M. Forster, John Galsworthy, and Henry James." In *Dostoevsky and English Modernism, 1900-1930*. New York: Cambridge University Press, 1999. Focuses on Galsworthy and other English writers who either admired Fyodor Dostoevski or feared him as a destructive literary force. Kaye analyzes these writers' misunderstandings of Dostoevski to better understand the nature of the modern English novel.

Ru, Yi-ling. *The Family Novel: Toward a Generic Definition*. New York: Peter Lang, 1992. Ru examines Galsworthy's *The Forsyte Saga* and novels by French writer Roger Martin du Gard and Chinese writer Pa Chin to define the distinct character of the family novel.

Sternlicht, Sanford. *John Galsworthy*. Boston: G. K. Hall, 1987. Chapter 3 describes *The Forsyte Saga* as Galsworthy's crowning achievement, an ironic account without heroes or epic battles and a fine portrait of the passing from power of England's upper-middle class.

Stevens, Earl. "John Galsworthy." In *British Winners of the Nobel Literary Prize*, edited by Walter Kidd. Norman: University of Oklahoma Press, 1973. Concludes that *The Forsyte Saga* alternates between satiric novel and lyric interlude and that Galsworthy seeks to teach readers to see the world more completely.

Whatmore, Petra. *"That Mysterious Thing": Family Concepts in "The Forsyte Saga," "To the Lighthouse," "Mrs. Dalloway," and "Ulysses."* Tübingen, Germany: Stauffenburg, 2001. Examines *The Forsyte Saga* and three other novels written in the 1920's that focus on fragmented families at the end of the Victorian era. Includes a discussion of the historical and political context of Galsworthy's novel, its narrative and stylistic elements, and its depiction of marriage, parenthood, and relationships outside the family.

Fortunata and Jacinta
Two Stories of Married Women

Author: Benito Pérez Galdós (1843-1920)
First published: Fortunata y Jacinta, 1886-1887 (English translation, 1973)
Type of work: Novel
Type of plot: Social chronicle
Time of plot: 1869-1875
Locale: Madrid

Principal characters:
FORTUNATA, a woman of the lower class
JUANITO SANTA CRUZ, her lover
MAXIMILIANO RUBÍN, her husband
JACINTA, Juanito's wife
MORENO ISLA, her admirer
COLONEL EVARISTO FEIJÓO, Fortunata's protector

The Story:

The Santa Cruz dry-goods store in Madrid, established in the eighteenth century, provides an income for Juanito Santa Cruz. Graduating from the university at the age of twenty-four, he is not yet ready to take his place in the family business. He wants to enjoy life, and Barbara Santa Cruz, his mother, spoils him. Her chief adviser is a former clerk, Placido Estupiñá, who smuggles goods into the city in his spare time.

At the home of a fellow student, Juanito meets the attractive Fortunata and takes her as his mistress. Shortly afterward, Estupiñá finds out about the affair, and Juanito's mother contracts for him a marriage with his beautiful but passive cousin, Jacinta. They are married in May, 1871. When they return from their honeymoon, Fortunata leaves Madrid.

Jacinta discovers in the passing years that she cannot have children. Learning some details of her husband's earlier affair with Fortunata, including the fact that his mistress bore him a son nicknamed Petusin, she wonders whether it is her duty to take care of the child. In the meantime, Juanito is told that Fortunata is back in Madrid. He immediately begins to look for her, but his search ends when a lung infection disables him for a long time.

Among Fortunata's admirers is the ill-favored and schizophrenic Maximiliano Rubín, the orphan of a goldsmith, who, like his two brothers, is subject to violent headaches. Thin and weak, he was reared by his Aunt Lupe, who allowed him to live in a world of his own imagination. While studying to become a pharmacist, he meets Fortunata at a friend's house. Her poverty affords her the opportunity to overlook his ugliness and to date him. When she confesses her past, he proposes marriage in order to redeem her.

Hearing of his plan, Aunt Lupe sends one of his brothers, a priest, to talk to Fortunata. The woman says frankly that Maximiliano is the only one of her lovers—except one now married—for whom she ever cared. The priest proposes that she spend some time in a home for wayward girls; if she benefits by the experience, he will agree to the marriage. After a term in the institution, Fortunata marries Maximiliano on a day when he is suffering from one of his worst headaches.

Knowing beforehand of the proposed marriage, Juanito takes a room in the boardinghouse that Fortunata and her husband are to occupy. At first he intendeds only to see Fortunata again, but on the night of the wedding her husband is ill, and Fortunata and Juanito resume their old intimacy. Maximiliano, finding out about the affair, quarrels with Juanito, who overpowers the puny pharmacist and sends him to the hospital with an injured larynx. Then Fortunata packs her belongings and leaves her husband.

Juan Pablo, the second of Maximiliano's brothers, spends his afternoons in one café or another with his cronies, among them the elderly Colonel Evaristo Feijóo. While watching the parade marking the restoration of the monarchy in 1874, one of the loiterers sees Juanito and Fortunata sharing a balcony. Through gossip, Jacinta learns of her husband's infidelity. When she accuses him, he arouses her sympathy for Fortunata by telling how badly she was treated by her husband. Nevertheless, he does promise to break off relations with the woman. His farewell message, with an enclosure of one thousand pesetas, so angers Fortunata that she goes to his house in order to create a scandal. The sight of Jacinta's gentle beauty tempers her anger, however, and while she is trying to decide what to do she sees Colonel Feijóo. He points out that, untrained as she is for any career, she has only three choices: go back to her husband, accept the attentions of any man with money to pay her, or take him as her protector.

She chooses Feijóo as her lover, at the same time planning to make her future secure after his death and to reinstate herself in the good graces of the Rubín family. On one occasion, Fortunata comes face-to-face with Jacinta, who does not know what her husband's former mistress looks like. Torn between a realization of Jacinta's beauty and goodness and her hatred for her as Juanito's wife, Fortunata blurts out her identity, much to Jacinta's confusion.

Only one woman present during the encounter knows what to do. Guillermina Pacheco asks Fortunata to come to see her the next day to discuss the situation. The frank conversation between the two women is overheard by Jacinta, who is in the next room. The cruelest blow to Jacinta is Fortunata's insistence that Juanito needs her, since she gave him the son his wife could never bear him. When Fortunata discovers the eavesdropper, her angry words show that she is still essentially of the lower class.

Later, Fortunata has a scene with Maximiliano, who is gradually losing his mind. At last he drives her out of the house. Before long, she and Juanito once again become lovers. Maximiliano tries to earn a living by working in a drugstore, but his mental state causes him to make dangerous mistakes in mixing drugs. His employer has two daughters. One is Aurora, the thirty-three-year-old widow of a Frenchman killed while fighting the Prussians in 1870. She wears clothes with a Parisian flair and soon catches the eye of Juanito, as Fortunata learns to her dismay.

In the meantime, Moreno Isla falls violently in love with Jacinta. He and Guillermina Pacheco, bribed by Moreno, try to convince her that her husband will never be faithful, but Jacinta gives Moreno no encouragement. At the same time

Aurora, for her own purposes, tries to convince Juanito that his wife is in love with another man.

Fortunata is pregnant and is therefore afraid to live with Maximiliano any longer. He talks constantly of a philosophy of death; afraid, she hides herself at Aunt Lupe's house. While looking for her, Maximiliano discovers proof that Juanito and Aurora are having an affair. He finally discovers his wife's hiding place after Estupiñá takes the news of Fortunata's baby son to the Santa Cruz household. No longer wanting to kill her, Maximiliano forces his way into Fortunata's room, where he tells her what he knows about Juanito and Aurora. Although the doctor orders her not to leave her bed, Fortunata rushes out to revenge herself on Jacinta's enemy and her own. The exertion causes her death. Before she dies, she sends a letter by Estupiñá to Jacinta. In the letter, she asks Jacinta to care for Juanito's son.

Being compelled to acknowledge his paternity is a blow to Juanito, for it loses him his wife's remaining esteem. He realizes sadly that his philandering brings him to old age in spirit while he is still young in years, with nothing but an empty and unhappy future before him.

Critical Evaluation:

Considered by some to be the greatest Spanish novelist after Miguel de Cervantes, Benito Pérez Galdós is known for his numerous historical novels and his treatment of nineteenth century Spain. In his contemporary novels, Pérez Galdós attempts to capture the flavor of Spanish life during a period of great turmoil and political change. In addition to a complex portrayal of nineteenth century Spanish life, Pérez Galdós's novels are rich in characterization and psychological subtlety. They are matched by few other novels of the time.

Pérez Galdós spent his childhood in the Canary Islands, where he was the youngest in a well-to-do family. In 1863, Pérez Galdós left for Madrid to study law at the University of Madrid. He failed, through lack of interest, his law course, but Pérez Galdós took an intense interest in the daily life of Madrid. An astute observer of life, he set out to pursue his interest in writing, which led him to work for a newspaper after his university days. He published his first novel in 1870, the start of a long and immensely productive career as a writer.

Fortunata and Jacinta is a massive novel in four volumes, which focuses on the lives, sufferings, and eventual reconciliation of two women of very different backgrounds and social statuses. The women are the lover and the wife of Juanito Santa Cruz. Both vie for his attention and loyalty. While *Fortunata and Jacinta* overflows with finely portrayed characters from nearly all strata of nineteenth century Spanish society, the core of the novel focuses on the subtly idealized, yet flesh-and-blood portrayal of the female protagonists as representatives of two opposing ideals. This opposition is set in a Christian framework, in which charity, compassion, and forgiveness are seen as the highest principles of a spiritual life.

Many of the characters in the novel are portrayed with great complexity and depth, but their purpose is primarily to act as foils for Fortunata and Jacinta. Probably the most complex character besides the two female protagonists is Maximiliano Rubín, or Maxi, who, despite his mental and physical weakness, appears to embody certain philosophical and ethical concerns of Pérez Galdós. These concerns are the overbearing effects of environment and heredity on a person's life. Maxi strives to overcome his inherited weaknesses, but he is fated to be thwarted at every turn by bad health and mental instability. Juanito, in contrast, is a character of little emotional depth, who lacks intelligence, sensitivity, or insight, and whose main function in the novel is to further the character development of the two protagonists.

The narrative complexity of *Fortunata and Jacinta* is typical of nineteenth century realist novels, whose aim is to provide the illusion of a complete vision of the actual life of the time and place portrayed. This aim accounts for the extensive background material presented in volume 1 of the novel. Readers may feel this material to be excessive, but they should take into consideration the fact that family history, references to actual events, political figures, places, streets, names, and other detailed information are all meant to provide the sense that readers are getting a true glimpse into Spanish society. These details also set the stage for the further development of the characters. Pérez Galdós, for instance, meticulously portrays Juanito as the indolent and spoiled child of doting upper-class parents. All his actions during the early chapters of volume 1 confirm that his behavior will cause suffering to Fortunata and Jacinta, although the relative flatness of his character prevents readers from assigning him anything but cursory blame for their pain.

The final chapter of volume 4 brings together the many tributaries of Pérez Galdós's tale, uniting Fortunata and Jacinta with a bond of love, understanding, and forgiveness. Fortunata's suffering ends in death, as readers suspect it must, while the barren Jacinta inherits the infant Fortunata has by Juanito. Despite the continual sufferings of both women they are redeemed, at least partially, by the resolution of their circumstances. As she nears death, Fortunata is seen to be capable of deep sympathy as well as of compassion for those who cause her to suffer and seems also to transcend her earthy nature.

On her deathbed, she accepts Jacinta's message of thanks through Guillermina, forgives even Juanito, then finally, in a delirium that resembles religious ecstasy, declares herself to be an angel, an "angel face," just like her infant.

With Jacinta's adoption of the infant after Fortunata's death, Jacinta at long last finds the joy that escaped her. She effectively bears a child, although through the womb of another woman. An association of Fortunata with the Christ figure is not out of the question, for in dying she brings life and hope. The final message of *Fortunata and Jacinta* appears to be a positive one in which disparate, often conflicting, personalities and beliefs are reconciled under the veil of a somewhat mystic ethic of compassion. The two former enemies, with death separating them, "one of them in visible life and the other in invisible life . . . may possibly have looked at each other from opposite banks and wished to embrace." Juanito, as obtuse as ever, finally receives his due from Jacinta, who consigns him to the role of a nothing, a husband who loses all respect from and influence over his wife. He becomes utterly superfluous, an appendage to his wife's existence.

The novel ends with Maxi finally being placed in an asylum for the insane. Even in this end there is hope, for it is in his confinement that Maxi, like all the others who suffer in Pérez Galdós's story, finds rest in the submission of his will "to whatever the world wishes to do with me." He, as have Fortunata and Jacinta, makes his peace with the world.

"Critical Evaluation" by Howard Giskin

Further Reading

Bell, T. E. *Galdós and Darwin.* Rochester, N.Y.: Tamesis, 2006. Traces the influence of Charles Darwin's evolutionary theories and other scientific concepts on Pérez Galdós's literary works.

Larsen, Kevin. *Cervantes and Galdós in "Fortunata y Jacinta": Tales of Impertinent Curiosity.* Lewiston, N.Y.: Edwin Mellen Press, 1999. Examines the influence of Miguel de Cervantes on Pérez Galdós's novel.

McGovern, Timothy Michael. *Dickens in Galdós.* New York: Peter Lang, 2000. Compares how Pérez Galdós and Charles Dickens criticize society by creating three types of characters—the religious ascetic, the miser, and the Lazarillo, a type of itinerant rogue. Includes bibliography and index.

Pattison, Walter T. *Benito Pérez Galdós.* Boston: Twayne, 1975. A concise and informative biography of Pérez Galdós. Chapter 7 dwells rather extensively on *Fortunata and Jacinta.*

Ribbans, Geoffrey. *Conflicts and Conciliations: The Evolution of Galdós's "Fortunata y Jacinta."* West Lafayette, Ind.: Purdue University Press, 1997. Chronicles the various stages of the novel's composition and discusses its structure, characters in family and society, and its depiction of time and space.

_____. "Contemporary History in the Structure and Characterization of *Fortunata y Jacinta.*" In *Galdós Studies,* edited by J. E. Varey. London: Tamesis Books, 1970. Elucidates Pérez Galdós's references to specific historical, political, and social events in nineteenth century Spain. Discusses the manner in which Pérez Galdós integrates fact and fiction.

Scott, Paddy. *Women in the Novels of Benito Pérez Galdós and Ecá de Queiroz.* Lewiston, N.Y.: Edwin Mellen Press, 2008. A feminist analysis of the depiction of women in Pérez Galdós's work, describing how the wives and mothers in his fiction are affected by education, work, religion, and consumerism.

Shoemaker, William H. *The Novelistic Art of Galdós.* 3 vols. Valencia, Spain: Albatros Ediciones Hispanofila, 1980-1982. Volume 1 offers a broad literary critique of Pérez Galdós's novels in their entirety; volume 2 examines each of the novels individually.

Turner, Harriet S. *Fortunata and Jacinta.* New York: Cambridge University Press, 1972. A thorough introduction to the novel, providing detailed discussions of the sociohistorical, structural, and metaphorical aspects of Pérez Galdós's masterwork.

The Fortunes of Nigel

Author: Sir Walter Scott (1771-1832)
First published: 1822
Type of work: Novel
Type of plot: Historical
Time of plot: Early seventeenth century
Locale: England

Principal characters:
NIGEL OLIFAUNT, the lord of Glenvarloch
RICHARD MONIPLIES, his servant
GEORGE HERIOT, a goldsmith and friend of Nigel's father
MARGARET RAMSAY, Heriot's goddaughter
THE EARL OF HUNTINGLEN, an old nobleman
LORD DALGARNO, his son
LADY HERMIONE, a relative of Nigel
DAME SUDDLECHOP, a gossip
TRAPBOIS, a usurer
MARTHA TRAPBOIS, his daughter
JAMES I, the king of England

The Story:

The threatened loss of his family estates in Scotland sends Nigel Olifaunt, the lord of Glenvarloch, and his servant, Richard Moniplies, to London. Their mission there is to petition King James I for the repayment of large loans made to the crown by Nigel's late father. After Richie Moniplies makes an unsuccessful attempt to deliver his master's petition, he is followed from the court by George Heriot, the royal goldsmith, who goes to Nigel and offers to help him gain favor with the king. Heriot gives his friendship with Nigel's late father as his motive. He succeeds in presenting Nigel's petition to the king. King James, in royal good humor, orders Heriot to provide Nigel with money needed to outfit himself properly for an appearance at court, so that he can speak in his own behalf. The king gives Heriot a small crown of jewels with instructions that the gems are to remain in Heriot's possession until the state repays him for the money he will lend to Nigel. The state's finances are seriously depleted, and the king is forced to do business by warrant.

While dining at Heriot's house the next day, Nigel meets Margaret Ramsay, Heriot's godchild and the daughter of David Ramsay, the royal clockmaker. Margaret promptly loses her heart to Nigel, but because he is a nobleman, she is too shy to talk with him. That same night, however, she commissions Dame Suddlechop, a local gossip, to investigate Nigel and his business. The Dame already knows that Nigel has powerful enemies in court, who are interested in seeing that he is prevented from taking rightful possession of his estates. On the promise of more money in the future, the old gossip agrees to learn all she can about Nigel and his affairs.

Dressed in clothing bought by money advanced by Heriot, Nigel goes to the king with his petition. At first, he has difficulty in gaining admittance, but at last, he manages to see the king. The king confesses that there are no funds available for the debt, but he makes a notation on the petition to the Scottish Exchequer and tells Nigel that perhaps he can borrow from moneylenders on the strength of the royal warrant. Nigel leaves the court with Heriot and the earl of Huntinglen, who befriends him because of his father's name.

Anticipating a session with the moneylenders, the three decide to have a paper drawn up, a document that will allow Nigel ample time to redeem his estates by means of the king's warrant. Trusting Heriot and the old earl to handle his business, Nigel devotes himself to becoming acquainted with the earl's young son, Lord Dalgarno. Pretending friendship, Dalgarno in reality begins a campaign to undermine Nigel's character and reputation and complete his financial ruin. Dalgarno himself hopes to gain possession of Nigel's estate.

Dalgarno takes Nigel to gaming houses and other questionable places until Nigel's reputation begins to suffer in the city and at court. At last, even faithful Richie asks for permission to leave his service and return to Scotland. Immediately after Richie's departure, Nigel receives an anonymous note, telling him of Dalgarno's plot to ruin him. At first, Nigel refuses to consider such a possibility, but at length he decides to investigate the charges. When he confronts Dalgarno in the park and accuses him of knavery, Dalgarno is so contemptuous of him that Nigel draws his sword and strikes Dalgarno. The young courtier is not injured. There is a severe penalty for drawing swords in the park, however, and Nigel is forced to flee in order to avoid arrest. He is befriended by a young man he met in a gaming house and is hidden in the house of an old usurer named Trapbois. His refuge is in Whitefriars, known as Alsatia, the haunt of bravos, bankrupts, bullyboys, and thieves.

Meanwhile, Margaret is trying to help the young Scottish lord. A mysterious lady stays apart in a secluded apartment in Heriot's house. She saw Nigel once during his first visit at the house. She is Lady Hermione, who is in seclusion following a tragic affair of the heart. Because she is extremely wealthy, Margaret begs her to help Nigel out of his difficulties. Lady Hermione reveals to Margaret that she is of the House of Glenvarloch and thus a distant relative of Nigel. When Margaret tells her of Dalgarno's plot to ruin Nigel, Lady Hermione gives her the money but warns her not to lose her heart to Nigel, for he is too highborn for a clockmaker's daughter.

Margaret arranges with an apprentice for Nigel's escape. The apprentice is willing to aid her because he is in love with Margaret and was advised by old Dame Suddlechop that he might win the girl's heart by helping Nigel. In the meantime, Nigel kills one of two Russians who murdered Trapbois. Nigel takes Trapbois's daughter Martha with him when he escapes from Alsatia with the help of the apprentice sent by Margaret.

Nigel sends Martha to the house of a ship chandler with whom he lodged for a time and then sets out to find the king and present his own account of the quarrel with Dalgarno. Martha has difficulty in gaining admittance to the house where Nigel sends her, for the ship chandler's wife has disappeared. She is discovered and protected by Richie Moniplies, who returned to London to look for his master and to help him. Nigel, in the meantime, tries to approach the king. James, believing that Nigel wants to kill him, calls out for help. His attendants seize Nigel and carry him off to the Tower. Dalgarno, one of the royal party, is only too glad to see Nigel imprisoned.

In his cell, Nigel is accused by Heriot of adultery with the ship chandler's wife and of duplicity in the disappearance of Martha. Nigel denies his guilt in both of these affairs. Heriot, while refusing to believe him, nevertheless says that he will again try to help Nigel for his dead father's sake, and he asks Nigel for the royal warrant. His plan is to collect the money from the state and satisfy the moneylenders who are pressing for the repayment of Nigel's loan. Nigel falls into despair when he discovers that the royal warrant has been taken from his baggage.

Through a noble friend, Nigel is cleared of the charge of treason—that is, his supposed attempt on the king's life. Nevertheless, he still has to stand trial for drawing his sword against Dalgarno. Richie goes to Nigel in his cell and promises to help his master out of his troubles.

In the meantime, the king receives a letter from the Lady Hermione, in which she charges that Dalgarno is the man who betrayed her. In an attempt to amend the wrongdoing, the king forces Dalgarno to marry Lady Hermione; after the ceremony, however, Dalgarno informs the king that he now possesses his wife's wealth and, through her, a claim upon the Glenvarloch estates. He announces that if the redemption money is not paid by noon of the following day, he will take possession of Nigel's property. Convinced at last that Nigel is the injured party in the affair with Dalgarno, the king informs Richie that his master will be restored to royal favor. Richie, armed with money given to him by Martha, pays the mortgage on Nigel's estates. After trying to show that the redemption papers were gained unlawfully, Dalgarno proceeds on his way to Scotland to claim the property; but on the way, he is killed by the same ruffian he hired to murder Trapbois some time before. His death restores to Lady Hermione the fortune that Dalgarno, as her husband, claimed. She gives a large portion of her wealth to Margaret and the rest to Nigel, her kinsman. Nigel and Margaret declare their love for each other and are married. During the ceremony, Richie appears with Martha, whom he married. Martha tells Nigel that her father stole his royal warrant, and by returning the paper to him, she makes his estates secure. In gratitude to Richie for his part in restoring honor in the court, the king makes the faithful servant a knight of the land.

Critical Evaluation:

In *The Fortunes of Nigel*, Sir Walter Scott surpasses even his former efforts to introduce dozens of characters and plots into one novel. Although the multiplicity of people and events and the use of Scottish dialect may make this novel a difficult one for some readers, the reward in the end is worth the effort. This novel is an exciting tale of intrigue and mystery, one of the great adventure stories in the language. As is also common in stories by Scott, the novel takes much of its romantic atmosphere and dramatic vigor from the author's use of many characters drawn from the lower levels of society. To balance these, Scott also presents in the figure of James I, king of England and Scotland, his finest historical portrait.

Since most of Scott's important work was completed in the first twenty-five years of the nineteenth century, he is often considered part of the Romantic literary movement. Rebelling against the formalism of the eighteenth century, this literary impulse advocated the natural expression of feelings, the value of nature against artifice, and the possibilities of life beyond the strict confines of rationalism. The diverse intellectual and literary trends within the Romantic movement make the classification of most authors problematic; there was a coherent movement, however, and it did stand for certain modes of expression and ideas.

Clearly, many of the features of Scott's novels and of *The Fortunes of Nigel* can be considered Romantic. Although he did not always succeed, he was interested in preserving and presenting the rhythms of the natural speech of his countrymen. His willingness to portray all the ranks of society, the loosely knit structure of the novel, the use of the past, the idealization of women, the intense sentiments—all these can be taken as Romantic features in Scott's work in general and in *The Fortunes of Nigel* in particular. At the same time, however, principles of rationalism, neoclassicism, and literary realism are clearly apparent in *The Fortunes of Nigel*. First, in the "Introductory Epistle" Scott attached to his novel, there is a defensive essay (written, significantly, in the form of a dialogue) that supports the didactic views of the literature of neoclassicism.

In fact, Scott's work stands at one of those junctures in the history of literature where various traditions meet, in mixtures of unpredictable and varying quality, only to separate again as historical and literary circumstances change; it can be said that realists and Romantics may claim Scott with justification. Alexandre Dumas, *père*, and James Fenimore Cooper were profoundly influenced by him, but so were Honoré de Balzac and Leo Tolstoy. In short, whatever the value of Scott's novels (and there has been much disagreement on that score), Scott is a seminal figure in literary history. Therefore, *The Fortunes of Nigel* can be judged not only as a historical novel but as a work influential in the history of the novel.

Scott's literary production may be divided into four parts: the early poetry, the initial group of the Waverley series, the later group of historical novels, and the novels after his financial collapse in 1826. It was during the middle period of the Waverley novels and the years immediately following that Scott did his best work. *The Fortunes of Nigel* falls into the late Waverley period. *The Fortunes of Nigel*, like the early Waverley novels, was highly successful. Although the book was priced out of the reach of the ordinary reader, it nevertheless sold ten thousand copies in the first printing.

In a manner characteristic of the Waverley series, *The Fortunes of Nigel* abounds in realistic detail. There is little of the excess and abstraction typical of the Romantic novel. In *The Fortunes of Nigel*, for example, an enormous variety of social strata are presented, the details of the characters' lives revealed, and their connections with other social groupings and classes dramatized. This sort of description is more exemplary of the realistic novel than of the Romantic. What separates *The Fortunes of Nigel* from the earlier Waverley group is the setting, which Scott moves from Scotland and the Scottish border to England. Although earlier readers and

critics seem to have preferred the original setting, Scott's portrait of James I won for him a much expanded audience south of the border.

Although the setting differs, the substance of the novel is similar to Scott's other work. *The Fortunes of Nigel* is about history—the social, personal, and political forces that compose history; the plot in *The Fortunes of Nigel*, however, is less vivid than the scenes of life, of social contrasts and collisions, which appear throughout the book. Since Nigel is exceedingly passive and is more an observer of the action surrounding him than an active principal in it, he shares the plot's comparative weakness. The weakness of this character and the incidental nature of the plot led some contemporary critics of Scott, in reviewing *The Fortunes of Nigel*, to summarize its stereotyped features. In 1822, the *Quarterly Review* remarked: "The poor passive hero is buffeted about in the usual manner, involved, as usual, in the chicaneries of civil process, and exposed to the dangers of a criminal execution, and rewarded by the hand of the heroine, such as she is, and the redemption of the mortgage on the family estate."

It is certainly true that Scott repeated himself from novel to novel. He wrote very rapidly, almost never reviewed or rewrote his own work, and was frequently guilty of poor and careless writing. At the same time, however, Scott was a master of describing social and historical clashes. Above all, he was concerned with the process of history—the confrontation between the old and the new. For example, in the opening pages of *The Fortunes of Nigel*, Scott draws a picture of the construction of a new palace by James I. As critics have remarked, the passage is designed to show the position of James I, a monarch poised between feudalism and mercantile capitalism, between Scotland and England, between the past and the present.

Scott is also highly sensitive to the English language and especially to the social and cultural contexts of dialect. In *The Fortunes of Nigel*, for example, he is able to switch fluently from Scots to English. Heriot, who uses formal English in his business transactions, finds himself speaking Scots when another character reminds him of home. The king himself uses an ornate, Latinized form in one social setting and then, for purposes of political image or personal satisfaction, returns to Scots or part Scots and part ornamented English.

The reputation of Scott has suffered an eclipse. Scott himself, in his introduction to *The Fortunes of Nigel*, shows an awareness of questions of his less-than-careful writing style—raised even in his own day—and tries to defend himself and his method of composition. Other critics, however, such as the Marxist George Lukacs, argue that Scott was a great novelist. The introduction of history into the writing of novels, the vivid portrayal of social types, and the depiction of profound social and historical conflict outweigh the stylistic and compositional faults of the novels, according to Lukacs. Nor can one ignore Scott's impact on his contemporaries and on the history of fiction.

"Critical Evaluation" by Howard Lee Hertz

Further Reading

Irvine, Robert P. "The State, the Domestic, and National Culture in the Waverley Novels." In *Enlightenment and Romance: Gender and Agency in Smollett and Scott*. New York: Peter Lang, 2000. Analyzes the fiction of Scott and Tobias Smollett within the context of the emergence of social sciences and the dominance of novels written by female writers in the eighteenth century. Describes how the authors adapted the feminine romance and the domestic novel to assert control over the narrative structure of their novels.

Johnson, Edgar. *Sir Walter Scott: The Great Unknown*. 2 vols. New York: Macmillan, 1970. The fullest biography of Scott. Contains one chapter on *The Fortunes of Nigel*. Includes notes, index, and bibliography.

Lauber, John. *Sir Walter Scott*. Rev. ed. Boston: Twayne, 1989. Introductory overview of Scott's life and works. Includes bibliography and index.

Robertson, Fiona. *Legitimate Histories: Scott, Gothic, and the Authorities of Fiction*. New York: Oxford University Press, 1994. Analyzes Scott's Waverly novels within the context of eighteenth and nineteenth century gothic literature; examines the novels' critical reception. Devotes a chapter to *The Fortunes of Nigel*.

Shaw, Harry E. *The Forms of Historical Fiction: Sir Walter Scott and His Successors*. Ithaca, N.Y.: Cornell University Press, 1983. Begins with an excellent analysis of historical fiction as a genre. Contains a thoughtful discussion of some of Scott's problems with his characterization. Includes bibliography and index.

_____, ed. *Critical Essays on Sir Walter Scott: The Waverley Novels*. New York: G. K. Hall, 1996. Collection of essays published between 1858 and 1996 about Scott's series of novels. Includes journalist Walter Bagehot's 1858 article about the Waverly novels and discussions of Scott's rationalism, storytelling and subversion of the literary form in his fiction, and what his work meant to Victorian readers.

Sutherland, John. *The Life of Walter Scott: A Critical Biography*. Malden, Mass.: Blackwell, 1995. Puts Scott's poetry and fiction in their biographical and historical contexts. Links *The Fortunes of Nigel* to Scott's visit to the 1821 coronation in London and to his growing indebtedness. Includes bibliography and notes.

Wilt, Judith. *Secret Leaves: The Novels of Sir Walter Scott*. Chicago: University of Chicago Press, 1985. Not an easy book, but with genuine insights into the hidden psychological mainsprings of Scott's fiction. Notes his fondness for changeling stories and brings out the variety and richness of his emotional portrayals.

The Forty Days of Musa Dagh

Author: Franz Werfel (1890-1945)
First published: Die vierzig Tage des Musa Dagh, 1933 (English translation, 1934)
Type of work: Novel
Type of plot: Historical
Time of plot: 1915
Locale: Near Antioch, Syria

Principal characters:
GABRIEL BAGRADIAN, an Armenian patriot
JULIETTE BAGRADIAN, his wife
STEPHAN BAGRADIAN, their son
TER HAIGASUN, an Armenian priest of the village of Yoghonoluk

The Story:

After twenty-three years spent in Paris, Gabriel Bagradian returns with his wife and child to his ancestral village of Yoghonoluk. He goes back to Turkey to settle the affairs of his dying brother, and after his brother's death, he stays on in the village to await the end of European hostilities.

One Sunday, his son's tutor tells him that officials came through the village collecting all passports. To learn what happened, Bagradian saddles a horse and starts for Antioch. There the kaimakam, or governor, gives only evasive answers about the passport incident. In a Turkish bath, Bagradian hears that the Turkish war minister ordered all Armenians disarmed and given menial work. From his Muslim friend Agha Rifaat Bereket, Bagradian learns that rich and prominent Armenians will soon be persecuted.

Bagradian is worried. On his return to Yoghonoluk, he begins to collect data on the number of men of fighting age in the vicinity. Ter Haigasun, the Gregorian priest, tells him one day that there was a mass arrest in Antioch. Bagradian begins a survey of Musa Dagh, a mountain that lies between the Armenian villages and the Mediterranean Sea. After having maps drawn of the terrain, Bagradian knows that the plateau with its natural fortifications offer a refuge for his people.

One day, a friendly Turkish policeman confides to Bagradian that in three days the village will be ordered to prepare for its trip into exile. Bagradian calls a meeting of the people. The Protestant pastor, Nokhudian, and his congregation vote to accept banishment, the rest of the population to defend Musa Dagh. Ter Haigasun is elected leader. The next morning, the young men under Bagradian's direction begin the construction of trenches and other defenses on Musa Dagh, and at night the people carry provisions up the mountain. Unfortunately there are not enough rifles to go around and very little ammunition, but the men of the village are augmented by army deserters who drift in from the desert. Eventually, there are sixty armed men in the community. On the third day, the convoy escort arrives. The village pretends to busy itself with preparations for the trip, but that night everyone but Pastor Nokhudian's flock secretly departs for Musa Dagh.

It takes five days for the Turks to discover Bagradian's mountain retreat, for the woods are so thick and the trenches dug so cleverly that the encampment is not visible from below. During that time the trenches are completed, posts assigned, and patterns for daily living established. Everyone is given a task, and the food of the community is held in common so that all might be treated fairly.

The first sortie ends in a victory for the holders of Musa Dagh. The four hundred regulars and gendarmes who attack without even seeking cover are quickly routed, and substantial booty of badly needed ammunition, boots, and uniforms is recovered. The second attack comes several days later. Turkish howitzers manage to do considerable damage, wounding six noncombatants in the town enclosure and setting the grain depot on fire. Sarkis Kilikian, commander of the south bastion, rigs up a catapult to hurl stones at the attackers. These cause a landslide, which kills or maims half the Turkish force. Young Stephan Bagradian and his friend Haik raid the Turkish gun emplacements. Sixteen of the defenders are killed.

Three days later, there are again signs of activity in the valley. The kaimakam imports families of Arabs to take over the Armenian houses and farms. On Musa Dagh, a Greek American adventurer, Gonzague Maris, who fled with the Armenians and who has since seduced Juliette Bagradian, tries to persuade her to flee with him under the protection his passport affords. She is undecided. She and her husband, Gabriel Bagradian, have grown apart in those troubled times; he is burdened with military duties, and she seems indifferent to his fate. Bagradian finds his only companionship in Iskuhi, with a refugee from Zeitun.

The next attack is carried out by two thousand trained Turkish soldiers. In fierce fighting, they capture the first line of trenches below the southern bastion. That night Bagradian orders his troops to counterattack, and the trenches are retaken. The defenders also set a fire that races down the mountain, driving the Turks into the valley. Musa Dagh is saved again.

Gonzague Maris begs Juliette several times to go away with him, but she does not have the courage to tell her husband that she is leaving him. Then Bagradian discovers the lovers together and takes his wife, half unconscious with a fever, back to her tent. Gonzague Maris disappears.

That same night, Stephan leaves Musa Dagh without permission to accompany his friend Haik, who is being sent to the American consul in Aleppo to ask for intervention on behalf of his people. Haik makes his way safely to Aleppo, but Stephan develops a fever and starts back to the mountain. On the way, the Turks capture and kill him. His body is thrown into the cemetery yard in Yoghonoluk where it is found by some old women who take it to his father. The last of the Bagradians is buried on Musa Dagh.

The next day, flocks grazing beyond the fortifications are captured by the Turks. There is now only enough food to last three or four more days. On the fortieth day on Musa Dagh, the people are suffering. It is their third day of famine. Gabriel plans one last desperate attack for that night, an attempt to reach the valley with his men, capture some high officials as hostages, and return to the mountain. That afternoon, however, as Ter Haigasun holds a service to petition God for help, Sarkis Kilikian and his deserters break into the town enclosure to steal ammunition and food. As they flee, they set fire to the buildings to cover their escape. The Turks take advantage of their desertion to capture the south bastion. Kilikian is brought back by deserters who feel it would be better to die with their own people than to be captured by the Turks. He is put to death.

As the Turks prepare to advance at dawn, a French cruiser drops its first shell into the valley. Its commander saw the fire in the town enclosure the day before. Approaching to investigate, he sees the enormous flag the Armenians are using as a distress signal. The Turks retreat into the valley. Bagradian leads the weary defenders to the coast and sees them safely aboard a cruiser and a troopship. Then he starts back up the mountain for a last view of his son's grave. Exhausted by his ordeal, he falls asleep halfway up the mountainside. When he awakens, the ships are already standing out at sea. He starts to signal them but changes his mind. He feels that his life is now complete. Up he climbs until he reaches his son's grave. There a bullet from a Turkish scout catches him in the temple. He falls on his son's grave, Stephan's cross on his heart.

Critical Evaluation:

When Franz Werfel arrived in the United States as an exile from Nazi Germany, his fame there had been established, based largely on the popularity of *The Forty Days of Musa Dagh*, a 1934 Book-of-the-Month Club selection and arguably Werfel's most powerful prose work. The Hollywood studio Metro-Goldwyn-Mayer acquired an option on making a film of the novel; the project was eventually abandoned, purportedly because of pressure exerted by the Turkish government.

For the Armenian people, *The Forty Days of Musa Dagh* became something of a national epic. An Armenian priest in New York is recorded to have preached that the novel invested his people with a soul. The financial assistance of the Armenian community in the United States made possible the transfer of Werfel's remains from Hollywood to Vienna in 1975, as well as, that same year, the holding of a Werfel symposium and the publication of a volume of his occasional writings.

The Forty Days of Musa Dagh almost single-handedly publicized the genocide of Turkey's Armenian population during World War I. Werfel had planned to write about the crime when he first learned of it while serving at the military press bureau in Vienna. However, it was not until 1930, when he encountered young Armenian refugees laboring in a carpet factory in Damascus, that the abstract number of more than one million victims became a disturbing reality for the novelist. Werfel immersed himself for two years in research, including a study of firsthand accounts, that resulted in the particular blend of historical re-creation and imaginative invention that marks *The Forty Days of Musa Dagh*.

The defense of Musa Dagh in 1915 was an actual event, and some of the novel's peripheral characters, such as the Turkish official Enver Pascha, were historical figures. Werfel's drawing on reality and the wealth of descriptive details, ranging from architecture to children's games to farming methods, lend the novel a compelling aura of authenticity.

As a creative writer, Werfel occasionally suited facts to his purposes. Sources differed, for example, on whether the Armenian contingent spent fifty-three or thirty-six days on the mountain. By indicating that the sojourn lasted forty days, Werfel links the incident to biblical events: the forty days of the flood, the forty days that Moses and Jesus fasted, and the forty years the Hebrews wandered in the desert following their liberation from bondage in Egypt. Other biblical associations in the novel include the destiny of Gabriel Bagradian to die, as did Moses, within sight of, though not actually entering, the promised land. Bagradian is a type modeled on Moses: an individual assimilated to a foreign culture and estranged from his own people who, through circumstance, reunites with them to guide them out of captivity. Significantly enough, Musa Dagh translates to "Mount of Moses." The piety of the Armenians of Musa Dagh is emphasized by their placing an altar at the center of their settlement.

Given the preponderance of biblical allusions in the novel, it is not surprising that the solutions to the political issues it raises are invariably spiritual ones. Werfel suggests that sacrifice—particularly that of father and son—is supremely efficacious. Some have criticized Werfel's symbolism as heavy-handed, for instance, in invoking the crucifixion in the deaths of Gabriel and Stephan Bagradian.

The fundamental conflict in the novel is evidently between godliness, signified by commitment to a transpersonal and transnational entity, and godlessness, an amoral and reductionistic pragmatism. An apocalyptic note—signifying the Day of Judgment and its separation of the "wheat," or the godly, and the "chaff," or the ungodly—is sounded by the titles of the novel's three parts, which are taken from the book of Revelations. It has been pointed out that Gabriel Bagradian is another example of the prodigal son in Werfel's writings: From an alienated life of worldly sophistication, he returns to his people and his roots and, in suffering and self-transcendence, ultimately finds fulfillment. Bagradian's personal drama is, moreover, played out in the context of the persecution of a religious minority by an atheistic political regime in the relentless pursuit of modernity, which, for Werfel, meant nationalism, racism, and progress merely for progress's sake. The "progress" promoted by the Young Turks, in Werfel's view, raised expectations among the Turkish people that could not be satisfied without violence.

Much of the attention *The Forty Days of Musa Dagh* has attracted concerns its foreshadowing of the Holocaust. Parallels between the mass murder of the Jews by the Third Reich and that of the Armenians as presented in the novel are striking: the clinical, bureaucratic nature of the Turkish execution of policy; the reluctance of Armenians to recognize their peril; and the acceptance of the official lie that the government's plan was one of resettlement. Nevertheless, critics debate the extent to which Werfel intended to be a prophet of the fate of his own people, the Jews.

Those who stress the topicality and prophetic nature of the novel claim that Werfel revealed his premonition when, on a lecture tour in Germany in 1932, pending the book's publication, he chose to read from it a chapter that included a plea by a German pastor on behalf of the Armenian people. Some have argued that there is no empirical evidence for Werfel's having gauged early on the extent of danger to European Jewry; they point to the fact that the novelist did not flee Europe until as late as 1940. Many consider the implications of Werfel's insights all the richer for their not having been calculated. In any case, critical consensus maintains that as an investigation into the historical phenomenon of genocide, *The Forty Days of Musa Dagh* is a novel of fundamental significance.

"Critical Evaluation" by Amy Spitalnick

Further Reading

Brender, Edwige. "'Neither as a Cowboy nor as a Gold-hunter, but Simply as a Refugee': Franz Werfel's Debate with His American Publishers, Translators, and Adapters." In *Exile and Otherness: New Approaches to the Experience of the Nazi Refugees*, edited by Alexander Stephan. New York: Peter Lang, 2006. Explores the lives and works of Austrian and German writers, artists, and intellectuals who fled the Nazis and settled in other countries. The chapter about Werfel discusses his experiences in the United States.

Heizer, Donna K. *Jewish-German Identity in the Orientalist Literature of Else Lasker-Schüler, Friedrich Wolf, and Franz Werfel*. Columbia, S.C.: Camden House, 1996. Examines the depiction of the East in the works of Werfel and two other authors. Analyzes *The Forty Days of Musa Dagh*, describing how Werfel uses the conflict between Turks and Armenians as a means of exploring his German-Jewish identity. Includes bibliography and index.

Jungk, Peter Stephan. "*Die vierzig Tage des Musa Dagh.*" In *Franz Werfel: An Austrian Writer Reassessed*, edited by Lothar Huber. New York: St. Martin's Press, 1989. A dra-matic, well-detailed account of the genesis of the novel. Portrays Werfel in a positive light. Jungk scripted and directed a film about Werfel for German television.

Keith-Smith, Brian. "The Concept of 'Gemeinschaft' in the Works of Franz Werfel and Lothar Schreyer." In *Franz Werfel: An Austrian Writer Reassessed*, edited by Lothar Huber. New York: St. Martin's Press, 1989. Elaborates on the importance of community in Werfel's work. Knowledge of German is helpful but not essential.

Kirby, Rachel. *The Culturally Complex Individual: Franz Werfel's Reflections on Minority Identity and Historical Depiction in "The Forty Days of Musa Dagh."* Lewisburg, Pa.: Bucknell University Press, 1999. Examines the themes of identity in Werfel's works, describing his changing views on the subject. Focuses on *The Forty Days of Musa Dagh*, discussing Werfel's treatment of identity and historical community and the reception and literary response to the novel.

Michaels, Jennifer. *Franz Werfel and the Critics*. Columbia, S.C.: Camden House, 1994. Identifies aspects of Werfel's work that have attracted critical interest. Shows how various trends in criticism have shaped Werfel's reputation as a writer. A clear and comprehensive presentation.

Minasian, Edward. *Musa Dagh: A Chronicle of the Armenian Genocide Factor in the Subsequent Suppression, by the Intervention of the United States Government, of the Movie Based on Franz Werfel's "The Forty Days of Musa Dagh."* Nashville, Tenn.: Cold Tree Press, 2007. Recounts the history of Werfel's novel, describing the book's creation, the successful reception of its English translation, and Metro-Goldwyn-Mayer's (MGM) plans to produce a film adaptation. However, the Turkish government protested the planned film, and the Turkish authorities, the U.S. State Department, and the Hays Office (the Hollywood censorship bureau) pressured MGM to cancel the project.

Steiman, Lionel B. *Franz Werfel: The Faith of an Exile from Prague to Beverly Hills*. Waterloo, Ont.: Wilfrid Laurier University Press, 1985. A penetrating analysis of Werfel's political and theological development in historical context. Generally critical of his faith and work.

Wagener, Hans. *Understanding Franz Werfel*. Columbia: University of South Carolina Press, 1993. Assesses Werfel's work from a literary, as well as historical, perspective. Readable and concise.

Foucault's Pendulum

Author: Umberto Eco (1932-   )
First published: Il pendolo di Foucault, 1988 (English translation, 1989)
Type of work: Novel
Type of plot: Satire
Time of plot: 1970-1984
Locale: Milan, Paris, and Rio de Janeiro

Principal characters:

CASAUBON, a historian employed by a Milan publishing firm

JACOPO BELBO, a senior editor at the firm and a former political activist

DIOTALLEVI, an editor interested in Jewish mysticism

GARRAMOND, owner of the publishing firm

COLONEL ARDENTI, the author of a book the firm considers for publication

AGILÈ, an aged occultist claiming to be the comte de Saint-Germain

INSPECTOR DI ANGELIS, a policeman investigating Ardenti's disappearance

LORENZO PELLIGRINI, a beautiful woman loved by Belbo

AMPARO, a beautiful Brazilian woman loved by Casaubon

LIA, Casaubon's wife

The Story:

Jacopo Belbo, the senior editor at a publishing house in Milan, Italy, is taken hostage by a shadowy group of occultists. These Diabolicals, as Belbo thinks of them, are convinced that he possesses a secret map or code. They are determined to get hold of it so they can complete the task they believe their society was set up to accomplish. Casaubon, the firm's junior editor, rushes to Paris, hoping to save Belbo's life and perhaps his own. He hides in the Musée des Arts et Métiers (Museum of Arts and Trades), where the famous pendulum of Léon Foucault is housed. Casaubon's investigations have led him to believe that the occult society will gather there at midnight that night, as the moment of the summer solstice approaches.

As he waits in hiding, Casaubon thinks over the events of the last dozen years: He first meets Belbo when in a Milan tavern that serves as a meeting place for students and workers of every political persuasion; it has always seemed to him to resemble Rick's bar from the 1942 film *Casablanca.* He is then a doctoral student in philology, writing a thesis on documents pertaining to the medieval Knights Templar. Belbo is reviewing a manuscript submitted by a retired army colonel that purports to solve the mystery of the Templars' lost treasure. Just as Casaubon is brought into the office, where he briefs Belbo and the other editor, Diotallevi, on the Templars, the manuscript's author disappears, and the three men of letters become caught up in a police investigation.

Casaubon leaves Italy shortly afterward, following a beauty named Amparo back to her native Brazil, where he

teaches for the next two years. Returning to Florence in the late 1970's, he is unable to secure a teaching position and therefore becomes a literary researcher, modeling his agency on that of Sam Spade, the detective hero of the 1941 film *The Maltese Falcon.* He is soon doing research for Belbo's firm and before long is a regular fixture in the editorial office. He marries and awaits the arrival of his first child. Then disaster strikes.

An adviser to the press, an old occultist who hints that he has been active for several hundred years, invites the editors to a Rosicrucian ritual in a country villa. They attend and witness the mysteries not forbidden to outsiders, but Belbo is shocked to learn that the old man is after his beautiful mistress and seems to have won her affection. Madly jealous, Belbo later decides to make the old man envy him. He therefore intimates that he has the secret map or code that seemed to have been lost when the colonel disappeared some years earlier.

Belbo soon regrets his rash claim. He had thought the search for this code was an intellectual game. The three editors devised rules on their own for deciphering the code and figuring out what they called "the plan." They never suspected that people would take the game so seriously that they were prepared to kill.

By the time Belbo disappears, Diotallevi is in the hospital. He is dying of cancer, half-convinced that the deadly cells multiplying in his body represent a sort of divine judgment on his efforts to crack the Kabbalistic code. Meanwhile,

Casaubon has decided that the new life growing in his wife's womb is far more magical and important than any occult plan. When he goes in search of Belbo, he is trying to protect both their safety and their sanity.

Critical Evaluation:

When summarized, the plot of *Foucault's Pendulum* sounds curiously similar to that of Dan Brown's *The Da Vinci Code* (2003). The resemblance has not escaped Umberto Eco, who once told a reporter, "I invented Dan Brown." By this he meant that he invented "the plan" and the paranoid interpretation of texts that makes conspiracies out of mere resemblances. He did not invent the story of the Templar treasure or the map to it; rather, he found that story in books such as *Holy Blood, Holy Grail* (1982), whose authors sued Brown unsuccessfully for copyright violation. Eco's novel warns against the kinds of crazy connections that Brown and his protagonist both make. He gives his protagonist, Casaubon, a name that alludes both to the Renaissance philologist Isaac Casaubon, who dated the occult works attributed to Hermes Trismegistus, and to a character in George Eliot's *Middlemarch* (1871-1872) who seeks a "key to all mythologies."

Following the success of his first and most famous novel, *Il nome della rosa* (1980; *The Name of the Rose*, 1983), Eco began a second mystery about the perils of reading. Like its predecessor, *Foucault's Pendulum* could be called a novel about death by reading: Just as the prejudices of an old librarian make reading dangerous for his monastic community in the former text, the obsessions of modern occultists threaten the lives of people who publish their favorite books in the latter text.

Though framed as a crime novel, *Foucault's Pendulum* has much in common with the occult literature it satirizes. The novel is organized into ten sections, corresponding to the ten emanations, or *sephirah*, on the Kabbalistic tree of life. It has 120 chapters, corresponding to the rulers, or archons, in some gnostic systems. Each chapter includes an epigraph from a book of occult learning. The characteristics of the emanations are incorporated into the novel's dialogue, as are the themes of the epigraphs, as form follows content.

As a book about books, *Foucault's Pendulum* is stronger on ideas and satire than on character and plot. Some reviewers, such as the novelist Salman Rushdie, have found it entirely lacking in these respects. Nevertheless, while Belbo and others are mainly mouthpieces for Eco's witticisms and insights, the senior editor has a compelling story. As Casaubon tries to learn about his mentor's whereabouts and motives, he accesses Belbo's primitive computer and reads files that recount memories, including those of a difficult childhood during the Fascist era. Belbo's personal story is remarkably similar to Eco's, and the most traumatic moments are retold very closely in Eco's final novel, *La misteriosa fiamma della Regina Loana* (2004; *The Mysterious Flame of Queen Loana: An Illustrated Novel*, 2005). When Casaubon has worked through Belbo's files, he and a reader can both understand much better why Belbo made the stand he took with the Parisian occultists and even why he chose the words he spoke in response to their demands. Reverting to the earthy dialect of his youth in the Italian Piedmont, he said, in effect, "Put a cork in it."

As a careful student of detective fiction, Eco has paid almost obsessive attention to the different time frames in the novel: The narrator remembers his past associations with Belbo as he waits for the midnight assembly in the museum; later, he commits his memories to or perhaps inputs them into Belbo's computer. The different time frames come together quite precisely at sunrise on Tuesday, June 26, 1984. In one of the lectures given at Harvard as *Six Walks in the Fictional Woods* (1994), Eco describes the research and planning that went into the novel's plot, as well as the inaccuracies that careful readers have discovered.

Eco told the same reporter that he regretted not having allowed the late Stanley Kubrick to turn the novel into a film. He had been appalled by the film version of *The Name of the Rose* (1986) and told Kubrick he would only cooperate on a film adaptation of *Foucault's Pendulum* if he could write the screenplay himself. Eco realized too late that Kubrick had a genius for turning ideas into images and might have given new power to the story.

Foucault's Pendulum features a finale that borders on phantasmagoria. As Belbo stands at the mercy of the occult elders, a parade of spirits enters the museum in a scene that recalls nothing so much as the Walpurgis Night in Johann Wolfgang von Goethe's *Faust: Ein Fragment* (pb. 1790; *Faust: A Fragment*, 1980). These are the spirits of all the occult hucksters whose work has claimed the attention of Belbo and his fellow editors, everyone from Edward Kelly, who lived in Elizabethan England, to Madame Blavatsky, who lived some three hundred years later. They are joined by all the loonies who have brought manuscripts to Belbo, including the much-searched-after colonel. The fun is in the names on the roll rather than the images the spirits project.

The pendulum in the book's title, a mechanism designed in the nineteenth century to demonstrate the rotation of the earth on its axis, takes on a sinister quality, like the pendulum of the Spanish Inquisition in Edgar Allan Poe's tale "The Pit and the Pendulum" (1842). It is also associated with the

Kabbalistic tree of life, as well as the cross of Jesus, when Belbo is bound to it by his occult inquisitors. Moreover, the inquisitorial apparatus is also associated (through allusions noted by Linda Hutcheon) with Michel Foucault and other postmodernists who, to Eco's way of thinking, have tortured a text to say whatever they want it to say. Since the Italian word *pendolo* is also slang for "penis," Belbo's slang retort to the gathered occultists (roughly translated "put a cork in it") has the force of authorial commentary.

Thomas Willard

Further Reading

Barranu, Manuela. "Eco and the Reading of the Second Level." In *Illuminating Eco: On the Boundaries of Interpretation*, edited by Charlotte Ross and Rochelle Sibley. Aldershot, England: Ashgate, 2004. Applies Eco's concept of "second-level" reading to identify formal properties in the novel. Includes a time chart placing episodes of the plot in chronological order.

Bennett, Helen. "The Limitations of Openness: *Foucault's Pendulum* and Kabbalah." In *Umberto Eco's Alternative: The Politics of Culture and the Ambiguities of Interpretation*, edited by Norma Bouchart and Veronica Pravadelli. New York: Peter Lang, 1998. Discusses the representation of Kabbalah in Eco's novel and relates the text to Kabbalistic traditions of textual interpretation.

Bondanella, Peter. *Umberto Eco and the Open Text: Semiotics, Fiction, Popular Culture*. New York: Cambridge University Press, 1997. Chapter 6 summarizes Eco's comments on "over-interpretation" and "paranoid interpretation" and discusses them in connection with *Foucault's Pendulum*.

Farronato, Cristina. *Eco's Chaosmos: From the Middle Ages to Postmodernity*. Toronto, Ont.: University of Toronto Press, 2003. Chapter 4 includes a section on readers' complicity in crime, as presented in *Foucault's Pendulum*. Chapter 7 continues the theme while considering Eco's adaptation of the whodunit form.

Francese, Joseph. *Socially Symbolic Acts: The Historicizing Fictions of Umberto Eco, Vincenzo Consolo, and Antonio Tabucchi*. Madison, N.J.: Fairleigh Dickinson University Press, 2006. The chapter on Eco discusses his theory of reading. A section is devoted to *Foucault's Pendulum* and the different kinds of reading that its characters demonstrate.

Hutcheon, Linda. "Irony-Clad Foucault." In *Reading Eco: An Anthology*, edited by Rocco Capozzi. Bloomington: Indiana University Press, 1997. Discusses Eco's response to Michel Foucault, the literary and cultural theorist.

Naparstek, Ben. "'I Invented Dan Brown.'" *Jerusalem Post*, December 13, 2007. Discusses Eco's reaction to Brown's *The Da Vinci Code*.

Rushdie, Salman. *Imaginary Homelands*. London: Penguin, 1991. Section 9 includes an essay on Eco's fiction. Rushdie much prefers *The Name of the Rose* to *Foucault's Pendulum*, which he finds "devoid of characterization" or humor.

The Foundation Trilogy

Author: Isaac Asimov (1920-1992)
First published: 1963; includes *Foundation*, 1951;
    Foundation and Empire, 1952; *Second Foundation*,
    1953
Type of work: Novels
Type of plot: Science fiction
Time of plot: More than twelve thousand years in the
    future
Locale: Galactic human empire

Principal characters:
GAAL DORNICK, a young psychohistorian
HARI SELDON, inventor of psychohistory
SALVOR HARDIN, mayor of Terminus
LIMMAR PONYETS, a Foundation trader
HOBER MALLOW, a Foundation trader
JORANE SUTT, the mayor's secretary
BEL RIOSE, an ambitious general of the dying Empire
LATHAN DEVERS, a young Foundation trader
DUCEM BARR, an authority on the Foundation
TORAN, son of a small trader on Haven
BAYTA, a discontented Foundation citizen and Toran's
    bride
THE MULE/MAGNIFICO, a mysterious conqueror of many
    worlds, who pretends to be his own fool
HAN PRITCHER, a Foundation spy
EBLING MIS, a Foundation scientist
BAIL CHANNIS, a capable Mule assistant
THE FIRST SPEAKER, leader of the Second Foundation
TORAN DARELL, a Foundation scientist
ARKADY DARELL, Toran's fourteen-year-old daughter
PELLEAS ANTHOR, a new arrival on Terminus
HOMIR MUNN, a librarian sent to Kalgan
LORD STETTIN, ruler of Kalgan
LADY CALLIA, Stettin's mistress
PREEM PALVER, a Trantor trading representative

The Story:

In *Foundation*, Gaal Dornick arrives on Trantor, the roofed-over planet that is the center of government for a Galactic Empire of 25 million planets, to work with Hari Seldon, the inventor of a predictive science called psychohistory. Psychohistory is able to predict far future events on an extremely large scale, but not to predict more localized events. Almost immediately, Seldon goes on trial for treason, because his calculations predict the fall of the Empire. Seldon escapes punishment by persuading the judges that everyone will benefit if he is allowed to set up the Foundation on the planet Terminus, on the edge of the galaxy, to compile a massive encyclopedia, the Encyclopedia Galactica, that will preserve all of human knowledge. Seldon then tells Dornick that the entire crisis has been manufactured so that 100,000 encyclopedists and their families will agree to leave Trantor for Terminus.

Fifty years later, Terminus is facing a crisis: It is under threat from ambitious rulers of nearby planets, one of whom,

the ruler of Anacreon, wants to annex Terminus. Anacreon has a rival, the planet Smyrno. Terminus has few mineral resources but much technology because of the high proportion of scientists that live there. No psychologists live on Terminus, because Seldon included none when he brought the encyclopedists there. During the crisis, Seldon appears in a "time vault" with prepared comments about a predicted crisis (later called a "Seldon crisis"); he announces that the encyclopedia project was a ruse concocted to influence history without any encyclopedist's knowledge—a necessary element of effective psychohistory. The lack of freedom of action is an essential part of a Seldon Crisis. Terminus, Seldon says, is an island of atomic power in an ocean of more primitive energy resources; the solution to their problem is obvious, but it is obvious only to Mayor Salvor Hardin, who has assumed control of Terminus.

Thirty years later, Hardin has solved the crisis by playing one barbarian planet against another, stoking each one's fears of the other gaining atomic control. He sells devices to everyone but reserves the science to a newly created religious order. When Anacreon attacks Terminus, the priests rebel. Seldon appears again and warns that regionalism is stronger than religion.

Fifty years later, religious science has allowed the Foundation to take over its barbarian neighbors. Some planets view technology as sacrilegious. One of them, Askone, has imprisoned a trader for meddling in local politics. Another trader, Limmar Ponyets, tricks the ruler into accepting a transmutation machine for turning base metals into gold and then blackmails him into allowing the import of Foundation machines.

About twenty-five years after this, religion in the Foundation has rigidified to the point that is has itself become a problem. To get rid of a rival, Jorane Sutt, the power behind the ruling mayor, sends a trader named Hober Mallow to investigate the disappearance of Foundation ships near the planet Korell. Mallow persuades the Korellian ruler to import Foundation atomic devices. Mallow traces the source of Korellian atomic handguns to Siwenna, where he discovers that atomic science has degenerated into ritual. On Terminus, Mallow is tried for the death of a priest he turned over to the Korellians, but he clears himself by proving the priest was a Korellian spy; Mallow is elected mayor. When Korell attacks the Foundation, their atomic devices begin to fail, and the Korellians rebel to regain their prosperity.

In *Foundation and Empire*, forty years later, Bel Riose, an ambitious and capable general of the dying Empire, is sent to conquer the Foundation. The Merchant Princes, who now rule the Foundation, have no idea how to withstand the assault but send a young trader, Lathan Devers, to be captured by Riose. The suspicious emperor sends Brodrig, his privy secretary, to keep track of Riose but Brodrig instead joins Riose to conquer the Foundation and restore the Empire. Ducem Barr, Riose's expert on the Foundation, escapes with Devers, and they take word to Trantor about Brodrig. They cannot get through bureaucratic barriers but learn that Brodrig and Riose have been arrested. An emperor cannot tolerate a strong general, lest he take over the Empire, and a weak general could not threaten the Foundation: Thus, the Foundation could not lose.

Toran and Bayta, just married, are sent from the planet Haven to Kalgan, which has just been conquered by the Mule, a mysterious leader to whom worlds surrender. They hope to instigate a war between the Mule and the Foundation. The couple rescues the Mule's fool, Magnifico, and flees with him and Han Pritcher, a Foundation spy. The Mule declares war on the Foundation and wins every battle, while

Seldon appears in the Time Vault to reveal that psychohistory has not foreseen this crisis. Toran, Bayta, scientist Ebling Mis, and Magnifico escape Haven before it falls. They travel to Trantor to search for the Second Foundation, the Foundation's last hope. Before the dying Mis can reveal the location of the Second Foundation, Bayta shoots him; she has figured out that Magnifico is the Mule. His secret weapon is his ability to adjust people's emotions, but he has left Bayta unadjusted because she already liked him without needing adjustment. The Mule resolves to keep looking for the Second Foundation, but his ability will die with him; like his namesake, he is sterile.

In *Second Foundation*, the Mule continues to search for the Second Foundation, with the help of an adjusted Han Pritcher and an unadjusted Bail Channis. The Second Foundation is said to be at "Star's End." Channis figures that Star's End must be Tazenda. He and Pritcher land on Rossem, where they are joined by the Mule, who reveals that he thinks Channis is a Second Foundation agent who would lead him into a Second Foundation trap. Channis admits that the Mule is right, and Rossem is the location of the Second Foundation. The first speaker of the Second Foundation enters to reveal that the Mule has been lured to Rossem so that Second Foundation psychologists can sow rebellion on Kalgan in his absence. In the Mule's confusion, the first speaker enters the Mule's mind and reconstructs his memories.

Pelleas Anthor arrives on Terminus and gathers a group of conspirators at the home of Dr. Toran Darell to explore the possibility that Second Foundation psychologists may be controlling their minds. Such a situation would be intolerable to them. A librarian named Homir Munn is sent to Kalgan to explore the Mule's palace for information on the Second Foundation's location. Darell's fourteen-year-old daughter Arkady stows away on Munn's ship. Meanwhile, Second Foundation psychologists discuss a flaw in Seldon's plan: Now that people know about the Second Foundation, they are failing to exercise their normal initiative, altering the course of history.

Arkady helps Munn gain permission to perform his research, but in the process Lord Stettin, the Kalgan ruler, decides to marry her. Arkady is saved by a trading representative from Trantor, Preem Palver. Palver and his wife take Arkady to Trantor. Lord Stettin's fleet attacks the Foundation but is finally defeated. In a final session in Dr. Darrell's home on Terminus, Munn says there is no Second Foundation, but an encephalograph reveals that his mind has been tampered with. Darell has invented a mental static machine that renders advanced minds helpless. He turns it on, and Munn collapses. With the machine, the Foundation can wipe out Second Foundation psychologists on Terminus, where Darell has deduced the Second Foundation is located. In a final interlude, the first speaker, revealed to be Preem Palver, further reveals that the plan has worked: Fifty psychologists have been sacrificed, but Selden's plan has been saved. The Second Foundation is located on Trantor, where it all began. "Stars end at Trantor."

Critical Evaluation:

The Foundation trilogy has become one of the texts on which the science-fiction future history subgenre is based, and its popularity validates its canonical status. The trilogy has sold millions of copies in many languages and has never been out of print. Its vision of a human galactic empire encompassing 25 million stars provided a broad canvas on which to paint human progress or downfall. It begins—like Edward Gibbons's *The History of the Decline and Fall of the Roman Empire* (1776-1788), on which the trilogy was modeled—with the impending dissolution of civilization and efforts to avert an ensuing dark age.

Donald Wollheim was a fellow member with Isaac Asimov of the Futurians (a seminal Brooklyn fan organization of the late 1930's and early 1940's), the editor of Ace Books, and then editor and publisher of DAW Books. In *The Universe Makers* (1971), Wollheim called the Foundation trilogy "the point of departure for the full cosmogony of science-fiction future history." The 1966 World Science Fiction Convention voted the trilogy "the greatest all-time science fiction series." Numerous scientists have attributed their interest in science to their early reading of the trilogy. These include theoretical physicist Michio Kaku and Nobel laureate Paul Krugman, who has said that he went into economics because it was the closest thing he could find to psychohistory.

A number of misconceptions arise from calling the work a "trilogy." It is a sequence of three books with a coherent topic: the fall of the Galactic Empire and efforts by Hari Seldon and his successors to shorten the period of barbarism that would follow from thirty thousand years to only one thousand years. However, none of the three books was orginally conceived as a single novel. The first book, *Foundation*, is made up of five novelettes, four of them written and published in *Astounding Science Fiction* over a period of three years. The first section of the book was written specifically for the publication of the book in 1951. The second book, *Foundation and Empire*, is composed of two novellas, written in 1944 and 1945 and published in *Astounding Science Fiction* in 1945. The third book, *Second Founda-*

tion, consists of two more novellas, written in 1947 and 1949 and published in *Astounding Science Fiction* in 1948 and 1949.

Before and during World War II, almost no science fiction was published in book form, and Asimov had no idea that he was writing anything but magazine fiction that would die with the issue of the magazine in which it was published. He was astonished after the war to find editors interested in reprinting his magazine stories in anthologies and a few publishers interested in publishing complete Asimov books. One of the publishers was Doubleday, whose editor, Lawrence Ashmead, asked Asimov for an original novel, rather than reprinted material. Asimov wrote *Pebble in the Sky* (1950), in which he imagined Earth's radioactivity increasing, shortening human lifespans and forcing humanity to seek a refuge among the stars that would ultimately lead to the Galactic Empire. Only a fan publisher, Gnome Press, was interested in *Foundation*, and Asimov published it there in 1951, followed by *Foundation and Empire* in 1952, and *Second Foundation* in 1953. Later, the books would be acquired and reprinted by Doubleday.

The problem with considering the trilogy as three coherent, sequential novels is that readers will fail to understand their creation properly if they are analyzed as novels. Asimov has recounted traveling on the subway as a twenty-one-year-old graduate student in chemistry at Columbia University, on his way to the office of *Astounding Science Fiction* editor John W. Campbell, Jr. He happened to open a book of plays by W. S. Gilbert and Arthur Sullivan and come across a picture from *Iolanthe: Or, The Peer and the Peri* (pr., pb. 1882) of the Fairy Queen throwing herself at the feet of Private Willis. The picture made him think of soldiers, military empires, the Roman Empire, and then of a Galactic Empire. By the time he reached Campbell's office, Asimov had a story in mind, and he and Campbell thrashed it out between them, including the theory of psychohistory. Asimov wrote the first two Foundation stories (the second and third published in the first book) in sequence. He wrote the others later on, interspersed between academic studies, military service, and other stories, but when he wrote the first two stories, he had nothing beyond them in mind, except a general outline of the overall narrative.

The stories compiled in the Foundation trilogy for Gnome Press publisher Marty Greenberg were each written to stand as a single entity, and whenever Asimov went back to them (he viewed any Foundation story he could produce as a sure sale to Campbell, and he wrote about them for the Science Fiction Writers of America in "There's Nothing Like a Good Foundation") he had to take the conclusion of the previous story as the starting point for the next one. The stories exist, then, like a series of tinker-toys, one linked logically to the previous one and all organized around several basic themes: the rise and fall of empires; the possibilities (and consequences) of predicting mass behavior and therefore being able to encourage one outcome over another; the impact on individual behavior of a science of prediction; the conflicts between barbarism and civilization and between emotion and reason; and the ways in which civilizations change. The trilogy's individual stories are best judged for how well, as a whole, they deal with these themes, how ingeniously they develop from their starting points, and how convincing they are. Asimov valued transparency and logic over character and style (the latter, he thought, militated against the former), and traditional literary analyses are likely to find his stories deficient.

Asimov was interested in studying history, but he instead decided to become a doctor, then was frustrated by his distaste for dissection and was sidetracked into studying chemistry. Nonetheless, his initial interest in history influenced the sequence of the stories as much as the manner of their creation, as they portray the solution of each generation's problem itself becoming a problem that the next generation must solve. The grip of the encyclopedists, for instance, must be broken by Mayor Hardin; the political power of the mayors must then be broken by Hober Mallow; the religious power of scientism must be broken by the traders; and the economic power of the traders must be modified by the incorporation of the independent traders.

The existence of psychohistory and Hari Seldon's appearances in the Time Vault raise the issue of determinism throughout the trilogy. Indeed, when Bel Riose says to Ducem Barr, "Then we stand clasped tightly in the forcing hand of the Goddess of Historical Necessity?" Barr corrects him: "Of Psycho-Historical Necessity." The stories, however, are determinedly antideterministic. Rational decisions reached by perceptive individuals prevail, not historical necessity. The Mule, an unpredictable mutation, upsets Seldon's plan, and the Second Foundation's psychologists, with their ability to shape minds and memories, must act to preserve some semblance of Seldon's goal to shorten the period of barbarism between galactic empires. If there is any element of necessity in the trilogy, it is the necessity to behave rationally rather than emotionally if civilized ends are to be achieved without resorting to violence. As a consequence, power often lurks behind the scenes, which may also have been Asimov's analysis of history.

In the end, Asimov's trilogy covered only some four hundred of the one thousand years between the fall of the Galactic Empire and the success of the Foundation Era. Asimov ran out of ideas after *Second Foundation*, and he found too difficult the effort of recapitulating everything that had gone before in each new story. He also had moved on to a new career as an instructor in biochemistry at Boston University, and had begun working on science textbooks and then science popularizations that would lead George G. Simpson of Harvard to call him "one of our natural wonders and national resources." Asimov continued to write science fiction, mostly short stories, but the only novels he published for a long while were some Lucky Starr juvenile novels, *The Caves of Steel* (1954), *The End of Eternity* (1955), and *The Naked Sun* (1957). After a fifteen-year silence (with the exception of the film novelization *Fantastic Voyage* in 1982), Asimov published *The Gods Themselves* (1972). This was followed by another ten-year gap. He returned to the science-fiction novel and the Foundation universe, at the insistence of Doubleday, with *Foundation's Edge* (1982), which became his first best seller. That success led to further Foundation novels, as well as robot novels (which had begun with *The Caves of Steel*) and an effort to interweave his Foundation and robot universes.

James Gunn

Further Reading

Asimov, Isaac. *I, Asimov: A Memoir*. New York: Doubleday, 1994. Individual essays about Asimov's life and experiences, and updates of his earlier autobiographies.

_____. *In Memory Yet Green: The Autobiography of Isaac Asimov, 1920-1954*. New York: Doubleday, 1979. The first volume of Asimov's mammoth autobiography, with accounts of his uneventful life and eventful works, researched from his own journals.

_____. *In Joy Still Felt: The Autobiography of Isaac Asimov, 1954-1978*. New York: Doubleday, 1980. The continuation of Asimov's autobiography.

Asimov, Janet Jeppson, ed. *It's Been a Good Life*. Amherst, N.Y.: Prometheus Books, 2002. A selection from Isaac Asimov's autobiographical works plus updates and an afterword about the author's death.

Asimov, Stanley, ed. *Yours, Isaac Asimov: A Lifetime of Letters*. New York: Doubleday, 1995. Asimov's correspondence, edited by his brother.

Gunn, James. *Isaac Asimov: The Foundations of Science Fiction* Rev. ed. Lanham, Md.: Scarecrow Press, 2005. A critical analysis of Asimov's life and works in the context of the publishing situation of the times.

Hassler, Donald M. *Isaac Asimov*. Mercer Island, Wash.:

Starmont House, 1991. Another insightful survey of Asimov's life and work.

Knight, Damon. "Asimov and Empire." In *In Search of Wonder.* Chicago: Advent, 1967. A fellow Futurian criticizes The *Foundation* Trilogy for relying too heavily on Gibbons's *The Decline and Fall of the Roman Empire.*

Olander, Joseph D., and Martin H. Greenberg, eds. *Isaac Asimov.* New York: Taplinger, 1977. Olander and Greenberg bring together a variety of essays about various aspects of Asimov's work, concluding with Asimov's unusual reaction to all the analyses.

The Fountainhead

Author: Ayn Rand (1905-1982)
First published: 1943
Type of work: Novel
Type of plot: Parable
Time of plot: 1922-1930's
Locale: New York City

Principal characters:
HOWARD ROARK, an architect
PETER KEATING, an architect
ELLSWORTH TOOHEY, a writer and social reformer
CATHERINE HALSEY, Keating's girlfriend and Toohey's niece
GUY FRANCON, the principal partner of the firm where Keating works
DOMINIQUE FRANCON, his daughter
GAIL WYNAND, a newspaper publisher

The Story:

Howard Roark is expelled from architectural school because he has no respect for copying the past. Peter Keating, one of the favorite students at the school, frequently persuades Roark to help him with his assignments. Roark decides to go to New York City to work for Henry Cameron, a once-respected but now renegade architect who shares Roark's ideals. Keating takes a job with the firm of Guy Francon, a powerful and influential architect who believes in copying classic buildings. After Cameron's business fails, Keating hires Roark, but the job does not last long. Francon fires Roark for his failure to draft an adaptation of one of Cameron's buildings; Roark continues to refuse to copy others' work.

Dominique Francon, Guy's daughter, visits the office. Her beauty immediately impresses Keating, and he remains interested in her even after discovering that she wrote a newspaper column in Gail Wynand's *Banner* in which she criticized one of his building designs. They later begin dating. Keating's longtime girlfriend, Catherine Halsey, announces that she wants to get married immediately; however, she agrees to wait. Keating knows that Halsey is the niece of Ellsworth Toohey, a *Banner* columnist who writes about architecture and many other topics. He refuses to use his relationship with Halsey to gain influence with Toohey.

Roark takes a job with another firm but learns that his designs will be combined with those of others. His employer uses most of Roark's drawing in a draft presented to one client, who says that it is the best of many designs that he saw but that it is somehow wrong. Roark seizes the drawing and marks over it, restoring his original work. The client hires Roark, inspiring Roark to start his own firm.

In an attempt to cement his position, Keating attempts to blackmail Lucius Heyer, Francon's partner, who does almost no work in the firm and is not respected by the employees. Heyer dies, leaving Keating his share in the firm because Keating once was kind to him. Keating wins a worldwide design contest, after getting Roark's assistance. He attempts to bribe Roark to remain silent about working on the design, but Roark says that Keating will be doing him a favor by not mentioning his assistance.

Roark's business fails because he is too selective in accepting commissions; he prefers not to work at all rather than to design buildings he does not believe in. He takes a job in a granite quarry owned by Guy Francon. Dominique sees him working in the quarry and is struck by his beauty and by the way he approaches his work. She purposely damages a piece of marble in her house and has him assess the damage. She then hires him to come back and repair the damage; however, he sends another worker. Later, he returns and rapes her. Soon thereafter, Roark receives a letter of inquiry from Roger Enright about designing a house, whereupon he leaves the quarry job.

Toohey writes a favorable column about Keating's work and asks to meet him, and then he suggests that Keating head a group of young architects. He also acknowledges Keating's engagement to Halsey. Dominique tells Keating that she no longer wants to see him because he is the best of what there is, and she does not approve of perfection. She sees plans for the Enright house, not knowing it is Roark's work or even that Roark is an architect, and tells Toohey that the man who designed it should not allow it to be built because it will not be appreciated. Roark agrees to go to a party because he knows that Dominique will be there and will not expect to see him. They pretend not to know each other. Afterward, she writes a column disparaging the Enright house, having found out that it is his design. She also persuades a potential client not to hire him. She goes to Roark's office and tells him that she will continue to try to destroy him. She wants him to own her, however, and she tells him that she will come to him every time she beats him. She continues to denigrate his work in her newspaper columns, and she persuades clients to use Keating instead.

Toohey convinces multimillionaire Hopton Stoddard to let Roark design an interdenominational temple for him and to give Roark a completely free hand in the design. Stoddard, a traditionalist, does not see the building until it is completed; he then refuses to open it. Stoddard sees it as inappropriate for a temple, in part because of the nude statue of Dominique that Roark commissions for it. Toohey persuades Stoddard to sue Roark; Toohey's plan all along was to destroy Roark's reputation. Stoddard wins the lawsuit, and Dominique is fired for testifying at the trial that the building should be destroyed, not because it is faulty but because it is too good.

Keating proposes marriage to Halsey, but Dominique proposes to him later that day and he accepts. Dominique tells Roark that she believes that he will be destroyed because he is too near perfection and that she will destroy herself before she is destroyed by others. About a year later, she agrees to sleep with the newspaper publisher Gail Wynand to get a commission for her husband, Keating. She and Wynand take a trip to Wynand's yacht, but they begin talking before they sleep together. They discover that they have similar ideas and agree to be married.

Toohey assembles mediocre workers in various professions and promotes their work because he believes in the value of the average. Keating's business declines. When he complains that Toohey promoted another architect, Toohey claims that Keating and the others are interchangeable. Desperate for work, Keating hires Roark to design a low-income housing project so that Keating can submit the plans to the government. Roark undertakes the project for the challenge; he knows that with his reputation he can never land a government contract. He makes Keating agree to construct the buildings exactly as designed.

Wynand and Dominique recognize the new project as Roark's work. Wynand and Roark become friends, and they take a trip on Wynand's yacht. When they return, Roark sees that other architects have been brought onto the housing project. When he sees that the buildings are different from his plans, he dynamites them, with Dominique's help. Wynand does everything he can to help Roark at his criminal trial, even though he knows that Roark's victory will cost him Dominique. Toohey manages to get a column opposing Roark into print. Wynand fires him, prompting a strike at the paper.

Dominique arranges for news of the affair between her and Roark to become public, and Wynand agrees to file for divorce. Roark wins his acquittal. Wynand closes the newspaper and then hires Roark to design a building for him; Wynand does this to symbolize his new freedom from trying to please people with his publications. Roark and Dominique marry.

Critical Evaluation:

Ayn Rand wrote *Atlas Shrugged* (1957) as a more complete exposition of the principles and ideas espoused in *The Fountainhead*. Both novels illustrate her philosophy of positive rational egoism, morality based on self-interest rather than on compassion for others. *The Fountainhead*'s heroes, including Howard Roark, Dominique Francon and, eventually, Gail Wynand, stand for their principles and refuse to conform. Wynand at first tries to offer what people want in his newspaper but later refuses to submit to Toohey and others, who want to promote the ideas of selfless service to others and lack of personal responsibility. Toohey and Keating are the primary antagonists. Toohey appears noble in his deflection of attention from himself; however, he seeks absolute power through manipulation of public opinion. He tells Halsey that people should not think; they should merely believe and serve others. Keating represents conformity for its own sake and pandering to popular opinion, values Rand clearly opposes.

As in *Atlas Shrugged*, the heroes are attractive: tall, physically fit, with strong faces. Roark and Dominique Francon receive glowing descriptions of their physical beauty. Roark's ideals are clear; Francon's are somewhat more puzzling. Her short speeches describing her goals are unclear, perhaps as

Rand intended. Francon claims to admire perfection, but at the same time she hates it because it is not appreciated by others; she buys artwork and destroys it.

The Fountainhead is a sweeping drama, drawing in a large number of characters with large roles and covering an array of events. Rand shifts her attention between characters, allowing various individuals to come forth at appropriate moments. Dominique, perhaps the most perplexing character, draws the others together. Her actions play off those of other characters and offer contrasts. She brings out the best in Peter Keating, making him doubt the value of conformity and also making him realize what Roark has to offer. She also aids Wynand in his journey toward fulfilling his personal ideas, rather than simply producing newspapers that cater to the lowest common denominator. In some ways she destroys the people with whom she comes in contact, but it is a creative destruction, allowing them to emerge stronger than before. She deliberately tries to ruin Roark because he is too good for an imperfect world, but her efforts against him, as she intends, make him stronger. Inevitably they end up together.

Rand uses various plot lines to make her points in a novel clearly intended more as a social message than as literature. Toohey is her primary villain. He appears benevolent and caring but promotes selflessness, which Rand sees as ultimately harmful because it teaches reliance on others. The result can only be mediocrity; in fact, Toohey deliberately promotes the work of mediocre artists, architects, and others. Catherine Halsey is a relatively minor character, but she is important for her frank admission that, in her job as a social worker, she has come to resent people who can improve themselves without her help. She also provides a foil for Keating and his personal ambition. Keating wants to be considered a great architect more than he actually wants to be one; Halsey appears selfless. Each time Keating gets close to Halsey, Dominique draws him away, thus helping him in his personal development by removing Halsey's influence on him.

The Fountainhead has been praised as a novel of ideas. In the 1940's, publication of such a novel by an American woman was relatively uncommon. Rand later abandoned the novelistic form, choosing instead to write directly on what she called the morality of reason. Rand had grown up in Russia and lived through the Bolshevik Revolution; this background led to her becoming a champion of capitalism in its purest forms. Her heroes are self-interested individuals who oppose the social reformers claiming to work for the public good.

A. J. Sobczak

Further Reading

Baker, James T. *Ayn Rand.* Boston: Twayne, 1987. An objective study of Rand's career. Includes brief descriptions and analyses of her major works of fiction and drama. One chapter succinctly describes the main themes and ideas expressed in her written work.

Branden, Barbara. *The Passion of Ayn Rand.* Garden City, N.J.: Doubleday, 1986. Branden's biography of Rand is based partly on her own association with Rand, including the extensive interviews she conducted with Rand while preparing the biographical sketch published in *Who Is Ayn Rand?* (below), and partly on interviews with more than two hundred people who discussed their relationships with Rand. Branden appears to have done substantial research in available documentary materials, but the absence of footnotes makes it impossible to pinpoint her sources of information.

Branden, Nathaniel, and Barbara Branden. *Who Is Ayn Rand?* New York: Random House, 1962. The Brandens were Rand's closest associates in the Objectivist movement until Rand broke with them in 1968. Barbara Branden's biographical essay is based upon information provided by Rand herself and thus reflects the version of her life that she wanted to present to the world. Nathaniel Branden's contributions include an examination of Rand's literary methodology, an analysis of the significance of her ideas for psychology, and the essay "The Moral Revolution in *Atlas Shrugged.*"

Den Uyl, Douglas J. *"The Fountainhead": An American Novel.* New York: Twayne, 1999. Analysis of the novel within the context of Rand's philosophy of Objectivism. Discusses the novel's Socratic roots, Rand's concern with the power of individualism and self-examination, and how each character represents a philosophical ideal or failing.

Gladstein, Mimi Reisel. *The New Ayn Rand Companion.* Rev. and expanded edition. Westport, Conn.: Greenwood Press, 1999. Provides biographical information, a summary of Rand's fiction and nonfiction, information about her characters, criticism of her writing, and a comprehensive bibliography. This revised edition contains updated biographical data and newly discovered writings published after her death.

Gladstein, Mimi Reisel, and Chris Matthew Sciabarra, eds. *Feminist Interpretations of Ayn Rand.* University Park: Pennsylvania State University Press, 1999. Collection of essays examining Rand's life and work from a feminist perspective. Includes pieces by feminist writers Susan Brownmiller and Camille Paglia.

Mayhew, Robert, ed. *Essays on Ayn Rand's "The Fountainhead."* Lanham, Md.: Lexington Books, 2007. Among other topics, the essays examine the history, publication, and critical reception of the novel; its film adaptation; the meaning of the rape scene and the dynamiting; and the novel's Aristotlean philosophy, depiction of the ideal man, and humor.

Peikoff, Leonard. *Objectivism: The Philosophy of Ayn Rand.* New York: E. P. Dutton, 1991. Based on the author's lectures on Rand's philosophy, which were authorized by Rand. Understanding Rand's philosophy is vital to understanding *The Fountainhead.*

Rand, Ayn. *For the New Intellectual: The Philosophy of Ayn Rand.* New York: Random House, 1961. Provides Rand's introduction to her philosophy. Separate chapters on individual works of fiction give excerpts from those works that illustrate her philosophy.

_____. *Philosophy: Who Needs It?* Indianapolis, Ind.: Bobbs-Merrill, 1982. Essays range in content from the basics of Rand's philosophy to its applications in social policy. Most were written between 1970 and 1975 and reflect contemporary events, her philosophy, and thoughts on her fiction.

The Four Horsemen of the Apocalypse

Author: Vicente Blasco Ibáñez (1867-1928)

First published: Los cuatro jinetes del Apocalipsis, 1916 (English translation, 1918)

Type of work: Novel

Type of plot: Historical

Time of plot: Early twentieth century

Locale: Argentina, Paris, and the front lines of World War I

Principal characters:

JULIO MADARIAGA, the intrepid owner of a successful cattle ranch in Argentina

MARCELO DESNOYERS, a French immigrant to Argentina who marries Madariaga's daughter, Luisa

JULIO DESNOYERS, Marcelo's son and heir

MARGUERITE LAURIER, Julio's lover

ÉTIENNE LAURIER, Marguerite's husband

The Story:

Julio Desnoyers's father, Marcelo, angered by his nation's participation in the Franco-Prussian War (1870-1871), immigrates to Argentina. There he helps a vital Spaniard named Julio Madariaga (nicknamed the Centaur because of his lust for life and his many illegitimate offspring) carve a ranch out of a wilderness. In the process, they defeat or win over the Indians, but eventually they build an empire and make a fortune. Desnoyers experiences the splendor of turn-of-the-century Argentina, with its multicultural population and its potential for growth and development. Eventually, Desnoyers marries Madariaga's daughter, Luisa, and oversees the financial management of the estate, converting where possible Madariaga's intensely personal and erratic methods to more methodical and efficient ones. The accidental death of Madariaga's only legitimate son leaves Desnoyers as Madariaga's principal heir, with a fortune at his disposal. His German brother-in-law, Karl Hartrott, elopes with Madariaga's second daughter, Elena, much to her father's consternation; after a period of ostracism, Karl finagles his way back to the ranch and into an inheritance. When Madariaga dies, the German and French sides of his family

decide to return to Europe. Desnoyers does so under pressure from his wife, who is disturbed that their daughter Chichi is growing up a wild savage, riding the range alongside her grandfather as if she were the son he lost.

The Hartrotts ingratiate themselves with the German nobility and assume the haughtiness and pretensions of the German aristocracy, while the Desnoyerses became an established part of Parisian society. A visit to their German relatives confirms the Desnoyerses' negative feelings about them. Desnoyers wastes a fortune on grand antiques sold at bargain prices in auctions and fills up a castle with ostentatious wealth, including a solid gold bathtub. His son Julio becomes a known roué and is invited to the best homes because of his skill at the tango, the most popular dance of the time; he is also the adulterous lover of many an aficionada of the tango. When, however, he meets Marguerite Laurier, everything changes, and Julio's artist's studio becomes the scene of a romance that promises to blossom into marriage, once a messy divorce is past.

Returning from a business trip to Argentina, Julio is disturbed at the dinner table conversations of the German travelers who look forward to war and blame others as the aggressors. He also notices that the behavior of the personnel of the German ship changes; instead of being courteous and eager to please, they are arrogant and commanding. Back home in Paris, he is disturbed that Marguerite is impressed with the good reports he earns as a fearless soldier; she cannot understand Julio's reluctance to join what for him is a foreign army.

Julio's father, Marcelo Desnoyers, disapproves of his son's profligate life and his affair with Marguerite, especially because her husband, Étienne Laurier, is one of his good friends. When news comes that Étienne is seriously injured, possibly blinded in battle, Marguerite abandons Julio and Paris. Later, when Julio traces her to a convalescent home, he finds her nursing her husband. Though she cannot deny her continued love for Julio, she finds a deeper commitment to a brave patriot who loves her dearly and whose sacrifice for his country demands her courageous support. Marcelo is pleased that the affair is over, but Julio, distraught, joins the French army and flings himself into conflict with an abandon that wins him the hearts of his comrades and the respect of his superiors.

When the rich of Paris flee south to escape the invading Germans, Marcelo travels north to protect his castle from looting. He assumes that civilized rules of confrontation will be in force and that civilians will go unmolested. Instead, he finds Germans executing civilians, raping young women, shooting babies, burning villages, defacing property, and engaging in wholesale looting. An encounter with a Hartrott offspring saves Marcelo from certain death, but cannot prevent him from having to endure German officers disporting themselves lewdly, defecating on his valuable furnishings, and participating in acts of perversion and sadism. As a landowner and victim, Marcelo cheers the French resurgence at the Battle of the Marne and makes his way safely back to Paris and security. Later, his growing pride in his son's heroism makes him seek out Argensola, his son's companion and manservant, and look with greater forgiveness on the indiscretions of Julio's youth. Through the influence of Senator Lacour, whose son René is engaged to his daughter Chichi, Marcelo visits Julio in the trenches and observes the nightmare of trench warfare at first hand. News of his son's injury makes him fear for Julio's life, and only shortly thereafter he receives news of his death. The old man's final trip to the front is toward the close of the war, as he seeks his son's name on a mass grave near the spot where he died. Marcelo realizes the futility of his wealth, for it was not able to prevent the loss of his son. His grief is mirrored in that of his sister-in-law, Elena, whose strong, unquestioning support of the German

cause results in the loss of two sons and the injury of a third. Only the young, among them Marcelo's daughter, Chichi, can look to the future with confidence.

Critical Evaluation:

Vicente Blasco Ibáñez is among the most widely read Spanish novelists, and *The Four Horsemen of the Apocalypse* is one of his most popular works. The 1921 Rudolph Valentino film and a 1962 World War II adaptation starring Glenn Ford further popularized the book. Its multicultural perspective, its warnings about the dangers of racism and of twisting logic to defend the indefensible, its prescience about World War II and the causes of modern conflagrations, and its antiwar sentiments based on realistic portraits of the horrors of war make *The Four Horsemen of the Apocalypse* relevant to ages beyond its own. Its underlying picaresque conventions, roguish young hero, and competent, yet somehow innocent, older hero lend it charm and interest, and its character studies of the way in which war transforms individuals and instills a spirit of self-sacrifice and fortitude are psychologically convincing.

The book's title is derived from the biblical book Revelation, which describes the four scourges that will afflict humanity at the end of time: Disease, War, Famine, and Death. Part 1 of the novel treats the life of the Desnoyers family before the onset of World War I; it ends with the Russian Tchernoff, the French-Argentine Julio Desnoyers, and the Spaniard Argensola discussing the suicide of a German woman and seeing her death as the beginning of the end. Drawing on memories of the famous engravings by Albrecht Dürer, they envision an apocalyptic beast, a blind force of evil, rising from the depths of the sea and threatening to engulf all humanity, with the four horsemen that signal its arrival brutally sweeping the earth ahead of it and bringing agony in "their merciless gallop of destruction."

In parts 2 and 3, Blasco Ibáñez demonstrates the fulfillment of that prophecy as war sweeps across Europe. Part 2 is a graphic and memorable portrait of the Battle of the Marne and of German brutality, which is given added force from the description of the aging Marcelo Desnoyers's incredulity at what he is witnessing. The details of slaughter, inhumanity, and torture are convincingly realistic, yet the point of view adds a touch of the surreal. Part 3 provides a closer look at twentieth century trench warfare, with its intricate maze of trenches, the horror of the mud and the rats, the insidiousness of the gases blown across from enemy lines, and the buzzing of bullets overhead. Again the description is intensified by the drama of a determined father braving the nightmare for a brief glimpse of his beloved son.

Blasco Ibáñez had been a political activist ever since his university years, and he endured imprisonment and exile for his outspoken political statements. *The Four Horsemen of the Apocalypse* is in keeping with this spirit of protest. The novel is a condemnation, not only of the World War I German military establishment and its barbaric methods of conducting warfare but also of the German people's inflated sense of superiority and the intellectuals and artists who perpetuated that myth of superiority and right to power. The novel was condemned as a heavy-handed tract by critics who disapproved of Blasco Ibáñez's life and politics and envied his financial success, but the work also reflects a deeply felt revulsion for war and a frighteningly accurate prophecy of the horrors of Nazism.

Blasco Ibáñez sets up a compelling contrast between the inhumanity of the war machine that leaves chaos, destruction, and despair in its wake and the constructive fervor of the lively, impassioned Spaniard Madariaga, who helps transform the Argentine pampas into thriving ranch land and whose prodigious reproductive powers reflect a love of life. Blasco Ibáñez also establishes the contrast between war and the civilized, cultured life of Paris, where artists and lovers thrive and where conflicts of opinions lead only to good-natured arguments over a bottle of wine. Against these life-affirming regions and peoples, the scenes of conquest and destruction seem completely senseless. Blasco Ibáñez has been praised for the realism of his portraits of war, but it is his portrait of peace that makes his images of war so horrifying.

Gina Macdonald

Further Reading

Anderson, Christopher L., and Paul C. Smith. *Vicente Blasco Ibáñez: An Annotated Bibliography, 1975-2002*. Newark, Del.: Juan de la Cuesta, 2005. Extensively annotated compilation of writings by and about Blasco Ibáñez.

Day, A. Grove, and Edgar Knowlton. *V. Blasco Ibáñez*. New York: Twayne, 1972. A survey of Blasco Ibáñez's life and canon that includes a discussion of his revolutionary influences, cosmopolitan experiences, interest in social protest and human psychology, glorification of Spain, and intense dislike of Germans.

Howells, William Dean. "The Fiction of Blasco Ibáñez." *Harper's* 131 (1915): 956-960. Howells, an American novelist and literary critic, praises Blasco Ibáñez's literary skill.

Oxford, Jeffrey Thomas. *Vicente Blasco Ibáñez: Color Symbolism in Selected Novels*. New York: Peter Lang, 1997. Analyzes the use of color in some of Blasco Ibáñez's novels, arguing that although he was a Naturalist, he often depicted life in a subjectively artificial way that belied the Naturalists' attempt to objectively portray reality.

Swain, James Q. *Vicente Blasco Ibáñez: General Study—Special Emphasis on Realistic Techniques*. Knoxville: University of Tennessee Press, 1959. One chapter focuses on the realistic images of war in *The Four Horsemen of the Apocalypse*.

Wedel, Alfred R. "Blasco Ibáñez's Antipathy Toward Germans." *Revista de Istorie si Teorie Literara* 35 (July-December, 1987): 3-4, 192-200. Discusses the negative portrait of Germans in *The Four Horsemen of the Apocalypse*.

Four Quartets

Author: T. S. Eliot (1888-1965)
First published: 1943
Type of work: Poetry

Four Quartets is T. S. Eliot's last book of nondramatic poetry. Each of the quartets, which were written over a period of eight years and published separately, has the same structure and helps develop cumulatively the same themes. Eliot said that transitions in poetry can be similar to those in a symphony or quartet, and that these quartets are written in a five-movement sonata form.

The personal and historical significance of the place names in the poems' titles are the points of departure for the themes developed in the first part of each quartet. The theme of "Burnt Norton"—an old Gloucestershire house—is the nature of time and personal memories and experience. "East Coker," which is the name of the English village from which Eliot's ancestor left for America in the seventeenth century, is a consideration of the meaning of history and an explanation of the idea of spiritual rebirth. "The Dry Salvages," a group of rocks off the coast of Massachusetts, which Eliot knew as a boy, continues the meditations on time and history and includes reflections on human endeavor and the nature of experience. These themes are all also present in "Little Gidding," whose title refers to an Anglican lay community founded by Nicholas Ferrar.

All the themes are present in each quartet with different emphases, and the subsidiary themes are directly related to the major ones. What distinguishes these poems from Eliot's earlier verse is that, in addition to the elements of surprise and rapid transition that mark his earlier works, these include transitional passages. The same symbols also occur in each of the quartets, and their multiple and shifting meanings are resolved in "Little Gidding."

In "Burnt Norton," Eliot writes, "What might have been and what has been/ Point to one end which is always present." Here there is no placing of experience in time ("do not call it fixity"); it is instead a "stillness," a point beyond experience "into the rose garden." To reach it requires the negation of flesh and spirit. Eliot repeatedly considers this way of purgation, which requires release from desire and compulsion. Meaningful experience is both in and out of time, but life is too full of distraction for this to be often attained. The description of that distraction is a vivid realization of the contemporary predicament: "Only a flicker/ Over the strained, time-ridden faces/ Distracted from distraction by distraction." The passage following these lines presents "the way down" toward the dark night of the soul, "desiccation of the world of sense." However, there are times in the realm of art when the moment can be prolonged "as a Chinese jar still/ Moves perpetually in its stillness." A further theme in the quartets, the nature and difficulty of poetic creation, creates a contrast to the image of the jar. The struggle with words that "decay with imprecision" introduces the Word, which is subject always to temptation. "Burnt Norton" ends with a repetition of the vision of hidden children laughing in the rose garden, a motif from the first movement. Such immediacy is contrasted with the usual bleakness of existence.

Time in "East Coker" involves the consideration of human history. This, the most despairing of the quartets, approaches complete and unredeemed bitterness. Eliot stresses the cyclic nature of life and experience. Fields give way to factories that crumble to dust, and the life cycle of humans and the earth is presented as if in a vision after the poet has gone down the dark lane into the somnolent village. The second section begins with a lyric on November, which is followed by a characteristic reversal: "That was a way of putting it . . ./ A periphrastic study in a wornout poetical fashion." The theme of the bitterness and deception of time mentioned in "Burnt Norton" is expanded here; the wisdom of old men is really folly, and "The only wisdom we can hope to acquire/ Is the wisdom of humility." The concrete description, which in these poems always either immediately follows or precedes the abstract thought, is that of the descent into subways that had been used as air-raid shelters during World War II. Thus negation and stillness are combined, and the necessity for "waiting" is introduced.

The fourth movement is a lyric on the Christian paradox of life in death and death in life. The symbols are those of a hospital with a wounded surgeon and a dying nurse, "Wherein, if we do well, we shall/ Die of the absolute paternal care." Fire and roses are multiple symbols of destruction and salvation, purgation and resurrection. After the cold fever of death there is purgatory, "Of which the flame is roses, and the smoke is briars." In the fifth section, Eliot despairs of poetic creation, which, at "every attempt/ Is a wholly new start" because the difficulties once conquered are no longer those that face the poet. The resolution of this dilemma is similar to that for the soul: "For us there is only the trying." The conclusion inverts the opening statement—"In my beginning is my end"—to become "In my end is my beginning."

The superb pictures of the Mississippi River and the Atlantic Ocean in "The Dry Salvages" show an increase in the music of the verse, which is sustained in "Little Gidding." The river is "a strong brown god" and the sea has "Many gods and many voices." The sea time "is not our time"; "time stops and is never ending." The lyric in section 2 speaks of the grief of shipwreck and of those things thought "most reliable" that are "therefore the fittest for renunciation." There is no end to this pain, only the possibility of prayer.

The pattern of the past with its content of meaningful experience is seen here in its historical perspective: "And approach to the meaning restores the experience/ In a different form, beyond any meaning/ We can assign to happiness." This passage connects with the reference to Krishna in section 3, one of the many allusions to and quotations of other authors in *Four Quartets*. The theory of time is drawn from the philosopher Heraclitus and part of the conclusion of "Little Gidding" from Dame Julian of Norwich. The rose and fire symbolism is reminiscent of Dante, whereas the conception of the dark night of the soul is that of St. John of the Cross. While awareness of these sources adds considerably to the enjoyment of the poems, Eliot integrates them so completely and controls their place in the poetry so perfectly, placing them where they have an exact significance, that the poems can be appreciated and understood without knowledge of source or influence. The poet Krishna is mentioned by name, however, and his words, "fare forward, voyagers" instead of "fare well" are important, as they indicate the essential release from desires and are an exhortation to unselfishness or selflessness.

Section 5 contains the meaning of the explanation of time's paradoxical aspects: " . . . But to apprehend/ The point of intersection of the timeless/ With time, is an occupation for the saint." The images of flowers, sunlight, and music, which have recurred throughout these poems, symbolize ordinary human experiences that, although fragmentary, nevertheless are "hints of grace": "The hint half guessed, the gift half understood, is Incarnation."

The resolution of themes in "Little Gidding" is accomplished by semirepetitive exposition and further development. The chapel at Little Gidding is a place "where prayer has been valid." Eliot also explains the many allusions to writers and saints and saints who were writers as " . . . the communication/ Of the dead is tongued with fire beyond the language of the living." The death of the four elements in section 2 opens the way to spiritual resurrection. This lyric is followed by the poet's meeting, after an air raid, with a "familiar compound ghost"—the shade of all his past teachers—who tells him of the grief and failure of old age "unless restored by that refining fire/ Where you must move in measure like a dancer." The historical theme is restated in the relationship of the present and the past as a reconciliation of opposites: "History may be servitude,/ History may be freedom," while "Whatever we inherit from the fortunate/ We have taken from the defeated." The solution of the dilemma of the burden of divine care for humanity, so bleakly felt in "East Coker," is here seen to be love, which binds us in our desires and alone is able to give the essential release from them.

The end of exploration, of the struggle with words and of all human actions "Will be to arrive where we started/ And to know the place for the first time." The moments of personal and historical experience are never lost:

> The moment of the rose and the moment
>   of the yew tree
> Are of equal duration. A people without history
> Is not redeemed from time, for history is a pattern
> Of timeless moments.

The way of purgation, which requires the whole being, has led to "complete simplicity" where "the fire and the rose are one."

For all its complexity, *Four Quartets* contains Eliot's most explicit poetry. The poems are specifically Christian, recording the progress of the soul toward salvation. The way in which the themes are at various levels interwoven to augment and illuminate one another, the control of language and rhythm, and the beauty and precision of the images have led some critics to call these quartets Eliot's finest achievement.

Further Reading

Cameron, Sharon. "'The Sea's Throat': T. S. Eliot's *Four Quartets.*" In *Impersonality: Seven Essays.* Chicago: University of Chicago Press, 2007. Cameron argues that the issue of personal identity is inconsequential to Eliot in this poem, in which he creates a voice that is "virtually anonymous."

Cooper, John Xiros. *The Cambridge Introduction to T. S. Eliot.* New York: Cambridge University Press, 2006. An introductory overview to Eliot's life and work, focusing on his poetry. Chapter 3 includes a fourteen-page discussion of *Four Quartets.*

Gardner, Helen Louise. *The Composition of "Four Quartets."* New York: Oxford University Press, 1978. Easily one of the best critics of Eliot's poetry, Gardner employs her ample resources in examining his process of composition. Gardner's work is a helpful summary of primary documents and includes many notes on versions of the text.

Kramer, Kenneth Paul. *Redeeming Time: T. S. Eliot's "Four Quartets."* Lanham, Md.: Cowley, 2007. Demonstrates how Eliot creates an interaction between the poem and its readers, and how this interaction promotes a genuine connection with the natural world, with others, and with the divine.

Lobb, Edward, ed. *Words in Time: New Essays on Eliot's "Four Quartets."* Ann Arbor: University of Michigan Press, 1993. A fine collection of ten essays by authors such as Denis Donoghue, Lyndall Gordon, and Louis L. Martz, which expands the discussion of Eliot's *Four Quartets.* Useful for new readers and scholars alike.

Moody, A. David, ed. *The Cambridge Companion to T. S. Eliot.* New York: Cambridge University Press, 1994. Collection of essays, including discussions of Eliot's life; Eliot as a philosopher, a social critic, and a product of America; and religion, literature, and society in Eliot's work. Also features the essay "*Four Quartets*: Music, Word, Meaning, and Value" by A. David Moody.

Raine, Craig. *T. S. Eliot.* New York: Oxford University Press, 2006. In this examination of Eliot's work, Raine maintains that "the buried life," or the failure of feeling, is a consistent theme in the poetry and plays. Chapter 4 contains an explication of *Four Quartets*.

Smith, Grover Cleveland. *T. S. Eliot's Poetry and Plays: A Study in Sources and Meaning*. 2d ed. Chicago: University of Chicago Press, 1974. A detailed and probing exploration of Eliot's clever use of allusions and quotations to express his spiritual and philosophical concerns. This book remains a standard critical work on Eliot's poetry and a good sourcebook for scholars.

Traversi, Derek Antona. *T. S. Eliot: The Longer Poems: "The Waste Land," "Ash Wednesday," "Four Quartets."*

London: Bodley Head, 1976. A scholarly, objective analysis of the *Four Quartets*. Traversi sees Eliot's poetry as a continuous whole and offers a detailed study of these poems on their own terms rather than primarily as expressions of a given ideology, Christian or otherwise.

Warner, Martin. *A Philosophical Study of T. S. Eliot's "Four Quartets."* Lewiston, N.Y.: Edwin Mellen Press, 1999. Warner, himself a philosopher, provides a detailed analysis of the poem's philosophy and places the work within the context of Eliot's intellectual and personal lives.

Frankenstein
Or, The Modern Prometheus

Author: Mary Wollstonecraft Shelley (1797-1851)
First published: 1818
Type of work: Novel
Type of plot: Gothic
Time of plot: Eighteenth century
Locale: Europe and the Arctic

Principal characters:
ROBERT WALTON, an explorer
VICTOR FRANKENSTEIN, an inventor
ELIZABETH, his foster sister
WILLIAM, his brother
JUSTINE, the Frankensteins' servant
HENRY CLERVAL, Victor's friend
THE MONSTER

The Story:

English explorer Robert Walton's ship is held fast in polar ice. As his company looks out over the empty ice field, they are astonished to see a sledge drawn by dogs speeding northward. The sledge driver looks huge and misshapen. At night, an ice floe carries to the ship another sledge with one dog and a man in weakened condition. When the newcomer learns that his is the second sledge sighted from the ship, he becomes agitated.

Walton is greatly attracted to the newcomer during his convalescence, and as the ship remains stuck in the ice, the men have leisure time to get acquainted. At last, after he has recovered somewhat from exposure and hunger, the man, Victor Frankenstein, tells Walton his story.

Victor is born into an aristocratic family in Geneva, Switzerland. As a playmate for their son, the parents adopt a lovely little girl, Elizabeth, of the same age. Victor and Elizabeth grow up as brother and sister. Much later another son, William, is born to the Frankensteins.

At an early age, Victor shows promise in the natural sciences. He devours the works of Paracelsus and Albertus

Magnus and thinks in his ignorance that they had been the real masters. When he grows older, his father decides to send him to the university at Ingolstadt. There, he soon learns all that his masters can teach him in the field of natural science. Engaged in brilliant and terrible research, he stumbles by chance on the secret of creating life. Once he has gained this knowledge, he cannot rest until he has employed it to create a living being. By haunting the butcher shops and dissecting rooms, he soon has the necessary raw materials. With great cunning, he fashions an eight-foot monster and endows him with life.

As soon as Victor creates his monster, however, he is subject to strange misgivings. During the night, the monster comes to his bed. At the sight of the horrible face, Victor shrieks and frightens the monster. Overcome by the horror of his act, he becomes ill with a brain fever. His best friend, Henry Clerval, arrives from Geneva and helps to nurse him through his illness. He cannot tell Clerval what he has done.

Terrible news then comes from Geneva. William, Victor's young brother, had been killed at the hand of a murderer. He was found strangled in a park, and a faithful family servant, Justine, was charged with the crime. Victor hurries to Geneva. At the trial, Justine tells a convincing story. She had been looking for William in the countryside and, returning after the city gates had been closed, had spent the night in a deserted hut; she cannot, however, explain how a miniature from William's neck came to be in her pocket. Victor and Elizabeth believe the girl's story, but despite all of their efforts, Justine is convicted and condemned.

Depressed by these tragic events, Victor goes hiking over the mountainous countryside. Far ahead on the glacier, he sees a strange, agile figure that fills him with horrible suspicions. Unable to overtake the figure, he sits down to rest. Suddenly, the monster appears before him. The creature demands that Victor listen to his story. The monster begins to tell him that when he left Victor's chambers in Ingolstadt, everyone he met screamed and ran from him. Wandering confusedly, the monster finally found shelter in an abandoned hovel adjoining a cottage. By great stealth, he remained there during daylight and at night sought berries for food. Through observation, he began to learn the ways of humankind. Feeling an urge to friendship, he brought wood to the cottage every day, but when he attempted to make friends with the cottagers, he was repulsed with such fear and fury that his heart became bitter toward all people. When he saw William playing in the park, he strangled the boy and took the miniature from his neck. Then during the night, he came upon Justine in the hut and put the picture in her pocket.

The monster now makes a horrible demand. He insists that Victor fashion a mate for him who will give him love and companionship. The monster threatens to ravage and kill at random if Victor refuses the request; but, if Victor agrees, the monster promises to take his mate to the wilds of South America, where they will never again be seen by humankind. It is a hard choice, but Victor feels that he must accept.

Victor leaves for England with his friend Clerval. After parting from his friend, he goes to the distant Orkney Islands and begins his task. He is almost ready to animate the gross mass of flesh when his conscience stops him. He cannot let the two monsters mate and spawn a race of monsters. He destroys his work. The monster is watching at a window. Angered to see his mate destroyed, he forces his way into the house and warns Victor that a terrible punishment will fall upon the young man on his wedding night. Then the monster escapes by sea. Later, to torment his maker, he fiendishly kills Clerval.

Victor is suspected of the crime. Released for lack of evidence, he returns to Geneva. He and Elizabeth are married there. Although Victor is armed and alert, the monster gets into the nuptial chamber and strangles the bride. Victor shoots at him, but he escapes again. Victor vows to follow the monster and kill him.

Weakened by exposure, Victor dies on Walton's ship in the ice—Elizabeth, William, Justine, and Clerval remain unavenged. The monster comes to the dead man's cabin, and Walton, stifling his fear, addresses the gigantic, hideous creature. Victor's is the greater crime, the monster says. He had created a man, a man without love or friend or soul. He deserves his punishment. The monster then vanishes over the ice field.

"The Story" by Bonnie Flaig

Critical Evaluation:

Frankenstein began as a short story written by Mary Wollstonecraft Shelley while she was on summer vacation in Switzerland with her husband, poet Percy Bysshe Shelley and with poet Lord Byron and physician-writer John William Polidori. The novel was first published anonymously in 1818 and was then followed by a revised version in 1831, crediting Mary Shelley as the author and including an autobiographical introduction that reflects on her life and on the novel's authorship.

The novel's themes center on the social and cultural aspects of society during Shelley's lifetime, including the movement away from the intellectually confining Enlightenment. The characters in the novel reflect the struggle against societal control. The monster, in particular, is an outcast from society, and the reader is able to empathize with his subsequent rage at being ostracized. Nature and science, opposing forces during this time period, are important themes shaping the novel.

Early nineteenth century society's views of human standards were associated with the natural sciences. Some literary critics suggest that nature and physiology, specifically anatomy and reproduction, are linked in literature. Irregularities in the human standard were therefore viewed as unacceptable by society, and through an innate reaction, these differences were rejected. Even though Frankenstein's monster develops language skills, emotion, and consciousness, he appears as a grotesque being and is spurned by society because he does not fit any ideal.

Shelley employs many stylistic techniques in *Frankenstein*. She uses explorer Robert Walton's epistolary communication with his sister as part of an outer frame structure that segues into a flashback of Victor Frankenstein's experiences leading up to and after the creation of the monster. First-person narrative is used in Walton's voice, while the core chapters offer Victor's personal narration. In addition, Shelley uses dialogue to provide the thoughts of other characters, such as the monster. Also evident are characteristics of gothic horror, including a foreboding setting, violent and mysterious events, and a decaying society.

Many themes in *Frankenstein* represent not only the social and political theories of Shelley's time but also those that followed. For example, Sigmund Freud's Oedipus complex can be seen in Victor's attempts to replace his deceased mother by "birthing" a being who represents her. Elaborating on this theory, psychoanalyst Jacques Lacan adds a pre-Oedipal stage, in which young children learn language through nonverbal communication. This stage is evident in Victor's attempt to learn the language of the sciences, and in the creature's attempt to seek knowledge about society and language. Victor and the creature are "doubles" (or mirrors) of each other because they are both struck with the inability to successfully communicate with society. This theme demonstrates the balance of the conscious and unconscious aspects of human behavior.

Another theme, the search by the novel's male protagonists for a teacher who will provide them political and social guidance, represents Lockean theory, which claims that education determines a person's level of value in society. For example, during a conversation with Victor, Walton denounces his lack of formal education, demonstrating his lack of a friend (or formal teacher) to lead him to enlightenment. Additionally, Victor acknowledges his father's lack of leadership in guiding his interest in the natural sciences.

Prior to the 1970's, most criticism about *Frankenstein* focused on Shelley's life and the story behind the novel's authorship and creation. As the novel received increased critical attention, evaluations started to focus on its storyline and characters as a reflection of the author. This change in focus was, in part, due to the emergence of feminist theory in the 1970's and 1980's, a theory that began to establish the academic value and significance of female writers. Critics have evaluated the work's lack of dominant female characters, but also have examined its attention to the idea of the Romantic artist.

Frankenstein has been further critiqued through the lens of gender. In the novel, the feminine is not central; rather, the novel features characters who have both masculine and feminine qualities. Furthermore, relationships between women figure in the novel, namely the relationship between Justine and Elizabeth. When Justine faces execution, the two establish a bond that begins during a brief conversation about their shared experiences. Female relationships were tenuous in Shelley's own life, too, particularly because of the premature death of her mother and her questionable relationship with her half-sister, Jane (later known as Claire), who was rumored to have had a child with Shelley's husband.

Frankenstein revolutionized the genres of gothic literature, science fiction, and horror stories, and elevated the status of the Romantic artist. Written by Shelley when she was only nineteen years old, the novel offers artistic flare, originality, and a maturity beyond Shelley's age. In the last decades of the twentieth century, this work reached a new status in critical evaluation. It remains an undisputed fictional masterpiece.

"Critical Evaluation" by Susan J. Sylvia

Further Reading

Allen, Graham. *Critical Issues—Mary Shelley.* New York: Palgrave Macmillan, 2008. A collection of essays that interpret each of Shelley's major works. Included is a discussion of *Frankenstein* that evaluates, among other topics, the inclusion of friendship in the novel.

Bloom, Harold, ed. *Mary Wollstonecraft Shelley.* New York: Bloom's Literary Criticism, 2009. The majority of the essays in this collection discuss various aspects of *Frankenstein*, including gender and language, racial discourse, and the boundaries of political community in the novel.

Engelstein, Stefani. *Anxious Anatomy: The Conception of the Human Form in Literary and Naturalist Discourse.* New York: State University of New York Press, 2008. This collection discusses the physiological and natural processes of the body, its role in reproduction and appropriate social connections, and how these theories apply to literature.

Garrett, Martin. *Mary Shelley.* New York: Oxford University Press, 2003. A biography providing a general overview for readers new to Shelley's work. Discusses her early formative years, and includes a rich collection of illustrations and excerpts from diaries and letters to enhance the text.

Higgins, David. *Frankenstein: Character Studies.* New York: Continuum, 2008. Examines the characters of Victor Frankenstein, Robert Walton, and the monster. Discusses how these characters are used to explore the novel's varied themes, including science, revolutionary politics, imperialism, and personal identity.

Hitchcock, Susan Tyler. *Frankenstein: A Cultural History.* New York: W. W. Norton, 2007. Chronicles the history of the Frankenstein myth, beginning with Shelley's novel through numerous stage, film, and television adaptations, to the ways the scientist and his monster continue to inhabit the public imagination.

Hoobler, Dorothy, and Thomas Hoobler. *The Monsters: Mary Shelley and the Curse of Frankenstein*. New York: Little, Brown, 2006. A biography describing the creation of *Frankenstein* and demonstrating how the themes of this novel correspond to the events of Shelley's life.

Morrison, Lucy, and Staci Stone. *A Mary Shelley Encyclopedia*. Westport, Conn.: Greenwood Press, 2003. This reference volume contains alphabetically arranged and cross-referenced entries providing information about Shelley's family, friends, homes, works, characters, literary influences, and themes, among other topics.

Smith, Johanna M., ed. *Frankenstein: Case Studies in Contemporary Criticism*. Boston: Bedford/St. Martin's Press, 2000. Essays define and discuss the novel through the lens of psychoanalytic, feminist, gender, Marxist, and cultural criticism.

Franny and Zooey

Author: J. D. Salinger (1919-2010)
First published: "Franny," 1955; "Zooey," 1957; linked stories, 1961
Type of work: Novel
Type of plot: Domestic realism
Time of plot: November, 1955
Locale: Princeton, New Jersey; Manhattan, New York City

Principal characters:
BESSIE GALLAGHER GLASS, the mother of seven children
FRANNY, her youngest daughter, a college student
ZOOEY, Franny's older brother, a television actor
BUDDY, their brother, a writing professor

The Story:

Franny Glass, a twenty-year-old college student, meets her weekend date, Lane Coutell, at the train station. She came to town for the big Yale football game at an unidentified Eastern Ivy League college where Lane is an undergraduate. She greets him enthusiastically, despite his spurious, narcissistic detachment. They immediately go to a trendy restaurant for lunch, where Lane digs into snails and frog legs and Franny leaves her chicken sandwich untouched. They smoke incessantly, while Lane speaks at length and with scarcely veiled pomposity of a recent paper he wrote on Gustave Flaubert. Franny grows paler as she tries to listen attentively. She finally explodes in a hushed rant against pedants, section men, pseudointellectuals, and shallow humanity in general. She tells him that she quit the theater group at school, which was her one great love, because she is so fed up with ego. Feeling undone, she flees to the ladies' room where, secluded in a vacant stall, she sobs freely for five minutes. She stops abruptly and clutches to her chest a small green book, as if it is her security blanket. She returns to the table determined to apologize and to salvage the weekend, but Lane notices her little book, *The Way of the Pilgrim*, and engages her in a discussion about it. Trying to appear casual, Franny tells him about the pilgrim's quest for enlightenment through praying without ceasing. Lane responds with condescending skepticism, which makes Franny angry again. As she again makes her way to the ladies' room, she faints.

Buddy Glass, the oldest living child of the Glass family and a rather eccentric writer and professor, relates the events of Franny's return home after her nervous collapse. He was not there, but he tells the story as a sort of "prose home movie" as gleaned from the primary players. Zooey Glass, Franny's twenty-five-year-old brother, sits in the tub in the Glass house in midtown Manhattan. He reads a four-year-old letter from his brother Buddy, which concerns Zooey's acting career, and whether or not he can tolerate the inherent phoniness of the trade. After Zooey finishes reading, he picks up a television script and studies it. He is soon interrupted by his mother, Bessie, who wants to give him something. Zooey grudgingly lets his mother in and finishes dressing for an afternoon appointment while carrying on a long, at times excruciatingly tense, conversation with her about Franny's breakdown. After much squabbling over that and other relatively inconsequential practical matters, Bessie leaves the bathroom with nothing decided except that a neighbor's psychologist will not be called in.

Franny comes home after the fainting incident and takes over the living room sofa, where she cries, refuses to eat, and continues to murmur the prayer "Lord Jesus Christ, have mercy on me." Zooey, at his mother's request, goes to see Franny and makes a long, unsuccessful attempt to rouse Franny from what seems to be a nervous breakdown. In rants he speaks of religion and Jesus, the search for enlightenment, the Glass family's brilliance, and the need for Franny to pull herself together and appreciate the nice things in the world. He advises her to strive for perfection on her own terms instead of criticizing the world or retreating into religion as a haven from it. He describes himself and her as spiritual freaks, which he blames on the religious teachings they received from their oldest brothers at a very early age. They are too aware to live in ignorant bliss, as do the masses, but live among them they must.

His tactless tirade sends Franny into an even deeper fit of sobbing. With a halfhearted apology, Zooey leaves the room and enters the bedroom that his brother Seymour shared with Buddy. It is the first time Zooey has entered the room since Seymour's suicide seven years earlier. On the back of the bedroom door are quotations from many of the world's most enlightened religious thinkers. After pondering those words for some time and reading a portion of Seymour's old diary, he rings Franny on Seymour's old private phone, pretending to be Buddy. A slip causes Franny to catch on that it is Zooey, but by that time he has told her that as an actress she must act on her own terms and disregard those of the ever-present, ignorant audience. Zooey uses the same metaphor of performing for the fat lady that Seymour used when they were children to inspire them to do their best. Carrying this metaphor further, Zooey tells Franny that everyone is that fat lady and that the fat lady is Jesus Christ. This revelation of interconnectedness allows Franny to find peace, and she falls into the deep sleep of renewal.

Critical Evaluation:

J. D. Salinger is generally regarded, critically or reverentially, as the preeminent literary force from the Beat era to capture the spirit of and speak to young Americans. Salinger's technique of presenting twentieth century American family relationships has been compared with the work of such authors as William Faulkner, Ernest Hemingway, and F. Scott Fitzgerald. Salinger was known primarily as a short-story writer when the novel *Franny and Zooey* was first published in two parts in *The New Yorker*. Salinger wrote "Franny" as a wedding gift for his wife, upon whom the title character is based. "Franny" also marked the beginning of what became Salinger's obsession with the Glass family.

Franny and Zooey are the youngest of seven brilliant children of a successful vaudevillian couple from the 1920's, Les Glass, who is Jewish, and his wife, Bessie Gallagher, who is Irish. The oldest and most brilliant of the children, Seymour, kills himself while on his second honeymoon, presumably because of an inability to reconcile childhood innocence with adulthood. The heir to Seymour's role as guru is Buddy, an author and writing instructor at a small college, who lives in modified, self-imposed hermitage. The character of Buddy is often identified as the alter ego of Salinger, who is known to be a heavily autobiographical writer and who was accused of being self-indulgent and preachy, especially in the later works introduced by *Franny and Zooey*.

With this novel, Salinger takes a marked turn from focusing on action, structure, and humor to a preoccupation with monologue, character development, and seriousness. The shift is underscored by a change from the omniscient third-person narrative voice in "Franny" to the first-person voice of Buddy, who tells the "Zooey" portion of the novel. It is here that discourse and extensive detail take the place of plot and structure. More than one-third of the novel takes place in bathrooms, and both stories cover only a very few hours of time. "Zooey" proceeds as if the narrator is looking through a randomly roving and pausing camera lens. By paying minimal attention to plot and attempting to present all objects with equal emphasis, Salinger tries gradually to reveal the complex nature and interconnectedness of otherwise static characters.

Salinger's work is mostly concerned with the various trials of adolescence: alienation, loss of innocence, the obscenity of modern life, the search for meaning, and the redeeming power of love. Franny is a typical Salinger character, seeking enlightenment, struggling against an onerous ego, and isolated by a hypersensitivity to her own shortcomings and those of others. There are differences, however, between Franny and Salinger's earlier protagonists, the most obvious being that Salinger for the first time uses a female character as spokesperson for this battle. The strong Judeo-Christian element in *Franny and Zooey* is a departure from Salinger's previous Zen-Buddhist point of view. Salinger appears to be taking a more general view of religion, not as a solution to the world's problems but rather as a means of learning to live with them and with oneself.

The overall theme of the novel is one of renewal, which is attained when the characters realize the unifying principle or interconnectedness of the universe. This realization is dependent on a dissolution of such opposites as phony and nice, bad and good, adulthood and childhood, knowledge and naïveté, boy and girl, us and them. The recurrent symbol of the little girl—which makes epiphanous appearances in Seymour's, Buddy's, and Zooey's lives, and whom Franny turns into as she makes her journey down the corridor to receive the ostensible Buddy's phone call—represents innocence and beauty. It is the loss of this innocence as they strive to connect with the unbearably ugly adult world that causes all of the Glass children in turn to go through a spiritual crisis. Seymour's fat lady—for whom he tells Zooey to shine his shoes and Franny to sing when they are child radio stars—represents that spiritual singleness of the universe. The fat lady is Everyman, and Everyman is Jesus Christ, or God, or Buddha, or Brahman. It is this realization that allows Franny to reconcile her views of self, ego, and the world and to resolve her spiritual crisis.

Some critics suggested that the resolution rings false and that when Salinger sets the Glasses apart from the rest of the world—in describing them as more handsome and more brilliant and more spiritually aware than other people—he is implying that only those with their intellectual and spiritual potential can search for the true way.

Beyond being impressively crafted and philosophically uplifting, *Franny and Zooey* presents Salinger's belief in the importance of spiritual seeking. As Zooey says in the closing scene, "the artist's only concern is to shoot for some kind of perfection, and *on his own terms*, not anyone else's."

Leslie Pendleton Myers

Further Reading

Alsen, Eberhard. *A Reader's Guide to J. D. Salinger.* Westport, Conn.: Greenwood Press, 2003. Provides a biographical essay, pointing out the autobiographical elements in Salinger's works, and insightful analysis of *Franny and Zooey* and other works.

Bloom, Harold, ed. *J. D. Salinger.* New ed. New York: Bloom's Literary Criticism, 2008. Collection of essays, including analyses of Salinger's novellas and short stories. Includes chronology, bibliography, and index.

French, Warren. *J. D. Salinger, Revisited.* Boston: Twayne, 1988. One of the most helpful and informative books on Salinger. French, who wrote an earlier book on the author, explains here how he changed his perspective on some of Salinger's works. In addition to offering a useful chronology and bibliography, French discusses the New Hampshire area, where Salinger and French lived, and makes enlightening comparisons of the stories to films. Includes notes, references, and index.

Laser, Marvin, and Norman Fruman. *Studies in J. D. Salinger: Reviews, Essays, and Critiques of "The Catcher in the Rye" and Other Fiction.* New York: Odyssey Press, 1963. A wonderful and diverse collection of analyses written at the time of Salinger's publications by some of the most recognized contemporary critics.

Lundquist, James. *J. D. Salinger.* New York: Frederick Ungar, 1979. A so-called New Criticism analysis that conflates Salinger's life with the lives of his characters and stories. The thorough chronology is very useful in this context.

Miller, James E., Jr. *J. D. Salinger.* Minneapolis: University of Minnesota Press, 1965. A concise, succinct, and accessible synopsis of Salinger's writing.

Wenke, John Paul. *J. D. Salinger: A Study of the Short Fiction.* Boston: Twayne, 1991. Traces the development of Salinger's short-story writing, analyzing *Franny and Zooey*, two short-story collections, and twenty-two uncollected stories.

Free Fall

Author: William Golding (1911-1993)
First published: 1959
Type of work: Novel
Type of plot: Bildungsroman
Time of plot: 1917-c. 1950
Locale: Southeast England

Principal characters:
SAMMY MOUNTJOY, a painter
BEATRICE IFOR, a former girlfriend of Sammy
ROWENA PRINGLE, a teacher
NICK SHALES, a teacher
MA, Sammy's mother
FR. WATTS-WATT, a clergyman, Sammy's guardian
PHILIP ARNOLD, a school friend
JOHNNY SPRAGG, a school friend
DR. HALDE, a member of the Gestapo
TAFFY, Sammy's wife

The Story:

Sammy Mountjoy, a well-known painter, reviews his past life to discover where his sense of guilt began and his innocence ended. He is convinced there was a moment of fall, when a choice freely made cost him his subsequent freedom of action. Several possible moments are examined, until a defining moment is discovered.

Sammy first examines his infancy. Born illegitimately, he lived with his obese, dirt-poor mother in a rural slum in Kent. It was an animal existence, however warm and sensuous. He enjoyed his infants' school, where his talent for drawing was first noticed, and then the boys' elementary school. Here he became a gang leader, vying against Johnny Spragg's gang. Aided by a manipulative friend, Philip Arnold, he set up a playground extortion racket that was soon discovered. Philip attended the local Church of England and dared Sammy to desecrate the altar by urinating on it. Sammy only managed a weak spit, but even then he was promptly pounced on by the verger, who hit him violently round the ear. As a result, Sammy needed hospitalization, during which time his mother died. The vicar, Father Watts-Watt, perhaps as a sign of atonement, became his guardian. For all his naughtiness, Sammy does not believe he lost his innocence during this period.

He analyzes next his time as an art student in London just before the outbreak of World War II. He was infatuated with Beatrice Ifor at school. She was also in London at a teacher training college; he determined to seduce her. His violent, obsessive nature frightened her, but eventually she yielded. Sammy was disappointed: He could find no personality in her, let alone the mystery he was seeking. Their lovemaking was disappointing, and he soon tired of her, although she was emotionally dependent on him. In the end he met Taffy at a Communist Party meeting, fell instantly in love with her, and abandoned Beatrice. In reviewing this part of his life, Sammy realizes his compulsive behavior was a sign that he had already lost his freedom: He was a driven man.

Sammy then explores a defining moment of insight that he had as a prisoner in a German prisoner of war camp. He was being interrogated by Dr. Halde about certain escape plans. Dr. Halde, a psychologist, was working for the Gestapo. Sammy did not know any of the details of the plan, but Dr. Halde knew that as an artist Sammy had intuitive insights and was not held by any strict morality. Before Sammy could articulate any such intuitions, he was placed in a completely dark cell. Sammy had been terrified of the dark since living at Father Watts-Watt's vicarage, and he was on the point of panic. He measured the cell to keep his sanity, but all the time his imagination was running riot. When he touched a wet soft mass in the center of the cell, he imagined it to be human organs, left perhaps when the ceiling descended and crushed a former inmate. At that point he broke down completely, crying "Help me! Help me!" This expression of utter helplessness and hopelessness became a death experience. When he was released, he felt resurrected, seeing everything quite differently. Life became a glory to him; his old self-centeredness was broken. This revelation enabled him to regain his schoolboy faith in the spiritual and to reject scientific materialism as a full explanation of life.

He now examines the powerful influence of two teachers in his losing faith. Miss Pringle taught religious education, and her lessons on the miraculous and transcendent events of the Bible thrilled him, but her attitude toward Sammy seemed to deny what she said. By contrast, Nick Shales, the science teacher, expressed a strictly logical and material view of life, and his kindness and generosity to his pupils won Sammy over. Sammy, however, felt that neither teacher touched a still-existing innocence within him.

One other episode at school is examined. During an art class, Sammy managed, almost by accident, to capture the inner character of one of the students sitting as a model, Beatrice. From then on Sammy's infatuation grew as he tried to recapture, unsuccessfully, that moment of artistic insight. On graduation day, the headmaster told Sammy he could achieve anything if he were willing to pay a high enough price, even though he would always be disappointed by what he got. As he went swimming that day, he made a conscious decision to have Beatrice. There lies the moment of fall and the loss of innocence.

Once the war ends, Sammy revisits Beatrice, Miss Pringle, and Nick, in the hope of communicating his new vision and perhaps to set the record straight. None of the three visits is successful. Beatrice is incurably insane and merely urinates over his shoes; Nick is dying; Miss Pringle rearranged her own reality to see herself as an early patron of Sammy. The past cannot be undone. Sammy's last memory is the final glimpse of the dark prison cell. He was in a broom cupboard, and the wet mass was a floor cloth. The Camp Commandant apologizes for Dr. Halde's behavior: "The Herr Doktor does not know about peoples."

Critical Evaluation:

Free Fall is the fourth novel of Sir William Golding. It is written not only in the genre of the novel of personal development but also in that of the *Künstlerroman*, the novel about artistic development and personality. As most of Golding's earlier novels, it is written in conscious dialectic to some other narrative, in this case Albert Camus's *La Chute* (1956; *The Fall*, 1957). Camus sees no possibility of regeneration or redemption after a fall; Golding does. There are other literary influences. Joyce Cary's *The Horse's Mouth* (1944) also is a first-person narrative by a painter; Golding's style is at times reminiscent of Cary's. L. P. Hartley's prizewinning novel *The Go-Between* was published only a few years previously (1953) and also deals with a boy's loss of innocence through sexual knowledge, though Leo is a much more passive protagonist than Sammy. Another influence is the great French text *À la recherche du temps perdu* (1913-1927; *Remembrance of Things Past*, 1922-1931) by Marcel Proust, a model for Sammy's search for significant moments of time buried in half-conscious memory.

The title suggests that the novel stands in a central literary tradition of exploration of the limits of freedom. Golding's achievement is to be able to restate such traditional material, often of a theological nature, in the language and thought of the post-World War II Western world. The novel also describes moments of revelation that define one's view of reality, the futility of material life without a spiritual or transcendent dimension, the nature of evil, and the correspondence of personal to social integration or disintegration. Perhaps new to this novel, for Golding, is an exploration of the relationship of guilt to forgiveness, and the way that conviction of guilt and the ability to forgive need conversion experiences. Golding seems to suggest that redemption can only be partial. Beatrice remains insane, with no hope of recovery. Sammy has to bear some, though not all, the guilt for this. Past time can be examined to find truth, but it cannot be remade.

Although Sammy is an artist, the novel's style is not altogether painterly. Much of the imagery is, in fact, religious and is Golding's way of expressing traditional theological concepts in contemporary concerns. Fire is one such example. The novel features the traditional symbolism of Pentecostal fire, the bringing of new spiritual life; less frequently it refers to hell. Fire is also related to the burning bush of Moses, both as miracle and as glory, and to Nick's placing a candle in a bell jar, symbolizing rationality, but also confinement, the death of the spirit. Other recurring religious images are of paradise, water, "fear and trembling," altars and temples, and Christ's temptations. The other image that is central to the novel and to all of Golding's fiction is that of darkness—from the dreadful panic of the cell to the "warm darkness" of Ma. Images of sickness, captivity, and cells/cellars can also be traced.

Episodes take on symbolic value as enacted images: the cell, the desecration of the altar, Sammy's waiting at red traffic lights on the way to Beatrice, for example. Surprisingly, only a few of Sammy's drawings are seen as images, the most obvious being the few hurried, uncredited lines that somehow capture the essence of Beatrice in a way no seduction could ever do. Names also take on symbolic force: Beatrice echoes Dante's inspirational love, but her surname, "if/or" suggests dislocation, lack of result. "Mountjoy" is ironic until his cell experience, where for the first time he does discover joy, but only by going through the depths.

Golding also uses little catch phrases, or leitmotifs, to encapsulate symbolic force—"the taste of potatoes" is one such, symbolizing the authenticity of felt experience. Another is "blue cornflowers." Both are clearly memory fragments.

Golding's narrative method is not to conduct a simple autobiographical plot line. Although he covers much of Sammy's life, there are numerous omissions. The novel is more an excavation, starting at the most obvious places. It is also like a treasure hunt, in which what is buried is only to be found at the end. One may guess where the treasure lies, but not predict the actual moment of discovery. The reader explores with Sammy. Perceptions are partly those of the adult Sammy looking back, partly those of Sammy as a child. Sammy the innocent, the unregenerate, and the regenerate are all represented. This helps Golding elicit a response from the reader that is neither too sympathetic nor too hostile to Sammy.

David Barratt

Further Reading

Babb, Howard S. *The Novels of William Golding*. Columbus: Ohio State University Press, 1970. One chapter is devoted to each novel. Babb's strength in writing on *Free Fall* is his introductory analysis of Golding's style.

Boyd, S. J. *The Novels of William Golding*. New York: St. Martin's Press, 1988. Boyd's volume is contemporaneous with the later novels of Golding and thus able to look back on the earlier ones with some hindsight. The quality of Sammy's love is central to Boyd's analysis.

Gindin, James. *William Golding*. New York: Macmillan, 1988. Sees Golding relating sinfulness to "becoming" in *Free Fall*. An economic, well-focused thematic discussion.

Kinkead-Weekes, Martin, and Ian Gregor. *William Golding: A Critical Study*. 3d rev. ed. London: Faber, 2002. A new edition of one of the standard critical accounts of Golding that features a biographical sketch by Golding's daughter, Judy Carver. Anticipates later criticisms of *Free Fall* being too reductionist by arguing that such criticisms are misconceived.

McCarron, Kevin. *William Golding.* 2d rev. ed. Tavistock, England: Northcote House/British Council, 2006. Introductory overview to Golding's life and works. Includes bibliography and index.

Redpath, Philip. *William Golding: A Structural Reading of His Fiction.* New York: Barnes & Noble, 1986. Examines the circular structure of *Free Fall* and Golding's other novels.

Tiger, Virginia. *William Golding: The Unmoved Target.* New York: Marion Boyars, 2003. An examination of Golding's novels in which Tiger draws upon her conversations and correspondence with the author to describe how these books explore themes of human destiny and vision. Devotes a chapter to an analysis of *Free Fall.*

Freedom or Death

Author: Nikos Kazantzakis (1883-1957)
First published: Ho Kapetan Michales, 1953 (English translation, 1956)
Type of work: Novel
Type of plot: Historical
Time of plot: 1889
Locale: Meghalo Kastro, Crete

Principal characters:
CAPTAIN MICHALES, the principal rebel
NURI BEY, a Turk, Michales's "blood brother"
KOSMAS, Michales's nephew
CAPTAIN POLYXIGIS, a rival Cretan
EMINÉ, Nuri's wife and later Polyxigis's wife
SEFAKAS, Michales's father
NOEMI (CHRYSULA), Kosmas's wife
TITYROS, Michales's brother
VANGELIO, Tityros's wife
MANUSAKAS, Michales's brother
THE PASHA OF MEGHALO KASTRO, leader of the Turks

The Story:

Captain Michales is obsessed with the ideal of freedom. He does not listen to his wife or to the elders of Meghalo Kastro. Turks, with the exception of Michales's boyhood friend Nuri Bey, are Michales's natural enemies. Counterbalancing this obsession is Michales's attraction to Nuri's wife, Eminé. He is enraptured by her beauty and enchanting voice, but he realizes that this attraction interferes with his total dedication to the liberation of Crete. Another problem is his heavy drinking bouts, which are usually followed by senseless cruelty toward Turks.

At the same gathering at which Eminé first captivates Michales, another Cretan fighter, Captain Polyxigis, also falls under her spell. It is Polyxigis who eventually wins Eminé's heart and becomes her lover. Michales is jealous of Polyxigis, although he respects him as a comrade in arms.

Polyxigis's success in winning Eminé does not stop Michales from trying to impress her. In a contest of strength, Michales wins a match over Nuri, who is devastated and feels ineffectual in the eyes of Eminé. Nuri becomes further humiliated in a fight with Michales's brother Manusakas. Although he manages to kill Manusakas, Nuri is permanently emasculated by a knife wound.

Michales, hearing of his brother's murder, renounces his childhood friendship with Nuri and vows revenge. When the opportune moment comes, however, he finds Nuri in a pathetic condition and relents. Nuri, who wanted to die in battle, loses his manhood, his wife, his friend, and his honor. He commits suicide. Nuri's death saddens Michales but emboldens Polyxigis to propose marriage to Eminé. He succeeds in converting her from Islam to Christianity.

The war intensifies. The Turks make major advances and pillage many towns, slaughtering the inhabitants. Michales with two hundred rebels and sixty-five monks defends the monastery of Arkadi for two days and nights against fifteen thousand Turks. In the midst of the fighting, Michales receives word that Eminé was captured by Turks. He and a group of his men rush off to rescue her. By the time he returns, the monastery is on the verge of collapse. He feels guilt and shame. He refuses to surrender in spite of the odds. All other officers and troops retreat except Michales and a few of his devoted followers.

Michales's dedication is infectious and transforms others. His brother Tityros, an ineffectual schoolteacher, gets involved in petty domestic rivalries that result in his killing his brother-in-law. His wife, Vangelio, heartbroken over her brother's death, kills herself. These events and his brother's influence spur a spiritual transformation in Tityros. He becomes a revolutionary.

Another transformation takes place in Kosmas, Michales's nephew. Kosmas is an intellectual who is studying at a German university. He surprises his family by coming home with Noemi, his Russian-Jewish wife. Upon their arrival, Sefakas, Kosmas's grandfather, dies. The family thinks it is time for Michales to retreat and to come home. Kosmas volunteers to go to the mountains to persuade his uncle to return. He carries letters from the family and from the elders of Crete that accept failure of the revolt and request Michales's return.

When he enters the trenches where Michales is valiantly fighting the Turks, Kosmas is strongly affected by his uncle's idealism. Instead of trying to persuade him to come back, he joins in the fighting. Shortly afterward, the young freedom fighter is captured and beheaded by the Turks.

When the Turks finally ram through the gate of the monastery, a Cretan fighter fires his pistol into an underground powder vault where six hundred women and children are hiding. All perish, together with everyone at the monastery, including the hundreds of Turks who had already entered.

Michales grabs his nephew's severed head by the hair and, raising it like a banner, charges the enemy roaring, "Freedom or . . ." Before he can finish the famous Cretan slogan, the Turkish bullets find their target.

Critical Evaluation:

Freedom or Death is a colorful story full of symbolic motifs. In it, Nikos Kazantzakis depicts his own experiences as a child in Meghalo Kastro. He recalled that in 1889 Christians in his village killed a prominent Turkish dignitary, which triggered a new Turkish massacre of Cretan civilians. "My mother, my sister, and I sat glued to one another," Kazantzakis said, "barricaded within our house." Turks outside cursed, broke down doors, and slaughtered Christians. His father, standing with a loaded musket and his long knife unsheathed, told the family he planned to slaughter them before they fell into Turkish hands.

Kazantzakis altered much of his personal history, yet many characters and episodes match real persons and events, and the character of Kosmas embodies Kazantzakis's poli-

tics and experiences as an expatriate. Kosmas, like Kazantzakis, studies in Germany, travels throughout Russia, and marries a Russian-Jewish girl. Kosmas, like Kazantzakis, is a follower of Henri-Louis Bergson and Friedrich Nietzsche and has Marxist tendencies.

Kazantzakis's central plot is derived from a famous Cretan folk song about a 1770 revolt led by a teacher named Dhaskaloyannis. With a band of eight hundred Sphakians, the hero held off twenty-five thousand Turkish regulars for several weeks. Both in the 1770 revolt and in the revolt of 1889 chronicled in *Freedom or Death*, the Russians promised assistance that they never delivered. Dhashkaloyannis surrendered but refused to sign a truce, stoically accepting torture and death.

In *Freedom or Death*, past and present, fact and fiction, art and life, and dream and reality are often indistinguishable. This is a reflection of both the Cretan sense of history and Kazantzakis's own interest in Freudian and Jungian conceptions of the interrelationship between the conscious and the unconscious. Characters in the novel may seem exaggerated, scenes overly dramatic, and people and events inflated, unreal, and larger than life. In this, the work reflects Cretan sensibility, a synthesis of mythology and reality. Greek mythology by its nature is a colorful and fantastic reflection of Greek views of humans, God, nature, and death. These are the primitive forces that generate mythology to inspire hope and relieve anxiety. Kazantzakis's *Freedom or Death* was created within that tradition.

Anthropomorphic and metaphorical characterization, including animal imagery, is dominant in the novel. Michales is referred to as wild boar, dragon, lion, bull, and minotaur. Kazantzakis describes various characters and situations in naturalistic terms, giving them animal vitality and raw qualities. Spring "leaps" onto the village like a man falling onto a woman, allowing no sleep. Michales is like an "earthquake" or "hard, knotty tree." His father Sefakas is like a "great oak tree." Kosmas is like a Cretan "rock."

A Christ metaphor appears, with Crete being crucified like Christ. The return of Christ is intimately associated with the prospect of a Crete free of Turkish domination. There are visions of the Greek king's son coming by sea to free Crete, like Christ coming on a cloud to establish his rule on earth. Michales on the mountaintop calls out to his few remaining followers that whoever dies for Immortal Crete is dying for Christ and will return with Christ to regenerate the island.

Kazantzakis presents a genre of sacrifice and martyrdom that does not come out of Marxist dialectics or intellectual inspiration but out of vital, sensual forces similar to the Christian faith. Kosmas, a socialist, dies not for an intellectually reasoned purpose but for a raw and visceral prompting of his soul, for the mythical Crete. Michales scorns the education of his nephew and brother. However, this anti-intellectualism is not an idiosyncratic characteristic; rather, it is a Cretan resentment of any activity that might diminish or call into question the individual's love affair with Crete.

By offering a visceral philosophy of action, Kazantzakis in a sophisticated manner leans toward a naturalistic free will as opposed to the Turk's Islamic fatalism. The pasha tells Michales to surrender because everything that happens in a war is already predestined. Michales, however, believes that human beings always win over fate if they persist to the death. Even when defeated they are ennobled, not degraded.

Michales is an individualistic, primitive, culture-bound, and primitively Christian being. Kazantzakis was able to blend such an odd number of sensibilities into one unified character because he was influenced by a variety of Western and Eastern philosophies, among them Marxism, Sigmund Freud's psychoanalysis, Carl Jung's collective unconscious, and Buddha's Nothing.

Dreams play an important part in *Freedom or Death* in shaping the reality of the townsfolk of Meghalo Kastro. Dreams are a means of justification for their personal beliefs, aspirations, and actions. The tavern keeper Vendusos dreams of the wine goddess who turns out to be the Virgin Mary. Efendina, a devout Muslim, dreams of pork and wine. Michales dreams of Eminé, the liberation of Crete, and his father.

Kosmas's dead father appears in his dreams to chastise, advise, and uplift his spirits, as well as to order him to take revenge on the Turks. Noemi, Kosmas's pregnant wife, dreams that grandfather Sefakas does not want her to have the baby; he kicks her in the stomach and she wakes up in a pool of blood after suffering a miscarriage. Indeed, there is a dreamlike quality to the novel. Dreams and harsh realities imperceptibly mingle. Ultimately, all dreams seem to originate from one spiritual source, the Cretan slogan of "Freedom or Death."

The similarity of dreams among the Cretans suggests the influence on Kazantzakis of Jung's belief in the collective unconscious underlying the history of struggle and oppression. Primitive ancestors, with all of their beastlike grandeur, stir within Michales and Kosmas and goad them to extraordinary sacrifices. The Cretan martyrs of past revolutions whisper in Cretan ears and recruit a fresh army of superhumans.

Cretans can easily become heroes, but these are not such antiheroes as James Joyce's Leopold Bloom, Franz Kafka's K., or Thomas Mann's Hans Castorp. Kazantzakis's insignificant characters become heroes because they are intoxicated

with an ideology and play out their madness to its ultimate degree. They are not ruled by history or fate. They may die but are never defeated. These heroes possess the qualities of positive humanism. They are quintessentially free because they believe in a myth.

Chogollah Maroufi

Further Reading

Anton, John. "Kazantzakis and the Tradition of the Tragic." *Journal of the Hellenic Diaspora* 10, no. 4 (Winter, 1983): 53-67. A clear exposition of Kazantzakis's understanding and use of the ancient notions of tragedy, which are discussed as they relate to his novels, including *Freedom or Death*.

Bien, Peter. *Kazantzakis: Politics of Spirit*. 2 vols. Princeton, N.J.: Princeton University Press, 1989-2007. The first volume focuses on the evolution of Kazantzakis's personal philosophy from 1906 up to the publication of *The Odyssey* in 1938. Volume 2 completes this definitive biography, describing the period of Kazantzakis's life in which he wrote *Zorba the Greek* and *The Last Temptation of Christ*.

_____. "O Kapetan Mihalis, an Epic (Romance?) Manqué." *Journal of Modern Greek Studies* 5, no. 2 (October, 1987): 153-173. A delightful and well-written analysis of the character of Captain Michales in *Freedom or Death*. Bien discusses the notions of romance in the novel.

Block, Adele. "Mythological Syncretism in the Works of Four Modern Novelists." *International Fiction Review* 8, no. 2 (Summer, 1991): 114-118. A useful analysis of the method by which Kazantzakis in *Freedom or Death* synthesizes various mythological motifs in a workable and unified system.

Dombrowski, Daniel A. *Kazantzakis and God*. Albany: State University of New York Press, 1997. Analyzes Kazantzakis's novels and other works to describe his religious vision, interpreting his ideas in terms of contemporary "process theology." Explains how Kazantzakis combined his ideas about God with a Darwinian belief in the evolution of all creatures—including God.

Dossor, Howard F. *The Existential Theology of Nikos Kazantzakis*. Wallingford, Pa.: Pendle Hill, 2001. Examines Kazantzakis's religious ideas, describing how the writer created a personal theology based upon his existential belief that human beings are mortal and must live as if they are heading toward death.

Gilevski, Paskal. "From Homer to Kazantzakis." *Macedo-*

nian Review 22, no. 2 (1992): 147-150. An interesting review and analysis of the connection between Kazantzakis's tragic hero Michales and the tragic mythological heroes of Homer's epics.

Levitt, Morton P. "*Freedom or Death* and Rebellion on Crete." In *The Cretan Glance: The World and Art of Kazantzakis.* Columbus: Ohio State University Press, 1980. An excellent exposition and evaluation of *Freedom or Death*. Levitt looks at this novel from historical, social, cultural, and philosophical perspectives.

Middleton, Darren J. N., and Peter Bien, eds. *God's Struggler: Religion in the Writings of Nikos Kazantzakis*. Macon, Ga.:

Mercer University Press, 1996. Collection of essays exploring the theme of religion in Kazantzakis's works, including a Greek Orthodox interpretation of his religious ideas, a discussion of mysticism in his writings, and an explanation of his "theology of struggle."

Owens, Lewis. *Creative Destruction: Nikos Kazantzakis and the Literature of Responsibility*. Macon, Ga.: Mercer University Press, 2003. Detailed study of Kazantzakis's writings, describing how he was influenced by the philosophy of Henri Bergson. According to Lewis, Kazantzakis believed destruction was a necessary prerequisite for renewed creative activity.

The French Lieutenant's Woman

Author: John Fowles (1926-2005)
First published: 1969
Type of work: Novel
Type of plot: Symbolic realism
Time of plot: 1867
Locale: Lyme Regis, Dorset, England

Principal characters:
SARAH WOODRUFF, a mysterious seduced-and-abandoned governess
CHARLES SMITHSON, a thirty-two-year-old London gentleman and amateur paleontologist
ERNESTINA FREEMAN, his twenty-one-year-old fiancé
AUNT TRANTER, a kindly spinster with whom Ernestina is staying
MARY, Aunt Tranter's maid
SAM, Charles's manservant
MRS. POULTENEY, a self-righteous prude who takes Sarah in to demonstrate her charity
DR. GROGAN, a scholarly bachelor physician
THE NARRATOR, an unnamed and mysterious spy

The Story:

Charles Smithson, a London gentleman on vacation in the south of England, goes for a walk with his fiancé, Ernestina Freeman, on the sea ramparts in Lyme Regis on the Dorset coast. They see a woman in a black coat and bonnet staring seaward from the very end of the quay, who, when warned of the danger, turns and gives Charles such a look of sadness that he never forgets it. He is further fascinated when Ernestina tells him the story of the woman, Sarah Woodruff, who, it is rumored, was seduced and abandoned by a shipwrecked naval officer she nursed back to health. Since then, she is called Tragedy or the French Lieutenant's Woman, a euphemism for "whore."

The next day, while Charles, an amateur paleontologist, is looking for fossils in an area known as the Undercliff, he once again sees Sarah, sleeping on a ledge beneath the path

where he walks, and he is struck by her appalling loneliness. When she suddenly awakens, startled, he can only apologize for his intrusion. After she runs away, he follows her and offers to walk her to town, but she refuses. On the following day, Charles sees Sarah again when he visits Mrs. Poulteney's, where Sarah was taken in as a kind of charity case. They share a look of understanding but do not indicate that they already met.

Later, Charles encounters Sarah on the Undercliff again and offers to help her get away from the self-righteous Mrs. Poulteney, but Sarah refuses, leaving Charles puzzled as to what keeps her in Lyme Regis. Charles talks to his physician and friend Dr. Grogan about his interest in Sarah, justifying it as only humanitarian, but Dr. Grogan thinks it is something more. The next time Charles meets with Sarah, she tells him that she was not seduced by the French Lieutenant but willingly gave herself to him in order to free herself from the restraints of Victorian expectations of women. Charles, disillusioned with Ernestina's simplicity and conformity to Victorian conventions, finds Sarah puzzling and irresistible.

Sarah asks Charles to meet her one more time. She then purposely gets herself discharged by Mrs. Poulteney. When Charles meets with Dr. Grogan again and talks to him about Sarah, Dr. Grogan warns him about Sarah's possibly trying to entrap him. Although Charles agrees with Dr. Grogan's advice that Dr. Grogan meet her instead of Charles, he leaves ahead of Grogan and finds Sarah in a barn. Interrupted by his manservant Sam and the maid Mary just as he is about to kiss Sarah, Charles gives her money on which to live. Sarah goes to Exeter, takes a hotel room, and sends Charles her address. Charles goes to London, gets drunk, and visits a prostitute, but gets sick and vomits when she tells him her name is Sarah.

On the way back to Lyme Regis, Charles decides to forget Sarah and return to Ernestina. Charles and Ernestina get married, Charles becomes a businessman, the couple has children, and Sarah is never heard from again. The narrator says, however, that this is not the real ending of the story but the one that Charles imagines and the most conventional one according to Victorian standards. What really happens, the narrator says, is that Charles stops at Exeter and goes to Sarah's hotel, where she is expecting him. Sarah subtly seduces Charles into her bed, and he discovers that she did not give herself sexually to the French Lieutenant but is a virgin. Sarah admits it, telling Charles it is part of her plan to exile herself from conventional expectations, and sends him away. Charles goes to a church and suddenly has an insight about Sarah as a real person, not as an ideal.

Charles writes a letter to Sarah telling her he wants to marry her, but his servant Sam does not deliver it. Charles breaks his engagement with Ernestina and goes back to the hotel, only to find Sarah gone. Barely escaping disastrous legal revenge by Ernestina's father, Charles looks everywhere for Sarah, even going to America, which he discovers is more suitable to his new sense of freedom than England. After a few years of searching, he receives word from Sam (who marries Mary, works in a shop, and feels guilty for not having delivered Charles's letter) that Sarah is living in London. Charles finds Sarah working as a secretary and model to the famous artist Dante Gabriel Rossetti. Sarah tells Charles that she will never marry him, but when he turns to leave, she introduces him to their daughter, Lalage, and they all embrace. The narrator of the novel, watching from across the way, sets his watch back fifteen minutes. The reader witnesses, for a second time, the meeting of Charles and Sarah.

This time, there is no daughter to reunite them. Although Sarah offers Charles an unmarried relationship, he leaves her to start his life over again.

Critical Evaluation:

The French Lieutenant's Woman became a best-selling novel both in England and America when it was first published. It was also the novel that made John Fowles's work of interest to academic critics because of its experimentation with narrative structure and style. The book is not only a historical novel, it is also a self-reflexive work about the Victorian novel, on which it is patterned. Although the primary action focuses on a triangle love relationship taking place in 1867, it is clear from the beginning that the narrator of the novel is a twentieth century man familiar with the conventions of the late nineteenth century novel genre as well as the cultural and intellectual changes that have taken place in the one hundred years between 1867 and 1967, when Fowles began writing the novel. Exploiting this historical perspective, the narrator, who places himself within the novel's action, parodies the conventions of the Victorian novel and creates a tension between the past and the present as well as between the nature of reality and the nature of fiction.

Much of the importance of this novel depends on its parody and play with novelistic conventions, including the many asides in which the narrator interferes with and comments on the action. A plot summary of the novel's nineteenth century story does not truly reflect its multilayered structure and sophisticated point of view. Not only does the narrator refer to the action from the perspective of having known such twentieth century figures as Sigmund Freud, Adolf Hitler, and Marshall McLuhan, he purposely places himself—a twentieth century man—within the story as an observer-voyeur, beginning with the first chapter, when he appears as a spy, looking through a telescope at Charles and Ernestina walking on the quay, and continuing to the last chapter when he sets his watch back fifteen minutes and creates an alternate ending to the novel, so that the book ends both conventionally and unconventionally. At one point in the novel, he even justifies his breaking of the illusion of reality by reminding readers that reality is not so real as they think; they do not even believe that their own past is quite real, he says, for it is dressed up, censored, fictionalized, and put away on a shelf. He concludes that the basic definition of human beings is that they are all in flight from reality.

In addition to the two alternate endings in the last two chapters, the novel also has a third possible ending that occurs in chapter 44, more than a hundred pages before the actual conclusion of the book. In this first ending, Charles does not go to Sarah's hotel and end up in her bed. Instead, he goes back to Ernestina and they get married and Charles never hears of Sarah again. The narrator says that although this may be a very traditional ending, it is not what "really" happened, only what Charles imagines happened. Indeed, this first ending is the most conventional ending, satisfying all the Victorian expectations of morality and social responsibility.

The central figure in *The French Lieutenant's Woman* is the mysterious Sarah, although Charles is the character caught in a moral, ethical, and social conflict. The basic question the narrator poses about Sarah is: "Who is Sarah? Out of what shadows does she come?" He says Charles is attracted to her not for herself, but for some emotion or some possibility that she symbolizes, that Sarah is more like a figure from myth than from actuality. Sarah is a symbol of the kind of woman who was not allowed to exist in the Victorian novel or Victorian society, or rather she embodies a kind of wish for a freedom that was not permitted. Sarah creates a fiction in which she may live a reality radically different from that in which society would force her to live. She transforms herself from the conventional Victorian female to a modern woman, cutting herself loose from society by a single act of defiance—an act that is a supreme bit of fiction. She was not, in fact, seduced. Realizing that she has transformed herself from human being to mythic and symbolic embodiment, Sarah says, "I am hardly human any more."

What Sarah symbolizes to Charles is the tension between desire and renunciation. She carries the promise of existential freedom long before Jean-Paul Sartre made that notion a popular one in twentieth century philosophy. The narrator provides an important clue to the basic tension in the novel when he says that Robert Louis Stevenson's *The Strange Case of Dr. Jekyll and Mr. Hyde* (1886) is the guidebook for the Victorian period. Conflict between physical desire and social expectations (between what Freud called the id and the superego) is the central theme of the novel. *The French Lieutenant's Woman* is, by extension, also about the unraveling of Victorian society and the beginnings of the modern period. The novel moves thematically from the biological sources of life in the fossils for which Charles searches in the Undercliff to the modern period's remaking of reality by the aesthete as suggested by Sarah's becoming a model for Dante Gabriel Rossetti. In this sense, Sarah is the first modern woman, one who insists on escaping biology and society and making herself in her own image. Similarly, Charles is the first modern man, caught in an existential dilemma before the word "existentialism" was ever coined.

Charles E. May

Further Reading

Acheson, James. *John Fowles.* New York: St. Martin's Press, 1998. An excellent introduction to Fowles's life and works, in which Acheson traces the development of his novels. Chapter 4 focuses on *The French Lieutenant's Woman.*

Aubrey, James R., ed. *John Fowles and Nature: Fourteen Perspectives on Landscape.* Madison, N.J.: Fairleigh Dickinson University Press, 1999. Four of these fourteen essays focus on Fowles's depiction of the Undercliff and other aspects of the natural landscape in *The French Lieutenant's Woman.*

Foster, Thomas C. *Understanding John Fowles.* Columbia: University of South Carolina Press, 1994. An accessible critical introduction to Fowles's principal works, including analysis of *The French Lieutenant's Woman* and other novels. Includes an annotated bibliography.

Huffaker, Robert. *John Fowles.* Boston: Twayne, 1980. A general introduction to Fowles's fiction. Focuses on the intrusive author, the novelist as character, and the alternative Victorian and modern endings of *The French Lieutenant's Woman.*

Lenz, Brooke. *John Fowles: Visionary and Voyeur.* Amsterdam: Rodopi, 2008. A feminist analysis, in which Lenz demonstrates how Fowles progressively creates female characters who subvert male voyeurism and create alternative narratives. Chapter 3 focuses on *The French Lieutenant's Woman.*

Olshen, Barry N. *John Fowles.* New York: Frederick Ungar, 1978. An introduction to Fowles's fiction, focusing on the basic themes in *The French Lieutenant's Woman*, including that of the breakup of Victorian culture and the rise of existential modernism.

Reynolds, Margaret, and Jonathan Noakes. *John Fowles: The Essential Guide.* New York: Vintage Books, 2003. A guide designed for students, teachers, and general readers, this volume contains an interview with Fowles and reading guides, reading activities, and information about contexts, comparisons, and complementary readings for three novels: *The Collector* (1963), *The Magus* (1965, 1977), and *The French Lieutenant's Woman.* Also includes a glossary and select bibliography.

Stephenson, William. *Fowles's "The French Lieutenant's Woman."* New York: Continuum, 2007. A reader's guide with information about the novel's contexts, language, style, form, and critical reception. Discusses how to read the novel and provides suggestions for further reading.

Warburton, Eileen. *John Fowles: A Life in Two Worlds.* New York: Viking Press, 2004. A thorough, entertaining, and well-reviewed biography. Warburton was given full access to Fowles's journals and personal papers and she presents many previously untold details of his life, most notably his thirty-seven-year love affair with his wife.

Wolfe, Peter. *John Fowles: Magus and Moralist.* Cranbury, N.J.: Bucknell University Press, 1976. Provides a useful summary of the critical reception of the book and discusses how the mystery of Sarah is crucial.

The French Revolution

Author: Thomas Carlyle (1795-1881)
First published: 1837
Type of work: History

Principal personages:
KING LOUIS XV
KING LOUIS XVI
QUEEN MARIE ANTOINETTE
DANTON
MARAT
ROBESPIERRE
TURGOT
NAPOLEON BONAPARTE
COUNT FERSEN, a Swedish admirer of Marie Antoinette

The French Revolution is a landmark in the history of nineteenth century English literature, the work that, after the comparative public failure of *Sartor Resartus* (1833-1834), helped to establish Thomas Carlyle. In its dramatic picture of the French Revolution it offers the reader an estimate of an event that disturbed and shocked the consciences of Carlyle's grandparents. It offers a measure of revolutionary and socially disruptive narrative, but it is neither optimistic and blindly trustful of progress (here Carlyle differed from Utilitarian friends) nor pessimistic and horrified, as Edmund Burke had been at the time of the revolution. Finally, and perhaps most important for readers, *The French Revolution* is a more successful self-realization for Carlyle than the comparatively nebulous explorations of ideas in *Sartor Resartus.* That earlier work presents Carlyle's ideas in a kind of cloud formation that conceals whatever terrain of fact and real human experience they float over; *The French Revolution* presents the same ideas in relation to and supported by a bewilderingly rich body of facts: the day-by-day events of the unsettling French years.

Impressive as Carlyle's method of digesting and arranging the body of facts is, still more memorable is the way he musters them in a readable narrative. Like an Old Testament prophet, Carlyle rides the hurricane and directs the storm of the fall of absolute monarchy in France. He produces not simply another history of a vexed period, full of rationalized

information. It is true of Carlyle that his view of one period of history is always on the verge of becoming a vision of all human history. The Frenchwomen who march on Versailles stand for the passionate outbreak of all oppressed human beings, and the sorrows of Marie Antoinette in the Conciergerie stand for the agonies of all trivial human beings carried to their doom by forces they cannot control.

It is possible to identify some of the means that Carlyle employs to create his apocalyptic vision—a vision, not of last things, but certainly of the forces that combine to drive history onward. The arrangement of the facts is rigorously chronological. The book begins with the death pangs of King Louis XV; these are represented as the death throes not simply of one aged monarch but of a regime that once justified itself but that had become a hollow shell. The book continues with an account of the suicidal follies of the young king, Louis XVI, and his pretty and thoughtless wife, Marie Antoinette. It notes the efforts of some of the king's ministers, Necker, Turgot, and others, to stem the advancing tide: to restore financial soundness and yet provide money for all who thought they had a right to spend it. Carlyle, often with a somewhat uneven pace, one that permits him to stop for angry or compassionate meditation when he wishes to point out the "inevitable" chain of disaster and struggle, continues his year-by-year and month-by-month account. He tells of the meeting of the Estates General, the Tennis Court Oath, the march on Versailles, the various attempts to frame a constitution, the degeneration of the relations between the royal couple and the Revolutionary Government, the royal family's attempted escape to Varennes, the successive decapitations of king and queen, the succession of leaders who could not lead but had to dictate by harangue and outright terror, and, finally, the end of the revolution at the hands of Napoleon Bonaparte, who brought order with a "whiff of grapeshot."

Carlyle, at the end of his work, speaks of a ship that finally is over the bar after much labor and peril from counter winds; and this is certainly the effect of his narrative. Despite its complexity, his story is the single account of a set of events that gives a full demonstration of the glories and horrors of revolution, a period of history that was inevitable but not, because of its inevitability, admirable.

In dramatizing a mighty and perilous passage that involved not the French nation alone but all humanity, Carlyle is able to transform his account of actual events into an apocalyptic statement about humanity that does not seem to belong to any particular time at all. He does so by means of his style of presentation and by passages of direct, explicit interpretation. Perhaps it is the style that is most decisive. Never before or since has a historian writing in English written a book like Carlyle's history. The narrative is couched in the present tense, wearing but hortatory; what happens is not in a safely distant past, but here and now. The sentimentality of the French philosophes and the ignorant and brutal enthusiasms of the mob threaten the readers, as Carlyle drags them through mountains of detail and event. Moreover, Carlyle frequently interrupts the forward movement of the narrative to harangue some of the chief actors in his story—Danton, Mirabeau, Marie Antoinette—and it seems possible that they may listen to him and escape what readers well know was their historical fate. Some of the harangues, of course, speak not to the historical personages but to readers and suggest that readers (even more than a century after the appearance of the book) may escape their historical fate, whatever it may be, if they will but listen to Carlyle. Or if readers may not escape it, they will understand it better after reading *The French Revolution*.

Implication becomes explicit in innumerable passages such as the following brief one:

Or, apart from all Transcendentalism, is it not a plain truth of sense, which the duller mind can even consider as a truism, that human things wholly are in continual movement, and action and reaction; working continually forward, phasis after phasis, by unalterable laws, towards prescribed issues? How often must readers say, and yet

not rightly lay to heart: The seed that is sown, it will spring! Given the summer's blossoming, then there is also given the autumnal withering: so is it ordered not with seedfields only, but with transactions, arrangements, philosophies, societies, French Revolutions, whatsoever man works with in this lower world.

A great body of French fact attests what the drifting clouds of *Sartor Resartus* suggested. It is the law of life that social forms become old clothes unless they are worn by the people who have some kind of faith: faith in duty, faith in silent work, faith in, finally, the transcendental, self-realizing movement of some force, some kind of deity which is realizing itself in the movements of human history and particularly in the great persons who rise above themselves and command the attention of the rest of humanity, pointing a finger to show the way all should go.

Carlyle devoted later books to such demonstration. Oliver Cromwell, Frederick the Great, and a whole company of great men in *On Heroes, Hero-Worship, and the Heroic in History* (1841)—all of these so exhort. The essential tragedy of the French Revolution, as Carlyle sees it, is that in it was a congeries of events that cried out for a hero and found only destruction and social chaos. It lacked, among other things, a contemporary such as Carlyle to annotate that chaos. The French people's loss, however, is the readers' gain. Upon their agonies Carlyle rests a view of history as a scroll of events always on the verge of parting and revealing to readers—in the heavens or in the depths of their beings—the essential divine plan.

Further Reading

Clubbe, John. "Carlyle as Epic Historian." In *Victorian Literature and Society*, edited by James R. Kincaid. Columbus: Ohio State University Press, 1984. Carlyle's reading of the *Iliad* in 1834 transformed his vision of what history could become. *The French Revolution*, subsequently, was envisioned as an epic.

Desaulniers, Mary. *Carlyle and the Economics of Terror: A Study of Revisionary Gothicism in "The French Revolution."* Montreal: McGill-Queen's University Press, 1995. An analysis of the book, focusing on its complex language. Desaulniers discusses some of the sources for the work, such as Aristotle, Johann Wolfgang von Goethe, and gothic romances; she argues that Carlyle used "revisionary gothicism" as a linguistic device to discuss economic and political issues.

Frye, Lowell T. "'Great Burke,' Thomas Carlyle, and the French Revolution." In *The French Revolution Debate in*

English Literature and Culture, edited by Lisa Plummer Crafton. Westport, Conn.: Greenwood Press, 1997. The French Revolution's ideas of democratic reform became a major topic of debate in late eighteenth and nineteenth century Britain. This collection of essays examines how various Britons responded to that debate, with Frye's essay focusing on Carlyle's and Edmund Burke's histories of the revolt.

Morrow, John. *Thomas Carlyle*. New York: Hambledon Continuum, 2006. Chronicles Carlyle's personal life and intellectual career and discusses his works.

Rosenberg, John D. "Carlyle and Historical Narration." *The Carlyle Annual* 10 (Spring, 1989): 14-20. Treats *The French Revolution* as an experiment in narrative form, an attempt to create a relevant literary structure.

Roy, G. Ross. "The French Reputation of Thomas Carlyle in the Nineteenth Century." In *Thomas Carlyle 1981: Papers Given at the International Thomas Carlyle Centenary Symposium*, edited by Horst W. Drescher. Frankfurt: Lang, 1983. Carlyle's relationship with Germany is well known, but his book on the French Revolution brought him to the attention of French readers. It was the first of his books to be translated.

Trela, D. J., and Rodger L. Tarr, eds. *The Critical Response to Thomas Carlyle's Major Works*. Westport, Conn.: Greenwood Press, 1997. Collection of reviews and essays about *The French Revolution* and Carlyle's other major works that date from the initial publication of Carlyle's works until the end of the twentieth century. The introduction discusses how Carlyle responded to his critics.

Friar Bacon and Friar Bungay

Author: Robert Greene (1558-1592)
First produced: c. 1589; first published, 1594
Type of work: Drama
Type of plot: Historical
Time of plot: Thirteenth century
Locale: England

Principal characters:
HENRY III, king of England
EDWARD, prince of Wales
LACY, earl of Lincoln
ROGER BACON, a Franciscan friar
BUNGAY, a Suffolk conjurer
JAQUES VANDERMAST, a German conjurer
ELINOR, princess of Castile
MARGARET, daughter of the keeper of Fressingfield Park

The Story:

When Prince Edward returns from hunting in a downcast mood, Lacy remarks on his lord's temper. It remains for Ralph, the court fool, to hit on the truth. The hunting party stopped for refreshments at the keeper's lodge in Fressingfield Park, and Prince Edward fell in love with Margaret, the keeper's daughter.

Plans are laid to win Margaret's love for Edward, but the maid is modest and will keep her virtue for her husband. Ralph proposes that Edward dress in the jester's motley and that Ralph dress as the prince. They will then go to Oxford and enlist the help of Friar Roger Bacon, since only magic will win over the girl. Lacy is to go to the fair at Harleston to spy on Margaret there and to press a suit on behalf of the prince.

At Oxford, Friar Bacon and his poor scholar Miles receive a deputation of learned doctors. Burden, their spokesman, asks about certain rumors they hear. It is said that Friar Bacon fashioned a great head of brass and with it he is going to raise a wall of brass around all of England. Bacon admits that he planned such a project. Burden doubts that even Friar Bacon can accomplish such a mighty deed.

To demonstrate his power, Friar Bacon has a devil bring a tavern host from Henley, a woman with whom Burden spent the previous day. Thus the doctors are convinced of Bacon's powers. At Harleston, Lacy approaches Margaret. Although the earl is dressed as a farmer, his manners are so elegant that Margaret is attracted to him. Lacy has a mind to press a suit in his own behalf.

At court, meanwhile, King Henry receives the king of Castile, his daughter Elinor, and the Emperor of Germany. Negotiations are under way to betroth Elinor to Prince Edward. The princess, having seen a portrait of Edward, is much inclined to love the prince. The emperor brings with him a German conjurer, Vandermast, to test his powers against the wise men of England. The royal party departs for Oxford to find Friar Bacon.

With the jester disguised as the prince and Edward disguised as a gentleman in waiting, the prince's party meets the friar and Miles at Oxford. An argument develops between Miles and the others. To save his scholar, Friar Bacon freezes Edward's sword in its scabbard. After rebuking the prince for trying to disguise himself, he invites Edward into his cell. There he lets the prince look into a magic glass that shows Margaret and Lacy at Fressingfield.

Friar Bungay is revealing the secret of Lacy's identity to Margaret as Edward watches from afar. Margaret is troubled, for she is in love with Lacy. When Lacy enters, he declares at once his desire to wed Margaret. Friar Bungay is about to perform the ceremony on the spot, but the anguished prince calls on Friar Bacon to stop the wedding. The friar obliges by striking Bungay mute and whisking him away to Oxford.

Edward, posting to Fressingfield in great haste, charges Lacy with treachery and threatens to kill him. Lacy admits his guilt and prepares to submit, but Margaret pleads valiantly for the cause of true love and begs Edward to kill her instead. Edward, marveling at his own weakness, changes his mind and gives his permission for Lacy to marry Margaret.

At Oxford, the emperor of Germany has Vandermast dispute with Friar Bungay. Bungay conjures up the tree that guards the Garden at Hesperides. In return Vandermast brings in Hercules and commands him to tear the branches from the tree. Triumphantly the German challenges Friar Bungay to make Hercules stop, but Bungay admits that he is vanquished. When Friar Bacon arrives, Hercules, to the emperor's chagrin, ceases his task immediately for fear of Bacon. To demonstrate the eminence of Oxford, Friar Bacon then forces Hercules to transport Vandermast back to Habsburg.

Two squires come to seek the hand of Margaret. Both are wealthy and insistent, and the keeper asks his daughter to choose between them. Margaret is evasive and puts off her answer for ten days, because she is sure Lacy will return by that time. After the squires leave, a messenger comes with a letter and a sack of gold. In the letter Margaret reads that Lacy chose to marry a Spanish lady-in-waiting to Princess Elinor, and he sends the gold as a dowry for her own wedding. In great grief, Margaret gives the gold to the messenger and vows to enter a convent.

Working in his cell, Friar Bacon is at the climax of his experiments, for with much labor he completes the brazen

head. Tired from wrestling with spirits, he lies down to sleep. Miles is to watch the head and wake his master as soon as it speaks. During the night the head makes a great noise and says, "Time is." Thinking those words unimportant, Miles rests on. The head makes more noise and says, "Time was." Again Miles does not arouse the friar. A third time the head speaks: "Time has been." Lightning flashes and a great hand appears and breaks the head with a hammer.

Then Miles awakens Friar Bacon, who knows at once that the blundering Miles ruined his work. No wall of brass will ever surround England. In his wrath the friar sends Miles to wander homeless with a devil to torment him. After he leaves Oxford, however, Miles makes the best of a bad situation. He gets on the devil's back and goes with him to Hell, where he is engaged as a tapster.

King Henry and the king of Castile are both pleased that Elinor and Edward make a match. Lacy, thinking still of Margaret, speaks so persuasively of her beauty that the king sanctions their marriage as well. Elinor is particularly gracious in suggesting a double wedding. The happy Lacy sets out for Fressingfield to seek his bride.

Friar Bacon breaks the sad news of the brazen head to Friar Bungay. As he finishes his tale, two young scholars come in to ask permission to look into Friar Bacon's glass; they want to see what their fathers are doing. The fathers, who are the two squires seeking Margaret's hand, are fighting a duel. As the sons watch, the squires are stabbed to death. The sons then fight and each mortally wounds the other. In sorrow, Friar Bacon breaks his magic glass.

In spite of her father's remonstrances, Margaret is preparing to enter a nunnery when Lacy rides up to claim his bride. Reproached for his cruel letter, he explains he wrote it to test her constancy. Margaret, yielding to his entreaties, accompanies him back to court. The double wedding is solemnized with royal pomp. Before the wedding feast Friar Bacon makes a prophecy of the future of England. He foresees a period of triumph and peace under a fair ruler who will exalt the glory of England over all other nations. Not understanding that reference to Queen Elizabeth, Henry calls the prophecy mystical and leads the guests to the dining hall.

Critical Evaluation:

Friar Bacon and Friar Bungay, a comical history play, is Robert Greene's most enduring work. It combines the romanticism and realism that are his hallmarks. The precise date of the play is unknown, so the play's relationship with Christopher Marlowe's *Doctor Faustus* (c. 1588) is unclear. Was Greene or Marlowe the borrower who drew upon the recent success of a fellow dramatist's conjuring play? Whichever came first, both works cater to the Elizabethans' curiosity about magic and sorcery, delight in theatrical horseplay, and pleasure in seeing ordinary people rise to power and influence. *Friar Bacon and Friar Bungay*, like *Doctor Faustus*, was frequently revived in the 1590's, two of many conjuring plays of the period.

Greene's main source was a mid-sixteenth century anonymous prose romance. The events in his drama of thirteenth century England are fictional, but there actually was a Roger Bacon at that time who allegedly practiced black magic at Oxford University (Greene's alma mater) and around whom legends developed. Despite Bacon's title, Bacon does not function as a churchman in the play, but is more like Merlin, the patriotic Arthurian sorcerer. Bacon's repentance speech late in the play reflects prevailing Elizabethan beliefs. Bacon's dalliances, however, unlike those of Faustus, are not frightening and do not lead to damnation, although they do cause deaths.

Noteworthy about *Friar Bacon and Friar Bungay* is how it brings together royalty, nobility, and commoners, preserving some traditional class barriers but breaking through others. Greene's idealistic portrait of a benevolently democratic aristocracy may reflect the outburst of patriotism in England following the 1588 defeat of the Spanish Armada. Indicative also of this nationalistic theme are Bacon's plan to build a protective brass wall around England and his humiliation of the German emperor's necromancer Jaques Vandermast.

Multiple plots are commonplace in Elizabethan comedies, and Greene's play is typical in this regard. Half of it is devoted to a presentation of Bacon's prodigious powers, which his foolish servant Miles partially thwarts. In his first appearance, with the visiting group of doubtful scholars, Bacon boasts of his skills. This prideful display announces his later troubles, but the magician does prove himself by evoking the devil and transporting the host of a pub to his cell. Later, he strikes his rival Bungay mute (to prevent him from marrying Lacy and Margaret). Then Bacon joins with Bungay in a conjuring contest against foreigners and commands the spirit of Hercules to carry Vandermast back to Germany. Bacon's one act of damnation is directed at Miles after the servant's ineptness destroys the friar's life work. When the devil comes for him, Miles, rather than being afraid, delights in the singular experience. The other half of the play revolves about the fair maid Margaret of Fressingfield, her multiple suitors, her loyalty to her love, and Prince Edward's magnanimity.

Edward at the start of the play is lovesick for Margaret, but seduction, not marriage, is his aim. Inhibited by his royal position, he relies upon his fool, Ralph, and friend, Lacy, to

advance his cause. When the plan fails, Edward denounces Lacy and Margaret but almost immediately reverses himself, recognizing his royal position and offering to give away Margaret in a wedding that will make her countess of Lincoln.

Friar Bacon and Friar Bungay is not as formless as it sometimes is said to be. The halves are linked by the presence of Bacon in both plots, but there are other, more important, parallels. The love story moves from joy through sadness to happiness, and the Bacon plot progresses from great heights to disaster and tragedy (the deaths of the suitors and their fathers) but again to joy. Further, in both plots, exceptional gifts (Bacon's magical abilities and Margaret's outstanding beauty) lead to misery that causes each to renounce the gift (he forsakes his magic, and she joins a convent). The play is a comedy, however, so everyone eventually is reconciled, and the last scene celebrates a double marriage and restoration of the natural order.

The critical assessment that Margaret is the first realistically portrayed and thoroughly believable female character in English drama has been superseded by the judgment that she is little more than a patient Griselda type. As such, substantive development of her personality would have been superfluous. She remains an interesting character. Her father respects her judgment regarding Lacy, deferring to her when the rival suitors—Lambert and Serlsby—ask him for her hand in marriage. She buys time with the rivals but later acts quickly—deciding to become a nun—after receiving Lacy's letter with news of his intention to marry another. When he comes to the convent, reveals that he only meant to test her, and asks her to marry, she renounces her vocation and agrees. Margaret's impulsiveness and the prince's sudden turnabout are not wholly credible, but these actions are in harmony with the rest of *Friar Bacon and Friar Bungay*, a romantic, not realistic, comedy.

"Critical Evaluation" by Gerald H. Strauss

Further Reading

Cartwright, Kent. "Robert Greene's *Friar Bacon and Friar Bungay*: The Commonwealth of the Present Moment." In *Theatre and Humanism: English Drama in the Sixteenth Century*. New York: Cambridge University Press, 1999. This analysis of Greene's play is included in a study of the roots of Renaissance drama, focusing on pre-Shakespearean plays written from 1490 through 1590.

Clemen, Wolfgang. *English Tragedy Before Shakespeare: The Development of Dramatic Speech*. Translated by T. S. Dorsch. New York: Barnes & Noble, 1961. Clemen concludes that the playwright does not maintain a "free and easy style," though he does praise the language of Miles and Simnel as being "robust and realistic."

Empson, William. *Some Versions of Pastoral*. New York: New Directions, 1974. This classic study shows that through the characterizations of Bacon and Margaret the playwright succeeds in developing a literary metaphor that likens magic and beauty and thus unifies the two plots.

Greene, Robert. *Friar Bacon and Friar Bungay*. Edited by Daniel Seltzer. Lincoln: University of Nebraska Press, 1963. Analysis of the play that deals with such matters as the problem of dating the play, Greene's use of his source, and occult science in the Renaissance.

Leggatt, Alexander. "Greene, *Friar Bacon and Friar Bungay*." In *Introduction to English Renaissance Comedy*. New York: St. Martin's Press, 1999. An analysis of Greene's play is included in this study of Renaissance comedy. Leggatt emphasizes the experimental nature of these plays and how they satirically mock the English court and city and country life.

Melnikoff, Kirk, and Edward Gieskes, eds. *Writing Robert Greene: Essays on England's First Notorious Professional Writer*. Burlington, Vt.: Ashgate, 2008. Several of the essays discuss Greene's plays and the theater of his day, including "From *Homo Academicus* to *Poeta Publicas*: Celebrity and Transversal Knowledge in Robert Greene's *Friar Bacon and Friar Bungay*" (c. 1589) by Bryan Reynolds and Henry S. Turner.

Muir, Kenneth. "Robert Greene as Dramatist." In *Essays on Shakespeare and Elizabethan Drama in Honor of Hardin Craig*, edited by Richard Hosley. Columbia: University of Missouri Press, 1962. Muir thinks Greene excelled as a prose writer, not as a playwright, but he respects the plotting of the play and shows how magic unifies it.

Parrott, Thomas Marc, and Robert Hamilton Ball. *A Short View of Elizabethan Drama*. New York: Charles Scribner's Sons, 1943. Despite its age, this remains an excellent critique of *Friar Bacon and Friar Bungay*.

Williams, Deanne. "*Friar Bacon and Friar Bungay* and the Rhetoric of Temporality." In *Reading the Medieval in Early Modern England*, edited by Gordon McMullan and David Matthews. New York: Cambridge University Press, 2007. Focuses on Greene's interpretation of medieval culture as reflected by the play.

Frithiof's Saga

Author: Esaias Tegnér (1782-1846)
First published: Frithiofs saga, 1825 (English translation, 1835)
Type of work: Poetry
Type of plot: Epic
Time of plot: Eleventh century
Locale: Scandinavia

Principal characters:
FRITHIOF, a Viking adventurer and fighter
INGEBORG, a noblewoman loved by Frithiof
HELGE and HALFDAN, brother kings in Scandinavia
HRING, a petty king married to Ingeborg

The Poem:

In the ancient days of Scandinavia lives a king named Bele who has two sons, Helge and Halfdan. King Bele also has a daughter, Ingeborg, who is very beautiful. As King Bele grows old and near death, he calls to him his friend of former days Thorsten Vikingsson, who has been loyal to the king in peace and in battle for many years and who is also near the end of his days. The king tells his sons of the help that Thorsten Vikingsson gave him in past days and warns them to keep the friendship of Thorsten's son, Frithiof.

Frithiof has grown up with the companionship of King Bele's daughter Ingeborg and her brothers. After the deaths of King Bele and old Thorsten, who are both laid to rest in burial mounds overlooking a fjord, the sons of Bele forget the warning that their father gave them, and their friendship toward Frithiof cools. When Frithiof, who has long loved Ingeborg, asks her brothers for her hand in marriage, they refuse his request. Frithiof, angered and humiliated, vows that he will have his revenge and that he never will carry out his father's request that he help the brother kings.

Not long thereafter, when King Hring makes war on the brothers, they send for Frithiof to help them. Frithiof, remembering his vow, continues to play at chess and ignores their summons. King Hring is successful in his campaign against the sons of Bele, and he makes them promise to give him Ingeborg as his wife. Meanwhile, Ingeborg has taken refuge in the temple of Balder. Frithiof, disdainful of the sanctity of the temple, visits her there, and they exchange rings, along with vows of love. Frithiof thus runs the risk of the god Balder's wrath.

To punish Frithiof for violating the temple, the brother kings send him to collect tribute from the inhabitants of the Faroe Islands. Frithiof, with his foster brother, sets sail for the Faroes in *Ellida*, the best ship in the north country. It is said of *Ellida* that it can even understand human speech.

During the voyage, a violent storm comes up and the ship almost founders. Frithiof breaks the gold ring he received from Ingeborg and gives the shards to his men, so that none of the crew might enter the kingdom of the sea goddess without gold. When the storm subsides—after the men conquer a pair of sea spirits riding against them on the backs of whales—the ship reaches the Faroe Islands in safety. Yarl Angantyr, ruler of the islands, lets the tribute be collected, and then Frithiof departs again for his homeland in Scandinavia.

Upon his return, Frithiof hears that the brother kings have burned his hall. He learns that the kings are celebrating the midsummer feast at the grove of Balder, and he goes there to confront them. He finds few people there, but among them are Helge and his queen, who is anointing the image of the god.

Frithiof throws the purse holding the tribute money he has collected into Helge's face, hitting him with such force that Helge's teeth are knocked out. Then, as he turns to leave, Frithiof sees on the arm of Helge's queen the great ring of gold he gave to Ingeborg when they exchanged vows. Frithiof snatches the ring from the queen's arm, and when she falls to the ground because of his violence, the god's image overturns into the sacred fire, which, blazing up, destroys the temple.

Helge pursues Frithiof to punish him, but Frithiof and his men have made pursuit on the sea impossible by damaging the royal ships. In his anger, Frithiof pulls with such might on the powerful oars of his ship that they break like kindling.

Frithiof's violence against Helge and his queen and his profanation of Balder's temple make the warrior an outcast from his homeland. A true son of the Vikings, he takes to the sea and battles with haughty sea kings, whom he slays. In spite of his outlawry, he permits traders to travel the seaways unmolested. When he has earned great glory as a fighter and much gold through his exploits, Frithiof seeks once again to return to his homeland in the north.

Disguising himself, he visits the land of the brother kings'

enemy, King Hring, who has long since married Ingeborg, Frithiof's beloved. Hring, recognizing Frithiof but not letting on that he does, commands that the warrior be seated next to him at the head of the table. Frithiof remains for some time in the hall of King Hring. Ingeborg, who has also recognized Frithiof, speaks but little to him, because she is now the wife of another man. She remembers that she and Frithiof once exchanged rings, and she is still in love with him.

During his stay with Hring, Frithiof saves the king and Ingeborg from death when their sleigh falls through some thin ice and into the water. Frithiof drags the sleigh, with its occupants and horses, back onto the surface of the ice. One day, while he and the king are alone in the woods, Frithiof is tempted to kill Hring while he sleeps, but he conquers his temptation and throws away his sword. Awaking, the king tells Frithiof, who is still disguised, that he has known from the first night who his guest is.

Frithiof wishes to leave the household of Hring, but the good king will not allow him to depart. Instead, Hring gives up Ingeborg to Frithiof and makes the warrior guardian of the kingdom. Soon afterward, Hring dies and Frithiof is named to succeed him on the throne. When Helge and Halfdan, the brother kings, go to war against their old enemy, they are defeated. Frithiof slays Helge in battle, and Halfdan is made to swear fealty to his conqueror.

Critical Evaluation:

A tale of ancient Scandinavia, *Frithiof's Saga* is told in a modern spirit by Esaias Tegnér. The old story is presented in a narrative poem of twenty-four cantos, each canto done in a different meter. Frithiof himself is more akin to a modern hero than he is to the great warriors of other Scandinavian tales. Tegnér's effort is similar to that of Alfred, Lord Tennyson, in that he attempts to shape the epic material of an ancient Norse story into nineteenth century poetic form. Although the poem lacks the simplicity and power of old Norse poetry, the imagery is memorable and the lyricism sweet and beautiful. Tegnér's long narrative poem displays an odd sort of virtuosity: The poem remains faithful to its ancient ancestor in theme and narrative detail, yet it is made up of a curious blend of Scandinavian and English images and rhetorical devices in twenty-four different meters.

Because of forces beyond their control, Frithiof and his beloved are parted, and Ingeborg marries another, King Hring. The hero gallantly respects the marriage, and the king to whom his beloved is married, by maintaining the proper courtly distance. *Frithiof's Saga* does not end tragically, however. Through Hring's benevolence, Frithiof and Ingeborg are reunited, and Frithiof satisfies his pride by defeating the brother kings. The magnificent reconciliation canto, rendered by Tegnér in blank verse, evokes the grandeur of Norse mythology and the theme of atonement.

Frithiof's Saga provided Tegnér with the opportunity to employ a pastiche of images and rhetorical devices. His rendering of each canto in a different meter demonstrates both virtuosity and preoccupation with the surfaces of poetry. Virtuosity for its own sake is no virtue, and it is regrettable that Tegnér did not choose to render his poem in a less obtrusive and more unified manner, for the work elevates style at the expense of content. Tegnér's use of imagery raises further concerns. For example, readers find the Norse blood-and-guts warrior amid Elizabethan roses and the lilies, nightingales, and vanished dreams of the English Romantics. The poem displays two or three obvious thefts from William Shakespeare, and perhaps another from Percy Bysshe Shelley. It may be that the Swedish poet wished to align his narrative poem with the English literary tradition. *Frithiof's Saga* was enormously successful when it appeared, becoming something of the poem of the Swedish people. It has been translated and read around the world.

Further Reading

Brandes, Georg Morris Cohen. *Creative Spirits of the Nineteenth Century.* Translated by Rasmus B. Anderson. 1923. Reprint. St. Clair Shores, Mich.: Scholarly Press, 1973. Includes an accessible discussion of Tegnér and his works that places *Frithiof's Saga* within its literary context.

Hilen, Andrew R. *Longfellow and Scandinavia: A Study of the Poet's Relationship with the Northern Languages and Literature.* 1947. Reprint. Hamden, Conn.: Archon Books, 1970. Explains the relationship between American poet Henry Wadsworth Longfellow and Tegnér, asserting that Tegnér was influential in the development of Longfellow's poetry.

Moffett, Judith, ed. and trans. *To the North! To the North! Five Swedish Poets of the Nineteenth Century.* Carbondale: Southern Illinois University Press, 2001. Features new English translations of some of Tegnér's poems, including *The Temptation of Frithiof*, book 19 of *Frithiof's Saga*. An introductory essay provides biographical information about the poet as well as critical discussion of his work.

Nolin, Bertil. "Tegnér: The Standard Bearer of Cultural Idealism." In *A History of Swedish Literature*, edited by Lars G. Warme. Lincoln: University of Nebraska Press, 1996. Provides an overview of the poet's life, an explanation of his cultural philosophy, and an analysis of his writing. Explains how during the late nineteenth century and much of the twentieth, Tegnér's work occupied a central position in Swedish cultural life, but it eventually was displaced by modernism and genres other than the verse narratives and meditative poetry that were Tegnér's specialty. A section about his verse narratives includes a discussion of *Frithiof's Saga*.

The Frogs

Author: Aristophanes (c. 450-c. 385 B.C.E.)
First transcribed: Batrachoi, 405 B.C.E. (English translation, 1780)
Type of work: Drama
Type of plot: Satire
Time of plot: Fifth century B.C.E.
Locale: Underworld

Principal characters:
BACCHUS, the god of wine and revelry
XANTHIAS, his slave
HERCULES, the mythological hero
CHARON, the ferryman of Hades
EURIPIDES, a famous Greek playwright
AESCHYLUS, another Greek dramatist

The Story:

Wishing to visit the underworld, Bacchus sets out with his slave, Xanthias, to visit Hercules, from whom the god of wine hopes to get directions for his visit to the lower regions. On the way, Xanthias grumbles and moans about his many bundles. Xanthias is actually being carried on a donkey, but

he complains until Bacchus loses patience and suggests that perhaps Xanthias would like to carry the donkey for a while.

Hercules, when consulted, suggests that Bacchus allow himself to be killed in order to arrive in the land of the dead. Bacchus wants to go there alive because he is anxious to see and to talk to the great playwrights; the critics tell him that all good writers are dead and gone. He is particularly anxious to meet Euripides. Hercules advises him to be content with the playwrights who are still alive. Bacchus argues that none of them is good enough. After getting directions from Hercules, he starts out, Xanthias still complaining about his bundles.

They come to the River Acheron and meet Charon, who ferries Bacchus across, insisting, however, that Bacchus row the boat; Xanthias walks around the margin of the stream because he dishonored himself by not volunteering for a naval victory. Xanthias tries to excuse himself on the grounds that he has sore eyes, but Charon refuses to listen.

While Bacchus and Xanthias talk to Charon, a chorus of frogs sets up a hoarse croaking, imitating the noisy plebeians at the theater with their senseless hooting. Bacchus sprains his back with his rowing and the frogs think his groans quite amusing.

Safely on the other side, Bacchus pays his fare and joins his slave. The two meet a monster, which Bacchus takes care to avoid until it turns into a beautiful woman. With difficulty, they find their way to the doorway of Pluto's realm, Xanthias still grumbling because of his heavy bundles.

At the entrance to Hades, Bacchus foolishly pretends to be Hercules—a mistake on his part, for Aeacus, the doorman, raises a clamor over the theft of Cerberus, the watchdog. When Aeacus threatens all sorts of punishments, Bacchus reveals who he really is. Xanthias accuses him of cowardice, but Bacchus stoutly denies the charge.

Bacchus and Xanthias decide to change characters. Xanthias pretends to be Hercules and Bacchus takes up the bundles his slave carries. When, however, servants of Proserpine enter and offer Xanthias a fine entertainment, Bacchus demands his legitimate character back.

Aeacus returns, eager to punish someone, and Xanthias gives him permission to beat Bacchus. Bacchus says that he is a deity and that he should therefore not be beaten. Xanthias counters by saying that since Bacchus is an immortal he need not mind the beating. Aeacus decides they both should be beaten soundly, and he finally decides to take them both to Pluto and Proserpine, to discover who is the deity. Aeacus says Bacchus is apparently a gentleman, and Xanthias agrees wholeheartedly, saying Bacchus does not do anything except carouse.

In Pluto's realm, they find two dead dramatists, Aeschylus and Euripides, fighting for favor. The rule in Hades is that the most famous man of any art or craft eats at Pluto's table until some more talented man in his field dies and comes to Hades. Aeschylus holds the seat Euripides is now claiming.

Aeacus says that the dramatists intend to measure their plays line for line by rules and compasses to determine the superior craftsman. The quarreling dramatists debate, accusing each of the other's faults. Aeschylus says he is at a disadvantage because Euripides' plays died with him and are present to help him, whereas his own plays still live on earth.

Bacchus offers to be the judge, whereupon each dramatist begins to defend himself. In the midst of their violent quarrel, Pluto appears. Bacchus orders each to recite from his own works. Euripides seems to have the worse of this contest, but Bacchus wisely refuses to judge so as not to make either playwright angry with him. Pluto wearily insists that he pick one winner and take his choice back with him to the upper world in order to stop needless rivalry in Hades.

At last, Bacchus votes for Aeschylus. Euripides complains at the choice. He is consoled, however, when Pluto says he might be sure of a good meal in the underworld, while Aeschylus will be burdened forever with the task of earning his living by his attempts to reform folly and evil in the world above.

Critical Evaluation:

The Frogs is deservedly one of the best-known plays of Aristophanes. It took the first prize for comedy on first being presented at an annual drama festival in Athens, and it continues over the centuries to retain much of its freshness and exuberance. As a depiction of the foibles and follies of men and gods alike, the play is great satirical fun. The high point of the comedy, however, is the witty debate between Aeschylus and Euripides as to which of them produced the better tragedies. Some knowledge is desirable of Aristophanes' opinions and the times in which he lived, of the Athenian crisis at the end of the Peloponnesian War, and of Aeschylus and Euripides.

The play starts with the absurdity that Bacchus braves the terrors of the underworld to bring Euripides back to life. On this conceit Aristophanes builds a farcical sequence of situations, all of which defy reason and probability. It is important to know that shortly before Aristophanes wrote *The Frogs*, *Bakchai* (405 B.C.E.; *The Bacchae*, 1781), Euripides' last play, was produced, in which Euripides portrayed Bacchus (Dionysus), who is both the god of wine and the god of the theater, as a powerful, mysterious, fearless, and vengeful being. It is therefore all the funnier that Aristophanes shows him as a weak, pedestrian, cowardly, and pacific god who is obviously flattered by Euripides and wants him brought back to life to continue the praise. The humor of the first half of *The Frogs* is devoted to exposing Bacchus as a fraud and, by implication, Euripides himself. *The Bacchae* was awarded first prize, posthumously; and the chorus of frogs in Aristophanes' comedy represents the popular clamor that greeted Euripides' play.

Having thoroughly routed Bacchus, Aristophanes brings Euripides and Aeschylus on stage to engage in comic debate. Euripides is depicted as an upstart in Hades. Recently dead, he tries to wrest the chair of honor from Aeschylus. Obviously, Aristophanes regarded Euripides as a base-born upstart in life as well, for the tragedian also appeared as a farcical character in *Acharnēs* (425 B.C.E.; *The Acharnians*, 1812) and *Thesmophoriazousai* (411 B.C.E.; *Thesmophoriazusae*, 1837), and he was made the butt of numerous jokes in other plays. The antagonism was largely due to Aristophanes' snobbery and conservatism, for he prided himself on coming from landed gentry.

Aristophanes thought that Euripides was partly responsible for the decline in Athenian politics and morality. There is no question that Euripides used tragedy to turn a light on current social issues and effect changes. This is the heart of the matter: The comic poet propagandized for conservatism, while the tragic poet urged reform. The importance of drama in Athenian life cannot be overemphasized. Public oratory and the theater were the only media, the only means of conveying propaganda to large audiences. Aristophanes' comments against Euripides are far more than mere fun or the prejudices of a clever conservative; in actuality they were part of a battle to control public opinion.

Some of the charges Aristophanes makes against Euripides in *The Frogs* could be leveled at himself as well. Impiety, near-colloquial verse, sordid passions, and characters who reason sophistically without any sincerity are all a part of his comic art. What Euripides had done in essence was to lessen the difference between tragedy and comedy; but what Aristophanes could not forgive was that Euripides tended to be a left-wing social reformer, tearing away at established institutions.

The truth is that Athenian politics and life did degenerate during Euripides' long career, but it would be as foolish to blame it on him as on Aristophanes. The real villains were those who initiated the Peloponnesian War and kept it going for twenty-seven years.

The Frogs can be read as a literary, social, or political tract by a very amusing dramatist. On the literary level, Euripides pokes fun at Aeschylus's bombast and theatricality, while Aeschylus ridicules Euripides' commonness of diction. When Aeschylus's lines of poetry are weighed against those of Euripides, the latter is shown quite literally to be a lightweight talent. Socially, Aeschylus is made to represent the old, heroic, patriotic virtues of Athens, whereas Euripides stands for the degenerate contemporary society. Aristophanes hints

that Euripides comes of lower-class people, and he states openly that his audience in Hades consists of felons, who love his sophistries.

Nevertheless, it is on the political plane that Aristophanes really indicts Euripides, suggesting that the demagogues learned their twisting logic from Euripides. In fact, the contest between Aeschylus and Euripides is finally settled over who offers the best advice politically. In this, Aeschylus wins hands down, and he is taken back to earth by Bacchus to teach the Athenians virtue. Aristophanes had no intention of playing fair. To him Euripides represented everything corrupt in Athenian society. Moreover, *The Frogs* was written in a time of crisis, when it was clear to many that Athens either had to make peace with Sparta or be ruled by her. The Peloponnesian War had yet one more year to go. In the middle of the play, Aristophanes makes a direct political plea to the audience, trying to convince Athenians so that they might avoid defeat. The wonder is that, given the author's bias and the times in which it was written, *The Frogs* is one of the most delightful comedies of any age.

"Critical Evaluation" by James Weigel, Jr.

Further Reading

Bowie, A. M. *Aristophanes: Myth, Ritual, and Comedy.* New York: Cambridge University Press, 1993. Presents criticism and interpretation of the mythic and ritualistic content of Aristophanes' comedies. Drawing from examples such as Dionysus's and Heracles' presence in *The Frogs*, Bowie considers the importance of mythology in Aristophanes' comedic plays in particular and in Greek drama in general.

Dover, Kenneth, ed. Introduction to *The Frogs*, by Aristophanes. New York: Oxford University Press, 1993. Dover's essay and commentary, which accompany Aristophanes' original text, offer a comprehensive overview of the structure and significance of the play.

Edmonds, Radcliffe G., III. "Descent to the Depths of Comedy: *The Frogs* of Aristophanes." In *Myths of the Underworld Journey: Plato, Aristophanes, and the "Orphic" Gold Tablets.* New York: Cambridge University Press, 2004. Edmonds's analysis focuses on how Aristophanes adapts the mythological tale of a journey to the underworld to create its satire.

Hall, Edith, and Amanda Wrigley, eds. *Aristophanes in Performance, 421 B.C.-A.D. 2007: Peace, Birds, and Frogs.* London: Legenda, 2007. A collection of papers originally delivered at a conference held in 2004. The papers discuss how Aristophanes' plays were staged at various times in

England, South Africa, France, and Italy, and analyze specified performances of *The Frogs, The Birds*, and *Peace*.

Harriott, Rosemary M. *Aristophanes, Poet and Dramatist*. Baltimore: Johns Hopkins University Press, 1986. Offers criticism and interpretation of Aristophanes' poems and plays. Sets *The Frogs* in the context of such other works as *The Clouds, The Knights*, and *The Birds*.

Lada-Richards, Ismene. *Initiating Dionysus: Ritual and Theatre in Aristophanes' "Frogs."* New York: Oxford University Press, 1999. Lada-Richards uses literary and anthropological approaches to examine how a member of Greek society would have viewed the play and Dionysus as a dramatic figure.

Littlefield, David J., ed. *Twentieth Century Interpretations of "The Frogs": A Collection of Critical Essays*. Englewood Cliffs, N.J.: Prentice-Hall, 1968. A collection of analytical papers examining Aristophanes' *The Frogs* in terms of style, characterization, dramatic theory, symbolism, and structure. Provides a spectrum of interpretations on the work's position in literature from classical times to the present.

Rothwell, Kenneth S., Jr. "The Literary Fragments of Aristophanes' *Knights, Wasps*, and *Frogs*." In *Nature, Culture, and the Origins of Greek Comedy: A Study of Animal Choruses*. New York: Cambridge University Press, 2007. Rothwell analyzes *The Frogs* and other comedies in which Aristophanes featured animal choruses. He maintains that these animal characters may be a conscious revival of an earlier Greek tradition of animal representation.

Silk, M. S. *Aristophanes and the Definition of Comedy*. New York: Oxford University Press, 2002. Silk looks at Aristophanes not merely as an ancient Greek dramatist but as one of the world's great poets. He analyzes *The Frogs* and the other plays to examine their language, style, lyric poetry, character, and structure.

Whitman, Cedric Hubbell. *Aristophanes and the Comic Hero*. Cambridge, Mass.: Harvard University Press, 1964. Explores Aristophanes' construction of heroes in his comedic plays and provides an overview of Aristophanic comedy. Considers the dramatist's lampooning of such contemporary figures in Greek society as the playwrights Euripides and Aeschylus in *The Frogs*.

From Here to Eternity

Author: James Jones (1921-1977)
First published: 1951
Type of work: Novel
Type of plot: Realism
Time of plot: Late 1941
Locale: Hawaii

Principal characters:
ROBERT E. LEE PREWITT, a U.S. Army bugler and boxer
MILTON ANTHONY WARDEN, an Army sergeant
ALMA SCHMIDT (LORENE), Prewitt's girlfriend and a prostitute
KAREN HOLMES, Captain Holmes's wife and Warden's lover
DANA HOLMES, an Army captain

The Story:

Robert E. Lee Prewitt, born in Kentucky and raised in the Great Depression as a hobo and on railcars, is a U.S. Army sergeant stationed in Hawaii in the Bugler Corps. After being passed over as first bugler despite his skill and experience—he has played a taps at Arlington National Cemetery—Prewitt decides to transfer to G Company. The transfer will cause him to lose his rank of sergeant and become a private, but he feels compelled to go through with it.

The head of G Company is Captain Holmes, who is also the head of the boxing team. He wants Prewitt, a talented welterweight boxer, to fight on the team. Prewitt refuses. He has given up boxing after accidentally blinding a sparring mate, thereby breaking a deathbed promise to his mother: He vowed never to hurt another person unless absolutely necessary. Holmes insists Prewitt fight. Prewitt continues to refuse. As a result, the members of the boxing team give him "the treatment," harsh physical discipline, in the hope of compelling him to fight.

Captain Holmes relies on First Sergeant Warden to run Company G for him, Holmes being more interested in making sure the regiment has a good boxing team than in company discipline and morale. Holmes's marriage to his wife Karen has become a sham. They have one son, but they are unable to have any more children. Holmes acquired a sexually transmitted disease, which he passed on to his wife, destroying her womb and requiring a hysterectomy. She no longer has much to do with her husband.

As Prewitt enters G Company, Warden begins an affair with Karen Holmes, the captain's wife. Karen has been the subject of rumors on the base: She has had an affair with at least one soldier, and it is popularly believed that she has had many such relationships. Warden is warned to stay away from Karen by Mess Sergeant Stark, who has had a relationship with the captain's wife himself and who is the source of many of the rumors about her.

Prewitt begins his stint as a private. He becomes friends with Maggio, an Italian from New York City. Prewitt and other privates write a blues song for the common soldier called the "Re-enlistment Blues." He also makes a trip to the brothels with Maggio. There, he meets a prostitute named Lorene; he later discovers that her real name is Alma Schmidt. They fall for each other immediately and spend the night in the brothel together feeling as if they were husband and wife. Alma has plans to move back to the mainland and settle down with the money she earns in the brothel, but she feels that Prewitt is beneath her. Because she was rejected by a rich man's son in her hometown, she believes that she must marry someone who is beyond reproach, not a common soldier. After a seduction, Prewitt moves in with Alma, who continues to work in the brothel as Lorene.

One night, a broke Prewitt tags along with Maggio to a gay bar. After plying the patrons for free drinks, Maggio and Prewitt accompany some of them back to a private apartment to continue drinking. Maggio gets drunk, runs out into the street, and, while Prewitt is trying to find him, gets into a fight with two military police officers. As a result, Maggio is thrown into the stockade.

Prewitt soon follows Maggio there. After fighting a private first class named Bloom, a middleweight in Holmes's boxing outfit, Prewitt knocks out a noncommissioned officer who pulled a knife on him. Prewitt spends more than three months in the stockade for this action.

The stockade is a place of brutality and cruelty. Guards beat the prisoners for minor offenses. They throw the prisoners into the "hole," a space of solitary confinement, and at one time beat a prisoner to death. One guard is reviled more than the others: Sergeant "Fatso" Judson. Prewitt resolves to kill Judson after he is released. Prewitt meets a mentor of Maggio, a prisoner named Jack Malloy, who orates on the na-

ture of society and the coming revolution. Maggio pretends to go insane and, after being transferred to a mental hospital and shipped to the mainland, is dishonorably discharged. Malloy escapes from the stockade.

Nine days after being released from the stockade, Prewitt goes to town and waits for Judson to leave a bar. He calls him over and offers to fight him. In the ensuing fight, Prewitt is wounded in the side but is able to stab Judson with a knife just below the sternum, killing him. Prewitt, injured and bleeding, flees to Alma's. Malloy is sought for the murder.

Warden spends a vacation with Holmes's wife but discovers they are not compatible. He returns to the barracks a man again alone.

Prewitt is now absent without leave (AWOL); he spends his days recovering from his wound, reading books, and drinking. On December 7, 1941, the Japanese bomb Pearl Harbor. As this trauma is absorbed by Prewitt, he realizes he is a soldier without an army and drinks steadily for over a week. Finally, he resolves to make his way back to G Company. On a golf course, he confronts some military police officers who suspect that he might be a spy and decide to take him to the jail. Prewitt tries to run away, but he is shot in the chest and dies in a sand trap.

Both Karen and Alma take a ship back to the mainland. Karen attracts the interest of a member of the Army Air Forces, and Alma romanticizes the story of Prewitt for Karen, explaining that Prewitt was a pilot in the Army Air Forces who was killed during the Japanese attack.

Critical Evaluation:

James Jones was born in 1921 in Robinson, Illinois. He joined the U.S. Army in 1939 and served in New York and Puerto Rico. In December, 1941, he was stationed in Hawaii, making him the only major American writer to witness the Japanese attack on Pearl Harbor. Jones won the National Book Award in 1951 and moved to France in 1959. He spent much of the rest of his life in Paris but identified as an American. He died in 1977. He wrote novels and short stories. Among his novels, the World War II trilogy—consisting of *From Here to Eternity*, *The Thin Red Line* (1962), and *Whistle* (1978)—is the most notable. *From Here to Eternity* is the novel for which he is mostly remembered. Film adaptations were made of *From Here to Eternity*, *The Thin Red Line*, and Jones's second novel, *Some Came Running* (1957).

In Jones's fiction, individuals find themselves fighting against faceless institutions and unstoppable natural forces to gain a sense of identity. In the novels, foot soldiers confront Army bureaucracy and incompetent officers. Known mostly as a writer of war fiction, Jones recycled many characters in his novels. For example, Prewitt, Warden, and Stark in *From Here to Eternity* all reappear as essentially the same characters with different names in *The Thin Red Line* and *Whistle*. This unity of character types and theme allows readers to approach each of Jones's novels as one element in a larger whole.

Realistic in its treatment of Army life, *From Here to Eternity* is considered Jones's best novel. It includes many vivid and memorable scenes, including those in which Prewitt fights against the Army machine for a sense of identity, its brutal stockade scenes, and finally the attack on Pearl Harbor. The text's realist effect may gain its force from the sheer length of the novel, which comprises some 850 pages.

The novel explores the need to achieve and maintain individuality within an institution, the Army, that denies that very individuality. Prewitt attempts to retain his autonomy by refusing to box for Captain Holmes. Warden attempts to accomplish the same thing by having an affair with the captain's wife. Maggio makes the attempt by fighting with a group of military police officers. By the end of the novel, these individuals are given no real status at all: Prewitt lies dead in a sand trap, Warden's relationship with Karen Holmes ends, and Maggio has deserted the Army and is in hiding on the mainland. By then, the Army has no time to search for him, having entered World War II.

The novel's structure, coupled with the song "Re-enlistment Blues," suggests the low stature of the individual. The novel is divided into five sections, each focused on a different aspect of Army life. In the first and shortest, "The Transfer," Prewitt joins G Company. The second, "The Company," introduces the people with whom Prewitt serves. The third, "The Women," introduces Alma. The fourth, "The Stockade," depicts Prewitt in the military prison, while the last, "Re-enlistment Blues," portrays him trying to rejoin his outfit after the Japanese bomb Pearl Harbor. These chapters are reflected in the song Prewitt cowrites, a song whose lyrics end the book. The song "Re-enlistment Blues" tells the story of a soldier who is paid out by the Army but is robbed after a night of pleasure with women and alcohol. Without his money, he is forced to reenlist. Prewitt's own struggles reflect this narrative, but his own reenlistment is not the result of needing money but rather of the Japanese bombing. Prewitt reenlists not for personal reasons but because the country does need him: Circumstances convince him that the individual does not matter.

Much of Jones's success in *From Here to Eternity* comes from his achievement in creating well-rounded, realistic characters. Maggio tries to achieve some individuality with humor and talk but ultimately is run out of the Army. Bloom,

a middleweight boxer, cannot accept not being part of the group of soldiers, so he kills himself. Karen Holmes, a women misunderstood by others, is rendered sympathetic by the personal tragedies she experiences. Alma's decision to become a prostitute cuts her off from her own emotions to such an extent that she cannot at first tell Prewitt she wants to marry him. After he dies, she is unable to face the truth of his demise and invents a romantic fiction of his heroic death to replace reality. These and other characters give the novel its depth.

Brett Conway

Further Reading

Aldrich, Nelson W., ed. *Writers at Work: The "Paris Review" Interviews*. New York: Viking Press, 1967. Includes an interview with Jones in which he discusses *From Here to Eternity* and other works.

Carter, Steven R. *James Jones: An American Literary Orientalist Master*. Urbana: University of Illinois Press, 1998. Focuses on Jones's representation of eastern cultures and their implications for his understanding of American identity.

Didion, Joan. *The White Album*. 1979. Reprint. New York: Farrar, Straus and Giroux, 1990. Personal account by the author of the extent to which the real Honolulu has been shaped for her by Jones's representation of it in *From Here to Eternity*.

Giles, James R. *James Jones*. Boston: Twayne, 1981. Detailed study of Jones's work.

Hassan, Ihab. *Radical Innocence: Studies in the Contemporary American Novel*. Princeton, N.J.: Princeton University Press, 1961. Examines the themes most prevalent in American literature written after World War II. Compares *From Here to Eternity* to other novels to place it within its literary context and lineage.

Jones, Peter G. *War and the Novelist*. Columbia: University of Missouri Press, 1976. Discusses the relationship between war and the form of the novel, particularly the ability of novels to represent the trauma at the heart of wartime experience.

Messenger, Christian K. *Sport and the Spirit of Play in Contemporary American Fiction*. New York: Columbia University Press, 1990. Discusses the role of boxing in *From Here to Eternity* and the role of sports in American literature.

Morris, Willie. *James Jones: A Friendship*. Garden City, N.Y.: Doubleday, 1978. Recounts the author's relationship with Jones.

The Fruit of the Tree

Author: Edith Wharton (1862-1937)
First published: 1907
Type of work: Novel
Type of plot: Social realism
Time of plot: Late nineteenth century
Locale: United States

Principal characters:
JOHN AMHERST, an assistant mill manager
BESSY WESTMORE, owner of the mills, and John's first wife
JUSTINE BRENT, John's second wife, a nurse
MR. LANGHOPE, Bessy's father
DR. WYANT, Justine's former suitor

The Story:

When Justine Brent, a nurse who is visiting Mrs. Harry Dressel at Hanaford, volunteers to care for Dillon, an operator who was injured at Westmore Mills, she is approached by John Amherst, the assistant manager of the mills. Amherst deplores the miserable living and working conditions of the mill workers and, since Dillon's accident was a result of these conditions, he wants to use his case to show the need for improvement to Bessy Westmore, the newly widowed owner of the mills who is due to make an inspection tour the following day.

The next day, Amherst conducts Bessy through the mills. Touched by Dillon's case, Bessy decides to stay at Hanaford for a while. She recalls that she and Justine attended school together before Justine's parents lost their wealth.

Bessy and Amherst make plans to improve the living conditions of the workers, and this association finally leads to their marriage. Amherst, hoping to make Westmore Mills a model of humanitarianism, is disillusioned to learn that Bessy is not willing to sacrifice the time or the money to accomplish this end.

Some time later, Justine comes to Lynbrook, the Amherst country house, to be a companion to Bessy, who is not feeling well. Amherst, meanwhile, spends most of his time at the mills in Hanaford. Bessy, to compensate for Amherst's long absences, begins to entertain lavishly, at the same time confiding her bitterness and loneliness to Justine. Later, Amherst decides to manage a friend's cotton mill in the South.

Justine writes to Amherst saying that Bessy needs him. Amherst replies that he will not return and, in a postscript, asks her not to permit Bessy to ride a particularly spirited horse they own. Bessy, learning of his request, later takes the horse out into the frost-covered countryside. There Bessy suffers an accident that seriously injures her spinal cord. She is taken home and looked after by Dr. Wyant, a local doctor whose proposal Justine refused some time before. A surgeon and various other consultants are also summoned. Bessy remains paralyzed after an operation; Justine knows that Bessy

will never recover. By this time, Amherst is on a business trip into a remote part of South America, and Bessy's father is in Europe.

One day, while Justine is caring for her, Bessy regains enough consciousness from her opiated state to plead with Justine to relieve her pain. Justine, convinced that she is doing the right thing, later gives Bessy an overdose of morphine. When Dr. Wyant comes into the room, Justine tells him that Bessy is dead. Dr. Wyant seems to sense what happened.

A year and a half later, Amherst is back at the Westmore Mills. Bessy left half her fortune to Cicely, her daughter by her first marriage, and the other half to Amherst. He lives at Hanaford and continues his plans of reconstruction. In the meantime, Justine is taking care of Cicely and an intimate friendship develops between the two. Later, when she goes to visit Mrs. Dressel in Hanaford, Justine meets Amherst again, a romance develops between them, and they are married. Cicely goes to live with her grandfather. Justine takes an active part in Amherst's work.

Dr. Wyant, who left Lynwood and married, now needs money, and he comes to Justine and threatens to expose her mercy killing of Bessy unless she arranges to have Amherst write him a letter of recommendation to Mr. Langhope, who can give him a responsible hospital post. Justine, realizing that Dr. Wyant is a narcotics addict, cannot in her conscience arrange a recommendation for him. When she goes out of the room, Amherst comes in. Learning that Dr. Wyant is in financial straits, Amherst writes him a letter of recommendation in gratitude for his services to Bessy. On her return, Justine tells her husband that Dr. Wyant is not qualified for the hospital post. Dr. Wyant, in retaliation, charges Justine with the mercy killing and leaves. Intellectually, Amherst approves of Justine. Emotionally, he is horrified at what she did. Their relationship becomes strained.

When Dr. Wyant is appointed to the hospital post, Amherst remembers the letter of recommendation. He knows that if

Mr. Langhope is told about Dr. Wyant's addiction to narcotics, the doctor will in turn disclose Justine's crime. Amherst tells Justine that if Mr. Langhope thinks that she was in love with Amherst when she killed Bessy, he and Justine will have to give up the mills, go away, and start a new life. Justine secretly goes to New York to see Mr. Langhope and tells him the truth about Dr. Wyant and herself. She then promises to disappear if Mr. Langhope will continue on his former terms with Amherst. Mr. Langhope agrees.

Justine, returning to Hanaford, tells Amherst that Mr. Langhope took the news very well. In the course of the following months, Amherst's horror of Justine's crime causes their relationship to deteriorate even more. At last, Justine goes to Michigan to resume her nursing career, thus fulfilling her promise to Mr. Langhope.

A year later, Cicely becomes ill. Mr. Langhope, realizing that she needs Justine's love, asks Justine to come back to Amherst so that she can be close to Cicely. When Amherst learns why Justine left him, he feels love for her and remorse for his attitude. They continue, however, to feel somewhat estranged.

About a year later, Amherst, speaking at the dedication of the mill workers' new recreational center, gives a stirring tribute to Bessy who, he says, drew up the plans herself. Justine realizes that Amherst is referring to the plans for a gymnasium that Bessy intended for her own pleasure at Lynbrook, in open defiance of Amherst's wishes. Although angry, Justine keeps Bessy's secret.

As they leave the dedication, Amherst tells Justine how good he feels about improved conditions at the mill. They walk away hand in hand.

Critical Evaluation:

It is clear from its opening scene that *The Fruit of the Tree* is about class conflict in the era of industrialization at the time around the beginning of the twentieth century. The novel opens with John Amherst, the idealistic assistant manager of the Westmore mills, standing over the hospital bedside of an injured worker. Amherst is determined to show the mills' new owner, Bessy Westmore, that this latest accident is the result of the brutality inherent in a factory system fueled by a profit motive. He wants to "awaken" Bessy, a pampered, unthinking member of a leisure class that wants generous profits supplied as unobtrusively as possible. Edith Wharton brings together the two classes, embodied in Amherst and Bessy, in a struggle over the improvement of the lives of the mill workers.

In depicting this class struggle, Wharton also brings together two kinds of narrative: social realism and love. Bessy is first drawn into Amherst's world. She comes to the ugly mill town; she tours the noisy, dirty mills; she weeps at the plight of the ill-treated, malnourished, and exhausted workers. Her sympathetic reactions, as well as her plans for a nursery and a night school, promise future reforms. The novel begins with Amherst guiding Bessy through rows of pounding machines, but it subtly turns its focus to the relationships between individual hearts and minds. Amherst is attracted to Bessy's physical beauty and charm, which he interprets as outward signs of her moral and spiritual beauty. He marries her, but this action pulls him away from Westmore more than it connects Bessy to it. Amherst's work at Westmore, although it is described as his life, takes place out of sight, away from and in conflict with his personal and domestic concerns at Lynbrook, Bessy's home.

Amherst attempts to resist Bessy's world of luxury, keeping himself aloof from her party guests and encouraging her to trim her expenses so that money can go into the mills. He views himself as caught between "sacrificing" the mills to his wife's need for luxury and "sacrificing" his wife to the mills. When they are not in the forefront of the novel, the Westmore mills serve as the influential backdrop for the rest of the story. The novel evolves into a troubled mixture of love story and social realism. The mills and the mill workers become little more than abstractions, points of contention between husband and wife, the yardstick by which they measure their failing marriage. Even after Bessy's death and Amherst's marriage to Justine Brent, a nurse whose heart and mind are more attuned to his, the work of improvement at Westmore has an abstract quality, uniting the two in the chill atmosphere of high principles.

Wharton uses the imagery of hands and machines to emphasize the dehumanizing atmosphere of the worlds of both the working and the leisure classes. The mill hands, such as Dillon's arm, are merely objects caught up in the great machine of industrialization. Bessy's world is equally mechanical and empty, despite its glittering sophistication and luxury. Amherst sees her world of ease as "mental and spiritual bondage," fearing that it "might draw him back into its revolutions as he had once seen a careless factory hand seized and dragged into a flying belt." Justine, too, recognizes the mechanical quality of Bessy's household, getting "a queer awed feeling that, whatever happened, a machine so perfectly adjusted would work on inexorably," despite Bessy's crippling injury. Existence itself becomes "the machinery of life."

Amherst is transformed from a truly revolutionary thinker viewed with suspicion by the upper class into a bland paternal figure who has settled "down into a kind of mechanical altruism" and who stands within the confines of the rich as he surveys the little kingdom that he has created. Early in the novel, Justine wonders about the "wings" that one sprouts "when one meets a pair of kindred shoulders," and wonders how well Amherst's are doing under the constrictive clothing of his new social position. By the end of the novel, Wharton reveals how much those wings have atrophied. When Amherst hears how Justine killed Bessy out of a sense of love and respect, a truly radical defiance of science and religion, he is horrified. His wings of mercy and radicalism have atrophied. He exacts a high price from Justine. His unspoken censure of Justine and his conveniently revisionist memory of a saintly Bessy are moral failings.

Despite the novel's sometimes radical critique of the factory world as brutalizing and the leisure world as empty and dehumanizing, the social import of *The Fruit of the Tree* is ultimately conservative. The narrative operates with a dual movement: It recognizes class conflict, but at the same time it attempts to efface that conflict. Real, and largely irreconcilable, social conflict is hidden behind the trappings of a love story in the same way that the real conditions of labor at Westmore are finally hidden behind flower beds and fresh paint for the dingy houses that line the grim streets of the mill town. The final irony of the novel is that Amherst mistakenly believes that Bessy was planning to build a "pleasure-house" for the mill workers when what she really wanted was an extravagant gymnasium for herself.

In this novel, Wharton responds to social concern about industrialization in America by turning polemic into fiction and using it not only to reflect that concern but also to manipulate it. She takes on the important but potentially dangerous subject of factory reform and then successfully transforms that material into something that will please the greatest number of people—a romance and a success story. She rewards Amherst with the fulfillment of his dreams, and she gives material improvements to the factory workers in return for their patient silence. The upper class, too, is happy. Its members have new outlets for their self-important philanthropic endeavors. The brutal factory system described so graphically at the beginning of the novel becomes a kind of extended family at the end. The happy ending for the Westmore workers helps to assuage the anxieties of a public increasingly aware of horrible factory conditions. The problems inherent in the new wealth of industrialization thus become more acceptable in the glow of upper-class philanthropy, love, and duty.

"Critical Evaluation" by Judith Burdan

Further Reading

Ammons, Elizabeth. *Edith Wharton's Argument with America*. Athens: University of Georgia Press, 1980. Comprehensive study of Wharton's fiction, focusing on her depiction of women and women's issues. Reads the novel as an attack on patriarchal power.

Bell, Millicent, ed. *The Cambridge Companion to Edith Wharton*. New York: Cambridge University Press, 1995. Collection of essays, including a critical history of Wharton's work, discussions of Wharton and race and the science of manners, and "*The Fruit of the Tree*: Justine and the Perils of Abstract Idealism" by James W. Tuttleton.

Carlin, Deborah. "To Form a More Imperfect Union: Gender, Tradition, and the Text in Wharton's *The Fruit of the Tree*." In *Edith Wharton: New Critical Essays*, edited by Alfred Bendixen and Annette Zilversmit. New York: Garland, 1992. Analyzes Miltonic echoes and Edenic allusions. Describes the way in which Wharton uses marital incompatibility in order to examine various other irreconcilable social issues.

Farwell, Tricia M. *Love and Death in Edith Wharton's Fiction*. New York: Peter Lang, 2006. An insightful look at Wharton's beliefs about the nature of love and the way they reflect her philosophical views, namely those of Plato and Charles Darwin. Wharton's own shifting feelings on the role of love in life are revealed in conjunction with the shifting role that love played for her fictional characters. Chapter 4 provides an analysis of *The Fruit of the Tree*.

Goodwyn, Janet. *Edith Wharton: Traveller in the Land of Letters*. New York: St. Martin's Press, 1990. Discusses Wharton's use of specific landscapes and explores her consistent concerns with ideas of place. Argues that the number of contentious issues Wharton covers in the novel leads to a confusion of aim and direction.

Lee, Hermione. *Edith Wharton*. New York: Knopf, 2007. An exhaustive study of Wharton's life, offering valuable insights and pointing out interesting analogies between her life and her fiction.

Wershoven, Carol. *The Female Intruder in the Novels of Edith Wharton*. Rutherford, N.J.: Fairleigh Dickinson University Press, 1982. Focuses on Wharton's disruptive and often defiant heroines. Sees two intruders in the novel who link the work's different subjects.

Wolff, Cynthia Griffin. *A Feast of Words: The Triumph of Edith Wharton*. New York: Oxford University Press, 1977. A superb psychological study of Wharton's life and artistic career. Perceives Justine's need to find fulfillment as a woman as a core issue of the work.

G

Gabriela, Clove and Cinnamon

Author: Jorge Amado (1912-2001)
First published: Gabriela, cravo e canela, 1958
　(English translation, 1962)
Type of work: Novel
Type of plot: Social realism
Time of plot: 1925-1926
Locale: Ilhéus, Bahia, Brazil

Principal characters:
GABRIELA, a beautiful young mulatto
NACIB SAAD, the Syrian-born proprietor of the Vesuvius
　Bar
MUNDINHO FALCÃO, a young cacao exporter and rising
　political reformer
COLONEL RAMIRO BASTOS, the rugged old political boss of
　Ilhéus
COLONEL MANUEL OF THE JAGUARS, a planter from the
　outlands
COLONEL JESUÍNO MENDONÇA, a cuckold
COLONEL AMÂNÇIO LEAL, a former bandit chief
PROFESSOR JOSUÉ, a young teacher
TONICO BASTOS, the most elegant man in Ilhéus and a
　ladykiller
COLONEL CARIOLANO RIBEIRO, a wealthy plantation
　owner
GLORIA, his mistress
FATHER BASÍLIO CERGUEIRA, a worldly priest
JOAO FULGÊNCIO, a good-natured skeptic
QUINQUANA and FLORZINHA DOS REIS, the spinster sisters
　of an old Ilhean family
DONA ARMINDA, Nacib Saad's neighbor and a widow

The Story:

In the mid-1920's, the Brazilian provinces are suffering under the political, social, and economic dominance of the *coroneis*. These "colonels," who run the local organization of both major political parties unchallenged, who dictate at whim all manners and morals, and who hold, often by violence, the huge estates that supply the money upon which all provincial life depends, are the direct administrators of a feudal society. They rule vast territories through a complicated system of allegiances built upon favors, kinship, and power. In the country around Ilhéus, a seacoast town in the province of Bahia, the grip of the colonels, given sinews by a boom in the international market for cacao, remains anachronistically strong. A challenge comes to that feudal order, as represented by the colonels, in the person of Mundinho Falcão, a

rich, energetic, progress-minded young man from Rio de Janeiro.

Unlike most of the colonels, who are self-made men, Falcão is the son of an illustrious family whose influence extends into the highest reaches of the national government. He exiles himself from the high life of Rio de Janeiro for three reasons: to make his own fortune, to forget a woman, and to accomplish needed social reforms. One of the colonels recently murdered his wife and her lover. The fact that she had a lover at all reveals some cracks in the old order. That no effort is made at first to punish the colonel, in observance of the region's unwritten law, indicates that, for the time being at least, the old order survives as an effective force.

Meanwhile, Nacib Saad, a fat, gentle Brazilian from Syria

and the owner of the Vesuvius Bar, loses his cook, whose appetizers and tidbits had largely accounted for his considerable success. Fortunately for him, however, a continuing drought in the backlands brings a steady stream of homeless migrants to Ilhéus looking for work. Nacib is becoming desperate when he discovers among them Gabriela, whose cinnamon-colored skin and scent of clove enhance her equal and prodigious talents for cooking food and making love. Gabriela represents a way of life that is older and more essentially Brazilian than any of the ways represented by either the colonels or Falcão. She embodies the idea of *convivência*— of varied and mingling races and classes mutually dissolving and living together in harmony and absolute democracy— that was a Brazilian tradition and ideal.

Falcão seeks to operate on the body of society, rechanneling its old systems into new ones, but Gabriela unconsciously operates upon its soul. Every man in town adores her and few of the women are jealous. When election time arrives, the colonels find their influence whittled away to the vanishing point. In a last attempt to save their ascendancy, the more reactionary of them attempts to arrange the assassination of a powerful political chief who defected to Falcão. The attempt fails, and Falcão's forces of reform are swept into office, not without his privately acknowledging, however, that his promised reforms are only temporary and have to lead to even greater changes.

Nacib's attempt to transform Gabriela into a married and respectably shod little bourgeoise ends in the discovery that her love is as naturally democratic as her ancestry. She has slept with any man in Ilhéus lucky enough to be handsome. As her husband, poor Nacib is shocked, but not for long. Gabriela still loves him, and he learns, too, in the course of a short estrangement that was disastrous for the business of the Vesuvius Bar, that he likewise still loves her. Wild and free, the mulatto woman is as unregimentable as she is desirable, as indomitable as she is beautiful. She finds herself no longer his unhappy wife but once again established as Nacib's happy cook and mistress. All other factions—the colonels' and Falcão's—are reunited in freedom to celebrate new prosperity and progress for Ilhéus. The colonel who shot his wife is sent, as testimony to a new reign of law, to prison.

Critical Evaluation:

Gabriela, Clove and Cinnamon is a complex novel that marks an important change in the direction of Jorge Amado's writing. The new direction represents a fresh, invigorating movement in twentieth century fiction in general. Earlier in his career, Amado favored novels in a political vein written in the mode of gritty realism. Starting with *Gabriela, Clove*

and Cinnamon, however, Amado's fictive canvases become brighter in tone, his plots more wildly imaginative (including frequent use of the supernatural), and his characters more varied and colorful. The development of the novel of realism, from Miguel de Cervantes through the great nineteenth century realists such as Leo Tolstoy and Gustave Flaubert, seems to have reached a climax with the modernists—Marcel Proust, James Joyce, and William Faulkner prominent among them. Thereafter, in the eyes of many readers and critics, a stagnation set in, not relieved until the appearance of the great Latin American Magical Realists such as Jorge Luis Borges and Gabriel García Márquez. Amado has earned a place among this latter group.

Although *Gabriela, Clove and Cinnamon* is a complex novel, it is not difficult reading. In contrast to many of the modernists, who often seem to design deliberately inaccessible fictive structures, most Magical Realists seem to take as a primary goal the ancient one of delighting and entertaining the reader. One senses that Amado is writing in much the same spirit as the authors of the chivalric romances that Cervantes so entertainingly parodies. Rather than Magical Realism—a term borrowed from art criticism and often misleading when applied to literature—the term "romance" better prepares readers for the style and technical strategies of Amado's later novels.

Gabriela is within the Romantic tradition; she would be out of place in a novel of traditional realism, which would emphasize her ordinariness. Amado's Gabriela, however, is extraordinary to the point of mythic proportions. Gabriela does not walk but "glides." She is not simply a capable cook and lover but is "perfect" as both. When she enters and smiles, the whole room glows; when she is unhappy, the whole world loses its zest for life. Professor Josué maintains that a prospective lover should not write for her a sonnet—a sophisticated, polished, and studied form—but a ballad, with its implications of raw emotions, passion, and violence. Subthemes of the novel include adultery, jealousy, and violent reprisal, the stuff of ballads and romances.

The novel is divided into chapters that alternate between the romantic crises of Gabriela and her associates and the political crises faced by Mundinho Falcão as he attempts to invade the entrenched power structure of Ilhéus. The principals in this latter plot line—Falcão, Colonel Ramiro Bastos, and Colonel Cariolano Ribeiro—are based, if not on specific historical individuals, on actual historical types. Amado provides richly detailed backgrounds for these characters, along with astute analyses of the economic, cultural, and political forces that shape them. This historical realism shows Amado augmenting the Romantic aspects of his work. *Gabriela,*

Clove and Cinnamon is every bit as political as the novels from the earlier phase of his career, but here he skillfully has it both ways: He teaches readers important political lessons while amusing them.

The two plot lines and the two goals—to teach and to entertain—are not mutually exclusive. Falcão is not part of a distant political establishment of which Gabriela and the denizens of her world are only vaguely aware. Falcão knows Gabriela and her husband, Nacib Saad, personally. More important, Falcão is touched by Gabriela's world of emotion and romance. How much of Falcão's drive to succeed, the readers might well ponder, derives from the fact that he fled to Ilhéus to make his fortune after an unhappy love affair? Is Colonel Bastos's stubborn clinging to power based on genuine convictions or on the same sort of irrational, ingrained self-centeredness that drives men to see their wives as property and to murder suspected adulterers?

Just as the actors in the political plot line are caught up in the passions of Gabriela's romance plot line, Gabriela is also affected by currents in the realistic political world. She makes her way to the city, for instance, as part of the historical movement of peasants from the countryside to urban areas, where they too often find their old mores and customs eroded. Hence, Gabriela begins to lose her zest for life—and the world around her likewise—when her husband insists that she wear shoes.

The action in the novel covers exactly one year, implying the cyclical nature of the changes besetting Gabriela's and Falcão's worlds. All are victims of change, just as all are in various ways instigators.

"Critical Evaluation" by Dennis Vannatta

Further Reading

Brower, Keith H., Earl E. Fitz, and Enrique Martínez-Vidal, eds. *Jorge Amado: New Critical Essays*. New York: Routledge, 2001. One of the essays, "*Gabriela, Clove and Cinnamon*: Rewriting the Discourse of the Native" by Joanna Courteau, focuses on the novel. Other essays provide a broader critical overview of Amado's work, while one recounts a visit by Amado and his wife to Pennsylvania State University in 1971.

Chamberlain, Bobby J. "Escape from the Tower: Women's Liberation in Amado's *Gabriela, cravo e canela*." In *Prismal/Cabral: Revista de Literatura Hispanica/Caderno AfroBrasileiro Asiatico Lustitano* 6 (Spring, 1981): 70-86. Discusses feminist issues in the novel. Chamberlain sees Gabriela as a victim of male power and a source of liberation.

Ellison, Fred P. *Brazil's New Novel*. Berkeley: University of California Press, 1954. Examines the political impulse of Amado's early novels. Useful for judging the change in Amado's writing represented by *Gabriela, Clove and Cinnamon*.

Hall, Linda B. "Jorge Amado: Women, Love, and Possession." *Southwest Review* 68 (Winter, 1983): 67-77. Describes male and female relationships in *Gabriela, Clove and Cinnamon* and other Amado novels.

Keating, L. Clark. "The Guys and Dolls of Jorge Amado." *Hispania* 66 (September, 1983): 340-344. Discusses *Gabriela, Clove and Cinnamon* in the context of other Amado novels in which the author's ultimate aim is to reform society. Amado's most frequent strategy is the use of heavy irony.

Martin, John, and Donna L. Bodegraven. "Mythical Patterns in Jorge Amado's *Gabriela, Clove and Cinnamon* and Bruno Barreto's Film *Gabriela*." In *Film and Literature: A Comparative Approach to Adaptation*, edited by Wendell Aycock and Michael Schoenecke. Lubbock: Texas Tech University Press, 1988. Focuses on the characterization of Gabriela and Nacib and the novel's sources in classical myth.

Robinett, Jane. *This Rough Magic: Technology in Latin American Fiction*. New York: Peter Lang, 1994. Amado is one of the writers whom Robinett includes in her examination of the relationship of technology to magical and political realities in Latin American literature. Includes a discussion of the representation of technology and of technology and women's place in *Gabriela, Clove and Cinnamon*.

Galileo

Author: Bertolt Brecht (1898-1956)
First produced: Leben des Galilei, first version, 1943; second version (in English), 1947; first published, 1952; revised, 1957 (English translation, 1960)
Type of work: Drama
Type of plot: Historical
Time of plot: 1609-1637
Locale: Florence, Padua, Rome, and Venice, Italy

Principal characters:
GALILEO GALILEI, an astronomer and a professor of mathematics
VIRGINIA, his daughter
LUDOVICO MARSILI, his pupil
ANDREA SARTI, Galileo's apprentice, his housekeeper's son
PRIULI, a curator
SAGREDO, Galileo's friend
LITTLE MONK, Galileo's disciple
BARBERINI, a Roman Catholic cardinal, and later Pope Urban VIII
BELLARMIN, a Roman Catholic cardinal
COSIMO DE MEDICI, Galileo's patron

The Story:

It is 1609, and the forty-six-year-old Galileo Galilei, a renowned if impoverished professor of mathematics at the University of Padua in Italy, is forced to live frugally and in humble surroundings despite his taste for luxury and good food. Through it all, he maintains an obvious love of learning. When his housekeeper's son, Andrea Sarti, brings in a model of the geocentric universe based on the ancient Ptolemaic system, Galileo patiently demonstrates how in actuality the earth orbits around the sun, as had been hypothesized by the Polish astronomer Nicolaus Copernicus.

A young aristocrat named Ludovico Marsili arrives, seeking a tutorship under Galileo. Marsili explains that he had seen primitive telescopes in Amsterdam, where they were being sold in the streets. Galileo sends Andrea out to purchase lenses for his own experiments with the device. He promises Priuli, the curator, that he will soon have something practical to offer the authorities in Venice.

Galileo gives a demonstration of his own improved telescope to the Venetian senators and arsenal artisans; afterward, he has his fourteen-year-old daughter, Virginia, present it to the city as a gift, to be copied and openly sold. Priuli tells Galileo that the gift will improve Galileo's financial situation. However, the curator visits Galileo and his friend Sagredo to complain that Galileo had deceived the city fathers. A ship from Holland had arrived in Venice and was about to unload a shipment of telescopes to be hawked cheaply on every street corner. After the curator's indignant exit, Galileo explains to Sagredo what his improved telescope has revealed to him: evidence that there is move-

ment in the previously believed fixed and rigid crystalline spheres of the universe. To Virginia and Sagredo, Galileo announces his intention to move to Florence and seek the patronage and protection of the wealthy and powerful Medici family.

In Florence, Galileo is quickly disappointed by the cautious and politic courtiers of Cosimo de Medici, who is but a boy of nine years. However, Galileo earns a temporary victory when Christopher Clavius, the chief astronomer at the Papal College in Rome, confirms Galileo's findings. Soon after, Galileo encounters Cardinal Barberini at a masked party and dinner at the home of Cardinal Bellarmin. Barberini (who will later become Pope Urban VIII), takes a practical view of Galileo's findings, which leads Galileo to believe that he has a strong ally at the papal court, despite the guarded manner in which Barberini expresses his support. At the same party, another Church leader, an inquisitor, urges Virginia to look after her father's spiritual well-being with a veiled hint that she should spy on him.

Galileo's growing renown wins for him many converts, including the Little Monk, who, when first confronting Galileo, strongly argues a humanitarian's case for not disseminating Galileo's Sun-centered theory of the solar system. The Little Monk's thirst for truth proves too powerful, however, and he is soon drawn into Galileo's inner circle.

Galileo remains content to study without publishing his findings. Then, just as his eyesight begins to fail from having repeatedly looked at the sun in his telescope, Galileo grows bolder. Word comes that the pope is dying and that his most likely successor would be Cardinal Barberini, which gives Galileo hope that the Church might be more receptive to his radical ideas. However, Galileo soon begins to pay a price for his dedication and relentless pursuit of evidence to prove his theories. His daughter is the first to suffer. Marsili, with stern warnings to Galileo about his revolutionary concepts, breaks off his eight-year engagement to her.

In the meantime, Galileo's radical ideas have become common knowledge in the Italian streets. Ballad singers and dancers enact in song and pantomime what the authorities consider the dangerously heretical and seditious notions of Galileo. In catchy choruses and engaging dances, they sing with raucous abandon that Galileo is a thinker bent on destroying the Bible. Indeed, friends and supporters, like Matti, an iron founder, try to warn Galileo. Gradually even they desert him.

Under pressure from the Church, Cosimo de Medici withdraws his protection, as does Pope Urban VIII, the former Cardinal Barberini, who instructs his cardinal inquisitor to threaten Galileo with torture to exact a confession of heresy and ultimately a recantation. To the dismay of his close followers, who await him at the Florentine ambassador's house in Rome, Galileo recants. The news is announced to his family and friends by the church bells of Saint Marcus, followed by the town crier's reading of the text of the recantation. Galileo, his abjuration done, sits quietly by himself, unnoticed among the commotion in the street, listening to the words of the crier.

Nearly nine years have passed since the recantation. Feeling betrayed, Galileo's disciples had long turned away from him. Only Virginia believes that her father had done the right thing and that he has saved himself from damnation. Galileo himself, still vigorous but nearly blind, remains a de facto prisoner of the Inquisition, under house arrest in a country villa near Florence, under the care and watchful eye of Virginia. Secretly, he works at night on his scientific opus. He hides his papers inside a globe.

Galileo wants to get his theoretical work out to the burgeoning European scientific community. His former apprentice, Andrea, visits him, reluctantly, to ask about his health. After admitting that he had recanted out of a fear of being tortured, Galileo commits the manuscript to Andrea's care. Andrea conveys the document across the Italian frontier on his way to Amsterdam, ironically even as a group of children harass an old woman by accusing her of being a witch, the very kind of superstitious excesses that Galileo's radical theories would ultimately end. Soon, Galileo's scientific opus, *Discorsi*, will be published and, in turn, will commence the golden age of science.

Critical Evaluation:

Bertolt Brecht, in *Galileo*, covers close to three decades in Galileo's life. Although the dramatic action is clearly grounded in a historic event, Brecht freely shapes those events into a coherent narrative designed to raise difficult and thorny questions about the relationship not only between science and religion but also between free thinkers and the oppressive social and political structures within which such radical thinkers are seen as dangerous and heretical. Although Brecht would revisit the play and essentially alter its thematic argument during his career, the basic elements of the story stayed relatively constant.

That there are two extant versions of *Galileo*, each worked on by Brecht, testifies to the play's central position within Brecht's canon. Indeed, Brecht was working on a third production at the time of his death. The play has a pivotal place in understanding Brecht's evolution as an artist who conceived of drama as a vehicle for promoting thought and encouraging action as a way to change corrupt social and political conditions outside the theater. For twenty years as an evolving experimental dramatist, the playwright returned to the dilemma suggested by the historic events surrounding Galileo's stand against the powerful Catholic Church of Baroque Italy.

The first version was written quickly in 1938 (in less than two weeks) and under enormous and immediate pressure. Brecht was in Switzerland and felt keenly the encroaching menace of the Third Reich. Later, after World War II, in 1947 in the United States, Brecht returned to the play in the wake of the unsettling implications of the bombings of Hiroshima and Nagasaki in Japan and the beginnings of the atomic age. Taken together, the two versions reveal Brecht's complicated vision of the position of truth in a vast material universe in which, as Galileo had first posited four hundred years earlier, humanity's central position had become laughingly absurd. Brecht, himself profoundly influenced by the argument of the Theater of the Absurd, found in Galileo the threshold figure who had first exposed the comforting superstitions of religion and the faith in a perfect universe designed and controlled by a creator God. However, Brecht's reading of the implications of science as it emerged and religion as it waned reveals his own deep-seated anxieties over the triumph of science. Together, the two readings of Galileo form Brecht's larger theme: the heroic individual willing to search for truth must ultimately accept the responsibility to the greater community.

Structurally, the two versions of the play are quite similar. In both versions, *Galileo* is a chronicle play that in structure and technique is reminiscent of the history plays of the English Renaissance. Brecht had freely adapted and produced one of these, Christopher Marlowe's *Edward II* (pr. c. 1592, pb. 1594), in 1924. To some extent, *Galileo* also resembles Brecht's epic theater pieces, but it is Brecht's only major and original example based on the life of an actual person. The play is divided into scenes or vignettes that cover several years, from 1609 to 1637, six years before Galileo's death in 1643. In the manner of the chronicle play, these vignettes are isolated episodes, not always linked in a causal way. Although the plot advances in chronological order, it is thus more like a composite or montage than a piece structured from logically interrelated parts. As in other epic theater plays, most of the individual vignettes contain a *gestus* or dramatic kernel, sometimes a line or phrase, around which the scene is built.

Brecht used the theater to teach rather than merely entertain. He had worked to prevent the audience from slipping into the traditional suspension of disbelief and getting "involved" with character and plot. *Galileo* thus mingles different styles and techniques to maintain distance from the audience. Although some scenes are relatively conventional, many scenes are more symbolic and expressionistic. Although Brecht himself felt that the play was too traditional in technique, these vignettes are both unconventional and highly imaginative. In scene 11, for example, during the investiture of Cardinal Barberini as Pope Urban VIII, Barberini, dressed in the outsized papal clothing, listens to the cardinal inquisitor who wants to silence Galileo as a heretic. By the time he is buried under the heavy clothing of his new office, Barberini's open-mindedness has become equally buried under the papal panoply, and he permits the inquisitor to proceed against Galileo. In the brief scene, to the growing annoyance of Barberini, there is a persistent off-stage shuffling of feet that the cardinal inquisitor claims belongs to a select gathering of the faithful; it also, however, suggests the aimless shuffling of humanity as ubiquitous and ignorant as locusts.

Other expressionistic passages occur in scene 9, in which a ballad singer spreads Galileo's theories to a carnival gathering, and, to a lesser extent, in scene 6, which occurs during a masquerade dance and dinner at the house of Cardinal Bellarmin. In both scenes, Brecht uses symbolic devices charged with implications for the protagonist. In scene 6, Bellarmin and Barberini wear masks, which they raise or lower as the situation requires; their actions suggest that they are astute and pragmatic politicians, quite capable of masking their true beliefs as the winds of necessity dictate. However, Galileo, as Barberini remarks, has no mask to hide behind; he deals not with policy with but scientific truth, which

makes him both vulnerable and defenseless. In scene 9, after the ballad singer has given a narrative account in song of the impact of Galileo's theories on the Church and society and after much riotous and irreverent behavior by many characters, a procession begins, led by a float supporting a huge figure of Galileo. The effigy holds a Bible with pages crossed out and mechanically turns its head from side to side to deny the infallibility of scripture. A voice then proclaims "Galileo, the Bible killer!"; this prompts the people to laugh with loud delight. It is a scene full of spectacle, unlike anything else in the play.

Although both versions of the play employ such Brechtian stage techniques to manipulate audience involvement, it is Brecht's thematic argument that changed radically. In the historic figure of Galileo, Brecht found a malleable character able to embody two significantly different readings of science that together reflect the changing cultural environment before and after World War II.

The initial version of the play (wr. 1938) tested the contentious debate inevitable when science confronts religion, or more specifically, the tension inevitable when observation and logic contend with faith and superstition. Brecht, himself in elective exile from Germany and observing the emergence of Nazi extremism and its manipulation of propaganda, saw Naziism's harsh suppression of any ideas that conflicted with its extreme social and political doctrines. For Brecht, the figure of Galileo embodies the daring and defiant spirit of truth and the courage that it takes to speak the truth in the face of entrenched and powerful resistance.

The defining symbol here for Brecht is the telescope itself: When Galileo invites reluctant authorities in Venice to simply peer into it, to look at the sky, to see for themselves the simple truth of his observations, they decline. Brecht exploits this tension between honest vision and willful blindness. Galileo has simply seen the truth of things. He is not responsible for the implications of his discoveries. Using the new pope as the antagonist, Brecht considers Galileo the voice of honesty and science, with its vested faith in observation and demonstration, as the search for that truth.

Galileo is far from a paragon of virtue—he attempts to claim credit for inventing the telescope, manipulates his trusting daughter, is vain and unattractively obsessed with money, and ultimately recants in the face of Vatican pressure. Brecht is not interested in idealizing the scientist—Galileo is compelled largely by self-interest. Galileo's capitulation before the Church and its barbaric threat of torture is seen not so much as cowardly as a complicated (and entirely understandable) strategy of survival and enlightened self-interest. When, in the closing scenes, Galileo, under de facto house arrest, secures the transmission of his controversial findings outside the reach of Rome—and when he secretly smuggles out his revolutionary manuscript through the agency of his former student—he emerges as the embattled spirit of defiance, disgraced and held in contempt by a world that could not perceive the stakes nor grasp science's eventual triumph. Four centuries later, however, audiences understand the implications of Galileo's heroic actions. In Galileo's final speech, Brecht clearly sees the *Discorsi* itself as a manifestation of the triumph of truth, a celebration of knowledge unfettered by context, of curiosity as its own reward, and of science as its grandest expression.

When Brecht revisited the play immediately after World War II, much in the world had changed, most prominently the cultural perception of science. The optimistic celebration of the courageous individual and the self-evident reward of investigation and the scientific endeavor were sorely tested by the troubling implications of Hiroshima. In the 1947 version, Galileo is far less courageous—Brecht does not emphasize the smuggled book (indeed its existence is revealed long before the closing scene and is thus denied its dramatic positioning). Rather, Galileo's harsh self-assessment of his motivations closes the play. That self-assessment stresses not so much how Galileo has failed science by kowtowing to the Vatican authorities but rather how he has failed the greater good, how in his narrow quest to understand the material universe he had allowed himself to lose sight of the scientist's ultimate responsibility to address the welfare of the human community—to ease human existence. Science, he reasons, must be more than contribution.

It is clear that Brecht brought to this reading of science his assessment of the work of those brilliant scientists, most prominently J. Robert Oppenheimer, who had pursued the creation of the atomic bomb as a grand-scale research project, disregarding the reality of its eventual use. Brecht alters the character of Galileo, and tarnishes the tragic aura of the first version of the play, to condemn the scientist as one who had squandered his considerable gifts and is guilty of the great sin of scientists since Faust: arrogance.

Brecht, in turn, softens the portrayal of the Church authorities and mitigates their antagonism. The speeches by Little Monk in scene 7, extolling the virtues of a Heaven in which God oversees all operations and ensures grandeur and purpose to the meanest of lives, are far more moving than any delivered by Galileo. In this version, Galileo ends a ruin of a man—what emerges with especial poignancy is the fate of the common folk, brought on stage in the carnival scene midway through the play. The audience inevitably feels sadness for the common rabble who, even as they recount with

such manic urgency the death of the Bible, have been left, unknowingly, in a material universe that will ultimately deny their lives meaning.

Thematically, then, the two readings of Galileo need to be taken together. The two readings of the historic Galileo create a single parable that addresses the question that has defined science since Galileo first peered through the telescope: What is the reward of knowledge? Brecht challenges his audience with a complicated and provocative answer: truth must be tempered with responsibility, knowledge is not self-justifying, and truth cannot exist in a consequence-free environment.

John W. Fiero; revised by Joseph Dewey

Further Reading

Esslin, Martin. *Brecht: The Man and His Work*. Rev. ed. Garden City, N.Y.: Anchor Books, 1971. A seminal study of Brecht that remains significant because of its insights into Brecht's own theories of drama and the relationship of his works to communist ideology.

Fuegi, John. *Bertolt Brecht: Chaos, According to Plan*. New York: Cambridge University Press, 1987. Offers a detailed chronology and reviews the production problems of the 1947 staging of the play with Charles Laughton in the title role. Includes a useful selective bibliography.

Gray, Ronald. *Brecht: The Dramatist*. New York: Cambridge University Press, 1976. An excellent introduction to Brecht, focusing exclusively on his plays, his dramatic theory, and his theater.

Hayman, Ronald. *Bertolt Brecht: The Plays*. Totowa, N.J.: Barnes & Noble, 1984. A short, succinct study by a major Brecht biographer. An excellent starting place for further study of Brecht's plays. Relates *Galileo* to Brecht's Marxist ideology, and discusses his practical reasons for writing the play.

Hill, Claude. *Bertolt Brecht*. Boston: Twayne, 1975. A good critical introduction to Brecht, with a chronology and bibliography. Focuses the discussion of *Galileo* on Brecht's artistic intention in the different versions of the play.

McNeill, Dougal. *The Many Lives of Galileo: Brecht, Theatre, and Translation's Political Unconscious*. New York: Peter Lang, 2005. A Marxist study of how the play was developed for the English-language stage. McNeill examines various English translations and productions by Charles Laughton, Howard Brenton, and David Hare.

Thomson, Peter, and Glendyr Sacks, eds. *The Cambridge Companion to Brecht*. 2d ed. New York: Cambridge University Press, 2006. Collection of essays offering numerous interpretations of Brecht's work, including examinations of Brecht and cabaret, music, and stage design; his work with the Berliner Ensemble; and key words in his theory and practice of theater. Chapter 10 discusses *Galileo*.

Unwin, Stephen. *A Guide to the Plays of Bertolt Brecht*. London: Methuen, 2005. Contains analyses of many of Brecht's plays, and discusses his theories of drama, his impact, and his legacy. Designed as an accessible introduction to Brecht for students, teachers, and other readers.

The Gambler

Author: Fyodor Dostoevski (1821-1881)
First published: Igrok, 1866 (English translation, 1887)
Type of work: Novel
Type of plot: Psychological realism
Time of plot: Mid-nineteenth century
Locale: Germany

Principal characters:
ALEXEY IVANOVITCH, a young gambler
THE GENERAL, a Russian aristocrat
POLINA, his stepdaughter
MADEMOISELLE BLANCHE, a French adventurer
THE MARQUIS DE GRIEUX, a factitious French nobleman
ASTLEY, a young English capitalist
ANTONIDA TARASEVITCHEVA, the General's wealthy old aunt

The Story:

Alexey Ivanovitch returns to Roulettenburg, a German resort, after two weeks in Paris. He is a tutor in the family of a Russian general who comes to the resort to repair his dwindling fortune. The General woos an apparently wealthy young Frenchwoman, Mademoiselle Blanche. Polina, the General's stepdaughter, is attracted to Mademoiselle Blanche's alleged distant relative, the Marquis de Grieux. Alexey is Polina's creature; he loves her and accepts any humiliation at her hands.

Alexey goes to the casino with money Polina gives him. After winning a tidy amount, he feels that his stay in Roulettenburg will affect his life seriously. Believing that he cannot lose at the gambling tables, Alexey tells Polina that hereafter he will gamble only for himself. Polina, however, aware of her power over Alexey, easily persuades him to share his winnings with her.

An affluent young English capitalist, Astley, comes to Roulettenburg and, much to the General's discomfort, diverts the attentions of Mlle Blanche, who is growing tired of waiting for the General's old aunt to die. The General telegraphs Moscow every day to inquire about the condition of the old lady, who, he is sure, will leave him a fortune.

It is soon evident that Astley is in love with Polina. Alexey, suspecting the French pair to be impostors, wants to get away from the machinations of Roulettenburg existence, but his love for Polina holds him. At the casino he loses a large amount of Polina's money; his possession of the money arouses renewed interest in the General on the part of Mlle Blanche. The General, it seems, is deeply in debt to de Grieux.

Unable to win with Polina's money, Alexey offers to win with his own and to lend her whatever she wants. Alexey hopes that he can win Polina by becoming wealthy through gambling. He confesses his ardent love for her, and when he tells her that he can even commit murder for her, she impishly orders him to speak in French to a stuffy German baroness who is passing by with her husband. After Alexey brashly insults the Germans, he is discharged by the General, despite his plea that he was mentally aberrant during the escapade. Alexey manages to maintain his self-respect when he tells the General, who apologizes to the baron for Alexey's behavior, that he is capable of making his own apologies, that as the son of a nobleman he objects to the General's patronizing treatment. The General, fearful of the consequences of Alexey's further impetuosities, unsuccessfully tries to mollify the youth.

De Grieux, as mediator, tells Alexey that any further indiscretion on his part might spoil the chances of the General's marriage to Mlle Blanche. He also promises that the General will reemploy Alexey soon and will continue, meanwhile, to pay him his salary. Alexey, however, chooses Astley to be his second in a duel with the baron. De Grieux then produces a letter from Polina asking Alexey to drop the matter. The young man obeys, although he knows for certain that Polina loves de Grieux.

Astley indirectly confirms Alexey's suspicions that Mlle Blanche and de Grieux are adventurers. During previous exploits at Roulettenburg, Mlle Blanche made advances to the baron and, at the direction of the baroness, was escorted out of the casino by the police. Alexey suspects the General of being indebted somehow to Mlle Blanche, and Polina of being involved with the French couple.

The General's old aunt, Antonida Tarasevitcheva, arrives from Moscow with a large retinue. Quite alive, she wickedly chides the General about his urgent solicitations and criticizes him for squandering his children's inheritance. The General is visibly shocked by her arrival. Accompanied by the General's party, the old lady visits the casino and wins fabulously at the gaming tables. In her triumph she gives money to her servants and to beggars.

Polina becomes more of an enigma to Alexey when she has him deliver a letter to Astley. Despite the General's pleas to the young tutor to prevent Antonida from gambling away her fortune, Alexey and the old lady frequent the casino together. Obsessed with the fever to win, she loses heavily. When she prepares to return to Moscow, she invites Polina to return with her, but Polina declines. Antonida, unable to resist one last try at the gambling tables, again loses heavily. She converts bonds into cash and again loses. The old lady now possesses nothing but land and the houses on it; she borrows money from Astley in order to return to Moscow.

The General's inheritance having been lost at roulette, Mlle Blanche and de Grieux break off relations with him and prepare to leave Roulettenburg. The General is a ruined man. Polina is distracted by her impending loss of de Grieux, but she is shaken out of her infatuation when de Grieux offers her consolation money from the proceeds of the General's property, which was mortgaged to de Grieux. In distress, Polina turns to Alexey, who goes to the casino and wins a fortune for her to hurl in de Grieux's face. She spends the night with Alexey in his hotel room. The next morning she takes his money, then throws it in his face. She flees to Astley. Alexey goes with Mlle Blanche to Paris, where he lives with her while she spends her winnings. Tired of the life of an adventuress, Mlle Blanche, persuaded by Alexey, decides to marry the General.

Now a confirmed gambler, Alexey returns to the gambling tables of the German resort towns. Once he goes to jail for debt. In Homburg he sees Astley, who tells him that Polina, recuperating from an illness, is in Switzerland with Astley's family. Meanwhile the General dies of a stroke in Paris, and Mlle Blanche receives his inheritance from Antonida, who dies in Moscow. Alexey regretfully reminds Astley of Polina's infatuation for de Grieux and is momentarily hopeful when Astley tells him that Polina sent him to Homburg to bring Alexey back to her. Alexey knows that he has no choice, really—he has given his heart and soul to gambling.

Critical Evaluation:

Fyodor Dostoevski was every bit as erratic, volatile, irresponsible, and contradictory in his personal life as any of his fictional characters. He created most of his works in the face of extreme pressure and adversity that, more often than not, were the product of his own actions. *The Gambler*, a novel he probably never wanted to write, resulted from such a self-created pressure, a situation as pathetic and comic as the book itself.

In 1865, in severe financial difficulties (a frequent condition), Dostoevski signed a contract with Stellovsky, an unscrupulous publisher, in which he agreed to furnish a new novel by November 1, 1866, or else grant Stellovsky the right to publish all of his works royalty-free for nine years. As of October 1, Dostoevski had nothing on paper. In desperation he hired a stenography student and began to dictate. It was one of the most important decisions of his life. Prodded by the shy, awed, but firm and sensible young lady, Anna Grigorievna Snitkina, Dostoevski completed the novel in less than a month and salvaged his financial future. He also acquired, in Anna, a second wife who put an efficiency and order into his life that considerably eased his last years and freed him to concentrate on the writing of his greatest works.

The intense pressure under which *The Gambler* was composed is no doubt one reason why, except for *Zapiski iz podpolya* (1864; *Notes from the Underground*, 1913), it is the most directly personal, even autobiographical, of his works of fiction. The primary motifs in *The Gambler* are frustrated love and compulsive gambling, two conditions that dominated Dostoevski's life in the years immediately preceding its writing. The book's narrator, Alexey Ivanovitch, resembles the Dostoevski of that period in many ways, and Polina Alexandrovna is a thinly disguised re-creation of Polina Suslova (note the names), a student half his age, whom he met in 1862 while on his first European trip. It was on this same tour that he also began to gamble. Thus, Alexey's experiences in Roulettenburg are loosely based on a confused and traumatic trip the novelist took with Polina Suslova in 1863. Consequently, the passions of love and gambling were inextricably bound in Dostoevski's mind and, in *The Gambler*, he renders them in all of their complexity.

These motifs, however, do not actually become central until quite late in the book. The first two-thirds of the novel concentrates on the seriocomic machinations of the general's party as they vie with one another and with old "Granny" Antonida Tarasevitcheva. Except for the narrator and Polina, the characters, even the colorful old lady, are one-dimensional, almost caricatures. The general is a sophisticated Russian quasi-aristocrat who, cut off from his native roots, is the easy, pathetic victim of all West European temptations. De Grieux is the stock French adventurer: stylish, cultivated, shallow, and corrupt. The Englishman, Astley, is likewise a national type: stolid, laconic, honest, and dull. Mlle Blanche is the French seductress: beautiful, coaxing, playful, free with sex and other people's money but essentially selfish and shrewd (it is she who finally ends up with Granny's money). Even Antonida is a stereotype: the headstrong, obstinate, outspoken, outrageous old woman.

If individually the characters are little more than clichés, however, collectively they provoke a colorful sequence of comic situations that make the first two-thirds of the novella exciting and amusing. Then, as Dostoevski comes to focus the book more intensely on Alexey and Polina, the other characters retreat into the background but continue to provide a grotesque comic counterpoint to the more serious antics of the principals.

The association of Alexey's love for Polina with his addiction to gambling is made early in the novel when she asks him to play roulette for her. Thus, from the beginning, Polina shows a dependence on Alexey, but, at that point in the novel, there is little he can do to help her. One of the most important, if subtle, movements in the book is the manner in which Alexey gradually ascends from the position of a disdained inferior to that of a sought-after superior who gains powers over the others—the general, de Grieux, and finally Polina—and then rapidly loses it all.

Ostensibly, Alexey's power derives initially from his role as the old woman's "adviser" and then from the fortune he wins gambling, but the real source of it probably lies in his lack of identity and commitment. Because he has little interest in appearances and social postures, he has a great advantage over the others. As they strive to protect and enhance their social, financial, and romantic positions in the group, Alexey moves around freely and unobtrusively, capitalizing on his associates' failures and weaknesses. He becomes progressively absorbed by his two passions, Polina and gambling; however, he cannot translate his advantages into permanent victory but must ultimately destroy himself pursuing these addictions.

Polina is a fascinating mixture of femme fatale and passionate victim. She loves Alexey yet feels a need to demean him. When he seriously expresses a willingness to kill himself for her, she reduces it to the comic by suggesting that he insult a German baron. She mocks his vow to "kill himself for her" but is excited by it. She fears being in his power but comes to him in her hour of need. In the novel's enigmatic climax, when she offers herself to him, her behavior is erratic, volatile, almost hysterical; she rapidly alternates between abjectly demeaning herself, stridently justifying her behavior, belittling and berating Alexey, and proclaiming her lasting love for him. Then, after spending the night with him, she flings the money into his face and flees.

Alexey is perhaps even more puzzling. He both loves and hates Polina. He abjectly submits to her every whim, yet he also wants dominance, perhaps both at the same time. His feelings for her are inevitably bound up with his gambling compulsions. At the point when she offers herself to him, he feels the need to rush out to the gaming table. As he feverishly plays, he forgets about her. After he wins, he hurries back and empties his pockets before her almost as an integral part of the lovemaking ritual. When she leaves him, he casually enters into an unexpected affair with Mlle Blanche and gives her free rein to dissipate his modest fortune, which she quickly does. Many critics have seen this sudden shift in his character as unlikely and, after considering the pressures on the author, have dismissed it as a quick and easy resolution to the story.

However, in the light of Dostoevski's association of Alexey's compulsive gambling with his love for Polina, the ending makes definite psychological sense. Rationally, the hero's love for Polina has as its object the consummation of the affair; the gambling is a way of quickly procuring the money necessary to support the romance. Alexey, however, is not essentially a rational creature but one driven by needs and emotions that he does not fully comprehend. It is the intensity of the experience of pursuing Polina, not the physical actuality of the woman, that really enraptures Alexey, and, likewise, it is the excitement and danger of gambling, and not the monetary outcome, that captivate him. It is even possible that, given his taste for self-humiliation, Alexey gambles to lose rather than to win. Having "won" Polina, he casts money at her to provoke her rejection of him; having won the fortune, he subconsciously wants it taken from him. Thus, in *The Gambler*, Dostoevski not only explores frustrated love and compulsive gambling but also analyzes the dynamics of psychological self-destruction, creating in Alexey a character type that was to become central in his most powerful novels.

"Critical Evaluation" by Keith Neilson

Further Reading

Frank, Joseph. *Dostoevsky: The Miraculous Years, 1865-1871*. Princeton, N.J.: Princeton University Press, 1995. The fourth book of a five-volume biography. Contains extensive biographical information and readings of the novels.

Hlybinny, Uladzimer. *Dostoevski's Image in Russia Today*. Belmont, Mass.: Nordland, 1975. Traces Dostoevski's life from childhood onward. Covers what is mostly unknown in Dostoevski's writing as well as what is popular. A large and complete book.

Jackson, Robert Louis. *The Art of Dostoevsky: Deliriums and Nocturnes*. Princeton, N.J.: Princeton University Press, 1981. An authority on Dostoevski examines the novels written in Dostoevski's last twenty years. Links the themes of the most important novels and gives an extended character description of Polina from *The Gambler*.

_____. *Dostoevsky's Quest for Form: A Study of His Philosophy of Art*. 2d ed. Bloomington, Ind.: Physsardt, 1978. Considers the contradiction between Dostoevski's working aesthetic and his higher aesthetic of true beauty. A mature and helpful study for the serious Dostoevski reader.

Leatherbarrow, W. J., ed. *The Cambridge Companion to Dostoevskii*. New York: Cambridge University Press, 2006. Collection of essays that examine the author's life and works, discussing his relationship to Russian folk heritage, money, the intelligentsia, psychology, religion, the family, and science, among other topics. Includes a chronology and bibliography.

McReynolds, Susan. *Redemption and the Merchant God: Dostoevsky's Economy of Salvation and Antisemitism*. Evanston, Ill.: Northwestern University Press, 2008. McReynolds argues that readers cannot fully understand Dostoevski's writings without understanding his obsession with the Jews. She analyzes not only the elements of anti-Semitism in his works but also his views of the Crucifixion, Resurrection, morality, and other aspects of Christian doctrine.

Scanlan, James P. *Dostoevsky the Thinker: A Philosophical Study*. Ithaca, N.Y.: Cornell University Press, 2002. Scanlan analyzes Dostoevski's novels, essays, letters, and notebooks in order to provide a comprehensive account of his philosophy, examining the weakness as well as the strength of Dostoevski's ideas. He concludes that Dostoevski's thought was shaped by anthropocentrism—a struggle to define the very essence of humanity.

Straus, Nina Pelikan. *Dostoevsky and the Woman Question: Rereadings at the End of a Century*. New York: St. Martin's Press, 1994. Straus argues that Dostoevski's compulsion to depict men's cruelties to women is an important part of his vision and his metaphysics. She maintains that Dostoevski attacks masculine notions of autonomy and that his works evolve toward "the death of the patriarchy." Chapter 2 is devoted to a discussion of *The Gambler*.

The Garden Party
And Other Stories

Author: Katherine Mansfield (1888-1923)
First published: 1922
Type of work: Short fiction

Katherine Mansfield revolutionized the short story genre by ending the predominant reliance upon traditional plot structure, instead relying more on a specific moment in time, expressed through image patterns. By doing this, Mansfield carried the short story genre away from formalistic structuring and helped to establish its credibility as a literary form.

This collection of short fiction contains the following stories: "At the Bay," "The Garden Party," "The Daughters of the Late Colonel," "Mr. and Mrs. Dove," "The Young Girl," "Life of Ma Parker," "Marriage à la Mode," "The Voyage," "Miss Brill," "Her First Ball," "The Singing Lesson," "The Stranger," "Bank Holiday," "An Ideal Family," and "The Lady's Maid."

The Garden Party centers on female protagonists and the roles they play in family and social structures. These female characters differ in both age and class, ranging between the ages of six and sixty-five years and belonging to lower-, middle-, and upper-class social groups. For example, in "The

Garden Party," the collection's title story, the female protagonist is approximately sixteen and is a member of aristocratic society, whereas in "Life of Ma Parker," the title character, a maid, belongs to the lower class and is perhaps fifty.

Not only does Mansfield like to juxtapose differences in class and in age, but she also likes to position fictional elements against one another. Characters, settings, and themes are juxtaposed in her short fiction. In "The Garden Party" two classes are juxtaposed: On one hand there is the affluent and aristocratic Sheridan family celebrating the new flowers in bloom, and on the other hand there is the poor family, less than two miles away from the Sheridan estate, that has just suffered the father's untimely death.

A feminist, Mansfield juxtaposes the roles of men and women in "At the Bay." She uses the character of Linda to address the idea that women need more than a husband and children to fulfill their lives. The story's narrative depicts Linda's growing realization that there is more to life than wifely and motherly duties. Increasingly evident within the story is her desire to take an active role in her own life.

Mansfield is a master of utilizing and implementing many literary techniques. A striking use of metaphor is apparent in Mansfield's short fiction. Her stories also tend to operate by means of the implied rather than the direct. Furthermore, she uses a voice that is influenced by the characters, experiments with point of view, employs the use of natural elements, and begins stories in medias res.

Mansfield uses voice to present a character accurately. If a character is a young woman or an adolescent, for example, voice conveys the character's young or adolescent feelings. If the narrator speaks from the consciousness of a young child, the words are short, to the point, and not complicated, like the language and speech patterns of an actual child. Thus does narrative voice help to give the reader a realistic impression of the character.

Mansfield also experiments with point of view. She uses first and third person viewpoints, standard to short fiction, yet she has also created a point of view peculiarly her own that seemingly derives from her gift of impersonation. Her early mimicking of family and acquaintances carries over in her fiction to her use of a multipersonal perspective. Writing from a multipersonal point of view also allows Mansfield to give readers an extended sense of time, in both a historical and an immediate sense. This point of view also allows Mansfield to extend the viewpoint of a story from that of a single character to that of an entire group. In "The Garden Party," the beginning viewpoint is that of Laura Sheridan; however, at the end of the story, the viewpoint has shifted to be inclusive of the entire family.

The use of natural elements is an essential component of Mansfield's narrative craft. She believes that natural elements, such as air, sea, and gardens, help to create one's existence. In "Bank Holiday," for example, the use of the wind is important. The characters are pushed by the wind and do not realize the role played by the wind in moving them to their ultimate destination. Another use of natural elements is in "The Voyage." During the night, the young girl Fenella is taken by sea from a place that is familiar to her and emerges in a new place at the beginning of a new day.

Another characteristic device used by Mansfield is beginning stories in medias res, for example, in "The Voyage" and "The Daughters of the Late Colonel." In "The Voyage," Fenella is whisked away from her father, and readers do not understand why until near the end of the story. Similarly, when "The Daughters of the Late Colonel" begins, the father has died and the daughters are indecisive as to how to behave. These in medias res beginnings emphasize endings in a way that typical plot structure does not.

Not only are Mansfield's short stories characterized by female protagonists, each story addresses a social or psychological issue, including class, loneliness, or despair. "Miss Brill," "The Voyage," "Life of Ma Parker," and "The Lady's Maid" are representations of different women's existences and their varying relationships with those around them. In "Miss Brill," for example, Mansfield brings to the reader's consciousness the struggle between the young and the old. Miss Brill is elderly and alone, so she is forced to become "an actress" in the lives of those around her. She is no more than an observer in the conversations and lives of others who are also in the park, and at the end of the story she is compelled to realize this. The mean and hurtful words of the young couple she encounters force her to recognize that she is an outsider and unappreciated. Upon her return home, Miss Brill begins returning her fur stole to its box and then seems to hear the fox whimpering. In actuality, Mansfield suggests that it is Miss Brill herself who is crying because she is not only alone but also without hope of ever being more than "an actress" in the lives of others.

Both female protagonists in "The Lady's Maid" and "Life of Ma Parker" exemplify women who have an undying commitment to those who surround them. Ellen in "The Lady's Maid" has previously declined a marriage proposal she received as a young girl in order to fulfill her obligation to her "lady." Ellen wants to marry but realizes unselfishly that it will not be such a good idea to leave alone a lady who cannot adequately take care of herself. Along with Ellen, Ma Parker also demonstrates a sense of commitment. She never once sheds a tear or thinks of herself when her husband dies of consumption or when seven of her thirteen children die. She exemplifies strength and a strong commitment to others. Eventually, she realizes that she needs to release her pent-up emotions and begin healing from the pain she has experienced over the years.

Other themes and issues brought forth by Mansfield in *The Garden Party* include those of suffering, loneliness, abandonment, denial of self-fulfillment, and, most important, death's effect on human consciousness.

The effect of death on human consciousness is the thread that connects most of the stories. According to Saralyn R. Daly, death is relevant to the human condition: "In each instance the characters are affected by a death, but it becomes clear that death is not central in the author's mind." In "The Stranger" and "Marriage à la Mode," the death that occurs is not of a human being but of a relationship. In both stories, the bond between husband and wife falls apart for one reason or another. In "The Stranger," the relationship deteriorates because Janey Hammond has emotionally shut herself off from her husband. In "Marriage à la Mode," the relationship falls apart because there is a communication gap between William and Isabel. In the early years of their marriage William is content and Isabel is not. They decide to move to appease her, and then the roles are reversed: William is unhappy and Isabel is ecstatic. Their relationship falls apart because they have failed to express their feelings to each other. What each of these stories suggests is that death comes in all forms and is capable of affecting everything and everyone. In many of Mansfield's stories, relationships die because people fail to acknowledge the needs of others.

To Mansfield, death is the beginning of a self-awakening process. In "The Daughters of the Late Colonel," the father's death leads the sisters to the discovery of how desperate their lives have been up to that point. As a result of the colonel's death, the sisters realize that they have been excluded from others and are lonely for companionship. After their father's death they are not able to communicate or socialize independently. Everything has been organized and dictated to them by their father, and now there is no one to tell them what to do.

All of the stories that belong to *The Garden Party* suggest that life needs to be examined and that everyone needs to pursue some sort of happiness, whether it be alone, in a relationship, or in practicing everyday rituals such as going to the park and listening to music. Each story presents a moment in which such happiness is either missing or attained, and together these tales reinforce the value of such moments by presenting them vividly and convincingly.

Tara Y. Carter and Mary Rohrberger

Further Reading

Atkinson, William. "Mrs. Sheridan's Masterstroke: Liminality in Katherine Mansfield's *The Garden Party*." *English Studies* 87, no. 1 (February, 2006): 53-61. Argues that Laura experiences two rites of passage: a rite of temporary status reversal, in which her connections to the middle class are loosened, and a rite of permanent passage, in which she returns to the status quo.

Bell, Barbara Currier. "Non-Identical Twins: Nature in 'The Garden Party' and 'The Grave.'" *Comparatist* 12 (May, 1988): 58-66. Examines the meaning of nature in both short stories. Provides insight into Mansfield's use of nature in most of her short fiction.

Bennett, Andrew. *Katherine Mansfield*. Tavistock, England: Northcote House/British Council, 2004. A concise introduction to Mansfield's work. Traces the connection between her life and her writing, focusing on issues of personal identity and her theories of impersonation.

Boddy, Gillian. *Katherine Mansfield: The Woman and the Writer*. New York: Penguin Books, 1988. An extensive biography of Mansfield. Discusses her life in the context of her writings and experiences.

Charters, Ann, ed. *The Story and Its Writer: An Introduction to Short Fiction*. 6th ed. Boston: Bedford/St. Martin's, 2003. Includes the text of "The Garden Party," Mansfield's essay about this story, and another essay by Willa Cather about Mansfield's short fiction.

Daly, Saralyn R. *Katherine Mansfield*. New York: Twayne, 1965. Chapter 6 is the most useful in terms of understanding themes and meanings; however the entire book lends insight into Mansfield as a writer.

Kaplan, Sydney Janet. *Katherine Mansfield and the Origins of Modernist Fiction*. Ithaca, N.Y.: Cornell University Press, 1991. Chapter 8 offers a useful tool for analysis of Mansfield's characters. Stresses that a feminist approach is applicable to the interpretation of her works.

New, W. H. *Reading Mansfield and Metaphors of Form*. Montreal: McGill-Queen's University Press, 1999. Examines the form of Mansfield's stories, arguing that they are "neither simple vehicles for conveying emotional states nor neutral representations of moments in time, but carefully crafted models of social and psychological conditions of understanding."

Rohrberger, Mary. *The Art of Katherine Mansfield*. Ann Arbor, Mich.: University Microfilms International, 1977. Chapters 4, 5, and 6 are principally concerned with explaining the themes and techniques used in *The Garden Party* and Mansfield's other short stories. Includes extensive bibliographic notes and index.

The Gardener's Dog

Author: Lope de Vega Carpio (1562-1635)
First published: El perro del hortelano, 1618 (English
    translation, 1903)
Type of work: Drama
Type of plot: Comedy of manners
Time of plot: Late sixteenth century
Locale: Naples

Principal characters:
DIANA, the countess of Belflor
TEODORO, her secretary
FABIO, a gentleman of Naples
MARCELLA,
DOROTEA, and
ANARDA, ladies-in-waiting
COUNT FEDERIGO, in love with Diana
THE MARQUIS RICCARDO, also in love with Diana
COUNT LODOVICO, an old nobleman
TRISTAN, Teodoro's lackey

The Story:

The countess Diana is enraged when she hears that a man was seen leaving the upper chambers of the palace. He threw his cap at the candle, snuffing out the only light so that he could not be identified. Diana sends for her ladies-in-waiting and questions them to learn who had been visited by a lover during the night. Dorotea and Anarda plead innocent but whisper to Diana that Marcella has a lover in the palace. He is Teodoro, secretary to the countess Diana herself. Marcella confesses her love but protests that it is a pure love. Teodoro wants to marry her. Diana gives her consent to the marriage but cautions Marcella to stay away from Teodoro until the wedding day; otherwise passion might consume honor. After her ladies leave her alone, Diana realizes that she, too, loves Teodoro, but since he is not highborn she cannot proclaim her love.

Teodoro, who had indeed been the man involved in the midnight escapade, fears that he will be found out and banished or executed, but he cannot get Marcella out of his heart. Tristan, his lackey, begs him to forget Marcella and never see her again lest Diana punish them; it is Tristan who threw the cap and snuffed out the candle so that his master would not be recognized while escaping. Soon afterward, Diana tricks Tristan into revealing his part in the affair; she also sends for Teodoro and subtly hints at her love for him in a letter she feigns is intended for someone else.

Marcella goes to Teodoro and tells him that Diana has blessed their betrothal. Confused, Teodoro takes Marcella in his arms just as Diana appears. When he thanks her for giving Marcella to him, their capricious mistress orders Marcella locked in her room to await her decision concerning the wedding. Then Diana again hints to Teodoro that she loves him, whereupon he renounces Marcella. He regrets rejecting Marcella, but he cannot put aside the lure of wealth and power

that will be his if Diana takes him for a husband. After Marcella is released from the locked room, Teodoro, meeting her, spurns her love and disgraces her. Marcella swears revenge on him and on Anarda, who has, as she learns, betrayed her and Teodoro to Diana because Anarda thinks Marcella has been encouraging Fabio, a gentleman with whom Anarda is in love. Marcella, meeting Fabio, offers him her love and greatly confuses that poor man by her words and actions.

When two noblemen, the Marquis Riccardo and Count Federigo, both beg for Diana's hand, she sends Teodoro to tell Riccardo that she chooses him for her husband. Deserted by the lovely countess before she is really his, Teodoro turns back to Marcella and tells her that he loves only her. At first she spurns him and declares she will marry Fabio, but at last love wins over jealousy. Falling into Teodoro's arms, she makes him forswear Diana forever. The lovers call their mistress a devil, an ass, and a bore, not knowing that Diana and Anarda are hidden nearby and listening to their conversation. When they suddenly appear, they frighten the lovers almost to death. Diana dictates a letter to Teodoro, in which she states that if a noble lady loves a man, he dare not love another. When she cautions him to interpret its meaning correctly, Teodoro again renounces Marcella and tells her to marry Fabio so as to please Diana.

Riccardo, appearing in answer to the summons from Diana, is told that Teodoro misunderstood her words and that she did not intend to marry him. Teodoro, believing then that his mistress truly loves him, declares his love for her. Instead of listening to his pleas, Diana berates him for daring to speak of love when he is lowborn and she a lady. As she does not intend to have him herself, he thereupon asks her for Marcella. Like the gardener's dog who will allow no other dog to eat what he himself does not want, she refuses to let Teodoro have Marcella. Instead, she strikes at Teodoro with her knife. He half-believes that she wounds him because she loves him, and, when she returns and wipes the blood from his wound, he is sure that it is love that makes her cruel to him.

Count Federigo and the Marquis Riccardo, hearing that Diana has wounded Teodoro, are convinced that he had threatened her honor, and they decide to have him killed. For their assassin they hire Teodoro's faithful lackey, Tristan, who takes their gold and then informs Teodoro of their plot. Tristan has other plans for helping his master. He learns of one Count Lodovico, who had lost a son named Teodoro twenty years before. The boy had been captured by the Moors and was never heard of again. Tristan plans to convince the old count that Teodoro is his long-lost son. Then Teodoro will have a family of birth and wealth and will be good enough to wed Diana. Teodoro, too honorable for such knavery, goes to Diana and tells her that he is going to Spain, to avoid both the death planned for him by her suitors and the torture he endures while in her presence. Diana, not knowing her own mind, alternately tells him to leave and to stay. When Marcella goes to Diana and asks for permission to accompany Teodoro to Spain, Diana tells the girl that she must marry Fabio.

Meanwhile, Tristan carries through his plot to make Count Lodovico think that Teodoro is his lost son, and the old man is delighted at the prospect of having his child returned to him. Before the old count sees Teodoro, Diana, knowing that her true love is to leave her, tells him at last that she loves him. Still she refuses to marry him because of his humble birth. When Count Lodovico appears with the announcement that Teodoro is his son, Diana opens her arms to Teodoro and says that they will be married that very night. Marcella, finally realizing that she can never have Teodoro, agrees to marry Fabio.

Teodoro, in one last attempt to save his honor, confesses to Diana that Tristan had tricked the old nobleman into believing that Teodoro is his own missing son. By that time, however, Diana has learned that love does not respect position. She declares that they will marry anyway and keep the secret between themselves and Tristan. Federigo and Riccardo confess their plot to have Teodoro killed, and Diana gives Dorotea to Tristan as his bride. So all ends well, with honor saved and love triumphant. The gardener's dog makes a final choice.

Critical Evaluation:

The Gardener's Dog has often been called Shakespearean in the style and manner of its seriocomic treatment of love. Indeed, this play is, perhaps, Lope de Vega Carpio's *A Mid-*

summer Night's Dream (pr. c. 1595-1596, pb. 1600). A dreamlike quality suffuses the action, as love turns into hate and back into love, affection turns to scorn, indifference turns to desire, sweet heroines turn vindictive, courtly lovers turn would-be murderers, lovers change partners, and confusion reigns supreme. Both audience and characters wonder what will happen next.

If, however, the treatment of love is Shakespearean, the treatment of illusion versus reality is closer to Luigi Pirandello. The play's conclusion hints that perhaps Teodoro becomes an actual count because everyone believes him to be one. The situation is an interesting reversal from that in Pirandello's *Enrico IV* (1922; *Henry IV*, 1923), where a character in his madness believes he is a king, while everyone around him, knowing him for what he really is, simply humors him. In Vega Carpio's play, only Teodoro, Tristan, and Diana know the facts of the matter, while the rest of the world believes it is paying court to a true count. The practical result in both cases is the same, however, whereby Vega Carpio may perhaps be suggesting that nobility is nothing more than a social convention and has no other basis than that people agree to honor its credentials, no matter how spurious.

This proposition may be self-evident to later ages, but in early seventeenth century Spain it was an assumption that struck at the heart of the social order, though admittedly, in not quite so revolutionary a manner as Vega Carpio's *Fuenteovejuna* (written 1611-1618, published 1619; *The Sheep-Well*, 1936). In fact, Teodoro's instant pedigree may have been less a social statement than simply a convenient dramatic device to bring Diana, the countess of Belflor, and her secretary together at last. For centuries, writers of comedy and romance have solved the problem of love between highborn and lowborn by revealing that the lowborn hero or heroine is actually highborn (having been, like the baby in Tristan's story, stolen in childhood by pirates, or else inadvertently mixed up with another baby). Vega Carpio's dramatic resolution is an interesting variation of this theme; nevertheless, he seems to accept the underlying premise that highborn and lowborn must not marry in defiance of convention.

For all the intriguing questions of reality and appearance in the play, the main focus is on the nature of love, on just what this universal yet incomprehensible phenomenon is. In the first act, Marcella sighs that love causes people to mount as if to heaven; in the second, she calls love "god of envy, god of hate!" As the play progresses, it dramatizes the often-asked questions as to how love originates, how it is affected by jealousy, how it causes people to behave, how it is affected by absence, what happens when it is frustrated by power or social convention, and how it affects a person's natural temperament.

The air of questioning and confusion that pervades the work is set at the very beginning of the first act. The second line of the play, "Who's there?" echoes the first line of *Hamlet, Prince of Denmark* (pr. c. 1600-1601, pb. 1603), a play also suffused with doubt and ambiguity of motive. Roused in the middle of the night by a mysterious noise, Diana and her ladies-in-waiting dash in and out and scurry around the stage, with only shadows and feathers as solid evidence of intruders. Was the disturbance a dream? Two figures are seen on stage on some unknown mission at the outset, but they disappear after breathlessly delivering only four short lines.

As the action progresses, more questions press for answers. Is it possible that Diana has no inclination at all toward Teodoro until she learns that he loves and is loved by Marcella? How much of Teodoro's love for Diana is based on true passion, and how much on his greed for wealth and station? If the latter is his predominant motivation, then how much sympathy does he deserve? Teodoro complains at great length of the extremes to which Diana's passions run and of her cruelty to him, yet his own treatment of Marcella is crass and heartless. He adores her at the beginning, shifts his love to Diana when the countess suggests her interest in him, comes whining back to his first love when Diana's attitude seems to change, and then unfeelingly spurns Marcella a second time when the wind of love once more blows his way. When, at the conclusion, Diana expresses some concern that her former secretary may have some lingering feelings for Marcella, the "count" loftily assures her, "Noblemen know no maidservants."

To help him develop his ideas on the range of love, Vega Carpio uses an unconventional dramatic device: a series of sonnets interspersed through the action and spoken by either Diana, Teodoro, or Marcella. Each sonnet develops a different aspect of love: Diana's first sonnet deals with the passion, jealousy, and frustration of love; Teodoro's deals with the nature of new love and with the conflicting feelings of affection, ambition, conscience, and cynicism it arouses; Marcella's deals with the constancy and permanency of love, despite all barriers and reverses. Other sonnets treat love's violence and cruelty, its cautions and terrors, and its black moments of despair. Counterpointed to these sonnets are other set speeches on love. In the Marquis Riccardo's speech to Diana, for instance, there is the conventional high-flown rhetoric of courtly love, as splendid as it is artificial: "Did I command gold . . . or the frozen tears of heaven . . . or mines of

oriental gems whose gleam has ploughed a furrow through the heaving hillocks of the sun, I would lay them at your feet, and delve beyond the confines of the light." Earlier in the play, Teodoro reveals that his love for Marcella is based on an idealized view of woman: "pure serenely crystallized, transparent like glass." Tristan, who often acts like Lear's fool in throwing the cold water of common sense on these romantic illusions, responds with a more realistic picture of women, one that emphasizes their defects instead of their glories. (Like many a fool, Tristan is resourceful, shrewd, and basically decent—he rebukes Teodoro for his treatment of Marcella—though he ultimately lacks the nobility that elevates his master at the end.)

In its overall conception, *The Gardener's Dog* is a highly mature example of dramatic art. Unlike the majority of contemporary plays, including Vega Carpio's own, it does not rely on villainous antagonists for its plot complications, but rather on the vagaries of love and the effects of this ennobling and exasperating passion. All of the important characters are drawn with a high degree of sympathy, though the playwright is not afraid to look unflinchingly at their defects. As long as the focus remains on love, the play remains a work of art. The quality begins to decline markedly in the third and final act when character development begins to slacken and the standard mechanics of plot contrivance take over. However, it would be charitable to forgive the prolific Vega Carpio for the absurdities of his dramatic resolution, for seldom have the many faces of love been presented so subtly and at the same time so entertainingly.

"Critical Evaluation" by Laurence Behrens

Further Reading

Dixon, Victor. Introduction to *The Dog in the Manger*, by Lope de Vega Carpio. Ottawa, Ont.: Dovehouse Editions, 1990. Extensive examination of the sources, structure, and characterization of the work. Explicates the action and discusses the complexity of plotting. Reviews Vega Carpio's intriguing resolution of the comedy.

Hayes, Francis C. *Lope de Vega*. New York: Twayne, 1967. Introductory overview, with separate chapters providing a brief biographical sketch, analysis of Vega Carpio's plays and nondramatic works, and commentary on the status of drama in Vega Carpio's lifetime. Classifies *The Gardener's Dog* as one of several works in which Vega Carpio uses stock devices to achieve humor.

Pring-Mill, R. D. F. Introduction to *Lope de Vega: Five Plays*, translated by Jill Booty. New York: Hill and Wang, 1961. Brief but insightful commentary on the play, highlighting Vega Carpio's use of irony, especially in the ending, where he reveals that honor as portrayed by the protagonists is no more than a sham.

Samson, Alexander, and Jonathan Thacker, eds. *A Companion to Lope de Vega*. Rochester, N.Y.: Tamesis, 2008. Twenty-one essays provide various interpretations of Vega Carpio's life and work. Includes discussions of Vega Carpio and the theater of Madrid, his religious drama, his chronicle memory plays, his comedies, and Vega Carpio as icon.

Vega Carpio, Lope de. *Four Plays*. New York: Charles Scribner's Sons, 1936. Includes an introduction by John Garrett Underhill and a critical essay by Jacinto Benavente, in which a practicing artist discusses technical aspects of *The Gardener's Dog* and Vega Carpio's accomplishments as a dramatist.

Wright, Elizabeth R. *Pilgrimage to Patronage: Lope de Vega and the Court of Philip III, 1598-1621*. Lewisburg, Pa.: Bucknell University Press, 2001. Chronicles how Vega Carpio used his publications and public appearances to win benefactors at the court of Philip III. Describes how his search for patrons shaped his literary work, and how the success of his plays altered the court's system of artistic patronage.

Gargantua and Pantagruel

Author: François Rabelais (c. 1494-1553)

First published: Gargantua et Pantagruel, 1567 (first complete edition); *Gargantua*, 1534 (English translation, 1653); *Pantagruel*, 1532 (English translation, 1653); *Tiers livre*, 1546 (*Third Book*, 1693); *Le Quart livre*, 1552 (*Fourth Book*, 1694); *Le Cinquiesme livre*, 1564 (*Fifth Book*, 1694)

Type of work: Novel

Type of plot: Mock-heroic

Time of plot: Renaissance

Locale: France

Principal characters:

GRANGOSIER, a giant king

GARGAMELLE, his wife

GARGANTUA, their son

PANTAGRUEL, the son of Gargantua

PANURGE, a clever rascal

FRIAR JOHN OF THE FUNNELS, a lusty monk

The Story:

Grangosier and Gargamelle are expecting a child. During the eleventh month of her pregnancy, Gargamelle eats too many tripes and then plays tag on the green. That afternoon, in a green meadow, Gargantua is born from his mother's left ear. Gargantua is a prodigy and, with his first breath, he begins to clamor for drink. To supply him with milk, 17,913 cows are needed. Tailors use nine hundred ells of linen to make his shirt and 1,105 ells of white broadcloth to make his breeches. Eleven hundred cowhides are used for the soles of his shoes.

At first, Gargantua's education is in the hands of two masters of the old school, Holofernes and Joberlin Bride. When Grangosier observes that his son is making no progress, however, he sends him to Paris to study with Ponocrates. Aside from some mishaps, as when he takes the bells from the tower of Notre Dame to tie around his horse's neck, Gargantua does much better with his studies in Paris.

Back home, a dispute arises. The bakers of Lerne refuse to sell cakes to the shepherds of Grangosier. In the quarrel, a shepherd fells a baker, and King Picrochole of Lerne invades the country. Grangosier bakes cartloads of cakes to appease Picrochole, but to no avail, for no one dares oppose Picrochole except doughty Friar John of the Funnels. Finally, Grangosier asks Gargantua to come to his aid. Gargantua fights valiantly. Cannonballs seem to him as grape seeds, and when he combs his hair, cannonballs drop out. After he conquers the army of Lerne, he generously sets all the prisoners free.

All of his helpers are rewarded well, and for Friar John Gargantua builds the famous Abbey of Theleme, where men and women are together, all can leave when they wish, and marriage and the accumulation of wealth are encouraged. When he is more than four hundred years old, Gargantua has a son, Pantagruel. A remarkable baby, Pantagruel is hairy as a bear at birth and of such great size that he costs the life of his mother. Gargantua is sorely vexed, between weeping for his wife and rejoicing for his son.

Pantagruel requires the services of 4,600 cows to nurse him. Once he gets an arm out of his swaddling clothes and, grasping the cow nursing him, eats the cow. Afterward, Pantagruel's arms are bound with anchor ropes. One day, the women forget to clean his face after nursing, and a bear comes and licks the drops of milk from the baby's face. By a great effort, Pantagruel breaks the ropes and eats the bear. In despair, Gargantua binds his son with four great chains, one of which is later used to bind Lucifer when he has the colic. Pantagruel, however, breaks the five-foot beam that constituted the footboard of his cradle and runs around with the cradle on his back.

Pantagruel shows great promise as a scholar. After a period of wandering, he settles down in Paris. There he is frequently called on to settle disputes between learned lawyers. One day he meets Panurge, a ragged young beggar. On speaking to him, Pantagruel receives answers in twelve known and unknown tongues. Pantagruel is greatly taken by this fluent beggar, and the two become great friends. Panurge is a merry fellow who knows 63 ways to make money and 214 ways to spend it.

Pantagruel learns that the Dipsodes have invaded the land of the Amaurots. Stirred by this danger to Utopia, he sets out by ship to do battle. By trickery and courage, Pantagruel overcomes the wicked giants. He marries their king, Anarchus, to an old lantern-carrying hag and makes the king a crier of green sauce. Now that the land of Dipsody is conquered, Pantagruel transports a colony of Utopians there, numbering 9,876,543,210 men, plus many women and children. All of these people are very fertile. Every nine months, each married woman bears seven children. In a short time, Dipsody is populated by virtuous Utopians.

For his services and friendship, Panurge is made Laird of Salmigondin. The revenue from this lairdship amounts to 6,789,106,789 gold royals a year, but Panurge manages to spend his income well in advance. Intending to settle down, Panurge begins to reflect seriously on marriage, and he consults his lord Pantagruel. They come to no conclusion in the matter because they get into an argument about the virtues of borrowing and lending money. Nevertheless, the flea in his ear keeps reminding Panurge of his contemplated marriage, and he sets off to seek other counsel.

Panurge consults the Sibyl of Panzoult, the poet Raminagrobis, Herr Tripa, and Friar John. When all the advice he receives proves contradictory, Panurge prevails on Pantagruel and Friar John to set out with him to consult the Oracle of the Holy Bottle. From Saint Malo, the party sails in twelve ships for the Holy Bottle, located in Upper India. The Portuguese sometimes take three years for that voyage, but Pantagruel and Panurge cut that time to one month by sailing across the Frozen Sea north of Canada.

The valiant company has many adventures on the way. On the Island of the Ennasins, they find a race of people with noses shaped like the ace of clubs. The people who live on the Island of Ruach eat and drink nothing but wind. At the Ringing Islands, they find a strange race of Siticines who long ago turned into birds. On Condemnation Island, they fall into the power of Gripe-men-all, Archduke of the Furred Law-cats, and Panurge is forced to solve a riddle before the travelers are given their freedom.

At last, they come to the island of the Holy Bottle. Guided by a Lantern from Lanternland, they come to a large vineyard planted by Bacchus himself. Then they go underground through a plastered vault and come to marble steps. Down they go, a hundred steps or more. Panurge is greatly afraid, but Friar John takes him by the collar and heartens him. At the bottom, they come to a great mosaic floor on which is shown the history of Bacchus. Finally, they are met by the priest Bacbuc, who is to conduct them to the Holy Bottle. Panurge kneels to kiss the rim of the fountain. Bacbuc throws something into the well, and the water begins to boil. When Panurge sings the prescribed ritual, the Holy Bottle pronounces one word, "trinc." Bacbuc looks up the word in a huge silver book. It means drink, a word declared to be the most gracious and intelligible she has ever heard from the Holy Bottle. Panurge takes the word as a sanction for his marriage.

Critical Evaluation:

Partly because France's greatest comic prose writer was a legend even in his own lifetime, most of the facts of François Rabelais's life remain hazy. A monk, doctor of medicine, and writer, Rabelais transferred from the Franciscan to the Benedictine order with the Pope's express permission, because the latter order was more tolerant and more scholarly. The year 1532 found him in Lyons, at that time the intellectual center of France, where he published his first creative work, *Pantagruel*. As a satirist and humanist, Rabelais labored between the two religious extremes of Roman Catholicism and Genevan Protestantism; he had the mixed blessings of being attacked by Julius Caesar Scaliger, St. Francis of Sales, and John Calvin. All of them warned against his heretical impiety. Rabelais was, first and last, an iconoclast, but he attempted to be moderate in his views and writings. This may have made Rabelais unpopular with his more radical contemporaries, such as Martin Luther and Ignatius Loyola, but it also made him one of the most durable and most humane comic writers. As indecorous as his writings are, they also reveal a relatively conservative spirit; they show a sense of proportion and of human limitation in outraging both.

In Rabelais, the spirit of comedy blends with the spirit of epic to produce a novel work without parallel or close precedent. The chronicles are quite inclusive, expressing the Renaissance ambition to explore and chart all realms of human experience and thought. The mood of the narrator matches the scope of the narration. Rabelais attributes his infinite exuberance to his literal and symbolic inebriation, which he invites his readers to share. His curiosity, interest in the things of this world, joy, and unpredictability are greatly enjoyable, as long as the reader is willing to be intoxicated by a distillation of strong wit and language. As a genre, the chronicles may be compared to other books of instruction so popular during the Renaissance—such as Niccolò Machiavelli's *Il principe* (wr. 1513, pb. 1532; *The Prince*, 1640); Baldassare Castiglione's *Il libro del cortegiano* (1528; *The Courtier*, 1561), and Roger Ascham's *The Schoolmaster* (1570). They also have been considered a parody of medieval adventure romances. *Gargantua and Pantagruel* includes history, fable, myth, drama, lyrics, comedy, burlesque, novel, and epic. Its sources include sculpture, jurisprudence, pedagogy, architecture, painting, medicine, physics, mathematics, astronomy, chemistry, theology, religion, music, aeronautics, agriculture, botany, athletics, and psychological counseling. All of these elements are thrown together with flair and abandon.

It is a consistency of mood that holds together this diverse and variegated work. That mood is not one of thoughtfulness, for Rabelais is no great thinker. The unifying idea, eternal in its simplicity, is the philosophy of Pantagruelism: "Do as Thou Wilt." The world of Pantagruel is a world in which no restrictions on sensual or intellectual exploration can be tolerated; excessive discipline is regarded as evil and inhuman. In true epicurean fashion, Rabelais has no patience for inhibitions. People live for too brief a time to allow themselves the luxury of denial. The Abbey of Theleme is the thematic center of the work, with its credo that instinct forms the only valid basis for morality and social structure. Rabelais ignores the dangers of the anarchy this credo implies; he is talking about the mind, not the body politic. The dullest thing imaginable is the unimaginative, conforming mind. His satirical pen is lifted against all who lessen freedom of any kind in any fashion: hypocrites, militarists, abusers of justice, pedants, and medieval scholastics.

The reader of these gigantic chronicles, then, must not expect a plot. Anything so regular is anathema to Pantagruelism. Readers also should realize that the characters themselves are not the focus of the author's art but are largely indistinguishable. One of the most amusing elements of the book is that they are also indistinguishably large; Pantagruel's mouth, described in book 2, chapter 32, one of the finest chapters in European literature, is, at times, large enough to contain kingdoms and mountain ranges, at other times, no larger than a dovecote. The exception is Panurge, the normal-size man. He is an unforgettable character who makes so strong an impression, even on the author, that he cannot be forgotten. The third, fourth, and fifth books, in fact, are based on his adventures—just as William Shakespeare's *The Merry Wives of Windsor* (pr. 1597, pb. 1602) was written to exploit the beloved character of Falstaff. Panurge is the heroic companion of Pantagruel, in the best epic tradition; he also has the cunning of Ulysses, the drunken mirth of Falstaff, the roguishness of Jack Wilton and Tyl Ulenspiegel (his numerous pockets filled with innumerable tricks), the cynical but lighthearted opportunism of Geoffrey Chaucer's Pardoner, the magic powers of Shakespeare's Puck or Ariel. He is the wise fool of Erasmus and King Lear, and a Socratic gadfly who bursts the pretensions and illusions of all he encounters. The chapter entitled "How Panurge Non-plussed the Englishman Who Argued by Signs" is a literary tour de force, concentrating into one vivid, raucous chapter the comic spirit forever to be known as Rabelaisian. Important in other ways are "How Pantagruel Met a Limousin Who Spoke Spurious French," for its attack on unfounded affectation; and Gargantua's letter to Pantagruel, expressing the entire range of Renaissance learning, juxtaposed with the chapter introducing Panurge, who personifies Renaissance wit.

Rabelais's chaotically inventive style, filled with puns, wordplay, and synonyms, as well as with neologisms of his own creation, makes him difficult to translate accurately. His language reflects the rich variety of sixteenth century France; as the first to observe invariable rules in the writing of French prose, he has been called the father of the French idiom. His syntax is flexible, supple, expansive, sparkling with vitality and the harmony of an ebullient character, complex, and original. Rabelais does for French vocabulary what Geoffrey Chaucer did for English, fortifying it with eclectically selected terms of the soil, mill, tavern, and market, as well as scholarly terms and phrases gleaned from nearly all languages. As his comic theme reflects the universal as well as the particular, Rabelais's language combines the provincial with the popular in a stew fit for the mouths of giants.

"Critical Evaluation" by Kenneth John Atchity

Further Reading

Berry, Alice Fiola. *The Charm of Catastrophe: A Study of Rabelais "Quart livre."* Chapel Hill: Department of Romance Languages, University of North Carolina, 2000. Analyzes *Le Quart Livre* of *Gargantua and Pantagruel*, the last novel published in Rabelais's lifetime, demonstrating how it expresses the elderly writer's despair over failing to achieve his youthful dreams.

Bowen, Barbara C. *Enter Rabelais, Laughing.* Nashville, Tenn.: Vanderbilt University Press, 1998. Focuses on the humor in Rabelais's work, describing why it was funny to his sixteenth century contemporaries and placing him within the tradition of Renaissance comic writings. Includes notes and bibliography.

Carron, Jean-Claude, ed. *François Rabelais: Critical Assessments.* Baltimore: Johns Hopkins University Press, 1995. A selection and revision of papers delivered at a 1991 symposium at the University of California, Los Angeles. Some of the papers examine realism, feminism, and cultural connections in Rabelais's works.

Chesney, Elizabeth A., and Marcel Tetel. *Rabelais Revisited.* New York: Twayne, 1993. Contains a good general introduction to the four novels definitely written by Rabelais and an annotated bibliography of important critical studies on Rabelais. Explores relationships between male and female characters in Rabelais's novels.

Febvre, Lucien. *The Problem of Unbelief in the Sixteenth Century: The Religion of Rabelais.* Translated by Beatrice Gottlieb. Cambridge, Mass.: Harvard University Press, 1982. Explores the many different representations of religious belief in Rabelais's writings. Demonstrates the need for modern scholars to avoid anachronistic interpretations of Renaissance treatments of religious topics.

Frame, Donald. *François Rabelais: A Study.* New York: Harcourt Brace Jovanovich, 1977. Clear, well-documented biography of Rabelais's life as a monk, medical doctor, and novelist. Summarizes general trends in the critical reception of Rabelais's works since the sixteenth century.

Gauna, Max. *The Rabelaisian Mythologies.* Madison, N.J.: Fairleigh Dickinson University Press, 1996. Rabelais described his novels as "mythologies," and this study analyzes the mythological elements in *Pantagruel, Gargantua, Tiers Livre,* and *Le Quart Livre.* Includes bibliography.

Greene, Thomas. *Rabelais: A Study in Comic Courage.* Englewood Cliffs, N.J.: Prentice-Hall, 1970. Thoughtful analysis of the coexistence of farce and high comedy in Rabelais's writings. Explains clearly how Rabelais uses laughter as an effective weapon for discrediting unsympathetic characters.

Screech, Michael A. *Rabelais.* Ithaca, N.Y.: Cornell University Press, 1979. Insightful, thorough study of Rabelais's four books. Discusses Rabelais's work in the light of Renaissance philosophy and theology, and examines his creative imitation of biblical, classical, medieval, and Renaissance sources.

Zegura, Elizabeth Chesney, ed. *The Rabelais Encyclopedia.* Westport, Conn.: Greenwood Press, 2004. Alphabetically arranged collection of articles about Rabelais's characters, references to Renaissance and historical figures, themes and allusions, and key influences upon his writing. Also features a chronology of major events in his life and literary career.

The Gates of Ivory

Author: Margaret Drabble (1939-   )
First published: 1991
Type of work: Novel
Type of plot: Symbolic realism
Time of plot: 1987-1989
Locale: London, Thailand, and Cambodia

Principal characters:
LIZ HEADLEAND, a psychiatrist living in London
ALIX BOWEN, one of Liz's close friends
ESTHER BREUER, an eccentric historian of Italian Renaissance art
STEPHEN COX, a friend of Liz and Alix, and a writer
HATTIE OSBORNE, a heavy-drinking casual friend of Stephen
MISS PORNTIP, a Thai beauty queen and entrepreneur who befriends Stephen
KONSTANTIN VASSILIOU, a globetrotting young photographer
ROBERT OXENHOLME, a government minister, and Esther's husband
MME SAVET AKRUN, a Thai woman who escaped from the Khmer Rouge
SIMON GRUNEWALD, an ethnologist and collector

The Story:

Liz Headleand, a London psychiatrist, receives a package from Southeast Asia containing a variety of scraps of writing and notes by her friend Stephen Cox, plus parts of two human finger bones, photographs, and other items. She consults her close friend Alix Bowen and continues to pore over the fragments, for she is half in love with Stephen and is worried. She contacts Hattie Osborne, a friend of Stephen who is living in his London flat while he is away. Hattie begins telling Liz what she knows about Stephen, who had left on a trip to Bangkok, Thailand, to research Pol Pot for a play he had been writing. No one knows how long he has been gone.

Months earlier, Stephen is sitting next to a former Thai beauty queen on his flight to Bangkok. Miss Porntip, now an entrepreneur, takes him under her wing after they arrive. Stephen soon meets Konstantin Vassiliou, a photographer, who introduces him to a network of foreign travelers and aid workers. Meanwhile, in London, Liz goes to a banquet to raise funds for the restoration of Asian temples at the invitation of her former husband. She sits with her friend Esther Breuer, an art historian, who is being wooed by government minister Robert Oxenholme.

In no time, Robert and Esther marry. At their wedding, Liz meets Simon Grunewald, an ethnologist who had met Stephen in Bangkok. He tries to help Liz understand the contents of the package that she received from Asia, and confirms that the package was posted in Cambodia.

Stephen and Konstantin travel to the Thai-Cambodian border to see the refugee camps. At one camp, Stephen meets Mme Savet Akrun, the woman Konstantin immortalized in a photograph of the refugees—the same photograph Liz had found in the package mailed from Southeast Asia. Stephen and Konstantin next fly to Hanoi to get passes to Ho Chi Minh Ville (formerly Saigon) and Cambodia. In Saigon they arrange a trip to include a Japanese photographer named Akira, with whom they eventually enter Cambodia and reach Phnom Penh. After Stephen has one unsuccessful outing into the countryside on Akira's motorcycle, the three of them drive into the countryside and are captured. Akira is separated from Stephen and Konstantin. Stephen gets a serious fever, and Konstantin leaves him to seek help. Stephen is brought back to partial health by a peasant nurse and is moved to a Khmer Rouge clinic. He falls ill again and dies.

Two years later, in London, Liz gathers together Stephen's friends and acquaintances. Still unable to find him, they all agree that someone should go to Asia to find him; Liz is chosen. She flies to Bangkok, and seeks Stephen's trail. The trail leads her to a refugee camp at the Cambodian border, where she meets Mme Akrun. She then travels to Hanoi and then Saigon, where her search ends: Gabriel Denham, an old friend of Liz, is making a film about Stephen and confirms to Liz that Stephen is dead—and he has proof. Liz then falls ill with toxic shock and is rescued and taken to Bangkok by Miss Porntip. Another of her former husbands, Charles Headleand, flies to Bangkok and brings her back to England. In London, Liz organizes a memorial service for Stephen.

Critical Evaluation:

The Radiant Way (1987), *A Natural Curiosity* (1989), and *The Gates of Ivory* form Margaret Drabble's powerful trilogy surveying English life in the 1980's. The two early novels center on the lives of three Englishwomen—Liz, Alix, and Esther—from their university days to late middle age, and reach out through families and acquaintances to all classes and facets of British society. *The Gates of Ivory* places the world of international violence—the horrors of the Khmer Rouge and the killing fields of Cambodia—in the lap of its English characters.

Drabble is a moral novelist, concerned with the personal, social, and political choices people make and with the relationships among these realms. As general editor of *The Oxford Companion to English Literature* (1985-), she has a strong sense of the traditions of English fiction as social commentary, which ranges from the writings of Jane Austen to those of Charles Dickens, Joseph Conrad, and John Galsworthy. The bulk of *The Gates of Ivory* comprises the richly detailed lives of the English, as families and generations interweave against the background of Prime Minister Margaret Thatcher's Great Britain.

In addition, *The Gates of Ivory* weaves together layers of metafiction and other narrative techniques to address the tumult of the modern world. Stephen's strange, unfocused pilgrimage into the Cambodian jungles is reminiscent of Joseph Conrad's *Heart of Darkness* (1899, serial; 1902, book), in which the protagonist's inner evil is soon discovered. However, Stephen, who dies of a fever, is not an evil character but a confused one stumbling toward the violent evil of Pol Pot and the Khmer Rouge in a vague attempt to understand and embrace such things in the world. Drabble frames Stephen's pilgrimage against the daily lives of her London characters.

The novel has two important framing devices. The title, the first frame, is taken from Homer's *Odyssey*, in which Penelope explains that dreams come to humankind through either gates of ivory or gates of horn—the former depicting false images of what will not come to pass and the latter made up of dreams that will become real. Stephen's dream of meeting Pol Pot and writing about him comes out of the ivory gates, supported by the exotic descriptions of his voyages through Bangkok, Hanoi, Saigon, and Phnom Penh, and into the jungles. The balance of the novel, with its domestic vision of lives lived in England—the dreams that become and are real—arrives through the gates of horn.

The second frame is a strong echo of Dickens's opening to *A Tale of Two Cities* (1859): "It was the best of times. It was the worst of times." Drabble speaks in her opening sentence of Good Time and Bad Time and carries this throughout the text, with Stephen entering the Bad Time when he is captured. She also speaks of how the Good and Bad Times exist simultaneously, with some communications existing between the two. For example, the Good Time includes the London dinner to raise funds for Asian temple restoration, the photograph of Mme Arkun used as a poster in England, and the Cambodian refugee children's settlement in England. The package of Stephen's jottings and the finger bones is a missive from the Bad Time, which starts the plot.

The prose methods depart in a number of ways from Drabble's earlier realistic fiction. In *The Gates of Ivory*, the author enters the story to list some possible plot twists and endings, and then tells readers that these twists and endings are not suitable. While the bulk of the narrative is omniscient, Hattie's self-centered, scatterbrained, and often-ironic narrative is in the first person and is a rich stew of gossip and sexual focus. The fragments of Stephen's writing from the package include bits of film scenarios, a short history of genocides, and some idealized romantic vignettes. On a number of occasions, Drabble simply lists, in single sentences, what might have happened to a character. These narrative possibilities are never closed off, indicating to the reader that much of reality cannot be known. Drabble also implies that traditional fiction's tidy closures are unrealistic.

The novel is rich in satire and irony as well, particularly clear when the narration moves into characters' thoughts. Drabble is a master of managing distance in her writing, so that at one moment the reader is immersed in the realistic drama of life and at the next moment feels pulled away to look at the comic folly of so much of the human condition.

The Gates of Ivory offers a comprehensive approach to history in the broadest sense. On one level, the novel is about the horrors of the Khmer Rouge and human suffering. On another level, the novel looks at social, political, and domestic life in a particular decade in England.

Peter Brigg

Further Reading

Bokat, Nicole Suzanne. *The Novels of Margaret Drabble: "This Freudian Family Nexus."* New York: Peter Lang, 1998. A psychobiography of Drabble that relates her life experience to the contents of her fiction. Also considers how her work approaches classic psychological determinism.

Brownley, Martine Watson. "Mothers and Capitalists in International Politics: Margaret Drabble's *The Gates of Ivory.*" In *Deferrals of Domain: Contemporary Women Novelists and the State.* New York: St. Martin's Press, 2000. Presents a sociopolitical analysis of *The Gates of Ivory* through the lens of feminist theory.

Knutsen, Karen Patrick. "Leaving Dr. Leavis: A Farewell to the Great Tradition? Margaret Drabble's *The Gates of Ivory.*" *English Studies* 77 (1996): 579-591. Knutsen argues that Drabble partially abandons her inheritance of social realism and uses postmodern techniques to pursue her goal of an "un-postmodern" moral critique of the contemporary world.

Leeming, Glenda. *Margaret Drabble.* Tavistock, England: Northcote House/British Council, 2006. A general and thoughtful book on Drabble's work. Chapter 7 deals with the trilogy ending in *The Gates of Ivory.*

Onega, Susana, ed. *Telling Histories: Narrativizing History, Historicizing Literature.* Amsterdam: Rodopi, 1995. This wide-ranging study of the way history appears in fiction and the way in which fiction critiques history leads up to studies of contemporary British writing, including the trilogy ending in *The Gates of Ivory.* Complex essays that place Drabble's work in perspective.

Rubenstein, Roberta. "Fragmented Bodies/Selves/Narratives: Margaret Drabble's Postmodern Turn." *Contemporary Literature* 35 (1994): 136-155. This article focuses on Drabble's use of illness, the maiming of the body, and metaphorical suggestions of human beings disintegrating to reflect how the larger world is losing meaning.

Sullivan, Mary Rose. "Margaret Drabble: Chronicler, Moralist, Artist." In *British Women Writing Fiction*, edited by Abby H. P. Werlock. Tuscaloosa: University of Alabama Press, 2000. Provides a short chronological analysis of Drabble's novels through *The Gates of Ivory.* Includes both a bibliography of critical works on Drabble and an extensive bibliography of her works, including her scholarly publications and short stories.

Wojcik-Andrews, Ian. *Margaret Drabble's Female Bildungsromane: Theory, Genre, and Gender.* New York: Peter Lang, 1995. This book approaches Drabble's novels of women's experience of growth and maturity through a variety of theoretical perspectives, including Marxist-feminist theory.

The Gaucho Martín Fierro

Author: José Hernández (1834-1886)
First published: part 1, *El gaucho Martín Fierro*, 1872; part 2, *La vuelta de Martín Fierro*, 1879 (English translation, 1935)
Type of work: Poetry
Type of plot: Adventure
Time of plot: Nineteenth century
Locale: Argentina

Principal characters:
MARTÍN FIERRO, the gaucho
CRUZ, his friend
PICARDIA, Cruz's son
TWO SONS OF MARTÍN FIERRO

The Poem:

Martín Fierro is a gaucho, born and raised on the rolling plains of Argentina. A gaucho is a mixture of the Spaniard and the Moor, transplanted to South America and mixed again with aboriginal Indians. He is God-fearing, brutal, superstitious, ignorant, lazy, and kind. His type is a passing one, but while he roams the plains he is a legend. Martín plays his guitar and sings his songs, songs that tell of his unhappiness and the sorrows of the gaucho all over the land.

Martín has a home and a wife and children to comfort him. He owns land and cattle and a snug house. He rides the plains and lives in peace with his neighbors. Then officers appear to take Martín and his neighbors away from their homes and families to serve the government in wars with the Indians. Martín is among those chosen because he did not vote when the judge was up for election, and the judge says that those who do not vote help the opposition. The government promises that the gauchos will serve only six months and then be replaced. Martín takes his horse and clothes and leaves his wife and children.

The men live in filth and poverty. Complaints bring a staking out and lashes with leather thongs. There are no arms; the colonel keeps the guns and ammunition locked up except when the Indians attack. The Indians come and go as they please, killing, plundering, and taking hostages. They pull babies from mothers' arms and kill them for sport. The Indians are not much worse than the officers, however. The men have no pay, no decent food. They wear rags, and rats crawl over them while they sleep.

At last, Martín escapes and returns to his home. There he finds his wife and sons gone, the house destroyed, the cattle and sheep sold by the government. Martín swears revenge and sets out to find his sons. He is soon in more trouble. He kills a black man in a fight. Another swaggering gaucho picks a quarrel and Martín kills him. These killings bring the police after him. They track him down and are about to kill him when one of their number joins him in fighting the others. Cruz, his new friend, fights so bravely that the two of them drive off or kill their attackers.

Cruz, telling Martín his story, sings it like a true gaucho. He lost his woman to the *commandante* of the army and so left his home. He, too, killed a man and was hunted by the law until an influential friend got him a pardon and a job with the police, but Cruz has no heart for the police. Seeing Martín prepared to fight against great odds, he decides to join him. The two resolve to leave the frontier and go to live among the Indians.

Martín and Cruz travel across the desert to the land of the savages. Before they can make friends and join a tribe, they are captured by a raiding party. For two years, they suffer tortures inflicted by the Indians; then they are allowed to pitch a tent and live together, still under guard. They have to ride with the savages on raids against the Christians. When smallpox ravages the tribe, Cruz gives his life by nursing a chief who has been kind to them.

Martín is alone once more. At last, he escapes from the Indians. He rescues a white woman who had been beaten with the bowels of her own baby son. After weeks of weary travel, they return to the plains, where Martín leaves the woman with a rancher and goes on his way. He knows by then that even the evils of the government are better than life with savage Indians.

Martín, returning to his homeland, learns that he is no longer wanted by the government. The judge who put him into the army is dead, and no one any longer cares about the black man and the gaucho he killed in fair fights. In his new freedom, he goes to a racing meet and there is reunited with two of his sons. From them, he learns that his wife is dead and that they had also been tortured and cheated by the government.

The older son sings his song first. He had been arrested and convicted for a killing that he did not do. Beaten, starved, abused, he spent a long time in the penitentiary. In his loneliness, he had had no friend to share his woes. He cautions all who hear his tale to keep away from the law, for the law is not for the gaucho.

The second son sings his song. An aunt died and left him some property. The judge appointed a tutor who robbed the boy of his inheritance and beat him and starved him. Penniless, Martín's second son roamed the land like a tramp until he was sent to the frontier with the army.

Father and sons sit singing and talking, when a stranger named Picardia appears and sings his song. Like the others, he was sent to serve in the army and endured the tortures of the wicked officials. At the end of his song, Picardia tells Martín that he is the son of Cruz, Martín's old friend. The friends celebrate the meeting with wine and song. While they sing, a black man joins them. He and Martín hold a singing match, a common thing among the gauchos. The African American sings that he is the brother of the black man Martín killed long years before, and that he will avenge the death. Before they can fight, other gauchos step between them and send Martín, his sons, and Picardia on their way.

They ride only a short distance together, then separate to seek new lives, each man alone. Before they depart, Martín gives the young men some advice out of his own experience. He tells them to be true to their friends, to give every man his due, to obey the law, and to never cheat. If ever a woman should win their hearts, they must treat her well and be true. The four scatter, each one taking a new name from that day on. Martín, ending his song, commends his words to gauchos everywhere, for they come from the wisdom of an old man. Then he lays down his guitar, never to sing again.

Critical Evaluation:

Although it is not well known in the English-speaking world, the tale of Martín Fierro has had great popularity in the South American countries, particularly in Argentina. Fierro gave hope to a people long oppressed by the government and cheated by corrupt officials. He became a legend, and his tale was repeated over and over again. José Hernández himself was identified with his hero, and everywhere he went he was idolized as the spokesman for the gaucho. It is said that much of the romantic appeal of the poem is lost in translation; nevertheless, the English version is musical, vigorous, and exciting.

The Gaucho Martín Fierro is the poetic epic of the gauchos who settled the rich Argentine pampas. An ocean of land, pancake flat, the pampa has fertile brown soil and may be the only area on earth where one can yoke oxen to a plow and slice a furrow for six hundred miles without turning up a stone. Before the Spaniards arrived, it was peopled by warlike, nomadic Indians. Its deep grass supported birds and ostriches; its only tree was the rugged ombu, later sung about by Argentine poets, including Hernández. Cattle and horses introduced by the first Spaniards increased at an amazing rate around the port town of Buenos Aires, on the ocean's edge, and a cowboy type known as gaucho began to ride the plains near the town. Slowly, the first gauchos pushed inland, rolling back the Indians, thus starting what was to be their historic role of settling Argentina. Gauchos also settled the "purple land" of Uruguay and the extensive Brazilian pampa of Rio Grande do Sul, but in Argentina they built a nation.

Usually of Spanish or mestizo blood, the gaucho lived on horseback in his sea of grass. He ate only meat, sometimes killing a steer simply to eat its tongue or to have a seat. He was nervous, restless, and almost always in motion. His weapons were a huge knife and the bolas that he twirled to capture steers or ostriches. His games were rough and on horseback; he was tough and ignorant and despised city folk. He drank "Paraguay Tea," or *yerba maté*, and danced the tango. His literature was the so-called gaucho poetry, redolent of the pampa, that was sung around campfires at night by illiterate minstrels known as *payadores*. The *payador* was a medieval European minstrel of Spanish origin, transplanted to the New World, his songs comprising a new, regional literature describing the various types of gaucho, such as the outlaw, the tracker, the tamer of horses, the lover, or the storyteller. This literary genre was to tinge all Argentine literature centuries later, even the drama, and from it came *The Gaucho Martín Fierro*.

A dichotomized Argentina grew during three centuries of colonialism under Spain. White bread was eaten only in "the Port," Buenos Aires, where an urban class dressed in European style and had more contact with Europe than with the semicivilized gauchos of their own country's interior. After Argentina became independent, early in the nineteenth century, an army of gauchos, led by Juan Manuel de Rosas, captured Buenos Aires. To symbolize the capture of the city by the country, Rosas's gauchos tied their horses in front of the Pink House, Argentina's presidential palace. For twenty-three years, Rosas dominated Buenos Aires, persecuting the intellectual class and forcing everyone to wear red, his favorite color.

One young intellectual, Domingo Sarmiento, went into exile and wrote the book *Facundo* (1845). In *Facundo*, the gaucho was criticized as Argentina's barbaric drawback. The title referred to Facundo Quiroga, a gaucho tyrant who ruled

La Rioja Province as head of a gaucho army flying a black death's-head flag of skull and crossbones. Sarmiento included a blueprint for a new Argentina, in which the gaucho would be tamed or replaced by European immigrants, the pampa fenced, railroads built, wheat planted, and higher-bred livestock introduced. Rosas finally fell in 1852, and Sarmiento and others lived to carry out Sarmiento's blueprint for a modernized Argentina.

Hernández was born on an Argentine *estancia*, or large ranch, in Rosas's day. He grew up among gauchos and Indians and loved their free way of life. He knew the gaucho thoroughly—his speech, folklore, psychology, heart, and soul. He also knew the pampa—its beauty, silence, climate, grass, sunrises, and sunsets. As the day of the gaucho began to wane, and Hernández realized that the antigaucho intellectuals were creating a new Argentina, he decided to tell the dying gaucho's story, to portray his manly virtues and his once-happy way of life.

The Gaucho Martín Fierro thus tells of the gaucho's passing. This took place after the 1850's, when the last wild Indian tribes were being pushed up against the setting sun and the Andes foothills. At the same time, the gaucho was being supplanted by progress in the form of barbed wire, railroads, immigrants, wheat, and the herds of purebred cattle and sheep and thoroughbred horses that have made Argentina famous. In telling the tragic story of Martín and his lost family and lost home, the poem includes many epic themes—the fight against injustice, against governmental power over individuals, and against nature and the yearning for lost freedom and lost loved ones during bitter years of exile in a strange country. It also contains such themes as a temporary flight to the land of a hated enemy and the rescue of a maiden in distress. Drenched with the pampa's earthiness, *The Gaucho Martín Fierro* gives pictures of the land and sky, the grass, the birds, and other creatures of the pampa, as well as of the gaucho himself, as symbolized by the redoubtable but bigoted Martín. The poem presents the life cycle of a group of people; the poetic style is brisk and clear, and the language is replete with gaucho vocabulary and flavor of speech. Martín's character projects itself over the poem: The reader can empathize with him for the loss of his home and family; for the lonely bitterness of his cruel military years fighting the raiding Indians on the far frontier; and for his sadness when he finally returns home to find his cabin abandoned, his wife and children gone, and only one familiar figure in sight, his old cat prowling unhappily around the well. *The Gaucho Martín Fierro* holds one's interest throughout most of its stanzas and stands at the summit of Argentine gaucho literature. It attracted attention in Spanish America, Brazil, and

Spain, where the noted Miguel de Unamuno y Jugo often read it aloud to his classes at the Spanish Oxford, Salamanca University.

Gauchos no longer roam the unfenced pampas. They are often only peons on a mechanized *estancia*, but still have nostalgic yearnings for the past. At night, around campfires, they often produce old copies of *The Gaucho Martín Fierro*, bound in calfskin. Gauchos speak of Martín himself as if he still lives and might, at any moment, flip open the cowhide door flap and walk in to sip *yerba maté* and sing his sorrows.

"Critical Evaluation" by William Freitas

Further Reading

Dabove, Juan Pablo. "*Martín Fierro*: Banditry and the Frontiers of the Voice." In *Nightmares of the Lettered City: Banditry and Literature in Latin America, 1816-1929*. Pittsburgh, Pa.: University of Pittsburgh Press, 2007. Focuses on the depiction of banditry in Hernández's poem and in other works of Latin American literature. Describes how this representation is related to the formation of nation states within the region.

Franco, Jean. *An Introduction to Spanish-American Literature*. New York: Cambridge University Press, 1969. Pages 77-82 relate the poem's plot and demonstrate how Hernández's masterpiece transcends the regional dimensions of the pampas to become a universal myth.

Geirola, Gustavo. "Eroticism and Homoeroticism in *Martín Fierro*." In *Bodies and Biases: Sexualities in Hispanic Cultures and Literatures*, edited by David William Foster and Roberto Reis. Minneapolis: University of Minnesota Press, 1996. Geirola's reading of the poem focuses on its depiction of sexuality and gender.

Hanway, Nancy. "The Injured Body: *Martín Fierro* and the Public Hygiene Movement." In *Embodying Argentina: Body, Space, and Nation in Nineteenth Century Narrative*. Jefferson, N.C.: McFarland, 2003. Hanway examines the relationship between the poem's theme of displacement and the nineteenth century debate over public hygiene. She also explores how the poem, and other works of Argentine literature written between 1850 and 1880, depict changing ideas about Argentine nationhood.

Lindstrom, Naomi. "Argentina." In *Handbook of Latin American Literature*, edited by David William Foster. 2d ed. New York: Garland, 1992. Shows that, despite its harsh criticism of the Argentine government's policy of waging war on the Indians in the pampas, this poem did not slow the campaign to convert the pampas to fenced private property.

Sommer, Doris. *Foundational Fictions: The National Romances of Latin America*. Berkeley: University of California Press, 1991. Compares the poem to José Mármol's novel *Amalia* (1851), and shows how the former projects an epic view of the Argentine nation as rooted in the ruggedness of the gaucho way of life.

Vogeley, Nancy. "The Figure of the Black *Payador* in *Martín Fierro*." *College Language Association Journal* 26, no. 1 (September, 1982): 34-48. Compares the unfavorable depiction of the black singer in *The Gaucho Martín Fierro* with the favorable depiction of the gaucho.

A General Introduction to Psychoanalysis

Author: Sigmund Freud (1856-1939)
First published: Vorlesungen zur Einführung in die Psychoanalyse, 1917 (English translation, 1920)
Type of work: Psychology

A General Introduction to Psychoanalysis, which could more properly be entitled "Introductory Lectures in Psychoanalysis," probably remains the most widely used and popular means of introducing Sigmund Freud's ideas of the psyche. Given during World War I, these lectures embody the results of Freud's analytical research between 1895 and 1910, when the basic groundwork was set for his revolutionary ideas about the role of the unconscious and the power of sexuality in the life of the mind. Freud undertook several other introductory surveys in later years, but these lectures remain the most concise and useful of the Freudian surveys. Although a veritable army of subsequent Freudian scholars and psychoanalysts have explicated the Viennese pioneer, none can replace Freud's own writings, for he is an excellent stylist and the power of his mind speaks in every paragraph, even in translation. Freud reproduces his own quest for meaning in these lectures and involves the reader in what is, among other things, one of the greatest detective stories ever written. Another device, which Freud employs here as elsewhere, is to have frequent recourse to dialogue between himself and an imaginary, quasi-hostile critic. With this rhetorical procedure, Freud succeeds in half convincing his readers even before he has begun to present his arguments in full.

In his first four lectures, Freud gives an analysis of the psychology of errors as a simple means of introducing what was at that time an extraordinary subject. The slip of the tongue or pen, misreading, forgetting, or mislaying things is often not due to chance but comes from something contrary to our rational intention that slips out and distorts speech or action. From the device of the errors that often are not what they appear, Freud turns in the next ten lectures to dreams. Freud is concerned to stress that his subject is not abnormal psychology, and that his analysis applies to all. It was because his patients spoke of dreams so often that Freud began this area of investigation. It was another radical idea, for the reading of dreams was tantamount to Gypsy soothsaying. According to Freud, the dream must be interpreted, for the manifest dream content always condenses, displaces, or elaborates the latent content and replaces feelings with visual images. In interpretation, the analyst ignores surface confusion and waits for the central theme to emerge from the dreamer's retelling. In sleep people regress; the conscious mind idles at its customary control, and the mind returns to something like the womb. Moreover, dreamers know the meaning of their dreams, but they generally do not know that they know. Freud maintains that all the manifest or surface content of the dream comes from experience of the previous waking day. Because dreamers fear the censor or dread reality, their minds distort and condense. Thus all dream material is symbolic. To someone who knows the environment and circumstances in which a dreamer has dreamed, interpretation is simple. Although, however, it is unclear to Freud at this time why certain elements are symbolic and others are not, he is convinced that the overwhelming number of dream symbols are sexual.

As Freud notes in his introduction, the greatest resistance to his work came because of his insistence on the importance of sexuality in the formation of character. In dreams, the male organ is represented by all pointed or elongated objects, fish and snakes, anything sharp, like a weapon. All hollows, apertures, and jewels represent the female organ. Birth is associated with water, and erection and intercourse with flying. Freud notes that all these associations can be found in folklore, legend, and jokes, and in daytime fantasies as well as in night dreams. So important is this material, he briefly suggests, that all conscious language, and thus rational thought, comes from the libido, or sexual hunger. In answer to his critics, Freud declares that these symbolic readings must not be applied mechanically; dreams require a sensitive and intelligent interpreter. Not all dreams are primarily sexual, though he insists that the oddest, most anxiety-ridden ones invariably are. The material in dreams is primitive in that it comes out of the childhood of the dreamer and perhaps the childhood of the race. Here Freud briefly suggests an idea that his quondam colleague, Carl G. Jung, was to make into a major tenet in his quite different analytical mode, in which he posited a racial unconsciousness within the psyche, as well as an individual one.

It is an untenable fallacy, Freud observes, to call children innocent, if it means innocent of sexuality. The child has not yet focused upon sex as reproduction, a situation that adults often fail to observe. The child is "polymorphously perverse," in Freud's phrase. In dreams people regress to childhood, for the unconscious is the repository of infantile mental life. What adults call evil in dream and intent is merely childlike. What becomes apparent here is Freud's calm expectation that human beings can understand and consequently control everything. Known to popular culture as an exponent of free love and a demoniac prophet of uncontrollable sex, Freud actually was one of the greatest of the nineteenth century rationalists. His whole life went into extending understanding, so that control and utilization might follow. Rather than being a prophet of doom, he is a scientist with perhaps too much faith in human perfectibility.

In the last portion of the book, a series of twelve lectures, Freud outlines his general theory of sexuality and neurosis. The whole science of psychoanalysis comes from the study of obsessional neurosis. In such a condition, the mind is taken over at times by seemingly useless and meaningless compulsions and forced to repeat trivial acts that nevertheless are endowed with unreasonable tension and anxiety. Through his work with Josef Breuer on hysteria—first through hypnosis and then through his own technique of free association—Freud found that patient after patient, in probing the past, came up with some event or situation over which the unconscious still brooded, causing neurosis in the present. Freud called this stumbling block a trauma, and he designed his analytical technique as a way of exploring and explaining this event to his patients, thus ridding them of the need to succumb to the trauma. Out of fear, patients will always resist such a probe, a situation that must be overcome by the analyst's seeking the patients' confidence and persuading them to participate in the quest themselves. Every neurosis contains such a trauma or fixation, Freud avers, though not every fixation need cause a neurosis. The mind could be described as two rooms: a large one crowded with unconscious feelings and memories, and a small preconscious room of control and censorship. (In later Freudian theory this metaphorical structure became the famous tripartite designation of id, ego, and superego.)

In the last lectures of this series, Freud describes the development of human sexuality as his analysis found it. Libido, or sex drive, is present in the child from the beginning, though unfocused. At first a child's libido is directed through sucking toward its mother's breast, which is the first object of sexual desire. Later the child is autoerotic, finding gratification for libido in exploring itself. Then the child becomes analytical, interested in objects and finding gratification in bowel movements, for example. From age seven on the child is latently mature, beginning to be concerned with adult or genital sex. The first object of love is the mother. Here Freud summarizes his famous analysis of the Oedipus myth, in which the hero is punished by society and the gods for killing his father and marrying his mother. This is the key myth in Western culture, Freud explains, because what society calls "maturity" consists of displacing the libidinal fixation from the mother and transferring it to another being of the opposite sex beyond the incest barrier. Those who cannot or will not do this revert to childlike sexuality, which in the adult is perversion.

In conclusion, Freud notes that psychoanalysis is only a superstructure, resting on some organic base (the electrochemistry of the brain) about which little is yet known. Psychoanalysis does not advocate free love or wild abandonment through destroying censorship. It seeks to free the libido from unhealthy repressions and re-educate the whole person for a responsible life in a world of adult maturity.

Further Reading

Elliott, Anthony, ed. *Freud 2000*. Cambridge, England: Polity Press, 1998. The essayists examine how Freud's theories apply to current issues in the social sciences and humanities.

Gay, Peter. *Freud: A Life for Our Time*. New York: W. W. Norton, 1988. Covers the whole of Freud's life. Devotes considerable attention to the history, techniques, implications, and applications of psychoanalysis. Includes some references to *A General Introduction to Psychoanalysis*.

Jones, Ernest. *The Life and Work of Sigmund Freud*. Edited by Lionel Trilling and Steven Marcus. 3 vols. New York: Basic Books, 1961. A superb reference for information on Freud. The discussion of *A General Introduction to Psychoanalysis* includes synopsis and information on its origin and creation.

Levin, Gerald. *Sigmund Freud*. Boston: Twayne, 1975. A concise yet efficient and thorough study of Freud. Includes biography, case histories, Freud's theory of literature, and discussions of several specific writings, including *A General Introduction to Psychoanalysis*.

McGlashan, Agnes M., and Christopher J. Reeve. *Sigmund Freud: Founder of Psychoanalysis*. New York: Praeger, 1970. A short account of the life of Freud through his work and theories; McGlashan focuses on Freud's biography as it is relevant to the advent of psychoanalysis. Includes illustrations.

Neu, Jerome, ed. *The Cambridge Companion to Freud*. New York: Cambridge University Press, 1991. Collection of essays analyzing various aspects of Freud's philosophy.

Timms, Edward, and Naomi Segal, eds. *Freud in Exile: Psychoanalysis and Its Vicissitudes*. New Haven, Conn.: Yale University Press, 1988. Articles discuss the Jewish origins of psychoanalysis, Freud's library, and the impact of psychoanalysis on art criticism. Contains five essays on the problems of translating Freud and a final section on the future of psychoanalysis.

The "Genius"

Author: Theodore Dreiser (1871-1945)
First published: 1915
Type of work: Novel
Type of plot: Naturalism
Time of plot: 1889-1914
Locale: Alexandria and Chicago, Illinois; New York

Principal characters:
EUGENE WITLA, the "genius"
THOMAS WITLA, his father, a sewing machine agent
SYLVIA and MYRTLE, his sisters
STELLA APPLETON, Eugene's first love
ANGELA BLUE, a schoolteacher and later Eugene's wife
MARGARET DUFF, a laundry worker and Eugene's first lover
RUBY KENNY, an artist's model
MIRIAM FINCH, a sculptor in New York
CHRISTINA CHANNING, a singer in New York
ANATOLE CHARLES, an art dealer
FRIEDA ROTH, a young woman in Alexandria
CARLOTTA WILSON, a gambler's wife
DANIEL SUMMERFIELD, the head of an advertising agency
OBADIAH KALVIN, the head of a publishing company
MARSHALL P. COLFAX, a publisher
FLORENCE J. WHITE, Eugene's associate and enemy
MRS. EMILY DALE, a wealthy socialite friend of Eugene
SUZANNE, her daughter
MRS. JOHNS, a Christian Science practitioner

The Story:

Eugene Witla, a sensitive seventeen-year-old boy, lives with his parents and two sisters in Alexandria, Illinois. Eugene has little idea of what he wants to do, although his aspirations are vaguely artistic. His father, a sewing machine agent and a respectable member of the middle class, gets him a job setting type for the local newspaper. He falls in love with a local girl named Stella Appleton, but even this does not keep him from leaving the small town and going to Chicago to seek his fortune.

In Chicago, Eugene at first supports himself by moving stoves, driving a laundry wagon, and collecting for a furniture company. While at the laundry, he meets the passionate young Margaret Duff and enters into his first real love affair. About this time, he also meets a schoolteacher named Angela Blue, a fair-haired, beautiful young woman who represents everything fine and elegant to impressionable young Eugene.

Eugene begins attending art classes at night at the Chicago Art Institute. He shows some talent, particularly in life drawing, for he seems to have a special sensitivity in conveying the beauty of the human form. He meets a model there, Ruby Kenny, who soon becomes his mistress. Ruby, like Margaret, is from the lower classes and makes her charms

easily available to men. Eugene finally leaves them both, preferring the finer and more fragile beauty of Angela, to whom he becomes engaged before he leaves Chicago to seek his artistic fortune in New York.

There, Eugene paints powerful and realistic pictures of what he sees in the city. From time to time, he sells a few of his paintings, and after several years, he becomes moderately successful. Some of the women he meets, like Miriam Finch and Christina Channing, begin to educate him in the knowledgeable polish of the New York art world. For a short time, he has a sophisticated affair with Christina that somewhat baffles him; despite his new elegance, he still thinks of Angela. Returning to the Midwest to visit her, he seduces her and then, feeling his responsibility, marries her and takes her back to New York. Angela feels that all her dreams of happiness have been fulfilled.

Eugene's work impresses Anatole Charles, the manager of a distinguished firm of art dealers in New York. Monsieur Charles holds an exhibit which is a great success and gives Eugene a reputation as a rising young artist. Full of enthusiasm, he and Angela go to Paris. The works he shows when he returns are not as successful and are judged less fresh and unusual. While in Paris, Eugene began to suffer from a vague malaise and lack of energy and purpose. He does not realize at the time that his marriage is causing him to feel uneasy and restless.

Eugene and Angela return to Alexandria for an inexpensive rest. While there, Eugene meets eighteen-year-old Frieda Roth, whom he finds all the more attractive because he is twenty-nine and Frieda represents a connection to youth and beauty. Angela is able to stop this relationship before it advances further than a few kisses. Eugene and Angela leave Alexandria and stay at several resorts until their money runs out. Angela then returns to her parents, while Eugene returns to New York to reestablish his reputation as an artist.

Eugene is still restless, however, and finds himself unable to paint. He takes a job doing manual labor for the railroad in a town near New York. There he meets and has a passionate affair with his landlady's married daughter, Carlotta Wilson. Angela hears of the affair and again reclaims Eugene. They decide to try to start again in New York.

Eugene works for a newspaper and then as art director for an advertising agency. When his superior there, Daniel Summerfield, breaks his promises and fails to pay him adequately, Eugene leaves for another job with the advertising department of the *North American Weekly*, under the directorship of Obadiah Kalvin. Successful there, he moves to Philadelphia to accept a higher paying job as head of advertising for all books and publications directed by Marshall P. Colfax. When Eugene is made a vice president, the other vice president, Florence J. White, becomes jealous.

Eugene becomes very successful, both financially and socially. His marriage is hollow, but both he and Angela accept the situation and cope fairly well. Although Eugene has money enough to retire and go back to painting, he desires greater financial success and loses the will to paint. His artistic lassitude is matched by the emotional emptiness of his marriage.

About this time, Eugene meets Mrs. Emily Dale, a rich socialite. They exchange visits and become friendly. One day, Mrs. Dale brings Suzanne, her eighteen-year-old daughter, to tea, and Eugene falls in love with her at first sight. All his yearning for beauty returns, and soon Eugene and Suzanne are meeting secretly. Although she is a cultured and sophisticated young woman, Suzanne is willing to enter into an affair with Eugene. Filled with romantic ideas about being an artist's mistress, she insists on telling her mother of her plans, for she is sure that her mother will approve. However, Mrs. Dale does not approve, and Angela, when she learns of the affair, decides that the only way to hold Eugene is to have a baby, despite the fact that doctors have warned her against having children. Angela, who has become a Christian Scien-

tist, believes that her firm faith and willpower will allow her to have a healthy child. Mrs. Dale takes her daughter to Canada to get her away from Eugene. When he tries to follow Suzanne to Canada, Mrs. Dale puts pressure on Florence and threatens the firm with scandal, whereupon Eugene is fired from his job. Having lost both his job and Suzanne, Eugene returns to comfort Angela during her ordeal.

Angela dies giving birth to a daughter, who is also named Angela. Eugene asks his sister Myrtle to come east to help him make a home for the child. In his desolation, Eugene begins to read about Christian Science, but he fails to find comfort or salvation in its message.

When Eugene and Suzanne meet by accident on the street two years later, they are both too self-conscious to acknowledge the other's presence. Living sanely with his daughter and Myrtle and her husband, Eugene begins to paint again. He has several shows, is sponsored again by Monsieur Charles, and again becomes a popular and fairly successful artist. He begins to weave romantic dreams around his daughter, Angela, thinking of the time when she will grow up and they can search for beauty together. In spite of his new awareness of human beings' inability to control their fate, and of the delusions that belief in beauty or belief in Christian Science represent, Eugene's emotional impulse toward beauty remains strong, and he continues to dream impossible dreams for himself and his daughter.

Critical Evaluation:

The "Genius" is generally conceded to be the weakest of Theodore Dreiser's major novels, but critical opinion differs as to whether it is a magnificent failure or simply a failure. Its weaknesses generally derive from the fact that Dreiser was too subjectively involved with his artistic protagonist to clarify his ideas. Although all of Dreiser's writings contain many transcriptions of direct experience, *The "Genius"* chronicles traumatic events that were recent personal history. In many aspects, Eugene Witla's artistic career closely parallels Dreiser's own—impoverished youth, odd jobs, modest artistic success, nervous breakdown, restoration, financial success, monetary and professional collapse, and, finally, serious artistic endeavors. More important, in terms of Dreiser's emotional identification with the story, is the fact that Eugene's marriage to Angela Blue—with all of its consequent disappointments, frustrations, hostilities, and psychic damage—is a thinly disguised rendering of his own drawn-out, agonized marriage to Sallie White.

If the extreme subjectivity of *The "Genius"* weakens the book artistically, however, it also makes it a vital document to anyone interested in Dreiser's life and works. The novel focuses on the tensions among three fundamental human elements: the urge to artistic creation, the sexual drive, and the corrupting influence of material success. For all of its complexity, inconsistency, redundancy, and confusion, at the center of *The "Genius"*—and what gives the novel its redeeming strength—is Eugene's prolonged and agonized attempt to reconcile those three forces.

In the opening segment of the book, Eugene is introduced to creative activity and sexuality almost simultaneously. His artistic impulse, like Dreiser's, is to portray life as realistically and graphically as possible. His vision of women, however, is idealistic: The perfect woman is beautiful, sensual, and "always eighteen." His sexual impulses are intensified by the fact that he seeks an impossibility and becomes increasingly frustrated in his effort to find that ideal—which recedes even further as he ages.

His situation is made more complicated and painful by his foolish marriage to Angela, the one woman for whom he feels, at best, a lukewarm sexual attraction. Initially, Angela represents America's small-town, conservative, hypocritical morality, especially in sexual matters. Her narrowness, provinciality, possessiveness, and domineering attitude toward Eugene frustrate both his artistic development and his personal fulfillment. When he begins to drift to other women, Angela becomes sexually aggressive in an attempt to save the marriage. In the novel's most absurd hypothesis, Dreiser ascribes Eugene's nervous breakdown to the excessive sexual activity Angela instigates.

Dreiser also blames Angela for Eugene's turn from artistic creativity to crass commercialism. It is at her prompting that Eugene puts his painting aside and becomes an advertising executive. It is suggested, therefore, that a curious alliance of sex, materialism, and middle-class morality have combined temporarily to suppress Eugene's creativity; his return to serious painting does not result from a repudiation of materialism but is the consequence, once again, of his sexual adventuring. Eugene's affair with the daughter of a rich and powerful socialite costs him his job, his fortune, and his social standing, but it also forces him back to the easel, where he apparently regains all of his creative powers quickly.

Dreiser demonstrates that even the strong-willed and talented are ultimately buffeted by forces over which they have little control. Despite his remarkable abilities and powerful drive, Eugene allows major decisions—whether to be an artist, to marry, to become a businessman, to return to painting—to be made for him by outside circumstances and internal impulses over which he chooses to exercise little conscious control. At the end of the book, there are hopeful hints—his painting, his "forgiveness" of Angela, his feelings

for his daughter—but the final image is that of an aged and unreconciled artist who feels no personal satisfaction, no social identification, or even a conviction that his own life and art have real value and meaning.

Further Reading

Cassuto, Leonard, and Clare Virginia Eby, eds. *The Cambridge Companion to Theodore Dreiser.* New York: Cambridge University Press, 2004. A collection of twelve essays focusing on the novelist's examination of American conflicts between materialistic longings and traditional values. Includes essays on Dreiser's style, Dreiser and women, and Dreiser and the ideology of upward mobility. The references to *The "Genius"* are listed in the index.

Gerber, Philip L. *Theodore Dreiser Revisited.* New York: Twayne, 1992. Concludes that Dreiser while writing *The "Genius"* was too close to the work's autobiographical elements (his own failing marriage and frustrating editorial work during the years 1898-1910) to shape a convincing story about his hero's conflicting artistic, materialistic, and sexual desires.

Gogol, Miriam, ed. *Theodore Dreiser: Beyond Naturalism.* New York: New York University Press, 1995. Ten essays interpret Dreiser from the perspectives of new historicism, poststructuralism, psychoanalysis, feminism, and other points of view. Gogol's introduction advances the argument that Dreiser was much more than a naturalist and deserves to be treated as a major author.

Juras, Uwe. *Pleasing to the "I": The Culture of Personality and Its Representations in Theodore Dreiser and F. Scott Fitzgerald.* New York: Peter Lang, 2006. Juras examines how the two authors depicted the newly emerging concept of personality, defined as the outward presentation of self, in their work. Includes a discussion of *The "Genius."*

Loving, Jerome. *The Last Titan: A Life of Theodore Dreiser.* Berkeley: University of California Press, 2005. This engrossing survey of the author's life and work is a welcome addition to Dreiser scholarship. Focuses on Dreiser's work, including his journalism, discussing the writers who influenced him and his place within American literature.

Lundquist, James. *Theodore Dreiser.* New York: Frederick Ungar, 1974. Suggests that in *The "Genius"* Dreiser begins to show an increased sympathy toward his characters, especially Eugene Witla, an artist struggling in a world that overvalues both material success and marital fidelity. Notes resemblances between Dreiser's cityscapes and Everett Shinn's paintings of the so-called Ashcan School.

Mencken, H. L. "A Literary Behemoth." In *Critical Essays on Theodore Dreiser*, edited by Donald Pizer. Boston: G. K. Hall, 1981. Reprint of Mencken's 1915 article, in which he rebukes Dreiser for piling on details in numbingly dull prose, but praises him for showing that spiritual corruption follows Eugene Witla's financial successes and that his inner conflicts add to his bitterness.

Swanberg, W. A. *Dreiser*. New York: Charles Scribner's Sons, 1965. Shows how thoroughly Dreiser based his main characters and episodes on his own acquaintances and experiences. Details efforts of the New York Society for the Suppression of Vice to censor Dreiser's alleged blasphemy and obscenity.

Warren, Robert Penn. *Homage to Theodore Dreiser*. New York: Random House, 1971. Castigates Dreiser for self-indulgence and self-vindication in *The "Genius"* and for naïvely believing that a collection of supposedly true details of his life would take on artistic form.

Georgics

Author: Vergil (70-19 B.C.E.)
First transcribed: c. 37-29 B.C.E. (English translation, 1589)
Type of work: Poetry

Vergil's *Georgics*, a long poetic work in four sections, was written at the request of the poet's patron, Maecenas, to bolster the Emperor Augustus's agricultural policy. It was essential to the progress of the Roman nation that farming be seen as a worthy and patriotic occupation for soldiers returning from military campaigns, and Vergil's work glorifies many aspects of country life. His poem is quite remarkable, for in it he manages to provide a considerable amount of what was, in his day, accurate information on the cultivation of crops and the care of animals, while maintaining a lofty tone that is far from the prosaic quality of the subject matter.

Vergil uses mythology extremely effectively, invoking the gods traditionally associated with agriculture at the beginning of each section and describing such ordinary phenomena as spring rains in metaphorical terms; the rain is Aether, the atmosphere's embrace of his wife, the earth. By referring to familiar deities, Vergil lifts details of the weather and conditions of the soil far above the realm of the mundane. His metaphorical language, his use of epic similes, and his references to the greatness of his country also contribute to making the *Georgics* fine poetry.

Each of the four sections deals with a specific problem of farming, but each also has a number of digressions that add interest and grandeur to the work as a whole. The first Georgic begins with a long invocation to the deities who control the growth of grain, vines, and olives and a special prayer to Julius Caesar, who has become a new divinity, with his own place among the constellations. The body of this section is devoted to the plowing, planting, and harvesting of crops and to the helpful knowledge that can be gained by study of the stars. Practical advice on the best time to plow and sow, on crop rotation, on fertilizing the soil, and on the tools needed by the farmer is enlivened by a majestic description of a storm, brief vignettes of farm life, and a description of the worship of the goddess Ceres at harvest time. A discussion of the changing appearance of the sun under different weather conditions leads to a description of the eclipse that was one of the disastrous omens that appeared at the time of the assassination of Julius Caesar. The conclusion of this section is a prayer that Augustus, Rome's new champion, may bring peace to the nation and allow farmers to return from the battlefield to their own lands.

The cultivation of the vine and the olive, staples of the Italian economy, is the central theme of the second Georgic, and Vergil makes the appropriate invocation to Bacchus, the wine god, as well as to the poet's patron, as this part of the poem opens. Perhaps the most memorable passages here are the poet's lines in praise of Italy, in which he cites the special virtues of each part of the country and evokes patriotic sentiments as he alludes to famous ruling families of past ages. Notable is the restatement of the pastoral ideal, Vergil's picture of the happy state of the farmers who live at peace on their own lands, far from the battlefield, the rule of law courts, and the frenzy of politics.

Even subjects such as the grafting of trees and the preparation of soil for the planting of seedlings are treated in majestic language, and the catalog of the virtues of the various wines of the country is equally poetic. John Milton learned much from this classical master about the evocative effect of place names.

Vergil's praise of country life at the end of this section is tied to his political aims; he asserts that it was through the efforts of the sturdy farmers of the past that Etruria and Rome won their first greatness, and he suggests that much of the fate of the new empire will rest on those who cultivate the Italian fields.

The third Georgic opens with a general statement on poetry. Vergil realizes that he is opening new doors in writing about fields and flocks; he also knows that the old myths have been repeated so often that they no longer lend luster to the poet. He hopes eventually to win fame for himself and for his homeland, Mantua, by describing the heroic exploits of Augustus Caesar and his army; but, meanwhile, he must follow Maecenas's request that he chronicle the domain of the wood nymphs, and he turns to a new topic, the breeding of horses and cattle. He pictures vividly the strength and grace of the thoroughbred horse, alert and eager for action as the mount of a great soldier. Vergil elevates the tone of his subject by alluding to the magnificent horsemen and charioteers among the Homeric heroes.

The nurture of sheep and goats forms another part of this section. The poet even suggests remedies for diseases that strike these animals, and he gives a moving and realistic description of a devastating plague among them, picturing their death agonies as the result of the avenging force of the fury Tisiphone, who drives slaughter and terror before her.

The fourth Georgic probably has provided the greatest pleasure for modern readers, who can share Vergil's fascination with the habits of bees more readily than his interest in various kinds of soil and methods of grafting. The poet relates the popular belief that the highly complex society of the bees results from a special blessing bestowed on them by Jupiter after they aided him when he was imprisoned in a cave; they alone of all the creatures live under law.

The poet has observed colonies of bees closely, and he describes with great accuracy their characteristic swarms and the battles between the "king" bees for supremacy. He suggests the best sweet-smelling plants for attracting the swarms to new hives and recommends the playing of cymbals to aid in drawing them toward their new homes. He also offers helpful hints about the flowers that make the best honey and mourns regretfully that he lacks time and space to speak of gardens.

The last half of this Georgic deals with the curious subject of spontaneous generation from corruption, a belief that has fascinated humankind as recently as the seventeenth century, when Francis Bacon discussed it in his *New Atlantis* (1627). There was a tradition, apparently quite widespread, that, should a whole colony of bees perish, a new swarm could be born from the corruption of the blood of a slaughtered bullock. Vergil explains this phenomenon by relating a mythological tale about a shepherd, Aristaeus, the son of Apollo and a sea nymph, who goes to the sea god Proteus to learn why his bees have died. He finds that the nymphs who mourn the deaths of Orpheus and Eurydice have brought about this misfortune, and he sacrifices four bulls to placate the spirits of the singer and his bride. A great cloud of bees arises from the carcasses of these animals, signifying the acceptability of the sacrifice; from that time on, hives were believed to be replenished in the same way.

The concluding lines of the fourth Georgic summarize the poet's achievement in this poem; he speaks a little apologetically about singing of the cultivation of fields, flocks, and trees while Caesar is winning great victories, and he identifies himself as the same writer who formerly sang of the shepherd Tityrus, in his *Eclogues* (43-37 B.C.E.).

While the *Aeneid* (c. 29-19 B.C.E.) is unquestionably Vergil's masterpiece, the *Georgics* perhaps reveals his remarkable poetic imagination even more fully. There are few successful didactic poems in Western literature, only a small number of which achieve the majestic tone of Vergil's work. Like all great practitioners of the genre, Vergil pays careful attention to the specifics of his subject, in this case farming, and his clear affection for the simple, unsullied lifestyle of the rural inhabitants of Italy shines forth in a work that allows him to transform the commonplace into the materials of great art. No doubt his patrons (including the emperor, Augustus) would have been exceedingly pleased to find such a compelling argument for the continuance of the agrarian lifestyle expressed in mellifluous language. The work stands with Lucretius's *De rerum natura* (c. 60 B.C.E.; *On the Nature of Things*, 1682) as one of the finest transformations of technical materials into poetry produced during the classical period in literature.

Were the work only a technical treatise, however, its appeal to succeeding generations would have long since faded. As numerous critics have pointed out, in the *Georgics*, Vergil transcends his subject to present to readers a more universal theme about humankind and the relationship of humanity to the natural world. Working as he often does on the principle of analogy, Vergil draws constant, if subtle, parallels between the farmer's life and that of all people: The cycle of life parallels the yearly cycle that the farmer repeats, working sometimes in cooperation with the world around him and sometimes against it, to forge a meaningful life and achieve a sense of happiness and accomplishment.

The work highlights the theme of regeneration and the symbiotic relationship between humans and the natural world. The work is also visionary in that it rises above the details of farming life to present a vision of "the function and value of human art." Seen in this light, the many details of the work, including the curious inclusion of the story of Aristaeus at the conclusion of the fourth book, become important keys to understanding the classical view of the art of living. More properly, perhaps, the *Georgics* suggests ways that one can make an art out of living.

Vergil's indirect method of presenting his theme is effective precisely because it is evocative rather than directive. The method has been practiced by many since that time but never with greater subtlety or technical skill.

"Critical Evaluation" by Laurence W. Mazzeno

Further Reading

Griffin, Jasper. *Virgil*. New York: Oxford University Press, 1986. A general introduction to Vergil's life and works. The third chapter examines the *Georgics* in detail and provides a good explanation of the important themes of labor and duty. Includes a bibliography and an index.

Nappa, Christopher. *Reading After Actium: Vergil's "Georgics," Octavian, and Rome*. Ann Arbor: University of Michigan Press, 2005. A book-by-book analysis of the *Georgics*. Describes Vergil's treatment of Octavian as one of the poem's students, who is given the chance to learn how to wield power, control Rome's resources, and prevent another civil war.

Perret, Jacques. "The *Georgics*." In *Virgil: A Collection of Critical Essays*, edited by Steele Commager. Englewood Cliffs, N.J.: Prentice-Hall, 1966. A concise examination of the *Georgics*. Discusses changes in Vergil's life and his poetry in the period in which he composed the *Georgics*. Provides a useful chronology of Vergil's life and relevant Roman history. Includes bibliography.

Slavitt, David R. *Virgil*. New Haven, Conn.: Yale University Press, 1991. A superior overview of Vergil's poetry. The second chapter discusses the *Georgics* and offers a rewarding analysis of the societal influences in the composition of the work, as well as discussing the poem's influence on ancient and modern literature. Includes index and bibliography.

Volk, Katharina. *The Poetics of Latin Didactic: Lucretius, Vergil, Ovid, Manilius*. New York: Oxford University Press, 2002. Analyzes the theory of poetics in the *Georgics* and four other works of didactic poetry. Chronicles the history of the genre and describes the characteristics of didactic poetry. Chapter 4 focuses on *Georgics*.

_____, ed. *Vergil's "Georgics."* New York: Oxford University Press, 2008. Collection of essays analyzing the work, including discussions of agriculture, tradition and meaning, authorial rhetoric, and myth and allusion in the *Georgics*. Volk's essay reviews scholarly approaches to the poem since the 1970's.

Wilkinson, L. P. *The Georgics of Virgil: A Critical Survey*. New York: Cambridge University Press, 1969. The standard work of criticism for the *Georgics*. Places the poems within their literary and historical context and provides an exhaustive scholarly analysis.

_____. *Virgil: The Georgics*. Harmondsworth, England: Penguin Books, 1982. Excellent translation of the four books. The introduction is a rewarding source for beginners; it summarizes Vergil's life and the political situation of the time, and discusses the *Georgics*'s place in literary tradition. Includes a bibliography and copious notes.

Germinal

Author: Émile Zola (1840-1902)
First published: 1885 (English translation, 1885)
Type of work: Novel
Type of plot: Naturalism
Time of plot: Nineteenth century
Locale: France

Principal characters:
ÉTIENNE LANTIER, a socialist laborer
VINCENT MAHEU or "BONNEMORT," a miner
MAHEUDE, his wife
CATHERINE MAHEU,
ZACHARIE MAHEU,
JEANLIN MAHEU, and
ALZIRE MAHEU, the Maheus' children
CHAVAL, another workman

The Story:

Étienne Lantier sets out to walk from Marchiennes to Montsou looking for work. On the way, he meets Vincent Maheu, another workman, called Bonnemort because of successive escapes from death in the mines. Nearing sixty years old, Bonnemort suffers a bad cough because of particles of dust from the mine pits. Bonnemort has a son whose family consists of seven children. Zacharie, the eldest son, twenty-one years old, Catherine, sixteen years old, and Jeanlin, eleven years old, work in the mines. In the morning, as they are dressing, they listened to the sounds of Levaque leaving the next-door apartment. Soon afterward, Bouteloup joins the Levaque woman. Philomène Levaque, the eldest daughter and Zacharie's mistress, coughs from her lung ailment. Such is the life of those who work in the mine pits.

Étienne is given a job in the mine. He descends the mine shaft along with Maheu, Zacharie, Chaval, Levaque, and Catherine. At first Étienne mistakes the last for a boy. During lunchtime, Chaval roughly forces the girl to kiss him. This act angers Étienne; the girl insists that the brute is not her lover. The head captain, Dansaert, comes with Monsieur Négrel, Monsieur Hennebeau's nephew, to inspect Étienne, the new worker. There is bitterness among the workers, danger lurking in the shafts, and so little pay that it is hardly worth working. Étienne, however, decides to stay in the mine.

M. Grégoire inherited from his grandfather a share in the Montsou mines. He lives in peace and luxury with his wife and only daughter, Cecile. A marriage has been arranged between Cecile and Négrel. One morning Maheude, Maheu's wife, and two of her small children go to the Grégoires to seek help. They are given warm clothing but no money, since the Grégoires believe working people will only spend money in drinking and nonsense. Maheude has to beg for some groceries and money from Maigrat, who keeps a shop and who will lend money if he receives a woman's caresses in return. He has Catherine in mind. Catherine, however, escapes him,

meets Chaval that night, and allows him to seduce her. Étienne witnesses the seduction and is disillusioned by the young girl.

Étienne so quickly and expertly adapts himself to the mine that he earns the respect of Maheu. He makes friends with the other workers. Only toward Chaval is he clandestinely hostile, for Catherine now openly shows herself as the man's mistress. At the place where Étienne lives, he chats with Souvarine, a friendly man who thinks that true social change can only be achieved through violent social revolution. Étienne discusses a new movement he has heard about from his friend Pluchart, a Lille mechanic. It is a Marxist movement to free the workers. Étienne comes to loathe the working conditions and the lives of the miners and their families, and he hopes to collect a fund to sustain the forthcoming strike. He discusses his plan with Rasseneur, with whom he boards.

After Zacharie marries his mistress Philomène, the mother of two of his children, Étienne comes to the Maheu household as a boarder. Night after night he urges them to accept his socialistic point of view. As the summer wears on, he gains prestige among the neighbors, and his fund grows. As the secretary, he draws a small fee and is able to put aside money for himself. He begins to take on airs.

The threat of a strike is provoked when the company changes the structure of the wages of the workers, essentially lowering wages. As a final blow to the Maheus, a cave-in strikes Jeanlin, leaving him a cripple. Catherine goes to live with Chaval, who has been accusing her of sleeping with Étienne. In December, the miners strike. While the Grégoires and the Hennebeaus are at lunch, arranging the plans for the marriage between Cecile and Négrel, the miners' delegation comes to see M. Hennebeau, but he refuses to give any concessions. The strike wears on through the weeks, while the workers slowly starve. Étienne preaches socialism, and the strikers listen; as their misery increases, they became more adamant in their resistance to M. Hennebeau. The endless weeks of strike at the Montsou mines end in a riot when the people advance to other pits to force the workers to quit their labors and join the strike. The mob destroys property throughout the day and rages against their starvation. Catherine remains faithful to Chaval, but when, during the riot, he turns renegade and runs to get the gendarmes, she deserts him to warn her comrades, especially Étienne.

Étienne goes into hiding, assisted by Jeanlin, who has become a street urchin and a thief. The Maheu family fares poorly. Crippled Alzire, one of the younger children, is dying of starvation. Everywhere neighbors quarrel fretfully over trifles. Étienne frequently slips into Maheu's house for a visit. For the most part, he wanders alone at night. After the strike has been in force for two months, there is a rumor that the company is bringing strikebreakers to the pits. Étienne begins to despair. He suggests to the Maheus that the strikers bargain with M. Hennebeau, but Maheude, who once had been so sensible and had resisted violence, shouts that they should not give in to the pressure of their demands.

One night at Rasseneur's, while Étienne is discussing matters with Souvarine, Chaval and Catherine enter. The animosity between Étienne and Chaval flares up, and they fight. Chaval is overpowered and orders Catherine not to follow him but to stay with Étienne. Left alone, Catherine and Étienne are embarrassed and confused. Étienne has no place to take the girl. It is not possible for her to go home, since Maheude could not forgive her for having deserted the family and for working during the strike. Resignedly, Catherine goes back to her lover.

After Catherine leaves, Étienne walks by the pits, where he is a witness to the murder of a guard by little Jeanlin. Étienne drags the body away and hides it. When the strikebreakers begin to work, the strikers storm the entrance to the pit and threaten the soldiers on guard. After a while, the soldiers fire into the mob. Maheu is among those killed. Twenty-five workers are wounded, and fourteen are dead. Company officials come to Montsou to settle the strike. The strikebreakers are sent away. Étienne's popularity ends. He brings Catherine home and begins to stay at Maheu's house again. The bleak house of mourning fills Étienne with remorse.

Souvarine resolves to leave Montsou. Before he goes, he sneaks into the pit and creates enough damage to cause a breakdown in the shafts. That same morning, Étienne and Catherine decide that they must go back to work. Chaval manages to be placed on the same work crew with Étienne and Catherine. Repeatedly the two men clash; Chaval still wants Catherine. Water begins rushing into the shaft. Chaval,

Étienne, and the rest are trapped below when the cage makes its last trip up and does not come down again. The people above wait and watch the mine slowly become flooded. Négrel sets about to rescue the entombed workers; as long as they are below, they must be assumed to be still alive. At last, he and a rescue party hear faint thumpings from the trapped workers. The men begin to dig. An explosion injures several of them and kills Zacharie.

Meanwhile, the trapped workers scatter, trying to find a place of safety. Étienne and Catherine come upon Chaval in the gallery to which he has climbed. There the animosity between the two men leads to a fight that ends when Étienne kills Chaval. Alone, the two lovers hear the rescuers' tapping. For days they continue to answer the tapping. Catherine dies before the men outside reach them. Étienne is still alive when help comes. After six weeks in a hospital, Étienne prepares to go to Paris, where more revolutionary work awaits him.

Critical Evaluation:

From the opening sentence through the final words of *Germinal*, Émile Zola sets a tone that is as relentless as it is bleak. His naturalism is clearly signaled by his opening paragraph, which depicts a solitary man trudging across a lifeless plain, buffeted by March winds that cut like ice and, subsequently, seem to echo with cries of famine and suffering. From this beginning, Zola propels the reader into a metaphorical abyss and devotes the first two (of seven) parts of the novel to a single day, during which the reader is given a panoramic view of the living and working conditions of Montsou.

The Voreux (voracious) mine is introduced. It is a ghoulish monster capable of devouring all who come in contact with it. Its awesomeness, first suggested by Bonnemort, who speaks of the mine as if it were a higher power to which all have surrendered, is reinforced by Étienne's observation that it appears to swallow men in large mouthfuls without taking the slightest notice. Then, once Étienne descends into its bowels, details accumulate and the mine emerges as an elaborate maze that deprives man and beast alike of air, light, and meaningful communication. Its ravenous appetite, no less than its inhospitable nature, makes it a force to be reckoned with even during its destruction following Souvarine's sabotage.

It quickly becomes clear, however, that the mine is not the enemy. The enemies are the board of directors (safely ensconced in Paris, who siphon off the mine's profits with little or no regard for the workers who have generated them) and the lack of class consciousness among the workers. The directors are worse than indifferent. They are calculating in their every move, restructuring wages just after learning that a strikers' contingency fund has been started and bringing in soldiers and Belgian workers with the clear intent of escalating the crisis brought about by the strike. Their heartlessness is not, however, aimed solely at the workers. They also take aim at M. Deneulin, the owner of the Jean-Bart mine, which they hope to add to their acquisitions. When, toward the end of the novel, Deneulin is forced to capitulate, Zola treats it as a death knell for independent entrepreneurs, destined to be picked off one by one by the "maw of capital."

Despite his obvious indignation regarding the aggregation of wealth, Zola tempers his view of the bourgeoisie when depicting its local representatives, which include the Grégoires, Deneulins, Hennebeaus, and Paul Négrel. They are not perpetrators of evil so much as they are flawed humans who also must answer to the soulless board of directors. They, like Étienne and his coworkers, are shown to be victims of social, psychological, historical, and economic forces which they have a "tormenting desire to see and yet a fear of seeing." In part, their reluctance to see is an unwillingness to confront their own powerlessness. On another level their reluctance is a function of their own complicity in the maintenance of the status quo. This complicity, however, is not limited to the upper class. The workers, too, have resigned themselves to their situation and actively compete against one another rather than working together to challenge those in authority.

To emphasize this point, Zola gives Étienne center stage for much of the novel. Being an outsider, he is not accustomed to things that the other miners take for granted. As a result, he not only has the capacity to feel outrage and horror but also the capacity to begin asking questions and seeking answers. His is not, as Zola repeatedly reminds the reader, an ideological campaign so much as it is a quest for understanding and justice. He reads constantly and seems, on occasion, to be testing out ideas. When he galvanizes the workers during the forest meeting, for example, he has no idea that he is essentially giving them license to embark on a rampage of wanton and purposeless destruction. Accordingly, he tries vainly to regain control or, at the very least, to redirect the miners' energies. This failing, he begins to doubt his own words and wonders whether the untutored masses can contribute to meaningful social change.

He cannot embrace Souvarine's advocacy of violent destruction of the existing system. He clearly believes that education and experience will lead individuals to truth. He detests violence, be it Souvarine's calculated sabotage or Jeanlin's capricious killing of the young soldier. It is for this reason that he maintains his resolve to promote socialism through trade unions and legislative initiatives.

His departure from Montsou marks the end of one part of his education. He has learned and taught as much as he can and must seek a new channel. The miners, too, have learned a great deal and are better prepared to work for social justice. The objective circumstances of their lives do not appear to have changed, and in many instances have clearly worsened, but one comes away with the feeling that the excesses and violence were necessary parts of their collective education. Significantly, the image of the miners germinating like good seeds with which Zola concludes the novel has already been introduced at two other critical junctures in the book. Its first occurrence comes in the third chapter of part 3, soon after Étienne moves in with the Maheus and begins trying to convert them. The second occurrence comes at the end of part 4, just prior to their storming of the neighboring mines. Each of these episodes teaches important lessons, as Maheude's prophecy of future vindication, just prior to the end of the novel, indicates. Maheude, who has suffered the most, also grows. She emerges at the end of the novel as clear-headed and pragmatic. Catherine and Lydie, by contrast, symbolize the compliant, abused female; they can be liberated only through death. Maheude survives and, even though she is forced to return to the mines, has a much better understanding of her responsibilities.

The book is not, therefore, simply a protest against the subjugation of the working class. It is also a direct appeal to the workers to band together, to stop killing one another on behalf of the rich, and to take responsible action in order to improve their lives. The conclusion is intentionally left ambiguous; a ray of hope emerges as Étienne leaves Montsou.

"Critical Evaluation" by C. Lynn Munro

Further Reading

Berg, William J., and Laurey K. Martin. *Émile Zola Revisited*. Boston: Twayne, 1992. Textual analysis of Zola's twenty-volume series the Rougon-Macquart. Discusses naturalism's debt to positivism. Devotes a major part of chapter 3 to a study of the ideological ambiguity of *Germinal* and explores Zola's functional use of imagery.

Brooks, Peter. "Zola's Combustion Chamber." In *Realist Vision*. New Haven, Conn.: Yale University Press, 2005. Zola's novels are among the works of literature and art that are examined in this study of the realist tradition in France and England during the nineteenth and twentieth centuries.

Brown, Frederick. *Zola: A Life*. New York: Farrar, Straus and Giroux, 1995. A detailed and extensive biography of Zola that discusses his fiction and the intellectual life of

France, of which he was an important part. Shows how Zola's naturalism was developed out of the intellectual and political ferment of his time; argues that this naturalism was a highly studied and artificial approach to reality.

Gallois, William. *Zola: The History of Capitalism*. New York: Peter Lang, 2000. Interprets the Rougon-Macquart novels as a history of capitalism, drawing connections between Zola's novels and the work of economists and sociologists Karl Marx, Max Weber, and Émile Durkheim. Includes bibliography and index.

Grant, Elliot M. *Émile Zola*. Boston: Twayne, 1966. Examines the historical context and the literary devices, such as color, symbolism, and anthropomorphism, used in *Germinal*. Provides a detailed critique of the major characters.

Haavik, Kristof Haakon. "*Germinal*: Life out of Death." In *In Mortal Combat: The Conflict of Life and Death in Zola's "Rougon-Macquart."* Birmingham, Ala.: Summa, 2000. Argues that life and death "are bitterly opposed forces" in the Rougon-Macquart, and the "epic struggle" between them is the "central unifying thread" of the series.

King, Graham. *Garden of Zola: Émile Zola and His Novels for English Readers*. London: Barrie & Jenkins, 1978. Explains some of the choices Zola made while writing *Germinal*. Concludes that there are no villains, only victims, and that the main character of *Germinal* is the community.

Nelson, Brian. *Zola and the Bourgeoisie*. London: Macmillan, 1983. Offers a structural analysis of Zola's treatment of the values of the capitalist class. *Germinal* figures prominently in the first part of the book's analysis.

_____, ed. *The Cambridge Companion to Émile Zola*. New York: Cambridge University Press, 2007. Collection of essays, including discussions of Zola and the nineteenth century, his depiction of society, sex, and gender, and "*Germinal*: The Gathering Storm" by David Baguley. Includes a summary of Zola's novels, a family tree of the Rougon-Macquarts, a bibliography, and an index.

Walker, Philip. *Zola*. London: Routledge & Kegan Paul, 1985. Compares *Germinal* to an intricately crafted fresco teeming with mythic imagery. Argues that Zola's blend of archetypal and historic forms is responsible for the book's epic grandeur and universality.

Germinie Lacerteux

Authors: Edmond de Goncourt (1822-1896) and Jules de Goncourt (1830-1870)
First published: 1865 (English translation, 1887)
Type of work: Novel
Type of plot: Naturalism
Time of plot: Nineteenth century
Locale: Paris

Principal characters:
GERMINIE LACERTEUX, a maidservant
MADEMOISELLE DE VARANDEUIL, Germinie's employer
MADAME JUPILLON, Germinie's friend
MONSIEUR JUPILLON, Madame Jupillon's son and Germinie's lover
MONSIEUR GAUTRUCHE, an artist

The Story:

When Germinie Lacerteux is left an orphan at the age of four, her sisters take care of her. At the age of fourteen, she is sent to Paris to live with an older sister who has settled with her husband in the city. Not wishing to pay for all the expenses of the child from their own meager income, the sister and her husband find Germinie a job as a waitress in a café. She has been working in the café for several months when she becomes pregnant. Germinie suffers many indignities at the hands of her relatives because she will not tell them that she has been raped by one of the waiters; they think she must have invited seduction. Her child is born dead, and giving birth almost kills Germinie. Finally, a retired actor takes pity on her and hires her as a maid and companion. For Germinie, this is a step up in the world, but the old actor dies within a few months. Germinie then fills a host of positions as maid to kept women and boarding school mistresses.

One day, Mademoiselle de Varandeuil's maid dies suddenly. Through the influence of her sister, Germinie is given the position. Mademoiselle de Varandeuil is an old maid whose father prevented her from being anything but a servant to him until his death, so that she now has few friends and acquaintances. Other members of her family have died, and she is an old woman. She has a sufficient income to live fairly comfortably, but she cannot afford many extravagances. In her old age, she needs someone to look after her, as much a companion as a maidservant.

For a time after her entry into Mademoiselle de Varandeuil's service, Germinie is a devoted Christian. She spends a great deal of time at church and goes to confession regularly. Through her devotions, she falls in love with a young priest, but he, sensing her state of mind, sends her to another confessor and refuses to speak to her. With that, Germinie's devotions cease.

Germinie's next devotion is to her sister's niece, who had been left in her care when the mother died. Germinie's happiness, however, is short-lived, for another sister takes the child to Africa. When word comes by letter that the child is ill and the sister's husband out of work, Germinie sends everything she can spare to aid the stricken child and the family that is taking care of her. After depriving herself of necessities for two years, Germinie learns that the child died shortly after leaving Paris and that the letters from her sister and her husband were a ruse to get Germinie's hard-earned money.

About that time, a dairy store opens very close to the house in which Germinie lives with Mademoiselle de Varandeuil. In her dealings with the store, Germinie finds a friend in Madame Jupillon, the proprietress. Madame Jupillon has a son, who is at a trade school learning to become a glove maker. Germinie is quite impressed by the youngster and often goes with his mother to see him on visiting days. One day, when Madame Jupillon is ill, Germinie goes to the school by herself. Upon arriving, she learns that the young man is in trouble because some questionable books have been found in his possession. Germinie helps him out of his difficulty, but when she tries to lecture him, she finds herself unable to do so.

Soon Germinie realizes that she has a great deal of affection for the young man, who is ten years her junior. In order to be near him and to have company, she spends a lot of time with the Jupillons, who take advantage of her willingness to help in the store. She is exceedingly jealous when the young man is attracted to a woman of notoriety, and she does everything she can to keep the two apart. By her actions, she leaves herself open to his advances.

Germinie is extremely happy as the lover of young Jupillon. She soon discovers, however, that Jupillon spends much time in the company of other women. To help keep him for herself, Germinie spends all of her money to buy him a place in which to open his own business, meanwhile providing him with an apartment of his own. Shortly after she did so

much for him, Germinie is turned away from Jupillon's door by another woman who has become his mistress. In the meantime, Germinie discovers she is pregnant and gives birth to a baby daughter. Because it is impossible to keep the child at home while acting as Mademoiselle de Varandeuil's maidservant, Germinie farms out the child. The death of the baby a few months later brings Germinie great sorrow.

Some time after she was turned out by Jupillon, the young man is unfortunate enough to be called for military service. He has no money to secure his release, but he knows that he can get the money from Germinie, who still loves him. After some trepidation, Germinie goes into debt to keep her false lover near her. She is compelled to borrow so much money that the bare interest on it takes everything she can spare from her small income.

As the years pass, Jupillon takes less and less interest in Germinie, so that she finally gives him up and turns to liquor for comfort. Drunkenness becomes her one joy, although she manages to keep the secret of her vice to herself; old Mademoiselle de Varandeuil never even guesses the truth. Everyone notices, however, that she becomes slovenly in her appearance and in her work. Mademoiselle de Varandeuil keeps her on only because the old woman cannot stand the thought of a new servant in the house. Germinie has two grave problems: She has no one to love, and she is miserably in debt because of a man who cares nothing for her.

When Germinie is approaching the age of forty, she meets a man in his fifties, a painter, and takes him as a lover. She does not love Gautruche except as an object upon which to lavish her pent-up affections. Before long, she feels much better, behaves much better, and is a better servant to her mistress. Gautruche, however, sees her only as a servant for himself, and he believes that she will be only too happy to leave her job and marry him. Much to his surprise, she refuses his offer of marriage, and the two part forever. Once again, Germinie is left with no one who cares for her or upon whom she can lavish her affections. In desperation, she begins picking up any man she can find on the streets. One night, as she roams Paris looking for a lover, she sees Jupillon. She follows him to a house and spends the night outside in the rain, while waiting for a chance to see him again. The next morning, she is desperately ill with pleurisy. She keeps on working in spite of her illness, but Mademoiselle de Varandeuil finally sends her to a hospital, where Germinie dies. After her death, all of her secrets become known, for everyone to whom she owed money attempts to collect from her employer. At first, Mademoiselle de Varandeuil is outraged; then she comes to realize the agony and frustration of Germinie's life and feels only pity for the wretched woman.

Critical Evaluation:

The Goncourt brothers, who are associated with the naturalist school in nineteenth century French fiction, were the first to create the documentary novel. Naturalist plots are frequently based on newspaper scandals and take place in brothels, hospitals, slums, and oppressive bourgeois interiors. Certain characters recur, among them hysterical women or prostitutes brought to ruin, disenchanted intellectuals, bachelors or unhappily married men, and hypocritical merchants. Typically, there is a wide range of discourse to ensure resemblance to reality. Naturalist novels are characterized by themes of disintegration and confusion as well as by ironic treatment of political and social institutions.

Germinie Lacerteux became a paradigm of naturalist texts. The novel documents the Goncourts' own interaction with the working class, recording the life of their maid, who had served them faithfully for years. They were shocked to learn of her life of debauchery and of her death in a workhouse. Creditors had tried to collect money she owed for liquor, and through those creditors and other townspeople the Goncourts discovered that she had squandered her money on young men. In addition to interviewing friends and coworkers, they read studies on hysteria, a diagnosis that became a blanket term for a number of symptoms in the nineteenth century. They also visited ragpickers' huts on the edge of the city and explored the dance halls while collecting material for *Germinie Lacerteux*.

In earlier novels, the Goncourt brothers had presented life as a series of discontinuous tableaux, and their characters had lacked personal history and been unattached to family or society. Because the Goncourts knew their maid, Rose, well, they were able to maintain continuity of character and story line in *Germinie Lacerteux*. The novel begins with an exposition of Germinie's childhood and describes the death of her parents and the hardship of poverty. A series of episodes follows, showing Germinie as a passive victim in society; the episodes include neglect by a sister, rape at fifteen, the stillbirth of a child, and her drifting from job to job before finally settling at the residence of Mademoiselle de Varandeuil. During the course of her education in life's miseries, Germinie learns to accept hard work and to expect exploitation.

The story also traces Germinie's quest for love. Her first love centers on religion. Catholicism provides a temporary outlet for her emotional needs, but her devotion is ultimately disappointed by her displaced and unrequited love for a priest. Germinie informally adopts her sister's niece, only to experience that loss as well. She acts as a foster mother to Monsieur Jupillon, but motherly love eventually turns to obsessive, romantic love, exacerbated by jealousy. Pregnancy brings only temporary joy, since she must hide her physical state from her mistress and give away her child. The decline of Germinie's personal circumstances is attributed to her consistently foiled attempts at love. Fate becomes a physiological imperative. Germinie's temperament is described as lymphatic, sluggish in thought and action; she is sensitive and anxious and has a need for love and maternity.

Rather than representing the simple opposition of illusion and reality, multiple realities coexist in the character of the protagonist. Germinie embodies the victim, the ideal servant, the obsessive lover, the alcoholic, and the thief. Although the novel appears to depict a simple psychological decline, on closer examination, the positive traits typical of her younger years continue to be revealed even as she lapses into despair. The concept of a multiple personality is demonstrated by the use of mirrors: Germinie is frequently confronted with her own image in the mirror and, in the end, recoils from her own reflection.

The story depicts class issues as well as individual psychology. The Goncourts do not limit misery to the lower classes. Mademoiselle de Varandeuil, who had been tormented by a tyrannical father, shares similar experiences—but not sympathy—with Germinie. The difference in social class makes a friendship between the two women impossible. Germinie learns that class distinctions form insurmountable barriers. The Goncourts demonstrate how poverty not only makes everyday survival difficult but also limits possibilities.

Germinie's psychological development, while played out in the artificial and corrupt atmosphere of Paris, is set against a natural backdrop. Nature's beauty heightens her bitterness, but nature also grows more ominous. The narrator emphasizes the sameness of the road of life and the gathering night of oblivion. At the end of the novel, funereal winter reigns. There are images of enclosure and there is absence of communication. The Goncourts are conscious of the stylistic possibilities of exhausting a place through detailed description. Both painters themselves, they likened the technique of description to that of mimetic painting.

Like many naturalist novels, *Germinie Lacerteux* does not contain documents such as newspaper articles or court records. Instead, dialogue and thought are transcribed, with little narrative or interpretive intervention. Free indirect discourse approximates the collective voice of the audience rather than the voice of an individual narrator. The language of the novel stresses corruption and depicts a society in its death throes. At the end of society, there are no more doctrines, and there one can find unusual, prodigious, free adventurers who risk everything in art and life.

Germinie Lacerteux is recognized as one of the first novels in the naturalist tradition; the novel draws a documentary portrait based on authentic observation and a record of existing conditions. In the preface, the Goncourts repudiate any desire to titillate with the graphic subject matter. Contemporaries were, however, shocked by the clinical descriptions of Germinie's sexuality and the realistic detail of lower class squalor. While the novel was condemned as pornography and only experienced mild popularity, *Germinie Lacerteux* became a model for Émile Zola and other great writers of the period.

"Critical Evaluation" by Pamela Pavliscak

Further Reading

Ashley, Katherine. *Edmond de Goncourt and the Novel: Naturalism and Decadence*. Amsterdam: Rodopi, 2005. Ashley analyzes Edmond's four solo novels, arguing that these books deviated from the strict naturalistic style that characterized the novels he wrote with his brother. She places Edmond's work within the larger context of late nineteenth century fin de siècle literature.

Auerbach, Erich. *Mimesis: The Representation of Reality in Western Literature*. Translated by Willard Trask. New York: Doubleday, 1953. Discusses the Goncourts as representatives of the naturalist school.

Baldick, Robert. *The Goncourts*. London: Bowes, 1960. A brief but excellent survey of the Goncourts' novels. Concentrates on biographical background to the novels. Explores major themes and aspects of the Goncourts' literary style. Cites *Germinie Lacerteux* as the precursor to the naturalist movement because the work concentrates on the lower classes. Asserts that the work served as a model for the Goncourts' own later novels.

Billy, Andre. *The Goncourt Brothers*. Translated by Margaret Shaw. New York: Horizon Press, 1960. The standard biography of the Goncourts. Elucidates events from which the novels emerged. Also offers contemporary reaction to their novels.

Cordova, Sarah Davies. "Spectacularisation or Transfiguration: *Germinie Lacerteux*." In *Paris Dances: Textual Choreographies in the Nineteenth-Century French Novel*. San Francisco: International Scholars, 1999. Analyzes dance as a cultural activity in nineteenth century France and the role it played in the era's literature, including the depiction of dance in *Germinie Lacerteux*.

Grant, Richard B. *The Goncourt Brothers*. New York: Twayne, 1972. Surveys the life and works of Jules and Edmond de Goncourt. Ordered chronologically, the book carefully integrates the lives of the authors with detailed stylistic and thematic analysis of all of their novels.

Nelson, Brian, ed. *Naturalism in the European Novel: New Critical Perspectives*. New York: Berg, 1992. Essays on the naturalist school in England, France, Germany, and Spain. Includes important discussions of the Goncourts' role in the literary development of social documentary.

Weir, David. "Decadence and Naturalism: The Goncourts' *Germinie Lacerteux*." In *Decadence and the Making of Modernism*. Amherst: University of Massachusetts Press, 1995. Weir analyzes novels by the Goncourts and other European authors to demonstrate how late nineteenth and early twentieth century decadence was a significant literary movement and an important link between Romanticism and modernism.

The Ghost Sonata

Author: August Strindberg (1849-1912)
First produced: *Spöksonaten*, 1908; first published, 1907 (English translation, 1916)
Type of work: Drama
Type of plot: Expressionism
Time of plot: c. 1900
Locale: Sweden

Principal characters:
THE OLD MAN, the eighty-year-old Jacob Hummel
THE STUDENT, a young man named Arkenholz
THE MILKMAID, an apparition who appears to the student
THE COLONEL
THE MUMMY, the Colonel's wife
THE YOUNG LADY, the Colonel's daughter, but really Hummel's daughter
JOHANSSON, Hummel's servant
BENGTSSON, the Colonel's footman

The Story:

The building superintendent's wife is sweeping and polishing brass while the Old Man, Director Hummel, sits in a wheelchair reading a newspaper. As a Milkmaid comes in and drinks from the fountain in front of the apartment building, a Student, "sleepless and unshaven," approaches and asks for the dipper. The Milkmaid reacts in terror, for she is an apparition and unaccustomed to being seen, and the Old Man stares at the Student in amazement because he cannot see the Milkmaid. Neither of them knows that the Student is a child born on a Sunday, which gives him special perceptions.

This puzzling tableau yields to a conversation between the Old Man and the Student. The Student, Arkenholz, is exhausted from having treated people who have been injured that night in a collapsing house. The Old Man's questions disclose that the Student is the son of a man who—so the Old Man says—had swindled him out of his life savings many years before. The Old Man, whose behavior and casual remarks suggest some mythic, timeless quality, has apparently contrived the Student's occasion for heroism as a ruse to meet him so that he can manipulate the Student into friendship and ultimately marriage with the daughter of the Colonel, who is actually the Old Man's daughter. To this end, the Old Man instructs the Student to attend a performance of Richard Wagner's opera *Die Walküre* (1856; *The Valkyrie*, 1877) that evening and to sit in a certain seat.

The Student agrees to these arrangements, all of which seem like the manipulations of an eighty-year-old man who admits that "I take an interest in people's destinies." The Old Man takes the Student by the hand, claims exhaustion from an "infinitely long life," and proclaims that their destinies are "intertwined through your father." The Student, repulsed by this intimacy, withdraws his hand and protests, "You're draining my strength, you're freezing me. What do you want of me?" What the Old Man wants is to perpetuate himself through the Student, who is young, vital, and a fit mate for the Old Man's daughter. The Student worries about these arrangements, wondering if they mean "some kind of pact," but the Old Man assures him that his motive is simply that all his life he has taken and that now, poised for an uncertain eternity, he wants to give.

The Old Man rather gleefully recites several bits of gossip. He reveals that a mysterious lady in black standing on the steps is the daughter of the superintendent's wife by a dead man, a former consul, whose body lay upstairs; this adulterous liaison is explained as the occasion by which the superintendent had been given his job. Furthermore, divulges the Old Man, the lady in black is having an affair with an aristocrat whose wife is not only giving him a divorce but throwing in an estate to be rid of him. The Old Man concludes by noting that the aristocrat pursuing the lady in black is a son-in-law of the dead man upstairs. After the Old Man's servant, Johansson, pushes him around the corner in his wheelchair, the Student learns from Johansson that the Old Man always wanted power and is afraid of only one thing: the Milkmaid.

Bengtsson, the Colonel's footman, gives Johansson his orders for the evening as they enter the Round Room on the ground floor. They are to serve the Colonel and his wife, the Mummy, a "ghost supper," so called because they have looked like ghosts for years. The Mummy, secluded in a closet, speaks childish parrot talk to Bengtsson when he opens her door. Bengtsson then points out to Johansson the "death screen" put up around a dying person. At this point, the Old Man arrives and the Mummy emerges to speak to him of their daughter, who sits next door in the Hyacinth Room, reading.

In the conversation that follows, the Old Man humiliates the Colonel by exposing all the pretensions in his life and revealing that he has bought up the Colonel's promissory notes. However, the Old Man is humiliated in turn by Bengtsson, who declares that years before in Hamburg the Old Man had "lured a girl out onto the ice to drown her, because she had witnessed a crime he was afraid would be discovered." At this disclosure, the Mummy demands all the notes and by stroking him on the back transforms Hummel into a parrot-speaker; she switches places with him in the closet and places the death screen before the closet door.

In the Hyacinth Room, the Student elaborates to the Young Lady on his love for hyacinths, finding in this flower "a replica of the universe" as its star flowers shoot up to become a veritable "globe of heaven." The Young Lady responds by criticizing her cook, a vampire like Hummel, and her maid, whose carelessness demands the Young Lady's regular attention. When the Young Man recounts an episode when his father had criticized all of his friends at the dinner table, "strip[ping] everybody naked, one after another, exposing all their falseness," he harangues the Young Lady with his own devotion to perfection and ends with the plea, "Alas! Alas for us all! Savior of the world, save us, we are perishing!" This unexpected verbal assault destroys the Young Lady, who crumples and dies as harp music accompanies the Student's tender elegy for her. The room then disappears and Arnold Böcklin's painting "The Island of the Dead" emerged in the background.

Critical Evaluation:

In a life charged with personal and spiritual obsessions, August Strindberg wrote three dozen plays, seven novels, six volumes of essays, three volumes of short stories, and a volume of poems. Most of these works reflect his extensive reading of the Bible, mythology, theosophy, Friedrich Nietzsche, and Emanuel Swedenborg, as well as much else that stimulated his creative impulses. *The Ghost Sonata* can be grouped with *Oväder* (1907; *Storm*, 1913), *Brända tomten* (1907; *After the Fire*, 1913), *Pelikanen* (1907; *The Pelican*, 1962), and *Svarta handsken* (1909; *The Black Glove*, 1916) as the third in a quintet of what Strindberg called chamber plays. The term "chamber play" was a reference to their analogies to musical forms, and they were written for Strindberg's Intimate Theater in Stockholm. He initially thought *The Ghost Supper* an appropriate title to evoke the central event of the play, but switched to *The Ghost Sonata* as proper for a play built around three scenes.

Strindberg preceded and influenced such playwrights as Eugene O'Neill, Samuel Beckett, and Edward Albee in his exploitation of expressionist techniques and in the use of settings, sound effects, and other devices to suggest states of mind. The apparition of the Milkmaid, for instance, prompts a reaction in Hummel that expresses his guilt over the events in Hamburg. For Hummel, the Milkmaid functions much as the Furies do in Greek tragedy, guilty consciences that drive their victims toward expiation. Other examples include the Mummy and the Colonel. The Mummy hides in her closet, dehumanized and reduced by the manipulative Old Man to a mere parrot of a person; the Colonel, with his spurious military title, his wig, and his mustache, collapses as a hollow man under Hummel's ruthless attack on his puffed-up self. When the Old Man himself is exposed, he succumbs to the Mummy's parrot speech as a sign of his own spiritual emptiness.

Vampirism and exploitation constitute the main theme of *The Ghost Sonata*. Johansson says of the Old Man that "he's like a horse thief, only with people. He steals them, in all kinds of ways." Hummel rides around, Johansson says, "like the great god Thor," destroying houses, killing his enemies, and forgiving nothing. In his younger days, he had been a Don Juan who was so clever that he got his women to leave when he had used them up. Hummel knows everyone's dark secrets, and his corrosive cynicism shows up in his talk about them, as when he reveals the identity of the lady in black.

The Old Man explains at the ghost supper that "Nature itself plants in human beings an instinct for hiding that which should be hidden" but that "sometimes the opportunity presents itself to reveal the deepest of secrets, to tear the mask off the imposter." That is what he has chosen to do at the ghost supper, "to pull up the weeds" and "settle the accounts"

so that the Student and the Young Lady can start afresh. It is too late, however, for the Old Man Hummel himself: The Mummy charms him into her parrot role and puts the death screen around him.

Ironically, it was the folly of the Student's father, to expose everyone's pretensions at a dinner party, that led to his incarceration in a madhouse. The Student has clearly inherited his father's inverted idealism and his disgust for a world that cannot live up to his standards of honesty and goodness. His tirade in the last minutes of the play condemns creation: "Why is it that the most beautiful flowers are so poisonous, the most poisonous? Damnation hangs over the whole of creation." Students of Strindberg's life see autobiographical elements in the Student's bitterness. Whatever its source in the author's creative impulses, *The Ghost Sonata* dramatizes with great power the dark and apocalyptic side of existence.

"Critical Evaluation" by Frank Day

Further Reading

Converse, Terry John. *The Psychology of the Grotesque in August Strindberg's "The Ghost Sonata."* Lewiston, N.Y.: Edwin Mellen Press, 1999. Provides a Jungian analysis of the play's grotesque vision.

Ekman, Hans-Göran. *Strindberg and the Five Senses: Studies in Strindberg's Chamber Plays.* Somerset, N.J.: Transaction, 2000. A critical analysis of *The Ghost Sonata* and three other plays written in 1907, focusing on their relation to Strindberg's obsession with the symbolic and dramatic function of the five senses in stage plays.

House, Poul, Sven Hakon Rossel, and Göran Stockenström, eds. *August Strindberg and the Other: New Critical Approaches.* Amsterdam: Rodopi, 2002. Collection of papers delivered at a 2000 conference, "Strindberg at the Millennium—Strindberg and the Other," interpreting the motif of "the other" and "otherness" in Strindberg's work.

Johnson, Walter. *August Strindberg.* Boston: Twayne, 1976. Introductory overview to Strindberg's life and works, with a useful bibliography, for beginning readers. The chapter entitled "Dramatist of Penetration and Representation" is helpful to understanding the chamber plays.

Mays, Milton A. "Strindberg's *Ghost Sonata*: Parodied Fairy Tale on Original Sin." *Modern Drama* 10, no. 2 (September, 1967): 189-194. An excellent explication of the manner in which Strindberg turns folkloric elements into allegories.

Meyer, Michael. *Strindberg.* New York: Random House, 1985. A long, well-written biography with excellent illustrations. One chapter is devoted to the chamber plays.

Robinson, Michael, ed. *The Cambridge Companion to August Strindberg*. New York: Cambridge University Press, 2009. Collection of essays analyzing Strindberg's work, placing it within the context of his life and times. Lynn R. Wilkinson's essay focuses on the chamber plays. Includes bibliography and index.

Törnqvist, Egil. *Strindberg's "The Ghost Sonata": From Text to Performance*. Amsterdam: Amsterdam University Press, 2000. Analyzes the text of the play, English transla-tions, and several stage productions, most notably a 1973 version directed by Ingmar Bergman. Provides contextual background for the play and assesses its influence on modern drama.

Williams, Raymond. "August Strindberg." In *Drama, from Ibsen to Eliot*. London: Chatto & Windus, 1952. Williams chooses five plays, including *The Ghost Sonata*, to trace the evolution of Strindberg's dramatic style and technique. An excellent commentary on Strindberg the artist.

Ghosts

Author: Henrik Ibsen (1828-1906)
First produced: **Gengangere**, 1882; first published, 1881 (English translation, 1885)
Type of work: Drama
Type of plot: Social realism
Time of plot: Nineteenth century
Locale: Rosenvold, Norway

Principal characters:
MRS. HELEN ALVING, a widow
OSWALD ALVING, her son, an artist
MANDERS, pastor of the parish
JACOB ENGSTRAND, a carpenter
REGINA ENGSTRAND, his daughter, in Mrs. Alving's service

The Story:

Pastor Manders calls on Mrs. Helen Alving on the eve of the tenth anniversary of her husband's death to discuss certain details concerning the opening of an orphanage in memory of her late husband. The pastor finds Mrs. Alving in the best of spirits, for her son Oswald, an artist, has returned from Paris to attend the dedication of the memorial to his father. Oswald, now twenty-six, has lived away from his parents since he was seven, and Mrs. Alving is delighted at the prospect of having her son spend the entire winter with her.

Oswald idealizes his father, for in her letters his mother portrays Captain Alving as a sort of hero. The boy's own memories of his father are confined to one incident in his childhood when his father took him on his knee and encouraged him to smoke a large meerschaum pipe. Upon his return home, Oswald takes a certain pride in lighting up his father's old pipe and parading in front of his mother and Pastor Manders.

Pastor Manders does not approve of smoking; in fact, he does not approve of anything that can even loosely be interpreted as sin. He does not approve of Oswald's bohemian way of life in Paris and blames Mrs. Alving for her son's ideas. He reminds Mrs. Alving that she came to him scarcely one year after having married, wanting to leave her husband, and that he sent her back to her duty. Pastor Manders considers this act the greatest moral victory of his life.

Mrs. Alving thinks it high time that the pastor knows the truth about her late husband. Years before, when he advised her to return to Captain Alving, the minister was aware of her husband's profligacy, but he did not know that the profligacy continued after his wife's return. Her relationship with her husband consisted principally of helping him into bed when he came home from one of his drinking bouts; on one occasion she came across him making love to her own maidservant. The most abominable aspect of her situation, and what she discovered soon after her marriage, was that her husband had contracted syphilis and that her son might have inherited the disease. Pastor Manders's religious influence and her own cowardice led Mrs. Alving to keep silent.

While Mrs. Alving and the minister talk, Oswald flirts in the adjoining dining room with the maid, Regina. To Mrs. Alving it sounds like the ghost of the flirtation she overheard years earlier between her husband and Regina's mother. Regina, ostensibly the daughter of a drunken carpenter named Jacob Engstrand, is actually the daughter of Captain Alving and the maidservant. It is that discovery that sent Mrs. Alving flying to Pastor Manders for solace and help. Engstrand was willing to turn Regina over to Mrs. Alving for her education and care, but now he plans to enlist her aid in the establishment of a seamen's home. Regina has other plans for herself and sees no reason why she should throw herself away on worthless and irresponsible sailors when she might, as she thinks, have the heir of a wealthy family.

Oswald, who is unaware of the blood relationship, wants to marry Regina. He confides to his mother that before he left Paris he went to a doctor because he felt listless and had lost his ambition to paint. The doctor commented on the sins of fathers. Oswald, knowing only the picture of his father that his mother's letters had given him, was furious and thinks he must have contracted venereal disease himself. He tells his mother that he wants to marry Regina and be happy for what remains of his life. Mrs. Alving realizes that at last she must tell the two young people the truth. Before she has a chance to do so, however, news comes that the orphanage that is to have been Captain Alving's memorial is on fire.

At the time the orphanage caught fire, Pastor Manders and Engstrand were in the carpenter shop nearby. After the fire, Engstrand accuses the pastor of dropping a lighted candle wick into some shavings. Although he is probably not guilty, Pastor Manders is anxious not to endanger his position in the community. When Engstrand offers to take the blame for the fire in return for money from the remainder of Captain Alving's fortune, with which he can build his sailors' home, the self-righteous pastor agrees to the blackmail and promises to help Engstrand.

Mrs. Alving tells Oswald and Regina about their father, explaining the nature of his illness and that his children might have inherited it. When she hears that she is really Alving's daughter, Regina is angry, feeling that she should have been reared and educated as a lady. Now, preferring to cast her lot with Engstrand, she leaves. Alone with his mother, Oswald reveals that symptoms of his inherited venereal disease are already evident, and that he is doomed to insanity. Mrs. Alving assures her son that she will always be by his side to take care of him. Oswald begs his mother to kill him and shows her the morphium he has brought with him, but Mrs. Alving is shocked. Mother and son are still talking at daybreak. When Mrs. Alving blows out the light, she is horrified to see Oswald begin to cry childishly for the sun.

Critical Evaluation:

Ghosts is Henrik Ibsen's effort to substitute the modern scientific concept of heredity for the Greek idea of fate. More important, it is a mordant attack on society and societal standards. In explicitly stating that these standards are responsible for Mrs. Alving's tragedy, Ibsen inflamed even the liberal sensibilities of his day. The play can still be read as a study in what has come to be known as the science of semantics—the disruptive effect caused when words or concepts are, in soci-

ety, divorced from the realities for which they are supposed to stand.

Frequently called the founder of modern drama, Ibsen, like Pablo Picasso in painting and Igor Stravinsky in music, was a dynamic innovator whose far-ranging experiments had a continuing influence on Western theater and culture. *Ghosts*, Ibsen's most celebrated, at one time even notorious, play, was the key document in his "social-realistic" period during the 1870's and 1880's. To some extent, the play obscured the fact that he was a protean writer whose social-realistic phase occupied only two decades of a career that spanned half a century, from 1849 to 1899, during which he explored many social, psychological, and metaphysical problems in a wide range of theatrical styles.

In the 1880's, however, *Ghosts* was a red flag to the conventional theater audience and a defiant banner for the avant-garde. Ibsen's earlier social play, *Et dukkehjem* (1879; *A Doll's House*, 1880), in which a woman leaves her husband to achieve maturity, found stout defenders but also excited denunciation (in fact, the playwright was forced to produce a happy ending, in which Nora stays home, for German consumption). The controversy was in large part responsible for the play's commercial success on stage and, even more emphatically, in book form. *Ghosts*, which deals with a woman who does stay home, was another matter, for this time the public concluded that the play was entirely too shocking, especially for its open treatment of venereal disease and its defense of unmarried cohabitation. Even the sales of Ibsen's earlier plays dropped off. One newspaper critic summed up the general opinion when he wrote, "The book has no place on the Christmas table of any Christian home." Eventually, the play became one of the pillars of literature.

One aspect of *Ghosts* is its attack on conventional morality. Pastor Manders embodies everything Ibsen hated in those conventions—the "ghosts" of the title. Manders is an unconscious hypocrite. Though he sees himself as a moral and ethical leader, he is motivated almost exclusively by fear of what others think of him. When he discusses the question of insuring the new orphanage, he states that he is not opposed to the principle of insurance—he himself is insured, and his parishioners insure themselves and their businesses—but he fears that by insuring the orphanage, his wealthier patrons may insist he is showing less reliance than he should on divine Providence. The decision not to insure the orphanage is based neither on an interpretation of God's will nor out of concern for the orphans but for fear of public opinion. To Ibsen, the conventional moral code is itself hypocritical, and those who adhere to it are neither morally nor spiritually motivated.

In the closing act, fear of what others may think proves to be Manders's undoing. After the orphanage burns to the ground, the unscrupulous, consciously hypocritical Engstrand convinces the pastor that he, Manders, caused the fire. Since Manders's sole concern is his reputation, when Engstrand "accepts" the blame for the fire (and it is clear that he set it), the greatly relieved Manders agrees to provide financial support for Engstrand's "Sailors' Home"—a "home" that will clearly be little more than a brothel. To save his own skin, the spiritual mentor agrees to underwrite immorality.

Hypocrisy and opportunism pervade the moral landscape of the play. Engstrand is an obvious and open hypocrite, a confidence man who persuades Manders that he is a worthy soul. Regina sets her cap for Oswald not because she loves him but because she wants to be taken to Paris; as a second string to her bow, she makes advances to Pastor Manders. Although Mrs. Alving is a thoroughly sympathetic character, she, too, played the hypocrite in the past, hiding the lifelong philanderings of her husband behind a wall of public respectability: The last stone in that wall was to have been the orphanage named in Captain Alving's honor; ironically, his real and more fitting memorial will be Engstrand's "Sailors' Home."

Ibsen believed that the moral code enforces hypocrisy, and that it ranges far beyond the reach of Mrs. Alving's house. When Manders suggests that men of means might object to insuring the orphanage, he suggests also (without himself understanding the implications of his statement) that these men, while speaking in spiritual terms, are interested in the orphanage solely for financial reasons; it will reduce the taxes they pay for charitable purposes. In an intense confrontation with Oswald (one of the scenes the audience of Ibsen's time found objectionable because Oswald defends unmarried cohabitation), Manders accuses Oswald of having moved in openly immoral circles in Paris, only to be told that Oswald has indeed seen a good deal of immorality abroad—when some of Manders's respectable parishioners have come to Paris to have their fling: "Then we had a chance of learning something, I can tell you."

The exposure of the conventional code in itself might have created a comedy, for Engstrand and Manders are in many ways comic figures, or it might have led to a serious problem play. There is, however, a second, more subtly stated theme, and in it lies the play's tragic momentum. According to Ibsen, understanding and exposing the conventions do not destroy them or their power to harm; the truth does not make one free in Ibsen's worlds.

Mrs. Alving is quite contemptuous of the conventional code. She sees herself as an emancipated woman who has freed herself of her past and, by recalling Oswald from Paris,

ensured her future happiness. In act 1, she seems in complete control of the situation; she is tranquil, confident, certain of herself. "And from tomorrow on," she tells Manders at the conclusion of the act, "I shall be free at last . . . . I shall forget that such a person as Alving ever lived in this house—there'll be no one here but my son and me." At that point, however, she and Manders hear Oswald running after the maid (unbeknown to him, his half sister) in an echo of the affair between Captain Alving and the maid who was Regina's mother. In the sad and bitter discussion that opens act 2, Mrs. Alving, no longer certain that the past can be put aside, states the second theme of the play explicitly: "We're all haunted in this world . . . by the ghosts of innumerable old prejudices and beliefs—half-forgotten cruelties and betrayals . . . and we can't get rid of them."

She does make several efforts to "get rid of them." When Oswald, guiltily confessing to her that he has acquired a venereal disease, speaks of the "joy of life" and the "joy of work," Mrs. Alving sees a pattern in the past that she had not discerned before. When she tells Oswald and Regina the truth about Captain Alving—that he was a drunkard and a philanderer all his life—she at long last has come to understand and excuse him, insisting that he had a "joy of life" in him for which his conventional environment could provide no outlet. The Captain's wasted life, she goes on to declare, was her own responsibility, because, instead of offering him "joy," she judged him by society's standards, thus driving him elsewhere—to one of the servants, among others. However, Mrs. Alving's final effort to face and thereby perhaps undo the past fails. Regina reacts with bitterness and leaves. Oswald, facing mental oblivion, is more alone than ever. As the curtain comes down, Captain Alving's legacy to Oswald, the last stage of venereal disease, strikes the boy as Mrs. Alving stares at the horror that is her life. Physically and spiritually, the past has destroyed both present and future.

Ghosts is a richly orchestrated play and remains one of the most complex and significant realistic dramas of the century. Its symbols—the rain that beats darkly on the large parlor window and represents the moral ghosts of the play, the sun that rises at the close to shine on Oswald's darkness—mesh closely with the action and with the themes of the play. Its structure, a gradual revelation of the past that is fully disclosed only at the final catastrophe, is clearly and firmly joined to the idea that the past enters into and destroys the present. This form, developed and perfected by Ibsen, was to be employed over and over again as his influence merged with other developments of the twentieth century.

"Critical Evaluation" by Max Halperen

Further Reading

Binding, Paul. *With Vine-Leaves in His Hair: The Role of the Artist in Ibsen's Plays*. Norwich, England: Norvik Press, 2006. Examines the character of the artist-rebel in *Ghosts* and four other Ibsen plays. Binding demonstrates how this character represents the tensions of contemporary society.

Clurman, Harold. *Ibsen*. New York: Collier Books, 1977. This introductory study provides the general reader with a good starting place to learn about Ibsen. Clurman, a renowned stage director, discusses the plays as theater, as well as literature. His analysis of *Ghosts* clarifies a misunderstanding about the play's title and explores at some length the motivations of the characters.

Fjelde, Rolf, ed. *Ibsen: A Collection of Critical Essays*. Englewood Cliffs, N.J.: Prentice-Hall, 1965. Sixteen essays that cover Ibsen's conception of truth, realism, and stage craftsmanship, among other topics. Includes Francis Fergusson's discussion of the realism, suspense, and tragic nature of *Ghosts*.

Ledger, Sally. *Henrik Ibsen*. 2d ed. Tavistock, England: Northcote House/British Council, 2008. Includes a close reading of *Ghosts*, placing the play within its cultural, historical, and intellectual contexts.

Lyons, Charles R., comp. *Critical Essays on Henrik Ibsen*. Boston: G. K. Hall, 1987. A thorough and useful volume of essays addressing, among other topics, realism and dramatic form in Ibsen's works. The remarks on *Ghosts* explore the use of asides, disease, and dramatic language.

McFarlane, James, ed. *The Cambridge Companion to Ibsen*. New York: Cambridge University Press, 1994. Sixteen essays on Ibsen's life and work provide a good resource. Chapters 9-13 discuss Ibsen's working methods and the stage history of the plays up through the age of film and television.

Moi, Toril. *Henrik Ibsen and the Birth of Modernism: Art, Theater, Philosophy*. New York: Oxford University Press, 2006. A reevaluation of Ibsen, in which Moi refutes the traditional definition of Ibsen as a realistic and naturalistic playwright and describes him as an early modernist. The references to *Ghosts* are listed in the index.

Robinson, Michael, ed. *Turning the Century: Centennial Essays on Ibsen*. Norwich, England: Norvik Press, 2006. Collection of the essays published in the journal *Scandinavica* during the past four decades, including discussions of Ibsen's style, language, and the reception of his plays in England. One of the essays analyzes *Ghosts*.

Valency, Maurice. *The Flower and the Castle: An Introduction to Modern Drama*. New York: Schocken Books, 1982. Readers interested in Ibsen as the founder of twentieth century drama will find rewarding material in this study, the first in Valency's modern drama series. The author devotes more than one hundred pages to Ibsen, and his comments on *Ghosts* are a good introduction to the play.

Giant

Author: Edna Ferber (1885-1968)
First published: 1952
Type of work: Novel
Type of plot: Regional
Time of plot: Mid-1920's to 1950's
Locale: Texas and Virginia

Principal characters:
JORDAN "BICK" BENEDICT III, owner of Reata Ranch
LESLIE LYNNTON BENEDICT, his wife
JORDAN "JORDY" BENEDICT IV and LUZ BENEDICT, their children
JETT RINK, a ranch hand who strikes oil
JUANA BENEDICT, Jordy's wife

The Story:

Texas is a vast, moneyed, and contradictory place. On this day, millionaires gather before attending a party to be hosted by the arrogant, nouveau riche, former ranch hand Jett Rink. At Reata Ranch, their giant kingdom of sorts, is the Benedict family—Jordan III, Leslie, their children Luz and Jordan IV, and Jordan's Mexican wife, Juana—neither of whom is enthusiastic about attending Rink's party. Jordan III, called Bick, is tall, blond, and dusty as he comes out from the corral.

Soon, the Benedicts and their guests adjourn to the ranch airfield to board Bick's private plane for the four-hundred-mile trip to Rink's party in Hermoso. Aboard the plane, talk is of oil leases and cattle, two basic components of Texas wealth. After arriving, everyone settles at the massive new hotel built by Rink, a place, as one person calls it, "almost majestically vulgar." The hotel is segregated: Only whites can be guests.

One guest of the Benedicts, a South American ambassador, is being refused admittance to Rink's party because hotel staff think he is Mexican. The Benedicts quickly intervene. Then, daughter-in-law Juana is turned away from the hotel beauty parlor because it "don't take Mexicans." At the party, an irate Jordy, Juana's husband, attacks Rink, but he is restrained by Rink's bodyguards and then beaten by them. Leslie, looking at Bick, says "It's caught up with us. It always does."

Twenty-five years earlier, Leslie and Bick first meet. Bick, in Virginia to buy a racehorse owned by Dr. Horace Lynnton, becomes intrigued by Leslie, the second of the doctor's three adult daughters, who is unusual, both in her dark-haired looks and in her opinions. She is outspoken and interested in politics, sociology, medicine, and literature. Unlike the Texas girls Bick has known, Leslie does not chatter about unimportant things or focus her conversation on what might be interesting to a man. At dinner, Bick is again surprised, as the women, especially Leslie, lead the conversation. Later, Leslie, who has always loved to read, gathers a number of books about Texas and reads all night. The next morning, she shows her newfound knowledge of Texas by stating "We really stole Texas, didn't we." Such statements are typical of Leslie, and Bick is offended.

After a whirlwind courtship, Leslie and Bick are married and travel to Texas. Without being able to speak Spanish, Leslie is at a disadvantage, but she wants to know about her new home and meet the people she will be living with. She is interested in the Mexican servants and their lives and begins to offend people, particularly her new husband, with her friendly attitude toward the servants. The Benedicts and their friends consider the servants to be nothing more than serfs.

Leslie then meets the boorish ranch hand Jett Rink, who is willing to show her aspects of Reata Ranch that others do not want her to see. Leslie has to face and learn to overcome the different wind, heat, and foods. She discovers that men talk only to other men and that the women, the wives, talk only amongst themselves. There seems to be no exchange between women and men because the men believe women could not be interested in, let alone understand, business or politics or other such topics. Ever curious, Leslie continues to visit and learn about the Mexican locals. From Rink, who becomes fascinated by Leslie, she learns that Mexicans are not regarded as white by the ranch owners.

Gradually, Leslie takes charge of her new home. When she becomes pregnant, she thrives. Energized, she works on restoring the old family home and travels through Texas. Leslie and Bick's first child, a boy, is born, and Leslie's name choice is rejected in favor of Jordan Benedict IV, nicknamed Jordy. One year later, Leslie gives birth to the couple's second child, a girl they name Luz. Daughter Luz is everything Jordy is not, both with her blond hair and with her fearless love of horseback riding.

Leslie returns to Virginia to see her family, the Lynntons, but does not fit in as she once did. Bick visits as well, full of excitement about the oil boom in Texas. Leslie happily returns to Reata, accompanied by her family, who are thrilled with the ranch and astonished by the magnitude of Texas. The more sedate Lynntons begin to adjust to the exuberant Texans. However, when Rink bursts into a family dinner, drunk and excited because he has struck oil, the situation turns ugly. Rink reaches for Leslie, touching the soft bow at her neck, provoking Bick to punch him and throw him off the ranch.

Years later, the children have grown. Texans begin to change their business focus from raising cattle to building oil derricks. Those who once lived on ranches move into the developing cities. The sound of machinery becomes louder than that of cowboys singing to cattle. Jordy learns how to run the Benedict ranch, but he does so unwillingly, for running a ranch is not what he wants to do with his life. He is determined to become a surgeon and work with a local Mexican doctor. At a wedding for one of the ranch workers, Jordy announces he has secretly married Juana.

Leslie and Luz, along with Jordy and Juana and their son, are traveling to visit a friend. They stop at a roadside diner along the way. Luz, who is blond, parks the car as the rest, who have dark hair and dark eyes, are turned away from the restaurant because its owner refuses to serve Mexicans. "It," racism, has faced them down, just as it will many times again. They all agree not to tell Bick about the incident until after Rink's party.

Critical Evaluation:

When it was published, Edna Ferber's *Giant* angered many Texans, who considered its representation of the excessive lifestyle and boundless wealth of the cattle and oil barons to be false and inaccurate. Many also believed Ferber unfairly characterized racists. Another cause of anger among readers was the depiction of the manipulation of Mexican votes during elections. As a result, Ferber received hundreds of letters criticizing the novel. Some letters were just angry; others were vicious and suggested that she be shot or lynched.

Ferber had been no stranger to controversy, or discrimination. The daughter of a Jewish shopkeeper, she remembered being subjected to anti-Semitism. Her novels, particularly *Cimarron* (1930) and, to a lesser degree, *Showboat* (1926), include the theme of racial prejudice. In *Giant* she exposes the racial prejudice against Mexican Americans in Texas. Before writing the novel, Ferber had read extensively on the state's history. Carey McWilliams's study of Mexican Americans, *North from Mexico: The Spanish-Speaking People of the U.S.* (1949), helped Ferber link Texas greed with the exploitation of Mexican Americans. Ferber also visited Texas. As she notes in an interview with *The New York Times*, published in 1952, she "drove over Texas, flew over it, visited ranches, talked to people." The novel includes descriptions of Texas "bigness," its varying landscapes, its cattle ranching, and its tradition of social gatherings. In addition, Ferber takes an almost comic look at how those persons unaccustomed to great wealth spend their money.

The plot is a page-turner, but its strength is in its characters and its theme of racism. Although the novel features three generations of the Benedict family, the focus is on Leslie Lynnton Benedict, an educated, Eastern-born outsider, who functions as a critical voice for what routinely happens yet is never spoken about. Although she tries, she never fits the stereotype of the wife of a Texas millionaire whose principal concerns are social gatherings and shopping. She is curious about all the people on and near the ranch, particularly the workers, and wants to help by improving health care and educational opportunities for them and their children. Leslie's father had remarked to Jordan "Bick" Benedict III, Leslie's husband, that Leslie was born out of her time and "would have been good in the Civil War, hiding slaves in the Underground." Her family's friendly attitude toward blacks who work for them is natural to Leslie, and she attempts to replicate this behavior with the Mexican servants and ranch hands. She is repulsed both by the Mexicans who cannot understand such care and kindness from an "Anglo" and by the Texans who see Mexicans as serfs.

Another important character is Jett Rink, the angry ranch hand who strikes oil on his tiny piece of land. Rink delights in causing trouble for the Benedicts, and he wants Leslie. His desires become unrestrained, and he becomes almost a caricature of the Texas oil barons with his blatant spending. With too much money and too few morals, Rink, also a racist, represents everything wrong with the new oil-rich Texas.

The racism represented in *Giant* was a common social reality, especially before World War II. One character, Angel Obregon, the son of a vaquero at the Benedict ranch, becomes Jordy Benedict's friend; however, he is never ac-

cepted as an equal. Angel joins the military, is killed in battle in the South Pacific, and is awarded the Congressional Medal of Honor. A white undertaker in Texas refuses to handle his funeral. The novel does show change, however, as Jordy becomes a doctor and helps the poor. He also marries Juana, the Mexican American granddaughter of Bick's ranch foreman.

Giant has remained in the public mind. It was made into a successful film in 1956, starring Elizabeth Taylor as Leslie, Rock Hudson as Bick, and James Dean as Rink. The film, which softened Ferber's focus on racism, was adored by Texans and nominated for an Academy Award for Best Picture. In 2009, writer-composer Michael John LaChiusa premiered *Giant*, the musical. Based on the novel, the musical focuses on prejudice, environmentalism, and the consequences of greed.

Ferber's *Giant* has a sound sociological basis. In some ways it is a study of the phenomenon that was Texas in the first half of the twentieth century. Millions of copies of the novel have been sold, reaching an audience who not only enjoys the story but is provoked, in both negative and positive ways, by Ferber's examination of a caste system based on money, exclusion, and race.

Marcia B. Dinneen

Further Reading

Baxter, Monique James. "*Giant* Helps America Recognize the Cost of Discrimination." In *Hollywood's West*, edited by Peter C. Rollins and John E. O'Connor. Lexington: University Press of Kentucky, 2005. Although this chapter discusses the film version of *Giant*, it examines how discrimination against Mexican Americans is central to the novel. Part of a larger study of Hollywood's representation of the American West.

Campbell, Donna. "'Written with a Hard and Ruthless Purpose.'" In *Middlebrow Moderns: Popular American Women Writers of the 1920's*, edited by Lisa Botshon, Meredith Goldsmith, and Joan Rubin. Boston: Northeastern University Press, 2003. Discusses *Giant* as a critique of racism, arguing that Texas embodies a caste system of exploitation and power. Part of a collection of essays looking at popular American women writers who were active in the 1920's.

Gilbert, Julie Goldsmith. *Ferber: Edna Ferber and Her Circle—A Biography*. New York: Applause, 1999. A well-researched biography that considers Ferber a romantic realist. Notes that although she was not opposed to working with the system, she created her own unique niche within it.

McMurtry, Larry. "Men Swaggered, Women Warred, Oil Flowed." *The New York Times*, September 29, 1996. Occasioned by the rerelease of the film *Giant* in 1996, novelist McMurtry describes Ferber's novel as slapdash and reflects on the "glorious flamboyance" that was the Texas of rich cattlemen and oil barons.

Prescott, Orville. "Books of the Times." Review of *Giant*, by Edna Ferber. *The New York Times*, September 30, 1952. Prescott, in a generally positive assessment of the novel, examines how Ferber satirizes Texans, Texas life, and the "cult of bigness."

Smyth, J. E. *Edna Ferber's Hollywood: American Fictions of Gender, Race, and History.* Austin: University of Texas Press, 2010. A look at the artistic and business partnership between Ferber and the Hollywood studios, who adapted her often controversial work into popular films. Explores the "research, writing, marketing, reception, and production histories of Hollywood's Ferber franchise."

_____. "Jim Crow, Jett Rink, and James Dean: Reconstructing Ferber's *Giant* (1952-1956)." *American Studies* 43, no. 3 (Fall, 2007): 5-27. Provides background on the writing of *Giant*, the racist attitudes of elite white Texans, and a discussion of Leslie Benedict, the novel's protagonist.

Watts, Eileen. "Edna Ferber, Jewish American Writer: Who Knew?" In *Modern Jewish Women Writers in America*, edited by Evelyn Avery. New York: Palgrave Macmillan, 2007. An essay interpreting Ferber's work from the perspective of her Jewish heritage is included in this collection devoted to the discussion of American women writers whose lives and work have been influenced by Judaism.

Giants in the Earth
A Saga of the Prairie

Author: O. E. Rölvaag (1876-1931)
First published: I de dage: Fortaëlling om Norske Nykommere i Amerika, 1924; *I de dage: Riket grundlægges*, 1925 (English translation, 1927)
Type of work: Novel
Type of plot: Regional
Time of plot: Late nineteenth century
Locale: The Dakotas

Principal characters:
PER HANSA, a Norwegian settler
BERET, his wife
OLE,
ANNA MARIE,
HANS KRISTIAN, and
PEDER VICTORIOUS, their children

The Story:

Per Hansa moves all his family and his possessions from Minnesota into the Dakota Territory. His family consists of his wife, Beret, and three children, Ole, Anna Marie, and Hans Kristian. Beret is fearful and sad, for she has been uprooted too often and the prairie country through which they travel seems bleak, lonely, and savage.

Per Hansa stakes out his claim near the family of Hans Olsa at Spring Creek. Then Beret announces that she is carrying another child. Money is scarce. Per Hansa faces overwhelming odds, and thoughts of the great risks he is taking keep him awake long after Beret and the children sleep. Being something of a poet, Per Hansa thinks at times that the land speaks to him, and he often watches and listens and forgets to keep to his work as he clears his land and builds his house. He labors from before dawn until after dark during those long, northern summer days.

When Indians come and drive away the settlers' cows, only Per Hansa has the courage to follow them. Only he has the sense to doctor a sick Indian. Beret mistrusts his wisdom and there are harsh words between them. The grateful Indian gives Per Hansa a pony. Then Per Hansa goes on a buying expedition and returns with many needed supplies and, what is more, news of coming settlers.

The next summer, Per Hansa discovers claim stakes that bear Irish names. The stakes are on his neighbor's land; the homesteaders have settled where others have already filed a claim. Secretly he removes the stakes and burns them, but not before Beret realizes what he is doing. She begins to worry over her husband's deed. Per Hansa sells some potatoes to people traveling through and awakens the slumbering jealousy of his neighbors.

In midsummer, more people arrive, the settlers who had

set out the stakes that Per Hansa burned. They call the Norwegians claim jumpers, but after a fight, they take up other land nearby. Per Hansa manages to sell some of his goods to them. That fall, more Norwegians come. The little community is thriving. Beret, however, depressed by the open spaces and her fear that her husband has done a bad thing, brews a dark remorse within herself. Day by day, she broods over her lonely life, and she covers her window at night because of her nameless fears. At least Per Hansa, on his infrequent trips around to different settlements, meets other people.

When winter comes, Per Hansa rests. He can sleep long hours while the winds blow outside, but his wife worries and frets. He begins to quarrel with her. Soon, however, he notices that his neighbors are suffering hardship and privation. The unmarried young men who settled near the Hansas are planning to desert the settlement. It requires all his ability to convince them to stay and to face the desolate, bitter winter to its end. The settlers begin to talk of a school that will move from house to house so that the parents might learn English along with the children.

During the winter, Per Hansa becomes lost in a blizzard, and only his tremendous strength and courage sees him and his oxen safely through the storm to the Tronders' settlement. The following day, forgetting how Beret must be worrying about him, he stays on and cuts a load of wood to take back home with him. His next expedition is to bargain with the Indians for furs. He suffers greatly from exposure and loses two toes through frostbite.

When spring comes, Per Hansa cannot wait to get into his fields to plant his wheat. His friends think he is planting too early, and so it seems, for snow falls the next day and freezing weather sets in. Determined not to lose heart, Per Hansa decides to plant potatoes in place of the wheat. Beret takes to her Bible, convinced that evil is working its way into their lives. Then, unexpectedly, their wheat comes up.

Another couple arrives. They are exhausted with travel, the wife saddened by the death of her son on the prairie. Per Hansa and Beret take them in. When they move on, greater despondency seizes Beret. She feels some doom is working its way closer and closer to her life.

That summer, grasshoppers destroy much of the grain. Most of Per Hansa's crop is saved, but Beret takes his good fortune only as a sign that the underground trolls, or evil spirits, are planning greater ruin for her and her husband.

In the following years, the scourge of the grasshoppers returns. Many of the settlers are ruined. Some starve; some go mad. One summer, a traveling Norwegian minister takes up residence with them to plan a religious service for the whole community. His coming works a change in Per Hansa's household. Per Hansa takes courage from it and consolation, but the reveries in Beret's mind grow deeper and stranger. Because it is the largest house in the district, the minister holds a communion service in Per Hansa's cabin. Disconnected parts of the service float all that week in Beret's head. Her mind is filled with strange fancies. She begins to think of Peder Victorious, her youngest child, who was born on the prairie, as a savior who will work their salvation. As autumn approaches, the great plains seem hungry for the blood and strength of those who have come to conquer them.

That winter, Hans Olsa freezes his legs and one hand. In spite of all that Per Hansa and the others do for their neighbor, Hans Olsa grows weaker. Beret stands beside him, predicting that he has not long to live. She puts into the sick man's mind the idea to send for the minister. Per Hansa thinks that Hans Olsa is weak in calling for a minister and that the way to throw off illness is to get out of bed and go to work. He has never spared himself nor has he spared his sons. He is the man able to go for the minister, but this time, he is unwilling to set out on a long winter journey. Hans Olsa is a good man; he does not need a minister to help him die. The weather itself is threatening. However, Per Hansa reconsiders. His sons are digging a tunnel through snow to the pigsty. Inside, his wife is preparing a meal for him. They watch as he takes down his skis and prepares to make the journey for the sake of his dying friend. He does not look back at his house or speak farewell to Beret as he starts out. So Per Hansa, on his errand of mercy, walks into the snowstorm. There death overtakes him.

Critical Evaluation:

O. E. Rölvaag was born in the Helgoland district of Norway and lived there until he was twenty years of age. He attended school irregularly; his ambition to become a poet, once broached in the family circle, brought a discouraging barrage of ridicule. At age fourteen, he left school entirely and went out with the Lofoten fishing fleet. He seemed destined to pursue this hard vocation all his life, and the prospect brought him little contentment. Although considered by his family as too stupid to learn, he read voraciously, both Norwegian and foreign authors. His reading gave him a view of the possibilities of life that made the existence to which he was bound seem intolerably circumscribed. When he had been a fisherman for five years, something occurred that forced him to a decision. The master of his boat, whom he greatly admired, offered to stake him to a boat of his own. Rölvaag realized that if he accepted the offer, he would never be anything but a fisherman, so he declined it and emigrated to America.

For three years he farmed for an uncle in South Dakota; then at the age of twenty-three, with great trepidation, he entered a preparatory school in Canton, South Dakota. Six years later, he was graduated *cum laude* from St. Olaf College. After a year of postgraduate study in Oslo, he took the chair of Norwegian literature at St. Olaf, which he held until his death.

By the time Rölvaag began work on *Giants in the Earth*, at age forty-seven, he had already written five novels, of which four had been published. All were written in Norwegian, published in Minneapolis, and read exclusively by the Norwegian-speaking population of the Midwest. All the works deal with aspects of the Norwegian settlement and appealed strongly to an audience of immigrants. *Giants in the Earth* is actually an English translation of two novels previously written in Norwegian: *I de dage* and *Riket grundlægges*. This novel and its sequel, *Peder Seier* (1928; *Peder Victorious*, 1929), spring from a European artistic tradition but treat matters utterly American. They are perhaps unique in both American and foreign literature.

The European and specifically Norwegian elements that distinguish *Giants in the Earth* are its orientation toward the psychology rather than the adventures of its characters and its strain of Nordic pessimism. The characters of Beret and Per Hansa illustrate two complementary facets in the psychology of the Norwegian settlers. In Per Hansa, the desire to own and work his own land, to "found a new kingdom," seems to feed on the hazards he encounters. The brute resistance of the soil, the violence of the weather, the plagues of grasshoppers, the danger from Indians, the dispute over the claim stakes only spur him on to greater feats of daring, endurance, and ingenuity. Every victory over misfortune makes him feel more lucky and fuels his dream of a prosperous life for himself and his children. Freed from the cramped spaces and conventions of an old culture, he embraces the necessities of the new life joyfully, trusting in his instinct for the fitness of things to help him establish a new order.

Beret, on the other hand, takes no joy in pioneer life and is instead deeply disturbed at having to leave an established way of life to confront the vast, unpeopled plains. Uprooted, she feels morally cast adrift, as if her ethical sense and her identity are attached to some physical place. Beret sees Per Hansa's exultant adaptability to pioneer life as evidence of the family's reversion to savagery. For a man to shelter with his livestock, to change his name or give his child a strange name, to parley with Indians, or to christen in the absence of a minister indicate to her a failure of conscience, a giving up of the hallmarks of civilization.

Yet, Beret, like Per Hansa, brings her worst troubles with her from home. Her growing despondency about Per Hansa and her neighbor's spiritual condition springs from her own sense of sin in having borne Ole out of wedlock. She sees herself as the deserving object of divine retribution; in her deranged state, she takes every escape from disaster as a sign that God has marked her for some still more awful punishment. The very openness that thrills Per Hansa with its endless potentialities fills her with dread: "Here, far off in the great stillness, where there was nothing to hide behind—here the punishment would fall!" Per, bearing her in his heart, is drawn down into her despair.

Ironically, it is only after Beret regains her courage and her faith through religious ministration and ceases to expect calamity from minute to minute that Per Hansa dies. It even seems as if she sends him out to die. From an aesthetic point of view, however, his death is necessary to the work itself. For all of its realism and modernity of tone, *Giants in the Earth* is a saga, and, as sagas must, it ends with the death of heroes. Per Hansa and Hans Olsa are heroes of epic stature, and like the heroes of old legend, they complement each other's virtues. They have loved each other from their youth, and in their prime, their strength and wit combine to carve a new home out of the wilderness. Like Beowulf braving Grendel, they sacrifice themselves in a last great struggle with the prairie before it succumbs to the plow and the fence. Thus "the great plain drinks the blood of Christian men and is satisfied." The deaths of Hans Olsa and Per Hansa signal the passing of the time of legend, when giants walked the earth, and one man could do the work of ten; they signal as well the beginning of a more comfortable time of clapboard houses and hot coffee and of heroes of a wholly different kind.

"Critical Evaluation" by Jan Kennedy Foster

Further Reading

Eddy, Sara. "'Wheat and Potatoes': Reconstructing Whiteness in O. E. Rölvaag's Immigrant Trilogy." *MELUS* 26, no. 1 (Spring, 2001): 129. Focuses on the complex relationship between Norwegian and Irish characters in *Giants in the Earth* and *Peder Victorious*.

Gross, David S. *No Place to Hide: Gothic Naturalism in O. E. Rölvaag*. Madison, N.J.: Fairleigh Dickinson University Press, 1993. Relates traditional gothic tradition to Rölvaag's use of the frontier as a gothic setting of terror and wonder, which is especially a problem for Beret. Includes treatment of frontier and immigrant life.

Haugtvedt, Erica. "Abandoned in America: Identity Dissonance and Ethnic Preservationism in *Giants in the Earth*." *MELUS* 33, no. 3 (Fall, 2008): 147-168. Explains how

Rölvaag is known for his advocacy of a culturally pluralistic America in which all ethnic groups would coexist. Examines how this philosophy applies to the depiction of ethnic identity in *Giants in the Earth* and the other novel in the immigrant trilogy.

Reiff, Raychel Haugrud. "Fighting the Trolls on the Dakota Plains: The Ecstasy and the Agony of Norwegian Immigrants' Lives in O. E. Rölvaag's *Giants in the Earth*." In *The Immigrant Experience in North American Literature: Carving out a Niche*, edited by Katherine B. Payant and Toby Rose. Westport, Conn.: Greenwood Press, 1999. Describes how Rölvaag depicts the lives of immigrants who seek to reconcile their Norwegian heritage with their new American lives.

Reigstad, Paul. *Rölvaag: His Life and Art*. Lincoln: University of Nebraska Press, 1972. Examines Rölvaag's novels in a biographical context, revealing the forces and influences that shaped his work. Relates the treatment of folklore, myth, and Norwegian religious beliefs and values to Rölvaag's early life and experiences in Norway, and the

plot incidents to his father-in-law's stories of Dakota frontier life. Analyzes where in the plot reminiscences are superseded by imagination.

Schultz, April. "To Lose the Unspeakable: Folklore and Landscape in O. E. Rölvaag's *Giants in the Earth*." In *Mapping American Culture*, edited by Wayne Franklin and Michael Steiner. Iowa City: University of Iowa Press, 1992. Examines how Rölvaag's use of landscape and its relationship to folk myths of the Norwegian immigrant community shape his plot.

Simonson, Harold P. *Prairies Within: The Tragic Trilogy of Ole Rölvaag*. Seattle: University of Washington Press, 1987. A good look at Beret, the central character, especially how her religious values and her fearful attitude toward frontier space affect all three novels.

Sledge, Martha. "Truth and Fact: The Rhetoric of Fiction and History in Immigrant Literature." *South Dakota Review* 29, no. 2 (Summer, 1991): 159-169. Compares Rölvaag's treatment of immigrant life to that of other Scandinavian writers.

The Gift of the Magi

Author: O. Henry (1862-1910)
First published: 1905
Type of work: Short fiction
Type of plot: Moral
Time of plot: Early twentieth century
Locale: New York City

Principal characters:
DELLA, a young housewife
JIM, her husband
MME SOFRONIE, proprietress of a hair goods shop

The Story:

Tomorrow is Christmas Day, and Della is distraught. The meager savings she managed to put aside to purchase a gift for her beloved husband is a mere $1.87. It is simply not enough for a present worthy of her Jim.

There were brighter days for this young, loving couple. Earlier, Jim managed to bring home thirty dollars a week. Now, with their income reduced to twenty dollars a week, there is nothing left after basic living expenses are met. Della managed to save her $1.87 by doggedly bullying the grocer, the vegetable man, and the butcher into giving her better prices. Lean living, however, has not dimmed the couple's devotion to one another. Jim returns home from his job punctually every evening to be greeted by Della's loving embrace.

Della simply cannot bear the thought of giving her hus-

band a shabby gift or no gift at all. She collapses in tears of frustration, but then inspiration strikes. After taking a long look at herself in a mirror, Della is reminded that her assets extend beyond the pittance she is hoarding. She catches sight of her long, flowing hair, the one worldly possession she takes pride in, and realizes that there is a way to accomplish her goal.

Della sheds a few tears for what will be her lost glory. Just as quickly, however, she represses her emotions, scoops up her old jacket and hat, and leaves the flat. Arriving at a shop whose sign reads MME SOFRONIE. HAIR GOODS OF ALL KINDS, Della inquires what the proprietress would pay for her hair. Coldly, Madame Sonofrie appraises Della's tresses with an experienced eye and hand and offers twenty dollars.

Without hesitation, Della submits to the shearing and walks out with money in hand. After two hours of joyful searching, Della finds the perfect gift for Jim.

If Della has one possession that means the world to her, Jim has one, too, a beautiful gold watch that belonged to his father and his grandfather before him. Jim does not display the watch willingly, however, for it hangs on an old leather strap instead of a suitable gold chain.

Jim will not have to be circumspect any longer about his watch; Della finds a platinum fob chain, simple in design and of exquisite quality, which will do justice to Jim's treasure. Thrilled that she procured a gift worthy of her husband, Della hurries home to repair the damage the shearing did.

After styling her short hair into curls that resemble those of a "truant schoolboy" or a "Coney Island chorus girl," Della readies the dinner things and sits down near the door. As she waits expectantly, gift in hand, she prays that he will still find her pretty.

Punctual as always, Jim arrives. As he steps inside the door, he freezes, his eyes on Della. Della cannot read his reaction. It does not seem to be anger, disapproval, surprise, or anything she might expect. He simply stares. She runs up to him and pleads with him not to be upset; she sold her hair so that she could give him a present for Christmas.

When Jim finally comes out of his stupor of disbelief, he takes Della into his arms. He admits that nothing could make him love her any less, but that if she will have a look at what he bought her for Christmas, she will understand his shock. He draws a package out of his overcoat pocket and hands it to her. Della quickly unwraps the parcel and lets out a shriek of joy that soon turns to tears, for Jim's gift to her is a pair of combs, side and back, tortoise shell with jeweled rims, which she long admired in a shop window. She never dreamed that she would actually be able to have them.

Once her tears subside, she reminds Jim, weakly, that her hair grows very fast. She brightens when she recalls that Jim did not yet see his present. She holds the fob out to him expectantly, reminding him that now he can look at the time a hundred times a day. Upon seeing Della's gift, Jim collapses on the couch and smiles at her. He suggests that they put their lovely Christmas gifts away for a while; he sold his watch to buy Della the combs.

Critical Evaluation:

When, in 1919, the O. Henry Memorial Award Prize Stories was inaugurated, the work of O. Henry was the standard by which other short stories were evaluated. In the space of about a decade, William Sidney Porter, writing under the pseudonym O. Henry, produced almost three hundred short stories. Wildly popular, his stories were both commercially successful and critically acclaimed from 1908 until 1930. Sadly, O. Henry's death in 1910 prevented him from enjoying the fruits of his labor and its attendant praise. Mercifully, perhaps, it also prevented him from witnessing the critical crucifixion his work endured from 1930 until around 1960.

O. Henry's stories were noted for their thoroughly American spirit. His stories were always sympathetic to the underdog, and his characters, rooted in the grind of making a living, managed to transcend their humdrum existence by dint of love, loyalty, and self-sacrifice. A smart-alecky, brash humor, which is also typically American, also fills his stories.

O. Henry's stories were once lauded as the highest form of short story, but his mechanized plot structure was considered contrived after 1930. Fraught with sentimentality, the stories rely heavily on the use of irony in their paradoxically predictable surprise endings. While there may have been a strong commercial and critical appetite for this work in pre-Depression America, after 1930 the critics' taste for it soured. A new era in literature was emerging; it was an era that had no use for the previous generation's moralism. Critically acclaimed short stories now embrace subtlety, indirectness, and the symbolic. Next to them, O. Henry's stories' overstatement, predictable plots, and clear moral messages are deemed shallow and nonintellectual.

"The Gift of the Magi" has endured as one of O. Henry's best-known stories. A tribute to the transcendent power of sacrificial love, the story extols the foolish impulsiveness of the two lovers as being rooted in a deeper wisdom, sacrificial giving.

Della and Jim are typical O. Henry characters; they are hard-working and poor, and their existence is full of struggle. They manage to transcend it, however, and they experience joy through the power of their love for one another. When the lovers, unbeknown to each other, sell the possessions most dear to their hearts because they hope to make each other happy, they unwittingly undercut the effectiveness of their gifts. Beyond the minor tragedy of the situation, however, is the larger gift underlying it. The joy and sustaining power of self-sacrificial love is the greatest gift of all, and that, ultimately, is the gift these two share.

"Critical Evaluation" by Kim Dickson Rogers

Further Reading

Blansfield, Karen Charmaine. *Cheap Rooms and Restless Hearts: A Study of Formula in the Urban Tales of William Sydney Porter.* Bowling Green, Ohio: Bowling Green State University Popular Press, 1988. Focuses on the predominant character types and plot patterns in O. Henry's urban short stories. Describes how his life experiences influenced his writing.

Bloom, Harold, ed. *O. Henry*. Broomal, Pa.: Chelsea House, 1999. Provides a biography of O. Henry as well as a thematic analysis and other information about "The Gift of the Magi."

Current-Garcia, Eugene. *O. Henry (William Sydney Porter)*. New York: Twayne, 1965. Includes a biography of O. Henry and a critical analysis of his work's structure and technical characteristics. Analyzes his popularity and the subsequent decline of his reputation. Discusses his influence on the development of the American short story.

_____. *O. Henry: A Study of the Short Fiction*. New York: Twayne, 1993. Provides an overview of O. Henry's life and short fiction, describing the influence of his childhood in North Carolina, of his experiences in Texas and at the border of Mexico, and of editor Harry Payton Steger on his writing. Offers excerpts from critical reviews of O. Henry's work.

Langford, Gerald. *Alias O. Henry: A Biography of William Sydney Porter*. New York: Macmillan, 1957. Analyzes the work as well as the life of the writer. Asserts that O. Henry's rightful place in American literature is that of a minor but classic writer.

Long, E. Hudson. *O. Henry: The Man and His Work*. Philadelphia: University of Pennsylvania Press, 1949. This biography makes a case for O. Henry as a "humorist, craftsman, and social historian." Long claims that O. Henry is properly understood and appreciated in the context of the times in which he lived and of the audience for which he wrote.

O'Connor, Richard. *O. Henry: The Legendary Life of William Porter*. Garden City, N.Y.: Doubleday, 1970. Traces the life of O. Henry from his boyhood in North Carolina through his Texas and Ohio prison years, and, finally, to New York. Vividly portrays the early twentieth century New York City evoked in his work.

Smith, C. Alphonso. *O. Henry*. Edgemont, Pa.: Chelsea House, 1980. Reprint. Garden City, N.Y.: Doubleday Page, 1916. A biography and analysis of O. Henry's work written by a professor who knew Henry. Written in 1916, during the height of Henry's popularity, this book reveals a great deal about late Victorian culture and literary tastes.

Gil Blas

Author: Alain-René Lesage (1668-1747)
First published: Histoire de Gil Blas de Santillane, 4 volumes, 1715, 1724, 1735 (*The History of Gil Blas of Santillane*, 1716, 1735)
Type of work: Novel
Type of plot: Picaresque
Time of plot: Seventeenth century
Locale: Spain

Principal characters:
GIL BLAS, a rogue
SCIPIO, his servant
DON ALPHONSO, his patron
DUKE OF LERMA, his employer and prime minister of Spain

The Story:

Blas of Santillane retires from the wars and marries a chambermaid no longer young. After the birth of Gil, the parents settle in Oviedo, where the father becomes a minor squire and the mother goes into service. Happily, Gil Perez, Gil Blas's uncle, is a canon in the town. He is three and a half feet high and enormously overweight. Without his aid, Gil Blas would never have received an education. Perez provides a tutor for his nephew, and at the age of seventeen, Gil Blas has studied the classics and some logic.

When the time comes for him to seek his fortune, the family sends Gil Blas to Salamanca to study. The uncle provides him with forty pistoles and a mule. Shortly after setting out, Gil Blas is foolish enough to join the train of a muleteer who concocts a story that he has been robbed of a hundred pistoles and threatens all of his passengers with arrest and torture. His purpose is to frighten the men away so that he can seduce the wife of one of the travelers. Gil Blas has some thought of helping the woman, but he flees upon the arrival of a police patrol.

Gil Blas is found in the woods by a band of ruffians who have an underground hideout nearby. Under Captain Rolando, they make Gil Blas their serving boy. After an unsuccessful escape attempt, he sets out to ingratiate himself with the captain. At the end of six months, he becomes a member of the gang and embarks on a career of robbery and murder. One day the robbers attack a coach, kill all the men, and capture a beautiful woman. She is well-born and modest, and Gil Blas resolves to rescue her. Waiting until the robbers are asleep, he ties up the cook and escapes with the woman, whose name, he learns, is Doña Mencia. Grateful for her rescue, she dresses Gil Blas in fine clothes and presents him with a bag of money. He goes on his way, comparatively rich and comfortable.

On his travels, he meets Fabricio, a former schoolmate who has become a barber. Scornful of Gil Blas's intention to study, Fabricio soon persuades him to go into service as a lackey. Gil Blas turns out to be well adapted to flattery and intrigue, and he soon becomes proficient by serving a variety of masters, among them Doctor Sangrado, a physician. The doctor's one remedy for all maladies is forced drinking of water and frequent bleeding. Gil Blas wins the doctor's esteem and is permitted to attend poor patients in his master's place. During an epidemic, he has a record as good as that of Sangrado; all of their patients die.

Another master is Don Matthias, a fashionable man about town. By means of a little judicious thievery and daring, Gil Blas finds his new life highly satisfying. Each day is spent in eating and polite conversation and every night in carousing. During this service, Gil Blas dresses in his master's clothes and tries to get a mistress among the titled ladies of the town. An old lady who arranges these affairs introduces him to a grand lady who is pining for a lover. Gil Blas is disillusioned when he goes with Don Matthias to the house of Arsenia, an actress, and finds that his grand lady is really a serving maid.

After Don Matthias is killed in a duel, Gil Blas attends Arsenia for a time. Later he goes into service in the household of Aurora, a virtuous young woman who grieves because a student named Lewis pays no attention to her charms. At Gil Blas's suggestion, Aurora disguises herself as a man and takes an apartment in the same house with Lewis. Striking up a friendship with him, Aurora skillfully leads him on. Then she receives him in her own house in her proper person, and soon Lewis and Aurora are married. Gil Blas leaves their service content with his part in the romance.

On the road again, Gil Blas is able to frustrate a band of robbers who had planned to kill Don Alphonso. Thus, he and the don begin a lasting friendship.

After losing a situation because he learns that the dueña has an ulcer on her back, Gil Blas next takes service with an archbishop. His work is to write out the homilies composed by the archbishop. After he wins his master's confidence, the churchman makes Gil Blas promise to tell him when his homilies show signs of degenerating in quality. After a stroke, the archbishop fails mentally, and Gil Blas tells him his homilies are not up to the usual standard. In his rage, the archbishop dismisses Gil Blas, who learns in this manner the folly of being too truthful.

Engaged as secretary by the duke of Lerma, prime minister of Spain, Gil Blas soon becomes the duke's confidential agent. Gil Blas is now in a position to sell favors, and his avarice grows apace with his success in court intrigue. During this successful period, he engages Scipio as his servant. Gil Blas's high position enables him to secure the governorship of Valencia for Don Alphonso.

Gil Blas becomes involved in a high court scandal. At the request of the prime minister, he acts as panderer for the prince of Spain, the heir apparent. About the same time, Scipio arranges a wealthy marriage for Gil Blas with the daughter of a rich goldsmith. One night, however, the king's spies catch Gil Blas conducting the prince to a house of pleasure, and Gil Blas is confined to prison. Faithful Scipio shares his imprisonment. After months of sickness, Gil Blas is released and exiled from Madrid. Fortunately, Don Alphonso gives Gil Blas a country estate at Lirias, and there he and Scipio settle to lead the simple lives of country gentlemen. Attracted by Antonia, the daughter of one of his farmers, Gil Blas marries, but his happiness is brief. After Antonia and his baby daughter die, Gil Blas becomes restless for new adventures. The prince is now king, and Gil Blas resolves to try court life again. He becomes an intimate of the new prime minister, Count Olivarez. Once again, he is employed to arrange a liaison for the king, a mission that turns out badly. Forced to resign, Gil Blas returns for good to Lirias. There, he marries again, to a girl named Dorothea. Now content, Gil Blas hopes for children whose education will provide amusement for his old age.

Critical Evaluation:

The history of the picaresque novel has been cyclical; the genre has appeared, disappeared, and reappeared sporadically throughout its history but traditionally reappears during periods when there is economic upheaval and marked social inequality. The picaresque novel addresses these inequities in a satiric, pseudoautobiographical mode, teaching not by moralizing but by offering the protagonist—the picaro—as a negative example.

The historical origin of the form is uncertain. Some critics believe it sprang initially from ancient mythologies, primarily the myth of Odysseus, while others pinpoint its beginnings in Spanish picaresque novels of the 1500's. Regardless of when the genre began, it remains characterized, if not defined, by a collection of elements. Often any novel that is constructed in an episodic format, features a first-person narrator, and is satiric may be considered picaresque. Also, the true picaresque novel combines elements of realism and idealism as the picaro moves from ignorance to knowledge as a student in the school of hard knocks. He or she may be a rogue, a scoundrel, and even a criminal, but the true picaro is no more than an initiated but still innocent youth trapped in a situation in which a choice must be made between survival and integrity. The picaro chooses the former.

The picaresque novel is a Spanish tradition. Writers in other countries have emulated the picaresque novel, however. The hallmark of the French picaresque novel is *Gil Blas*, which is modeled on its Spanish predecessors. In honor of the novel's sources and to maintain credibility, Alain-René Lesage set his work in Spain; however, he wrote the novel in his native French. The novel's formality of language sets it apart from the tradition of the colloquial charm of the typical picaresque novel, with its lower-class cast of characters and its high-flown parody of the language of the rich and educated. Additionally, the work is tediously long, something many picaresque novels are not; *Gil Blas* is constructed in two volumes of incessant repetition of events and types.

Gil Blas may also be considered different from the typical picaresque novel in that its protagonist is not a poverty-stricken creature who will survive and maintain at all costs. Obviously influenced by his contemporary, Jean-Jacques Rousseau, Lesage develops his character into a semirespectable courtier, modifying the picaresque model of a lowly reprobate who must use his wits to live. Lesage's character thus "transcends" picarism and is endowed with the gifts of middle-class respectability. The protagonist also develops his native abilities, his patience, and his ability to choose his words carefully.

Although the work is a reaction to social inequality and is set in Spain within a picaresque framework, it cannot be considered pure picaresque. The ideas and tone are French, and the protagonist is little more than the prototype of Rousseau's "natural man," who is also imbued with middle-class morality. From the initial separation instructions of his parents to "go honestly through the world" and "not to lay [his] hands on other people's property" to his pious reversal in prison, Gil Blas is not a typical picaro. The true picaro, while

he or she may pretend to be redeemed, is not destined for sainthood or aristocracy in any form. He or she is only waiting for the next sucker to wander by.

The basic picaresque quality missing in *Gil Blas* is longing. The protagonist begins his journey not from need but with money for school and the good wishes of his family. Although the protagonist's subsequent adventures are tainted with misfortune, the reader feels little empathy with the plight of Gil Blas. It is assumed he could return to his native village and be welcomed with open arms. Alienation, stemming from a life begun in poverty, is pervasive in the picaresque tradition. Such alienation is absent in *Gil Blas*.

One quality that Gil Blas shares with the typical picaro is his skill at manipulation. Although it gives him no joy, Gil Blas is an adept role player. His is a world of disguises, and his troubles begin whenever he fails to see the person behind each mask, for few people in his world are what they seem to be. He rationalizes his roguish behavior as a means of coping, but, in nonpicaresque fashion, he suffers from guilt and remorse at every turn. When the situation threatens his moral code or the work to be done becomes too dirty, he delegates it to his servant and alter ego, Scipio.

Gil Blas's divergence from a moral course happens only once, when he is aligned with the duke of Lerma. The character has difficulty acknowledging his dark side, and the tale grows complex as Gil Blas the character debates with Gil Blas the narrator. His personality assumes the duality of an existence within the plot simultaneous to a satiric detachment from it.

In service to the duke, Gil Blas's morality is threatened by his greed. He is lured by avarice into a world of bribery and solicitation until he becomes a different person and is eventually required to compensate for his digression. The salvation for the character and boredom for the reader is an ethical reversal during his political imprisonment. There, the character undergoes a symbolic moral rebirth and vows that he prefers exile in a hermitage to a life of amoral prosperity. Thus, Gil Blas is whisked, a changed man, away to the throne of a Rousseauistic natural aristocracy.

According to Alexander Blackburn, renowned critic of the picaresque, Lesage, in this novel, has converted the picaresque into a novel of manners. The novel may be considered an accurate history of prerevolutionary France and the fall of the feudal plutocracy, but it should not be considered picaresque. Although many of the characters are rogues and scoundrels, Gil Blas is too inherently moral to be a picaro.

"Critical Evaluation" by Joyce Duncan

Further Reading

Alter, Robert. *Rogue's Progress: Studies in the Picaresque Novel.* Cambridge, Mass.: Harvard University Press, 1964. One of the better-known works on the picaresque novel. Discusses the variety of the genre. Contains an extended discussion of *Gil Blas.*

Bjornson, Richard. *The Picaresque Hero in European Fiction.* Madison: University of Wisconsin Press, 1977. Includes a thorough treatment of *Gil Blas* as the epitome of the genre in French. Traces the history of the picaresque from its conception in Spain to the books of Tobias Smollett in England.

Blackburn, Alexander. *The Myth of the Picaro.* Chapel Hill: University of North Carolina Press, 1979. Blackburn, considered a definitive expert on the picaresque, traces the recurrence of the genre from 1554 to 1954.

Chandler, Frank Wadleigh. *The Literature of Roguery.* New York: Burt Franklin, 1958. Although dated, this work is a thorough examination of the picaresque genre.

Gutiérrez, Ellen Turner. *The Reception of the Picaresque in the French, English, and German Traditions.* New York: Peter Lang, 1995. Traces the development of the picaresque novel from its origins in Spain through its adaptation as a genre in France, England, and Germany. Includes a discussion of *Gil Blas.*

Monteser, Frederick. *The Picaresque Element in Western Literature.* Tuscaloosa: University of Alabama Press, 1975. A study of the history and evolution of the picaresque. By examining a variety of examples, the author attempts to locate important elements.

Rivers, Kenneth T., ed. *A Survey of French Literature*: Vol. 3, *The Eighteenth Century.* New rev. 3d ed. Newburyport, Mass.: Focus/R. Pullins, 2005. This is a French-language anthology, but it contains an English-language introduction discussing trends in eighteenth century French literature and a short biography of Lesage in English, as well as an abridged excerpt of *Gil Blas* in French.

Spencer, Samia I., ed. *Writers of the French Enlightenment.* Vol. 313-314 in *Dictionary of Literary Biography.* Detroit, Mich.: Thomson Gale, 2005. Volume 1 of this two-volume survey of French literature includes an essay on Lesage, featuring biographical information, a discussion of his writings and critical reception, and a bibliography.

The Gilded Age
A Tale of Today

Authors: Mark Twain (1835-1910) and Charles Dudley
Warner (1829-1900)
First published: 1873
Type of work: Novel
Type of plot: Satire
Time of plot: Late 1840's to early 1870's
Locale: United States

Principal characters:
SQUIRE HAWKINS, an impoverished but proud southerner
WASHINGTON HAWKINS, his guileless and impractical son
LAURA HAWKINS, his daughter
CLAY HAWKINS, his adopted son
COLONEL BERIAH SELLERS, an improvident optimist
PHILIP STERLING, a young engineer
HARRY BRIERLY, his friend
SENATOR ABNER DILWORTHY, a corrupt member of
Congress
RUTH BOLTON, a Quaker

The Story:

Squire Hawkins of Obedstown, Tennessee, receives a letter from Colonel Beriah Sellers asking Hawkins to come to Missouri with his wife, Nancy, and their two children, Emily and Washington. Moved by the Colonel's eloquent account of opportunities to be found in the new territory, the family travels west. On the journey, they stop at a house where a young child is mourning the death of his mother. Feeling compassion for the orphan, Hawkins offers to adopt him. His name is Henry Clay.

The travelers board the *Boreas*, a steamboat headed up the Mississippi. The *Boreas* begins to race with another, rival steamboat, the *Amaranth*. The boiler on the *Amaranth* explodes, causing a fire on board and killing or injuring scores of passengers. As the *Boreas* rescues survivors, Hawkins finds a stray child, Laura, whose parents apparently have died. The Hawkinses, although now burdened with four children, find hope in the promise of Tennessee lands that they still own and adopt Laura.

After a tiresome journey, they reach their new home, a log cabin surrounded by a dozen or so other ramshackle dwellings. There Colonel Sellers helps the Hawkinses start their new life. However, Squire Hawkins does not prosper as he has hoped; rather, he makes and loses several fortunes.

Ten years later, Colonel Sellers is living in Hawkeye, a town some distance away. Squire Hawkins, by this time, is impoverished. Clay has gone off to find work, and Laura, now a beautiful young girl, volunteers to do so. Washington and Emily cannot decide what to do. Clay brings money to the destitute family and pays Washington's stagecoach fare to Hawkeye, where he finds Colonel Sellers as poorly off as the Hawkins family. Colonel Sellers, however, is a magnificent talker. His fireless stove becomes a secret invention, his meager turnip dinner a feast, his barren house a mansion, and under the spell of his words, Washington's dismal prospects are changed to expectations of a glowing future. Colonel Sellers speaks confidentially of private deals with New York bankers and the Rothschilds. He confides that he is working on a patent medicine that will bring him a fortune. Sellers takes Washington to the real estate office of General Boswell. It is arranged that the young man will live with the Boswells while working for the general. Before long, he falls in love with Boswell's daughter Louise.

Squire Hawkins dies, leaving his family only the lands in Tennessee. Among his papers, Laura finds some letters from a Major Lackland, who apparently came across a man believed to be Laura's father. Before Hawkins can get in touch with the man, he disappears. Laura's doubtful parentage makes her an object of scorn in the region.

Meanwhile, two young New Yorkers, Philip Sterling and Harry Brierly, set out for Missouri to work as construction engineers for a railroad company. In St. Louis, they meet Sellers, who entertains them with boasts about his investments and treats them to drinks and cigars. When he shows embarrassment, pretending to have lost his money, Philip relieves him by paying the bill.

In Philadelphia, Ruth Bolton, the daughter of Eli and Margaret Bolton, both Quakers, receives a letter from Philip. Rebelling against the rules of the Friends, Ruth tells her parents that she wants to do something different, perhaps study medicine.

Sellers continues to befriend the two young men in St. Louis. He goes so far as to suggest that the railroad should be built through Stone's Landing, a small village not along the route planned for the road. Like Sellers, Harry is a man of imagination. When their money runs out, Harry and Philip go to an engineer's camp near Hawkeye, and the Colonel joins them to plan the city to be built there.

Philip and Harry arrive in Hawkeye eight years after the death of Squire Hawkins. The Civil War has been fought; the Hawkinses are still supported by Clay, and Laura has become a beauty. During the war, she married a Colonel George Selby, who, already married, deserted her when his regiment was transferred. After that calamity, she turned her eye upon Harry Brierly, who fell in love with her.

When Senator Abner Dilworthy goes to Hawkeye to investigate Colonel Sellers's petition for funds to improve the area, he meets Washington Hawkins. Thinking Washington a fine young man, the senator takes him on as an unpaid secretary. Laura charms Dilworthy to such an extent that he invites her to visit his family in Washington, D.C.

Ruth is in school at Fallkill, where she stays with a family named Montague. On their way to New York, Philip and Harry stop to see her. Philip is disappointed with the manner in which Ruth accepts him. Alice Montague is kinder to him; Ruth seemed too attentive to Harry. In Washington, D.C., Harry sees the appropriation for Stone's Landing passed by Congress. When the New York office sends no money with which to pay the workers at Stone's Landing, Harry goes to New York to investigate. Speculation is everywhere; even Mr. Bolton decides to buy some land near the railroad in Pennsylvania. Unfortunately, Harry learns that the bribes to obtain the congressional appropriation have been so costly that there is no money left to pay for the work at Stone's Landing. Hired by Mr. Bolton, Philip goes to develop the natural resources of a tract of land in Ilium, Pennsylvania. He becomes a frequent visitor at the Boltons'.

Senator Dilworthy invites Laura to come to Washington, where she immediately becomes a belle—much to Harry's consternation. Many people believe her an heir. The senator attempts to use her influence in getting congressmen to vote in favor of a bill in which he is interested. At a party, Laura sees Colonel Selby, who has come to Washington to claim reimbursement for some cotton destroyed during the war. When the former lovers meet, Laura knows that she still loves Selby and the two begin to be seen together. When Selby leaves Washington and Laura, she follows him to a New York hotel, where she shoots him.

The opening of the Ilium coal mine finds Philip and Harry hard at work. Before they locate the main vein, however, Mr. Bolton goes bankrupt and surrenders all his property to his creditors. Philip is able to buy the Ilium tract. Ruth, now graduated from medical school, goes to work in a Philadelphia hospital. Harry is in New York, a witness at Laura's murder trial. Philip, hoping to read law in a squire's office, visits the Montagues in Fallkill. Mr. Montague, seeing value in Philip's mine, offers to finance a further excavation.

Laura's trial attracts much attention. Claiming that she is insane, her lawyer tries to show that her mind has been deranged from the time she lost her parents in the steamboat fire.

Senator Dilworthy's bill, a measure to establish a university for African Americans on the Hawkins land in Tennessee, has been for some time in committee. Washington and Sellers expect to make a fortune when the bill passes. Then Dilworthy, up for reelection, attempts to buy votes and is exposed, and his bill is defeated on the floor of the Senate. Washington and Sellers are crestfallen.

Laura is acquitted of the murder charge. Penniless, she tries to begin a lecture tour, but on her first appearance, she finds only an empty auditorium. On the streets, she is attacked by angry citizens and driven home to a cold room, where she dies of a broken heart.

Philip finally finds coal in his shaft, but his elation subsides when a telegram from the Boltons tells him that Ruth is gravely ill. He hurries to her bedside, where his loving presence brings her back to life and to him.

Critical Evaluation:

The Gilded Age, as opposed to a golden age, is an excellent portrait of the American post-Civil War years, a period for which Mark Twain and Charles Dudley Warner's title has become a name. Lacking a cohesive plot, the novel derives its unity from its satiric purpose and ironic tone. These begin with the preface, which lampoons contemporary fictional practices, and continue by satirizing formulaic fiction, economic speculation, political corruption, fraudulent piety, visionaries, exploiters, confidence men, and the get-rich-quick mentality. The book is considered one of the best sources for an understanding of the economic boom years during the administration of President Ulysses S. Grant.

Reportedly, when Twain and Warner, essayist and editor of the *Hartford Courant*, were ridiculing the contemporary sentimental novels their wives were reading, the women taunted them to write something better. Although both were seasoned writers, neither had attempted a novel before. Twain turned out the first eleven chapters and Warner the next twelve. For the remaining forty, they alternated small and large units, then patched them together to make the book, completing it in about three months. Of the total, Twain claimed thirty-three chapters and parts of three others. He contributed most of the frontier episodes and Warner most of

those concerning the East, the two parts interwoven by the theme of speculation, by Senator Dilworthy's moves between the West and the East, by the trip to Missouri of Philip Sterling and Harry Brierly, by travels to Washington, D.C., and by Laura Hawkins. Twain's portion was reworked into a successful play. The numerous stock situations—the adopted child searching for a father hinted to be aristocratic, the villainous seducer, the false marriage, the steamboat disaster, the adopted child becoming more helpful to his parents than the natural child, the reliable Philip contrasted with the foppish Harry, a heroine saved from grave illness, the beautiful wronged woman turned vengeful, the industrious young man finally earning wealth—were intended to burlesque the fiction that was then popular. Similarly, the obscure mottoes, contributed by the Hartford philologist James Hammond Trumbull, parody the contemporary practice of heading chapters with erudite quotations suggestive of moral profundity. Adding the mottoes' translations in 1899 provided a basis for extending the copyright.

Many reviewers have judged Twain's opening chapters, drawn almost completely from his own family history, to be the best part of the book. Squire Hawkins and his wife Nancy, with their children Washington and Emily, move from Tennessee to Missouri as did John and Jane Clemens with Samuel's older siblings, Orion, Pamela, Margaret, and Benjamin. The Tennessee land that represents false expectations to Hawkins held the same meaning for Twain's father. The delightful but unreliable Colonel Beriah Sellers was, Twain said, a close portrayal of his mother's cousin, James Lampton. Beyond making use of the family history, the authors drew many characters and episodes in the novel as clear parodies of contemporary well-known persons and events. Laura's story is based on the historical Laura D. Fair, whose insanity plea in 1870 extended the notoriety of her having shot her lover. Senator Dilworthy's escapades reenact the vote-buying scandal of Senator Samuel C. Pomeroy of Kansas, which made news in January, 1873. William M. Weed and Mr. Fairoaks were readily recognized by the contemporary audience as, respectively, William M. "Boss" Tweed of Tammany Hall and Representative Oakes Ames, scandalously exposed for bribing congressmen to fund and then control watered railroad stock. The many topical allusions recognizable to readers of 1873 make the novel a *roman à clef*. Land development speculation and other ambitious schemes were so widespread, however, as were religious cant and hypocrisy motivated by an ethics of greed, that the satire is effective even without identification of all the allusions to actual chicanery.

Social satire gives the novel its dominant theme. The displacement of democratic ideals—those of Thomas Jefferson, Benjamin Franklin, and Thomas Paine—stressing integrity of character and virtuous industry, by dreams of bonanzas that would repeat the robber barons' leaps to luxury represented to Twain and Warner the national evil that supported the Old World idea that one's worth could be measured by one's birth and wealth instead of by one's values and honest achievement. Thus, only the honest work of Philip Sterling and Clay Hawkins is rewarded with material success. Their education for useful work and their genuinely humanitarian motives contrast with the illusory ambitions toward wealth and station that corrupt Washington and Laura into becoming tools of the scoundrels. Laura's expectations from reading sentimental novels, especially those concerning an aristocratic father and a dashing lover, prime her for the seduction and betrayal by Colonel Selby, who embodies the authors' bitter distaste for the myth of southern chivalry. This theme of appearance contrasted with reality is captured in Colonel Sellers's insistence, as his family and guest suffer from the chill, that one needs only the appearance of heat, not the actual heat itself. The contrast plays out in the perversions of the legal system at Laura's trial: the self-serving bases for choosing jurors, the manipulations of the defense attorney, the corrupt politician-judge, and the misuse of the insanity plea.

The preference for appearance over reality also governs the absurdities of the social-caste system of Washington, D.C. The book's title emphasizes the difference between the truly golden and what only appears to be. The book helped establish Twain as a satirist of corrupted American political and religious institutions. It sold thirty-five thousand copies before the panic of 1873 reduced sales—a panic caused by the speculation it burlesqued.

"Critical Evaluation" by Carolyn F. Dickinson

Further Reading

Ashton, Susanna. *Collaborators in Literary America, 1870-1920.* New York: Palgrave Macmillan, 2003. Focuses on Mark Twain's collaboration with Charles Dudley Warner to write *The Gilded Age.* Analyzes how this book and other collaborative novels of the late nineteenth and early twentieth centuries were instrumental in defining the nature of authorship.

Camfield, Gregg. *The Oxford Companion to Mark Twain.* New York: Oxford University Press, 2003. Collection of about three hundred original essays on individual works, themes, characters, language, subjects that interested Twain, and other topics. Includes an appendix on researching Twain, which lists useful secondary sources, and an annotated bibliography of Twain's novels, plays, poems, and other writings.

Emerson, Everett. *Mark Twain: A Literary Life.* Philadelphia: University of Pennsylvania Press, 2000. A complete revision of Emerson's *The Authentic Mark Twain* (1984), this masterful study traces the development of Twain's writing against the events in his life and provides illuminating discussions of many individual works.

French, Bryant Morey. *Mark Twain and "The Gilded Age."* Dallas, Tex.: Southern Methodist University Press, 1965. Still the definitive study of *The Gilded Age.* Identifies the events, persons, and practices that the novel satirizes. Includes a bibliography and illustrations.

Gerber, John. *Mark Twain.* Boston: Twayne, 1988. Offers a full account of the background for *The Gilded Age* and an evaluation of its significance in Twain's development as a writer of fiction. Includes bibliography.

Rasmussen, R. Kent. *Critical Companion to Mark Twain: A Literary Reference to His Life and Work.* 2 vols. New York: Facts On File, 2007. A revised and significantly expanded edition of Rasmussen's *Mark Twain A to Z* (1995), with alphabetically arranged entries about the plots, characters, places, and other subjects relating to Twain's writings and life. The revised edition features extended analytical essays on Twain's major works, an expanded and fully annotated bibliography of books about Twain, and a glossary explaining unusual words in Twain's vocabulary.

Zheng, Da. "Economy of Insanity: *The Gilded Age.*" In *Moral Economy and American Realistic Novels.* New York: Peter Lang, 1996. Analyzes *The Gilded Age* and other realistic novels, describing their depiction of insanity, attention-seeking, lack of sympathy, and other aspects of American society. Discusses Twain and the other writers' ambivalence toward capitalism and their desire for a moral economy based on sanity, brotherhood, and modesty.

Gilead

Author: Marilynne Robinson (1943-   )
First published: 2004
Type of work: Novel
Type of plot: Epistolary
Time of plot: 1956
Locale: Gilead, Iowa

Principal characters:
THE REVEREND JOHN AMES, protagonist and narrator
LOUISA AMES, the narrator's first wife
FATHER (JOHN AMES), the narrator's father
GRANDFATHER (JOHN AMES), the narrator's paternal grandfather
LILA AMES, the narrator's second wife
ROBERT BOUGHTON, a minister, and Reverend Ames's closest friend
JOHN AMES BOUGHTON, his son

The Story:

The Reverend John Ames is dying. This is not a surprising circumstance for a person who is seventy-six years old. Neither is it a depressing one, for Ames, the longtime pastor of the small Congregational church in Gilead, Iowa, has every hope of Heaven. However, Ames has a young wife and a six-year-old son, both of whom he adores and dreads to leave. Although there is little he can do to provide a financial inheritance for his small family, he does intend to leave a long letter of family history and moral instruction to guide his small son as he nears adulthood. His letter tells his life story, and the story of his family.

The Ames family's history centers on Grandfather John Ames, a young man in 1830's Maine who has a vision of Christ in chains, summoning him to Kansas to fight for abolition. Once there, grandfather, also a minister, rides with John Brown, preaches about just war—sometimes with a pistol in his belt—and being too old to fight, serves as a chaplain for the Union forces during the American Civil War. After the war, he shepherds a congregation composed almost entirely of women and children who have lost sons, husbands, and fathers in the war. Ames's father, John Ames, is sickened by the militancy of Grandfather Ames, and rejects it. Father Ames becomes a pacifist and leaves grandfather's church to worship with the Quakers.

Later, when John Ames (the future reverend) is only two years old, father becomes a minister in Gilead, and his now-widowed grandfather joins the family there. Gilead is important to the family for the role it had played prior to the Civil War as a haven for John Brown and his cohorts, and as a stop on the Underground Railroad.

Ames's childhood memories are colored by the uneasy peace brokered by his father and grandfather. However, as grandfather grows ever more eccentric, hard feelings persist and he returns to Kansas to live as an itinerant preacher. When word reaches the family that the old man has died, Ames, now twelve years old, and his father set out on a difficult journey to find and tend to the grave. It is a treacherous trip, during which father and son come close to starvation. In the hardscrabble territory of Kansas, though, Ames witnesses the peace father is finally able to make with the memory of grandfather.

Ames, now grown up, marries his childhood playmate Louisa, only to lose her and their newborn baby when he is just twenty-five years old. He continues as a bachelor for four decades, ministering to his parishioners but remaining quite lonely. Now sixty-seven years old, a mysterious, uneducated, thirty-two-year-old woman named Lila appears at the Pentecost Sunday service and quite unexpectedly captures his heart. He baptizes her, and she, finding no better way to thank him, proposes marriage. Lila's inexplicable but obviously difficult past stands as an important reminder to Ames of the power of transforming grace. She and Ames become a devoted couple and the parents of a boy.

Robert Boughton is the minister of the Presbyterian church, and Ames's closest friend. Though now a widower and in poor health as well, Boughton had enjoyed a long marriage. He is the father of eight children and has many grandchildren. Ames values this friendship highly but has struggled over the years with jealousy, at times finding it impossible to be in Boughton's home, full of children. Boughton, sensitive to Ames's pain, names his youngest son John Ames Boughton—for Ames—and asks him to be the boy's godfather. Ames accepts, though the gesture intensifies rather than soothes his sorrow. This child, nicknamed Jack, soon becomes a source of grief for his own family as well. He is a prankster and a thief and ultimately fathers an illegitimate child whom he abandons to poverty and death. He disappears from Gilead and rejects communication with his family for twenty years, but inexplicably returns during the summer of 1956.

Having been the subject of many of Jack's often cruel cons, Ames cannot bring himself to trust Jack. His feelings intensify as Jack, who is the same age as Lila, begins to pay particular attention to her and their son. When Jack brings the boy a baseball and mitt and teaches him to play catch, something Ames is no longer well enough to do himself, Ames becomes jealous and fearful that Jack will take advantage of his family after his death. However, Jack's return to Gilead has nothing to do with Ames's family.

Jack has fallen in love with a black woman in St. Louis, Missouri, and has fathered a son with her. They are unable to legally marry, however, because of antimiscegenation laws. The woman has returned to her family in Memphis, Tennessee, and Jack is desperately searching for a community where he can make a home for them. Jack is disappointed to find that Gilead is no longer the bastion of racial equality it once was. When he confides all this to Ames, Ames is finally able to see the man that Jack has become and gives the blessing that Jack yearns for and which his own family cannot seem to supply.

As Ames remembers his past, he reevaluates it, considering his grandfather and father in the light of his own paternity. He wrestles his way to forgiveness as he encounters the threat that he perceives in Jack. He ponders theological questions as he considers his grandfather's militancy and his father's pacifism and the prodigal nature of his namesake, Jack. He finds grace in the care of his congregation but especially in the devotion of his wife. In the many ordinary moments of life—his son soaring on a rope swing; the cat, Soapy, stretching itself; the sun filling the church sanctuary at dawn—he finds beauty and wonder.

Critical Evaluation:

Marilynne Robinson's novels have achieved critical acclaim: *Housekeeping* (1980) won a Hemingway Foundation/PEN Award for best first novel and was nominated for a Pulitzer Prize in fiction. *Gilead* won the Pulitzer Prize, a National Book Critics Circle Award, and an Ambassador Book Award. Her third novel, *Home* (2008), was a finalist for the National Book Award. Robinson also is known for her articles, book reviews, interviews, and outstanding nonfiction, including *Mother Country: Britain, the Welfare State, and Nuclear Pollution* (1989) and *The Death of Adam: Essays on Modern Thought* (1998).

Epistolary novels, such as *Gilead*, tend to be static. Action can lose its immediacy because that action must be conveyed in the form of a letter from one character to another. Additionally, virtuous protagonists, especially clergymen, often appear flat and uninteresting. It is a great credit, then, to

Robinson that she masterfully turns these liabilities to her advantage. By employing the second-person narrator, inherent in letter form, Robinson creates not distance but an intimacy with her reader just as her character John Ames attempts to do with his son. As Ames sets on paper his memories, delights, worries, and experience, the reader takes in, as Ames's son presumably will one day, the complex and thoughtful inner life of a man struggling to live so that his actions are consistent with his understanding of Christian spirituality.

Because Robinson is able to expose the full humanity of Ames without sentimentality, readers are given not a wearisome stereotype but a rich and compelling protagonist. The pace of the novel suits this intimate portrait, resembling a long, companionable walk one might take with a close friend. In addition, Robinson, an outstanding prose stylist, captures not only midwestern vernacular but also Old Testament cadences and Melvillean metaphors.

Gilead does not follow a typical linear plot line but rather the stream-of-consciousness musings of its intelligent, endearing, elderly protagonist, the Reverend Ames. There are no chapter breaks, only spacing to indicate a new entry in the journal-like letter. Within this format, the story of Ames's family and childhood; the story of the Boughton family, especially Jack; and the story of Ames's personal struggles, flow around each other. This fluid narrative, however, belies a largely invisible substructure. Ames's digressions from family history to personal introspection, from astute observations to theological pondering, allow Robinson to contrast one father/son conflict against another and to juxtapose abstract ethical standards against deeply personal moral struggles. Such intricate layering gives each memory or encounter added metaphysical weight. This happens in numerous small ways, but can be seen in one large division of the novel.

In the first half, Ames tells the story of going with his father to search out his grandfather's grave. It is a wilderness experience both physically and emotionally. The focus shifts in the last half of the novel to the dilemma surrounding Jack Boughton's return. This is a wilderness of another sort but an equally frightening one. Ames's conflict with Jack is complicated by not only his bitterness at being childless for so many years but also his guilt that he has somehow failed Jack as well. Because he is dying, Ames believes he also will fail his young son. Ames must struggle toward resolution of these intertwined issues to emerge from this last wilderness of his life.

An obvious theme, examined in multiple ways in the novel, is the relationship of fathers and sons. Closely related to this is an exploration of the prodigal son. The conflict Ames has with Jack probes how both the religious person and the reprobate wrestle with moral tensions. Robinson makes the reader feel the intensity and significance of these tensions. Additionally, by setting *Gilead* in 1956, between World War II and the Vietnam War, between Jim Crow and the Civil Rights movement, and between a predominantly Christian worldview and a postmodern one, Robinson explores the complexities of war and pacifism, faith and doubt, and racial equality and racism. Considered fiercely calm, grave, and lucid, *Gilead* is a significant late twentieth century work both stylistically and thematically.

Susan T. Larson

Further Reading

Gardner, Thomas. "This Poor Gray Ember of Creation." *Books and Culture* 11, no. 2 (March/April, 2005): 15. Gardner's brief, readable review concerns Robinson's writing style, including her skillful use of metaphor.

Johnson, Sarah Anne. "Waiting for Gilead: Twenty-four Years After Her Masterpiece, *Housekeeping*, Writer and Thinker Marilynne Robinson Dazzles Critics and Fans with a Second Magnificent Novel." *The Writer* 118, no. 4 (April, 2005): 22. Johnson places *Gilead* within the context of Robinson's earlier novel, *Housekeeping*, and includes an interview with Robinson, providing insight into both novels.

Miner, Valerie. "Iowa Meditations." *Women's Review of Books* 22, no. 3 (December, 2004): 19. This brief but useful article by another novelist provides a detailed summary of *Gilead*.

Painter, Rebecca M. "Virtue in Marilynne Robinson's *Gilead*." *Analecta Husserliana* 96 (2008): 93-112. Argues that *Gilead* is a "remarkable" novel "for daring to focus on the interior life and spirituality of a presumably dull literary figure, a man of virtue."

Robinson, Marilynne. "Interview with Marilynne Robinson," by Sarah Fay. *Paris Review* 186 (Fall, 2008). An excellent overview of Robinson's work, including *Gilead*. Discusses the novel's origins, Robinson's major themes and ideas, and the writing process.

Wood, James. "Acts of Devotion." *The New York Times Book Review*, November 28, 2004. Woods skillfully delineates in this lengthy review what makes *Gilead* such a powerful novel and how it differs from much current fiction.

Giles Goat-Boy
Or, The Revised New Syllabus

Author: John Barth (1930-   )
First published: 1966
Type of work: Novel
Type of plot: Fantasy
Time of plot: A time like the 1960's
Locale: New Tammany College

Principal characters:
GEORGE GILES, also called Billy Bocksfuss
MAXIMILIAN SPIELMAN, his tutor
VIRGINIA HECTOR, his mother
GEORGE HERROLD, a person who saved George's life when he was an infant
ANASTASIA STOKER, loved by George
MAURICE STOKER, the husband of Anastasia
PETER GREENE, a friend of George
CROAKER, a brutish exchange student and football hero
EBLIS EIERKOPF, former Bonifacist scientist who lives with Croaker and rides on his shoulders
HAROLD BRAY, who claims to be a Grand Tutor

The Story:

Billy Bocksfuss lives contentedly in the goat barns of New Tammany College, thinking he is a goat and the child of Maximilian "Max" Spielman, his keeper and tutor, and a goat named Mary V. Appenzeller. One day, after killing his best friend, a goat named Redfern's Tommy, Billy learns that he is human. For his human name, he chooses George, after George Herrold, the man who found him as an infant on a booklift leading into the belly of WESCAC (West Campus Automatic Computer), the giant computer that runs New Tammany College. In a way, George's father is WESCAC, for George resulted from an experiment in which WESCAC collected samples of human sperm to produce the GILES, Grand-Tutorial Ideal, Laboratory Eugenical Specimen.

In rescuing the baby, George Herrold was partly EATen by WESCAC. EAT stands for Electro-encephalic Amplification and Transmission, a means of disrupting brain waves and thus killing people; its first test was against the Amaterasu, against whom New Tammany College still fought after it had defeated Siegfrieder College in Campus Riot II. Max and Eblis Eierkopf pushed the EAT button, killing thousands of Amaterasus, something for which Max feels great remorse. Only partially EATen when he rescued the infant, George Herrold still lives but acts like a child.

George learns about sex from watching students make love around the goat barns. He learns about love from Max and from a woman he calls Lady Creamhair, who feeds him peanut butter sandwiches and tells him stories such as "The Three Billy Goats Gruff." Later, he discovers she is Virginia Hector, his mother, but first he decides that her concern for him is sexual and acts accordingly, to his later shame.

At the age of twenty-two, George sets out to achieve what he feels is his destiny and to fulfill his assignment, "Pass All Fail All." Only a Grand Tutor can enter WESCAC's belly unEATen. Since he had come from WESCAC's belly by means of the booklift, he thinks he is destined to be a Grand Tutor. As Grand Tutor, he intends to enter WESCAC's belly, destroy its AIM (Automatic Implementation Mechanism), and thus prevent Campus Riot III. One night, awakening to the sound of Max blowing the shofar, he leaves the goat barns, walking toward the central campus of New Tammany College. When George reaches a fork in the road and Max tries to get him to return to the barns, he plunges through the woods, determined to continue. George Herrold and Max accompany George. They reach a river with a washed-out bridge. There, George Herrold drowns trying to cross to Anastasia Stoker, who stands on the other side displaying her nude body and shouting, "Croaker," attempting to lure Croaker, a gigantic, primitive exchange student who has run amok. Anastasia was brought up as Virginia's daughter. Anastasia, however, is not Virginia's biological child. After George Herrold drowns, Croaker comes, takes George on his back, crosses the river, and rapes Anastasia. George then recrosses the river on Croaker's back, gets Max, and brings him to the other side.

Maurice Stoker, Anastasia's husband, then comes with his troopers on motorcycles and takes Anastasia, George, and George Herrold's body to the Power House, which Stoker runs. The Power House supplies the power for WESCAC and New Tammany College, which is engaged

in the Quiet Riot with the Nikolayans and EASCAC, the Nikolayan equivalent of WESCAC. George enjoys the chaos in the Power House. He attends a party that Stoker throws at which, during George Herrold's funeral service, George "services" Anastasia.

The next morning, George, riding Croaker, finds Max near a wrecked motorcycle. George puts Max on Croaker, and George starts riding the motorcycle toward the main campus of New Tammany College, when they meet Peter Greene, owner of many industries and businesses, including Greene Timber and Plastics, a company that is destroying the forests of New Tammany College. Greene, who is hitchhiking, accompanies the travelers to the main campus.

Arriving the last day of Carnival, they attend a performance of *The Tragedy of Taliped Decanus*, about the dean who kills his father and marries his mother. Toward the performance's end, Max disappears, having been arrested for the murder of Herman Hermann, the Siegfrieder leader of the Bonifacists during Campus Riot II, who had been working as one of Stoker's troopers. At the performance's end, Harold Bray flies from the sky and announces that he is the new Grand Tutor. George protests that Bray is an impostor.

After spending the night with Eblis Eierkopf, who feels that WESCAC is the real Grand Tutor, George successfully endures the Trial by Turnstile and goes successfully through Scrapegoat Grate. Then, he receives his assignment, "*To Be Done At Once, In No Time*," to "*Fix the Clock*," "*End the Boundary Dispute*," "*Overcome Your Infirmity*," "*See Through Your Ladyship*," "*Re-Place the Founder's Scroll*," "*Pass the Finals*," and "*Present Your ID-Card, Appropriately Signed, to the Proper Authority*." In the course of trying to complete his assignment, George creates chaos on the New Tammany campus and brings his college and the Nikolayans to the verge of Campus Riot III. He then enters WESCAC's belly, along with Bray, and when he emerges, he sees that all is ruined.

Arrested, George spends forty weeks imprisoned in the Nether Campus. When he emerges, he tries to correct the problems he caused earlier. He enters WESCAC's belly a second time. When he emerges, he is almost lynched. Later, George enters the belly for a third time, now locked in a sexual embrace with Anastasia. When they emerge, Virginia, who has gone insane, greets them with the word, "*A-plus*." George pronounces her his first graduate.

Briefly going to the goat barns with Anastasia, George returns to campus with a goat, Tom's Tommy's Tom, who attacks Bray, driving him from New Tammany College at the exact time that Max is being shafted for the murder to which he has confessed. In a "Posttape," George says that at the age of thirty-three and one-third, again in the Nether Campus, he dictates his story to WESCAC and the book about his adventures results. He feels that he will eventually be shafted and that it does not matter whether or not people believe his story.

Critical Evaluation:

Giles Goat-Boy came from what John Barth called the Ur-Myth, or the myth of the hero, that he read about in *The Hero: A Study in Tradition, Drama, and Myth* by Fitzroy Richard Somerset, fourth baron (1956) and *The Hero With a Thousand Faces* (1949) by Joseph Campbell. *Giles Goat-Boy* follows Campbell's description of the pattern of the mythic hero. Giles's journey parallels those of the heroes Campbell treats, including Odysseus, Aeneas, and Jesus. The mythic hero's adventure includes a humble birth or infancy that belies the hero's great origins, a journey to the underworld, and a triumphant return.

George's comic adventures parody the hero's quest and satirize many prominent people and events of the twentieth century. Max, for example, is partially modeled on Albert Einstein and J. Robert Oppenheimer. A character called Lucius "Lucky" Rexford is largely modeled on John F. Kennedy; Campus Riot II is modeled on World War II; the Quiet Riot, on the Cold War; and New Tammany College, on the United States. Barth combines topical satire and allusion with perhaps the most universal story known to humanity— the hero's journey—to produce a book of epic proportions.

In addition to the story itself, *Giles Goat-Boy* employs metafictional devices reminiscent of earlier works by Barth. A "Publisher's Disclaimer" by the "Editor-in-Chief," for example, contains statements by four editors arguing whether the book should be published. Included also are a "Cover-Letter to the Editors and publisher" by "This regenerate Seeker after Answers, J.B.," a "Posttape," a "Postscript to the Posttape," and a "footnote to the Postscript to the Posttape"—all by Barth himself, in which he creates the fiction that Barth is an editor of a manuscript given to him by one Giles [,] Stoker, son of George Giles and Anastasia, but that parts of the manuscript got mixed with one of Barth's own. The manuscript causes him, the frame story goes, to give up his career as a writer to pursue the truths in it. The manuscript itself may or may not have been put on tape by WESCAC. The Posttape tends to contradict everything toward which the manuscript points, the Postscript to the Posttape questions all that the Posttape says, and the Footnote casts doubt on the authenticity of the Postscript. The art of fiction humbly emulates the life of academe.

Barth plays numerous other jokes on the reader. For example, the play about Taliped Decanus is a highly comical retelling of the story of Oedipus. Taliped, like Oedipus, means "swollen-footed" or "club-footed," and decanus means "dean," the university-world equivalent of rex, or king. George Giles's life in many ways parallels and parodies Oedipus's life. Barth often uses names jokingly. Giles is the name of the seventh century patron saint of cripples; George Giles limps because his foot was damaged when, as an infant, he was put in the booklift. Bocksfuss means goat's foot, again referring to George's limp. Eblis Eierkopf means devilish egghead. He eats eggs, is bald, and is thoroughly committed to science, to the exclusion of human values. Unlike Max, he feels no remorse at having pushed the EAT button. Peter Greene becomes the Gilesian parody of Saint Peter; he is the anything-but-saintly founder of the Gilesian church. Maurice Stoker, as his last name implies, is a Satan figure. Once, when George enters the library, he finds a woman reading a book that probably is *Giles Goat-Boy*; she seems to be up to the exact place at which George finds her reading.

In addition to the book's humor, there is an element of seriousness: George is a definite hero. When faced with a dilemma, such as the one he encounters at the fork in the road, he unhesitatingly creates a third choice by making his own path between the two forks. He achieves his destiny to "Pass All Fail All." Like the typical hero, he snatches victory from the jaws of defeat, but the victory is ambiguous and may not be a victory at all. Like Jesus and other saviors, he descends into the nether regions, achieves a victory there, rises from the land of the dead, and works what at least seem to be miracles. Critics interpret his three descents into WESCAC's belly as involving George's visions, first of diversity (a Western concept), second of unity (an Eastern view), and, finally, of the interdependence of opposites (a synthesis). In the end, George leaves a disputed legacy further complicated by disputes between his disciples. Thus, *Giles Goat-Boy* is a parody of the New Testament, recounting the life of what may or may not be the Grand Tutor of New Tammany College who came to campus to show students the way to Commencement Gate.

"Critical Evaluation" by Richard Tuerk

Further Reading

Clavier, Berndt. *John Barth and Postmodernism: Spatiality, Travel, Montage.* New York: Peter Lang, 2007. Clavier analyzes Barth's work from a perspective of postmodernism and metafiction, focusing on theories of space and subjectivity. He argues that the form of montage is a possible model for understanding Barth's fiction.

Harris, Charles B. *Passionate Virtuosity: The Fiction of John*

Barth. Champaign: University of Illinois Press, 1983. Harris views the novel as a search for unity, in which Barth speaks the unspeakable.

Lindsay, Alan. *Death in the Funhouse: John Barth and Poststructuralist Aesthetics.* New York: Peter Lang, 1995. Lindsay's analysis of Barth's work focuses on the author's middle and late texts, demonstrating the complexity and perpetual quest for pleasure in Barth's postmodern fiction.

Madsen, Deborah L. "John Barth's *Giles Goat-Boy* and Post-Romantic Allegory." In *Allegory in America: From Puritanism to Postmodernism.* New York: St. Martin's Press, 1996. Madsen's survey of American allegorical literature concludes with a chapter on *Giles Goat-Boy.* She analyzes how Barth and earlier writers have used allegory and how allegory relates to the myth of American exceptionalism.

Safer, Elaine B. *The Contemporary American Comic Epic: The Novels of Barth, Pynchon, Gaddis, and Kesey.* Detroit, Mich.: Wayne State University Press, 1988. Safer

treats elements of the absurd and the parody of Emersonian ideas of education in the novel.

Scholes, Robert. *Fabulation and Metafiction.* Champaign: University of Illinois Press, 1979. Contains a pioneering treatment of the novel. Scholes sees the book as a combination of philosophy and myth.

Scott, Steven D. *The Gamefulness of American Postmodernism: John Barth and Louise Erdrich.* New York: Peter Lang, 2000. Scott applies postmodernist theories to analyze Barth's work. He theorizes on the motifs of play and game in American postmodernist fiction generally, eventually focusing on "gamefulness" in the writings of Barth and Erdrich.

Tobin, Patricia. *John Barth and the Anxiety of Continuance.* Philadelphia: University of Pennsylvania Press, 1992. Tobin sees George Giles as a poet-as-hero; she focuses on the Oedipus story as a source for the novel.

Walkiewicz, E. P. *John Barth.* Boston: Twayne, 1986. Walkiewicz treats the novel in terms of myth, satire, and parody and discusses the idea of repetition within it.

The Gilgamesh Epic

Author: Unknown
First published: c. 2000 B.C.E. (English translation, 1917)
Type of work: Poetry
Type of plot: Adventure
Time of plot: Antiquity
Locale: The ancient world

Principal characters:
GILGAMESH, the ruler of Uruk
ENGIDU, his companion
ANU, the chief god
ISHTAR, the divinity of fertility
UTNAPISHTIM, a man who found the secret of life
UR-SHANABI, the boatman on the waters of death
NINSUN, a goddess
SIDURI, the divine cup-bearer
KHUMBABA, a dragon

The Poem:

Gilgamesh is the wisest, strongest, and most handsome of mortals, for he is two-thirds god and one-third man. As king of the city-state of Uruk he builds a monumental wall around the city, but in doing so he overworks the city's inhabitants unmercifully, to the point where they pray to the gods for relief.

The god Anu hears their plea and calls the goddess Aruru to fashion another demigod like Gilgamesh in order that the two heroes might fight and thus give Uruk peace. Aruru creates the warrior Engidu out of clay and sends him to live among the animals of the hills. A hunter of Uruk finds Engidu and in terror reports his existence to Gilgamesh. Gilgamesh

advises the hunter to take a priest to Engidu's watering place to lure Engidu to the joys of civilization and away from his animal life. The priest initiates Engidu into civilization with her body, her bread, and her wine. Having forsaken his animal existence, Engidu and the priest start for Uruk. On their arrival she tells him of the strength and wisdom of Gilgamesh and of how Gilgamesh told the goddess Ninsun about his dreams of meeting Engidu, his equal, in combat.

Engidu challenges Gilgamesh by barring his way to the temple. An earth-shaking fight ensues in which Gilgamesh stops Engidu's onslaught. Engidu praises Gilgamesh's strength and the two enemies became inseparable friends. Gilgamesh informs Engidu of his wish to conquer the terrible monster, Khumbaba, and challenges him to go along. Engidu replies that the undertaking is full of peril for both. Gilgamesh answers that Engidu's fear of death deprives him of his might. At last Engidu agrees to go with his friend. Gilgamesh then goes to the elders and they, like Engidu, warn him of the perils he will encounter. Seeing his determination, the elders give him their blessing. Gilgamesh then goes to Ninsun and she also warns him of the great dangers, but to no avail. Then she takes Engidu aside and tells him to give Gilgamesh special protection.

Upon climbing the cedar mountain to reach Khumbaba, Gilgamesh relates three terrible dreams to Engidu, who shores up Gilgamesh's spirit by placing a favorable interpretation on them. On reaching the gate to the cedar wood where Khumbaba resides, the pair are stopped by the watchman, who possesses seven magic mantles. The two heroes succeed in overcoming him. Accidentally, Engidu touches the magic portal of the gate; immediately he feels faint and weak, as if afraid of death. The champions enter the cedar wood and, with the aid of the sun god, slay Khumbaba.

Upon their return to Uruk after their victory, the goddess Ishtar falls in love with Gilgamesh and asks him to be her consort. Gilgamesh, being wiser than her previous consorts, recalls all of the evil things she did to her earlier lovers. Ishtar then angrily ascends to heaven and reports his scornful refusal to Anu. Threatening to destroy humanity, she forces Anu to create a monster bull that will kill Gilgamesh.

Anu forms the bull and sends it to Uruk. After it slays five hundred warriors in two snorts, Engidu jumps on its back while Gilgamesh drives his sword into its neck. Engidu then throws the bull's thighbone in Ishtar's face, and Gilgamesh holds a feast of victory in his palace.

Engidu, still ailing from touching the portal to the cedar wood, curses those who showed him civilization. He relates his nightmares to Gilgamesh, grows fainthearted, and fears death. Since Engidu was cursed by touching the gate, he dies. Gilgamesh mourns his friend six days and nights; on the seventh he leaves Uruk to cross the steppes in search of Utnapishtim, the mortal who discovered the secret of life.

Upon reaching the mountain named Mashu, he finds scorpion men guarding the entrance to the underground passage. They receive him cordially when they learn he is seeking Utnapishtim, but they warn him that no one has ever found a way through the mountain.

Gilgamesh travels the twelve miles through the mountain in pitch darkness, and at last he enters a garden. There he finds Siduri, the cup-bearing goddess, who remarks on his haggard condition. Gilgamesh explains that his woeful appearance has been caused by the loss of Engidu, and that he seeks Utnapishtim. The goddess advises him to live in pleasure at home and warns him of the dangers ahead.

Gilgamesh continues ahead, seeking the boatman Ur-Shanabi, who might possibly take him across the waters of death. On finding Ur-Shanabi's stone coffers, Gilgamesh breaks them in anger, but he makes up for them by presenting the boatman with huge poles. Ur-Shanabi then ferries Gilgamesh across the waters of death.

Utnapishtim, meeting Gilgamesh on the shore, also speaks of his haggard condition. Gilgamesh tells him about the loss of Engidu and his own search for the secret of life. Utnapishtim replies that nothing is made to last forever, that life is transient, and that death is part of the inevitable process.

Gilgamesh then asks how Utnapishtim found the secret of eternal life, and Utnapishtim tells him the story of the Great Flood. Utnapishtim was told in a dream of the gods' plans to flood the land. So he built an ark and put his family and all kinds of animals on it. When the flood came, he and those on the ark survived, and when the flood subsided he found himself on Mount Nisser. After the waters had returned to their normal level, he gave thanks to the gods, and in return the god Ea blessed him and his wife with the secret of life everlasting.

After finishing his story Utnapishtim advises Gilgamesh to return home, and before he leaves, Ur-Shanabi bathes Gilgamesh and clothes him in a robe that would remain clean as long as he lived. As Gilgamesh is leaving, Utnapishtim gives him the secret of life, a magic plant that grows at the bottom of the waters of death. However, as Gilgamesh bathes in a pool on his way home, an evil serpent eats the plant.

On arriving home Gilgamesh goes to Ninsun to inquire how he can reach Engidu in the land of the dead. Although Ninsun directs him, he fails in his attempt because he breaks some of the taboos that she has laid out for him. Deeply disappointed, he makes one final appeal to the god Ea, the lord of the depths of the waters, and Engidu is brought forth. Gilgamesh asks Engidu what happens after death, and Engidu lays bare the full terrors of the afterworld. Worms, neglect, and disrespect are the lot of the dead.

Critical Evaluation:

The Sumerian tale of *Gilgamesh* is the oldest to have survived into the modern era. Thus the greatest value of *Gilgamesh* is that it opens a window for modern readers into their collective past. The tale's content reveals much about humanity's earliest social and religious concerns, while its form reveals equivalent insights about the relationship between instruction and entertainment in an oral culture.

The story of *Gilgamesh* reveals both a desire to commemorate the hero's greatness and an obligation to learn from his flaws. The first thing the audience learns from the story is that Gilgamesh builds protective walls around the city, a great gift to his society. When the audience next learns that the king has been abusive to the young men of the city and has deflowered young maidens, their disapproval of these acts is tempered by their initial approval of his great accomplishment. Overall, the early portions of the story demonstrate that the abiding criterion for judgment is not the happiness of the individual, even if that individual is the king, but the good of society as a whole. When Gilgamesh exercises the kingly privilege in deflowering maidens, his actions may be legal, but they fail to provide any benefit for Uruk and are therefore condemned. Thus does the audience learn that greatness entails responsibility, not just strength.

Crucial to the lesson of the story is Gilgamesh's status as two-thirds god, one-third human. Kings are more than human and therefore are revered; yet at the same time kings are imperfect, so that as they learn, their growth will serve as a model for the improvement of their subjects. One special feature of *Gilgamesh* is its introduction of an additional intermediary between the king and his people, Engidu. Precisely because the hero is so far above his subjects, he needs to befriend someone who is thoroughly human, though possessing heroic strength; only in this way can the audience achieve an emotional identification, or at least a profound empathy, with the hero. They can never quite see themselves as Gilgamesh, but they can see themselves as Engidu, standing by the hero's side, supporting him, making possible his glorious triumphs. Thus when the pair are confronted by the Bull of Heaven, it is Engidu who leaps upon him, allowing Gilgamesh to make the killing blow. Gilgamesh gains a triumph, but Engidu shares in the moment—and the audience shares in both.

Nevertheless, Engidu is mortal. His death motivates the greatest feat of *Gilgamesh*, the hero's quest for the secret of immortality. In his desperation, in his willingness to commit all of his strength to his search, and most of all in his willingness to share the secret of renewed youth with the people of Uruk once he has obtained it, Gilgamesh displays the true nobility of the heroic character. It is his failure in this final quest, not his ability to triumph over Khumbaba or the Bull of Heaven, that stays with the audience and teaches the final lesson of the story. If even the greatest hero of them all cannot escape his destiny, if every man and woman is doomed someday to die, then perhaps each member of the audience who hears the Gilgamesh story has done the right thing, simply by choosing life. For if the city is to thrive, its citizens must accept the will of the gods, obey the will of the king, and strive not for more than can be granted but for such happiness as is their lot. In a society such as Uruk's, whose religion offers no travel after death to some promised land of gardens and fountains, such a lesson is the only one that can lead to success.

Nevertheless, Gilgamesh's desire for immortality is not totally denigrated. It is what separates the long series of forgotten kings in Uruk from the heroic figure who earns the title role in his own story. When Gilgamesh expresses the desire to set his name in brick where no man's name has ever appeared, he is articulating a yearning shared by many. This approval is clear in the large proportion of the story that is given over to the campaign against Khumbaba. This is Gilgamesh's great triumph, the fulfillment of his desire to do what no man has ever done. Modern speculation is that this section of the tale is based on an actual expedition—perhaps one led by the historical king Gilgamesh—across the desert, into the mountains, which brought tons of precious wood back to the city and perhaps even enabled the building of the walls and temples so proudly referred to at the beginning and end of the tale.

Finally, the form of the Gilgamesh story also reveals much about the special demands of oral composition and performance. Speeches with vital plot or thematic content are repeated, to ensure that the audience gets the message or to underscore the importance of the event. In a world without written communication, messengers typically repeated back what they had been told in order to make sure they had heard correctly; when this feature is incorporated into the world of the story, it provides additional connection between the tale and its audience. Formulaic phrases are also repeated, often accumulating great power. The best example of this feature of oral composition occurs during Gilgamesh's trip through the darkness of the mountain tunnel between his world and the world of the gods, when the hero travels many leagues with "darkness ahead of him and darkness behind him."

"Critical Evaluation" by Hartley S. Spatt

Further Reading

Ackerman, Susan. *When Heroes Love: The Ambiguity of Eros in the Stories of Gilgamesh and David.* New York: Columbia University Press, 2005. Ackerman analyzes the sexual relationships of Gilgamesh and Engidu, and of David and Jonathan in the biblical story, and describes how these relationships provide a new understanding of sexuality and gender in ancient Near Eastern literature.

Damrosch, David. *The Buried Book: The Loss and Rediscovery of the Great Epic of Gilgamesh.* New York: H. Holt,

2007. Damrosch recounts the origins of the epic, placing it within the context of ancient Mesopotamian court life, and chronicles the epic's eventual recovery and translation in the nineteenth century.

Gardner, John, and John Maier, trans. *Gilgamesh.* New York: Vintage Books, 1985. Each column of the actual tablets is translated, then supplemented by numerous parallel texts. An appendix analyzes the tablets in more detail, demonstrating the extreme difficulty of establishing any single version of *Gilgamesh.*

George, A. R. *The Babylonian "Gilgamesh Epic": Introduction, Critical Edition, and Cuneiform Texts.* 2 vols. New York: Oxford University Press, 2003. This edition of the epic contains fragments from the cuneiform texts that are published here for the first time. George provides a detailed analysis of the work and an introduction placing it in its literary and historical contexts.

Heidel, Alexander. *The Gilgamesh Epic and Old Testament Parallels.* 2d ed. Chicago: University of Chicago Press, 1973. This is the first, and still one of the clearest, studies of the close links between Sumerian and Hebrew tales of natural heroism and supernatural disaster.

Moran, William L. *The Most Magic Word: Essays on Babylonian and Biblical Literature.* Edited by Ronald S. Hendel. Washington, D.C.: Catholic Biblical Association of America, 2002. This collection features four essays on the Gilgamesh epic, including one discussing Gilgamesh's acceptance of his own humanity and another on the humanization of his companion Engidu.

Sandars, N. K., trans. *The Epic of Gilgamesh.* Harmondsworth, England: Penguin, 1960. This is the standard text version of the epic, rendered as a continuous, compelling story. Although this version's exact readings have been superseded in many cases by later discoveries, it remains one of the best attempts at recapturing the original audience's experience of the epic.

Tigay, Jeffrey H. *The Evolution of the Gilgamesh Epic.* Philadelphia: University of Pennsylvania Press, 1982. Tigay demonstrates that numerous differences among the various redactions of the Gilgamesh saga resulted in significantly different versions of the story; therefore, he argues, translations that combine passages from separate versions in order to achieve a more readable story distort the saga.

Girl with a Pearl Earring

Author: Tracy Chevalier (1962-   )
First published: 1999
Type of work: Novel
Type of plot: Historical
Time of plot: 1664-1666 and 1676
Locale: Delft, the Netherlands

Principal characters:
GRIET, a maid
JOHANNES VERMEER, a painter
CATHARINA, his wife
MARIA THINS, Catharina's mother
MAERTGE,
CORNELIA,
ALEYDIS,
LISBETH, and
JOHANNES, the Vermeer children
TANNEKE, the family's housekeeper
PIETER, a butcher's son
PIETER VAN RUIJVEN, Vermeer's patron
ANTONIO VAN LEEUWENHOEK, Vermeer's friend

The Story:

After her father is blinded by an explosion at a kiln factory, sixteen-year-old Griet has to begin work as a maid in the household of painter Johannes Vermeer. Her wages will help sustain her newly poor family. The Vermeer household includes Catharina, Vermeer's pregnant wife, who dislikes Griet on sight; Maria Thins, Catharina's powerful mother;

and five children—Maertge, Lisbeth, Cornelia, Aleydis, and baby Johannes. Griet immediately suspects that Cornelia will be a difficult child.

The family housekeeper, Tanneke, explains to Griet her duties as a maid, including washing, ironing, mending, cooking, shopping, and, most important, cleaning Vermeer's studio. Griet is instructed to be extremely careful and to not move anything out of place. Griet thinks how difficult this could be, trying to dust under objects set up for painting, but she works out a method, using her arm and hand to measure distances between objects as she removes them. Vermeer approves of her cleaning.

Vermeer is working on a painting of the wife of his patron, Pieter van Ruijven. She is dressed in a yellow mantle trimmed with ermine and wearing a pearl necklace and pearl earrings. Griet is fascinated by the painting and yearns to know the painter.

On Sunday, her first day off (and the only one she will have each week), Griet visits her parents, who ply her with questions about the house and the painter. Griet describes the painting in detail to her father.

One day, Vermeer's friend Antonio van Leeuwenhoek arrives with a strange box that he identifies as a camera obscura. Vermeer shows Griet how it operates, and encourages her to look through it. He says it is a tool to help him see things better, and she comes to understand that he sees things in a way others do not.

Meantime, Griet has become friendly with Pieter, a butcher's son. One day, he tells her that the plague has struck the neighborhood where her parents live, and that her sister, Agnes, is ill. On another Sunday, she visits her brother, Franz, in the kiln factory where he is working as an apprentice. She learns that the difficult circumstances under which he works are punishment for his inappropriate attentions to the owner's wife.

Vermeer's painting of van Ruijven's wife is finished, and everyone is satisfied with it. The painting is taken from the home before Griet can get a final look at it. Van Ruijven, whose eye has been on Griet for some time, manages to corner her one day, but he is stymied in his attempts by the kindly van Leeuwenhoek, who keeps van Ruijven away from her.

Vermeer begins to paint again; his next subject is the baker's daughter. For this work, he secretly asks Griet to assist him, first by buying colors at the apothecary and then by grinding pigments. He also shows her how a painting is created. The two work closely together, but her assistance is kept secret from the rest of the household. Family members, especially Catharina, would be jealous if they knew of the maid's privileged position.

Pieter, the butcher's son, is now a serious suitor, interested in Griet's hand. He goes to her family's church and is invited by Griet's parents to Sunday dinners. Griet repels his advances, though, telling him that at age seventeen, she is not ready.

Vermeer finishes the painting of the baker's daughter and begins another painting for van Ruijven. At one point, Griet sees something she thinks is not right in the painting and dares to change the folds of the drapery left in position for the model. Despite the seriousness of her actions, Vermeer nevertheless agrees with the change and remarks that he has learned something from her.

Cornelia has played several mean tricks on Griet. This time, she secretly places her mother's tortoise-shell combs among Griet's belongings. Griet finds the objects and, horrified of being accused of theft, requests Vermeer's help in identifying the true culprit, Cornelia. Soon, she is punished. Griet now feels indebted to Vermeer, but is disappointed that he has not yet revealed to Catharina her assistance in his work. Still, Griet now has an identity in the household, and she grows even closer to Vermeer, so much so that her brother Franz says he can see that she wants him.

Vermeer next decides to paint Griet, at van Ruijven's insistence. In preparation for the pose, she is asked to remove her maid's cap to show her hair, but she refuses to do so. Instead, she creates a turban with pieces of blue and gold cloth. As the painting proceeds, both she and Vermeer conclude that something is missing. She dreads the decision she knows is coming—that she wear Catharina's pearl earring. Griet is at first reluctant, because she realizes it will mean the end for her in the household. She cannot refuse the master, though, so she pierces her own ear. Vermeer inserts the earring, then insists she wear both pieces.

Catharina and Cornelia come to the studio to view the finished painting. Catharina explodes in a rage, infuriated that a maid should wear her beloved earrings. She picks up a palette knife and moves forward to slash the painting, but Vermeer stops her. Griet leaves the house.

It is now ten years later, and Griet is married to Pieter and has two little boys, one named Jan, for Vermeer. Griet learns that Vermeer has died. In the years after working in the Vermeer household, Griet has not seen the painter, except from a distance. In her maturity she has decided that he cared more for the painting than he did for her.

One day, the Vermeer's housekeeper, Tanneke, requests Griet's presence at the Vermeer house so that Catharina—reluctantly—can fulfill her late husband's wish: for Griet to have the pearl earrings. Griet takes them but, knowing they are inappropriate for a butcher's wife, sells them for twenty guilders.

Critical Evaluation:

In the postmodern era, a number of historical figures have been re-created in literature and film. With the novel, most authors begin their stories with the famous person and work back to the work of art. Tracy Chevalier reverses this process, beginning with the painting and working back to the artist. Her focus, however, is not on the painter Vermeer, but on the painting—*Girl with a Pearl Earring* (c. 1665).

Chevalier's methodology was to examine the famous painting and to infer from it aspects of the model's character. Because historians agree that Vermeer often used servants as his models, Chevalier had devised a fictional servant named Griet for her story. After closely examining the painting, Chevalier formed her story around the incongruity displayed in the painting: Griet is a servant wearing an unusual headdress and luminous pearl earrings. Her wide eyes stare provocatively at the painter (or viewer), and her half-open mouth is sexually suggestive.

Griet lives by a strict Protestant moral and social code and is uncomfortable in the Catholic household of her employer. Properly cognizant of the mores of her position, she refuses to take off her maid's cap for her sitting with Vermeer.

Griet, too, is on the verge of a sexual awakening, a subtle development by Chevalier that is one of the beauties of this coming-of-age novel. While the attentions of Pieter, the butcher's son, do not awaken her sexuality, and van Ruijven's attentions repulse her, she is attracted by Vermeer's presence and artistry. She is too inexperienced to understand where her fascination might lead, but gradually her feelings grow from simple awe to admiration for Vermeer's talent to a real emotional investment as she becomes virtually his collaborator. When he inserts the pearl earring into her newly pierced ear, the consummation is complete.

The character of Vermeer is a mystery, just as the actual Vermeer remains a mystery to historians. The few facts known about his life are that he fathered eleven children, painted thirty-six paintings, and died at the age of forty-three. Chevalier wisely refrains from providing a more fleshed-out character, allowing Vermeer to be seen only from Griet's perspective. There are, however, glimpses of the man: He disappoints Griet by not acknowledging her assistance to Catharina, but he recognizes her native intelligence and intuitive artistic sense. Despite their close working relationship, he maintains his distance from her and seems to view her only as a servant. However, his gift of the earrings in his will is a marvelous touch by Chevalier. Griet had long ago decided that she meant nothing to him, but the gift contradicts

that perception. It indicates that his feelings for her had been deep.

Chevalier also presents a realistic and authentic picture of the town of Delft in the seventeenth century. The city itself takes shape, pulsing with activity. Chevalier accurately depicts Market Square and its stalls, the canals, the churches, and the neighborhood where Griet's family lives. Chevalier also cleverly includes detailed descriptions of several Vermeer paintings, as told by Griet to her blind father. Other items that add to the novel's verisimilitude are a celebratory birth feast, with Vermeer wearing a paternity cap; the experience with the camera obscura, which some historians believe Vermeer used for his work; the existence of the plague and its effects; and the making of Delft tiles.

Joyce E. Henry

Further Reading

Andres, Sophia. "From Camelot to Hyde Park: The Lady of Shalott's Pre-Raphaelite Postmodernism in A. S. Byatt and Tracy Chevalier." *Victorians Institute Journal* 34 (2006): 7-37. Examines Chevalier's talent from a feminist perspective, looking at her blending of history and fiction and her giving voice to women in paintings.

Baker, Barbaraz, ed. *The Way We Write: Interviews with Award-Winning Writers*. New York: Continuum, 2006. A collection of interviews with novelists, playwrights, and others, including Chevalier, who discuss their methods of writing. Chevalier comments about her interest in history, her use of the first person, and the balancing act between fact and fiction.

Cibelli, Deborah H. "*Girl with a Pearl Earring*: Painting, Reality, Fiction." *Journal of Popular Culture* 37, no. 4 (May, 1994): 383-392. Discusses Chevalier's methodological assumptions and the use of historical accounts of Vermeer's art and Dutch culture. Concludes that Chevalier's approach to creating a novel from a specific painting is unique.

Strout, Cushing. "Fact, Fiction, and Vermeer." *Sewanee Review* 109, no. 2 (2001): ixvi-ixix. A brief, positive review of the novel in which Strout notes the religious and class differences and praises Chevalier for her intelligent methods of fictionalizing history.